MANAGEMENT OF BANKING AND FINANCIAL SERVICES

THIRD EDITION

Padmalatha Suresh
Adjunct Faculty
Indian Institute of Management Kozhikode
and
Visiting Faculty
Indian Institute of Management Indore

Justin Paul
Professor
Graduate School of Business, University of Puerto Rico
San Juan, PR, USA
(Formerly, faculty member, University of Washington)

PEARSON

Delhi • Chennai

Assistant Editor—Acquisitions: Varun Goenka
Editor—Production: Nikhil Rakshit

ISBN: 978-93-325-0747-0

First Impression, 2014
Fourth Impression, 2015
Fifth Impression

Published by Pearson India Education Services Pvt Ltd, CIN: U72200TN2005PTC057128,formerly known as TutorVista Global Pvt Ltd, licensee of Pearson Education in South Asia.

Head Office: 7th Floor, Knowledge Boulevard, A-8 (A), Sector 62, Noida 201 309, UP, India.
Registered Office: Module G4, Ground Floor, Elnet Software City, TS-140,Block 2 and 9, Rajiv Gandhi Salai, Taramani, Chennai 600 113, Tamil Nadu, India.Fax: 080-30461003,Phone: 080-30461060
www.pearson.co.in, Email: companysecretary.india@pearson.com

Compositor: PageTech Publishing Services Pvt. Ltd.

Printer: Anand Sons

CONTENTS

FOREWORD

Mrs. Padmalatha Suresh and Dr Justin Paul have written an extremely useful book on banking. Banking industry has undergone far-reaching changes in the recent period as a result of the banking reforms initiated in 1991–92. Among other things, banking reforms focused on the deregulation of the interest rate structure, introduction of prudential norms and imparting greater competition by allowing new banks and by permitting private participation up to a limit in public sector banks. Even as banks are required to fulfill certain socio-economic goals, they have to remain viable and efficient.

The introduction of the various measures which formed part of the banking sector reforms has had an impact on the way banks perform their functions. Conformity to the new prudential norms requires that banks manage their liabilities and assets in ways different from those practiced earlier. With the deregulation of the interest rate structure, banks have to pay attention to the interest rate risk besides the usual credit risk. The change in the exchange rate regime calls for banks to pay attention to exchange rate risk. These and many other problems have been dealt with lucidly by the authors in this book. The authors are eminently suited to write a book of this type. They have an excellent academic background. The also have the practical experience of dealing with banking issues at various levels. The book fulfills a need and I am sure it will be welcomed by students of banking as well as executives in the banking industry.

(C. Rangarajan)
Chairman
Economic Advisory Council to the
Prime Minister
and
Former Governor
Reserve Bank of India

PREFACE TO THE THIRD EDITION

"My other piece of advice, Copperfield", said Mr Micawber, "you know. Annual income twenty pounds, annual expenditure nineteen nineteen six, result happiness. Annual income twenty pounds, annual expenditure twenty pounds ought and six, result misery. The blossom is blighted, the leaf is withered, the god of day goes down upon the dreary scene, and—and, in short, you are for ever floored. As I am!"
[Charles Dickens, 'David Copperfield' (1849–1850 [1950]), Chapter 12, p. 185.]

More winds of change have swept over national landscapes since our second edition. What began as a credit crisis in the banking industry fanned itself into a wildfire, smothering nations under the burden of debt. What was true for Mr Micawber was true for powerful sovereigns as well!

'Banks, regulators, governments, and the entire global financial system are still finding ways to deal with the after-shocks of the crisis, and to avert new ones in future.' This sentence from the second edition is still valid at the time of the third edition!

What's New?

The financial crisis of 2007 had thrown 'risk management' into sharp relief. The sovereign crisis that soon followed and continues to this day in various countries had led to pronounced global economic slowdown. The third edition in its introductory chapter deals with the future of the banking industry in the context of the global financial and economic crisis that has taken its toll on sovereign powers. It has updated chapters on advanced topics on 'credit risk management' that discusses various models of credit risk measurement and management. 'Risk management', of course, occupies centre-stage, and risks faced by the banking industry from its investment (market risk), solvency (capital), interest rate volatility and adequate liquidity have to be measured and managed. All the chapters have been rigorously updated and revamped to help users of the book understand how these risks can be managed.

How the book has been organized

With risk management in sharp focus, the book is reorganized to enable the modern banker, academician, or student to recognize risks in banking and financial services, and take decisions to achieve the most favourable risk-return trade-offs.

The book is divided into two major sections—'Management of Banks' and 'Management of Financial Services'. Chapter 1 is an introduction to the changing dynamics of one of the most regulated industries in the world. Chapters 2 to 12 examine various facets of managerial and risk management aspects of banking in detail. The remaining chapters—13 to 23—deal with management of financial services that banks offer. Wherever relevant, aspects of financial markets, co-banking institutions and legal and regulatory reforms impacting banking and financial services have been highlighted.

New features in this edition

- All chapters have been substantially updated and revised. Portions of some chapters have been completely rewritten to make them contemporary.
- New chapters have been added to address contemporary issues in the industry.
- More case studies and live examples have been provided in most chapters.
- Additional problems and research questions have been added to many chapters to provide students the opportunity to work with data and circumstances that would help them understand basic concepts better.
- All web references have been provided for further research work by academics.
- More topics have been included for possible research by interested students.
- A notable feature of this book is that the topics presented in this book would be found in advanced textbooks on banking and finance. However, the explanations and illustrations are aimed at those with no basic knowledge of both banking and financial concepts. Most concepts are explained in simple terms with the aid of diagrams, figures, and simple worked out examples. The technical details/advanced concepts related to each chapter are provided as annexures.

In short, the book, written by practitioners turned consultants/academicians, uniquely focuses on managerial issues in the banking and financial services industry. The book offers something unique for various types of target audiences. For those seeking knowledge of banking and financial services, the book explains basic concepts underlying the key banking activities in very simple terms, and demonstrates how banks make financial decisions. For practitioners, the book enables building a sound conceptual foundation that will help them evaluate the overall organizational impact of decisions in their area of expertise, as well as provides tips to trade off between risk and return. Additionally, the book provides the big picture for managing the entire bank, since each chapter in the book is based on a strategic function of the bank, and addresses the basic concepts and application of these concepts in modern day management of banking and financial services. It is also interesting that the section on 'basic concepts' (presented as Section I) of each chapter has not undergone much change. This only implies that basic tenets and objectives of the banking and financial services industry have not changed. What do change are the applications of the basic concepts and their evolution to suit the environment in which they operate.

Padmalatha Suresh

Justin Paul

PREFACE

Banking and financial services have been written about, debated and discussed so much over the years that one would wonder what unique contribution another book would have to make to the subject. A few years ago, even we would have found another book on this subject unnecessary. However, after teaching the subject for over six years at various management schools, we found that we could make a valuable contribution to the existing presentation of the subject by bringing together a distinctive conceptual and managerial flavor to understanding this dynamic industry. Our long years as practitioners in the industry also helped us tremendously in this venture.

Today, the winds of change are sweeping through the landscape of the banking and financial services in the country. The industry is simultaneously consolidating and diversifying in an increasingly deregulated environment. Multiple pressures fuelled by rapid globalization, competition nurtured by customer awareness and expectations of the highest levels of service aided by sophisticated tools and techniques of analysis, threats of security invasion and fraud in an era dominated by technology, demands for transparency and the regulators' overdrive to capital efficiency or asset quality, and the complexity of issues in managing financial institutions have grown exponentially. These issues have been addressed in this book.

This book is divided into six parts. Part I provides an overview of the environment in the banking and financial services sector. Part II describes the banking structure, dealing extensively with analysing banks' financial statements, sources and uses of bank funds, with a comprehensive coverage of the leading function. Part III details risk management in banks—credit risk, market risk, capital adequacy and risk measurement techniques. Part IV introduces international banking, while Part V deals with some contemporary issues in bank management such as high-tech banking, cash management and consolidation of the financial sector through mergers and acquisitions. Part VI and the appendices contain useful pedagogical tools—case studies and multiple-choice questions. This book is also special in that each chapter has sections on basic concepts and the application of these concepts in banking practice. An instructor's tool kit for teaching each chapter is also available on the Web site.

Through this book, we aspire to provide valuable takeaways for all segments of readers: for practitioners, the book will help evaluate the overall impact of their decisions on the organization as a whole, as also the critical trade-offs between risk and return; students will find the book useful to build a conceptual and practice-oriented foundation at one go; academics would find the book a useful reference guide.

We express our heartfelt gratitude to the Pearson Education team, without whom the book would have remained a dream.

Justin Paul

Padmalatha Suresh

ACKNOWLEDGEMENTS

I would like to thank my parents, Mr. Balakrishnan and Mrs Meenakshi, for instilling the right values and providing me the opportunities; my guru, Shri Kamakshi Baba, whose grace has guided this work; my husband, S. Suresh and my children, Anagha and Abhinav, for their unswerving and enthusiastic support; all my teachers—at school, college and IIM Ahmadabad—who opened the gateway to acquiring knowledge; and the versatile veterans under whom I learnt banking in practice.

My humble gratitude to Dr C. Rangarajan, whose foreword to the first edition of this book placed me on cloud nine, and Dr A. H. Kalro, whose invitation to teach banking at IIM Kozhikode helped me begin this wonderful voyage.

As with the previous edition, I gratefully acknowledge the contribution of the entire Pearson team who patiently spent several painstaking hours over telephone and mail, to fine tune the book's quality and make it error free. Their commitment to this project, in spite of their busy schedule, has been commendable and exemplary.

—Padmalatha Suresh

Several experts deserve to be thanked for their comments and help extended to the first and second edition of this book. We owe a deep debt of gratitude to M. Venugopalan (Chairman, Federal Bank) who formally released this book at a function held in Cochin, Kerala. A partial list of others, who have been a source of inspiration for this work and those who had given comments on different chapters include:

M. V. Nair (Chairman, Union Bank of India)
Dr V. A. Joseph (Chairman, South Indian Bank)
Professor Thomas Paul (National Institute of Bank Management)
Dr Hiroshi Kurimoto (President, Nagoya University of Commerce and Business, Japan)
Krishna Mohan Nandiraju and Mayur Udermani (Ex students, IIM)
V. S. R. Moorthy (Former GM, Union Bank)
S. Harikumar (Oriental Bank of Commerce)
Jeomoan Kuriaon (Wells Fargo Bank)

—Justin Paul

ABOUT THE AUTHORS

Padmalatha Suresh is an alumnus of the IIM Ahmadabad. She also holds a degree in LLB and CAIIB. She has more than two decades of industry experience at senior levels, primarily in the banking, and briefly in the IT sector. Her long exposure to the banking sector has enabled her to evaluate banking and financing strategies, risk entailments and options for redressing them as also commentate on banking, in general, and infrastructure finance, in particular.

She is an independent finance consultant and Director, DMS Financial Services Pvt. Ltd, a firm specializing in strategic financial consultancy, outsourcing of financial services, corporate training and recruitment in the finance area. She is a visiting/adjunct professor of finance at the Indian Institute of Managements and other reputed B-Schools, where she teaches the courses on bank management and infrastructure financing. She also teaches at executive and management development programs. She has edited a popular professional reference book titled *Project Finance: Concepts and Applications*. Her several articles on banking and infrastructure financing have been published in popular business dailies, magazines, and refereed journals in India and abroad. Her views/interviews on banking and infrastructure financing issues have been published in leading business magazines.

Justin Paul is a professor at Graduate School of Business, University of Puerto Rico, San Juan, USA. He has served as Department chairperson at Indian Institute of Management (IIM) and has also taught full courses at Grenoble Eco Le De Management, France and ISM University, Lithuania (Europe). He has been a visiting professor at University of Washington M. Foster Business School, University of Puget Sound-Seattle, St.Martin's University-USA, Meiji University-Tokyo, Goethe University-Germany and SP Jain Institute of Management, Dubai. He has been a speaker, trainer and consultant to many organizations including the governments and conducted corporate training programs in Oman, Mauritius, India, China and Japan. He has been as a Ph.D examiner and director on the board of studies various of institutes.

In addition to this book, he is known as author/co-author of books—*Business Environment and International Marketing*, *Export-Import Management and International Business* published by McGraw-Hill, Oxford University Press and PHI, respectively. A consistent rank holder, he holds two masters degrees, two postgraduate diplomas, an FDP-SS (Germany) and a doctorate from Indian Institute of Technology (IIT) Bombay. He has also received international awards for research papers and case studies instituted by American Society for Competitiveness, Emerald Publishers, Indian Banks Association and Association of Indian Management Scholars.

He has hands-on experience of working with two commercial banks before joining academic world and has been recognized as role model and achiever by *The Hindu, Manorama TV* and *Careers and Campuses* magazine. He has published over 20 papers in international journals and presented papers at the conferences organized/hosted by University of San Francisco, Fudan University-Shanghai, Indiana University of Pennsylvania, University of Stirling-UK, Asian Academy of Management, Waseda University-Tokyo in the recent past. He has also undergone a case writing training program organized by London Business School. He has also served as reviewer of research papers for Academy of International Business, USA, *International Journal of Commerce and Business*, *International Journal of Bank Marketing and Management Review*. He has widely traveled in over 50 countries. His Web site is www.drjustinpaul.com and contact email is profjust@gmail.com.

CHAPTER ONE

Managing Banking and Financial Services—Current Issues and Future Challenges

CHAPTER STRUCTURE

KEY TAKEAWAYS FROM THE CHAPTER

- Understand the present state of the global financial system.
- Understand the basic causes behind the global financial crisis of 2007.
- Learn how macro economic factors can affect financial stability.
- Learn how financial stability can be achieved through better regulation.
- Understand how the Indian financial system is organized.
- Understand the various types and characteristics of financial markets.
- Learn about the evolution of the Indian financial system.
- Understand the impact of the financial sector reforms.
- Take a look at the future challenges in the global and Indian financial systems.

SECTION I

THE SETTING

'Leading up to Janet Yellen's January 6 confirmation vote, the Federal Reserve recently announced that it will taper back its bond-buying program, known as quantitative easing. This was encouraging news for inflation hawks, if barely so. Right now, the Fed buys $85 billion worth of mortgage-backed securities and Treasury bonds every month from financial firms. These firms, flush with cash from the Fed, then diffuse those dollars throughout the economy through loans and other financial activities. Going forward, the Fed will roll back its monthly purchases from $85 billion to $75 billion, or roughly 11 percent.'

...Ryan Young in The Washington Times, January 1, 2014[1]

'Japan's Central bank has promised to unleash a massive programme of quantitative easing—worth $1.4tn (£923bn) that will double the country's money supply—in a drastic bid to restore the economy to health and banish the deflation that has dogged the country for more than a decade.

As part of a new set of policies known as Abenomics, formulated by Japan's new prime minister Shinzo Abe, the Bank of Japan will buy ¥7tn (£46bn) of government bonds each month using electronically created money, with the aim of rekindling demand and pushing up prices and wages.'

...Heather Stewart in The Guardian, April 4, 2013[2]

'.... the Cypriot banks' high exposure to bad Greek debt meant that when Greece negotiated a debt write-off—the so-called 'haircut'—for its struggling financial institutes in February 2012, Cyprus took a severe blow.

Downgraded by the big rating agencies, Cypriot banks were cut off from the international financial markets and only kept alive through infusions from the European Central Bank (ECB). But the central bankers in Frankfurt threatened to withhold even these emergency funds unless Cyprus agreed to a deal, so Nicosia budged, accepting to raise around 5.8 billion euros to qualify for a 10 billion euro bailout.'

...Michael Steininger in The CS Monitor, March 29, 2013[3]

Welcome to the world—post the financial crisis that began in 2007-08

SECTION II

THE GLOBAL FINANCIAL SYSTEM—CURRENT ISSUES

It has been nearly half a decade since the global financial crisis began. The global financial system continues to be under pressure, as are governments and key economic indicators of most countries. The global economies are in the grip of vicious cycles as depicted in Diagram 1.

While advanced economies at the centre of the financial crisis reel under high debt loads and marked slowdown, the emerging economies also face a slowdown in spite of rapid credit expansion or export led growth. The Bank for International Settlements (BIS, www.bis.org in its 82nd annual report), categorizes the ongoing challenges as those pertaining to (a) structural adjustment, (b) monetary and fiscal policy risks, and (c) financial reform.

Another paper from BIS[4] categorizes financial crises into banking, currency and sovereign debt crises. Recent research shows that during the period 1970 – 2011, currency crises occurred most frequently (218), followed by banking crises (147) and sovereign debt crises (66).

Since the first quarter of 2010, sovereign debt tensions and their impact on banks and economies have dominated. Sovereign debt crises have been more pronounced in the euro area. How is sovereign risk related to the banking and currency crises? Box 1.1 explains.

DIAGRAM 1 VICIOUS CYCLES AND THE BURDEN ON CENTRAL BANKS.

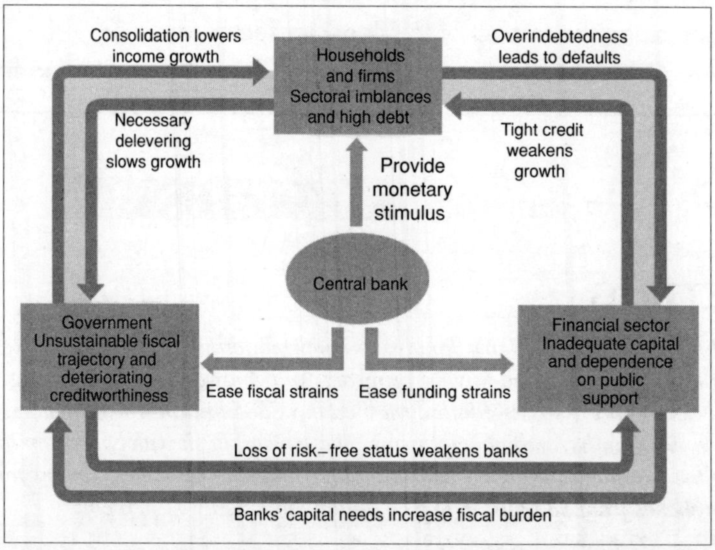

Source: Bank for International Settlements, 82nd annual report, p. 8, Graph 1.1, accessed at www.bis.org

BOX 1.1 THE BANKING CRISIS–SOVEREIGN CRISIS NEXUS EXPLAINED

The recent global financial crisis and the consequent deepening of the euro debt crisis clearly indicate the interdependencies between banks and sovereign risk. Several research studies have found a link between the fiscal and financial distress. Discussing the transmission channels during the fiscal and financial turmoil, Reinhart and Rogoff (2011) present a set of four stylized facts. First, private and public debt booms ahead of banking crises. Second, banking crises, both home-grown and imported, usually accompany or lead sovereign debt crises. Third, public borrowing increases sharply ahead of sovereign debt crises; moreover, it turns out that the government has additional 'hidden debts' (domestic public debt and contingent private debt). Fourth, the composition of debt shifts towards the short term before both debt and banking crises. Further, a default may take place if the financial crisis ignites a currency crash that impairs the sovereign's ability to repay foreign currency debt.

The bailout of banks by their respective countries during the recent global financial crisis has led to a shift of credit risk from the financial sector to national governments and led to an increase in sovereign risk (Acharya, *et al*, 2010).

However, historically, the transmission of distress has often moved from sovereign to banks with sovereign defaults triggering bank crises (Caprio and Honahan 2008). The anaemic economic growth combined with high debt-to-GDP ratio has led to frequent downgrades of the sovereign ratings of euro area [Greece, Ireland, Italy, Portugal and Spain (GIIPS)] countries by credit rating agencies. With an increase in sovereign debt risk, banks were also affected as they were the major holders of sovereign bonds.

There are multiple channels through which the increase in sovereign risk feeds into the banks' funding costs: (i) losses on holdings of government debt weaken banks' balance sheets, increasing their riskiness and making funding more costly and difficult to obtain; (ii) higher sovereign risk reduces the value of the collateral which banks can use to raise wholesale funding and central bank liquidity; (iii) sovereign downgrades generally flow through to lower ratings for domestic banks, increasing their wholesale funding costs and potentially impairing their market access; and (iv) a weakening of the sovereign reduces the funding benefits that banks derive from implicit and explicit government guarantees (CGFS-BIS 2011).

The interdependency between the sovereign and their banks can be clearly seen for euro area GIIPS countries, as both sovereign and bank risk (largest bank in the respective country), as measured by CDS spreads, tend to move together during the crisis.

The sovereign and banking stress increased as investors' concerns about the political situation in Greece and the implications of the difficulties experienced by the Spanish banking system were compounded by a perceived lack of cohesion among governments in upgrading the crisis management mechanisms in the euro area.

References

Acharya, Viral V, Drechsler, I and Schnabl, (2011), 'A Pyrrhic Victory? Bank Bailouts and Sovereign Credit Risk', NBER. Working Papers 17136, National Bureau of Economic Research.

Barth, James R, Apanard Prabha and Greg Yun, 2012, *The Eurozone Financial Crisis: Role of Interdependencies between Bank and Sovereign Risk*', Journal of Financial Economic Policy, vol. 4.

Caprio, Gerard and Patrick Honahan 2008, 'Banking Crisis', Center for Development Economics, Williams College.

CGFS-BIS, 2011, *The Impact of Sovereign Credit Risk on Bank Funding Conditions*, CGFS Papers No. 43, Bank for International Settlements.

Rogoff, Kenneth S and Carmen M. Reinhart, (2011), *A Decade of Debt*, NBER Working Paper 16827, National Bureau of Economic Research.

Source: Extract from RBI, Report on Trend and Progress of Banking in India 2011–12, Box II.2, pages 18, 19. The charts in this box have not been reproduced here.

A Rewind to the Financial Crisis of 2007–08

Set in 2009, no discourse on 'banks', and more so, 'managing banks', can begin without reference to the credit market turmoil of 2007. The global crisis spared no country—developed or developing. With many countries' financial systems still grappling with the after-shocks of what began as a sub-prime lending crisis in the United States, it comes as no surprise that voluminous literature already exists on the causes of and lessons from the crisis, as well as remedial action taken by governments and regulators in various countries.

We will discuss the events that led to the crisis in detail elsewhere in this book. However, what is more important is the way forward. The financial system is the lifeline of any economy. It is therefore only natural that the 'future' of banking is hotly debated topic at not only banking forums but also at every congregation of professionals from various walks of life.

The term 'paradigm shift' is now being applied to banking as well. The question is—what does this 'shift' constitute? Will it mean jettisoning the old model of banking and adopting a completely new one? Or, would it signify fine tuning existing banking practices so that 'crisis management' is strengthened through effective anticipation and preventive action?

The Causes of the Crisis

Several arguments/theories/events have been cited as the causes of the 2007 crisis. But, there seems to be consensus on one possible over arching cause—lack of adequate attention from monetary authorities and regulators to certain factors that were shaping the global financial system when the crisis happened. Three groups of mutually reinforcing factors were then contributing to increased 'systemic' risk. They were as follows:

- Lower interest rates caused by worldwide macroeconomic imbalances over the last decade, inducing heightened risk taking and contributing to extremely high asset prices—the asset price 'bubble'.
- Changing structure of the financial sector and rapid pace of financial innovation over the last two decades, and the failure of 'risk management' to match up to the new demands.
- Failure to adequately regulate highly leveraged financial institutions.

Macroeconomic and Financial Stability—Understanding the Linkages

Studies of economic cycles show that 'booms' and 'busts' are typical of market-driven systems. 'Depressions', 'recessions' and 'market crashes' have all happened and passed into history, leaving behind painful memories, case studies and vital practical lessons to be learnt.

How are a country's macroeconomic developments and financial stability related? Figure 1.1[5] depicts the linkages between shocks in the real sectors of the economy and the financial sector.

Let us understand the figure using the example of the global crisis of 2007. The shock to the US economy began as an asset bubble in the real estate (housing) sector, caused by banks lending to sub-prime (less than creditworthy) borrowers.[6] The delinquency of such borrowers led to credit and interest rate risk[7] for banks involved in the lending. Since many of these banks, by this time, had 'securitized' the loans[8] and transferred the risks to other banks/entities, and the underlying asset prices had fallen drastically, liquidity in the market dried up. Funding available in the market also dwindled, partly because there was no liquidity and, also due to banks being wary of lending to other borrowers/banks which needed funding.[9] The high degree of interlinkages in the various markets led to a rapid transmission of the crisis from one segment to other segments. Ultimately, many banks 'and other institutions' balance sheets[10] were affected. Taken together, the combined effect of various risks reflected in the aggregate loss distribution, which can be mapped back to the adverse impact on bank lending and the economy.

FIGURE 1.1 INTERRELATIONSHIPS BETWEEN MACROECONOMIC DEVELOPMENTS AND FINANCIAL STABILITY

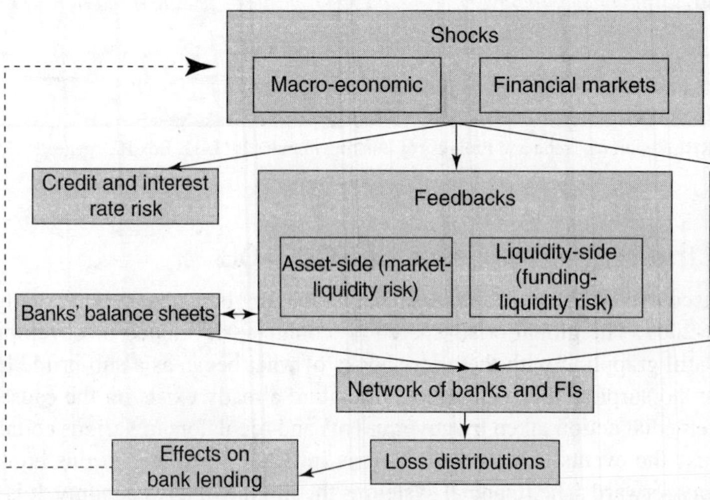

Source: Haldane, Andrew; Hall, Simon and Pezzini, Silvia (2007). A New Approach to Assessing Risks to Financial Stability; Financial Stability, Paper No. 2; www.bankofengland.co.uk

In this case, since several banks and other institutions around the world were involved as 'buyers' or 'insurers' or 'traders' of credit risk, a number of other countries' financial systems were adversely affected. Hence, the United States sub-prime mortgage market triggered a credit market crisis at the global level, the depth of whose adverse effects are being estimated even in 2009–2010.

How do we define 'financial stability'? There is no single definition for financial stability (and the term 'systemic risk' which is used in tandem). Hence, the term takes on contextual meaning, signifying smooth functioning of the financial system, both under normal and stressed conditions.[11]

The recent credit crisis, like others before it, has thrown up several issues and challenges for banks and other financial institutions, as well as central banks and regulators. However, all stakeholders agree on one thing—recovery of the global financial system depends on restoration of 'TRUST'.

The Role of 'Trust' in Financial Stability

The global crisis witnessed the crumbling of the very foundation of a sound financial system—TRUST.

There was a 'massive breakdown of trust across the entire financial system—trust in banks and non banks, trust in central banks and other regulators, trust in credit rating agencies, trust in investment advisors, trust in brokers, dealers and traders, and trust in the financial markets, if not in the market system itself'.[12]

The loss of trust, coupled with failure of banking behemoths and lack of transparency, led to great fear and uncertainty. Which were the banks/institutions that could withstand losses? Can the potential losses be estimated with certainty? Were there lurking risks in the system that could explode in the future? Frightening questions—with no reassuring answers—resulted in unprecedented panic. Banks that had liquidity, hoarded it. Banks that did not have liquidity faced doomsday, since they got no help from the distrusting markets. The financial markets nearly went into a deep freeze. Long-standing financial institutions that had appeared rock solid quietly folded up. Lack of trust had almost brought the entire chain of financial intermediation to a standstill.

The Role of Regulation in Ensuring Financial Stability

The G20 Working Group on 'enhancing sound regulation and strengthening transparency' (Working Group I), in its report[13] dated 25 March 2009, has reiterated the paramount importance of robust financial regulation in each country based on effective global standards for financial stability in future. The report has acknowledged the role of regulation as the first line of defence against financial instability. It sums up the cause of the financial crisis: 'In hindsight, policy makers, regulators and supervisors in advanced countries did not act to stem excessive risk taking or to take into account the inter-connectedness of the activities of regulated and non-regulated institutions and markets'.

Experts have identified some of the areas that were given inadequate attention as the following:

a. *The 'perimeter' of regulation.* In deciding which institutions and practices should be regulated and to what extent, the regulators had overlooked that some institutions outside their purview were taking on excessive risks, and that some of these risks were not 'visible' or 'detectable'.

b. *Procyclical practices.* Booms in the economy lead to higher confidence levels both among borrowers and lenders. As a consequence, lenders become lax about credit standards and borrowers turn overconfident about the potential of projects they invest in. When the economy is on the downturn, banks become wary and tighten lending standards and pull back liquidity.

c. *Information gaps about risk and where they were distributed in the financial system.* This happened in the case of financially engineered products, where credit risk transfer was done in a distributed manner. Though the principle of 'structuring' was to transfer risk to those parties who could best bear them, the rapid increase in demand for such high-yielding products led to lower transparency. As a result, most sellers and the buyers of these products lacked adequate understanding of what they were selling or buying, thus exposing themselves to greater risks.

d. *Lack of cross-border information flow and co-operation among regulators in various countries.* There was no harmonization of national regulatory policies and legal frameworks in various countries, even though risks were being transferred across countries.

e. *Provision of liquidity by regulators* in the event of crisis.

It is, therefore, clear that the regulatory framework needs considerable strengthening. The stark lessons from the crisis will ensure that adequate regulation will be receiving significant attention in future.

The Objectives of Financial Regulation

According to an IMF Working Paper,[14] there are two vital objectives of financial regulation, as depicted in Figure 1.2.

We have already seen how the failure of financial institutions can have a wider impact on financial markets and macroeconomic stability. However, even a weak financial system can have adverse effects on economic growth and stability. Individual banks or financial institutions would not be able to assess the overall economic impact of bank level business decisions. Hence, regulation is used to mitigate such systemic risks.

As seen in Figure 1.2, systemic risks can be macro or micro in nature. Both types of risks, in essence, are interrelated.

When risks taken by various banks/institutions in the economy have a correlated negative impact across other institutions, the financial system as a whole gets weakened and economic growth is adversely affected. This is macro systemic risk, and the credit crisis of 2007 is an example of this risk.

In micro-systemic risk, the failure of one bank or institution has an adverse impact on the financial system as a whole. For example, failure of one bank can cause a loss of confidence and trigger a run on other banks, even those that are fundamentally sound.

FIGURE 1.2 OBJECTIVES OF FINANCIAL REGULATION

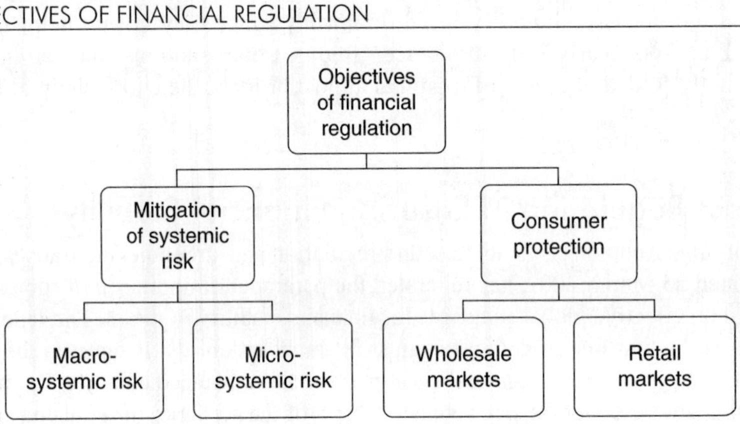

FIGURE 1.3 TOOLS OF FINANCIAL REGULATION

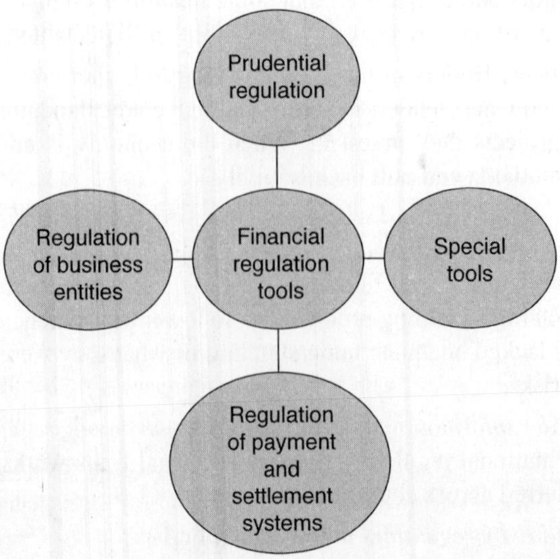

How are the objectives of mitigating systemic risks and customer protection related and regulated? The following examples illustrate the facts:

- In financial markets, the sellers of financial products (say, deposit accounts or insurance services) have more information than the buyers (customers of banks, insurance, etc.). Hence, regulation is required to establish rules and procedures for disclosure of information or limit risk by placing a cap on the amount that can be invested in certain products.
- In retail markets, it is necessary for the regulator/regulation to ensure that the provider of financial services is in good financial health, since the payoff to the customers (*e.g.*, repayment of deposits, insurance proceeds, and so on) is dependent on it.
- In wholesale markets, say in the case of securities, the sellers of securities have more information than the investors. Hence, more disclosures by way of information given in prospectuses or stiff penal clauses to restrain undesirable practices, such as insider trading are required. More transparency can be achieved through regulation.

According to the IMF paper, quoted above, financial regulation can be done using four broad tools (*see* Figure 1.3). These are as follows:

- Prudential regulation typically sets out regulatory prescriptions for maintaining capital or liquidity or credit quality. The regulation seeks proactive remedial action.[15]
- Specialized tools in the hands of central banks and other regulators are the role of 'lender of last resort'(LOLR) or deposit insurance.[16]
- Regulation of payment and settlement systems is vital for ensuring post-trade transactions in financial contracts are managed well.[17]
- Business regulation aims to regulate activities of financial market participants through regulation of trading activity and financial market products.[18]

Financial Stability—the Over-arching Agenda for the Future

One of the key lessons from the crisis is that financial stability does not automatically follow price stability or macroeconomic stability. In an increasingly globalizing world, a threat to financial stability in any country could trigger a series of responses that jeopardize the financial stability of other countries. Hence, 'financial stability' will, in future, have to be looked at as an explicit objective, rather than an implicit objective of economic policy and growth.

A lot of discussion has already taken place at the highest levels in international forums, and these discussions are forming the basis for new or altered regulation or supervisory guidance. Some of the significant actions already taken include strengthening the Basel 2 capital framework,[19] developing global standards for liquidity risk management,[20] strengthening supervision of cross-border financial conglomerates, reviewing international accounting standards,[21] strengthening the functioning of credit rating agencies,[22] rationalizing compensation structures and extending the scope of regulation to cover non-banking financial institutions.[23] (See Box 1.2, for the role of non-banking financial institutions—also called 'shadow banking system' in the financial crisis.)

BOX 1.2 ROLE OF THE 'SHADOW BANKING SYSTEM' IN THE FINANCIAL CRISIS

Internationally, the non-banking financial institutions are also termed 'other financial intermediaries' (OFI). They typically include, among others, pension funds, securities dealers, investment funds, finance, leasing and factoring companies and asset management companies. They can also include the less understood special investment vehicles (SIVs), conduits, money market funds, monolines, investment banks, hedge funds and other non-banking financial services.[24] Since many of these operations are opaque, these entities are sometimes categorized as part of a 'shadow banking system'.

In the run up to the financial crisis of 2007, many of these shadow banks, which were typically bank subsidiaries or associates, capitalized on regulatory gaps. They raised short-term funds in the market, such as 'commercial paper' and invested in illiquid, long-term assets, such as sub-prime mortgages or other SIVs. The danger with this approach was that if the assets failed to return cash flows (from repayments and interest), the short-term borrowings could not be repaid. The shadow banks, being outside the banking system, did not have access to the 'lender of last resort' protection from the central banks. Thus, if the market turned illiquid, these entities could become insolvent.

Unfortunately, the worst scenario materialized. The sub-prime assets failed to return cash flows and the shadow banks scrambled for liquidity to refinance the short-term liabilities. The liquidity in the market too, soon dried up and many of these entities were forced to declare bankruptcy. The contagion spread to the parent banks as well, as the credit risk in sub-prime mortgages, and the market risk in structured products rapidly turned into a systemic liquidity risk. Since many international banks were involved in shadow banking activities, the US centred sub-prime crisis snowballed into a major global financial credit and liquidity crisis.

The Financial Stability Board (FSB)[25], in April 2012, defined shadow banking system as 'Credit intermediation involving entities and activities outside the regular banking system'.

At the Cannes Summit in November 2011, the G-20 leaders agreed to strengthen the oversight and regulation of the shadow banking system and endorsed the FSB's initial recommendations with a work plan to their further development in the course of 2012. The FSB has adopted a two-pronged approach. First, the FSB will enhance the monitoring framework by continuing its annual monitoring exercise to assess global trends and risks, with more jurisdictions participating in the exercise. Second, the FSB will develop recommendations to strengthen the regulation of the shadow banking system, wherever necessary, to mitigate the potential systemic risks.

In April 2012, the FSB in its report on shadow banking system to the G-20 leaders reviewed the progress made.

Does India Have Shadow Banking System?

In India and certain other countries like Turkey, Indonesia, Argentina, Russia and Saudi Arabia, the non-banking financial assets remained below 20 per cent of GDP at the end of 2012. However, the sector showed rapid growth, though from a low base, in some of these jurisdictions, including India. In the Indian context, the Non-Banking Finance Companies (NBFCs) are regulated by the Reserve Bank and all types of Mutual Funds (MFs) are regulated by the Securities and Exchange Board of India (SEBI). As such, India does not have shadow banking entities, in the formal financial system with potential for creating systemic instability. However, a large number of non-bank financial entities function in the unorganized sector (unincorporated entities outside the purview of regulatory perimeter), whose collective size and profile of activities need to be gauged to ensure that they do not pose any threat to the 'trust'in and 'stability' of India's financial system.

Source: Various documents from RBI, FSB.

The encouraging signal emerging from global deliberations is the recognition that international co-operation is key to resolve crises of such proportion. The various working groups constituted by the G-20 have emphasized that future regulation and supervision must reinforce risk management capacity of financial institutions. Greater transparency and lower regulatory 'arbitrage' (defined later in this chapter) have also been insisted upon. A major outcome is the establishment of a new Financial Stability Board (FSB) to be operated by the International Monetary Fund (IMF), with strengthened mandate that includes all large countries of the world.

SECTION III

THE INDIAN FINANCIAL SYSTEM—AN OVERVIEW

Financial Stability in India

The financial system of any country has two important segments—the financial markets and the financial intermediaries.[26]

The turmoil in the global financial system has triggered introspection and discussion on the stability of the Indian financial system. Some have termed the fact that India has not faced any financial crisis so far as a consequence of deregulation as 'remarkable', while others attribute it to the 'correctness of 'judgement' that reforms to global standards need to be adjusted to local conditions'.[27] The relative insulation of India could also appear 'fortuitous', since the credit derivatives market is in an embryonic stage and the originate-to-distribute model in India is not comparable to that in developed markets, or 'conservative', since regulatory guidelines on securitization do not permit immediate profit recognition or the reforms were not speeded up through bold and drastic steps as in other countries.

However, the fact remains that the Indian financial sector has matured since the financial reforms were instituted. What we see today is a reasonably sophisticated and robust system delivering a diverse range of financial services, efficiently and profitably. With deregulation, the operational and functional autonomy of financial institutions has increased and, so has their participation in various financial market segments in the face of heightened international competition. It is also moving towards the goal of financial inclusion by accelerating growth momentum while containing risk and emphasizing on 'financial stability'.

In order to understand the challenges and issues confronting, the Indian banking system in the present context, it is necessary to understand the structure and evolution of the Indian financial system.

One way of understanding the financial market structure is to look at its components. Table 1.1 classifies financial markets into broad components and lists their typical characteristics. The table also indicates the broad aspects of regulation in each market, as well as the depth of the market in India.

TABLE 1.1 CHARACTERISTICS OF FINANCIAL MARKETS

Type of Market	Purpose	Operators	Typical Regulator	Regulator in India	Depth of Market[28] in India
Money market.	Short-term finance	Banks, government, mutual funds, financial institutions, insurance companies and corporate companies.	Central bank	Reserve Bank of India (RBI) (under clause 45 (W) of RBI Amendment Act, 2006).	Reasonably deep
Capital market.	Long-term finance	Companies, banks, financial institutions, mutual funds and exchanges.	Capital market regulator	Securities and Exchange Board of India (SEBI)— under SEBI Act, 1992; Securities Contracts (Regulation) Act, 1956 and Depositories Act, 1996.	Equity markets and its related derivative segments are quite deep and liquid. But corporate bond market is quite shallow.
Foreign exchange market.	Foreign currency operations.	Companies, banks and authorized dealers (AD).	Central bank	RBI[29]	quite developed and deep.
Government securities market.	Short- and long-term finance.	Government, banks and primary dealers[30].	Central bank	RBI[31]	Well-developed and deep.
Credit market	Short- and long-term finance.	Banks, financial institutions and non-banking financial institutions.	Central bank	RBI	Reasonably well-developed, except credit derivatives market.

Table 1.2 outlines the typical instruments, their salient features, and some of issues to be resolved in each market.

TABLE 1.2 TYPICAL FINANCIAL INSTRUMENTS IN INDIA—SALIENT FEATURES

Market Type	Typical Instruments	Exchange Traded or OTC[32]	Typical Derivatives	Issues
Money market	Instruments[33] with maturities of one year or less: • Inter-bank call money • Market repo • Collateralized borrowing and lending obligations (CBLO) • Commercial paper (CP) • Certificates of deposit (CD)	Electronic trading platforms for call, market repo, CBLO, OTC for call, CP, CD. Settlement over RTGS (Real time gross settlement) on electronic platform.	Derivative products—Interest rate swaps/forward rate agreements[34]. Trades in swap market OTC. Interest rate futures reactivated in August 2009,	1. Little growth in medium-term money market. 2. Assessment with IOSCO[35] principles reveal existence of critical regulatory and accountability gaps.
Capital market	Equities and bonds	Operation of equity markets through stock exchanges.	Related derivatives	1. Equity and derivative markets well-developed and functioning smoothly. 2. However, corporate bond market yet to take off. 3. The private placement segment is growing, but lacks transparency. 4. Overlap of responsibilities between Government and SEBI. 5. Tightened risk-management practices.

(Continued)

TABLE 1.2 (CONTINUED)

Market Type	Typical Instruments	Exchange Traded or OTC	Typical Derivatives	Issues
Foreign exchange market	Spot currencies	Operated by banks and authorized dealers— screen based and brokered trading.	Forwards, swaps, options. Currency futures introduced.	1. No risk based capital requirements in place for full-fledged money changers. 2. More transparency required in derivatives reporting by non bank financial entities. 3. Forward trading subject to settlement risks. 4. Trading in off shore locations by global investors interested in the 'India' asset class not regulated. 5. Assessment on IOSCO principles reveals gaps in areas relating to operational independence and accountability and detection of manipulation and unfair trade practices.
Government securities market	Both short (money market) and long-term securities.	Auction system for issue of securities, electronic platform for trading, OTC and exchange traded.		Lack of transparency in primary dealers' and foreign entities' trading positions.
Credit market[36]	Wholesale and retail banking and financial services products.	Through financial intermediaries.	Derivatives used in risk management and for generating income. Credit derivatives yet to be introduced.	Issues will be discussed in detail in the following chapters of the book.

To summarize, Figure 1.4 depicts the manner in which the financial system is regulated at present.

FIGURE 1.4 REGULATORY STRUCTURE OF THE INDIAN FINANCIAL SYSTEM

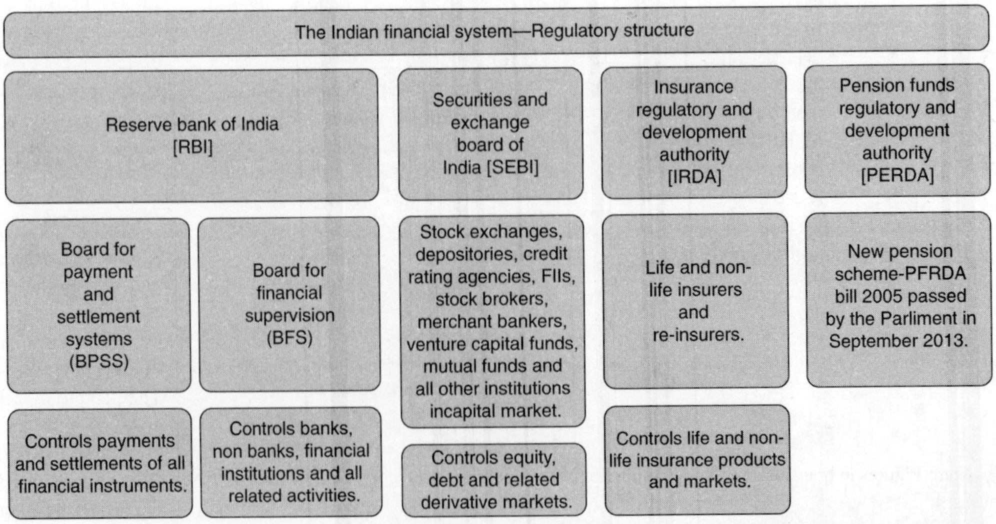

SECTION IV

THE INDIAN BANKING SYSTEM—AN OVERVIEW

Though the capital market size has expanded substantially since financial liberalization, the Indian financial system is dominated by financial intermediaries.[37] The commercial banking sector holds the major share (about 60 per cent) of the total assets of the financial intermediaries, which comprise of commercial banks, urban co-operative banks, rural financial institutions, non-banking finance companies, housing finance companies, development financial institutions, mutual funds and the insurance sectors.

The Bank Market Structure in India

The bank market structure in India can be broadly classified into: (a) commercial banks; (b) financial institutions; (c) non-banking finance companies; and (d) co-operative credit institutions. (See Figures 1.5A to 1.5G).

FIGURE 1.5 THE BANK MARKET STRUCTURE IN INDIA

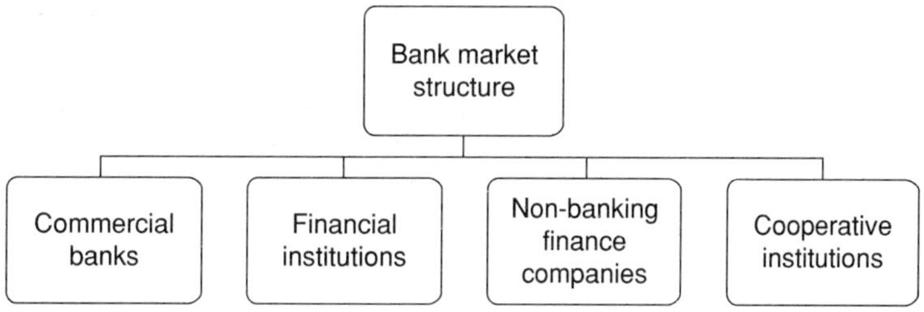

FIGURE 1.5A THE COMMERCIAL BANKING SYSTEM

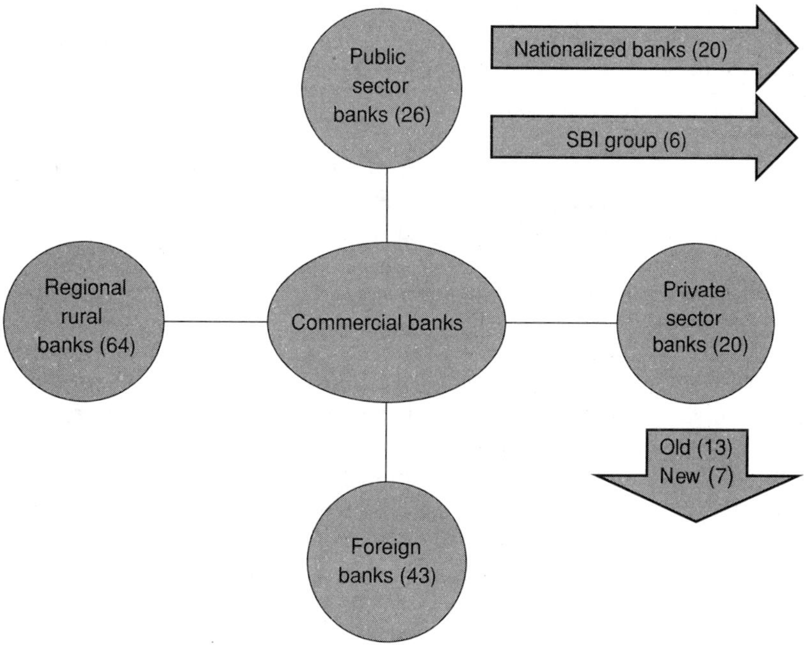

Note: Figures in brackets signify the number of banks under each category. All data pertain to March, 2013.

Source: RBI database.

Who Owns the Commercial Banks in India?

Public Sector Banks At the end of March 2013, there were 26 public sector banks in India, comprising of State Bank of India and its associate banks (6), and 20 nationalized banks (including IDBI Bank Ltd).

The public sector banks in India are regulated by statutes of the Parliament and some important provisions under section 51 of the Banking Regulation Act, 1949.

Specifically, the regulations are as follows:

- State Bank of India regulated by the State Bank of India Act, 1955.
- Subsidiary banks of State Bank of India regulated by State Bank of India (Subsidiary Banks) Act, 1959.
- Nationalized banks regulated by Banking companies (Acquisition and Transfer of Undertakings) Act, 1970 and 1980.

The statutes also stipulate that the central government is mandated to hold a minimum shareholding of 51 per cent in nationalized banks and 55 per cent in State Bank of India (SBI). In turn, SBI will have to hold a minimum 51 per cent of the shareholding in its subsidiaries. Another stipulation is that foreign investment in any form cannot exceed 20 per cent of the total paid up capital of the public sector banks.

From 1984–1985, there have been three distinct 'phases' of equity infusion by the government into public sector banks. In the period up to 1992–1993, all nationalized banks were capitalized without any predetermined norm. Over the next couple of years, (up to 1993–1995), when the first phase of financial reforms were under way, some 'weak' nationalized banks were put on a recovery path and in the following years, the government, as owner, had to improve banks' capital position to levels stipulated by the Basel Accords. In 2006–2007, banks were allowed to raise capital from the public through equity issues. The relevant Acts were amended to permit banks raise capital to a level not exceeding 49 per cent of their equity base.

The Board of public sector banks comprises of whole time directors—chairman, managing director(s), executive directors, government nominee directors, RBI's nominee directors, workmen and non workmen directors and other elected directors.

Private Sector Banks At the end of March 2013, there were 20 private sector banks in India, of which 13 are classified as 'old' and the remaining 7 as are classified as 'new' private sector banks.

The broad underlying principle in permitting the private sector to own and operate banks is to ensure that ownership and control is well-diversified and sound corporate governance principles are observed. New private sector banks can initially enter the market with a capital of ₹200 crores, which should be increased to ₹300 crores over the following three years. No single entity or group can have shareholding or control (direct or indirect) more than 10 per cent of paid-up equity capital of the bank. The aggregate foreign investment[38] in an Indian private sector bank cannot exceed 74 per cent and at least 26 per cent of the paid-up capital should be held by resident Indians at all times.

There are two distinctly observable categories among the private sector banks—the new banks—aggressive, professionalized and the fastest growing, and the old private sector banks—typically smaller, with a specific regional bias and less than satisfactory performance.

Foreign Banks Foreign banks are required to invest an assigned capital of USD 25 million upfront at the time of opening their first branch in India. They can operate in India in one of the following three ways: (1) through branches, (2) through wholly-owned subsidiaries, and (3) through subsidiaries with maximum aggregate foreign investment of 74 per cent in a private sector bank. Hence, foreign banks can have an asset share, equity stake and FII investment in the Indian banking system. In a move to foster globalization, the RBI announced a two-phase road map for the presence of foreign banks in 2005. In the first phase, 2005–2009, foreign banks were allowed to establish wholly-owned subsidiaries in India (minimum capital requirement of ₹300 crores and maintain capital adequacy of 10 per cent), or spin off existing operations into a subsidiary. The second phase, due to commence in April 2009, was intended to consider extension of national treatment to wholly-owned subsidiaries, dilution of stake and permitting mergers and acquisitions with private sector banks in India. These measures would also entail amendments to the Banking Regulation Act, 1949.

Regional Rural Banks (RRBs) The RRBs were created for rural credit delivery and to ensure financial inclusion. Their capital base is held by the central government, relevant state government and the commercial bank that 'sponsors' them, in the ratio of 50:15:35, respectively. Recent policy initiatives include recapitalization and amalgamation of RRBs with their sponsor banks. So far, there have been two broad phases in the amalgamation of RRBs. In the first phase (September 2005–March 2010), RRBs of the same sponsor banks within a state were amalgamated bringing down their number to 82 from 196. In the second and ongoing phase, starting from October 2012, geographically contiguous RRBs within a state under different sponsor banks would be amalgamated to have just one RRB in medium-sized states and two/three RRBs in large states. In the current phase, 31 RRBs have been amalgamated into 13 new RRBs within 9 states to bring down their effective number to 64.

However, an issue that is considered to hamper performance efficiency of RRBs is the multiplicity of control—RBI is the banking regulator, while NABARD[39] is the supervisor with limited supervisory powers.

FIGURE 1.5B NON-BANKING FINANCIAL INSTITUTIONS (NBFI)–THE COMPONENTS

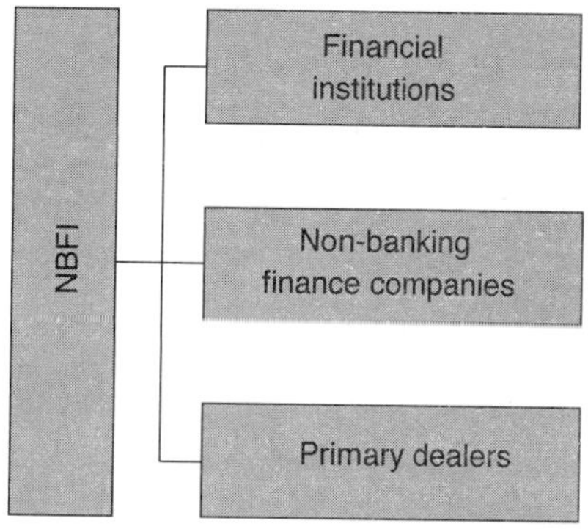

Non-banking Financial Institutions (NBFIs) are a heterogeneous group of institutions that cater to a wide range of financial requirements. They can broadly be grouped as financial institutions (FIs), non-banking financial companies (NBFCs) and primary dealers (PDs). The structure of these components is described in the following paragraphs.

FIGURE 1.5C FINANCIAL INSTITUTIONS' STRUCTURE

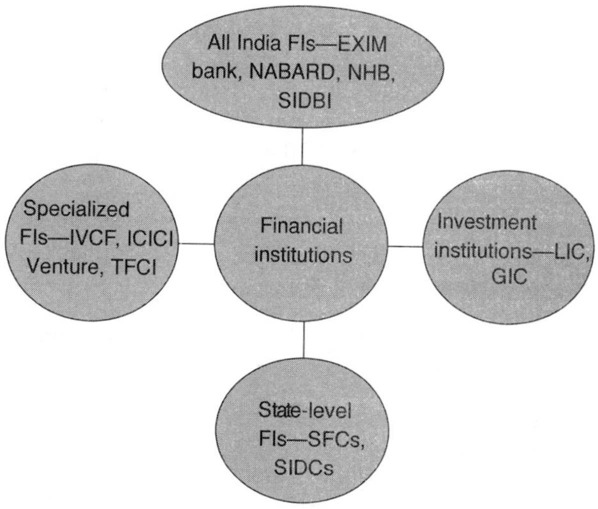

The 'financial institutions' (FIs) fall under the category of 'Non-banking Financial Institutions (NBFI)[40] that complement banks in providing a wide range of financial services to a variety of customers and stakeholders. While banks primarily provide payment and other liquidity related services, the NBFIs offer equity and risk-based products. However, this distinction is blurring now, as some financial institutions convert themselves into banks and 'financial integration' proceeds at a rapid pace.[41]

Based on their major line of activity, the four all-India financial institutions are classified into: (1) term-lending institutions (EXIM Bank), which invests in projects directly through investments and loans; and (2) refinancing institutions (NABARD, SIDBI and NHB). The refinancing institutions extend refinance to both banks as well as other NBFIs. Specifically, however, NABARD extends refinance and other facilities for agriculture and allied activities, SIDBI for the micro, small and medium enterprises (MSME) sector and NHB for the housing sector. Table 1.3 provides the ownership of these financial institutions

TABLE 1.3 ALL INDIA FINANCIAL INSTITUTIONS – OWNERSHIP

(As at End of March 2013)

Institution	**Ownership**	**Per Cent**
(1)	(2)	(3)
EXIM Bank	Government of India	100
NABARD	Government of India	99.3
	Resrve Bank of India	0.7
NHB	Resrve Bank of India	100
SIDBI*	Public Scetor Banks	62.5
	Insurance Companies	21.9
	Financial Institutions	5.3
	Others	10.3

*Three major shareholders of SIDBI are: IDBI Bank Ltd. (19.2%), State Bank of India (15.5%), and Life Insurance Corporation of India (14.4%).

Investment institutions, such as LIC and GIC deploy their resources for long-term investment. After the Insurance Regulatory and Development Authority came into being in 1999, the sector—both life and non-life—have been thrown open for private and foreign participation.

State/regional level financial institutions comprise of State financial corporations (SFCs) and State Industrial and development corporations (SIDCs).

Some institutions, including a few from those listed above, have been notified as 'public financial institutions' by the Government of India under the Companies Act, 1956. Of these, a few have ceased operations (such as the Industrial Investment Bank of India), while some others have been converted into NBFCs (see the discussion on NBFCs, below). Examples of FIs converted into NBFC-ND-SI (see definition, below) are Industrial Finance Corporation of India (IFCI) and Tourism Finance Corporation of India (TFCI).

The RBI Act 1934 was amended in January 1997 to bring in a comprehensive legislative framework for regulating NBFCs. The amendment called for compulsory registration and maintenance of minimum 'net owned funds' (NOF[42]—the concept of 'capital' for NBFCs), for all NBFCs and conferred powers on RBI to determine policies and issue directions to NBFCs.

The two major categories of NBFCs in India are the deposit taking (NBFC-D) (from the public) and non-deposit taking (NBFC-ND) NBFCs. Housing Finance Companies (HFC) are considered a special type of NBFC. The residuary non-banking finance companies—RNBC, also accepts deposits from the public. Earlier, RNBCs held almost 90 per cent of all NBFC deposits, but their business model was found unviable. Hence, RNBCs were required to migrate to other business models. The two existing RNBCs would be exiting the present business model by repaying their liabilities by 2015. Non-deposit taking NBFCs have been further bifurcated into NBFC-ND and NBFC-ND-SI, as shown in Figure 1.5D. 'SI' stands for 'systemically important'. Understandably, NBFCs with asset size of over ₹100 crores are classified in this category.

While deposit taking NBFCs (NBFC-D) were subject to some prudential regulation since 1963, the non-deposit taking institutions (NBFC-ND) were almost unregulated. As 'systemic risk' became frequently used term and began threatening the stability of financial systems, RBI designated those NBFCs with asset size of over ₹100 crores as 'systemically important' (NBFC-ND-SI), due to their linkages with money markets, equity markets, banks and financial institutions and brought them under a specific regulatory framework (capital adequacy and exposure norms[43]) from April 1, 2007. NBFC-ND-SI is the fastest growing segment of NBFCs, growing at a compound rate of 28 per cent between 2006 and 2008. They raise resources[44] primarily from issue of debentures, borrowings from banks and other financial institutions and issue of commercial paper (a money market instrument, discussed in a later chapter). This category of NFBCs is closely monitored by RBI due to their systemic importance.

Figure 1.5E also shows another classification of NBFCs according to their asset profile. Across NBFC categories, asset finance companies (AFC) hold the largest share in total assets/liabilities (above 70 per cent). They are followed by loan companies (LC) with about 30 per cent.

FIGURE 1.5D NBFC STRUCTURE BASED ON LIABILITIES

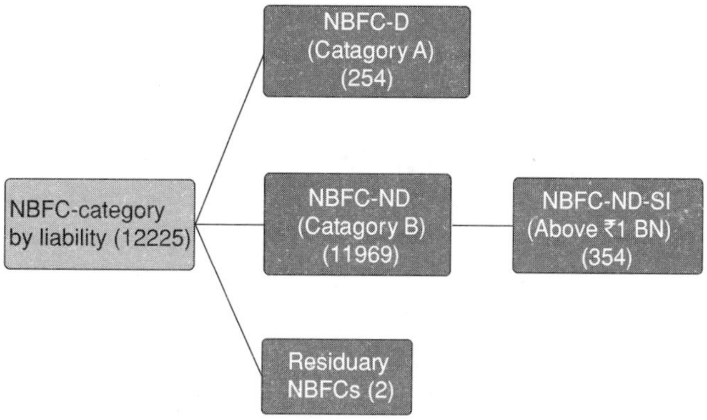

Note: Figures in brackets indicate the number of institutions at the end of March 2013. Note that NBFC-ND-SI constitutes only about 2.9 per cent of NBFC-ND by number, but account for about 95 per cent of business.

Source: RBI database (figures as of March, 2013).

FIGURE 1.5E NBFC STRUCTURE BASED ON ACTIVITY

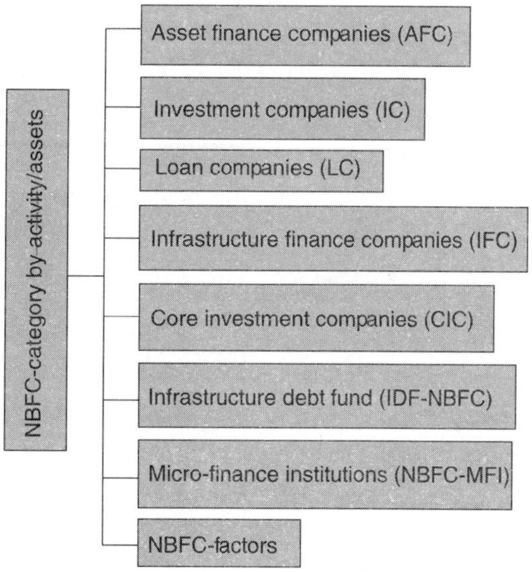

It can be gauged from the above discussion that NBFCs, especially NBFC-NDs, do not have access to low-cost sources of funds like the banks do.[45] Therefore, to compensate for high cost of funds, a significant segment of NBFC-ND companies have adopted a capital market based business model, such as providing loans against shares or financing public issues. While this is a model where high yields are possible, the risks are also higher.

Housing finance companies (HFC) are special types of NBFCs. When the National Housing Bank (NHB), one of the all India financial institutions (described earlier) was set up in 1988, there were about 400 housing finance companies regulated by the RBI that financed only 20 per cent of the population's home financing needs. The remaining 80 per cent was being financed through informal sources. Housing Development Finance Corporation (HDFC) was the largest housing finance company. The housing finance market has grown stupendously since then, with many banks and other institutions entering the sector. The NHB is the regulator and supervisor of HFCs.

There are further regulatory challenges in this fast growing segment.

For example, RBI's Panel for financial regulation and supervision classifies NBFCs into a third set of broad categories[46]:

1. Stand-alone NBFCs.
2. NBFCs that are subsidiaries/associates/joint ventures of banking companies.

3. NBFCs and banks under the same parent company, *i.e.*, 'sister companies'.
4. NBFCs that are subsidiaries/associates of non-financial companies.

FIGURE 1.5F PRIMARY DEALERS (PD)[47] OPERATING IN FINANCIAL MARKETS

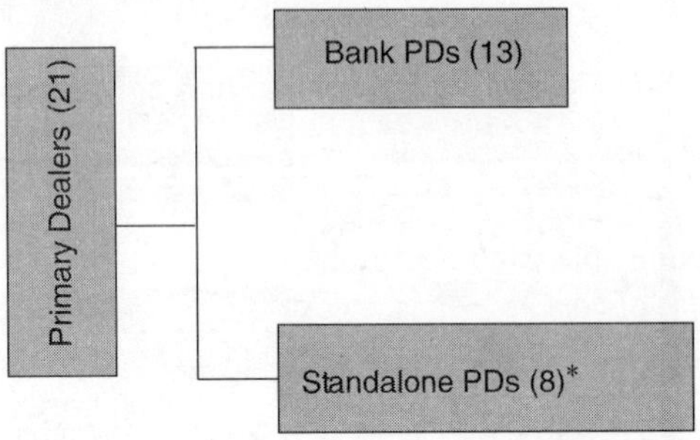

*The 8 stand alone PDs are STCI Primary Dealer Ltd., SBI DFHI Ltd., ICICI Securities Primary Dealer Ltd., PNB Gilts Ltd., Morgan Stanley India Primary Dealer Pvt. Ltd., Nomura Fixed Income Securities Pvt. Ltd., Deutsche Securities India Pvt. Ltd., and Goldman Sachs.

Note: Figures in brackets indicate the number at the end of March 2013. Bank PDs are run by banks. Standalone PDs are also called non-bank PDs and are registered as NBFCs under Section 45 1A of the RBI Act, 1934.

Source: RBI database.

FIGURE 1.5G STRUCTURE OF THE CO-OPERATIVE BANKING SECTOR (AS AT END-MARCH, 2013)

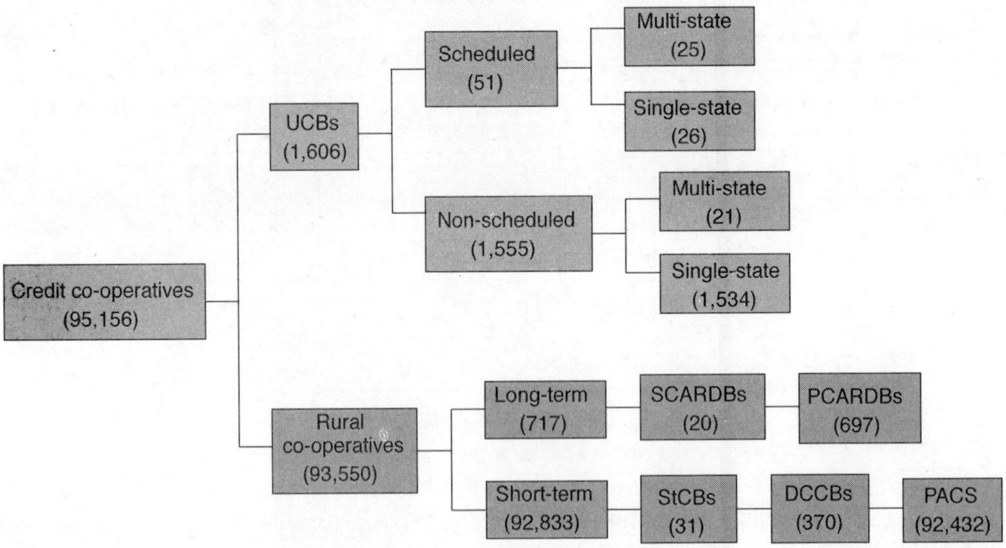

StCBs: State Co-operative Banks; DCCBs: District Central Co-operative Banks; PACS: Primary Agricultural Credit Societies: SCARDBs: State Co-operative Agriculture and Rural Development Banks; PCARDBs: Primary Co-operative Agriculture and Rural Development Banks.

Notes: 1. Figures in parentheses indicate the number of institutions at end-March 2013, for UCBs and at end-March 2012, for rural co-operatives.
2. For rural co-operatives, the number of co-operatives refers to reporting co-operatives.

Note: Tier 1 UCBs includes: (i) banks with deposits below ₹100 crore, whose branches are located in a single district; (ii) banks with deposits below ₹100 crore having branches in more than one district, provided the branches are in contiguous districts and deposits and advances of branches in one district separately constitute at least 95 per cent of the total deposits and advances respectively of the bank; and (iii) banks with deposits below ₹100 crore, whose branches were originally in a single district, but subsequently, became multi-district due to reorganization of the district. All other UCBs are classified as Tier 2.

Source: RBI, Report on Trend and Progress of Banking in India, 2012–13, Chart V.1, p. 93.

Co-operative Credit Institutions India has a large number and broad range of rural financial service providers—with formal financial institutions/banks at one extreme, informal providers such as money lenders or traders at the other extreme and between these two, a large number of semi formal providers. The 'formal' providers include rural and semi urban branches of commercial banks, regional rural banks, rural co-operative banks and primary agricultural credit societies (PACS). The 'semi-formal' sector is characterized by self-help groups (SHGs) with bank linkages and the micro-finance institutions (MFIs).

The co-operative sector was conceived as the first formal institutional channel for credit delivery to rural India. It has been regarded as a key instrument for achieving the 'financial inclusion' objective. The urban co-operative banks (UCBs) are an important channel for financial inclusion in the semi-urban and urban areas, especially for the middle- and low-income customers.

Though these institutions play a critical role in the financial sector, their commercial viability and financial soundness are seen as areas of concern. The size of the rural and co-operative sector is small when compared with the commercial banking sector. However, there are certain issues that have to be resolved if these institutions have to function efficiently.

A key issue that hampers efficiency is that these institutions' operations are overseen by both the RBI/NABARD and the relevant state governments, which leads to multiplicity of control. According to the committee on financial sector assessment (CFSA, 2009), the dual control is 'the single most important regulatory and supervisory weakness' in the co-operative banking sector.

Another issue causing concern is the management and governance of these institutions. Since, only borrowers are members, co-operatives could tend to frame and pursue borrower-oriented policies. Many co-operatives function as banks without proper licences. Further, directors are appointed mostly on political affiliation and rarely on merit. To introduce best practices and professional governance, the CFSA recommends (Chapter II, page 174) that co-operatives in India be modelled on the lines operated by the World Council for Credit Unions (WOCCU).[48]

The rural cooperative credit structure is shown in Figure 1.5G.

The RBI adopted a multi-layered regulatory and supervisory strategy aimed at the consolidation of UCBs by way of merger/amalgamation of viable UCBs and the exit of unviable banks for the revival of this sector, which led to a gradual reduction in the number of UCBs. The closures of UCBs were due to various reasons such as high non-performing advances, negative net-worth, deterioration in financial health, non-compliance with RBI guidelines, frauds, affairs conducted in a manner detrimental to the interests of depositors, misappropriation of funds, sanctioning of loans in excess of permissible limit, sanctioning of loans to the entity in which directors have interest, etc. The total number of UCBs as at the end of March 2013 stood at 1606 as against 1618 as at the end of March 2012. The progress of consolidation of UCBs is shown in Table 1.4.

TABLE 1.4 PROGRESS IN CONSOLIDATION OF URBAN COOPERATIVE BANKS (UCB)

	Number of UCBs				
Financial Year (FY)	**Operational as on the Last Day of Previous FY**	**Merged During FY**	**Cancellation of Licenses Rejection of Applications for License***	**Closed During FY (5) = (3) + (4)**	**Operational as on the Last Day of Current FY**
(1)	(2)	(3)	(4)	(5)	(6)
2008–09	1.770	22	27	49	1.721
2009–10	1.721	13	34	47	1.674
2010–11	1.674	13	16	29	1.645
2011–12	1.645	14	13	27	1.618
2012–13	1.618	3	9	12	1.606

*Rejection of application of the existing urban co-operative credit societies for license.

Source: RBI – Financial Stability Report, December 2013, p. 43 and Table 2.10.

Box 1.3 summarizes the major findings and recommendations of an Expert Committee on the short-term cooperative credit structure.

BOX 1.3 SHORT-TERM CO-OPERATIVE CREDIT STRUCTURE—FINDINGS AND RECOMMENDATIONS

Under-capitalization is one of the major problems afflicting the co-operative credit institutions.

Even after capital infusion to strengthen co-operative banks in July, 2013, 23 unlicensed banks in four states were unable to meet the licensing criteria as issuing of licences to these institutions is contingent upon their attaining minimum risk-weighted capital ratio of 4 per cent.

Against this backdrop, the Reserve Bank constituted an Expert Committee to examine the 3-Tier Short-term Co-operative Credit Structure (Chairman: Dr Prakash Bakshi) with a set of objectives: (i) to have a relook at the functioning of the Short-term Co-operative Credit Structure (STCCS) from the point of view of the role played by them in providing agricultural credit; (ii) to identify Central Co-operative Banks (CCBs) and State Co-operative Banks (StCBs) which may not remain sustainable in the long-run even if some of them have met the diluted licensing criteria; (iii) to suggest appropriate mechanisms for consolidating by way of amalgamation, merger, takeover, liquidation and delayering; and (iv) to suggest proactive measures to be taken by co-operative banks and various stakeholders.

The Committee submitted its report to the Reserve Bank in January 2013.

The major findings and recommendations of the Committee are:

Findings:

- STCCS's share in providing agricultural credit dipped to 17 per cent at the aggregate level.
- STCCS, which was primarily constituted for providing agricultural credit must provide at least 15 per cent of the agriculture credit requirements in its operational area, gradually increasing to at least 30 per cent. Around 40 per cent of the loans provided by PACS and almost half the loans provided by CCBs are for non-agricultural purposes. PACS and CCBs were not performing the role for which they were constituted.
- About 209 of the 370 CCBs would require additional capital aggregating to ₹65 billion in four years to attain 9 per cent CRAR by 2016–17.
- Almost two-third of the deposits with StCBs is deposits made by CCBs in the form of term deposits for maintaining their SLR and CRR requirements. However, StCBs lend far higher amounts to the same CCBs and also invest in loans which have generally resulted in higher NPAs, thus putting the SLR and CRR deposits made by CCBs at risk.

Recommendations made by the committee are in the following broad areas:

- The co-operative credit institutions should fulfil the purpose for which they were constituted, namely, provide agricultural credit in rural areas. Penalties/deterrents are proposed for not fulfilling this primary objective.
- To enable the institutions to mobilize funds and disburse loans to meet these objectives, Amendments to the State Co-operative Societies Acts, rules and by-laws would be necessary in each state with regard to the definition of active members.
- The RBI would define the composition of capital for these institutions to enable meeting their objectives.
- The Banking Regulation Act needs to be amended to give direct and overriding authority to the Reserve Bank over any other law for superseding the Board or removing any director on the board of a StCB.
- CCBs and StCBs need to be covered by the Banking Ombudsman or a similar mechanism that may be developed by the Reserve Bank with NABARD.

An Implementation Committee has been constituted with members from NABARD and the Reserve Bank for expeditious implementation of these recommendations.

The implementation of these recommendations is likely to strengthen rural co-operative credit institutions.

Reference

NABARD (2013), Report of the Committee to Examine Three-tier Short-term Co-operative Credit Structure, January, 2013.

Source: RBI, Report on Trend and Progress of Banking in India 2012–13, Box 5.2, p. 111, 112.

Figure 1.6 shows the ways in which financial conglomerates can be organized.

In the 'universal bank' model, all financial operations are conducted within a single corporate entity. In the 'operating subsidiary' model, operations are conducted as subsidiaries of a financial institution. In the 'holding company' model, financial operations are carried out by distinct entities (such as banks, mutual funds, insurance, NBFCs and HFCs), each with separate capital and management, but together owned by a single institution (financial or non-financial).

The current model used in India is the 'operating subsidiary' model. There are no universal banks in India.

FIGURE 1.6 ALTERNATE ORGANIZATIONS FOR FINANCIAL CONGLOMERATES

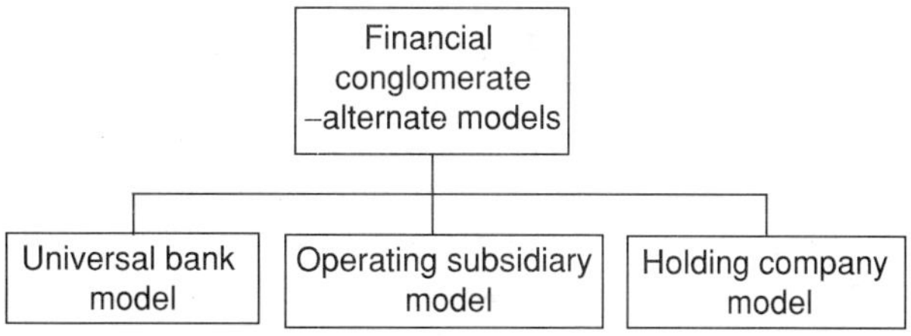

Evolution of Indian Banking

The evolution of the Indian banking system can be categorized into four distinct phases:

- The pre-Independence (pre-1947) phase
- 1947–67
- 1967 to 1991–92
- 1991–92 (financial sector reforms) and beyond

In the pre-Independence phase, there were no entry norms and several banks were established. The Swadeshi Movement was instrumental for establishment of some banks that are in existence even today. This phase, marked by two World Wars and the Great Depression, also saw several banks failing. Most of the banks that failed were either too small to withstand global pressures or were mismanaged by directors, managers and practices of inter-connected lending or had combined trading and banking functions. Partly in response to the bank failures, the RBI was set up in 1935.[49] However, due to the presence of a dominating unorganized sector (money lenders, etc.) and the lack of a sound regulatory framework, RBI's control over banks was limited.

In the post-Independence era, the Banking Companies Act (now called, 'the Banking Regulation Act') was enacted in 1949, primarily to address the issue of banking failures. It also empowered the RBI to regulate and control the banking sector. The RBI could improve the safety and soundness of the banking sector by enabling weak banks to amalgamate or liquidate. Deposit insurance was introduced to increase depositors' confidence in the banking system. Efforts were made through branch expansion of the State Bank of India to include more rural areas in the banking ambit. However, the nexus between banks and big industrial houses resulted in very little credit percolating down to the common man or to small industries and agriculture. RBI's micro controls to ensure adequate credit to productive sectors resulted in a complex structure of regulated interest rates.

1967 to 1991–92 saw the tightening of social controls over the banking sector. To ensure equitable credit flow to the agriculture and small sectors, directed lending to 'priority sectors' was introduced. This period also saw the nationalization of major banks. This period was marked by rapid expansion in bank branches and, also an increase in lending to the priority sectors. However, the expansion in branches and credit was made without regard to banks' profitability or asset quality. Credit to medium and large industries was more difficult to get due to strict targets for priority sector lending, stringent norms for lending to the 'non-priority' sectors and high statutory pre-emption (cash reserve ratio and statutory liquidity ratio). At the end of this phase, banks had accumulated a staggering amount of assets that gave no income to the bank (known today as 'non-performing' assets) and were low on profitability, efficiency and productivity.

'Until the beginning of the 1990s, the state of the financial sector in India could be described as a classic example of 'financial repression'.[50] The characteristic features of this state were manifested in the following forms:

- Administered and regulated interest rates.
- Large amount of resources drained away from productive lending by high rates of CRR and SLR.
- Extensive micro-regulation of flow of funds between banks.
- Limited disclosure and opaque accounting practices.
- Dominant public ownership with decreasing efficiency and productivity.
- Low capital and high level of non-performing loans.
- High investment in government securities, enabling high government borrowings at administered or concessional interest rates.
- Stringent barriers to entry of new and more efficient players into the banking sector.
- Restrained access of the private sector to bank credit, especially in the absence of other avenues for external financing.

During this period, the capital and foreign exchange markets also lacked depth. While the capital market reeled under complex regulations with little transparency or depth in secondary market trading, stringent controls, opaqueness and malpractices characterized the foreign exchange market. The Monetary Policy's subservience to the fiscal policy[51] had effectively blocked the development of the financial system. A serious balance of payments problem was in the offing. Foreign exchange reserves were hardly sufficient to cover three weeks' imports. Gold reserves were swapped and India went in for a loan from the International Monetary Fund (IMF).

The year of 1991–1992 saw the dawn of one of the most productive phases in India's banking history.

The RBI (report on currency and finance) divides this phase into two sub phases: 1991–92 to 1997–98 and 1997–98 and beyond. In the first sub phase, against the backdrop of a balance of payments problem, the need was felt for a vibrant and competitive banking and financial sector. The government of India constituted a high-powered committee on the financial system (CFS) under the chairmanship of Shri M. Narasimham. Popularly known as the 'Narasimham Committee', it made wide ranging recommendations that formed the basis of financial sector reforms. *Annexure I* lists the salient features of the committee's recommendations, widely acknowledged as the very foundation of the country's financial sector reforms process.

The approach to reforms was guided by the 'Pancha Sutra' or five principles: (1) cautious and sequenced reform measures; (2) introduction of reinforcing norms; (3) introduction of complementary reforms across relevant sectors—monetary, fiscal, external and financial; (4) development of financial institutions; and (5) development and integration of financial markets.

A major highlight of the first sub-phase was the improved profitability, competitiveness, capital position and asset quality of most banks. However, banks also developed a risk aversion that translated into slower credit growth, especially to the agriculture sector.

The early part of the second sub-phase, 1997–98 onwards, saw a push towards prudential norms in line with international best practices. By this time, new private sector banks had also been allowed to operate, which implied that existing banks had to turn more competitive. The thrust veered towards improving credit delivery and customer service, strengthening corporate governance practices and the urban co-operative banking sector and promoting financial inclusion, while taking appropriate measures to enable banks to recover non-performing loans. Banks were able to achieve a sharp decrease in non-performing assets (loans and investments). The asset quality improvement manifested itself in better capital adequacy. This phase has also been witnessing increasing use of technology by banks and customers alike.

To speed up financial sector reforms, the government of India set up a high level committee in 2007 (report published in 2009), under the Chairmanship of Prof. Raghuram Rajan. The terms of reference of the committee were as follows[52]:

a. To identify the emerging challenges in meeting the financing needs of the Indian economy in the coming decade and to identify real sector reforms that would allow those needs to be more easily met by the financial sector.
b. To examine the performance of various segments of the financial sector and identify changes that will allow it to meet the needs of the real sector.
c. To identify changes in the regulatory and the supervisory infrastructure that can better allow the financial sector to play its role while ensuring that risks are contained.
d. To identify changes in other areas of the economy, including the conduct of monetary and fiscal policy and the operation of the legal system and the educational system that could help the financial sector function more effectively.

Annexure 2 presents the 35 proposals made by the committee in summarized form. The proposals are grouped under the following broad heads:

a. Macroeconomic framework and financial sector development (2)
b. Broadening access to finance (4)
c. Levelling the playing field (6)
d. Creating more efficient and liquid markets (7)
e. Creating a growth friendly regulatory framework (9)
f. Creating a robust infrastructure for credit (7)

The numbers in brackets indicate the number of proposals under each head. It can be seen that the committee emphasizes on improving the regulatory framework, an important ingredient of financial stability.

The committee also offers its views on three critical aspects of economic growth for India—financing infrastructure growth, financing old age pensions and information generation. The report, in its conclusion, 'places inclusion, growth and stability as the three objectives of any reform process and fortunately, these objectives are not in contradiction. With the right reforms, the financial sector can be an enormous source of job creation both directly and indirectly through the enterprise and consumption it can support with financing. Without reforms, however, the financial sector could become an increasing source of risk, as the mismatches between the capacity and needs of the real economy and the capabilities of the financial sector widen. Not only would the lost opportunities be large, but the consequences for the economy could be devastating'.

Annexure III outlines the major policy and legal reforms (related to the banking/financial sector) that took place in India since 1991–1992.

The Way Forward...

The Indian financial sector may have come through the financial crisis of 2007 relatively unscathed. But, there is much more that needs to be done. There are several challenges to financial stability and the most critical of them have been articulated by the RBI governor.[53] In doing so, he has drawn from global experience.

According to him, the first challenge is, 'defining and measuring' financial stability. A second challenge is, determining who takes the responsibility for financial stability—will it be the central bank, the banks, other regulators and the government as well? While it is recognized that 'risk management' at all levels in the financial sector has to take precedence, the challenge remains as to where risk management amounts to 'conservativeness'. Yet another challenge is the massive and continuing reforms that should go in to create an effective and efficient 'regulatory architecture' that ensures financial stability. And finally, there is the constant tension between fiscal and monetary policies that could impair financial stability if left unchecked.

CHAPTER SUMMARY

- It has been nearly half a decade since the global financial crisis began. The global financial system continues to be under pressure, as are governments and key economic indicators of most countries. Since the first quarter of 2010, sovereign debt tensions and their impact on banks and economies have dominated. Sovereign debt crises have been more pronounced in the euro area. The bailout of banks by their respective countries during the recent global financial crisis has led to a shift of credit risk from the financial sector to national governments and led to an increase in sovereign risk.
- The global financial crisis of 2007 has spared no country—developed or developing. With many countries' financial systems still grappling with the after-shocks of what began as a sub-prime lending crisis in the United States, it comes as no surprise that voluminous literature already exists on the causes of and lessons from the crisis, as well as remedial action taken by governments and regulators in various countries.
- Several arguments/theories/events have been cited as the causes of the 2007 crisis. But there seems to be consensus on one possible over-arching cause—lack of adequate attention from monetary authorities and regulators to certain factors that were shaping the global financial system when the crisis happened.
- There is no single definition for financial stability. Hence, the term takes on contextual meaning, signifying smooth functioning of the financial system, both under normal and stressed conditions.
- The 2007 credit crisis, like others before it, has thrown up several issues and challenges for banks and other financial institutions, as well as central banks and regulators. However, all stakeholders agree on one thing—recovery of the global financial system depends on restoration of 'TRUST'.
- The G20 Working Group on 'enhancing sound regulation and strengthening transparency' (Working Group I), in its report dated March 25, 2009, has reiterated the paramount importance of robust financial regulation in each country based on effective global standards for financial stability in future. The report has acknowledged the role of regulation as the first line of defence against financial instability.
- Some of the significant actions already initiated include strengthening the Basel 2 capital framework, developing global standards for liquidity risk management, strengthening supervision of cross-border financial conglomerates, reviewing international accounting standards, strengthening the functioning of credit rating agencies, rationalizing compensation structures and extending the scope of regulation to cover non-banking financial institutions.
- The turmoil in the global financial system has triggered introspection and discussion on the stability of the Indian financial system.
- In order to understand the challenges and issues confronting the Indian banking system in the present context, it is necessary to understand the structure and evolution of the Indian financial system.
- Though the capital market size has expanded substantially since financial liberalization, the Indian financial system is dominated by financial intermediaries. The commercial banking sector holds the major share (about 60 per cent) of the total assets of the financial intermediaries, which comprise of commercial banks, urban co-operative banks, rural financial institutions, non-banking finance companies, housing finance companies, development financial institutions, mutual funds and the insurance sectors.

- The evolution of the Indian banking system can be categorized into four distinct phases: (1) The pre-Independence (pre-1947) phase, (2) 1947 to 1967, (3) 1967 to 1991–1992 and (4) 1991 to 1992 (financial sector reforms) and beyond.
- The RBI (Report on currency and finance) divides the last phase into two sub-phases: 1991–1992 to 1997–1998 and 1997–1998 and beyond. In the first sub-phase, against the backdrop of a balance of payments problem, the need was felt for a vibrant and competitive banking and financial sector. The Government of India constituted a high-powered committee on the financial system (CFS) under the chairmanship of Shri M. Narasimham. Popularly known as the 'Narasimham Committee', it made wide ranging recommendations that formed the basis of financial sector reforms.
- To speed up financial sector reforms, the Government of India has set up a high level committee in 2007 (report published in 2009), under the Chairmanship of Prof. Raghuram Rajan. The committee emphasizes on improving the regulatory framework, an important ingredient of financial stability.
- The Raghuram Rajan Committee also offers its views on three critical aspects of economic growth for India—financing infrastructure growth, financing old age pensions and information generation.

TEST YOUR UNDERSTANDING

1. Why did the European Central Bank decide to bail out Greece and other countries?
2. What is the difference between the bail out of Greece and that of Cyprus? Why did the central bank take a different stance in the case of Cyprus?
3. What is quantitative easing (QE)? Has it helped the US Fed in financial stability?
4. Why and how did signals of QE tapers affect the emerging markets?
5. What were the major causes of the global financial crisis of 2007?
6. Who is to be blamed for the financial crisis–banks or regulators?
7. Why did US banks lend to sub-prime borrowers?
8. How are macro economic developments linked to financial institutions?
9. Relate the following financial instruments to the different markets: (1) money market, (2) capital market, (3) foreign exchange market, (4) government securities market and (5) credit market.

   a. Commercial paper
   b. Certificates of deposit
   c. Equity shares
   d. Cheque
   e. Demand draft
   f. Treasury bills
   g. Forward exchange contract
   h. 10 year government bonds
   i. Corporate bonds
   j. Housing loans/mortgages
10. Relate the following transactions to (a) the respective markets and (b) the respective regulators in India.
    a. The Indian government issues securities in the market to cover a budget deficit
    b. An Indian blue chip company issues new shares in the market to fund its future expansion
    c. An Indian bank invests in bonds issued by a corporate body in India
    d. An Indian bank borrows funds abroad
    e. A foreign bank in India buys Indian government securities
    f. An Indian company sells its equity holdings in an Indian blue chip company
    g. An Indian bank invests in the 'initial public offering' of an Indian pharmaceutical company
    h. An Indian bank sells insurance products to a deposit customer
11. Why are non-banking financial companies valuable to the financial system? Can their failure cause systemic risks?
12. Why does lack of liquidity cause financial institutions to fail? If the financial institution had adequate liquidity, but made a loss on its operations during a year, what are the chances that it would fail?
13. Relate the following transactions to the spot or forward markets.
    a. An Indian bank sells USD 1 million to a customer
    b. A foreign bank buys ₹1 crore
    c. A foreign bank agrees to sell USD 1 million of Indian rupees three months later at a price agreed upon today
    d. An Indian bank agrees to buy USD 1 million after three months at a price agreed upon today
14. Why are credit co-operatives valuable to the Indian financial system and economic growth?

TOPICS FOR FURTHER DISCUSSION

- What are the interlinkages between banking crises, currency crises and sovereign crises? How close are the interlinkages?
- Would international financial cooperation alone ensure financial stability? What are the other factors that contribute to global financial stability?
- Visit the International Monetary Fund website (www.imf.org). What are the financial soundness indicators prescribed by the IMF? Do these indicators ensure financial stability?
- India has faced banking and financial crisis in the past. How were these crises managed and why did they not have the large adverse impact that such crises created in other countries?

ANNEXURE I

BANKING SECTOR REFORMS

The Narasimham Committee I

The banking sector reforms in the 1990s in India were based on the report of the committee headed by Mr M. Narasimham in 1991. Major recommendations of the committee were as follows:

- There should be no bar to new banks being set up in the private sector, provided they have the start up capital and other requirements prescribed by the Reserve Bank of India.
- The government should indicate that there would be no further nationalization of banks and there should not be difference in treatment between public sector banks and private sector banks.
- The banking system should evolve towards a broad pattern consisting of three or four large banks, including the State Bank of India which could become international in character; eight to ten national banks with a network of branches throughout the country engaged in universal banking; local banks whose operations would be generally confined to a specified region and lastly, rural banks to cater to rural areas.
- There should be an assets reconstruction fund (ARF) which could take over from the banks and financial institutions a portion of their bad and doubtful debts at a discount, the level of discount being determined by independent auditors on the basis of clearly defined guidelines. The ARF, according to the committee, should be provided with special powers for recovery, somewhat broader than those contained in Sections 29–32 of the State Financial Corporation Act, 1951. The capital of the ARF should be subscribed to by the public sector banks and the financial institutions.
- The banks and the financial institutions should be authorized to recover bad debts through the special tribunals and based on the valuation given in respect of each asset by a panel of at least two independent auditors.
- The public sector banks with profitable operations should be allowed to tap the capital market for enhancement of their share capital. Subscribers to such issues could be mutual funds, profitable public sector undertakings (PSUs) and the employees of the institutions besides the general public.
- Branch licensing should be abolished and the option of opening branches or closing of branches other than rural branches should be left to the commercial judgment of the individual banks. Further, the internal organization of banks is best left to the judgment of the management of the individual banks.
- There should be phased reduction of the CRR and the SLR.
- Banks should adhere to prescribed capital adequacy ratio (CAR) and should attain a CAR of 8 per cent by 1998.
- A board for financial supervision should be set up to oversee the operations of the banks.
- Banks should conform to prudential income recognition norms of provisioning against bad and doubtful debts and ensure transparency in maintaining balance sheets.
- There should be speedy computerization of the banking industry.

According to the committee, foreign banks should be subjected to the same requirements as are applicable to Indian banks and RBI policies should be more liberal in respect of allowing the foreign banks to open branches or subsidiaries. Joint ventures between foreign banks and Indian banks should also be permitted particularly in regard to merchant banking, investment banking, leasing and other newer forms of financial services. Priority sector lending by banks should be reduced from 40 per cent to 10 per cent of their total credit.

The committee recommended phasing out concessional interest rates. The committee was of the view that the present structure of administered interest rates was highly complex and rigid and proposed that interest rates be further deregulated so as to reflect emerging market conditions. Premature moves to market-determined interest rates could, as experience abroad has shown, pose the danger of excessive bank lending at highly nominal rates to borrowers of dubious credit worthiness, the committee observed.

Most of the recommendations of the committee have since been implemented. Meanwhile, keeping in view the changing global scenario after the setting up of the WTO and the need for more efficient, competitive and broad-based banking sector, the government has set up another committee, once again headed by Mr Narasimhan.

The Narasimham Committee II

The Narasimham Committee, in its second report on banking sector reforms, submitted in April 1998, made a series of sweeping recommendations. The report covers an entire gamut of issues ranging from bank mergers and the creation of globalized banks to bank closures, recasting bank boards and revamping banking legislations.

The major recommendations of the committee were as follows:

- Concept of 'narrow banking' should be tried out to rehabilitate weak banks. If this was not successful, the issue of closure should be examined. Narrow banking, according to the committee, implies that weak banks should not be permitted to invest their funds anywhere except in government securities as these were absolutely safe and risk-free.
- Two or three large Indian banks should be given an international character.
- Small local banks should be confined to states or a cluster of districts in order to serve local trade, small industry and agriculture.
- The committee has also commented on the government's role in public sector banks by observing that government ownership has become an instrument of management. Such micro-management of banks is not conducive to the enhancement of autonomy and flexibility.
- Functions of boards and management need to be reviewed so that the boards remain responsible for enhancing shareholder value through formulation of corporate strategy.
- There is a need to review minimum prescriptions for capital adequacy. In this regard, the committee recommended that minimum CAR be raised to 10 per cent by 2002. Most of the banks have a CAR of 11 per cent or higher.
- The committee also felt a need to lay down prudential and disclosure norms and sound procedures for the purpose of supervision and regulation.
- There should be an integration of NBFC's lending activities into the financial system.
- There is a need for public sector banks to speed up computerization and focus on relationship banking.
- A review of recruitment procedures, training and remuneration policies in public sector banks should be carried out.
- Threat of action by vigilance and other investigative authorities, even in the case of commercial decisions creates low morale. The committee recommended that this issue be addressed in right earnest.
- Need for professionalizing and depoliticizing of bank boards.
- The Banking Service Recruitment Boards should be abolished.

ANNEXURE II

COMMITTEE ON FINANCIAL SECTOR REFORMS—2009: MAIN PROPOSALS OF THE RAGHURAM RAJAN COMMITTEE[52]

The Macroeconomic Framework

Proposal 1: The RBI should formally have a single objective to stay close to a low inflation number or within a range, in the medium term and move steadily to a single instrument, the short-term interest rate (repo and reverse repo) to achieve it.

Proposal 2: Steadily open up investment in the rupee corporate and government bond markets to foreign investors after a clear monetary policy framework is in place.

Broadening Access to Finance

Proposal 3: Allow more entry to private well-governed deposit-taking small finance banks offsetting their higher risk from being geographically focused by requiring higher capital adequacy norms, a strict prohibition on related party transactions and lower allowable concentration norms (loans as a share of capital that can be made to one party). Make significant efforts to create the supervisory capacity to deliver the greater monitoring these banks will need initially, and put in place a tough prompt corrective action regime that ensures these banks do not become public charges.

Proposal 4: Liberalize the banking correspondent regulation so that a wide range of local agents can serve to extend financial services. Use technology both to reduce costs and to limit fraud and misrepresentation.

Proposal 5: Offer priority sector loan certificates (PSLC) to all entities that lend to eligible categories in the priority sector. Allow banks that undershoot their priority sector obligations to buy the PSLC and submit it towards fulfilment of their target.

Proposal 6: Liberalize the interest rate that institutions can charge, ensuring credit reaches the poor, but require (a) full transparency on the actual effective annualized interest cost of a loan to the borrower, (b) periodic public disclosure of maximum and average interest rates charged by the lender to the priority sector and (c) only loans that stay within a margin of local estimated costs of lending to the poor be eligible for PSLCs.

Levelling the Playing Field

Proposal 7: Sell small under performing public sector banks, possibly to another bank or to a strategic investor, to gain experience with the process and gauge outcomes.

Proposal 8: Create stronger boards for large public sector banks, with more power to outside shareholders (including possibly a private sector strategic investor), devolving the power to appoint and compensate top executives to the board.

Proposal 9: After starting the process of strengthening boards, delink the banks from additional government oversight, including the Central Vigilance Commission and Parliament, with the justification that with government-controlled boards governing the banks, a second layer of oversight is not needed. Further ways to justify reduced government oversight is to create bank holding companies where the government only has a direct stake in the holding company. Another is to bring the direct government stake below 50 per cent, perhaps through divestment to other public sector entities or provident funds, so that the government (broadly defined) has control, but the government (narrowly defined) cannot be considered the owner.

Proposal 10: Be more liberal in allowing takeovers and mergers, including domestically incorporated subsidiaries of foreign banks.

Proposal 11: Free banks to set up branches and ATMs anywhere.

Proposal 12: Allow holding company structures, with a parent holding company owning regulated subsidiaries. The holding company should be supervised by the Financial Sector Oversight Agency, with each regulated subsidiary supervised by the appropriate regulator. The holding company should be well diversified if it owns a bank. The holding company structure is shown in the following figure:

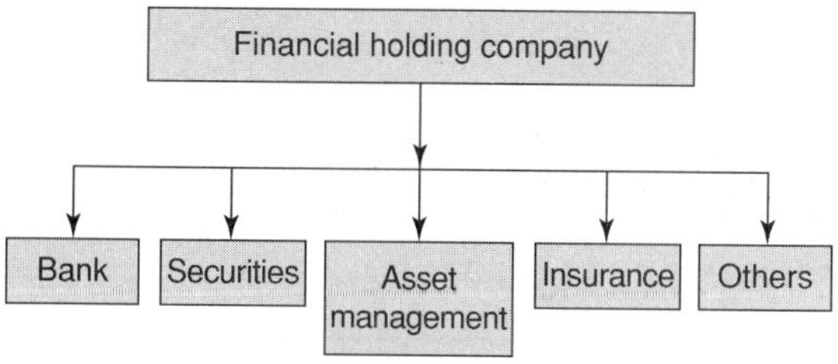

Creating More Efficient and Liquid Markets

Proposal 13: Bring all regulation of trading under the Securities and Exchange Board of India (SEBI).

Proposal 14: Encourage the introduction of markets that are currently missing, such as exchange traded interest rate and exchange rate derivatives.

Proposal 15: Stop creating investor uncertainty by banning markets. If market manipulation is the worry, take direct action against those suspected of manipulation.

Proposal 16: Create the concept of one consolidated membership of an exchange for qualified investors (instead of the current need to obtain memberships for each product traded). Consolidated membership should confer the right to trade all the exchange's products on a unified trading screen with consolidated margining.

Proposal 17: Encourage the setting up of 'professional' markets and exchanges with a higher-order size, that are restricted to sophisticated investors (based on net worth and financial knowledge), where more sophisticated products can be traded.

Proposal 18: Create a more innovation friendly environment, speeding up the process by which products are approved by focusing primarily on concerns of systemic risk, fraud, contract enforcement, transparency and inappropriate sales practices. The threshold for allowing products on professional exchanges (see Proposal 16) or over the counter markets should be lower so that experimentation can take place.

Proposal 19: Allow greater participation of foreign investors in domestic markets as in Proposal 2. Increase participation of domestic investors by reducing the extent to which regulators restrict an institutional investor's choice of investments. Move gradually instead to a 'prudent man' principle where the institutional investor is allowed to exercise judgement based on what a prudent man might deem to be appropriate investments. Emphasize in providing access to suitable equity linked products to the broader population as part of the inclusion agenda.

Creating a Growth Friendly Regulatory Environment

Proposal 20: Rewrite financial sector regulation with only clear objectives and regulatory principles outlined.

Proposal 21: Parliament, through the finance ministry and based on expert opinions as well as the principles enshrined in legislation, should set a specific remit for each regulator every five years. Every year, each regulator should report to a standing committee (possibly the standing committee on finance), explaining in its annual report the progress it has made on meeting the remit. The interactions should be made public. In addition, to ensure there are more direct checks on the regulator in a system that is less rule-bound, the committee recommends Proposal 22.

Proposal 22: Regulatory actions should be subject to appeal to the financial sector appellate tribunal, which will be set up along the lines of, and subsume, the securities appellate tribunal.

Proposal 23: Supervision of all deposit-taking institutions must come under the RBI. Situations where responsibility is shared, such as with the state registrar of cooperative societies should gradually cease. The RBI will have to increase supervisory capacity to take on this task. The committee recognizes that this involves constitutional issues but nevertheless recommends a thorough overhaul of the system of shared responsibility.

Proposal 24: The Ministry of Corporate Affairs (MCA) should review accounts of unlisted companies, while SEBI should review accounts of listed companies.

Proposal 25: A Financial Sector Oversight Agency (FSOA) should be set up by statute. The FSOA's focus will be both macro-prudential as well as supervisory; the FSOA will develop periodic assessments of macroeconomic risks, risk concentrations, as well as risk exposures in the economy; it will monitor the functioning of large, systemically important and financial conglomerates; anticipating potential risks, it will initiate balanced supervisory action by the concerned regulators to address those risks and will address and defuse inter-regulatory conflicts.

Proposal 26: The committee recommends setting up a working group on financial sector reforms with the finance minister as the chairman. The main focus of this working group would be to shepherd financial sector reforms.

Proposal 27: Set up an office of the financial ombudsman (OFO), incorporating all such offices in existing regulators, to serve as an interface between the household and industry.

Proposal 28: The committee recommends strengthening the capacity of the Deposit Insurance and Credit Guarantee Corporation (DICGC) to both monitor risk and resolve a failing bank, instilling a more explicit system of prompt corrective action (see Proposal 3) and making deposit insurance premia more risk-based.

Creating a Robust Infrastructure for Credit

Proposal 29: Expedite the process of creating a unique national ID number with biometric identification.

Proposal 30: The committee recommends movement from a system where information is shared primarily amongst institutional credit providers on the basis of reciprocity to a system of subscription, where information is collected from more sources and a subscriber gets access to data subject to verification of 'need to know and authorization to use' of the subscriber by the credit bureau. This will also require rethinking the incentives of providers to share information and a judicious mix of payments as well as mandatory requirements for information sharing will have to be developed.

Proposal 31: Ongoing efforts to improve land registration and titling-including full cadastral mapping of land, reconciling various registries, forcing compulsory registration of all land transactions, computerizing land records and providing easy remote access to land records-should be expedited, with the centre playing a role in facilitating pilots and sharing experience of best practices. The committee also suggests the possibility of special law courts to clear the backlog of land disputes to be examined.

Proposal 32: Restrictions on tenancy should be re-examined so that tenancy can be formalized in contracts, which can then serve as the basis for borrowing.

Proposal 33: The powers of SRFAESI that are currently conferred only on banks, public financial institutions and housing finance companies should be extended to all institutional lenders.

Proposal 34: Encourage the entry of more well-capitalized ARCs, including ones with foreign backing.

Proposal 35: The committee outlines a number of desirable attributes of a bankruptcy code in the Indian context, many of which are aligned with the recommendations of the Irani Committee. It suggests an expedited move to legislate the needed amendments to company law.

ANNEXURE III

SELECT MAJOR POLICY AND LEGAL REFORMS SINCE 1991–92

Year	Banking/Financial Policy Reform	Legal Reform
1992	Prudential norms for income recognition, asset classification and provisioning norms for advances and for capital adequacy introduced in a phased manner.	
1993	Guidelines for entry of private sector banks released. Process for phased reduction in SLR put in place. The SLR was progressively reduced from its peak of 38.5 per cent in 1992 to the then statutory minimum of 25 per cent in 1997. CRR was progressively reduced from the high of 15 per cent in 1993. Process of interest rate deregulation begins, in respect of both bank deposits and lending.	The recovery of debts due to banks and financial institutions Act enacted. This paved the way for establishment of debt recovery tribunals (DRTs) to enable speedy adjudication and recovery of non-performing loans. The State Bank of India Act amended to throw its shareholding open to public. Amendments made to the banking companies (Acquisition and Transfer of Undertakings Act, 1970/1980), to permit nationalized banks direct access to capital markets to mobilize public shareholding.
1994	The Board for Financial Supervision (BFS) set up within the RBI to provide effective and integrated supervision over the banking system, financial institutions, non banking financial companies and para banking institutions.	
1995	Banking Ombudsman Scheme introduced under the Banking Regulation Act, 1949.	
1997	Stringent norms for assessing permissible bank finance for eligible borrowers phased out.	
2000	Capital to risk weighted assets ratio (CRAR) raised to 9 per cent against the international norm of 8 per cent. First liquidity adjustment facility (LAF) introduced under the RBI's open market operations (OMO).	
2001	Increase in FDI limit in private sector banks to 49 per cent.	
2002		Securitization and reconstruction of financial assets and enforcement of Security Interest Act, 2002 (SARFAESI Act) promulgated[6] Prevention of Money Laundering Act (PMLA), 2002, empowers banks to combat the menace of crime-related money. Multi State Cooperative Societies Act, 2002, empowers the central government issue directives to cooperatives in public interest, even superseding Board decisions, if warranted.

2003	Concept of benchmark prime lending rate (BPLR) introduced for transparent pricing of loans.	SARFAESI Act extended to cooperative banks through a notification. Negotiable instruments (NI) (amendments and miscellaneous provisions) Act, 2002, (effective 2003) expands definition of 'cheque' (as in NI Act, 1881) to include 'electronic cheque' and 'cheque truncation'.
2004	Increase in FDI limit in private sector banks from 49 per cent to 74 per cent. Risk based supervision (RBS) approach initiated to monitor each institution according to its risk profile real time gross settlement (RTGS) system operationalized for settlement of transactions.	
2005	Comprehensive policy framework for governance of private sector banks. Roadmap drawn up for presence of foreign banks in India. State level task force for urban cooperative banks (TAFCUB) set up to overcome dual control issues over urban cooperative banks. Introduction of 'no frills' accounts (with nil or low minimum balances) to ensure financial inclusion. National electronic fund transfer (NEFT) introduced.	Credit Information Companies Act, 2005, provides regulation of credit information companies.
2006	Business facilitator/business correspondent (BC) model introduced to include services of non-governmental organizations (NGOs), micro-finance institutions (MFIs) and other civil society organizations as intermediaries for providing banking services. Banking code and standard board of India (BCBSI) brings out code of banks' commitment to customers. BCBSI is a collaborative effort between the RBI and the banking industry to promote sound banking practices, increase transparency and instil trust in customers.	RBI (Amendment) Act, 2006, provides RBI flexibility in deciding reserve requirements[55] for banks and also confers comprehensive powers to regulate money and government securities markets. Section 42 of the Banking Regulation Act amended to remove ceiling (20 per cent) and floor (3 per cent) on the cash reserve ratio (CRR). Banking Companies (Acquisition and transfer of undertakings) and Financial Institutions Laws (Amendment) Act, 2006, specifies corporate governance norms for the banking sector. Government Securities Act, 2006, empowers RBI to hold and transfer government securities more efficiently.
2007	Banks allowed to take up pension fund management (PFM) through subsidiaries.	The Banking Companies (Amendment) Act, 2007, provides RBI with the power to specify statutory liquidity ratio (SLR) without any floor. Section 24 of the Banking Regulation Act amended to permit this. The Securities Contract (Amendment) Regulation (SR) Act, 2007, amends SR Act, 1956, to provide legal framework to trade in securitized debt, including mortgage-backed securities. The Government Securities Act (GS Act), 2006, replaces the Public Debt Act, 1944, and repealed the Indian Securities Act, 1920. The new Act has more investor friendly provisions. The Payments and Settlements Act, 2007, gives RBI wide supervisory and regulatory powers in respect of the payment systems.
2008	Second LAF reintroduced for better liquidity management by RBI. Banking code for medium and small enterprises (MSE) customers released, intended to give fillip to banks' positive commitment to this sector.	Regulations framed under Payments and Settlements Act, 2007, Board for Regulation and Supervision of Payment and Settlements Regulations, 2008 and Payment and Settlements Systems Regulations, 2008.
2011	Deregulation of interest rates on savings bank deposits and certain categories of non-resident deposits.	
2011	Marginal Standing Facility (MSF) introduced for enhanced liquidity.	

2012	Bank rate aligned to Marginal Standing Facility (MSF) rate (*Details can be found in the next chapter*).	
2012	Priority sector guidelines revised.	
2012	New bank applications called for to enhance financial inclusion.	Final guidelines after the amendment Banking Regulation Act.
2012	Roadmap and guidelines for Basel III implementation.	
2012	Compensation guidelines for private sector and foreign banks issued – governance, risk based and disclosure norms will be in line with the Basel committee proposals.	
2012	Factoring Regulation Act, 2012.	The Act provides a regulatory framework under which factors would be required to register with the Reserve Bank.
2012	The Financial Sector Legislative Reforms Commission (FSLRC) was set up by the Government of India to make the laws governing the financial sector compatible with a growing, globalized and modernizing economy; and to reflect the lessons of the global financial crisis.	The Commission has proposed changes in the landscape of financial sector. The proposals cover consumer protections, dedicated and unified resolution authority, inter- regulatory coordination, development function and providing independence to the regulators/ central bank with accountability. The Commission has envisaged a regulatory framework where governance standards for regulated entities will not depend on the form of organization of the financial firm, such as, co-operatives, private Indian firms, foreign firms and public sector firms.
2012	Mandatory prior approval from RBI for acquiring five per cent or more of the share capital of a banking company. The notification confers power to RBI to impose conditions as it deems necessary while granting such approvals.	Provisions have been made in the Banking Regulation Act, 1949. This has been effected by an amendment notified by the Government of India vide Banking Law Amendments Act, 2012.
2013	Guidelines for setting up of Wholly-owned subsidiaries by foreign banks.	
2013	Banking Laws Amendment Act, 2013.	The Act gives RBI powers to supersede the board of directors of a banking company subject to a total period of 12 months and appoint an administrator till alternate arrangements are made. It also confers power to raise the ceiling on voting rights from 10 to 26 per cent in a phased manner. Stipulates prior approval of RBI for acquisition of 5 per cent or more shares or voting rights in a banking company.
2013	The Enforcement of Security Interest and Recovery of Debt Laws (Amendment) Act, 2012.	The Act amends the Securitization and Reconstruction of Financial Assets and Enforcement of Security Interest Act, 2002 (SARFAESI Act) and the Recovery of Debts Due to Banks and Financial Institutions Act, 1993 (RDDBFI Act).
2013	National Housing Bank Amendment Bill, 2012.	It seeks to amend the National Housing Bank (NHB) Act, 1987. The Bill provides for transfer of shareholding of the RBI in NHB to the Central Government to avoid conflict of ownership and regulatory role. To ensure uniform control over non-banking financial companies including housing finance companies, powers related to registration and regulation over housing finance companies are proposed to be transferred to the Reserve Bank. NHB will concentrate on supervision and financing of such institutions.
2013	The Micro Finance Institutions (Development and Regulation) Bill, 2012.	To provide a statutory framework for promotion, development, regulation and orderly growth of micro finance institutions (MFI) and thereby facilitate financial inclusion.

Sources: RBI reports on currency and finance—various years.

RBI reports on trend and progress of banking in India—various years.

ENDNOTES

1. News item accessed at http://www.washingtontimes.com/news/2014/jan/1/young-stop-the-money-presses/, on January 2, 2014.
2. News item accessed at http://www.theguardian.com/business/2013/apr/04/japan-quantitative-easing-70bn, on January 2, 2014.
3. Accessed at http://www.csmonitor.com/World/Europe/2013/0329/What-s-behind-the-bailout-crisis-in-Cyprus, on January 2, 2014.
4. BIS, Monetary and Economic department, 'Financial crises and bank funding: recent experience in the euro area', by Adrian van Rixtel and Gabriele Gasperini, Working paper no. 406, March 2013.
5. RBI, March 2009, 'India's financial sector—an assessment', Volume III, Advisory panel on financial stability assessment and stress testing, committee on financial sector assessment (CFSA), Government of India and RBI, chart 1.1, page 32.
6. 'Creditworthiness' of borrowers is discussed in detail in the chapters on lending.
7. 'Credit risk' and 'interest rate risk' are discussed in detail in the Chapters 'Managing Credit Risk' and 'Risk Management in Banks', respectively.
8. 'Securitization' and 'credit derivatives' are discussed in detail in the Chapter 'Managing Credit Risk'.
9. 'Liquidity risk' is discussed in detail in the Chapter 'Risk Management in Banks'.
10. Analysis of banks' financial statements is discussed in the relevant chapter.
11. The Reserve Bank of India (RBI), in its 'Report of trend and progress of banking in India, 2007–2008' clarifies, 'While under normal conditions, the financial system can be considered to be stable if it is generally free from imbalances, in periods of stress, financial stability would depend on the ability of financial markets (in terms of infrastructure and organization) and participants in these markets (intermediaries, investors and financial providers) not only to absorb shocks, but also to work properly (*i.e.*, without major/lasting disruptions) when confronted with an unexpected shock of any nature (such as burst, bubble or terrorist attacks)'. (Chapter VII, page 253)
12. RBI Monthly Bulletin, October 2009, Speech by the RBI governor Dr D Subbarao, 'Financial Stability—Issues and Challenges', page 1698.
13. Final report of the G 20 Working Group I, March 25, 2009. The G 20 comprises of the following countries—Argentina, Australia, Brazil, Canada, China, EU, France, Germany, India, Indonesia, Italy, Japan, Mexico, Russia, Saudi Arabia, South Africa, South Korea, Turkey, the United Kingdom and the United States. The Working Group was constituted to review and make recommendations that will strengthen international regulatory standards, enhance transparency in global financial markets and ensure all financial markets, products and participants are appropriately regulated or subject to oversight.
14. International Monetary Fund (IMF) Working Paper (WP/09/70), April 2009, 'Financial Stability and the Role of Central Banks: Lessons from the crisis', prepared by Erlend W Nier.
15. Chapters on 'Credit risk', 'Investments', 'Capital' and 'Risk management' explain this role in detail.
16. These tools are described in the Chapters on 'Monetary policy' and 'Sources of bank funds'.
17. This aspect is discussed in the Chapter on 'Retail banking'.
18. These aspects are dealt with throughout the book wherever relevant.
19. The Basel 2 framework is discussed in the Chapter 'Capital—Risk, Regulation and Adequacy'.
20. Discussed in the Chapter 'Risk Management in Banks'.
21. Discussed in chapters relating to 'Banks' Financial Statements' and 'Risk Management in Banks'.
22. The role of credit rating is discussed in the chapter related to 'Bank lending'.
23. Discussed later in this chapter in relation to India.
24. Most of these terms are defined in related chapters in the book.
25. The Financial Stability Board (FSB) (www.financialstabilityboard.org) is hosted by the Bank for International Settlements (BIS) (www.bis.org). The FSB has been established to coordinate at the international level the work of national financial authorities and international standard setting bodies and to develop and promote the implementation of effective regulatory, supervisory and other financial sector policies.
26. For a discussion on the primary differences between financial markets and intermediaries, see chapters 'Monetary policy tools for bank management' and 'The lending function'.
27. Speech delivered by Dr K C Chakraborty, Deputy Governor, RBI, on August 31, 2009, titled 'Banking and finance in India: Developments, issues and prospects', accessed at www.rbi.org.in
28. 'Market depth' is a concept related to its 'liquidity'. An asset that can be easily bought or sold in the market is termed 'liquid'. Hence 'cash' is the most liquid asset. In terms of financial instruments, liquidity signifies the extent to which a financial asset can be bought and sold in the market without affecting its price. In terms of the market, 'depth' signifies the ability of the market to sustain large orders without impacting the price of securities being traded in the market.
29. The RBI regulates the foreign exchange markets. The Foreign Exchange Dealers' Association of India (FEDAI) frames rules for conduct of foreign exchange business. Settlement of transactions are done through Central Clearing Corporation of India Ltd. (CCIL).
30. Though open to individual investors, the government securities market is largely wholesale in nature. The major investors are banks, insurance companies, primary dealers, pension funds and foreign institutional investors (FII). At the end of September 2009, there were 19 primary dealers, of which 11 were banks (Bank-PDs) and the remaining eight stand-alone primary dealers registered as NBFCs under section 45IA of the RBI Act, 1934.

31. Though RBI is the regulator, where instruments are listed/traded on stock exchanges, they come under SEBI's purview. The Fixed Income Money Market and Derivatives Association of India (FIMMDA) and the primary dealers (PD) also have important roles in the market.
32. OTC—Over the counter (market trading)—as contrasted with 'traded on a recognized exchange'.
33. Described in Chapter 'Monetary Policy Tools for Bank Management'.
34. Described in Chapter 'Risk Management in Banks'.
35. IOSCO—International Organization of Securities Commissions—is part of the 'joint forum' of international financial regulators. IOSCO's members are the regulators of the world's securities and derivatives markets. Its stated objectives are to maintain just, efficient and sound markets through international co-operation, information exchange, establishment of standards and surveillance of international transactions and mutual assistance to promote integrity of markets. More information on IOSCO is provided in Chapter 'Sources of Funds'. The IOSCO 'principles' can be accessed at www.iosco.org
36. The major portion of this book will be devoted to this market.
37. The function and parts of a financial system are described in the Chapter 'Monetary Policy Tools for Bank Management'.
38. Includes foreign direct investment (FDI), foreign institutional investors (FII) (24–49 per cent) and non-resident Indians (NRI) (5–24 per cent).
39. NABARD—National Bank for Agriculture and Rural Development—is an all India development financial institution (DFI)—see Figure 1.5B.
40. The major intermediaries included under this group in India are development finance institutions (DFI), insurance companies, non-banking finance companies (NBFC), primary dealers (PD) and capital market intermediaries such as mutual funds (MF). Internationally, NBFIs are also called 'other financial intermediaries' (OFIs) that took a good share of the blame for the 2007 financial crisis. (See Box 1.2).
41. For example, banks can today deal in other financial products, such as insurance or mutual funds.
42. Briefly, NOF for NBFCs is measured as the total of paid up capital and free reserves less intangible assets, such as accumulated losses and deferred revenue expenditure. This figure is further adjusted by netting off investments and loans and advances to subsidiaries, companies in the same group and investments in excess of 10 per cent (of owned fund) in other NBFCs.
43. 'Exposure norms' are discussed in the chapter on 'Bank Lending'.
44. When the financial crisis of 2007 caused tight liquidity in the markets, NBFCs were severely impacted. To ease the stress on liquidity, RBI permitted some temporary measures, such as permitting NBFC-ND-SI to (a) raise foreign currency borrowings through approval route (discussed in the chapter 'Sources of bank funds'), (b) relax SLR maintenance, (c) borrow from banks at reduced risk weights, (d) issue perpetual debt instruments, (e) deferred stricter capital adequacy maintenance norms and (f) access a special 'lender of last resort' facility from RBI.
45. See chapter on 'Banks' Sources of Funds'.
46. CFSA, March 2009, volume II, page 185.
47. Primary Dealers (PD) deal in the government securities market—both in its primary and secondary segments. The PDs typically have a standing arrangement with RBI based on the execution of an undertaking and the authorization letter issued by RBI. They are registered with Securities and Exchange Board of India (SEBI) and are members of self-regulatory organizations (SROs) like Primary Dealers Association of India (PDAI) and Fixed Income Money Market and Derivatives Association (FIMMDA).
48. The WOCCU is the global trade association and development agency for credit unions, and is headquartered in Madison, Wisconsin, USA, with offices in Washington and program offices worldwide. Its current membership is 186 million people from 54,000 credit unions spread across 97 countries. It promotes sustainable development of credit unions and other financial co-operatives with a stated vision to 'improve people's lives' through credit unions, translating into 'empowering people through access to high quality and affordable financial services'. WOCCU works with national governments to improve legislation and regulation and runs 'technical assistance programs' to introduce new tools and technologies to improve credit unions' performance. The council is funded by government agency and foundation grants, member dues and annual gifts from supporters. More details can be accessed at www.woccu.org
49. Interestingly, central banks in most other countries in the world, including the United States, were set up to address the problem of bank failures.
50. Mohan, Rakesh, 2007, 'India's financial sector reforms: fostering growth while containing risk', Address by Dr Mohan, Deputy Governor, RBI, at Yale university on 3 December 2007, accessed at www.rbi.org.in
51. During the 1980s, the fiscal deficit was met through issue of ad hoc treasury bills. This caused expansion in money supply. Interest rate regulation, high reserve requirements and stringent credit rationing were used as the means to restrict expansion in money supply. For more on money supply and monetary policy, please refer to the Chapter 'Monetary Policy Tools for Bank Management'.
52. 'A hundred small steps', Report of the committee on financial sector reforms, Planning commission, Government of India, 2009, accessed at www.planningcommission.nic.in
53. 'Financial stability: Issues and challenges', Speech by D Subbarao, Governor, RBI, at the FICCI-IBA annual conference, September 2009, accessed at www.rbi.org.in

CHAPTER TWO

Monetary Policy—Implications for Bank Management

CHAPTER STRUCTURE

KEY TAKEAWAYS FROM THE CHAPTER

- Understand the role of central bank and monetary policy in economic growth.
- Understand why banks hold reserves.
- Learn about the tools of monetary policy.
- Understand how the monetary policy impacts banking operations and management.

SECTION I

BASIC CONCEPTS

A Macroeconomic View

The primary objective of a country's government is to achieve economic stability and growth. Hence, macroeconomic policies will typically target and monitor three basic indicators: prices, employment and balance of payments. Such monitoring is done through two fundamental pillars of macroeconomic policy—the fiscal and monetary policies.

The fiscal policy targets two major parameters: tax receipts and government expenditure. While taxes are garnered through the mechanism of tax rates that can be varied by the government from time to time, government expenditure is planned and monitored through the annual and long-term plans formulated by the government.

The monetary policy targets the vital parameters that determine the liquidity and capital formation in the economy, as seen in the pictorial depiction given in Figure 2.1, and is formulated by the Central Bank of the country.

FIGURE 2.1 VITAL PARAMETERS THAT DETERMINE LIQUIDITY AND CAPITAL FORMATION IN THE ECONOMY

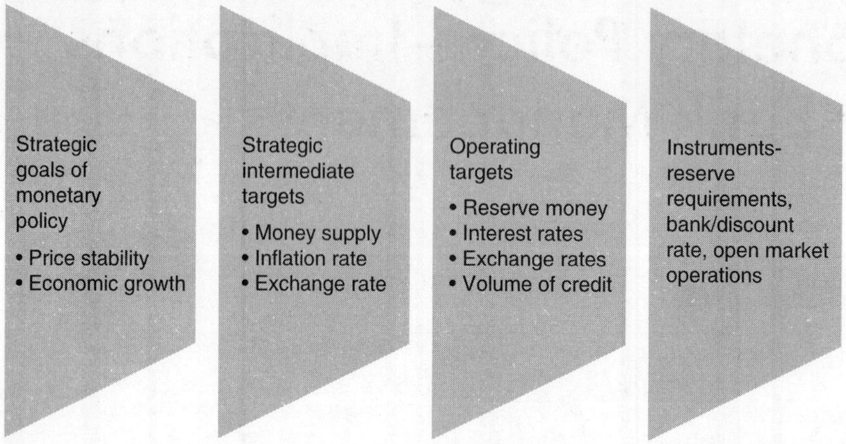

In the 1930s, John Maynard Keynes focussed attention on the use of fiscal policy to manage business cycles, and this emphasis continued well into the 1960s. However, Keynes' theory could not provide satisfactory answers to the worldwide stagflation of the 1970s. Further, some governments, for political reasons, were more inclined to run deficits than surpluses. The rapid changes in the economic and business environments could not be adequately supported by legislative processes or policies. In contrast, the monetary policy, formulated by the central banks, appeared more insulated from political pressures, and hence was seen as being able to impose more economic restraint. Since the 1980s, policy makers have come to rely more on the monetary policy to manage the business cycle and achieve price stability.

Theoretically, monetary policies rest on a simple identity that economists know too well:

$$M 3 V 5 P 3 Q$$

In this equation, M equals money supply, V the velocity or turnover of money, P the price level and Q the quantity of output. Simply stated, the economic output or the GDP, measured in monetary terms, equals the amount of money in circulation times the frequency with which the money changes hands. Hence, in essence, both sides of this equation represent the nominal GDP.

This deceptively simple-looking equation, however, raises pertinent questions.

- What is money?
- What determines money supply?
- How do we measure money supply?
- What should be the basis of monetary policy?

A deeper understanding of and clarity in respect of the above concepts will help effective use of the equation for policy formulation.

Money 'Money' is generally defined as anything that people are willing to accept in payment for goods and services or to pay off debts—in other words, money is generally an acceptable medium of exchange, usable by all, with standardized quality, durable, divisible and easy to transport. 'Currency', therefore, is undeniably 'money'.

Money has other characteristics as well.

- It is a 'store of value'. This implies that money is a measure of 'value', and can be held for future use. However, in times of inflation, 'money' retained as 'currency', could lose 'real' value.

TEASE THE CONCEPT

What is the difference between 'money'—defined as currencies and an alternative financial asset, say a money market instrument or physical assets such as real estate?

- It is a 'unit of accounting'.
- It is a 'standard for deferred payment'. This implies that for a transaction done today, payment could be made later.
- It is the 'means of final payment'. This is a characteristic unique to money.

TEASE THE CONCEPT

Are the following 'money'?

- Cheques
- Travellers' cheques
- Debit cards
- Demand deposit accounts
- Credit cards
- Gift coupons, tokens, which can also be exchanged for goods and services

Money Supply Money supply is the total quantity of money in the economy. While we will look at the various measurement parameters adopted by central banks a little later, in the narrow sense, 'money supply' is defined as the currency in circulation in the economy plus demand deposits[1] with banks.

Only the central bank has the power to authorize creation of 'currency' (notes and coins) that we carry around in our wallets. Banks, however, can 'create' deposits (and credit).

How are banks able to create deposits? The simple example given in the Box 2.1 illustrates this iterative process.

Why do banks not lend all the deposits that they get? Banks are obligated to pay depositors as and when they demand repayment of their deposits. Any demur on the part of a bank to repay deposits would cause panic among the depositors, and the bank would be dubbed unsafe. Hence, reserves ensure 'liquidity' for the bank. Most central banks, therefore, insist that a portion of the liabilities of banks be kept as 'reserve', either as cash or balances with the central bank or as near cash securities.

BOX 2.1 HOW BANKS CREATE DEPOSITS/CREDIT—THE CONCEPT OF THE MONEY MULTIPLIER

Let us look at a highly simplified example.

Suppose, an individual X deposits ₹100 of currency into his demand deposit account in Bank A. Although Bank A is obligated to repay ₹100 on demand to X or any other third party designated by X, the Bank, for commercial reasons, will probably lend a sizeable portion—say ₹80 of the deposit to another person, say Y. Now, X has a demand deposit of ₹100 and Y has currency worth ₹80. In other words, Bank A has increased the 'money supply' to ₹180 on a base of ₹100. In this case, ₹100 is called the 'monetary base'. The iterative process starts here. Y will either deposit the loan ₹80 in his Bank B or pay to a third party who will, in turn, deposit the amount with Bank B. In any case, a new demand deposit of ₹80 is created. If we assume that all banks lend 80 per cent of the amount they take in as demand deposits and all money thus lent is redeposited in full into a bank, Bank B will lend ₹64 to say, Z, who in turn, deposits this amount with Bank C. The iterations can be represented as follows:

$$\text{Money supply} = 100 + [4/5]\ 3\ 100 + [4/5]\ 3\ [4/5]\ 3\ 100 + \cdots \text{ and so on.}$$

The process can be recognized as a Geometric Progression (GP) whose summation would be 100/[1 2 4/5], or 100/0.20 5 100 3 5 5 500.

Let us now sum up our calculations as follows:

Bank	Deposits Received	Loans Made	Required Reserves
A	100	80	20
B	80	64	16
C	64	51.2	12.8 … and so on
Final amount (all banks)	500	400	100

It is thus seen that the initial deposit of ₹100 has created ₹500 deposits or 400 of credit in the banking system. In other words, 'money supply' can be calculated by multiplying the monetary base by the inverse of the leakage', which is the proportion of deposits that the banks have retained with themselves. The inverse of the 'leakage', in this case 5, is called the 'money multiplier'.[2]

TEASE THE CONCEPT

- What happens to the money multiplier if the leakage is (a) 25 per cent or (b) 10 per cent?
- What will be the impact on money supply if, instead of depositing the entire loan amount into another bank, X, Y, Z and others in the example above, retain 5 per cent of the loan amount as cash?

In most countries, the central bank sets the 'reserve requirements', thus, placing a cap on the ability of banks to create credit. Although banks almost always hold reserves in excess of statutory requirement, the size of this excess is quite small. Excess reserves maintained with the central bank impose a cost on banks that equals earnings foregone on the amount by which required reserves exceed the reserves that banks would voluntarily hold in order to conduct their business. This practice of setting aside a portion of the bank's deposits to meet liabilities is also called 'fractional reserve banking'.[3]

Therefore, it is evident that the size of the monetary base and the level of leakage determine the money supply in the economy. The central bank can control the monetary base and strongly influence the leakage.

A typical central bank's balance sheet has the following components:

Liabilities	**Assets**
Currency (about 80 per cent)	Government securities (about 80 per cent)
Deposits from banks (about 20 per cent)	Foreign exchange (about 10 per cent)
(these are the reserves maintained by banks)	Gold (about 10 per cent)

The total liabilities of the central bank constitute the 'monetary base'.

Measuring Money Supply There are three broad measures economists use when looking at the money supply: M1, a narrow measure of money's function as a medium of exchange; M2, a broader measure that also reflects money's function as a store of value; and M3, a still broader measure that covers items regarded as close substitutes of money. The indicators that measure money supply, though conceptually similar, differ in nomenclature and composition from country to country. Basically, all countries measure their money supply through a 'narrow money' and 'broad money' definition. While the narrow money definition restricts itself to money held for immediate transactions, such as notes and coins with the public, and transaction accounts (*e.g.*, demand deposits) held with banks, the broad money concept includes time deposits as well as other forms of money supply defined by the central bank.

For example, in the United Kingdom, narrow money is termed M0—this is simply the total stock of notes and coins in circulation plus the commercial bankers' operational deposits held with the Bank of England. Broad money is termed as M4 and includes M0 plus sterling deposits held by the UK residents at bank and building societies. Broad money (or M4), therefore, comprises both the deposits lodged into accounts by people wanting to save, together with deposits created by commercial banks and building societies through their lending activities.

In the United States, monetary measures are defined as follows:

- M0: The total of all coins and paper cash in circulation.
- M1: M0 + the amount in checking or demand deposit accounts.
- M2: M1 + other various savings account types, money market accounts and certificate of deposit (CD) accounts of below USD 100,000.
- M3: M2 + all other CDs, deposits of eurodollars and repurchase agreements.

Central Bank Tools to Regulate Money Supply

Most central banks use three primary tools to influence money supply in the economy.

First, the central bank determines 'reserve requirements'. We have seen in the simple example in the previous box that the 'leakage' or 'reserves' impact the credit creation ability of banks. When the central bank decreases the reserve requirement, the money multiplier increases, and, thus, money supply expands. Remember that the money supply identity is the product of the monetary base and the money multiplier.

Conversely, by increasing the reserve requirement, the central bank causes the money multiplier to fall, thus contracting money supply. Alteration in the reserve requirement can have an immediate impact on the availability of credit in the economy, through effecting a change in the money multiplier.

The second tool is the 'discount rate' or 'bank rate'. Banks can borrow directly from the central bank through the 'discount window'. The term 'discount window' originated with the practice of banks selling loans or short-term notes to the central bank at a discount. Such loans or 'refinancing' from the central bank add directly to the existing monetary base by increasing bank reserves thus leading to an expansion in money supply. The central bank periodically determines the size of the discount—which is called the 'discount rate'. The 'discount rate' is also called the 'bank rate' since this is the rate at which banks borrow from the central bank. By lowering this rate, the central bank makes borrowing more attractive to banks, and by increasing this rate and making funds dearer, it attempts to discourage banks from borrowing. Typically increase or decrease of the bank rate is considered a 'signal' for banks to raise or lower their interest rates. Higher interest rates are expected to discourage credit growth in the economy, since it is assumed that borrowers will borrow less or desist from borrowing when interest rates rise. Therefore, in such cases, a hike in the bank rate is designed to restrict money supply.[4]

The third, and in many cases, the most important tool of the central bank is 'open-market operations' (OMOs). The central bank influences the money supply in the economy by buying or selling bonds and other financial instruments in the open market. When the central bank, say, buys government securities from banks and other parties, it injects liquidity into the economy and, thus, increases the monetary base. When the central bank sells securities, it absorbs liquidity and, thus, reduces the monetary base. OMOs are the primary policy instruments of central banks of developed countries, and are becoming increasingly important in developing countries. OMOs are a form of indirect control over the reserves in the banking system, as contrasted with the direct control exercised by, say, the cash reserve ratio (CRR). Developing indirect controls is vital to the process of economic development. As markets in globalized economies grow and expand, market forces seek to unleash their potential and direct controls start losing their efficacy. However, for OMOs to become an important part of the monetary policy, market infrastructure needs to be revamped, and the existing tools of monetary policy would need to undergo some modifications.

It is, therefore, evident that the central bank can regulate the money supply in the economy by changing the money multiplier (changing the reserve requirements) or by changing the monetary base (altering bank rates or through OMOs).

To summarize, the three tools of Monetary Policy operate as shown in Table 2.1.

TABLE 2.1 OPERATION AND IMPACT OF THE THREE TOOLS OF MONETARY POLICY

Central Bank Action	Expected Impact on Banks	Expected Impact on Monetary Base/Money Multiplier	Expected Impact on Money Supply
Increase discount rate	Borrowings by banks decrease	Monetary base decreases	Money supply decreases
Decrease discount rate	Borrowings by banks increase	Monetary base increases	Money supply increases
Increase reserve requirements	Higher leakage	Money multiplier decreases	Money supply decreases
Decrease reserve requirements	Lower leakage	Money multiplier increases	Money supply increases
Open market purchases	Injection of liquidity	Monetary base increases	Money supply increases
Open market sales	Absorption of liquidity	Monetary base decreases	Money supply decreases

The Impact of OMOs on Other Tools of Monetary Policy

OMOs can typically be conducted in an 'active' or 'passive' manner. Under active OMOs, the central bank aims at a predetermined quantity of reserves, and allows the interest rates (the price of these reserves) to fluctuate freely. This approach is typically used in countries where the interbank or secondary markets are less efficient. Many central banks in developed and developing countries with sophisticated markets, however, prefer the passive approach, in which a predetermined interest rate is aimed at, while allowing the reserves to fluctuate.

However, when OMOs are used as a primary policy instrument, the use of other instruments, such as discount (bank) rate and the CRR, becomes more selective and restricted. Why does this happen?

Let us first consider the bank rate. Effective OMOs also presupposes that banks' access to central bank funds needs to be restricted. The discount rate should, therefore, be pegged at a level that makes it unattractive for banks to borrow from the central bank. In some countries, penalties and restrictive clauses are used to limit banks' access to central bank funds. Of course, these restrictions and penalties should be flexible enough to permit short-term adjustments to banks' liquidity when the need arises, or serve long-term emergency funding requirements in a distress situation.

Reserve requirements in the nature of CRR are considered 'basic' compared with the level of sophistication that OMOs demand of the market. Central bank in several developed countries impose minimal or no reserve requirements on their banks. However, reserve requirements are still used in many instances as a way of enhancing the efficacy of OMOs and regulating money supply in the short term. They are seen to be particularly useful where the central bank has to adjust banks' liquidity rapidly or signal the need for expansion or contraction of money supply.

Central Bank Signaling Through the 'Policy Rate'

Most central banks announce their policy stance through a single rate—the 'Policy rate'. The Policy rate could be a target for a market interest rate (*e.g.*, the overnight interbank market interest rate). Or it could take the form of an official rate of a central bank operation or facility, such as the Bank rate or Repo rate. Central banks running exchange rate-based regimes with no capital controls may not be able to set policy interest rates.

Their exchange rates/capital flows determine the money market and other interest rates within their countries. Thus, the factors determining choice of an appropriate policy rate for central banks to signal their operational measures are the functionality and controllability of the official policy rate.

Popularity of the 'Repo' Rate as the Policy Rate

The widespread use of OMOs has given rise to active 'Repo' markets in many countries. In Repo (the abbreviated form for 'Repurchase agreements') transactions, securities are exchanged for cash, with an agreement to repurchase the securities at a later date. The securities form the collateral for the 'cash loan', and the cash form the collateral for the securities loan. The securities typically used are sovereign debt instruments, private sector debt instruments, such as commercial paper or mortgage-backed securities (MBS) or equity. As repos are short maturity (varying between overnight and 1 year) collateralized instruments, repo markets have strong linkages with other short-term markets, such as inter-bank and money markets, as also with derivatives and securities markets. Another positive feature of an active repo market is that it helps to enhance liquidity in the underlying securities, thus, leading to an active secondary market (*see* Box 2.2).

BOX 2.2 HOW DO REPOS WORK?

A repurchase agreement or repo, is a sale of securities for cash with a commitment to repurchase them at a specified price at a future date.

The repurchase agreement by itself is simply a collateralized loan. However, the operation resembles a spot purchase + forward sale of a bond. Representing the transaction in the form of an equation would clarify:

Repo = spot purchase + forward sale of a bond

Now, we know that

Forward sale = spot sale of bond + lending money to settlement date

Therefore, the earlier equation stands modified as

Repo = spot purchase + spot sale + lending money

Since the net effect of spot purchase and sale would be null, repo is similar to 'lending money'. See the pictorial depiction shown below.

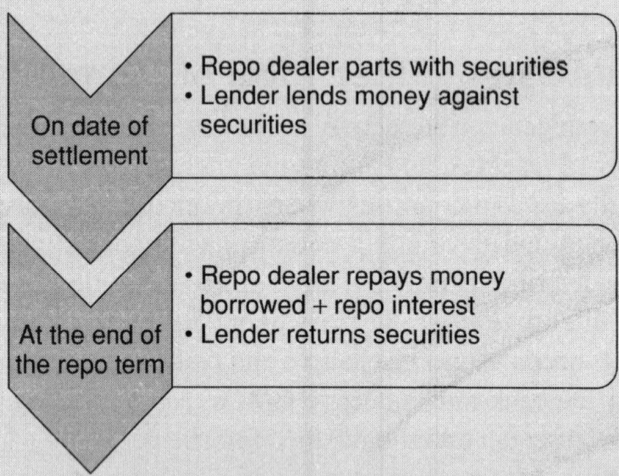

The lenders are typically banks, money market funds, corporations, etc., while the dealers or borrowers would typically be banks or securities dealers or other market participants permitted to deal in repos. The securities are typically government securities and other securities approved by the respective regulatory authorities.

The predominant form of repo is the 'overnight repo', where the duration of the loan is one day. Term repos can have maturities of up to 1 year.

A 'reverse repo' is the exact opposite of a repo transaction. The transaction labels are usually determined from the dealer's standpoint—hence when the dealer 'borrows', it is a 'repo' (the borrowing is at the 'repo rate') and if the dealer 'lends', the transaction is a 'reverse repo'.

For example, assume the repo rate to be 9 per cent and the reverse repo rate to be 7 per cent. Since we are viewing the transaction from the dealer's perspective, 9 per cent would be the rate the dealer would earn when he lends money and 'buys' securities. When the securities are delivered in the reverse repo transaction, the dealer effectively 'sells' the securities to receive money at a cost, which is the reverse repo rate. The difference is the dealer's earnings from the collateralized loan transaction.

It is, therefore, clear that interest rate on repos is the rate at which the dealer compensates the lender for temporary use of money, and should be related to other money market interest rates as well. Usually, the securities pledged in a repo are valued at current market prices plus accrued interest (on coupon-bearing securities), less a small 'haircut' (discount) to reduce the lender's market risk exposure. The longer the term and the riskier and less liquid the securities pledged for a repo transaction, the larger will be the 'haircut' to protect the lender against fall in the security price. Therefore, repos are 'marked to market' periodically, and if the prices of the securities pledged have dropped, the borrower would have to pledge additional collateral.

Interest income from repos is usually determined as follows:

Repo interest income 5 amount of loan 3 current repo rate 3 no. of days/360

(Note that 360 days a year is assumed by convention)

To illustrate, an overnight loan of ₹1 crore to a dealer at a repo rate of 9 per cent would yield interest income of ₹2,500 by the above formula. Under a continuing contract repo, the rate would change everyday. Hence, the interest income would be calculated for each day the funds were lent, and total interest would be paid to the lender when the contract period ends.

In such a case, the yield on repurchase agreements is represented by the following equation:

$$\text{Yield } (Y_r) \; 5 \; [(RP_m \; 2 \; RP_s)/RP_s] \; 3 \; (360/t_d)$$

where, Yield Y_r is an annualized percentage, assuming a 360 day year by convention,
RP_m is the repurchase price of the securities (selling price + interest paid on the repurchase agreement),
RP_s is the selling price of the securities, and
t_d is the number of days until maturity of the repo.

To illustrate the above, assume a bank enters a reverse repo agreeing to buy treasury bills from another market participant at a price of ₹1 crore, with an agreement to sell back the securities at a price of ₹1,00,09,000 (interest being ₹9,000) after 5 days. The yield on the repo transaction to the bank is calculated as follows:

$$Y_r \; 5 \; [(1{,}00{,}09{,}000 \; 2 \; 1{,}00{,}00{,}000)/1{,}00{,}00{,}000] \; 3 \; (360/5) \; 5 \; 6.48 \text{ per cent}$$

How are repos useful as a monetary policy instrument? Their attractiveness stems from the fact that the features of repo contracts are well-suited to influence the interest rates in the economy, through impacting two of the main channels of monetary policy—controlling liquidity in money markets and signalling to markets the desired interest rate levels.

Repos and reverse repos are often used by central banks to offset short-term fluctuations in bank reserves. They are also used for adjusting large liquidity imbalances arising out of, say, large capital inflows or outflows. Repos can be used for various maturities, though they are predominantly used for short-term transactions (including overnight transactions). Outright purchases and sales of government securities in the secondary market forms an important part of the repo market in many countries.

Box 2.3 briefly outlines the effects of the recent sub-prime crisis[5] on the monetary policy of the USA.

BOX 2.3 THE SUB-PRIME CRISIS AND USA'S MONETARY POLICY

The deterioration of the sub-prime mortgage market became apparent in 2006, and continued into 2007. Hedge fund failures and write downs by investment banks stemmed primarily from the collapse of the MBS market, and other related financial derivatives. However, when, as a consequence, the money markets and interbank markets were affected, the stability of short-term funding markets was shaken.

Under normal circumstances, the central bank would have injected liquidity into the banking system by resorting to open market operations and lending through its discount window. However, the Federal Reserve faced unusual challenges while attempting to use its monetary policy tools under distress conditions.

Under the OMO, the Federal Reserve injects liquidity into the market at a rate close to the target rate set by the Federal Open Market Committee (FOMC). In the open market, the Federal Reserve trades with 'primary dealers (PDs)', who in turn distribute the liquidity to the interbank money market, and thus to the other sectors of the economy. However, in turbulent times like those witnessed during 2007, there was a marked reluctance for banks to lend to one another in the inter-bank market, thus leading to a credit crunch and an economic slowdown.

The fed lowered its discount rate substantially to attract banks to borrow from it. While such a move should have made borrowing more attractive, under the present distress conditions banks seemed reluctant to borrow from the central bank. A possible explanation for this behaviour could be the fear of signalling to the market that the borrowing banks' liquidity had been substantially affected, thus, reducing their ability to borrow from the market.

To offset the strain in the term funding market, the Federal Reserve introduced, at the end of 2007, a term auction facility (TAF), and followed it up with two more lending facilities in March 2008—the term securities lending facility (TSLF) and a primary dealer credit facility (PDCF)—to promote liquidity in the financial market. These facilities have been discontinued since 2011, after the crisis situation improved.

The new facilities do not increase the total reserves in the system. To maintain the federal funds rate at the target level, every TAF auction is offset by the Federal Reserve through a matching transaction in the open market.

Source: Federal Reserve documents.

The Monetary Ratios

We can now propose some simple ratios to determine the reserve ratios, currency ratios and money multiplier for M1 in an economy.[6]

1. The reserve ratio can be measured as = (reserves/bank's demand liabilities), where the bank's reserves would be the total of the cash that banks hold in their vaults and their deposits with the central bank, and bank's demand liabilities would include all deposits payable on demand and travellers' cheques.[7]
2. The currency ratio can be measured as = (currency in the hands of the public/bank's demand liabilities), where the currency can also be calculated from the central bank financial statements as the 'monetary base' less 'bank reserves'.
3. The money multiplier for 'narrow money' can, therefore, be measured as = (M1 or narrow money/bank's demand liabilities as defined in [1], above).
4. Similarly, taking into account time liabilities and other components of 'broad money' would enable us to calculate the money multiplier for broad money, M3.

Other Factors that Impact Monetary Base and Bank Reserves

The central bank can change the monetary base deliberately through any of the tools described above. However, monetary base can also change due to other factors as well without any intervention by the central bank. Such factors could be:

- **Refinance or Discount windows.** Most central banks perform the function of a 'lender of last resort', *i.e.*, they provide additional liquidity to banks through the discount or refinancing windows. Refinancing is made on the request of the borrowing bank, and the central bank has little control over the demand for refinancing at a particular point of time. Refinancing has the effect of increasing the monetary base and bank reserves. However, in practice, central banks do change, albeit infrequently, the terms and rates of such refinance, to encourage or discourage banks from seeking refinance.
- **Securitization.** Securitization of assets has the same effect as refinancing on the monetary base and reserves. Though central banks have the power to fine tune the terms of securitization in the long run, the additional liquidity in the system arising out of securitization of assets does affect the money supply in the short term.
- **Foreign exchange transactions.** Central banks, sometimes, buy and sell foreign exchange. From a bank in the same country, such purchase of foreign currency not only increases 'definitive money',[8] but also has the effect of increasing the monetary base and the bank's reserves.
- **Central Bank 'Float'.** A cheque deposited with the collecting banker in clearing, gives rise to a provisional liability in the central bank's books (provided the cheque is not dishonoured), which is matched by a provisional asset—items in the process of collection—which the central bank would get from the paying bank when the cheque is cleared. During this period, the collecting bank's reserves increase (the paying banker has not lost its deposit yet), and so does the reserves of the banking system by a corresponding amount. When the cheque is finally paid, the reserves of the banking system return to their original level. Since funds are constantly flowing through the clearing system, it is to be expected that the amount of items in process of collection will always exceed the amount of deferred credit items. The difference between the two amounts or the amount by which collection items exceed the deferred credit items is called the central bank's 'float'. This float is an additional source of reserves to the banking system, and since it is subject to daily fluctuations, the central bank may not have direct control over it.
- **Defensive open-market operations.** When the monetary base or reserves change as a result of any of the above factors, the central banks typically conduct OMOs to offset this effect. For instance, if the government were to spend ₹100 crore out of its funds, there is bound to be monetary expansion. However, the central bank can absorb the additional liquidity by an open market sale of the same amount. This is called a 'defensive open-market operation'. In contrast, the central bank can conduct OMOs to effect a change in the monetary base or reserves. This is known as a 'dynamic open-market operation'.

SECTION II

APPLICATION OF THE MONETARY POLICY TOOLS IN INDIA

The Monetary Base in India

A summary of the Reserve Bank of India's assets and liabilities as on January 2014 is shown in Table 2.2. It can be seen that the balance sheet structure is largely similar to the typical central bank's balance sheet shown in Section I. The aggregate liabilities of the RBI will give an idea of the monetary base of the country. The detailed annual report of the RBI can be accessed at www.rbi.org.in

TABLE 2.2 RESERVE BANK OF INDIA—A SUMMARY OF LIABILITIES AND ASSETS

(₹ in Billion)

	2013	2014		Variation	
	Jan. 18	Jan. 10	Jan. 17	Week	Year
Item	1	2	3	4	5
Notes Issued	**11,467.36**	**12,600.36**	**12,709.97**	**109.61**	**1,242.61**
Notes in Circulation	11,467.22	12,600.26	12,709.82	109.56	1,242.60
Notes held in Banking Department	0.14	0.10	0.15	0.05	0.01
Deposits					
Central Government	122.37	79.80	219.06	139.26	96.69
Market Stabilization Scheme	–	–	–	–	–
State Governments	0.42	0.42	0.42	–	–
Scheduled Commercial Banks	2,989.98	3,205.14	3,188.40	–16.73	198.43
Scheduled State Co-operative Banks	32.29	33.38	32.46	–0.93	0.16
Other Banks	143.84	160.35	160.16	–0.19	16.31
Others	118.90	163.53	161.22	–2.31	42.32
Other Liabilities	6,971.18	8,800.86	8,572.47	–228.39	1,601.29
Total Liabilities/Assets	**21,846.35**	**25,043.84**	**25,044.16**	**0.32**	**3,197.81**
Foreign Currency Assets	14,156.60	16,604.66	16,373.85	–230.81	2,217.24
Gold Coin and Bullion	1,491.03	1,220.89	1,220.89	–	–270.14
Rupee Securities (including Treasury Bills)	5,862.21	6,459.70	6,700.60	240.90	838.39
Loans and Advances					
Central Government	–	–	–	–	–
State Governments	1.55	19.74	5.36	–14.38	3.80
NABARD	–	–	–	–	–
Scheduled Commercial Banks	243.94	414.28	433.93	19.65	189.99
Scheduled State Co-operative Banks	–	–	–	–	–
Industrial Development Bank of India	–	–	–	–	–
Export-Import Bank of India	–	–	–	–	–
Others	22.92	62.31	70.85	8.53	47.93
Bills Purchased and Discounted					
Commercial	–	–	–	–	–
Treasury	–	–	–	–	–
Investments	13.20	13.20	13.20	–	–
Other Assets	54.90	249.06	225.49	–23.56	170.60

Notes: 1. Includes foreign securities balances held abroad and investments in foreign shares/bonds. This also includes investments in foreign currency denominated bonds issued by IIFC (UK) since 20 March 2009.

2. Effective October 17, 1990, gold is valued close to international market price.

3. Excludes investments in foreign shares and bonds and in Government of India rupee securities.

Source: RBI Weekly Statistical Supplement, dated January 24, 2014, accessed at www.rbi.org.in

Measuring Money Supply in India[9]

In India, in accordance with the recommendations of the RBI's Working Group on Money Supply (June 1998), the definition of money supply (termed 'new monetary aggregates') had been altered to adhere to the 'residency concept', in line with the best of international practices. The residency basis of compilation of monetary aggregates implies that non-resident deposit flows would not be included in money supply, *i.e.*, capital flows in the form of non-resident repatriable foreign currency fixed liabilities with the Indian banking system, such as the balances under the Foreign Currency Non-resident Repatriable (Banks) Scheme [FCNR(B)] and Resurgent India Bonds (RIB) would not be included in money supply computation.

Four measures of money supply termed 'new monetary aggregates', are being compiled in India on the basis of the banking sector's balance sheet, in conformity with the norms of progressive liquidity: M0 (the monetary base), M1 (narrow money), M2 and M3 (broad money).

M0 constitutes 'reserve money' maintained by banks with the central banks under the fractional reserve banking system. In specific terms, M0 is measured as follows:

M0 = currency in circulation + bankers' deposits with the RBI + 'other' deposits with the RBI.

The concept of 'narrow money' is similar to that adopted by other countries, and is represented as follows:

M1 = currency with the public + demand deposits with the banking system + 'other' deposits with the RBI.

restated,

M1 = currency with the public + current deposits with the banking system + demand liabilities portion of savings deposits with the banking system + 'other' deposits with RBI.

The components of M2 and M3 are as follows:

M2 = M1 + time liabilities portion of savings deposits with the banking system + CDs issued by banks + term deposits [excluding FCNR(B) deposits] with a contractual maturity of up to and including 1 year with the banking system.

restated,

M2 = currency with the public + current deposits with the banking system + savings deposits with the banking system + CDs issued by banks + term deposits [excluding FCNR(B) deposits] with a contractual maturity of up to and including 1 year with the banking system.

and,

M3 = M2 + term deposits [excluding FCNR (B) deposits] with a contractual maturity of over 1 year with the banking system + call borrowings from non depository financial corporations by the banking system.

The following points need to be noted:

- Currency with the public includes notes and coins of all denominations in circulation, but excludes cash in hand with banks.
- Demand deposits with the banking system implies demand deposits with commercial and co-operative banks, but excludes interbank deposits.
- 'Other deposits' with the RBI include current deposits of foreign central banks, financial institutions and quasi-financial institutions operating in India, and others such as the IMF and the IBRD.

Box 2.4 elaborates upon the differences between the new and old series of money supply in India.

BOX 2.4 DIFFERENCES BETWEEN THE NEW AND OLD SERIES OF MONEY SUPPLY

The new series of broad money (NM3) differs from the old series (M3) by a magnitude comprising FCNR(B) deposits and RIBs, and banks' pension and provident funds. Compilation of monetary aggregates on residency basis is in line with the best of international practices. Repatriable foreign currency fixed non-resident deposits (FCNR(B) deposits and RIBs in the Indian context) are excluded from money supply computation because they are BOP-related and do not constitute part of domestic demand for money.

This does not imply that RIBs and FCNR(B) deposits with the banking system in India do not affect money supply. If a bank sells foreign currency to the RBI, net foreign currency assets of the RBI increase, with a corresponding rise in the rupee value of reserve money. Since an increase in reserve money raises money supply in subsequent rounds of credit creation, FCNR(B) deposits and RIBs influence money supply.

If the RBI sterilizes the additional liquidity created by purchase of foreign currency from the banks by selling government securities from its portfolio, then this would not impact the reserve money and hence the money supply. The only effect is that FCNR(B) and RIBs would add to the net foreign currency assets of the RBI, with a corresponding reduction in government securities in the RBI balance sheet.

From the view of the country's balance of payments (BOP), FCNR(B) deposits and RIBs constitute liabilities under the banking capital account and commercial borrowing account, respectively.

Pension and provident funds are essentially a portfolio of assets created to provide old age and retirement benefits. As they differ from deposits redeemable for cash at face value plus accrued interest, they need to be excluded from monetary aggregates in line with international practices.

Source: www.rbi.org.in. RBI, 2000, 'New Monetary and Liquidity Aggregates'.

Apart from the four new monetary aggregates, the Working Group has also proposed three 'liquidity aggregates' in conformity with the norm of progressivity in terms of liquidity, as follows:

L1 = M3 + all deposits with post office savings banks, excluding National Savings Certificates,
L2 = L1 + term deposits with term lending institutions and refinancing institutions (FIs) + term borrowings by FIs + CDs issued by FIs, and
L3 = L2 + public deposits of non-banking financial companies.

It is evident from the above discussion that not all money is equal, at least from the perspective of monetary authorities and the monetary policies. While money in transaction deposits like current or savings deposits gets spent fairly quickly, funds invested in term deposits or CDs remain with the banks for some time. Thus, the impact upon the economy and the banking system of creating ₹1 crore in current deposits and ₹1 crore in term deposits is quite different. However, central banks cannot control where the money goes in the financial system. Further, recent financial innovations, such as money market accounts or credit cards, which finance transactions in a big way, do not figure in the conventional definition of money.

Hence, most countries, including India, adopt broad money aggregates, such as M3 as the basis for arriving at policy measures. Table 2.3 shows the components and sources of money supply in India up to January 2014.

TABLE 2.3 COMPONENTS AND SOURCES OF MONEY SUPPLY—JANUARY 2014

Item	Outstanding Amount (₹ in Billion) Jan 10, 2014	FY Variations (%)		Y-o-Y Variations (%)	
		2012–13	2013–14	Jan 11, 2013	Jan 10, 2014
1	2	3	4	5	6
Reserve Money (M_0)*	**16,277**	**3.7**	**7.4**	**2.0**	**10.0**
Reserve Money (Adjusted)*		5.9	6.9	10.0	10.6
Broad Money (M_3)	92,848	10.1	10.8	12.9	14.5
Main Components of M_3					
Currency with the Public	12,264	8.5	7.1	11.0	10.5
Aggregate Deposits	80,561	10.4	11.4	13.2	15.1
of which: Demand Deposits	7,586	–3.5	1.6	1.5	10.6
Time Deposits	72,975	12.2	12.5	14.6	15.6
Main Sources of M_3					
Net Bank Credit of Government	29,914	11.9	10.5	16.8	12.7
Bank Credit to Commercial Sector	62,111	9.6	9.6	16.3	14.3
Net Foreign Assets of the Banking Sector	18,735	5.3	14.5	6.5	15.3
NM_3(money supply net of FCNR (B) effect)	**90,955**	**9.8**	**8.8**	**13.3**	**12.4**

*: Data for reserve money pertain to January 17, 2014.
Note: Data of provisional.
Source: RBI, Macroeconomic and Monetary Developments, January 28, 2014, Table IV.I, page 19.

Operation of Reserve Requirements in India[10]

From the foregoing discussion, it is obvious that reserve requirements are mandatory if the liquidity in the banking system is to be preserved, and if even a single instance of default in repayment to depositors is to be avoided. All such reserves to be maintained as a legal requirement are termed 'Primary Reserves'.

There are legal reserve requirements under Section 42(1) of the RBI Act, 1934, stipulating that banks maintain a CRR on their liabilities. In addition, banks are bound under Section 24 of the Banking Regulation (BR) Act, 1949, to maintain a portion of these liabilities in cash or near cash form, termed the statutory liquidity ratio (SLR).

As the nomenclature implies, the CRR is maintained as cash reserves, while the SLR is maintained in liquid, near cash instruments. While the aim of the CRR is to take care of immediate liquidity needs, there is a two-fold objective for the SLR: to provide profitability along with liquidity, since the funds would be parked in interest yielding government and other approved securities; and to augment the government's borrowing program.

In the earlier simplified example of the Money Multiplier, it is seen that the fractional reserve requirement (the equivalent of CRR/SLR) is determined by the central bank as a percentage of deposits garnered by the bank. In reality, banks have varied sources of funds, as we will learn in a subsequent chapter. Hence, the CRR and SLR are prescribed as a minimum percentage of 'net demand and time liabilities' (NDTL) of each bank. Since the actual maintenance of the reserves is based on the NDTL, it is necessary to understand the constituents of NDTL and the method of calculating the actual reserves. Figure 2.2 shows the trend in growth in money supply, reserve money (*see* Box 2.5).

FIGURE 2.2 MONEY SUPPLY, RESERVE MONEY GROWTH AND THE MONEY MULTIPLIER IN INDIA

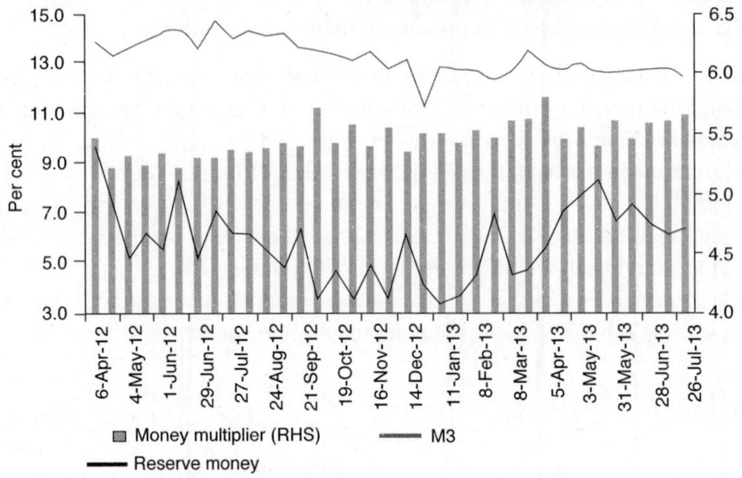

Source: RBI Annual Report, March 2013, Chart II.29, page 40

BOX 2.5 THE DEBATE OVER RELEVANCE OF CRR

Should CRR continue as an instrument of Monetary Policy in India? This debate was sparked off once again in September 2012.

Those who argue that CRR should go have expressed the following views:

i. It curbs banks' ability to lend.
ii. Funds blocked in CRR yield no return.
iii. Banks face a disadvantage compared with mutual funds, non-banking finance companies (NBFCs), and insurance companies, which are not subject to CRR.
iv. The Narasimham Committee-1 mandated a sharp reduction in the CRR and SLR.
v. The argument was reiterated by the Raghuram Rajan committee report on financial sector reforms in 2009.

However, those in support of CRR feel that the tool helps monetary policy achieve some important objectives:

i. It fulfills an important regulatory function in countries like India where the Open Market Operations (OMO) face some structural rigidities.
ii. The CRR can be an effective short-term tool to check inflation by varying money supply.
iii. Banks should view the zero interest on CRR balances as a fee paid to the RBI for its supervisory function.
iv. Banks alone can mobilize low-cost savings and current account deposits. Mutual funds, NBFCs, and insurance companies do not have access to such funds. So, banks have to ensure liquidity at all times and CRR is an effective tool to ensure liquidity.

Experts also feel that such pertinent questions should be raised in respect of the SLR and government bond holdings of banks, that do not yield high returns.

Net Demand and Time Liabilities

Bank liabilities can be broadly classified into external and internal liabilities. While equity, reserves and provisions are the internal liabilities, external liabilities are those that the bank owes to outsiders. External liabilities can be further classified into 'liabilities to the banking system' and 'liabilities to others'.

NDTL is broadly those liabilities of banks in India, which have been sourced from the 'banking system' and 'others'. It is to be noted that liabilities of overseas branches will be excluded since these branches operate under the jurisdiction of the countries in which they are located. Therefore, to grasp the concept and computation of NDTL, it is necessary to know what constitutes the banking system, assets with the banking system, demand and time liabilities to be reckoned for NDTL and how the reserves are calculated and maintained by banks.

Annexure I answers the following questions:

- What constitutes the banking system in India?
- Which type of institutions are excluded from the banking system?
- What are 'assets with the banking system'?
- What are the demand liabilities to be considered while computing the NDTL?
- What are the time liabilities to be considered while computing the NDTL?
- What are the 'other demand and time liabilities (ODTL)' to be considered while computing the NDTL?
- What are the liabilities to be excluded while computing the NDTL?
- What are the categories of liabilities exempted for calculation of reserve requirements under the CRR and SLR?
- How are the reserves calculated and maintained by banks?

In case of doubt or dispute in classification of liabilities, the RBI has the power to decide on the classification under section 18(2) of the BR Act.

Operation of the Bank Rate in India

The Section 49 of the Reserve Bank of India Act, 1934 requires the Reserve Bank to make public (from time-to-time) the standard rate at which it is prepared to buy or re-discount bills of exchange or other commercial papers eligible for purchase under that Act. Since, discounting/re-discounting by the Reserve Bank remained in disuse, the Bank Rate has not been active. Moreover, even for the conduct of monetary policy, instead of changing the Bank Rate, monetary policy signalling was done through modulations in the reverse repo rate and the repo rate under the Liquidity Adjustment Facility (LAF) (till May 3, 2011) and the policy repo rate under the revised operating procedure of monetary policy (from May 3, 2011 onwards). *As a result, the Bank Rate had remained unchanged at 6 per cent since April 2003.* Effective from February 13, 2012, the Bank Rate has been aligned with the Marginal Standing Facility (MSF) rate. (*See also* Box 2.6 "Changes in operating procedure of Monetary Policy", below). The MSF, standing at 100 bps above the policy repo rate, is now regarded as serving the purpose of the Bank rate.

Being the 'discount rate' (see also the earlier discussion on 'discount rate' or 'bank rate' under the sub heading 'Central Bank tools to regulate Money supply'), or the rate at which the central bank lends to commercial banks, the bank rate should essentially be higher than the policy repo rate. Thus, the bank rate was aligned to the MSF, which was pegged at 100 bps over the repo rate. The RBI has clarified that this is 'a one time adjustment not to be construed as a monetary policy action'. The alignment with the MSF also implies that all rates specifically linked to the bank rate, such as penal interest levied on shortfall in reserves kept by commercial banks with the RBI, will now be linked to the MSF and revised accordingly.

BOX 2.6 CHANGES IN THE OPERATING PROCEDURE OF MONETARY POLICY

Since initiation of financial sector reforms in the early 1990s, and the development of the money market, the operating procedure of the Monetary Policy in India has undergone significant changes. In 2000, the LAF emerged as the principal operating procedure of the Monetary Policy, with the repo and reverse repo rates as the key instruments for signalling the stance of the Policy. The LAF had been supported by other instruments such as the CRR, OMO, and the MSS.

However, the aftermath of the financial crisis brought in large volatility in capital flows and fluctuations in government's cash balances. These developments impacted liquidity management by the RBI.

In 2010, the RBI decided to review the operating procedure of the Monetary Policy, and constituted a Working Group (Chairman: Shri Deepak Mohanty).

Based on the Group's recommendations, the Monetary Policy statement for 2011–12 effected the following changes in the operating procedures:

i. The weighted average overnight call money rate would be the operating target of the Monetary Policy.
ii. The repo rate will be the one independently varying policy rate.
iii. Under the MSF, commercial banks can borrow overnight upto 1% of their NDTL (now, revised to 2% of NDTL).

Open Market Operations in India

In order to tackle uncertainty in financial markets, the RBI, in the late 1990s, decided to accept private placement of government securities with the purpose of off loading them into the market through active OMOs. This measure effectively met the large borrowing requirements of the government, without putting pressure on interest rates and paved the way for RBI to use the bank rate, repo rate and the reserve requirements in conjunction with the OMOs for meeting short-term monetary policy objectives.

The Liquidity Adjustment Facility (LAF), introduced in 2000, operates through repos and reverse repos to set the corridor for money market interest rates. Both repo and reverse repo rates are fixed by the RBI, with the spread between the two rates determined by the central bank based on market conditions and other relevant factors.

The LAF has settled into predominantly a fixed rate overnight auction, though repo auctions can be conducted at variable or fixed rates for overnight or longer terms. The second LAF introduced in November 2005 enables market participants fine tune liquidity management. LAF operations are supplemented by RBI's standing facilities linked to the repo rate, in the form of export credit refinance to banks and standing liquidity facility to PDs.

The move towards indirect instruments of monetary control (the CRR, *e.g.*, is a direct instrument of monetary control) has provided greater flexibility to the regulator, not only in fixing and adjusting policy rates, but also in monitoring them on a daily basis.

In addition, the central bank also aims at developing a repo market outside the LAF for both bank and non-bank participants, serving multiple purposes providing a stable collateralized funding alternative, promoting smooth transition of the call/notice money market into a pure interbank market and adding depth to the underlying government securities market.[11]

Repo Market Instruments Outside the LAF

1. **Collateralized borrowing and lending obligations:** Under the collateralized borrowing and lending obligations (CBLO), participants can lend and borrow funds, against the security of government securities, including treasury bills, for maturity periods ranging from 1–90 days (with flexibility up to 1 year). Transactions can be carried out in this market by banks, financial institutions, insurance companies, mutual funds, PDs, non-banking financial companies (NBFCs), non-government pension funds and corporate participants. Clearing Corporation of India Limited (CCIL), which developed and introduced the instruments in 2003, provides the electronic dealing platform for transactions, through the Indian financial network (INFINEN), a closed user group for members of the negotiated dealing system who maintain current accounts with the RBI, and through the Internet for other participants. Borrowing limits for each borrower is fixed by CCIL at the beginning of every day, based on the securities deposited by the borrower, and after applying appropriate hair cuts on the marked to market securities. CCIL guarantees settlement of transactions in CBLO. The operations in CBLO do not attract cash reserve requirements and unencumbered securities can be included as part of SLR requirements.
2. **Market repo:** From 2003, non-banking financial companies, insurance companies, housing finance companies and mutual funds could access the repo markets, and later on, non-scheduled urban co-operative banks and listed companies with gilt accounts with scheduled commercial banks were also permitted to transact in this market. Their participation serves to broaden the government securities market (market repos are currently restricted to the government securities market). Controls to ensure transparency in transactions and delivery versus payment) have been built into the system.

Both the CBLO and market repos have helped in aligning short-term money market rates to the repo and reverse repo rates in the LAF, as Figure 2.3 shows. It is also to be noted that repo markets outside the LAF have banks, PDs and corporates as major borrowers of funds supplied typically by mutual funds and insurance companies.

It can be seen from Figure 2.3 that the corridor has a fixed width of 200 bps with the repo rate in the middle of the corridor. The width of the corridor can be changed by the RBI. It is also evident, that CP and CD rates rule higher when liquidity conditions are tight, and tend towards the MSF rate (equivalent to the Bank rate) when liquidity conditions improve. A similar trend is seen in call money rates within the corridor of MDF-repo-reverse repo rate (reverse repo rate is aet at 100 bps lower than the repo rate by the RBI).

The Market Stabilization Scheme (MSS-2004) It has been designed to lend more flexibility to liquidity management. Increasing capital inflows into India has necessitated managing their impact on liquidity. However, since external capital flows could be volatile, the central bank would have to make choices for day to day exchange rate and monetary management. When the central bank intervenes in the foreign exchange market

FIGURE 2.3 MOVEMENT IN MONEY MARKET RATES

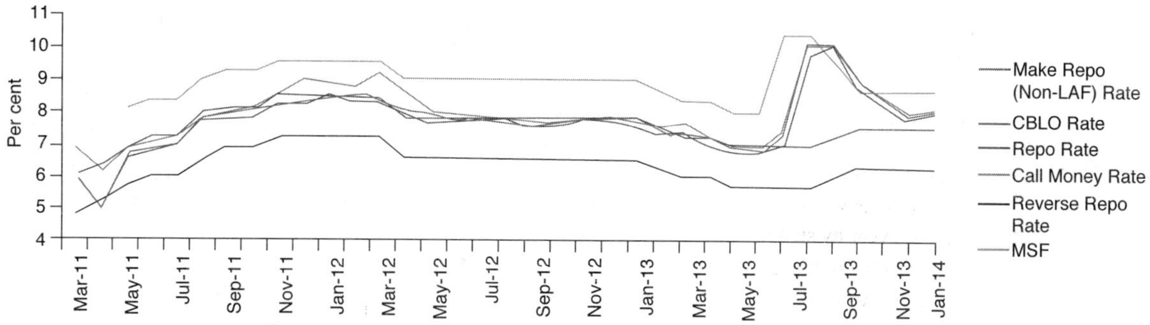

Note: CP WADR denotes Commercial Paper-Weighted average discount rate; CD WAEIR denotes Certificates of Deposit-Weighted average effective interest rate.
Source: RBI, Macroeconomic and Monetary Developments, January 2014, Chart V.4, page 25.

through purchase of foreign exchange, it injects liquidity into the system through corresponding sale of domestic currency. Similarly, when the central bank sells foreign exchange, liquidity is absorbed from the system. It is possible that such operations cause unanticipated expansion or contraction of money supply, which may not necessarily be consistent with the prevailing monetary policy stance. The central bank, therefore, looks at neutralizing such impact on money supply, partly or wholly. This process is termed 'sterilization'. OMO operations are commonly used as instruments of sterilization. However, while the liquidity impact of capital inflows have been managed using the LAF and the OMO, the process ended up depleting the stock of government securities held by the RBI. In response to this situation, the MSS was launched in agreement with the Government of India. Under this scheme, the government would issue treasury bills or dated securities in addition to the normal borrowing requirements, with the purpose of absorbing liquidity from the system. The MSS securities would be treated and serviced like other marketable government securities, but would be maintained and operated in separate accounts by the RBI. The amount held in this account would be appropriated only for the redemption or buy back of securities under MSS. Generally, short-term instruments are preferred for MSS operations to provide flexibility in liquidity management. The ceiling for outstanding balance under the MSS for the fiscal year 2012–13 has been fixed at ₹50,000 crore by the RBI. Thus, there has been no change in the ceiling amount over the last fiscal year.

SECTION III

MONETARY POLICY TOOLS IN SELECT COUNTRIES

The United States of America[12]

Monetary Policy Tool 1—Reserve Requirements Reserve requirements are the portion of deposits that banks may not lend and have to keep either on hand or on deposit at a Federal Reserve Bank. Within limits specified by law, the Board of Governors has sole authority over changes in reserve requirements. All depository institutions including commercial banks, savings banks, savings and loan associations, credit unions, US branches and agencies of foreign banks, etc. are required to maintain reserves of 3–10 per cent on transaction deposits. Table 2.4 shows the reserve requirement stipulated by the Fed.

TABLE 2.4 RESERVE REQUIREMENTS

Liability Type	Requirement	
	% of Liabilities	Effective Date
Net transaction accounts[1]		
USD 0–12.4 million[2]	0	12-27-12
More than USD 12.4–79.5 million[3]	3	12-27-12
More than USD 79.5 million	10	12-27-12
Non-personal time deposits	0	12-27-90
Euro-currency liabilities	0	12-27-90

Source: http://www.federalreserve.gov/monetarypolicy/reservereq.htm, accessed December 23, 2012.

Note: Required reserves must be held in the form of vault cash and if vault cash is insufficient, also in the form of a deposit maintained with a Federal Reserve Bank. An institution that is a member of the Federal Reserve System (FRS) must hold that deposit directly with a Reserve Bank; an institution that is not a member of the System can maintain that deposit directly with a Reserve Bank or with another institution in a pass-through relationship.

1. Total transaction accounts consists of demand deposits, automatic transfer service (ATS) accounts, NOW accounts, share draft accounts, telephone or pre-authorized transfer accounts, ineligible bankers acceptances, and obligations issued by affiliates maturing in seven days or less. Net transaction accounts are total transaction accounts less amounts due from other depository institutions and less cash items in the process of collection.
2. The amount of net transaction accounts subject to a reserve requirement ratio of zero percent (the 'exemption amount') is adjusted each year by statute.
3. The amount of net transaction accounts subject to a reserve requirement ratio of 3 per cent is the 'low-reserve tranche'.
4. The federal reserve banks pay interest on required reserve balances—balances held at reserve banks to satisfy reserve requirements and on excess balances—balances held in excess of required reserve balances and contractual clearing balances. The interest rate paid on required reserve balances is determined by the Board and is intended to eliminate effectively the implicit tax that reserve requirements used to impose on depository institutions. The interest rate paid on excess balances is also determined by the Board and gives the Federal Reserve an additional tool for the conduct of monetary policy.

The Federal Reserve changes reserve requirements for monetary policy purposes only infrequently. The transactions-account reserve requirement is applied to deposits over a 2-week period: a bank's average reserves over the period ending every other Wednesday must equal the required percentage of its average deposits in the 2-week period ending the Monday 16 days earlier. Banks receive credit in one 2-week period for small amounts of excess reserves they held in the previous period; similarly, a small deficiency in one period may be made up with excess reserves in the following period. Banks that fail to meet their reserve requirements can be subject to financial penalties.

Monetary Policy Tool 2—The Discount Rate The Federal Reserve Banks offer three discount window programs to depository institutions: primary credit, secondary credit and seasonal credit, each with its own interest rate. All discount window loans are fully secured.

Under the primary credit program, loans are extended for a very short term (usually overnight) to depository institutions in generally sound financial condition. Depository institutions that are not eligible for primary credit may apply for secondary credit to meet short-term liquidity needs or to resolve severe financial difficulties. Seasonal credit is extended to relatively small depository institutions that have recurring intra-year fluctuations in funding needs, such as banks in agricultural or seasonal resort communities.

The discount rate charged for primary credit (the primary credit rate) is set above the usual level of short-term market interest rates. (Because primary credit is the Federal Reserve's main discount window program, the Federal Reserve at times uses the term 'discount rate' to mean the primary credit rate.) The discount rate on secondary credit is above the rate on primary credit. The discount rate for seasonal credit is an average of selected market rates. Discount rates are established by each Reserve Bank's board of directors, subject to the review and determination of the Board of Governors of the Federal Reserve System. The discount rates for the three lending programs are, in most cases, the same across all Reserve Banks.

The current rates (beginning February 19, 2010) are 0.75 per cent for primary credit, 1.25 per cent for secondary credit, and 0.20 per cent for seasonal credit.

Monetary Policy Tool 3—Open Market Operations In open market operations, purchases and sales of US Treasury and federal agency securities—are the Federal Reserve's principal tool for implementing monetary policy. The short-term objective for open market operations is specified by the FOMC. This objective can be a desired quantity of reserves or a desired price (the federal funds rate). The federal funds rate is the interest rate at which depository institutions lend balances at the Federal Reserve to other depository institutions overnight.

The Federal Reserve's objective for open market operations has varied over the years. During the 1980s, the focus gradually shifted towards attaining a specified level of the federal funds rate. Beginning 1995, the FOMC began to explicitly state its target level for the federal funds rate. Since February 2000, the FOMC states its assessment of the risks to the attainment of its long-run goals of price stability and sustainable economic growth. It is noteworthy that the intended federal funds rate has been on a decreasing trend since 2006, and is at 0–0.25 per cent since December 2008.

Other Tools of Monetary Policy

Term Asset-Backed Securities Loan Facility (TALF) The TALF is a funding facility instituted to help market participants meet the credit needs of households and small businesses by supporting the issuance of asset-backed securities (ABS) collateralized by loans of various types to consumers and businesses of all sizes. Under the TALF, the Federal Reserve Bank of New York (FRBNY) will lend up to $200 billion on a non-recourse[13] basis to holders of certain AAA-rated ABS backed by newly and recently originated consumer and small business loans. The FRBNY will lend an amount equal to the market value of the ABS less a haircut and will be secured at all times by the ABS. The US Treasury Department—under the Troubled Assets Relief Program (TARP) of the Emergency Economic Stabilization Act of 2008—will provide $20 billion of credit protection[14] to the FRBNY in connection with the TALF.

Term Deposit Facility (TDF) The term deposits provide a new tool by which the Federal Reserve manages the aggregate quantity of reserve balances held by depository institutions. Funds placed in term deposits are removed from the accounts of participating institutions for the life of the term deposit and, thereby, drain reserve balances from the banking system. The Reserve Banks will offer term deposits through the TDF, and all institutions that are eligible to receive earnings on their balances at the Reserve Banks may participate in the term deposit program.

Maturity Extension Program and Reinvestment Policy Under this program, the Federal Reserve intends to sell or redeem a total of $667 billion of shorter-term treasury securities by the end of 2012 and use the proceeds to buy longer-term treasury securities. This will extend the average maturity of the securities in the Federal Reserve's portfolio. By reducing the supply of longer-term treasury securities in the market, this action is expected to put downward pressure on longer-term interest rates, including rates on financial assets that investors consider to be close substitutes for longer-term treasury securities. The reduction in longer-term interest rates, in turn, will contribute to a broad easing in financial market conditions that will provide additional stimulus to support the economic recovery.

Discontinued Policy Tools During the financial crisis, the Federal Reserve established several facilities to provide liquidity directly to borrowers and investors in key credit markets. As the performance of financial markets has improved, the Federal Reserve has wound down some of the programs. The Money Market Investor Funding Facility expired on October 30, 2009, and the Asset-Backed Commercial Paper Money Market Mutual Fund Liquidity Facility, the Commercial Paper Funding Facility, the Primary Dealer Credit Facility, and the Term Securities Lending Facility were closed on February 1, 2010. Also, the final Term Auction Facility auction was conducted on March 8, 2010.

Canada[15]

Canada imposes no minimum reserve on its banks. Its central bank, the Bank of Canada (BOC), freely lends overnight at its bank rate to ensure that payment orders between banks will clear. That sets an upper limit on overnight rates. It also pays interest on any clearing balances that banks hold at the BOC at a rate 0.5 percentage point below the bank rate. That sets a floor on overnight rates. Volatility in the money market rate is effectively limited to within this operating range.

The BOC target rate is the midpoint of the range. In order to steer the overnight rate towards its target, the BOC conducts OMOs similar to those used by the Federal Reserve. To compensate for variations in clearing balances caused by federal government inflows and outflows, on a daily basis the BOC offers to buy or sell government balances at the BOC on an auction basis to a select group of securities dealers.

When the bank changes the target for the overnight rate, it sends a clear signal about the direction in which it wants short-term interest rates to move. These changes usually lead to changes in the prime rate at commercial banks, which serves as a benchmark for many of their loans. These changes can not only indirectly affect mortgage rates and the interest paid to consumers on bank accounts and other savings, but also the exchange rate of the Canadian dollar. The target for the overnight rate has been at 3 per cent from April 2008 up to September 2008.

The Eurosystem[16]

The eurosystem comprises the European Central Bank (ECB) and the national central banks (NCBs) of the European Union (EU) countries that have adopted the euro (The euro area). Since 1 January 1999, the ECB has been responsible for conducting monetary policy for the euro area that at present comprises of 18 member countries. A statute established both the ECB and the European System of Central Banks (ESCB). The ESCB comprises the ECB and the NCBs of all EU member states whether they have adopted the euro or not. The ECB is the core of the eurosystem and the ESCB. The eurosystem and the ESCB will co-exist as long as there are EU member states outside the euro area.

Monetary policy tools used to achieve this objective through steering short-term interest rates are as follows: (1) minimum reserve requirements; (2) open market operations; and (3) standing facilities. By influencing the amount of liquidity available in the eurosystem, the level of short-term rates in the money market is regulated.

Monetary Policy Tool 1—Minimum Reserve Requirements All credit institutions[17] in the system are required to hold minimum reserves in separate accounts with the NCBs over a specified maintenance period (around a month). The Eurosystem pays a short-term interest rate on these accounts. The reserve requirement of each institution is determined in relation to elements of its balance sheet. Compliance with the reserve requirement is determined on the basis of the institutions' average daily reserve holdings over a maintenance period of about one month. The reserve maintenance periods start on the settlement day of the Main Refinancing Operation (MRO). The required reserve holdings are remunerated at a level corresponding to the average interest rate over the maintenance period of the MROs of the eurosystem.

The minimum reserve requirements take three forms—Reserve coefficients, Standardized deduction, and Lump-Sum allowance.

Reserve Coefficients

As from the maintenance period starting on	Overnight deposits, deposits with agreed maturity or period of notice up to 2 years, debt securities issued with maturity up to 2 years, money market paper	Deposits with agreed maturity or period of notice over 2 years, repos, debt securities issued with maturity over 2 years
1st Jan. 1999	2%	0%
18th Jan. 2012	1%	0%

Source: The table has been accessed from the ECB website.

Note: Liabilities *vis-à-vis* other credit institutions subject to the Eurosystem's minimum reserve requirements, the ECB and Euro area national central banks are excluded from the reserve base.

Standardized Deductions

As from the maintenance period starting on	Debt securities issued with maturity upto 2 years	Money market paper
1st Jan. 1999	10%	10%
24th Jan. 2000	30%	30%

Source: The table has been accessed from ECB website.

Note: If a credit institution subject to the Eurosystem's minimum reserve requirements can not provide evidence of its interbank liabilities in the form of debt securities issued with a maturity up to 2 years and money market paper, the ECB allows the institution to apply a standardized deduction to the aforementioned liabilities.

Lump-Sum Allowance

As from the maintenance period starting on	
1st Jan. 1999	€1,000,00

Source: The table has been accessed from the ECB website.

Note: The Lump-Sum allowance should be deducted by each credit institution from the amount of its reserve requirement.

Monetary Policy Tool 2—Open Market Operations OMOs, coordinated by the ECB, but carried out by NCBs, take four distinct forms: Open market operations play an important role in steering interest rates, managing the liquidity situation in the market and signalling the monetary policy stance. Five types of instruments are used. The most important instrument is reverse transactions, which are applicable on the basis of repurchase agreements or collateralized loans. The other instruments used are outright transactions, issuance of debt certificates, foreign exchange swaps and collection of fixed-term deposits.

- Main refinancing operations (MROs) to provide liquidity, with a frequency and maturity of 1 week.
- Longer term refinancing operations (LTROs) to provide liquidity, however with a longer frequency of a month and maturity of 3 months. Through MROs and LTROs, the Eurosystem lends funds to banks for short periods, secured by collateral. Longer-term refinancing operations that are conducted at irregular intervals or with other maturities, *e.g.*, the length of one maintenance period, 6 months, 12 months or 36 months are also possible. These operations aim to provide counter parties with additional longer-term refinancing. As a rule, the Eurosystem does not signal to the market by means of these operations. Main refinancing operations are carried out at a fixed rate of 0.75%, effective July 2012.
- Fine tuning operations (FTOs) as and when warranted to smooth the effects of unexpected liquidity imbalances on interest rates, and
- Structural operations through reverse transactions, outright transactions and issuing debt certificates.

Monetary Policy Tool 3—Standing Facilities The two standing facilities—a marginal lending facility and a deposit facility—offered by the Eurosystem set boundaries for overnight market rates by providing and absorbing liquidity. As their names imply, the marginal lending facility allows credit institutions to obtain overnight liquidity from the NCBs against the security of eligible assets, while the deposit facility enables credit institutions to make overnight deposits with the NCBs. These two facilities form a corridor—the lending facility forming the ceiling rate for the corridor and the deposit facility forming the floor rate—around the minimum bid rate and, therefore, set limits on the fluctuations in the short-term money market rates. Effective July 2012, the marginal lending facility carried a rate of 1.50%, while the deposit facility carried no interest (*see* Table 2.4).

TABLE 2.4 OVERVIEW ON EUROSYSTEM OPEN MARKET OPERATIONS AND STANDING FACILITIES[18]

Monetary Policy Operations	Types of Transactions		Maturity	Frequency	Procedure
	Liquidity-providing	**Liquidity-absorbing**			
Open market operations					
Main refinancing operations	Reverse transactions	–	1 week	Weekly	Standard tenders
Longer-term refinancing operations	Reverse transactions	–	3 months	Monthly	Standard tenders
Fine-tuning operations	Reverse transactions	Reverse transactions	Non-standardized	Non-regular	Quick tenders
	Foreign exchange swaps	Collection of fixed-term deposits	–	–	Bilateral procedures
		Foreign exchange swaps	–	–	–
Structural operations	Reverse transactions	Issuance of debt certificates	Standardized/ non-standardized	Regular and non-regular	Standard tenders
	Outright purchases	Outright sales	–	Non-regular	Bilateral Procedures
Standing facilities					
Marginal lending facility	Reverse transactions	–	Overnight	Access at the discretion of counter parties.	
Deposit facility	–	Deposits	Overnight	Access at the discretion of counter parties.	

This procedure also applies to irregular longer-term refinancing operations with longer maturities.

Source: http://www.ecb.europa.eu/mopo/implement/intro/html/index.en.html, accessed on December 25, 2012.

Other Developed and Developing Countries

Table 2.5 summarizes the key aspects of monetary tools in operation in select developed and developing countries.

TABLE 2.5 KEY ASPECTS OF MONETARY TOOLS IN OPERATION IN SELECT DEVELOPED AND DEVELOPING COUNTRIES

	Australia	UK	Switzerland	Sweden	Singapore	Japan	Brazil
Central bank	Reserve Bank of Australia	Bank of England	Swiss National Bank	Sveriges Riksbank	Monetary Authority of Singapore	Bank of Japan	Central Bank of Brazil
Key policy rate	Target cash rate	Official bank rate paid on commercial bank reserves.	3-month LIBOR	Overnight repo rate	Exchange rate	Uncollateralized overnight call rate.	Selic rate- interest rate on overnight interbank loans collateralized on federal debt instruments.
Operational target	Interbank cash rate	Overnight interest rates in line with bank's official rate.	Target range for 3-month LIBOR	Overnight repo rate target	S$NEER maintained within policy band	Uncollateralized overnight call rate.	Selic rate
Standing facilities	Yes	Yes	Yes	Yes	Yes	Yes	Yes
Form and maturity	Loans/ deposit; overnight.	Loans/unsecured deposits; overnight	Loans	Loan/ deposit; overnight	Loan/deposit; overnight	Fixed term loan; one day	Lending and deposit facilities, 2 days.
Pricing method	Fixed margin above/below target cash rate.	Official bank rate + or 2100 bps	Call money rate + 200 bps	Repo rate + or 275 bps	Overnight rate determined at morning auction + or 250 bps	Basic loan rate.	Security collateral price accepted by central bank repurchase agreements
Corridor width	50 bps	200 bps	NA	150 bps	100 bps	NA	Seltic rate + or 2 80 bps.
Reserve requirements	No	No; but voluntary contractual reserves targets	Yes	No	Yes. Cash balances with central bank.	Yes	Yes. Banks divided in Groups A and B
Reserve ratios	NA	NA	2.5% of applicable liabilities to the reserve base.	NA	Domestic currency: 3%. Minimum cash balance 3% of liabilities base	Domestic currency 20.521.3%; foreign currency 0.522.5%	45% on demand deposits.
Maintenance period	NA	1 month	1 month	NA	2 weeks.	1 month	2 weeks
Remuneration on excess reserves	NA	Reserves remunerated at bank rate; Excess reserves remunerated based on range set by the bank.	No	NA	No	No	No. But additional reserve of 8% on demand deposits remunerated.
Open market operations	Yes	Yes	Yes	Yes	Yes	Yes	Yes
Main operations			Repo	Repo			
functions	Liquidity injection and withdrawal.	Enable reserve holding banks meet reserve targets in aggregate.	Liquidity injection and absorption.	Influence market rates.	Exchange rate intervention.	Long term funds supply operations; short-term funds supply and absorbing operations.	Adjust market liquidity to maintain overnight interest rate close to target.

(*Continued*)

TABLE 2.5 (CONTINUED)

	Australia	UK	Switzerland	Sweden	Singapore	Japan	Brazil
Types of operations	Repo and reverse repo	Short-term fixed rate repos; long-term variable rate repos; outright purchases of gilts and foreign currency bonds; overnight fixed rate fine tuning repo.		Repos	FX spot	Outright purchase long-term Japan govt. bonds; purchase of govt. bonds, treasury bills, CP with repurchase agreement against pooled collateral; outright sale of bills, govt bonds, treasury bills with repurchase agreement.	Repurchase agreements using national treasury securities as collateral.
Maturity of operations	1 day to about 180 days	Short-term repos—1 week; long-term repos—3, 6, 9, 12 months	Around 1 week	1 week	Spot	Short-term funds supply-overnight to 1 year;	Short-term operations-1 to 20 days; Long-term operations, 5 month and 7 month repos.
Frequency of operations	Daily	Short-term weekly; long term monthly; gilts one lender per month.	Daily	Weekly	Discretionary	Short-term funds supply-about twice a day	Short-term-daily; Long term-weekly
Other discretionary operations	Yes	Yes. Various contingency measures.	Yes. FTOs	Yes. FTOs	Yes. Monetary management operations.	No	Yes
Functions	Liquidity injection and withdrawal.		Liquidity injection and absorption.	Stabilizing overnight rate.	Liquidity injection and absorption.		Structural operations; securities lending; managing liquidity for future operations.
Types of operations	Outright transactions, foreign exchange swaps.		Auctions	Loan/deposit; Repo rate + or 2 10 bps.	Repo; FX swaps; direct lending and borrowing, uncollateralized.		Outright operations; associated repos.
Maturity of operations	1–90 days		1 day	Overnight	Up to 1 year		Associated repos: overnight; outright operations: non standardized.
Frequency of operations	Several times a month.		Intermittent	Almost every day.	Daily		Not regular

(Continued)

TABLE 2.5 (CONTINUED)

	Australia	UK	Switzerland	Sweden	Singapore	Japan	Brazil
Use of standing facilities/ discount window	Overnight repo facility through which banks can access cash at penal rate of 25 bps over cash rate.	Available every day at margin of + or 2100 bps.	Overnight special rates repo transactions to bridge short-term liquidity bottlenecks.	Available every day at margin of + or 275 bps to repo rate.	Available to primary dealer banks at + or 250 bps over reference over-night rate.	Borrowing overnight from central bank at about 25 bps over target rate.	Standing facilities implemented through repos and reverse repos of two working days' maturity. Discount window provides costless intraday credit for payment systems operations.

CHAPTER SUMMARY

- The ability of banks to create money is constrained by the reserves they would have to maintain. The central banks can control the creation of money and thus the money supply, by controlling the reserve requirements from the banking system.
- In an economy in which all payments are made through the banking system, by cheques, the total quantity of money (deposits/credit) is the inverse of the reserve ratio times the monetary base (definitive money).
- The total liabilities of the central bank constitute the 'monetary base'.
- There are three broad measures economists use when looking at the money supply: M1, a narrow measure of money's function as a medium of exchange; M2, a broader measure that also reflects money's function as a store of value; *i.e.*, and M3, a still broader measure that covers items regarded as close substitutes of money. The indicators that measure money supply, though conceptually similar, differ in nomenclature and composition from country to country.
- Most central banks use three primary tools to influence money supply in the economy—the reserve requirements, the bank rate or discount rate and OMOs. However, when OMOs are used as a primary policy instrument, the use of other instruments, such as discount (bank) rate and the CRR becomes more selective and restricted.
- Reserve requirements in the nature of CRR are considered 'basic' compared with the level of sophistication that OMOs demand of the market. Central bank in several developed countries impose minimal or no reserve requirements on their banks. However, reserve requirements are still used in many instances as a way of enhancing the efficacy of OMOs and regulating money supply in the short term.
- The widespread use of OMOs has given rise to active 'repo' markets in many countries. The attractiveness of repos stems from the fact that the features of repo contracts are well suited to influence the interest rates in the economy, through impacting two of the main channels of monetary policy—controlling liquidity in money markets and signalling to markets the desired interest rate levels.
- The central bank can change the monetary base deliberately through any of the tools described above. However, monetary base can also change due to other factors as well, without any intervention by the central bank, such as refinance or discount windows, securitization, foreign exchange transactions, central bank 'float', defensive OMOs, to name a few.
- In India, the definition of money supply adheres to the 'residency concept', in line with best international practices. The residency basis of compilation of monetary aggregates implies that non-resident deposit flows would not be included in money supply, *i.e.*, capital flows in the form of non-resident repatriable foreign currency fixed liabilities with the Indian banking system.
- All financial institutions in India, which are into lending and investment operations are required to maintain a specified amount of reserves as cash/bank balances with the central bank and as investment in approved securities. All such reserves that are to be maintained as a legal requirement are termed 'primary reserves'. In the Indian context, these reserve requirements are categorized as the CRR and SLR. The CRR and the SLR are prescribed as a minimum percentage of 'net demand and time liabilities' (NDTL) of each bank operating in India.
- The LAF, introduced in 2000, operates through repos and reverse repos to set the corridor for money market interest rates. Both repo and reverse repo rates are fixed by the RBI, with the spread between the two rates determined by the central bank based on market conditions and other relevant factors.
- Repo market instruments also exist outside the LAF, such as CBLO, Market Repo and the MSS.

TEST YOUR UNDERSTANDING

1. Define the various money supply measures. What is the rationale for these different measures of money supply?
2. What are the goals of monetary policy in India? How well have they been achieved in recent times? If the goals have not been achieved satisfactorily, what are the reasons?
3. What is the difference between an outright open market transaction and a Repo? Why are OMOs being increasingly used as the primary monetary policy tool?
4. The NDTL of a bank operating in India on the reporting Friday dated 12 August 2009, is computed as ₹20,000 crore.
   a. When does the maintenance period for the CRR and the SLR begin?
   b. The CRR is to be maintained at 5 per cent, and the minimum CRR to be maintained on a daily basis is at 70 per cent. The bank expects that its internal surplus funds will amount to ₹500 crore during the first 6 days of the maintenance period, ₹600 crore during the next 5 days of the maintenance period and ₹500 crore for the remaining days of the maintenance period. What is the amount of funds the bank should mobilize to maintain the CRR without attracting penalty?
   c. If short-term interest rates are expected to rule at 4 per cent for the first 7 days of the maintenance period, 4.5 per cent during the next 3 days of the maintenance period and at 6 per cent thereafter, and the bank decides to borrow, what would be the interest outgo?
   d. If the penal provisions are as described in the annexure to this chapter, would the bank decide to pay the penalty or borrow to meet the CRR requirements?
5. A bank's liabilities comprises deposits amounting to ₹2,000 crore and an equity of ₹200 crore. On this liability base, the bank has to maintain a CRR of 5 per cent and an SLR of 25 per cent. If the bank can earn an average yield of 15 per cent on its loanable funds and its fixed expenses, including manpower expenses, amount to about 7 per cent of its deposits, what should be the average rate of interest the bank can pay on its deposits, if it wants to earn a profit of ₹20 crore for a period of 1 year? Assume that income on investments, along with interest earned on CRR and SLR investments, amounts to 22 per cent of the total income. Also assume that the balance sheet data given above are all averages applicable for the entire period.
6. A bank has an equity base of ₹700 crore. If the CRR is to be maintained at 5 per cent and the SLR at 25 per cent, what is the number of branches the bank can sustain given the following expectations?
   a. Average cash and bank balance per branch ₹1 crore.
   b. Average fixed cost per branch ₹3 crore.
   c. Average deposits per branch ₹100 crore.
   d. Capital to assets ratio of 10.

   Also, compute the level of fund-based business the bank can achieve.
7. What is the difference between a repo and reverse repo transaction?
8. A bank enters into a repo agreement in which it agrees to buy approved securities from an authorized dealer at a price of ₹1,49,25,000, with an agreement to pay back at a price of ₹1,50,00,000. What is the yield on the repo if it has (a) a 5 day maturity and (b) a 15 day maturity?
9. What is likely to happen to: (a) deposits with the banking system; and (b) interest rates in each of the following transactions?

   The central bank decreases CRR by 1 percentage point.

   The central bank increases CRR by 1.5 percentage points.

   The central bank sells government securities of ₹5 crore to the banking system.

   The central bank buys government securities of ₹10 crore from the banking system.
10. Assume that the RBI injects ₹60,000 crore liquidity into the banking system and that the current CRR is at 7 per cent. If there are no other leakages of funds from the banking system, how much of new deposits can the banking system create? If subsequently, the RBI withdraws ₹40,000 crore liquidity from the same banking system. What will be the current level of deposits with the banking system?

TOPICS FOR FURTHER DISCUSSION

- Study the monetary policies of the RBI of the last few years.
- What has been the stance of the RBI in respect of CRR and SLR requirements?
- Do you find any significant policy shifts in the usage of the three tools of monetary policy—*reserve requirements, bank rate and OMOs?*

- If such shifts have taken place, why have they been necessitated?
- What has been the impact of such shifts on banks?
- Go to the RBI website www.rbi.org.in and study the latest money market and LAF operations. What inferences can you draw from the transactions about what RBI is trying to achieve on the liquidity front?
- Study the way monetary policies are formulated and the stance of these policies in various countries. What similarities/dissimilarities do you notice with the manner in which RBI conducts Monetary Policy?

ANNEXURE I

COMPUTATION OF THE NDTL FOR THE BANKING SYSTEM IN INDIA[19]

What Constitutes the Banking System in India?

The banking system (for the purpose of CRR/SLR maintenance) includes the State Bank of India and its subsidiaries, the nationalized banks, co-operative banks, all private sector banks, foreign banks operating in India and any financial institution notified by the central government, such as PDs.

The banking system excludes the Reserve Bank of India, EXIM bank, NABARD, SIDBI and other similar financial institutions and primary credit societies, co-operative land mortgage/development banks and foreign banks having no branches in India, as well as Regional Rural banks.

What Constitute the 'Assets with the Banking Systems'?

'Assets with the banking system' include balances with the banking system in current accounts; balances with banks and notified financial institutions in other accounts; funds made available to the banking system by way of loans or deposits repayable at call or short notice of a fortnight or less and loans other than money at call and short notice made available to the banking system. Any other amounts due from banking system which cannot be classified under any of the above items are also to be taken as assets with the banking system.

What are the Demand and Time Liabilities to be Included for Computing NDTL?

Demand Liabilities Demand liabilities' include all liabilities which are payable on demand and they include:

- current deposits,
- demand liabilities portion of savings bank deposits,
- margins held against letters of credit/guarantees,
- balances in overdue fixed deposits, cash certificates and cumulative/recurring deposits,
- outstanding telegraphic transfers, mail transfer, demand drafts (DDs),
- unclaimed deposits,
- credit balances in the cash credit account, and
- deposits held as security for advances which are payable on demand.

Time Liabilities Time liabilities are those which are payable otherwise than on demand and they include:

- fixed deposits, cash certificates, cumulative and recurring deposits,
- time liabilities portion of savings bank deposits,
- staff security deposits,
- margin held against letters of credit if not payable on demand,
- deposits held as securities for advances which are not payable on demand, and
- Gold deposits.

Some Special Cases

- Loans/borrowings from abroad by banks in India will be considered as 'liabilities to others' and will be subject to reserve requirements.
- Money at call and short notice from outside the banking system should be shown against 'liability to others'.
- When a bank accepts funds from a client under its remittance facilities scheme, it becomes a liability (liability to others) in its books. The liability of the bank accepting funds will extinguish only when the correspondent bank honours the drafts issued by the accepting bank to its customers. The balance amount in respect of the drafts issued by the accepting bank on its correspondent bank under the remittance facilities scheme and remaining unpaid should be reflected in the accepting bank's books as an outside liability and the same should also be taken into account for computation of the NDTL for CRR/SLR purpose.
- The amount received by correspondent banks will be classified as 'liability to the banking system'.
- Upper Tier-2 instruments raised abroad will be included for computing reserves.
- Cash collaterals received under collateralized derivative transactions should be included in the bank's DTL/NDTL for the purpose of reserve requirements as these are in the nature of 'outside liabilities'.

Other Demand and Time Liabilities (ODTL) ODTL include the following:

- Interest accrued on deposits, bills payable, unpaid dividends, suspense account balances representing amounts due to other banks or public, net credit balances in branch adjustment account and any amounts due to the 'banking system' which are not in the nature of deposits or borrowing. Such liabilities may arise due to items like collection of bills on behalf of other banks, interest due to other banks and so on. If a bank cannot segregate from the total of ODTL the liabilities to the banking system, the entire ODTL may be shown against 'other demand and time liabilities, and average CRR is required to be maintained on it.
- Participation certificate issued to other banks.
- The balances outstanding in the blocked account pertaining to segregated outstanding credit entries for more than 5 years in the inter-branch adjustment account.
- The margin money on bills purchased/discounted.
- Gold borrowed by banks from abroad.
- Cash collaterals received under collateralized derivative transactions.

What are the Liabilities to be Excluded While Computing the NDTL?

Liabilities not to be Included for DTL/NDTL Computation The following will not form part of liabilities for the purpose of the CRR:

- Paid-up capital, reserves, any credit balance in the profit and loss account of the bank, amount availed of as refinance from the RBI and apex financial institutions like EXIM Bank, NABARD, NHB and SIDBI.
- Amount of provision for income tax in excess of the actual/estimated liabilities.
- Amount received from DICGC towards claims and held by banks pending adjustments and amount received from ECGC by invoking the guarantee.
- Amount received from insurance company on ad-hoc settlement of claims pending judgement of the court.
- Amount received from the court receiver.
- The liabilities arising on account of utilization of limits under banker's acceptance facility.
- The amount received by correspondent banks has to be shown as 'liability to the banking system' by them and not as 'liability to others' and this liability could be netted off by the correspondent banks against the interbank assets. Likewise sums placed by banks issuing drafts/interest/dividend warrants are to be treated as 'assets with banking system' in their books and can be netted off from their interbank liabilities.
- Interbank term deposits/term borrowing liabilities of original maturity of 15 days and above and up to 1 year, along with interest accrued on these deposits.
- Net unrealized gain/loss from derivatives transactions.
- Other items as specified by RBI periodically.

What are the Categories of Liabilities Exempted from Maintenance of Reserve Requirements? Exempted Categories

Banks are exempted from maintaining CRR on the following liabilities:

- Liabilities to the banking system in India as computed under Clause (d) of the Explanation to Section 42(1) of the RBI Act, 1934.
- Credit balances in ACU (USD) Accounts.
- Transactions in CBLO with CCIL.
- Demand and time liabilities in respect of their offshore banking units.

Banks are not required to include inter-bank term deposits/term borrowing liabilities of original maturities of 15 days and above and up to 1 year in 'liabilities to the banking system'. Similarly banks should exclude their interbank assets of term deposits and term lending of original maturity of 15 days and above and up to 1 year in 'assets with the banking system' for the purpose of maintenance of the CRR. This concession is not available for maintenance of the SLR.

How are Bank Reserves Calculated and Maintained with the RBI?

Conceptually, NDTL is the aggregate of liabilities to others and net interbank liabilities (NIBL), where

NIBL = liabilities of the banking system LESS assets with the banking system.

Here, three different cases may arise: interbank assets are equal to, greater than or less than interbank liabilities. Since NIBL has to be a positive figure, it is added to the liabilities to others only where interbank assets are less than interbank liabilities. In case they are equal, the net effect is zero, and in case the difference is negative, *i.e.*, interbank assets are greater than interbank liabilities, the net effect will be ignored in computing NDTL (see Illustration 2.1).

ILLUSTRATION 2.1

Bank A has computed its 'liabilities to others' at ₹1000 crores. What will its NDTL be if its inter-bank liabilities are at ₹300 crores, but its interbank assets stand at (a) ₹300 crore, (b) ₹400 crore, and (c) ₹200 crore?

Solution:

NDTL = Liabilities to others + NIBL (interbank liabilities 2 interbank assets)

a. NDTL = 1000 + [300 2 300] = 1000
b. NDTL = 1000 + (300 2 400) = 1000 (NIBL is negative, hence ignored)
c. NDTL = 1000 + (300 2 200) = 1000 + 100 = 1100

Reporting Friday and Reservable Liabilities

It is now clear that the quantum of primary reserves to be maintained is based on the computation of the NDTL. The next question is how is the maintenance actually done and at what periodicity? In India, NDTL is measured every alternate Friday by banks. These Fridays are termed 'Reporting Fridays'. If the reporting Friday is declared a holiday, then the previous working day is considered for fixing the NDTL.

The maintenance period based on the reporting Friday commences after a fortnight. In other words, the reserve requirement based on the NDTL on the reporting Friday, commences only a fortnight after the reporting Friday. This is to enable large banks with far-flung branches to obtain and consolidate balance sheet data, with which the actual NDTL would be worked out.

From the level of NDTL obtained on the reporting Friday, each bank deducts those liabilities exempted from maintenance of statutory reserves (as announced by the RBI from time to time). The balance of NDTL after such deductions is called the 'reservable liabilities' (RL). The prescribed rate of CRR is applied on the RL to arrive at the actual amount of reserves to be maintained.

Sometimes, RBI will identify some liabilities, which qualify for a differential CRR, or are exempted from reserve requirements altogether for a specified period. Such a measure would motivate banks to source these liabilities, in the interest of economic growth. In such cases, such differential rates will be applied on the components of RL.

Composition of CRR

The CRR has to be maintained only as:

- deposits with the RBI, or
- cash balances in the 'Currency chest'.

The 'Currency chest' is maintained at individual bank premises, but is deemed to be part of the RBI. Cash deposited with the currency chest is deemed to have been deposited with the RBI.

CRR Maintenance Period

Once the cash reserve requirement is assessed based on the NDTL as on a reporting Friday, banks have to maintain the calculated cash balance with RBI for the period of a fortnight. However, during this period, banks have the flexibility of distributing the reserve maintenance depending upon their intra-period cash flows. According to the latest directives, banks are required to maintain minimum CRR balances up to 70 per cent of the total CRR requirement on all days of the fortnight. However, on the last day of the fortnight, the total amount of reserves required for fulfilling the CRR requirement has to be maintained without fail.

For instance, if a bank's per day CRR requirement for a fortnight is ₹100 crore, then the bank should have maintained $100 \times 14 =$ ₹1,400 crore at the end of the fortnight. In accordance with the flexibility permitted, the bank could maintain ₹70 crore or more on the first 13 days of the fortnight. However, on the last day of the fortnight, the shortfall over ₹1,400 crore of the aggregate cash reserves maintained so far, should be imperatively made up. If the shortfall persists on the 14th day, the bank is considered a defaulter in meeting the CRR, and is penalized.

The bank is also penalized if the bank had failed to observe the minimum level of CRR on any of the days during the relevant fortnight, even if there is no shortfall in the CRR on an average basis for the whole fortnight.

Illustration 2.2 depicts the mode of reserve maintenance.

ILLUSTRATION 2.2

Assume that Bank A had arrived at a cash reserve requirement of ₹50 crore based on, say, data obtained on the reporting Friday dated 26 June 2009. This implies that total reserves to be maintained by the Bank for the maintenance period commencing 3 July 2009, should be $50 \times 14 =$ ₹700 crore.

Assume that Bank A has been maintaining ₹35 crore per day for the first 13 days of the fortnight. The amount to be maintained by the Bank on the 14th day would be $(700 - 35 \times 13) =$ ₹245 crore.

Failure to maintain a minimum of ₹35 crore per day even if at the end of the fortnight, the total maintenance amounts to ₹700 crore, as well as failure to maintain the aggregate reserve of ₹700 crore will attract the penal provisions of RBI.

Penal Provisions

The importance of holding reserves at the bank and economy levels has already been emphasized. The implications of flouting the reserve requirements by individual banks will be felt on the monetary position of the entire country. Hence, the RBI proposes deterrent penal provisions.

The guidelines in force state that 'In cases of default in maintenance of CRR requirement on a daily basis, which is presently 70 per cent of the total cash reserve ratio requirement, penal interest will be recovered for that day at the rate of 3 per cent per annum above the bank rate on the amount by which the amount actually maintained falls short of the prescribed minimum on that day and if the shortfall continues on the next succeeding day/s, penal interest will be recovered at a rate of 5 per cent per annum above the bank rate'. In case of default in CRR maintenance on average basis, penal interest will be as stipulated under Section 42 of the RBI Act.

Statutory Liquidity Ratio

Assets maintained as cash, though lending liquidity to banking operations do not contribute much to profitability. To satisfy the need for both liquidity and profitability, RBI has proposed the SLR, which in essence, stipulates a minimum investment by banks in near cash items. There are three basic objectives of the SLR:

- Control money supply for credit purposes,
- Channel bank investments into government securities and
- Ensure solvency of banks.

In addition to the cash reserve requirements, all banks in India are required to maintain SLR up to a maximum of 40 per cent of their demand and time liabilities. The SLR is to be maintained in the following forms:

a. in cash or
b. in gold, valued at a price not exceeding the current market price, or,
   in unencumbered investments in specified instruments called 'SLR securities' (*see* Box 2.7).

The present rate at which SLR is to be maintained is 25 per cent. The computation of NDTL for SLR is similar to the procedure followed for arriving at the CRR that there is one point of difference. Banks are required to include inter-bank term deposits and term borrowing liabilities of original maturities of 15 days up to 1 year under the head 'Liabilities to the banking system'. Similarly, inter-bank assets such as term deposits and term lending of original maturity of 15 days up to 1 year in 'Assets with the banking system'. (Note that, both the above-mentioned liabilities and assets are excluded for the calculation of CRR.)

Classification and Valuation of Approved Securities for SLR

An illustrative list of securities eligible to be reckoned as SLR investments is presented in Box 2.7. The box also lists some types of securities that are not eligible to be classified under SLR investments.

Valuation of these and other securities forming part of banks' investment portfolio will be dealt with in detail in the chapter on Investments.

As in the case of CRR, the RBI is empowered to exempt any liability from maintenance of statutory reserves, or can specify a differential rate for certain liabilities.

Under the MSF scheme introduced by the RBI with effect from May 09, 2011, banks can borrow up to 2 per cent of their respective NDTL outstanding at the end of the second preceding fortnight from April 17, 2012. Additionally, banks can continue to access overnight funds under this facility against their excess SLR holdings. In the event, the banks' SLR holding falls below the statutory requirement up to 2 per cent of their NDTL, banks need not seek a specific waiver for default in SLR compliance.

Maintenance Period

The maintenance period of SLR is similar to that of CRR, a fortnight beginning one fortnight after the reporting Friday. The reporting Friday is common for both the CRR and SLR.

BOX 2.7 SOME TYPES OF SECURITIES APPROVED AS SLR INVESTMENTS

i. Dated securities as given by RBI.
ii. All treasury bills already issued, and to be issued in future, by the Government of India.
iii. Dated securities to be issued in future by the Government of India under the market borrowing programme and under the market stabilization scheme.
iv. State development loans to be issued in future by the State Governments under their market borrowing programme.
v. Any other instrument as notified in future by RBI for SLR status.

Securities *not eligible for classification under SLR include* some special securities, such as oil bonds, fertilizer bonds, bonds issued to Unit Trust of India, IFCI Ltd., Food Corporation of India, Industrial Investment Bank of India Ltd., the erstwhile Industrial Development Bank of India and the erstwhile Shipping Development Finance Corporation.

Source: www.rbi.org.in

However, unlike the CRR, there is no flexibility permitted in SLR maintenance, which implies that 100 per cent of the SLR has to be maintained on a daily basis.

Penalties

If a bank fails to maintain the required amount of SLR even for a day, it would have to pay to RBI in respect of that day of default, on the amount of shortfall, penal interest at the rate of 3 per cent per annum above the bank rate. If the default continues, the penal interest may be increased to a rate of 5 per cent per annum above the bank rate for the number of days of shortfall.

ENDNOTES

1. Demand deposits' are, as the nomenclature implies, deposits repayable to the depositor on demand. In India, this category includes 'savings bank' and 'current' deposit accounts.
2. The money multiplier is not to be confused with the income multiplier, which is also important to fiscal policy.
3. Critics of fractional reserve banking allege that maintaining reserves may not altogether eliminate banking panics. If banking assets are insufficient to compensate all depositors, the liquidity risk would still remain.
4. However, critics of the bank rate argue that the bank rate could influence the 'cost of credit', but has no bearing on the 'availability of credit'.
5. The sub-prime crisis is described more completely in the chapter on 'credit risk.'
6. Meir Kohn, *Financial Institutions and Markets*, (New Delhi: Tata McGraw-Hill), 808.
7. Travellers 'cheques' (also DDs and bankers' cheques) are usually added to the definition of 'money' since they represent money already lying with banks pending payment.
8. Money not convertible into anything else—real money—is called 'definitive money'. For example, you cannot take rupees to the central bank and demand payment in 'real money'. In exchange, all you will receive is rupees for the same amount. A normal function of most central banks is provision of definitive money to the economy. Money of this type, which exists by an order of the government or 'fiat' alone, is called 'fiat money'.
9. Based on RBI, 2000, 'New Monetary and Liquidity Aggregates', RBI Bulletin, November 16, 2000.
10. Based on guidelines issued by RBI in its 'Master Circular on CRR and SLR', dated July 1, 2013.

11. A good source for the basic concepts of repos is the RBI report on repurchase agreements that can be accessed at www.rbi.org.in
12. *Source*: www.federalreserve.gov, the website of the Federal Reserve Board, Washington.
13. 'Non-recourse' signifies that the lender looks only to the cash flows from the asset pool and not to the originators for servicing the debt (interest + principal payments). More on this form of lending can be found in the chapters on Credit Risk (Chapters 8 and 9).
14. 'Credit protection' is discussed under Chapters 8 and 9.
15. *Source:* Bank of Canada Web site
16. *Source:* www.ecb.int
17. Include banks and savings banks who take deposits from the public and create credit out of the repayable funds.
18. http://www.ecb.europa.eu/mopo/implement/intro/html/index.en.html accessed on December 25, 2012.
19. *Source:* RBI 'Master Circular on CRR and SLR', dated July 1, 2013.

CHAPTER THREE

Banks' Financial Statements

CHAPTER STRUCTURE

Section I Basic Concepts
Section II Financial Statements of Banks Operating in India
Section III Analyzing Banks' Financial Statements
Chapter Summary
Test Your Understanding
Topics for Further Discussion
Annexures I, II, III, IV, V

KEY TAKEAWAYS FROM THE CHAPTER

- Learn how banks' financial statements are different.
- Understand the components of banks' financial statements.
- Learn to analyse banks' financial statements.
- Understand how inter-bank comparisons are carried out.
- Understand the KPIs for banks.

SECTION I

BASIC CONCEPTS

A bank's financial statements are quite different from those of a firm in any other industry. A cursory analysis of the balance sheet and income statement of any bank would confirm this statement. In their roles as financial intermediaries, banks have to take considerable financial risks, and their financial statements merely reflect these risks.

Examine the latest financial statements of a commercial bank and compare the components with a manufacturing or a trading company. You will notice several interesting points of differences. For example, to understand and analyze a bank's financial statements, you will have to first understand, why:

- The sources of funds are primarily short-term in nature, payable on demand or with short-term maturities. (Depositors can renegotiate the term deposit rates as market interest rates change.)
- The financial leverage is very high, in other words, the equity base is very low. (This is risky and can lead to earnings volatility.)
- The proportion of fixed assets is very low and, so is the operating leverage. (Operating leverage is the ratio of fixed costs to total costs. It can also be defined as the % change in operating income for a given % change in revenue.)

- A high proportion of bank funds are invested in loans and advances or investments, all of which are subject to interest rate volatility.

Furthermore, when deposit rates change, the cost of funds also changes, which in turn would impact the pricing of bank assets.

Thus, there seem to be considerable risks embedded in banking operations—high financial risk due to the high leverage, high interest rate risk, which would affect profitability, and high liquidity risk, which might endanger the solvency of the bank. In order to understand these risks, it is necessary to learn to read and analyze the financial statements of a bank. Let us, therefore, explore the nature of each item on the financial statement in some detail.[1]

Bank Liabilities

Sources of bank funds are classified according to the type of debt and equity components. The various debt instruments are differentiated on the basis of the maturity (interest rate), cheque writing and other facilities, the insurance they carry and their tradability in the markets. Till about a few decades back, the banking industry in many countries was highly regulated and did not exhibit much discretion in fixing interest rates. The industry has been deregulated progressively and banks can now compete globally by quoting viable interest rates on almost all their liabilities. It is now common for large banks to tap global markets for long-term debt and debentures.

The following constitute the major part of a bank's liability accounts, which represent sources of funds for the bank. In addition, in most major economies, various forms of regulation and legislation protect these accounts.

Net Worth The net worth of a bank is measured by the aggregate of its share capital, reserves and surplus. In any enterprise, capital is required to absorb unexpected losses. A bank typically sustains losses when the value of its assets is eroded—leading to fall in profitability due to loss of income. The loss in liquidity when the value of assets is eroded may even threaten the very existence of the bank.

Deposits The primary source of borrowed funds for a typical bank is 'deposits'—predominantly raised from the public. We will see in subsequent chapters the rationale and implications of banks garnering household, corporate and government savings in order to channelize them to deficit sectors in the economy, thus, leading to capital formation.

Deposits are grouped for transaction as well as balance sheet purposes based on purpose and maturity. They are broadly classified as deposits payable on demand and deposits payable after a specified period. Deposits payable on demand are generally called, 'transaction deposits' and in India, they take on the nomenclature of 'savings' and 'current' deposits. In some countries, such as the United States, such demand deposits are also called 'checking accounts' since these accounts can be transacted through cheques. Deposits payable after a specified time period are called 'term deposits'.

Borrowings Banks can borrow from the markets, both domestic and overseas, other institutions and banks, and from the central bank. Such borrowings, typically contribute a lower proportion to the banks' total sources of funds. Generally, borrowings are used to shore up the liquidity position or create specific assets.

TEASE THE CONCEPT

How are the debt instruments for a bank are different from the debt instruments available to a manufacturing or trading firm?

Bank Assets

As financial intermediaries, banks typically trade in credit, thus, leading to economic growth. The funds mobilized from various sectors in the economy are deployed into productive sectors of the economy. The credit, thus, deployed forms the most important asset on banks' balance sheets. Banks also aid economic growth by investing in securities issued through the financial markets and government. 'Investments', therefore, form another major asset on banks' balance sheets.

Cash holding by banks would comprise cash in the banks' vault and deposits with the country's central banks used to meet regulatory requirements, clearing house requirements and other uses. In spite of the importance of mitigating liquidity risk, banks prefer not to hold significant amounts of cash due to the possible loss of profitability.

Therefore, though cash does not form a significant proportion of banks' balance sheets, the importance of liquidity for banks cannot be underestimated.

TEASE THE CONCEPT

Is the cash holding of a bank really a liquid asset?

Investments Investment securities help banks in several ways. They help to meet liquidity needs, earn interest, take advantage of interest rate movements and are a part of the banks' treasury functions. At the time of investment, banks must be able to decide on the objective of buying the designated securities—whether the securities are to be held to maturity or are meant for short-term investments under the 'held for trading' or 'available for sale' categories.

Investment securities' attractiveness stems from the risk-return trade-off—good securities with low default risks are available at relatively low transaction and administrative costs, yielding good returns. Liquidity risks can be offset by investing in short-term securities, ranging from overnight to 1 year, which can be sold at a price very close to the acquisition cost. For the additional liquidity, banks are willing to sacrifice higher returns that are possible in long-term investment securities.

Treasury income could be one of the major sources of income for banks if they adopt prudent investment policies.

Loans and Advances This category of assets is the most important for banks because it defines their roles as financial intermediaries and impacts their profitability to a large extent. These assets also carry a high level of default risk and each asset or class of assets exhibits unique characteristics that render generalizations and monitoring difficult. For example, banks negotiate loans with borrowers whose businesses are widely different, and the loan terms for whom vary on all respects—amount, price, source of repayment, use of loan amount or type of collateral. Maturities could range from a few days (loans repayable on demand) to long-term loans (loans for real estate or infrastructure) ranging from 10–15 years. The price of the loans, or interest rates, may be fixed for the loan tenure, or may be floating—varying as market rates change. Repayment terms could be different for different loans—paid in equal installments, or principal and interest paid separately, or paid at the end of the loan period in one lump sum.

TEASE THE CONCEPT

Are loans and advances liquid assets?

Fixed Assets In sharp contrast to other industrial and service sectors, banks own relatively few fixed assets. Compared to non-financial firms, banks operate with lower fixed costs and exhibit lower operating leverage.

Contingent Liabilities

A contingent liability is an off-balance sheet item. How is it different from a liability on the balance sheet?

A liability arises out of a *present* obligation as a result of past events. Further, settlement of a liability is expected to result in an outflow of resources, by way of payments to creditors.

A contingent liability, on the other hand, is a *possible* obligation, which could arise depending on whether some uncertain future event occurs. It could also arise where there is a present obligation, but payment is not probable or the amount cannot be measured reliably.

In the case of banks, contingent liabilities can generate substantial income in good times. A major contributor to contingent liabilities is the non-funded business that banks take on, such as issue of letters of credit, opening letters of guarantee and derivatives dealing.

The major risk in contingent liabilities is the counter party default risk. In the event of the counter party failing to honour his commitment, the liability will crystallize into a fund-based liability for the bank. Relatively higher fees for these services offset the higher risk.

Though not forming part of the balance sheet, the contingent liabilities of banks will have to be examined thoroughly to identify potential risks to the bank's profitability and sustainability.

The Income Statement

The income statements of banks clearly reflect the financial nature of the banking business. The bulk of revenue is generated from interest on advances and investments. However, an analysis of the trend in income generation by banks shows a gradual upward shift in the proportion of non-interest income, reflecting the gravitation of modern banking business towards fee-based services.

The income statement starts with interest income from advances and investments (comparable to the 'revenues' figure in a non-financial firm). Interest payments on deposits and borrowings (comparable to 'direct costs' of a non-financial firm) are deducted from interest income to arrive at net interest income (NII). The NII is an important measure of profitability for banks and is used for calculating the 'spread'. The NII can be likened to 'gross profit' or 'contribution' in a non-financial firm.

It is desirable that the NII be substantial enough to generate a surplus after overhead expenses and taxes. The other major source of income—non-interest or fee-based income—is set off against non-interest expenses, which represent overhead costs. Typically, the non-interest income would be less than the overhead costs, leading to a net negative figure that is known as the 'burden'. From the burden, provisions for loan and other losses are deducted. These provisions are estimates made by the bank management about the likelihood of default in loan repayments or investment losses. The resultant figure would be the *operating income* of the bank. Where applicable, profit or loss from sale of long-term securities or assets is set off against the operating income to arrive at the net operating income before taxes. Net income or profit after taxes is arrived after deducting taxes and other adjustments, if any. Therefore, conceptually, a bank's net income is dependent on the following variables:

- NII
- Burden (non-interest income, LESS overhead expenses)[2]
- Provisions for loan losses and market risk
- Profit or loss from sale of securities and/or assets
- Taxes

Presented differently, the sources of a bank's income are interest earned from advances and investments, fee-based or non-interest income and profit from sale of long-term securities and other assets. The expenses of a bank comprise interest paid on deposits and borrowings, overhead expenses, provisions for loan losses and market risk and loss on sale of long-term securities and other assets.

A bank's efficiency ratio is defined as the ratio of overhead expenses to the total of NII and non-interest income. The burden and efficiency ratio indicate how well the bank controls its overhead expenses.

TEASE THE CONCEPT

Should the efficiency ratio be low or high to increase bank's profitability?

Other Income As pointed out earlier, banks are increasing their earnings through fee-based services, such as fund transfers and remittances, custodial services, collections, government business, agency business, opening letters of credit, issuing letters of guarantee and dealing in derivative markets.

Interest Expended This represents variable cost for the bank. However, due to the variety of borrowed sources of funds in terms of tenure, price and covenants, keeping this cost in check is a challenge for banks. Banks typically operate on narrow spreads, and any increase in interest expended is bound to erode profits, unless matched by commensurate growth in income generated by assets.

SECTION II

FINANCIAL STATEMENTS OF BANKS OPERATING IN INDIA

Comparing financial statements of banks operating in India will reveal that all of them are almost identically structured. This is because the banks in India have to prepare their financial statements in accordance with the third schedule of Section 29 of the Banking Regulation Act. A typical bank's balance sheet has 12 schedules, with Schedules 13–16 being allocated to the income statement (Tables 3.1 and 3.2). Accordingly, a uniform pattern of financial statement presentation and disclosures is followed.

TABLE 3.1 A TYPICAL BANK'S BALANCE SHEET—INDIA

Schedule	Liabilities	Schedule	Assets
01	Capital	06	Cash and balances with the RBI
02	Reserves and surplus	07	Balances with banks and money at call and short notice
03	Deposits	08	Investments
04	Borrowings	09	Advances
05	Other liabilities and provisions	10	Fixed assets
12	Contingent liabilities	11	Other assets

TABLE 3.2 INCOME STATEMENT

Schedule	Income	Schedule	Expenses
13	Interest earned	15	Interest expended
14	Other income	16	Operating expenses

Source: RBI Reserve Bank of India.

Schedules 17 and 18 typically relate to Notes to Accounts or provisions and contingencies and Significant Accounting Policies. The RBI requires other mandatory disclosures as well.

Bank Liabilities

Capital Banks have to show the authorized, subscribed and paid-up capital under this head. The RBI guidelines for the minimum capital to be held by banks in India—both private and foreign—are shown in Box 3.1.

BOX 3.1 RBI GUIDELINES—MINIMUM CAPITAL REQUIREMENTS

The capital requirement of existing private sector banks should be on par with the entry capital requirement for new private sector banks prescribed in the RBI guidelines of 3 January 2001, which is initially ₹200 crore, with a commitment to increase to ₹300 crore within 3 years. In order to meet this requirement, all banks in private sector should have a net worth of ₹300 crore at all times. The banks which are yet to achieve the required level of net worth will have to submit a time-bound programme for capital augmentation to the RBI. Where the net worth declines to a level below ₹300 crore, it should be restored to ₹300 crore within a reasonable time.[3]

Foreign banks are allowed to operate through branches. The 'tests of entry' criteria are applied also to branches of foreign banks. Besides these, the RBI examines dealings of the foreign bank with Indian parties, international and home country ranking wherever available, international presence, economic and trade relations with the home country and supervisory standards prevalent in the home country. The RBI also insists on prior consent of the home country regulator and ensures that the laws of the home country do not discriminate in any way against banks incorporated in India. A new foreign bank is required to bring in minimum assigned capital of USD 25 million, of which USD 10 million shall be brought in at the time of opening each of the first two branches and the balance USD 5 million at the time of opening of the third branch. All the foreign banks are required to maintain a minimum Capital Adequacy Ratio of 9 per cent on the aggregate risk-weighted assets of their Indian operations. It is important to get the home regulators' consent even in the case of opening a representative office, as once presence is allowed, it may be construed that the bank has fulfilled the 'tests of entry'.[4]

The Banking Laws (Amendment) Bill, 2012, was passed by both houses of Parliament in December 2012 to amend the Banking Regulation Act, 1949, the Banking Companies (Acquisition and Transfer of Undertakings) Act, 1970, the Banking Companies (Acquisition and Transfer of Undertakings) Act, 1980 and to make consequential amendments in certain other enactments.

This development is expected to impact ownership and management of Banks in India. The finance ministry has suggested (in December 2012) that the level of capital requirement start with as little as ₹30–40 crore for local banks to promote financial inclusion and increase the amount of capital as the region of operation of the bank-widens. The capital requirement would be higher than for local banks. Similarly, for banks with nationwide operations, the requirement may be ₹500–1000 crore of minimum capital.

The Banking Bill also allows foreign banks to set up subsidiaries in India. The hike in the cap on voting rights is expected to result in renewed investor interest in PSU banks.

Source: RBI

Reserves and Surplus Typically, Indian banks have to include the following components under this head.

Statutory reserves: Under Section 17(1) of the Banking Regulation Act, 1949, every banking company incorporated in India shall create a reserve fund out of the balance of profit each year as disclosed in the profit and loss account. Such transfer to the reserve fund will be before any dividend is declared, the amount being equivalent to not less than 20 per cent of the profit.[5]

Capital reserves: Excess depreciation on investments, or profit on sale of permanent investments or assets, are some of the surpluses that will be carried to the capital reserve account. This reserve will not include any amount that can be freely distributed through the profit and loss account.

Share premium: This will include any premium on the issue of share capital by the bank.

Revenue and other reserves: This will comprise all other reserves not included above. Excess provision on depreciation on investments will have to be appropriated to the 'Investment Reserve' account.[6]

Balance in profit and loss account: This contains the balance of profit after appropriations.

Deposits The balance sheet of a bank operating in India will show the following classifications.

Demand deposits: These would include balances in 'current' accounts and term deposits, which have fallen due for payment but not paid to the depositor. The bank will pay no interest on these balances. Current deposits are typically used as operating accounts for business transactions.

Savings deposits: These deposits are meant primarily to tap household savings. Hence, most of the depositors operating such accounts, in which balances are payable on demand, would be individuals. Trusts are also permitted to open and operate savings accounts. However, the RBI prohibits certain incorporated bodies from operating savings accounts.

Term deposits: Banks accept deposits with maturity periods ranging from 15 days to 10 years. The upper limit of 10 years can be relaxed in special cases such as disputed deposits or where minors are involved. Term deposits typically take the form of Fixed Deposits (FD), Recurring Deposits (RD), Reinvestment Deposits (RDP), Cash Certificates, Certificates of Deposits (CD), deposits under various schemes conceived and marketed by individual banks or deposits mobilized from Non-Resident Indians, under the nomenclatures such as NRE, NRO and FCNR deposits.

The types of deposits described above (except savings deposits) will be bifurcated into those from banks and from others. Deposits from banks are retained for various purposes and include deposits from the entire Indian banking system as well as co-operative banks and foreign banks, which may or may not operate in the country.

Internationally active banks in India will also present the deposit balances segregated into deposits collected by domestic branches and those raised by overseas branches.

Borrowings In its balance sheet, a bank operating in India would show 'borrowings' under two categories—borrowings in India and 'borrowings outside India'.

Borrowings in India would include 'refinance' from the RBI or other apex institutions, such as NABARD, SIDBI and other such refinancing agencies, against advances already disbursed. Borrowings from the money market–including the call money market–and other long-term markets would be reflected under borrowings from other banks or institutions, depending on the source of such borrowings.

Other Liabilities and Provisions These categories of liabilities are typically grouped as follows.

Bills payable: These constitute the floating liabilities of banks arising out of fee-based services rendered by banks for funds transfer, such as demand drafts, bankers' cheques and travellers' cheques.

Inter-office adjustments: The net credit balance will be included under 'liabilities'.

Interest accrued: Interest accrued on deposits and borrowings, which are due for payment, would be included in the balances outstanding under deposits or borrowings. Interest accrued but not due for payment will get reflected under this head.

Others: Importantly, this head would reflect the provisions made for income tax, bad debts and depreciation in securities. Other liabilities that cannot be grouped under any other head, such as unclaimed dividends, provisions or funds earmarked for specific purposes, and unexpired discount are also classified under this head.

Some banks include 'proposed dividend' as a separate category under 'other liabilities'.

Bank Assets

The following broad categories of assets are typically detailed in Indian banks' balance sheets:

- Cash and balances with the RBI
- Balances with banks and money at call and short notice
- Investments
- Advances
- Fixed assets
- Other assets

Cash and Balances with the RBI All cash assets of the bank are listed under this head, and this would be the most liquid part of the balance sheet.

Cash is held to meet deposit withdrawals, day-to-day expenses and credit drawal demands.

- 'Cash' includes cash in hand and cash in the vault, including foreign currency notes and cash balances at overseas branches of the bank.
- 'Balances with the RBI' are held to meet the statutory 'cash reserve requirements' (CRR) forming part of the fractional reserve-banking concept. The RBI has also permitted the operation of 'currency chests' at select banks. The currency chest is maintained at the premises of the approved banks, but the cash balances in the currency chest are reckoned as tantamount to balances kept with the RBI, as also meeting the statutory requirements.

Balances with Banks and Money at Call and Short Notice Under this head, banks separately disclose the balances they hold with other banks in various deposit accounts, in and outside India. These balances are held for various purposes, including settlements under clearing house operations, and include all balances with banks, including co-operative banks. However, domestic branches holding balances with the foreign branches of the same bank will be regarded as 'inter-branch balances' and not reckoned for inclusion under this head.

All lending to the inter-bank call money market is shown under the head 'money at call and short notice'. Loans made outside India, classified as 'call loans' in those markets are also included under this head. These short-term assets serve as 'near-cash' and form an additional line of defence against liquidity risks along with the CRR and statutory liquidity reserves (SLR).

Investments In times of soft interest rates, investments yield substantial incomes to banks.

To minimize the risks of indiscriminate investments by Indian banks, the RBI has drawn up a set of guidelines under which banks' investments in India will be slotted into six baskets depending on the nature of the security. These are as follows:

- Government securities
- Approved securities
- Shares
- Debentures and bonds
- Subsidiaries and/or joint ventures
- Other investments

Banks can also invest in overseas markets, where the categories would include foreign government securities, subsidiaries and/or joint ventures and other investments.

The SLR requirements would form part of the investment portfolio of the bank, which is intended to be, along with the CRR, part of the reserves serving as a hedge against liquidity risk.

Further, as a hedge against interest rate risks in the market, the RBI guidelines specify that all approved investments should be categorized into 'permanent' and 'current' investments, in a flexible proportion.

Under the current category, securities will be periodically marked to market. While appreciation in value is ignored, any depreciation is provided for.

Loans and Advances Indian banks classify their loan assets in three ways—by nature of credit facility granted, by security arrangements and by sector. The numerical total of 'advances' under all three categories is the same, since the same data has been presented in three different ways.

Presentation format I: By nature of credit facility

- Bills purchased and discounted: This head depicts the outstanding under this type of advance irrespective of the type of bills—clean/documentary/supply/foreign/domestic.
- Cash credits, overdrafts and loans repayable on demand: As the nomenclature suggests, these are loans to be repaid on demand irrespective of whether a due date is mentioned or not. Both financing and cash credit bills are essentially short-term advances.
- Term loans: All outstanding balances of loans granted for a specific period usually for more than 12 months are shown under this head. These loans are repayable only on due dates, not on demand.

Presentation format II: By security arrangements

- Secured by tangible assets, both prime and collateral.
- Covered by bank/government guarantee: Balances under advances within India and granted abroad, covered by guarantees of Indian or foreign governments or by agencies such as Export Credit Guarantee Corporation of India, are included under this head.
- Unsecured advances: These are not covered by tangible securities or government/institutional guarantees, or do not fall under the above-mentioned categories.

Presentation format III: By sector

- Priority sectors: These represent advances to sectors classified as such by the RBI. Most of these sectors, under the prevailing guidelines, have specific norms for directed lending.
- Public sector advances: These are loans/advances made to central and state government, and other government undertakings. However, any advance made to a public sector unit, eligible to be classified as priority sector, would be included under priority sector advances.
- Banks: These include all advances made to the banking sector and to the co-operative banks.
- Others: These constitute the advances made to the corporate sector and all other residual advances.

The total outstanding advances presented in the balance sheet represent 'Net bank credit'. 'Gross bank credit' is arrived at by adding the figure of bills rediscounted by bank with SIDBI or IDBI.[7]

Fixed Assets Indian banks classify 'fixed assets' on their balance sheets into the following categories:

- Premises (including land)
- Other fixed assets (including furniture and fixtures)
- Assets on lease

Costs of the assets are adjusted for additions, deletions or write offs during the year, and the net block after depreciation is presented in the balance sheet.

Other Assets These are residual assets of relatively small magnitude.

In Indian banks' balance sheets, they take the following forms (only major heads listed):

- Interest accrued: This consists of interest accrued, but not due on investments and advances, and interest accrued, but not collected on investments. Even under advances, only interest accrued on bills purchased or discounted will be included under this head. This is because interest on loans, cash credits or overdrafts gets debited to the respective accounts and is shown as outstanding advances in the balance sheet. Hence, the major component under this head would be interest accrued on investments.
- Inter-office adjustments: The debit balance, if any, in the inter-office accounts, will appear here. As a measure of prudence, the RBI has advised banks to make 100 per cent provision for the net debit position in inter-branch accounts, arising out of unreconciled entries.
- Advance tax paid/tax deducted at source
- Stationery and stamps
- Non-banking assets acquired in satisfaction of claims: Immovable property or tangible assets acquired by the bank in satisfaction of its claim on others are listed under this head.
- Others: These may contain the accumulated losses. Hence, while analyzing banks' financial statements, it would be prudent to scan this head to detect any erosion of net worth.

Contingent Liabilities Generally, contingent liabilities are shown under the following broad heads.

- Claims against the bank not acknowledged as debts.
- Liability for partly paid investments.
- Liability on account of outstanding forward exchange contracts.
- Guarantees given on behalf of outside constituents—in India and outside India (data to be furnished separately).
- Acceptances, endorsements and other obligations.
- Currency swaps.
- Interest rate swaps, currency options and interest rate futures.
- Other items for which the bank is contingently liable.

As stated already, contingent liabilities are non-fund-based and can become fund-based if the liability crystallizes and, therefore, carry inherent risks. (These risks are discussed in the appropriate context in subsequent chapters.)

Income Statement of Indian Banks

Income

Interest earned Interest earned is categorized as follows:

- Interest/discount on advances/bills: Banks charge interest on almost all types of advances. However, they discount certain types of bills, implying that the bank charges are taken upfront. Both categories of income are included under this head.
- Income from investments: The dividend and interest income earned from the bank's investment portfolio are included under this head.
- Interest on balances with the RBI and other inter-bank funds: Interest earned from sources, such as balances kept with the RBI deposits with other banks, and call loans, are included under this head.
- Others: All other types of interest/discount income that do not fall in any of the above categories will find a place under this head.

Other income The head 'other income' contains the following classifications:

- Commission, exchange and brokerage: All the types of fee-based income described above fall under this category.
- Profit/loss on sale of investments: The net position of gains or losses from sale of securities (held to maturity) is shown under this head.
- Profit/loss on revaluation of investments: The net position on revaluation of investments is shown here. Any loss will be shown as a deduction.
- Profit/loss on sale of building and other assets: The net position of gains or losses from sale of fixed assets including gold and silver will be shown under this head.
- Profit on exchange transactions: All income earned through foreign exchange dealings, except the interest earned, will be shown under this head. The income recorded here will be after setting off losses on exchange transactions.
- Income earned by way of dividends: These will be applicable to dividends earned from subsidiaries, joint ventures or companies in which the bank has invested.
- Miscellaneous income: All residual income arising out of miscellaneous sources, such as income from bank-owned property, security charges and recoveries of godown rents will be shown under this head. However, if any type of income exceeds 1 per cent of the bank's total income, details of such income have to be disclosed in the form of notes.

Expenses

Interest expended: The income statement lists three categories of interest expenses, based on the source of liabilities.

- Interest on deposits: This head will include interest paid on all types of deposits raised from the public, other banks and institutions.

- Interest on RBI/inter-bank borrowings: This head includes interest/discount on borrowings/refinance from other banks/RBI.
- Other interest: This would include interest on subordinated debt or borrowings/refinance from other financial institutions.

Operating expenses: These expenses are typically the overheads and other expenses necessary for a bank to function. They are categorized as follows:

- Payments to and provisions for employees
- Rent, taxes and lighting
- Printing and stationery
- Advertisement and publicity
- Depreciation on bank's property
- Directors' fees, allowances and expenses
- Auditors' fees and expenses
- Law charges
- Postage, telephone, etc.
- Repairs and maintenance
- Insurance
- Other expenses: If any one category exceeds 1 per cent of total expenses, details of the expenses will have to be provided separately.

Provisions and contingencies: Provisions made for loan losses, taxes and diminution in the value of investments will be included under this head.

Other Disclosures to be Made by Banks in India

In India, of late, there has been a notable shift towards more transparency and disclosures in the financial statements of banks.

Banks are required to disclose additional information as part of annual financial statements as specified in RBI instructions, revised periodically. The latest directive (in July 2013), has stipulated the 'minimum' disclosures in the 'Notes to Accounts' of banks' financial statements (*see* Box 3.2).

BOX 3.2 MINIMUM DISCLOSURES TO BE MADE IN 'NOTES TO ACCOUNTS' OF BANKS' FINANCIAL STATEMENTS[8]

1. Common equity—Tier I capital ratio
2. Tier I capital ratio
3. Tier II capital ratio and total capital ratio
4. Percentage of shareholding of the Government of India in the nationalized banks.
5. Amount of equity capital raised
6. Amount of additional Tier I capilal raised by issue of IPDI and PNCPS.
7. Amount raised by issue of Tier II instruments.
8. Gross and net value of investments,
9. Provisions made towards depreciation in the value of investments.
10. Movement of provisions held towards depreciation on investments.
11. Repo transactions
12. Non-SLR Investment Portfolio—Issuer composition and non-performing investments shown separately.
13. Sale and transfers from Held To Maturity (HTM) category.
14. Forward Rate Agreement/Interest Rate Swap

15. Exchange traded interest rate derivatives—classified by instrument
16. Disclosures on risk exposure in derivatives—qualitative and quantitative
17. Percentage of Net Non-Performing Assets (NPAs) to net advances
18. Movements in NPAs
19. Amount and movement of provisions made towards NPAs.
20. Details of loan assets restructured—under Corporate Debt Restructuring (CDR) Scheme, Small Medium Enterprises (SME) and others.
21. Details financial assets sold to a Securitization/Reconstruction Company (SC/RC) for asset reconstruction.
22. Details of non-performing asset purchased/sold.
23. Provisions on standard assets
24. Interest income as a percentage to working funds.
25. Non-interest income as a percentage to working funds.
26. Operating profit as a percentage to working funds.
27. Return on Assets
28. Business (deposits plus advances) per employee
29. Profit per employee
30. Maturity pattern of Assets—Loans and advances, investments and foreign currency assets
31. Maturity pattern of Liabilities—Deposits, Borrowings, foreign currency liabilities
32. Exposure to Real Estate Sector
33. Exposure to Capital Market—Investment in equity shares, etc.
34. Risk category wise country exposure
35. Details of single borrower/group borrower limit exceeded by the bank.
36. Unsecured advances
37. Disclosure of penalties imposed by RBI.
38. Disclosures in respect of the Accounting Standards (AS) where the RBI has issued guidelines—AS 5, 9, 15—relating to net profit/loss for the period, revenue recognition, and employee benefits.
39. Segment reporting—AS 17
40. Related party disclosure—AS 18
41. Consolidated financial statements—AS 21
42. Accounting for taxes on income—AS 22
43. Accounting for investment in associates—AS 23
44. Other disclosures as required under the relevant AS.
45. Disclosure of 'Provisions and Contingencies'
46. Disclosure on floating provision
47. Disclosure on draw down from reserves.
48. Disclosure of complaints
49. Disclosure of Letter of Comforts (LOCs) issued by banks.
50. Provisioning coverage ratio
51. Bancassurance business
52. Concentration of deposits, advance, exposures and NPAs
53. Sector-wise NPAs
54. Movement of NPAs
55. Overseas assets, NPAs and revenue
56. Off balance sheet Special Purpose Vehicles (SPVs) sponsored
57. Unamortized pension and gratuity liabilities
58. Disclosures on remuneration
59. Disclosures relating to securitization
60. Credit Default Swaps (CDS)
61. Other disclosures as required by Basel III

The formats for disclosure under each of the above heads can be found in the RBI's Master Circular titled 'Disclosure in Financial Statements—Notes to Accounts', dated July 1, 2013, and RBI Master Circular—Basel III Capital Regulations dated July 1, 2013.

Under 'significant accounting policies', banks are required to provide information on the basis of accounting expenses and incomes, investments, foreign exchange transactions, advances, fixed assets and net profit.

Banks are also required to present cash flow statements, accounts of subsidiaries and consolidated financial statements. In addition, some private sector banks also present their accounts under the US generally accepted accounting principles (US GAAP).

Under Section 31 of the Banking Regulation Act, 1949, banks are required to submit their financial statements along with the auditor's report to the RBI.

SECTION III

ANALYZING BANKS' FINANCIAL STATEMENTS

How do we compare banks? Which is the larger bank—the one whose average assets are larger than other banks or the one whose total income (interest plus non-interest income) is the highest?

The answer depends on what metrics we use to measure size. Traditional models of bank performance are based on the return on assets (ROA) approach. Some others such as CAMELS rating models (see *Annexure I*) follow a rating approach based on various parameters. *Annexure II* provides an illustrative list of key performance indicators (KPIs) that would enable to evaluate bank performance on various parameters. There are also more sophisticated models based on risk rating criteria (see *Annexure III*).

In this section, we will present a basic framework that will help analyse an individual bank's financial health, as well as compare performance across banks. This framework is based on the DuPont System of Financial Analysis and adaptations made by David Cole in 1972.[9]

This simple procedure helps evaluate the source and magnitude of bank profits in relation to the selected risks of banking business.

Timothy Koch and S. Macdonald[10] have used the Cole model to perform an analysis of the return on equity (ROE). Since a bank's market performance and sustainability are paramount in the long term, the model starts with ROE as the aggregate profit measure and decomposes it progressively into its component ratios to determine the strengths of an individual bank's performance, or compare its performance with other banks.

IMPORTANT NOTE

While using balance sheet figures with income statement figures, the balance sheet figures should be averaged.

Step 1 ROE = Net income/average total equity = NI/E

NI/E can be rewritten as

(Net income/Average total assets) × (Average total assets/Average total equity), *i.e.*, ROA × EM

What is the significance of the equity multiplier (EM)? See Box 3.3.

BOX 3.3 SIGNIFICANCE OF THE EM

Consider two banks, both with ₹100 crore in asset values and identical asset qualities but with different liability compositions. Bank X has a liability composition with ₹90 crore in debt and ₹10 crore in equity. Bank Y has a liability composition of ₹95 crore in debt and ₹5 crore in equity.

The EMs of the two banks are as follows:

Bank X: 100 ÷ 10 = 10

Bank Y: 100 ÷ 5 = 20

CASE 1

Assume that both banks have an ROA of 1

Then the ROE of the two banks would be

Bank X: 1 × 10 = 10

Bank Y: 1 × 20 = 20

This implies that, in spite of identical asset values and quality, Bank Y is able to earn a better ROE, simply because of a higher EM.

CASE 2

Assume both banks have a negative ROA = 21

The ROE of the two banks would now be

Bank X: 21 3 10 5 210

Bank Y: 21 3 20 5 220

We now notice that the decrease in Bank Y's profits is more than that of Bank X's profits—despite the asset values and quality still being identical—because of the higher EM of Bank Y.

What, then, is the nature of the EM? It is a measure of the bank's financial leverage—a higher financial leverage works to the firm's advantage by boosting the ROE when earnings are positive. However, leverage is a double-edged sword—when the firm records negative earnings, the fall in ROE is greater.

TEASE THE CONCEPT

What does the inverse of the EM represent and measure?

Step 2 Net income (NI) = Total revenue (R) − Total expenses (E) − Taxes (T)

Here, R represents interest plus non-interest income plus profit on sale of investments and E represents interest expenses, overhead expenses and provisions.

The effect of dividing both sides of the above equation by total average assets (TA) is to 'decompose' ROA:

$$NI/TA = (R/TA) - (E/TA) - (T/TA)$$

In other words,

$$ROA = \text{Asset utilization} - \text{Expense ratio} - \text{Tax ratio}$$

This implies that maximizing asset utilization and minimizing the expense ratio and taxes can maximize ROA.

Step 3 Revenue (R) can be further decomposed into

R = Interest Income (II) + Non-interest income (OI) ± Net profit/loss on sale of securities (PS).

Dividing throughout by average total assets (TA), as in Step 2

$$R/TA = (II/TA) + (OI/TA) + (PS/TA)$$

In other words,

Asset utilization = Yield on assets + Non-interest income rate + Profit rate on sale of securities

TEASE THE CONCEPT

Will two banks having identical asset base also have identical yield on assets?

Step 4 Similarly, Expenses (E) can also be further decomposed.

$$E = \text{Interest expenses} + \text{Overhead expenses} + \text{Provisions}$$

Again dividing throughout by average total assets

$$E/TA = (IE/TA) + (OH/TA) + (P/TA)$$

Here, IE/TA represents cost of funds for the bank and OH/TA represents the overhead expense rate. The provision rate signifies, to a large extent, the asset quality for the bank. The lower these ratios, the better will be the profitability of the bank.

Box 3.4 outlines some common strategies to control non-interest (overhead) expenses of banks.

BOX 3.4 SOME COMMON STRATEGIES TO CONTROL BANKS' NON-INTEREST EXPENSES

- Identify redundant expenses and eliminate them.
- Change product or service pricing to increase volumes or increase revenues at the existing volume.
- Study workflow processes and increase operating efficiency by maintaining current level of products and services at reduced costs or maintain the current costs but increase the level of products and services.
- Increase non-interest income so that they exceed non-interest expenses.

In this manner, every aspect of the bank's operations can be examined for analysis and decision-making.

To sum up,

ROE = ROA × EM

ROE = (Asset utilization − Expense ratio − Taxes) × EM

Stated differently,

$$\begin{aligned} \text{ROE} &= (\text{NI/assets}) \times (\text{assets/equity}) \\ &= (\text{NI/revenue}) \times (\text{revenue/assets}) \times (\text{assets/equity}) \\ &= \text{Profit margin} \times \text{asset utilization} \times \text{EM} \end{aligned}$$

where the profit margin can reflect

- expense control,
- tax management,
- effectiveness of pricing strategies and
- effectiveness of marketing.

And asset utilization is affected by

- mix of loans,
- investments and
- liquidity.

The EM is a measure of capital structure.

Where banks have high proportion of non-interest income, the bank's operating performance will have to be viewed differently.

For example, the following ratio is used by analysts to assess a banks' operating performance. The lower this

(Non-interest expenses or overheads – Non-interest income)/Net interest margin

ratio, the better is the perception of the bank's performance.

Annexure IV to this chapter provides a Du Pont analysis of profitability of banks in India, while *Annexure V* outlines the changes in International Accounting Standards for banking operations, and Code of Good Practices on Transparency in Monetary and Financial Policies of the International Monetary Fund.

CHAPTER SUMMARY

- A bank's financial statements are quite different from those of a firm in any other industry. In their roles as financial intermediaries, banks have to take considerable financial risks, and their financial statements merely reflect these risks.
- A few striking characteristics of the financial structure of banks would be revealed from an analysis of any bank's financial statements.
  - The sources of funds are primarily short-term in nature, payable on demand or with short-term maturities. Depositors can renegotiate the term deposit rates as market interest rates change.
  - The financial leverage is very high, in other words, the equity base is very low. This is risky and can lead to earnings volatility.
  - The proportion of fixed assets is very low.
  - A high proportion of bank funds is invested in loans and advances or investments, all of which are subject to interest rate volatility.
  - Besides, when deposit rates change, the consequent impact on the cost of funds could create problems with the pricing or portfolio of assets.
  - Operating leverage is relatively low due to the comparatively lower fixed costs.
  - Each of the above characteristics gives rise to significant risks in bank management. The income statement of banks clearly reflects the financial nature of banking business. The bulk of revenue is generated from interest on advances and investments. However, an analysis of the trend in income generation by banks shows a gradual upward shift in the proportion of the non-interest income, reflecting the gravitation of modern banking business towards fee-based services.
- Conceptually, a bank's net income is dependent on the following variables:
  - NII
  - Burden (non-interest income LESS overhead expenses)
  - Provisions for loan losses and market risk
  - Profit or loss from sale of securities and/or assets
  - Taxes

- Banks operating in India exhibit almost identically structured financial statements. This is because banks in India will have to prepare their financial statements in accordance with the third schedule of Section 29 of the Banking Regulation Act. A typical bank's Balance Sheet has 12 schedules, with Schedules 13–16 being allocated to the Income Statement. Accordingly, a uniform pattern of financial statement presentation and disclosures is followed.
- Traditional models of bank performance are based on the ROA approach. Some others such as CAMELS rating models follow a rating approach based on various parameters. There are also more sophisticated models based on risk rating criteria.

TEST YOUR UNDERSTANDING

1. Which of the following is NOT an asset on a bank's balance sheet?
   a. Cash in hand and balances with banks
   b. Reserves
   c. Loans and advances
   d. Investments
2. Which of these is found in a bank's income statement?
   a. Cash in hand and balances with banks
   b. Provisions for loan losses
   c. Deposits
   d. Borrowings
3. Net interest income is:
   a. Interest on loans and advances minus other income
   b. Interest on loans and advances plus interest on investments minus interest on deposits and borrowings
   c. Average interest rate earned on loans and investments less average interest paid on deposits and borrowings
   d. Interest on loans and advances plus interest on investment minus other income minus taxes
4. When we use ratios to analyze bank performance, we should:
   a. Use KPIs pertaining to a single year
   b. Compare year-end figures of both income statement and balance sheet
   c. Compare average figures of both income statement and balance sheet
   d. Compare year-end figures of income statement and average figures from the balance sheet
5. A bank's equity multiplier reflects:
   a. Financial risk
   b. Management control of expenses
   c. Liquidity risk
   d. Operating leverage
6. A bank's ROE has been falling over the last three years. On decomposition of the ROE, it is found that the ROA is increasing, and the equity multiplier is decreasing. This implies that:
   a. Investors should not invest in the bank
   b. The bank is earning less per Re of assets
   c. The bank is lowering its financial risk
   d. The bank is increasing its risk
7. When a bank increases its outside liabilities, other things remaining constant, the bank's equity multiplier will:
   a. Increase
   b. Decrease
   c. There will be no change in the equity multiplier
8. A bank holds 60% of its assets as liquid securities. This implies that:
   a. The bank's cost of funds is high
   b. The bank's cost of funds is low
   c. The bank's yield on assets is low
   d. The bank's yield on assets is high
   e. The bank will have high profits

9. In the case of a typical bank, which balance sheet accounts would be affected by the following transactions? You have to indicate at least two accounts for each transaction.
   a. A opens a deposit account with ₹1 lakh. The funds are loaned in the call money market for a week.
   b. Bank B contracts the services of its investment-banking arm for its initial public offer of shares to the market. The bank plans to use these funds to make loans to long-term infrastructure projects.
   c. Just as C, a residential complex promoter, pays off his loan taken from the bank for construction, D, an engineer with a multinational company, takes a home loan.
   d. Bank E raises ₹10 lakh in the call money market to grant a 3-month overdraft to its valuable customer, F.

10. Arrange the following information on Bank X into its income statement. Label and place each item in the appropriate category, in the appropriate order, and compute the bank's net income (₹ in lakh).

Commission, exchange and brokerage received	32,271
Income on investments	2,23,431
Interest paid on deposits	3,57,477
Payments to and provisions for employees	1,25,307
Interest paid on RBI/inter-bank borrowings	2,867
Interest/discount received on advances/bills (net of interest tax)	2,92,019
Income from leasing/hire purchase	603
Interest paid—others	13,181
Profit on exchange transactions—net	12,381
Rent, taxes, lighting	13,374
Insurance	2,538
Law charges	80
Profit on sale of land, building and other assets	66
Miscellaneous income	23,318
Auditor's fees and expenses	856
Printing and stationery	1,017
Profit on sale of investments—net	20,139
Depreciation on bank's property	6,591
Income by way of dividends from subsidiaries	3,001
Advertisement and publicity	333
Interest earned—others	38
Directors' fees, allowances and expenses	14
Miscellaneous income	23,318
Repairs and maintenance	2,469
Other expenses	12,782
Postage, telegram, telephone and other communication expenses	1,597
Interest received on balances with the RBI and other inter-bank funds	46,339

11. For the above bank, average balance sheet figures (average of previous year's and current year's balances) are given below (₹ in lakh).
    a. Decompose the bank's ROE and analyze the bank's profitability.
    b. Compute a few key performance ratios and interpret them, assuming that the ratios you compute are indicative of the past trend.

Capital	57,787	Cash and balances with the RBI	3,88,636
Reserves and surplus	2,23,658	Balances with banks and money at a call and short notice	9,28,488
Deposits	59,06,953	Investments	21,44,546
Borrowings	1,46,625	Advances	27,83,177
Other liabilities and provisions	3,08,882	Fixed assets	64,965
Total liabilities	66,43,905	Other assets	3,34,093
		Total liabilities	66,43,905

12. Is there a liquidity risk for a bank in the following circumstances? Indicate 'YES' or 'NO' and substantiate your answer.
    a. A bank's 'core deposits' form 20 per cent of its total assets.
    b. About 85 per cent of the bank's investments are to be held till maturity.
    c. A bank's demand deposits form 80 per cent of its total deposits.
    d. More than 60 per cent of the bank's advances will be repaid over the next 7 years.
    e. Sixty per cent of the bank's advances are short-term advances given for speculation in shares.
    f. Loans for purchase of cars form 70 per cent of the bank's advances portfolio. All of them will be repaid within 2 years.

TOPICS FOR FURTHER DISCUSSION

- Compare the financial statements of (1) a private sector bank, (2) a nationalized bank and (3) a foreign bank.
- What are the differences, if any, in presentation of the financial statements?
- Analyze the profitability ratios. Do you see any striking differences in the way each of these banks do business? Why do you think such differences exist?
- Analyze the asset—liability composition of these banks. Do you see any striking differences in the composition of assets and liabilities in each bank category? Why do you think such differences exist?
- Compare the financial statements of (a) a large and (b) a small private or public sector bank. Compute the KPIs and interpret them. Do you see any size-related differences in the KPIs?
- What financial ratios best capture each of the aspects of the CAMELS ratings?
- What do you notice about the contingent liabilities in each bank? Do these contingent liabilities pose any risk to these banks?

ANNEXURE I

CAMELS RATINGS

Regulators, analysts and investors have to periodically assess the financial condition of each bank. Banks are rated on various parameters, based on financial and non-financial performance. One of the popularly used assessments goes by the acronym CAMELS, where each letter refers to a specific category of performance.

C—Capital adequacy: This indicates the bank's capacity to maintain capital commensurate with the nature and extent of all types of risks, as also the ability of the bank's managers to identify, measure, monitor and control these risks.

A—Asset quality: This measure reflects the magnitude of credit risk prevailing in the bank due to its composition and quality of loans, advances, investments and off-balance sheet activities.

M—Management quality: Signalling the ability of the board of directors and senior managers to identify, measure, monitor and control risks associated with banking, this qualitative measure uses risk management policies and processes as indicators of sound management.

E—Earnings: This indicator not only shows the amount of and the trend in earnings but also analyses the robustness of expected earnings growth in future.

L—Liquidity: This measure takes into account the adequacy of the bank's current and potential sources of liquidity, including the strength of its funds management practices.

S—Sensitivity to market risk: This is a recent addition to the ratings parameters and reflects the degree to which changes in interest rates, exchange rates, commodity prices and equity prices can affect earnings and, hence, the bank's capital.

The components of the CAMELS rating system comprise of both objective and subjective parameters. Some illustrative components are as follows:

- Capital adequacy
  - Size of the bank
  - Volume of inferior quality assets

- Bank's growth experience, plans and prospects
- Quality of capital
- Retained earnings
- Access to capital markets
- Non-ledger assets and sound values not shown on books (real property at nominal values, charge-offs with firm recovery values and tax adjustments)

■ Asset quality

- Volume of classifications
- Special mention loans—ratios and trends
- Level, trend and comparison of non-accrual and renegotiated loans
- Volume of concentrations
- Volume and character of insider transactions

■ Management factors

- Technical competence, leadership of middle and senior management
- Compliance with banking laws and regulations
- Adequacy and compliance with internal policies
- Tendencies towards self-dealing
- Ability to plan and respond to changing circumstances
- Demonstrated willingness to serve the legitimate credit needs of the community
- Adequacy of directors
- Existence and adequacy of qualified staff and programmes

■ Earnings

- ROA compared to peer group averages and bank's own trends
- Material components and income and expenses—compare to peers and bank's own trends
- Adequacy of provisions for loan losses
- Quality of earnings
- Dividend payout ratio in relation to the adequacy of bank capital

■ Liquidity

- Adequacy of liquidity sources compared to present and future needs
- Availability of assets readily convertible to cash without undue loss
- Access to money markets
- Level of diversification of funding sources (on- and off-balance sheet)
- Degree of reliance on short-term volatile sources of funds
- Trend and stability of deposits
- Ability to securitize and sell certain pools of assets
- Management competence to identify, measure, monitor and control liquidity position

■ Sensitivity to market risk

- Sensitivity of the financial institution's net earnings or the economic value of its capital to changes in interest rates under various scenarios and stress environments
- Volume, composition and volatility of any foreign exchange or other trading positions taken by the financial institution
- Actual or potential volatility of earnings or capital because of any changes in market valuation of trading portfolios or financial instruments
- Ability of management to identify, measure, monitor and control interest rate risk as well as price and foreign exchange risk wherever applicable and material to an institution

Internationally, and in India, these ratings are used by regulators to determine the supervision policies for individual banks. Ratings are assigned for each component in addition to the overall rating of a bank's financial condition. The ratings are assigned on a scale from 1 to 5. Banks with ratings of 1 or 2 are considered to present few, if any, supervisory concerns, while banks with ratings of 3, 4 or 5 present moderate to extreme degrees of supervisory concern.

The rating analysis and interpretation are typically done along the following lines.

Rating Analysis	Rating Analysis Interpretation
1.0–1.4	*Strong:* Sound in every respect, no supervisory responses required.
1.6–2.4	*Satisfactory:* Fundamentally sound with modest correctable weakness.
2.6–3.4	*Fair (watch category):* Combination of weaknesses if not redressed will become severe. Watch category—requires more than normal supervision.
3.6–4.4	*Marginal (some risk of failure):* Immoderate weakness unless properly addressed could impair future viability of the bank. Needs close supervision.
4.6–5.0	*Unsatisfactory (high degree of failure evident):* High risk of failure in the near term. Under constant supervision/cease and desist order.

CAMELS Ratings Applied to Banks in India

The main instrument of supervision in India is the periodical on-site inspection of banks supplemented by off-site monitoring and surveillance. Since 1995, on-site inspections are based on the CAMELS[11] model and aim at achieving the following objectives:

- Evaluation of bank's safety and soundness
- Appraisal of the quality of board and top management
- Ensuring compliance with prudential regulations
- Identifying the areas where corrective action is required to strengthen the bank
- Appraisal of soundness of bank's assets

- Analysis of key financial factors, such as capital, earnings, and liquidity and bank's solvency
- Assessment of the quality of its management team and evaluation of the bank's policies, systems of management, internal operations and control
- Review of compliance with banking laws and regulations as well as supervisory guidance conveyed on specific policies

Financial performance parameters have typically been developed along the dimensions of this framework. These are typically used for peer comparison and benchmarking, regulatory reporting and shareholder reporting purposes. Some banks have also linked these parameters to the individual performance review process and compensation of its employees. However, these financial measures are primarily lag indicators, a post-mortem view of the business, rather than lead indicators that assess the bank's ability to create value in the future.

Domestic banks are rated on the CAMELS model while foreign banks are rated on the CACS model (capital adequacy, assets quality, compliance and systems). The frequency of inspections is generally annual, which can be increased/decreased depending on the financial position, methods of operation and compliance record of the bank.

Weights of Various Parameters Under the CAMELS/CALCS Model

	CAMELS	CALCS
Capital Adequacy	18	18
Asset Quality	18	18
Management	18	–
Earnings	10	–
Liquidity	18	18
Compliance	–	26
System and Control	18	20

Source: RBI, June 2012, report of high level steering committee on 'Review of Supervisory Processes for Commercial Banks', page 34.

Note: The CACS model mentioned in an earlier paragraph was subsequently modified to CALCS to include 'liquidity' as a measure.

The risk profile of each bank draws upon a wide range of sources of information, besides the CAMELS rating, such as off-site surveillance and monitoring (OSMOS) data, market intelligence reports, ad-hoc data from external and internal auditors, information from other domestic and overseas supervisors, on-site findings and sanctions applied. The data inputs are assessed for their significance and quality before being fed into the risk profile. All outliers, *i.e.*, banks, which fall outside the normal distribution based on characteristics, such as profitability, new business activity and balance sheet growth are identified and investigated on a regular basis. The risk profile is constantly updated.

The key components of the risk profile document are

- CAMELS rating with trends
- Narrative description of key risk features captured under each CAMELS component
- Summary of key business risks including volatility of trends in key business risk factors
- Monitorable action plan and bank's progress to date
- Strength, weaknesses, opportunities, threats (SWOT) analysis
- Sensitivity analysis

In December 2009, a Working Group on OSMOS, redevelopment, reviewed the OSMOS structure and suggested XBRL (Extensible Business Reporting Language) adoption for the returns.

The CAMELS rating system and other supervision processes, according to the RBI, were not adequately risk focussed or forward-looking to the required extent. In the context of the risks that have emerged after the global financial crisis of 2008, the need for a revamped supervisory rating system was felt. A high level steering committee submitted its report in June 2012 after a review of the supervisory processes in commercial banks.

Accordingly, the RBI proposes to replace CAMELS with INROADS (Indian Risk-Oriented and Dynamic Rating System) from the next round of Annual Financial Inspection (AFI), in 2013. The following table shows the likely changes in banking supervision.

The Changing Landscape of Banking Supervision

- CAMELS rating system to be phased out, as it lacks forward-looking assessment and merely represents banks' performance.
- New system, INROADS, to capture the risks that may cause a bank to fail.
- The AFI report to be fast-tracked.
- Single-point contact at the RBI to bridge regulatory gap.
- Information-sharing agreements with overseas regulators on cards.

Source: Business Standard, December 28, 2012, accessed at http://www.business-standard.com/india/news/rbi-sets-stage-forbank-supervision-overhaul/486292/ on December 29, 2012.

The proposed supervisory process would be as follows:

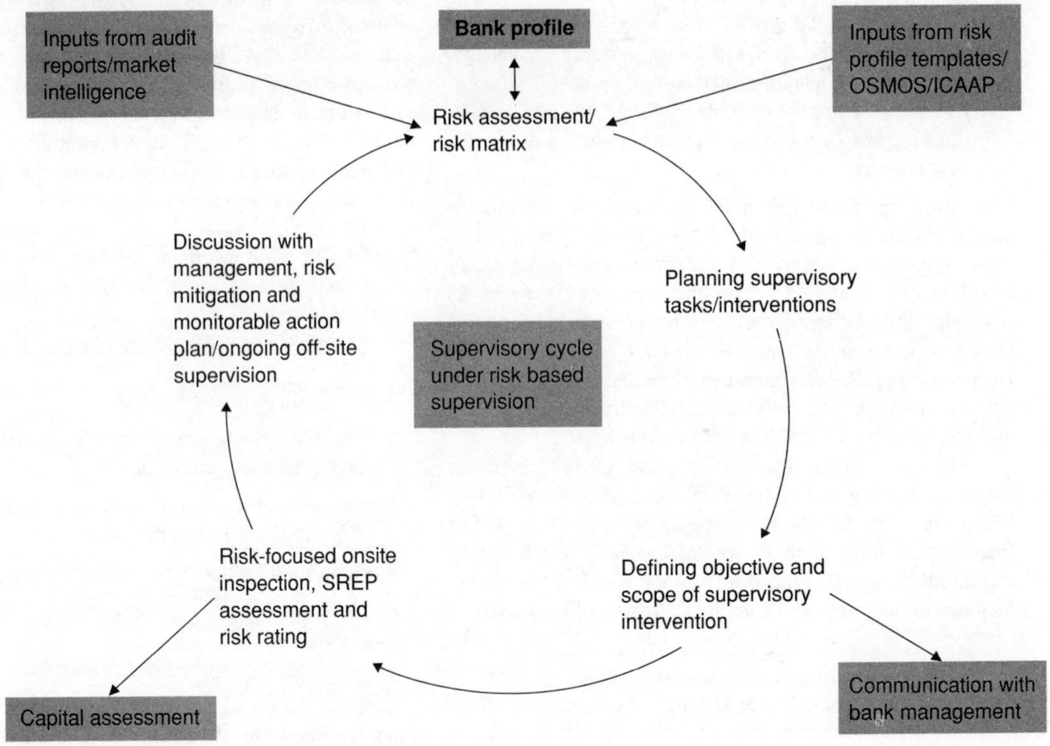

Source: RBI, June 2012, report of high level steering committee on 'Review of supervisory processes for commercial banks', p. 23.

The RBI report points out that the present rating does not capture the risks that could cause a bank to fail. The committee had identified the risk groups that could determine the risk of unexpected losses in a bank, as:

- Credit risk,
- Market risk,
- Operational risk,
- Liquidity risk, and
- Pillar 2 risk (Supervisory risk).

Based on the above, a 'probability of failure' for the bank would be arrived at. Based on a relative and approximate probability of failure vis-à-vis the risk of failure, the supervisory ratings would be allotted as follows:

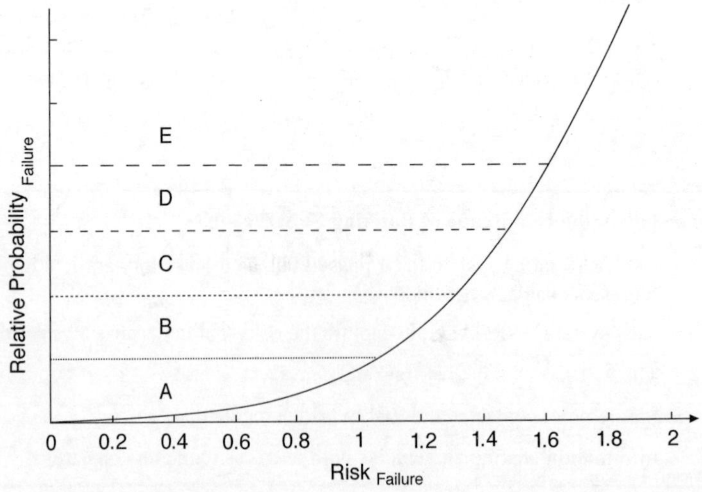

Source: RBI, June 2012, report of high level steering committee on Review of Supervisory Processes for Commercial Banks, p. 40.

The RBI proposes to enter into mutual regulatory cooperation agreements with regulators of other countries to gather information about Indian banks operating overseas. The RBI has already signed agreements with about 15 countries. The central bank is also planning to create a single-point contact for each bank.

SELECT REFERENCES

1. Federal Reserve documents for CAMELS ratings.
2. RBI, 'Seven Years of OSMOS—Looking Back and Way Forward.' *RBI Bulletin*, 16 December 2002, Department of Banking Supervision, RBI Central Office, Mumbai.
3. Sahajwala, Ranjana and Paul Van den Bergh, 'Supervisory Risk Assessment and Early Warning Systems.' Basel Committee on Banking Supervision Working Paper No. 4 (2000), Bank for International Settlements, Basel, Switzerland.

ANNEXURE II

KEY PERFORMANCE INDICATORS (KPI) FOR BANKS

Important Note for Calculating and Interpreting KPIs

KPIs given below are essentially financial ratios. For meaningful interpretation of these ratios, they must be calculated in a consistent manner, and compared with past trends or benchmarked with industry peers. The magnitude of the ratio depends on the value of the numerator and denominator, and if either of them is not correctly represented, the interpretation could be misleading.

While calculating ratios the following aspects should be considered:

1. Are we comparing a balance sheet figure with an income statement figure? The balance sheet figure is a 'stock' figure and the income statement figure is a 'flow' figure and to make them comparable, the balance sheet figure should be taken as an average figure. The average can be computed as the average of year-end figures or quarterly figures if available.
2. A single ratio cannot be interpreted meaningfully. Trends in ratios should be traced and interpreted. What has caused the changes in the ratio? Is it the numerator or the denominator? What are the implications of these changes?
3. If only a single ratio is available, then benchmarking against industry average, or peer comparison would yield meaningful insights. Choosing the peer group for comparison should be done carefully.
4. Accounting figures may camouflage details, and computing ratios mechanically might not lead to proper interpretation. Notes to accounts would provide more detailed information on the financial statement figures and would help in improved understanding of the implications of the ratios.

External factors that affect the performance of financial institutions include:

- Technology changes
- Competition
- Regulation
- Government policies (fiscal and monetary policy)

Bank management cannot control these factors. The best they can do is to try to anticipate future changes and position the institution to best take advantage of these changes.

Managers of banks, can however, control many internal factors. The KPIs will, therefore, focus on these controllable factors, some of which are

- Operating efficiency
- Expense control
- Tax management
- Liquidity
- Risk

It is important to note that while calculating ratios, all balance sheet figures should be averaged.

Efficiency and Expense Control Ratios

These ratios describe how well the financial institution controls expenses relative to producing revenues and how productive employees are in terms of generating income, managing assets and handling accounts.

Description	Numerator	Denominator	Interpretation/Remarks
Operating efficiency	Total operating expenses	Total assets	The lower this ratio, the more efficient the bank.
Cost of funds	Total interest expenses	Total deposit and non-deposit borrowings	The lower this ratio, the lower the variable cost for the bank.

Efficiency (cost–income) ratio	Non-interest income	Net total income	Net total income will be NII 1 other income. Shows the share of non-interest income in total income. Though some schools of thought seem to think that the higher the ratio, the more profitable the bank, since most of this income comprises fees-based services, such services are not without risks to banks.
Overhead efficiency (burden) ratio	Non-interest income	Non-interest expenses	A variant of this ratio would be non-interest income LESS non-interest expenses in the numerator. (Typically, non-interest income will be less than non-interest expenses overhands.)
Income productivity per employee	Net-income after taxes	Number of full time equivalent employees	
Break even volume of incremental cost per employee	Cost per employee	Net-interest margin (NIM)	NIM = Net-interest income/Total earning assets
Tax ratio	Total income tax payments	Income before taxes	
Tax ratio (2)	Provision for tax	Total equity	
Tax ratio (3)	Taxes paid	Total assets	

Liquidity

It is mandatory that banks meet investors' demands for liquidity. However, there is a trade-off since more liquid assets generally yield lower returns.

The following ratios describe the institutions' liquidity position.

Description	Numerator	Denominator	Interpretation/Remarks
Demand-to-time deposits	Total demand deposits	Total time deposits	The higher this ratio, the more the need for liquidity for the bank.
Demand deposits ratio	Total demand deposits	Total assets	The higher this ratio, the more the need to invest in liquid assets for the bank.
Non-deposit borrowing ratio	Non-deposit borrowings	Total assets	The higher the ratio, the higher the probability of default risk or reputation risk for the bank.
Credit—asset ratio	Total credit extended	Total assets	The more this ratio for the bank, the higher the risk of counter party default
Net loans—asset ratio	Total credit LESS provisions made	Total assets	When comparing the preceding ratio with this, the larger the difference between the two ratios, the less healthy the bank's credit portfolio.
Short-term investments—total assets ratio	Investment in money market instruments and other short-term assets	Total assets	The higher this ratio, the more liquid is the bank's asset portfolio. However, it is likely that a very liquid portfolio may be at the cost of profitability.
SLR investment—total investment ratio	SLR investments	Total investments	SLR investments are essentially liquid. Hence, the higher the ratio, the higher the liquidity in the bank.

Cash to demand deposits ratio	Cash and bank balances including call money	Demand deposits	The higher the ratio, the higher the liquidity of the bank. Hence, the probability that the bank defaults on its payment obligations is low.
Cash to total deposits	Cash and bank balances	Total deposits	Akin to the CRR. A variant to this ratio is including call money to cash in the numerator.
Cash to total	Cash and bank balances including call money	Total assets	The higher the ratio, the higher the liquidity of the asset portfolio; however, this may lead to low profitability.

Risk

Financial institutions face many risks including losses on loans and losses on investments. Financial institution managers must limit these risks in order to avoid failure of the institution (bankruptcy).

The following ratios provide some information concerning the risk of the institution.

Description	Numerator	Denominator	Interpretation/Remarks
Equity Multiplier	Total assets	Equity	Discussed at length in the chapter.
Equity ratio	Equity	Total assets	Inverse of the EM. Shows how many assets can default before the equity is eroded. The higher the ratio, the less risky the bank.
Capital adequacy ratio[12]	Total capital	Risk-weighted assets	
Adjusted capital adequacy	Total capital LESS net NPAs[13]	Risk-weighted assets LESS net NPAs	
Provision ratio	Loan loss provisions	Total assets	
Net NPA to assets ratio	Net NPAs	Total asset	
Net NPAs to equity ratio	Net NPAs	Equity	
Average risk-weighted assets	Risk-weighted assets	Total assets	
Incremental risk of asset portfolio	Incremental risk-weighted assets	Incremental total assets	A trend would indicate the bank's propensity to take risk

Profitability

Description	Numerator	Denominator	Interpretation/Remarks
ROE[14]	Net profit	Equity	Measures the return to shareholders.
ROA	Net profit	Total assets	ROA measures efficiency or how well the institution is using its assets to generate income.
Profit margin	Net profit	Total income	
Asset utilization	Total income	Total assets	ROE can be decomposed into profit margin 3 asset utilization 3 EM.
Yield on assets	Interest income earned	Total earning assets	
Interest cost to assets ratio	Interest expenses	Total assets	
Cost of funds	Interest expenses	Interest beaming deposits + borrowings	
Earnings per share	Net profit	Number of equity shares	

P/E ratio	Share price	Earnings per share (EPS)	
Net operating margin	Total operating income LESS total operating expenses	Total assets	Represents bank's operational efficiency. What portion of the bank's revenues flow through to net income?
Yield spread	Per cent yield on interest earning assets less per cent cost on interest-besting funds		This is comparable to 'contribution margin' and provides insight into profitability of banking operations.
Net interest margin (NIM)	Total interest income LESS total interest expense.	Total assets	
Interest before security gains or losses (IBSG)	Income before security gains or losses	Total assets	Similar to ROA, except that securities gains or losses are added back into net income. This removes the effects of portfolio manipulation by bank managers.

Breaking down ROE as shown in Section III can help us determine problem areas for the bank.

Valuation of a Bank—Some Pointers

1. The Price to Book Value (P/BV) multiple is frequently used to value banks. The rationale is that the growth in business value of a bank is closely related to its BV, unlike in other businesses. There are two reasons for this:
   a. The bank uses leverage to boost its return to equity holders, and the ratio reflects the capital it has for future growth. The ratio also reflects the flexibility offered by its regulatory ratios.
   b. The net worth of the bank is comprised of relatively liquid assets, since the bank has to hold more liquidity to carry on business. In cases of bank mergers that generate intangible value, analysts use P/TBV multiples, TBV denoting the 'Tangible Book Value' of the bank.
2. The Dividend Discount model is also used prevalently to value banks. In this model, a bank's expected dividend flows in future are discounted by its cost of equity. Alternatively, a constant growth model could be assumed. In both cases, the implicit assumption is that the credit quality of the bank's assets would not fluctuate, even in a downturn.

SELECT REFERENCES

1. Various Federal Reserve documents
2. RBI documents
3. IMF documents

ANNEXURE III

SOME ALTERNATIVE MODELS FOR BANK FINANCIAL STATEMENT ANALYSIS

Measures Based on Total Operating Revenue

In using 'total assets' as the denominator for calculating performance measures, as we have done in Section III, we have ignored the fact that off-balance sheet items—contingent liabilities—have the potential of turning into unsolicited 'assets' for banks. Further, they also have the potential to generate substantial income for banks (classified as 'non-interest income'). To circumvent this 'omission', it has been suggested[15] that performance measures may be calculated using 'total operating revenue' as the denominator rather than 'total assets'. Here, 'total operating revenue' represents both interest and non-interest income. However, non-recurring revenues, such as securities gains or losses, are to be excluded in computing total operating revenue.

Stock Market-Based Performance Measures

Investors are less concerned about historical ratios such as ROE or ROA, since these indictors do not convey the extent of cash flows to investors in the form of dividends and stock market prices. Thus, over the period in question, investors can assess how profitable their investment in the bank was through this simple ratio.

$$\text{Market return to stockholders} = \{[P(t) - P(t-1)] + D\}/P(t-1)$$

where

P(t) is the stock price at the end of the period,

P($t-1$) is the stock price at the beginning of the period, and

D is the cash dividend paid plus reinvestment income during the period.

Other common ratios used by investors and analysis are:

1. EPS = Net income after taxes/No. of outstanding shares
2. Price to earnings (P/E ratio) = Stock price/EPS
3. Price to book value = Stock price/Book value per share
4. Market value of equity (MVE) = Market value of assets LESS market value of liabilities, or stock price × number of outstanding shares

Customer-Centric Performance Measures

Looking beyond financial measures, banks use indicators such as market share, customer profitability, customer retention, customer satisfaction, as well as internal productivity indicators, such as business per employee and employee satisfaction. Many banks also measure profitability in terms of business segments (*e.g.*, corporate, retail), customer segments (small and medium enterprise, personal segments, corporate and institutional borrowers) by types of depositors or by delivery system (ATMs, branch, Internet banking).

Profitability by Line of Business

■ RAROC/RORAC analysis

RAROC refers to risk-adjusted return on capital and is represented as (Risk-Adjusted Income/Capital).

RORAC refers to return on risk-adjusted capital and is calculated as (Income/Risk-Adjusted Capital).

Though the above are the theoretical definitions, these terms are often used interchangeably.

'Risk-adjusted income' implies that net revenues have been arrived at after deducting expenses and expected losses. Some banks also deduct a 'capital charge' from the return to assess the 'economic capital'.

'Risk-adjusted capital' represents capital necessary to compensate earnings volatility.

■ Internal funds transfer pricing

Funds transfer pricing (FTP) is a management control technique used to calculate the true NII component of profitability of business units, products, portfolios and customers. FTP helps build the income statement for each of these items by calculating the cost of funding assets and the credit for funds provided in the form of deposits.

Conceptually, funds-generating businesses are seen as originating funds to be sold in an internal capital market to funds-using businesses. The 'transfer price' used to value these transferred funds is the rate at which the bank can buy or sell funds in the external capital market. For a bank branch or profit centre, which is using up funds for its business, the balance sheet would consist of the loans generated on the 'asset' side, and funds 'purchased' from the transfer funds 'pool' on the 'liability' side. Similarly, a funds-generating unit would show funds 'sold' to the transfer pool as its asset, while 'deposits' would form the liabilities. In this case, the NII of the unit would be the 'spread' between the transfer pool rate received on funds sold to the pool, and the rates paid on deposits. Thus, the transfer price has helped bifurcate the overall NII of the bank into two segments—one from asset origination and the other from liability origination.

Although many banks had been using a 'pooled funds approach' to assign interest rates, most banks now use a 'matched maturity approach'.[16]

A 'Risk Index'-Based Approach

We have seen that the ROA is one of the most widely accepted measures of overall bank performance. However, the ROA is not a static measure—it varies with credit risk, interest rate risk, liquidity risk and other risks[17] inherent in banking business. The variability (or volatility) in the ROA is typically measured by the standard deviation—either over time for an individual bank or across various banks at any point in time. A combination of the three important factors—ROA, EM (both of which determine the ROE, as described in Section III of this chapter) and the standard deviation of the ROA (the risk measure)—is called the 'Risk Index' (RI). This measure was proposed by Hannan and Hanweck [18] in their 1988 paper, and expresses the RI as:

RI = (Expected value of ROA + Capital to assets ratio)/ Standard deviation (σ) of ROA

Note that the capital to asset ratio is the inverse of the EM described in Section III, and is a measure of book value solvency of a bank. RI, therefore, can be interpreted as a measure of the extent to which a bank's accounting earnings can fall till its book value turns negative.

It follows that higher values of RI indicate lower risk of insolvency—implying a higher level of book value of equity—relative to the potential shocks to the earnings of a bank. Thus, banks with risky asset portfolios can remain solvent as long as they are well capitalized.

In their quoted paper, Hannan and Hanweck also derive a probability of book value insolvency (PI) expressed in terms of the RI as:

$$PI = 1/2\ (RI)^2$$

However, the above measure is different from the measures of market value solvency.

The RI measure derives its appeal from the use of ROA, the most widely accepted and understood accounting measure of banks' overall performance, the standard deviation of ROA, which is an accepted measure of risk, and book 'capital adequacy' that approximates a banks' solvency.

Banking Stability Map (RBI)

The Banking Stability Map and Indicator (BSI) present an overall assessment of changes in underlying conditions and risk factors that have a bearing on stability of the banking sector during a period. The following ratios are used for construction of each composite index:

Indicators Used for Construction of Banking Stability Map and Banking Stability Indicator				
Dimension	**Ratios**			
Soundness	CRAR	Tier-I Capital to Tier-II Capital	Leverage ratio as Total Assets to Capital and Reserves	
Asset-Quality	Net NPAs to Total Advances	Gross NPAs to Total Advances	Sub-Standard Advances to gross NPAs	Restructured Standard-Advances to Standard Advances
Profitability	Return on Assets	Net Interest Margin	Growth in Profit	
Liquidity	Liquid Assets to Total Assets	Customer Deposits to Total Assets	Non-Bank-Advances to Customer Deposits	Deposits maturing within 1-year to Total Deposits
Efficiency	Cost to Income	Business (Credit+Deposits) to staff expenses		Staff Expenses to Total Expenses

Source: RBI, Financial Stability Report, December 2012, p. 72.

SELECT REFERENCES

1. Koch, Timothy and Scott S. MacDonald, *Bank Management*, Chapter 4 (4th edn. The Dryden Press, 2000), USA.
2. Rao, Jammi and Kalpana Prabhu, '*RAROC—A Performance Measurement Tool.*' (2001), available at http://www.iciciresearchcentre.org.

ANNEXURE IV

ANALYSIS OF PROFITABILITY—A DU PONT ANALYSIS OF BANK GROUPS IN INDIA[19]

With the advent of complex financial products, banks' business has expanded in recent years beyond the traditional financial intermediation process. Also, off-balance sheet exposure of banks has witnessed a significant increase in recent years.

In recent years, significant variation in profitability has been observed among bank groups. It was observed that, generally profitability of foreign banks was higher than that of other bank groups. Some past studies on profitability of Indian banks concluded that higher profitability of foreign banks could be attributed to their access to low cost CASA deposits, diversification of income as well as higher 'other income'. During 2011–12, foreign banks accounted for close to 12 per cent of the total net profit of SCBs. As against this, their share in total assets of Indian banking sector stood at 7 per cent (see Figures 3.1 and 3.2).

In order to understand the sources of profitability across bank groups, RoE analysis and Du Pont analysis have been carried out taking the bank group-wise data for 2011–12. The RoE analysis decomposes the profitability of banks into two components, *i.e.*, profitability of bank assets, as captured by RoA and leverage, captured by the ratio of total average assets to total average equity.

Table 3.3 shows that the higher RoE for SBI group and the nationalized banks was associated with higher leverage, while for new private sector banks, the higher ROE was attributable to higher return on assets and relatively lower leverage. Among the bank groups, foreign banks had the highest return on assets combined with the lowest leverage ratio.

However, on the whole, return on assets of the Indian Banking system is lower compared to the banking system in select countries among the emerging economies, but is well ahead of the advanced economies. Table 3.4 shows the comparison.

FIGURE 3.1 NET PROFIT AS PERCENTAGE OF AVERAGE TOTAL ASSETS

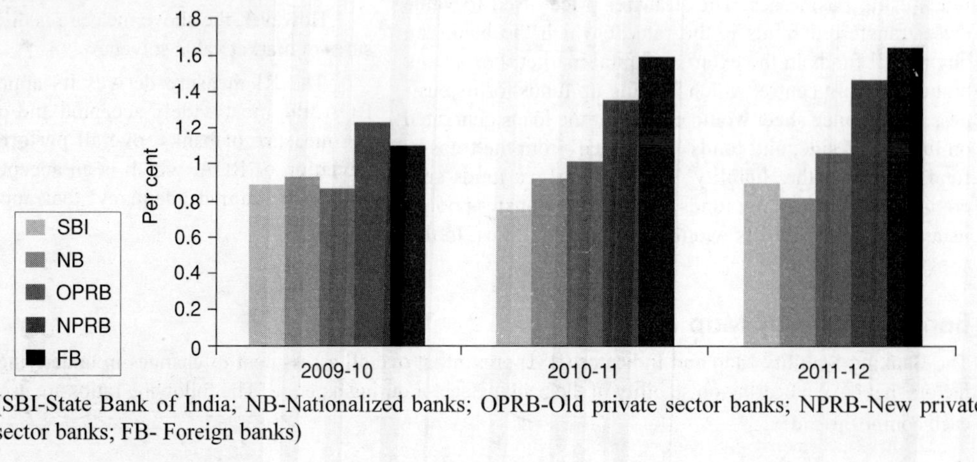

(SBI-State Bank of India; NB-Nationalized banks; OPRB-Old private sector banks; NPRB-New private sector banks; FB- Foreign banks)

FIGURE 3.2 PROFITABILITY OF BANK GROUPS AND THEIR SHARE IN TOTAL ASSETS, 2011–12

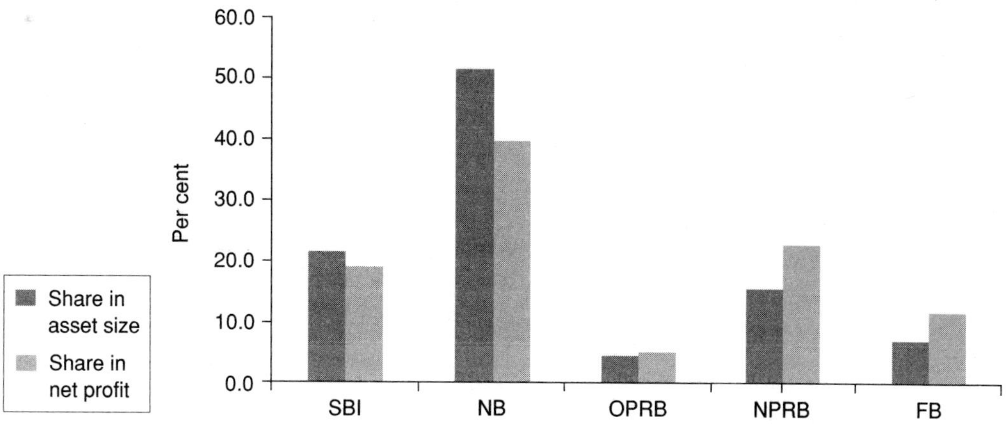

TABLE 3.3 ROE ANALYSIS—BANK GROUPS, 2011–12

Bank Group	Return on Equity	Profitability of Assets	Leverage	Capital to Assets Ratio
1	2	3	4	5
SBI group	16	0.91	17.58	0.07
Nationalized banks	15.05	0.87	17.37	0.4
old private sector banks	15.18	1.15	13.23	0.35
New private sector banks	15.27	1.57	9.27	0.27
Foreign banks	10.79	1.75	6.15	6.95

The Figure 3.3 shows the leverage ratios in advanced economies and emerging economies. The Indian banks have relatively lower leverage compared to the banking systems of both advanced and emerging economies.

The capital to assets ratio further corroborates the findings of RoE analysis. At end of March 2012, this ratio was highest for foreign banks in India, indicating their better capital position *vis-à-vis* other bank groups.

Du Pont analysis further decomposes profitability of banks into two components, *viz.*, asset utilization and cost management. Better profit of banks can be attributed to better asset utilization or better cost management or both simultaneously. According to the Du Pont analysis results summarized in Table 3.5, foreign banks showed the highest RoA in 2011–12 among bank groups, mainly on account of better asset utilization, though their operating expenses to assets ratio (indicator of cost management) was also higher when compared to other bank groups. This result corroborates the findings of past studies according to which foreign banks' higher profitability could be attributed to better fund management practices.

The operating efficiency of Indian banks improved during 2011–12, as measured by the Cost to Income ratio (operating expenses/total income). However, Net Interest Margin (NIM) also an efficiency indicator, dipped during the year. Figure 3.4 shows the results.

The Net Interest Margin (NIM)—An Important Indicator of Banking Efficiency and Profitability

The NIM, operating expenses and 'other income' are crucial in determining profitability of banks. The NIM indicates the margin taken by the banking sector while carrying on banking business. In India, during the last one decade, the NIM was in the range 2.5–3.1 per cent. The NIM, which witnessed a declining trend during the period 2004–10, improved during 2010–11. The NIM of the Indian banking sector continues to be higher than some of the emerging market economies of the world. The NIM can be decomposed into

a. The NIM from core banking business, (*i.e.*, calculated as the difference between interest income from loans and advances minus interest expenses on deposits as a per cent of average total assets), and
b. The NIM from others (*i.e.*, mainly the difference between all other interest income and interest expenses divided by average total assets).

The NIM from core banking business in India witnessed substantial increase during the last decade. In contrast, the NIM from others witnessed a decline, leaving the total NIM more or less stable during the same period. The increase in the NIM from core banking business, though a profitability indicator for banks, can also be interpreted to imply that the cost of

TABLE 3.4 RETURN ON ASSETS OF BANKS IN SELECT COUNTRIES (%)

Country	2007	2008	2009	2010	2011	2012
Advanced Economies						
France	–	0.1	0.3	0.6	0.4	–
Germany	0.3	–0.1	0.2	0.4	–	–
Greece	1.0	0.2	–0.1	–0.6	–2.0	–
Italy	0.8	0.3	0.3	0.3	–0.9	–
Japan	0.5	0.3	–0.3	0.2	0.3	
Portugal	1.1	0.3	0.4	0.5	–0.3	0.1
Spain	1.1	0.8	0.6	0.5	0.2	–
United Kingdom	0.4	–0.4	0.1	0.1	0.1	–
United States	1.2	–0.1	–0.1	0.9	1.2	1.0
Emerging and Developing Economies						
Russia	3.0	1.8	0.7	1.9	2.5	–
China	0.9	1.0	0.9	1.10	1.3	–
India	0.9	1.0	1.0	0.9	1.0	1.0
Malaysia	1.5	1.5	1.2	1.5	1.5	1.6
Brazil	3.5	1.6	2.4	3.2	1.5	1.4
Mexico	2.3	1.4	1.5	1.8	1.5	1.8

Note: Not available.

2011 data for Japan and Greece pertain to September.

2012 data for Portugal, US, India, Malaysia and Brazil pertain to June and for Mexico pertain to March.

Sources: Compiled from Finacial Soundness Indicators. IMF; RBI, Trends and Progress of Banking in India, 2011–12, Table II.1, p. 13.

financial intermediation increased in the economy during the last decade (see Chart A in Figure 3.5).

Therefore, it is important to increase 'other income' and reduce operating expenses as ratio of assets in the interest of profitability. The operating expenses to total average assets witnessed a declining trend during the last one decade mainly owing to the cost effective technological advancements. However, 'other income' to total average assets also witnessed a declining trend during the last one decade. Thus, it may be important for the Indian banking sector to improve 'other income'. (see Chart B in Figure 3.5)

However, spreads (difference between yields on advances and investments and cost of funds) narrowed during 2011–12 due to higher increase in cost of funds as compared with the increase in yields on advances and investments. Among bank groups in India, foreign banks showed lower cost of funds due to the high proportion of Current Account Savings Account (CASA) deposits held by them. Figure XX shows the trends in growth of cost of funds and yields.

Off Balance Sheet (OBS) Exposures—Contingent Liabilities of Banks in India: Earlier, we have seen the important role 'other income' plays in bank profitability. One of the main sources of other income is OBS.

The financial crisis of 2007–08 has brought into focus the role of contingent liabilities of banks in both banks' profitability as well as risks. Figure 3.7 shows the growth in contingent liabilities of banks in India and their relative size to banks' total balance sheet size.

Contingent liabilities are usually viewed with concern as their exact impact on the soundness of the banking system can not be accurately determined. In the event of default, an OBS exposure can extensively damage financial stability. This was demonstrated by the global financial crisis in the recent past.

During the last ten years, the OBS of the banking sector witnessed substantial growth, especially that of new private sector banks and foreign banks. With the onset of the global financial turmoil, the policy on the OBS was tightened in August 2008. Resultantly, there was a decline in the OBS of the banking sector in 2008–09 and 2009–10. However, with the onset of recovery, the OBS of the banking sector again witnessed positive growth in 2010–11 and 2011–12.

Major Components of OBS (Contingent Liabilities)

Letter of Credit A letter of credit (LC) is defined as 'an arrangement by means of which bank acting at the request of

FIGURE 3.3 LEVERAGE IN THE BANKING SYSTEM—SELECT ECONOMIES

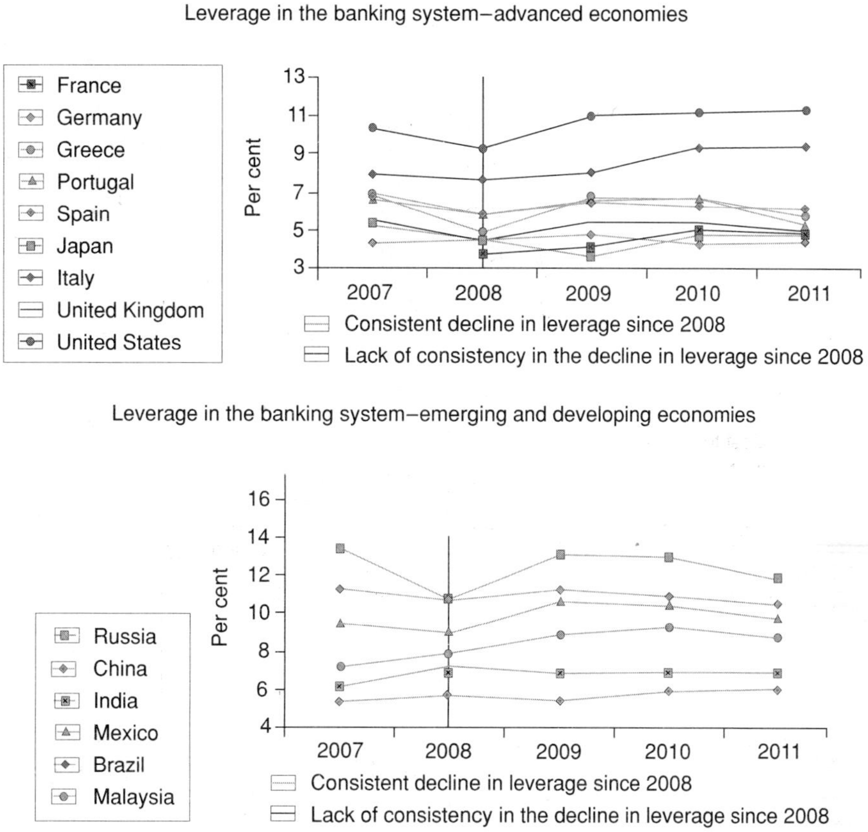

Note: 2011 data for Japan and Greece pertain to September 2011. 2007 data for France is not available.
Sources: RBI, Trends and Progress of Banking in India, 2011–12, Chart II.5, p. 16.

TABLE 3.5 ROA ANALYSIS—ASSET UTILIZATION AND COST MANAGEMENT BANK GROUPS IN INDIA, 2011–12

Bank Group	Asset Utilization	Cost Management
1	2	3
SBI group	2.85	1.95
Nationalized banks	2.35	1.48
Old private sector banks	3.06	1.91
New private sector banks	3.81	2.24
Foreign banks	4.27	2.52

the customer, undertakes to pay a third party a predetermined amount by a given date, according to agreed stipulations and against presentation of stipulated documents'. *The bank earns a specific amount of commission when it deals with an LC on behalf of its customer.* (More on LCs in the Chapter on 'International Banking')

Bank Guarantee A contract of guarantee is a contract to perform the promise, or discharge the liability of a third person in the case of his default. The person who gives the guarantee is called the surety, the person in respect of whose default the guarantee is given is called the principal debtor and the person to whom the guarantee is given is called the creditor. *Here, the bank acts as the surety and earns a commission.* (More on letters of Guarantee in Chapter 6).

Payment and Clearing Operations This is one of the most important fee-based services of the banking system. A cheque is the most common form of payment system used by banks. Apart from cheque, which is a paper-based payment mechanism, transfer of funds can also be made through electronic payments and funds transfer mechanisms, such as telegraphic transfers, 'electronic credit transfers, electronic debit transfers, electronic fund transfer and, more recently, the Real Time Gross Settlement System (RTGS).[20] (More on payment and clearing operations disaussed in the chapter titled 'High-tech Banking').

FIGURE 3.4 TREND IN EFFICIENCY INDICATORS—BANKS IN INDIA

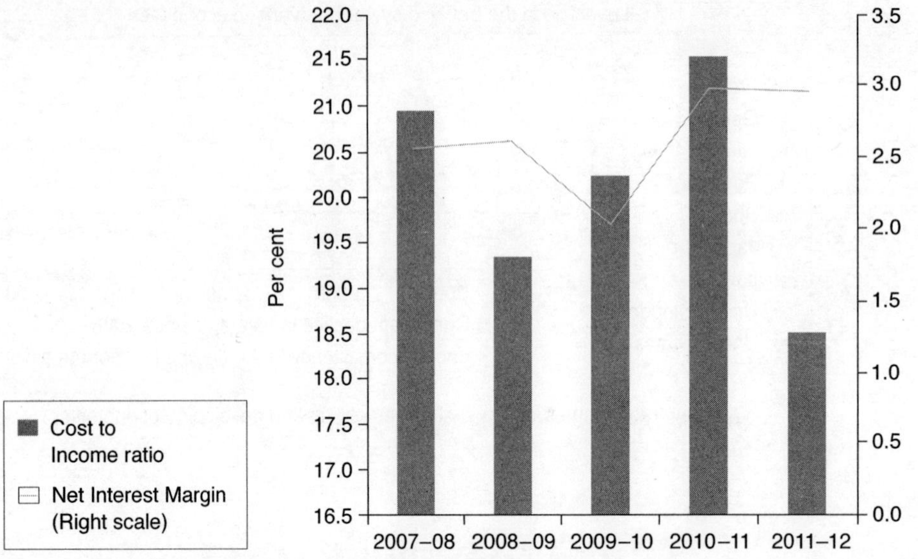

Source: RBI, Trends and Progress of Banking in India, 2011–12, Chart IV.7, p. 64.

FIGURE 3.5 TRENDS IN THE NIM, OPERATING EXPENSES AND OTHER INCOME—BANKS IN INDIA, 2002–2011

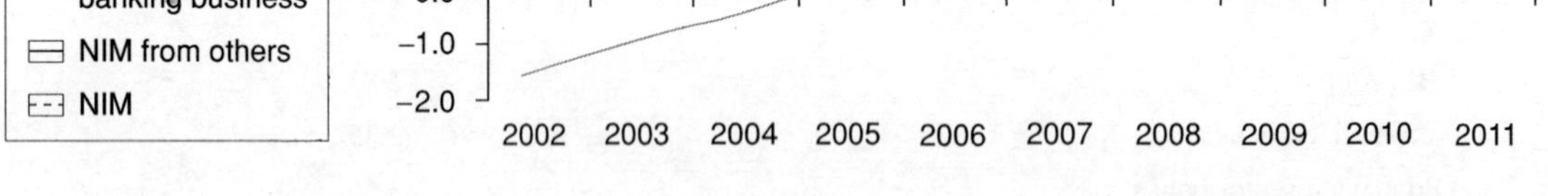

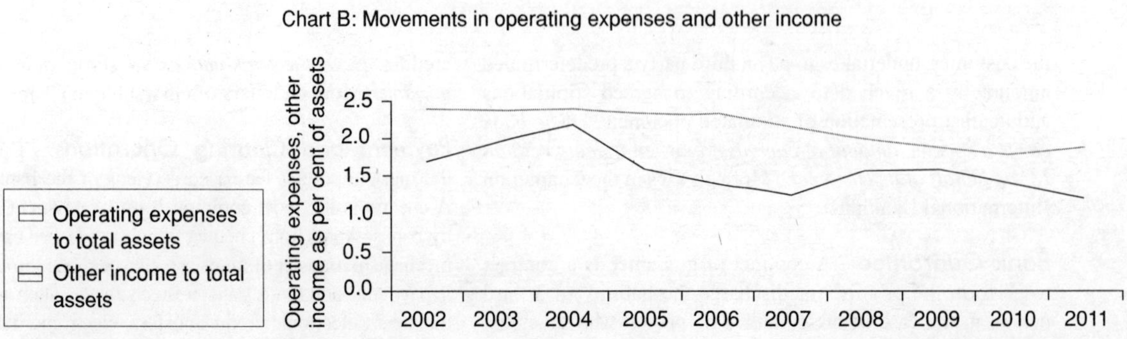

Source: RBI, Trends and Progress of Banking in India, 2010–11, Box IV.3, p. 73.

FIGURE 3.6 TRENDS IN COST OF FUNDS AND YIELDS—BANK GROUPS IN INDIA, 2011–12

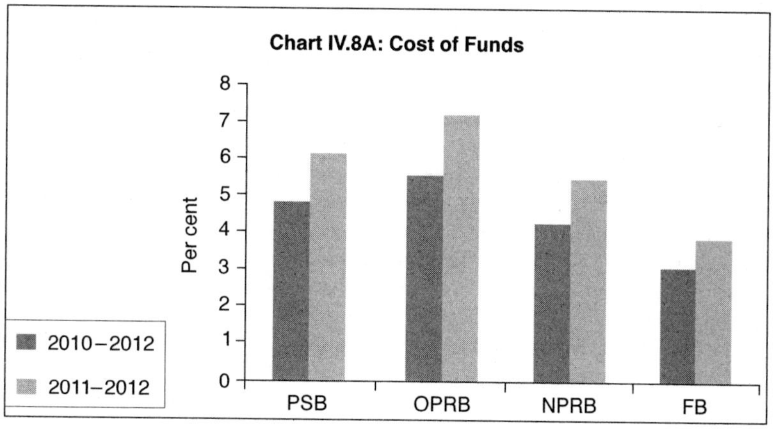

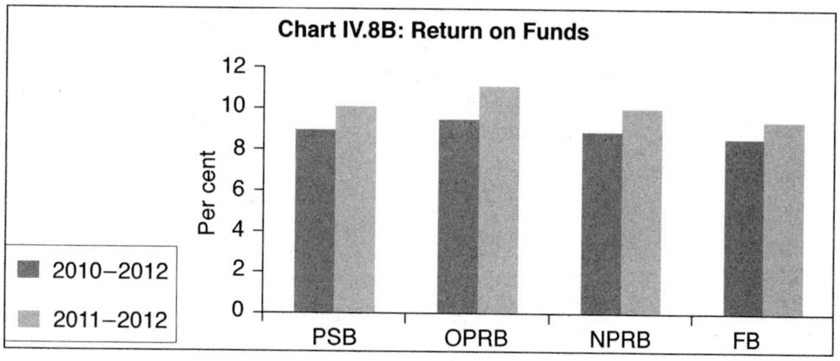

Source: RBI, Trends and Progress of Banking in India, 2011–12, p. 65.

FIGURE 3.7 CONTINGENT LIABILITIES AS PROPORTION OF TOTAL LIABILITIES/ASSETS OF BANK GROUPS IN INDIA

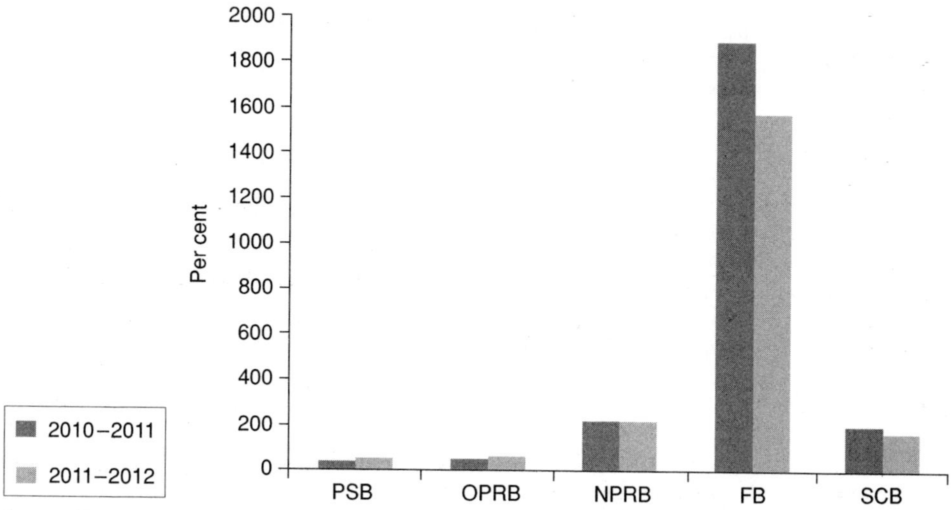

Source: RBI, Trends and Progress of Banking in India, 2011–12, Chart IV.6, p. 61.

Forward Exchange Contracts and Other Derivatives

A forward exchange contract is a contract between two parties (the bank and the customer). One party contracts to sell and the other party contracts to buy, one currency for another, at an agreed future date, at a rate of exchange, which is fixed at the time the contract is entered into.

This is basically a tool that enables customers to hedge their foreign exchange (forex) exposure. Banks offer two types of foreign exchange contracts. In a special option Forward Exchange Contract (FEC), a rate is quoted to the customer for an agreed validity period where the customer can take up the booked rate during the specified period. Customers who are unsure of the expected payment or receipt dates usually request this type of contract. The second is a fixed date FEC in which a rate is normally quoted for a fixed maturity date where the customer is required to take up the FEC on the maturity date of the contact. Customers who are certain of their expected payment or receipt dates usually request this type of contract.

Many banks also deal in derivatives. These are discussed in the chapter on 'Risk Management'.

Fluctuations in the exchange rate and also the higher interest rate environment increase the demand for forward contracts from the customers of banks, which is the biggest component of the OBS exposure of the banking sector. As the economy grows, the demand for such risk management services from the banking sector also increases. On the other side, from the point of view of banks, OBS exposures, which are basically fee-based services, increase the gross income although at a higher level of risk. Thus, if the risk appetite of a particular bank is high, it has an incentive to accumulate OBS exposures to reap more fee income.

The role of the OBS in generating 'other income' was examined by the RBI using regression analysis. Results indicated that 1 per cent increase in OBS exposures increases 'other income' of the banking sector by 0.08 per cent. Thus, banks have an incentive to accumulate OBS exposures to earn more income and therefore, profit.

Other Sources of Non-Interest Income Most of the banks have expanded their fee-based services to selling of insurance policies, mutual fund products and cash management services. Popular forms of fee-based businesses are

1. Fees from insurance business
2. Credit/debit cards—apart from fees, credit cards loans also earn higher spreads than other assets. Debit cards are even more lucrative, as they generate fees at virtually no risk.
3. Mutual fund distribution

ANNEXURE V

CHANGES IN INTERNATIONAL ACCOUNTING STANDARDS AND CODE OF GOOD PRACTICES ON TRANSPARENCY IN MONETARY AND FINANCIAL POLICIES—THE INTERNATIONAL MONETARY FUND

The International Accounting Standards Committee (IASC) and the International Organization of Securities Commissions (IOSCO) agreed in 1995 on a programme of work to prepare a set of accounting standards that could be accepted internationally. In accordance with the programme, the IASC completed an agreed set of standards at the end of 1998.

The committee reviewed the standards from the perspective of banking supervisors and has limited its review to those standards that have a significant effect on banks.

One of the important International Financial Reporting Standards applicable to banks and similar financial institutions relate to IAS 30, which deals with disclosures in banks' financial statements. IAS 30 was introduced in August 1990, operationalized in 1991 and reformatted in 1994. After being amended to IAS 39 (Financial instruments recognition and measurement), it was superceded by IFRS 7 (International Financial Reporting Standard 7) 'financial instrument disclosures', effective 1 January 2007. In effect, the project on bank disclosures was carried over from IASC and merged into the project on IFRS 7. IAS 39 is being superseded by IFRS 9—Financial instruments—for annual periods beginning on or after January 1, 2015.

On 5 March 2009, the IASB has issued *Improving Disclosures About Financial Instruments (Amendments to IFRS 7)*. The amendments require enhanced disclosures about fair value measurements and liquidity risk, in the light of the global financial crisis of 2007–2008. For more on the latest accounting standards impacting banks, a good resource is the IASB website, http://www.iasb.com. The Websites of the big accounting firms of the world also give comprehensive information on IFRS 7. IAS 39 is being superseded by IFRS 9— Financial instruments—for annual periods beginning on or after January 1, 2015.

Code of Good Practices on Transparency in Monetary and Financial Policies—The International Monetary fund (2000)

The objective of developing the code of good practices was in the context of strengthening the international monetary and financial system.

The IMF, in cooperation with the Bank for International Settlements, and in consultation with a representative group of central banks, financial agencies, other relevant international and regional organizations, and selected academic experts, developed a code of transparency practices for monetary and financial policies.

The design of the good transparency practices in the Code rests on two principles. First, monetary and financial policies can be made more effective if the public knows the goals and instruments of policy and if the authorities make a credible commitment to meeting them. Second, good governance calls for central banks and financial agencies to be accountable, particularly where the monetary and financial authorities are granted a high degree of autonomy.

The Code contains a list of broad principles related to transparency for monetary and financial policies that central banks and financial agencies should seek to achieve. As a guide to their implementation, the IMF, in consultation with central banks, has prepared a supporting document to the Code. The Supporting Document provides a fuller description of each of the transparency practices of the Code, the rationale of the practices in the context of transparency, examples of how the transparency practices are applied by central banks and financial agencies (including alternative ways to achieve the objective), and some considerations in implementation.

The Code and the supporting documents can be viewed at http://www.imf.org.

SELECT REFERENCES

1. Basel Committee on Banking Supervision, 'Report to G7 Finance Ministers and Central Bank Governors on International Accounting Standards.' (2002), Bank for International Settlements, Basel, Switzerland.
2. http://www.iasb.org
3. http://www.iasplus.com
4. http://www.imf.org

ENDNOTES

1. The basic nature of banking business is similar in all countries. Only nomenclatures and disclosures may differ.
2. The burden will be a negative figure in most banks. Hence, the burden is measured as a ratio with the denominator as total assets—the lower the absolute difference in the numerator, the more profitable the bank.
3. Excerpt from *RBI: Guidelines on Ownership and Governance in Private Sector Banks, dated 28 February 2005.*
4. RBI, 2002. *Core Principles for Effective Banking Supervision—An Assessment of the Position in India.*
5. Section 17 of the Banking Regulation Act reads as follows: Reserve Fund—(1) Every banking company incorporated in India shall create a reserve fund and [* * *] shall, out of the balance of profit of each year as disclosed in the profit and loss account prepared under Section 29 and before any dividend is declared, transfer to the reserve fund, a sum equivalent to not less than twenty per cent of such profit. (1A) Notwithstanding anything contained in sub-section (1), the central government may, on the recommendation of the Reserve Bank and having regard to the adequacy of the paid-up capital and reserves of a banking company in relation to its deposit liabilities, declare by order in writing that the provisions of sub-section (1) shall not apply to the banking company for such period as may be specified in the order:

   Provided that no such order shall be made unless, at the time it is made, the amount in the reserve fund under sub-section (1), together with the amount in the share premium account is not less than the paid-up capital of the banking company.
6. For a discussion on the 'Investment Reserve', please refer to Chapter on 'Investments'.
7. Bills rediscounted with SIDBI/IDBI are reflected in the balance sheet as a contra entry. It therefore forms part of the 'contingent assets'. The amount presents credit extended to a borrower, in which the bank has subsequently rediscounted the bills financed against with these apex institutions under a special scheme meant for the purpose. Hence, such rediscounted amounts do not get reflected in the balance sheet under 'advances.'
8. The concepts related to the disclosures in the list are dealt with in detail in subsequent chapters.
9. This approach is followed in 'Bank Management', Chapter 4, by Timothy Koch and Scott Macdonald, 4th edition, The Dryden Press, USA.
10. *Ibid.*
11. Also called 'CRAMELs' (capital adequacy, risk, asset quality, management, earnings, liquidity, and systems).
12. Refer chapter on 'Capital Risk Regulation and Adequacy'.
13. Represents 'non-performing assets', where payment of interest or repayment of principal is in arrears. For more details, refer to chapter on 'Credit Risk'. Net NPAs = Gross NPAs LESS Provisions.
14. For an analysis of the ROE in its decomposed form, refer to Section III of this chapter.
15. David Cates [1996], quoted in Koch, Timothy and Scott Macdonald Bank Management, Chapter 4, 4th ed. (2000). The Dryden Press.
16. We will discuss more on these approaches in the section on 'Loan Pricing'.

17. The terms 'credit risk', 'liquidity risk' and 'interest rate risk' are explained comprehensively in later chapters.
18. Hannan, Timothy H & Hanweck, Gerald A, 1988. 'Bank Insolvency Risk and the Market for Large Certificates of Deposit,' Journal of Money, Credit and Banking, Blackwell Publishing, vol. 20(2), pages 203–11, May.
19. Major portions of this annexure are extracted from RBI, Trends and Progress of Banking in India, 2011–12, Box IV.1, page 63.
20. For more detail on these modes of funds transfer, visit www.rbi.org.in.

CHAPTER FOUR

Sources of Bank Funds

CHAPTER STRUCTURE

KEY TAKEAWAYS FROM THE CHAPTER

- Understand the nature of bank liabilities.
- Learn about the nature of bank deposits.
- Understand deposit pricing strategies.
- Learn about non-deposit funding sources of banks.
- Understand the legal aspects of deposits in India.

SECTION I

BASIC CONCEPTS

We have seen in earlier chapters that banks, in their role as financial intermediaries, provide the vital link between savers and users of funds in the economy.

The ability of a bank to attract money from customers and businesses is a vital signal of the bank's acceptance in the market. In today's competitive environment, where returns from the capital markets or mutual funds are more attractive, banks find liability management a challenge. Banks have to constantly innovate—whether it is in product development or customer service.

Liability management plays a critical role in the risk—return profile of banks. In the present deregulated environment, banks have to balance profitability and risks while deciding on their liability mix. For example, if banks price their liabilities higher to lure more depositors, their interest expenses would rise. Further, the deposit rates are also subject to change, which lead to interest rate risk. Deposits could be withdrawn at any time, leading to liquidity risk for the bank. The bank would have created assets out of these deposits and in the event of sudden withdrawal of the deposits, the bank would also be subject to a refinancing risk.

We have seen in an earlier chapter that 'deposits' are the primary sources of funds for banks. The other sources of funds for banks are 'equity and reserves' and 'borrowings'.

The sources of funds as described above form the basis for creation of assets by the bank and are hence responsible for the bank's profit and growth. Therefore, it would be prudent for the bank to base its funds requirement and mobilization on some relevant parameters, such as:

1. **Maturity:** Deposit holders in a bank are a diverse lot. They are from divergent backgrounds, from small depositors to large corporations, financial institutions and governments. They have different needs and planning horizons and would require their savings back at different points in time. Each instrument would have to be priced differently, in terms of the prevailing regulations and the bank's strategy. The maturity of each debt instrument is vital for the bank, since it has to plan for repayment at the end of the period with no risk of default. Further, it has to forecast the interest rates that could prevail at the end of the period.
2. **Cost of funds:** Investors look for reasonable return on their investments when they put their savings into a bank. However, the bank should consider the yield from investing these funds in assets such as loans or investments, so that its target profit can be achieved.
3. **Tax implications:** Depositors would prefer to look at post-tax cash flows from their investments. Even if the bank prefers to borrow from a particular source, the availability of funds would be determined by tax rules in force.
4. **Regulatory framework:** Regulations in force would very often determine the attractiveness of one source of funds over the other.
5. **Market conditions:** The prevailing sentiment in the market and the investors' attitude towards risk would predominantly determine the amount of funds that would flow into banks.

It is, therefore, evident that a host of dynamic factors would determine the availability and cost of bank funds at any point of time. Preferences and investment objectives of depositors are changing over time and hence, banks may not be able to source the type of funds that they desire in the market.

In the following sections, we will look at the features of bank deposits and other non-deposit borrowings.

SECTION II

BANK LIABILITIES—DEPOSITS

Bank deposits are differentiated by the type of deposit customer, the tenure of the deposit and its cost to the bank. On the basis of these parameters, deposits can be broadly classified as follows:

1. **Transaction accounts or payment deposits:** These deposits, repayable by the bank on demand from the depositor, represent one of the primary services offered by banks. They can be bifurcated into non-interest bearing and interest bearing demand deposits. Such deposits facilitate transfer of funds by the deposit holder to third parties, primarily through cheques[1] and other forms of funds transfer. Cheques are attractive because they provide easy and formal verification and are readily accepted as a recognized mode of payment.

   Non-interest bearing demand deposits are typically held by individuals, businesses or the government. Explicit interest payments on these deposits are prohibited in most countries. However, there are no regulations restraining banks from prescribing minimum balances or transaction charges. Corporate customers prefer these accounts for ease of operation. These are generally large deposits and can be quite volatile sources of funds for the bank.

   Interest bearing demand deposits are preferred by individuals or certain types of organizations. Similar to the non-interest bearing accounts, these deposits are also used for the purpose of transactions by the deposit holders and a major portion of these deposits is likely to be volatile. They are called 'savings' accounts in some countries (as in India), since the depositors park their earnings in these accounts to be used for routine and other payments. These deposits carry a low rate of interest (in many countries, this rate of interest is prescribed by the regulator).

2. **Term deposits:** These are a form of 'debt investment' for a customer, who is willing to lend money to the bank for a specified period of time. In return, the customer receives a stream of cash flows in the form of interest. These deposits typically pay higher interest. A popular variant of large term deposits is the certificate of deposit (CD) (see Box 4.1).

Box 4.1 describes some of the prominent types of deposit accounts in select countries.

BOX 4.1 FEATURES OF DEPOSIT ACCOUNTS IN SELECT COUNTRIES

The USA

In the early 1970s, in New England, hybrid checking—savings accounts called negotiable order of withdrawal (NOW) accounts were introduced. These were meant to be interest bearing savings deposits that required the customer to give notice to the bank before withdrawing funds. However, the notice requirement is not insisted upon and the NOW is being used like any other checking account.

In the US, most banks predominantly offer three different transaction accounts—demand deposit accounts (DDAs), interest bearing NOW accounts or automatic transfer from savings (ATS) accounts and money market deposit accounts (MMDAs). Investors seeking relatively low risk investment that can easily be converted into cash go in for CDs. Banks differentiate between these deposits on parameters, such as the minimum balance required, the number of transfers/cheques permitted and the interest rate paid. All deposits are insured by the Federal Deposit Insurance Corporation (FDIC) up to USD 100,000 per account.

DDAs are non-interest bearing checking accounts, predominantly held by commercial units, though individuals and the government can also hold such accounts.

A NOW account is an interest bearing demand deposit. An ATS account is similar to a NOW account, with the difference that in the ATS account a customer has both the DDA and savings accounts, with the balance in the DDA account being brought down to 'nil' at the end of each day through transfer of funds from the savings account. NOW accounts are priced competitively and can be held only by individuals and non-profit organizations.

MMDAs were primarily introduced to enable banks compete with money market mutual funds offered by large brokerage houses. These are basically 'term' deposits and not transaction accounts. Though the average size of an MMDA account could be much larger than a transaction account, cheque usage and transactions are limited.

A CD is a special type of deposit account with a bank that typically offers a higher rate of interest than regular savings account. In a CD, a fixed sum of money, usually large, is invested for a fixed period of time and in exchange, the bank pays interest typically at regular intervals. Though CDs were designed to pay a fixed interest rate until maturity, they now pay variable rates as well. Further, CDs can be issued with special features, such as 'call' provisions. Zero coupon CDs ensure long-term funds for banks without periodical interest pay outs. Some banks also issue CDs with yields linked to a stock market index such as S&P 500 to lure investors who could otherwise take their money out of banks.

The UK

The predominant types of deposit accounts are:

- Current account, which provides a cheque-book but usually pays no interest.

These accounts are primarily used for paying bills.

- Deposit account, which pays interest and is used primarily for short-term saving.
- Investment or savings account, which pays a higher rate of interest and is used primarily for long-term saving. Notice of withdrawal must be given in writing.

Australia

'Deposits' include transaction and non-transaction deposit accounts and CDs.

Canada

The predominant types of deposit accounts are savings and cheque accounts, term deposits and guaranteed investment certificates (GICs). GICs are term investments that require depositors to lock in their investment for a set length of time. GICs generally pay higher rates of interest than term deposits, but are often not redeemable before maturity. The Canada Deposit Insurance Corporation (CDIC) insures eligible deposits up to a limit of USD 100,000 per depositor in each member institution.

Source: Web sites of the Countries' Central Banks.

Protecting the Depositor—Deposit Insurance

Deposit insurance is a measure taken by banks in most countries to protect small depositors' savings, either fully or in part, against any possible risk of a bank not being able to return their savings to these depositors. Deposit insurance institutions are mostly government-established and managed and may or may not form part of a country's central bank.

The US was the first country to initiate an official deposit insurance scheme, triggered by a banking crisis during the Great Depression in 1934. [As of end June 2013, 112 countries had some form of explicit deposit insurance. Another 41 countries were actively considering implementation of explicit deposit insurance.]

Many of the deposit insurance agencies are members of the International Association of Deposit Insurers (IADI). This organization was established in 2002 to promote deposit insurance, help countries without deposit insurance schemes to establish their own institutions for this purpose and promote knowledge and experience exchange between deposit insurers in various countries. Box 4.2 provides details on IADI and principles of deposit insurance.

BOX 4.2 THE INTERNATIONAL ASSOCIATION OF DEPOSIT INSURERS (IADI)

Introduction to IADI

IADI was founded on 6 May 2002. It is a non-profit organization, constituted under Swiss law.

The genesis of IADI was the Working Group on Deposit Insurance established by the Financial Stability Forum (FSF)[2] in 2000.

The IADI has four categories of participation—Members, Associates, Observers, and Partners. In January, 2014, IADI has 73 members. Members are entities/countries that, under law or agreement, have a deposit insurance system and have been approved for membership by IADI.

Associates are entities that do not fulfil all the criteria to be a Member, but are considering the establishment of a deposit insurance system, or are part of a financial safety net and have a direct interest in the effectiveness of a deposit insurance system.

Observers are not-for-profit entities such as international organizations which do not fulfil the criteria to be an Associate but have a direct interest in the effectiveness of deposit insurance systems.

Partners are not-for-profit entities such as international institutions that enter into a cooperative arrangement with the Association in the pursuit and furtherance of the Objects of the Association.

The IADI-BCBS Core Principles for Effective Deposit Insurance Systems

The financial crisis of 2008 prompted the Basel Committee on Banking Supervision (BCBS)[3] and the International Association of Deposit Insurers (IADI) to collaborate for developing an internationally applicable set of 'Core Principles'. The IADI 'Core principles for effective deposit insurance systems' served as the basis for the new set of core principles.

The document sets the following preconditions for an effective deposit insurance system:

- An ongoing assessment of the economy and banking system;
- Sound governance of agencies comprising the financial system safety net;
- Strong prudential regulation and supervision; and
- A well developed legal framework and accounting and disclosure regime.

The 18 Core Principles are broadly categorized into ten groups as given below:

a. Setting objectives (Principles 1 and 2)
   i. **Principle 1** sets out 'Public Policy objectives' that should primarily focus on financial system stability and depositor protection.
   ii. **Principle 2** deals with 'mitigating moral hazard'.

b. Mandates and powers (Principles 3 and 4)
   i. **Principle 3** elaborates on the consistency between public policy objectives and the 'mandate'—powers and responsibilities given to the deposit insurer.
   ii. **Principle 4** specifies that some 'powers' that deposit insurers should be equipped with, such as the power to finance reimbursements, enter into contracts, set internal operating budgets and procedures, and access timely and accurate information to ensure that they can meet their obligations to depositors promptly.

c. Governance (Principle 5)
   i. **Principle 5** emphasizes 'governance' aspects such as operational independence, transparency, accountability and insulation from undue political and industry influences, in order to function effectively.

d. Relationships with other safety-net participants and cross-border issues (Principles 6 and 7)
   i. **Principle 6** describes the nature of 'relationships with other safety net participants'. Close coordination and sharing of information should be part of the framework.
   ii. **Principle 7** deals with 'cross border issues' where deposit insurers in different jurisdictions and foreign participants are involved.

e. Membership and coverage (Principles 8 and 10)
   i. **Principle 8** suggests 'compulsory membership' for all financial institutions accepting deposits from small depositors and those most in need of such protection.
   ii. **Principle 9** deals with 'coverage' issues such as legal definition of insurable deposit, or quick determination of level of coverage, which could be limited but should cover the large majority of depositors to meet public policy objectives.
   iii. **Principle 10** suggests quick 'transitioning from a blanket guarantee to a limited coverage deposit insurance system' to avoid moral hazard issues during the transition period.

f. Funding (Principle 11)
   i. **Principle 11** deals with the 'funding' aspects of the system to ensure prompt reimbursement of depositors' claims. The primary responsibility for paying the cost of deposit insurance should be borne by banks. Where deposit insurance used risk adjusted differential premium systems, the criteria and administrative aspects should be made transparent.

g. Public awareness (Principle 12)
   i. **Principle 12** deals with ongoing information to the public about the limitations and benefits of the deposit insurance system, in order to create 'public awareness'.

h. Selected legal issues (Principles 13 and 14)
   i. **Principle 13** deals with 'legal protection' to the deposit insurer for decisions and actions taken in 'good faith'
   ii. **Principle 14** 'dealing with parties at fault in a bank failure', states that the deposit insurer should be provided with the power to seek legal redress against those parties at fault in a bank failure.

i. Failure resolution (Principles 15 and 16)
   i. **Principle 15** emphasizes on 'early detection and timely intervention and resolution' of troubled banks.
   ii. **Principle 16** calls for 'effective resolution processes' to facilitate the deposit insurer's ability to meet its obligations.

j. Reimbursing depositors and recoveries (Principles 17 and 18)
   i. **Principle 17** emphasizes on 'reimbursing depositors' promptly in conditions under which the reimbursement is to be made. Depositors should be informed of their legal right to reimbursement, the coverage limit, the time frame over which payments will be made, and so on.
   ii. **Principle 18** deals with 'recoveries' by the deposit insurer from the failed bank's assets.

Source: www.iadi.org, for an introduction to IADI and BIS and IADI, core principles for effective deposit insurance systems, June 2009, accessed at www.iadi.org on January 3, 2012, and January 29, 2014.

Deposit insurance is being increasingly used by governments as a tool to ensure the stability of the banking system of their countries and protect bank depositors from incurring large losses due to bank failures. Actually, almost all countries have some kind of financial safety nets in place to protect depositors. These could take the form of bank regulation and supervision, lender of last resort facilities from the central bank, bank insolvency resolution procedures or explicit and implicit deposit insurance. Although deposit insurance is used as a popular tool, its desirability is debated by many economists who point to the moral hazard problems and the accompanying excessive risk being taken by banks.

However, between creation of possible 'moral hazard' by deposit insurance systems and financial stability, the choice is clear. Financial stability has to be preserved at any cost, this fact was highlighted by the recent financial crisis.

The Financial Stability Board's 'Thematic Review of Deposit Insurance Systems' (DIS) published in February 2012, throws up interesting facts and comparisons, post the financial crisis of 2007–08. Some of these are given below:

1. Explicit deposit insurance has become the preferred choice of most countries. Australia, Palestine, and Mongalia are some of the latest countries to establish an explicit deposit insurance system. China and South Africa have confirmed their plans to introduce deposit insurance. However, Saudi Arabia is not convinced about introducing a deposit insurance system in the country.
2. Those countries with explicit deposit insurance systems (including India) are broadly in conformity with the 'Core Principles for effective deposit insurance systems' issued by BCBS and IADI (see Box 4.2).
3. Some of the areas of divergence from the core principles are observed in the following countries:
   a. In some countries like Switzerland, certain non-bank institutions taking deposits from the public and participating in the national payments system are not covered by the domestic DIS.
   b. In some jurisdictions (*e.g.*, Germany, Japan, United States), the coverage limits—both in terms of the proportion of depositors covered and the value of deposits covered are relatively high. The report notes that although a high coverage level reduces the incentives for depositors to run, adequate controls are needed to ensure a proper balance between financial stability and market discipline.
   c. In the case of Switzerland, the existence of a system-wide limit of CHF 6 billion on the total amount of contributions by participating members in the DIS could create the perception in times of stress that some insured deposits would not be reimbursed in the event of a (large) bank failure.
   d. The payout systems vary significantly from country to country, such as, the institution that triggers a claim for payment or the speed of depositor reimbursement. In Germany, the institutional protection schemes do

not have any arrangements to reimburse depositors because they protect their member institutions against insolvency and liquidation. In Switzerland, depositor reimbursement is the responsibility of the failed bank's liquidator as opposed to the deposit insurance agency (DIA).

e. The starting date used to set the payout timeframes also differs. Adequate payout arrangements—such as early information access via a single customer view—are the practice in the United States. Some countries such as the Netherlands, Singapore and the United Kingdom have shifted from a net to a gross payout basis, *i.e.*, the insured deposits will not be offset against the depositor's liabilities owed to the failed bank.
f. The mandates of DISs in FSB member jurisdictions are generally well defined and formalized, and may be broadly classified into four categories:
    i. Narrow mandate systems that are only responsible for the reimbursement of insured deposits ('paybox' mandate)—such as in Australia, Germany, Hong Kong, India, Netherlands, Singapore, Switzerland;
    ii. A 'paybox plus' mandate, where the deposit insurer has additional responsibilities such as resolution functions—such as in Argentina, Brazil, United Kingdom;
    iii. A 'loss minimizer' mandate, where the insurer actively engages in the selection from a full suite of appropriate least-cost resolution strategies—such as in Canada, France, Indonesia, Italy, Japan, Mexico, Russia, Spain, Turkey; and
    iv. A 'risk minimizer' mandate, where the insurer has comprehensive risk minimization functions that include a full suite of resolution powers as well as prudential oversight responsibilities—such as in Korea, United States.

The mandates of certain DISs have been expanded or clarified following the financial crisis:

g. The composition of the governing body varies across countries and generally reflects a variety of safety net participants and relevant stakeholders. However, some DIAs are dominated by representatives from the government (*e.g.*, Russia), the banking industry (*e.g.*, Argentina, Brazil, Germany, Italy, Switzerland), or the supervisor.
h. The provision of cross-border deposit insurance is concentrated primarily in those countries within the European Economic Area. However, even in countries not extending protection to overseas deposits, local depositors in foreign-owned bank branches may still be eligible for protection by the foreign (home authority) DIS.
i. Some countries run multiple DISs, *e.g.*, Brazil, Canada, Germany, Italy, Japan, United States.
j. While the global trend is towards establishing DIS with ex-ante funds, some countries such as Australia, Italy, Netherlands, Switzerland, and the United Kingdom are presently supported solely by an ex-post funding system.

What happens when an insured bank fails? The insuring agency typically has the following options in the event of bank failure[4]: It can invite bids from healthy banks for the sale of the failed bank, in which case the insured depositors' accounts will be shifted to the new bank rather than being paid off by the agency; it can give financial assistance to the bank interested in acquiring the failed bank, so that depositors of the failed bank can start having accounts with the acquiring bank; it can transfer all insured deposits to a healthy bank; it can take charge and manage the operations of the failed bank till it finds a suitable buyer or it can pay off the depositors up to the maximum allowed.

Deposit Insurance in India

The Deposit Insurance Corporation (DIC), established under the Deposit Insurance Act, 1961, came into being in 1962, following two bank failures (Laxmi Bank and the Palai Central Bank). *India was the second country in the world to introduce the Scheme—the first being the United States in 1934*. Initially, the system covered exclusively the commercial banks. In 1968, cooperative banks with a minimum size operating in states having pertinent legislation was included in the system. In 1975, coverage was extended to rural banks as well. In 1978, the deposit insurance and credit guarantee functions were integrated to form the Deposit Insurance and Credit Guarantee Corporation (DICGC). But over time the credit guarantee schemes were delinked. The coverage limits have been changed in time as follows: initially ₹1,500; ₹5,000 in 1968; ₹10,000 in 1970; ₹20,000 in 1976; ₹30,000 in 1980 and ₹1,00,000 since 1 May 1993. The system is administered officially. Certificates of deposit, government, inter-bank and illegal deposits are not covered. More information on the operational aspects of the scheme is available at www.dicgc.org.

The RBI's annual report for 2012–13 presents the following information:

a. The number of registered insured banks at the end of March, 2013 stood at 2167, comprising of 89 commercial banks, 67 regional rural banks, 4 local area banks, and 2007 cooperative banks.

FIGURE 4.1 COMPARISON OF ABSOLUTE LEVEL AND PER CENT OF PER CAPITA GDP–INDIA WITH SELECT COUNTRIES

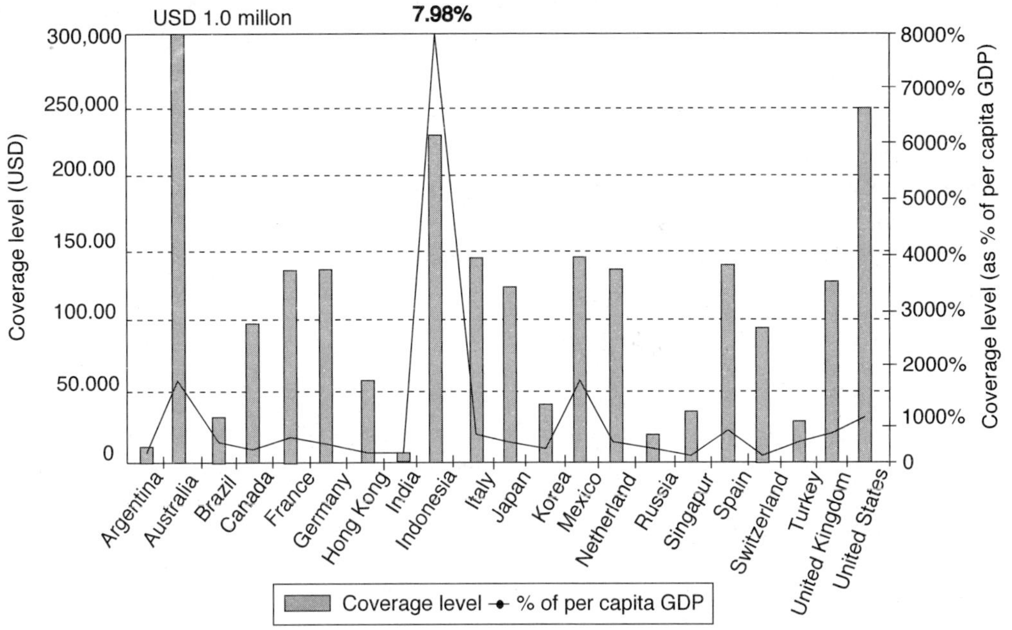

Note: See Table 5 in Annex C for details. Figures for Germany only include the statutory DIS. The absolute coverage level for Australia was A$1 million per account-holder per authorized deposit-taking institution as of year-end 2010, but the authorities introduced a new ceiling of A$250,000 as from February 1, 2012.

Sources: 1. 2012, Financial Stability Board, 'Thematic Review on Deposit Insurance Systems', accessed at www.financialstabilityboard.org
2. National Authorities, World Bank.

b. The 1393 million fully protected accounts form 94 per cent of the total 1482 million accounts in the banking system. The international benchmark in this respect is 80 per cent.
c. Insured deposits amounted to ₹21,584 billion. This constituted 33 per cent of assessable deposits against the international benchmark of 20–40 per cent.
d. At the March 2013 level, the insurance cover is 1.45 times India's per capita income. Figure 4.1 compares India's deposit insurance cover with that of other countries at the end of 2010.
e. The deposit insurance fund (DIF) is built through transfer of the Deposit insurance Corporation's surplus—excess of income (primarily premium received from insured banks, interest income from investments and cash recovery out of assets of failed banks) over expenses, each year. This fund is used for settlement of claims of depositors of banks going into liquidation/reconstruction/amalgamation, etc.

SECTION III

PRICING DEPOSIT SERVICES

The Need to Price with Precision

The pricing of deposits and related services assumes great importance in the present deregulated and highly competitive environment, where deposit rate ceilings do not exist. However, banks have to monitor the cost of their funding sources carefully for the following reasons:

- Changes in cost of funds would require changes in asset yields to maintain spreads
- Changes in cost of funds could alter the liability mix of banks and expose the bank to liquidity constraints
- Changes in cost of funds could render the bank less competitive in the market

It is, therefore, imperative that banks understand how to measure the cost of their funding sources and accordingly price their assets in order to ensure a desired level of profitability. This is done through a pricing policy.

The pricing policy of a bank is typically a written document that lays down guidelines for evaluating deposit sources and pricing them effectively. Generally, the following key aspects would be considered before arriving at a pricing decision:

- Servicing costs versus minimum balance requirements
- Deposit volumes and their costs in relation to profits
- Lending and investment avenues and compensating balances
- Relationship with customers
- Promotional pricing, if new products are being considered
- Product differentiation in a competitive market

Therefore, measuring the cost of funds should take into account both explicit and implicit costs associated with sourcing the deposits.

The explicit costs would be interest payments on the deposits and giveaways and gifts to promote the deposit product. However, even in non-interest bearing transaction deposits, where no explicit interest is paid out, there are implicit costs, such as a provision of services like free cheque books to the customer and added convenience for customer transactions, such as provision and maintenance of ATMs and branch offices. To compensate for these transaction costs, some banks levy fees depending on the frequency of cheque usage or ATM usage or prescribe a minimum balance maintenance in customers' accounts. Table 4.1 depicts some typical explicit and implicit prices and their impact on bank revenues and costs.

TABLE 4.1 EXPLICIT AND IMPLICIT PRICES AND THEIR IMPACT ON BANK REVENUES AND COSTS

Bank Cash Flows	Explicit Prices	Implicit Prices
Bank costs	Interest payments	Below cost services (*e.g.*, free cheque book issue)
	Gifts to customers	More convenience to customers such as branch offices, ATMs and business hours
Bank revenues	Service fees such as charges per cheque issued	Minimum balance requirements
	Other fees such as on overdrafts	Restrictions such as limited cheque writing privileges

Developing a sound deposit pricing methodology is gaining greater importance since banks have to look more to non-core sources for funding their assets. One reason for this is the intense market competition and the other is the changing asset profile of banks that requires sources with different maturities and risk profiles.

The traditional approach to deposit pricing was a 'supply–side' approach. Deposit rates reflected what competition was paying for similar products and what the bank could 'afford'. The most serious drawback of this approach was that it ignored both customer needs and the underlying demand elasticity of deposits. This resulted in specialized competitors like investment banks targeting the most desirable customer segments through product offerings that combine rate and convenience—products that banks could barely match.

Most banks have now, therefore, shifted to the 'demand side' approach. This view considers the degree to which customer demand varies with the deposit rate offered. This demand elasticity is analyzed and quantified by major products, geographies or customer segments.

For example, deposit rates could be computed separately for large time deposits, non-transaction (excluding large time) deposits and transaction deposits. This allows the evaluation of deposit pricing strategy for these three different classes of deposit investors.

Recent research[5] indicates that in reality, deposit customers are fairly tolerant of price changes. The cited report also notes that 'if they (banks) had more flexibility to price retail products without sparking widespread customer defections, they could boost their bottom-line retail earnings by as much as 5–7 per cent'. The research also found that 'checking account' customers rated convenience, service quality and relationship with the bank over price increases. More than one-third of these customers were unable to even recall when the last price change occurred and in the end, just 2 per cent of all customers moved their accounts to another bank.

Such analysis could help banks avoid raising rates (and lowering profitability) to attract deposits in customer segments which are known to be price inelastic. Or the information could help in fine tuning the deposit prices in customer segments where better rates would be a deciding factor for a customer to keep deposits in or move them out of a bank. Better informed tradeoffs would enable better use of resources to improve service or convenience than to raise deposit rates.

There are also other drivers to deposit growth. Exogenous factors such as macroeconomic factors or movements in the financial markets may impact the flow of deposits in and out of the banking system. Banks can do little in influencing these factors. However, they need to understand the nature of these flows. For example, when the interest rates are ruling high, customers would gravitate to high interest paying deposits (transitioning from checking accounts which would pay lower) or to the markets. When interest rates move southward, investors may prefer to invest in short-term instruments, such as savings deposits or money market accounts. Such trends can be forecasted reasonably accurately and blended into the pricing strategy of the bank.

The second factor driving deposit growth is endogenous. Banks can attract more deposits by appropriate promotion and pricing strategies and by reflecting a robust value proposition for the long-term. Best practice banks are increasingly analyzing customer price elasticities by product, to enable specific quantification of the potential volume and revenue impact associated with a given price position.[6] The cited article[7] adds, 'Such an analysis reveals an "area of indifference" around the average market price for each product. Within this zone, consumers are apparently indifferent to small pricing changes. Outside this zone, demand rises dramatically in response to rate increases and then flattens out again. Above a certain point, higher rates do not have a commensurate impact on balances'.

An important point to be noted here is that proper deposit pricing will have a positive effect on the growth of net interest income and net interest margin. Some common practices adopted by banks for improving profitability while pricing deposits are:

- Setting deposit prices in keeping with the deposit origination cost. For example, the origination cost of two deposits of say, ₹100 crores and ₹10 crores may be almost the same, but the larger deposit can provide an opportunity for the bank to create an asset that is 10 times larger. Therefore, the pricing could be based on the deposit amount.
- Paying higher rates for longer term deposits. This again depends on the nature of assets the bank wants to create.
- Banks prefer adding interest to principal or paying interest by automatic transfer to another internal account, to issue periodic interest payments to the customer. The latter practice is less expensive.

Some Commonly Used Approaches to Deposit Pricing

1. *Cost Plus Margin Deposit Pricing*

This type of pricing encourages banks to determine the deposit rate as one that would be adequate to cover all costs of offering the service, plus a small profit margin. Banks incur costs such as personnel and management time, material and automation in offering each deposit service. In a deregulated environment, the pressure is on banks' profitability in terms of higher cost of funds, thinning net interest margins and higher cost of customer solicitation and retention. If deposit pricing is not related to banks' costs in extending deposit services, the bank could end up exacerbating the pressure on profitability.

Thus, the price of deposit services would typically conform to the following 'cost plus deposit pricing' formula:

Unit price charged to the customer per deposit service = Operating expense per unit of deposit service + Estimated overhead expense allocated to deposit function + Planned profit from each deposit unit

Relating deposit prices to costs as above has encouraged banks to match prices and costs more closely and allocate prices to many services that were earlier rendered free. Thus, in most countries today, banks levy fees for excessive withdrawals from transaction deposits, customer balance enquiries, cheques returned without being paid, stop payment orders, ATM operations and so on and also prescribe required minimum deposit balances.

2. *Market Penetration Deposit Pricing*

This pricing strategy is typically aimed at high growth markets in which the bank is determined to garner a large market share. Therefore, banks are tempted to offer either high interest rates, well above the market level or charge customer fees well below the market standards. Bank managers expect that the large sources of funds and the associated loan business and investment opportunities would offset thinner spreads. Because it is usually costly for a customer to move certain kinds of deposits such as payment accounts, the lower fees on certain deposits initially attracted through penetration pricing which may eventually be raised to a cost-recovery or profit-making level.

3. *Conditional Pricing*

Conditional pricing can be used by banks as a tool to attract the types of depositors they want as customers. Under this pricing technique, the bank will post a schedule of interest rates or fees for deposits based on size of deposits or account activity. Typically, larger volume deposits carry higher interest rates or lower fees. This strategy is mostly designed to encourage customers to hold high average deposit balances for a given period of time, which, in turn, could be invested in earning assets.

An added advantage of this pricing strategy is that the customer chooses a deposit plan suitable for the customer and not for the bank. This selection process serves as a signal to the markets and the bank itself regarding the behaviour and cost of its deposits.

The following hypothetical example would serve to illustrate how two banks use conditional pricing to attract a certain class of deposit customers.

Bank X		**Bank Y**	
Transaction deposits with cheque facility		Transaction deposits with cheque facility	
Minimum operating balance	₹10,000	Minimum operating balance	₹10,000
If minimum daily balance is:		If minimum daily balance is	
₹1 lakh or more	No service fee	₹80,000 or more	No service fee
₹50,000– ₹1 lakh	₹50 per month	Less than ₹80,000	₹50 per month
₹30,000– ₹50,000	₹75 per month	If ATM transactions or number of cheques issued exceed 10 in a month and the balance falls below ₹80,000	₹10 per debit
If collected monthly balance averages ₹1.2 lakhs, no fee will be charged			
No limit to number of cheques that can be issued			

Savings Accounts		**Savings Accounts**	
Minimum balance	₹5,000	Minimum balance	₹5,000
If the balance is ₹25,000 or more	No service fee	₹10,000 or more	No service fee
Less than ₹25,000	₹10 per month	Less than ₹10,000	₹7 per month
Fee for more than two withdrawals per month	₹5 per debit	Fee for more than three withdrawals per month	₹5 per debit

In the above example, Bank X seems to prefer relatively low activity but high balance transaction and savings accounts, while Bank Y is not averse to smaller accounts. This is evident from the way the service fees are structured. Generally, larger volume deposits carry higher interest returns to the depositor or are assessed lower service charges, encouraging customers to hold high average deposit balances which give the bank more funds to invest in earning assets.

In such cases, banks' deposit pricing policy is typically sensitive to the customer segments that each bank plans to serve and the costs incurred by the banks in serving different customer segments.

4. *Upscale Target Pricing*

Upscale target pricing is the use of carefully but aggressively designed deposit advertising programs and deposit pricing schemes to appeal to customers with higher levels of income or net worth, such as business owners and managers, doctors, lawyers and other high income households. The customers being targeted are price sensitive and therefore could respond quickly to the price differentials.

5. *Relationship Pricing*

Relationship pricing typically ensures that the bank's best customers get the best pricing. It involves basing fees charged to a customer not only on the number of services that the customer purchases from the bank, but also on the intensity of use of these services. The objective is to forge a strong relationship with the customer by selling 'convenience' (through multiple services) and thus prevent the customer from moving away from the bank only on pricing concerns. Theoretically, relationship pricing is perceived as promoting customer loyalty to the bank, thus rendering the customer relatively insensitive to prices or other charges.

In all the above deposit pricing approaches, the key parameter that banks should be able to determine is their costs.

At times of sluggish deposit growth, the temptation for banks is to increase rates offered on special deposits such as CDs or new account introductions. Such strategies to increase deposit inflows would put pressure on the banks' cost of funds and also trigger a market-wide rate war. However, over a period of time, it is possible that the increased rates would not translate into overall increase in deposits or in market share. On the other hand, the banks may be left with increased cost of funds eating into their already thin spreads.

Therefore, before hiking interest rates on some classes of deposits or going on an aggressive campaign to mobilize new deposits, there are two types of analysis that should be considered. The analysis should quantify the actual cost of new deposits and the cost of protecting existing deposits. Such analysis is typically done using the following suggested approaches—the marginal cost of funds approach and the new cost of funds approach.[8]

The historical average cost rate is called break even because the bank must earn at least this rate on its earning assets (primarily loans and securities) just to meet the total operating costs of raising borrowed funds and the bank's stockholders' required rate of return. Therefore, the bank will know the lowest rate of return that it can afford to earn on assets it might wish to acquire.

Marginal Cost of Funds Approach

Assume that Bank J has a deposit base of ₹1,000 crores, of which about ₹250 crores comprises premium deposits perceived as rate sensitive. The bank pays 5 per cent per annum on these deposits at present.

A competitor, Bank L, announces that it is prepared to pay 6 per cent on premium deposits. The objective of the competitor, of course, is to garner more deposit market share.

Should Bank J respond to the threat and revise its deposit rate?

If Bank J does not match the 100 bps rate rise, it would probably lose a portion of its deposits to Bank L. The options before Bank J are to increase the rate on the entire rate-sensitive component of ₹250 crores or leave the present rate unchanged and replace the lost deposits. Of course, Bank J has a range of options between the two extremes. For example, it could raise the rate by 50 or 75 bps instead of 100 bps. The question would be: At what cost can it replace the lost deposits as compared to increasing the rate on the entire ₹250 crores component? In short, the effective cost of protecting these balances should be compared with the incremental cost of alternative funding sources to replenish the lost funds.

An illustration of the likely impact of two extreme options is presented as follows:

	Balance (₹ in Crores)	Rate Per Cent	Expense
Initial rate	250	5	12.5
Pricing option 1	250	6	15
Pricing option 2	200	5	10
Marginal cost/benefit	250	1	25
Marginal cost			0.1 or 10%

According to the above calculations, if Bank J does not raise the rate to 6 per cent, it is likely to lose ₹50 crores of its deposit base. However, it will save ₹5 crores in annual interest expense. The marginal cost of holding on to the ₹50 crores is therefore 10 per cent (₹5 crores/₹50 crores).

It doesn't seem logical, does it? How can it cost 10 per cent to hold to a deposit that at present costs only 5 per cent to the bank?

The answer to this question is the key to making intelligent pricing decisions on rate sensitive deposit accounts.

There are actually two different costs associated with increasing the deposit rate to 6 per cent. First, Bank J must pay 6 per cent on the rate sensitive deposits of ₹50 crores that it expects to lose. This works out to an annual cost of ₹3 crores. Second, Bank J must also pay an additional 1 per cent to the remaining customers (₹200 crores) in the rate-sensitive segment. This amounts to an additional cost of ₹2 crores. This additional cost will have to be incurred even though the probability that these customers would shift their deposits out of Bank J was minimal. Hence, the total additional expense for the bank aggregates to ₹5 crores.

Now that Bank J knows that the 'marginal cost' of holding on to ₹50 crores of deposit is ₹5 crores in annual interest expense, which works out to an annual interest cost of 10 per cent, it can decide on whether to raise the rates.

Of course, the bank will not be able to make the decision based on one scenario alone. Hence, it may want to look at various scenarios of interest rate increases ranging from 0 per cent to even more than 1 per cent if it wants to be very aggressive. It may also want to relate various probabilities of loss of deposits under each of the interest rate scenarios. Typically, the following table would result from the analysis.

Expected Deposit Loss Protected (per cent)	Probable Rate Increases (per cent)		
	0.50	0.75	1.0
10	10.00	12.50	15.0
20	7.50	8.75	10.0
30	6.67	7.50	8.33
40	6.25	6.88	7.50
50	6.00	6.50	7.0

The above table identifies the effective marginal cost associated with increasing deposit rates with the objective of minimizing flight of deposits from the bank. For example, the incremental cost of increasing deposit rate by 0.75 per cent to protect the most volatile 20 per cent of the balances is 8.75 per cent. This effective cost is calculated as shown earlier and should be compared with the incremental cost of alternate funding sources for the bank. That is, if Bank J is likely to lose 30 per cent of its deposits due to the competitor's offering of 1 per cent more and can replace these funds at 8.33 per cent or less, it will be better off financially than paying 1 per cent more on the entire rate-sensitive account base.

Another interpretation of the table is that as the proportion of non-rate sensitive customers in a segment increases, so does the marginal cost of paying up to retain rate sensitive customers in the segment.

This interpretation would explain why a bank would be more likely to push up its rates for CDs in a rising rate environment, rather than on its transaction accounts. The CD customers are perceived as more rate sensitive. And the more the rate sensitive customers in a segment, the less are the non-rate sensitive customers that will receive a higher rate determined in order to retain the rate sensitive customers.

The second issue that arises in the above analysis is the worth of the customers' relationship to the bank. Using the table generated above with different rate scenarios and expected protection of deposit loss, a new question can be formed: If the bank fails to match the 6 per cent rate being offered by the competitor, what could be the maximum deposit loss? Let us assume that 20 per cent of Bank J's customers in the segment threaten to withdraw their deposits if the bank did not match the competitor's offering. Would the bank be willing to increase the rate to keep them? Or what if 40 per cent were to demand a rate hike? The bank's decision would depend on how much these deposit relationships are worth to the bank, since for retaining 20 per cent or 40 per cent of its customers, the bank is actually willing to pay up to 10 per cent or 7.5 per cent, as the case may be.

A strategy that can be employed here is convincing the rate sensitive customers to move their balances into some other account in the same bank. For example, the bank can convince the customers wanting higher interest income to move to, say, higher yielding short-term deposits. Let us assume that these instruments yield an average of 5.75 per cent. The customers would be satisfied, as they are earning more on their deposits. Bank J will also be happy that it need not incur the marginal cost ranging from 6.5 per cent to 12.5 per cent to retain the relationship with these customers.

A third issue is that the bank should be satisfied that the yields it receives on assets supported by the ₹250 crores deposit accounts is more than the marginal cost of retaining rate sensitive deposits. This implies that the bank's average yield on assets should be more than 7 per cent to 15 per cent, if the deposit rate increase contemplated is 1 per cent. For example, if only 20 per cent of the customers were rate sensitive in the segment and the bank fears that its comparable asset yield may be less than 10 per cent (see table above), it will be better off selling the assets and using the sale proceeds to fund the outgo of deposits. It is to be noted that the asset yields being used in the comparison would be net of any adjustments and servicing costs. For example, the yield on a credit card may dip from, say, 20 per cent to 12 per cent after adjusting for operational costs and charge offs.

New Cost of Funds Analysis

Let us now assume that Bank J wants to offer a new deposit product at 5.75 per cent to expand its market share. The bank is interested in tapping entirely new deposit clientele and not in conversion from its existing deposit base. The bank reviews the performance of the new product after 2 months and finds that only about a quarter of the deposits mobilized were fresh ones, the remaining being existing deposits of the bank converted to the new scheme.

The bank can use the marginal costing method as outlined above to analyse the effectiveness of the pricing strategy in attracting new customers. If the strategy has resulted more in conversions from the bank's own existing deposit base that had earlier been sourced at a much lower cost, the bank may end up paying more as marginal cost for the new deposits, as well as merely retaining the existing market share rather than growing it. In this case too, the marginal cost of new money should be compared to the incremental cost of alternative funding sources.

Another approach helps in setting the interest rate that banks can offer for new accounts. Let us assume that Bank J now estimates that it can raise fresh deposits of ₹25 crores from the market if it offered the rate of 6 per cent offered by Bank L. Bank J also estimates that if it beat the competitor's offering by 0.5 per cent, *i.e.*, it offered an interest rate of 6.5 per cent, it can double the fresh deposit inflow to ₹50 crores. If Bank J pushed up the deposit rate further to 7 per cent, the fresh deposit inflow estimate would swell to ₹75 crores, while at 7.5 per cent and 8 per cent, the fresh deposits would increase to ₹100 crores and ₹150 crores, respectively.

The new deposits can be used by Bank J to invest in assets that would have an average yield of 10 per cent.

The following table illustrates the analysis using marginal cost to choose the optimum interest rate that can be offered to deposit customers.

Expected New Deposit Inflow (₹ in Crores)	Average Interest Bank wants to Pay on the New Funds	Annual Interest Expenses on New Funds Raised (₹ in Crores)	Marginal Cost of New Deposit	Marginal Cost as % of Incremental New Funds (Marginal Cost Rate)	Expected Return (Marginal Revenue) From Investing the New Funds	Return Less Marginal Cost (%)	Spread[9] Earned on New Funds (After Interest Cost is Met)
25	6.0	1.5	1.5	6	10	4	1
50	6.5	3.25	1.75	7	10	3	1.75
75	7.0	5.25	2.0	8	10	2	2.25
100	7.5	7.5	2.25	9	10	1	2.5
125	8.0	10.0	2.5	10	10	0	2.5
150	8.5	12.75	2.75	11	10	–1	2.25

It can be observed from the above table that the bank is able to improve its profits as long as marginal revenue exceeds the marginal cost up to a deposit interest rate of 7.5 to 8 per cent. At this point, the spread is highest at ₹2.5 crores. Beyond this point, even if the bank raises deposit rates to garner more deposits, it cannot benefit, since the average yield is estimated at 10 per cent.

Note that with the above analysis, we have gone a step further and incorporated loan or asset pricing into deposit pricing.

BOX 4.3 RELATIONSHIP BETWEEN DEPOSIT GROWTH AND BANK STOCK PRICES[10]

Research has indicated that deposit growth has a significant impact on bank stock prices. What could be the reasons for this relationship?

One, deposits lower a bank's risk. Core deposits, which include transaction and savings accounts, time deposits and money market accounts, are a cheap source of funding. As a result, banks with a high percentage of core funding don't have to take as much risk in their loan portfolio to generate a strong return.

Two, growing deposits help the balance sheet since equity need not be added, as in the case of loans. Banks have to raise adequate equity before they make loans.

Three, a high proportion of transaction accounts is an advantage to the bank. Transaction accounts (commonly known as CASA (Current account savings account) in India act as 'hub' accounts in most retail banking relationships. Industry studies show that banks are more successful in cross-selling additional financial products to their transaction account customers. The typical customer views the transaction account as the core of his banking relationship. Hence, banks get better deposits and a much larger role with these customers than with mortgages or CDs.

Finally, industry experts believe that deposits are universally valuable regardless of the environment and in most rate environments, deposit growth can pay exponentially.

Deposits and Interest Rate Risk[11]

Even in the 1990s, banks considered 'core' deposits insensitive to interest rate movements. However, a declining interest rate environment thereafter threw up some challenges. Bank customers started looking for alternate investment avenues and banks were forced to revisit their pricing strategies. Analysts are now of the opinion that bank deposits carry some interest rate risk, measuring which is not easy in practice.

In theory, measurement of interest rate risk of deposit liabilities is similar to the techniques used for the measurement of bond investments. The steps to be followed are forecasting cash flows, balances and interest;

discounting future cash flows to arrive at the present value; calculating duration[12] and interest rate elasticity; and stress testing. However, the application of bond valuation methodologies to deposits would require added assumptions or information due to some unique features of bank deposits.[13]

Box 4.4 presents the similarities and differences between bonds and bank deposits.

BOX 4.4 COMPARATIVE FEATURES OF BONDS AND BANK DEPOSITS

Similarities

- Both bonds and deposits are financial instruments. They form part of the holders' assets and makers' liabilities.
- Both create interest income to the holder and interest expense to the maker.
- Bonds and some classes of deposits have a predetermined maturity date.
- Both have economic value, whether traded or not in the financial markets.
- Both can carry embedded options.

Differences

- Typically, banks are holders of bonds and makers of deposits.
- Hence, both impact the financial performance and condition of banks in similar but opposite directions (since bonds are typically assets and deposits are liabilities).
- Deposits can have stated maturity dates and also be payable on demand.

Before looking to quantify interest rate risk, we should appreciate a fundamental difference between banks and other financial firms—that under deposit insurance, banks issue a class of liabilities for which most balances are fully insured by most governments across the world. The resulting market structure could create complications for the implementation of risk management models.

First, deposit insurance insulates the deposit investor from the credit risks of the bank, which are assumed by the deposit insurer. In essence, when a bank issues a deposit it engages in two transactions: it issues a risk-free (government insured) liability to a depositor and it purchases an insurance contract from the insurer to cover the credit risks associated with the priority position of the deposit claim. Thus, the economic value of a deposit depends upon the market yield on a comparable risk-free claim, as well as the pricing of deposit insurance relative to the market pricing of credit risk.

Second, for small depositors, bank search and switch costs, convenience value, information costs and simply limited alternatives make adjusting to changing market conditions difficult.[14]

The impact of interest rate changes on a bank can be viewed from two possible perspectives—the earnings perspective and the capital perspective.

For viewing the impact from an earnings perspective, we should remember that bank deposits include some that have no direct interest cost for the bank and some that bear interest at rates that could have been administered by managerial decisions not directly linked to market rate movements. Also, research finds that retail deposit markets are characterized by sluggish behaviour in both interest rates and deposit issuance in response to changing market conditions. Since, by definition, competitive markets respond immediately and completely to changing circumstances, it appears that there is no comparable competitively priced instrument that could be used as a reference for deposit profit.

Hence, to measure the 'earnings-at-risk' related to deposits, the way in which deposit interest expense reacts to changes in market rates must be known (or assumed). Some movements in market rates may be too insignificant to have any perceptible impact on deposit interest rates, while other market rate movements may be large enough to influence managerial pricing of deposit rates. Such changes in pricing are bound to impact both the deposit balances with and the cost of deposits for the bank.

From the longer term perspective, while demand deposits, by definition, are repayable on demand, much of these deposits could also be held as 'idle balances' by customers who prefer convenience or financial security or liquidity. These idle balances form part of the 'core deposits' for the bank. Interestingly, research has found that banks' access to such core deposits forms one of the foundations of 'relationship lending', where banks can afford to fund their key borrowers at less than market rates, in order to sustain their relationship.[15]

Since all types of deposits do not react in a similar fashion to market rate changes, current interest rate shocks translate into changes in profitability over time thus impacting the bank's 'value'. From the 'capital' perspective, the current economic value of deposits held by a bank is typically measured by the current interest rate paid on the deposits and the cost of alternative funding sources for the bank based on assumptions of maturity or repayment of these balances. For better understanding, if we treat demand deposits as continuously-maturing financial contracts, the existence and magnitude of current deposit base is an indicator of profitable deposit growth in future. Hence, 'equity at risk' related to deposits for the bank would be measured by the current economic value of its core deposits and estimates of how the core deposits would change with changes in market rates.

SECTION IV

BANK LIABILITIES—NON-DEPOSIT SOURCES

Over the last three decades or so, banks have been increasingly turning to non-deposit funding sources (also called 'wholesale funding' sources).

For example, in the United States of America, prior to the 1970s, domestic deposits made up 80 per cent or more of total bank assets. In the 1970s, however, financial markets changed in response to inflation and higher interest rates, resulting in banks taking on larger amounts of non-deposit liabilities. By 1980, domestic deposits made up only 64 per cent of total assets. During the 1990s, banks' reliance on domestic deposits for funding continued to decrease as banks increased their usage of borrowed funds, foreign deposits and other liabilities. At the end of 2000, the ratio of domestic deposits to total assets stood at 55.6 per cent. Banks had come to rely more heavily on foreign deposits, fed funds, repurchase agreements, Federal Home Loan Bank (FHLB) advances (described in *Annexure I*) and other forms of borrowing than they did during the first few decades of the FDIC's existence.[16]

The Funding Gap

The funding gap is calculated as the difference between current and projected credit and deposit flows. If the difference shows the projected need for credit exceeding the expected deposit flows, the bank has to raise additional resources either from deposit or non-deposit sources. If the difference shows the projected credit requirements falling short of resources, the bank will have to find profitable investment avenues for the surplus resources.

Assume, Bank X has made the following projections for the ensuing week:

- New credit offtake: ₹300 crores
- Drawings by existing borrowers from credit sanctions already made, but not utilized: ₹500 crores
- New deposits inflow: ₹700 crores
- Planned investments in government and corporate securities: ₹400 crores

The projected funding gap for Bank X would be:

Need for funds = 300 + 500 + 400 = ₹1,200 crores

less

Deposit funds expected = ₹700 crores

The funding gap for Bank X for the following week is expected to be ₹500 crores.

If Bank X wants to bridge the funding gap with non-deposit sources, it would have to weigh the following factors in choosing among the various options available.

- The relative cost of each funding source.
- The relative risk of each funding source.
- The period for which the funding is required.
- The size of Bank X.
- The regulations governing each of the funding sources being considered.

Other factors held constant, management will seek out the lowest cost non-deposit funding sources available, subject to availability and the expected interest rate risk.

Let us further assume that Bank X has the following options to bridge the funding gap of ₹500 crores.

Alternative Funding Source	Market Interest Rate (per cent)	Cost of Access (per cent)
Central bank funds	6.0	0.10
CDs	8.0	0.20
Foreign funds	10.0	0.30
Other money market funds	6.5	0.25

If Bank X plans to raise ₹600 crores this week, of which ₹500 crores will be used to meet the investment and loan commitments made, the effective annual cost of each of the sources would work out as follows:

Alternate Sources of Funds	Market Rate	Cost of Access	Effective Cost of Funds*
Central bank funds	0.06	0.001	0.0732
CDs	0.08	0.002	0.0984
Foreign funds	0.1	0.003	0.1236
Commercial paper	0.085	0.005	0.108
Other money market funds	0.065	0.0025	0.081

*Effective cost of funds is worked out as = [(market rate × 600) + (cost of access × 600)]/500

Bank X will have to compare the effective cost of each type of funds with the cost of getting fresh deposits in the market and the yield it expects to earn on deployment of the funds into loans and investments. It can also consider a mix of various sources of funds, subject to availability and other factors listed above.

The Indian Scenario[17]

The economic slowdown was reflected in the balance sheet expansion of commercial banks that showed 15.1 per cent growth during 2012–13, noticeably lower than the growth of 18.8 per cent during 2010–11. The deceleration was more pronounced in the growth rate of credit. Deposit growth moderated at 15.1 per cent after a sharp fall in the previous year. It is noteworthy that the growth rate of deposits in 2011–12 had been the lowest in the past 10 years.

At the end of March 2013, deposits constituted more than three-fourths of the total liabilities of the banking sector. Demand deposit growth—constituting savings and current deposits (CASA)—showed an increase, and stood at about one-third of total deposits. CASA constitute low cost funding sources for banks, and therefore, an increase in CASA helps in boosting banks' profitability

The increase in CASA growth in 2012–13 over 2011–12 was most perceptible for new private sector banks—at 18.5 per cent, this was the highest among all bank groups (*See* Figures 4.2). According to the RBI, this could be attributed to improved competition among banks in attracting savings deposits following the deregulation of the savings deposit rate.

FIGURE 4.2 GROWTH IN CASA DEPOSITS AND SHARE OF SAVINGS DEPOSITS IN TOTAL DEPOSITS—BY BANK GROUPS

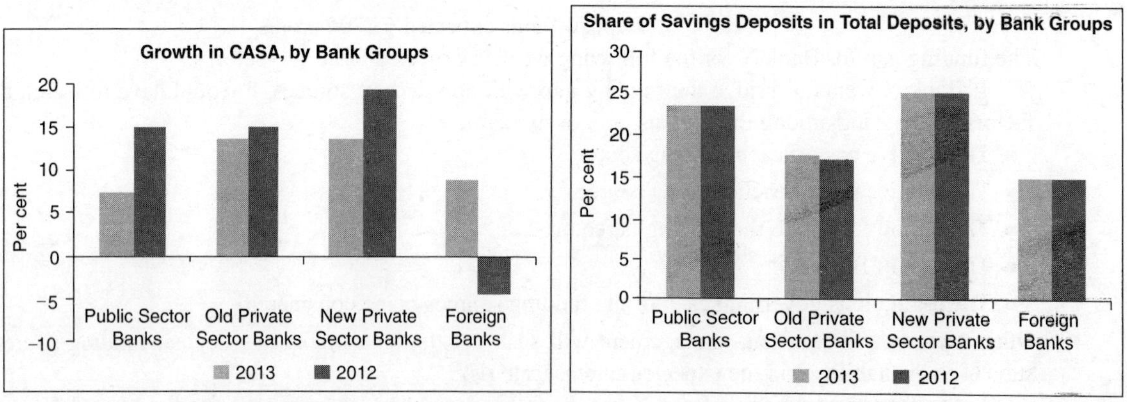

Source: RBI, Report of Trends and Progress of Banking in India, 2012–13, Chart IV.4, p. 56.

RBI attributes the higher proportions to the fact that number of private sector banks revised their savings bank deposits rates upwards after the deregulation of savings bank interest rate in October 2011. Box 4.5 explains the rationale behind deregulation of savings bank interest rates.

Deposit growth during 2012–13 outstripped credit growth, primarily due to the build-up of Foreign Currency Non-Resident (FCNR) deposits. However, without the FCNR effect, deposit growth lagged credit growth as seen in Figure 4.3.

FIGURE 4.3 CREDIT-DEPOSIT GROWTH DIVERGENCE

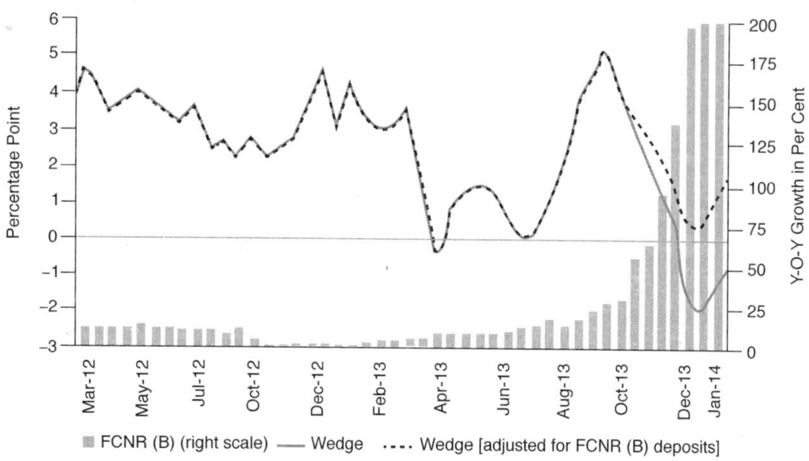

Source: RBI, Macroeconomic and Monetary Indicators, 3rd Quarter Review, January 2014, chart IV.7, p. 21.

BOX 4.5 DEREGULATION OF SAVINGS BANK DEPOSIT INTEREST RATE—THE RATIONALE

The progress of financial reforms that was begun in the early 1990s included almost complete deregulation of interest rates. The only interest rates that continued to be regulated were the savings and current deposit interest rates. While current deposit rates were kept at 'zero', savings deposit rate changes were announced by the RBI as and when required. In October 2011, interest rates on savings deposits were deregulated, which implied that banks were free to fix rates based on their business requirements.

The arguments in favour of interest rate deregulation on savings deposits are summarized below:

1. Market determined rates can be set by banks.
2. Regulated savings deposit interest rates had made these deposits unattractive and also adversely affected the transmission of monetary policy.
3. It can be seen from the Tables showing the composition of deposits, that savings deposits constitute almost a quarter of the total deposits of banks in India. Continuing to regulate the interest rates on these deposits could impede product innovation and competitiveness among banks.

The issues raised against the deregulation were as follows:

1. Savings deposits constituted a substantial source of low cost funds to banks. A large portion of the savings deposits are being treated as 'core' deposits, and hence are suitable for financing long term assets. It was feared that deregulation might lead to unhealthy price war among banks, resulting in major shifts in such deposits and asset liability mismatches.
2. Small depositors might be hit if banks consider savings bank deposits as 'high cost' source of funds due to price competition. Banks would then discourage small deposits due to the associated high transaction costs.
3. On the other hand, if interest on savings deposits are reduced, small investors and pension earners might be affected
4. Product innovation might result in banks introducing complex products, which may not be easily understood by small savers. Complex products may also lead to misleading and mis-selling of deposit products.

The deregulation came into effect with the following two conditions:

1. Each bank should offer uniform interest rates on savings deposit balances up to ₹1 lakh, irrespective of the amount in the deposit account.
2. For savings deposit balances over ₹1 lakh, a bank may provide differential rates of interest. However, there should be no discrimination from customer to customer on interest rates for similar amounts.

Source: Summarized from RBI Annual Report 2011–12, p.79.

RBI had to take some exceptional measures to stem a rapid depreciation of the rupee during July-August, 2013. This led to a tightening in money market rates. The weighted average effective interest rate (WAEIR) of Certificates of Deposit (CD) peaked to 11.2 per cent in the early part of September, 2013. As markets returned to normalcy and liquidity conditions improved, rates declined whereas volumes increased. Similarly, Commercial Paper (CP) issues hit a two year low in July 2013. The weighted average discount rate (WADR) also touched a high of 11.9 per cent at end-August, 2013. Subsequently, the volume of issuances picked up and rates declined leading to an increase in amount of CPs.

Non-deposit Sources of Funds

The share of Non-deposit sources of funds (listed under "Borrowings" in banks' balance sheets) decreased sharply during 2012–13. Interestingly, most of the increase in borrowings was in the form of short-term sources or in the range of 1–3 years (*Trend and Progress of Banking in India*, 2012–13, *Tables* IV.1, IV.6, *pages* 55 and 59).

One of the primary reasons for the slackening of growth in non-deposit sources was the decrease in credit growth, which, in turn could be related to the slowdown in economic growth.

Since 2007–08, there has been a noticeable decline in the international borrowings by Indian banks. The decelerating trend was attributed to negative global developments. The trend was reversed in 2012–13, when total international liabilities of banks in India grew significantly. However, international assets of these banks remained almost unchanged. Table 4.2A shows the trend in international liabilities of Indian banks over the last two years while Table 4.2B shows the sectors that have been responsible for the increase.

Table 4.2 A shows significant increase in American Depository Receipts/Global Depository Receipts (ADR/GDR)[18] issued by domestic banks, followed by equities of banks held by non-resident Indians.

TABLE 4.2A TREND IN THE GROWTH OF INTERNATIONAL LIABILITIES OF BANKS IN INDIA (₹ IN BILLION)

	Amount Outstanding (as at end-March)		**Percentage Variation**	
Liability Type	**2012**	**2013**	**2011–12**	**2012–13**
1. Deposits and Loans	4,472 (79.0)	5,274 (77.2)	18.2	17.9
2. Own Issues of Securities/Binds	56 (1.0)	58 (0.8)	23.0	3.1
3. Other Liabilities	1.133 (20.0)	1,503 (22.0)	– 18.3	32.7
a. ADRs/GDRs	271 (4.8)	393 (5.8)	– 21.8	45.1
b. Equities of banks held by non-residents	536 (9.5)	714 (10.4)	– 26.8	33.2
c. Capital/remittable profits of foreign banks in India and other unclassified international liabilities	326 (5.8)	396 (5.8)	5.8	21.4
Total International Liabilities	**5,661 (100.0)**	**6,835 (100.0)**	**8.6**	**20.7**

Notes: 1. Figures in parentheses are percentages to total.
2. Percentage variation could be slightly different as absolute numbers have been rounded off to ₹ billion.

Sources: 1. Based on LBS (locational banking statistics) Statements.
2. RBI report on Trend and Progress of Banking in India, 2012–13, Table IV.2, p. 57.

TABLE 4.2B INTERNATIONAL LIABILITIES—BREAK UP BY SECTOR (₹ IN BILLION)

	Amount Outstanding		**Percentage Variation**	
Residual Maturity/Sector	**2012**	**2013**	**2011–12**	**2012–13**
1	2	3	4	5
Total Consolidated International Claims	**2,809 (100.0)**	**8,312 (100.0)**	**14.0**	**17.9**
1. Maturity-wise				
a. Short-term (residual maturity of less than one year)	1,832 (65.2)	2,153 (65.0)	19.0	17.5
b. Long-term (residual maturity of one year and above)	924 (32.9)	1.100 (33.2)	5.9	19.1
c. Unallocated	54 (1.9)	59 (1.8)	1.7	10.1
2. Sector-wise				
a. Bank	1,286 (45.8)	1,383 (41.8)	17.8	7.6
b. Non-Bank Public	19 (0.7)	31 (0.9)	114.1	66.2
c. Non-Bank Private	1,505 (53.6)	1,898 (57.3)	10.3	26.1

Notes: 1. Figures in parentheses are percentages to total.
2. Unallocated residual maturity comprises maturity not applicable (*e.g.*, for equities) and maturity information not available from reporting bank branches.
3. The 'Bank' sector includes official monetary institutions (*e.g.*, IFC, ECB, etc.) and central banks.
4. Prior to the quarter ended March 2005, non-bank public sector comprised of companies/institutions other than banks in which shareholding of State/Central Governments was at least 51 per cent, including State/Central Government and its departments. From the March 2005 quarter, the 'Non-bank public' sector comprises only State/Central Government and its departments and, accordingly, all other entities excluding banks are classified under 'Non-bank private sector'.
5. Percentage variation could be slightly different as absolute numbers have been rounded off to ₹ billion.

Sources: 1. Based on CBS (consolidated banking statistics) Statements—Immediate country risk basis.
2. RBI, Trend and Progress of Banking in India, 2012–13, Table IV.4, p. 58.

The break-up of international liabilities by sector (Table 4.2B) shows a shift towards the private non-banking sector. According to the RBI, this is reflective of the weak performance of the global banking sector in the recent years. The shift was primarily from the US and advanced European economies, such as the UK and Germany, towards South-East Asian economies, such as Hong Kong and Singapore, as also the UAE (*See RBI, Trend and Progress of Banking in India*, 2012–13, *Table* IV.5, *page* 59). RBI opines that this shift could have been partly a fallout of the uncertain economic environment prevailing in most advanced economies in the period following the global financial and sovereign debt crises.

Cost of Funds

What is the impact of these shifts in bank liability composition on banks' profitability? Table 4.3 provides the answer.

The growth in deposits and borrowings of banks has come at a huge cost. Interest expended on deposits and borrowings rose sharply during 2012–13 compared to the previous year. The most obvious reasons for the increase in cost of funds are the preponderance of term deposits, rise in high cost retail deposits, and increase in borrowings in certain bank groups.

Though both cost and return on funds increased for almost all bank groups, spreads are seen to be falling, primarily because of the higher cost at which funds were being sourced. Among bank groups, some interesting observations are as follows:

a. Indian public sector and private sector banks have the highest cost of deposits, while the cost is relatively low for foreign banks.
b. However, cost of borrowings is comparable for public sector and foreign banks.
c. The return on funds for foreign banks is comparable (or sometimes relatively less) than Indian banks. The advantage of lower cost of funds has therefore not translated into a substantial increase in spread.

TABLE 4.3 COST OF FUNDS AND SPREAD (%)—BY BANK GROUP

Sl. No.	Bank Group/Year	Cost of Deposits	Cost of Borrowings	Cost of Funds	Return on Advances	Return on Investments	Return on Funds	Spread
1	2	3	4	5	6	7	8	9 = (8.5)
1	Public Sector Banks							
	2011–12	6.36	2.80	6.06	10.31	7.54	9.52	3.46
	2012–12	6.63	2.45	6.27	10.08	7.60	9.38	3.11
	1.1 Nationalized Banks*							
	2011–12	6.51	2.77	6.22	10.32	7.43	9.49	3.27
	2012–13	6.74	2.37	6.39	10.16	7.42	9.36	2.97
	1.2 SBI Group							
	2011–12	5.97	2.85	5.66	10.27	7.80	9.60	3.94
	2012–13	6.37	2.58	5.96	9.90	8.08	9.42	3.46
2	Private Sector Banks							
	2011–12	6.43	2.92	5.84	11.06	7.26	9.73	3.89
	2012–13	6.72	3.33	6.12	11.52	7.28	10.02	3.91
	2.1 Old Private Sector Banks							
	2011–12	7.24	4.34	7.10	11.98	7.37	10.47	3.37
	2012–13	7.46	4.33	7.27	12.15	7.49	10.62	3.35
	2.2 New Private Sector Banks							
	2011–12	6.14	2.81	5.45	10.77	7.23	9.51	4.06
	2012–13	6.45	3.24	5.77	11.33	7.22	9.85	4.08
3	Foreign Banks							
	2011–12	4.34	2.78	3.88	9.61	8.02	8.87	4.99
	2012–13	4.67	2.78	4.05	9.55	8.13	8.89	4.84
4	All SCBs							
	2011–12	6.28	2.83	5.90	10.42	7.52	9.53	3.63
	2012–13	6.57	2.76	6.12	10.33	7.57	9.49	3.36

Notes: 1. Cost of Deposits = Interest paid on deposits/Average of current and previous year's deposits.
2. Cost of Borrowings = Interest paid on borrowings/Average of current and previous year's borrowings.
3. Cost of Funds = (Interest paid on deposits + Interest paid on borrowings)/(Average of current and previous year's deposits plus borrowings).
4. Return on Advances = Interest earned on advances/Average of current and previous year's advances.
5. Return on Investments = Interest carned on Investments/Average of current and previous year's Investments.
6. Return on Funds = (Interest earned on advances + Interest earned on Investments)/(Average of current and previous year's advances plus Investments).
7. * Includes IDBI Bank Ltd.

Source: RBI, Trend and Progress of Banking in India, 2012-13, Table IV.9, p. 62.

The RBI has provided explicit guidelines on mobilizing certain types of non-deposit sources such as: (a) call and notice money; (b) external commercial borrowing (ECB); and (c) a special type of refinance such as 'export refinance'. The salient features are summarized in *Annexure I*.

Are Non-Deposit Sources More Costly and Risky? Borrowings from the market are generally perceived to be more expensive than deposit sources. Where banks tend to rely on borrowings to fund their lending operations, they are exposed to market risks—the cost of such borrowings and their availability may also fluctuate. In contrast, there are quite a large number of deposit customers who put an extremely high value on the safety and accessibility of insured deposits and keep their money with banks even when alternate investments offer more attractive returns.

Generally depositors, whose deposits with banks are insured, may not be very concerned about the financial health of the bank they invest in. However, other lenders who do not enjoy insurance protection would seek interest rates commensurate with the risk profile of the borrowing bank and also expect the bank to match market interest rates.

However, apart from the cost aspect, wholesale funding is not without its risks. Non-deposit sources lack the stability of deposit, especially core deposit sources. Banks accessing wholesale funding markets must develop the capability to not only access the appropriate type of funds at short notice, but also repay them on due date. This implies that these banks would have to ensure back up measures, such as short-term investment in government securities, which can be sold at short notice. Such measures may affect the banks' profitability since liquid securities yield lower returns. Banks may also have to invest in personnel with the requisite expertise in managing sourcing and repayment of such funds in the market.

On the other hand, such wholesale borrowings may be cheaper at the margin than deposits, even if the rates paid on non-deposit funds are actually higher. One reason would be the lower transaction costs for raising bulk wholesale funds, which banks often raise with a mere phone call. In doing so, banks save on branch, personnel and system costs. Another reason would be that banks need not alter their deposit rates for accessing wholesale funds. As discussed in the earlier section, if a bank has to attract more deposits only by offering higher rates, the overall cost of funds for the bank might increase substantially.

In fact, banks have been finding new funding sources from the money markets, long term and international markets. Of late, loan sale[19] (such as securitization) mechanisms have also become a popular means of augmenting banks' liquidity. Moreover, banks active in the non-deposit funding market are increasingly finding that some wholesale fund lenders are willing to sculpt their repayment schedule to banks' cash inflows from asset liquidation.

SECTION V

BANK DEPOSITS IN INDIA—SOME IMPORTANT LEGAL ASPECTS

'Banking' Defined

Banking is defined under Section 5(b) of the Banking Regulation Act, 1949. It means 'accepting, for the purpose of lending or investment, deposits of money from the public, repayable on demand or otherwise and withdrawable by cheque, draft, order or otherwise'. Some important interpretations follow from the above definition.

- 'Banking' means performing two essential functions of: (a) accepting deposits from the public; and (b) lending or investing the deposits. It, therefore, follows that if the purpose of accepting deposits is not to lend or invest, it cannot be called 'banking business'. For example, companies accepting deposits from the public for financing their business cannot be said to be doing banking business.
- The banker accepts deposits of 'money' from the 'public' that offers its money as deposit. But it is not mandatory that the banker has to accept all such deposits offered. The banker can refuse to accept money from undesirable elements of society such as thieves, smugglers or terrorists.
- The deposit could be payable on demand (such as transaction deposits, savings deposits) or payable after a fixed term as in the case of term deposits. The essential point to note here is that the bank need not repay the deposit without a 'demand' being made by the depositor, even after expiry of the contracted period of deposit. Withdrawal of deposit balances are to be done through cheques, drafts, etc. This implies that a written demand is necessary to end the contract and seek repayment of the depositor's balances.

It is thus clear that accepting deposits and maintaining deposit accounts is the core activity of any bank.

Annexure II provides a brief overview of some of the important legal provisions that affect banking operations in India.

Who is a Customer?

You will be surprised to know that the term 'customer' of a bank is not defined by law. Typically, any person or entity transacting with a bank through a deposit or borrowing account is considered its customer.

From a summary of past important judicial decisions, the following characteristics can be attributed to a customer.

- A customer is one who maintains a deposit account with the bank.
- Duration of the account is immaterial.
- State of the account, that is whether it is in debit or credit, is immaterial.
- Banker–customer relationship would exist even between two banks if one maintains accounts with the other and cheques, etc. are collected through that account.
- Merely visiting a bank frequently for purchasing a draft or for encashing a cheque, etc. does not confer on the visitor the status of a customer, *i.e.*, maintenance of a deposit account is mandatory to be eligible to be termed a 'customer'.
- A customer of one branch does not automatically become a customer of another branch of the same bank where he does not maintain an account.
- Even an agreement to open an account would make a prospective depositor a customer of the bank.

In modern banking, the vital determinant of the 'customer' status of a person or entity is the nature of dealings with the bank. Such dealings should be in the nature of 'banking business'. Accordingly, the person or entity that does not deal with the bank in respect of its core banking functions—accepting deposits and lending or investing the deposits—but avails of other services from the bank, is not deemed a 'customer'.

TEASE THE CONCEPT

Which of the following transactions indicate that X is a customer of Bank A?

- deposits cash with Bank A to be credited to the Insurance company on whose behalf A accepts payments.
- deposits cash to purchase a demand draft from Bank A.
- X brings a cheque in his name to Bank A for encashment.
- X brings a cheque in his name to Bank A for crediting to his savings account with A.
- X deposits documents in Bank A's safe deposit vault.

The primary relationship between a banker and customer is therefore of 'debtor and creditor'. However, under special circumstances and on the customer's request, the banker can also act as 'trustee' (*e.g.*, holding a designated deposit of the customer for the purpose of paying a third person or holding the customer's valuables in safe deposit lockers) or as an 'agent' (*e.g.*, buying and selling securities on behalf of the customer, making insurance and utilities payments on due date as specified by the customer).

Who is Eligible to be a Customer?

In their role as financial intermediaries, banks are bound to accept public savings as deposits. However, they can enter into legally valid contracts for this purpose only with certain sections of the society.

Thus, deposit accounts can be opened only by those who (a) are capable of entering into a valid contract, (b) follow the banks' prescribed procedures while entering into the contract and (c) accepts the banks' terms and conditions while doing so. Thus, banks retain the right to reject an application for opening deposit accounts.

The legal position of some special classes of banks' customers is outlined in *Annexure III*.

General Guidelines for Opening Deposit Accounts

The importance of proper introduction and verification of new deposit accounts has been embodied in the Know Your Customer (KYC) guidelines of the RBI.[20] These guidelines advise banks to put in place systems and procedures to prevent financial frauds, identify money laundering and suspicious or criminal activities and for scrutiny/monitoring of large value cash transactions, including transactions in foreign currency.

The KYC guidelines of the RBI are modelled on international best practices. Both the World Bank and the IMF have been involved in international efforts to strengthen financial sector supervision and promote good governance, in an effort to reducing financial crime and enhancing the integrity of the international financial system. Since 2001, anti-money laundering (AML) and combating the financing of terrorism (CFT) measures have come into sharper focus. Both the World Bank and the IMF have worked closely with the Financial Action Task Force (FATF) on money, the standard setting body in this area, to develop a methodology for assessing the observance of international standards on the legal, institutional and operational framework for AML–CFT.

The BCBS, International Association of Insurance Supervisors (IAIS) and International Organization of Securities Commissioners (IOSCO) have each issued broad supervisory standards and guidelines on a wide range of supervisory issues, including money laundering as it relates to banking, insurance and securities. FATF incorporates those standards and guidelines in its 40 recommendations.

Salient features of the international and the RBI guidelines on AML and KYC are presented in *Annexure IV*.

Termination of Banker–Customer Relationship

The banker–customer relationship is determined by the contract between them. The relationship can be terminated by any one of them, by giving notice of the intention to terminate to the other party.

Apart from the stated intention, compulsions of law may also force the banker to terminate the relationship.

The rights and obligations of the banker in this respect are summarized below. A banker can terminate his relationship with the customer (with due notice) under the following circumstances:

- When the customer directs the banker in writing to close his deposit and other accounts with the bank.
- When the account has not been operated for a long time and the customer is not traceable in spite of the banker's efforts. Such deposit balances are usually parked in an 'unclaimed deposit' account and the account is closed. If the depositor is traced later, the balance (net of applicable charges) can be paid after verification.
- When the banker finds the customer's dealings no longer satisfactory—say, the customer is convicted for forgery or fails to keep up commitments to repay loans and overdrafts.
- When the banker is informed of the customer's death.
- When the banker receives proof of the customer's insanity.
- When the customer is insolvent or goes into liquidation.
- When the banker receives a garnishee order[21] from the court.

Types of Deposit Accounts

1. *Term Deposit Accounts*

At the time of entering into the deposit contract, the customer agrees to retain the deposit amount for a fixed term with the bank. This type of deposit is called a 'term' deposit. The term of the deposit is chosen by the depositor according to his convenience.

Term deposit accounts can be opened by individuals/partnership firms/private and public limited companies/HUFs/specified associates/societies/trusts, etc.

The rate of interest on such deposits would vary from bank to bank in the present deregulated environment. The interest rates on these deposits can be 'fixed' (fixed for the entire term at the time of entering into the contract) or 'floating' (fixed in relation to a varying benchmark rate at the time of entering into the contract).

Banks can offer various innovative schemes to suit the needs of the customer segments they serve. How they design these deposit schemes will be outlined in the next section with illustrative examples.

The term deposit account is opened on a written request from the depositor in a prescribed format. The term deposit 'receipt' from the bank acknowledges receipt of the depositors' funds into the bank.

Other salient features related to term deposits are as follows:

- Existing term deposits can be renewed before maturity at the depositor's request, without any penalty provided the period of renewal is longer than the period of the original deposit.
- Though interest is payable at the contracted rate on maturity of the term deposit, banks can pay quarterly or half-yearly interest on request by the depositor.
- Beyond maturity date, term deposits held with the bank are classified as 'overdue deposits'. Legally, interest ceases to accrue on overdue term deposits. However, banks have the discretion to allow interest if the entire deposit amount or a part of it is renewed from the date of maturity till some future date. The rate of interest prevailing on the maturity date would be applicable on the renewal, with the proviso that such interest will not exceed the appropriate rate for the period for which the deposit is to be renewed.
- Banks have the discretion to pay the term deposit before the due date. However, if large deposits are withdrawn before maturity, the bank's asset liability management[22] may be adversely impacted. Similarly, loan may be granted to the depositor against the security of the term deposit.
- In the case of deposits in joint names, all the depositors should agree for premature payment or loan against the term deposit.

2. *Current Deposits*

Current deposits are part of the demand deposit portfolio of the bank, with the primary objective of providing 'convenience' of operation to the customer. It is essentially a running and actively operated account, with very little restriction on the number and amount of drawings. They are part of 'demand deposits', since the banker is obligated to repay these liabilities on demand from the customer.

Current accounts can be opened by individuals/partnership firms/private and public limited companies/HUFs/specified associates/societies/trusts, etc.

The primary objective of operating a current deposit for these types of customers is 'convenience', since it dispenses with the risk of handling cash.

Since the bank satisfies the 'convenience' need of such depositors by undertaking payment and collection services on a daily basis, the 'transaction costs' for the bank are quite substantial. For example, the frequent transactions in the current account would entail personnel and system costs of a high order. Hence, it is customary for banks not to pay any interest on current account balances. In fact, the RBI specifically prohibits payment of any interest on current account balances.

Many banks insist on 'compensating balances' meant to offset the transaction costs involved. Some banks deliberately discourage non-remunerative accounts where the balances maintained are too low to compensate the transaction cost involved. Some banks apply graded service charges for the range of services offered.

For borrower–depositors, loans and advances are not disbursed as cash, but routed through the current account. Thus, there is a close link between current account depositors and borrowers for a bank. Hence, banks use the current account as a disciplining tool for its credit customers as well.

Typically, banks carry out due diligence before opening current accounts. Banks in India usually insist that the account holder declare all the credit limits availed at other banks. The account opening bank not only verifies the customer's bonafides before opening the account, but also insists on 'no objection certificates' from the customer's other bankers.

3. *Savings Deposits*

Savings deposits or savings bank (SB) accounts are targeted at those customers who wish to save a part of their current income and also earn from such savings. Savings bank accounts can be opened by any eligible person/persons and certain organizations/agencies (as advised by the RBI from time to time).

Since the scheme is meant for a major part of the country's populace, the central bank continues to regulate the interest rates offered by banks on such deposits.

Some of the salient features are as follows:

- Many banks place restrictions on the number of withdrawals per period.
- Minimum balances are prescribed by many banks, primarily to offset the cost of maintaining and servicing such deposits.
- Savings accounts cannot be opened in the name of a trading or business firm. Similarly, government departments, bodies receiving government grants/subsidies, municipal corporations, panchayat samitis, state housing boards, water and sewerage boards, state text book publishing corporation, metropolitan development authority and state or district level co-operative housing societies are some of the other entities prohibited from opening SB accounts.

4. *Certificates of Deposit*

CDs were introduced in 1989 in India with the objective of further widening the range of money market instruments and giving investors greater flexibility in deployment of their short-term surplus funds.

CDs are negotiable money market instruments issued in dematerialized form or as usance promissory notes for funds deposited at a bank (or at certain designated financial institutions) for a specified period. Guidelines for issue of CDs are governed by periodic directives issued by the RBI.[23]

Banks can issue CDs with a minimum amount of ₹1 lakh per subscriber and can be issued in multiples of ₹1 lakh. CDs can be issued to individuals, corporations, companies, trusts, funds, associations and also to non-resident Indians (non-repatriable and cannot be endorsed to another NRI in the secondary market).

Since CDs are money market instruments, their maturity cannot exceed 1 year. The minimum period of issue would be not less than 7 days.

CDs are to be issued at a discount on face value. Banks can also issue floating rate CDs, with interest rates to be reset periodically based on a predetermined formula indicating the spread over an objective, transparent and market-based benchmark. There is no minimum lock in period and CDs are freely transferable by endorsement and delivery (or as applicable to demat securities).

The funds flowing in from issue of CDs are subject to reserve requirements[24] (Cash Reserve Ratio and Statutory Liquidity Ratio). It is also to be noted that banks cannot grant loans against CDs or buy their own CDs back before maturity.

5. ***Deposit Schemes for Non-Resident Indians (NRIs)***

In order to make deposits under the schemes intended for NRIs, a depositor should meet any one of the following criteria.

- He should be an Indian citizen staying in a foreign country either for employment or for carrying on business or vocation or for any other purpose, under circumstances indicating an indefinite period of stay outside India.
- He should be an Indian citizen working in a foreign country with international organizations such as the United Nations and the IMF.
- He should be an employee of the Indian central or state government or a public sector unit in India, deputed to a foreign country on a temporary assignment.
- He should be a person of Indian origin. A person is considered to be of Indian origin if he has held an Indian passport at any time in the past or he or either of his parents or any of his grandparents were Indian citizens or his/her spouse is an Indian citizen or of Indian origin.
- Overseas corporate bodies (OCBs) can also maintain deposit accounts with Indian banks. An OCB is defined as a company, partnership firm, society or any other corporate body, owned directly or indirectly to the extent of at least 60 per cent by NRIs. It also includes trusts in which at least 60 per cent irrevocable beneficial interest is held by NRIs.

SECTION VI

DESIGN OF DEPOSIT SCHEMES—SOME ILLUSTRATIONS

The principles underlying the concept of 'time value of money'[25] are prevalently used in designing deposit schemes. Simply stated, the future value is the value of an investment today at some period in future, while the 'present value' is the value today of cash flow receivable at some period in future.

Recurring Deposit Scheme (RD)

General Features Under the scheme, a fixed sum agreed upon by the banker and customer will be deposited every month for a pre-determined period. At the end of the period, the depositor will be paid the total amount of deposit installments with interest. Minimum and maximum deposit periods are usually 12 and 120 months, respectively.

Advantages to the Depositor This is intended to be a variant of the savings deposit account with the objective of inculcating regular savings habit.

Calculating the Maturity Amount While operating these accounts, banks should ensure that the effective interest rates on such accounts are identical with those being paid for other similar deposits.

To arrive at the amount on maturity, the future value of annuity should be computed as follows:

$$\text{Maturity of RD} = \text{RD installment } (\text{FVIFA}_{n,k})$$

where, n and k are the number of periods and the rate of interest, respectively.

ILLUSTRATION 4.1

What is the maturity value of a monthly recurring deposit of ₹1,000 per month for 12 months, if the contracted interest at 9 per cent per annum is compounded quarterly?

$$\text{Effective Rate}^{26} = \left(1 + \frac{0.09}{4}\right) - 1 = 9.31\ \%$$

Therefore the monthly interest rate = 0.78%

$$\text{Maturity value} = FVA_n = A[FVIFA_{n,k}]^{27}$$
$$= A\left[\frac{(1+k)^n - 1}{k}\right]$$
$$= 1000\left[\frac{(1+0.0078)^{12} - 1}{0.0078}\right]$$
$$= 1000 + 12.53 = ₹12.530$$

Reinvestment Deposit Scheme

General Features In this scheme, a lump sum amount is invested for a fixed period and repaid with interest on maturity. Interest on the deposit is reinvested at the end of each quarter and hence, there is interest on interest. The minimum and maximum durations for such schemes are generally 6 and 120 months, respectively, though the (minimum) period could differ among banks.

Advantages to the Depositor The depositor can withdraw the interest plus the principal at the end of the tenure. Since the interest is not withdrawn during the deposit period, the maturity value would be higher than in the case of similar schemes.

Calculating the Maturity Amount The maturity amount in a re-investment scheme would be the initial deposit multiplied by the effective rate.

$$\text{Maturity amount} = \text{Initial deposit } (1 + r)^n$$

where, $r = \text{Effective rate} = \left(1 + \frac{k}{m}\right)^m = 1$

$n = \text{Number of years}$

ILLUSTRATION 4.2

Bank B offers the following interest rates on its term deposits—8.5 per cent for one year, 10 per cent for 2 years and 12 per cent for 3 years. What will be the maturity amount for an investment of ₹1,00,000 for a period of 2 years, if the depositor does not want periodic interest to be paid out during the period and the bank reinvests the amount quarterly?

The amount at the end of the re-investment period would be = 100,000 $(1 + r)^2$

On quarterly re-investment, the effective rate for 2 years would be

$$= \left(1 + \frac{0.10}{4}\right)^4 - 1 = 10.38$$

Hence, the maturity amount = 1,00,000 $(1 = 0.1038)^2$ = ₹1,21,840

Fixed Deposit Scheme

General Features Under this scheme, a specific amount is deposited for a fixed term during which the amount cannot generally be withdrawn. However, at the request of the depositor, interest can be paid out on a monthly/quarterly/half-yearly/annual basis. Since interest on term deposits is payable at quarterly (or longer) rests, for monthly deposit schemes, interest is calculated for the quarter and paid monthly at discounted value.

Advantages to Depositor Depositors seeking regular income from their fixed investment would prefer this scheme.

Calculating the Interest Rate to be Quoted By periodically withdrawing the interest, the depositor can actually earn a return on this interest amount by reinvesting it. Moreover, if monthly interest is withdrawn for reinvestment, the returns earned will be more than those for a quarterly repayment. To recognize this, the interest rate that is paid for a monthly withdrawal scheme should be such that on reinvestment it shall not yield more than the quarterly returns. That is,

Quarterly interest paid out $Y = X(1 + r/6) + X(1 + r/12) + X$

where, X = Monthly interest amount

r = Reinvestment rate for the monthly interest

Simplifying the above equation by multiplying by 4.

$$4X\left(1+\frac{r}{6}\right)+4X\left(1+\frac{r}{12}\right)+4X=4Y$$

$$12X+4X\left(\frac{r}{6}+\frac{r}{12}\right)+4Y$$

$$12X+4X\frac{3r}{12}+4Y$$

$$X(12+r)=4Y$$

$$X=\frac{4Y}{12+r}$$

Thus,

$$\text{Discounted monthly interest} = \frac{P \times R}{(12+r)}$$

where, P = Principal/fixed deposit amount

R = Contracted interest rate

r = Reinvestment rate for the monthly interest

In the above expression, it can be observed that the first month's interest amount is re-invested for 2 months and the second month's interest for 1 month. To these amounts, when the third month's interest is added, it should give interest that equals the quarterly interest amount.

ILLUSTRATION 4.3

A 2-year fixed deposit of ₹50,000 with Bank L carries a contracted interest rate of 10.5 per cent.

(a) What should be the interest amounts if payment is made on a quarterly, half-yearly and annual basis?

(b) What would be the effective interest rate if the interest is withdrawn every month and transferred to the savings bank account? Assume a re-investment rate at .04.

Solution:

a. Quarterly interest amount = 50,000 × 0.105/4 = ₹1,312.50

Half-yearly interest amount = 50,000 × 0.105/2 = ₹2,625

Annual interest amount = 50,000 × 0.105 = ₹5,250

b. Discount monthly interest $= \frac{50{,}000 \times 0.105}{(12 + 0.04)} =$ ₹436.04

Thus, the effective interest rate that the bank pays on the ₹50,000 FD, if the interest amounts are withdrawn every month will be 10.46 per cent (*i.e.*, 436.04 = 12/50,000).

It can also be inferred from the above illustration that the interest that can be paid for a monthly withdrawal FD scheme will be slightly lower to the rate paid for the other interest payment periods.

Cash Certificates

General Features This is a variation of the re-investment deposit scheme, where the maturity value will be a pre-determined lump sum. The amount of initial deposit will be the issue price of the cash certificate and will be computed based on the maturity amount or the face value of the cash certificate and the tenure of the deposit. The interest is re-invested quarterly and hence, there will be interest on interest. The minimum and maximum maturity periods are generally similar to the re-investment scheme.

The issue price can be arrived at using the 'present value' principle.

Issue price = PV = Face Value ($PVIFA_{n,k}$)[28]

ILLUSTRATION 4.4

A depositor requires ₹1 lakh after 1 year. If the current interest rate is 12 per cent per annum what should be the issue price of the cash certificate that would give the investor the required amount in a year's time?

$$\text{Effective Rate } (r) = \left(1+\frac{k}{m}\right)^m - 1$$

$$= \left(1+\frac{0.12}{4}\right)^4 - 1 = 12.50\%$$

Issue price (PV) for ₹1,00,000 = Face value ($PVIE_{n,k}$)

$$= \frac{100}{(1+k)^n} \times 1000$$

$$= \frac{100}{(1+0.1255)} \times 1000 = ₹88,850$$

Therefore, for obtaining ₹1 lakh after a year, the depositor will have to invest ₹88,850 at present.

CHAPTER SUMMARY

- Liability management plays a critical role in the risk-return profile of banks. In the present deregulated environment, banks have to balance profitability and risks while deciding on their liability mix.
- 'Deposits' are the primary source of funds for banks. The other sources of funds for banks are 'equity and reserves' and borrowings. 'These sources of funds form the basis for creation of assets by the bank and are hence responsible for the bank's profit and growth. Therefore, it would be prudent for the bank to base its funds requirement and mobilization on some relevant parameter such as (a) maturity, (b) cost of funds, (c) tax implications, (d) regulatory framework and (e) market conditions.
- Bank deposits are differentiated by the type of deposit customer, the tenure of the deposit and its cost to the bank. On the basis of these parameters, deposits can be broadly classified as transaction accounts or payment deposits and term deposits. Transaction accounts can be further classified into interest bearing and non-interest bearing deposits. A popular variant of large term deposits is CDs.
- Deposit insurance is a measure taken by banks in most countries to protect small depositors' savings, either fully or in part, against any possible risk of a bank not being able to return their savings to these depositors. Deposit insurance is being increasingly used by governments as a tool to ensure the stability of the banking system of their countries and protect bank depositors from incurring large losses due to bank failures.
- The pricing of deposits and related services assumes great importance in the present deregulated and highly competitive environment where deposit rate ceilings do not exist. It is, therefore, imperative that banks understand how to measure the cost of their funding sources and accordingly price their assets in order to ensure a desired level of profitability. This is done through a pricing policy.
- Analysis of depositors' profile and preferences would help banks avoid raising rates (and lowering profitability) to attract depositors in customer segments which are known to be price inelastic. Second, the information could help in fine tuning deposit prices in customer segments where better rates would be a deciding factor for a customer to keep deposits in or move them out of a bank. Better informed tradeoffs would enable better use of resources to improve service or convenience than to raise deposit rates. Proper deposit pricing will have a positive effect on the growth of net interest income and net interest margin.
- Some common pricing methodologies adopted by banks for improving profitability while pricing deposits are: (a) cost plus margin pricing, (b) market penetration deposit pricing, (c) conditional pricing, (d) upscale target pricing, and (e) relationship pricing and so on.
- Further, before hiking interest rates on some classes of deposits or going on an aggressive: campaign to mobilize new deposits, two types of analysis are typically considered. The analysis quantifies (a) the actual cost of new deposits and (b) the cost of protecting existing deposits. Such analysis is typically done using the following approaches—the marginal cost of funds approach and the new cost of funds approach.
- In theory, measurement of interest rate risk of deposit liabilities is similar to the techniques used for the measurement of bond investments. The steps to be followed are: (a) forecasting cash flows, balances and interest, (b) discounting future cash flows to arrive at the present value, (c) calculating duration[29] and interest rate elasticity and (d) stress testing. However, in practice, such application would require added assumptions or information due to some unique features of bank deposits.
- Last three decades or so, banks have been increasingly turning to non-deposit funding sources (also called 'wholesale funding' sources). The funding gap that is generally calculated as the difference between current and projected credit and deposit flows is bridged though additional resources either from deposit or non-deposit sources. Banks

have been finding new funding sources from the money markets, long-term and international markets. Of late, loan sale (such as 'securitization') mechanisms have also become a popular means of augmenting banks' 'liquidity'.

- In India, 'Banking' is defined under Section 5(b) of the Banking Regulation Act, 1949. The provisions of the Act make it clear that accepting deposits and maintaining deposit accounts is the core activity of any bank. The primary relationship between banker and customer is therefore of 'debtor and creditor'. However, under special circumstances and on the customer's request, the banker can also act as 'trustee' or as an 'agent'. The banker–customer relationship is determined by the contract between them. The relationship can be terminated by any one of them, by giving notice of the intention to terminate to the other party.
- The importance of proper introduction and verification of new deposit accounts has been embodied in the KYC guidelines of the RBI. These guidelines advise banks to put in place systems and procedures to prevent financial frauds, identify money laundering and suspicious or criminal activities and for scrutiny/monitoring of large value cash transactions, including transactions in foreign currency. The KYC guidelines of the RBI are modelled on the international best practices.
- The principles underlying the concept of 'time value of money' are prevalently used in designing deposit schemes of banks.

TEST YOUR UNDERSTANDING

1. Bank U has the following schedule of fees for its savings and current accounts.
    a. If the average monthly account balance is over ₹10,000, there are no charges levied for withdrawals by cheque. The monthly service charges are also waived.
    c. If the average monthly account balance is between ₹5,000 and ₹10,000, a charge of ₹5 is levied for every withdrawal by cheque. The bank also levies a monthly service charge of ₹50.
    d. If the average monthly account balance falls below ₹5,000, the charge per withdrawal by cheque is ₹10. Further, the monthly service charge is ₹100.

    What is the type of deposit pricing that Bank U is resorting to? What is the strategic objective of Bank U in imple menting this pricing schedule? What could be the problems with such a pricing strategy in a country like India?
2. Rank the following bank liabilities according to their typical levels of liquidity risk. The highest rank is to be awarded to the liability with the highest liquidity risk.
    a. Transaction/Current deposits
    b. Term deposits
    c. Certificates of deposit
    d. Savings deposits
    e. Borrowings from banks
    f. Borrowings from bond markets
    g. Equity
    h. Borrowings in foreign currency
3. If you were to rank the liabilities shown in question 2 in the order of their interest rate risk, would the ranking change? What would be the changes in the ranking?
4. If you were to rank the liabilities shown in question 2 in the order of their cost to the bank, how do you think the ranking would change? Give reasons.
5. Bank N expects to attract fresh term deposits with 2 years maturity and renew existing deposits if it offers the following interest rates per annum—at 6 per cent ₹5 crores, at 6.5 per cent ₹10 crores, at 7 per cent ₹16 crores, at 7.5 per cent ₹20 crores and at 8 per cent ₹23 crores. The bank looks to an average yield of 9 per cent on investing these deposits in new loans or market investments. What is the optimum deposit rate the bank should offer if it wants to maximize its profit?
6. Bank M requires that its savings account depositors maintain a minimum balance of ₹5,000. The services offered costs the bank ₹3 per depositor per month and the bank estimates a monthly cost of ₹2 per depositor in overhead expenses. The bank requires a minimum profit of ₹2 per month on such transactions.
    a. What should be the monthly fee that the bank charges its savings account customers?
    b. The bank further estimates that it saves about 2 per cent in operating expenses for each ₹1,000 held as deposits above the minimum balance of ₹5,000. What would be the appropriate fee for a customer holding an average minimum balance of ₹15,000?

7. Why is introduction necessary to open a current account with an Indian bank? Is introduction necessary for opening a savings account with an Indian bank under the following circumstances?
   a. Where no cheque operations are permitted.
   b. Where only withdrawals by cheque are permitted.
   c. Where both deposit of and withdrawal by cheques is permitted, including deposit of other instruments.
8. A CD with a face value of ₹1 crore and a term of 6 months is issued at a discounted price of ₹97,08,740. The bank incurs a stamp duty of 0.15 per cent per quarter on the transaction. Further, the bank has to maintain a reserve of 5 per cent as cash reserve on this amount as per central bank directives, on which it will earn no interest.
   a. What is the cost to the bank for issuing the CD?
   b. What is the return to the investor in the CD?
9. In which of the following situations should a bank use the marginal cost of funds approach?
   a. Calculating the bank's profitability.
   b. Deciding whether to tap fresh deposits or borrow from the market.
   c. Calculating the rate to be charged for a new loan.
   d. Calculating the profitability of a customer to the bank.
10. Bank V has a liability mix consisting of deposits and equity only. Average deposits of the bank amount to ₹16,000 crores and average equity to ₹2,000 crores. The bank has to maintain reserves of 30 per cent on the deposits. The remaining funds can be deployed as credit and investment in securities on which the bank earns an average yield of 12 per cent per annum. Income on investments, including interest on reserves, is about 20 per cent of the bank's total income. The overhead expenses of the bank amount to about 6 per cent of average deposits. If the bank wants to earn a profit of ₹200 crores for the year, what should be the rate the bank can pay on its deposits?

TOPICS FOR FURTHER DISCUSSION

- Take a sample of banks (private sector, public sector and foreign banks in India) and examine how their liability mix has changed over the last few years. What has been the impact on the cost of funds for these banks and their profitability?
- Analyze the non-deposit sources of funds of the above banks. Which source is the cheapest for the bank? Which source is the most risky for the bank? Take into consideration both liquidity and interest rate risks.
- Examine the maturity pattern of deposits as given in the above banks' balance sheets as part of 'notes on accounts'. Is there a marked shift in the maturity pattern? Is there a significant difference in the shift among bank categories—private sector, public sector and foreign banks? What conclusions could be drawn from the results?

ANNEXURE I

SOME IMPORTANT NON-DEPOSIT FUNDING SOURCES FOR BANKS IN INDIA AND THE USA

Indian Banks

Call/Notice Money[30]

This is a money market instrument. The money market is a market for short-term (maturities from 1 day to 1 year) financial assets.

Money market instruments are considered 'near cash' investments since they are highly liquid. They also carry the advantages of the ability to be turned over at a low cost, with borrowing and lending rates being determined by demand and supply of funds in the market.

The call/notice money market forms an important segment of the Indian money market under the call money market, funds are transacted on overnight basis and under the notice money market, funds are transacted for the period between 2 days and 14 days.[31]

- Participants in call/notice money market currently include banks (excluding regional rural banks), all cooperative banks (other than land development banks) and primary dealers (PDs), both as borrowers and lenders.
- In the case of banks borrowing in this market, the outstanding borrowing should not exceed 100 per cent of the bank's capital funds (tier 1 + tier 2 capital),[32] on a fortnightly average basis.
- In the case of banks lending in this market, the fortnightly average lending should not exceed 25 per cent of the banks' capital funds.
- Non-bank institutions cannot operate in this market (w.e.f. 6 August, 2005).

- Interest rates are market-determined and their calculation is to be based on FIMMDA's (Fixed Income Money Market and Derivatives Association of India) Handbook of Market Practices.

External Commercial Borrowings, Foreign Currency Convertible Bonds and Foreign Currency Exchangeable Bonds[33]

ECBs are typically commercial loans in the form of bank loans, buyers' credit, suppliers' credit[34] or securitized instruments such as floating rate notes and fixed rate bonds, taken from non-resident lenders with a minimum maturity of 3 years.

Foreign Currency Convertible Bonds (FCCBs) are bonds issued by an Indian company expressed in foreign currency, whose principal and interest payments are also in foreign currency. They are convertible to ordinary shares of the issuing company in accordance with the rules in force. The policy for FCCBs is similar to the policy for ECBs.

Foreign Currency Exchangeable Bonds (FCEBs) are bonds expressed in foreign currency, whose principal and interest payments are also in foreign currency. They are issued by an 'issuing company', subscribed to by residents outside India and exchangeable into equity shares of another company, called the 'Offered company', in accordance with the rules in force. The guidelines and rules governing ECBs are also applicable to FCEBs. (For more details, the RBI Circular may be referred to).

ECBs can be accessed through two routes, the automatic and approval routes.

The salient features of ECBs are summarized in Table 4.4.

TABLE 4.4 SALIENT FEATURES OF ECB/FCCB/FCEB—RBI GUIDELINES

Feature	ECBs Through Automatic Route	ECBs Through Approval Route
Basic	Do not require approval from Government of India or the RBI.	Require approval from the Government of India or the RBI.
Who can borrow?	1. Companies registered under the Companies Act, 1956, and infrastructure finance companies (IFCs). 2. Units in special economic zones (SEZ). 3. Non-governmental organizations (NGOs) 'and micro finance institutions (MFI)' involved in micro finance with good borrowing track record. 4. Small Industries Development Bank of India (SIDBI). 5. Micro Finance Institutions (MFI).	1. Financial institutions dealing exclusively with infrastructure or export finance, such as IDFC, IL&FS, Power Finance Corporation, Power Trading Corporation, IRCON and EXIM Bank. 2. Banks and financial institutions which had participated in the textile or steel sector restructuring package as approved by the Government are permitted to the extent of their investment in the package and assessment by the RBI. 3. ECB with minimum average maturity of 5 years by non-banking financial companies (NBFCs) from multilateral financial institutions, reputable regional financial institutions, official export credit agencies and international banks to finance infrastructure projects 4. FCCBs by housing finance companies satisfying certain criteria. 5. Special purpose vehicles or any other entity notified by the RBI set up to finance infrastructure companies/projects exclusively. 6. Financially sound multi-state co-operative societies engaged in manufacturing activity. 7. Special Economic Zone (SEZ) and development of National Manufacturing Investment Zones (NMIZ) developers providing specified infrastructure facilities. 8. All cases falling outside the purview of the automatic route limits

(Continued)

TABLE 4.5 (CONTINUED)

Feature	ECBs Through Automatic Route	ECBs Through Approval Route
Who cannot borrow?	1. Financial intermediaries such as banks, financial institutions (FIs), housing finance companies and non-banking financial companies (NBFCs) 2. Individuals, trusts and non-profit organizations	Not applicable
Who can lend?	1. Recognized international banks 2. International capital markets 3. Multilateral financial institutions such as IFC, ADB, CDC, etc. 4. Export credit agencies (ECAs) 5. Equipment suppliers 6. Foreign collaborators 7. Foreign equity holders, subject to certain norms. 8. Overseas organizations subject to certificate of due diligence from an eligible overseas bank. 9. Individual lenders in recognized countries subject to certificate of due diligence from an eligible overseas bank.	Similar to the automatic route.
Amount and maturity	1. The maximum amount by a corporate body (other than hotels, hospitals and software companies) is USD 750 million or equivalent during a financial year NBFC–IFCs and AFCs. 2. Hotels, hospitals and software companies in the services sector can raise up to USD 200 million, provided the amount is not for land acquisition can raise upto 75 per cent of their owned funds. 3. NGOs in micro finance can raise upto USD 10 million ECBs 4. ECB upto USD 20 million can have call/put option provided the minimum average maturity of 3 years is complied with before exercising the option. 5. All eligible borrowers can avail of ECBs in Indian Rupees, subject to rules in force.	1. Corporate borrowers availing of ECB beyond USD 750 million in the financial year. Corporate borrowers in the services sectors can borrow over USD 200 million for permitted end uses.
All in cost ceilings (over 6 month LIBOR)	Include rate of interest, other fees and expenses in foreign currency except commitment fee, pre-payment fee and fees payable in Indian Rupees, but excludes payment of withholding tax in Rupees (reviewed by RBI periodically).	Similar to automatic route.
End use permitted	1. Investment such as import of capital goods, implementation of new projects, modernization/expansion of existing production units in the industrial and infrastructure sectors and specific services (as defined and reviewed periodically by the RBI), including payment for spectrum allocation in the telecom sector. 2. Overseas direct investment in joint ventures (JV)/wholly owned subsidiaries (WOS). 3. First stage acquisition of shares and mandatory second stage offer to public under the Government's disinvestment programme of public sector units. 4. Interest during construction reckoned as part of project cost for Indian companies in the infrastructure sector. 5. Lending to self help groups or micro credit/micro finance. 6. Payment for spectrum allocation. 7. Non-Banking Finance Companies (NBFCs) for lending to infrastructure sectors. 8. Capital expenditure for maintenance and operation of toll systems for roads and highways, included in the project cost. 9. Refinancing of Bridge Finance by International Companies.	Similar to automatic route. Additionally: 1. Infrastructure companies are permitted to refinance rupee loans from the domestic banking system, subject to certain conditions. 2. Short term bridge finance for Infrastructure companies provided the bridge loan would be replaced with a long term ECB. 3. Working capital loans for Civil aviation/airline companies subject to certain conditions and also subject to repayment of ECB out of foreign currency earnings alone. 4. Manufacturing and infrastructure companies with consistent foreign exchange earnings can refinance rupee loans for capital expenditure through ECBs. 5. Others sectors as specified by the RBI.

(Continued)

TABLE 4.4 (CONTINUED)

Feature	ECBs Through Automatic Route	ECBs Through Approval Route
End use prohibited	1. On-lending or investment in capital market or acquiring a company in India by a corporate. 2. Real estate 3. Working capital, general corporate purpose and repayment of existing Rupee loans.	Similar to the automatic route.
Bank guarantees/ letters of comfort/ standby LCs/etc.	Prohibited	May be considered on a case by case basis.
Debt service	Through the designated bank	Through the designated bank
Procedure	1. Borrowers enter into loan agreement complying with ECB guidelines with recognized lender. 2. The borrower must obtain a loan registration number (LRN) from the RBI before drawing down the ECB.	Application to RBI with necessary documents.
ECB proceeds	Can be parked overseas until actual requirement in India and invested in the following liquid assets: (a) deposits or CDs or other products offered by banks rated investment grade (b) deposits with overseas branch of an Indian bank: (c) treasury bills and other rated money market instruments. In short, investment has to be made in liquid instruments.	Similar to the automatic route.
Prepayment of ECB	Permitted up to USD 500 million by banks without prior approval of RBI subject to compliance with the stipulated minimum average maturity period.	1. Prepayment of ECB up to USD 500 million may be allowed by the bank without prior approval of the RBI, subject to compliance with the stipulated minimum average maturity period. 2. Pre-payment of ECB for amounts exceeding USD 500 million would be considered by the RBI under the approval route.
Security	Left to the agreement between the borrower and lender. However, creation of charge over immovable assets and financial securities, such as shares, in favour of the overseas lender, is subject to Foreign Exchange Management Act (FEMA) regulations.	Similar to automatic route.

Source: RBI 'Master Circular on External Commercial Borrowings and Trade Credits' dated 1 July, 2009, and subsequent amendment dated 9 December, 2009.

Export Refinance from the RBI[35]

There is another important and prevalent source of wholesale funds for banks—refinancing. Various institutions offer refinancing for credit extended by banks to sectors of the economy identified as critical or priority. For example, apex institutions such as Small Industries Development Bank of India (SIDBI), National Bank for Agriculture and Rural Development (NABARD) and Infrastructure Development Finance Corporation (IDFC) provide refinance to banks making loans to the SME, agriculture and infrastructure sectors, respectively. Banks have the option of sourcing funds from the refinancing agencies when they have extended credit to eligible borrowers in these sectors.

The RBI provides export credit refinance facility to banks under Section 17(3A) of the Reserve Bank of India Act, 1934, in order to encourage banks to extend more credit to exporters. This facility is given on the basis of banks' eligible outstanding rupee export credit both at the pre-shipment and post-shipment stages. The quantum of refinance is fixed from time to time based on the stance of monetary and credit policy of the RBI. However, export credit deployed in foreign currency (PCFC) would not be refinanced against. Banks can also rediscount export bills with Export Import Bank of India (EXIM Bank).

Banks can take refinance to the extent of 50 per cent of the outstanding export credit eligible for refinance on a specified date (at the end of the second preceding fortnight). The refinance is priced at the repo rate[36] under the liquidity adjustment facility (LAF). The amount of refinance can be repaid to the RBI on specified dates that, in any case, cannot exceed 180 days. The RBI grants the refinance against a demand promissory note from the bank seeking the funds, which, in any case, has to be a minimum of ₹1 lakh or multiples of this amount. Banks would be penalized if they are found to: (a) utilize refinance that exceeds the total amount of export credit given to borrowers or (b) misreport or miscalculate the amount of the eligible refinance or (c) do not repay the refinance within the stipulated time period or (d) delay reporting excess utilization to the RBI.

Some Non-Deposit Sources of Bank Funds in the USA[37]

IRA and KEOGH Plans These are long-term sources of funds for banks. They act as custodians for personal pension plans that individuals may use to defer federal income taxes on contributions and subsequent investment earnings. Both IRAs are allowed under the Taxpayer Relief Act of 1997.

Federal Funds Federal funds are short-term unsecured transfers of immediately available funds between depository institutions for one business day (*i.e.*, overnight loans). Federal funds are best suited for institutions short of reserves to meet their legal reserve requirements or to satisfy customer loan demand. It satisfies this demand by tapping immediately usable funds. Deposits held by the US banks at Federal Reserve Banks, deposits with correspondent banks and demand deposit balances of security dealers and governments are also used for short-term funding.

Borrowing from the Federal Reserve This is seen as a viable alternative to the Federal funds market. There are three types of loans available based on the bank's needs. Each type of loan comes at a different price. They could take the form of: (a) adjustment credit, where the loan is for a few days only and is intended to provide immediate aid in meeting statutory reserve requirements, (b) seasonal credit, where the loan has a longer maturity and is meant for banks with seasonal swings in business and (c) extended credit, where the loan is intended for banks experiencing longer-term funding problems.

Repurchase Agreements Repurchase agreements contract to sell (typically high quality and usually government securities) securities temporarily by a borrower of funds to a lender of funds with the borrower agreeing to buy back the securities at a predetermined price on an agreed date in the future. These could take the form of overnight loans, term loans or continuing contracts. These agreements are collateralized loans and thus, the lender is not exposed to credit risk as they are with federal funds transactions. They are therefore seen as low cost and low risk way of borrowing funds for short periods of time (usually 3 or 4 days). They are low risk because they are collateralized by the securities that are sold as part of the agreement.

Non-Deposit Funds These are money market liabilities purchased for relatively short time periods to adjust liquidity demands. The use of these purchased funds came into existence due to tight money periods in which deposit rate ceilings caused banks to develop alternative sources of funds. Unlike deposit funds, these are exempt from federal reserve requirements, interest rate ceilings and FDIC insurance assessments.

Negotiable CDs These were initially developed to attract large corporate deposits and savings from wealthy individuals. They are interest-bearing receipts evidencing deposit of funds in the bank for a specified time period, at a specified interest rate. However, since they also have the legal attributes of deposits, negotiable CDs are considered 'hybrid' accounts. There are four identifiable types of negotiable CDs: (a) domestic CDs issued by domestic banks in the US, (b) Euro CDs, being dollar-denominated CDs issued outside the US and (c) Yankee CDs issued by foreign banks in the US and (d) thrift CDs issued by large savings loans and other non-banks in the US. Moreover, these funds are highly interest rate sensitive and are often withdrawn on maturity, unless management aggressively bids in terms of yield to keep the CDs.

Discount Window Advances The 12 regional Federal Reserves operate discount windows[38] from which banks can borrow (subject to Regulation A rules). A discount window loan must be secured by collateral acceptable to a Federal Reserve (usually US government securities). Most banks keep government securities in the vaults of the Federal Reserve for this purpose. The Federal Reserve Bank will also accept some government agency securities and high-grade commercial paper as collateral.

Eurocurrency Deposits These were originally developed in Western Europe to provide liquid funds for financial institutions to lend to one another or to customers. These are dollar-denominated deposits placed in banks outside US territory. Many Eurodollar deposits arise from US balance-of-payments deficits that give foreigners claims on US assets and form the need to pay in dollars for some international commodities (such as oil) mostly denominated in US dollars.

Bankers' Acceptances These are time drafts drawn on a bank by either an exporter or importer to finance international business transactions. The bank may discount the acceptance in the money market to (in effect) finance the transaction.

Commercial Papers These are high quality short-term debt obligations (unsecured promissory notes) issued by corporations with strong credit ratings to meet the firm's working capital needs. Banks can issue such paper through their affiliated or holding companies. Typically, the maturities range from 3 or 4 days to 9 months.

Federal Home Loan Bank Borrowings Under the Financial Institutions Reform, Recovery and Enforcement Act (FIRREA) of 1989, FHLBs can provide discount window services to banks. FHLBs function as special lending facilities for the housing finance industry. These government-sponsored enterprises increase the liquidity of mortgage markets by lending against the security of banks' mortgage portfolios. These loans are very popular as funding sources, because of their stability and the below-market lending rates offered.

Long-Term Non-Deposit Sources These include mortgages to fund the construction of new buildings, capital notes and debentures. Generally, the interest costs on these funds, though substantially higher than money market loans, are more stable.

ANNEXURE II

SOME IMPORTANT LEGAL PROVISIONS RELEVANT FOR BANKERS

- The RBI Act, 1934 envisages major functions for the RBI as a central banker, a promoter and a regulator.
- The Banking Regulations Act, 1949 primarily deals with the administrative and functional aspects of governance of banks. The act also confers the RBI with powers of supervision over commercial banks.
- The Negotiable Instruments (NI) Act, 1881 is acclaimed as one of the most comprehensive and well-drafted enactments that have stood the test of time with only 25 minor revisions. The NI Act defines the nature, functions and limitations of several negotiable instruments with comprehensive coverage of cheques. It demarcates the rights and obligations of various parties to negotiable instruments and offers transactional clarity to minimize the areas of disputes between parties. The Act also lays down the procedure for claims against dishonour of instruments and punishments for breach of legal provisions. A later amendment titled Negotiable Instruments (Amendments and Miscellaneous Provisions) Act, 2002 addresses various issues emerging out of e-commerce and tightens the prosecution procedure for dishonour of cheques.
- The Companies Act, 1956 is important for banks, since companies incorporated under the Act form the major customers for banks.
- The Indian Contract Act, 1872 is of great relevance as bankers have to enter into relationships with their customers as debtors, creditors, agents or bailee. The Act determines the capacity of parties to the contracts and validity of transactions arising out of contracts. The Act also covers special contracts such as contracts of guarantee, bailments, pledge and agency.
- The I.T. Act 2000 is relevant for banks since it addresses issues emerging out of electronic banking transactions and provides protection against possible abuse and misuse of services.
- The Limitation Act, 1963 aims to prevent unduly stale legal claims and reduce long-winded court procedures. It is necessary for bankers to protect their documents from getting time barred, since legal remedy also lapses with the expiry of the limitation period. The Act also provides some safeguards to protect the documents from getting time barred.
- The Indian Stamp Act, 1899 seeks to raise revenue by making payment of stamp duty statutory to establish validity of certain transactions. The Act is important for banks as certain unstamped documents are inadmissible as evidence in a court of law.
- The Registration Act, 1908 is aimed at preserving and protecting title to property. The Act imposes serious disqualifications and penalties for non-observance of regulations. It also determines the priority of validity of transactions based on their registration. Banks must take into account various aspects of the Act for opening of accounts, execution of documents and enforcing securities.
- The Transfer of Property Act, 1882 sets out the rights and liabilities of the transferor and transferee in respect of various transactions. Since the transfer of interests and rights involves registration and payment of stamp duty, this law should be read along with the Registration Act and the Indian Stamp Act. Mortgage of immoveable property is one of the popular modes of obtaining security and hence, bankers have to ensure compliance with the provisions of this Act.
- The Sale of Goods Act, 1930 deals with rights and obligations of sellers and buyers apart from conditions and warranties covering the sale of goods. The provisions of this Act are relevant to bankers who often act as agents for collecting bills accompanied by documents of title to goods and as holder for value while discounting the bills. The Act also offers remedies for breach of agreements of sale.
- The Consumer Protection Act, 1986 (as amended in December 2002), protects the interests of the consumers and establishes dispute redressal agencies at district, state and national levels. A bank customer can be considered a 'consumer' since banking services are hired for consideration. The growing awareness among customers of their rights and responsibilities, fixed by the Act on banks for deficiency of service, have made it important for banks to be informed of the various provisions of the Act.
- International laws pertaining to international trade and commerce are necessary tools for banks to operate in the present globalized environment.
- Securitization and Reconstruction of Financial Assets and Enforcement of Security Interest Act, 2002 empowers the banks to seize the assets of non-performing advances and securitize the assets to realize the dues.
- The Prevention of Money Laundering Act, 2002 makes it obligatory for banks to verify and maintain records of identity pertaining to all its customers for prescribed value of transactions. The Act lays rigorous punishments for aiding and promoting domestic and international crimes.
- The Competition Act, 2002 was enacted to address market realignment strategies of large companies. The important provisions of the Act could influence the business strategy of banks.

ANNEXURE III

A SUMMARY OF IMPORTANT LEGAL ASPECTS OF BANK DEPOSITS IN INDIA

How Banks in India Have to Deal with Some Special Classes of Bank Customers

- Under the Indian Contract Act, 1872, a 'minor' (one who has not completed 18 years of age) cannot enter into a valid contract and such a contract, even if entered into, is considered void. A contract for supply of goods and services necessary for the minor to live, however, is a valid contract. All other contracts can be repudiated by the minor. Therefore, banks should be extremely cautious while opening and operating accounts on behalf of minors. Even if the bank opens the minor's deposit account after following all the prescribed legal procedures, care should be taken to ensure that no 'overdraft'[39] is permitted in such an account. If such a loan is granted, even inadvertently, the bank has no legal remedy for recovery. Even if the assets of the minor are charged to the bank, the legal remedy is non-existent since the minor cannot enter into a contract to charge his assets. Similarly, even if the advance granted to the minor is backed by a counterparty guarantee, the contract of guarantee is invalid on the grounds that the contract between the debtor and the creditor (minor) itself is invalid. However, if a minor posing as a major enters into the contract and later seeks to nullify the contract on the grounds of his having been a minor at the time of entering the contract, the minor is liable to restore to the bank the benefits derived by him under the false contract[40] The bank should also be cautious while dealing with a negotiable instrument, in which a minor is one of the signatories. Under Section 26 of the Negotiable Instruments Act, a minor can issue or negotiate a cheque or Bill of Exchange, but cannot be sued in respect of the instrument.
- A married woman can enter into a valid contract and the husband cannot be made liable for her actions except under the following circumstances—a loan is taken with the husband's consent and authority, or the loan has been taken to supply the wife with necessities for her sustenance, since the husband has failed in his duty to provide her with basic amenities. While entering into a contract with a married woman, the banker should ascertain that she has assets of her own.
- The banker should enter into a contract with a 'pardanashin' woman only after taking precautions to establish her identity.
- In the case of illiterate persons, bankers take thumb impressions in lieu of signatures, along with photographs of depositors as proof of identity.
- The banker should avoid opening an account in the name of a person of unsound mind. According to the Indian Contract Act, a contract with a person of unsound mind is invalid. If a person has been sane while entering into the contract with the bank, but turns insane later, the banker should suspend all operations in the account subsequent to the customer's lunacy. Operations can be resumed only on receiving proof of sanity or is served with an order of the court.
- The banker should also take precautions while opening accounts in the names of Trustees. According to Section 3 of the Indian Trusts Act, 1882, a 'Trust' is an obligation annexed to the ownership of property and arising out of a confidence reposed in and accepted by the owner for the benefit of another. The author of the trust is the person who reposes the confidence and the 'trustee' is the person in whom the confidence is reposed. The person for whose benefit the trust is formed is called the 'beneficiary'. A trust is formed through a document called the 'trust deed'. The banker should thoroughly scrutinize the trust deed to ascertain that the trustees are authorized to act in the interest of the beneficiaries. The trustees can borrow or mortgage the trust property only if the trust deed specifically confers such powers on them.
- The banker should also take precautions while opening and operating accounts in the name of a joint Hindu family. The banker should be familiar with the provisions of the Hindu Law and Succession Act while doing so.

SELECT REFERENCE

Varshney, P. N. (2004), *Banking Law and Practice*, Chapters 3, 4 and 5. New Delhi: Sultan Chand & Sons.

ANNEXURE IV

ANTI-MONEY LAUNDERING AND KNOW YOUR CUSTOMER GUIDELINES—INTERNATIONAL BEST PRACTICES[41] AND GUIDELINES FOR INDIAN BANKS[42]

Ill-Effects of Money Laundering on the Economy

Money laundering can have potentially negative consequences for a country's macro-economic performance, can impose welfare losses and may also have negative cross-border externalities. It can distort allocation of economic resources and distribution of wealth. In most cases, it is costly and difficult to detect and eradicate.

Some manifestations of the economic impact of money laundering could be as follows:

- Impaired banking system soundness
- Potentially large fiscal liabilities
- Reduced ability to attract foreign investment
- Increased volatility of international capital flows and exchange rates
- Difficulty in national tax collection and law enforcement.

More seriously, over and above the direct abuse of the financial system, the country runs a reputation risk in international circles, which, in turn, could impair global willingness to conduct business (such as foreign investment into the country and banking correspondent relationships) with that country.

Overall, the 'trust' that underpins the development and existence of vibrant financial markets would be adversely affected. Effective functioning of financial markets is heavily based on the fundamental expectation that high professional, legal and ethical standards would be observed and enforced. A reputation for integrity—soundness, honesty and adherence to standards and codes—is one of the most valued assets by global investors and financial institutions. Money laundering and terrorist financing would compromise the reputation of financial institutions, undermine investors' trust in those institutions and therefore, ultimately weaken the financial system.

The Anatomy of Money Laundering and Terrorism Financing[43]

What is the link between money laundering and terrorist financing? The techniques used to launder money are essentially the same as those used to conceal the sources of terrorist financing. The origin of funds used in terrorist financing may be legitimate, or from criminal activities. The danger lies not in the origin, but in disguising the source of terrorist financing, which implies that these concealed sources of funds remain available for future terrorist financing. Terrorists too would want their use of funds concealed so that the financing goes undetected.

While criminal activities and the funds they generate could be captured by a country's legal or anti money laundering framework, the 'legitimate' sources pose more challenges. These 'legitimate' sources may include donations or gifts of cash or other assets to organizations or charities, which in turn could be a façade to support terrorist activities. Hence special laws and measures have to be brought in to tackle these legitimate sources as well.

Whatever be the illegal means of sourcing the funds, money launderers follow the 'process' of placement, layering and integration in the process of turning illicit proceeds into apparently legal money or goods.

Simply, the process money launderers follow, is shown in the following Chart:

The Processes of Money Laundering and Terrorism Financing

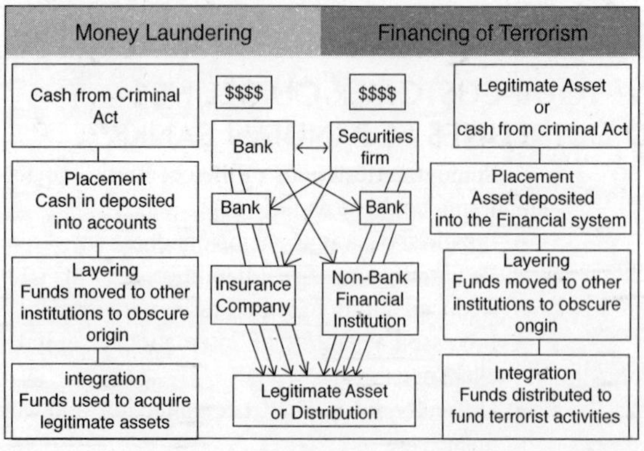

Source: World Bank, Schott, Paul Allen, 2006, Reference guide to anti money laundering and combating the financing of terrorism, second edition, pp. 1–8.

It is clear from the Chart that the first stop for the illegal money is the financial system, usually financial intermediaries like banks. The most ubiquitous method is to deposit large amounts of cash, broken into smaller amounts, into various fictitious accounts spread over different banks/ bank branches. Parts of the cash then find their way into other parts of the financial system, as insurance contracts or investment in securities.

It is therefore not surprising that to check money laundering and its deleterious consequences, banks need to have watertight regulations and supervision.

International Standards to Deal with Money Laundering and Terrorism Financing

Money laundering can be simply defined as 'transfer of illegally obtained money or investments through an outside party to conceal the true source'.[44] Money launderers may also operate outside financial systems—*e.g.*, through alternative remittance systems.

The World Bank and the IMF have been working closely since 2001 with the FATF[41] on money laundering, the standard setting body in this area, to develop a methodology for assessing the observance of international standards on the legal, institutional and operational framework for AML and CFT.

The FATF standards draw on and complement a wide range of United Nations (UN) conventions and resolutions that promote international cooperation in preventing and containing drug trafficking, organized crime, corruption and efforts to finance terrorism.

The FATF has been taking important steps to protect the international financial system from abuse. In the recently concluded FATF plenary held at Paris in February 2013, some additional measures were initiated:

- Two public documents were produced as part of its ongoing work to identify jurisdictions that may pose a risk to the international financial system[45].
- Discussions were held on adopting new Methodology for Assessing Technical Compliance with the FATF Recommendations and the Effectiveness of AML/CFT Systems.
- The Guidance on Anti-Money Laundering and Counter Terrorist Financing Measures and Financial Inclusion was updated.
- Guidance on conducting National Risk Assessment was approved and published.
- OSCE (Organization for Security and cooperation in Europe) was invited as Observer.
- The global challenges in supervision and enforcement were discussed.

In addition, all financial supervisory standards have core principles to enhance KYC rules, suspicious transactions reporting and other due diligence requirements that help to support AML–CFT regimes.

The BCBS, IAIS and IOSCO have each issued broad supervisory standards and guidelines on a wide range of supervisory issues, including money laundering as it relates to banking, insurance and securities.

The contents of the above mentioned standards and guidelines are summarized in the following section. It is noteworthy that FATF has incorporated these standards and guidelines in its 40 recommendations.

The Basel Committee Guidelines The BCBS has issued three documents covering money laundering issues.

1. **Statement on prevention of criminal use of the banking system for the purpose of money laundering**

This statement contains essentially four principles that should be used by banking institutions.

- Proper customer identification.
- High ethical standards and compliance with laws and regulations.
- Cooperation with law enforcement authorities.
- Policies and procedures to be used to adhere to the statement.

2. **Core principles for effective banking supervision**

These principles set out a comprehensive blueprint for supervisory issues, which cover a wide range of topics. Core Principle 15 deals with money laundering by stipulating that bank supervisors must determine that banks have adequate policies and procedures in place, including strict KYC rules.

3. **Customer due diligence for banks**

This paper provides extensive guidance on appropriate standards for banks to use in identifying their customers. The paper was issued in response to a number of deficiencies noted on a global basis with regard to the KYC procedures noted above. In addition, the standards go beyond the fight against money laundering and are intended to help protect banks in terms of safety and soundness.

IAIS Guidelines This association has issued its Guidance Paper 5, 'Anti-Money Laundering Guidance Notes for Insurance Supervisors and Insurance Entities', which parallels the BCBS's statement on prevention.

It contains four principles that should be followed by insurance entities;

- Comply with anti-money laundering laws.
- Have KYC procedures in place.
- Cooperate with all law enforcement authorities.
- Have internal anti-money laundering policies, procedures and training programs for employees.

International Organization of Securities Commissioners (IOSCO) Guidelines IOSCO in its 'Resolution on Money Laundering' proposes seven specific areas for security regulators in individual countries to consider while establishing requirements for firms under their jurisdiction.

- The extent of customer identifying information with a view towards enhancing the ability of authorities to identify and prosecute money launderers.
- The adequacy of record-keeping requirements to reconstruct financial transactions.
- Whether an appropriate manner is used to address the reporting of suspicious transactions.
- What procedures are in place to prevent criminals from obtaining control of securities businesses and to share information with foreign counterparts.
- Whether means are appropriate for monitoring compliance procedures designed to deter and detect money laundering.
- The use of cash and cash equivalents in securities transactions, including documentation to reconstruct transactions.
- Whether means are appropriate to share information to combat money laundering.

Salient Features of the RBI's KYC Norms[46]

Central banks of most countries, including the RBI, have been reiterating the need for banks to 'know' their customers. In November 2004, the RBI issued revised KYC guidelines in line with the recommendations made by the FATF on AML standards and CFT. Banks were required to frame their KYC policies with the approval of their boards and ensure compliance with its provisions by 31 December 2005.

The salient features of the policy relate to the procedure prescribed with regard to customer acceptance, customer identification, risk management and monitoring as required under Prevention of Money Laundering Act (PMLA), 2002. Additionally, banks had to follow the provisions of the Foreign Contribution (Regulation) Act, 1976 in respect of acceptance of foreign donations on behalf of associations/organizations maintaining accounts with them.

The objective of KYC/AML/CFT guidelines is to prevent banks from being used, intentionally or unintentionally, by criminal elements for money laundering or terrorist financing activities. KYC procedures also enable banks to know/understand their customers and their financial dealings better which in turn help them manage their risks prudently.

For the purpose of KYC policy, a 'Customer' is defined as:

- a person or entity that maintains an account and/or has a business relationship with the bank,
- one on whose behalf the account is maintained (*i.e.* the beneficial owner). ' Beneficial Owner' means the natural person who ultimately owns or controls a client and or the person on whose behalf a transaction is being conducted, and includes a person who exercises ultimate effective control over a juridical person],
- beneficiaries of transactions conducted by professional intermediaries, such as Stock Brokers, Chartered Accountants, Solicitors, etc. as permitted under the law, and
- any person or entity connected with a financial transaction which can pose significant reputational or other risks to the bank, say, a wire transfer or issue of a high value demand draft as a single transaction.

The RBI has given general guidelines on the subject and specific procedural guidelines for strict adherence by banks.

The general guidelines stipulate that:

a. Customer information is kept confidential and not divulged for cross selling or any other purpose.
b. Remittances of funds by demand drafts, mail or telegraphic transfer, issue of travelers' cheques and other modes of funds transfer exceeding Rupees fifty thousands should be done only through debit of the customers' account and not against cash payment.
c. Instruments such as cheques, demand drafts, etc. presented beyond three months from their date of issue should not be paid by banks (effective April 1, 2012).
d. Banks should strictly adhere to the provisions of Foreign Contribution (Regulation) Act, 2010, where applicable.

RBI stipulates that Banks' KYC policies should incorporate the following key aspects: [a] Customer Acceptance policy [CAP], [b] Customer identification procedures [CIP], [c] monitoring of transactions, and [d] risk management. [Detailed description of these aspects can be found in the quoted RBI circular].

The other procedural guidelines can be accessed from the quoted RBI circular.

Introduction of New Depositors

Opening an account with a bank signifies the beginning of the banker–customer relationship. The special features of this relationship impose obligations and responsibilities on both parties. More so in the case of bankers, whose vigilance in opening of and operations in the accounts would entitle them to legal protection under Section 131 of the Negotiable Instruments Act, 1881 (the NI Act).

The NI Act governs payment and collection of negotiable instruments and provides certain kinds of rights, liabilities (obligations) and protection to the issuers/drawers, payees, endorsees, drawers, collecting banks and paying/drawer banks that will be available, only if the bank makes or receives payment of a cheque/draft payable to order in 'due course'. Any payment or collection of a negotiable instrument is deemed to be in 'due course' only when the bank has, for its customer, acted without negligence and in good faith.

The due diligence process, while opening a deposit account will involve verifying the person's identity, address, occupation and source of income. An important part of the process is obtaining introduction of the prospective depositor from a person acceptable to the bank.

Why is Introduction Necessary?

- To gain protection for the banker under Section 131 of the NI Act.
- To enable proper identification of the person opening an account and ensure that the customer can be traced later if required.
- To guard against accounts being opened by socially undesirable persons or in fictitious names with the objective of, inter alia, to deposit unaccounted money.

'Proper' Introduction

- Generally an account is opened only after a meeting between the banker and the prospective customer.
- The prospective depositor has to be 'introduced' by an existing account holder or a respectable member of the local community, who is also a customer or well known to the bank. The guidelines indicate that the introducer should have been the bank's customer for at least 6 months, during which interval the bank should have been satisfied with the conduct of the introducer's account. This is required for opening all types of deposit accounts.
- The bank should additionally take steps to ascertain the identity of its depositors and not rely solely on the credentials presented by the introducer. The above duty of the banker was reiterated by the Madras High Court, when it ruled that the bank had indeed been negligent in making its own investigation into the depositor's antecedents.[47]
- Generally, the bank's employees are discouraged from providing the introduction for new accounts.
- In cases where the introducer is not able to be physically present to introduce the account, a confirmation of the introduction should be obtained in writing. It is advisable to allow operations in the new account, only after the bank is convinced about the antecedents of the new depositor.
- Some of the key risks for the bank in opening accounts without proper introduction are as follows.

  The banker will lose statutory protection under Section 131 of the NI Act. Briefly stated, under this section, the collecting banker for cheques, bills and other negotiable instruments whose title is defective, will not be liable to the true owner of the instrument, provided the banker has acted in good faith and without negligence. The banker stands to lose this vital protection if the account holder sends a forged or stolen instrument for collection and it transpires that the miscreant had been allowed to open the account without proper introduction. In such cases, the banker remains liable to the true owner of such instruments.

  In case the bank allows an overdraft[48] in a deposit account that has not been properly introduced, the bank has to bear the credit risk[49] if the overdraft is not repaid.

  In case the banker has permitted, without proper verification, an 'undischarged insolvent'[50] to open a deposit account, the balances in this account run the risk of attachment by the court.

Other Procedures for Opening Deposit Accounts

- It is mandatory to obtain recent photographs of the deposit account holders at the time of opening almost all new accounts, except where exempted by the guidelines in force.[51] The photographs have to be affixed on the account opening forms submitted by the new customers.

- Specimen signatures of the persons, authorized to operate the accounts and sign cheques and other instruments, have to be obtained and preserved. Every transaction in the account has to be scrutinized by the bank to ensure that it is the account holder who is authorizing the transaction. In case the signature on the instrument authorizing a transaction is different from the specimen signature, the bank can refuse to go through with the transaction.
- Genuine address of the account holders should be verified at the time of opening the account and updated periodically.
- Other safeguards include obtaining the PAN/GIR number of the new deposit customer and completion of account opening documentation formalities at the bank.
- Deposit accounts can be opened by an individual in his own name (known as an account in a single name) or by more than one individual in their own names (known as a joint account). Savings bank account can also be opened by a minor, jointly with natural guardian or with mother as the guardian (known as a minor's account). Minors above the age of 14 will also be allowed to open and operate savings bank account independently.
- When a bank opens a 'joint' account, any of the following mandates will have to be provided to the bank for disposal of the balance in the deposit accounts—'either or survivor' or 'anyone or survivor/s'. Any modification in the mandate can be carried out only with the consent of all the account holders. 'Either or survivor' accounts will be held by two persons and in the event of death of any of the account holders, the balance will be paid to the survivor. Where the account is held by more than two persons, 'anyone or survivor/s' mandate will operate. The exception to this is the joint deposit account on behalf of a minor, where only the natural guardian can operate the account.

Nomination Facility for Deposit Accounts

The Banking Laws Amendment Act, 1983 inserted a new Section 45 ZA in the Banking Regulation Act, 1949 to provide for nomination by bank deposit holders.

Legal Status of Nominee Does the nominee become the absolute owner of the deposit money received under the nomination on death of the principal depositor? What is the status of legal heirs in the face of nomination?

These are some of the questions that arise when depositors are required to make a nomination in respect of the deposit amounts held by them with banks.

A Supreme Court judgement[52] makes the position of the nominee clear:

'A mere nomination made … does not have the effect of conferring on the nominee any beneficial interest in the amount payable. The nomination only indicates the hand which is authorized to receive the amount …. The amount, however, can be claimed by the heirs … in accordance with the Law of Succession governing them'.

It is thus clear that the nominee cannot become the absolute owner of the amount received by him. The law of succession will have to ultimately prevail.

Other points to be noted in respect of nomination of deposit accounts are as follows:

- A single depositor or many depositors (in the case of joint accounts) together, can nominate a person to whom, in the event of death of the deposit customers, the balance in the deposit account may be paid. The nominee's right to receive these balances arises only after the death of all the depositors.
- Only individuals can be nominees. This implies that organizational bodies such as associations, trusts or their office bearers cannot be designated nominees.
- The nominee has the right to receive the deposit amount to the exclusion of all other interested persons. The nominee can also request the bank to close a term deposit before maturity.[53]
- If the nominee is a minor, the depositors can name any person to receive the deposit amount in the event of the depositors' death while the nominee continues to be a minor.
- The nomination can be varied or cancelled by the depositor/s at any time. In the case of a joint account, all depositors should agree in writing to the change in nomination.
- Once it makes payment to the designated nominee after due diligence, the bank is fully discharged from its liability in respect of the deposit. Such payment shall not be bound by any claim made by a person other than the nominee.
- Mere renewal of the deposit does not cancel nomination or cause any variation in the nomination.
- Nomination facility is available to all types of deposit accounts irrespective of the nomenclatures used by different banks.
- If the customer prefers not to nominate, the fact should be recorded.
- Nomination rules apply to cases where the bank is operating as a trustee or agent, as for example, articles entrusted to the bank for safe custody. For example, while releasing contents of safe deposit lockers to the nominee or nominees and surviving hirers, banks need not open sealed/closed packets found in the locker. In case the locker has been hired jointly, on the death of any one of the joint hirers, the contents of the locker can be removed (jointly by the nominee and the survivors) after an inventory is taken. Thereafter, the nominee and surviving hirer(s) may still keep the entire contents with the same bank, if they so desire by entering into a fresh contract for hiring a locker.

SELECT REFERENCES

1. Indian Institute of Bankers, 2005, 'Legal Aspects of Banking operations', Chapter 1, Macmillan India Ltd, New Delhi.
2. Varshney, P N, 2004, 'Banking Law and Practice', Chapters 3, 4, and 5, Sultan Chand & Sons, New Delhi.

ENDNOTES

1. Since cheques are used primarily for transfer of funds, these are also called 'checking accounts' in some countries.
2. The FSF was founded in 1999 by the G7 Finance Ministers and Central Bank Governors as a new structure for enhancing cooperation among the various national and international supervisory bodies and international financial institutions so as to promote stability in the international financial system. In November 2008, leaders of G20 countries called for a larger membership of the FSF. In April 2009, an expanded FSF was established as the Financial Stability Board (FSB) with the objective of promoting financial stability. The FSB functions from the Bank for International Settlements (BIS) in Basel, Switzerland. (www.financialstabilityboard.org)
3. More on the BCBS can be found in the chapter 'Capital – Risk, Regulation and Adequacy' and on www.bis.org
4. Simply stated, 'bank failure' is the inability of a bank to meet its credit obligations. In other words, the bank does not have liquid funds to pay off its debts (deposits, barrowings) when demanded or on maturity.
5. Vishy Cvsa, Alexandru M. Degeratu and Rebecca L. Ott-Wadhawan, 'Bank Deposits Get Interesting', *The Mckinsey Quarterly*, No. 2 (2002): 10–13.
6. Rick Spitler, Sherief Meleis and Phil Vaccaro, 'Pricing with Precision', *Banking Strategies*, Vol. LXXVIII, No. V (September/October 2002).
7. *Ibid.*
8. Based on the approaches suggested by Darling, George K, of the Darling Consulting Group, Inc, in 'Now is not the time', published in 'Bank Asset Liability Management', February 2006, Vol 22, No. 2, pages 1 and 2.
9. Spread is calculated as the difference between total revenue (deposit inflow 10 per cent the average yield on deployment of the new funds) Less total cost (deposit inflow average interest the bank will pay on the new funds).
10. Summarized from Milligan, Jack, 'Growing the Bank', Bank Director Magazine, 2nd Quarter, 2006.
11. One way to define interest rate risk is 'the gain/loss arising due to sensitivity of interest income/interest expenses or values of assets/liabilities to fluctuations in interest rates'.
12. More on duration concepts and interest rate risk management can be found in the Chapter on 'Risk Management'.
13. Olson Research Associates, Inc, 'Deposits: Measuring Interest rate risk?', A/L Benchmarks Communicator, March 1999, Issue No. 4.
14. Hutchison, Dave, 2003. 'Value and Duration in Retail Financial Markets: The Economics of Bank Deposits', HYPERLINK "http://www.westga.edu" www.westga.edu
15. Berlin, Mitchell, and Mester, Loretta J, 1998, 'Deposits and relationship lending', Working Paper No. 98-22, Research Department, Federal Reserve Bank of Philadelphia, page 30.
16. Shibut, Lynn, 2002, 'Should Bank liability structure influence deposit insurance pricing?', Working Paper 2002-01, FDIC, page 6.
17. *Sources:* RBI documents.
18. An ADR is a negotiable security that enables a non-US company to trade in the US financial markets. They are denominated in USD, and pay dividends in USD. They are traded like regular shares on the American stock exchanges. For more on ADRs, http://www.tradingadr.com/ is a good resource. GDRs are very similar to ADRs. They are usually listed on European exchanges. Both are negotiable instruments, and both entail delivery of shares of an Indian company to a bank in India, which in turn instructs an overseas depository bank (ODB) to issue the ADR/GDR. After redemption of the ADR/ GDR, the underlying shares can be sold in India by the company issuing these shares.
19. 'Loan Sale' is discussed in detail in the Chapter titled 'Credit Risk—An Overview'.
20. The latest guidelines have been issued by RBI on 1 July, 2009. The document titled 'Master Circular—Know Your Customer (KYC) norms/Anti-Money Laundering (AML) standards/Combating of Financing of Terrorism (CFT)/Obligation of banks under PMLA, 2002', can be accessed at www.rbi.org.in.
21. A garnishee order is issued under Order 21, Rule 46 of the Code of Civil Procedure, 1908. It is issued at the behest of a creditor for recovery of his debt from the account holder. On receipt of the order, the account of the customer with the bank gets suspended and the bank cannot make any subsequent payments from the account.
22. Please refer to Chapter on 'Risk Management' for more discussion on 'asset liability management'.
23. Latest RBI guidelines for issue of CDs were issued on 1 July, 2009.
24. For more detailed discussion on 'reserve requirements', please refer to Chapter titled 'Monetary Policy—Implications for Bank Management'.

25. The concept of 'time value of money' is one of the most important concepts in financial theory. All basic textbooks of financial theory would typically carry tables that show the future value and present value interest factors for a given interest/discount rate and number of periods.

26. Apart from the annual compounding, if the interest is compounded monthly/quarterly/half-yearly, the effective rate of interest for such periods will be different from the nominal rate quoted. Given the nominal contracted rate, the effective rate can be computed as:

$$r = (1 + k - m)m - 1$$

where, r = Effective rate

k = Nominal rate

m = Frequency of compounding per year

For instance, if the nominal contracted rate of interest on a 2-year term deposit is 9.5 per cent and if the interest amount is compounded on a quarterly basis then the effective rate works out to

$$r = \left(1 + \frac{0.095}{4}\right)^m - 1 = 9.84\%$$

27. These are commonly used abbreviations for Future Value of an Annuity after n years (FVAn) and Future Value Interest Factor of an Annuity (FVIFAn, k)], where n and k represent the number of years of the Annuity and the relevant interest rate. The values of FVIFA for given values of n and k can be obtained from tables available in any standard text book on financial theory.

28. Under the 'time value of money' concept, these are accepted abbreviations for present value (PV) and present value interest factor annuity (PVIFAn, k) for n years at interest rate k. Present value tables would be available for given values of n and k in all standard text books of financial theory.

29. 'Monetary Policy—Implications for Bank Management'.

30. RBI, 'Master Circular on Call/Notice Money Market operations' (July 1, 2013).

31. 'Call Money' means deals in overnight funds, while 'Notice Money' means deals in funds for 2-14 days and 'Term Money' means deals in funds for 15 days-1 year.

32. Banks capital funds are discussed in detail in the Chapter titled 'Capital-Risk, Regulation and Adequacy'.

33. On the basis of the RBI 'Master Circular on External Commercial Borrowings and Trade Credits' (July, 2013) and subsequent revision dated.

34. Suppliers' credit relates to credit for imports into India extended by the overseas supplier, while buyers' credit refers to loans for payment of imports into India arranged by the importer from a bank or financial institution outside India for maturity of less than 3 years.

35. RBI, 'Master Circular on Export Credit Refinance Facility' (July 2, 2012).

36. Repo and reverse repos are discussed in more detail in the chapter titled "Monetary Policy: Implications for Bank Management'.

37. *Source:* Various Federal Reserve websites.

38. More on 'discount windows' of the central bank can be found in the chapter titled 'Monetary Policies: Implications for Bank Management'.

39. 'Overdrafts' are in the nature of loans and are discussed in detail in the Chapter titled Banks in India—Credit Delivery Legal Aspects of Lending.

40. *In Thiru Arooran Sugars Ltd vs State Bank of India*, the High Court based its verdict on Section 65 of the Indian Contract Act, which states as follows: 'When an agreement is discovered to be void or when a contract becomes void, any person who has received any advantage under such agreement or contract is bound to restore it or make compensation for it to the person from whom he received it'.

41. The World Bank, IMF, 'Financial Sector Assessment: A Handbook', Chapter 8 (2005): 207. The footnote to this definition on page 220 of the handbook elaborates thus: 'Definitions of money laundering have been adopted in common vocabulary (see the Oxford English Dictionary (1989): 702). FATF defines money laundering as the processing of criminal proceeds to disguise their illegal origin and the IOSCO defines it as a wide range of activities and processes intended to obscure the source of illegally obtained money and to create the appearance that it has originated from a legitimate source'.

42. *Source*: RBI Master Circular "Maintenance of Deposit Accounts", dated August 11, 2005.

43. *Source*: World Bank, Schott, Paul Allen, 2006, Reference guide to anti money laundering and combating the financing of terrorism, second edition.

44. The World Bank, IMF, 2005, 'Financial Sector Assessment: A Handbook', Chapter 8, page 207. The footnote to this definition on page 220 of the Handbook elaborates thus: 'Definitions of money laundering have been adopted in common vocabulary (see Oxford English Dictionary, 1989, 702). FATF defines money laundering as the processing of criminal proceeds to disguise their illegal origin, and the International Organization of Securities Commissions [IOSCO] defines it as a wide range of activities and processes intended to obscure the source of illegally obtained money and to create the appearance that it has originated from a legitimate source'.

45. These can be accessed at FATF Public Statement on jurisdictions with strategic anti-money laundering and combating the financing of terrorism (AML/CFT) deficiencies.

46. RBI, 2013, 'Master Circular on Know Your Customer (KYC) norms/Anti-Money Laundering (AML) standards/Combating of Financing of Terrorism (CFT)/Obligation of banks under Prevention of Money Laundering Act, (PMLA), 2002', dated July 1, 2013.

47. Indian bank vs Catholic Syrian Bank, TN Law Notes Journal (1980): 23. In this case, a well-known customer of the bank had introduced the applicant, who desired to open a current account. The bank had relied on the oral introduction by its customer and made no independent enquiries about the bonafides of the new depositor. The Madras High Court held that the bank had been negligent in securing proper introduction of the applicant.
48. Overdrafts are discussed in more detail in the chapter titled Banks in India—Credit Delivery and Legal Aspects of Lending'.
49. Credit risk is discussed in detail in the Chapter titled, 'Managing Credit Risk—An Overview.
50. An 'undischarged insolvent' is an entity that has been declared insolvent. All the assets or funds of the insolvent are attached by the court, until the entity is fully discharged of liabilities.
51. Some examples of accounts exempted from affixing photographs on account opening forms are savings bank accounts without cheque facility, term deposits of ₹10,000 or less, bank's employees, banks and government departments.
52. Sarbati Devi vs Usha Devi, (AIR 1984 S C 346). This case was decided by the Supreme Court in connection with nomination made in respect of an insurance policy. A similar judgment was passed in a more recent case between Shri Vishin N Khanchandani and other vs Vidya Lachmandas Khanchandani and other (JT 2000 (a) SC 321) in respect of the legal position of a nominee to national savings certificates.
53. Smt. Parvati vs Central Bank of India (1989)(2) Bank CLR 194. In this case, the Allahabad High Court permitted premature encashment of a fixed deposit by a nominee on the grounds that Section 45 Z – A(2) confers 'all rights of the depositor in relation to the deposit on the nominee.

CHAPTER FIVE

Uses of Bank Funds—The Lending Function

CHAPTER STRUCTURE

Section I Basic Concepts
Section II The Credit Process
Section III Financial Appraisal for Credit Decisions
Section IV Fund Based, Non Fund Based and Asset Based Lending
Section V Loan Pricing and Customer Profitability Analysis
Chapter Summary
Test Your Understanding
Topics for Further Discussion
Annexures I, II, III, IV

KEY TAKEAWAYS FROM THE CHAPTER

- Understand why banks lend.
- Learn how banks lend—Principles of lending.
- Understand the process of making a loan from start to finish.
- Learn the fundamentals of credit appraisal.
- Understand how loans are priced.
- Understand how banks choose profitable customers.

SECTION I

BASIC CONCEPTS

Introduction

Assume that you have ₹10 lakh with you and that a dear friend approaches you with a request to lend him ₹10 lakh for a business he wishes to start. You need the money for buying a house in a year's time, and your friend agrees that he will return the money at the time you require it, out of the profits he generates from the business. A year goes by. You have negotiated the price of the house you want to buy, and ask your dear friend to repay the ₹10 lakh he took from you. You remind him of his assurance that he would repay you out of the profits from his business. Listed below are a few possible scenarios.

- Your friend repays the loan in full and thanks you profusely for your timely help.
- Your friend regrets that the business did not generate the expected profit, and he will be able to repay only ₹5 lakh immediately. He assures you that he would repay the remaining amount within another year if the business improves as expected.
- Your friend gives you the story of how the project did not take off, and therefore he would be unable to repay even a small part of the total amount borrowed.

In the first case, you are happy that you could help your friend in need and do not envisage the other two possible outcomes. However, what if any of the latter two events happened? You would have lost your savings as well as the dream house. You regret having trusted your friend and his judgment about the prospects of his business. You regret not having had asked for more information about the project and its likelihood of success. You regret not having called your friend periodically to find out how the business venture was progressing.

In short, you could probably have avoided the unpleasant situation of your friend having to renege on his promise to you if you had had more information on the project, its risks and prospects; written a formal contract, enforceable in a court of law; instituted safeguards by way of terms and conditions and monitored the project cash flows periodically.

Let us consider another scenario. You have now invested your hard-earned savings of ₹10 lakh in a bank. Your dear friend approaches the same bank and requests a loan of ₹10 lakh for his business venture. What does the bank do? It calls for 'information'—about your friend, his antecedents, his previous track record in business and honouring commitments, the nature and scope of his new venture, the nature of the industry, the market, the technology, proposed suppliers and buyers and how much he is willing to invest in the business if the bank were to grant him his request. The bank compares the information he gives with that available with it in respect of similar business ventures, and determines the probability of success. The bank lends your friend the money if it is satisfied that the ₹10 lakh will be repaid on the contracted date. At the end of 1 year, with your dream house almost finalized, you go to the bank and ask for your money back. The bank repays you without demur and with interest for the period for which your money had been lent to the bank. At the end of the same year, your friend would have repaid the bank in full; or repaid only a part of the amount borrowed since the business did not yield the expected returns or repaid nothing, since the project had not taken off as expected. However, unlike in the first scenario, where you were likely to be put to partial or total loss, you have not been affected by your friend's business success or failure.

Why is this so? The bank, as the financial intermediary, has assumed the risks you would have faced had you lent to your friend directly. Not only that, the risks in lending to your friend has not deterred the bank from assuring you of liquidity for your deposits—you could get back your ₹10 lakh when you demanded it back, irrespective of whether your friend had repaid the bank at that time.

Banks' Role as Financial Intermediaries

Banks have a crucial role to play in the financial system of any country. The prime objective of the financial system is to channel surpluses arising in the economy through the activities of households, corporate houses and the government, into deficit units in the economy, again in the form of households, corporate houses and the government.

The financial system comprises 'financial markets' and 'financial intermediaries'.

The financial markets function as 'brokers' that bring the surplus and deficit units together for mutual benefit. However, the risk of lending to deficit units is borne largely by the surplus units themselves.[1]

The financial intermediaries, on the other hand, create 'assets' out of the surpluses of the economy. In doing so, they assume the risk of lending to the deficit sectors. Not only that, they assure liquidity to the surplus units who have entrusted their savings to them. Last but not least, they reduce risk with low information costs. To illustrate this aspect, let us go back to scenario two in the above example of lending to a friend. If you had to gather all the information before deciding to lend to your friend, it would have been a costly exercise. But banks can gather the information at much lower costs because (1) they have the expertise; (2) they have the experience to back their decision of lending to a similar or the same industry; (3) they have ready access to current information on the borrowers' cash flows through observing transactions in the accounts; (4) various deposit resources are pooled to form large loans, making which are relatively cheaper for banks; (5) borrowers value their ongoing relationship with the banks and hence part with information more readily and on a regular basis; and (6) diversification of deposits over many independent assets is possible for banks.

Hence, financial intermediaries serve three useful purposes:

- They mitigate the default risk of deficit units when surplus units lend to them.
- They ensure liquidity of savings by surplus units.
- They lower information costs.

Figure 5.1 illustrates the flow of funds through the financial system.

FIGURE 5.1 FLOW OF FUNDS THROUGH THE FINANCIAL SYSTEM

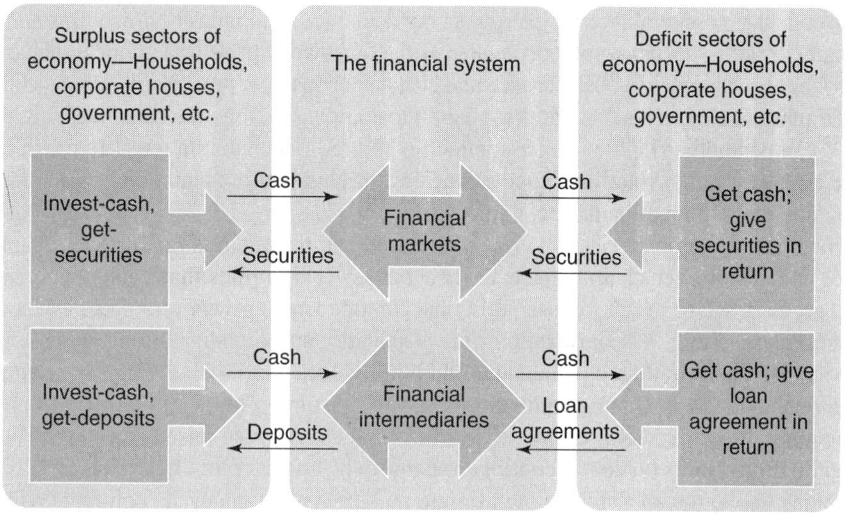

Gains from Lending

Let us assume that your friend's project, if a success, could generate ₹1 crore of annual net profit. Your deposit with the bank earns an interest of ₹1 lakh at 10 per cent interest per annum. What has the bank done? Your investment, currently earning ₹1 lakh, has been converted into an asset that has the potential of earning ₹1 crore per year! Thus, there is a net addition to the total income of the economy by ₹90 lakh per annum. The bank has also saved you substantial transaction costs—information, contracting, monitoring—if you had invested directly in the project as in scenario above, thus maximizing the net income addition to the economy. However, net addition to national income can be maximized only if bank lending is 'efficient'—lending should be at competitive prices, at minimum transaction costs, and the financial system should be 'integrated'[2] A financial system is said to be integrated if similar loans can be made on similar terms everywhere in the economy.

Apart from adding to the entire economy's income, lending also adds profits to individual banks. A bank can lend profitably only if it is able to take on and manage credit risk that arises from the quality of the borrower and his business. The bank also has to contend with the impact of fluctuations in interest and exchange rates on profits, as well as the liquidity risk posed by mismatch in the maturities of its liabilities and assets.[3]

Who Needs Credit?

Banks extend credit to different categories of borrowers for different purposes. For most of these borrowers, bank credit is the primary and cheapest source of debt financing. Both the demand and supply sides of the economy need bank credit. Consumers of goods and services constitute the demand side of the economy, and they require bank credit to enable them acquire assets such as consumer durables, housing or for plain consumption. On the supply side, the need for credit arises from the corporate and government sectors engaged in manufacturing, trading and services. These sectors require bank credit for capital investment in long-term projects and for day-to-day operations.

In more common terms, financing the demand side of the economy, the large class of consumers, is called retail banking (also termed mass banking). Financing the supply side of the economy, which is more customized in nature and calls for specialized skills, is called wholesale banking or corporate banking or class banking.

In this chapter, we will look primarily at wholesale banking or corporate banking concepts, features and practices, since these are one of the most specialized in any banking organization.

Features of Bank Credit

For a bank, good loans are its most profitable assets. And any loan is 'good' till the borrower defaults in repayment. In its role as a financial intermediary, the direct assumption of financial risk is the bank's defining characteristic.

Consequently, banks have to look for higher returns. Returns come in the direct form of loan interest, or in the indirect form of fee-based ancillary services. Further, the borrowers may also contribute to generation of deposits, which, in turn, can be invested by the bank. The most prominent risk in lending is default risk (known as credit risk), which can arise due to several factors. Borrowers may default due to industry downturns and business cycles (such as in real estate) or due to specific problems related to the borrowers' firms or activities, such as mismanagement, problems with labour, technological obsolescence and change in consumer preferences. Banks, therefore, make it a practice to set aside substantial reserves (called 'provisions') to compensate for anticipated losses due to credit risk.[4]

There can be another kind of risk associated with credit decisions-interest rate risk.[5] Fluctuations in interest rates give rise to earnings volatility. Loan maturities, pricing and the methods of principal repayments all impact the timing and magnitude of banks' cash inflows.

Keeping these prominent risks in view, risk-based capital standards require that banks maintain a stipulated amount of capital for every loan created in their books.[6] This implies that banks choosing to lend to a specific borrower, group or sector must mobilize additional capital to keep growing. Banks have sought to circumvent these requirements by resorting to 'securitization'[7] or 'off-balance sheet lending arrangements'. Under 'off-balance sheet lending', the bank does not directly extend credit but involves itself with the borrower either as an underwriter for arranging financing (as in 'Loan syndications'[8]), or by issuing a letter of credit to import inventory rather than finance acquisition of inventory. In both cases, the bank earns a 'fee-based income' for its services, but creates a 'contingent liability' in its books.[9] A contingent liability is, however, not free of risks. If the borrower defaults, the bank becomes liable, *i.e.*, the bank's obligation to make payment under the contract arises from the happening of a contingent event.

Types of Lending

Broadly, three types of lending can be identified:

- **Fund-based lending:** This is the most direct form of lending. It is granted as a loan or advance with an actual outflow of cash to the borrower by the bank. In most cases, such lending is supported by prime and/or collateral securities.[10]
- **Non-fund-based lending:** There are no funds outlays for the bank at the time of entering into an agreement with a counterparty on behalf of the bank's customer. However, such arrangements may crystallize into fund-based advances for the bank if the customer fails to fulfil the terms of his contract with the counterparty. Most 'contingent liabilities' of the bank, more prominently, letters of credit (LCs) and bank guarantees (BGs), fall under this category.
- **Asset-based lending:** This is an emerging category of bank lending. In this type of lending, the bank looks primarily or solely to the earning capacity of the asset being financed, for servicing its debt. In most cases, the bank will have limited or no recourse to the borrower. Specialized lending practices, such as securitization or project finance fall under this category.

Fund-based advances can be further classified based on the tenure of the loans.[11] The traditional approach is to make the following distinction: short-term loans, long-term loans and revolving credits. We will examine the basic features of these loans in the following paragraphs.

Short-Term Loans Typically, these are loans with maturities of 1 year or less. Most of these loans are granted with the primary purpose of financing working capital needs of the borrower, resulting from temporary build up of inventories and receivables. In the case of such loans, repayments would flow out of conversion of current assets to cash.

Sometimes, seasonal lines of credit are granted to borrowers whose businesses are subjected to seasonal sales cycles, and hence, periodic peaking of inventory and other current assets. The amount of credit is made available based on the estimated peak and non-peak funding requirements of the borrowers. The borrowers draw upon the seasonal lines of credit during periods of peak production to meet seasonal demand, and repay the loans as inventories are liquidated and cash flows from sales come in. Interest accrues only on the amounts drawn down from the line of credit.

Both the above types of loans are generally made as 'secured loans'. This implies that the banks make the loans based on the strength of underlying securities, such as inventories, receivables and other current assets. Such securities, the values of which directly affect the amount that can be granted as loan, are called 'prime securities'. The other type of securities backing the loan repayments is 'collateral securities'. Such securities are not directly linked to the operations of the borrower, but are offered either in lieu of or along with prime securities, as a cushion against probable default by the borrower. The idea is that banks can liquidate these securities in the event of default and realize the amount due under the loan agreement.

A third category of short-term loans, granted for 'special purposes', may or may not be secured. Such loans are called 'unsecured loans'. They may arise due to a host of reasons, including temporary but unexpected or unusual increases in current assets, or a temporary cash crunch in the borrower's firm. Such requests are considered as falling outside the borrower's estimated needs for short-term working capital financing, and, depending on the borrower's creditworthiness, may be granted as 'temporary' or 'ad hoc' loans. These loans are often granted with terms and conditions different from those applicable to the assessed working capital needs of the borrower. Such loans may require full payment of interest and principal at maturity, *i.e.*, a 'bullet'. The term for such loans is determined by estimating the time at which the borrower can generate cash flows to make the repayment. The risk in these loans arises from a change in the assumed circumstances on which the decision to grant the loans were based.

Long-Term Loans Bank lending, which used to traditionally focus on 'short-term' loans, started looking at lending for periods longer than a year only from the 1930s onwards. These are called 'term loans' and have the following characteristics:

- Original maturities of more than 1 year.
- Repayments are structured based on future cash flows rather than on liquidation of short-term assets.
- The primary purpose of these loans could be acquisition of fixed assets (versus current assets in the case of short-term loans), or funding expansion/modernization/diversification plans of the borrower's firm.
- The term loans may be used as substitutes for equity or for financing permanent working capital needs.
- Typically, these loans are fully disbursed at inception, and principal and interest are repaid depending on the borrower's capacity to generate operating cash flows.
- The amount and structure of these loans will closely match the transaction being financed.
- Mostly, the securities for the term loans will be the bank's claims on assets purchased from the term loan proceeds.
- Though banks do not customarily lend for very long periods,[12] the maximum tenure (maturity) of term loans is 10 years, the average ranging between 3 and 5 years.

Thus, long-term loans are generally structured to be more adaptable to borrowers' specific requirements.

Revolving Credits Revolving credits offer the most flexibility to borrowers. Assessed to meet the borrowers' requirements over a period of 1 year or more, revolving credits permit drawings from the line of credit at any time, and similarly, repay the whole or part of the outstanding loans as and when cash inflows happen in the borrowers' firms. The revolving credit is usually a secured loan, with terms and conditions as applicable to other types of loans. The amount of revolving facility granted will be based on the assessed need of borrowers, underlying securities and borrowers' creditworthiness.

In rare cases, revolving loans are structured to convert to term loans or automatically renew on maturity. The automatic renewal facility, termed the 'evergreen' facility, continues till the borrower gives notice of termination. Such arrangements, needless to say, will put the banks more at risk of default than the other two types of lending.

SECTION II

THE CREDIT PROCESS

The risks involved in lending render it imperative that banks should have systems and controls that enable bank managers to take credit decisions after objectively evaluating risk-return trade offs. Whether it is consumer or commercial lending, credit decisions impact the profitability of banks, and ultimately their competitiveness and survival in the industry.

Credit decisions are by no means easy. The credit officer has to deal with conflicting objectives of increasing the loan portfolio (his targets) while maintaining loan quality (the risks inherent in the loan portfolio as well as in individual loans). He also has to balance these objectives with the bank's profitability and market value objectives, liquidity requirements and constraints of capital. He should be able to investigate and appraise the risks inherent in every opportunity to lend, and take decisions that will fit in with the overall strategy of the bank. Above all, he should not take or lead the bank to a wrong credit decision.

Despite the availability of tools and techniques and a huge body of knowledge to support decision-making, credit decisions are largely judgmental. However well versed the credit officer is in appraising and lending to risky projects, his contribution may not suit the bank if his decisions do not fall in line with the overall strategy of the bank. Therefore, apart from their expertise in credit appraisal, the strategic role of credit officers assumes utmost importance.

Constituents of the Credit Process[13]

The Loan Policy To ensure alignment of individual goals of credit officers to the bank's overall goals, banks formulate 'loan policies'. These are written documents, authorized by individual bank's Board of Directors, that formalize and set guidelines for lending to be followed by decision-makers in the bank.

The loan policy specifies the bank's overall strategy for lending, identifies loan qualities and parameters, and lays down procedures for appraising, sanctioning, granting, documenting and reviewing loans. Loan policies emerge from and are fine-tuned by past experience of individual banks in extending credit, and the best practices followed in the industry. While supervising bank operations, regulators examine banks' documented loan policies to ensure that existing lending practices conform to the organization's objectives and acceptable guidelines. The stance taken by individual bank managements determines the extent and form of risk that the bank would be willing to take.

Box 5.1 outlines the major components of a typical loan policy.

BOX 5.1 MAJOR COMPONENTS OF A TYPICAL LOAN POLICY DOCUMENT

Loan objectives

Within the regulatory prescriptions, the loan objectives will communicate to credit officers and other decision-makers, the bank's priorities among the conflicting objectives of liquidity, profitability, increasing business volumes, and risk and asset quality.

Volume and mix of loans

How much of the loan portfolio is to be channelled into specific industries, sectors or geographical areas, will be communicated in this section. It may also specify composition of the loan portfolio by size of loans, pricing of loans or securities. In many countries, especially developing economies, regulators stipulate targets for directed lending to certain critical sectors.

Loan evaluation procedures

Generally, uniform credit appraisal procedures are prescribed throughout the bank. The procedures would deal with all issues ranging from establishing suitability of the loan to the bank's overall strategy and risk taking ability, to selection of borrowers, market and project risk appraisal criteria, financial statement analysis, structuring of loan agreements, documentation and post-sanction monitoring.

Credit administration

Lending involves more risks than any other banking activity. Hence, banks are careful to ensure that credit decisions are taken by experienced and knowledgeable officers, with decision-making authority as decided by the top management or the board from time to time. The loan policy should indicate the credit sanctioning powers of the officers at various hierarchical levels of the bank. Due diligence should also ensure that officers do not overstep limits fixed for their levels. Similarly, if limits fixed for decision-making are too low and conservative, the top management may have to spend more time on decision-making. If limits are too high at every level, the bank may expose itself to heightened risks.

Credit files

Credit files are important documented and updated material used for both decision-making and continuous evaluation. Sometimes, the loan policy specifically mentions the mandatory format in which information in the credit files is to be maintained.

Lending rates

The interest charged should reflect the credit risk in a loan. The policy may also state the returns expected for each risk group of borrowers in the bank, and specifies risk limits up to which the bank can lend. It can also specify the credit scoring system to be adopted to fix the lending rates, and circumstances under which fixed and floating rates of interest can be charged to the borrower.

The other parameters that a loan policy may specify are (1) type of collateral the bank can accept as security for the loans; (2) the extent to which the security should cover the advances made; (3) nature of margins/compensating balances[14] to be maintained by various classes of borrowers; (4) limits up to which the bank can expose itself to certain sectors and borrower groups; (5) credit monitoring system that would be operative after the loan is disbursed; (6) credit to deposit ratios that the bank needs to maintain; (7) incentive schemes for loan officers; (8) loan agreement and other communication practices; (9) procedure for rescheduling/restructuring loans; (10) role of credit department in the bank; (11) role of recovery department in the bank; and (12) role of legal department in the bank.

The loan policy establishes the 'credit culture' that is unique to each bank. Adherence to the guidelines of the loan policy is reviewed by credit monitoring committees, and the need for periodic revision is also suggested, in keeping with the dynamic environment.

Business Development and Initial Recommendations Within the broad framework of the loan policy of the bank, and based on the bank's goals in building its loan asset portfolio, credit officers seek to reinforce the relationship with existing customers, build new clientele and cross sell non-credit services. Though every employee of the bank, from the front office personnel to the top management, is responsible for overall business development, credit development requires a more focused approach. For one, not every prospective customer can be invited to be a borrower. There are enormous risks attached to making a bad loan than bypassing an opportunity for making a good loan.

Therefore, business development efforts for credit expansion should preferably begin with market research and detailed credit investigation. The outcome of this research will be reflected in the annual business plan of the bank, which would specify the broad industries, or areas where the bank would like to expand, and the extent to which the bank would like exposure to each industry or area.

Based on the plan, the bank embarks upon publicity for its proposed credit products in the case of retail lending, or special campaigns for attracting target customers. In the case of corporate borrowers, the credit officers formulate call programs. Once prospective credit customers are identified, credit officers try to obtain formal loan requests from these customers. The loan requests, once found acceptable in principle, would be processed further based on various documents called for, such as the prospective borrower's financial statements, credit reports, the relevant project report and the legal resolution to borrow.

Sufficient information is sought from the prospective borrower to analyze creditworthiness. Credit appraisal is essentially an analysis of the risks or vulnerabilities in respect of the borrower and his business. The risks are analyzed with a view to determining how each of them, individually or in combination, can affect the debt servicing capacity of the borrower. A typical credit appraisal would deal with the following issues.

- What are the risks inherent in the borrower's business? These risks are classified into market-related risks, technology-related risks, environment-related risks and so on.
- What are the antecedents of the borrower? What is his reputation and integrity? How is his track record?
- What are the financial risks inherent in the borrower's business? Is the project economically viable? Is the project financially feasible?
- What risks are inherent in the operations of the business?
- What have the managers of the borrower firm done to mitigate these risks?
- Does the bank want to lend to this borrower in spite of the risks? If so, what steps should the bank take to ensure that debt repayments are not hampered?
- What risks will the bank have to take if it decides to fund the borrower? How does the bank propose to mitigate these risks?

The first three questions focus on appraisal of the borrower, his firm, the project for which he has sought funds and his capacity to repay. The next two questions enable the credit analyst to examine the internal management and operations of the firm. The analysis leads to a decision–to lend or not to lend? Once the analyst decides to recommend lending, the safeguards in and structure of the loan agreement has to be put in place.

Traditionally, key risk factors were analyzed using pragmatic considerations, such as creditworthiness of the borrower, security offered, prospects of the firm and longevity of the relationship. These were considered the 'canons of lending', and were addressed as the 'five Cs', (capacity, capital, collateral, conditions, character) or remembered through mnemonics such as 'CCC'[15] (capital, character, capability) or 'PARTS'[16] (purpose, amount, repayment, terms, security), or 'CAMPARI'[17] (character, ability, means, purpose, amount, repayment, insurance).

In all these models, the inherent assumption was that the borrower's past would be indicative of the future, an assumption that may not hold well in a highly dynamic or volatile environment.

Modern credit analysis uses the traditional concepts in making subjective evaluation, along with wide use of financial ratios and risk evaluation models to determine if a borrower is creditworthy. The accent on risk evaluation implies that the banker lends only if he is satisfied that risks are mitigated to ensure that the borrower's future cash flows (and hence debt service) will not be affected.

Broad Steps to Credit Analysis

Step 1—Building the 'credit file': The first step to effective credit analysis is gathering information to build the 'credit file'. The preliminary information so obtained would throw light on the borrower's antecedents, his credit history and track record. If the project is a Greenfield project, the credit officer will have to do a thorough research into various aspects of the project, as well as into the borrower's financial and managerial capacity to make the project a success. If the borrower is an existing one, seeking additional credit, the information would be readily available with the credit officer. The credit file is an important tool box for the credit officer. It should contain all pertinent information on the borrower, including call report summaries, past and present financial statements, cash flow projections and plans for the future, relevant credit reports, details of insurance coverage, fixed and other assets, collateral values and security documents. The file for an existing borrower should also contain copies of past loan agreements, comments by prior loan officers and all correspondence with the customer. In the case of long standing borrowers, such credit files may run into several volumes. It is advisable for the credit officer to peruse all the volumes of the credit file before embarking on credit analysis.

Why is this step so important? One of the most vital factors in lending is assessing the borrower's willingness and desire to repay the loan. The most sophisticated credit analysis cannot measure and, therefore, cannot establish beyond doubt the borrower's intention to repay. The extensive information in the credit file will enable the credit officer to examine the borrower's track record in repayment, and help in forming an opinion about the borrower's future repayment intention and potential.

Step 2—Project and financial appraisal: Once the preliminary investigation is done, the internal and external factors, such as management integrity and capability, the company's performance and market value and the industry characteristics are evaluated.

One of the important activities at this stage is financial analysis. An illustrative list of inputs and activities is as follows:

- Past financial statements. While the borrower's audited financial statements are typically the starting point/ many banks additionally ask for financial statements presented in the bank's own format. Typically, past financial statements pertain to the last 2–3 years, along with estimates for the current year.
- Cash flow statements. This statement would reveal the usage of own and borrowed funds by the borrower.
- The above data from the borrower enables the credit officer to analyze the liquidity position of the borrower/ his firm. Adequate liquidity is a vital indicator of the borrower's financial health to the bank, as loss of liquidity through delayed cash flows or diversion of short-term funds or leakage in cash, is bound to adversely affect the borrower's repayment capacity. Liquidity is assessed through a set of financial ratios. Most banks recast the financial statements of the borrower to reveal the true picture—for example, banks remove ageing receivables or slow moving/obsolete inventory from current assets. Hence, more detailed information is sought from the borrower before the financial statements are analyzed.
- The financial risk of an entity is measured by the debt it has incurred in the course of business compared with the owner's stake. Banks generally stipulate maximum debt to value ratios for various categories of borrowers, beyond which the borrowers will have to increase their stake in the business to avail more bank credit. Credit officers look more to the 'tangible net worth' on the borrower's books as the measure of owner's stake in the business. 'Tangible net worth' represents the net worth less intangible assets, such as losses or goodwill.
- Once the borrower's current financial health is gauged, the projections are examined. The borrower's debt servicing capacity is determined by assessing the quality of cash flow projections given by the borrower. The experienced credit analyst questions the borrower's projections, especially the sales projections, till he satisfies

himself that they are indeed realistic, achievable, and more importantly, the cash flows are sufficient to service the debt (principal + interest). Further, sensitivity analyses are carried out on the projections to test the strength of the underlying assumptions and assess the impact on debt service capacity under various stress conditions. While every scenario cannot be adequately tested, the worst case scenario will indicate the most pessimistic outcome for the bank and it is then for the bank to decide whether it wants to undertake the risk.

- Even the most scientifically done projections cannot predict the onslaught of future uncertainties. Hence, the lender looks for a secondary source of repayment, which is provided by the collateral securities. The credit officer evaluates the strength of the collateral securities to determine the amount that can be recovered by liquidating these securities in the worst possible scenario. It is to be noted that loans should not be made based on the strength of the collateral securities alone. The securities should be treated as the second line of defence and not the raison-d'etre of the loan itself.

Step 3—Qualitative analysis: Integrity is the most important quality that the banker looks for in a borrower, and the most difficult to measure. So is assessment of the quality of the management team. However, lenders will have to make qualitative assessment of the borrower on most of the criteria mentioned in *Annexure I*, by evolving suitable measures. Many poor credit decisions have been the result of not knowing enough about the customer.

Step 4—Due diligence: Bypassing due diligence can be very costly for a bank. Many loans have run into problems since bankers did not take this step seriously. This is a time-consuming activity but well worth the effort. Due diligence can include checking on the borrower's address (if a new borrower), pre-approval inspections of the borrower's workplace, and interviews with the borrower's competitors, suppliers, customers and employees. A comprehensive due diligence can also include reviews of technology used by the borrower, planned capital expenditures, other obligations to outsiders, credit reports from other debtors, the internal management control and information system, industrial relations, employee compensation and benefits, and environmental audit. Disclosure of contingent liabilities by the borrower is an essential part of due diligence, since any such contingent claim on the borrower would directly impact the assessed debt service capacity.

Step 5—Risk assessment: A key function of the credit officer is to identify and analyze the key risks associated with the proposed credit. All potential internal and external risks are to be identified and their severity assessed in terms of how these risks would impact the borrower's future cash flows and hence the debt service capacity. The risk assessment would form an important input for structuring the credit facility and the terms of the loan agreement.

A sample risk classification grid has been presented in *Annexure I.* Why do we need risk classification criteria? They are necessary to assist lending officers in assessing the degree of default risk in a proposed loan. They also set standards for arriving at loan pricing decisions and terms of the loan agreement commensurate with the risk of loss. Once constructed, the classification can be used for comparisons over time periods for the same borrower, or can be standardized for comparisons of different loans. It is, however, important to note that the most sophisticated risk classification criteria cannot substitute the experienced judgment of the credit officer. The risk classification criteria are to be used to determine the relevance and impact of identified factors and construct a framework to examine their applicability to specific loans.

Credit rating agencies play an important role in assessing risk of bank loans. As recommended by Basel II, (*see Chapter 11 'Capital-risk, Regulation and Adequacy'*) external ratings are required for calibrating regulatory capital requirement. In the 'standardized' approach for credit risk and market risk, the risk weight of bank exposures are aligned to the external ratings of the exposures. Even in the advanced approaches, external ratings will be used by banks for assessing the efficacy of their own internal assessments. *Annexure II* provides an overview of credit rating agencies in India and their role in assessing risk, and its location and distribution in the financial system.

Step 6—Making the recommendation: Finally, based on a thorough analysis of the project, the borrower and the market, and after examining the 'fit' of the credit with the 'loan policy', the credit officer makes his recommendations to consider the loan favourably or reject it outright. Sometimes, in the case of clients with a long history of relationship with the bank, even if the criteria for consideration of the current proposal fall short of expectations, the credit officer can suggest procedures to improve the borrower's financial condition and the repayment prospects. If warranted, the credit officer can also call for a revised credit proposal from the borrower. After a preliminary negotiation with the borrower, the credit officer's recommendations would specify the credit terms, including loan amount, maturity, pricing, repayment schedule, description of prime and collateral securities and the required terms and conditions for the borrower's compliance.

Credit Delivery and Administration Who takes the decision to lend? Depending on the size of the bank, the loan size and type of exposures planned, the final decision to lend may be taken by an authorized layer of the bank. Typically, banks fix 'discretionary limits'—monetary ceilings up to which personnel at each level can take credit decisions—for each layer of authority starting from credit officers themselves to branch heads to senior and top management at the corporate office, including the Board of Directors. These 'discretionary limits' become larger as they move up the organizational hierarchy. For example, in some banks, the credit officer may have the least discretionary limit. Any request for a loan amount over and above this limit will have to be referred to the next higher layer, say the branch head, for his decision. Where the loan amount exceeds the branch head's or territorial head's discretion, the request is referred to the corporate office, where decision-makers can be individual senior or top management officials or a committee of such officials. Many times, large credit exposures are referred to a top management committee for a joint decision to be later ratified by the Board. Some critical exposures are referred to the Board for a decision.

For all decision-makers above the level of loan officers, the loan officer's appraisal forms the very basis of decision-making. Hence, the loan officer's role in the credit decision-making process is extremely critical. Many banks create a separate channel in the hierarchy for grooming and equipping credit officers with the essential attitude and skills for the lending function.

The hierarchical levels over and above the credit officer merely review the recommendations made by the credit officer, and add their insights and comments before making the decision. It is not necessary that a favourable recommendation from a credit officer after extensive research has to be approved by the ultimate decision-maker. Accountability demands at every level of the bank require that the decision-making authority forms an independent opinion of the borrower's creditworthiness and takes decisions accordingly in the best interests of the bank.

Some very large banks have a centralized 'underwriting department'. This corporate service essentially sources new business for the bank and manages select existing relationships. For these select customers, this centralized department processes the credit request and conveys approval 'in principle', in order to cut the process and time required for a sanction through the regular process. Many large banks use customized software to evaluate credit requests. However, as already emphasized, sophisticated tools can be used as aids, and not as substitutes, for the credit officer's or the credit sanctioning authority's judgment.

Once a loan is approved, the officer communicates the sanction to the borrower through a formal 'sanction letter'. The sanction letter is generally in the form of a 'loan agreement', to be signed by the borrower(s) and guarantors, if any. The loan agreement contains the following essential features:

- Nature/type of credit facility.
- Interest/discount/charges as applicable.
- Repayment terms.
- Stipulations regarding end use of each facility.
- Additional fees applicable such as processing fees, closing fees or commitment fees.
- Prime security for each credit facility.
- Full description of the collateral securities.
- Details of personal/third party guarantees.
- Covenants—terms and conditions under which the loan facilities are being granted.
- Events of default and penal provisions.

Loan Documentation Different types of borrowers and different types of security interests necessitate loan documentation procedures that would be valid in a court of law. Accordingly, once the loan agreement is signed, the borrowers and guarantors execute the loan documents. The security interest is said to be 'perfected' when the bank's claim on the borrower's assets forming the security is senior to that of any other creditor.

If the borrower defaults on a secured loan, the bank has the right to take possession of the assets and liquidate them to recover its dues. Proper loan documentation secures this right.

Terms and Conditions of Lending These are very important ingredients of any loan agreement. The bank derives control over the borrower's operations and also mitigates the risks of lending through this part of the loan agreement. The terms and conditions comprise of three distinct portions:

- **Conditions precedent:** These are requirements that a borrower should satisfy before the bank acquires the legal obligation to disburse the loan amount. Some illustrative and commonly used conditions precedent are auditor's certificate for having brought in the committed capital amount, relevant legal opinions sought for and board resolution to borrow. An important condition precedent is a material adverse change clause that covers the financial statements and projections. The clause protects the bank in the event of a material change occurring after the loan is sanctioned but prior to disbursement, which may jeopardize the bank's chances of recovery of its dues from the borrower.
- **Representations and warranties:** The assumptions based on which credit appraisal is done and the bank has agreed to lend money, emanate from the information the borrower himself provides to the bank. In executing the loan agreement, the borrower is assumed to confirm the truth and accuracy of the information provided to the bank. Any misrepresentation constitutes an event of default and renders the agreement invalid. The principal representations and warranties include the following:
    - All information provided, including financial statements, is true and correct.
    - The borrower is authorized by law to carry on the business.
    - The signatories to the loan agreement are authorized to do so, and their commitment is legal and binding.
    - All statutory obligations, such as payments of taxes, have been met.
    - There are no major legal proceedings pending or threatened against the borrower.
    - There are no factual omissions or misstatements in the information provided.
    - Collateral and prime securities are unencumbered.

The third and most negotiated part of the loan agreement is the 'covenants' of the borrower.

These are the operative part of the terms and conditions, and set standards and codes of conduct for the borrower's future business, as long as the borrower is indebted to the bank. The covenants are used by astute credit officers to mitigate the risks of the borrower's business, in order that credit risk is mitigated for the bank. Covenants are sacred, and any violation will be treated as an 'event of default'. They normally take two distinct forms—'affirmative' and 'negative'.

- Affirmative covenants are those actions the borrower should take to legally and ethically carry on the business. Illustrations of affirmative covenants include the following:
    - Ensuring that the funds are applied for the purpose for which they were intended.
    - The indicators ensuring financial health, such as a strong current ratio, a safe debt to equity ratio, appreciable sales growth and a healthy return on equity (ROE).
    - Ensuring that proper records and controls are maintained within the firm.
    - Ensuring compliance with the law, and reporting requirements required under statute.
    - Ensuring compliance with information requirements by the bank, and periodic reporting of financial and operating performance.
    - Ensuring that the prime and collateral securities are adequately insured.
    - Ensuring that property, fixed assets and other assets belonging to the borrower's firm are properly maintained.
    - The bank will retain its right of inspecting the assets offered as security at any time, without prior notice.
- Negative covenants place clear and significant restrictions on the borrower's activities. Such covenants are intended to pre-empt managerial decisions that may adversely impact cash flows and hence jeopardize the borrower's debt service capacity. Borrowers would generally be more inclined to negotiate negative covenants, since they may be perceived as restricting operational autonomy. Some typical negative covenants are as follows:
    - Limiting further capital expenditure.
    - Limiting investment of funds.
    - Restricting additional outside liabilities.
    - Restricting investment in subsidiaries, other businesses.
    - Restricting sale of assets, subsidiaries.
    - Restricting dividend payouts.
    - Restricting prepayment of other debts.
    - Limits on debt in the capital structure.
    - Restrictions on mergers or share repurchase.

- Restriction on starting or carrying on other business.
- Restriction on encumbering assets (negative lien).

The last restriction, negative lien,[18] is a covenant that is widely used by banks to prevent the borrower from creating encumbrances on assets, so as to benefit other creditors.

The bank may employ these restrictions and limitations selectively, to ensure that the risks in the borrower's business are mitigated. The ultimate objective of these restrictions is to ensure that the borrower's financial health is not impaired, and the bank's dues are paid on time.

Events of Default Such events, when they happen, may trigger the end of the banker–borrower relationship. An illustrative list of situations that may lead to an event of default include the following:

- Failure to repay principal when due.
- Failure to service interest payments on due dates.
- Failure to honour a covenant.
- Misrepresentation of facts.
- Reneging on declarations made under representations and warranties.
- Diversion of funds without bank's knowledge to other creditors or other accounts of the borrower.
- Change in management or ownership structure.
- Bankruptcy or liquidation proceedings.
- Falsification or tampering with records.
- Impairment of collateral, or entering into invalid agreements.
- Material adverse changes that drastically change the assumptions under which the loan agreement was entered into.
- All other force majeure events that imperil debt service.

The happening of which event of default may signify the end of the banker–borrower relationship is left for the banker to decide on the merits of each case. Under certain circumstances, where the risks of such events are considered less significant, the loan agreement can provide the borrower a grace period within which to rectify the breach of a covenant. In case the borrower is unable to rectify the breach within the grace period, the bank can downgrade or recall the advances made; agree for the take over of the borrowing account by another bank; or, if the borrower is not in a position to repay the bank's dues, enforce the securities and liquidate the outstanding advance.

In case of the third scenario given above, the bank will initially set off any unencumbered deposits of the borrower[19] or cash margins[20] against the advances outstanding. It will then sell off the securities to realize its dues or invoke the outside guarantees till the advance is completely liquidated.

Since the banker–borrower relationship is generally considered valuable by both parties, banks do not act in haste in the event of default.

Updating the Credit File and Periodic Follow-Up The credit file has to be continuously updated throughout the above process. Further, once the loan is disbursed, the following activities have to be carried out either by the credit officer himself or a team designated for the purpose:

- Process loan payments and send reminders in case loan payments are received late. The simple practice of reminding the borrower for every payment not received on due date, would ensure that defaults are noticed on time by the bank and timely action taken in case defaults persist, ultimately preventing a credit risk to the bank.
- The borrower will have to submit updates of financial performance periodically or as per the accounting practices in force. The bank can call for financial data at any point of time if it feels that the borrower's financial health deserves mid-course scrutiny.
- The bank can call on the borrower at any time, even without prior intimation. When the bank's representative visits the borrower, the primary objective will be to ensure that the borrower's activities are in accordance with the bank's expectations.

Credit Review and Monitoring This is the most important step in credit management, and one that lends value to bank financing. Banks that have succeeded in credit management, and hence reduction of credit risk, are those that have separated credit review and monitoring from credit analysis, execution and administration.

The credit review and monitoring process is typically bifurcated into the distinct functions of monitoring the performance of existing loans and problem accounts.

Monitoring performance of existing loans is done in two ways. One is a continuous monitoring of the transactions in the accounts of the borrower. This is best done at the office from which the credit has been disbursed. The credit officers at the disbursing office have to be alert to symptoms exhibited by day-to-day operations in the borrower's loan account, and send warning signals to the borrower if they detect signs of incipient deterioration of financial health or misdemeanour.[21] The second type of monitoring will be done through external or internal audit teams, and will be periodic or continuous, depending on the size of credit exposures or the importance of the credit disbursing office in the bank. The deficiencies in loan documentation or conduct uncovered by the audit team will have to be rectified by the credit team. The deficiency could be rectified simply by getting signatures on loan documents or filing the required statutory returns for perfecting the security. If the audit team points out violation of any loan covenant, then the credit team can persuade the borrower to fall in line.

However, what causes most concern would be deterioration in the financial condition of the borrower, which is manifested as the inability of the borrower to meet debt service requirements. Such accounts would be put on a 'watch list' and monitored closely, so that they do not turn 'non-performing'.[22] Sometimes, banks will have to modify the repayment terms in order to increase the probability of repayment. Such modified terms include restructuring interest and principal payments to suit the current cash flows of the borrower, or lengthening maturity of the loans. In such cases, the bank may also seek additional securities or additional capital from the borrower to compensate for the increased credit risk. It would be prudent to separate the loans under restructuring from the general credit stream, so that monitoring would be made more intense. Similarly, a separate set of specialists would man the credit monitoring or restructuring function.

In some cases, the borrower's financial condition deteriorates to such an extent that the loan will have to be 'recalled'. In such cases, liquidation of assets or take over by another bank willing to take on the risk will be considered. It is more likely that the former action will have to be instituted. If all other avenues of restructuring and forbearance fail, the bank would resort to legal action. Once legal action is under way, the borrower loses the option to restructure the loans or be rehabilitated back to financial health. At this stage, many borrowers opt for 'out of court settlement', thus avoiding long and protracted legal hassles.

SECTION III

FINANCIAL APPRAISAL FOR CREDIT DECISIONS

Though several qualitative factors play a role in a credit decision, a major influencing factor is the financial health of the borrower as brought out by the financial appraisal. We have seen in the previous section that the credit officer uses techniques, such as financial ratio analysis, cash flow analysis and sensitivity analysis to assess the achievability of the projections. How these techniques are employed in appraising various categories of loans will be dealt with in this section.

Financial Ratio Analysis

Most large banks begin financial analysis with a standardized spreadsheet or format, where the balance sheet and income statement data, past and future, are rearranged in a consistent format to facilitate comparison over time and benchmark with industry standards. The rearrangement, and sometimes reclassification, is necessary not only for consistency but also for throwing up potential risks to the borrower's financial health.

Most credit analysts use five broad categories of ratios—liquidity, profitability, leverage, operating and valuation. Liquidity ratios indicate the borrower's ability to meet short-term obligations, continue operations and remain solvent. Profitability ratios indicate the earning potential and its impact on shareholders' returns. Leverage ratios indicate the financial risk in the firm as evidenced by its capital structure and the consequent impact on earnings volatility. Operating ratios demonstrate how efficiently the assets are being utilized to generate revenue. Finally, valuation ratios extend beyond historical accounting measures to depict a realistic 'value' of the borrower. An illustrative list of commonly used financial ratios is presented in *Annexure III*.

Common Size Ratio Comparisons

Many banks may additionally use common size ratio comparisons. Such comparisons are valuable since they are independent of firm size, thus facilitating inter-firm comparisons in the same industry or line of business. However, the analysis should be able to spot the outliers, such as firms whose financial structure is vastly different from the typical firm in the industry. For example, a firm with leased assets would show a different asset ratio in an industry in which firms typically own substantial fixed assets. Hence, common size analysis is generally used along with ratio analysis as described above, to lead to better insights about the borrowing firm's financial strength.

Cash Flow Analysis

While the income statement of the borrower provides vital information, it also contains accounting adjustments and non-cash expenses. To get a clearer picture of the borrower's capacity to repay, the bank will have to convert the income statement into a cash flow statement, or call for a cash flow statement from the borrower.

Typically, the statement of cash flows is divided into four parts—cash from operating activities, cash from investing activities, cash from financing activities and cash. The intent is to distinguish between accounting profits as measured by net income in the income statement and the firm's various activities that affect cash flows, but are not reported in the income statement. *Annexure IV* provides a methodology to reconcile the income statement to its cash equivalent. The vital analysis here is to determine how much cash is generated from the firm's activities, and whether it is sufficient to cover loan repayments and interest payments. It is expected that a firm with prudent financial management would repay short-term loans from liquidating inventories and receivables, and long-term loans from surpluses after meeting financing costs, increase in net working capital (NWC) and capital expenditure.

SECTION IV

FUND BASED, NON-FUND BASED AND ASSET BASED LENDING—FEATURES AND POPULAR FORMS

Though classified under the single nomenclature—loan—on the bank's balance sheet, every loan or class of loans is unique. Each loan or type of loan has distinguishing features based on the purpose, the collateral, the repayment period and the borrower profile. We will examine the predominant characteristics of some popular loan types from the points of view of the borrower as well as the credit officer.

Fund Based Lending

Loans for Working Capital

Banks are generally considered primary lenders to working capital requirements of firms, small and large. The rationale for banks having built up considerable expertise in funding short-term working capital is explained by the nature of bank liabilities, which are essentially short-term in nature.

A firm's Net Working Capital (NWC) is measured as the difference between its current assets and current liabilities. If a firm's working capital is positive, it implies that its current assets exceed its current liabilities, *i.e.*, its current assets have been partly financed by 'spontaneous liabilities', such as trade creditors, and short-term bank debt and other current debt, and partly by long-term funds, including equity. A positive NWC is construed as a sign of healthy liquidity in the firm, since it is assumed that the liquidation of current assets at any point of time would enable the firm to pay off its current creditors fully.

Every firm begins by investing cash in current assets. Manufacturing firms invest in raw material that would be converted to finished goods to be sold in the market. Retail firms invest in merchandize for display at their showrooms. Service firms need cash for operations and office supplies. Almost all firms encourage credit sales to stimulate growth. Thus, there is a time lag between the investment of cash and the realization of cash from sales. The longer the firm takes to complete the cash-to-cash or 'working capital' cycle, the longer the firm has to wait to get back its cash investment. During this time lag, operations have to continue. The firm will have to continue investing in raw material or merchandize or day-to-day expenses. Where will the cash for this investment come from? As noted earlier, cash for operations will have to come from external creditors or internal generation. Working capital management is, therefore, a continuous process.

Each type of business depends on appropriate financing methods to stimulate investment and growth. Some firms depend on trade credit[23] to finance the current assets—that is, they defer payment for inputs, in agreement with the supplier, for a specified number of days within which they hope to realize cash from sales. Some firms additionally defer expenses till the cash comes in from sales. However, the majority of firms depend on bank debt to manage the need for working capital. Thus, bank debt is a predominant source of funding working capital for all types of businesses and borrowers.

How much can a bank lend for working capital? The amount of loan will depend on the envisaged 'working capital gap' (WCG), determined by the borrower's decision to take trade credit offered, or defer payment of certain accrued expenses. In balance sheet terms, this would represent the projected current assets less current liabilities, without bank borrowings being taken into account. The working capital gap represents the borrower's need for cash for uninterrupted operations, after taking into account sources of funds available in the natural course of business also called 'spontaneous liabilities'. The bank, however, will not finance the entire working capital gap. It will expect that the borrower brings in his stake to fund the gap. This is called the 'margin'. Bank debt will, therefore, typically amount to the working capital gap less the margin.

Many businesses find that their working capital fluctuates over time. The reasons could be unexpected fluctuations in demand, changes in market dynamics or seasonality. Of these, seasonal sales are the easiest to predict, and firms build up inventories temporarily and incur higher operating expenses in time for the peak sales season. During the off-season, working capital needs increase since the inventory has already been invested in, peak sales have not taken place and cash flow from receivables will happen only when the inventories are liquidated. If seasonal patterns are discernible, the bank assesses working capital needs as 'peak level' and 'non-peak level'. Thus, two sets of working capital assessments would be required.

An important point to be noted here is that most firms have a stable level of working capital in the system, irrespective of seasonal and other fluctuations. In other words, just as fixed assets are at a predictable level, there are always some inventories, accounts receivable and other current assets that form a permanent part of the business. The only difference between the fixed assets and these 'permanent' current assets is that the latter changes its composition, as and when inventories are sold off and replaced, accounts receivable are realized and replaced with fresh ones, and so on. This 'permanent' working capital need, every year, is approximately equivalent to the minimum level of current assets minus the minimum level of current liabilities, without taking into consideration short-term bank debt and installments of long-term debt repayable in the short term (within the next 12 months). This difference reflects the requirement of long-term debt or equity financing for the 'permanent' current assets. It is important for borrowing firms and banks to be able to assess such 'permanent' working capital requirements and fund them with long-term investment. The increase over this 'permanent' working capital base due to sales growth would be financed through short-term credit from banks.

Working capital loans are structured as loans against the prime securities of inventories and/or book debts or as credit limits against bills raised on buyers of the goods and services of the borrowing firm. The price of the loan (the interest rate charged) depends on the additional securities available as collateral, and the credit score rating[24] of the borrower. The repayment of the loan should closely match the working capital cycle, and the covenants should be able to mitigate the risks and vulnerabilities in the borrower's business and financials.

It is extremely important for the bank and the borrower to assess the working capital requirements accurately. A mistake often made by inexperienced credit officers is granting a loan for a larger amount or for a longer maturity than what is required, especially to 'first class' customers. In a purpose-oriented loan, such as for working capital, irrespective of the standing of or relationship with the borrower, it is imperative to estimate funding needs accurately in order to help the borrower's business and minimize the bank's risks. Both under- and overestimation have their pitfalls. If the working capital need is overestimated, the borrower may not use the additional money judiciously, or may purchase assets over which the bank does not have lien.[25] If the working capital is underestimated, the borrower may face a liquidity crunch during the operational cycle and may have to re-approach the bank for additional loan or borrow from outside sources at exorbitant rates. In both cases, the bank faces default risk by the borrower.

Loans for Capital Expenditure and Industrial Credit

Firms need to invest periodically in capital assets to expand, modernize or diversify their business. In such cases, their credit needs will extend beyond a year. 'Term loans' are the preferred choice in such cases—with maturities of more than 1 year, repayment spread over the life of the asset or depending on the repaying capacity of the borrower. Most term loans are granted for purposes, such as a permanent increase in working capital (as discussed earlier) or for purchase of fixed assets or to finance start up costs for a new project. They generally carry maturities ranging from over 1–7 years. Though banks can, in theory, finance longer maturities, in practice they do not find it prudent to do so, because of the typically short- to medium-term maturity of bank liabilities. Lending for longer maturities may create a mismatch between asset and liability maturities and lead to a liquidity problem in banks.[26]

Since repayment runs into several years, the bank's decision to lend would be based more on the long-term cash generation capacity of the borrower firm or the assets being invested in. The benchmark ratio used predominantly is the debt service coverage ratio (DSCR),[27] the minimum desirable level generally pegged at 2. The bank typically would require collateral for long-term lending, more as a secondary source for repayment in case of borrower default.

The characteristics of term loans are determined by the use of the loan amount. In the case of a term loan for purchase of a capital asset, the cost of the asset less a suitable margin is disbursed in full (in most cases direct to the supplier of the equipment) after the loan agreement is executed. The repayment terms are a function of the useful life of the asset, and the borrower's capacity to generate cash flows sufficient to service the debt. The interest charged reflects the bank's perception of the default risk of the borrower and the collateral liquidation value over the duration of the loan. The covenants are more stringent than for working capital loans, since term loans extend over several years, and the borrowers may tend to dilute the negotiated terms. From the bank's side too, the credit officer who was instrumental in getting the loan sanctioned may no longer be available, and loan agreements may become unenforceable for lack of clarity.

Term loan repayments and interest payments could be structured in any of the following ways:

- Repayments in fully amortized equal annual/half yearly/quarterly installment. Each periodic repayment will include interest and principal in varying amounts. The installment are treated as annuities and equated to the present value of principal plus interest to arrive at the installment. Interest is recovered in full in every installment, and the remaining amount of the installment is taken towards principal repayment. As the principal gets repaid, the interest component, calculated on declining principal balances, decreases, and the principal component increases. Thus, in this method, the amount of payment per period remains constant, but the composition of the payment (principal and interest) varies from payment to payment.
- Repayment of principal in equal installments over the designated period, with interest calculated separately on declining balances. In this case, the amount of debt service will vary from period to period. In contrast to the annualized method of repayment, each periodic payment in this mode will vary, but the amount of principal will remain constant.
- Occasionally, the loan agreement may call for 'balloon repayments'. In this case, the borrower is required to service only the periodic interest over the period of the loan. The entire principal amount becomes due only on maturity (also called a 'bullet loan'). The difference between a 'bullet' and 'balloon' repayments is that in the case of 'bullet repayment' 100 per cent of the principal is due only at maturity while in the latter case, the credit (interest and principal) gets partially repaid during the term and presents lumpy repayment at maturity.
- In rare cases, a variation of the above method is used. The principal and interest are amortized over a very long period, say 25 to 30 years. At the end of the period, the remaining principal amount is repaid in full.
- For construction loans or project loans, the agreed amount is released in stages, as and when progress is shown in construction/the project.

Loan Syndication[28]

Large projects need enormous funding requirements. It may not be possible for one bank to finance the project requirements, from the viewpoint of both capital regulations and the risk of exposure. For the banks arranging the syndication and participating in it, syndication can be a source of substantial fee income as well. In essence, arranging a syndicated loan allows the lead bank to meet its borrower's demand for loan commitments without having to bear the market and credit risk alone, and also earn non-interest income in the process.

Syndicated loans are credits granted by a group of banks to a borrower. They are hybrid instruments combining features of relationship lending and publicly traded debt. They allow the sharing of credit risk between various financial institutions without the disclosure and marketing burden that bond issuers face.

Syndicated credits are a very significant source of international financing, with signings of international syndicated loan facilities accounting for no less than a third of all international financing, including bond, commercial paper and equity issues. Increasing trends of privatizations in emerging markets have enabled banks, utilities and transportation and mining companies from these regions to displace sovereigns as the major borrowers. However, and understandably so, the amount of international syndicated loan facilities, showed a decline since 2007. Quarters 2 and 3 of 2009 have shown a slight pick up, indicating confidence returning to the market (*Source*: BIS locational statistics, December 2009).

In a syndicated loan, two or more banks agree jointly to make a loan to a borrower. Every syndicate member has a separate claim on the debtor, although there is a single loan agreement contract. The creditors can be divided into two groups. The first group consists of senior syndicate members and is led by one or several lenders, typically acting as mandated arrangers, arrangers, lead managers or agents. These senior banks are appointed by the borrower to bring together the syndicate of banks prepared to lend money at the terms specified by the loan. The syndicate is formed around the arrangers—often the borrower's relationship banks—who retain a portion of the loan and look for junior participants. The junior banks, typically bearing manager or participant titles, form the second group of creditors. Their number and identity may vary according to the size, complexity and pricing of the loan as well as the willingness of the borrower to increase the range of its banking relationships. These bank roles have been enumerated above in decreasing order of 'seniority', and the hierarchy plays a decisive role in determining the syndicate composition, negotiating the pricing and administering the facility.

Junior banks typically earn just a margin and no fees. However, they may find it advantageous to participate in a syndicated loan—they may lack origination capability in certain types of transactions, geographical areas or industrial sectors, or a desire to cut down on origination costs. For these banks participation is also relationship building with the borrower who may reward them later with more profitable and prestigious business opportunities.

The Box 5.2 shows an illustrative structure of fees in a syndicated loan.

It is not mandatory that the lead arranger has to take a share in the credit exposure to the borrower. However, lead banks in practice do take a major share in credit exposures since their participation sends a strong signal to other participants that the borrower is creditworthy.

The mandated arrangers run two types of risks in syndication, assuming that the arrangers intend taking a major share in the syndicate's credit exposure. One is a 'syndication risk', arising out of under-subscription by participating banks in the syndicate. The credit requirements that have not been tied up will have to be entirely taken up by the lead bank/s. Once the syndicate is formed, the participating banks, including the arrangers, take on the credit risk—the risk that the borrower may default on debt service.

Therefore, before taking a decision to bid for the mandate, the relationship bank will have to do a thorough appraisal of the project and its prospects.

BOX 5.2 STRUCTURE OF FEES IN A SYNDICATED LOAN[29]

Fee	Type	Remarks
Arrangement fee	Front-end	Also called praecipium. Received and retained by the lead arrangers in return for putting the deal together.
Legal fee	Front-end	Remuneration of the legal adviser.
Underwriting fee	Front-end	Price of the commitment to obtain financing during the first level of syndication.
Participation fee	Front-end	Received by the senior participants.
Facility fee	Per annum	Payable to banks in return for providing the facility, whether it is used or not.
Commitment fee	Per annum charged on undrawn part	Paid as long as the facility is not used, to compensate the lender for tying up the capital corresponding to the commitment.
Utilization fee	Per annum charged on drawn part	Boosts the lender's yield: enables the borrower to announce a lower spread to the market than what is actually being paid, as the utilization fee does not always need to be publicized.
Agency fee	Per annum	Remuneration of the agent bank's services.
Conduct fee	Front-end	Remuneration of the conduct bank*
Prepayment fee	One-off if prepayment	Penalty for prepayment.

*The institution through which payments are channelled with a view to avoiding payment of withholding tax. One important consideration for borrowers consenting to their loans being traded on the secondary market is avoiding withholding tax in the country where the loan is deposited.

Source: BIS Quarterly Review, December 2004, p. 80.

Loans for Agriculture

Loans for agriculture are similar to other types of loans in the following respects:

- Most of the loans for agriculture are short-term loans.
- Agriculture being seasonal in nature, the norms for seasonal industries are applicable.

- They can be likened to working capital loans, in that the loan is used for purchase of inventory, such as seeds, fertilizer and pesticides, and also to pay operating costs.
- The sales are realized when the harvested crops are sold in the market.
- Long-term loans for agriculture are given for investment in land, equipment or livestock.
- Loans are paid out of cash flows arising from sale of crops harvested or produced from livestock.

The fundamental difference between loans for agriculture and other loans arises from the fact that agriculture is a vital national priority in many developed and developing countries. The governments and central banks of these countries have framed policies and institutional support systems to ensure that banks are involved in lending to this important sector, even when it appears that the sector may incur losses for a particular period.

Therefore, though loans for agriculture are to be assessed on similar lines as other loans, they are to be treated differently in terms of the outcome of such lending. Most countries have framed elaborate policies and institutional framework to ensure that agriculture and its allied activities are supported by banks.

Loans to Consumers or Retail Lending

Individual consumers generally seek bank finance to purchase durable goods, education, medical care, housing and other expenses. The average loan per borrower is small in relation to the bank's lending to corporate or business borrowers. Most loans have repayment periods ranging from 1–5 years, can be longer in the case of housing loans, carry fixed interest rates and are repaid in equal installments. Individual consumers are generally seen as more prone to defaulting on loan repayment commitments than corporate borrowers. Interest rates on consumer loans are, thus, higher to compensate for the higher default risk. However, the loss to the bank when an individual customer defaults is not as great as when a corporate borrower does.

Consumer loans can also be classified based on repayment terms as installments loans, credit cards and non-installments loans. Installments loans have a fixed periodic repayment schedule, which requires that a portion of both principal and interest are paid periodically. Payments on credit cards vary with the amount utilized. Non-installments loans are special purpose loans, in which the individual expects a large cash inflow at a particular point of time that will enable him repay the debt entirely. An example of this would be a bridge loan for paying an advance for purchase of a new house, which will be repaid once the old house is sold off.

Banks are increasingly resorting to retail lending to take advantage of increased consumer spending and also because pools of such assets can be securitized thus leading to removal of default risk and greater liquidity for the banks, which, in turn, would lead to improved profitability.

The latter part of this book deals with retail lending while securitization is discussed in the chapters on 'Credit Risk'

Non-fund Based Lending

LCs and BGs (BGs or letters of guarantee—LGs) are the common forms of non-fund-based credit limits granted to borrowers to carry on their business. They are non-fund based since there is no outlay of funds for the bank at the time of granting the facility. The income earned from these services is classified under non-interest income.

The fact that this type of credit is granted with no funds disbursement at the outset, does not render it free of credit risk. LCs and BGs are off-balance sheet exposures for the bank, but they carry equal or more risks than on balance sheet credit exposures. Their risk arises from the fact that the bank is called upon to pay the counter party or beneficiary, if the applicant or borrower fails to pay. The liability of the bank to the counter party is determined by the relevant statute and the bank will have to pay the agreed amount to the counter party without demur. It is then left to the bank to proceed legally or otherwise against the borrower or applicant to recover the loss.

It is, thus, evident that the bank will have to assess any request for non-fund based credit with the same rigour as it assesses the fund-based credit request. The default risk of the borrower remains, whether the bank has exposed itself to fund-based or non-fund-based credit.

The features of LCs and BGs are discussed in detail in subsequent chapters.

Asset Based Lending

Loans for Infrastructure—Project Finance

Project finance is a prominent form of 'Asset-based lending' (*see* Section I). Simply put, project finance involves the creation of a legally independent project company, with equity from one or more sponsoring firms, and non- or limited recourse debt, for the purpose of investing in a single purpose, industrial asset.[30]

Structuring a project finance deal entails substantial transaction costs in the nature of fees to lawyers, consultants and financial advisors, apart from obtaining necessary permits and environmental clearances. A deal could typically take 5–7 years to structure, since it also involves identifying and entering into suitable contracts with construction companies, suppliers of equipment and inputs, purchasers of output, operating companies and tying up the financing with various capital providers. Project companies are characterized by their highly leveraged structures with mean debts as high as 70 per cent, and the remaining equity contributed by the group of sponsoring firms in the form of either equity or quasi equity (subordinated debt), debt being non-recourse to the sponsors. The debt is also termed 'project recourse' since debt service depends exclusively on project cash flows.

A predominant share of project finance comes from banks in the form of debt, syndicated loans, or through subscription to bond issues of project companies. The risks for the lender are high, since the bank has limited or no recourse to the sponsor, unlike in conventional corporate financing. Thus, there are several supplementary credit arrangements that characterize project financing.

The primary mode of credit delivery is through term loans. The challenge in credit appraisal lies in the credit officer and the decision maker understanding the project and its risks in detail and instituting suitable risk mitigation measures for ensuring timely debt service.

SECTION V

LOAN PRICING AND CUSTOMER PROFITABILITY ANALYSIS

Till about a decade ago, banks in many countries were regulated in respect of interest rates they could charge to borrowers. But in today's environment of deregulated interest rates and intense price competition for credit services to worthy customers, banks will have to price suitably not only to garner profit margins, but also to balance risk—return tradeoffs and ensure market presence. Declining interest spreads have forced banks to re-examine their revenue generation and cost control practices.

Let us link loan pricing to pricing of a product. How is the selling price of a tangible product determined? First, the selling price should cover variable costs. Then it should cover a portion of the fixed costs. Thereafter, it should yield a net positive return at a rate commensurate with the firm's policy and market expectation.

We have seen in the chapter on 'Banks' Financial Statements' that the 'interest earned by banks on loans, advances and investments' is the equivalent of 'revenues' earned by a non-financial firm. The variable costs for our financial product—the loan—are the cost of the bank's liabilities. The fixed costs include the transaction servicing costs plus a portion of the overheads utilized for maintaining and monitoring the account. The bank's desired profit margin corresponds to the profit margin inbuilt into the selling price of a good or service.

However, there are two important points of difference between product pricing and loan pricing, especially for wholesale loans.

- Every loan has a unique risk profile, which will have to be quantified and built into the price. This implies that, unlike non-financial firms, a single price cannot be fitted to a product line.
- The price also depends on the profitability of the customer to the bank. Hence, loans to two borrowers with identical risk profiles may have to carry different prices. This is sometimes referred to as 'relationship pricing'.

It is, therefore, evident that proper pricing of a loan is more complex and non-standardized than pricing of a product or service.

It also follows that, for every loan, at the minimum,

$$\text{Loan price} = \text{cost of funds} + \text{servicing costs} + \text{risk premium} + \text{desired profit margin}$$

Banks are confronted with several issues related to pricing. How should they rate the risk profile of customers for pricing? Should they make variable rate loans or fixed rate loans? What should be the prime rate quoted for good borrowers? Can they increase loan prices and still retain customers? How should fee income derived from the borrowers be adjusted in the loan price? Is the price being quoted on par with the market? If a customer's relationship with the bank undergoes a change, how should prices be adjusted, and with what repercussions?

Many banks use a generalized customer profitability analysis framework to resolve these issues. The vital question that arises here is: how do banks reconcile strategic decisions regarding deposit and loan mix and overall profitability with pricing decisions for individual customers, based on a framework?

We will build a step by step a basic loan pricing model in the following paragraphs and then refine it to take into account relationship pricing.

Step 1: Arrive at Cost of Funds

The objective here is to ensure that the loan price covers variable costs. This serves as the most basic model for pricing the loan.

Loan price = cost of funds + desired profit margin[31]

The issue here is: What is the cost of funds? Is it the average cost of the bank's sources of funds—deposits and borrowings, or is it the cost of funds that the bank requires to source to make the loan? The answer to this is a function of the investment policy the bank follows[32], and is crucial in ensuring that the bank does not make a gross loss on the loan transaction.

We will define this with Illustration 5.1.

ILLUSTRATION 5.1

The maturity profile of Bank A is depicted in the Table 5.1. The bank's first class customer wants an additional loan of ₹50 crore to be repaid over the next 3 years. The bank seeks to have a net profit margin of 3 per cent on all its transactions. What should be the minimum interest rate ft proposes to the customer?

TABLE 5.1 THE MATURITY PROFILE OF BANK A

Maturity of Liability	Liability Amount	Rate (per cent)
Nil	10	0
6 months	25	5
1 year	25	9
2 years	10	11
3 years	20	12
Over 3 years	10	13
Total	**100**	

Average cost of funds = 8.30 per cent

Case 1

Loan price = average cost of funds + profit margin
= 8.30 + 3.00
= 11.30 per cent

Case 2

Suppose the bank has invested its surplus funds in long-term investments, and has to borrow in the market to meet the request for the loan. Funds with a maturity of three years are available at 12 per cent. Therefore, the loan price will be,

Loan price = cost of funds with matching maturity + profit margin
= 12 + 3 = 15 per cent

Interpretation of the results in Case 1 and Case 2

The bank quotes 11.30 per cent or 15 per cent depending on its sources of funds for the loan. The questions here are: would the first class customer of the bank be willing to pay 15 per cent if the bank has to source funds with matching maturity from the market? How does this rate compare with that other banks quote for similar loans? If the bank wants to satisfy and retain its customer; it could end up making a loss or settling for less profit on the transaction.

Step 2: Determine Servicing Costs for the Customer

The following are typically assessed for each customer.

- Identify the full list of services used by the customer. This list would include services related to the credit and non-credit facilities the customer avails from the bank. Examples of non-credit services would be the activity in the demand deposit accounts maintained by the customer (especially the zero cost deposits), usage of security/custodial services, or payment-related services such as transfers or LCs.
- Assess the cost of providing each service. The bank's cost accounting system can be of help, but there can be wide variations in the way banks allocate overheads.
- Multiply the unit cost with the extent to which such non-credit services are availed. For example, if it is assessed by a bank that it costs ₹10 to make a payment transfer, and the customer has used this service 500 times during the year; the cost for the customer works out to ₹5,000.
- Cost of credit services depends on the loan size and forms a major portion of the servicing costs. They include loan administration expenses, of which a large share is contributed by personnel, processing or delivery costs.

Most banks calculate these costs as a percentage of the loan size.

Step 3: Assess Default Risk and Enforceability of Securities

One of the basic methods of assessing default risk is a credit scoring system. A typical credit scoring system includes many of the risk classification criteria listed in *Annexure I*. The borrower whose loan is being processed is rated on these criteria not only for deciding on sanction of the loan, but also with a view to assigning a value to the risk the bank would face if it lent to the borrower.

Based on the risk value assigned to the borrower, banks build models to assess the probability of default, arising out of the bank's prior experience with borrowers having similar risk profiles. Assessing probability of default (PD) is a rigorous exercise involving statistical techniques and is discussed in detail in the chapters on 'Credit Risk'. The bank then puts a value to the enforceability and strength of the securities the bank holds or proposes to hold for the loan. Thus, the probable loss given default is also assessed.

Assigning these probabilities to the loan amount and interest recoverable, the bank computes the risk premium that will fit the borrower.

When there is no probability of default, the bank would receive the return it desires, or the rate contracted with the borrower. Let us assume that this rate is 15 per cent. Thus, at 100 per cent probability of repayment, the expected rate would be p 3 r, where p is the probability of repayment and r the contracted rate.

When there is a probability of default, the expected rate would be the aggregate of the following.

(a) The probability of repayment × the contracted rate Plus

(b) The probability of default × the irrecoverable portion of the advance, expressed as a rate.

Expressed as an equation, the expected rate would be:

$$E(r) = P(R) + P(D) \times (\{R(P + Pr)/P\} - 1)$$

where $E(r)$ is the expected rate
$P(R)$ is the probability of recovery
r is the contracted rate of interest
$P(D)$ is the probability of default
P is the principal amount
R is the recovery rate in the event of default

Illustration 5.2 gives one such simple methodology.

ILLUSTRATION 5.2

Bank A of Illustration 5.1 has made a risk assessment of the borrower and is confident that there is a 95 per cent probability of the borrower repaying the principal and interest as scheduled. It also makes a conservative estimate that in case of default, the bank can recover about 85 per cent of the principal and interest due. The bank feels that it cannot quote a rate lower than 14 per cent on the loan. What should be the rate it quotes to the borrower to include the default risk? Let us assume that the bank's cost of funds is 12 per cent and the servicing costs are at 0.25 per cent.

Solution

Though the bank intends quoting the rate of 14 per cent, it may not realize 14 per cent since there is a default risk attached to the borrower. The expected rate can be computed using the above equation:

$$E(r) = 0.95 \times 0.14 + 0.05\times (\{5000\ (1 + 0.14) \times 0.85\}/5000\} - 1)$$
$$E(r) = 13.3 + (-0.031) = 13.269$$

This implies that the bank will effectively obtain a return of 13.27 per cent from a loan contracted to yield 14 per cent. The difference between the contracted rate and the expected rate 0.731 can be taken as a measure of the risk premium.

Thus, the bank will have to price the loan to this borrower at a minimum of 12 (cost of funds) + 0.25 (servicing costs) + 0.731 (risk premium) + 3 (desired profit), that is, at 15.98 per cent.

An alternate method of arriving at the risk premium would be to assume the expected rate as the sum of cost of funds, servicing cost and the desired profit, that is, 15.25 per cent and solve for r. The difference between 15.25 per cent and r can be taken as a measure of the risk premium. The results from the two methods may not be identical, but will be comparable. 'Risk' measures can at best be indicative, and the bank can take a decision on the interest rate to be charged based on its relationship with the customer and the market demand for funds.

Step 4: Fixing the Profit Margin

One approach that can be used to set the profit margin for loan transactions is to use the ROE as a determinant. The ROE is generally set based on market expectations and shareholders' required returns.

We have already seen that ROE = ROA × EM

Therefore, ROA or net return on assets will be the product of ROE and the inverse of the equity multiplier (EM), which is represented by the term 'equity/assets', a measure of capital adequacy of the bank.

Illustration 5.3 will make the point clear.

ILLUSTRATION 5.3

If the bank in the Illustrations 5.1 and 5.2 desires to give its shareholders a return of 20 per cent, its assets amount to ₹10,000 crore, and its capital amounts to ₹1,000 crore, what should be the profit margin it should target for the borrower seeking ₹50 crore of credit, assuming that its cost of funds and servicing costs remain at the levels described above, and the risk premium is 0.731 as calculated above?

$$\text{Desired return} = 0.20 \times 1000/10000 = 0.02$$

Therefore, the bank should target a minimum return or profit of 2 per cent on the transaction. The bank already has proposed a return of 3 per cent which is profitable for the bank.

The steps discussed above are the basics that the bank should grapple with while pricing its loans. While the bank may have little influence over the cost of funds and servicing costs, it can adjust the risk premium and desired profit depending on the relationship it has with the individual borrower, the industry in which the borrowing firm operates, and the market rates for comparable loans.

Some More Models of Loan Pricing

Fixed Versus Floating Rates When the interest rates are relatively stable and the yield curve slopes upward, banks would be willing to lend at fixed interest rates, above the rates they pay for shorter term liabilities. In an environment where rates are volatile, and banks have to source funds from the market at varying interest rates, they would prefer to lend on floating rates and for shorter maturities. In effect, floating rate loans transfer the interest rate risk from the bank to the borrower. Though this appears desirable, it may result in heightened credit risk for the bank. The rationale is as follows: rising interest rates increase the borrower's interest expense, which, if not met out of operating cash flows or the borrower's own funds, may lead to a shortfall in debt service.

It is evident that most borrowers would prefer fixed rate loans, due to the predictable cash flows for debt service, and allow the banks to bear the interest rate risk. If banks want to encourage borrowers to agree for floating rate pricing, they typically offer two alternatives.

- In the first floating rate pricing alternative, banks may set the floating rate at a level below the corresponding fixed rate. The bank charges a 'term premium' to cover the risk on fixed rate loans. The size of the discount and the premium will have to depend on the bank's cost of funds and the required rate of return.
- In the second pricing alternative, banks set an interest rate cap on the floating rate loans to limit the possible increase in interest payments. The cap may be applicable for any interval or for the entire maturity of the loan. The borrower pays the negotiated floating rate till the cap is reached. The inherent risk to banks lies in the market interest rates breaching this cap.

Typically, the floating rate structure works well when linked to a reliable benchmark reference rate, representing the rate structure in the economy. The most widely used reference rates are the London Inter Bank Offered Rate (LIBOR)[33] and the prime rate (US markets).

The Box 5.3 outlines the concept of 'benchmark rates' and how they are fixed by various countries.

BOX 5.3 BENCHMARK RATES—MIBOR, AND THE LIBOR SCANDAL

We have understood the importance of a 'benchmark rate', to which interest rates and other rates in the economy are usually aligned with. How are these 'benchmark rates' decided upon? Who fixes them?

In advanced economies, all rates in the economy are based on the movements in a benchmark rate such as the LIBOR (London Inter Bank Offered Rate) or the 'Prime rate' of the USA. In India, however, different markets have different benchmark rates, and this led to banks finding it difficult to match the pricing of their liabilities and assets. This in turn, led to interest rate risk, and ultimately had an effect on banks' profitability. (*We will learn more on 'interest rate risk' in banks in the chapter on 'Bank risk management'*)

The LIBOR—The benchmark and the manipulation

LIBOR, since the 1960s, had been considered one of the most popular benchmark rates used by banks, securities houses and investors to gauge the cost of unsecured borrowing in the London interbank market. It was seen as the reference rate for the majority of financial products such as interest rate swaps (*see chapter on 'Bank risk management'*), corporate loans and residential mortgage loans.

The LIBOR is calculated each day by Thomson Reuters and is published by the British Bankers' Association (BBA). Eighteen major International banks in the UK submit to Thomson Reuters their cost of borrowing unsecured funds for 15 periods of time in 10 currencies. The highest and lowest submissions are discarded and the average of the remaining submissions is taken to compute LIBOR for the given day. The LIBOR calculation and fixation therefore involves a 'polling' methodology.

The LIBOR was considered a 'market determined reference rate' since it was not derived from real rates but based on the estimates of the bank market. However, the well respected and widely used reference rate came under a cloud when it came to light that the major banks that polled the rates had also resorted to influencing the rates. The bankers had succeeded in engineering the benchmark rate by nudging their own banks' submissions up or down in small increments to benefit their trading book (*the concept of 'trading book' is discussed in the chapter on 'Capital- risk, regulation and adequacy'*) from 2005 onwards. For example, the banks had lowered their rate submissions to provide a healthier picture of their financial health, particularly at the height of the financial crisis during 2008–09. In June 2012, when a large bank like Barclays admitted the misconduct, that some of its derivatives traders were found to have attempted to rig this key rate, it was fined 290 million pounds. The scandal forced both Barclays chief executive Bob Diamond and chairman Marcus Agius to resign.

The incident not only sent shock waves through the financial world but, also highlighted the need for regulatory reforms in the fixation of the LIBOR benchmarks. A committee was set up under the Financial Services Authority (FSA) to review the framework for setting the LIBOR. The committee's final report, submitted in September 2012, has suggested a 10-point plan for comprehensive reforms to the LIBOR that has been accepted by the UK government.

The major reforms/recommendations include the following:

- The LIBOR should be included under regulated activities under the Financial Services and Markets Act, 2000 (Regulated Activities) Order 2001,
- The BBA should transfer responsibility for LIBOR to a new administrator,
- Submitting banks should make explicit and clear use of transaction data to corroborate their submissions,
- The BBA, and in due course, the new Administrator, should cease the compilation and publication of LIBOR for those currencies and tenors for which there is insufficient trade data. This will result in decline of number of published rates from 150 to 20.

The controversy had added further uncertainty to the global financial system and reduced market confidence in key benchmark rates and the banking system.

The revelations about the LIBOR have also sparked off wider debate over how other benchmark rates and indices are calculated. The Benchmark rates already under scrutiny are the oil spot prices by the IOSCO (International Organization of Securities Commissions), and other financial benchmarks such as the Euro Inter Bank Offered Rate (EURIBOR) by the European Commission.

The Indian Benchmark Rate—MIBOR

In India, MIBOR (Mumbai Interbank Offered Rate), tailored after LIBOR, was introduced in 1998 as the key money market rate that corporates and banks use to hedge their risks and bet on interest rate movements. It was meant to be a tool to switch from fixed to floating rates or vice versa to either earn more from loans or pay less on debt, depending on the view on interest rates. The Mibor is currently used for majority of deals involving interest rate swaps, forward rate agreements, floating rate debentures and term deposits. However, its application is very limited compared with Libor, which had been used as a global benchmark for interest rates

The benchmark is computed by the National Stock Exchange of India (NSE). The MIBOR is currently a polled benchmark. The rate is arrived at by a poll of 30 banks, which is conducted by the National Stock Exchange (NSE) every morning. The panel of banks currently includes a mix of public sector banks including State Bank of India, Central Bank of India and Indian Bank; private sector banks including Axis Bank Ltd, HDFC Bank Ltd, and ICICI Bank Ltd; foreign banks including Citibank NA and Deutsche Bank; and primary dealers including ICICI Securities Ltd and PNB Gilts Ltd. The rate is the average of all the quotes given by the banks, though the outliers are ignored while arriving at the average. While MIBOR is not as widely used as LIBOR, the rate is taken as reference in the interest rate swap market. MIBOR is an index that is calculated every day, serving the purpose of providing a reference rate to which various entities can benchmark their short term interest rates. The rates are published at various platforms everyday such as the NSE website and news agencies. News agencies currently publish the overnight rate at 9.55 am, while rates for 14 days, 1 month and 3 months are put out at 12.15 pm.

The other benchmarks include MIFOR (used in forward rate agreements and interest rate derivatives) and those related to government bonds, triple-A papers, etc, The rate that is decided by the central bank every day around noon is the dollar-rupee reference rate which, besides local currency futures bourses, is largely used by offshore traders betting on the rupee in non-deliverable forwards—a market that is not officially acknowledged by RBI.

However, after the LIBOR scandal, the RBI and commercial banks have been discussing gradually moving away from 'polled' rates that may be prone to manipulation, to 'traded' rates for calculating the daily benchmarks in the money and currency markets.

Sources: RBI, Report on Trend and Progress of Banking in India, 2011–12; articles from the Economic times, various dates, 2013.

Pricing Floating Loans Once the benchmark rate is determined, the bank can develop and use prime rate-based[34] pricing models. Sub-prime lending is resorted to only in exceptional cases. In pricing most loans, a mark up over the prime rate is stipulated. As the market-determined or bank-determined prime moves up or down, the interest rates charged to the borrower also increase or decrease. The mark ups are based on a credit rating of the borrower, and are modelled to take care of the risks in lending to the particular borrower.

There are two basic methods for loading the mark ups on the prime rate—through an additive method and a multiplicative method-termed 'prime plus' and 'prime times', respectively. For instance, if the loan price is indicated as 'prime + 3', the borrower will have to pay interest at 300 basis points (bps) over the prime rate. As the prime rate changes, 300 bps (or 3 per cent) will be added on to the prime rate to arrive at the loan price for the borrower. The 300 bps reflect the bank's perception of the creditworthiness of the borrower. The more the default risk in a loan, the higher will be the additive factor over the prime rate.

The 'prime-times' method is a variation of the prime plus method, where the additive factor is replaced by a multiplicative factor. The extent to which this factor exceeds unity is a measure of the credit risk of the borrower. If the multiplicative factor is less than unity, the bank is pricing the loan sub-prime. For instance, if the bank wants to charge 300 bps above a prime rate of 10 per cent using the multiplicative model, the adjustment factor will be 1.3, *i.e*, 13/10.

In practice, banks fix a mark up based on the risk and other factors, and then arrive at the premium (in case of the additive model), or the adjustment factor (in case of the multiplicative model). Though both methods will have to lead to the same loan price at the time they are fixed, the impact of fluctuations in prime rate may lead to different loan prices as Illustration 5.4 demonstrates.

ILLUSTRATION 5.4

The bank cited in the foregoing illustrations wants to charge floating rates for its borrower since it expects interest rate volatility in the near future. The present prime rate is 10 per cent. The bank wants to charge a premium of 400 bps over the prime rate. Which method of arriving at the floating rate should it use—prime plus or prime times? Which pricing method would benefit the bank more when the prime rate

(a) moves up by 100 bps

(b) falls by 100 bps

Solution

Base Case

The prime rate is at 10 per cent.
Since the premium desired is 400 bps, by the additive method, the loan price would be = 10 + 4 = 14 per cent.
If the multiplicative method is used, the adjustment factor would be = 14/10 = 1.4.
Therefore, by the multiplicative method, the loan price would be similar to the additive method, that is, 10 × 1.4 = 14 per cent.

Case 1

The prime rate moves up by 100 bps, *i.e.*, to 11 per cent.
The loan price by the prime plus method would now be = 11 + 4 = 15 per cent.
The loan price by the prime times method would now be = 11 × 1.4 = 15.4 per cent.

Case 2

The prime rate falls by 100 bps, *i.e.*, to 9 per cent.
The loan price by the prime plus method would now be = 9 + 4 = 13 per cent.
The loan price by the prime times method would now be = 9 × 1.4 = 12.6 per cent.

Interpretation of the results

While the loan price is identical for a given prime rate under the two methods, when the prime rate increases, the prime times method is seen to yield a higher return for the bank. When the prime rate falls, the prime plus method is more beneficial to the bank.

Therefore, in a rising interest rate environment, banks may gain more returns by adopting the prime times method for arriving at floating rates. Conversely, in a falling interest rate regime, floating rates may be arrived at using the prime plus method.

Hedging and Matched Funding As described above, many borrowers prefer fixed rate loans. If banks have to make fixed rate loans in deference to borrower preferences, they attempt to control loss of profits due to interest rate volatility by using interest rate swaps or futures, or by matched funding.

In interest rate swaps, fixed rate payments are made in return for floating rate receipts. It is also possible to directly buy interest rate caps. With futures, it is possible to make fixed rate loans and hedge against potential losses from higher borrowing costs in future. This can be achieved by selling futures contracts or buying put options on futures.

In matched funding, loans are made with sources of funds with identical maturities. For example, the bank will source a deposit of 1 year maturity to fund a loan of identical maturity and amount. In the ideal situation, the bank can avoid interest rate risk on this transaction if there is a positive spread between the loan price and the cost of the deposit, and the interest payments also coincide. In large banks, the transfer pricing systems can be used flexibly for matched funding.

The Price Leadership Model The basic model described above makes the assumption that the bank knows its costs accurately, and can estimate probability of default and recovery rate for each borrower or class of borrowers. The basic model also fails to build in the effects of competition—the more intense the competition, the less the profit margin. These factors had led to the concept of 'price leadership' in banking, where a base or reference rate was established by banks. This rate was traditionally the lowest rate charged by banks to its most creditworthy customers on short-term or working capital loans. The actual loan rate charged to a borrower would be this base rate plus a suitable mark up, to compensate for the risk. Assigning the appropriate risk premium is one of the most difficult aspects of loan pricing, and many banks use a credit scoring system, basing their assessment on a grading of the risk factors.

Cost Benefit Loan Pricing It is a practice for many banks to base their loan rates on the base reference rate, the LIBOR or the prime rate. Some banks have also developed sophisticated loan pricing systems that determine whether their loan prices fully compensate for all the costs and risks involved in lending. One of these systems assesses the costs and benefits of the pricing model using the following steps.

Employ sensitivity analysis to estimate the total revenue that a loan would generate under different interest rates and charges.

Estimate the net loanable funds turnover.

Estimate the before tax yield from the loan by dividing the estimated revenue from the loans by the net amount loanable funds utilized by the borrowers.

This method is defined by the Illustration 5.5.

ILLUSTRATION 5.5

A borrower of a bank is sanctioned a ₹10 crore credit limit, but utilizes only ₹8 crore on an average at contracted rate of 20 per cent. The borrower will have to pay a commitment fee of 0.5 per cent on the unused portion of the credit limit. Additionally, the bank insists that the customer maintains a margin (a deposit or compensating balance) of 20 per cent for the utilized portion of the credit limit and 5 per cent for the unutilized portion. Reserve requirements imposed by the central bank stand at 10 per cent of the deposits.

(a) Estimated loan revenue = revenue from credit limit utilized + revenue from unutilized credit limit
= ₹8 crore × 0.20 + ₹2 crore × 0.005
= ₹1.6 crore + ₹1 lakh
= ₹1.61 crore

(b) Estimated bank funds outlay for the borrower = utilized credit limit less (i) compensating balance/margin requirement and (ii) reserve requirement.
= ₹8 crore − (₹8 crore × 0.2 + ₹2 crore × 0.05 + 0.10 {₹8 crore × 0.2 + ₹2 crore × 0.05})
= ₹8 crore − (₹1.7 crore + ₹17 lakh)
= ₹6.13 crore

c. Estimated before tax yield to the bank from this loan
= estimated loan revenue/estimated funds outlay
= ₹1.61 crore/₹6.13crore
= 26.26 per cent

In this case, the bank should decide whether the before tax yield of 26.26 per cent is sufficient to cover its cost of funds, servicing costs, the risk inherent in the loan and the desired profit margin.

Customer Profitability Analysis Periodically, or every time a borrower approaches the bank with a request for modifications in loan terms, a customer profitability analysis should be carried out by the bank. The analysis is used to evaluate whether the net gains from a borrower's transactions with the bank are in line with the bank's profit expectations. The procedure involves comparing revenues generated by the borrower with the associated costs, and ultimately with the bank's profit goal. Although the analysis is discussed here in respect of borrowers, the procedure can be used to evaluate the efficacy of non-credit activities as well.

The steps in analyzing customer profitability are typically as follows:

Step 1 Identify all the services used by the customer—deposit services, loans availed, payment services, services relating to transfer of funds, custodial services and other fee-based services.

Step 2 Identify the cost of providing each service. Generally, unit costs can be derived from the bank's cost accounting system. The bank's services can be bifurcated into credit-related and non-credit-related services.

Step 3 Cost estimates for non-credit-related services can be obtained by multiplying the unit cost of each service by the corresponding activity level.

Step 4 The major portion of costs is in respect of credit-related services. The bank incurs actual cash expenses in interest payment towards the source of funds for the loan, and the costs for credit analysis and execution. The latter includes personnel and overhead costs, including cash outgo for sending bills for collection, processing payments, maintaining collateral and updating documentation. It may be computed as a fixed percentage of the loan amount.

Step 5 The credit-related expenses has a non-cash component—the allocation of default risk expense. The bank's risk rating system is used in categorizing loans in terms of their potential for default risk, and the likely magnitude of such default. Some banks build in the default risk into the loan price as we have seen earlier in the basic model.

Step 6 Assess the revenues generated by the relationship with the borrower. The borrower could have deposit balances with the bank, either as a depositor or by way of compensating balances. To estimate the income from interest-bearing deposits, the bank deducts the average transactions 'float'[35] and the mandatory 'reserve requirements' from the average deposit balances held during the period of analysis. It then applies a 'notional interest rate' on the balances to estimate the earnings potential of the customer's deposit balances.[36] The opportunity cost of compensating balances varies directly with the interest rate levels, and hence, corporate borrowers do not prefer this mode of cash retention by the bank.

Step 7 Assess the fee-based income generated. Fees are generally charged on a per service basis. In the case of credit relationships, banks charge upfront fees for processing the loan application and making funds available (regardless of whether the funds are utilized by the borrower); commitment fees for the unutilized portion of the credit limit; and conversion fee, in case there is a rescheduling of the loan repayment terms.

Step 8 Assess the revenue from loans.

Illustration 5.6 describes the process.

ILLUSTRATION 5.6

Our bank in the examples given earlier has been requested by the customer to make the loan of ₹50 crore at the interest rate of 10 per cent. The borrower argues that the negotiated rate will be justified since compensating balances are being maintained with the bank in accordance with the loan agreement. The bank is looking for a target return of 14.4 per cent on the transaction, taking into account the risk factors in the loan and the ROE.

The terms of the proposed loan agreement (if the bank decides to lend) would be:

- Amount of short-term loan: ₹50 crore.
- Fees: 0.15 per cent processing fee: 1 per cent on unutilized loan amount as commitment fee.
- Compensating balances: 3 per cent of loan + 2 per cent of actual borrowing.

The customer uses the following services during the year for which the transaction costs are given alongside.

Nature of Service	Number of Transactions	Cost per Transaction (₹)
Items in transit	15,000	0.20
Demand deposit transactions	5,000	6.00
Payment transfers	500	2.00

Other information relating to the customer's loan and deposit transactions are as follows:

Average loan outstanding	₹42 crore
Credit administration costs	1 per cent
Credit risk expenses	1 per cent
Cost of funds	6.5 per cent
Average yield on the short-term investment	7 per cent
Required reserve ratio	10 per cent
Average demand deposit balance	₹1 crore
Average float in ₹	₹50 lakh

Would the bank meet its targeted profit if it were to lend to this borrower at 10 per cent?

Expenses

Description	Number of Transaction	Unit Cost	Total Expenses
Items in transit	15,000	0.2	3,000
Demand deposit transaction	5,000	6	30,000
Payment transfers	500	2	1,000
			34,000

Loan Expenses		**Average Balance**	
Credit administration expenses	0.01	42,00,00,000	42,00,000
Credit risk expenses	0.01	42,00,00,000	42,00,000
Cost of funds	0.065	42,00,00,000	2,73,00,000
Total expenses			3,57,34,000
Target profit 14.4 per cent of ₹42 crore		6,04,80,000	

Revenues	Rate	Average Balances	Revenues
Loan interest	0.1	42,00,00,000	4,20,00,000
Commitment fee	0.1	8,00,00,000	80,00,000
Upfront processing fee	0.015	50,00,00,000	75,00,000
Investment revenue*	0.07	45,00,000	3,15,000
Total revenue			5,78,15,000
LESS expenses			3,57,34,000
Profit			2,20,81,000

*Investment revenue calculated as follows:

Actual demand deposit balances	1,00,00,000
Less float	50,00,000
Collected balances	50,00,000
Less reserve requirement @ 10 per cent	5,00,000
Investible balance	45,00,000

Compare the profit generated by the customer with the target profit. The actual profit falls short by ₹3.84 crore. One reason is that the customer has not maintained compensating balances in accordance with the loan agreement. Against the stipulated compensating balances of ₹2.34 crore, the customer has maintained only ₹1 crore. However, even if the stipulated compensating balances had been maintained, the account would not have yielded the targeted profit for the bank. Hence, the bank has to rethink its relationship with the customer: Is it worth acceding to the customer's request and making less than targeted profit on the transaction? What should be the renegotiated interest rate if the bank wants to achieve targeted profit? If the customer does not agree to the renegotiated interest rate, what other compensating factors can be stipulated? Or can the relationship be terminated?

CHAPTER SUMMARY

- Banks have a crucial role to play in the financial system of any country. The prime objective of the financial system is to channel surpluses arising in the economy, into deficit units. The financial system comprises of 'financial markets' and 'financial intermediaries'. The financial markets function as 'brokers' that bring the surplus and deficit units together for mutual benefit. However, the risk of lending to deficit units is borne largely by the surplus units themselves. The financial intermediaries, on the other hand, create 'assets' out of the surpluses of the economy.
- Financial intermediaries serve three useful purposes—they mitigate the default risk of deficit units when surplus units lend to them, they ensure liquidity of savings by surplus units and they lower information costs.
- A bank can tend profitably only if it is able to take on and manage credit risk that arises from the quality of the borrower and his business. The bank also has to contend with the impact of fluctuations in interest and exchange rates on profits, as well as the liquidity risk posed by mismatch in the maturities of its liabilities and assets.
- Banks extend credit to different categories of borrowers for different purposes. For most of these borrowers, bank credit is the primary and cheapest source of debt. Financing the demand side of the economy, the large class of consumers, is called retail banking (also termed mass banking). Financing the supply side of the economy, which is more customized in nature and calls for specialized skills, is called Wholesale banking or corporate banking or class banking.
- For assuming financial risks, banks have to look for higher returns. Returns come in the direct form of loan interest, or in the indirect form of fee-based ancillary services. The most prominent risk in lending is default risk. There can be another kind of risk associated with credit decisions—interest rate risk.
- Broadly, there are three types of lending—fund-based, non-fund-based and asset-based. Fund-based advances can be further classified based on the tenure of the loans into (1) short-term loans, (2) long-term loans and (3) revolving credits.
- Credit decisions are by no means easy. Apart from their expertise in credit appraisal, the strategic role of credit officers assumes utmost importance.
- The 'credit process' has the following constituents—(1) the loan policy; (2) business development; (3) credit analysis, which includes steps such as building the credit file, project appraisal, financial appraisal, qualitative analysis, due diligence and risk assessment; (4) the initial recommendation based on the analysis; (5) credit delivery and administration, which includes important steps, such as loan documentation, stipulating the terms and conditions of lending, framing the positive and negative covenants, specifying the events of default and finally updating the credit file and following up periodically and credit review and monitoring, which is typically bifurcated into monitoring performance of existing loans and problem accounts.
- Though several qualitative factors play a role in a credit decision, a major influencing factor is the financial health of the borrower as brought out by the financial appraisal. The credit officer uses techniques, such as financial ratio analysis, cash flow analysis and sensitivity analysis to assess the achievability of the projections. Five broad categories of financial ratios are used—liquidity, profitability leverage, operating and valuation.
- Though classified under the single nomenclature—loans—every loan or class of loans is unique. Each type of loan has distinguishing features-based factors, such as the purpose, the collateral, the repayment period and the borrower profile. Examples of popular loans are working capital loans, industrial credit, term loans for capital expenditure, syndicated loans, agriculture, loans, project finance, retail lending and non-fund based credit.

- In the present environment of deregulated interest rates and intense price competition for credit services to worthy customers, banks will have to price suitably not only to garner profit margins, but also to balance risk—return tradeoffs and ensure market presence. Since every loan has a unique risk profile and every borrower enjoys a unique relationship with the bank, proper pricing of a loan is more complex and non-standardized than pricing of a product or service.
- For 'every loan', at the minimum, Loan price = cost of funds + servicing costs + risk premium + desired profit margin.
- For pricing floating loans, banks fix a mark up based on the risk and other factors, and then arrive at the premium (in case of the additive model) or the adjustment factor (in case of the multiplicative model).
- Many borrowers prefer fixed rate loans. If banks have to make fixed rate loans in deference to borrower preferences, they attempt to control loss of profits due to interest rate volatility by using interest rate swaps or futures, or by matched funding.
- Periodically, or every time a borrower approaches the bank with a request for modifications in loan terms, a customer profitability analysis should be carried out by the bank. The analysis is used to evaluate whether the net gains from a borrower's transactions with the bank are in line with the bank's profit expectations. The procedure involves comparing revenues generated by the borrower with the associated costs, and ultimately with the bank's profit goal.

TEST YOUR UNDERSTANDING

1. Why can't banks lend without a written loan policy?
2. How do banks frame covenants for lending? What factors do they base the covenants on?
3. Why do banks need specialized schemes of lending for each sector of economic activity? What would happen if lending procedures were standardized and rigid?
4. Why should credit needs of a borrower be assessed accurately? What would happen if the borrower's needs are (a) over-assessed (b) under-assessed?
5. A firm 'S' started its relationship with Bank 'B' with a demand deposit of ₹2 lakh. At the end of the year, the deposit had been overdrawn by ₹1 lakh. From the financial statement given below, establish the reasons for this: (₹ in lakh).

	Beginning of the Year	**End of the Year**
Fixed assets	7.5	12
Inventories	2	3.5
Receivables—book debts	3.8	3.5
Bills receivable	1.0	1.3
Trade creditors	2.5	3.3
Share capital	2.5	3.0
Share premium	Nil	0.25

   The profit before depreciation and tax was ₹2.5 lakh. Tax rate is at 40 per cent. Assume depreciation at 20 per cent on the outstanding fixed assets. The firm intends paying 15 per cent dividend on its year-end capital.

   Would you, as a bank manager, consider converting the overdraft into a working capital loan?

   What are some of the covenants you would stipulate?

6. What is the effective annual interest rate on each of the following loans? The amount of loan, in all cases, is ₹5 lakh, and the interest rate is 12 per cent.
   a. The loan is repayable in 3 years, principal payable in 36 equal installments and interest on declining balances.
   b. The loan is repayable in 4 years, in equal monthly installments.
   c. The loan is repayable with simple interest every year, at the end of 2 years. The entire amount of principal is payable at the end of the second year.
7. The promoters of a successful chain of restaurants approach you, the credit officer of a bank pursuing aggressive credit policies, for the following loans. Which of the loans would you consider favourably, and which would you reject? Give reasons for your decisions. What type of loan would you grant in each of the cases you have decided favourably upon? Also provide the risk mitigation measures you would put in place for each type of loan you are considering favourably. (Each situation is to be treated independently).
   a. The restaurant wants a working capital loan to finance its inventory predominantly consisting of vegetables, cheese and milk. The inventory may be transferred from the local sourcing headquarters (situated near your bank) to any of the restaurants in the city and suburbs.
   b. The restaurant wants to buy new cars for all the promoters.

c. The restaurant wants to invest in the firm supplying cheese and vegetables and seeks bank finance for the investment.
d. The restaurant wants bank finance to pay off the long-term mortgage loan used to buy the premises in which all the restaurants are located.
e. The restaurant wants bank finance to buy new, state-of-the-art cooking equipment for all its restaurants.
f. The restaurant has tied up for venture capital funding for its new posh up market chain and wants interim bank finance till the funding comes through.
g. The restaurant has run into cash flow problems and wants bank finance to pay employee's salaries.

8. From the following information relating to a bank, arrive at the prime rate (base rate) on which the bank would base the interest rates on loans.

Details (per cent)	
Capital adequacy Ratio	10
Reserve requirements	15
Cost of capital	12
Cost of deposits	
Demand deposits*	3
Term deposits	6

*Fifty per cent of demand deposits are interest-free deposits.

Ratio of demand to term deposit is 1:2

The bank has a credit scoring system to rate borrowers and uses the system to fix lending rates as given below.

Category	Rate	Proportion
A	At prime	0.40
B	At prime + 100 bps	0.40
C	At prime + 200 bps	0.20

The bank also earns an interest of 3 per cent on 50 per cent of the reserves.

The bank's total working funds consists of only capital and deposits. The management requires a net profit margin of 4 per cent.

9. A borrower approaches you, the credit officer, to amend the agreement in respect of the loan of ₹10 lakh sanctioned to him. He prefers you to price the loan at 15 per cent and completely waive the requirement of compensating balances. The loan agreement stipulates an interest rate of 13 per cent with compensating balances of 20 per cent of the loan amount.
a. What is the effective cost to the borrower of each alternative?
b. What is the effective return to the bank of each alternative, if the bank has to maintain a 15 per cent reserve requirement on its liabilities?
c. Which pricing scheme will be preferred by the bank and why?

TOPICS FOR FURTHER DISCUSSION

- Why does collateral alone not justify credit extension?
- What are the primary sources of income for a bank from a borrower? In today's changing scenarios which of these is more valuable and why?
- During a credit crunch, would non-fund-based lending increase or decrease? Why?
- What were the causes of the sub prime crisis that began in 2007? What kinds of banks were worst affected? What kinds of banks remained relatively unaffected? Why?

SELECT REFERENCES

1. Federal Reserve Bank of New York, 'The Credit Process: A Guide for Small Business Owners', accessed at http://www.ny.frb.org/education/addpub/credit.html
2. Harvard Business School. 1993 *Note on Bank Loans.* Boston: Harvard Business School Publishing.
3. Kohn, Meir. 1999. *Financial Institutions and Markets,* Chapter 2, New Delhi: Tata McGraw Hill Publishing Company Ltd, 27–47.

ANNEXURE I

RISK CLASSIFICATION CRITERIA

For a corporate borrower or a large project, risks can be endogenous or exogenous to the firm. Endogenous risks arise due to factors internal to the firm and its operations, and exogenous risks arise due to macroeconomic and other factors outside the firm that nevertheless impact the firm's operations, existence and success.

A key skill required in credit appraisal is the ability to identify risks, assess their severity on the firm's value and ensure they are mitigated so that the lender is comfortable with the credit risk.[37]

Many banks rate customers for risk internally, either qualitatively or through internally developed models. However, with the advent of Basel 2 regulations[38], banks feel the need to calibrate the credit risk in their books in a better manner. Hence, credit rating agencies such as CRISIL, ICRA and CARE have commenced rating bank loans. Credit risk in such cases would be measured by the ratings accorded to the proposed credit exposures by the rating agencies.

In spite of the role of external credit rating agencies, banks would have to develop internal risk rating systems to rate borrowers, since banks are in close proximity with the borrowers to collect more relevant information for decision making. The factors to be considered for such risk analysis can be synthesized from the rating agencies' models, and customized for individual banks and borrowers.

A typical risk management system should therefore take into account the following factors.

Principal Factors

The Borrower/Management

Integrity	Net worth	Previous history/track record	Group and Associate firms
Managerial capacity	Qualifications and experience	Stake	Risk-taking ability
Credit report	Market reputation	Succession plan	Endurance during bad times

The Firm/Project

General characteristics

- Constitution-proprietary versus partnership versus limited liability companies
- Product characteristics-differentiation, substitutes, patents, brand creation, technology (stable or fast changing), etc.
- Vulnerability to uncontrollable/unpredictable events (acts of God)
- Control over availability and prices of supplies and raw materials
- Scope in terms of both markets and products
- Availability of labour/power/other utilities
- Is the product subject to selective credit control?

Management team

- Industry experience
- Managerial breadth and qualifications
- Managerial depth and turnover rate
- Calibre and structure of board
- Management reputation
- Management controls proposed
- Forward planning and vision

Financial condition

- Business plan projections and critical assumptions made
- Borrower's/owner's stake
- Cash flow projections
- Leverage ratios
- Quality of assets
- Profitability ratios
- Shareholder value added
- DSCR over project/loan period
- NPV/IRR over project period
- Value of the firm as a going concern

Capital sources–Equity

- Access to private/public markets
- Borrower's/owner's personal equity
- Breadth of ownership

Capital sources–Debt

- Long-term/short-term
- Ease of a[u16]ccess to private and public markets or just private markets

Commercial Bank Relationships

Financial reporting

- Reputation/stature of audit firm
- Accounting practices proposed/existing

Industry

Structure and economics

- Competition
- Government policy-regulation/legislation
- Importance of industry to economy
- Degree of control by industry participants over demand and selling prices
- Industry's dependency on government/other industries
- Is the industry on any reservation list?
- Import substitute/export potential

Maturity

- Stage in industry's life cycle
- Ease of entry
- First mover advantage
- Rate of capacity additions
- Technology

- Rate of technological obsolescence
- Does the market need the product in this form?
- Are disruptive innovations likely?

Stability

- Sensitivity to business cycles
- Sensitivity to credit cycles
- Supply/demand balance
- Vulnerability to technological innovation
- Vulnerability to production changes
- Vulnerability to distribution changes
- Vulnerability to changes in consumption patterns/customer preferences

Risk Modifiers

Types of agreements

- Revolving credits
- Term loans
- Other loans
- Security provisions
- Restrictive covenants
- Repayment/amortization provisions
- Quality and reputation of other lenders

Types of collaterals

- Floating and fixed assets-market value
- Valuation considerations
- Marketability of securities
- Quality of floating and fixed assets
- Quality of inventories
- Condition of fixed assets and marketability
- Legal considerations
- Perfection of liens
- Enforceability of securities

Guarantees

- Collateralized
- Enforceability
- Status of guarantors

ANNEXURE II

THE IMPORTANCE AND ROLE OF CREDIT RATING AGENCIES (CRAS)[39]

A 'credit rating' is merely an informed indication of the probability that interest and principal on a debt instrument may not be paid on time as agreed to in the contract between the creditor and the borrower. It is therefore an estimate of the 'probability of default' on a debt instrument. When the risk assessment introduced in Annexure I is conducted by a credit rating institution with the requisite expertise and credibility, the efficiency of the market is assumed to increase by reducing information asymmetry. This in turn, results in lower costs for both borrowers and lenders

Credit rating agencies convey the 'probability of default' through simple alphanumeric symbols. In this context, it should be understood that the company which borrows the money is not being rated. The credit rating is applicable to the credit instrument to be used for fund raising. However, from the criteria being used for rating or risk assessment (as in Annexure I) the soundness and reliability of the organization seeking the debt can also be determined.

Therefore, credit rating is a mechanism through which an independent agency assesses the credit quality of the debt instrument based on various sources of information.

History of Credit Rating

Credit rating is not a new concept. The earliest known credit rating was done by John Moody in 1909, through rating of US railroad bonds. Over the next century, the process of credit rating evolved into a formal and acceptable mode of assessing credit quality, not only of simple debt instruments but also of complex derivative products and national economies. There are three major international credit rating agencies at present—Standard & Poor's (S&P), Moody's and Fitch – who share the bulk of the USD 5 billion rating business globally. There are also over 60 local or regional credit rating agencies all over the world who hold a much smaller share in the business.

Credit Rating in India

Credit rating in India began in 1987 with the establishment of CRISIL Ltd (The Credit Rating Information Services of India). Initially it was promoted by premier financial institutions such as ICICI, HDFC, UTI, SBI, LIC and the Asian Development Bank (ADB). Since 2005, CRISIL is an S&P company, the strategic alliance with S&P since 1996 culminating in S&P acquiring majority control.

All credit rating companies are governed by Securities and Exchange Board of India (Credit Rating Agencies) Regulations, 1999. The regulation provides detailed requirements that a rating agency needs to fulfil to be registered with the Securities and Exchange Board of India (SEBI).

The six credit rating agencies registered with SEBI (as given in SEBI notification in October 2012) are

1. CRISIL Ltd. : www.crisil.com
2. India Ratings and Research Pvt. Ltd. (formerly Fitch ratings India Pvt. Ltd., and a 100 per cent subsidiary of Fitch ratings) : www.indiaratings.co.in
3. ICRA Ltd. (promoted by IFCI and now controlled by Moody's) : www.icra.in
4. CARE Ltd. (Credit Analysis and Research Ltd., promoted by IDBI) : www.careratings.com
5. Brickworks India Pvt. Ltd. (the most recent) : www.brickworkratings.in
6. SME rating agency of India Ltd. (SMERA—joint venture between SIDBI (www.sidbi.com), Dun and Bradstreet Information Services India Pvt. Ltd. (www.dnb.co.in) and leading banks in India : www.smera.in

SEBI regulations for CRAs are designed to ensure the following criteria:

a. Only credible institutions enter the business of credit rating. This is ensured through stringent entry norms and fulfilment of eligibility criteria,
b. Through well-defined rules and obligations, it is ensured that credit rating is done in an objective manner and the agencies issue fair opinions,
c. Investors have widespread and easy access to ratings through a clear rating dissemination process,
d. The applicant institution should be registered as a company under the Companies Act, 1956 with a minimum net worth of ₹5 crore.

How are Ratings Conveyed?

Prior to July 2011, each Credit Rating Agency (CRA) had its unique set of symbols and definitions for rating long term and short-term instruments. To facilitate easy understanding of the rating symbols and their interpretation by investors, and to achieve high standards of integrity and fairness in ratings, SEBI instructed CRAs to use standard symbols and definitions for credit ratings.

In keeping with international practices, the standardized symbols used by CRAs at present pertain to the following types of instruments:

a. Long-term debt instruments;
b. Short-term debt instruments;
c. Long-term structured finance instruments; (Structured finance instruments are described in the Chapters on 'Credit Risk');
d. Short-term structured finance instruments;
e. Long-term mutual fund schemes; and
f. Short-term mutual fund schemes. (Mutual funds are described in the chapter on 'Mutual funds')

Rating symbols and definitions being currently used by all CRAs in India are as given in Tables 1 to 6.

TABLE 1 RATINGS FOR LONG-TERM DEBT INSTRUMENTS (LONG-TERM SIGNIFIES INSTRUMENTS WITH ORIGINAL MATURITY EXCEEDING ONE YEAR)

Rating Symbol	What the Symbol Denotes?
AAA	The highest degree of safety regarding timely servicing of financial obligations, and the lowest credit risk.
AA	High degree of safety regarding timely servicing of financial obligations and very low credit risk.
A	Adequate degree of safety regarding timely servicing of financial obligation, and carry low credit risk.
BBB	Moderate degree of safety regarding timely servicing of financial obligations, and carry moderate credit risk.
BB	Moderate risk of default regarding timely servicing of financial obligations.
B	High risk of default regarding timely servicing of financial obligations.
C	Very high risk of default regarding timely servicing of financial obligations.
D	In default or are expected to be in default soon.
Modifiers '+' or '–'	Can be suffixed to ratings AA to C. They signify the comparative standing within the category.

TABLE 2 RATINGS FOR SHORT-TERM DEBT INSTRUMENTS (SHORT-TERM SIGNIFIES INSTRUMENTS WITH ORIGINAL MATURITY UP TO ONE YEAR)

Rating Symbol	What the Symbol Denotes?
A1	Very strong degree of safety regarding timely payment of financial obligations, and the lowest credit risk.
A2	Strong degree of safety regarding timely payment of financial obligations and low credit risk.
A3	Moderate degree of safety regarding timely payment of financial obligation, and higher credit risk than the above two categories.
A4	Minimal degree of safety regarding timely payment of financial obligations, very high credit risk, and susceptible to default.
D	In default or are expected to be in default on maturity.
Modifiers '+' or '–'	Can be suffixed to ratings A1 to A4. They signify the comparative standing within the category.

TABLE 3 RATINGS FOR LONG TERM STRUCTURED FINANCE INSTRUMENTS (LONG TERM SIGNIFIES INSTRUMENTS WITH ORIGINAL MATURITY EXCEEDING ONE YEAR)

Rating Symbol	What the Symbol Denotes?
AAA(SO)	The highest degree of safety regarding timely servicing of financial obligations, and the lowest credit risk.
AA(SO)	High degree of safety regarding timely servicing of financial obligations and very low credit risk.
A(SO)	Adequate degree of safety regarding timely servicing of financial obligation, and carry low credit risk.
BBB(SO)	Moderate degree of safety regarding timely servicing of financial obligations, and carry moderate credit risk.
BB(SO)	Moderate risk of default regarding timely servicing of financial obligations.
B(SO)	High risk of default regarding timely servicing of financial obligations.
C(SO)	Very high risk of default regarding timely servicing of financial obligations.
D(SO)	In default or are expected to be in default soon.
Modifiers '+' or '–'	Can be suffixed to ratings AA(SO) to C(SO). They signify the comparative standing within the category.

TABLE 4 RATINGS FOR SHORT TERM STRUCTURED FINANCE INSTRUMENTS (SHORT TERM SIGNIFIES INSTRUMENTS WITH ORIGINAL MATURITY UP TO ONE YEAR)

Rating Symbol	What the Symbol Denotes?
A1(SO)	Very strong degree of safety regarding timely payment of financial obligations, and the lowest credit risk.
A2(SO)	Strong degree of safety regarding timely payment of financial obligations and low credit risk.
A3(SO)	Moderate degree of safety regarding timely payment of financial obligation, and higher credit risk than the above two categories.
A4(SO)	Minimal degree of safety regarding timely payment of financial obligations, very high credit risk, and susceptible to default.
D(SO)	In default or are expected to be in default on maturity.
Modifiers '+' or '–'	Can be suffixed to ratings A1(SO) to A4(SO). They signify the comparative standing within the category .

TABLE 5 RATINGS FOR LONG TERM DEBT MUTUAL FUND SCHEMES (LONG TERM SIGNIFIES DEBT MUTUAL FUND SCHEMES WITH ORIGINAL MATURITY EXCEEDING ONE YEAR)

Rating Symbol	What the Symbol Denotes?
AAAmfs	The highest degree of safety regarding timely receipt of payments from investments made.
AAmfs	High degree of safety regarding timely receipt of payments from investments made.
Amfs	Adequate degree of safety regarding timely receipt of payments from investments made.
BBBmfs	Moderate degree of safety regarding timely receipt of payments from investments made.
BBmfs	Moderate risk of default regarding timely receipt of payments from investments made.
Bmfs	High risk of default regarding timely receipt of payments from investments made.
Cmfs	Very high risk of default regarding timely receipt of payments from investments made.
Modifiers '+' or '–'	Can be suffixed to ratings AAmfs to Cmfs. They signify the comparative standing within the category.

TABLE 6 RATINGS FOR SHORT TERM DEBT MUTUAL FUND SCHEMES (SHORT TERM SIGNIFIES DEBT MUTUAL FUND SCHEMES WITH ORIGINAL MATURITY EXCEEDING ONE YEAR)

Rating Symbol	What the Symbol Denotes?
A1mfs	Very strong degree of safety regarding timely receipt of payments from investments made.
A2mfs	Strong degree of safety regarding timely receipt of payments from investments made.
A3mfs	Moderate degree of safety regarding timely receipt of payments from investments made.
A4mfs	Minimal degree of safety regarding timely receipt of payments from investments made.
Modifiers '+' or '–'	Can be suffixed to ratings A1mfs to A4mfs. They signify the comparative standing within the category.

In order to differentiate the rating of one CRA from the other, the regulations prescribe that the rating agency's first name is given as prefix for each rating. For example, a long term debt instrument rated AAA by CRISIL will be denoted as CRISILAAA, and a short term mutual fund scheme rated A1 by CARE will be denoted as CAREA1mfs, and so on

Who Uses the Ratings?

Investors in securities and other financial obligations can use the rating reports, which give detailed information and analytical judgements on the issuer's business and financial risk profile. This assists investors in taking more informed investment decisions, calibrated to their own risk-return preferences. In the case of investment in complex securitized instruments (securitization and securitized instruments are described in the chapter on 'Credit risk'), an independent assessment of the risks involved in the instruments by a credit rating agency acts as useful inputs to investors. CRAs also play a monitoring role when they track the performance of the securitized transaction and evaluate the corresponding impact on the riskiness of the instruments. Ratings also help banks in assigning risk weights to loans and other exposures, as required by the Basel Accord

Issuers of debt and other instruments rely on credit ratings as an important tool to access investors and gain a wider investor base. In many cases, successful placement of bond and other issues requires at least one rating from a recognized CRA. Rating also enables issuers price their issues competitively. Rating of the debt determines the price of the debt—banks and the market charge higher interest rates on lower rated loans. In this context, please recall the discussion on loan pricing in Section V of this chapter

Bank loan ratings, though not mandatory under the Basel norms, helps *banks* save capital. If a bank chooses not to rate the loans it makes, the bank would have to provide 100% of the loan amount as capital, even if the loan has been made to an extremely creditworthy borrower. The chapter on 'Capital-risk, regulation and adequacy', shows the impact of unrated and rated loans on the capital requirement of banks. On the other hand, the bank loans of a large number of hitherto unrated companies are now being rated. This development holds significant potential for further development of domestic debt markets, since transparent credit rating of a large pool of mid sized companies introduces into the public domain easily accessible credit information.

Regulators use credit ratings, or permit ratings to be used, for regulatory purposes. For example, under the Basel II capital framework of the Basel Committee on Banking Supervision, banking regulators can accredit credit rating agencies based on specified criteria to assign risk weights for calculation of regulatory capital of banks. You can find more details on regulatory capital and risk weights in the Chapter titled 'Capital-risk, regulation and adequacy'. Further, some regulators (such as IRDA and PFRDA) have incorporated ratings into the investment guidelines for the entities they regulate. Ratings are intended to provide an additional layer of comfort to the regulators in their assessment of product risks and overall systemic risks.

Multiple Ratings–Multiple Regulators?

Rating agencies rate various financial products and instruments: both short and long term. These products and instruments could be regulated by different regulators, as we have seen in Chapter 1. Some of the ratings are mandatory, while others are regulatory or prescriptive. An illustrative list of products/instruments, and the related regulators is given below:

Regulator	Product/Instrument Being Rated
SEBI	Public/Rights/listed issue of bonds
	IPO grading
	Capital protection oriented funds and other specialized capital market instruments
RBI	Commercial paper
	Bank loans (for the purpose of Basel norms for regulatory capital)
	Security receipts (for NAV calculation)
	Securitized instruments -Pass through certificates (for the purpose of Basel norms for regulatory capital)

	Fixed deposits by Non banking finance companies (NBFC) and Housing finance companies (HFC)
	Banks' investments in unrated non SLR securities
IRDA	Investments by insurance companies
Government of India/ PFRDA	Provident Fund investments

The Rating Framework

Since credit rating assesses the relative credit risk (risk of default) of the instrument being rated, the process of rating of debt instruments is similar to the framework bank credit officers employ, as described earlier in the text of this chapter.

Default occurs when the committed debt service payments or obligations are not fulfilled on due dates. This simply means that the cash generation capacity of the borrower through operations should be able to support the debt service obligations over the tenor of the debt instrument. The framework therefore involves assessing the Business risk, Technology risk, Operational risk, Industry risk, Market risk, Economic risk, Financial risk and Management risk, as done in credit appraisal.

The Rating Process

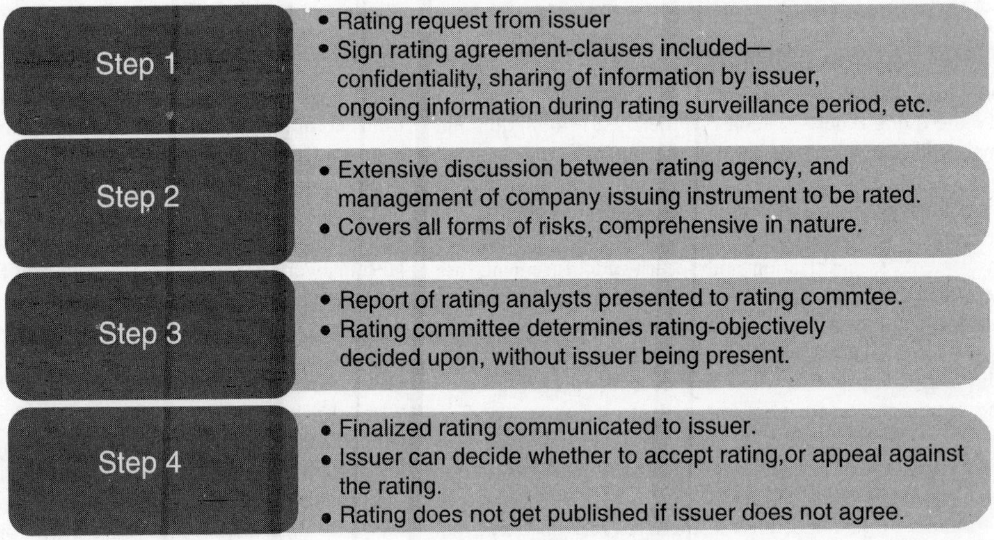

Rating Methodology

For example, CRISIL's credit rating methodology (for manufacturing companies) is summarized below (http://crisil.com/Ratings/SectorMethodology/MethodologyDocs/CRISIL-Ratings-crieria-manufacturing-cos_2007.pdf):

Step	Analysis	Key Factors Analyzed
1	Business risk–Industry risk	Macroeconomic factors, Industry structure, demand-supply, growth prospects, profitability, market size, competition, cyclicality, regulatory environment.
2	Business risk–Market position	Competitive advantage, market share, distribution strengths, pricing power, brand strength, SWOT analysis, etc.
3	Business risk–operating efficiency	Capacity utilization, cost structure, technological factors, labour relations, access to resources, flexible production and R&D capabilities, backward and forward integration.
4	Financial risk–accounting quality	Accounting policies, reporting and disclosures, and adjustments.
5	Financial risk–existing and future financial position	Capital structure, profitability, debt protection ratios, off balance sheet obligations, liquidity, working capital management, sensitivities.
6	Financial risk–cash flow adequacy	Working capital needs, sources and uses of funds, cash accruals to service debt payments, capital expenditure plans and funding.

7	Financial risk–financial flexibility	Bank limits, utilization, access to capital markets, cash and marketable securities, relationship with bankers, contingency plans, etc.
8	Management risk–integrity	Track record, reputation in markets, adherence to law and regulations, intra group transactions.
9	Management risk–risk appetite	Attitude to business risk, risk management practices, growth plans, unrelated diversification, etc.
10	Management risk–competence	Consistency of performance, track record, success of past strategies, succession plans, senior management quality, ability to attract and retain talent, experience in managing downturns.
11	Management risk–governance practices	Board composition and oversight, transparency and disclosure, shareholder value creation and equitable treatment.
12	Project risk	If new project.
13	External support	Government, group, parent company
14	Long term rating	Based on Steps 1 to 13 long term rating and rating outlook
15	Short term rating	Current liquidity position, size of short term debt, maximum short term debt capacity, mapping long term rating to short-term rating.

Similarly, CRISIL and other rating companies have rating methodologies to suit different types of industries, financial instruments and products. Detailed description of these criteria and methodologies can be found on the related CRA's website Chart 5.1 depicts the above risk analysis in a general form.

CHART 5.1 ANALYTICS BEHIND CREDIT RATING

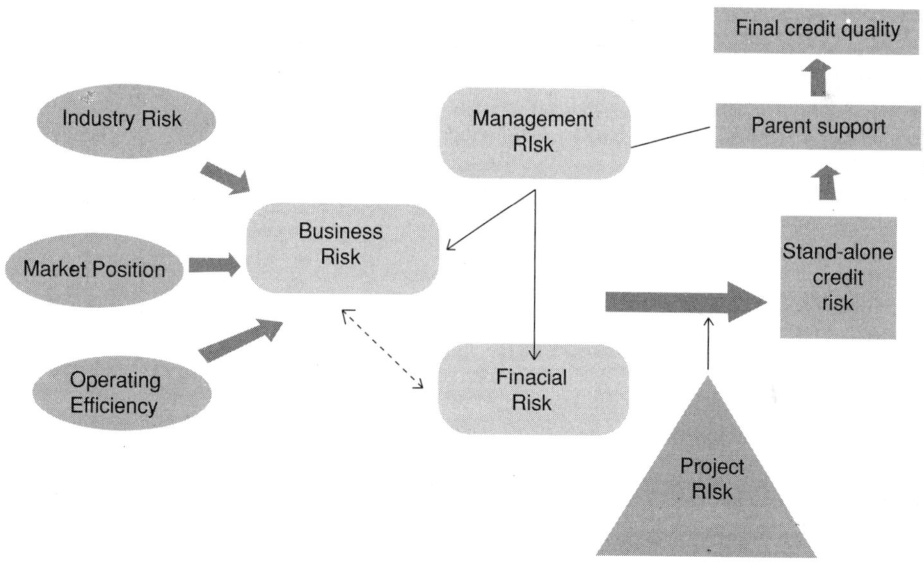

Source: Ministry of Finance, Capital Markets Division, Government of India, December 2009, Report of the committee on comprehensive regulation for credit rating agencies, Chart 4.1, page 20.

Two methodologies commonly used by agencies for assigning credit ratings are: A) Through The Cycle (TTC) methodology; and B) Point In Time (PIT) approach.

TTC methodology has two aspects: a focus on the permanent component of default risk and rating change policy. This methodology disregards short term fluctuations in default risk. It filters out the temporary component of default risk and retains only the permanent, long term and structural component. Only substantial changes in the permanent component of default risk lead to rating migrations (downgrades and upgrades in rating).

In contrast, PIT approach ensures change in credit rating immediately as the fortunes change irrespective of the cause. The basic difference between these two approaches perhaps lies on the relative weight that is assigned to the temporary and permanent components of credit quality. The relative weights are influenced by the time horizons for which the rating is valid. For example, for a one year horizon, the temporary component may get more weightage than for longer time horizons.

Non Rating Activities that Credit Rating Agencies Undertake

SEBI permits rating agencies to undertake the following activities, without compromising on the quality of rating or giving in to vested or conflicting interests:

1. Rating the Economy/Country
2. Company Research:
   a. Risk consulting—primarily for banks and financial institutions, in the areas of internal ratings, operational risk evaluation and calculation of regulatory capital,
   b. Funds research—Research on mutual funds' performance, and fixed income securities research,
   c. Advisory services—Developing policy frameworks, bid process management, Public private partnership (PPP) consulting, creating enabling environment for Indian business, etc.
3. Knowledge process outsourcing (KPO)

What Does Credit Rating by the Agencies Really Convey?

Credit rating by an agency is merely an indicator of the credit risk that could arise if the bank lent to the borrower. It reflects the opinion of the agency and does not amount to a recommendation to lend. The rating confines itself to the debt repaying capacity of the borrower, and does not consider the interplay of other risks inherent in the external and internal environment of the borrower, such as interest rate risk, liquidity risk, exchange rate risk and so on. Further, the rating is specific to the loan being granted, and is not tantamount to a rating of the borrowing entity.

For example, the website of CRISIL clearly mentions the following

'CRISIL's credit ratings are:

- An opinion on probability of default on the rated obligation.
- Forward looking.
- Specific to the obligation being rated.

But they are not:

- A comment on the issuer's general performance.
- An indication of the potential price of the issuers' bonds or equity shares.
- Indicative of the suitability of the issue to the investor.
- A recommendation to buy/sell/hold a particular security.
- A statutory or non-statutory audit of the issuer.
- An opinion on the associates, affiliates, or group companies, or the promoters, directors, or officers of the issuer. (http://crisil.com/ratings/credit-ratings.html).

Another limitation is that Credit Ratings are typically ordinal in nature—for example we know that a rating of BB has a higher likelihood of default than BBB, but we do not know how much higher. It is not until each rating is assigned a probability of default that we can say how much more risky a BB rated instrument is thus making the system cardinal, which is more useful for pricing an instrument. Calibration of ratings to default probabilities is again a difficult task.

International Regulations for Credit Rating Agencies

IOSCO (International Organization of Securities Commissions : www.iosco.org), the leading international policy forum for securities regulators, is recognized as the global standard setter for securities regulation. The organization's membership regulates more than 95 per cent of the world's securities markets in 115 jurisdictions and it continues to expand. One of its key objectives is investor protection on a global basis.

In December 2012, IOSCO has published two reports on Credit rating agencies—the final report on

Credit Rating Agencies: Internal Controls Designed to Ensure the Integrity of the Credit Rating Process and Procedures to Manage Conflicts of Interest, and a consultation report on *Supervisory Colleges for Credit Rating Agencies.*

Both reports form part of IOSCO's effort to improve the integrity of credit rating agencies (CRAs), as part of the global effort to enhance investor protection and the fairness, efficiency and transparency of securities markets.

The final report quoted above will form the basis of IOSCO's ongoing review and revision of the *IOSCO Code of Conduct fundamentals for CRAs* (called the 'Code'). The Code broadly addresses the areas of (a) quality and integrity of the rating process, (b) CRAs' independence and avoidance of conflict of interest, (c) CRAs' responsibilities to the investing public and issuers, and (d) disclosure of the code and communication with market participants.

The review is aimed at ensuring the Code remains relevant as the international standard for self governance. The Code was last revised after the 2008 financial crisis raised concerns about the quality of credit ratings and credit rating methodologies, the timeliness of adjustments to credit ratings, the integrity of the credit rating process, and how conflicts of interest are managed by CRAs.

An objective of the report is to increase public understanding of the internal workings of CRAs, and to enable CRAs to compare their internal controls and procedures with those of their peers. It is aimed at helping users of ratings draw their own conclusions about an individual CRA's controls and procedures, and thereby help the users make informed decisions with respect to their reliance on credit ratings.

The Sub Prime Crisis—a Failure of the Rating Agencies?

All the top credit rating agencies of the world are under a cloud in the wake of the financial meltdown. They have been accused of being too slow in alerting investors of the risks of investments based on high risk subprime loans.

Most countries are now considering stricter regulation on the rating agencies and the way they do business.

The European commission has, in November 2008, published a series of proposals that include banning ratings agencies from doing consulting work for clients who they also rate, and calling for greater disclosure of how the ratings are arrived at. The Commission has also suggested that if the agency did not have sufficient reliable information to rate, they should not be allowed to rate the security. Other proposals include having at least three independent directors on the boards of rating agencies, whose compensation was not linked to business performance, and publishing annual transparency reports.

Australia has proposed a 'licensed self regulatory system' for credit rating agencies, who would be required to adhere to the code of conduct developed by IOSCO. The code of conduct had been updated in 2008 to reflect the lessons from the sub prime crisis.

Banks' Internal Credit Appraisal and External Credit Rating

In spite of the role of external credit rating agencies, banks would have to develop internal risk rating systems to rate borrowers, since banks are in close proximity with the borrowers to collect more relevant information for decision making. The factors to be considered for such risk analysis can be synthesized from the rating agencies' models, and customized for individual banks and borrowers.

ANNEXURE III

CREDIT APPRAISAL—SOME COMMONLY USED FINANCIAL RATIOS

Liquidity Ratios

The liquidity ratios reflect the sufficiency of cash (liquid funds) in the firm to meet its liabilities. Those liabilities maturing for payment within the next 12 months are termed current liabilities. Such liabilities will be paid through generating cash and other liquid assets (called 'current assets') through the working capital operating cycle, typically within the next 12 months. The borrower with weak liquidity is generally not considered a good credit risk.

Description	Numerator	Denominator	Remarks/Interpretation
Current ratio	Current assets	Current liabilities	A current ratio of 2 indicates that the current assets in the form of cash, inventory and receivables are sufficient to pay twice over the current liabilities falling due for payment in the next 12 months. A higher ratio may be viewed favourably by the bank. However, a very large ratio implies that a substantial amount of the long-term funds or owner's stake is locked up in current assets, which may not always be profitable for the borrower. The ratio indicates the general ability of the firm to meet its current liabilities over a period. But it does not indicate the liquidity in the firm to meet immediate liabilities. For example, with a current ratio of 5, the firm may still fall short of meeting an immediate liability, since most of the current assets are locked up in say work in process inventory or slow moving goods or ageing receivables. Hence, in the case of borrowers with high current ratios, the bank will also have to carefully verify the speed with which inventory turns over or how quickly receivables get collected. On the other hand, with a current ratio of just 1, a firm with highly liquid assets can meet immediate liabilities with ease. The bank generally asks the borrower with a low current ratio to improve it by injecting fresh long-term funds or by profit plough back. A slip in the ratio is usually not viewed kindly by lending banks.
Quick ratio or Acid test ratio	Current assets Less inventory or Cash + accounts receivable	Current liabilities (including bank borrowings against inventory)	In a crisis, it may be difficult to dispose off the inventory of a firm. Hence, inventory and other less liquid current assets are excluded to determine a conservative measure of liquid funds of the borrower. A ratio of 1 or more than 1 is considered satisfactory.

Net working capital (NWC)	Current assets Less current liabilities	(No denominator since the NWC is an absolute figure).	The NWC is a measure of owner's stake or long-term liquid fund in the firm. It has a close relationship with the current ratio. When current ratio equals 1, the NWC is zero. When current ratio is more than 1, NWC is positive; and when current ratio falls below unity, NWC is negative. Negative NWC implies that the lending bank is running a more than normal financial risk in respect of the borrower.
Other measures used to determine liquidity	Ageing schedule of accounts receivables, inventory turnover, etc.		

Leverage Ratios

These ratios reflect the financial risk inherent in the borrower firm. Higher debt probably implies higher profitability in some cases, but also implies higher potential earnings volatility and higher risk of insolvency. The bank needs to assess the leverage of the borrower from the viewpoint of debt service, the firm size and industry practices. Some common ratios employed in the analysis are as follows.

Description	Numerator	Denominator	Interpretation
Debt—equity ratio	Total outside liabilities (long- + short-term liabilities)	Tangible net worth (generally equity + reserves—intangible assets)	The ratio is intended to measure the long-term solvency of the firm. As the firm grows and becomes more profitable, the ratio should decrease, indicating lower debt component in the capital structure for the existing business. The ratio also indicates the relative stakes of the capital holders of the firm—debt holders versus equity holders. The larger the ratio, the greater the financial risk of the firm. However, how large the ratio can be depends on factors such as industry characteristics, (also see Table 5.2 for a hypothetical example) risk bearing capacity of the firm, etc. The bank also has to view this ratio in conjunction with the current ratio to ensure that there is no imminent danger of the firm getting into liquidity problems while meeting liabilities.
Long-term liabilities ratio	Long-term debt	Tangible net worth	When the firm embarks on new projects with substantial capital expenditure, and cash inflows over a fairly long period of time, this ratio would indicate the long-term solvency of the firm. Many banks consider this ratio at market values over the useful life of the project, in which case, the market value of debt is expected to decrease as repayments are made, and the market value of equity increases as the project takes off and yields more profits to the firm.

Interest coverage	Earnings before interest and taxes (EBIT)	Interest expense	The larger the ratio, the better for the bank, since it indicates the number of times the EBIT is larger than the interest due to the bank and other lenders. In other words, it indicates by how much the EBIT can fall before the borrower is unable to meet interest payments to the bank and other lenders. A large ratio signifies a cushioning effect on interest payments in the case of a fall in the EBIT.
Debt service coverage ratio (DSCR)	EBIT + depreciation + principal repayment on existing and proposed loans or EBITDA–taxes paid–capital expenditure–incremental net working capital	Principal repayments + interest payments	This and its variations are one of the most important ratios for assessing the debt service capacity of the firm or its new project over a period of time. The ratio measures the number of times the firm can pay its debt commitments with current earnings. Typically, lenders insist on a DSCR of at least 2. The DSCR is calculated every year over the life of the loan or project to assess the cash generating and repayment capacity. The bank may not be comfortable with a lower than 2 DSCR in any year during the period for which the loan has been given.
Net fixed assets to tangible net worth	Net fixed assets (gross fixed assets less depreciation)	Tangible net worth	This ratio indicates how much of the firm's least liquid assets have been financed by net worth. It also serves as a variation of the EM, and shows how much of the owners' funds have gone into financing fixed assets. A higher ratio also means that more fixed assets have been financed from debt rather than by internal generation. The ratio is, therefore, a measure of risk inherent in the borrower firm.
Dividend payout	Cash dividends paid	Net profit after tax	The more the dividends paid, the happier the equity holders are. However, more dividends also mean less cash available as retained earnings. Typically, a bank is wary of high dividend payouts by the borrower. The less the equity, the more the risk for the lending bank, and the less the internal generation available for new projects, the more the demand for bank debt.

TABLE 5.2 ILLUSTRATION OF IMPLICATIONS OF A DEBT-EQUITY RATIO HIGHER THAN THE INDUSTRY AVERAGE

	Year 1 Firm X	Industry average	Year 2 Firm X	Industry Average
Total investment	100	100	100	100
Debt equity ratio	4	1.5	4	1.5
Debt	80	60	80	60
Equity	20	40	20	40
EBIT	20	20	10	10

(Continued)

TABLE 5.2 (CONTINUED)

	Year 1 Firm X	Industry average	Year 2 Firm X	Industry Average
Profitability (EBIT/value)	20%	20%	10%	10%
Interest at 14 per cent	11.2	8.4	11.2	8.4
PBT	8.8	11.6	(1.2) loss	1.6
Tax at 50 per cent	4.4	5.8	Loss	0.8
PAT	4.4	5.8	Loss	0.8
ROE	22%	14.25%	Loss	2%

The simple example shows that:

a. if the profitability of the firm exceeds the interest cost in good times (in year 1, the EBIT/value for the firm is 20 per cent, while the interest cost is 14 per cent), the ROE of the firm will be higher than the industry average.

b. In bad times, however, when the profitability of the firm plummets below the interest cost, the industry ends up making a small profit, while the firm makes a loss. Everything else being equal, it is the interest cost that is responsible for the loss of the highly levered firm.

Profitability Ratios

The bank expects the borrowing firm to conduct its business prudently, mitigate risks, be cost effective and thus generate enough profits to cover long-term debt obligations; taxes and other statutory payments; pay reasonable dividends to equity holders; and thereafter leave a surplus for plough back into reserves or invest in high yielding projects. The important profitability ratios for the bank as lender are as follows:

Description	Numerator	Denominator	Interpretation
ROE	Net income	Average total equity	We have seen that the ROE is a combination of two components-ROA and the EM.[40]
ROA	Net income	Average total assets	The more the assets have been worked for higher returns, the higher the ROE. Further, ROA is the product of the profit margin, a measure of expense control and asset utilization, the gross yield on assets.[41]
Return on capital employed (ROCE), more commonly known as return on investment (ROI)	EBIT	Average capital employed (tangible net worth + term liabilities + current liabilities)	A variation of the ROA, this ratio is useful for inter-firm comparison. The denominator can also be expressed as 'total assets less intangible assets'. (known as operating assets).
Sales growth	Change in sales	Last period's sales	A simple and efficient indicator of topline growth. Any credit analysis has to begin with assessing how realistic the projections of sales growth are. Trends in sales growth of the firm as well as the industry are good benchmarks for this assessment.
Gross profit ratio	Net sales-cost of goods sold (COGS)	Net sales	This ratio measures the manufacturing efficiency in the case of manufacturing firms, and the direct contribution from sales in other firms.
Operating profit ratio	Gross profit-operating expenses	Net sales	This ratio measures operational efficiency.

Operating or Activity Ratios

Activity or turnover ratios measure the operational efficiency and the liquidity of the current assets of the borrower firm.

Description	Numerator	Denominator	Interpretation
Days' cash Inventory turnover	Cash Sales or COGS	Average daily sales Average inventory	Indicates the availability of the most liquid asset-cash. Higher ratio indicates better inventory/working capital management and more profitability. Lower ratio should be examined with care-is it due to depressed sales, non-saleable stocks or excess inventory?
Debtors' velocity	Average receivables outstanding	Average daily sales	This ratio is also known as 'debtors' turnover' or 'average collection period'. It indicates the average number of days required to convert sales into cash. The actual collection period so obtained is to be compared with the firm's credit policy to establish the firm's ability to collect on its receivables. Lower the period, the quicker the cash inflow. However, a longer collection period than estimated will be a cause for concern for the bank, since repayments depend on how soon cash is realized from sales. If cash is not realized by the borrower on time, it is likely that the firm will approach the bank for more infusion of working capital. If the trend persists over a period, unless there is fresh infusion of funds, liquidity problems will result, which may also lead to profit erosion. The bank will have to take note of longer than estimated collection periods and ascertain the reasons, which could be (1) reduction in demand due to poor quality of goods sold (serious for the bank); (2) general recession in the industry (should the bank lend more to tide over the phase?); (3) poor collection mechanism (bank to insist on improvement); and (4) default/financial problems of one or more major buyers (bank may have to lend more till buyer pays up) and reckless credit policy of the firm (bank to insist on remedial action).
Creditors velocity (also known as 'creditors' turnover ratio', or 'average payment period')	Average outstanding of accounts payable	Average daily purchases	This ratio is generally computed for bills payable and creditors for goods, and indicates the time lag between a purchase and its payment. The more credit availed from its suppliers, the less a firm requires bank credit. Trade credit is available more freely, based on market reputation and the firm's relationship with the supplier. However, the cost conscious firm should be able to estimate the cost of availing such trade credit and compare it with the cost of availing bank credit. Further, if the firm is taking longer than the allowed period to pay its creditors, the bank should look into the firm's liquidity position and its reputation in the market. A longer than permitted credit period could indicate diversion of short-term funds, poor sales, inventory pile up or poor collection of accounts receivables. Prolonged default in trade payments may endanger the supply of raw material to the borrower.

Sales to net fixed assets	Sales	Net fixed assets	This is another turnover ratio, which indicates how efficiently the fixed assets are used to generate production and hence sales.
Number of days' cash to cash asset cycle	Days' cash + number of days of debtors outstanding + number of days of inventory outstanding		Approximates the actual working capital cycle of the firm and can be compared with the estimated cash cycle based on which the credit has been assessed.

Valuation Ratios

What is the real value of the borrower? The financial definition of 'value' is the 'present value of future cash flows'. The future potential of the firm is a major determinant of the market perception of the firm, and hence its 'market value'. This is particularly true of the value of publicly traded firms. The bank is interested in the value of a firm both in view of its ongoing relationship as well as the prospects of problem-free debt service.

Description	Numerator	Denominator	Interpretation
Book value per share	Book value of equity	Number of outstanding shares.	If shares are trading below book value, the question is-why is the market perception so low? Are asset values overstated?
Price/earnings ratio	Market value of share	Net income.	This is an important ratio for the bank. The borrower's share prices are an indicator of the market perception of future performance. Net income is tied to the past, and is influenced by the accounting practices. The bank also has to consider how the industry averages are in respect of this ratio.
Price/sales ratio	Market capitalization = current share price × outstanding number of shares	Average sales over the last 1 year.	
Liquidation value	Market value of firm = market value of equity + market value of debt	Liquidation value of assets.	This is an important measure for the bank. Research has shown that firms destroy value if liquidation value consistently remains above market value. Under such circumstances, the bank may want the borrower to divest the business unit that is value destroying.

ANNEXURE IV

INCOME STATEMENT-BASED CASH FLOW ANALYSIS

Cash flow to firm = cash flow from operations + cash flow from investments + cash flow from financing

How do we arrive at the cash flow of a firm from its income statement and balance sheet? Table 5.3 demonstrates this.

TABLE 5.3 CASH FLOW OF A FIRM CALCULATED FROM INCOME STATEMENT AND BALANCE SHEET

Cash Flow Item	Income Statement Source	Balance Sheet Adjustment	What Do the Adjustments Reflect?
Cash sales	Sales revenue	*Less:* Increase in accounts receivable	Borrower's sales growth; Credit policy of the firm
Less: Cash purchases	Cost of goods sold	*Less:* Inventory Plus: Increase in accounts payable	Inventory turnover; Inventory policy; Trade relationships; Market reputation

(Continued)

TABLE 5.3 (CONTINUED)

Cash Flow Item	Income Statement Source	Balance Sheet Adjustment	What Do the Adjustments Reflect?
Equals: Cash gross profit	Gross profit		
Less: Cash operating expenses	Operating expenses	*Less:* Increase in prepaid expenses *Plus:* Decrease in accrued expenses	Operating expense payment policies; Accounting methods
Add: Depreciation	Depreciation		
Add: Other cash income	Other income		
Less: Other cash expenses	Other expenses		
Less: Interest paid	Interest costs	*Less:* Increase in other current assets Plus: Increase in other current liabilities	
Equals: Cash profit before taxes	Profit before taxes		
Less: Cash taxes paid	Tax	*Add:* Taxes payable Add: Deferred taxes	Accounting methods; tax laws
Cash flow from operations	Profit after tax		Operating efficiency
Less: Cash used for capital expenditure			Capital expenditure. investment decision
Less: Increase in cash used for working capital			Working capital management
Equals: Cash flow from investments			
Less: Cash used to pay loan principal			
Less: Dividends paid			Dividend policy
Equals: Cash used for financing			
Add: Increase in short-term debt and long-term debt			
Add: Increase in new equity			Capital structure policies
Add: Increase in non-current liabilities			
Equals: Cash from financing			

ENDNOTES

1. Some authors call investment in financial markets 'direct lending' by investors, and deposits with banks as 'indirect lending'.
2. Kohn, Meir (1999). Financial Institutions and Markets, Chapter 2, pp. 27–47. Tata McGraw-Hill: New Delhi.
3. A more detailed discussion on these risks is found in the chapter on 'Risk Management'.
4. Discussed in detail in the chapter 'Managing Credit Risk–An Overview'.
5. Discussed in detail in the chapter on 'Risk Management'.
6. Discussed in detail in the chapter on 'Capital—Risk, Regulation and Adequacy'.
7. Discussed in detail in the chapter on 'Managing Credit Risk—An Overview'.
8. Discussed in Section IV of this chapter.
9. Also see chapter on 'Banks Financial Statements'.
10. Discussed in detail in the chapters on 'Credit'.
11. Though it is a practice to use the two terms 'loans' and 'advances' interchangeably, the difference in meanings is brought out by the following definitions: A 'loan' or

'loan commitment' is a formal agreement between a bank and its borrower, whereby the bank agrees to provide a fixed amount of credit for a specified period, subject to certain terms and conditions, with or without securities. An 'advance' is a payment made to a borrower under a loan agreement.

12. Banks do not lend for very long terms since the sources of their funds are essentially short term in nature. Borrowing short and lending long would lead to an asset-liability mismatch. More on this in the chapter on 'Risk Management'.
13. Based on the approach followed by Timothy W. Koch and S. Scott MacDonald in Bank Management, Chapter 15, pp. 617-623, 4th ed. The Dryden Press, USA.
14. Deposits that need to be maintained by the borrower as a condition for getting the bank loan.
15. First used by Lloyds Bank
16. First used by TSB Bank
17. First used by Barclays Bank and Natwest Bank
18. A 'negative lien' prohibits the customer from disposing of or dealing with a property or asset for which full payment has not been made.
19. This is called the 'right of set off' and is discussed in the chapter on 'Banks in India—Credit Delivery and Legal Aspects of Lending'.
20. A portion of the amount required will have to be brought in by the borrower as 'margin'. Generally, such margins are maintained as 'cash margins' or as investments in risk free, near cash securities. In case of liquidation or non payment, the cash margins are set off against the outstanding advance amount, to reduce the bank's exposure.
21. For a detailed discussion on 'incipient sickness,' refer to chapter on 'Credit Monitoring, Sickness and Rehabilitation'.
22. For a regulatory definition of 'non-performing' loans, see chapter 'Managing Credit Risk—An Overview'.
23. Trade credit is not entirely without cost. For example, a firm may have negotiated the following terms with its supplier: a 2 per cent discount if the purchase is paid for within 10 days, the total credit period not to exceed 30 days. The firm will have to calculate the implied cost of this arrangement and compare it with cost of bank or other funding sources, to arrive at a cost-effective working capital financing program.
24. Refer to Section V on 'Loan Pricing' for more on credit scoring of borrowers.
25. For a description of 'banker's lien' please refer the next chapter on 'Banks in India—Credit Delivery and Legal Aspects of Lending'.
26. For more discussion on 'asset-liability mismatch', please see the chapter on 'Risk Management in Banks'.
27. See *Annexure II* of this chapter for a definition of the DSCR.
28. Gadanecz, Blaise (2004). 'The Syndicated Loan Market: Structure, Development and Implications,' BIS Quarterly Review, December, pp. 75-89.
29. Ibid., p. 80
30. Esty, Benjamin C (2004). 'Why Study Large Projects? An Introduction to Research on Project Finance', European Financial Management, vol. 10, no. 2, pp. 213–224.
31. In this context, the word 'profit margin' implies the target net profit margin that the bank wants after meeting all operating and fixed costs.
32. 'Asset management' and 'liability management' concepts are explained in detail in the chapter on in the context of liquidity risk management.
33. London Inter Bank Offered Rate (LIBOR) represents the rate of interest at which banks could borrow funds from other banks, in marketable sizes, in the London interbank market. It is fixed daily by the British Bankers' Association.
34. Use of the term 'prime rate' here is not to be confused with the 'Prime rate' of the US markets. In this context, prime rate is the lowest rate the bank charges its first class borrowers, and can be taken as the benchmark rate where one does not exist. Such a prime rate can vary from bank to bank, while the prime of the US is market determined similar to LIBOR.
35. Uncollected or pipeline funds appearing as part of customer's deposit balances with the bank.
36. There is some debate over what this rate should be based on. According to one view, this rate should reflect the customer's opportunity cost of funds; according to another, the rate should be the average interest yield on earning assets.
37. Credit risk is the probability that a bank borrower or counter party will fail to meet its obligations in accordance with agreed terms, and is discussed in detail in the chapters on 'Credit Risk'.
38. Basel 2 regulations and their impact on the need for credit ratings are discussed in detail in chapters on 'Credit risk' and 'Capital—Risk, Regulation and Adequacy'.
39. Ministry of Finance, Capital Markets Division, Government of India, December 2009, Report of the committee on comprehensive regulation for credit rating agencies, www.sebi.gov.in, www.rbi.org.in, and the websites of the credit rating agencies mentioned in the Annexure.
40. *See* chapter on 'Banks' Financial Statements'.
41. *Ibid.*

CHAPTER SIX

Banks in India—Credit Delivery and Legal Aspects of Lending

CHAPTER STRUCTURE

KEY TAKEAWAYS FROM THE CHAPTER

- Know the types of borrowers in India.
- Learn about some types of credit that banks in India extend to borrowers.
- Learn about the forms in which the credit is given.
- Know the precautions banks should take while lending.
- Understand how the law helps the bank in enforcing securities.

SECTION I

MODES OF CREDIT DELIVERY

We have seen the basic principles and processes of the lending function in the previous chapter. The concepts discussed in the chapter have universal applicability. We will learn in this chapter how these concepts are applied by Indian banks.

Typical credit delivery modes used by Indian banks are summarized in Table 6.1.

The features of each of these credit delivery modes are designed to help the borrower carry on operations without interruption, simultaneously facilitating recovery of the debt for the lending bank. The terms and conditions, the rights and privileges of the bank and borrower differ in each case, as described below.

Annexure I provides an overview of the methods of lending prevalently used by Indian banks for various purpose-oriented loans.

TABLE 6.1 TYPICAL CREDIT DELIVERY MODES USED BY INDIAN BANKS

Purpose	Security	Mode of Credit Delivery
Working capital	Inventory	Cash credit, working capital demand loan (WCDL), overdraft, commercial paper, letters of credit (LCs)—inland and foreign.
	Book debts	Cash credit, WCDL.
	Receivables	Bills purchased/discounted—inland and foreign.
Capital expenditure	Capital assets	Term loan, consortium advance, multiple banking arrangement, loan syndication.
Consumer loans	Assets purchased under loan	Short-term loans, mortgage loans in case of housing.

Cash Credit

The cash credit system used to be the dominant mode of lending and the most preferred by borrowers. However, this mode of credit delivery is gradually being replaced by the short-term loan for reasons that will be discussed below.

Under the cash credit system, the bank specifies a credit limit for the borrower. The credit limit is backed by prime securities in the nature of inventories or book debts or receivables, and collaterals and guarantees, if the bank so insists.

The cash credit account is almost a mirror image of the 'current deposit account', and is operated in quite the same manner, except that the balances in the cash credit account are predominantly debit balances. The customer withdraws funds from the account for operating expenses, and deposits the cash inflows, primarily by way of sales. The bank generally stipulates that the account should be 'brought to credit' periodically, the periodicity of such credit depending on the cash-to-cash cycle. Hence, the sum of the credits in the account should practically reflect the 'sales' achievement of the firm for the period. This can be verified by the bank by periodically calling for the borrower's sales revenue data. The bank can also question the borrower when there is a substantial difference between the actual sales achievement of the borrower and the sum of 'credits' into the cash credit account. Such a discrepancy should be taken seriously by the lending bank since it could imply that the borrower is diverting bank funds either to long-term uses or for purposes other than those for which such funds were intended. Such practices could ultimately jeopardize the bank's chances of recovering the amount lent.

The bank also levies a 'commitment charge' on the unutilized portion of the cash credit limit. The magnitude of the commitment charge reflects the bank's opportunity cost of earmarking a portion of its liabilities for the loan assets created for the borrower.[1]

While the cash credit system provides great flexibility and operational convenience to borrowers, it leads to higher transaction costs for the bank, in the form of monitoring and opportunity costs. In the present competitive and profit-focused environment, the banks may find the system cumbersome and costly to operate.

Hence, to usher in discipline in the funds utilization of large borrowers and in still efficient funds management in banks, the loan system for delivery of bank credit was introduced in the mid 1990s. Though the new system is mandatory for borrowers enjoying working capital limits of over ₹10 crore from the banking system, the central bank encourages all borrowers to adopt the system. The system stipulates that the assessed working capital requirements of the borrower will be delivered as two components—a loan component, called the WCDL, constituting not less than 80 per cent of the assessed credit limit, with the ubiquitous cash credit component forming the remaining 20 per cent.

Loan System for Delivery of Bank Credit—The Working Capital Demand Loan

RBI Guidelines—Loan component and cash credit component*

Banks may change the composition of working capital finance by increasing the cash credit component beyond 20 per cent or increasing the loan component beyond 80 per cent, where warranted.

- Each component should be priced[2] appropriately, taking into account the impact of such decisions on banks' cash and liquidity management.
- A higher loan component can be granted by the bank within the overall assessed credit limits. Hence, a higher loan component would entail a corresponding reduction in the cash credit component of the total credit limit.
- Banks may persuade borrowers with working capital (fund-based) credit limit of less than ₹10 crore to adopt the loan system by offering an incentive in the form of lower rate of interest on the 'loan component' as compared to the 'cash credit component'. The actual percentage of 'loan component' in these cases may be mutually negotiated.

**Source*: RBI, 2012, Master Circular: Loans and Advances—Statutory and other restrictions, dated July 2, 2012. Page 41, point 2.3.16.

- In cyclical, seasonal or inherently volatile industries, strict application of the loan system may affect the borrowers. Hence, banks may exempt such borrowers from the loan system of credit delivery, with their Board of Directors' approval.

The repayment of these loans will be periodical, within the assessed period for which the credit limit has been granted. For example, the bank may want the WCDL repaid every quarter, with a replenishment of the limit for the next quarter, within the overall credit limit. The periodicity of the WCDL being 'brought to credit', like the cash credit, will be closely linked to the working capital cycle of the borrower.

Therefore, the WCDL is a more disciplined version of the cash credit system, with more advantages for the lending bank.

Overdrafts

Overdrafts are like cash credits because they are permitted as withdrawals over and above the borrower's credit balance in his current account. But overdrafts are unlike cash credits in that they are not purpose-oriented. The bank may grant an overdraft to satisfy urgent credit requirements of a borrower against a collateral security or personal guarantee.

The contract of an overdraft can be express or implied. In the case of an express contract for an overdraft, the customer approaches the bank with a request, which is appraised by the bank, the primary requisite being the track record of the borrower and his integrity. In some cases, when the overdraft is requested as a continuing facility, suitable collateral security is taken. The bank can also stipulate the number of times the account should be 'brought to credit' or minimum repayments into the account, during the period for which the overdraft is granted.

Since the credit is not purpose-oriented, and the securities may or may not be tangible, the risks are greater. Therefore, the interest rate on the overdraft account is normally fixed higher than that for other loan accounts.

An implied overdraft is created when the customer overdraws on the balance in his account, and the bank does not dishonour the payment. Can the bank charge interest on such overdrawn balances? Is the customer liable to repay, since there is no express contract between the bank and the customer? The Bombay High Court has decreed that an implied contract of overdraft arises when the customer overdraws on his account, and he is liable to compensate for the bank's outlay of funds with interest, as well as repay the amount overdrawn.[3]

Can an implied contract of overdraft be terminated by the bank without giving the customer reasonable notice? The Gujarat High Court has ruled that the bank cannot unilaterally terminate the contract, even if it is called a 'temporary overdraft'.[4]

Bills Finance

This is one of the very important modes of credit delivery. Typically 'bill financing' occurs when bills of exchange (BOE) (as defined in *Annexure I*) drawn by the borrower or by counter parties on the borrower, are discounted by the bank. On the basis of payment obligations on the part of the bank, the methods of bills finance can be classified into the following:

- Purchase of bills
- Discounting of bills
- Drawee bill acceptance
- Bills co-acceptance

In all these cases, the banker takes on an obligation, with the only difference that the first two are fund-based facilities and the remaining two are non-fund based.

The fund-based facilities—purchase of bills and discounting of bills arising out of sale of goods or services—score over cash credit and other types of working capital finance on the following counts:

- Bills ensure a definite payment date.
- The transactions underlying raising the bill can be easily identified and tracked.
- Bills are backed by legal provisions, leading to better control.
- Bills are negotiable instruments, *i.e.*, any person to whom the bill is transferred in accordance with the provisions of the Negotiable Instruments Act, would be entitled to receive the amount of the bill.

Bills purchased and discounted by banks fall under one of the following categories:

- Clean bills
- Documentary bills
- Supply bills

Clean Bills This is a bill of exchange not supported by any documents of title to goods,[5] since the seller has already delivered the goods and the documents to the buyer. Clean bills are also drawn to effect discharge of a debt or claim. Clean bills are treated like unsecured advances by banks, since their realization depends on the honesty and creditworthiness of the counter parties.

Documentary Bills A bill of exchange accompanied by documents of title to goods is a documentary bill. The goods have been despatched by the seller but the transfer of documents of title to goods has not yet taken place. Examples of documents of title to goods are lorry receipts, railway receipts, airway bills and bills of lading. Documentary bills are considered safer than other types of bills since they are backed by the security of documents of title to the goods, and they are either made in favour of the bank or endorsed in favour of the bank thus enabling the bank to liquidate the goods and realize its debt, in case the bill is not paid.

There are two types of documentary bills—documentary demand bills or documents against payment (D/P) and documentary usance bills or documents against acceptance (D/A).

D/P bills are similar to cash sales in that the buyer has to pay the bank before collecting the documents and taking delivery of the goods. In this type of transaction, the seller draws the bill on the buyer and sends the bill to his bank along with the documents of title to goods, instructing the bank to hand over the bill and documents only when the buyer pays for the goods.

D/A bills are similar to credit sales with a specified credit period or usance period. The usance bill is supported by documents of goods and bears the instruction to the bank that the documents can be delivered to the buyer if he 'accepts' the bill in writing. The bank finances the seller against the 'accepted' bill and holds the accepted bill till it is paid on the specified date. On the due date, the bill is presented for payment and the credit is adjusted.

It is easy to see why banks consider D/P bills safer than D/A bills. A usance bill turns into a 'clean' bill, since once the buyer accepts the bill, the documents are delivered and the buyer takes possession of the goods. Thereafter, the bank will have to depend solely on the 'acceptance' of the buyer, till the bill is paid. Hence banks should be cautious while purchasing or discounting bills on D/A basis.

Supply Bills These bills do not fall in the ambit of the Negotiable Instruments Act. They are in the nature of 'debts' and can be assigned in favour of the bank.

Supply bills are raised when the buyer is the government or a large corporation. In this case, the seller or supplier delivers the goods against a specified 'work order', and produces documents evidencing despatch of goods, such as a railway receipt or a bill of lading. These goods have to be inspected by the buyer, and once he is satisfied, an invoice is raised on the buyer. The supplier submits the invoice along with the buyer's certification of acceptance of the goods to the bank for financing, till the invoice is processed by the buyer and payment is received.

Banks take care to lend against supply bills only to borrowers who have a proven track record of supplies to the government or large corporations. The charge is only an 'assignment' (see the next section for definition of assignment) and, therefore, advances against supply bills are 'clean' advances—the bank may not realize the full amount of the bill due to a counterclaim or set off by the government.

Precautions to be Taken While Purchasing/Discounting Bills

- The facility should be granted only to creditworthy borrowers
- The bank being able to realize the amounts advanced against bills depends on the drawee's ability to pay. Hence, banks should obtain credit reports on the buyers before agreeing to purchase or discount bills drawn on them. The bank can choose not to advance against bills drawn on certain buyers or categories of buyers. The bank can also fix maximum amounts up to which it will purchase/discount bills drawn on specific buyers (called drawee-wise limits).
- The genuineness of the transactions should be verified before advancing against bills. A gist of the RBI guidelines issued in this respect is provided in Box 6.1.

BOX 6.1 RBI GUIDELINES ON DISCOUNTING/REDISCOUNTING[6] OF BILLS BY BANKS

The salient features of RBI's guidelines to banks while purchasing/discounting/negotiating/rediscounting of genuine commercial/trade bills are summarized below.

1. Sanction of credit limits for working capital and bills to borrowers should be done after proper appraisal of their credit needs and in accordance with the loan policy approved by their Board of Directors.
2. RBI recommends that banks clearly lay down a bills discounting policy approved by their Board of Directors, consistent with their policy of sanctioning of working capital limits. In this case, the procedure for Board approval should include banks' core operating process from the time the bills are tendered till these are realized. Banks should also

review their core operating processes and simplify the procedure in respect of bills financing, where feasible. RBI also urges banks to take advantage of improved computer/communication network like structured financial messaging system, wherever available, and adopt the system of 'value dating' of their clients' accounts to mimimize problems, such as late realization of bills.

3. Banks should open LCs and purchase/discount/negotiate bills under LCs only in respect of genuine commercial and trade transactions of their borrowers who have been sanctioned regular bank credit facilities. This effectively implies that banks should not extend fund-based (including bills financing) or non-fund based facilities like opening of LCs, providing guarantees and acceptances to non-constituent borrower or/and non-constituent member of a consortium/ multiple banking arrangement.
4. Bank Guarantee (BG) or Letter of Credit (LC) can be issued by scheduled commercial banks to clients of co-operative banks against counter guarantee of the co-operative bank, and subject to rules in force. It is also important that the co-operative bank requesting for these facilities demonstrates existence of sound credit appraisal and monitoring systems and a robust KYC process, which has been employed to assess the client.
5. However, irrespective of who has issued the LC, the bills arising out of the LC transaction would have to be discounted only by the bank with whom the exporter has credit facilities. This is to ensure that the bank sanctioning credit facilities to the exporter is not deprived of income and business growth.
6. While purchasing/discounting/negotiating bills under LCs or otherwise, banks should establish genuineness of underlying transactions/documents.
7. The practice of drawing BOE with 'without recourse' clause, and issuing LCs bearing the legend 'without recourse' should be discouraged because such notations deprive the negotiating bank of the right of recourse it has against the drawer under the Negotiable Instruments Act. Banks should not, therefore, open LCs and purchase/discount/negotiate bills bearing the 'without recourse' clause.
8. Accommodation bills—that is, bills not supported by genuine trade transactions—should not be purchased/discounted/negotiated by banks.
9. Banks should be careful while discounting bills drawn by front finance companies set up by large industrial groups on other group companies.
10. Bills rediscounts should be restricted to usance bills held by other banks. Banks should not rediscount bills earlier discounted by non-bank financial companies except in respect of bills arising from sale of light commercial vehicles and two/three wheelers.
11. Banks can discount bills of services sector, after ensuring that actual services are rendered and accommodation bills are not discounted. Services sector bills are not eligible for rediscounting. Further, providing finance against discounting of services sector bills should be treated as 'unsecured advance'.
12. RBI notes the need to promote 'payment discipline' in bills financing. One measure suggested is that all corporate and other constituent borrowers having turnover above threshold level as fixed by the bank's Board of Directors should be mandated to disclose 'aging schedule' of their overdue payables in their periodical returns submitted to banks.
13. Bills discounted/rediscounted cannot be used as collateral for repo transactions by banks.

Source: RBI, 2012, Master Circular: Loans and Advances—Statutory and other restrictions, dated July 1, 2013, pp. 36–39, point 2.3.11.

Advances Against Bills Sent on Collection

The bank advances against bills that are in the process of collection, after retaining a suitable margin. In all the above cases—purchase, discount and advances against collection of bills—the bank becomes 'holder in due course'[7] for the bills.

Drawee Bills In the earlier cases, the drawer of the bill, who is the seller, is financed by the bank. When the bank finances the buyer, the drawee, the buyer's bank itself discounts the bills and sends the amount to the seller. This has the effect of financing the purchases of the buyer. The buyer's bank grants an 'acceptance credit' to the buyer and accepts bills up to this limit. In short, drawee bills finance purchase of inputs and raw materials, while drawer bills (in the cases discussed above) finance receivables.

Annexure II outlines the broad guidelines to banks in India for reclassifying financial statement items for the purpose of credit appraisal.

Pricing of Loans

Banks in India are given the freedom to price loans with the objective of sustaining their profitability. However, for certain classes of borrowers, the interest rates will have to conform to the periodic RBI directives, the latest directive having been issued on July 1, 2013.[8]

The Base Rate system for computing minimum interest rate was introduced by the RBI from July 1, 2010. The basic premises supporting the base rate calculation is shown in Box. 6.2

BOX 6.2 HOW THE BASE RATE IS CALCULATED?

Base Rate = a + b + c + d, where

a. Cost of Deposits / Funds = D_{cost} (benchmark)

b. Negative Carry on CRR and SLR = $\left[\left[\frac{\{D_{cost} - (SLR * T_r)\}}{\{1-(CRR + SLR)\}}\right] * 100\right] - D_{cost}$

c. Unallocatable Overhead Cost = $\left(\frac{U_c}{D_{ply}}\right) * 100$

d. Average Return on Net Worth = $\left[\left(\frac{NP}{NW}\right) * \left(\frac{NW}{D_{ply}}\right)\right] * 100$

Where

D_{cost} = *Cost of Deposits/Funds*

D = Total Deposits = Time Deposits + Current Deposits + Saving Deposits

D_{ply} = *Deployable Deposits = Total Deposits less Share of Deposiis locked as CRR and SLR balances.*

*i.e., = D * [1 − (CRR + SLR)]*

CRR = Cash Reserve Ratio

SLR = Statutory Liquidity Ratio

T_r = *364 day T-Bill Rate*

U_c = *Unallocatable Overhead Cost*

NP = Net Profit

NW = Net Worth = Capital + Free Reserves

What is Negative Carry on CRR and SLR?

Negative carry on CRR and SLR balances arises because the return on CRR balances is nil, while the return on SLR balances (proxied using the 364-day Treasury Bill rate) is lower than the cost of deposits. Negative carry on CRR and SLR is arrived at in three steps. In the first step, return on SLR investment was calculated using 364-day Treasury Bills. In the second step, effective cost was calculated by taking the ratio (expressed as a percentage) of cost of deposits (adjusted for return on SLR investment) and deployable deposits (total deposits less the deposits locked as CRR and SLR balances). In the third step, negative carry cost on SLR and CRR was arrived at by taking the difference between the effective cost and the cost of deposits.

Unallocatable Overhead Cost: Calculated by taking the ratio (expressed as a percentage) of unallocated overhead cost and deployable deposits.

Average Return on Net Worth: The product of net profit to net worth ratio and net worth to deployable deposits ratio expressed as a percentage.

Comment on the base rate methodology: In chapter 5 we considered loan price as comprising of four factors, the aggregation of which would determine the interest rate to be charged to the borrower/the loan. These four factors were cost of funds, servicing costs, risk premium and required profit margin.

How does the base rate calculation take into account the above factors?

a. D cost amounts to the cost of funds
b. Negative carry on CRR and SLR is an adjustment to the cost of funds
c. Unallocatable overhead cost amounts to servicing cost
d. Average return on net worth represents the required profit margin.

What is missing in the formula therefore is the risk premium, which is unique to the borrower or the credit, for which there are various methodologies, as we will learn in subsequent chapters on credit risk.

Source: RBI Master Circular on interest rates on advances, dated July 1. 2013, Annexure I, pages 11, 12

Points to be noted about the base rate calculations, as given in the above quoted RBI circular are as follows:

1. Base rate shall include those elements of the lending rates that are common across all categories of borrowers (*i.e.*, cost of funds, servicing costs and required margin).

2. Banks may choose any benchmark (rate) to arrive at the base rate for a specific tenor. This benchmark rate has to disclosed.
3. Banks can use *any other methodology* considered appropriate, provided it is consistent and transparent.
4. The actual lending rates charged to the borrower will be with reference to the base rate, after the bank adds appropriate customer specific charges (*can be presumed as risk premium applicable to customer*). The actual lending rate should be consistent and transparent.
5. Each bank can have only ONE base rate. Any benchmark can be chosen by a bank to arrive at the single base rate, which should be disclosed.
6. Changes in base rate would be applied across all existing loans linked to the base rate.
7. Base rate will be the minimum lending rate for all loans, and banks cannot lend below the base rate.
8. The base rate should be reviewed at least once a quarter by the Asset Liability Management committee (ALCO-described in the chapter on 'Bank risk management').
9. The base rate and changes to the base rate should be displayed on banks' websites and at all bank branches. Minimum and maximum lending rates should be additionally conveyed to RBI every quarter.
10. Banks would continue to have the freedom to offer loans on fixed or floating rates. If the bank chooses to lend at fixed rates and the rate thus conveyed to the borrower falls below the base rate due to quarterly changes in base rate, it would not be construed as violation of RBI stipulations.
11. The base rate could also serve as the reference benchmark rate for floating rate loan products. External market benchmark rates, if chosen as the reference rate, should be equal to or above the base rate.
12. Penal interest can be charged in accordance with banks' internal policies for reasons such as repayment default, non-submission of financial statements, etc., on loans above ₹25000.
13. The loan agreement should incorporate a clause that enables banks to alter and charge applicable interest rates periodically, in conformity with RBI directives.
14. Interest will be charged at monthly rests (with effect from April, 2002).

SECTION II

LEGAL ASPECTS OF LENDING

We have seen in the earlier chapter on 'Banks' Financial Statements' that loans and advances can be classified by security arrangements into 'secured', 'covered by bank/government guarantees' and 'unsecured' loans.

What are Unsecured Loans?

If a loan is not backed by any tangible security, except the personal guarantee of the borrower himself or a third party, the loan is classified as 'unsecured'. In the event of borrower default, the bank will be ranked an unsecured creditor and gets no seniority in claiming against any property of the borrower. Hence, banks generally do not create unsecured loans unless the borrower is well established, has a track record of integrity and prompt repayments, and the bank has confidence in the borrower's future solvency, otherwise called 'creditworthiness'.

A notable exception is those loans covered by guarantees of the government or other banks. Balances under advances within India and granted abroad, covered by guarantees of Indian or foreign governments, or by agencies such as ECGC, are categorized under 'advances covered by bank/government guarantees' and are not considered unsecured.

What are Secured Loans?

A major portion of bank loans and advances fall under this category. Though a bank lends only to creditworthy borrowers, tangible securities are sought for the credit extended, over and above the assessed 'creditworthiness' of the borrower. This is to safeguard the bank's interest in the worst case scenario.

Secured loans are backed by tangible assets in the form of 'floating' or 'fixed' assets. Examples of floating assets are current assets, where the composition of the assets keeps changing over a specified period of time, the amount secured being constant. Examples of fixed assets are plant and machinery or land and buildings, whose composition cannot be altered in the short term without substantial investment. In some categories of advances, documents and commodities also form part of tangible securities.

As discussed earlier in this chapter, the securities can be 'prime' or 'collateral' in nature.

Securities and Their Features Can the banker accept any asset offered by the borrower as security for the advances made? Some basic safeguards observed while accepting assets as securities would help the bank recover most of its dues in the event of default.

Safeguard 1—Ensure adequate 'margin': For a bank, 'margin' signifies the difference between the market value of the security and the amount of advance granted against it. For example, if the bank has sanctioned ₹75 lakh as advance against a security worth ₹1 crore, the bank has a margin of ₹25 lakh (100 − 75 = ₹25 lakh). The rationale for adequate margin stems from the following factors:

- The market value of the security may fluctuate in future. If the market value falls, but the amount of advance remains the same, the bank's security cover may be eroded.
- The interest to be paid on the advances enlarges the dues to the bank over a period of time. Even if the borrower defaults on interest payments, the value of securities held should cover the total dues to the bank.
- The quantum of margin varies with types of securities and the customers who offer these securities. For example, the margin against an essential commodity with stable demand and prices would be different from the margin against a commodity whose prices and demand fluctuate widely. The margin against prime property offered as security would be less than the margin against company shares offered as securities. The margins stipulated for advances made to first class customers of the bank may be lower than for an advance made to a first generation entrepreneur's start up venture.

Safeguard 2—Easy marketability: In case of default, the security should have wide and ready marketability, to enable the bank sell off the security and realize its dues. For example, gold or jewels held as security are more liquid since they have wider marketability than, say, real estate.

Safeguard 3—Documentation: The bank's security interest is evidenced by legally valid documents that are executed by the borrower. These documents have to be periodically reviewed, especially in the case of securities for long-term loans or revolving credits, to ensure that the documents are kept enforceable and the legal limitation period for such agreements does not render the agreements invalid.

Some commonly accepted securities and their relative merits are discussed in *Annexure III*.

What is a 'Security'?

Though commonly used by bankers, 'security' is not defined in any act. The Provincial Insolvency Act defines a 'secured creditor' as one who holds a mortgage, lien or charge on the property of a debtor, as security for a debt due from the debtor. In banking parlance, securities accepted by banks fall into the following categories:

- Pledge
- Hypothecation
- Assignment
- Lien
- Mortgage

When the bank accepts different securities in respect of loans granted, the bank is said to have a 'charge' over the assets which constitute these securities.

We will now elaborate upon the various types of securities and their features.

Pledge: Section 172 of the Indian Contracts Act, 1872, defines 'pledge' as 'bailment of goods as security for payment of a debt or performance of a promise'. The bank (pledgee) enters into an explicit contract of pledge with the borrower (pledgor), under which the securities are delivered to the bank. Such delivery of possession can be actual or constructive. Thus, a pledge implies (a) bailment[9] of goods, and (b) that the objective of bailment is to hold goods as security for the payment of a debt or performance of a promise.

The primary advantage of pledge is that the goods are in the 'possession' of the bank thus preventing security dilution by the borrower. However, the bank would find holding goods of various borrowers under pledge a cumbersome exercise, since the bank, as the pledgee, has to take reasonable care of the goods and any loss has to be compensated to the borrower. This entails higher monitoring and inspection costs for the bank.

The disadvantages cited above, along with the risks associated with the nature of the goods under pledge,[10] have rendered this type of security unpopular.

Hypothecation: This is one of the most popular methods of creating security interest for banks, and is characteristic of the banking industry. Interestingly, 'hypothecation' is not governed by any identifiable Act in law. Simply defined, hypothecation is a legal transaction involving movable assets, amounting to an 'equitable charge' on the assets. The difficulties of holding the security in the bank's custody are removed in hypothecation, as the security interest is created without transferring the possession of assets to the bank. In hypothecation, the security remains in the possession of the borrower, and is charged in favour of the bank through documents executed by the borrower. The documents contain a clause that obligates the borrower to give possession of the goods to the bank on demand. Once possession over the goods is relinquished by the borrower, hypothecation becomes similar to pledge.[11]

How does hypothecation differ from 'pledge' and 'mortgage'? Box 6.3 explains in brief.

BOX 6.3 HYPOTHECATION DIFFERENTIATED

	Hypothecation	**Pledge**	**Mortgage**
Who holds the goods	Borrower[12]	With bank/constructive possession	With owner
Transfer of interest	Not done; bank has certain rights/charge over goods	To bank	To bank
Delivery of goods/property	Constructive	Actual	Constructive
Enforcement of security	With consent of borrower[13]	Bank can sell and recover dues	Through intervention of court
Types of goods	Existing and to be manufactured goods; present and future debts; immovable plant and machinery	Existing goods	Immovable property

Though the cumbersome procedures under pledge are eliminated by the process of hypothecation, the latter is more risky for the bank. Since the securities are in the borrower's possession, the borrower can fail to give possession to the bank on demand, or sell the securities without the bank's knowledge, or borrow from another bank on the strength of the same securities. In this respect, advances under hypothecation are as risky as unsecured or clean advances.

The bank will therefore have to take the following precautions:

- Credit limits with hypothecation should be sanctioned only after ascertaining the creditworthiness and integrity of the borrower.
- Only fully paid stocks will be hypothecated to the bank.[14]
- The bank has the unrestricted right of inspection of stocks and the related books of the borrower. Such inspection should be done periodically to ensure that the stocks under hypothecation provide adequate cushion for the advances. In the process, the bank should also eliminate slow moving and obsolete stocks while estimating security coverage.
- Stocks should be fully insured against fire and other risks as specified by the bank.
- The borrower should submit a statement of stocks at the periodicity specified by the bank, based on which the drawing power under the credit facility will be determined.
- The borrower should also declare in the above statement that the borrower has clear title to the stocks and that slow moving or obsolete stocks have been excluded.
- To prevent the borrower hypothecating the same stocks to another lender, the borrower should display in a prominent place in his premises/factory/godown the fact that the stocks are hypothecated to the credit-disbursing bank.
- If the borrower is a limited company incorporated under the Indian Companies Act, the hypothecation should be registered with the Registrar of Companies under Section 125 of the Companies Act, 1956, within 30 days of signing the documents. This aspect will be discussed in detail under the heading 'charge'.
- To enforce its claim, it is essential for the bank to take possession of the hypothecated property on its own or through the court. If the bank fails to take possession and seeks a simple money decree from the court, then the bank is presumed to have relinquished its right as hypothecatee.[15]

TEASE THE CONCEPT

If a vehicle hypothecated to a bank under vehicle loan is involved in an accident, and the passengers are injured, will the bank be liable for compensation to the victims?

An interesting point in this connection is the position of the 'guarantor' to the loan given by a bank to its borrower, who sells goods hypothecated to the bank without the bank's knowledge and does not repay the debt owed to the bank.

Under the above circumstances, the question is whether the guarantor is discharged from his liability since the goods were sold without the guarantor's consent (section 141 of the Contracts Act). Since the rights and obligations of a hypothecator and the hypothecatee are not defined precisely under a specific Act, courts have so far taken different and sometimes, opposing stances regarding the rights and obligations of various parties under hypothecation.[16]

Assignment: Borrowers 'assign' actionable claims to the bank. Section 130 of the Transfer of Property Act, 1882, permits an assignment to anyone except a judge, legal practitioner or an officer of the court of justice. Section 3 of the act defines actionable claim as 'a claim to any debt, other than a debt secured by mortgage of immovable property or by hypothecation or pledge of movable property, or to any beneficial interest in movable property not in the possession, either actual or constructive, of the claimant, which the civil courts recognize as affording ground for relief, whether such debt or beneficial interest be existing, accruing, conditional or contingent'.

What are the actionable claims a borrower can assign to a bank?

- Book debts
- Money due from government departments or semi-government organizations.
- Life insurance policies

Assignment takes two forms—(1) legal assignment; and (2) equitable assignment. A legal assignment, which is in writing by the assignor, constitutes an absolute transfer of the actionable claim. The assignor also informs his debtors of the assignee's interest, which is followed up by the assignee seeking confirmation from the debtors of the balances assigned. In the case of equitable assignment, the above conditions are absent.

The bank gets absolute right over the funds assigned to it. Once the borrower assigns his claims to the bank, other creditors of the borrower cannot get priority over the bank in the realization of their dues from the assigned debts.

TEASE THE CONCEPT

Life insurance policies carry nominations in favour of close relatives. If a life insurance policy is assigned to the bank as security for a debt, what is the legal position of the nominees?

Bankers' Lien: This is one of the most important rights of the lending bank. 'Lien' is the right of the bank to retain the securities given by the borrower until the debt due is fully repaid.

Lien is of two kinds—general lien and particular lien. Section 171 of the Indian Contracts Act, 1972, confers the right of general lien on the bank, stated as 'Bankers...may, in the absence of a contract to the contrary, retain as a security for a general balance of account, any goods bailed to them.' In the case of a particular lien, specific securities are earmarked for a specific debt. Once the debt is satisfied, the lien ceases to have effect. Example of a particular lien is that marked on a fixed deposit against which a loan has been taken. Once the loan is repaid, the fixed deposit becomes unencumbered.

The distinguishing features of the bankers' right of general lien are the following:

- The general lien can be exercised by the bank only on 'all the goods and securities entrusted to it in its capacity as 'banker' and in the absence of a contract inconsistent with the right of lien'. Circumstances under which the banker cannot exercise the right of general lien are one of the following:
  - The goods and securities have been entrusted to the banker as a 'trustee' or an 'agent' of the customer.
  - The goods and securities have been entrusted for a specific purpose.
- A banker's lien is tantamount to an 'implied pledge'. It confers upon the bank the right to sell the goods and securities in case the borrower defaults. Since this right resembles a pledge, the lien is called an 'implied pledge'. The bank can sell the securities to realize its dues after giving proper notice to the borrower.
- The right of lien is conferred by the Indian Contract Act, and therefore, tacitly understood by both banker and borrower. However, as a precaution, banks take a letter of lien from the borrowers acknowledging the right of lien over securities for existing as well as future loans.
- The right of lien extends to securities and goods belonging solely to the borrower and does not include securities owned jointly with others.

- If no contract to the contrary exists, the bank can exercise its lien over the securities remaining even after the loan, for which they were pledged, are repaid by the borrower. The bank can also exercise its general lien in respect of a customer's obligation as a guarantor, and retain the security offered by him for a loan granted on a personal basis, even after the loan has been fully repaid.

The following are the exceptions to the right of general lien:

- Goods entrusted for safe custody: A customer's documents, ornaments and other valuables deposited with the bank for safe custody or as trustee, is a contract inconsistent with the right of lien.
- Securities earmarked for a specific purpose: Customers may sometimes entrust the bank with shares or BOE, meant for a specific purpose, say, for sale or for honouring another liability, which contract is inconsistent with the right of lien.
- Sometimes, the banker's general lien may be replaced by a particular lien due to certain special circumstances. The right of the banker is interpreted by what is written by the banker in respect of the security rather than the printed word.
- The bank has no lien over securities left with the bank by oversight or negligence by the borrower.
- The bank cannot exercise right of lien over securities given to the bank as collateral for a loan, before such loan is actually granted or disbursed.
- The bank's right of lien extends only to securities and goods and not to money deposited with the bank, or the borrower's credit balances. In the latter case, the bank can exercise its right of 'set off'.

What is 'Right of Set Off'? The bank's right of set off enables it to adjust the credit balance (or deposit) in one account of a customer with the debit balance (or loan) in another account of the same customer. For example, if a customer has a term deposit of ₹2 lakh, and he owes ₹3 lakh to the bank, the bank can combine both the accounts, set off the deposit amount against the loan amount, and claim the remaining ₹1 lakh from the customer. The right of set off can be exercised under the following conditions:

- The accounts must be in the same name.
- The accounts must also be in the same right. This implies that the deposit funds are held by the customer in the same right or capacity in which he owes funds to the bank in the loan account. The underlying principle is that funds belonging to someone else, but standing in the name of the borrower, should not be used to satisfy the borrower's dues to the bank. For example, in the case of a proprietary firm, the accounts in the borrower's personal name and the firm's name are considered to be in the same right. In the case of a partnership firm, the firm's accounts and the personal accounts of the partners cannot be considered to be in the same right, except if the partners have specifically undertaken joint and several liabilities for the firm's debt with the bank.
- The right of set off can be exercised only in respect of debts already due for payment, and not for future debts or contingent debts.
- The exact amount of debt due should be ascertainable. For instance, if X stands guarantee for a loan due from Y to the bank, X's liability cannot be exactly determined till Y defaults. Therefore, till X's liability is determined, the bank cannot set off the credit balance in X's deposit account against the dues.
- The bank cannot exercise the right of set off if there is an express contract which is inconsistent with such a right.
- The bank can combine the accounts of the customer at various branches of the same bank at its discretion for exercising the right.
- In case of a garnishee order[17] against a customer, the bank can first exercise its right of set off and then surrender the remaining amount to the judgment creditor.

The bank has another right—the right of appropriation of payments received from the borrower, where the latter has taken more than one loan from the bank, or has more than one account with the same bank. This right is governed by Sections 59 to 61 of the Indian Contract Act, 1872, by which the bank can appropriate payments received to debts that have already fallen due for payment. Payments should first be appropriated towards interest and then towards principal repayments, unless there is a contract to the contrary. The rule derived from the famous Clayton's case[18] is of substantial practical application to banks. According to this landmark ruling, credits to loan accounts would adjust or set off debits in the chronological order. Further, in case of death, retirement or insolvency of a partner of a firm, the then existing debt of the firm is set off by subsequent credit inflows to the account. The bank thus loses its right to claim the debt from the assets of the outgoing partner, and may have to suffer a loss if the remaining debt cannot be recovered from other partners. Hence, to prevent the operation of the rule in Clayton's case, the bank closes the existing account of the firm, and reopens in the name of the reconstituted firm.

BOX 6.4 SOME CASE LAWS SUMMARIZED–BANKERS' LIEN AND SET OFF

In *Vijay Kumar vs M/s Jullundur Body Builders, Delhi and others [AIR 1981, Delhi 126]*, Syndicate Bank issued a bank guarantee on behalf of its customer. As security for the bank guarantee, the customer deposited two fixed deposit receipts, duly discharged, with a covering letter stating that the deposits can remain with the bank as long as any amount was due to it from the customer. However, the bank officer made an entry on the reverse of the deposit receipts, implying that the deposits served as security only during the validity period of the bank guarantee. When the bank guarantee was discharged, the bank claimed its right of general lien on the deposits. However, the Delhi High Court ruled that the bank had only particular lien since the officer's comments on the reverse of the deposit receipts were explicit and specific, while the covering letter from the customer was on a printed format.

However, the Supreme Court had a different view in the same case. In AIR 1992, SC 1066, the Supreme Court upheld the right of bankers' lien and right of set-off, holding that these are of mercantile custom and are judiciously recognized. It was held that 'The bank has general lien over all forms of securities or negotiable instruments deposited by or on behalf of the customer in the ordinary course of banking business and that the general lien is valuable right of the banker judicially recognized and in the absence of an agreement to the contrary, a Banker has a general lien over such securities or bills received from a customer in the ordinary course of banking business and has a right to use the proceeds in respect of any balance that may be due from the customer by way of a reduction of customer's debit balance. In case the bank gave a guarantee on the basis of the two FDRs it cannot be said that a banker had only a limited particular lien and not a general lien on the two FDRs. It was hence held that what is attached is the money in deposit amount. The banker as a garnishee, when an attachment notice is served has to go before the court and obtain suitable directions for safeguarding its interest'

In *Brahmayya vs. K P Thangavelu Nadar [AIR 1956, Madras 570]*, the Madras High Court has explained the rationale thus: 'When goods are deposited with or securities are placed in the custody of a bank, it would be correct to speak of rights of the bank over the securities or goods as lien, because the ownership of the goods or securities would continue to remain in the customer. But when moneys are deposited in a bank as fixed deposit, the ownership of the moneys passes to the bank and the right of the bank over the money lodged with it would not be really a lien at all. It would be more correct to speak of it as a right of set off or adjustment'

The court can interfere in the exercise of the Bank's Lien. *In Purewal and Associates and another vs. Punjab National Bank and others (AIR 1993, SC 954)* the debtor failed to pay dues to the bank which resulted in denial of bank's services to him. The Supreme Court of India ordered that the bank shall allow the operation of one current account which will be free from the incidence of the Banker's lien claimed by the bank so as to enable the debtor to carry on its day to day business transactions etc. and the liberty was given to bank to institute other proceedings for the recovery of its dues.

In City *Union Bank Ltd.vs.Thangarajan (2003)46 SCL 237 (Mad)*, certain principles with respect to Banker's lien were reiterated. The bank gets a general lien in respect of all securities of the customer including negotiable instruments and FDR s, but only to the extent to which the customer is liable. If the bank fails to return the balance, and the customer suffers a loss thereby, the bank will be liable to pay damages to the customer. In the quoted case the Court based its decision on the principle that in order to invoke a lien by the bank, there should exist mutuality between the bank and the customer *i.e.*, when they mutually exist between the same parties and between them in the same capacity. Retaining the customer's properties beyond his liability is unauthorized and would attract liability to the bank for damages.

Banker's Lien is not available against Term Deposit Receipt in Joint Names when the debt is due only from one of the depositors In *State Bank of India vs. Javed Akhtar Hussain and others, AIR 1993, Bom.87,* the bank obtained a decree against applicant and non-applicant who stood as a surety to the non-applicant No.1. After a decree was passed, the non-applicant No. 2 deposited a sum of ₹32,793 in TDR No. 856671 with the appellants in joint names of himself and his wife in another branch of the same bank. They were also having RD account. The applicant bank retained lien on both these accounts without exhausting any remedy against non-applicant No.1. The Court held that the action of keeping lien was a sort of *suomuto act* exercised by the Bank even without giving notice to the non-applicant No. 2 and his wife. The applicant could have moved the court for passing orders in respect of the amounts invested in TDR and RD accounts. However, it was ruled that the action of the bank in keeping lien over both these accounts was unilateral and high-handed.

A banker's right of set off cannot be exercised after the money in his hands has been validly assigned or in any case after he has been notified of the fact of an assignment.(*Official Liquidator, Hanuman Bank Ltd. vs. K.P.T. Nadar and Others 26 Comp.Cas. 81*)

In Punjab National Bank vs. Arunamal Durgadas, AIR 1960 Punj.632 State Bank of India vs. Javed Akhtar Hussain, AIR 1993 Bombay, 87, certain essentials to exercising the right of set off were indicated. It was established that: (1) Mutuality is essential to the validity of a right of exercising set-off (2) It must be between the same periods.

Source: Supreme court website www.supremecourtofindia.nic.in, and www.legalserviceindia.com

Mortgage: Section 58 of the Transfer of Property Act, 1882, defines a mortgage as 'the transfer of interest in specific immovable property for the purpose of securing the payment of money advanced or to be advanced by way of loan, on existing or future debt or the performance of an engagement, which may give rise to a pecuniary liability'.

The transferor of the property is the 'mortgagor'. The entity to whom the transfer takes place is the 'mortgagee'. The document through which mortgage takes effect is the 'mortgage deed'.

From the definition, it follows that there are two important ingredients to a mortgage—(a) the transfer of interest in the mortgaged asset, and (b) the transfer is to create a security for the amount paid or to be paid by the bank as loan.

The following points about mortgage are to be noted:

- Transfer of 'interest' differs from 'sale' where there is a transfer of ownership. Transfer of interest implies that only some rights of the owner are transferred, and some are retained with the owner. For example, the right of redemption of mortgaged property is retained with the owner. Once the amount due to the bank (principal and interest) is repaid, the interest in the property is restored to the owner. Similarly, the bank, as the mortgagee, does not become the absolute owner due to the transfer of interest, but only has the right to recover its dues from selling the mortgaged property.
- Every co-owner or joint owner of the property is entitled to mortgage his share of the property.
- The mortgaged property should be specific, and identified by features such as location, size, boundaries and distinguishing features.
- Transfer of property in discharge of a debt is not a mortgage. Transfer of interest in the property should be to secure an existing or future loan, or to ensure the performance of an obligation which results in monetary obligation.
- It is not necessary that the actual possession of the property be transferred to the bank.

The Transfer of Property Act recognizes six types of mortgages. They are as follows:

- *Simple mortgage [Section 58(b)]*. In this type of mortgage, the bank is not in possession of the property, but registration is mandatory irrespective of the amount of loan for which the property is the security. Further, the bank is not entitled to any income out of rents or profits of the mortgaged property, and the bank cannot sell the property for recovering its dues without the permission of the court.
- *Mortgage by way of conditional sale [Section 58(c)]*. Banks do not prefer this type of mortgage since there is no personal covenant for debt service, and the bank cannot look to other assets of the mortgagor if there is a shortfall in security coverage. Under this transaction, there is an 'ostensible' (not real) sale of the mortgaged property to the bank. If the debt is not repaid on due date, the bank can approach the court for foreclosure, which implies causing the borrower to lose his right of redemption of the property.
- *Usufructuary mortgage [Section 58(d)]*. Banks do not prefer this mode of mortgage, because, as in the earlier case, there is no personal covenant on the borrower for debt service. However, the bank is in 'legal possession' of the property, by which it can receive rent and profits from the property and appropriate them to the debt payable by the borrower. If the borrower fails to redeem the property within 30 years through the court, the bank becomes the absolute owner.
- *English mortgage [Section 58(e)]*. There is an absolute transfer of property to the bank, with the provision that full repayment of the debt will entitle the borrower to redeem the property. In case of security shortfall, the bank can look to the personal assets of the borrower for full liquidation of its dues.
- *Equitable mortgage or mortgage by deposit of title deeds [Section 58(f)]*. This is by far the most preferred type of mortgage by banks in India. Though this mortgage can be effected only in the towns notified by the government, the territorial restriction is applicable not to the location of the property, but where the title deeds are delivered by the borrower to the bank. 'Title deeds' are documents or instruments that enable the owner of the property to enjoy the right to peaceful and absolute possession of the property described in the documents. To create this mortgage, the owner or joint owners of the property should personally deposit the original title deeds with the bank at the notified centres, with the intention of creating a security for the loan taken from the bank. There are no registration or stamp charges involved in many Indian states and creation of the mortgage is least time consuming. The risks for the bank could arise in respect of the authenticity of the documents and the borrower's standing in respect of the property. For example, if the borrower mortgages the property for which he holds the original title deeds as trustee, the claim of the beneficiary under trust will prevail over any equitable mortgage. The bank should also conduct a physical inspection of the property and verify the authenticity of factors like the boundaries and market value before accepting the security.

Box 6.5 summarizes some Supreme Court decisions in respect of equitable mortgages.

BOX 6.5 EQUITABLE MORTGAGE: WHAT THE SUPREME COURT DECIDED

There are three important requirements for an equitable mortgage: (a) debt, (b) deposit of title deeds of the property and (c) the intention that the title deeds will be the security for the debt.

In *K J Nathan vs. S V Maruthi Rao (ATR 1965, SC 430)*, it was opined that, 'Whether there is an intention that the deeds shall be security for the debt is a question of fact in each case... there is no presumption of law that the mere depositing title deeds constitutes a mortgage, for no such presumption has been laid down, either in the Evidence Act or in the Transfer of Property Act'...

In *United Bank of India vs. Lekheram sonaram and comp.(AIR 1965, SC 1591)*, it was stated that 'But if the parties choose to reduce the contract to writing (with all terms and conditions) such document requires registration under Section 17 of Indian Registration Act 1908. If a document of this character is not registered it cannot be used in evidence at all and the transaction itself cannot be proved by oral evidence either'.

Further, in *Deb Dutt Seal vs. Raman Lal Phumsa (AIR 1970, SC 659)*, the Supreme court ruled... When the debtor deposits with the creditor, title deeds of his property with interest to create a security, the law implies a contract between the parties to create a mortgage and no registered instrument is required under Section 59 as in other classes of mortgage.

Source: Supreme Court's web site.

- *Anomalous mortgage [Section 58(g)]*. A mortgage that does not fall into any of the categories discussed above is an anomalous mortgage. Such mortgages can also be combinations of two types of mortgages, such as a combination of simple and usufructuary mortgages, depending on the custom and local usage.

Charge: This is a word that can commonly be used to describe any form of security for debt, whether the borrower is an individual, partnership firm, private or public limited company or the government.

More specifically, charges registered, under the Companies Act, 1956 include rigorous provisions, and can generally be classified into a 'fixed charge' and a 'floating charge'.

A 'fixed charge' (not to be confused with 'fixed assets') is a specific charge over designated properties of the company. It gives the bank the right to sell the assets and appropriate the sale value to the debt due from the company.

A 'floating charge' (a) 'floats' over the present and future property of the company (including those under fixed charge) and is not attached to any specific asset or assets; (b) does not restrict the company from selling the assets under charge or assigning them as security for loans from other parties; and (c) could crystallize into a fixed charge upon the happening of an event or contingency, such as liquidation of the company. It is important to note that when the floating charge becomes fixed, it constitutes a charge on all properties and assets belonging to the company, and gains seniority over all subsequent fixed charges, unsecured creditors and money advanced to the liquidator.

It is, therefore, evident that, in order for the bank to be the senior creditor, it will have to ensure seniority in claims over the bank's assets as well. This purpose is achieved by registering the bank's charge with the Registrar of Companies under Section 125 of the Companies Act, 1956. Such registration of charge will have to be done within 30 days of execution of the loan agreement, and can be extended up to 60 days with a penal provision.

What are the consequences of non-registration of charge by the bank? In the event of the company going into liquidation, the bank's debt, otherwise ranked senior to all other creditors' claims, will now be treated as unsecured, and will rank low as an unsecured creditor at the time of settlement of claims. It is to be noted that in spite of non-registration of charge, the bank's debt is recoverable and the securities are enforceable, as long as the company is a going concern. The bank gets ranked as an unsecured creditor only in case of company liquidation. A more serious consequence would be when a junior creditor moves up to senior position at the time of enforcement of securities, merely by virtue of having filed its charge with the registrar of companies before the senior creditor did. This is in accordance with the provisions contained in Section 126, which clarifies that notice of charge registered by the bank under Section 125 will be reckoned from the date of registration and not from the date of creation of the charge. It is also mandatory that every time there is a change in the loan agreement, a modification charge is filed with the registrar of companies within 30 days of such modification taking effect.

The bank should also verify prior fixed and floating charges on the assets charged to it by the borrowing company before specifying the security backing in its loan agreement. For example, if the borrowing company had made a debenture issue, secured by floating charge on all the company's assets, with a specific clause prohibiting creation of any charge senior to ranking on par with debenture holders, then the bank cannot gain a senior creditor position in spite of registering its charge on time. If the bank still finds lending to this company profitable, it should stipulate suitable covenants that would compensate for a likely shortfall in security backing for its advances to the company.

Box 6.6 presents an illustrative checklist of the precautions bankers should take while lending to a company.

A detailed description of the provisions of law relating to registration of charges can be found in Sections 124 to 145 of the Companies Act, 1956.

BOX 6.6 ILLUSTRATIVE CHECKLIST FOR BANKS LENDING TO COMPANIES

1. A company is a legal entity. Check the Certificate of Incorporation. When and where was the company incorporated? Where is the Registered Office? This is important since all communication to the company should be addressed to the registered office.
2. Ask for the Certificate to commence business. Any contract entered into by the company before this date will not be binding on the company, nor can the company exercise its borrowing powers before this date.
3. What are the objects of the company's incorporation as embodied in its Memorandum of Association? Is the present line of business in keeping with the objects?
4. Scrutinize the Memorandum of Association. The capital clause indicates how much equity the company can mobilize either from its promoters or the public. Are the capital projections of the company in keeping with the boundaries set down in this clause?
5. Are the company's lines of business as defined in the Memorandum? If there are deviations, have the necessary changes been made in the Memorandum in the manner prescribed by Company Law? Any attempted departure from the clauses will be 'ultra vires', even if assented to by all board members. The object clause of the Memorandum usually contains a blanket clause—'and to do all such other things as are incidental or conducive or as the company may think conducive to the attainment of the above objects'. Companies tend to construe these words as widening the scope of the object clause. For example, offering guarantee for the loans availed by another company under the plea that such an act would widen the scope of achieving the main objects of the company, would not be expressly permitted by the Memorandum. If the bank overlooks these lapses, it could run a risk of loss in case of default.
6. What is the composition of the Board? Are there sufficient independent directors? How are decisions made?
7. Scrutinize the Articles of Association. Are the directors acting within their powers? Do they have the capacity to borrow from the bank?
8. What is the limit up to which the company can borrow? This is different from the borrowing powers of directors. While borrowing powers of directors can be amended by suitable resolutions, the borrowing power of the company would be embedded in the Articles of Association, and cannot be violated.
9. Refer to the Articles of Association to ensure that the officials executing loan documents are indeed authorized to do so.
10. Ask for copies of all relevant resolutions passed at general body meetings—such as for borrowing, mortgaging property, etc.
11. Ensure creation/modification of charge on the property of the company as prescribed by the Companies Act. Note that a registered charge takes priority over an unregistered charge, registered charges take priority from date of creation (though constructive notice arises from date of registration), and a registered floating charge with no restrictive clause ranks after a subsequent (or prior) specific registered charge.
12. If a company is named as guarantor for a loan, scrutinize the Memorandum and Articles of Association to ascertain whether the company is authorized to give such guarantees.

CHAPTER SUMMARY

- The features of each of the credit delivery modes in India are designed to help the borrower carry on operations without interruption, simultaneously facilitating recovery of the debt for the lending bank. The terms and conditions, the rights and privileges of the bank and borrower differ in each case.
- Under the cash credit system, the bank specifies a credit limit for the borrower. The credit limit is backed by prime, securities in the nature of inventories or book debts or receivables, and collaterals and guarantees, if the bank so insists. To usher in discipline in the funds utilization of large borrowers, and instil efficient funds management in banks, the loan system for delivery of bank credit had been introduced in the mid 1990s. The system stipulates that the assessed working capital requirements of the borrower will be delivered as two components—a loan component, called the WCDL, constituting not less than 80 per cent of the assessed credit limit, with the cash credit component forming the remaining 20 per cent.
- The bank may grant an overdraft to satisfy urgent credit requirements of a borrower against a collateral security or personal guarantee. The contract of an overdraft can be express or implied.

- Bill financing' occurs when BOE drawn by the borrower or by counter parties on the borrower are discounted by the bank. Bills purchased and discounted by banks are in the form of clean bills, documentary bills or supply bills.
- If a loan is not backed by any tangible security; except the personal guarantee of the borrower himself or a third party, the loan is classified as 'unsecured'. Secured loans are backed by tangible assets in the form of 'floating' or 'fixed' assets. Observing some basic safeguards, such as (a) ensuring adequate margin; (b) ensuring easy marketability and (c) proper documentation while accepting assets as securities would help the bank recover most of its dues in the event of default
- Though commonly used by bankers, 'security' is not defined in any act. Securities accepted by banks fall into the categories of (a) pledge, (b) hypothecation, (c) assignment, (d) lien, (e) mortgage, and (f) charge.

TEST YOUR UNDERSTANDING

1. Which of the following statements are true?
   a. Documents of title to goods are negotiable instruments.
   b. Supply bills are BOE
   c. A bill of exchange is an unconditional direction to the drawer to pay a certain amount.
   d. Bills purchase facility is granted by the bank in the case of DP bills.
   e. Endorsement means signing the bill of exchange for transfer.
   f. Documentary bill means a bill accompanied by documents of title to goods.
2. Which of the following statements are false?
   a. Simple mortgage is created by an instrument in writing.
   b. Mortgage by deposit of title deeds is always required to be registered.
   c. All successive mortgages created over a property will rank equally at the time of liquidation.
   d. The owner of the goods cannot pledge the goods
   e. Hypothecation is an implied pledge in cases where constructive possession of goods is given.
   f. 'Charge' is any form of security for debt.
3. Can you list the differences between 'charge' and 'mortgage'?
4. J Industries Ltd wants to fund its new capital acquisition and working capital through bank finance. The cost of the expansion plan is given below:
   a. Plant and machinery: ₹500 lakh
   b. Building and site development: ₹75 lakh
   c. Other expenditure: ₹25 lakh

   The company requires current assets of ₹620 lakh during this period, the split up for which is as follows:

   Inventory: ₹300 lakh
   Receivables: ₹180 lakh
   Cash and others: ₹140 lakh

   Fill in the following table to assess the structure of working capital finance, if current liabilities amount to ₹70 lakh and the bill finance required is ₹40 lakh. Assume the bank wants a margin of 25 per cent for all the modes of financing it extends to the borrower.

Margin on capital expenditure will be @ 25 per cent on long-term assets.

(A) Long-term assets will include only specific immoveable property being considered for expansion =

(B) Margin = 0.25 × (A) =

(C) Bank finance for capital expenditure = (A) − (B) =

(D) Permissible bank finance (PBF) for working capital = 0.75 × (current assets − current liabilities) =

(E) Margin for working capital = ₹620 less (D)

Structuring limits

(F) WCDL = 0.8 × (D)

(G) CC = 0.2 × (D) = amount of CC available for inventory

(H) Balance of inventory to be financed = inventory − (G) =

(I) Amount of WCDL used for bills financing = ₹40 lakh

(J) Hence, WCDL available for funding remaining inventory and other debtors = (F) − (I) =

TOPICS FOR FURTHER DISCUSSION

- Take up the financial statements of any Indian company and try to do a credit appraisal, placing yourself in the shoes of the credit officer assessing the company's financial health and other factors. Under what conditions would you sanction credit limits to the company? (Tip: Do an analysis of risk factors).
- What would be the special covenants you would incorporate while lending to SMEs in India?

SELECT REFERENCES

1. Indian Institute of Banking and Finance, 2005, *Legal Aspects of Banking Operations*, chapters, 12–19, Macmillan India Ltd, 197–285. (N. Delhi)
2. RBI, 2009, *Master Circular: Loans and Advances—Statutory and other Restrictions*, dated 1 July 2009.
3. RBI, 2009, *Master Circular—Interest Rates on Advances*, dated 1 July 2009.
4. Supreme Court of India Web site—http://supremecourtofindia.nic.in
5. Varshney, P R, 2004, *Banking Law and Practice*, Chapters 15–18, Sultan Chand & Sons, 4.18–4.129. (N. Delhi).

ANNEXURE I

TYPES OF BORROWERS AND MODES OF LENDING

Who Can Borrow from Banks?

Typically, there are six types of borrowers to whom banks can lend. They are as follows:

- *Individuals*. Any individual who is competent to enter into a contract.[19]
- *Partnership firms*. These are firms governed by the Indian Partnership Act, 1932. The most relevant clause for banks is Section 19 of the act, which deals with the implied authority of a partner as an agent of the firm, and also states that a partner cannot mortgage the firm's property unless expressly authorized to do so.
- *Hindu Undivided Family (HUF)*. This is a law created by custom and has to be interpreted according to two prevalent schools of thought—the Dayabhag and Mitakshara. Succession among Hindus is governed by the Hindu Succession Act, 1956. The bank should ensure that the 'Karta' of a HUF borrows only for the joint family's benefit. Similarly, all adult members are jointly and severally liable for borrowings.
- *Companies*. These are to be registered under Section 11 of the Companies Act, 1956. The bank has to verify that the 'Memorandum of Association' of the company permits it to carry on the business for which credit limits are sought. Similarly, the borrowing powers of the company are determined by the articles of association.
- *Statutory corporations*. These are governed by the acts under which they were established.
- *Trusts and co-operative societies*. Trusts are governed by the Indian Trusts Act, 1882, and the bank should ensure that the credit is within the legal framework. Clubs, societies and co-operative societies have to be registered under the Companies Act, 1956, the Societies Registration Act or the Co-operative Societies Act. The bank should examine the by-laws and other applicable regulations to determine the eligibility of these organizations to seek bank credit.

In this section, we will look at the methodologies adopted by Indian banks to assess the various types of credit requirements of borrowers. Recognizing the need for banks to be competitive, both in the domestic and international markets, the RBI has now given banks the autonomy to evolve their own internal methods for appraisal and assessment of credit requirements. While credit appraisal closely follows the framework presented in the previous chapter, the methods of lending have been customized for various categories of borrowers, depending on the purpose, their contribution to the economy and their developmental needs.

Banks in India have traditionally been lenders for working capital needs of borrowers, with the financial institutions having been slated for the role of term lenders. The composition of liabilities and assets of banks and financial institutions, as two different categories of financial intermediaries, also varied to suit the purpose for which they were formed. The financial sector reforms and progressive privatization, consolidation and globalization of the banking sector have now led to the blurring of the distinction between banks and financial institutions. In the present context, Indian banks have almost taken over the functions of the financial institutions, and have also made a foray into financial services in a big way.

Banks are now are expected to lay down, through their Boards, transparent policies and guidelines for credit dispensation, in respect of each broad category of economic activity, keeping in view the credit exposure norms and various other guidelines issued by the RBI from time to time. Some of the currently applicable guidelines and practices are detailed in the following paragraphs.

Working Capital Finance

Banks generally use one of the following methods to assess the working capital financing requirements of borrowers.

Projected Turnover Method This method is generally used for assessing working capital finance requirements in case of borrowers whose fund-based working capital requirements are less than ₹2 crore. According to this method, the working capital requirement would be assessed at 25 per cent of the projected turnover to be shared between the borrower and the bank, *i.e.*, borrower contributing 5 per cent of the turnover as net working capital (NWC) and bank providing finance at a minimum of 20 per cent of the turnover. Alternatively, the banks may use the traditional method of assessment, using the working capital or cash-to-cash cycle to determine credit requirements. If the credit requirement based on traditional processing cycle is higher than that assessed on projected turnover, the bank may, at its discretion, sanction the former as the credit limit, as the borrower can be financed up to a minimum of 20 per cent of the projected annual turnover of the firm.

The simplicity of the procedure is intended to speed up credit sanctions for small and needy borrowers and does not amount to dilution of the assessment of the borrower's creditworthiness. Credit appraisal has to be carried out on the lines discussed in the previous chapter. It is also important to verify how reasonable the borrower's projections are. Hence, the bank should call for annual statements of accounts and other documents, such as returns filed with sales-tax/revenue authorities, and ensure that the estimated growth during the year is realistic.

Illustration 6.1 will clarify the computation.

ILLUSTRATION 6.1

Borrower: ABC Limited	(₹ in Lakh)
1. Projected turnover for the coming year	60.00
2. Gross working capital [assessed at 25 per cent of (1)] less	15.00
3. Borrower's margin (a minimum of 5 per cent of (1) or projected NWC, whichever is higher) (Assume 5 per cent)	3.00
4. PBF (2) − (3)	12.00

Case 1

In case the borrower has projected an NWC (current assets less current liabilities) of say, 7 lakh, the PBF will reduce to ₹8 lakh.

Case 2

In case the borrower's operating cycle is such that the actual working capital requirement would be ₹20 lakh, and the bank is convinced that this is an accurate reflection of the borrower's operations, the PBF can be increased, after deducting the requisite margin.

The borrower can be permitted to draw against the credit limits after instituting the usual safeguards to ensure that the bank finance will be used for the purpose intended. Banks will have to ensure regular and timely submission of monthly statements of stocks, receivables, etc., by the borrowers and also periodical verification by credit officers of these statements with physical stocks.

The Permissible Bank Finance Method This method is generally applied by banks to working capital limits of over ₹2 crore.

The earlier prescription regarding maximum permissible bank finance (MPBF), based on a minimum current ratio of 1.33:1, recommended by the Tandon Working Group has been withdrawn. Banks are now free to decide on the minimum current ratio and determine the working capital requirements according to their perception of the borrowers and their credit needs. Banks may adopt any of the following methods:

- The turnover method, as prevalent for small borrowers may be used as a tool of assessment for this segment as well.
- Banks may use the cash flow projections now increasingly adopted by major corporate borrowers.
- Bank may even retain the concept of the MPBF with necessary modifications.

The basic framework for arriving at the PBF will be on the lines shown below (Table 6.2).

Some ratios generally calculated to assess the reasonableness of the projections and the borrowers' capacity to repay.

- NWC/TCA
- Bank borrowings/TCA
- Sundry creditors/TCA
- Other current liabilities/TCA
- Inventories/sales (no. of days)
- Receivables to sales (no. of days)
- Trade creditors/purchases (no. of days)

Cash Budget Method This method is prevalently applied to borrowers with fund-based limits of over ₹10 crore from the banking system. Optional to all borrowers in industry, trade and service sectors, this method is preferred by borrowers in the construction industry and other seasonal industries.

TABLE 6.2 THE BASIC FRAMEWORK FOR ARRIVING AT THE PERMISSIBLE BANK FINANCE

Description	Previous Year	Current Year (estimated)	Next Year (projected)	Remarks
Total current assets (TCA)				Are the current assets marketable? Have the slow moving, obsolete stocks been eliminated? Have margins deposited for non-funded facilities such as LCs and bank guarantees been included in current assets? Has the non-current portion[20] of investments been removed from the current assets? Have the ageing receivables[21] been deducted? Have receivables under LCs been excluded from current asset?[22] Have the projections been done based on reasonable, realistic assumptions?

(Continued)

TABLE 6.2 (CONTINUED)

Description	Previous Year	Current Year (estimated)	Next Year (projected)	Remarks
Current liabilities (other than bank finance for working capital) (CL)				Have the spontaneous CL such as trade creditors and expenses payable, been projected with reasonable assumptions into the future? If there are major changes in these policies, have they been probed and the reasonableness of the projections established? Have ICDs and other short-term borrowings from 'others' been included under current liabilities? Have term loan installments due for payment in the next 12 months been excluded from current liabilities?
Working capital gap (WCG) (TCA − CL)				This is the actual funding gap for the firm.
NWC				Two computations of NWC should be compared: (1) 25 per cent (or any suitable margin stipulated by the bank) of the WCG, and (2) the NWC projected by the borrower in the financial statements as TCA − total CL (including bank borrowings). The higher of the above two figures will form the NWC for computing the PBF.
PBF				WCG − NWC (higher of (1) and (2), above).

Under this method, the amount of working capital finance is determined from the projected monthly cash flows, and not from the projected levels of assets and liabilities. The permissible bank finance will be restricted to the peak level gap between cash inflows and outflows in the cash flow projections. This method is preferred in cases where cash flows would fluctuate within a short time frame, and an 'averaging' of production and sales parameters (as in the case of PBF method) may lead to anomalies in the requirements and utilization of bank finance.

The cash flow budgets, after scrutiny by the credit officer, may be presented in the following manner to arrive at the funding gap as shown in Table 6.3.

TABLE 6.3 THE CASH BUDGET

No.	Description
1.	Total cash outflows from operations
2.	Total cash inflows to operations
3.	Cash gap in operations
4.	LESS: Cash to be brought in from other sources—for example, cash surplus under non-business operations/capital accounts/sundry items
5.	Net CASH GAP from operations (3−4)

The maximum bank finance for working capital requirements would be the peak 'gap' of the four quarters. Funds may be drawn by the borrower in accordance with the monthly or quarterly cash deficit in the projected cash flow statement, after reporting the actual cash flows during the preceding period. In case of a likely significant change in cash flows, the borrower will have to submit a revised cash flow budget for that period. However, borrowings will be capped by the assessed 'gap', though flexibility within this ceiling is permitted.

Fixing the Working Capital Credit Limit

Once the quantum of eligible bank finance is determined by any of the above methods, the bank will have to fix the amount of credit that it will extend to the borrower. How does the bank arrive at the credit limit appropriate to specific portions of the working capital cycle? Some illustrative situations are presented as following.

Situation 1: The borrower seeks working capital finance against raw material inventory, which needs to be stocked for 2 months. The value of this inventory is assumed at ₹1 crore. The borrower gets market credit for the inventory, creditors for which at any point in time show a balance of ₹25 lakh. The limit is structured as a percentage of the fully paid inventory that the borrower holds in one working capital cycle at any point of time.

The eligible bank finance against raw material inventory can, therefore, be only ₹75 lakh (to avoid double financing). Of this amount, the borrower is expected to bring in a margin of 20 per cent, or ₹15 lakh. Hence, assuming that the projected NWC of the borrower is not higher than ₹15 lakh, the bank will finance up to a credit limit of ₹60 lakh.

Situation 2: The borrower seeks working capital finance against inventory and receivables in the form of book debts. Let us assume that the borrower in Situation 1 has work in progress (WIP) and finished goods inventories of ₹2 crore and book debts amounting to ₹50 lakh outstanding at any point of time. After ascertaining that these inventories and book debts are current, marketable and realizable, the bank fixes appropriate margins of, say, 25 per cent for inventories and 50 per cent for book debts. Accordingly, against inventories of ₹3 crore (inclusive of raw material), the bank would fix a credit limit of 75 per cent amounting to ₹2.25 crore, and against book debts of ₹50 lakh the borrower would be eligible for ₹25 lakh as credit limit. Thus the bank would finance up to ₹2.75 crore of working capital.

Financing Receivables

Receivables can be in the form of book debts or 'bills'. Book debts are generally included as part of the assessed overall credit limits. However, bills are considered 'self liquidating' instruments and are financed separately.

BOE are 'negotiable instruments',[23] which arise out of commercial transactions both in inland and foreign trade. They are instruments in writing, containing an unconditional order signed by the maker (seller) directing a person (buyer) to pay certain amount only to certain person (bank).

When the creditor or seller of the goods draws a Bill on the debtor or the buyer, he has two options to realize the revenue from the sale—(a) he could send the bill for collection through the seller's bank, or (b) he could sell it or discount it with the bank, which has sanctioned him credit limits against such transactions. The bank can, therefore, easily assess the credit requirements of the borrower against goods or services sold by him against such BOE. The bank may sometimes agree to purchase or discount bills drawn on specified counter parties alone.

Financing Capital and Non-Operating Expenditure

Except working capital, all other requirements are met by banks through installment credit, *i.e.*, the loan is repaid by the borrower in periodic installments over a pre-specified period. Such loans are also called 'term loans', and are generally used to finance projects or asset purchases. Banks in India follow similar steps outlined in the previous chapter while appraising requests for term loans. DCF[24] valuation methodologies are applied to assess the financial viability of most projects in the medium-and long-term. The debt service coverage ratio is an important criterion for the decision to lend.

SELECT REFERENCE

1. Indian Institute of Banking and Finance (2004). *Legal Aspects of Banking Operations,* Unit 16, 2005 Reprint. Macmillan, 248–256. N. Delhi.

ANNEXURE II

RECLASSIFICATION OF BORROWERS' FINANCIAL STATEMENTS FOR CREDIT APPRAISAL

	Companies Act	RBI Guidelines	Rationale
Liabilities			
Share Capital	All kinds of share capital like equity, redeemable and irredeemable preference shares.	Excludes preference shares.	The repayment obligation in redeemable preference shares is certain and time bound. Hence, it is preferable to treat these as debt rather than equity.

Note: 1. Preference share capital enjoys priority over equity in respect of claims on dividend and repayments.
2. Since 1988, companies are not permitted to issue irredeemable preference shares. Redeemable preference shares can be issued with redemption period not exceeding 10 years.

	Companies Act	RBI Guidelines	Rationale
Liabilities			
Reserves	All kinds of reserves including revaluation, reserve for tax, bad debts, depreciation.	Excludes depreciation reserve, revaluation reserve, reserve for income tax, bad debts.	These are provisions for expected contingencies and do not represent cash flows to the company. These should be classified under 'provisions'.
Secured and Unsecured loans	All loans secured by fixed assets, current assets grouped under 'secured.' All other borrowings grouped under 'unsecured'.	To reclassify based on repayment period of loan.	To ensure that short-term liabilities are adequately covered by short-term assets.
CL and provisions	Can be reported as consolidated figure under 'sundry creditors'.	To call for detailed break up of current liabilities, particularly into 'trade creditors' and 'expenses payable'.	To ensure that pressing short-term liabilities can be paid on demand.

Assets			
Fixed Assets	Can include assets such as goodwill, patents, trade-marks copyrights.	These assets have to be classified under 'intangible assets'.	These assets are intangible in nature and cannot be employed in debt service. In the event of forced sale, they may not have any value.
Investments	All investments, including those in subsidiaries, associate firms, are included under this head.	Only investments in: (a) government securities, (b) bank deposits, and (c) trade-related investments are included under 'current assets' in the reclassified balance sheet. All other investments are classified under 'other non-current assets'.	Investments are looked upon as a source of liquidity for the firm. Investments in subsidiaries, etc. are not liquid investments, and may not be related to the borrower's main line of activity. However, a watch will have to be kept over such investments to ensure that short-term liabilities or bank funds are not diverted into those investment avenues.
Current assets and loans and advances	All current assets, including slow moving, obsolete inventory, spares, ageing receivables advances to staff, directors, etc. are included	Exclude consumable/non-consumable spares, slow moving, obsolete inventory, receivables outstanding for more than 6 months, and advances to staff and directors without a specified repayment program.	Inventory and receivables will have to be liquidated in the event of default. Further, loans in which cash flows by way of repayment are not certain do not provide liquidity to the company, and, hence, to the bank.
Miscellaneous expenditure	Loss, preliminary expenses, pre-operative expenses, deferred revenue expenditure are included under this head.	These should be classified as 'intangible' assets.	The presence of these items on the balance sheet signifies erosion in net worth. Capitalization of expenses lead to overstatement of profits, and do not yield any cash in the event of liquidation.

Source: RBI documents.

ANNEXURE III

SOME COMMON SECURITIES FOR BANK LOANS

Land/Real Estate

Merits

- It is generally assumed that land is a good security, since the market value keeps increasing in most places.
- It cannot be hidden or shifted by a borrower with fraudulent intent.

Demerits

- Though the value in most places is assumed to be increasing, actual valuation of land, especially in the face of sale for liquidation of an advance, would be difficult.
- Even if a reasonable value is ascribed to the land, actual sale may not materialize easily.
- Even if a suitable buyer is found, the realized value may be lower than the expected value.
- The legal procedures for ascertaining title to the land is cumbersome, and extreme vigilance is required on the part of the bank to detect and avert fraudulent practices.
- Charges have to be filed in time by the bank, a lapse in which will render the security unenforceable.
- Care has to be exercised to ensure that the land value is not eroded during the time it remains as security with the bank, due to either the actions of the borrower or force majeure events.

Goods

Merits

- Goods in reasonable condition can be easily sold, even if the value realized is lower than market value.
- Most goods can be valued easily.
- Generally, advances against goods are short-term in nature, hence, the resale risk for the banker is reduced. However, in case of easily perishable goods, care should be taken to ensure that such sale happens before the goods lose substantial value.
- Creating a charge on the security is relatively less cumbersome.

Demerits

- Certain goods depreciate in value very quickly and therefore cannot be accepted as security.
- Certain consumer goods exhibit fluctuations in demand and prices.
- Goods stored in large numbers are difficult to verify. Hence, a borrower with malafide intentions can mislead a bank in respect of the security value.
- It is difficult to physically verify the presence and value of some goods like oil and paints.

- The borrower can store goods at various locations, rendering value assessment difficult.
- The borrower can include slow moving or obsolete stocks in the list of securities, which will be difficult to offload at the time of liquidation.

Documents of Title to Goods

Examples of documents of title to goods: bill of lading, railway/lorry/airway receipts, warehouse certificates and delivery orders.

Merits

- There is no necessity to verify the underlying goods as the documents form a good security
- The documents can be transferred by endorsement and delivery. Hence, the rightful holder of the documents can transfer the goods along with the title to such goods through mere transfer of the documents.
- The procedures for creating and holding the securities are relatively simple.
- All goods have to be insured; hence, the bank has a back up in case of a mishap.
- In some cases, the bank releases documents of title to goods to the borrower before payment is made, after obtaining a letter of trust (also called 'trust receipt (TR)') from the borrower. Execution of the TR obligates the borrower to hold the proceeds of sale of the goods under the TR 'in trust' for the bank. Another significant advantage is that the goods under TR (or the sale proceeds of such goods) are not available to the official receiver in case the borrower becomes insolvent.

Demerits

- Forged and altered documents may be presented by borrowers with fraudulent intentions.
- The documents are not 'negotiable' as in the Negotiable Instruments Act. Hence, the holder cannot get a better title than the transferor.
- Under the Sale of Goods Act, 1930, an unpaid vendor has the right to stop the goods in transit. If this is done, the documents lose their value as security.
- If the documents contain any onerous clauses regarding the condition of goods received, the bank's security interest may be jeopardized.

Stocks and Shares

Merits

- Value of quoted shares can be easily ascertained.
- Shares of stable companies do not exhibit wide fluctuations in the short term, and hence the security value can be stabilized in the short term
- Simple procedures are involved in including shares as securities.
- Quoted shares are easily sold on the exchange to realize the security value.
- The dividends yielded by holding shares can also be appropriated to the balances in the loan account.

Demerits

- The principal demerit is the volatility possible in individual share values. The bank normally compensates for such events by stipulating a larger than usual margin and basing the loan amount on a notional value rather than the current market value.
- The bank should be wary of lending against partly paid shares since the bank may have to pay the remaining calls, and in view of the restricted marketability of such shares.

Debentures

These are debt instruments issued by companies, mostly bearing fixed interest payments at regular intervals. They are generally secured by the assets of the company issuing the instruments.

Merits

- Being debt instruments, they do not witness volatility in values.
- They can be easily transferred or sold.
- Bearer debentures are fully negotiable.

Demerits

- If interest on the debentures is not serviced regularly, the marketability would be affected.
- In times of increasing interest rates, the debenture price would decrease.

Fixed Deposit

Banks usually permit depositors to borrow against their own term deposits. This is one of the most secured advances for the bank, since the security needs no valuation or verification of title.

However, the security is enforceable only if the loan is granted in accordance with the norms. To illustrate: (a) the advance can be granted only to the person(s) in whose name(s) the term deposit stands; (b) no loan should be granted against fixed deposits of other banks;[25] (c) the bank should immediately mark its 'lien' over the deposit to avoid payment of the deposit amount before the loan is adjusted fully and (d) no loan should be granted against fixed deposits in the name of a minor.

SELECT REFERENCES

1. Indian Institute of Banking and Finance (2004). *Legal Aspects of Banking Operations*, unit 16, Delhi: MacMillan, 208–220.
2. Varshney, P N (2004). *Banking Law and Practice*, 20th ed. Chapter 17, New Delhi: Sultan Chand & Sons, 4.71–4.113.

ENDNOTES

1. RBI guidelines state that banks can decide upon the commitment charge on unutilized credit limits need not be imposed on the following types of loan accounts: (1) sick/weak units, (2) export credit, (3) inland bills financing and (4) loans to other banks and financial institutions subject to the 'Guidelines on Fair Practices Code for lenders' issued by the RBI on 5 May 2003.
2. See Section on 'Loan Pricing and Customer Profitability Analysis' in Chapter 'Uses of Bank Funds—The Lending Function'.
3. In the case of *Bank of Maharashtra vs United Construction Company and others (1986, 60 comp cases, 183 (Bom))*, a customer overdrew on his account. There was no express contract of an overdraft. When the bank demanded repayment with interest, the customer refused to pay the interest. The bank filed a suit for recovery of the overdrawn amount with interest.
4. In the case of *Indian Overseas Bank vs M/s Narain Prasad Govindlal Patel (AIR 1980, Guj 158)*, a firm continued enjoying an overdraft of ₹5,000 with the bank for 4 years. There was no contract, no documents and no security to back the facility. The bank unilaterally decided to terminate the facility without due notice to the customer, and dishonoured a cheque issued by the customer on the grounds of 'insufficient funds' even though honouring the cheque would have maintained the balance well within the overdraft amount of ₹5,000. The firm claimed damages for wrongful dishonour of the cheque.
5. 'Documents of title to goods' are defined under Section 2(4) of the Sale of Goods Act, 1930. The essential features are (1) the mere possession of these documents creates a right to possess the goods represented by the documents, (2) goods represented by the documents can be transferred by endorsement and/or delivery of the documents, (3) the person to whom the documents are transferred can take delivery of the goods in his own right, and (4) they are 'quasi-negotiable instruments—though appearing to be negotiable instruments, the bona fide transferee for value can be affected by defects in the title of the transferor.
6. To promote active bill and discount market in India, the RBI introduced the Bills Rediscounting Scheme under Section 17(2)(a) of the RBI Act. In 1981, the RBI stopped rediscounting bills under the scheme and permitted banks to rediscount bills with one another as well as financial institutions, such as LIC, UTI, ECGC and others approved under the scheme. The Discount and Finance House of India can rediscount these rediscounted bills, thus promoting activity in the discount market.
7. 'Holder in due course' is any person or bank who, for consideration, becomes the possessor of the bill, and is entitled to all the rights of the holder of the bill, or the seller of goods.
8. *Source*: RBI, (2009) 'Master Circular—Interest Rate on Advances', July 1, 2013.
9. Section 148 of the Indian Contracts Act defines bailment as 'delivery of goods from one person to another for some purpose upon the contract that the goods be returned when the purpose is accomplished'. Thus, the two important requirements of bailment are delivery of goods and return of goods.
10. For example, if perishable commodities, such as vegetables or medicines, with specific expiry dates form the prime security for a loan, it will not be prudent if the bank insists on a pledge.
11. 'In hypothecation, the possession of the property is retained by the owner and certain rights in that movable property are transferred to the person in whose favour the property is hypothecated. But, in a pledge, the possession of goods also passes to the pledge by way of security though the possession may be constructive' (*AIR 1988, A.P. 18=(1987) to Andhra Law Times 360 in the case of State of A.P. and another vs Andhra Bank Ltd.*).
12. 'In a sense, the borrower in the case of hypothecated goods has actual physical possession of the goods as agent, as it were, of the bank and in that limited sense, hypothecated goods are also not only constructively but actually in the possession of the bank.' (*M/s. Gopal Singh Hira Singh vs Punjab National Bank AIR 1976, Delhi, 115*)
13. '..., so far as the movables actually covered by the hypothecation deeds are concerned, there can be no doubt the Bank is entitled to retain possession and also exercise the right of private sale'. (*Shri Yellamma Cotton Woollen & Silk Mills and Co. Ltd., Bank of Maharashtra Ltd., Pune, vs Official Liquidator, AIR 1969 – Mysore 280=1970; 40 Company Cases 460*)
14. The rights of the unpaid seller of goods hypothecated to a bank was discussed in the *Punjab National Bank vs Lakshmi Card Clothing and Manufacturing Ltd and another (1978 T N Law Notes Journal, p. 89)*.
15. As decreed in M/s Gopal Singh Hira Singh vs. Punjab National Bank (AIR 1976, Delhi 115), and in Syndicate Bank vs. Official Liquidator Prashant Engineering Company P. Ltd. (1986) 59 Comp Cases 301.
16. In *Karnataka Bank Ltd. vs. Gajanan Shankarrao Kulkarni and another (AIR 1977 Karnataka 14)* it was held that 'a mere passive inactivity or passive negligence on the part of the creditor in failing to realize the debt from the security is not sufficient in itself to discharge a surety, as the surety can himself avoid the consequences of such passivity by paying the debt and getting subrogated to the rights of the creditor'. However, in an opposite view in *State Bank of India vs. Quality Bread Factory and Other* (*AIR 1983 Punjab & Haryana 244*), it was held that it was immaterial whether the goods were under bank's custody as pledgee or hypothecated to the bank. In both cases, the bank has constructive possession. Hence, the surety stands discharged to the extent of the value of the security lost or parted, without the consent of the surety, more so, since the Indian Contract Act does not specify that this principle applies only to a pledge.
17. A garnishee order is issued under Order 21, Rule 46 of the Code of Civil Procedure, 1908. If a debtor fails to pay his creditor, the latter may apply to the court to serve a garnishee order on the debtor's banker. The order attaches debts not secured by a negotiable instrument. The creditor at whose behest the order has been issued is the 'judgment creditor'.

18. Devaynes vs Noble (1816) I Mer 529, 572.
19. Under the Indian Contracts Act, minors, individuals of unsound mind and insolvent individuals cannot enter into a contract.
20. Banks generally classify the following investments under current assets-unencumbered fixed deposits with banks, government securities and investments in money market instruments for the purpose of parking short-term surpluses. All other investments, such as ICDs, shares and debentures, investment in subsidiaries and associates and so on, can be classified as 'non-current assets'.
21. In view of the national priority accorded to the export sector, export receivables are included in current assets for arriving at the PBF, but excluded for the purpose of stipulating the minimum NWC. This implies that almost 100 per cent of the export receivables will be financed by the bank.
22. The facility for negotiation of demand or usance bills drawn under letters of credit is generally excluded from the computation of PBF. Therefore, receivables in the form of bills (inland and export) under LCs is not included under current assets. Correspondingly, bank borrowings in the form of bills to be negotiated under LCs need not be included as part of the projected bank finance under 'current liabilities'. However, bills negotiated under LCs will form part of the bank's 'contingent liabilities'.
23. A bill of exchange is defined under Section 5 of the Negotiable Instruments Act, 1881. Sections 7, 8, 9, 10, 14, 15, 30, 32, 35, 79 and 80 of the act define various characteristics of bills of exchange.
24. 'Discounted cash flow' (DCF) methodologies are based on the principle of the 'time value of money' and are prevalently used to evaluate term loan requests. The popularly used techniques are the net present value, internal rate of return and profitability index also called benefit cost ratio. Non-DCF methodologies include the payback period method and accounting rate of return methods.
25. The bank which holds the fixed deposit holds a 'general lien' on the deposit. Hence, even if the lending bank informs the deposit holding bank of the proposed loan, the latter may refuse to even mark the lien in favour of the lending bank.

CHAPTER SEVEN

Credit Monitoring, Sickness and Rehabilitation

CHAPTER STRUCTURE

KEY TAKEAWAYS FROM THE CHAPTER

- Understand why credit needs to be monitored after disbursal.
- Learn to recognise symptoms of sickness/triggers of financial distress.
- Analyse whether to nurse or not to nurse.
- Understand how rehabilitation packages are framed.

SECTION I

BASIC CONCEPTS

The Need for Credit Review and Monitoring

From the previous chapters, it is evident that 'credit management' in a bank consists of two distinct processes—before and after the credit sanction is made. After the credit sanction is made, and the loan is disbursed to the borrower, it is important to ensure that the principal and interest are fully recovered. Loan review is, therefore, a vital post-sanction process.

Loan review helps in the following:

- Continuously checking if the loan policy is being adhered to.
- Identifying problem accounts even at the incipient stage.
- Assessing the bank's exposure to credit risk.[1]
- Assessing the bank's future capital requirements.[2]

A sound credit review process is necessary for the long-term sustenance of the bank. Once a credit is granted, it is the responsibility of the business unit, along with a credit administration support team, to ensure that the credit limit is being operated well, credit files, financial information and other information are updated periodically and the account is 'monitored', to ensure that the debt is serviced on time.

An effective credit monitoring system will have to include measures to ensure the following:

- The bank should periodically obtain and scrutinize the current financial statements of the borrower.
- Systems should be in place to ensure that covenants are complied with, and any violation is immediately noticed.
- The system should periodically ensure that the security coverage for the advances granted is not diluted.
- Payment defaults under the loan contract should be immediately noticed.
- Loans with the potential to run into problems should be classified in time to institute remedial action.

While individual borrowers should be subjected to intense monitoring, banks also need to put in place a system for monitoring the overall composition and quality of the credit portfolio.

It is seen that many problem credits reveal basic weaknesses in the credit granting and monitoring processes. A strong internal credit control process can, in many cases, offset the shortcomings in external factors such as the economy or the specific industry. It also follows that the monitoring policy need not be uniform, and can instead provide more frequent reviews and financial updates for riskier clients. Thus, rather than dedicating equal time to all credit transactions, review and monitoring time could be allocated to high risk and/or very large loans.

The structure of the credit review process would have to periodically examine the assumptions on which every loan was appraised and granted, and whether these assumptions have changed materially enough to endanger the debt-servicing capacity of the borrower. Typically, all or most of the following aspects are reviewed for every loan till it is repaid in full.

- Developments in the economy that may have an impact on the industry in which the borrower operates.
- Developments in the industry or sector in which the borrower operates.
- The borrower's financial health. Is the credit adequate? Has the borrower over-or under-borrowed? Can the borrower sustain debt service without default?
- The borrower's payment record in this and other loans so far.
- The quality, condition and value of the prime and collateral securities.
- The completeness of loan documentation, and developments in law governing the instruments effecting credit delivery.
- Adherence to loan covenants. Is there a danger of violating one or more of these? How critical are these violations for the debt service and the long-term relationship with the borrower?

Some borrowers may default on debt service due to factors out of their control. In such cases, the bank may have to reschedule the debt service requirements and alter some of the covenants, if necessary.

Central banks of most countries have devised country-specific definitions and control systems to tackle 'sick' borrowers. There are three categories of sickness that could afflict borrowers.

- Sickness at birth—the project itself has become infeasible either due to faulty assumptions or a change in environment.
- Induced sickness—caused by management in competencies or willful default.
- Genuine sickness—where the circumstances leading to sickness are beyond the borrowers' control, and has happened in spite of the borrowers' sincere efforts to avert the situation.

When the borrower turns 'sick', the bank will have to investigate (a) the reasons for sickness, and whether remedial measures can revive the ailing firm; (b) the rationale for categorizing the borrower as 'sick'; (c) the risks involved in rehabilitating the borrowing firm and (d) in case the bank decides to rehabilitate, the requirements for such revival in the form of additional financing, government support, management inputs or upgraded technology.

Triggers of Financial Distress

When does a firm face financial distress? Financial failure occurs when there is a prolonged period of lack of profitability. The most marked among the manifestations of lack of profitability is the decay in the cash inflows. Due to this decay, even though the firm's balance sheet could show a healthy level of current and fixed assets, the firm would be unable to meet its current liabilities. An example of such a situation is when the firm has a high level of receivables, but these are not realizable. Or, inventories look high but the quality is poor and items are non-moving, and due to low profitability the firm does not write them off. Or, due to continuous losses, the firm does not provide adequate depreciation, and the fixed asset balances seem high. In fact, in these cases, the assets are rapidly losing market value, which is not reflected in the balance sheet. Thus, a situation finally arises when the firm's assets are not all realizable, the cash flows are thinning out, and revenues have not been covering expenses over a period of time.

If such a state prolongs, economic failure could occur—the rates of return from investments drop below the cost of capital (COC), and the market value of liabilities exceeds the market value of assets. The result is 'insolvency'.

There are several factors that lead to financial distress in firms. Any of the risk factors listed in Annexure I of Chapter 5 could turn a reality, and cause a firm to fail. The factors could range from fundamental changes in the way firms do business, to sweeping changes in the economy, industry and markets. The reasons could also be endogenous to the firm, such as loss of major contracts or customers, growth without adequate capital, superior competition, management incompetence or poor financial management.

Lending banks would, therefore, be concerned with tackling the following crucial issues:

- What are the signals of financial distress?
- Can banks detect signs of distress early enough, and initiate remedial action, so that bank funds do not turn irrecoverable?
- Can financial failure be predicted?

Financial Distress Models—The Altman's Z-Score

Typically, the statistical tools used to predict financial distress are regression and discriminant analysis. Regression analysis uses past data to forecast values of dependent variables. Discriminant analysis classifies data into predetermined groups by generating an index. The model most popular with bankers and analysts, apart from ad hoc models, is the Altman's[3] Z-score model. Since it has been thoroughly tested and widely accepted, the model scores over various others that have been subsequently developed and used for predicting bankruptcy.[3]

The discriminant function Z was found to be:

$$Z = 1.2X_1 + 1.4X_2 + 3.3X_3 + 0.6X_4 + 1.0X_5$$

where X_1 = working capital/total assets (%)

X_2 = retained earnings/total assets (%)

X_3 = EBIT/total assets (%)

X_4 = market value of equity/book value of debt (%)

X_5 = sales to total assets (times)

The firm is classified as 'financially sound' if $Z > 2.99$ and 'financially distressed' or 'bankrupt' if $Z < 1.81$.

What are the model's attributes that lead to its continued validity in most cases? The model is based on two important concepts of corporate finance—operating leverage and asset utilization. A high degree of operating leverage implies that a small change in sales results in a relatively large change in net operating income. Lenders are aware of the pitfalls of financing firms with high operating leverage—they should be convinced that the borrowers can withstand recessions or sudden dips in sales. Asset utilization suffers when too many assets are held on the firm's balance sheet, disproportionate to the operating requirements and the sales generated. It is noteworthy that the model has total assets as the denominator in four out of the five variables. Box 7.1 on the next page provides a connective insight into the variables constituting the model.

However, the Z-score model makes two basic assumptions. One, that the firm's equity is publicly traded and second, that it is a firm engaged in manufacturing activities.

Hence, it became necessary to look for alternate models that predict financial distress in non-manufacturing or emerging market settings.

Some Alternate Models Predicting Financial Distress

The following are some alternate models that predict financial distress:

- The ZETA score[4] enables banks to appraise the risks involved in firms outside the manufacturing sector. The score is reported to provide warning signals 3–5 years prior to bankruptcy (against 2 years for Z score). It considers variables such as (a) return on assets (ROA), (b) earnings stability, (c) debt service, (d) cumulative profitability, (e) current ratio, (f) capitalization, and (g) size of the business as indicated by total tangible assets. An increase in the score is a positive signal.[5]
- Often, in emerging economies, it is not possible to build a model based on a sample from that country because of the lack of credit experience there. To deal with this problem, Altman, Hartzell and Peck (1995) have modified the original Altman's Z-score model to create the Emerging Market Scoring (EMS) model.[6] One such EMS model is the Emerging Markets Corporate Bonds Scoring System.[7] The model can be applied to both manufacturing and non-manufacturing companies, as well as privately held and publicly owned firms. In this case, an EM score is first developed as being equal to $6.56X_1 + 3.26X_2 + 6.72X_3 + 1.05X_4 + 3.25$, where $+X_1$ is defined as working the capital/total assets, $+X_2$ is defined as retained earnings/total assets, $+X_3$

is defined as operating income/total assets and $+X_4$ is defined as the book value of equity/total liabilities. The EM score is modified based on critical factors such as the firm's vulnerability to currency devaluation, its industry environment, and its competitive position in the industry. The resulting analyst modified rating is compared with the actual bond rating, if any, and other special features such as high quality collateral or guarantees, the sovereign rating, etc. should be factored in.

BOX 7.1 THE ALTMAN'S *Z*-SCORE MODEL—SIGNIFICANCE OF INDICATORS

Assume, *e.g.*, a firm with a high operating leverage.

- When sales decline, sales/assets also declines. Because of the high operating leverage, earnings before interest and taxes (EBIT) falls, leading to a fall in the EBIT/assets ratio.
- When EBIT falls, it drives down the retained earnings, and, thus, the ratio of retained earning/total assets.
- A fall in retained earnings is linked to the working capital and, therefore, the working capital/total assets fall.
- The market does not perceive the declines in key ratios in a favourable light, and the market value of equity falls. The book value of debt remaining relatively unchanged, the ratio market value of equity/book value of debt decreases.
- The decline in market value of equity causes a dip in the firm value and an increase in the financial leverage of the firm. This implies higher financial risk to the firm, and, hence, a higher probability of distress.
- The above chain of events is encapsulated in a decline in the *Z* score.

- Influenced by the use of discriminant analysis in Altman's model, subsequent researchers used logit analysis, probit analysis and linear probability models to improve the accuracy of predicting distress.[8]
- The multinomial logit technique has been used to build models to distinguish between financially distressed firms that survive and financially distressed firms that ultimately go bankrupt.
- Other researchers have proposed a 'gambler's ruin' approach to predict bankruptcies. This approach combines the net liquidation value (total asset liquidation value less total liabilities) with the net cash flows (cash inflows less cash outflows). Other things being equal, the model predicts that the lower the net liquidation value, the smaller the net cash flows, and the higher the volatility of these cash flows, the higher would be the probability of firm failure.[9]
- Neural networks[10] are also increasingly being used in predicting financial distress.
- From the early 2000s, some other models in bankruptcy prediction are reported to have shown good performance. An example is a hybrid model combining 'genetic programming and rough sets', the approach taken in a 2002 paper by McKee and Lensberg[11]. Another approach is the Multidimensional scaling approach proposed in a 2001 paper by Mar–Molinero and Serrano–Cinca[12], reported to bypass the shortcomings of models based on discriminant analysis, logit techniques or neural network models.

An illustrative list of warning signs that banks should look out for is provided in *Annexure I*.

The Workout Function

A loan is considered 'impaired' if, based on the current situation, it appears probable that the bank will be unable to collect all the amount due (both prinicipal and interest) from the borrower, in accordance with the terms of the loan agreement. The purpose of credit review and monitoring is to watch out for warning signals, identify 'troubled' or 'sick' loans, document the findings, revise credit ratings, if necessary, and, finally, classify the credit exposures under the appropriate categories for purpose of making 'provisions' against expected losses.[13]

The aims of establishing a separate workout function are primarily to examine whether the credit granted is performing as expected and, if not performing according to expectations, classify problem credits appropriately, and, second, to explore possible solutions to resolve the problem. Generally, banks have two choices for the workout—restructure the problem loan or liquidate it.

The skills, procedures and processes necessary for running a workout organization are fundamentally different from those relevant to credit appraisal, sanction and monitoring. The problem loans are classified into appropriate risk categories, and the workout procedure is decided. Though the line banker knows the problem credit better, the loan workout department is constituted with better expertise and experience in solving credit problems. Banks without a separate workout function could see a rise in credit defaults. If this happens, the quality of credit origination and appraisal could also slacken.

An independent workout function must do well the following four things[14]:

- It should establish clear rules for using a traditional workout process. Sometimes, a lower-cost, streamlined collection process via letters and phone calls would be sufficient to rectify the default. Successful banks may have four or five separate processes, depending on cost and potential for collection.
- It should prioritize loan workout effort according to the urgency of the situation, the possible economic impact and the probability of success in order to achieve high recovery rates. While it is necessary for loan workout to be reactive to day-to-day crises, it is also equally important to set clear priorities based on bottom-line impact.
- The loan workout function should assemble the best skills. Each situation will require a specific skill or combination of skills, such as real estate, legal, credit assessment, financial analysis, merchant banking, collateral evaluation and basic project management among them. The bank's systems should allow for flexibility to build an appropriate team from internal or external resources.
- The loan workout should assess available alternatives using analytically driven decision rules. The basic choices facing a bank—restructuring, loan sales, foreclosures, or 'do nothing'—should be evaluated according to the net present value (NPV) of each option multiplied by its probability of success. Such analyses should take into account all costs, including operating and carrying costs, as well as ROA (if any).

Banks often centralize the workout function to ensure that state-of-the-art methodologies are used to monitor overall risk response, and to create an environment to improve decision making without diffusing accountability. A well-designed central authority can provide maintenance and monitoring of limit systems and portfolio concentration; an early warning system authorized to place clients on the watch list; industry and micro-economic analysis to identify optimal portfolio composition and secondary market evaluation and trading capability.

The workout officers examine the updated credit file, and meet with the borrower to explore if the 'impaired' credit can be revived and the firm rehabilitated. If the firm's operations could be made viable after restructuring, the loan will be restructured with modified terms and some 'sacrifices' on the part of the bank.

SECTION II

CREDIT INFORMATION COMPANIES IN INDIA[15]

We have understood the importance of building credit files (credit information on borrowers) from Chapter 6. It is not uncommon for a single borrower to required different types of credit facilities from various branches of the same branch, nor is it uncommon for borrowers/customers to bank with multiple banks. We have also seen earlier that a key deciding factor for banks to grant loans is the integrity of the borrower, which can be interpreted from the borrower's track record of borrowings and timely repayments. Conversely, lack of credit history is an impediment to smooth credit flow, since inadequate information could lead to misleading conclusions about a borrower's creditworthiness or the pricing of a loan to such a borrower. In the absence of an industry-wide common information system, appraising a borrower's creditworthiness could be a subjective exercise.

In recognition of the vital need for credit information across the industry, a scheme for disclosure of information regarding defaulting borrowers of banks and financial institutions was introduced in 1994. In order to facilitate sharing of credit and borrower related information, the Credit Information Bureau (India) Limited (CIBIL) was set up in 2000, which took over the functions of dissemination of information relating to defaulting borrowers from the RBI. The Credit Information Companies (Regulation) Act was enacted in 2005 to facilitate the setting up of credit information companies.

The Government and the RBI have framed rules and regulations for implementation of the Act, with specific provisions for protecting individual borrower's rights and obligations. The rules and regulations were notified on December 14, 2006 in terms of the provisions of the Act.

Credit Information Companies (CIC) help lenders assess creditworthiness of individual borrowers and their ability to pay back loans, by collating data on the borrower's track record of timely repayment of loans and other forms of credit availed of. They collect personal financial data from financial institutions and others, which helps in modelling price discrimination, taking into account the individual borrower's credit rating and past behaviour. The information is aggregated and made available on request to companies/banks which have shared the data, for the purpose of credit assessment and credit scoring. The credit history of a borrower spans all the financial institutions the borrower has dealt with in the past, which helps the bank seeking the information to speed up credit decisions. CIBIL, for instance, collects (monthly), collates and disseminates credit information pertaining to both commercial and consumer borrowers to a closed group of member banks, financial institutions, non banking finance companies, housing finance companies and credit card companies.

Data sharing is reciprocal, which implies that only members who have shared credit data are eligible to access credit information reports from CIBIL.

CIBIL and Loan Approval

CIBIL's products, especially the CIBIL Trans Union Score and the Credit Information Report (CIR) are important to the loan approval process in banks. The credit score helps banks quickly determine, who they would like to evaluate further to provide credit. The CIBIL Trans Union Score ranges from 300 to 900. CIBIL data indicates that loan providers prefer a credit scores which are greater than 700.

Once the bank decides which set of loan applicants to evaluate, it analyzes the CIR in order to determine the applicant's eligibility. Eligibility basically means the applicants ability to take additional debt and repay additional outflows given their current commitments.

Post completion of these first 2 steps the bank requests other relevant documents from the borrower in order to finally sanction the loan.

Other Credit Information Companies in India

The banks and the financial institutions can submit details of wilful defaulters, borrowers on whom suits have been filed for recovery and other default data to a credit information company, which has obtained certificate of registration from RBI in terms of Section 5 of the Credit Information Companies (Regulation) Act, 2005 and of which the bank is a member. The following companies have been recognized by RBI and CICs and certificates of registration have been granted;

1. Credit Information Bureau (India) Ltd. (www.cibil.com)
2. Experian Credit Information company of India Pvt. Ltd. (www.experian.in)
3. Equifax Credit Information Services Pvt. Ltd. (www.equifax.co.in)
4. High Mark Credit Information Services Pvt. Ltd. (www.highmark.in)

DEBT RESTRUCTURING AND REHABILITATION OF SICK FIRMS IN INDIA—THE WORKOUT FUNCTION

Source: RBI Master circular titled 'Prudential norms on income recognition, asset classification and provisioning pertaining to advances" dated July 1, 2013, and various relevant RBI guidelines and circulars.

Companies on the verge of liquidation had to seek protection under the Sick Industrial Companies (Special Provisions) Act, 1985, administered by the Board for Industrial and Financial Reconstruction (BIFR). As of 2001, debt restructuring in India could be achieved through one of two modes—contractual, or court-based. Neither the contractual restructuring nor the court-based restructuring automatically insulated the company against suits or other action by creditors. Thus, BIFR though aimed at rehabilitating industrial enterprises, failed to achieve its objective. Moreover, it did not help banks and the financial institutions to recover their debts.

The process of workout of troubled loans—restructuring and rehabilitation—has been revamped since 2003. We will see how the process operates in *Annexure II*.

Box 7.2 provides an illustrative list of warning signals of incipient sickness.

BOX 7.2 AN ILLUSTRATIVE LIST OF WARNING SIGNALS OF INCIPIENT SICKNESS

- Continuous irregularities in cash credit/overdraft accounts—inability to maintain stipulated margin on continuous basis, or funds drawn from the account frequently exceeding sanctioned limits, or periodical interest debited remaining unrealized;
- Outstanding balance in cash credit account remaining continuously at the maximum;
- Failure to make timely payment of installments of principal and interest on term loans;
- Complaints from suppliers of raw materials, water, power, etc., about non-payment of bills;
- Non-submission or undue delay in submission or submission of incorrect stock statements and other control statements;
- Attempts to divert sale proceeds through accounts with other banks;
- Downward trend in credit summations;

- Frequent return of cheques or bills;
- Steep decline in production figures;
- Downward trends in sales and fall in profits;
- Rising level of inventories, which may include large proportion of slow or non-moving items;
- Larger and longer outstanding in receivables;
- Longer period of credit allowed on sale documents negotiated through the bank and frequent return by the customers of the same; also allowing large discount on sales;
- Failure to pay statutory liabilities;
- Diversion of bank funds for purposes other than running the firm;
- Not furnishing the required information/data on operations in time and non-cooperation or discrepancies noticed during routine stock and other inspections by the bank.
- Unreasonable/wide variations in sales/receivables levels.
- Delay in meeting commitments towards payments of installments due, crystallized liabilities under LC/BGs, etc.
- Diverting/routing of receivables through non-lending banks.

The bank office familiar with the day-to-day operations in the accounts exhibiting any of the above symptoms should be able to grasp the significance of these warning signals and initiate timely corrective measures. Such measures may include providing timely financial assistance based on the assessed need, and seeking help from the workout specialists at designated offices of the bank.

What is Restructuring?

As part of their workout function for troubled loans, banks grant concessions on credit facilities granted to borrowers facing financial difficulty due to economic or legal reasons. These are concessions, which banks would otherwise not consideron the credit facilities granted to borrowers. Under such circumstances, the borrower's account that is under the workout, is termed a 'restructured account'.

Restructuring would normally involve modification of terms of the advances/securities, which would generally include, among others, alteration of repayment period/repayable amount/the amount of installments/rate of interest (due to reasons other than competitive reasons). (However, extension in repayment tenor of a floating rate loan on reset of interest rate, so as to keep the EMI unchanged provided it is applied to a class of accounts uniformly will not render the account to be classified as 'Restructured account'. In other words, extension or deferment of EMIs to individual borrowers as against to an entire class, would render the accounts to be classified as 'restructured accounts'.)

RBI guidelines for restructuring fall under the following broad categories:

- Restructuring of advances to industrial units.
- Restructuring of advances to industrial units under the Corporate Debt Restructuring (CDR) mechanism.
- Restructuring of advances to Small and Medium Enterprises (SME).
- Restructuring of all other advances.

It can be seen that in the above categories of guidelines, the differentiation is based on whether a borrower is involved in industrial or non industrial activity. The institutional mechanism for accounts restructured under CDR (for both industrial and non industrial borrowers) has been made specific and elaborate.

Criteria for Considering Restructuring

All eligible advances/borrowing accounts classified under various asset classification categories—such as 'standard', 'sub standard' and 'doubtful' – can be restructured provided they satisfy certain criteria. (For an understanding of the asset classification categories, you may refer to the chapters on 'Credit risk')

- The most important criterion for deciding whether to restructure a borrower's account would be the financial viability after the restructuring package is implemented. The restructuring package should demonstrate reasonable certainty of repayment from the borrower. The viability should be determined by the banks—based on the acceptable viability benchmarks. Box 7.3 contains the viability benchmarks suggested by RBI's draft guidelines for the 'review of prudential guidelines on restructuring of advances by banks and financial institutions' published on its website on July 1, 2013. Where an account is not found viable, banks should accelerate the recovery measures.

BOX 7.3 BROAD BENCHMARKS FOR THE VIABILITY PARAMETERS (ILLUSTRATIVE LIST BY RBI—JULY 2013)

- Return on capital employed should be at least equivalent to 5 year government security yield plus 2%.
- The debt service coverage ratio should be greater than 1.25 within the 5 years period in which the unit should become viable and on year to year basis the ratio should be above 1. The normal debt service coverage ratio for 10 years repayment period should be around 1.33.
- The benchmark gap between internal rate of return and cost of capital should be at least 1 per cent.
- Operating and cash break even points should be worked out and they should be comparable with the industry norms.
- Trends of the company based on historical data and future projections should be comparable with the industry. Thus behaviour of past and future EBIDTA should be studied and compared with industry average.
- Loan Life Ratio (LLR), as defined below should be 1.4, which would give a cushion of 40 Per cent to the amount of loan to be serviced.

$$\text{LLR} = \frac{\text{Present value of total available cash flow (ACF) during the loan life period (Including interest and principal)}}{\text{Maximum amount of loan}}$$

- Banks cannot reschedule/restructure/renegotiate borrowers' accounts with retrospective effect. While a restructuring proposal is under consideration, the usual asset classification norms (as above) would continue to apply. The asset classification status as on the date of approval of the restructured package would be relevant to decide the asset classification status of the account after restructuring/rescheduling/renegotiation. In case there is undue delay in sanctioning a restructuring package and in the meantime the asset quality of the account deteriorates, it would be a matter of supervisory concern.
- Typically, restructuring entails changes in the prevailing loan agreement. Since the loan agreement is a legal document, changes require a formal process. However, restructuring can be initiated by a bank in deserving cases subject to customer agreeing to the new terms and conditions.
- Borrowers indulging in frauds and malfeasance will not be eligible for restructuring. Where wilful default is suspected, banks may review the account and implement a restructuring package and being satisfied that the borrower is in a position to rectify the wilful default. The restructuring of such cases may be done with Board's approval, and if restructuring under the CDR Mechanism, the package should be formulated with the approval of the core group only. (Please see Annexure II for an overview of the CDR mechanism)
- Cases under BIFR are not eligible for restructuring without the express approval of BIFR.

Relief Measures under Restructuring

Some typical measures/concessions that are provided to troubled borrowers' accounts under the restructuring package are as follows:

- A part of the outstanding principal amount can be converted into debt at lower rates or equity instruments as part of restructuring.
- Unpaid interest can be converted into a 'funded interest term loan' (FITL) to be repaid in installments under the package.
- The FITL can also be converted into other debt or equity instruments.
- Other relief measures under special circumstances spelt out by RBI.

Valuation of Restructured Advances

The restructuring package by banks typically envisages reduction in the rate of interest and/or rescheduling repayment of principal amount. It is evident that these measures will result in diminution in the fair value of the advance. Such diminution in value is an economic loss for the bank and will impact the bank's market value of equity. It is, therefore, necessary for banks to measure such diminution in the fair value of the advance and make provisions for it by debit to Profit & Loss Account. This provision should be held in addition to the provisions as per existing provisioning norms (*Please refer to the chapter on 'Credit risk'*), and in an account distinct from that for normal provisions.

The erosion in the fair value of the advance is computed as the difference between the fair value of the loan before and after restructuring. Fair value of the loan before restructuring will be the present value (PV) of cash flows from interest payments at the existing rate (charged on the advance before restructuring) and the principal repayments, discounted at a rate equal to the bank's base rate as on the date of restructuring plus the appropriate term premium and credit risk premium for the borrower category on the date of restructuring. Fair value of the loan after restructuring will be computed as the present value of cash flows from interest payments at the revised rate charged on the advance due to restructuring and the principal repayments, discounted at a rate equal to the bank's base rate as on the date of restructuring plus the appropriate term premium and credit risk premium for the borrower category on the date of restructuring.

The diminution in the fair value should be re-computed on each balance sheet date till the restructured payments are fully paid. The revised annual calculations are meant to capture the changes in the fair value due to changes in the base rate (or discount rate).

The restructuring package should be formulated and implemented within a short time period as stipulated by RBI, so that there is no further erosion in the asset value.

The RBI reiterates in its various guidelines that the basic objective of restructuring is to preserve economic value of units, not ever-greening of problem accounts. This can be achieved by banks and the borrowers only by careful assessment of the viability, quick detection of weaknesses in accounts and a time-bound implementation of restructuring packages.

CHAPTER SUMMARY

- 'Credit management' in a bank consists of two distinct processes—before and after the credit sanction is made. A sound credit review process is necessary for the long-term sustenance of the bank. Once a credit is granted, it is the responsibility of the business unit, along with a credit administration support team, to ensure that the credit limit is being operated well. Once the credit is disbursed, credit flies, financial information and other information will have to be updated periodically, and the account 'monitored', to ensure that the debt is serviced on time. The monitoring policy need not be uniform, and can instead provide more frequent reviews and financial updates for riskier clients.
- When a borrower turns 'sick', the bank will have to investigate (a) the reasons for sickness, and whether remedial measures can revive the ailing firm; (b) the rationale for categorizing the borrower as 'sick'; (c) the risks involved in rehabilitating the borrowing firm and (d) in case the bank decides to rehabilitate, the requirements for such revival in the form of additional financing, government support, management inputs or upgraded technology.
- It is crucial for lending banks to be able to identify the signals of financial distress, detect them early enough and initiate remedial action, so that bank funds do not turn irrecoverable.
- The model to predict financial distress of firms most popular with bankers and analysts, apart from ad hoc models, is the Altman's *Z*-score model. Since it has been thoroughly tested and widely accepted, the model scores over various others that have been subsequently developed and used for predicting bankruptcy.
- The aims of establishing a separate workout function are primarily to examine whether the credit granted is performing as expected and if not performing according to expectations, classify problem credits appropriately, and second, to explore possible solutions to resolve the problem. Generally, banks have two choices for the workout—restructure the problem loan or liquidate it.
- The RBI has proposed various rehabilitation/workout schemes for distressed assets as well as for large corporate borrowers (CDR).

TEST YOUR UNDERSTANDING

1. An over-levered Firm A, financed by Bank X, started making cash losses. Bank X found the firm potentially viable and hence decided to rehabilitate the firm. One year after implementation of the rehabilitation package, the following developments were noticed in the firm's financial statements.
   a. Firm A generated quite a large amount of cash in that year
   b. Total current liabilities of Firm A decreased
   c. There was a fall in the amount of long-term assets

   Give the reasons for the above phenomena
2. Why is it a prudent policy to separate credit appraisal and sanctioning from the workout function?

3. You are the banker to Firm B and notice the following features of the firm's cash flows. Explain how each of these observations could endanger the bank's ability to collect its dues from Firm B.
   a. The firm has used the money given by your bank for working capital to buy plant and machinery.
   b. The firm's COC and ROA is 15 per cent.
   c. 'Notes to accounts' shows considerable exposure to currency and interest rate swaps, to hedge the firm's export activity.
   d. 'Notes to accounts' shows a large possible write down in asset value, which has not been carried out in the current year.
   e. The firm's contingent liabilities are almost equal to the firm's balance sheet size.
   f. The firm's operations also show investments in joint ventures and off balance sheet special-purpose vehicles.
   g. The firm had taken over a firm in the same line of activity a year ago.
   h. The firm has certain long-term contract deals for which revenue is getting booked in the current year.

TOPICS FOR FURTHER DISCUSSION

- What is the function of MIS in credit management? What kind of control systems should a bank have to ensure that credit management is done in a proper manner?
- What are the circumstances under which the lender may fail to perform a financial analysis of the borrower? Why is financial analysis so vital to credit management?
- Develop a checklist for credit reviews in a typical bank.

ANNEXURE I

WARNING SIGNS THAT BANKS SHOULD LOOK OUT FOR—AN ILLUSTRATIVE CHECKLIST

Warning Signs Endogenous to the Firm

1. **Management related**
   - Lacks technical expertise for the project/running the firm.
   - Failure to control costs.
   - Poor capacity utilization.
   - Improper inventory and receivables management—accumulation of inventory, inefficient collection machinery.
   - Inability to anticipate problems and take effective remedial measures.
   - Failure to anticipate competition, and loss of competitive edge.
   - Diversion of funds, siphoning off funds by management for personal or uses other than for the business.
   - Indulging in fraudulent or speculative transactions, such as hoarding of finished goods in anticipation of a price increase, clandestine sale of goods at a premium.
   - Disagreements/conflicts among promoters/directors/managers.
   - Improper delegation of duties, or one person dominating decision-making.
   - Owners have stake in more than one business, and they no longer take pride in the business the bank has financed.
   - Managers' salaries show sharp reduction.
   - Management is unwilling to provide budgets, projects or interim information.
   - The owners/managers of the firm do not know the present position the firm is in, and in what direction it has to head in the future.
   - Frequent changes in senior management.
   - The Board of Directors does not participate effectively.
   - Management lacks depth.
   - Resignation of key personnel.
   - Non-compliance with covenants or excessive negotiation of covenants.
   - Management not able to or unwilling to explain unusual off-balance sheet items.
   - Visits by the bank to the borrowing firm's place of business reveals deterioration in the general appearance of the premises.
2. **Technology related**
   - Adopting processes that have not been tested on a commercial scale, or requiring major modifications after implementation.
   - Choice of obsolete process or technology.
   - Wrong choice of technology or collaboration—one that may not be suited to or succeed in the conditions prevailing in the country/state where the firm is located.
   - Unsuitable or non-optimal location of the firm.
   - Design of plant of an uneconomic size.
   - Choice of faulty or unsuitable equipment, without verifying the credentials and capacity of the supplier.
   - Production bottlenecks arising from improper balancing of plant and equipment.
   - Inadequate maintenance of plant and machinery, leading to frequent breakdowns and production losses.
   - Unusually high production wastages.
   - Failure to take cognizance of environmental factors while locating the firm.

- Inadequate quality control procedures, leading to product rejections by customers.
- Inappropriate choice of product mix while deciding on plant and machinery.
- Factory operating well below capacity.
- Adoption of obsolete production methods.

3. **Product related**
   - Overestimation of demand for products of the firm.
   - Orders slowing down in comparison with previous years, and in relation to the orders received by competitors.
   - The borrower changes suppliers frequently.
   - Inventory to one customer increases.
   - Concentration shifts from major well-known customer to one of lesser stature.
   - The firm loses an important supplier or customer.
   - Demand for product falls.
   - Obsolete product distribution methods are still adopted by the firm.
   - The firm still supplies to troubled customers and industries.
   - The product is priced improperly.
   - Increasing sales discounts or sales returns.
   - Large orders have been booked at fixed prices under inflationary conditions.
   - Ineffective marketing set up.
   - Unscrupulous sales and purchase practices.
   - Improper launch of new products.
   - Overestimation of demand for products, both existing and new.

4. **Financial management related**
   - Underestimating project costs at the time of project planning and implementation.
   - Inadequate working capital due to diversion of funds or faulty estimation of requirements.
   - Inappropriate costing methods for product pricing.
   - Financial risk due to high leverage.
   - A liberal dividend policy even under adverse circumstances.
   - Application of bank funds for purposes other than those for which they were intended.
   - Deferring payment of payables and creditors frequently.
   - Unusual items appear in the financial statements.
   - Negative trends in key indicators such as sales, gross and net profits.
   - Slow down in collection of accounts receivables, and increase in the age of debtors.
   - Where the owners have multiple businesses, intercompany payables and receivables are not being explained satisfactorily.
   - Substantial reduction in cash balances, overdrawn cash balances or uncollected cash during normally liquid periods.
   - Inability to avail of trade discounts, either because of poor inventory turnover or the supplier refusing trade discounts.
   - Deferred payment of statutory liabilities.
   - Creditors are not completely paid out at the end of the working capital cycle.
   - Interim results either not provided at all or provided incomplete.
   - Late release of financial statements to banks and investors.
   - Suppliers cut back favourable terms.
   - Accumulation of creditors and debtors, with no satisfactory explanation from the borrower.
   - Large and frequent loans are made to or from managers and affiliates.
   - The bank overestimates the seasonal peaks and troughs, and lends excessively.
   - The firm is unable to repay bank debt from internal generation, and rotates or restructures bank debt for repayment.
   - Large customers' creditworthiness has not been investigated by the firm.
   - The firm has over-expanded without adequate working capital.
   - Financial controls are weak.
   - Excessive investment in fixed assets, not matched by sales and profit growth.
   - Sale proceeds from fixed assets and other securities used to fund working capital.
   - Sale of a profitable division or product line.
   - The firm has not been making deposits in trust funds in time, such as pension and provident funds.
   - There are unexplained significant variances in key result areas as compared to the previous years or budget.
   - The credit limits are always utilized to the brim, and the firm approaches the bank frequently for ad hoc increases in credit limits.
   - Increase in off-balance sheet investments, not adequately explained by the management.

Warning Signs Exogenous to the Firm

1. **At the project implementation stage**
   - Currency risk—if the project depends heavily on imported equipment. Adverse changes in exchange rates may result in steep increases in the project cost.
   - Upward revision of import duties or excise duties may escalate the project cost.
   - Delay in receipt of approvals for the project from the government and other statutory bodies.
   - Delay in sanction of term loans from FIs and banks.
   - Force major events—acts of God.

2. **At the production stage**
   - Non-availability or limited availability of raw material and other inputs.

- Power cuts.
- Transport bottlenecks.
- Delay in supply of critical components by sub-contractors.
- Bottlenecks arising from monsoons and other acts of God.
- Technological innovation may lead to production process becoming obsolete.

3. **At the sales/marketing stage**
   - Delay in commissioning downstream projects intended for purchase of project's output.
   - Withdrawal or reduction in the degree of protection by the government.
   - Market is saturated since the entry barriers are low and competition is catching up.
   - Price undercutting by other established firms with more financial muscle.
   - Availability of cheaper substitutes in the market.
   - General economic downturn.

4. **Financial Management**
   - Non-availability of adequate credit from banks due to policy measures of the central bank/government.
   - Inordinate delay in release of adequate funding by banks and other funding agencies.

SELECT REFERENCES

1. Morton Glantz. *Managing Bank Risk*, Chapter 9, pp. 299–330 (Academic Press, 2003) USA.
2. RBI, 'Guidelines for Rehabilitation of Sick Small Scale Industrial Units',dated 16 January 2002.

ANNEXURE II

The following paragraphs summarizes the salient features of RBI's Framework for revitalizing distressed assets in the economy (dated February 26, 2014) (*Source: RBI web site*).

1. Borrowing accounts showing incipient stress would be categorized by banks as Special Mention Accounts (SMA). The category was introduced in 2002.
2. The SMA category would contain three sub categories as follows:
   a. SMA-0 Principal or interest payment not overdue for more than 30 days but account showing signs of incipient stress. Box 7.4 provides an illustrative list of signs of stress for classifying a borrowing account as SMA-0 (as given in the Annexure of the RBI circular dated February 26, 2014 quoted above).
   b. SMA-1 Principal or interest payment overdue between 31-60 days.
   c. SMA-2 Principal or interest payment overdue between 61-90 days.
3. RBI has set up a Central Repository of Information on Large Credits (CRILC) would be set up to collect, store and disseminate credit data to lenders. Banks would be reporting credit information, including classification of an account as SMA to CRILC relating to borrowers having aggregate fund based and non-fund based exposure of ₹50 million and above.
4. Once a bank reports a borrower classified as SMA-2, a committee called Joint Lenders' Forum (JLF) would be mandatorily formed if the aggregate exposure of lenders to that borrower exceeds ₹1000 million. JLF can also be formed for exposures less than ₹1000 million or when the borrower is classified under SMA-0 or SMA-1.
5. Where multiple banks are involved in extending credit to the borrower classified under SMA, the consortium leader (where the borrowing limits have been given by a formally constituted consortium of lenders) or the lender with the highest aggregate exposure (in the case of a multiple banking arrangement, which is less formal than a consortium), will convene the JLF to facilitate exchange of credit information.
6. The JLF would formulate and sign an Agreement (called the JLF agreement) that would set the broad guidelines for the forum's functioning. Specifically, the JLF would address the manner in which the borrower can rectify the irregularities or weaknesses observed in the conduct of the account. Other relevant stakeholders such as central/state Government or project authorities could also be invited to JLF deliberations.
7. The JLF would arrive at a Corrective Action Plan (CAP). The objective would be to find an early and feasible solution to preserve the economic value of the underlying assets of the borrowers and the loans extended.
8. The options under CAP would typically include (a) Rectification, or (b) Restructuring, or (c) Recovery.
9. If the option of 'Rectification' is chosen, the plan would focus on obtaining a specific commitment from the borrower to regularize the account, so that it emerges out of the SMA category and does not worsen to a Non performing Asset (NPA, the concept of which will be discussed in subsequent chapters). The commitment should be supported with identifiable cash flows within the required time period and without involving any loss or sacrifice on the part of the existing lenders. If the existing promoters are not in a position to bring in additional money or take any measures to regularize the account, the possibility of getting some other equity/strategic investors to the company would be explored by the JLF in consultation with the borrower. These measures are intended to turnaround the entity/company without any change in terms and conditions of the loan. The JLF may also consider providing need based additional finance to the borrower, if considered necessary.
10. The option of 'restructuring' is considered where the borrower's business is viable and the borrower is not a wilful defaulter, *i.e.*, there is no diversion of funds, fraud or malfeasance, etc. At this stage, commitment from promoters

for extending their personal guarantees along with their net worth statement supported by copies of legal titles to assets may be obtained along with a declaration that they would not undertake any transaction that would alienate assets without the permission of the JLF. Any deviation from the commitment by the borrowers affecting the security/recover ability of the loans may be treated as a valid factor for initiating recovery process. For this action to be sustainable, the lenders in the JLF would sign an Inter Creditor Agreement (ICA) and also require the borrower to sign the Debtor Creditor Agreement (DCA) which would provide the legal basis for any restructuring process. The formats used by the Corporate Debt Restructuring (CDR) mechanism (see the later part of this Annexure) for ICA and DCA could be customized and used. Under the ICA, both secured and unsecured creditors have to agree to the final restructuring package.

11. Further, a 'stand still' clause could be stipulated in the DCA to enable smooth process of restructuring. A 'stand still' agreement is an important element of the DCA. The agreement is binding for the period from the date of DCA to the date of approval of restructuring 'package. Under this clause, both the debtor and creditor(s) shall agree to a legally binding 'stand-still' whereby both the parties commit themselves not to take recourse to any other legal action during the period. This would be necessary to undertake the debt restructuring exercise without any outside intervention, judicial or otherwise. However, the stand-still clause will be applicable only to any civil action either by the borrower or any lender against the other party and will not cover any criminal action. Further, during the stand-still period, outstanding foreign exchange forward contracts, derivative products, etc., can be crystallized, provided the borrower agrees to such crystallization. The borrower will additionally undertake that during the stand-still period the documents will stand extended for the purpose of limitation and also that the borrower will not approach any other authority for any relief and the directors of the borrowing company will not resign from the Board of Directors during the standstill period. However, even when the 'stand-still' clause is in operation the borrower can make interim payments to the lenders.
12. If the options of rectification or restructuring are not found feasible, 'Recovery' is the final option. The JLF may decide the best recovery process to be followed, among the various legal and other recovery options available, with a view to optimizing the efforts and results.
13. The decisions agreed upon by a minimum of 75% of creditors by value and 60%of creditors by number in the JLF would be considered as the basis for proceeding with the restructuring of the account, and will be binding on all lenders under the terms of the ICA. However, if the JLF decides to proceed with recovery, the minimum criteria for binding decision, if any, under any relevant laws/Acts would be applicable.
14. The JLF is required to arrive at an agreement on the option to be adopted for CAP within 30 days from (i) the date of an account being reported as SMA-2 by one or more lender, or (ii) receipt of request from the borrower to form a JLF, with substantiated grounds, if it senses imminent stress. The JLF should sign off the detailed final CAP within the next 30 days from the date of arriving at such an agreement.
15. If the JLF has decided on 'Rectification' or 'Restructuring' as the course of action, but the borrower fails to perform according to the terms agreed upon, the JLF should initiate 'Recovery'.
16. If the JLF decides to restructure an account independent of the CDR mechanism described below, a Techno Economic Viability (TEV) study should be conducted. If the borrower's business is found viable, the restructuring package should be finalized within 30 days from the date of the final CAP. The TEV and the package should be evaluated by an Independent Evaluation Committee (IEC), comprising of eligible experts. The experts will evaluate the viability and the fairness of the package within 30 days. After the independent evaluation, the package will have to be approved within 15 days for implementation.
17. The time limit for finalizing a suitable restructuring package for accounts with aggregate exposure of less than ₹5000 million would be 15 days.
18. All time limits specified by RBI are the maximum time that can be taken for finalization of the workout package.
19. Wilful defaulters will normally not be eligible for restructuring. However, the JLF may review the reasons for classification of the borrower as a wilful defaulter and satisfy itself that the borrower is in a position to rectify the wilful default. The decision to restructure such cases should however also have the approvals of the board/s of individual bank/s within the JLF who have classified the borrower as wilful defaulter.
20. The viability of the account should be determined by the JLF based on acceptable viability benchmarks determined by them. Illustratively, the parameters may include the Debt Equity Ratio, Debt Service Coverage Ratio, Liquidity/Current Ratio and the amount of provision required due to the erosion of the value of the restructured advance, etc. Further, the JLF may consider the benchmarks for the viability parameters adopted by the CDR mechanism.
21. Both under JLF and CDR mechanism, the restructuring package should also stipulate the time line during which certain viability milestones (*e.g.*, improvement in certain financial ratios after a period of time, say, 6 months or 1 year and so on) would be achieved. The JLF must periodically review the account for achievement/non-achievement of milestones and should consider initiating suitable measures including appropriate recovery measures.
22. The general principle of restructuring should be that the shareholders bear the first loss rather than the debt holders. With this principle in view and also to ensure more participation by promoters, JLF/CDR may consider the following options when a loan is restructured: (a) Possibility of transferring equity of the company by promoters to the lenders to compensate for their sacrifices; (b) Promoters infusing more equity into their companies; (c) Transfer of the promoters' holdings to a security trustee or an escrow arrangement till turnaround of company. This will enable a change in management control, should lenders favour it.

23. For restructuring exposures to listed companies, lenders may be compensated up front for their loss/sacrifice (diminution in fair value of account in net present value terms) by way of issuance of equities of the company up front, subject to the regulations and statutory requirements. In such cases, the restructuring agreement shall not incorporate any 'right of recompense' (recovery of 'sacrifice' by the lender) clause. However, if the lenders' sacrifice is not fully compensated by way of issuance of equities, the right of recompense clause may be incorporated to the extent of shortfall. For unlisted companies, the JLF will have option of either getting equities issued or incorporate suitable 'right to recompense' clause.
24. Banks that fail to report SMA status of the accounts to CRILC or conceal the actual status of the accounts will be subjected to accelerated provisioning (over and above the current provision requirements, as seen in subsequent chapters) for these accounts and/or other supervisory actions by RBI.
25. Higher provisions will also have to made for wilful defaulters and 'non cooperative borrowers'. (A non-cooperative borrower is broadly one who does not provide necessary information required by a lender to assess its financial health even after 2 reminders; or denies access to securities etc. as per terms of sanction or does not comply with other terms of loan agreements within stipulated period; or is hostile/indifferent/in denial mode to negotiate with the bank on repayment issues; or plays for time by giving false impression that some solution is on horizon; or resorts to vexatious tactics such as litigation to thwart timely resolution of the interest of the lender/s. The borrowers will be given 30 days' notice to clarify their stand before their names are reported as non-cooperative borrowers to CRILC. The definitions and penalties can be found in the RBI instructions.

BOX 7.4 ILLUSTRATIVE LIST OF SIGNS OF STRESS FOR CATEGORIZING AN ACCOUNT AS SMA-0

1. Delay of 90 days or more in (a) submission of stock statement / other stipulated operating control statements or (b) credit monitoring or financial statements or (c)non-renewal of facilities based on audited financials.
2. Actual sales/operating profits falling short of projections accepted for loan sanction by 40% or more; or a single event of non-cooperation/prevention from conduct of stock audits by banks; or reduction of Drawing Power (DP) by 20% or more after a stock audit; or evidence of diversion of funds for unapproved purpose; or drop in internal risk rating by 2 or more notches in a single review.
3. Return of 3 or more cheques (or electronic debit instructions) issued by borrower in 30 days on grounds of non-availability of balance/DP in the account or return of 3 or more bills / cheques discounted or sent under collection by the borrower.
4. Development of Deferred Payment Guarantee (DPG) installments or Letters of Credit (LCs) or invocation of Bank Guarantees (BGs) and its non-payment within 30 days.
5. Third request for extension of time either for creation or perfection of securities as against time specified in original sanction terms or for compliance with any other terms and conditions of sanction.
6. Increase in frequency of overdrafts in current accounts.
7. The borrower reporting stress in the business and financials.
8. Promoter(s) pledging/selling their shares in the borrower company due to financial stress.

Source: RBI, Framework for Revitalizing Distressed Assets in the Economy – Guidelines on Joint Lenders' Forum (JLF) and Corrective Action Plan (CAP), dated February 26, 2014 (Annexure)

ILLUSTRATION 1

The outstanding advance in the cash credit account of a borrower firm on the date of implementation of the rehabilitation package is ₹60 lacs. The Drawing Power [DP] evidenced by the stock statements, as well as the actual stocks available to cover the advance is ₹20 lacs. The firm started incurring cash losses continuously since 2004. The total interest charged in the account since April 2004 upto the implementation of the relief package is ₹32 lacs.

Step 1: Compare the outstanding advance on the date of implementation of the relief package with the DP on that date. The difference is the irregularity in the cash credit account. Thus,

A. Outstanding advance on date of rehabilitation	₹60 Lakhs
B. *Less*: Drawing Power available	₹20 Lakhs
C. Total irregularity on date of implementation [A – B]	₹40 Lakhs

Step 2: Compute the interest charged to the cash credit account from the year the firm started showing continuous cash losses, up to the date of the relief package. If this interest exceeds the total irregularity in Step 1, the entire irregularity in the account is to be treated as 'interest irregularity' and converted into a funded interest term loan [FITL]. If less, the amount by which the total irregularity exceeds the interest irregularity would be treated as unsecured principal, and converted into a Working Capital Term Loan [WCTL].

D. Interest charged from the year of cash losses	₹32 Lakhs
E. Difference to be treated as 'principal irregularity' [C – D]	₹ 8 Lakhs
F. The interest irregularity portion to be converted into FITL	₹32 Lakhs
G. The principal irregularity portion to be converted into WCTL	₹ 8 Lakhs

Relief and Concessions from Other Agencies/Institutions

Apart from banks and other lenders, rehabilitation calls for sacrifices from the state and central governments, as well as the management of beleaguered firm itself. An indicative list of such relief measures is provided in Box 7.5.

BOX 7.5 AN ILLUSTRATIVE LIST OF CONCESSIONS AND RELIEF MEASURES THAT CAN BE SOUGHT FOR FROM THE GOVERNMENTS AND THE MANAGEMENT

State Government

- Sales tax loans at low rates of interest;
- Government guarantee for fresh advances from the bank;
- Preferential treatment for power supply, and uninterrupted power supply;
- Rescheduling of payments due for power;
- Duties/levies of the state government waived or provided at a concession;
- Speedier resolution of labour disputes;
- Market support for products to be produced by the firm under rehabilitation;
- Equity contribution, where possible, etc.

Central government

- Exemption from or reduction of central excise;
- For firms operating in industries catering to public interest, budgetary support through equity or interest free loans
- Adequate market support and price preferences, etc.

Sacrifice from the management

- Waiver or reduction of remuneration;
- Foregoing interest on loans made to the firm;
- Agreeing to reconstitution of Board, if necessary;
- Agreeing for additional collateral, etc.

Sacrifice from Labour

- Agreeing to retrenchment of surplus workers;
- Phasing out retrenchment compensation;
- Agreeing not to make fresh demands till the firm is rehabilitated, etc.

Rights of The Rehabilitating Bank

There are two important rights of the bank rehabilitating a sick firm – the right of 'review' and the right of 'recompense'.

The Right of Review enables the bank to re-assess the assumptions under which the rehabilitation has been embarked upon, and revise conditions of sanction if the actual cash flows of the firm are different from the expected cash flows. For example, the bank can revise the interest rates upward [since they have been lowered to aid the rehabilitation process] if the cash flows from the firm justify the increase, or the base rate increases.

The Right of Recompense entitles the bank to recoup the interest and other monetary 'sacrifices'—such *as reduction in interest rate, funding of interest at reduced rates, conversion of principal/interest into non-convertible debt instruments at lower interest rates, waiver of principal/interest dues, conversion into WCTL, and additional finance*—made by the bank, once the firm is rehabilitated, and begins generating adequate positive cash flows.

Corporate Debt Restructuring [CDR][16]—Salient Features

The CDR Scheme, originally proposed in 2001, was revised for implementation in 2002 based on the recommendations made by the Working Group under the Chairmanship of Shri Vepa Kamesam, Deputy Governor, RBI.

Objectives of the Scheme The objectives of the scheme are:

- Ensuring timely and transparent mechanism for restructuring debts of those corporate entities facing problems, for the benefit of all concerned.
- Preserving viable corporate entities affected by internal and external factors.
- Minimizing losses to creditors and other stakeholders through an orderly and coordinated restructuring programme.

Features The features of the scheme are as follows:

- The scheme operates as a voluntary, non-statutory system.
- It covers all corporate borrowing accounts, whether under multiple banking, syndication or consortium arrangements. However, it will not apply to accounts involving only one FI/bank.
- It is based on the principle of 'super majority'.
- It is applicable to accounts where the minimum outstanding credit exposure is over ₹10 crores.[17]
- Cases pending under the BIFR and the Debt Recovery Tribunal are also considered for CD, if such accounts are very large and have been recommended by the CDR Core Group.
- Cases of willful default, frauds and malfeasance are excluded from the CDR scheme.
- Two categories of debt restructuring are provided. Accounts classified as 'standard' and 'sub-standard' in the books of the lenders, will be restructured under the first category (Category 1). Accounts that are classified as 'doubtful' in the books of the lenders would be restructured under the second category (Category 2).
- The accounts where recovery suits have been filed by the lenders against the company, may be eligible for consideration under the CDR system provided,

the initiative to resolve the case under the CDR system is taken by at least 75 per cent of the lenders (by value). In addition, the supporting creditors should constitute at least 60 per cent of the number of creditors.[18]

- OTS would be allowed under the revised guidelines (2005) to make the exit option more flexible.
- Details of CDR during the year should be disclosed in the banks' financial statements under 'Notes on Accounts'.
- The accounting treatment of accounts restructured under CDR system, including accounts classified as 'doubtful' under Category 2 CDR, would be governed by the prudential norms indicated in RBI's Master Circular dated July 2, 2012.

The Methodology The methodology is similar to the rehabilitation schemes operated for the SME sector.

- Extending the repayment period of loans.
- Converting the unserviced interest portion into term loans.
- Reducing the rate of interest on outstanding advances.

The CDR Structure The mechanism operates with a three-tier structure, consisting of the following:

- **The CDR standing forum:** The CDR standing forum would be the representative general body of all FIs and banks participating in the CDR system. It is suggested by the RBI that all FIs and banks should participate in the system in their own interest. The CDR standing forum will be a self-empowered body, which will lay down policies and guidelines and monitor the progress of CDR. The forum will also provide an official platform for both creditors and borrowers (by consultation) to amicably and collectively evolve policies and guidelines for working out debt-restructuring plans in the interests of all stakeholders. A CDR core group will be carved out of the CDR standing forum to assist the forum in convening the meetings and taking decisions relating to policy, on behalf of the forum. The CDR core group would lay down the policies and guidelines to be followed by the CDR empowered group and CDR cell for debt restructuring. These guidelines shall also suitably address the operational difficulties experienced in the functioning of the CDR empowered group. The CDR core group shall also prescribe the timelines for processing of cases referred to the CDR system and decide on the modalities for enforcement of the time frame. The CDR core group shall also lay down guidelines to ensure that over-optimistic projections are not assumed while preparing/approving restructuring proposals.

- **The CDR empowered group:** This group is the decision-making body for individual cases of restructuring. If the group decides, after studying the preliminary feasibility report, that the restructuring is feasible and the borrower firm is potentially viable, the detailed restructuring package will be worked out by the CDR cell along with the lead lending institution. The time frame allowed for the decision to restructure is 90 days, which, at a maximum, can be 180 days. While approving the restructuring package, the group will also indicate acceptable viability benchmarks such as, ROCE (return on capital employed), DSCR (debt service coverage ratio), the gap between the IRR (internal rate of return) and the COC, and the extent of 'sacrifice'. If restructuring is not found viable at this stage, the creditors would be free to initiate recovery proceedings.

- **The CDR cell:** The CDR standing forum and the CDR empowered group will be assisted by a CDR cell in all their functions. The cell will carry out the initial appraisal of the rehabilitation proposals received from borrowers/lenders, and make its recommendations to the CDR empowered group, within 1 month. If restructuring is found feasible, the CDR cell will prepare a detailed rehabilitation plan with the help of lenders and, if necessary, outside experts. If restructuring is not considered feasible, the lenders may start action for recovery of their dues.

The Legal Issues The legal issues are as follows:

- The debtor–creditor agreement (DCA) and the inter-creditor agreement (ICA) provide the legal basis to the CDR mechanism.
- All participants in the CDR mechanism through their membership of the standing forum shall have to enter into a legally binding agreement, with necessary enforcement and penal clauses, to operate the system through laid-down policies and guidelines.
- The ICA signed by the creditors would be a legally binding agreement, with enforcement and penal clauses. The creditors commit themselves under the agreement to abide by the requirements and process of CDR. Further, if 75 per cent of creditors by value and 60 per cent of creditors by number agree to a restructuring package, the decision would be binding on all creditors to an existing debt. The agreement will be initially valid for a period of 3 years and subject to renewal for further periods of 3 years, thereafter. It is to be noted that foreign lenders are not a part of the CDR system.
- An important element of the DCA is the 'stand-still' agreement binding on both parties for 90 days or 180 days. Under this clause, both parties commit to a stand-still—implying that the parties would not resort to any other legal action during this period.
- However, the standstill clause will not be applicable to criminal action against any of the counter parties. Further, during the standstill period, issues like outstanding foreign exchange forward contracts, and derivative products can be crystallized, provided the

borrower is agreeable to such crystallization. The borrower will additionally undertake that during the stand-still period the documents will stand extended for the purpose of limitation and also that he will not approach any other authority for any relief and the directors of the borrowing company will not resign from the Board.

- All CDR approved packages must incorporate creditors' right to accelerate repayment and borrowers' right to pre-pay. The right of recompense should be based on certain performance criteria to be decided by the Standing Forum.

ANNEXURE III

CASE STUDIES: DEBT RESTRUCTURED UNDER CDR

A Look at how the Scheme has Worked in India

The data in Tables 7.1 and 7.2 show that the scheme has worked quite well so far.

At the end of December 2013, 259 companies were being restructured under the Scheme, with an outstanding debt of about ₹207635 crore.

Of these, the Infrastructure sector has accounted for a major share of about 20%.This is primarily due to CDR Group having approved the debt restructuring of Infrastructure projects/ companies such as Sasan Power (₹11000 crore), Suzlon (₹11000 crore), Gammon India (₹13500 crore) through the CDR mechanism. More significantly, the share of infrastructure companies has increased from about 2% (and 2 companies) in March 2009, to above 8% from 22 companies, thus reflecting the problems this vital sector is currently passing through.

In this Annexure, we will also study how a few companies could turn round in a short span, aided by the package under the CDR Scheme.

TABLE 7.1 CASES UNDER CDR–STATUS AT THE END OF DECEMBER 2013

Total References Received by CDR Cell		Cases Rejected before Admission or Approval		Cases Under Consideration of CDR EG		Total Cases Approved		Cases Withdrawn on Account of Package Failure		Cases Exited Successfully		Live Cases in CDR	
(1)		(2)		(3)		(4)		(5)		(6)		(7)	
No. of cases	Aggregate Debt	No. of cases	Aggregate Debt	No. of cases	Aggregate Debt	No. of cases	Aggregate Debt	No. of cases	Aggregate Debt	No. of cases	Aggregate Debt	No. of cases	Aggregate Debt
605	407656	105	52866	57	65492	443	289298	115	29038	69	52625	259	207635

Source: www.cdrindia.org

TABLE 7.2 DISTRIBUTION OF LIVE CASES UNDER CDR (BY INDUSTRY) AT THE END OF DECEMBER 2013

Sl. No.	Industry	No.	Aggregate Debt (₹ in Crores)	Debt in %
1	Infrastructure	22	40761	19.63
2	Iron and Steel	45	37214	17.92
3	Power	15	26309	12.67
4	Textiles	44	19636	9.46
5	Telecom	5	10785	5.19

(Continued)

TABLE 7.2 (CONTINUED)

Sl. No.	Industry	No.	Aggregate Debt (₹ in Crores)	Debt in %
6	NBFC	5	6976	3.36
7	Ship-Breaking/Ship Building	3	6753	3.25
8	Construction	6	6558	3.16
9	Pharmaceuticals	9	6429	3.10
10	Petrochemicals	2	4852	2.34
11	Sugar	17	4799	2.31
12	Hospitality	10	4805	2.31
13	Cement	8	4569	2.20
14	Paper/Packaging	14	4198	2.02
15	Computers	2	3124	1.50
16	Fertilizers	5	2738	1.32
17	Electrical	1	2117	1.02
18	Storage Media	1	2054	0.99
19	Automobiles	2	1729	0.83
20	Manufacture	5	1696	0.82
21	Ceramic Tiles	3	1362	0.66
22	Chemicals	5	1152	0.55
23	Logistic	1	1083	0.52
24	Service	2	778	0.37
25	Engineering	4	685	0.33
26	Coke and Coal	2	606	0.29
27	Auto Components	3	601	0.29
28	Agro	1	599	0.29
29	Cables	3	579	0.28
30	Forgings	1	490	0.24
31	Glass	1	404	0.19
32	Metals (Non-ferrous Metals)	1	200	0.10
33	Electronies	1	177	0.09
34	Other (Jewe, Liquor, edible oil etc.)	1	152	0.07
35	Hospital and Healthcare	2	134	0.06
36	Processing	1	133	0.06
37	Rubber	1	113	0.05
38	Dairy	1	97	0.05
39	Food and Food	1	69	0.03
40	Education	1	60	0.03
41	Irrigation	1	33	0.02
42	Plastic	1	26	0.01
	Total	**259**	**207635**	**100.00**

Source: www.cdrindia.org

Case Study I: India Cements Ltd

Need for Restructuring When India Cements Ltd submitted a CDR proposal to the FIs at the end of 2002, it had stated that the bunching up of debt repayments over the next few years and inadequate cash flow generation was making it difficult for the company to meet its obligations.

On 31 March 2002, India Cements' total outstanding debt was ₹1,793 crores made up of ₹447 crores of term loans, ₹759 crores of debentures, ₹164 crores of short-term unsecured loans, ₹363 crores of working capital cash credit/overdraft and ₹60 crores of public deposits. With earnings before interest, depreciation, tax and amortization of ₹83 crores, it would have been hardly able to meet its debt and preference capital obligations of ₹729 crores for the year (including repayment and interest).

India Cements Debt Restructuring India Cements mandated HSBC Securities and Capital Markets (India) Pvt. Ltd as exclusive adviser in the restructuring process. As part of the debt-restructuring exercise, India Cements agreed to divest its entire stake in Visaka Cement Industry Ltd. and other non-core assets, which expected to yield ₹410 crores net of debt and interest outstanding of ₹190 crores in Visaka.

The Debt-Restructuring Proposal[19] According to the debt-restructuring proposal, India Cements would use the proceeds from the sale of Visaka Cement to settle the debt in that company and then settle certain loans and interest and pressing creditors. It also created a contingency fund to meet any shortfall in Visaka's divestment realization. The balance bank borrowings were to be restructured along with term debt such that the entire outstanding debt had a moratorium of 3 years on principal repayments, with an overall tenor of 10 years for principal and interest payments and a yield to maturity of 11 per cent, achieved through a ballooning of interest rates from 2 per cent for FY2003 to 50 per cent for FY2012.

Accordingly, the debt repayment schedule of India Cements and Visaka together was estimated at ₹779 crores in 2002–2003, ₹449 crores in 2003–2004, ₹459 crores in 2004–2005, ₹500 crores in 2005–2006, ₹206 crores in 2006–2007 and ₹116 crores in 2007–2008. However, the projected operating cash flows for these years, at ₹31 crores, ₹117 crores, ₹215 crores, ₹371 crores, ₹470 crores and ₹376 crores for 2007–2008, indicated the company's inability to meet its debt obligations. Post-restructuring, India Cements expected to register a net loss of ₹57 crores for 2002–2003, and a net profit of ₹7 crores the next year. The net profit was projected to increase to ₹31 crores in 2004–2005, ₹75 crores in 2005–2006, ₹52 crores in 2006–2007, ₹26 crores in 2007–2008, ₹14 crores in 2008–2009, ₹10 crores in 2009–2010, ₹20 crores in 2010–2011 and ₹42 crores in 2011–2012.

Plan Under the CDR[20] In a debt-restructuring plan cleared by the CDR Forum of FIs and banks, the company had committed to the following:

- Sell off its non-core assets by March 2004, including ICL Shipping Ltd and real estate assets, to raise about ₹60 crores.
- Cut 1,000 jobs through a voluntary retirement scheme costing ₹50 crores, but estimated to save ₹10 crores per year.
- Two-year moratorium on repayments.
- Back-ended payments after the 2-year period with interest rates under different categories ranging between 3 per cent and 18.5 per cent.

The ₹1,706 crores debt-restructuring proposal was cleared by 30 odd lenders comprising banks and FIs, the progress of which would be monitored by Industrial Development Bank of India.

As per the debt-restructuring proposal approved by the lenders, the cut-off date for the package was 1 January 2003. All debts excluding deposits from the public would be restructured. There would be multiple options available to the lenders with different exit options and yields. Additional working capital would be released to the company on assessing requirements.

India Cements Post-CDR[21] Partly due to the restructuring and partly due to the booming cement market, India Cements has managed to post record profits up to December 2009. Table 7.3 shows the progress.

The net profit of ₹112.59 crores for the quarter ended 30 June 2006 is the highest ever profit made by the company. The good demand for cement and the favourable prices are expected to last for about 2–3 years, according to the company sources. Aided by this trend, the company wiped out its accumulated losses by the third quarter of 2006.

At the time of restructuring, the company's total debt stood at ₹1,280 crores, of which about ₹500 crores would come under the CDR scheme. India Cements hoped to repay a substantial portion of this high-cost debt during the year, thus, bringing down its average cost of borrowings from 10.5 per cent. The debt equity stood at 1.4 in March 2007, and fell to 0.6 in March 2009.

TABLE 7.3 INDIA CEMENTS—KEY FINANCIAL INDICATORS—QUARTERS ENDED JUNE 2005 AND 2006

	Quarter Ended June 2006	(₹ in Crores) June 2005	2008–09
Net sales	561.82	452.09	3359.09
Other income	5.43	0.89	115.41
Total expenditure	369.29	382.24	2431.70
Operating profit	170.96	70.74	1043.20
Interest	38.89	5.21	112.15
Net profit	112.59	5.21	432.18

Source: www.indiacements.co.in

CASE STUDY II: PRIVATE EQUITY AND CDR

Kitply Industries[22]

When India Debt Management, a group company of Hong Kong-based ADM Capital, infused ₹120 crores of private equity into the ailing Kitply Industries in April 2008, it heralded a new trend in the CDR mechanism. It signified not only restructuring but also a change of management at the plywood firm that owns the popular brand Kitply.

The private equity funds brought in will be used partly to repay the lenders to Kitply and partly to revive its operations. The company had outstanding loans of ₹500 crores to about 15 lenders. The company's operations were hit due to an earlier slowdown in the economy and a family dispute over management control.

The restructuring of Kitply was referred in 2006 to the CDR forum. The restructuring package proposes that ₹75–80 crores would be used to repay the lenders, while the balance ₹40–45 crores would be infused as equity into the company. While some of the lenders have already sold their loans to Asset Restructuring Company of India (Arcil), other lenders like ICICI Bank, SBI and IFCI would continue as lenders. Loans to the company are backed by 1,500 acres of land in Raipur, where the plant is also located.

Lenders would be issued non-convertible debentures of ₹40 crores. Pawan Goenka, the promoter, would bring in about ₹10 crores. In the wake of private equity infusion, shareholding pattern of Kitply Industries will change. Restructuring the company's outstanding bank debt would be done by Kotak Mahindra Bank.

CASE STUDY III: WOCKHARDT LTD[23]

Wockhardt Ltd., a pharmaceutical and biotechnology company headquartered in Mumbai, was founded by HabilKhorakiwala in the early 1960s. The company went public in 1992. The following few years witnessed the company's transformation from a local firm to a global player, with significant presence in the USA, Europe and India. Its major product lines were formulations, bio-pharamaceuticals, nutrition products, vaccines and pharmaceutical ingredients. It had 158 patents granted worldwide, and had a multi ethnic workforce of more than 8000.

Rise and fall of Wockhardt

Between 2001 and 2008 the company's sales and operating profits grew 5 times, while the stock prices increased 3 times. It acquired seven international companies at a cost of about USD 22 billion. During this period, the company's debt had also increased steeply, from ₹3 billion to ₹42 billion.

Two significant acquisitions made just before the financial crisis of 2007 broke were Pinewood Labs of Ireland for $150 mn in 2006 and Negma Labs of France for a sum of $ 265 mn. The latter was the largest deal that the company had entered into since its inception. These acquisitions were financed primarily through foreign currency convertible bonds. Major unsecured lenders (FCCB holders) were BNY Corporate Trustees Services Ltd., Barclays Capital Services Ltd., US Hedge fund QVT Fund LP, Quintessence Fund LP, Bank of Nova Scotia and Sun Pharma Global Inc.

Wockhardt was also involved in the use of complex derivatives to get itself a better exchange ratio. These derivatives were constructed in a manner that allowed the company to make gains on its foreign receivables. However, the derivatives were structured to work favourably only in healthy economic conditions. As a result, during the time of economic turmoil in 2008 these derivatives were the source of major losses to the company.

In February 2008, Wockhardt had huge debt on its balance sheet, while its sales slowed, and the company had to withdraw its IPO on account of cold response from the market. Wockhardt had initiated steps to derive cost benefits, move easier products into India, and increase its profits. But even before the benefits of these measures could concretize, the financial markets across the world started cracking in the second half of 2008. The company had issued FCCBs worth USD 140.6 million in anticipation of share prices reaching a level where the bondholders would convert to shares, thus reducing the debt burden. But that was not to be.

At the end of 2008, the company was struggling to find sources to repay FCCBs of ₹1324 crore due in September 2009 and ₹1048 crore due in 2010. Compounding the debt problem were the mark-to-market and derivative losses of about ₹581 crore. December 2008 saw the company posting a net loss of ₹139 crore for the financial year.

CDR workout for Wockhardt

The company approached the CDR Cell through ICICI Bank and availed approval for its scheme on July 4, 2009. The scheme (effective from April 15, 2009) covered most outstanding liabilities except certain FCCBs and disputed derivative contract liabilities.

Major secured Indian lenders were ICICI Bank, SBI, IDBI, IOB, BOI, PNB, HDFC Bank, and ING Vysya.

Under the approved CDR scheme, the company allotted approx. 153 mn preference shares to the CDR lenders valued cumulatively at ₹666.4 mn. These Non-convertible (NCCRPS) and Optionally-convertible (OCCRPS) Cumulative, Redeemable Preference Shares would be convertible in 2015 and redeemable in 2018.

A few of the FCCB holders were not satisfied with the CDR scheme, and filed a winding up petition against the company.

In response, the company assured the Court and its bond-holders that it would honour its loan repayment obligations, seeking permission to divest its nutrition business to the French company DANONE. It further assured that sale proceeds from this divestment would be primarily utilized towards repaying its FCCB holders. It also signed an undertaking in the court with an explicit time-table to repay its creditors. In case of failure to adhere, the court would appoint an official liquidator to divest the company's assets to recover dues of the aggrieved (bond holders) lenders. The management's resolve to turnaround the company was demonstrated when it complied with the court and deposited ₹1.15 bn, in accordance with the mandated schedule.

After paying bondholders a tranche of ₹200 crore in August 2012, Wockhardt planned to exit the CDR process.

The year 2012 saw Wockhardt's shares soar nearly 350 per cent to record highs, lifting its market value to USD 2.45 billion. The operating results were also encouraging –23 per cent sales growth in the first quarter of 2012–13, and a net debt to equity ratio now below 1, reduced from 5.5 times in March 2010. The EBIDTA stood at ₹502 crore at end June 2012, growing by 61 per cent and represented 10th consecutive quarter of sequential growth.

The financial highlights posted by Wockhardt on its website in February 2013 look promising:

- Free Cash Flow from operations in excess of ₹275 crores in Q3FY13 and above ₹800 crores for 9MFY13.
- Exit from CDR on target.
- Total Debt repaid during the year in excess of ₹1600 crores till date.
- Net interest cost stand at around 4.2 per cent on an annualized basis (at around 3.4 per cent for Q3FY13 on an annualized basis).
- Net Debt to Equity now stands below 0.50:1.

ENDNOTES

1. For a definition of credit risk, please see Chapter on 'Credit Risk'.
2. For a detailed discussion on the subject, please see chapter on 'Capital-Risk, Regulation and Adequacy'.
3. Edward Altman, E. L., 'Financial Ratios, Discriminant Analysis and the Prediction of Corporate Bankruptcy,' *The Journal of Finance*, 23, (1968): 589–609. The original model was built with data from 66 sample firms, of which half had filed for bankruptcy. The database constituted firms with assets of over $1 million, with less than $25 million in sales, and engaged in manufacturing activity. However, the model is reported to provide a satisfactory degree of accuracy in predicting failure in non-manufacturing firms as well.
4. Edward Altman, R. Haldeman and P. Narayanan, 'Zeta Analysis: A New Model to Identify Bankruptcy Risk of Corporations ', *Journal of Banking and Finance*, 1, no. 1, (1977): 29–54.
5. This model is a proprietary model for subscribers to Zeta Services, Inc.
6. Edward Altman, J. Hartzell and M. Peck, 'Emerging Markets Corporate Bonds: A Scoring System', Salomon Brothers Inc, New York, (1995), quoted in Altman, E. I., 'Predicting Financial Distress of Companies: Revisiting the *Z* Score and Zeta Models', Paper prepared for Korean Institute of Finance Conference on Bank Credit Risk (2000).
7. Please see for full discussion of the model, Hartzell, John, Pack, Mathew, Altman, Edward I and Heine, Max L, 'Emerging Market Corporate Bonds—A Scoring System', Salomon Brothers Emerging markets corporate bonds research, 1995.
8. Ohlson (1980), Zavgren (1983) and Zmijewski (1984) quoted by Morton Glantz (2003) in Managing Bank Risk, Chapter 9, 308. Academic Press.
9. *Ibid.*
10. Neural networks' are computer systems and programmes that can retain data in patterns, process information and learn from the processing experience, much like the human brain.
11. McKee, T.E., Lensberg, T., 2002. Genetic programming and rough sets: A hybrid approach to bankruptcy classification, European Journal of Operational Research 138 (2) 436–451.
12. Mar–Molinero, C., Serrano-Cinca, C., 2001. Bank failure: a multidimensional scaling approach, European Journal of Finance 7 (2) 165–183.
13. For more on 'impaired loans', please see Chapter on 'Credit Risk'.
14. Wuffli, Peter A. and David A. Hunt, 'Fixing the Credit Problem', *The McKinsey Quarterly*, no. 2, (1993).
15. Sources: RBI Master Circular on Wilful Defaulters, July 1, 2013; websites of credit information companies.
16. RBI, 'Corporate Debt Restructuring (CDR)', dated 5 February 2003. The latest guidelines can be found in RBI Master Circulars dated July 1, 2013.
17. Revised from ₹20 crores in 2005 through RBI's 'Revised Guidelines on Corporate Debt Restructuring Mechanism', dated 10 November 2005. This and other revisions were carried out based on a review of the Scheme in 2004 by a Special Group headed by Smt. S. Gopinath, Deputy Governor, RBI.
18. This and other revisions were carried out based on a review of the scheme in 2004 by a special group headed by Smt. S. Gopinath, Deputy Governor, RBI.
19. Data and information from Business Line dated December 13, 2002. 'India Cements has to pay up ₹779 crore debt this fiscal—Submits debt revamp proposal

to Fis', at http://www.blonnet.com/2002/12/13/stories/2002121301950200.htm.

20. Data and information from Business Line dated 19 May 2003, 'To Raise ₹800 cr. to Retire debt—India Cements Plans to Sell Visaka, Raasi', at http://www.blonnet.com/2003/05/19/stories/2003051901430300.htm.
21. 'India Cements Posts Record net Profit at ₹112 Cr', Business Line dated July 18, 2006, at http://www.thehindubusinessline.com/2006/07/18/stories/2006071804620100.htm.
22. *Source*: The Economic Times, dated 2 April 2008.
23. *Sources:* www.moneycontrol.com, www.wockhardt.com, and various newspaper articles.

CHAPTER EIGHT

Managing Credit Risk—An Overview

CHAPTER STRUCTURE

KEY TAKEAWAYS FROM THE CHAPTER

- Understand the concept of credit risk.
- Know how credit risk arises.
- Learn about credit risk mitigation techniques, such as securitization, covered bonds and credit derivatives.
- Understand the Basel Committee's role.
- Gain knowledge about the prudential norms for asset classification, income recognition and provisioning.

SECTION I

BASIC CONCEPTS

Banks grant credit to produce profits. In the process, they also assume and accept risks. In evaluating risk, banks should assess the likely downside scenarios and their possible impact on the borrowers and their debt servicing capacity.

Two types of losses are possible in respect of any borrower or borrower class—expected losses (EL) and unexpected losses (UL). EL can be budgeted for, and provisions held to offset their adverse effects on the bank's balance sheet. EL could arise from the risks in the industry in which the borrower operates, the business risks associated with the borrower firm, its track record of payments and future potential to generate cash flows. UL, being unpredictable, have to be cushioned by holding adequate capital. In this chapter, we will concentrate on the process by which banks identify and provide for EL.[1]

Banks can utilize the structure of the borrowers' transactions, collateral and guarantees to mitigate identified and inherent risks, but none of these can substitute for comprehensive assessment of borrowers' repayment capacity or compensate for inadequate information or monitoring. Any action of credit enforcement (recalling the advances made or instituting foreclosure proceedings, including legal proceedings) may only serve to erode the already thin profit margins on the transactions.

Expected Versus Unexpected Loss

Although credit losses are typically dependent on time and economic conditions, it is theoretically possible to arrive at a statistically measured long run average loss level. Assume, *e.g.*, that based on historical performance, a bank expects around 1 per cent of its loans to default every year, with an average recovery rate of 50 per cent. In that case, the bank's EL for a credit portfolio of ₹1,000 crores is ₹5 crores (*i.e.*, ₹1,000 crores × 1 per cent × 50 per cent). EL is, therefore, seen to be based on three parameters:

- The likelihood that default will take place over a specified time horizon (probability of default or PD).[2]
- The amount owed by the counter party at the moment of default (exposure at default or EAD).
- The fraction of the exposure and net of any recoveries, which will be lost following a default event (loss given default or LGD).[3]

Since PD is normally specified on a 1 year basis, the product of these three factors is the 1 year EL.

$$EL = PD \times EAD \times LGD$$

EL can be aggregated at the level of individual loans or the entire credit portfolio. It is also both customer- and facility-specific, since two different loans to the same customer can have very different ELs due to differences in EAD and/or LGD.

It is important to note that EL (and credit quality) does not by itself constitute risk—if losses turned out as expected, they represent the anticipated 'cost' of being in business. In any case, their impact is being factored into loan pricing[4] and provisions. Credit risk, in fact, emerges from adverse variations in the actual loss levels, which give rise to the so-called UL. As described in a later chapter, the need for bank capital arises from the need to cushion against UL or loss volatility. Statistically, UL is simply the standard deviation of EL as shown in Figure 8.1.[5]

FIGURE 8.1 EXPECTED AND UNEXPECTED LOSSES

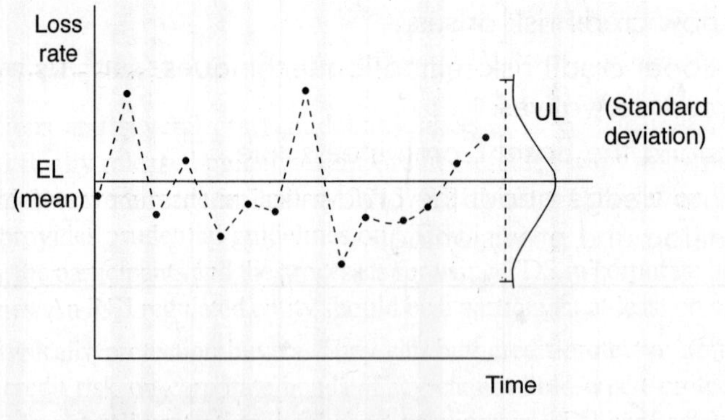

Source: World Bank Working Paper.

Defining Credit Risk[6]

Credit risk is most simply defined as the probability that a bank borrower or counter party will fail to meet its obligations in accordance with agreed terms.

The effective management of credit risk is a critical component of a comprehensive approach to risk management and essential to the long-term success of any banking organization. The goal of credit risk management should be maximizing a bank's risk-adjusted rate of return by maintaining credit risk exposure within acceptable parameters.

It follows that a bank needs to manage the following:

- The risk in individual credits or transactions (discussed extensively in the foregoing chapters).
- The credit risk inherent in the entire portfolio.
- The relationships between credit risk and other risks.

The elements of credit risk can, therefore, be grouped in the following manner[7] (*see* Figure 8.2):

FIGURE 8.2 ELEMENTS OF CREDIT RISK

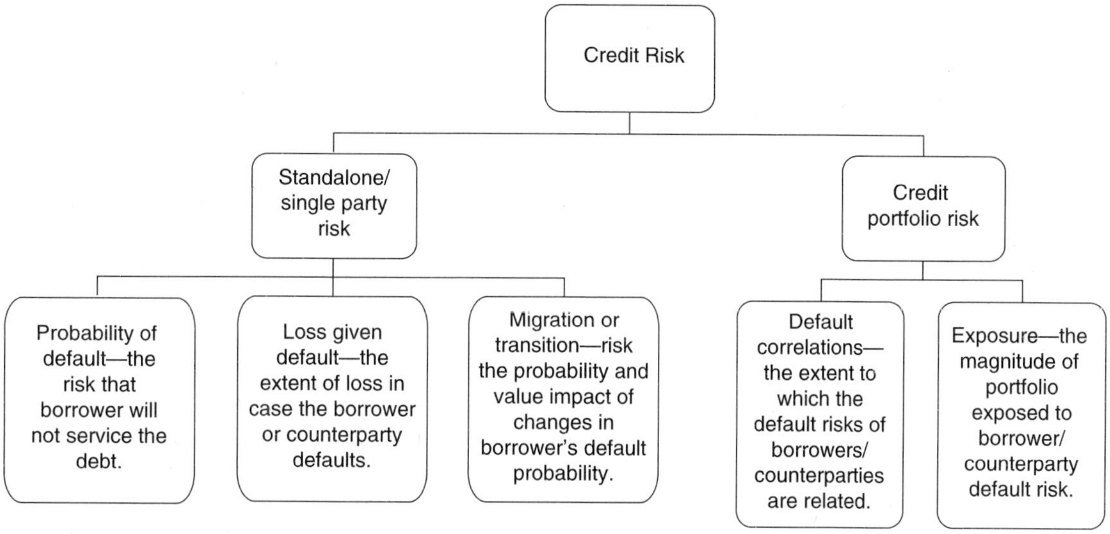

We will discuss these aspects in the ensuing paragraphs and in the next chapter.

Credit Risk of the Portfolio From our earlier discussions, it would be evident that managing the credit portfolio of a bank involves a higher level of risk-reward decisions than managing a portfolio of market investments. This is due to the fact that there is limited upside risk and unlimited downside risk in bank lending (in contrast to market investments, which hold limited downside risk, but unlimited upside risk).

For example, when a bank makes a 'good' loan that is repaid in full on the due date, what the bank has received are only the interest payments and principal repayments due to it. The bank cannot demand a share of the substantial cash flows that the business has managed to generate with the help of bank funds. On the other hand, if the business fails, the bank's earnings take a direct hit—the bank suffers along with the borrower. The bank could price 'risky' borrowers higher to compensate for the risk of failure.[8] But market dynamics would limit the extent of the risk premium that the bank can charge.

Often, a bank develops expertise in financing a particular activity or industry and increases its credit exposure to this sector to leverage its capabilities. If this sector collapses, for some force majeure reason, it drags the bank's fortunes down with it.

Thus, it is evident that a bank could be vulnerable to two factors—one, it may not be able to price its loan to compensate fully for the risk and two, its concentration in a specific industry or economic activity could render the bank susceptible to risks inherent in that industry.

It follows that the loan policy of a bank should be able to structure policies and procedures that ensure that credit exposures to various sectors and regions are adequately diversified to maximise the return on the loan portfolio of the bank. Such a task is too daunting for individual banks' portfolio managers and requires the intervention of the central banks of the countries. In most countries, central banks propose optimal 'exposure norms' for various industries and activities from time to time. Such exposure norms not only pre-empt banks intending to invest excessively in similar firms, but also try to balance the risk-reward relationship for banks in the country.

The Relationship Between Credit and Other Risks While loans are the largest source of credit risk and exposure to credit risk continues to be a leading source of problems, there are other sources of credit risk throughout the activities of a bank, in the banking and trading books and on and off its balance sheet. For example, a bank could face credit (or counter party default) risk in various financial instruments other than loans, such as in:

(a) acceptances, (b) inter-bank transactions, (c) trade financing, (d) foreign exchange transactions, (e) financial futures, swaps, bonds, equities, options, and (f) in the extension of commitments and guarantees and the settlement of transactions.[9]

The Basel Committee's Principles of Credit Risk Management[10]

Annexure 1 presents a summary of the sound practices set out by the Basel Committee to specifically address the following areas: (a) establishing an appropriate credit risk environment, (b) operating under a sound credit granting process, (c) maintaining an appropriate credit administration, measurement and monitoring process and (d) ensuring adequate controls over credit risks. Although specific credit risk management practices may differ among banks depending upon the nature and complexity of their credit activities, a comprehensive credit risk management program should address these four areas. These practices should also be applied in conjunction with sound practices related to the assessment of asset quality, the adequacy of provisions and reserves and the disclosure of credit risk.

Classifying 'Impaired' Loans International accounting practices set forth standards for estimating the impairment of a loan for general financial reporting purposes. Regulators are expected to follow these standards 'to the letter' for determining the provisions and allowances for loan losses. According to these standards, a loan is 'impaired' when, based on current information and events, it is probable that the creditor will be unable to collect all amounts (interest and principal) due in line with the terms of the loan agreement. Such assets are also called 'criticized' assets.

Typically, the impaired assets are categorized as follows:

- Special mentioned loans: These loans are assessed as 'inherently weak'. The credit risks may be minor, but may involve 'unwarranted risk'. Such credits contain weaknesses, such as an inadequate loan agreement or poor condition of or control over collateral or deficient loan documentation or evidence of imprudent lending practices. Adverse market conditions in future may unfavourably impact the operations or the financials of the borrower firm, but may not endanger liquidation of assets held as security. The special mentioned loans carry more than normal risks which, had they been present when the credit was appraised, would have led to rejection of the credit request.
- Sub-standard assets: These assets are seen to have well-defined weaknesses that may jeopardize liquidation of the debt, since they are not fully protected by the borrower's financial condition or the collateral given as security. The bank is likely to sustain a loss if the defects are not corrected.
- Doubtful assets: These assets contain all the weaknesses of a sub-standard asset and, additionally, recovery of the debt in full is quite remote. Auditors may insist on a write down of the asset through a charge to loan loss reserves or a write off of a portion of the asset or they may call for additional capital allocation. Any portion of the balance outstanding in the loan, which is uncovered by the market value of the collateral, may be identified as uncollectible and written off.
- Loss assets: All identified losses have to be charged off. Uncollectible loans with such little value that their continuance as bankable assets is not warranted are generally charged off. Losses are expensed in the same period in which they are written off.
- Partially charged off loans: Though credit exposures contain weaknesses that render them uncollectible in full, some portion of the outstanding loan could be collected if the collateral is marketable and in good condition. Hence, the secured portion is not written off, while the unsecured portion of the loan is charged off.
- Income accrual on impaired loans is discontinued from the time they are classified.

Loan Workouts and Going to Court for Recovery

The workout function has been discussed in detail in the previous chapter. In the case of a restructured loan, the ability of the borrower to repay the loan on modified terms is focused upon. The loan will be classified under the 'impaired' category if, even after restructuring, there arise weaknesses that tend to jeopardize repayment on the modified terms.

In some developed countries like the US, regulatory rules do not require that banks restructuring a loan grant excessive concessions to the borrower during the period of restructuring.[11]

If all other forms of renegotiation between the bank and the borrower fail, the bank approaches the court to enforce recovery of dues. In some cases, 'Debtor-in-Possession' (DIP) financing is also done while the suit against the borrower is pending at the court. DIP financing is considered attractive by banks where such provision exists, since it is done only under the order of the court, which is empowered to give a priority position on the bankruptcy estate to the lender. Some alternatives for DIP financing include receivables backed credit, factoring and loans against equipment or inventory. The DIP loan is repaid from the following sources:

- cash flows from operations,
- liquidation of the collateral,
- the firm turns viable and the new lender refinances the DIP loan, and
- the DIP loan is taken over by a new DIP lender.

Credit Risk Models

Ever since Markowitz developed his pioneering Portfolio Analysis Model in 1950, quantitative models of portfolio management have been widely used in financial analysis, especially in analysis of equity portfolios. Over the last few decades, equity analysts have been successfully using portfolio management models to quantify default risks in a portfolio of assets. The objective of these methods is to maximize the portfolio's returns while reining in risk within acceptable levels.[12] This maximization involves balancing of risks and returns within a portfolio, asset by asset and group of assets by group of assets.[13]

However, similar models are not widely used for debt portfolios because of the greater analytical and empirical difficulties involved.

- Debt defaults can happen all of a sudden and once they happen, the risk can increase very quickly.
- We have seen the risk premium associated with the borrower or borrower class is inbuilt into the loan pricing. If the borrower risk has been misjudged, the loan would not be priced appropriately, implying further erosion in the bank's already thin margins on lending.
- It is also pertinent to remember here that the lenders—the banks—themselves are highly leveraged entities. History is replete with instances where lenders have been destroyed by the combination of financial and default risks.

The truth is that 'risk' cannot be wished away, insured away, hedged away or structured away. Risk can merely be allocated or transferred, but ultimately the risk has to be borne by somebody. Hence, lenders try to diversify their credit risks, for they know that they cannot do business if they eliminate risks altogether. How can lenders diversify their risk? By avoiding 'concentration' of credit.

The Basel Committee[14] has identified 'credit concentrations' as the single most important cause of major credit problems. Credit concentrations are viewed as any exposure where the potential losses are large relative to the bank's capital, its total assets or where adequate measures exist and the bank's overall risk level. Concentrations of credit and, hence, risk can occur when the bank's portfolio contains a high level of direct or indirect credit to: (a) a single borrower, (b) a group of associated borrowers, (c) a specific industry or economic activity, (d) a geographic region, (e) a specific country or a group of inter-related countries, (f) a type of credit facility, or (g) a specific type of security. Sometimes, concentrations can also arise from credits with similar maturities or from inter-linkages within the portfolio.

Relatively large losses[15] may reflect not only large exposures, but also the potential for unusually high percentage losses given default.

Credit concentrations can further be grouped into two broad categories.[16]

- Conventional credit concentrations would include concentrations of credits to single borrowers or counter parties, a group of connected counter parties and sectors or industries, such as commercial real estate and oil and gas.
- Concentrations based on common or co-related risk factors reflect subtler or more situation-specific factors and often can only be uncovered through analysis, such as correlations between market and credit risks and their correlation with liquidity risk. Such interplay of risks can produce substantial losses.

Why do banks permit concentrations in their credit portfolios? The Basel Committee cites the following reasons:[17] 'First, in developing their business strategy, most banks face an inherent trade-off between choosing to specialize in a few key areas with the goal of achieving a market leadership position and diversifying their income streams, especially when they are engaged in some volatile market segments. This trade-off has been exacerbated by intensified competition among banks and non-banks alike for traditional banking activities, such as providing credit to investment grade corporations. Concentrations appear most frequently to arise because banks identify 'hot' and rapidly growing industries and use overly optimistic assumptions about an industry's future prospects, especially asset appreciation and the potential to earn above-average fees and/or spreads. Banks seem most susceptible to overlooking the dangers in such situations when they are focused on asset growth or market share'.

Until recently, such 'concentrations' could be measured only after the credit exposures had been created. Of late, finance literature has produced a variety of models that attempt to measure default risk.

While most of the methodologies are seen to work adequately in practice, research indicates that some issues are still not tackled by the models in respect of bank lending such as predicting macro-economic cycles and industry shocks (systematic or exogenous default risk) and hedging strategies.

Basel Committee – Proposals for Measuring and Controlling Credit Concentration risk

The need for a comprehensive framework to measure and aggregate banks' exposures to a single counter party, or related counter parties, prompted the Basel Committee, in March 2013, to propose measures in a consultative document (http://www.bis.org/publ/bcbs246.pdf). Box 8.1 shows the salient features of the measures proposed by the Basel committee for measuring and controlling large exposures (concentration risk). (The guidelines to banks in India for treatment of large exposures is described in Section IV of this chapter)

This framework was designed to complement the Committee's risk based capital framework (which can be found in the chapter 'Capital – risk, regulation and adequacy'). The risk based capital framework did not explicitly consider concentration risk while calculating capital requirements of banks – that is, the risk of large losses resulting from an unexpected default of a single large counter party or related group of counter parties.

The proposed framework is expected to contribute to increased stability of the financial system, especially after the experiences of the global financial crisis of 2007–08. One key lesson from the crisis was that material losses in one 'Systemically Important Financial Institution' (SIFI) can trigger concerns about the solvency of other SIFIs, with potentially catastrophic consequences for global financial stability—investors can withdraw from banks with risky exposures, or from institutions that hedge these risky exposures such as insurance companies.

The document also includes sectoral and geographical concentration of credit and asset exposures, as well as reliance on concentrated funding sources (as mentioned in the chapter 'Sources of Bank Funds'). However, sovereign exposures are not included in the current proposals

BOX 8.1 BASEL COMMITTEE CONSULTATIVE DOCUMENT—SUPERVISORY FRAMEWORK FOR MEASURING AND CONTROLLING LARGE EXPOSURES—SALIENT FEATURES OF PROPOSALS MADE

The proposals aim at integrating the risk based capital standards (as in the Chapter 'Capital—risk, regulation and adequacy') with the framework on credit concentration risk. However, for sharper focus on concentration risk, some deviations from the risk based capital standards have also been proposed.

In some cases, additional rigor or clarity in the proposed could seem like a deviation, which however does not entail revised calculations of regulatory capital by banks. These proposals under the large exposures framework relate to (a) non derivatives off balance sheet commitments; (b) eligible collateral/ protection providers for credit risk mitigation; (c) financial collaterals—approach to recognition of credit risk mitigation; (d) scope of exposures in the trading book, excluding options and offsetting positions (Please refer to Chapter 'Capital—risk, regulation and adequacy' for definition of trading book.)

There are some proposals that deviate widely from the risk based capital framework, and hence calculations of capital would have to be revised by banks. These proposals relate to: (a) collateral haircuts and structured finance products under credit risk mitigation; and (b) securities financing transactions.

The areas of no deviation from the risk based capital standards are in: (a) definition and components of the core capital of banks, (b) measurement of 'exposure' value; (c) treatment of specific provisions; (d) measurement of exposure value for debt and equity instruments, swaps, futures, forwards and credit derivatives; and (e) OTC derivative transactions.

A 'look through approach' has been proposed to help banks identify the underlying assets and the relevant counter parties while investing in transactions with single or multiple counter parties. In the absence of look-through, it would be impossible to identify the true concentration risk to a single counter party, and banks could easily avoid large exposure limits by investing in multiple transactions with identical underlying assets.

The decision tree provided by the Basel proposal for the Look Through Approach (LTA) is shown in the figure:

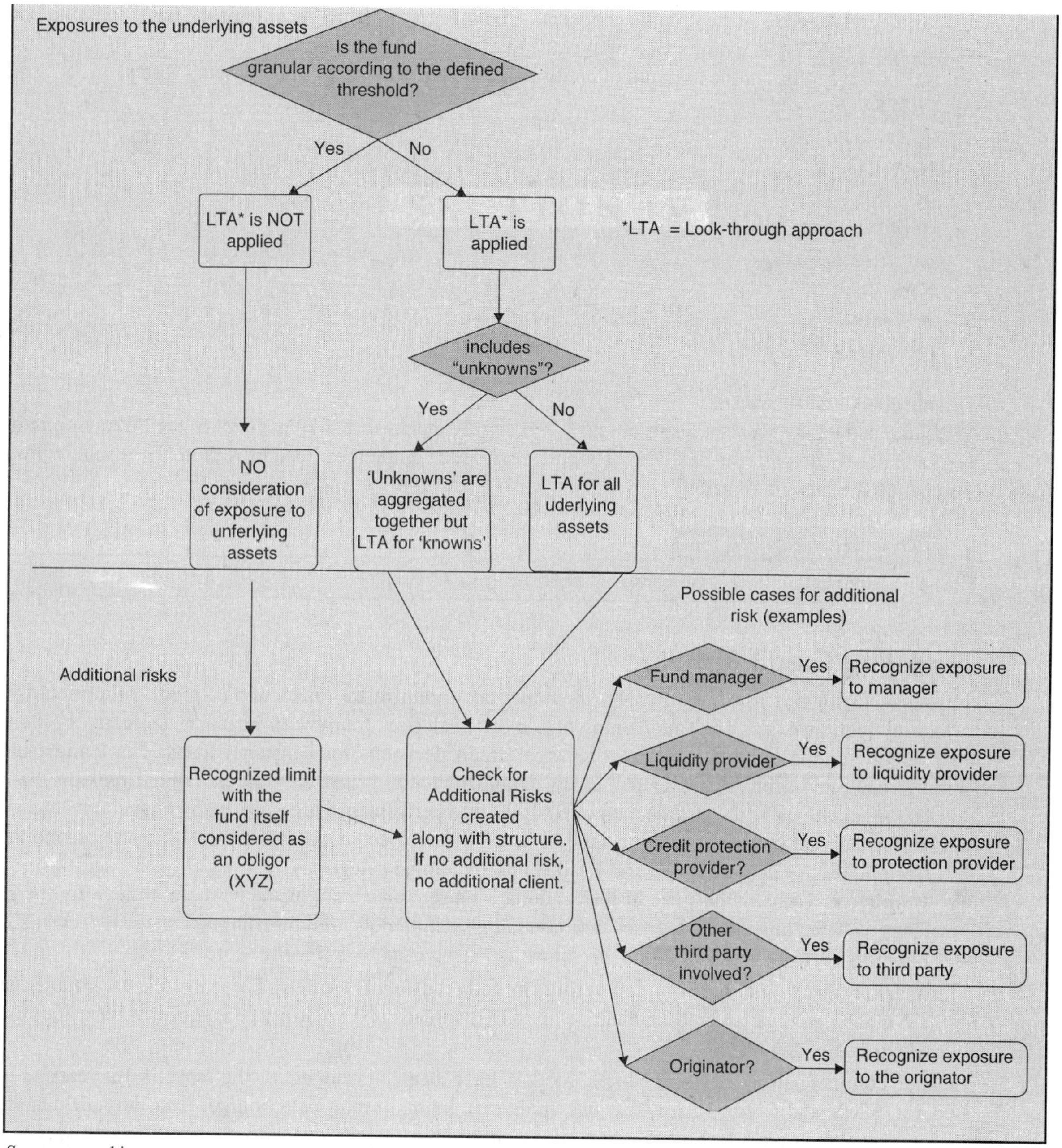

Source: www.bis.org

SECTION II

MEASURING CREDIT RISK—INTRODUCTION TO SOME POPULAR CREDIT RISK MODELS

A Basic Model

A simple method of estimating credit risk is to assess the impact of non-performing asset (NPA) write offs on the bank's profits. This can be achieved through dividing the 'profit before taxes' (PBT) by the NPAs. Here, PBT is more relevant since losses written-off typically enjoy tax shields.

Another method of presenting this concept is to work from the net income of the bank and treat both the net income and the NPAs as a proportion of average total assets of the bank.

Accordingly, this simple measure of credit risk can be presented in the following forms:

i. PBT/TA

NPA/TA

or

ii. (PAT/[1 − t])/TA

NPA/TA

or simply,

iii. PBT/NPA

Interpretation of the result

If the above measure yields a result of say, 0.7, it simply means that if 70 per cent of the NPAs turn into 'loss assets' and are written off, the bank's PBT would be eroded completely. For this reason, the resultant proportion is also called the 'margin of safety'.

TEASE THE CONCEPT

Which is safer for the bank—the above measure being lower or higher?

Modeling Credit Risk

Financial institutions have traditionally attempted to minimize the incidence of credit risk primarily through a loan-by-loan analysis. The foundations of a more analytical framework began in the early 1960s when the first 'credit scoring' models were built to assist credit decisions for consumer loans. The lending institutions initially classified debtors/counter parties on default potential based only on an ordinal ranking. By the mid-1980s, particularly with the introduction of RAROC as a performance measure, many financial institutions began calibrating each credit score to a particular PD[18] to estimate expected losses (EL) and ultimately economic capital.

Techniques to calculate PD can be divided into two broad categories.

1. **Empirical:** These models use historical default rates associated with each 'score' to identify the characteristics of defaulting counter parties. Traditionally, such models used discriminant analysis (such as *Z* scores), but more recently logit or probit regressions are being used to define the score 'S'[19]
2. **Market-based (also known as structural or reduced-form) models:** These models use counter party market data (*e.g.*, bond or credit default swap (CDS) spreads and volatility of equity market value) to infer the likelihood of default.

Several commercial credit value-at-risk models have been developed in the last 10–15 years (*e.g.*, Credit Metrics, KMV and Credit Risk+) that use credit risk inputs (credit data, market data, obligor data and issue/facility data) to derive a loss distribution, by assuming that correlations across borrowers arise due to common dependence on a set of 'systematic risk factors' (typically, variables representing the state of the economy). Sophisticated banks generally use these models for active portfolio-level credit management (particularly, for large corporate loans) by identifying risk concentrations and opportunities for diversification through debt instruments and credit derivatives.

Table 8.1 classifies popular models according to the approach adopted by them.

TABLE 8.1[20] INDUSTRY-SPONSORED CREDIT VALUE-AT-RISK (VaR) MODELS

Approach	Sponsor	Model
Credit migration approach	J P Morgan	CreditMetrics
	McKinsey	CreditPortfolio
Option pricing approach	KMV Corporation	KMV (Kealhofer/McQuown/Vasicek)
Actuarial approach	CSFB (Credit Suisse first Boston)	CreditRisk+
Reduced form approach		Jarrow/Turnbull
		Duffie/Singleton

Table 8.2 compares these approaches on various parameters.

TABLE 8.2[21] COMPARISON OF CREDIT RISK MODELS ON VARIOUS PARAMETERS

	Credit Migration Approach		Contingent Claim Approach	Actuarial Approach	Reduced-form Approach
Software	CreditMetrics	CreditPortfolio-view	KMV	CreditRisk+	Kamakura
Definition of risk	ΔMarket value	ΔMarket value	Market Value	Default losses	Default losses
Credit events	Downgrade/default	Downgrade/default	Δ Continuous default probabilities (EDFs)	Δ Actuarial default rate	Δ Default intensity
Risk drivers	Equity returns	Macro-factors	Asset values	Expected default rates	Hazard rate
Transition probabilities	Constant	Driven by macro factors	Driven by: ■ Individual term structure of EDF ■ Asset value process	N/A	N/A
Correlation of credit events	Standard multivariate normal distribution (equity-factor model)	Conditional default probabilities function of macro-factors	Standard multivariate normal asset returns (asset factor model)	Conditional default probabilities function of common risk factors	Conditional default probabilities function of macro-factors
Recovery rates	Random (beta distribution)	Random (empirical distribution)	Random (beta distribution)	Loss given default deterministic	Loss given default deterministic
Interest rates	Constant	Constant	Constant	Constant	Stochastic
Numerical approach	Simulation/analytic Econometric	Simulation econometric	Analytic/simulation econometric	Analytic	Tree-based/simulation econometric

Source: BIS Working Paper, 2005.

In addition, several *academic models* have been developed, which can be categorized into two. The models in the first category adopt an *exogenous* default-trigger value of assets. In contrast, the models in the second category derive the decision to default *endogenously*, as part of the borrower's internal problems and are, therefore, a function of borrower characteristics.[22]

A description of the approaches to credit risk measurement and the popular models can be found in the next chapter.

SECTION III

CREDIT RISK TRANSFERS—SECURITIZATION, LOAN SALES, COVERED BONDS AND CREDIT DERIVATIVES

Hedging reduces portfolio risk by offsetting one risk against another. Diversification reduces risk because risks are uncorrelated. How portfolio hedges are structured will vary according to the bank's goals on hedging credit risk.

Till even about a decade ago, banks had to expand their loan portfolios for growing their business and keep these assets in their books till they were completely liquidated. In the present scenario, banks still grow their business by expanding loan assets, but these assets are sold off to other agencies or of floaded in the secondary loan market. In this manner, banks get risky loans off their books. Such loan sales provide liquidity to the selling banks and also represent a valuable portfolio management tool, which minimizes risk through diversification.

Some prominent forms of loan sales include the following.

- Syndication: We have seen this as a form of credit in Chapter 5. The manner in which syndication is conducted spreads the credit risk in the transaction among the banks in the syndicate. Let us assume a borrower wants a loan of ₹10,000 crores for a large project. If Bank X is nominated as the lead bank for the syndication, X will negotiate the documents with the borrower and solicit a group of banks to share the credit exposure. X will generally hold the maximum exposure, though this is not mandatory. Bank X claims a fee for its efforts in syndication.

- Novation: In the above example, Bank X assigns its rights to one or more buyer banks. These buyer banks then become original signatories to the loan agreement. Thus, the borrower would have contracted with Bank X for the ₹10,000 crores loan. Post novation, Bank X would hold, say, ₹2,000 crores of credit exposure to the borrower and the three buyer banks, say A, B and C, would hold the remaining ₹8,000 crores share among themselves in a mutually agreed proportion. Unlike syndication, A, B and C would enter into separate loan agreements with the borrower.
- Participation: In this case, Bank X transfers to other participating banks A, B and C the right to receive pro rata payments from the borrower. Typically, the seller of the participation—Bank X—will have to consult A, B and C before agreeing to changes in the terms of the loan (principal, interest, repayment terms, guarantees, collaterals, interest rate, fees and other covenants).
- Securitization: This is one of the most popular and prominent forms of loan sale. The critical factor is finding a homogeneous pool of loan assets that generate a predictable stream of future cash flows.

Simply stated, securitization involves the transfer of assets and other credit exposures from the 'originator' (the bank) through pooling and re-packaging by a special purpose vehicle (SPV) into securities that can be sold to investors. It involves legally isolating the underlying exposures from the originating bank. A 'true sale' or 'traditional securitization' happens where the assets are actually transferred from the originator's balance-sheet to the issuer of the securities. For instance, a bank makes auto loans and sells these loans to a SPE or SPV that structures these assets into a homogeneous asset pool. The SPE retains the loan as collateral, sells the pool to investors and pays the bank for the loans bought from it with the proceeds from the sale of securities.

At the end of the tenure of the securitization, the residual assets are passed on to the investors. If the asset quality deteriorates, the investors have to bear the loss. The investors receive variable coupon payments depending upon the risk they decide to bear. The investors who are ready to take the first loss get the maximum spread. The originator, in this fashion, has passed on the risk associated with the assets to the investor.

Figure 8.3 depicts a typical securitization process.

Securitization can be seen as the method of turning un-tradable and illiquid assets into various types of securities, which can then be sold to different investors with different risk appetites. These different types of securities with different inherent risks are known as the 'tranches'. Technically, securitization is defined as a transaction involving one or more underlying credit exposures from which tranches that reflect different degrees of credit risk are created. Credit exposures may include loans, commitments and receivables. It may take the form of a security or of an unfunded credit derivative (to be explained later). The payments to investors depend upon the performance of specified underlying credit exposures. The salient features of securitization are outlined in *Annexure II* of this chapter.

The securities sold to investors are called 'asset-backed securities' (ABS), since they are backed by the homogeneous pool of underlying assets. Originators of ABS usually want to sell loans 'without recourse'.[23] Hence, investors usually safeguard their interests through three mechanisms—(a) over collateralization, (b) senior/subordinated structures, and (3) credit enhancement.

- 'Over collateralization', as the nomenclature implies, involves structuring a collateral pool to ensure cash flow in excess of the amount required to pay the principal and interest on the securities.
- In the 'senior/subordinated structures', the issuer of securities sells two categories of certificates—senior and junior—both secured by the same collateral pool. The senior certificates are usually taken by investors,

FIGURE 8.3 A TYPICAL SECURITIZATION PROCESS

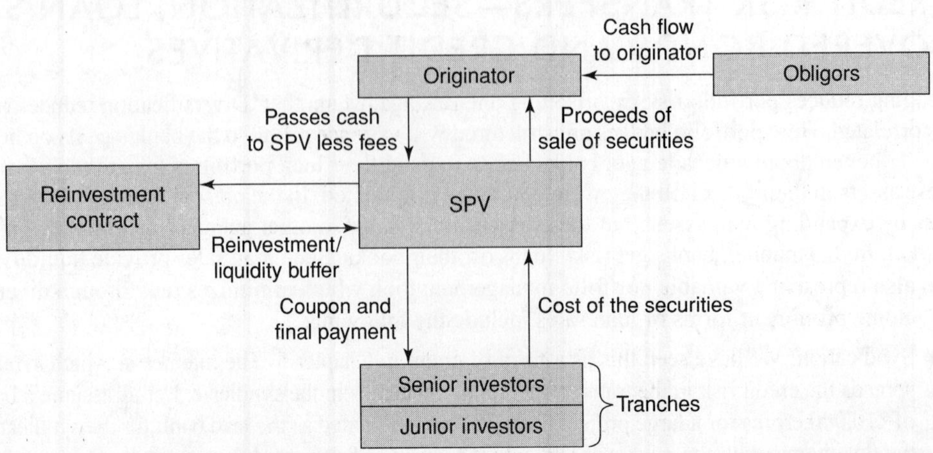

Source: RBI Guidelines on Securitization.

while the originator itself may purchase the junior certificates. The cash flows from the collateral are first allocated to make payments to senior holders and the residual cash flows are allocated to junior holders. In other words, the actual losses should not exceed the promised payments to subordinated certificate holders. Therefore, the larger the component of junior holders, the greater the protection for senior investors.

- 'Credit enhancements', such as letters of credit are used to cover losses in the collateral. A bank other than the originating bank issues the letter of credit, generally covering a certain proportion of the loss on the pool (comparable to historical losses plus a margin) for a fee.

Thus, securitization is seen to benefit banks by providing liquidity to banks' loan portfolios and mitigating credit risk by removing assets from banks' books. Other spin offs include a possible lowering of interest rate risk and profitability enhancement through better asset turnover and fee-based income.

Box 8.2 provides an overview of collateralized debt obligations (CDOs) and compares them with securitization.

BOX 8.2 WHAT ARE CDOs/CBOs/CLOs?

These are the fastest growing segment of the securitization market. Banks resort to securitization with the following predominant motives-sourcing cheaper funds, attaining higher regulatory capital, better asset—liability management and reduced NPAs or under-performing assets.

Where the originating bank transfers a pool of loans, the bonds that emerge are called 'collateralized loan obligations' (CLOs). Where the bank transfers a portfolio of bonds and securitizes the same, the resulting securitized bonds are termed 'collateralized bond obligations' (CBOs). A generic name given to both these is 'CDOs'. Some banks even securitize their equity investments—calling them 'collateralized investment obligations' (CIOs).

Difference between securitization and CDO structures

Though the essential nature of the structures are similar, securitization in its generic form and issuing CBO/CLO at the instance of banks, differ in respect of the following.

- For typical securitizations the primary objective is liquidity, while in the case of CBO/CLOs, the objectives could be capital relief, risk transfer, arbitraging profits or balance sheet optimization.
- While securitizations of, say, mortgage portfolios or auto loan portfolios could have thousands of obligors, CDO pools typically have only 100–200 loans.
- The loans/bonds are mostly heterogeneous in CDOs, whereas the securitized assets are typically homogeneous pools. The originator of CDOs might try to bunch together uncorrelated loans to provide the benefits of a diversified portfolio.
- Most CDO structures use a tranched and multi-layered structure with a substantial amount of residual interest retained by the originator.
- Generally, CDO issues will use a reinvestment period and an amortization period. Some tranches might have a 'soft bullet' repayment (a bullet repayment that is not guaranteed by any third party).
- Arbitraging is a common practice in the CDO market, where larger banks buy out loans from smaller ones and securitize them, earning arbitrage revenues in the process. There is a class of CDOs called arbitrage CDOs where the originating bank buys loans/bonds from the market and securitizes the same for gaining an advantage on the rates. Since the motive of such securitizations is arbitraging, such CDOs are called arbitrage CLOs/CBOs. To distinguish these from the ones where a bank securitizes its own receivables, the latter are sometimes referred to as 'balance sheet CLOs/CBOs'.

Yet another upcoming variety of CLOs is 'synthetic CLOs'. Here the originating bank merely securitizes the credit risk[24] and retains the loans on its balance sheet. Synthetic CLOs repackage the underlying loans into cash flows that suit the needs of the investors and are not dependant on the repayment structure of the underlying loans.

To summarize, CDOs could fall into two basic categories: balance sheet CDOs and arbitrage CDOs. In the case of balance sheet CDOs, loans are actually transferred from the balance sheet of the originator and therefore impact the originating bank's balance sheet. In the case of arbitrage CDOs, the originator merely 'buys' loans or bonds or asset-backed securities from the market, pools and securitizes them as a repackaged entity. The prime objective of balance sheet CDOs is to reduce risk and regulatory capital, while the purpose of arbitrage CDOs is to make profits from arbitrage.

Balance sheet CDOs could be further classified into cash flow CDOs and synthetic CDOs based on the nature of their assets.

In the case of 'cash flow CDOs', the assets are acquired for cash. The originating bank transfers a portfolio of loans into an SPV. 'Master trust' structures are commonly employed in CDOs to enable the bank to keep transferring loans into the pool on a regular basis without having to do complex documentation for every transfer. In view of the varied repayment structure of commercial loans, cash flow CDOs typically repay through bullet repayments and, hence, have a reinvestment period, during which the cash flows from repayments are reinvested.

However, a synthetic CDO primarily acquires 'synthetic' assets by selling 'protection'[25] rather than buying assets for cash. Hence, the funding requirement for a synthetic CDO is much lower than that for a cash flow CDO. The amount [illegible]f cash raised is limited only to the extent of expected and unexpected losses (EL and UL) in the portfolio of synthetic assets, such [illegible] the highest of the cash liabilities can get an investment grade rating. Once the senior most cash liability obtains [illegible] grade [illegible], the synthetic CDO does not raise more cash—it merely raises a synthetic 'liability' by buying protection fro[illegible]-sen[illegible]r swap provider. A typical structure in a synthetic CDO is illustrated in Figure 8.4. Clearly, the three different 'tranches [illegible] different risk characteristics.

FIGURE 8.4 TYPICAL STRUCTURE OF A SYNTHETIC CDO

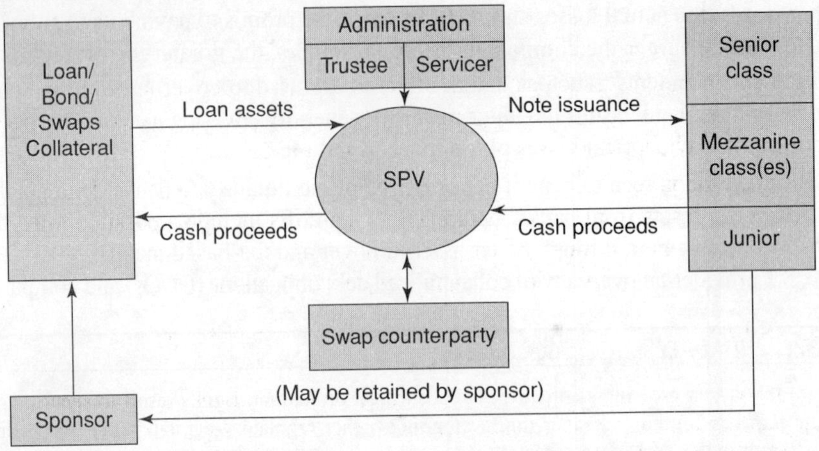

Source: RBI, 2003, 'Draft Guidelines for Introduction of Credit Derivatives in India', Figure 6 (26 March 2003): 11.

TEASE THE CONCEPT

Why would banks be tempted to sell only their best assets under the securitization process?

Let us now sum up the alternatives discussed so far in respect of a bank that has to deal with credit risk in its loan portfolio.

a. It can continue to hold the loans, assess the EL periodically, take preventive or remedial measures to reduce the risk of loss or make a provision on the EL and allocate capital for UL.
b. It can diversify its loan portfolio with several small loans to different counter parties, so that a few expected defaults may not lead to earnings volatility.
c. It can negotiate a loan sale for the whole or part of the loan amount and incur the costs associated with the loan sale.

In resorting to the first alternative—(a) the bank runs the risk of earnings erosion if the provisions are substantial in value. It is not always easy to diversify the portfolio as in alternative; (b) since the bank's operations, driven by its own internal skills and external competition, may not be able to balance the portfolio as optimally as it would like to. Further, a highly diversified portfolio is no complete hedge against borrower defaults and could lead to high transaction costs. Beyond diversification, banks look to sell off or securitize the loans as in the alternative; and (c) and this approach is seen to work well for standardized payment schedules and homogeneous credit risk characteristics. Commercial and industrial loans exhibit varied credit risk characteristics and can be sold or securitized through the CDO route as described above. In many cases, the banks themselves may not want the loans or more specifically, the 'borrowers' off their balance sheets and may merely want to hedge against the credit risk inherent in the loan transaction.

Covered Bonds

Covered bonds are not a new concept. They have been around for over 200 years, with a striking 'zero' default record! They have historically been associated with Germany—Pfandbriefe and Denmark–realkreditobligatione

Covered bonds are a hybrid between asset-backed securities/mortgage backed securities and normal secured corporate bonds, and serve as an instrument of refinancing, primarily used by mortgage lenders. Unlike secured corporate bonds which provide recourse against the issuer, covered bonds provide a bankruptcy-protected recourse against the assets of the issuer (Collateral Pool) too. Unlike mortgage backed securities which merely provide recourse against the Collateral Pool, covered bonds provide an additional recourse against the issuer too.

Covered bonds can therefore be defined as fixed income instruments that are unconditional obligations of the issuer, but containing an additional recourse against assets of a specified 'cover pool', the rights over which are protected, either by legislation or by using special legal devices, such that investors in the covered bonds have bankruptcy-protected claim against such cover pool.

Covered bonds are essentially used to raise liquidity through a bond issue, backed by a pool of assets. They combine the features of securitization and corporate bonds (debt instruments, more about which can be found in later chapters).

Typical covered bond issue process and cash payment structures are shown in Figures 8.5 and 8.6.

FIGURE 8.5 AT THE TIME OF ISSUING A COVERED BOND

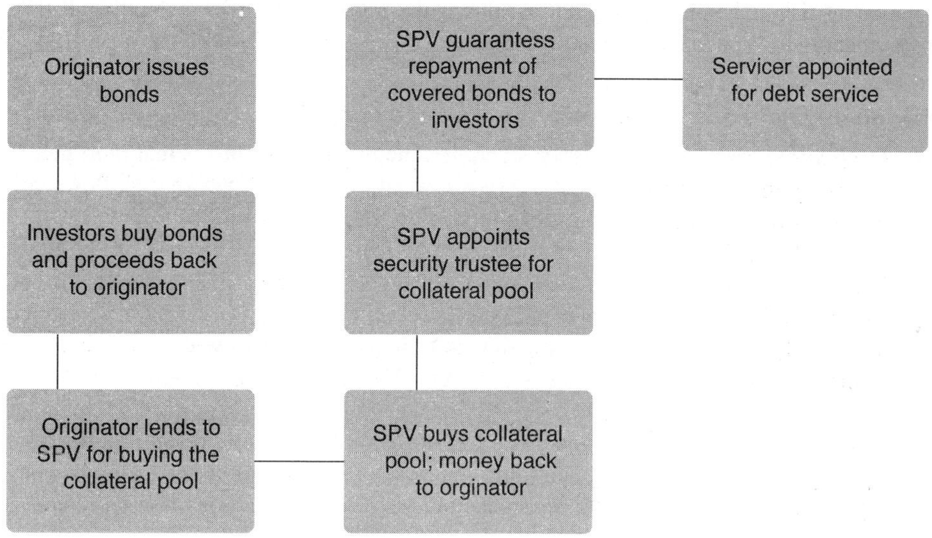

FIGURE 8.6 FLOW OF CASH PAYMENTS IN A STRUCTURED COVERED BOND

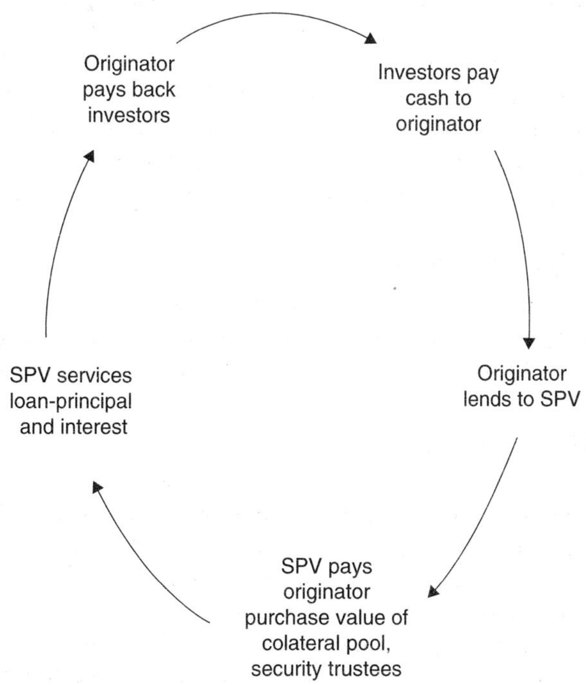

It can be understood from the diagrammatic representations that the covered bond, like a securitized asset, is backed by a pool of identifiable assets usually with a level of over collateralization. But there are many points of difference that add up to making covered bonds a viable alternative to securitization.

Traditionally, covered bonds have been used in mortgage refinancing. However, unlike in traditional Mortgage backed securities (MBS), where the pool of underlying mortgages is static, the pool underlying covered bonds is a dynamic pool. Hence the generic structure of covered bonds resembles secured bonds.

Unlike securitization, which does not depend on the rating of the issuer, covered bonds do depend on ratings, but have additional advantage of 'ring fenced', high quality assets to back the pool. The quality of underlying asset pool in covered bonds is laid down by specific legislation or common law of the country.

Covered bonds are shown on the balance sheet of the originator, who is therefore subject to default risk and prepayment risk of bondholders. Contrast this with securitization, where the default risk of the assets (and the prepayment risk) is passed on to the investors, and the assets are taken off the originator's balance sheet.

How do originators/issuers benefit from covered bonds?

- *Originators are able to get higher leverage.* The rationale for this is that mortgage lending, where covered bonds are the most prevalent, is low risk, low return business, where cash flows are recovered over a long period in time. Hence, for mortgage lenders to get a higher return on their equity, higher leverage is the preferred tool. This fact has been recognized by regulators too. Higher leverage also implies that originators have to constantly seek additional sources of funds. Covered bonds provide one such additional source of funds. The leverage that a covered bond issue can command is directly linked to the quality of underlying assets and the extent of over collateralization. Hence, originators will be able to raise funds only to the extent of the economic capital that the pool requires. (*The concept of 'economic capital' is discussed in detail in the chapter 'Capital—risk, regulation and adequacy'*)
- *Originators can get better ratings for the covered bond issue than their own ratings.* This is due to the fact that the 'cover pool' of assets that will form the security for the covered bonds would be high quality assets, whose quality would either be stipulated by law or stated in specific legislations.
- *Lower cost to originator as a direct result of better ratings.*
- *Originators can achieve better asset liability matches (asset liability matching is discussed in the chapter 'Bank risk management').* In a covered bond program there may be asset liability mismatches. The underlying asset is a long term mortgage asset (with a maturity typically greater than 10 years), while covered bonds may be issued with short term or medium term maturities. This would mean that the normal asset amortization alone may be insufficient to pay the bonds on time. While evaluating the asset-liability mismatches, there are two risks that are taken into consideration: (a) asset risk; and (b) cash flow risk. These are dealt with while structuring of the transaction. Thereafter, reliance is placed on the debt service capacity of the issuer. Over and above these, the issuer may need liquidity facility provider to meet the covered bond maturities. The less the magnitude of the asset liability mismatch, the higher the rating for the bonds.
- *Originators' exposure to the capital market yields better reputation.* Further the accountability to the capital market brings in better governance, discipline and best practices to the originator.

How do covered bonds benefit the borrowers/investors?

If covered bonds are able to bring down the cost of mortgage refinancing, the same would eventually translate into lower mortgage lending costs. In addition, covered bonds result into standardization of mortgage lending procedures and underwriting norms—all of which make pricing of mortgages far more transparent.

How do covered bonds benefit the economy?

Integration of capital markets with mortgage markets is an important step in the economic development of a country. Securitization is an extreme form of transforming illiquid assets into tradable securities in the capital market. However, post the 2007 crisis, the securitization model was seen as creating problems of moral hazard and adverse selection. As a device of capital market funding, covered bonds are mid-way between securitization and straight corporate bonds, since they combine the benefits of both.

One of the biggest advantages of covered bonds in future will be the liquidity requirements under Basel III (*Please see chapter 'Capital—risk, regulation and adequacy'*). Basel III proposes to impose a Liquidity Coverage Ratio requirement for banks according to which banks are to maintain at least 30 days' cash flows in 'highly liquid assets'. Covered bonds of a certain rating would qualify as liquid assets for this requirement.

About 32 countries have already passed laws in respect of covered bonds. The National Housing bank (NHB) of India is actively considering introducing covered bonds in the country's residential mortgage market. A working group submitted its report on the subject in October 2012. A draft National Housing Bank Covered Bonds Regulations, 2012, has also been proposed in the report.

Comparing Securitization and Covered Bonds

Table 8.3 compares securitization and covered bonds on various parameters

TABLE 8.3 COVERED BONDS VS SECURITIZATION

	Covered Bonds	**Securitization**
Purpose	Increase liquidity	Increase liquidity, risk management, off balance sheet
Risk transfer	The originator continues to absorb default risk as well as prepayment risk of the pool. To achieve a partial transfer of prepayment risk, there may be a call option embedded in the covered bonds.	The originator does not absorb default risk above the credit support agreed; prepayment risk is usually transferred entirely to investors
Legal structure	Direct and unconditional obligation of the issuer, backed by creation of security interest. Assets may or may not be parked with a distinct entity; bankruptcy remoteness is achieved either due to specific law or by common law principles. In structured covered bond structures, there may be a replica of a true sale, followed by guarantee from an SPV that acquires title by virtue of the true sale.	True sale of assets to a distinct entity; bankruptcy remoteness is achieved by isolation of assets.
Asset pool characteristics	Mostly dynamic. Originator is allowed to manage the pool as long as the required "covers" are ensured from a common pool of cover assets, there may be multiple issuances.	Mostly static. Except in case of master trusts, the investors make investment in an identifiable pool of assets. Generally, from a single pool of assets, there is only issuance.
Maturity matching	From out of a dynamic pool, securities may be issued over a period of time. Usually, covered bonds are 'programs', that is, series of issuance from a series of dynamic and replenishing mortgage pool.	Typically, securities are matched with the cash flows from the pool. When the static pool is paid off, the securities are redeemed.
Debt service to investors	Interest and principal are paid from the general cash flows of the issuer.	Interest and principal are paid from the asset pool, No recourse to originator in case of default.
Prepayment risk	In view of the managed nature of the pool, prepayment of loans does not affect investors, except to the extent of call option embedded in the bonds.	Prepayment of underlying loans is passed on to investors; hence investors take prepayment risk
Nature of credit enhancement	Over-collateralization inherent in the cover pool, that is, excess of the cover assets over the outstanding funding.	Overcollateralization is one of the credit enhancement forms. Other forms of credit enhancement include excess spread, subordination, etc.
Classes of securities	Usually a single class of bonds is issued. There may be multiple time tranches, each having hard or soft bullet maturity.	Most transactions come up in tranches—with different classes of securities,different risk and returns.
Ratings dependence on issuer rating	Theoretically, though the securities are those of the originator, bankruptcy-proofing and the value of 'cover assets', usually warrants higher ratings.	AAA ratings are given usually to senior-most classes, based on adequacy of credit enhancement from the lower classes.
Balance sheet treatment	On balance sheet	Typically off balance sheet
Impact on regulatory capital	Will be treated as on balance sheet exposures calling for regulatory capital maintenance.	Regulatory capital to be maintained in case residual risks are borne by originator

Source: National Housing Bank, October 2012, Report of the working group for promoting RMBS and other alternative capital market instruments—Covered Bonds, pp. 98, 99; accessed at www.nhb.org.in.

Box 8.3 provides an overview of the legislation governing covered bonds in select countries.

BOX 8.3 LEGISLATION ON COVERED BONDS – SELECT COUNTRIES

Legislation on covered bonds—select countries

The USA

The Covered Bonds Bill, 2011 provides for different Covered Bonds Regulators for different categories of issuers that may be an insurer, a bank holding company, any NBFC, etc.

A wide range of assets including residential assets as well as commercial assets qualify as eligible assets. Also, the Cover Pool may be comprised of ancillary assets and substitute assets. A loan will not qualify as eligible asset if it is delinquent for more than 60 consecutive days. The Bill stipulates minimum over-collateralization requirements to be established.

Singapore

In Singapore, the Monetary Authority of Singapore came up with Proposed Consultation Paper on Covered Bonds Issuance by Banks incorporated in Singapore in March, 2012. According to the proposal, Covered Bond holders will have dual recourse against the issuing bank as well as the Cover pool. Further, the aggregate value of assets in the cover pool is to be capped at 2 per cent of the value of the total assets of the bank. Only residential mortgage loans and the derivatives held for the purpose of hedging risks arising from issuing covered bonds are proposed as eligible constituents of the Cover Pool. A minimum over-collateralization of 103 per cent and a LTV (Loan to Value Ratio) of 80 per cent have also been proposed.

The UK

The Regulated Covered Bonds Regulations 2008 (amended periodically) constitute the regulatory framework for Covered Bonds in the United Kingdom (UK). The Asset Pool should consist of eligible property (*e.g.*, loans to registered social landlord, loans to a project company for specified projects, etc. or any interest in eligible assets specified in any one of the classes: public sector assets, residential mortgage assets and commercial mortgage assets) which shall be situated in particular areas only.

Europe

The European covered bond council (ECBC) has stipulated criteria that issuers will have to satisfy, and the 'covered bond label convention'—as the legislation will be called—is likely to be passed.

Source: National Housing Bank, October 2012, Report of the Working group for promoting RMBS and other alternative capital market instruments—Covered Bonds, pp. 98, 99, accessed at www.nhb.org.im, and The covered bond report, November 2011, accessed at www.coveredbondreport.com

Credit Derivatives

Due to the difficulties experienced by bankers with alternative methods of dealing with credit risk, another alternative has emerged: 'credit derivatives'—a more specialized way to insure against credit-related losses.

Credit derivatives are an effective means of protecting against credit risk. They come in many shapes and sizes, but all serve the same purpose. Simply stated, a credit derivative is a security with a pay-off linked to a credit related event, such as borrower default, credit rating downgrades or a structural change in a security containing credit risk.

There are different types of credit derivatives, but we will take a brief look in this section at the commonly used derivatives. Some analysts classify credit derivatives into two categories in terms of how they are valued or priced, namely 'replication' products and 'default' products. Replication products, as the name suggests, replicate the money market transactions, such as credit spread options, while default products, such as credit default swaps (CDS) are priced on the basis of the PD of the asset whose risk is being transferred, the exposure at risk and the expected recovery rate. Another common classification is on the basis of performance—'protection like' products (*e.g.*, credit default options and CDS) and 'exchange like' products (*e.g.*, total return swaps).

In credit derivatives, there is a party (or a bank) trying to transfer credit risk, called protection buyer and there is a counter party (another bank) trying to acquire credit risk, called protection seller. C[illegible] credit derivatives market has become a trading market. Trades in credit derivatives are taken to be proxies for trades in actual loans or bonds of the reference entity and the borrower. For example, a bank willing to acquire exposure in a particular borrower would sell protection with reference to the borrower, while a bank wanting to hedge the risk of lending to the same borrower will buy protection.

Credit derivatives are typically *unfunded*—the protection seller is not required to put in any money upfront. The protection buyer generally pays a periodic premium. However, the credit derivative may be *funded* in some cases. For example, the protection buyer may require the protection seller to pre-pay the entire notional value of the contract upfront (as in the case of a 'credit-linked note' (CLN) discussed later in this section).

As is typical of derivatives, a credit derivative does not require either of the parties—the protection seller or protection buyer—to actually hold the reference asset (the credit that is being hedged). Thus, a bank may buy protection for an exposure it has taken or has not taken, irrespective of the amount or term of the actual exposure. It, therefore, follows that the amount of compensation claimed under a credit derivative may not be related to the actual losses suffered by the protection buyer.

When a credit event (as specified in the contract between the protection buyer and seller) takes place, there are two ways of settlement—*cash* and *physical*. In a cash settlement, the reference asset will be valued and the difference between its par and fair value will be paid by the protection seller. In the case of physical settlement, the protection seller would acquire the defaulted asset for its full par.

Box 8.4 provides an insight into the evolution of credit derivatives.

BOX 8.4 EVOLUTION OF CREDIT DERIVATIVES[26]

In March 1993, *Global Finance* carried a feature on J. P. Morgan, Merrill Lynch and Bankers Trust, which were already then marketing some form of credit derivatives. This article also prophesied, quite rightly, that credit derivatives could, within a few years, rival the USD 40 trillion market for interest rate swaps.

In November 1993, *Investment Dealers* Digest carried an article titled 'Derivatives Pros Snubbed on Latest Exotic Product' which claimed that a number of private credit derivative deals had been seen in the market but it was doubted if they were ever completed. The article also said that Standard and Poor's had refused to rate credit derivative products and this refusal may put a permanent damper on the fledgling market. One commentator quoted in the article said: 'It (credit derivatives) is like Russian roulette. It doesn't make a difference if there's only one bullet: If you get it you die'.

Almost 3 years later, *Euromoney* reported (March 1996 'Credit Derivatives Get Cracking') that a lot of credit derivatives deals were already happening. The article was optimistic: 'The potential of credit derivatives is immense. There are hundreds of possible applications: for commercial banks which want to change the risk profile of their loan books, for investment banks managing huge bond and derivatives portfolios, for manufacturing companies over-exposed to a single customer, for equity investors in project finance deals with unacceptable sovereign risk, for institutional investors that have unusual risk appetites (or just want to speculate) and even for employees worried about the safety of their deferred remuneration. The potential uses are so widespread that some market participants argue that credit derivatives could eventually outstrip all other derivative products in size and importance'.

Some significant milestones in the development of credit derivatives have been as follows:

- 1992: Credit derivatives emerge. ISDA[27] first uses the term 'credit derivatives' to describe a new exotic type of over-the-counter contract.
- 1993: KMV introduces the first version of its Portfolio Manager model, the first credit portfolio model.
- 1994: Credit derivatives market begins to evolve. There are doubts expressed by some.
- September 1996: The first CLO of UK's National Westminster Bank.
- April 1997: J P Morgan launches Credit Metrics.
- October 1997: Credit Suisse launches CreditRisk+
- December 1997: The first synthetic securitization, JP Morgan's BISTRO deal.
- July 1999: Credit derivative definitions issued by ISDA.

Why Do Banks Use Credit Derivatives?

- They are an easy and cost-effective means to hedge portfolio risk.
- They permit substantial flexibility and hence increase the portfolio efficiency. For instance, the bank may have made a loan with 5-year maturity, but may be concerned with the risk over the next 2-year period only. The credit derivative permits the bank to allocate this risk to another party. The bank also effectively creates a 2-year security with many of the pricing characteristics of the 5-year loan. There are thus endless possibilities to create and structure flexible credit derivatives.

- They can be used to hedge against interest rate risks.
- Credit derivatives are often more efficient than loan sales since some investors who are unwilling to participate in the loan sales market are more willing to acquire credit derivatives.
- The bank transferring its credit risk may not want its actions to be visible to its borrowers and competitors and hence may want to use credit derivatives.
- Loan sales call for substantial information sharing among participants and the bank is likely to incur higher administrative costs and more obligations.

The popular credit risk transfer instruments can be summarized in Figure 8.7.

FIGURE 8.7 CATEGORIZATION OF CREDIT RISK TRANSFER INSTRUMENTS

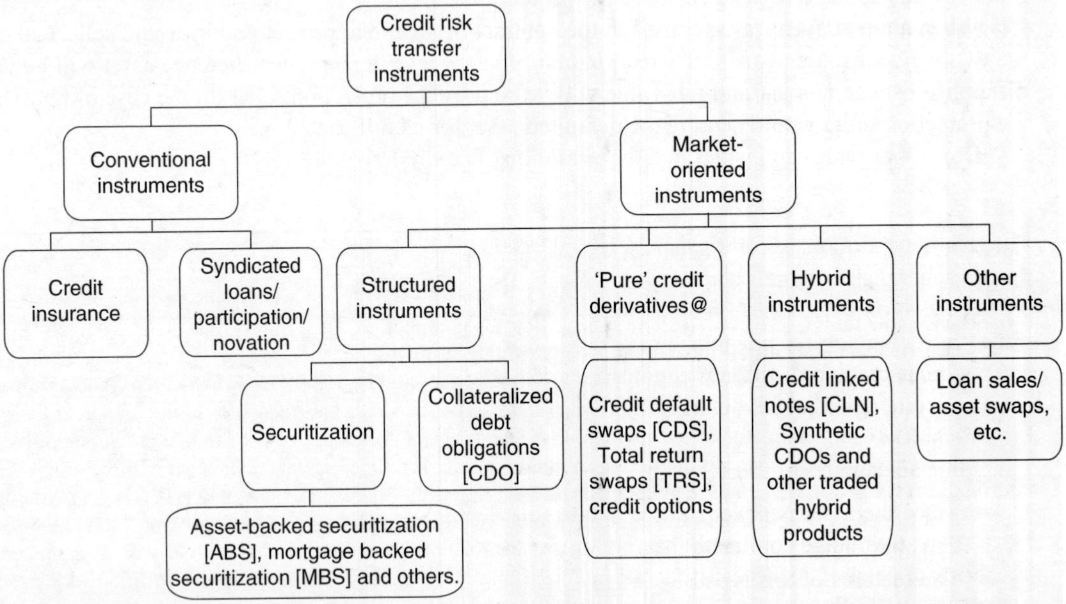

Note: @ 'Pure' credit derivatives are those whose prices can be used to price other credit risk bearing instruments. The next chapter outlines the basic methodologies for pricing credit derivatives.

Some Basic Credit Derivative Structures

There are many kinds of credit derivatives and to enumerate and describe them would be beyond the scope of this book. Further, most credit derivatives, like other derivatives, can be 'structured' to meet the specific requirements of the protection buyers and sellers.

However, we briefly describe some popular types of credit derivatives as follows:

1. **Loan portfolio swap[28]:** Banks swap loan portfolios to diversify their credit exposures to a particular industry or activity. For instance, if Bank X has more real estate loans in its portfolio and Bank Y has more loans to technology firms, X and Y can agree to swap payments received on a basket of each bank's loan exposures.
2. **Total return swap:** This is one of the most popular credit derivative instruments. The steps involved in the swap are as follows:
   - Bank A has made 5-year loan to firm XYZ. The bank would like to hedge its credit risk on the loan. Bank A is called the 'beneficiary' or the 'protection buyer'.
   - In terms of the swap agreement, Bank A agrees to pay Bank B, who is called the 'guarantor' or 'protection seller', the 'total return' on the 'reference asset', in this case, the loan to XYZ. The 'total return' comprises of all contractual payments on the loan, plus any appreciation in the market value of the reference asset.
   - The swap arrangement is completed when Bank B agrees to pay a particular rate (which would include a 'spread' and an allowance for loan value depreciation) to Bank A. This rate is generally fixed based on a reference rate such as the London Inter Bank Offered Rate (LIBOR). Now, in effect Bank B has a

'synthetic' ownership of the reference asset, since it has agreed to bear the risks and rewards of such ownership over the swap period. Bank B, therefore, assumes the credit risk and receives a 'risk premium' for doing so. The greater the credit risk, the higher the risk premium.

- On the date of a specified payment or when the derivative matures or on the happening of a specified event, such as default, the contract terminates. Any depreciation or appreciation in the amortized value of the reference asset (the loan to XYZ) is arrived at as the difference between the notional principal amount of the reference asset and the dealer price.
- If the dealer price is less than the notional principal amount on the date of contract termination, Bank B must pay the difference to Bank A, absorbing any loss due to the decline in credit quality of the reference asset.

To sum up, the protection buyer makes payments based on the total returns from the reference asset—the loan to XYZ—as seen in Figure 8.8.

FIGURE 8.8 TOTAL RETURN SWAP

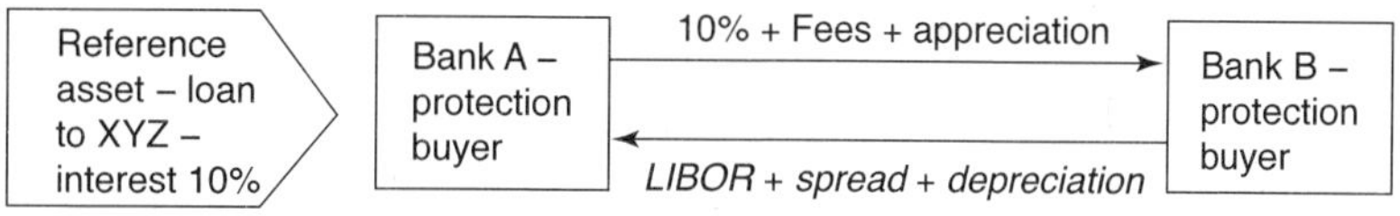

The total returns include contractual payments on the loan plus appreciation of the loan value. In return, the protection seller makes regular contracted payments, fixed or floating, which include a spread over funding costs plus the depreciation value (the 'protection'). Both parties make payments based on the same notional amount. The protection seller gets the advantage of returns without holding the asset on its balance sheet. The protection buyer can negotiate credit protection without having to liquidate the underlying asset. In floating rate contracts, not only is interest rate risk hedged, but also the risk of deterioration of credit quality (which can occur even where there is no default).

Some advantages of the TR swap are as follows:

- Since the asset is never transferred, the bank seeking protection can diversify its credit risk without the need to divulge confidential information on the borrower.
- The features of this type of credit protection are seen to have lower administration costs, as compared to loan liquidation.
- Banks with high funding levels can take advantage of other banks' lower cost balance sheets through such TR swaps. This facilitates diversification of the user's asset portfolio as well.
- The maturity of a TR Swap does not have to match the maturity of the underlying asset. Therefore, the protection seller in a swap with maturity less than that of the underlying asset may benefit from the 'positive carry' associated with being able to roll forward short-term synthetic financing of a longer-term investment. The protection buyer (TR payer) may benefit from being able to purchase protection for a limited period without having to liquidate the asset permanently. At the maturity of a TR Swap whose term is less than that of the reference asset, the protection seller has the option to reinvest in that asset (by continuing to own it) or to sell it at the market price.
- Other applications of TR Swaps include making new asset classes accessible to investors for whom administrative complexity or lending group restrictions imposed by borrowers have traditionally presented barriers to entry. Recently, insurance companies and levered fund managers have made use of TR Swaps to access bank loan markets.

3. **Credit default swap (CDS):** The CDS provides protection against specific credit-related events and, hence, bears more resemblance to a financial bank guarantee or a standby letter of credit, than to a 'swap'. Under this agreement, the protection buyer (Bank A in our earlier example) pays the protection seller (Bank B) only a fixed periodic amount over the life of the agreement.

   Figure 8.9 illustrates the mechanics of a CDS. The following chapter provides an overview of the mechanics of pricing and trading in the CDS.

   The steps in which a basic CDS proceeds are as follows:

- Bank A agrees to pay a fee to Bank B for being guarantor or protection seller. The fee amounts to a specified number of basis points on the value of the reference asset (the loan made by Bank A).

FIGURE 8.9 BASIC CREDIT DEFAULT SWAP

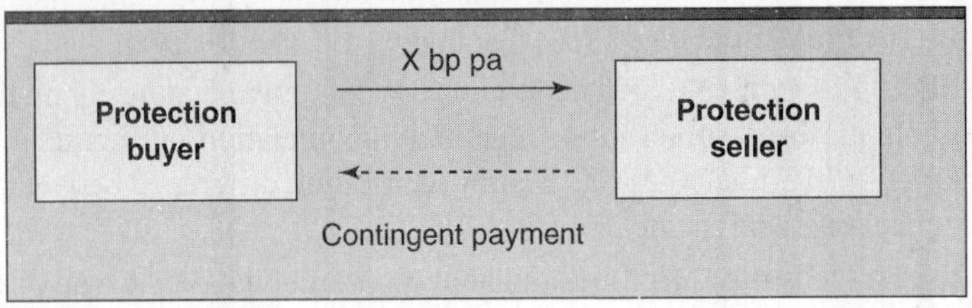

Source: The J.P. Morgan Guide to Credit Derivatives, 13.

- Bank B agrees to pay a pre-determined, market value based amount (usually a percentage of the value of the reference asset) in the event of credit default. The 'event of default' is rigorously defined in the contract—it could take the form of verifiable events such as bankruptcy, payment default or can amount to a specific amount of loss sustained by the protection seeker due to the credit ('materiality threshold'). Bank B is not required to make any payment unless there is a default within the period of the swap.
- The amount to be paid by Bank B, post-default, will be defined in the contract. This amount usually represents the difference between the reference asset's initial principal and the actual market value of the defaulted reference asset. The amount is settled through the 'cash settlement' mechanism.[29]

To lower the cost of protection in a credit swap, contingent credit swaps are employed. Contingent credit swaps are hybrid credit derivatives which, in addition to the occurrence of a credit event, require an additional trigger. Such a trigger could typically be tied to the occurrence of a credit event with respect to another reference asset or a material movement in equity prices, commodity prices or interest rates. The credit protection provided by a contingent credit swap, being weaker, is cheaper than that provided under a regular credit swap.

4. **Credit risk options:** These options provide the protection buyer a valuable hedge against interest rate risk, primarily arising out of a downgrade in a borrower's credit rating. Consider this example. When Bank A entered into a loan agreement with firm XYZ, the firm had an investment grade rating and the loan price was fixed accordingly on floating terms. However, in a year's time, firm XYZ witnessed a slide in its credit rating, due to various factors. This implies that Bank A will have to raise the risk premium and run the risk of default by XYZ or retain the contracted rate and take on higher risk. The third option available to Bank A is to enter into a contract with Bank B, the protection seller. Bank B writes a simple European option with a fixed maturity, agreeing to compensate Bank A for the decline in credit quality due to the lower credit rating of XYZ.

   Credit options can also be put or call options on the price of either a floating rate note bond or loan. In this case, the credit put (or call) option grants the option buyer the right, but not the obligation, to sell to (or buy from) the option seller a specified floating rate reference asset at a pre-specified price (the 'strike price'). Settlement may be on a cash or physical basis.

   The other settlement method is for the protection buyer to make physical delivery of a portfolio of specified deliverable obligations in return for payment of their face amount. Deliverable obligations may be the reference obligation or one of a broad class of obligations meeting certain specifications, such as any senior unsecured claim against the reference entity.
5. **Credit intermediation swap:** In a credit intermediation swap, one creditworthy bank serves as an intermediary between two smaller banks to alleviate credit concerns in the swap transaction. For example, let us assume two small regional banks are keen on entering into a swap contract with each other. Both of them do not have much market presence or credibility and are not convinced of each other's capability of honouring the respective commitments under the swap. The two small banks, therefore, invite a large prime bank with national/international presence to guarantee the swap. The two smaller banks can either pay to the large bank at floating rate and receive fixed rate in return or pay at fixed rate and receive floating rate. The difference between the rates received and paid forms the income for the large bank for accepting the credit risk of the two smaller banks.
6. **Dynamic credit swap:** An important innovation in credit derivatives is the dynamic credit swap. The protection buyer pays a fixed fee, either up front or periodically, which once set does not vary with the size of the protection provided. The protection buyer will only incur default losses if the swap counter party and the protection seller fail. This dual credit effect means that the credit quality of the protection buyer's position is at a level better than the quality of either of its individual counter parties. Also, assuming uncorrelated counter parties, the probability of a joint default is small.

Foreign currency denominated exposure may also be hedged using a dynamic credit swap where a creditor is owed an amount denominated in a foreign currency. This is analogous to the credit exposure in a cross-currency swap.

7. **Credit spread derivatives:** Credit spread is the difference between the interest rates of risk-free government securities and risky debt[30] in the market. Let us assume that interest rates move consistently with the market. That is, a one per cent change in government securities rate leads to a similar change in the debt market. If this is so, any difference between the two rates could be attributed to credit risk for the risky debt. Derivatives written on this spread are credit spread options/forwards/swaps.

   For example, a 'credit spread call' is a call option on credit spreads. If the spread increases, the value of the call increases and pays off if the credit spread at maturity exceeds the strike price of the call option.

   The 'asset swap package' consists of a credit-risky instrument (with any payment characteristics) and a corresponding derivative contract. The contract exchanges the cash flows of the credit-risky instrument for a floating rate cash flow stream.[31] Credit options may be American, European or multi-European. Their structure may transfer default risk or credit spread risk or both.

   Credit options have found favour with investors and banks for the following reasons:

   - Institutional investors see credit options as a means of increasing yields, especially when credit spreads are thin and they find themselves underinvested. These investors prefer to bear the risk of owning (in a put option) or losing (in a call option) an asset at a predetermined price in future and collect current income commensurate with the risk taken.
   - Banks, with their highly leveraged balance sheets, prefer credit options since they are off-balance sheet. Further, the credit options and credit swaps are structured to trigger payments upon the happening of a specific event, which help in mitigating credit exposure risk.
   - Such options are also attractive for portfolios that are forced to sell deteriorating assets. Options are structured to reduce the risk of forced sales at distressed prices and consequently enable the portfolio manager to own assets of marginal credit quality at lower risk. Where the cost of such protection is less than the benefit in terms of increased yield from weaker credits, a distinct improvement in portfolio risk-adjusted returns can be achieved.
   - Borrowers also find options useful for locking in future borrowing costs without impacting their balance sheets. Prior to the advent of credit derivatives, borrowers had to issue debt immediately, even if they had no requirement for the entire amount of debt all at once. The unutilized debt could be invested in other liquid assets, till the requirement for funds came up. This had the adverse effect of inflating the current balance sheet and exposing the issuer to reinvestment risk and often, negative carry.[32] Today, issuers can enter into credit options on their own name and lock in future borrowing costs with certainty.

8. **Credit linked notes (CLN):** This is a funded credit derivative where the protection buyer requires the protection seller to make upfront payments. In return, the protection buyer issues a note called 'CLN'. The CLN is largely similar to any other bond or note. The simplest form of a CLN is represented by a standard note with an embedded CDS. These are typically issued by a trust or SPE. The steps in issuing CLNs are as follows:

   - The bank seeking to issue CLNs (Bank A) sets up an SPE, in the form of a 'trust'. The CLNs are intended to protect Bank A in the event the borrower firm XYZ is unable to repay its debt to the bank.
   - Investors or other banks (say, Bank B) buy into these trusts and receive a CLN for a fixed period, say, 3 years.
   - The trust offers a steady stream of fixed payments to Bank B over the 3-year period. These payments constitute interest plus a risk premium. The total return on the notes is linked to the market value of the underlying pool of debt securities.
   - Bank A invests the funds received from Bank B in relatively risk-free securities, including highly rated corporate bonds.
   - If, during the 3-year period of the CLN, firm XYZ keeps up regular payments to Bank A, it returns the investment made by Bank B.
   - If firm XYZ defaults in payment, Bank A compensates its possible loss by liquidating the risk-free security investments. Bank B receives firm XYZ's debt, which could have turned unsecured or worthless.

   Issuers find CLNs attractive, because the 'risk' attached to a particular borrower is hedged and, therefore, the immediate need for more regulatory capital is avoided. The investing banks find CLNs attractive, because they are able to find a pool of leveraged securities, which could give them good income.

CLNs are used in several ways in practice. Four typical situations[33] are presented as follows:

a. Bank A has credit exposure to a firm S in a specific industry/sector. Institution C, an institutional investor, cannot, by policy or regulation, gain direct exposure to the industry that S is in, but is interested in reaping the benefits of such exposure. C therefore enters into a CLN contract with Bank A, by which A sells a note to C with underlying exposure equal to the face value of the reference asset S. In return, A receives from C, at the beginning of the contract, the face value of S in cash. In compensation, A pays to C a predetermined interest and some credit risk premium. In case of a credit event experienced by S during the contract period, A pays C the recovery proceeds of S. If the recovery value of S is less than what C paid for the asset, C suffers a loss. In case there is no credit event during the contract period, Bank A pays back to institution C the entire principal.
b. The situation above is also applicable to any investor who wants to sell protection to Bank A through a CDS, but is unable to or does not want to access the credit derivatives market.
c. Another common way to use a CLN is in buying protection. Bank A in the example above, the originator of the reference asset S, could buy protection from Bank B through a CLN, where A gets the value of the reference asset upfront (and pays interest and premium to the protection seller B). In a second case, Bank B could have sold protection through a CDS to A. Bank B now wants to guard itself against counter party risk, hence initiates a CLN contract with institution C or another Bank D. If the reference asset defaults, Bank A gets compensated as in example (a) above and Bank B makes the contingent payment on the default swap, which has already been compensated by the CLN. Thus, the CLN functions like insurance in both cases.
d. Special purpose entities (SPEs) or trusts set up in the context of the CLN (as shown in Figure 8.10) are prevalently used in the case of synthetic CDOs (to be discussed in the next chapter).

9. **Credit linked deposits/credit linked certificates of deposit:** Credit linked deposits (CLDs) are structured deposits with embedded default swaps. Conceptually, they can be thought of as deposits along with a default swap that the investor sells to the deposit taker. The default contingency can be based on a variety of underlying assets, including a specific corporate loan or security, a portfolio of loans or securities or sovereign debt instruments or even a portfolio of contracts which give rise to credit exposure. If necessary, the structure can include an interest rate or foreign exchange swap to create cash flows required by investors. In effect, the depositor is selling protection on the reference obligation and earning a premium in the form of a yield spread over plain deposits. If a credit event occurs during the tenure of the CLD, the deposit is paid and the investor would get the deliverable obligation instead of the deposit amount. Figure 8.11 shows the structure of a simple CLD.
10. **Repackaged notes:** Repackaging involves placing securities and derivatives in a SPV which then issues customized notes that are backed by the instruments placed. The difference between repackaged notes and CLDs is that while CLDs are default swaps embedded in deposits/notes, repackaged notes are issued against collateral—which typically would include cash collateral (bonds/loans/cash) and derivative contracts. Another feature of repackaged notes is that any issue by the SPV has recourse only to the collateral of that issue (Figure 8.12).

FIGURE 8.10 THE STRUCTURE OF A CLN

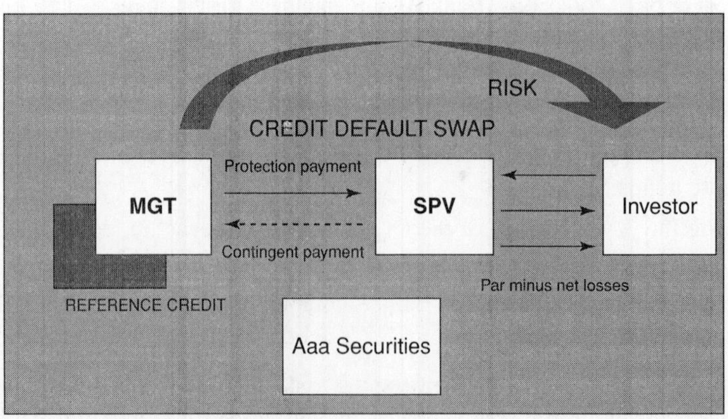

Source: The J.P. Morgan Guide to Credit Derivatives, 25.

FIGURE 8.11 STRUCTURE OF A CLD

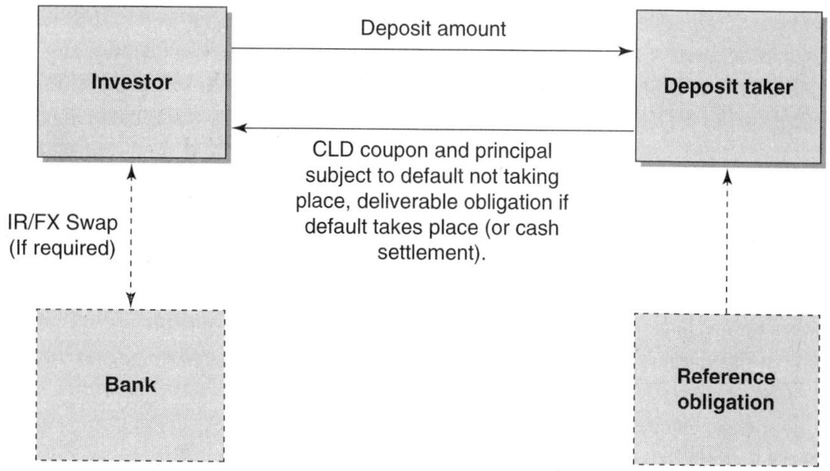

Source: RBI, 'Draft Guidelines for Introduction of Credit Derivatives in India', Figure 4 (26 March 2003): 9.

FIGURE 8.12 TRANSACTIONS UNDER A REPACKAGED NOTE

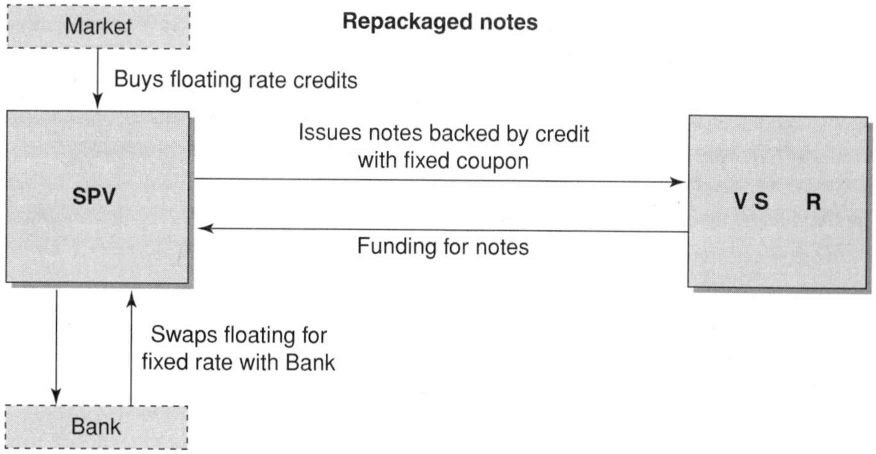

Source: RBI, 'Draft Guidelines for Introduction of Credit Derivatives in India', Figure 5 (26 March 2003): 10.

11. **Basket default swap:** A credit derivative may be with reference to a single reference asset or a portfolio of reference assets. Accordingly, it is termed a single credit derivative or a portfolio credit derivative. In a portfolio derivative, the protection seller is exposed to the risk of one or more components of the portfolio (to the extent of the notional value of the transaction).

    A variant of a portfolio trade is a basket default swap. In this type of swap, there would be a bunch of assets, usually homogeneous. Let us assume that the swap is for the first to default in the basket. The protection seller sells protection on the whole basket, but once there is one default in the basket, the transaction is settled and closed. If the assets in the basket are uncorrelated, this allows the protection seller to leverage himself—his losses are limited to only one default but he actually takes exposure on all the names in the basket. And for the protection buyer, assuming the probability of the second default in a basket is quite low, he actually buys protection for the entire basket but paying a price which is much lower than the sum of individual prices in the basket.

    Likewise, there might be a second-to-default or nth to default basket swaps. Box 8.5 sets out the operational requirements for credit derivatives as envisaged by the Basel Committee on Banking Supervision.[34]

BOX 8.5 OPERATIONAL REQUIREMENTS FOR CREDIT DERIVATIVES

In order for protection from a credit derivative to be recognized, the following conditions must be satisfied:

- The credit events specified by the contracting parties must at a minimum include:
  - a failure to pay the amounts due according to reference asset specified in the contract,
  - a reduction in the rate or amount of interest payable or the amount of scheduled interest accruals,
  - a reduction in the amount of principal or premium payable at maturity or at scheduled redemption dates and
  - a change in the ranking in the priority of payment of any obligation, causing the subordination of such obligation.
- Contracts allowing for cash settlement are recognized for capital purposes provided a robust valuation process is in place in order to estimate loss reliably. Further, there must be a clearly specified period for obtaining post-credit-event valuations of the reference asset, typically not more than 30 days.
- The credit protection must be legally enforceable in all relevant jurisdictions.
- Default events must be triggered by any material event, *e.g.*, failure to make payment over a certain period or filing for bankruptcy or protection from creditors.
- The grace period in the credit derivative contract must not be longer than the grace period agreed upon under the loan agreement.
- The protection purchaser must have the right/ability to transfer the underlying exposure to protection provider, if required for settlement.
- The identity of the parties responsible for determining whether a credit event has occurred must be clearly defined. This determination must not be the sole responsibility of the protection seller. The protection buyer must have the right/ability to inform the protection provider of the occurrence of a credit event.
- Where there is an asset mismatch[35] between the exposure and the reference asset, then:
  - the reference and underlying assets must be issued by the same obligor (*i.e.*, the same legal entity) and
  - the reference asset must rank pari passu or more junior than the underlying asset and legally effective cross-reference clauses (*e.g.*, cross-default or cross-acceleration clauses) must apply.
- Where a bank buying credit protection through a total return swap records the net payments received on the swap as net income, but does not record offsetting deterioration in the value of the asset that is protected (either through reductions in fair value or by an addition to reserves) the credit protection will not be recognized.
- CLN issued by the bank will be treated as cash collateralized transactions.
- Credit protection given by the following will be recognized.
  - Sovereign entities, PSEs and banks with a lower risk weight than the obligor.
  - Corporates (including insurance companies) including parental guarantees rated A or better.

Source: www.bis.org

SECTION IV

TREATMENT OF CREDIT RISK IN INDIA—SOME IMPORTANT EXPOSURE NORMS, PRUDENTIAL NORMS FOR ASSET CLASSIFICATION, INCOME RECOGNITION AND PROVISIONING

Some Important Exposure Norms[36]

In the earlier section, we have learnt that central banks try to limit credit risk concentration in their banking system by limiting exposure to certain sectors or activities.

Exposure is defined as including credit exposure (funded and non-funded credit limits) and investment exposure (including underwriting and similar commitments) as well as certain types of investments in companies. Exposure is taken to be the higher of sanctioned limits or outstanding advances. In the case of term loans that have been fully drawn up to the sanctioned limit, the outstanding will be considered the 'exposure'.

Computing the credit exposure of derivative products (most of these would be denoted as 'contingent liabilities' on banks' balance sheets) such as interest rate and foreign exchange derivative transactions, and gold, will have to be done using the 'Current exposure method'. Netting of mark to market (MTM) values arising on these transactions is not permitted by RBI. Therefore, the gross positive MTM value of such contracts should be considered both for exposure and capital adequacy calculations (*Capital adequacy is discussed in detail in the chapter 'Capital- risk, regulation and adequacy'*). In simple terms, the credit exposure equivalent of an off balance sheet transaction using the current exposure method is equal to *Current credit exposure + future potential credit exposure* of the contracts supporting the off balance sheet transactions.

'Current credit exposure' is the sum of positive MTM values of the contracts. It is therefore obvious that these values require periodical recalculation.

'Potential future credit exposure' is determined by multiplying the notional principal amount of each of these contracts(irrespective of whether the contract has a zero, positive or negative mark-to-market value) by the relevant add-on factor indicated in the quoted circular (page 5) according to the nature and residual maturity of the instrument.

Credit exposure comprises of the following:

- All types of funded and non-funded credit limits.
- Facilities extended by way of equipment leasing, hire purchase finance and factoring services. Under 'credit exposure', detailed guidelines are issued for industry/sector exposures, capital markets, financing equity and investment in shares including Initial Public Offerings and various other activities.

Investment exposure comprises of the following:

- Investments in shares and debentures of companies acquired through direct subscription, development arising out of underwriting obligations or purchased from secondary markets or on conversion of debt into equity.
- Investment in PSU bonds through direct subscription, development arising out of underwriting obligations or purchase made in the secondary market.
- Investments in commercial papers (CPs) issued by corporate bodies/public sector units.
- The Securitization and Reconstruction of Financial Assets and Enforcement of Security Interest Act, 2002, provides, among others, sale of financial assets by banks/FIs to securitization companies (SCs)/reconstruction companies (RCs). Banks'/FIs' investments in debentures/bonds/security receipts/pass-through certificates (PTCs) issued by a securitization company (SC)/reconstruction company (RC) as compensation consequent upon sale of financial assets will constitute exposure on the SC/RC. (As only a few SC/RC are being set up now, banks'/ FIs' exposure on SC/RC through their investments in debentures/bonds/security receipts/PTCs issued by the SC/RC may go beyond their prudential exposure ceiling). In view of the extraordinary nature of event, banks/ FIs will be allowed, in the initial years, to exceed prudential exposure ceiling on a case-to-case basis.
- Investments made in bonds/debentures of companies guaranteed by public financial institutions as given in the cited circular. Guarantees issued by the Public Financial Institutions (PFI) to corporate bonds are also treated as 'exposure'.

The concept of 'group' and the identification of borrowers belonging to a specific 'group' are to be based on the perception of the bank. The guiding principles should however be commonality of management and effective control. The RBI has specifically warned banks against splits in 'groups' being engineered to circumvent the exposure norms.

The salient features of the 'exposure norms' proposed by the RBI are given as follows:

- The exposure ceiling limits applicable from 1 April 2002, computed based on the capital funds in India[37] would be 15 per cent of capital funds (tier 1 + tier 2) in case of single borrower and 40 per cent in the case of a borrower group. However, in case of specified oil companies, the exposure limit to a single borrower can be 25 per cent of capital funds.
- Credit exposure to a borrower group can exceed the exposure norm of 40 per cent of the bank's capital funds by an additional 10 per cent (up to 50 per cent), if the additional credit exposure is to infrastructure projects. Similarly, exposure to a single borrower may exceed the norm of 15 per cent by 5 per cent (up to 20 per cent) if the additional credit exposure is to the infrastructure sector. (*Annexure I of the Master circular quoted above provides the list of sectors under 'Infrastructure'*)
- In addition to the above exposures, banks may enhance exposure to a borrower up to a further 5 per cent of capital funds in exceptional circumstances, with the approval of their Board of Directors.
- The exposures should be disclosed in the banks' financial statements under 'Notes on Accounts'.
- Exposures to NBFC and NBFC-AFC are capped at 15 per cent and 20 per cent respectively. However, relaxation may be considered if the NBFC uses the funds for lending to infrastructure sector.

- Exemptions to the above exposure norms can be made in the case of (a) rehabilitation of sick/weak industrial units, (b) Food credit (allocated directly by the RBI), (c) advances fully guaranteed by the Government of India, (d) banks' exposure to the National Bank for Agriculture and Rural Development (NABARD), and (e) advances granted against the security of the banks' own term deposits, on which the banks hold specific lien.
- Exposure norms for specific sectors have also been outlined by the RBI in the cited circular, which can be accessed at www.rbi.org.in.

Prudential Norms for Asset Classification, Income Recognition and Provisioning[38]

To correspond with the classification of loans discussed in Section I, RBI instructs all banks in India to classify assets under certain categories. 'Non-performing' assets (NPAs) are the broad equivalent of 'impaired' assets discussed in Section I. The RBI has provided detailed guidelines for asset classification, the salient features of which are presented below.

What are NPAs? An asset, including a leased asset, becomes non-performing when it ceases to generate income for the bank. An NPA is a loan or an advance where

- Interest and/or installment of principal remain 'overdue'[39] for a period of more than 90 days in respect of a term loan.
- The account remains 'out of order'[40] in respect of an overdraft/cash credit (OD/CC).
- The bill remains overdue for a period of more than 90 days in the case of bills purchased and discounted.
- A loan granted for short duration crops will be treated as NPA, if the installment of principal or interest thereon remains overdue for two crop seasons.
- A loan granted for long duration crops will be treated as NPA, if the installment of principal or interest thereon remains overdue for one crop season.
- The amount of liquidity facility[41] remains outstanding for more than 90 days, in respect of a securitization transaction (undertaken in terms of guidelines on securitization dated 1 February 2006.)
- Derivative contracts, whose overdue receivables represent positive mark to market value, remaining unpaid for 90 days from the due date for payment.

Additionally, banks should, classify an account as NPA only if the interest charged during any quarter is not serviced fully within 90 days from the end of the quarter.

Income Recognition

Income Recognition—Policy The policy for income recognition has to be objective and based on the record of recovery. In line with international best practices, income from NPAs is not to be recognized on accrual basis but is booked as income only when it is actually received. Therefore, banks should not charge and take to income account interest on any NPA,[42] including government guaranteed (advance).

Reversal of Income If any advance, including bills purchased and discounted becomes an 'NPA' as at close of any year, the unrealized interest accrued and credited to income account in the previous year should be reversed or provided for. This will apply to government guaranteed accounts also. Similarly, uncollected fees, commission and other income that have accrued in the NPAs during past periods should be reversed or provided for.

Leased Assets The unrealized finance charge component of finance income[43] on the leased asset, accrued and credited to income account before the asset became non-performing, should be reversed or provided for in the current accounting period.

Appropriation of Recovery in NPAs Interest realized on NPAs may be taken to income account provided the credits in the accounts towards interest are not out of fresh/additional credit facilities sanctioned to the borrower.

Asset Classification

Categories of NPAs Banks in India are required to classify NPAs into the following three categories based on (a) the period for which the asset has remained non-performing and (b) the realizability of the dues.

i. Sub-standard assets
ii. Doubtful assets
iii. Loss assets

Sub-standard assets: With effect from 31 March 2005, a sub-standard asset would be one, which has remained NPA for a period less than or equal to 12 months. The following features are exhibited by sub-standard assets: the current net worth of the borrower/guarantor or the current market value of the security charged is not enough to ensure recovery of the dues to the banks in full and the asset has well-defined credit weaknesses that jeopardize the liquidation of the debt and are characterized by the distinct possibility that the banks will sustain some loss, if deficiencies are not corrected.

Doubtful assets: With effect from 31 March 2005, an asset would be classified as doubtful if it has remained in the sub-standard category for a period of 12 months.

A loan classified as doubtful has all the weaknesses inherent in assets that were classified as sub-standard, with the added characteristic that the weaknesses make collection or liquidation in full—on the basis of currently known facts, conditions and values—highly questionable and improbable.

Loss assets: A loss asset is one which is considered uncollectible and of such little value that its continuance as a bankable asset is not warranted—although there may be some salvage or recovery value. Also, these assets would have been identified as 'loss assets' by the bank or internal or external auditors or the RBI inspection, but the amount would not have been written off wholly.

Treatment of some special situations is outlined in Box 8.6.

BOX 8.6 HOW DO WE TREAT THE FOLLOWING UNDER THE ASSET CLASSIFICATION NORMS?

Accounts with temporary deficiencies

Some assets display operational deficiencies such as inadequate drawing power; non-submission of stock statements, non-renewal of limits on due date or excess drawings over the limit. When should banks classify accounts exhibiting these characteristics as NPAs?

- When the outstanding in the account is based on stock statements more than 3 months old.
- If such irregular drawings are permitted in the account for 90 days continuously, even though the firm is functioning or the borrower's financial health is satisfactory.
- When an account enjoying regular or ad hoc credit limits has not been reviewed/renewed within 180 days from the due date/date of ad hoc sanction.

In such cases, if arrears of interest and principal are paid by the borrower subsequently, the account may be upgraded to 'standard'[44] category.

Accounts regularized near about the balance sheet date

Where a solitary or a few credits are recorded just before the balance sheet date in a borrowal account and the account exhibits inherent credit weaknesses based on the current available data, it should be classified an NPA.

Asset classification to be borrower-wise and not facility-wise

Even if one credit facility among many such credit facilities granted to a borrower is to be treated as NPA, the entire borrowing account has to be classified as NPA.

Advances under consortium arrangements

Asset classification of accounts under consortium should be based on the record of recovery of the individual member banks and other aspects having a bearing on the recoverability of the advances.

Accounts where there is erosion in the value of security/frauds committed by borrowers

In such cases of serious credit impairment, it will not be prudent to put these accounts through various stages of asset classification and the asset should be straightaway classified as a doubtful or loss asset as appropriate.

- Erosion in the value of security can be reckoned as significant when the realizable value of the security is less than 50 per cent of the value assessed by the bank or accepted by the RBI at the time of last inspection. Such NPAs may be straightaway classified under doubtful category and provisioning should be made as applicable to doubtful assets.
- If the realizable value of the security, as assessed by the bank/the RBI is less than 10 per cent of the outstanding in the borrowal account, the existence of security should be ignored and the asset should be straightaway classified as a loss asset. It may be either written off or fully provided for by the bank.

Advances against term deposits, National Savings Certificates (NSCs), Kisan Vikas Patra (KVP)/Indira Vikas Patra (IVP)
Advances against term deposits, NSCs eligible for surrender; IVPs, KVPs and life policies need not be treated as NPAs. However, advances against gold ornaments, government securities and all other securities are not covered by this exemption.

Loans with moratorium for payment of interest

- In cases where the loan agreement incorporates a moratorium for payment of interest, interest becomes 'due' only after completion of the moratorium or gestation period. Therefore, such interest does not become overdue and hence is not termed an NPA during the moratorium period. However, the advance becomes overdue if interest remains uncollected after the specified due date.
- In the case of housing loan or similar advances granted to staff members where interest is payable after recovery of principal, interest need not be considered as overdue from the first quarter onwards. Such loans/advances should be classified as an NPA only when there is a default in repayment of principal installment or payment of interest on the specified due dates.

Agricultural advances (some salient features)

- A loan granted for short duration crops (with crop season less than 1 year) will be treated as an NPA, if the installment of principal or interest thereon remains overdue for two crop seasons.
- A loan granted for long duration crops (those with crop season longer than 1 year) will be treated as an NPA, if the installment of principal or interest thereon remains overdue for one crop season (period up to harvesting of the crop).
- Where natural calamities impair the repaying capacity of agricultural borrowers, banks may decide on appropriate relief measures—conversion of the short-term production loan into a term loan; or rescheduling repayment or sanctioning a fresh short-term loan (subject to RBI directives).
- In such cases of conversion or re-schedulement, the term loan as well as fresh short-term loan may be treated as current dues and need not be classified as NPA.

Government-guaranteed advances
Overdue credit facilities backed by central government guarantee may be treated as an NPA only if the government repudiates its guarantee when invoked. However, in respect of state government guaranteed exposures, with effect from the year ending 31 March 2006, state government-guaranteed advances and investments in state government guaranteed securities would attract asset classification and provisioning norms if interest and/or principal or any other amount due to the bank remains overdue for more than 90 days.

Source: RBI 'Master Circular—Prudential Norms on Income Recognition, Asset Classification and Provisioning Pertaining to Advances' (July 2, 2012). More details can be found in this Master Circular, which can be accessed at www.rbi.org.in.

Provisioning Norms

Adequate provisions have to be made for impaired loans or 'NPA', classified as given in the foregoing paragraphs. Taking into account the time lag between an account becoming doubtful of recovery, its recognition as an impaired loan, the realization of the security charged to the bank and the likely erosion over time in the value of this security, banks should classify impaired loans into 'sub-standard', 'doubtful' and 'loss' assets and make provisions against these.

Loss assets should be written off or 100 per cent provided for.

Doubtful Assets

- Provision of 100 per cent to the extent the advance is not covered by the realizable value of the security (to which the bank has a valid recourse).
- That portion of the advances covered by realizable value of the security will be provided for at rates ranging from 25 per cent to 100 per cent on the following basis:

Period for which the advance has remained in 'doubtful' category	Provision requirement (per cent) (for the secured portion)
Up to 1 year	25
1 to 3 years	40
More than 3 years	100

Sub-standard Assets A general provision of 15 per cent on total outstanding should be made (without making any allowance for ECGC guarantee cover and securities available). The 'unsecured exposures'[45] identified as 'sub-standard' would attract additional provision of 10 per cent thus constituting 25 per cent on the outstanding balance. However, where banks have proposed additional safeguards such as escrow accounts for debt service in the case of lending to infrastructure projects, provisions on infrastructure loans classified as 'sub standard' will be at 20 per cent (and not 25 per cent applicable to other loans). The precondition for lower provisioning would be that banks have put in place an appropriate mechanism to escrow the cash flows and also hold a clear and valid legal claim on these cash flows.

What is an 'Unsecured' Exposure? RBI defines an 'unsecured' exposure as one where the realisable value of the security, as assessed by the bank/approved valuers/Reserve Bank's inspecting officers, is not more than 10 percent, of the outstanding exposure. 'Exposure' shall include all funded and non-funded exposures (including underwriting and similar commitments). 'Security' will mean tangible security properly discharged to the bank and will not include intangible securities like guarantees (including State government guarantees), comfort letters etc.

Standard Assets Under the existing norms, banks should make a general provision of a minimum of 0.25 per cent—1 per cent on standard assets on global loan portfolio basis. Within this framework, standard assets in specific sectors would attract lower or higher provisions. For example, provisions on loans to agriculture and SME sectors would be at 0.25 per cent. (For more details, the RBI's ongoing instructions in this regard would be a good source. It may be noted that by revising the standard asset provisioning upward or downward, RBI, in effect, signals to banks on the risk involved in financing the relevant sectors). Advances to commercial real estate sector would attract a provision of 1 per cent, indicating that standard assets in this sector have higher risk, due to market volatility.

Similarly, housing loans at 'teaser' rates attract a higher provision of 2 per cent. What is a 'teaser' rate and why is it considered risky? Teaser rates on housing loans have become a competitive pricing practice among banks, where the loan is granted at comparatively lower interest rates in the first few years, after which rates are reset at higher rates, which effectively is the appropriate lending rate. RBI is concerned that some borrowers may find it difficult to service the loans at the higher rates, and that many banks, at the time initial credit appraisal, do not take into account the repaying capacity of the borrower at higher rates. However, the provision requirement would be reduced to 0.4 per cent if the housing loans granted at teaser rates remain 'standard' assets after one year from the date of repricing to higher lending rates 'Restructured' advances classified as standard assets will attract a provision of 2 per cent in the first two years after restructuring All other loans and advances not included the categories mentioned above would attract a provision of 0.40 per cent. However, these provisions need not be included for arriving at net NPAs and will be presented as 'Contingent Provisions against Standard Assets' under 'Other Liabilities and Provisions—Others' in Schedule 5 of the balance sheet.

Floating Provisions[46] Internal policies approved by the Banks' Board would determine the level of floating provisions. Such provisions will have to be separately held for 'advances' and 'investments' and would be used only under 'extraordinary circumstances', as dictated in the policy and after approval from RBI.

To facilitate banks' Boards to evolve suitable policies in this regard, RBI has clarified that the 'extra-ordinary circumstances' refer to losses which do not arise in the normal course of business, and are exceptional and non-recurring in nature. According to RBI, these extra-ordinary circumstances could broadly fall under three categories viz. General, Market and Credit. Under general category, there can be situations where bank faces unexpected loss due to events such as civil unrest or collapse of currency in a country. Natural calamities and pandemics may also be included in the general category. Market category would include events such as a general melt down in the markets, which affects the entire financial system. Among the credit category, only exceptional credit losses would be considered as an extra-ordinary circumstance. For instance, expenses and other charges incurred by banks due to implementation of the Agricultural debt waiver and debt relief scheme, 2008, (announced by the Central Government, which exempted many farmers from repaying loans) would have to be set off against floating provisions.

Disclosures on floating provisions would be found in the 'notes on accounts' to the balance sheet as (a) opening balance in the floating provisions account, (b) the quantum of floating provisions made in the accounting year, (c) purpose and amount of draw down made during the accounting year, and (d) closing balance in the floating provisions account.

Banks can also make additional provisions over and above the provisioning rate mentioned for NPAs with Board approval, where the excess provisioning is deemed appropriate. However, the policy has to be clearly spelt out and show consistency over the years.

The guidelines for provisions under special circumstances such as (a) provisions on leased assets, (b) provisions on advances under rehabilitation, (c) provisions on advances against bank term deposits, NSCs eligible for surrender, IVPs, KVPs and Life policies, as well as advances against gold ornaments, government and all other securities, (d) take out finance, (e) reserve for exchange rate fluctuation account (RE-RFA), (f) provision for country risk and (g) provisioning for sale of financial asset to SC/RC are provided in the quoted RBI circular, point 5.9.

Writing-Off NPAs Provisions made for NPAs are not eligible for tax deductions. However, tax benefits can be claimed for writing off advances.

Illustration 8.1 demonstrates the impact of provisioning and write-off on banks' profits.

ILLUSTRATION 8.1

Profit before provisions for Bank Y is ₹500 crores. If the tax rate is 30 per cent, what will be the impact of the following actions on Bank Y's: (a) profits, and (b) capital base?

- Make a provision of ₹250 crores for NPAs.
- Provide ₹200 crores for NPAs and write-off the remaining ₹50 crores.

Option 1. Provide ₹250 crores for NPAs.

Profit before provision	₹500 crores
Less provision for NPAs	₹250 crores
PBT	₹250 crores
Less tax at 30 per cent	₹150 crores (since provision for NPAs is not tax deductible, tax calculated at 30 per cent of ₹500 crores.)

* NBV = Book value LESS provisions held.

Profit after tax	**₹100 crores**

Option 2: Provide ₹200 crores for NPAs and write off ₹50 crores.

Profit before provision	₹500 crores
Less provision for NPAs	₹200 crores
Less write-off	₹50 crores
PBT	₹250 crores
Less tax @ 30 per cent	₹135 crores (since write-offs are tax deductible, tax to be calculated on PBT + provisions = ₹450 crores)
Profit after tax	**₹115 crores**

Interpretation

Option 2 yields more profits after tax and hence would augment the capital base more than Option 1.

Calculation of NPA levels for reporting to RBI—see Box 8.7

BOX 8.7 CALCULATING NPA LEVELS – THE REPORTING FORMAT

(To be reported in ₹ crore up to two decimals)

Sl. No.	Description	Amount
1	Standard advances	
2	Gross NPAs*	
3	Gross Advances ** (1 + 2)	
4	Gross NPAs as per cent of Gross advances (2/3)	
5	Total deductions:	
	(i) Provisions held in the case of NPA Accounts as per asset classification (including additional Provisions for NPAs at higher than prescribed rates).	
	(ii) DICGC / ECGC claims received and held pending adjustment	
	(iii) Part payment received and kept in Suspense Account or any other similar account	
	(iv) Balance in Sundries Account (Interest Capitalization - Restructured Accounts), in respect of NPA Accounts	
	*(v) Floating Provisions****	
	(vi) Provisions in lieu of diminution in the fair value of restructured accounts classified as NPAs	
	(vii) Provisions in lieu of diminution in the fair value of restructured accounts classified as standard assets	
6	Net Advances [3 – 5(i + ii + iii + iv + v + vi + vii)]	
7	Net NPAs [2 – 5(i + ii + iii + iv + v + vi)]	
8	Net NPAs as per cent of Net advances (7/6)	
*	Principal dues of NPAs plus Funded Interest Term Loan (FITL) where the corresponding contra credit is parked in Sundries Account (Interest Capitalization - Restructured Accounts), in respect of NPA Accounts.	
**	For the purpose of this Statement, 'Gross Advances' mean all outstanding loans and advances including advances for which refinance has been received but excluding rediscounted bills, and advances written off at Head Office level (Technical write off).	
***	Floating Provisions would be deducted while calculating Net NPAs, to the extent, banks have exercised this option, over utilizing it towards Tier II capital.	

The Provisioning Coverage Ratio (PCR)

The PCR is calculated as the ratio of Provisions (specific + floating) to Gross NPAs. The Gross NPA position for calculation of the ratio is the position as on September 30, 2010. The PCR indicates the funds available with a bank to cover loan losses. RBI stipulates that banks in India should hold a PCR of not less than 70 per cent.

The rationale for the PCR is that banks should build provisioning and capital buffers in good times, that is, when profits are healthy, so that the buffer can be used to absorb losses in a downturn. The buffer is called a 'countercyclical provisioning buffer' and has to be held till international norms in this respect are finalized.

SECTION V

TREATMENT OF CREDIT RISK IN INDIA—SECURITIZATION AND CREDIT DERIVATIVES

Securitization—The Act

With effect from 23 April 2003, 'The Securitization Companies and Reconstruction Companies (Reserve Bank) Guidelines and Directions, 2003' are operational in India. These guidelines and directions apply to SC/RC registered with the Reserve Bank of India under Section 3 of the Securitization and Reconstruction of Financial Assets and Enforcement of Security Interest Act, 2002.

The salient features of the Securitization Act are listed as follows:

- Incorporation of SPVs, namely, securitization company and reconstruction company.
- Securitization of financial assets.
- Funding of securitization.
- Asset reconstruction.
- Enforcing security interest,*i.e.*, taking over the assets given as security for the loan.
- Establishment of a central registry for regulating and registering securitization transactions: One objective of the Securitization Act is to provide for the enforcement of security interest, that is, taking possession of the assets given as security for the loan. Section 13 of the Securitization Act contains elaborate provisions for a lender (referred to as 'secured creditor') to take possession of the security given by the borrower.
- Offences and penalties.
- Boiler-plate provisions.
- Dilution of provisions of the SICA.[47]
- Banks can sell the following financial assets to the securitization company.
  - An NPA, including a non-performing bond/debenture.
  - A 'Standard Asset'[48] where
    i. the asset is under consortium/multiple banking arrangements
    ii. at least 75 per cent by value of the asset is classified as NPA in the books of other banks/FIs and
    iii. at least 75 per cent (by value) of the banks/FIs who are under the consortium/multiple banking arrangements agree to the sale of the asset to SC/RC.

The Securitization and Reconstruction of Financial Assets and Enforcement of Security Interest Act, 2002 (SRFAESI Act) allows acquisition of financial assets by SC/RC from any bank/FI on mutually agreed terms and conditions. The salient features of the Act relevant to banks and those relating to securitization and reconstruction companies are described in various notifications of the RBI.[49]

Securitization—the Guidelines

The RBI published its Final Guidelines on securitization in May, 2012, proposing minimum risk retention (MRR) and minimum holding period (MHP) for securitization transactions. One of the unique moves by the RBI is removing the distinction that the market currently enjoys between bilateral or direct assignments and securitizations, and laying down separate standards for securitization and direct assignments

The salient features of the guidelines on securitization and direct assignment are as given in RBI Master circular "Prudential norms on Income recognition, Asset classification and provisioning" dated July 1, 2013, have been summarized below

Salient Features of the Current Guidelines on Securitization

1. When a financial asset is sold by one bank to the SC/RC, it should have the effect of taking the asset off the selling bank's books, 'without recourse' to the selling bank. This means that the entire credit risk is also transferred to the SC/RC.
2. The Board of the selling bank should lay down policies and guidelines in respect of the following aspects of the asset sale, such as, identification of assets to be sold, the procedure for selling the identified assets, realistic valuation of the identified assets and delegation of powers for deciding on selling the identified asset.
3. After the sale of the identified asset to the SC/RC, the selling bank should not assume any operational, legal or other types of risks relating to the sold asset.
4. Banks can decide to accept or reject the purchase price for the identified asset offered by the SC/RC. In the case of multiple banking arrangements/consortium lending, if 75 per cent of the banks in the arrangement decide to accept the offer, the remaining banks would be obligated to accept the offer as well. However, transfer of the asset cannot be made to the SC/RC at a 'contingent' price, since this would imply that in the event of a shortfall in realization by the SC/RC, the banks would have to bear a part of the shortfall.
5. Banks can receive cash or bonds or debentures as sale consideration for the assets sold to the SC/RC. In case the sale consideration is by bonds/debentures, the selling bank would show these bonds/debentures as 'investments' in its books. Similarly, banks' investments in security receipts, Pass through Certificates (PTC) or other bonds/debentures issued by an SC/RC would be shown under 'investments' in the banks' books.

6. If a bank sells an asset to the SC/RC at a price less than the Net Book Value (NBV—defined as book value less provisions held), the shortfall should be debited to the Income statement of the same year. If, on the other hand, the asset is sold for a value higher than the NBV, the excess provision will be kept aside to meet any shortfall or loss arising out of sale by the bank of other assets to SC/RC.
7. A bank can invest in the security receipts or pass through certificates issued by the SC/RC arising out of sale of its own assets to the SC/RC. The sale will then be valued in the bank's books as the lower of the redemption value of the security receipts/PTC, or the NBV of the asset sold.
8. The securities issued by the SC/RC should contain the following features:
   a. The securities must be for a term of less than six years
   b. The securities must carry a rate of interest higher than the prevailing bank rate + 150 basis point
   c. The securities must be secured by a legally created charge on the assets being transferred/sold
   d. The securities must be repaid in full or in part if the underlying asset is sold by the SC/RC before maturity
   e. The commitment of the SC/RC to redeem the securities must be unconditional (not linked to realization of asset value)
   f. If the investor in the security receipts transfers ownership to a third party, the SC/RC should be kept informed
9. The instruments (debentures/bonds) received by banks as sale consideration for financial assets sold to SC/RC, or those instruments issued by SC/RC in which banks have invested, will both be treated as 'non SLR securities'. Hence the valuation and other norms will be applicable to these instruments as for non SLR securities. (We will be studying the valuation of non SLR securities in the chapter on 'Market risk')
10. All securitization transactions have to be disclosed in the 'Notes on Accounts' in banks' balance sheets.
11. SC/RC can also act as agents for recovery for a fee, in the case of those assets that banks do not want to sell, but merely recover the outstanding advances. When the SC/RC acts as recovery agent, the assets under recovery will continue to be held in the banks' books. The amounts recovered will be credited to the banks' loan account, and therefore, appropriate provision for these assets will also be held by the banks themselves.

Sale of Assets by Banks Not Involving SC/RC

Salient Features of Direct Assignment Guidelines of RBI

In Figure 8.7 presented in Section III of this chapter, we see a category of credit risk transfer instruments labelled 'other instruments', examples of which are loan sales or asset swaps.

Banks can sell off their loans/financial assets, especially their non performing assets, without involving a securitization process or an SC/RC, to other banks willing to buy the same, when an active secondary market for loans exists in the economy. In effect, loans and non performing assets are now being treated as liquid securities that can be valued and traded in the inter bank market.

RBI has issued guidelines to banks for sale and purchase of financial assets from one another. The players involved in the direct sale and purchase of loans in the secondary loan market would be banks, financial institutions and the non banking finance companies (NBFCs).

The eligible asset would be a financial asset, including assets under multiple or consortium banking arrangements, and would be a non performing advance or investment in the books of the selling bank The salient features of the guidelines on direct sale and purchase of non performing financial assets are given below.

1. The bank intending to sell or purchase non performing financial assets direct from other financial institutions should have a Board approved policy in place. The policy should specify how to identify the assets to be purchased or sold, the procedure for such purchase or sale, valuation process for the assets based on estimated future cash flows from repayments and recovery prospects, decision making powers at each level of the bank, and the related accounting policies. The Board should also ensure that the bank has adequately skilled personnel, systems and procedures for risk mitigation are present to make the sale or purchase deals, so that the bank adds value to its financial health.
2. For the purpose of selling non performing assets in the secondary market, the NPA should have remained as NPA in the books of the selling bank for at least two years. The bank that purchases the NPA (or NPFA–non performing financial asset) should hold the asset in its books for at least 15 months before selling it to other banks. The asset cannot be however sold back to the bank from which it was purchased.

3. Banks selling non performing assets should compute the net present value (NPV) of the estimated cash flows associated with the realizable value of the securities available to support the asset, net of cost of realization. The estimated cash flows are typically expected to flow in within a three year period, with at least 10 per cent of the cash flow being realized in the first year, followed by 5 per cent in each of the following half years, with full recovery being achieved in three years. The net present value thus computed would be the floor of the sale price.
4. The purchase or sale of non performing assets should be 'without recourse'. This implies that the entire credit risk associated with the non performing assets should be transferred to the purchasing bank. For the selling bank, the asset should be taken off its books, with no residual liability or risk. This effectively means that credit enhancements or liquidity facilities (as in the case of securitization) would not be a part of these transactions. Banks are free to accept or reject offers based on the price being quoted for the asset. However, a sale to another bank cannot be made at a 'contingent' price, where, in the event of shortfall in realization by the purchasing bank, the selling bank would have to bear a portion of the shortfall.
5. The sale of assets should be made only on 'cash' basis—the entire sale consideration should be received up-front and the asset be taken off the selling bank's books.
6. Selling or purchasing homogeneous pools of retail NPAs can be done on a portfolio basis, provided each of the NPAs in the pool has remained non performing for at least two years in the books of the selling bank. For the purchasing bank, the pool would be treated as a single asset.
7. Though the assets being sold are non performing, the purchasing bank can classify them as 'standard' assets in its books for a period of 90 days from the purchase date. After this period, the classification of the asset will depend on the record of recovery in the books of the purchasing bank in accordance with the cash flows estimates while purchasing the asset. For example, any restructuring or rescheduling of the repayment schedule or the estimated cash flow of the non performing asset by the purchasing bank would render the account to be classified as non performing.
8. Once a non performing financial asset is sold, the asset will be removed from the selling bank's books. If the sale is at a price below the Net Book Value (NBV= book value less provisions held), the shortfall should be debited to the Income statement of that year. If the sales is for a value higher than the NBV, the excess provision will be retained and used to meet the shortfall or loss on account of sale of other non performing assets.
9. Once the asset is included in the books of the purchasing bank, provision has to be made on the purchased asset appropriate to its asset classification status. The 'exposure' norms discussed earlier would be applicable to the addition of the non performing asset to the purchasing bank's portfolio.
10. Sale and purchase of non performing financial assets will have to be disclosed in the Notes on Accounts to the banks' balance sheets.

Comparison of Guidelines—Securitization vs Direct Assignment

The similarities:

- Both require assignment of the assets to be sold, and both constitute true sale.
- Both ensure bankruptcy remoteness.
- Both can have multiple investors.
- Minimum Holding Period (MHP) is applicable to both.
- Both exhibit bankruptcy remoteness, though in slightly different ways.
- Investors are exposed to the underlying financial assets and their risks in both.
- Both are treated as off balance sheet transactions, subject to certain conditions.

The points where the operational guidelines are different are as follows:

- Securitization requires a special purpose vehicle to be created, while direct assignment does not need one.
- While multiple investors can participate in both, in the case of direct assignment, the multiple investors should also be the joint owners.
- In the case of securitization, investors purchase securities issued by the SPV, while in the case of direct assignment, investors purchase the underlying pool of assets.
- An important point of distinction is that credit enhancements are possible in securitization, while no credit enhancement is possible in a direct assignment.

- The securities are rated in their respective tranches in the case of securitization, while in direct assignment the investor buys a pool of loans, which may or may not be rated.
- Upfront cash payment is mandatory in direct assignment, while it is optional in securitization.
- Since the investors deal with purchase of financial assets in the case of direct assignment, due diligence has to be carried out by the investors themselves; in the case of securitization, the investors do not have recourse to the originator, and hence have to evaluate the cash flows from the securities issued by the SPV.
- Securitization guidelines stipulate a cap of 20 per cent on the extent of investment; there are no such restrictions in the case of direct assignment.
- In the investors' books, the accounting would be done as for securities under securitization; but would be shown as 'loans' under direct assignment.
- Due to the above point, Mark to Market (MTM) requirements are applicable for securities issued under a securitization; MTM is not relevant for direct assignment.
- Under direct assignment capital is freed for the selling bank; while under securitization, the originating bank can be asked to give first loss support, in which case, regulatory capital has to be maintained.
- The pricing of loans in direct assignment can be negotiated and fixed between the purchasing and selling banks; in the case of securitization, the pricing of the securities depend on their rating.
- There are certain unresolved tax related issues in the case of securitization; there are no tax issues in the case of direct assignment since assets are directly bought and sold by banks.

It is evident from the above, that both securitization and direct assignment have benefits and disadvantages to investors and originators. However, direct assignments seem easier to operationalize.

Securitization—The Indian Experience

Securitization is not new to India. It has been used since 1992. In the early years, originators directly sold consumer loan pools to buyers and also acted as servicers to collect the periodic loan and interest payments. The late 1990s saw the emergence of liquid and transferable securities backed by the pool receivables—Pass Through Certification (PTCs as they are commonly known).

The Indian securitization market is dominated by the following asset classes:

a. Asset Backed Securitizations (ABS) continued to remain the major asset class in FY 2013, dominated by commercial vehicles including two and three wheeler loans, car loans, micro-finance loans, SME loans, gold loans and others. Microfinance loans increased their share substantially during the FY 2013.
b. Residential mortgage-backed securities (RMBS).
c. Single loan CLO and loan sell offs (LSO).

It is noteworthy that there has been no default in any of the transactions.

In India, issuers have typically been private sector banks, foreign banks and non-banking financial companies with the underlying assets being mostly retail and corporate loans. Public sector banks are yet to enter securitization in a big way.

The Indian securitization market exhibits some unique characteristics, a few of which are listed as follows:

a. Credit enhancements to senior notes are usually provided through a cash reserve or guarantee by a highly rated institution.
b. Most investments in securitized instruments are held till maturity.
c. PTCs are not tradable securities. Since, the secondary market for securitized instruments is almost non-existent, almost all issues are privately placed.
d. The predominant investors in securitized instruments are mutual funds, insurance companies and some private sector banks.
e. In many countries where a robust market for securitization exists, ratings of securitized instruments are based on timely payment of interest. However, in India ratings are based on timely payment of principal as well as interest.

Figure 8.13 traces the growth of the securitization market over the years, mentioning specific landmark deals.

FIGURE 8.13 TRACING SECURITIZATION GROWTH—LANDMARK DEALS

1992
- First auto loan securitization—Citibank and GIC mutual fund—₹16 crore
- First securitization of property receivables

1999
- L&T securitizes future lease rentals to raise capital for power plant—₹409 crore
- First securitization of personal loans—Citibank—₹284.1 crore
- ICICI securitizs assets of ₹27.5 croroe

2001
- First offshore securitization backed by aircraft purchase receivables—Jet Airways—₹1600 crore
- First Mortgage-backed securitization [MBS]—NHB and HDFC—₹59.7 crore
- First sales tax deferrals securitization by Maharashtra Govt.—₹150 crore

2002
- First power receivables securitization—Karnataka State Eletricity Board—₹194 crore
- First CDO of corporate loans by ICICI bank

2003
- First floating rate loan securitization—Citigroup—₹281 crore

2004
- First revolving securitiation of working capital facilities to SMEs—Citibank

2005
- First sovereign lease receivables securitization by Indian Railway Finance Corporation—₹196 crore

2006
- RBI's guidelines for securitization of standard assets

2007
- Largest auto loan securitization—ICICI bank—₹1929.9 crore

The trend of deceleration in securitizations after the financial crisis was reversed in FY 2012. While ABS and RMBS grew substantially, the issuance of LSO reduced. The primary reason for the growth of ABS during FY 2012 was due to a greater share of micro-finance loan pools. Shriram Transport Finance Company, SREI Equipment Finance, Indiabulls Financial Services Ltd., Sundaram Finance and Shriram City Union Finance were the largest Originators in FY 2012, altogether contributing to over 60 per cent of the total number of ABS issuances. Banks continued to be a key investor segment, but stayed away from being originators.

Table 8.4 shows the trend in growth of securitization in India in various segments from 2009 to 2012.

TABLE 8.4 TREND IN SECURITIZATION—2009–2012

	FY2009		FY2010		FY2011		FY2012	
	Amount	**Share**	**Amount**	**Share**	**Amount**	**Share**	**Amount**	**Share**
ABS	13,581	25%	21,497	50%	21,819	69%	26,071	71%
RMBS	3,291	6%	6,254	14%	5,029	16%	7,680	21%
Total Retail Securitization	16,872	31%	27,751	64%	26,848	84%	33,751	92%
LSO	35,608	66%	14,581	34%	4,441	14%	2,217	6%
Others	1,160	2%	787	2%	536	2%	635	2%
Overall total	**53,640**	**100%**	**43,118**	**100%**	**31,825**	**100%**	**36,603**	**100%**
Growth	(16%)		(20%)		(26%)		15%	

Source: ICRA, May 2012, Update on Indian securitization market, Table 1, P. 2, accessed at www.icra.in

Note: LSO indicates Securitization of individual corporate loans or loan sell-off.

Some typical features exhibited by the Indian securitization market during FY 2012 were as follows:

a. Key originators were NBFCs, while key investors were banks—mostly private sector banks and foreign banks. The originators also functioned as servicers. (*Please refer to Figure 8.4 and Annexure II of this chapter for the servicers' role*)

b. While the market seemed to prefer AAA rated securities, other ratings also found a market over the last two years.

c. The average tenure of an ABS ranged from 18 to 24 months, while that of an MBS from 6 to 8 years. However, taken on a door-to-door basis, the tenure for an ABS was 40 to 60 months, while that for an MBS was 12 to 20 years.

d. In the case of ABS, the investors typically get a fixed yield, while MBS investors look to floating yields that are linked to pool yields or to external benchmarks.

e. The credit enhancements provided for transactions were more in the nature of cash collateral, excess interest spread (EIS) or principal subordination, since most of the transactions were at 'par' for obtaining priority sector benefit on loans (in accordance with RBI instructions issued in January 2011). All the RMBS transactions during FY 2012 were at par due to the volatility in interest rates, which affects the cash flows

f. Securitizations at a 'premium' formed only about 10 per cent of the total of ABS and RMBS, exhibiting a sharp decline from 37 per cent in FY 2010.

g. It can be seen from Table 8.4 that LSO issuance has decelerated significantly since FY2011. LSO transactions were largely short-term in nature and the Originator would typically disburse the loan with the specific intention of securitizing it soon after the disbursement. ICRA, in its report, assesses that RBI's guidelines (summarized above)—specially, the requirement of Minimum Holding Period (MHP) of 9 to 12 months could have created a potential interest rate risk for the Originator and adversely affected the LSO issuance volume. Moreover, Mutual Funds, the key investor segment in LSOs in the past, were less active in the market owing to low secondary market liquidity for PTCs, and the prohibition on investment by liquid funds in debt with tenure longer than 91 days.

Chart 8.1 shows the market's preference for direct assignment and par structures.

CHART 8.1 SECURITIZATION MARKET IN INDIA (2008–2012)—CHANGING PREFERENCES IN THE ABS AND RMBS MARKETS

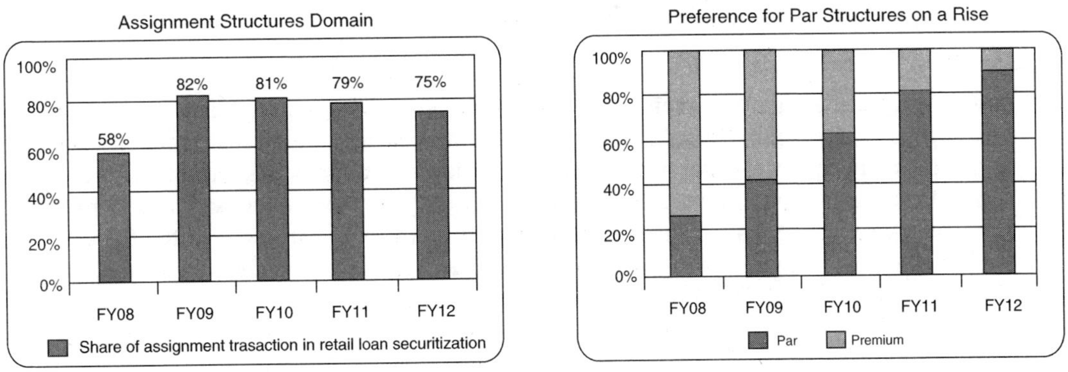

(A) (B)

Source: Presentation made by Kalpesh Gada, ICRA, May 2012, slide No 9, accessed at www.vinodkothari.com.

The issues to be resolved before the securitization market achieves a stable state in the Indian context are as follows:

a. Tax issues on securitized instruments.

b. The prohibition on credit enhancements and the stipulation of MRR is expected to reduce direct assignments.

c. Attracting more originators and investors into the market.

Changes in the Market During 2013—Highlights

- Some important changes in the regulatory framework during 2012–13 were related to the following aspects (the regulatory changes have been outlined in earlier paragraphs).
  - No credit enhancements for direct assignments (DA)– implies that originators cannot provide credit enhancement in any form in a DA transaction.
  - Minimum Holding Period (MHP) – Originators have to hold the assets for a minimum period before securitizing them. Minimum holding period varies with the original maturity of the loan and its repayment frequency; For example, for a monthly repayment frequency, the MHP is 3,6, and 12 months for original maturity of loans of up to 2 years, greater than 2 years but up to 5 years, and greater than 5 years, respectively.

- Minimum Retention Requirement (MRR) – Originators are expected to have a minimum stake in the transaction (in the form of subordination, equity tranche or cash collateral). Minimum retention requirement will depend on the original maturity of the loans in the pool. For example, MRR is 5% or 10% of the total book value of loans being securitized for original loan maturity of up to 2 years or greater than 2 years, respectively.

- CRISIL notes in its review of the securitization market (http://crisil.com/Ratings/Commentary/CommentaryDocs/CRISIL-ratings_indian-securitization-market-review_2012–13.pdf) that the change in the regulatory framework has led to an improvement in the quality of assets with increase in average seasoning, reduction in pool yield, and change in vehicle mix.
- However, Issuance volume fell by 20% in FY2013 to ₹30,250 crore. This decline was mainly because single corporate loan securitizations [also known as Single Loan Collateralized Loan Obligations (CLOs) or Loan Sell-Offs (LSOs)] completely stopped while some bilateral loan pool assignments were done on an unrated basis. The volume of securitization of retail loans (both Asset-Backed Securitization or ABS, and Residential Mortgage-Backed Securitization or RMBS, cumulatively) declined by 14% in FY2013.
- Both CRISIL and ICRA note that Asset backed securities (ABS) issuances continue to dominate with commercial vehicles (CV) preferred as the prominent asset class for securitization; - New asset classes like gold loan receivables and micro, small and medium enterprises (MSME) loan receivables have also been seen. New investor classes like insurance and wealth management clients have shown preference for securitization paper
- The number of originators increased during 2012–13 from 46 (in the previous year) to 51.
- Microfinance institutions (MFIs) continued to access securitization markets to meet their funding needs; - 27 MFIs had taken the securitization route during 2012–13 as compared to 23 the previous year. MFIs seemed to prefer participation in multi-originator transactions.
- A milestone in India's securitization market was reached when the first listed securitization instrument in the Indian market was rated by CRISIL; the PTCs issued in the transaction were backed by microfinance loan receivables and were listed on the Bombay Stock Exchange (BSE).
- The market volumes, however, remain susceptible to regulatory and legal changes. For instance, the introduction of a tax on income distributed by special purpose vehicles (SPVs) could impact market activity in 2013–14.

Developments that would impact securitization in the near future.

Source: websites of CRISIL, ICRA

1. ICRA expects the market dynamics to alter following the clarity in the taxation regime for securitization, brought in by the Union Budget 2013-14. The new tax treatment would enable mutual funds to invest in securitization transactions. However, the step could be detrimental for banks, since there could be a proportionate disallowance of expenses incurred in respect of such investment—thus having a significant impact on the post-tax yield on the transactions. Consequently, 2013-14 could witness a return of direct assignments as the chosen route for acquiring PSL assets by banks, new transaction structures in securitization to minimise the taxation impact and MFs re-starting investments in securitization.
2. In July 2013, the Reserve Bank of India (RBI) released guidelines for reset of credit enhancement (CE) in securitization transactions. While these guidelines are currently applicable only to banks as originators, similar guidelines are soon expected for non-banking financial companies and housing finance companies. The guidelines may improve the economics of securitization, since funds locked while providing Credit Enhancement (CE) will be released partially to the originators. Importantly, release of CE will benefit originators by providing capital relief, given that the outstanding CE is adjusted against the available Tier-I and -II capital.
3. Some changes being noticed in the market are the (a) shift to PTCs that are now preferred over Direct assignment after the latter was prohibited from using credit enhancements; (b) improvement in the quality of securitized assets, driven by the new priority sector norms (as per the revised PSL guidelines, bank's investment in securitization transaction will qualify for priority sector assets if the underlying assets qualify for priority sector treatment and the interest rate charged to the borrower by the originator does not exceed investing bank's base rate plus eight per cent per annum.) ; (c) facilitation of listing of securitized instruments on stock exchanges due to enhanced disclosure requirements stipulated in the revised guidelines being consistent with the listing requirements prescribed by the stock exchanges ; and (d) the Micro Finance Institution (MFI) Bill, which, once passed in Parliament,will reduce the risk of political intervention to the NBFC-MFIs, and increase investor and lender confidence in the sector.

Some commonly used measures and metrics in securitization:

Source: CRISIL website : accessed at http://crisil.com/Ratings/Commentary/CommentaryDocs/ABS-MBS-BOOK.pdf, pages 13, 14, 15

1. Originator: The bank or finance company that has originated the pool of receivables.
2. Pool principal: The sum of principal outstanding for all loans present in the pool at the time of securitization.
3. Pool cash flows: The sum of principal and interest outstanding for all loans present in the pool at the time of securitization.
4. Future payouts: The total obligation towards the PTC holders or the acquirer at the time of securitization.
5. Structure: Structure of a transaction can either be at par or at a premium, depending on whether the pool principal is sold at par or ata premium to investors. In case of transactions with Interest Only (IO) strips, or Deferred Purchase Consideration (DPC), it is suitably mentioned. Also mentioned is any other structural feature present in the transaction, for example par with turbo amortization etc.
6. Asset class: The asset(s) that back the securitized receivables.
7. Pool duration: The weighted average balance maturity of cash flows in months. Pool cash flows are taken as weights for the purpose of calculating the average. In MBS transactions, principal amounts are used as weights.
8. Weighted Average Seasoning (WAS): Indicates the weighted average seasoning (in months) of the pool at the time of securitization.
9. Weighted Average Loan to Value (WAL): The weighted average Loan to Value (LTV) ratio of the pool at the time of securitization.
10. Weighted Average Yield (WAY): The pool yield at the time of securitization.
11. Average yield: The current pool yield, calculated as the Internal Rate of Return (IRR) of the pool cash flows.
12. Overdue composition: Indicates the proportion of cash flows pertaining to current contracts, one-month overdue contracts and soon at the time of securitization.
13. Weighted Average Residual Maturity (WAM): The weighted average balance maturity of PTC/Acquirer payouts in months. Monthly payouts to PTC holders/acquirer are taken as weights for the purpose of calculating the average.
14. Deferred Purchase Consideration (DPC) as percentage of pool cash flows: The deferred purchase consideration (DPC) is carved out of the interest portion of the pool available after servicing interest on the PTCs/acquirer's principal balance. It is expressed as a percentage of total pool cash flows.
15. Credit collateral as percentage of pool cash flows: The credit collateral stipulated at the time of securitization/outstanding as on date as a percentage of future pool cash flows. In case of Mortgage Backed Securities (MBS) transactions, the credit collateral is expressed as a percentage of pool principal.
16. First loss as percentage of pool cash flows: The first loss credit facility stipulated at the time of securitization as a percentage of total pool cash flows. In case of Mortgage Backed Securities (MBS) transactions, the first loss credit facility is expressed as a percentage of pool principal.
17. Second loss as percentage of pool cash flows: The second loss credit facility stipulated at the time of securitization as a percentage of total pool cash flows. In case of Mortgage Backed Securities (MBS) transactions, the second loss credit facility is expressed as a percentage of pool principal.
18. Liquidity facility as percentage of pool cash flows: Indicates the liquidity support available to the transaction, expressed as a percentage of pool cash flows. Some transactions also have an advance payment mechanism, wherein monthly payouts are funded by the liquidity facility, which will be reflected in a high level of utilization of liquidity facility. In case of Mortgage Backed Securities(MBS) transactions, the liquidity facility is expressed as a percentage of pool principal.
19. Excess Interest Spread (EIS) as percentage of pool cash flows: The embedded cushion available in a transaction on account of the differential between the pool yield and pass-through rate. This is only available in par structures and is expressed as a percentage of the pool cash flows. However, in a few structures, this cushion is diluted as the spread is utilized to make certain payouts like charge-offs, servicing fees, fees to liquidity provider etc. In such cases the actual cushion available to investors due to EIS may be lower than the amount stated herein. In case of Mortgage Backed Securities (MBS) transactions, the EIS is expressed as a percentage of pool principal.

More such terms and measures can be accessed in the CRISIL document mentioned above

Securitization Companies in India

There are at present 14 securitization companies in India, owned by public sector banks, private sector banks and private or corporate groups. (Table 8.5)

TABLE 8.5 SECURITIZATION COMPANIES IN INDIA

Sl. No.	Name of Company	Major Sponsors (Owners)
1	Asset Reconstruction Company (India) Ltd, (ARCIL) (www.arcil.co.in)	SBI, IDBI, ICICI, PNB
2	Assets care & Reconstruction Enterprise Ltd (Formerly Assets Care Enterprise Ltd.) (ACRE) (www.acreindia.co)	IFCI, PNB, Tourism Finance, Bank of Baroda, LIC, UBI
3	ASREC (India) Ltd, (www.asrecindia.co.in)	Allahabad Bank, Bank of India, Andhra Bank, Indian Bank, LIC, Deutsche Bank
4	Pegasus Assets Reconstruction Pvt. Ltd. (www.pegasus-arc.com)	Bhimjyani Family, Rakesh Jhunjhunwala, L. Sanghvi + Family
5	Alchemist Asset Reconstruction Company Limited (Formerly Dhir&Dhir Asset Reconstruction & Securitization Company Ltd.) (www.alchemistarc.com)	Alok Dhir, Sanjiv Gupta, Shivashish Chatterjee, L. P. Dhir
6	International Asset Reconstruction Company Pvt. Ltd. (www.iarc.co.in)	HDFC Bank Ltd, Tata Capital Ltd, City Union Bank, Arun Duggal, ICICI, Standard Bank, FMO
7	Reliance Asset Reconstruction Company Ltd. (www.rarcl.com)	Reliance Capital, Corporation Bank, Indian Bank, GIC, Dacecroft Ltd, Blue Ridge
8	Pridhvi Asset Reconstruction and Securitization Company Ltd. (www.paras.org.in)	Dr Divi + Family, M. S. R. Prasad + Family, M. Rajya Lakhsmi, PNB
9	Phoenix ARC Pvt. Ltd. (www.phoenixarc.co.in)	Kotak Mahindra Prime, Kotak Mahindra Investments, others
10	Invent Assets Securitization & Reconstruction Private Limited	Not available
11	JM Financial Asset Reconstruction Company Limited (www.jmfinancial.in)	JM Financial, Narotam Sekhsaria, Indian Overseas Bank, Valiant Mauritius
12	India SME Asset Reconstruction Company Limited (ISARC) (www.isarc.in)	SIDBI, SIDNI Venture, Bank of Baroda, United Bank of India
13	Edelweiss Asset Reconstruction Company Limited	Edelweiss Capital, Reeta Kuhad, Vineet Kashyap, Alok Tandon, Aakanksha Management, Apian Finance
14	UV Asset Reconstruction Company Limited (www.uvarcl.com)	Shilpi Sharma, P. J. Vincent, Central Bank of India, B. B Choudhary

Source: RBI database and company websites, Association of ARCs in India (www.arcindia.co.in)

Study of the financial performance of Asset Reconstruction Companies shows that all of them (with published results) have been making profits, though the profit margin is quite thin, for RBI instructions in securitization companies, please refer Circulars in RBI website.

Credit Derivatives in India[50]

After protracted deliberations and several draft guidelines since 2005 on the introduction of Credit Default Swaps(CDS) in India, RBI finally released guidelines on Credit Default Swaps in corporate bonds in November 2011. Revisions to the guideline were made in January 2013. RBI Master Circular on 'Basel III Capital Regulations' dated July 1, 2013, provides prudential guidelines on CDS.

RBI guidelines specify the participants and the processes for using CDS in corporate bonds. The participants can be of the following categories. An RBI regulated entity should be a participant at least on one side of the transaction.

a. **Users:** The users are typically protection buyers. They can buy credit protection (buy CDS contracts) only to hedge the underlying credit risk on corporate bonds. They cannot hold credit protection without hedging the underlying asset. They cannot sell protection (hold short positions in CDS contracts). They can exit their CDS 'bought' contract by unwinding it with the original counter party, or by assigning it in favour of the buyer of the underlying bonds. The 'User' categories named by RBI comprise of Commercial Banks, Primary Dealers, NBFCs, Mutual Funds, Insurance Companies, Housing Finance Companies, Provident Funds, Listed Corporates, All India Financial Institutions namely, Export Import Bank of India (EXIM), National Bank for Agriculture and Rural Development (NABARD), National Housing Bank (NHB) and Small Industries Development Bank of India (SIDBI), Foreign Institutional Investors (FIIs) and any other institution specifically permitted by the Reserve Bank
b. **Market makers:** RBI permits certain entities to quote—both buy and/or sell—CDS spreads. (*The following chapter gives more details on the fixing of CDS spreads*). These entities, who would be permitted to buy protection without having the underlying bonds include Commercial Banks, stand alone Primary Dealers (PDs), Non-Banking

Financial Companies (NBFCs) having sound financials and good track record in providing credit facilities and any other institution specifically permitted by the Reserve Bank. In addition, Insurance companies and Mutual Funds would be permitted as market-makers subject to their having strong financials and risk management capabilities as prescribed and permitted by their respective regulators, IRDA and SEBI[51] . The eligibility norms for market makers are detailed in the quoted RBI guidelines, and the list of market makers can be accessed from the RBI website.

Eligible Underlying Assets for CDS—Deliverable Obligations or Reference Assets

- Rated corporate bonds—both listed and unlisted.
- Unrated corporate bonds in the case of SPVs set up by infrastructure companies (the rationale for setting up SPVs to hold infrastructure assets in the case of Public Private Partnerships – PPP-in the infrastructure sector has been outlined in the Chapter 'Uses of bank funds—the lending function').
- Money market securities (securities with original maturity up to one year) such as Commercial Paper, Certificates of Deposit, Non-convertible debentures.
- Reference assets should be in dematerialized form only.

Other Requirements to be Fulfilled

- The users (except FIIs) and the market makers should be resident entities.
- The contract should clearly define the identity of parties responsible for determining whether a credit event has occurred.
- The reference asset and the deliverable obligation should be to a resident and denominated in Indian Rupees.
- The CDS contract should be denominated and settled in Indian Rupees.
- Asset backed securities, mortgage backed securities, convertible bonds and bonds with call or put options (Please refer to Chapter 'Bank risk management' for details on options) cannot form the reference assets/ deliverable obligations.
- Interest receivable cannot form the underlying asset for CDS.
- The CDS contract should represent a direct claim on the protection seller. The contract should be irrevocable—there must be no clause in the contract that allows the protection seller to unilaterally cancel the contract, unless the protection buyer defaults under the terms of the contract.
- The CDS contract should not have any clause that may prevent the protection seller from making the credit event payment on time—after occurrence of the credit event and completion of necessary formalities in terms of the contract.
- The protection seller can have no recourse to the protection buyer for credit-event losses.
- Dealing in any structured financial product with CDS as one of the components is not permitted.
- Dealing in a derivative product where the CDS itself is an underlying asset is not permitted.

Credit Events and Settlement

The credit events specified in the CDS contract typically cover *Bankruptcy, Failure to pay, Repudiation/moratorium, Obligation acceleration, Obligation default, Restructuring approved under Board for Industrial and Financial Reconstruction (BIFR) and Corporate Debt Restructuring (CDR) mechanism and corporate bond restructuring*. The contracting parties to a CDS may include all or any of the approved credit events. Further, the definition of various credit events should be clearly defined in the bilateral Master Agreement prepared by FIMMDA.

A Determination Committee (DC), formed by the market participant (of which at 25 per cent will be drawn from the 'users') and FIMMDA, will be based in India and will deliberate and resolve CDS related issues such as Credit Events, CDS Auctions, Succession Events, Substitute Reference Obligations, etc. The decisions of the Committee would be binding on CDS market participants.

The settlement method, to be determined and documented in the CDS agreement, can be one of the following—physical, cash or auction. (More on these settlement methods can be found in the following chapter 'Credit risk—Advanced topics'). Where the CDS transaction involves 'users, physical settlement is mandatory. Where the CDS transaction involves market makers, any of the above three methods can be used. As their names suggest,

- 'Physical' settlement would require the protection buyers to transfer any of the deliverable obligations against the receipt of the full notional or face value of the reference asset;
- 'Cash' settlement would require the protection seller to pay the protection buyer an amount equivalent to the loss resulting from the credit event of the reference asset;
- 'Auction' settlement would require the intervention of the Determination committee, and would be decided on a case to case basis.

The RBI guidelines also mention other aspects such as accounting, pricing of CDS (FIMMDA would publish a daily CDS curve), and prudential norms for risk exposures and capital adequacy of market participants.

Would the Guidelines Energize the Credit Risk Transfer Market in India?

It is noteworthy that after the guidelines came into force, only 3 CDS transactions have happened upto end 2012.

The first two transactions involved IDBI Bank and ICICI Bank in December 2011. IDBI Bank underwrote two CDS deals of ₹5 crore each in respect of Rural Electrification Corporation (REC) and Indian Railways finance corporation (IRFC) bonds held by ICICI Bank. Both deals were for one year. The details of the third deal were not available.

The lukewarm response to the much awaited CDS guidelines has been attributed to the following factors:

a. CDS is restricted to the Indian corporate bond market, which is shallow and illiquid.
b. The corporate bond market today is dominated by AAA rated bonds, with few takers for lower rated bonds. The highest rated bonds do not require protection against default
c. The guidelines are perceived as too restrictive. Speculation, an essential ingredient of a liquid market, is not permitted.
d. Most of the bonds are being held to maturity. (*Please refer to the chapter 'Market risk' for an explanation of 'held to maturity'*). Hence they are not available for trading or marking to market. Derivative transactions are required only where the securities are actively traded
e. Other players such as Mutual funds or Insurance companies cannot be market makers under the present guidelines. This has further restricted the market
f. An acceptable operational framework for all participants is still not present. The market in its present form is dominated by banks. A heterogeneous market is necessary for CDS to grow
g. Globally, most CDS trades are for a tenure of over 3 years. In a short term instrument such as Commercial Paper, which RBI has permitted as an underlying asset, the probability of default is perceived to be low, and it may be costly to hedge through CDS.
h. Since India does not have an active or deep corporate bond market, it is difficult to develop a CDS market only for corporate bonds.

CHAPTER SUMMARY

- Two types of losses are possible in respect of any borrower or borrower class—expected and unexpected losses or EL and UL. EL can be budgeted for and provisions held to offset their adverse effects on the bank's balance sheet. UL, being unpredictable, have to be cushioned by holding adequate capital.
- Credit risk is most simply defined as the probability that a bank borrower or counter party will fail to meet its obligations in accordance with agreed terms.
- A bank needs to manage (a) the risk in individual credits or transactions, (b) the credit risk inherent in the entire portfolio and (c) the relationships between credit risk and other risks.
- Although specific credit risk management practices may differ among banks depending upon the nature and complexity of their credit activities, a comprehensive credit risk management program will address these four areas. (a) Establishing an appropriate credit risk environment, (b) operating under a sound credit granting process, (c) maintaining an appropriate credit administration, measurement and monitoring process and (d) ensuring adequate controls over credit risk. These practices should also be applied in conjunction with sound practices related to the assessment of asset quality, the adequacy of provisions and reserves and the disclosure of credit risk.
- International accounting practices set forth standards for estimating the impairment of a loan for general financial reporting purposes. Regulators are expected to follow these standards 'to the letter' for determining the provisions and allowances for loan losses. According to these standards, a loan is 'impaired' when, based on current information and events, it is probable that the creditor will be unable to collect all amounts (interest and principal) due in line with the terms of the loan agreement. Such assets are also called 'criticized' or 'non-performing' (in India) assets.
- Assessment of credit risk for individual borrowers and for a loan portfolio is an important task, for which various models are available, ranging from simple ones to banks' internal models to industry-sponsored models.
- Loan sales provide liquidity to the selling banks and also represent a valuable portfolio management tool, which minimizes risk through diversification. Some prominent forms of loan sales include (a) syndication, (b) novation, (c) participation and (d) securitization.
- Covered bonds are a hybrid between asset-backed securities/ mortgage backed securities and normal secured corporate bonds, and serve as an instrument of refinancing, primarily used by mortgage lenders. Unlike secured corporate bonds which provide recourse against the issuer, covered bonds provide a bankruptcy-protected recourse against the assets of the issuer (Collateral Pool) too. Unlike mortgage backed securities which merely provide recourse against the Collateral Pool, covered bonds provide an additional recourse against the issuer too.

- A credit derivative is a security with a pay-off linked to a credit-related event, such as borrower default, credit rating downgrades or a structural change in a security containing credit risk. In credit derivatives, there is a party (or a bank) trying to transfer credit risk, called a protection buyer and there is a counter party (another bank) trying to acquire credit risk, called a protection seller.
- Credit derivatives are typically unfunded. The protection buyer generally pays a periodic premium. However, the credit derivative may be funded in some cases. Some popular forms of credit derivatives include (a) loan default swaps, (b) total return swaps, (c) CDS, (d) credit risk options, (e) credit intermediation swaps, (f) dynamic credit swaps, (g) credit spread derivatives, (h) CLNs, (i) CLDs, (j) repackaged notes and (k) basket default swaps.
- For Indian banks, the RBI has provided detailed guidelines for 'exposure norms' to avoid credit concentration and for asset classification, income recognition and provisioning for credit risk. Assets are classified into (a) standard, (b) sub-standard, (c) doubtful and (d) loss, and provisions are made accordingly.

TEST YOUR UNDERSTANDING

1. How do the following help in credit risk mitigation?
   a. Loan covenants
   b. Credit scoring/risk rating system
   c. Credit risk models
2. Why do banks move loans off their balance sheets? What are the motivations for and risks involved in off-balance sheet transactions of banks?
3. Can each of the following types of loans be easily securitized? Give reasons.
   a. Agricultural loans
   b. Credit card loans
   c. Loans to professionals
   d. Home loans
   e. Vehicle loans
   f. Loans for capital expenditure
4. J bank has written off some loss assets. Which of the following is true?
   a. Its total assets and total liabilities decrease by that amount.
   b. Its total liabilities and capital decrease by that amount.
   c. Its total assets, total liabilities and capital decrease by that amount.
   d. Its total assets and capital decrease by that amount.
   e. Its total liabilities and capital increase by that amount.
5. Rank the following according to the degree of credit risk (highest credit risk = 1, lowest credit risk = 4)
   a. Advances against hypothecation of inventory and receivables
   b. Advances against pledge of inventory
   c. Advances against gold
   d. Underwriting commitments
6. The following data relate to K Bank.
   a. Margin of safety 0.75
   b. Return on assets (ROA) 9 per cent
   c. Total assets ₹2,000 crores
   d. Tax rate 40 per cent

   What is the level of NPAs of K Bank?
7. S Bank's profits before provisioning for NPAs is at ₹300 crores. The bank has total assets of ₹7,000 crores and its NPAs form 6 per cent of total assets. Which of the following actions should the bank take in that year to maximize its return to shareholders? (Assume tax rate of 40 per cent).
   a. Make a provision of 50 per cent of NPAs
   b. Write off 25 per cent of NPAs
8. What do we mean by the term 'securitization is non-recourse'? Who bears the risk in non-recourse lending?
9. What is the role of the 'SPV' in securitization?
10. How is 'securitization' of receivables different from 'factoring' of receivables?
11. The following table represents the balance sheet of Bank A before securitizing some of its assets. Can you fill in the balance sheet format alongside that indicates the balance sheet position after securitization? Assume that the pool of securitized assets have been sold at par. (₹ in crores).

Before Securitization		After Securitization	
Liabilities	Assets	Liabilities	Assets
Equity 5	Cash 10		
Other Liabilities 105	Assets for Securitization 80		
	Other assets 20		
Total 110	Total 110	Total 110	Total 110

12. How is a Credit Default Swap different from an insurance contract?

TOPICS FOR FURTHER DISCUSSION

- What factors would bankers consider before deciding to use credit derivatives? Can you evolve a checklist?
- Why do you think SPEs are used for issuing ABS? Why do the banks, which originate these assets, not issue these securities themselves?
- How has the ISDA standardized credit derivative transactions?
- Study the corporate debt restructuring scheme of the Reserve Bank of India. Would banks prefer to use this mechanism to restructure potentially viable corporate bodies or would they prefer to securitize loans that need restructuring?
- What should be the enabling factors for covered bonds to be successful in India?
- What are the risks that RBI perceives in introducing CDS for bank loans in India?

SELECT REFERENCES

1. Harvard Business School, *An Overview of Credit Derivatives*, rev. (12 March 1999), Harvard Business School Publishing.
2. JP Morgan and Risk Metrics Group, *The J P Morgan Guide to Credit Derivatives*. Risk Publications, U. S.

ANNEXURE I

BASEL COMMITTEE—PRINCIPLES FOR THE ASSESSMENT OF BANKS' MANAGEMENT OF CREDIT RISK

(*Source*: 'Principles for the Management of Credit Risk,' Basel Committee on Banking Supervision, pp. 3–4 September, 2000 accessed at www.bis.org)

Establishing an Appropriate Credit Risk Environment

- **Principle 1:** The board of directors should have responsibility for approving and periodically (at least annually) reviewing the credit risk strategy and significant credit risk policies of the bank. The strategy should reflect the bank's tolerance for risk and the level of profitability the bank expects to achieve for incurring various credit risks.
- **Principle 2:** Senior management should have the responsibility for implementing the credit risk strategy approved by the board of directors and for developing policies and procedures for identifying, measuring, monitoring and controlling credit risk. Such policies and procedures should address credit risk in all of the bank's activities and at both the individual credit and portfolio levels.
- **Principle 3:** Banks should identify and manage credit risk inherent in all products and activities. Banks should ensure that the risks of products and activities new to them are subject to adequate risk management procedures and controls before being introduced or undertaken and approved in advance by the board of directors or its appropriate committee.

Operating Under a Sound Credit-Granting Process

- **Principle 4:** Banks must operate within sound and well-defined credit-granting criteria. These criteria should include a clear indication of the bank's target market and a thorough understanding of the borrower or counter party, as well as the purpose and structure of the credit and its source of repayment.
- **Principle 5:** Banks should establish overall credit limits at the level of individual borrowers and counter parties and groups of connected counter parties that aggregate in a comparable and meaningful manner of different types of exposures, both in the banking and trading book and on- and off-balance sheet.
- **Principle 6:** Banks should have a clearly established process in place for approving new credits as well as the amendment, renewal and re-financing of existing credits.
- **Principle 7:** All extensions of credit must be made on an arm's length basis. In particular, credits to related companies and individuals must be authorized on an exception basis, monitored with particular care and other appropriate steps taken to control or mitigate the risks of non-arm's length lending.

Maintaining an Appropriate Credit Administration, Measurement and Monitoring Process

- **Principle 8:** Banks should have in place a system for the ongoing administration of their various credit risk-bearing portfolios.

- **Principle 9:** Banks must have in place a system for monitoring the condition of individual credits, including determining the adequacy of provisions and reserves.
- **Principle 10:** Banks are encouraged to develop and utilise an internal risk rating system in managing credit risk. The rating system should be consistent with the nature, size and complexity of a bank's activities.
- **Principle 11:** Banks must have information systems and analytical techniques that enable management to measure the credit risk inherent in all on- and off-balance sheet activities. The management information system should provide adequate information on the composition of the credit portfolio, including identification of any concentrations of risk.
- **Principle 12:** Banks must have in place a system for monitoring the overall composition and quality of the credit portfolio.
- **Principle 13:** Banks should take into consideration potential future changes in economic conditions when assessing individual credits and their credit portfolios and should assess their credit risk exposures under stressful conditions.

Ensuring Adequate Controls over Credit Risk

- **Principle 14:** Banks must establish a system of independent and ongoing assessment of the bank's credit risk management processes and the results of such reviews should be communicated directly to the board of directors and senior management.
- **Principle 15:** Banks must ensure that the credit-granting function is being properly managed and that credit exposures are within levels consistent with prudential standards and internal limits. Banks should establish and enforce internal controls and other practices to ensure that exceptions to policies, procedures and limits are reported in a timely manner to the appropriate level of management for action.
- **Principle 16:** Banks must have a system in place for early remedial action on deteriorating credits, managing problem credits and similar workout situations.

The Role of Supervisors

- **Principle 17:** Supervisors should require that banks have an effective system in place to identify, measure, monitor and control credit risk as part of an overall approach to risk management. Supervisors should conduct an independent evaluation of a bank's strategies, policies, procedures and practices related to the granting of credit and the ongoing management of the portfolio. Supervisors should consider setting prudential limits to restrict bank exposures to single borrowers or groups of connected counter parties.

The Basle Committee has also published in 2011 and 2012, documents in respect of counter party credit risk, which can be accessed at www.bis.org

ANNEXURE II

SALIENT FEATURES OF SECURITIZATION

The Concept

The concept is not new. 'Securitization', broadly defined, is simply the conversion of a typically illiquid 'financial relationship' into a tradable and liquid transaction. For example, trade debt on a firm's balance sheet is illiquid and signifies among others, the relationship between the firm and its suppliers. The debt is converted into a liquid transaction (instrument) in the market when it is issued as Commercial Paper (CP). The issue of 'equity shares' as a tradable instrument signifying ownership of a firm, is another example.

In today's capital markets, however, 'securitization' is synonymous with ABS—where illiquid assets (loans) on a firm's balance sheet are transformed into traded instruments by pooling the firm's interest in future cash flows from the assets, transferring these claims to another specially created entity that would use the future cash flows to pay off investors over time. Thus, securitization has enabled movement of assets from the less efficient debt markets to the more efficient capital markets, resulting in lower funding costs.

However, there is a key difference between an ABS and a typical capital market security. To the investor, the capital market security signals exposure to the issuer's business, whereas the ABS is no more than exposure to a pool of assets and has no connection with the business risks of the originator.[52]

The Key Players in ABS

The asset originator: Typically, this would be a bank which transfers a pool of loan assets to the securitization entity. However, it may continue to service the assets—for instance, if a pool of retail loans have been securitized, the bank may continue to collect the payments from the borrowers and pass it on to the securitization vehicle.

The issuer or the SPE: The securitization vehicle is created as a special purpose entity. It is created for the limited purpose of acquiring the underlying assets, issuing securities and other related activities.

Rating agencies: They are responsible for rating the multiple 'tranches' with different risk profiles, to help investors choose securities in keeping with their risk appetite.

Trustee: The trustee holds the securitization cash flows in separate accounts, and alerts investors and rating agencies in events of default or covenant breaches.

The underwriter: The primary responsibility of structuring the securitization—pricing and marketing the multiple tranches so that the issue is attractive to various classes of potential investors—rests with the underwriter.

The administrator: There is an important role for administrators in the CDO and Asset Backed Commercial Paper (ABCP) products. They actively manage, trade and monitor the respective loan pools.

The servicer: Typically, the servicer is also the asset originator and hence would be responsible for day to day portfolio administration, including collecting and temporarily reinvesting asset cash flows, where required.

Credit enhancement provider: In order to make the issue more attractive to investors and provide the tranches with better credit ratings, credit enhancement providers extend support.

Liquidity facility provider: Typically, liquidity support is provided to adjust for short-term lags between expected cash inflows from the underlying assets and the payment obligations under the securitization structure. Such liquidity access could be provided by financial institutions in the form of a commitment to lend or a commitment to purchase assets.

Figure 8.14 depicts the basic steps in a typical securitization deal

FIGURE 8.14 BASIC STEPS IN SECURITIZATION

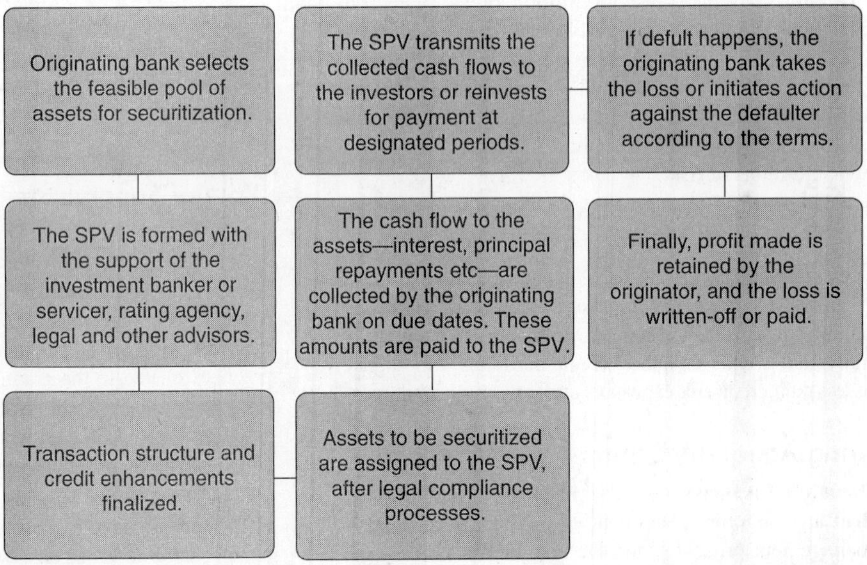

The Cash Flows and Economics in Securitization

Let us assume that Bank A has identified an asset pool of ₹100 crores for securitization.

1. Assume that this pool is being transferred at par value to an SPV—*i.e.*, the outstanding principal amount of the loans in the pool, ₹100 crores.
2. The SPV would also have to receive interest on the principal. This interest rate would be the weighted average interest rate of the loans in the pool. Let us assume the interest at 10 per cent per year.
3. Now the SPV has to pay for the asset pool it holds. It does so by issuing securities. These securities will be rated (by credit rating agencies) depending on the cash flows that the asset pool is capable of generating.
4. These cash flows will be used to repay the investors who have bought the securities issued by the SPV. It has to be noted here that Bank A will not have any claim on the cash flows (except to receive them and pass them on to the SPV), nor will the investors have any claim over Bank A's assets in case of a shortfall in cash flows (except to the extent of credit support Bank A would be providing, where agreed upon).
5. The securities are then structured into multiple tranches—typically, senior, mezzanine and junior (with hybrid classifications such as sub senior or sub junior) or any other nomenclature to convey differentiated priority of cash flows to investors in the pool. In our pool with ₹100 crores of Bank A's assets, let us assume that the description of the tranches are as follows: senior – 90 per cent, mezzanine – 7 per cent and junior – 3 per cent. This implies that if losses occur in the asset pool, the junior tranche will absorb the first 3 per cent. If losses exceed 3 per cent, the mezzanine tranche will absorb up to 10 per cent (3 per cent + 7 per cent). Only if losses in the asset pool exceed 10 per cent, will the cash flows to the senior investors be impaired. This 10 per cent (in this case) cushion against losses will enable the senior tranche to be highly rated by the rating agencies, the mezzanine tranche would get a lower rating, and many times, the most junior tranche may be unrated, since the risk of loss is very high. Typically, the unrated tranche is retained by the originating Bank A.
6. Understandably, since the risk of each tranche differs, the return would also be different. The senior tranche, which is perceived to be safe, would earn the lowest, while the junior tranche, perceived to be highly risky, would earn the highest yield. In other words, the cost of issue of the tranches to the SPV would depend on the risk of each tranche. Let us assume that the weighted average cost to the SPV is 8 per cent.
7. The SPV is only a conduit (in other words, a bankruptcy remote vehicle) and, therefore, requires an entity to carry out the functions of collecting the cash flow streams from the original borrowers in the asset pool and servicing the investors. Many times, these functions are taken on by Bank A itself, for a fee or servicing the investors can be done by a separate servicing firm. Let us assume that the fee for servicing is 70 bps per annum (that is, .07 per cent).
8. Recollect that the weighted average interest that the pool earned when it was transferred to the SPV was 10 per cent. We have seen now that the pool pays an average interest + fee of 8 + .07 = 8.07 per cent. The difference between the two rates, 1.93 per cent, is called the 'excess spread'. This

'residual interest' may be retained by the originator, Bank A or sold to willing investors.

9. Hence, at the end of the securitization transaction, Bank A has got the following cash flows: (a) upfront cash flow of ₹100 crores or ₹97 crores in case the junior tranche bearing the first loss of ₹3 crores has been retained by the Bank (in both cases, the transaction takes the assets off its balance sheet and provides liquidity) and (b) the residual interest, representing the excess cash after paying investors.
10. For the investors, especially in the more senior tranches, the transaction has assured periodic cash flows.

ENDNOTES

1. The need for banks to hold capital as a cushion against 'UL' will be dealt with in detail in the Chapter 'Capital—Risk, Regulation and Adequacy'.
2. Note that the Z score described in the previous chapter attempts to measure the probability of default typically over a 1 year horizon.
3. Also defined simply as the value of the loan outstanding less the market (realizable) value of collateral held by the bank.
4. See Chapter on 'The Lending Function' for more on loan pricing.
5. Constantinos Stephanouand Juan Carlos Mendoza, 'Credit Risk Measurement under Basel II: An Overview and Implementation Issues for Developing Countries',*World Bank Policy Research Working Paper* 3556, Fig. 1 (2005): 7
6. Basel Committee on Banking Supervision, *Principles for the Management of Credit Risk* (September 2000): 1.
7. The grouping is as proposed by Peter Crosbie in 'Modeling Default Risk', published by KMV Corporation, Document no 999-0000-031, Revision 2.1.0 (1999):1–2.
8. See chapter on 'The Lending Function' for more on loan pricing.
9. A further particular instance of credit risk relates to the process of settling financial transactions. If one side of a transaction is settled but the other fails, a loss may be incurred that is equal to the principal amount of the transaction. Even if one party is simply late in settling, then the other party may incur a loss relating to missed investment opportunities. 'Settlement risk' (*i.e.*, the risk that the completion or settlement of a financial transaction will fail to take place as expected) thus includes elements of liquidity, market, operational and reputation risk as well as credit risk. The level of risk is determined by the particular arrangements for settlement. Factors in such arrangements that have a bearing on credit risk include: the timing of the exchange of value, payment/settlement finality and the role of intermediaries and clearing houses.
10. Basel Committee on Banking Supervision, 'Principles for the Management of Credit Risk', (September 2000): 3–4.
11. We have seen in the previous chapter that in India, restructuring invariably involves 'sacrifices' on the part of banks.
12. Basically, the model works like this. Assume a lower return-to-risk asset is swapped for a higher return-to-risk asset. This improves the return of the overall portfolio with no addition to risk. The process of an asset being swapped out of a portfolio implies that the concentration of risk in the portfolio is being reduced, *i.e.*, risk is being 'diversified'. The reverse applies when an asset is swapped into the portfolio. Thus, the returns to risk increases for the low return asset and decreases for the high return asset, until the assets' return to risk ratios converge. At this point, where further swaps that raise returns will also raise risk, the portfolio has reached its optimal level. (*Source*: Morton Glantz, 'Managing Bank Risk', Chapter 9, (Florida: Academic Press, 2003): 299–330.
13. Morton Glantz, 'Managing Bank Risk', Chapter 9, (Florida: Academic Press, 2005): 299–330.
14. Basel Committee on Banking Supervision, 'Principles for the Management of Credit Risk', (September 2000): 18.
15. We have seen earlier in this chapter that ELs are equal to the exposure times the percentage loss given the event of default times the probability of loss. Hence, actual losses would be the product of the first two factors alone.
16. Ibid., 22.
17. Ibid., 23.
18. Until Basel II formalized the use of PD, this concept was often called Expected Default Frequency (EDF)).
19. Please refer the previous chapter for a discussion on these models.
20. Table derived by author from presentation material by Michel Crouhy, 'Credit Risk Assessment: A Comparative Study of Different Methods', at seminar on 'Global Risk Management Practices and Emerging Market's Particular Issues' at Moscow, (15–16 June, 2004).
21. Ibid., 15.
22. Nikola A Tarashev, 'An Empirical Evaluation of Structural Credit Risk Models', BIS Working Papers no. 179, *Bank for International Settlements*, (July 2005): 5–8.
23. 'Without recourse' implies that the issuer of security or the investors will have no recourse to the originator if there is shortfall in asset value at the end of the tenure of the securitized asset. The issuer/investor will have to look solely at the cash flows from the securitized assets for their return.
24. For more on transfer of credit risk, please see the section on 'Credit Derivatives'.
25. Ibid.
26. http://www.credit-derv.com/evolution.htm
27. ISDA-The International Swaps and Derivatives Association.
28. A 'swap' is an agreement in which two parties (called counter parties) agree to exchange periodic payments. The amount of payments exchanged is based on a notional principal amount. A swap can be viewed as a package of forward contracts, with more liquidity and longer maturity than typical forward contracts.
29. The other settlement method is for the protection buyer to make physical delivery of a portfolio of specified deliverable obligations in return for payment of their face amount. Deliverable obligations may be the

reference obligation or one of a broad class of obligations meeting certain specifications, such as any senior unsecured claim against the reference entity.

30. Called 'risky debt' because there is a possibility that the debt may not be repaid in full.
31. This is done through a complex method. The put buyer pays a premium for the right to sell to the put seller a specified reference asset and simultaneously enters into a swap in which the put seller pays the coupons on the reference asset and receives 3 or 6 month LIBOR plus a predetermined spread (the 'strike spread'). The put seller makes an up-front payment of par for this combined package upon exercise.
32. 'Negative carry' is the loss in income due to investing funds obtained at higher cost in lower yielding investments to ensure liquidity.
33. Christian Bluhm, et al., 'An Introduction to Credit Risk Modeling,' Chapter 7, 'Credit Derivatives', ISBN 1-58488-326-X, Chapman&Hall/CRC (2003).
34. Basel Committee on Banking Supervision, 'Consultative Paper: The Standardised Approach to Credit Risk', (January 2001): 33–34.
35. An asset mismatch occurs when a credit protection contract refers to an instrument that is not the same as the exposure being hedged.
36. RBI, 'Master Circular—Exposure Norms', (July 1, 2013).
37. As defined by the RBI under capital adequacy standards (please see chapter on 'Capital—Risk, Regulation and Adequacy') and as per published accounts at the end of the previous financial year. Exposures cannot be taken in anticipation of capital infusion at a future date.
38. RBI 'Master Circular—Prudential Norms on Income Recognition, Asset Classification and Provisioning Pertaining to Advances', July 1, 2013.
39. Any amount due to the bank under any credit facility is 'overdue' if it is not paid on the due date fixed by the bank.
40. An account should be treated as 'out of order' if the outstanding balance remains continuously in excess of the sanctioned limit/drawing power. In cases where the outstanding balance in the principal operating account is less than the sanctioned limit/drawing power, but there are no credits continuously for 90 days as on the date of balance sheet or credits are not enough to cover the interest debited during the same period, these accounts should be treated as 'out of order'.
41. 'Liquidity facilities' enable the securitization vehicles to assure investors of timely payments. These include smoothening of timing differences between payment of interest and principal on pooled assets and payments due to investors
42. Interest on advances against term deposits, NSCs, IVPs, KVPs and life policies may be taken to income account on the due date, provided adequate margin is available in the accounts. Fees and commissions earned by the banks as a result of renegotiations or rescheduling of outstanding debts should be recognized on an accrual basis over the period of time covered by the renegotiated or rescheduled extension of credit. If government guaranteed advances become NPAs, the interest on such advances should not be taken to income account unless the interest has been realized.
43. As defined in 'AS 19—Leases' issued by the Council of the Institute of Chartered Accountants of India (ICAI).
44. A 'standard' account is not an NPA. It carries normal business risks, the securities are sufficient to cover the advances made and the firm is currently meeting its interest and principal repayment obligations.
45. Unsecured exposure is defined as an exposure where the realizable value of the security, as assessed by the bank/ approved valuers/Reserve Bank's inspecting officers, is not more than 10 per cent, ab-initio, of the outstanding advances. 'Exposure' shall include all funded and non-funded exposures (including underwriting and similar commitments). 'Security' will mean tangible security properly discharged to the bank and will not include intangible securities like guarantees and comfort letters.
46. Considering that higher loan loss provisioning adds to the overall financial strength of the banks and the stability of the financial sector, banks are urged to voluntarily set apart provisions much above the minimum prudential levels as a desirable practice. RBI has been monitoring the accounting treatment of such floating provisions and issuing guidelines from time to time. At the G20 meet in London held in April 2009, the Group agreed to initiate several measures to strengthen the international frameworks for prudential regulation. The Financial Stability Board (FSB), the Basel Committee on Banking Supervision (BCBS) and Committee on Global Financial System (CGFS), along with various accounting bodies, would be working on the proposal to build buffers of capital and reserves in good times, so that the risk to financial stability can be mitigated when conditions worsen. The RBI proposes to issue fresh instructions based on the international recommendations.
47. SICA—Sick Industrial Companies Act—which has since been repealed.
48. Guidelines on 'Securitization of Standard Assets' issued by the RBI on 24 January, 2006.
49. For the salient features of the Act relevant to banks, please refer 'Annexure to RBI Guidelines to Banks/ FIs on sale of SC/RC (created under the Securitization and Reconstruction of Financial Assets and Enforcement of Security Interest Act, 2002) and related issues', and for the salient features relevant to securitization and reconstruction companies, please refer to RBI, Notification dated 23 April 2003, 'The Securitization Companies and Reconstruction Companies (Reserve Bank) Guidelines and Directions, 2003', as well as subsequent notification and amendments. All the resources can be accessed at www.rbi.org.in. Including RBI master circular "Prudential norms on Income recognition, Asset classification and provisioning" dated July 1, 2013.
50. RBI, 2011, 'Guidelines on Credit Default Swaps for corporate bonds', dated May 23, 2011, and 'Prudential guidelines on credit default swaps', dated November 30, 2011. RBI, 2013, Revised guidelines on CDS for corporate Bonds, dated January 7, 2013.
51. In November 2012, SEBI permitted Mutual funds to enter the CDS market only as 'users' – protection buyers
52. Frank J Fabozzi, and Vinod Kothari, 'Securitization: The Tool of Financial Transformation,' Yale ICF Working Paper no. 07–07, downloaded from http://ssrn.com (31 March 2008)

CHAPTER NINE

Managing Credit Risk—Advanced Topics

CHAPTER STRUCTURE

KEY TAKEAWAYS FROM THE CHAPTER

- Understand the issues in measuring credit risk.
- Understand how credit risk is measured through quantitative models.
- Find out how the popular industry sponsored credit risk models work.
- Understand how credit derivatives are priced and traded in developed markets.
- Understand how the global credit crisis happened.
- Learn about the use of 'big data' and business simulation.

SECTION I

BASIC CONCEPTS

Traditional methods, such as the Altman's Z score and other credit scoring models (described in the previous chapters) try to estimate the probability of default (PD), rather than potential losses in the event of default (LGD). The traditional methods define a firm's credit risk in the context of its 'failure'—bankruptcy, liquidation or default. They ignore the possibility that the 'credit quality' of a loan or portfolio of loans could undergo a mere 'upgrade' or 'downgrade' as described in the classification of loans in the previous chapter.

The credit risk of a single borrower/client is the basis of all risk modelling. In addition, credit risk models should also capture the 'concentration risk' arising out of portfolio diversification and correlations between assets in the portfolio.

Recall from the previous chapter that the expected loss (EL) for a bank, arising from a single borrower or a credit portfolio is the product of three factors—Probability of default (PD), loss given default (LGD) and exposure at default (EAD).

Typically, therefore, credit risk models are expected to generate (1) loss distributions for the default risk of a single borrower and (2) portfolio value distributions for migration (upgrades and downgrades of a borrower's creditworthiness) and default risks. It follows that all models require some common inputs, such as (1) information on the borrower(s), (2) credit exposures to these borrowers, (3) recovery rates (or LGD) and (4) default correlations (derived from asset correlations) to assess concentration risk in the credit portfolio.

Credit risk models have a wide range of applications. They are prevalently used for

a. Assessing the 'EL' of a single borrower.
b. Measuring the 'economic capital'[1] of a financial institution
c. Estimating credit concentration risk
d. Optimizing the bank's asset portfolio
e. Pricing credit instruments based on the risk profile

Figure 9.1 generalizes the components of credit risk models:

FIGURE 9.1 COMPONENTS OF CREDIT RISK MODELS

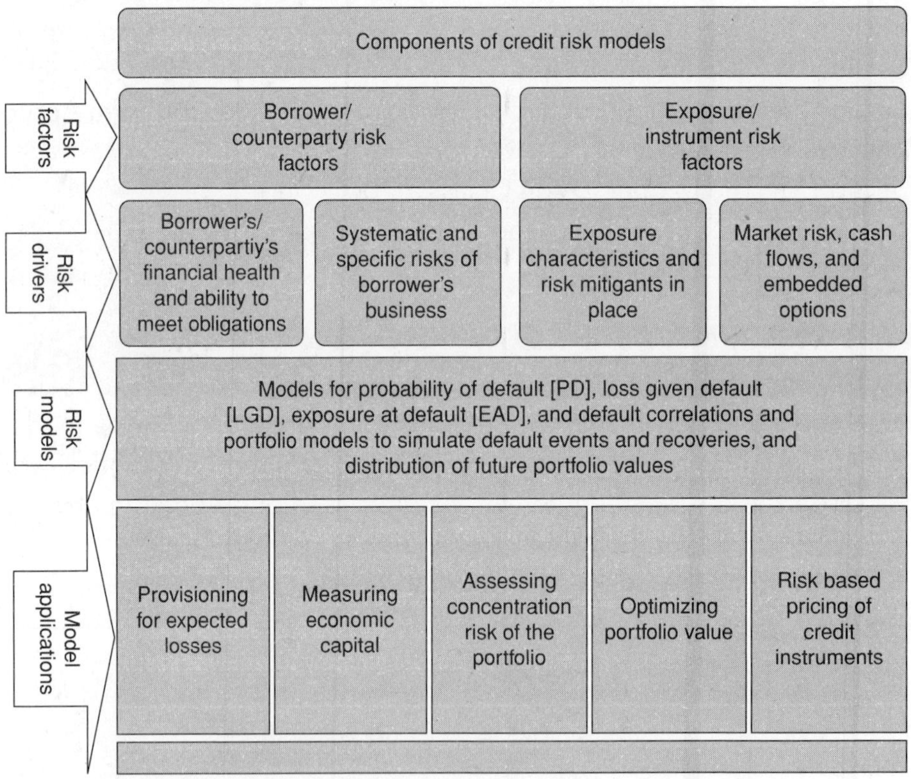

Estimating PD, EAD and LGD—The Issues

Recall our discussion on 'Loan pricing' in an earlier chapter, where we used a simplified model to estimate the risk premium to be embedded in the loan price, analogous to the EL formula above. In that model, we had assumed that the PD had to be estimated for the borrower, taking into account various risk factors, and superimposed on the recovery rate (RR) (in the event of default), and the likely exposure of the bank to the borrower over the period (assumed as 1 year). The shortfall in the contracted rate arising out of the borrower's default probability was called the 'risk premium'. This was analogous to the 'EL' and, therefore, had to be compensated. The bank did this by simply adding the 'risk premium' to the loan price. In this case, we had assumed that the EAD and LGD remained constant at the estimated levels.

However, in practice, the above view is too simplistic. There are various issues in estimating the risk factors. Let us look at each of the values that define EL.

1. Assigning a PD to each customer in a bank's credit portfolio is far from easy. One way to assess the PD is based on the fact that a default has occurred according to the bank's internal definition or a legal definition adopted by the bank—*i.e.*, the borrower has exceeded some default threshold. Alternatively, a credit rating migration approach can be used.
2. There are two commonly used approaches to estimate default probabilities. One is to base the estimate on historical default experience—market data based on credit spreads of traded products or internally generated data, or use models, such as the KMV and others—which will be described later on in this chapter. A second approach is to associate default probabilities with credit ratings (described in an earlier chapter)—either internally generated customer ratings or those provided by external credit rating agencies, such as CRISIL (or S&P). The process of assigning a default probability to a rating is called 'calibration'.
3. The EAD is the quantity of exposure of the bank to the borrower. This is not merely the 'outstanding' amount in the bank's books, as we assumed in the case of loan pricing in the earlier chapter. In fact, the EAD comprises two major parts—'outstandings' and 'commitments'. The 'outstandings' represent the portion of the loan already drawn by the borrower, and is shown as a funded exposure on the bank's assets. In case of default, the bank will stand exposed to the total amount of the 'outstandings'. In the time before default, the borrower is also likely to have 'commitments' (undrawn portion of the bank's promised credit limit to the borrower). These commitments can again be classified into 'undrawn' and 'drawn'. Historical default studies shows that borrowers tend to draw quickly on committed lines of credit in times of financial distress. Hence, the EAD should also include the 'drawn' portion of the commitment at the time of default. Since the borrower has the 'right' but not the 'obligation' to draw on undrawn commitments (the embedded 'option'), we can consider the proportion of drawn to undrawn commitments as a random variable. Therefore, now EAD becomes the aggregate of the outstanding exposure + a fraction of the undrawn commitment likely to be drawn prior to default. In practice, banks will calculate this fraction as a function of the borrower's creditworthiness and the type of credit facility.
4. One approach to estimate EAD is to assume it as being equal to 'current exposure + 'Loan Equivalency Factor (LEF)' × unutilized portion of the limit'.[2] The LEF is the portion of the unutilized credit limit expected to be drawn down before default, and depends on the type of facility and the credit rating just before default, as stated in the preceding paragraph. The cited World Bank paper provides a simple method to approximate LEF as shown in Figure 9.2.[3]
5. In the case of derivatives, the potential future exposure depends on the movement in the credit quality/value of the underlying asset, and this is estimated using simulation techniques.

FIGURE 9.2 ONE METHOD OF APPROXIMATING LEF

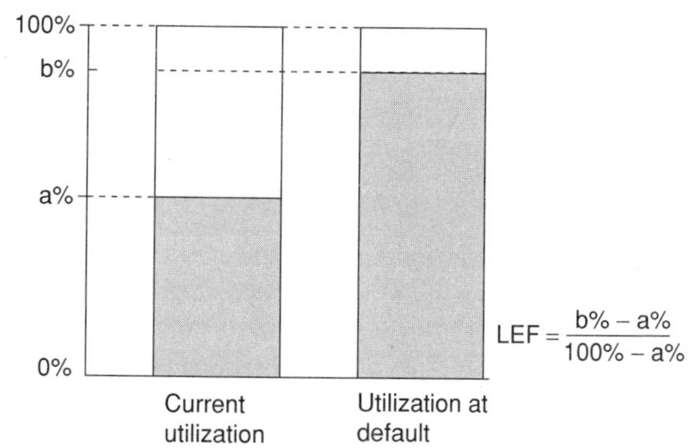

Source: Wold Bank Policy, Research Working Paper.

6. Modelling EAD should also take into account the 'covenants' attached to the loan document. Most of these covenants represent 'embedded options' for the borrower or the bank. For example, a covenant may require that the borrower provides additional collateral security in times of impending financial distress. In such a case, the borrower firm will have more information about its likelihood of default than the bank, which watches for signals of incipient distress (as described in an earlier chapter). In cases where banks are permitted by the covenants to close undrawn commitments based on predefined early indicators of default, the banks have to move quickly before the borrower draws on the undrawn commitments. This aspect will be discussed in detail in the subsequent chapter on 'Capital Adequacy' and the Basel Committee regulations.
7. The LGD is simply the proportion of EAD lost in case of default, and is typically estimated as (1–recovery rate)—*i.e.*, the actual 'loss' to the bank in case of default by the borrower. However, recovery rate (RR) is not static—it depends on the 'quality' of the collaterals (in case of decline in economic growth, the value of these securities could decline) and the 'seniority' of the bank's claim on the borrower's assets. Additionally, 'recovery' could also entail 'financial cost' (such as interest income lost due to time taken for recovery or the cost of 'workout' as discussed in a previous chapter). In reality, therefore, the LGD is modelled as the 'expected severity' of the loss in the event of default.
8. According to Schuermann,[4] there are three broad methods to measure LGD.
   a. Market LGD, which can be computed directly from market prices or trades of defaulted bonds or loans;
   b. Workout LGD that depends on the magnitude and timing of the cash flows (including costs) from the workout process. LGD can be computed under this method as EAD less recovery plus workout costs incurred expressed as a percentage of EAD. Since the recovery process can be long winded, the cash flows should be expressed in present value (PV) terms. The question then arises as to what the appropriate discount rate should be. According to Schuermann, the discount rate could be that for an asset of similar risk, or the bank's own hurdle rate. In practice, workout LGD is the most popular, especially with banks with prior experience in such defaults; and
   c. Implied Market LGD that is derived from prices of fixed income and credit derivatives, using a theoretical asset pricing model.
9. Approaches to modelling LGD are evolving rapidly. The initial models identified the factors driving the LGD values, including the correlation between PD and LGD. Schuermann's paper quoted above belongs to the 'first generation' models, as does Altman (et al)'s 2005 paper.[5] The 'second wave' of models developed and empirically applied frameworks to quantify the correlation between PD and LGD. The current stream of models derives concepts to stress LGDs in economic downturns, as in the events happening since 2007. There is a need to now calculate a 'downturn LGD' (BLGD). The Basel committee on Banking Supervision has proposed such a model in its 2006 comprehensive version of the revised framework,[6] and the Federal Reserve uses a simple model to arrive at the BLGD[7]:

$$BLGD = 0.08 + 0.92\ ELGD$$

   where ELGD is the 'expected LGD'.
   The above linear relationship between BLGD and ELGD, however, does not take into account the degree to which the risk segments are exposed to 'systematic risks'.

Why Do We Need Credit Risk Models?

There are important differences between market risk[8] and credit risk. While market risk is the risk of adverse price movements in equity, foreign currency, bonds, etc., credit risk is the risk of adverse price movements due to changes in credit events, such as borrower or counter party defaults or credit rating downgrades. These risks are also called 'market VaR' and 'credit VaR', the term VaR denoting 'Value at Risk', a technique to measure risk.

First, the portfolio distribution for credit VaR hardly conforms to the normal distribution. Credit returns tend to be highly skewed—while lenders' benefits are limited when there is an upgrade in credit quality, their losses are substantial in the case of downgrade or default, as shown in Figure 9.3.

FIGURE 9.3 COMPARISON OF DISTRIBUTION OF CREDIT RETURNS AND MARKET RETURNS

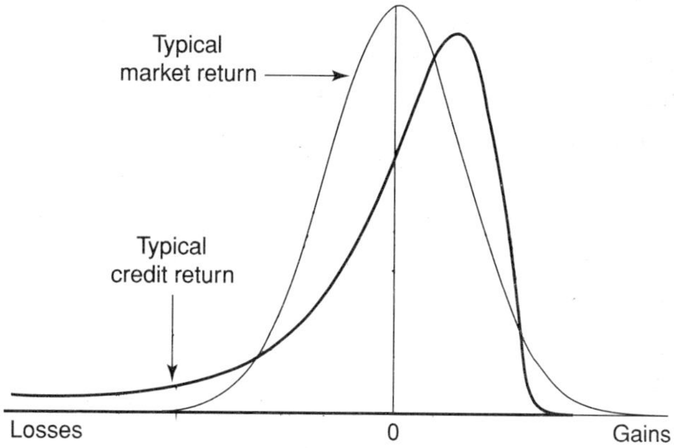

Second, market VaR can be directly calculated based on daily/periodic price fluctuations. However, measuring portfolio effect due to credit diversification is more complex than for market risk. To measure this effect, estimates of correlations in credit quality changes among all pairs of borrowers/counter parties have to be obtained. However, these correlations are not readily observable, and several assumptions are required for such correlation estimates.

Third, though the default probability of a borrower or counter party can be likened to 'asset volatility' in market risk, credit risk is more complicated. Take the instance of currency risk, an important market risk. One of the ways of arriving at the rate volatility is to observe the fluctuations in the currency over a period of time, and compute a reasonable estimate of the currency's volatility. However, a borrower's history may indicate nothing about the probability of future default; in fact, in many cases, the very fact that the lender stays exposed to the borrower signifies no prior default!

Credit risk models are valuable since they provide users and decision makers with insights that are not otherwise available or can be gathered only at a prohibitive cost. A credit risk model should be able to guide the decision-making manager on allocating scarce capital to various loan assets, so that the bank's risk-return trade off is optimized. Optimization, of course, does not imply 'risk elimination'—it means achieving the targeted or maximum return at minimum risk.

Banks typically have a diversified portfolio of assets. Most credit risk models compare risk-return characteristics between individual assets or businesses in order to quantify the diversification of risks and ensure that the bank is well diversified.

A good credit risk management model is expected to generate the outputs as given in Figure 9.4.

FIGURE 9.4 OUTPUTS OF A CREDIT RISK MODEL

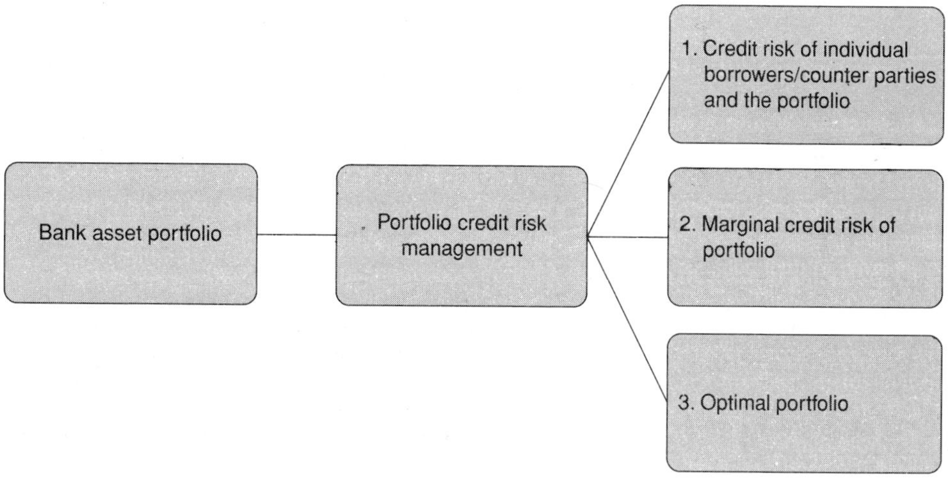

1. Credit risk of portfolio in Figure 9.4 indicates the output defining the probability distribution of losses due to credit risk.
2. The marginal credit risk of the portfolio in Figure 9.4 depicts how the risk-return trade off would change if an incremental (marginal) asset is added to the portfolio. This output helps bank managers to decide on new investment options for the bank and the price that can be paid for the opportunity.
3. The optimal portfolio is the optimal mix of assets that the bank should have at that point in time.

Every credit risk model is built on certain assumptions and, therefore, may not be able to generate all the outputs as above. Further, they cannot be used mechanically for predictions, since they are constructed mostly out of historical data. The outputs of the models are useful tools for decision making, but cannot substitute judgment and experience of bank managers.

Credit Risk Models—Best Practice Industry Models

Credit risk has been recognized as the largest source of risk to banks. The increasing focus of measuring credit risk through models—internal to banks and industry-sponsored—can be attributed to the following:

a. Substantial research has been carried out and advanced analytical methods have been evolved for formulating and implementing credit risk models;
b. The 'economic capital' of a bank is aligned closely to the bank's credit risk. Hence, efficient allocation of capital within a bank presupposes accurate quantification of credit risk, and better understanding of the impact of credit concentration and diversification on the bank's asset portfolio on the bank's capital requirements.[9]
c. The other incentives flowing from credit risk measurement include better pricing of credit due to better valuation of financial contracts, and better management of funds, due to accurate assessment of risk and diversification benefits.
d. Regulatory developments, such as the Basel II Capital Accord[10] have necessitated use of risk models.

The previous chapter lists some industry-sponsored credit risk models, based on approaches, such as the 'credit migration approach', 'option pricing approach', (these two classes of models are called 'structural models'), the 'actuarial approach' and the 'reduced-form approach'.

The above models can also be classified as given in Figure 9.5. This classification is based on the approach adopted by the model for credit risk measurement.

FIGURE 9.5 CLASSIFICATION OF SOME INDUSTRY-SPONSORED BEST PRACTICE CREDIT RISK MODELS

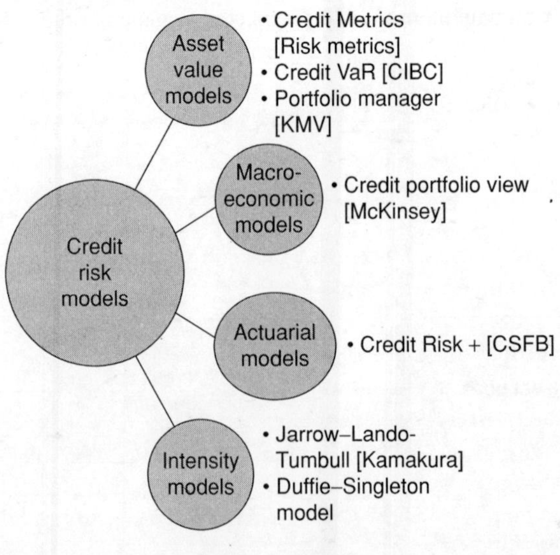

In the following sections, we will provide an overview of each of the above approaches.

SECTION II

SELECT APPROACHES AND MODELS—THE CREDIT MIGRATION APPROACH

The Credit Migration Approach (Used by Credit Metrics™[11])

We have seen that credit quality can vary over time. 'Credit migration' is analyzed as the probability of moving from one credit quality to another, including default, within a specified time horizon, usually a year.

'Credit Metrics™', the most well-known credit migration model, builds upon a broad body of research[12] that applies migration analysis to credit risk measurement. The model computes the full (1 year) forward distribution of values for a loan portfolio, where the changes in values are assumed as due to credit migration alone, while interest rates are assumed to evolve in a deterministic manner. 'Credit VaR'[13] is then derived as a percentile of the distribution corresponding to the desired confidence level.

Though we have earlier drawn the distinction between 'market' and 'credit' risks in order to isolate them and deal with them, the real world picture is different. For example, credit risk could arise due to volatility in currency movements, in which case, we have to capture market risk components as well in the credit risk models. The credit risk models are being increasingly refined to account for the impact of market risks.

However, as a first step, it would help to understand how the basic credit migration approach works for measuring credit risk.

Step 1: Assessing Real World Probabilities of Default—The Transition Matrix Credit rating agencies periodically construct, from historical data, a 'transition matrix', which shows the probability of an existing (rated) loan getting upgraded or downgraded or defaulting during a specified period in time (typically 1 year). The matrix is usually presented in the way as shown in Table 9.1. (in the case of S&P, CRISIL[14]):

TABLE 9.1 CRISIL's AVERAGE 1-YEAR TRANSITION RATES

Rating	Sample Size	AAA	AA	A	BBB	BB	B	C	D
AAA	647	97.4%	2.6%	0.0%	0.0%	0.0%	0.0%	0.0%	0.0%
AA	1457	2.3%	90.3%	6.3%	0.6%	0.4%	0.1%	0.0%	0.0%
A	1447	0.0%	3.9%	82.7%	7.2%	4.4%	0.2%	0.7%	0.9%
BBB	635	0.0%	0.3%	5.5%	73.7%	13.9%	1.3%	2.0%	3.3%
BB	341	0.0%	0.6%	0.0%	2.3%	74.8%	1.8%	5.3%	15.2%
B	34	0.0%	0.0%	0.0%	5.9%	0.0%	55.9%	8.8%	29.4%
C	81	0.0%	0.0%	0.0%	1.2%	0.0%	0.0%	70.4%	28.4%
Total	4642								

Source: CRISIL Ratings

Each cell in the above matrix contains a probability. The rating categories in the columns of the matrix signify the expected credit rating 1 year in the future. The rating categories in the rows of the matrix show current credit ratings.

For example, the probability in the cell AA-AAA will signify the chances of a loan, currently assigned an AA rating, upgrading to AAA over the ensuing year. Similarly, the probability in the cell A-BBB will signify the chances that a loan, currently rated A, downgrades to BBB over the next 1 year. The highlighted cells AAA-AAA, AA-AA and so on, therefore, signify the probability that the loan stays in the same category. These probabilities are 'real world probabilities'[15] as they have been calculated from historical data. For example, the transition matrix given by CRISIL in the reference provided has been constructed out of data over the period 1992–2007.[16]

Box 9.1 explains the distinction between 'real world' and 'risk neutral' probabilities, and their usage in credit risk analysis.

BOX 9.1 REAL WORLD VERSUS RISK NEUTRAL PROBABILITIES

Table 9.2 shows the average cumulative default rates estimated by CRISIL[17] for rated credit instruments.

TABLE 9.2 CRISIL AVERAGE CUMULATIVE DEFAULT RATES (WITHDRAWAL-ADJUSTED)

Rating	Sample Size	1-Year	2-Year	3-Year
AAA	419	0.00%	0.00%	0.00%
AA	593	0.00%	0.22%	0.22%
A	239	0.42%	1.03%	1.97%
BBB	86	3.49%	5.42%	8.47%
Investment grade (AAA to BBB)	1337	0.30%	0.63%	0.99%
Speculative grade	84	15.48%	20.58%	20.58%

Source: CRISIL ratings

From Table 9.2, we can infer that the probability of an A-rated loan defaulting in 1 year is .42 per cent, in 2 years is 1.03 per cent and in 3 years is 1.97 per cent. These are 'real world' probabilities, estimated from historical data—in the above case, data from 2000 to 2007.

Now let us assume that an A-rated loan is priced 100 bps (fixed) over the bank's Prime lending rate (the rate at which it lends to 'risk free' borrowers). Assuming a zero RR from the loan in case of default, the PD would be given by the equation $1 - [1/(1 + r)^n]$, where r denotes the premium over the risk-free rate and n the number of periods. Using this equation, the estimated probabilities of default would be 1 per cent, 1.97 per cent and 2.94 per cent for 1, 2 and 3 years, respectively.

Compare these probabilities with the historical probabilities of default in Table 9.2. Are the results inconsistent? They are not.

To understand the concept, we should note that the value of a risk-free loan is higher than the value of an A-rated loan that carries some element of risk. In other words, (1) the expected cash flow from the A-rated loan at the end of 3 years would be 2.94 per cent less than the expected cash flow from a risk-free loan at the end of 3 years, and (2) both cash flows would be discounted at the same rate in a risk neutral world, *i.e.*, at the prime lending rate or risk-free rate.

The above is analogous to stating that (1) the expected cash flow from the A-rated loan at the end of 3 years is 1.97 per cent less than the expected cash flow from a risk-free loan at the end of 3 years, and (2) the appropriate discount rate for the A-rated loan's expected cash flow is about 0.32 per cent higher than the discount rate applicable to the risk-free loan's cash flow—because a 0.32 per cent increase in the discount rate leads to the A-rated loan's value being reduced by the difference between the risk neutral and real world PD, *i.e.*, 1.97 per cent and 2.94 per cent, which is 0.97 per cent over 3 years or 0.32 per cent per year.

It, therefore, follows that 1.97 per cent is a correct estimate of the real world PD, if the correct discount rate to be used for the debt cash flow in the real world is 0.32 per cent higher than in the risk neutral world. The increase in the discount rate seems reasonable as A-rated loans have been perceived to have higher systematic risks—when the economy does badly, they are more likely to default.[18]

The question, therefore, is—which PD is appropriate for credit risk analysis—the real world or the risk neutral one?

Typically, analysts use risk neutral default probabilities while pricing credit derivatives or estimating the impact of credit risk on the pricing of instruments such as in the calculation of the PV of the cost of default (since risk neutral valuation is commonly used in the analysis). Real world probabilities are commonly used in scenario analysis as for estimating Credit VaR (to estimate potential future losses in the event of default).

The information contained in transition matrices provided by renowned credit rating agencies is considered robust and useful and is being used as the starting point for modelling credit risk. However, there are certain criticisms, the most obvious of them being that these transition probabilities only reflect averages over several years, and lack the predictive ability to determine how serious or benign the forthcoming year's credit transitions would be. To address this shortcoming, smaller historical periods are sometimes chosen to reflect the most likely current scenario, and transition matrices constructed. Another method used to improve the predictive ability is to model the relationship between transition of credit defaults and select macroeconomic variables, say, industrial production.

However, it has to be recognized here that predicting the PD or downgrade/upgrade in credit quality is a difficult task in practice. Hence, it would be prudent to stress test the portfolio under a variety of transition assumptions.

In many cases, banks develop their own transition matrices based on their borrowers' profile, since the probabilities provided by rating agencies are average statistics obtained from a heterogeneous sample of firms, with varying business cycles.

Step 2: Specifying the Credit Risk Horizon The risk horizon is typically taken to be 1 year, as assumed by the transition matrix. This is a convenient assumption, but can be an arbitrary one.[19] It should be noted here that the transition matrix should be estimated for the same time interval over which the credit risk is being assessed. For example, a semi annual risk horizon would use a semi annual transition matrix.[20]

Step 3: Revaluing the Loan In this step, we calculate the value of the loan at the end of the risk horizon. However, since there are eight possible ratings in the transition matrix, we have to estimate eight values of the same loan. This estimation has to be done within two broad, mutually exclusive assumptions.

a. In the worst case, if the loan defaults over the horizon, some recovery would be possible based on the available collaterals.
b. Alternatively, the loan can simply move between the ratings—an 'upgrade' or a 'downgrade'. In the second case, we need to revalue the loan based on the rating to which it migrates.

Assume that credit risk is being assessed for one large, long-term loan.

a. In the worst case of default, we require two important inputs—the 'seniority' of the loan and the 'recovery' in case of default. The likely value of the loan will depend on how much can be recovered, say, by enforcing securities offered for the loan, which, in turn will depend on the 'seniority' of the loan, the mean recovery rate and the volatility (standard deviation) of the RR. The Credit Metrics technical document provides the Table 9.3[21]:

TABLE 9.3 RECOVERY RATES BY SENIORITY CLASS (PER CENT OF FACE VALUE—'PAR')

Seniority class	Mean (%)	Standard Deviation (%)
Senior secured	53.80	26.86
Senior unsecured	51.13	25.45
Senior subordinated	38.52	23.81
Subordinated	32.74	20.18
Junior subordinated	17.09	10.90

Source: Carty and Liberman [96a]—Moody's Investors Service

Table 9.3 can be interpreted easily. If the loan or bond is 'senior secured', its mean recovery in default would be 53.8 per cent of its face value, *i.e.*, for a loan of, say, ₹100 crore, the average recovery would be ₹53.80 crore, with a volatility (standard deviation) of 26.86 per cent.

See Box 9.2 for further discussion on the relationship between the PD and recovery rates.

BOX 9.2 RELATIONSHIP BETWEEN PROBABILITY OF DEFAULT AND RECOVERY RATE

From our discussion earlier in this chapter, we know that EL under credit risk is calculated as the product of three factors—PD, LGD and EAD. RR is 1 – LGD.

While credit risk literature abounds with work on estimating PD, much less attention has been devoted to estimation of RR and its relationship with PD[22]. However, empirical evidence seems to suggest that: (1) recovery rates can be volatile; and (2) they tend to decrease (or LGDs increase) when PD increases, say, due to economic downturns.

However, many credit risk models continue to work with simplifying assumptions based on static losses for a given type of debt as in Table 9.3. It should also be noted that credit VaR models such as the one being discussed, treat RR and PD as two independent variables.

b. In case of an expected upgrade or downgrade in credit rating, *i.e.*, if a BBB-rated loan moves up to A or moves down to BB over the risk horizon, the 'value' of the loan would also change. The magnitude of this change can be assessed by estimating the forward zero curves[23] for each rating category, stated as of the risk horizon, going up to the maturity of the loan. Table 9.4 shows a sample of 1-year forward zero curves by rating category.[24]

We can now revalue the loan using forward rates as above, and the promised cash flows from the loan over the risk horizon for the appropriate rating category. The result of this exercise would be a distribution of loan values over all the rating categories.

TABLE 9.4 EXAMPLE 1-YEAR FORWARD ZERO CURVES BY CREDIT RATING CATEGORY (PER CENT)

Category	Year 1	Year 2	Year 3	Year 4
AAA	3.60	4.17	4.73	5.12
AA	3.65	4.22	4.78	5.17
A	3.72	4.32	4.93	5.32
BBB	4.10	4.67	5.25	5.63
BB	5.55	6.02	6.78	7.27
B	6.05	7.02	8.03	8.52
CCC	15.05	15.02	14.03	13.52

Source: CreditMetrics technical document

Step 4: Estimating Credit Risk The probabilities of migration of a single-rated loan to other categories from Step 1, and the result of the calculation in Step 3 would enable us calculate the expected value (mean) of the loan over the risk horizon, as well as the volatility (standard deviation). This standard deviation is the measure of 'credit risk' of the loan.

Another way to estimate the credit risk is to use 'percentile levels'. For example, if we determine the 5th percentile level for the loan portfolio, it denotes the level below which the portfolio value will fall with probability 5 per cent. For large portfolios, percentile levels are more meaningful. This is also called the *Credit VaR*.

Illustration 9.1 clarifies the methodology through a numerical example.

ILLUSTRATION 9.1

Estimating the credit risk of a single loan exposure

The problem

Using the Credit Migration approach, calculate the Credit Risk (Credit VaR) of a senior secured loan of ₹100 crore, to be repaid in 5 years, at an annual interest rate of 10 per cent.

Key inputs and assumptions

1. Risk horizon is 1 year
2. CRISIL's credit transition matrix given in Table 9.1 will be used.
3. The current credit rating for this senior secured loan is 'A'
4. The recovery rates and the 1-year forward zero curves as given in step 3 above would be used in the calculations
5. For calculation convenience, it can be assumed here that the principal is paid at the end of 5 years, while the annual interest of ₹10 crore is paid every year.

Step 1 Using the transition matrix, recovery rates and the forward curves given above, we will estimate the credit risk of the loan over the risk horizon.

We first determine the cash flows over the loan period—₹10 crore every year at the end of next 4 years as interest, and ₹110 crore at the end of the 5th year, including principal payment. This is similar to a straightforward bond valuation. The Credit Metrics document mentions that, among others, the methodology is applicable to bank loans as for bonds.

Using the forward rates applicable to an A-rated loan, we determine the value of the loan over the risk horizon. The discount rates are taken from the earlier 1-year forward zero curve as applicable to an A-rated instrument, and calculated as follows:

$$\text{Loan value} = 10 + 10/(1 + 3.72\%) + 10/(1 + 4.32\%)^2 + 10/(1 + 4.93\%)^3 + 110/(1 + 5.32\%)^4$$

That is, loan value = ₹126.89 crore over the next 1 year

Now let us calculate the value of the loan, assuming it downgrades to BBB. The loan value will be calculated as follows:

$$\text{Loan value} = 10 + 10/(1 + 4.10\%) + 10/(1 + 4.67\%)^2 + 10/(1 + 5.25\%)^3 + 110/(1 + 5.63\%)^4$$

That is loan value now changes to ₹125.67 crore, showing erosion in value due to the downgrade.

Continuing this exercise for all rating categories, we arrive at the possible 1 year forward values of the loan for all rating categories as in Table 9.5.

TABLE 9.5 ONE-YEAR FORWARD VALUES OF THE LOAN FOR ALL RATING CATEGORIES

Year-end Rating	Possible Loan Value
AAA	127.66
AA	127.46
A	126.89
BBB	125.67
BB	119.66
B	115.41
CCC	99.232
Default	53.8

The default value is the mean value in default for a senior secured loan of ₹100 crore (53.8 per cent of ₹100 crore) as given in Table 9.3 containing recovery rates. Also from the same table, the standard deviation of the RR is 26.86 per cent.

Step 2 With the above inputs, we can calculate the volatility in loan value due to credit quality changes, using Table 9.6. Note that the probabilities of rating migrations have been obtained from CRISIL's transition matrix in Table 9.1.

TABLE 9.6 VOLATILITY IN LOAN VALUE DUE TO CREDIT RATING CHANGES

Year-end Rating	Probability of State#	Forward Loan Value	Probability × Loan Value	Difference in Value from Mean	Probability × Difference Squared
AAA	0	127.66	0	2.03	0
AA	0.039	127.46	4.97	1.83	0.13
A	0.827	126.89	104.94	1.26	1.31
BBB	0.072	125.67	9.05	0.04	0.00
BB	0.044	119.66	5.27	−5.97	1.57
B	0.002	115.41	0.23	−10.22	0.21
CCC	0.007	99.23	0.69	−26.40	4.88
Default	0.009	53.80	0.48	−71.83	46.44

Mean = ₹125.61 crore

Variance = 54.53

Standard deviation = ₹7.38 crore

Obtained from transition matrix

We have now obtained one measure of credit risk—the standard deviation. The mean is calculated as an expected loan value using the probabilities of migration, and the standard deviation measures the dispersion of the likely loan values from the mean. ₹7.38 crore is, therefore, one measure of the absolute amount of the credit risk in the loan of ₹100 crore.

However, this value of credit risk has not taken into consideration the volatility (standard deviation) in the recovery rate. The RR in case of default was assumed to be the mean value of ₹53.80 crore, but this amount of recovery is uncertain since the volatility was estimated at 26.86 per cent. This uncertainty has to also find a place in our estimate of credit risk. The Credit Metrics technical document uses the following formula to include the volatility in RR in case of default[25]:

$$\sigma_T = \sqrt{\sum_{i=1}^{S} P_1 (\mu_i^2 + \sigma_i^2) - \mu_T^2} \quad \text{where } \mu_T = \sum_{i=1}^{S} p_i \mu_i$$

Accordingly, the standard deviation of the default state is included in the calculation. In the other cases of downgrade and upgrade, this volatility is assumed to be 0. This implies that in Table 9.6, the last term under 'D', 46.44, should be added to the product of the PD (.009) and the square of the standard deviation of default, that is, 26.86^2. This yields a higher standard deviation of ₹7.81 crore, amounting to a 5.7 per cent increase in volatility.

The revised Table 9.7 is shown as follows:

TABLE 9.7 REVISED VOLATILITY

Year-end Rating	ProbAbility of State#	Forward Loan Value	Probability × Loan Value	Difference in Value from Mean	Probability × Difference Squared	Probability × Difference Squared-with Volatility in RR
AAA	0	127.66	0	2.03	0	0
AA	0.039	127.46	4.97	1.83	0.13	0.13
A	0.827	126.89	104.94	1.26	1.31	1.31
BBB	0.072	125.67	9.05	0.04	0.00	0.00
BB	0.044	119.66	5.27	−5.97	1.57	1.57
B	0.002	115.41	0.23	−10.22	0.21	0.21
CCC	0.007	99.23	0.69	−26.40	4.88	4.88
Default	0.009	53.80	0.48	−71.83	46.44	52.93
	1		125.63		54.53	61.02
	# Obtained from transition matrix			Standard deviation	7.38	7.81

We should note here that we have considered the volatility of only the RR in case of default to arrive at a measure of the credit risk. This implies that we are assuming that there is zero volatility or uncertainty in the upgrade and downgrade states. However, this cannot be true in a practical situation—the volatility in each rating would be determined by the credit 'spreads' within each rating category. (The Credit Metrics technical document is aware of this shortcoming, arising out of non-availability of data to determine what portion of the credit spread volatility is due to 'systematic' factors, and what portion is diversifiable.)

Calculating credit risk using the percentile level—the credit VaR

If we want to ascertain the level below which our loan value will fall with a probability of say, 1 per cent, we can use the values generated by Table 9.7. Let us move upwards in the probability column (generated by the transition matrix), stopping at the point where the probability becomes 1 per cent. In our transition matrix, we see that for an A-rated loan, the PD is 0.9 per cent, and the probability that it moves to CCC is 0.7 per cent. The joint probability of being in default or in the CCC state is, therefore, 1.6 per cent, which is more than 1 per cent. Hence, we read off the value from the CCC row—99,33. This is the first percentile level value, which is ₹26.40 crore lower than the expected (mean) loan value.

Calculating credit VaR

The changes in the forward value of the A-rated loan is shown in Table 9.8.

TABLE 9.8 CHANGES IN FORWARD VALUE OF THE LOAN

Year-end Rating	Probability of State#	Forward Loan Value	Change in Value	Probability × Change in Value	Square of Change in Value − Mean × Probability
AAA	0	127.66	0.77	0	0
AA	0.039	127.46	0.57	0.022	0.13
A	0.827	126.89	0	0.000	1.31
BBB	0.072	125.67	−1.22	−0.088	0.00

(*Continued*)

TABLE 9.8 (CONTINUED)

BB	0.044	119.66	−7.23	−0.318	1.57
B	0.002	115.41	−11.48	−0.023	0.21
CCC	0.007	99.23	−27.66	−0.194	4.88
Default	0.009	53.80	−73.09	−0.658	46.44
			Mean	−1.258	
				Variance	54.53
				Standard Deviation	7.38

We can see that this distribution of changes in loan value under various rating changes shows long downside tails, the variance and standard deviation of the distribution remaining the same. In the earlier paragraph, we calculated the first percentile at 99.23. The corresponding first percentile of the distribution of change in loan value is −27.66, which is the credit VaR.

(However, if we assume a normal distribution for the change in loan value distribution, the credit VaR at the first percentile would be much lower at −18.46)[26]

Calculation of Portfolio Risk[27]

The methodology in the Illustration 9.1 can be extended and employed to assess the credit risk in a portfolio of loans with the bank. The approach is described in detail in the Credit Metrics technical document.

In brief, the methodology for a two loan portfolio would be as follows:

Step 1 Describe the basic features of both loans—their tenor, credit rating, amount and interest rate.

Step 2 Describe the transition matrix and the risk horizon—the same transition matrix can be used. The risk horizon has to be the same for the portfolio being described.

Step 3 Just as in the one loan case above, we need to specify the year end values for both loans using the relevant forward rate curves, and the probabilities of achieving these values (from the transition matrix).

Step 4 Calculate joint probabilities for all rating categories—if there are eight rating categories, the matrix will have 8 × 8 = 64 values—each reflecting a joint probability for the loans. The joint probability is calculated simply by multiplying individual probabilities for each scenario. For example, the joint probability that two loans retain their original ratings is the product of the probabilities that each retains its original rating.

Step 5 The two loans can be revalued as in the single loan case above, and then combined as the sum of individual values for each rating class. There would be 64 such combined values (assuming eight rating categories).

Step 6 The portfolio standard deviation is calculated in the same manner as for a single loan. However, there will now be 64 probability states against 8 in the single loan case. The percentile level can also be computed in a manner similar to the case of a single loan.

Step 7 However, the above method of calculating joint probabilities will be valid only for those cases where the loans/assets are not correlated. If there is any kind of dependence between the borrowers, the method of calculating joint probabilities will have to take the correlation into consideration. It has been shown that the overall credit VaR is quite sensitive to correlations, which could arise from borrowing firms being in the same industry/sector, or vary with the state of the economy. Hence, where asset returns are correlated, joint migration probabilities have to be arrived at. To achieve this, Credit Metrics estimates the correlations between equity returns of the two borrowers. It has to be noted here that equity returns are being used as a proxy for asset returns, since asset returns are not directly observable. In effect, this is equivalent to assuming that the firm is entirely financed by equity.

Step 8 Assuming that the joint normalized return distribution is bivariate normal,[28] arrive at the credit quality thresholds for each credit rating in the transition matrix. The same procedure is repeated for arriving at the joint rating probabilities for all combinations in the transition matrix related to the two borrowers.

Step 9 The probability of joint defaults as a function of asset return correlations is then obtained.

The above procedure, as well as the Monte Carlo simulation that is used in practice for large portfolios, is described in detail in the Credit Metrics technical document.

Credit Manager—We have seen in the earlier chapter that the interplay of credit and market risks is a significant source of risk to banks. Risk Metrics has devised the Credit Manager to deliver portfolio credit risk management across multiple asset classes, such as bonds, credit derivatives and traditional credit exposures. The methodology is similar to the Credit Metrics methodology described above.

Counter party credit exposure models—We have also seen earlier the influence of counter parties on credit risk. A counter party default would have consequences similar to borrower default. One challenge in arriving at exposures in respect of counter parties is the way OTC transactions are structured or customized. For example. Estimation of credit exposure to derivatives counter parties involves issues such as (a) determination of the replacement cost of a particular transaction at a given point in time involves modeling risk factors, and pricing the instrument; (b) modeling netting and margining arrangements between counter parties; (c) consolidation of exposures at any level of the portfolio to enable limit and exposure management, and so on. Risk Metrics' counter party credit exposure models aim to address a broad spectrum of risks.

Details on the above models can be accessed at www.msci.com

The Credit Migration Approach (Used by CreditPortfolioView)

Credit Portfolio View (CPV) was developed by McKinsey and Company based on two papers by Thomas C Wilson[29], then Principal consultant at McKinsey and company.

In summary, CPV is a ratings-based portfolio model used to define the relationship between macroeconomic cycles and credit risk in a bank's portfolio. It is based on the observation that default and migration probabilities downgrade when the economy worsens (*i.e.*, defaults increase), and the contrary happens when the economy strengthens. The model simulates joint conditional distribution of default and migration probabilities for non-investment grade (non-IG) borrowers (whose default probabilities are more sensitive to credit cycles, which are assumed to follow business cycles closely, than those of highly rated borrowers) in different industries and for each country, conditional on the value of macroeconomic factors, such as follows:

- Unemployment rate
- GDP growth rate
- Level of long-term interest rates
- Foreign exchange rates
- Government expenditure
- Aggregate savings rate

CPV calls these 'conditional migration probabilities' for a particular year, since it is constructed conditional on the economic conditions of that year. It should be noted here that the previous model, Credit Metrics, used 'unconditional migration probabilities', which is the average of conditional probabilities sampled over several years.

Thomas C Wilson[30] points out that this approach differs from others in that it models the actual, discrete loss distribution (as opposed to using normal distributions or mean variance approximations); the losses or gains are measured on a default/no default basis for illiquid credit exposures as well as liquid secondary market positions, and retail lending, such as mortgages and overdrafts; the loss distributions are driven by the state of the economy, since most of the systematic risk in a portfolio has been found to arise from economic cycles; and the approach is based on a multi-factor systematic risk that is closer to reality, while other models capture default correlations based on a single systematic risk factor.

The model follows three essential steps:

Step 1 Determine the state of the economy.

Step 2 Estimate the PD of customers/customer segments.

Step 3 Arrive at the loss distribution.

Illustration[31] 9.2 would help in understanding the methodology through a simple numerical example.

ILLUSTRATION 9.2

Credit portfolio view basic methodology

(Based on Thomas Wilson's paper-portfolio credit risk—October 1998)

Step 1 The states of the economy

State	GDP	PD%
Growth	1	33.33
Normal	0	33.33
Recession	−1	33.33

Step 2 Assume two customers/customer segments, X and Y, for simplicity

Customers have different risk profiles

State	Customer X—Medium Risk—PD	Customer Y—High Risk—PD
Growth	2.5	0.75
Normal	3	3.5
Recession	4.5	5

Note that we assume that the high-risk customer has lower likelihood of defaulting when the economy is growing.

Step 3 Arrive at the loss distribution

There are four possibilities in each state of the economy—X defaults, Y defaults, both X and Y default, or there is no default

Assume loss in case of default as ₹100 in the case of both X and Y

Growth State of Economy				
Scenario	Loss if X defaults	Loss if Y defaults	Loss if X and Y default	PD
X defaults	−100	0	−100	0.83
Y defaults	0	−100	−100	0.25
Both X and Y default	−100	−100	−200	0.01
No default	0	0	0	32.24
				33.33

Normal State of Economy				
Scenario	Loss if X defaults	Loss if Y defaults	Loss if X and Y default	PD
X defaults	−100	0	−100	1.00
Y defaults	0	−100	−100	1.17
Both X and Y default	−100	−100	−200	0.03
No default	0	0	0	31.13
				33.33

Recession State of Economy				
Scenario	Loss if X defaults	Loss if Y defaults	Loss if X and Y default	PD
X defaults	−100	0	−100	1.50
Y defaults	0	−100	−100	1.67
Both X and Y default	−100	−100	−200	0.07
No default	0	0	0	30.09
				33.33

Here, we have assumed that X and Y are independent of each other, that is, correlation = 0

FIGURE 9.6 PROBABILITY OF LOSS ACROSS ALL STATES OF THE ECONOMY

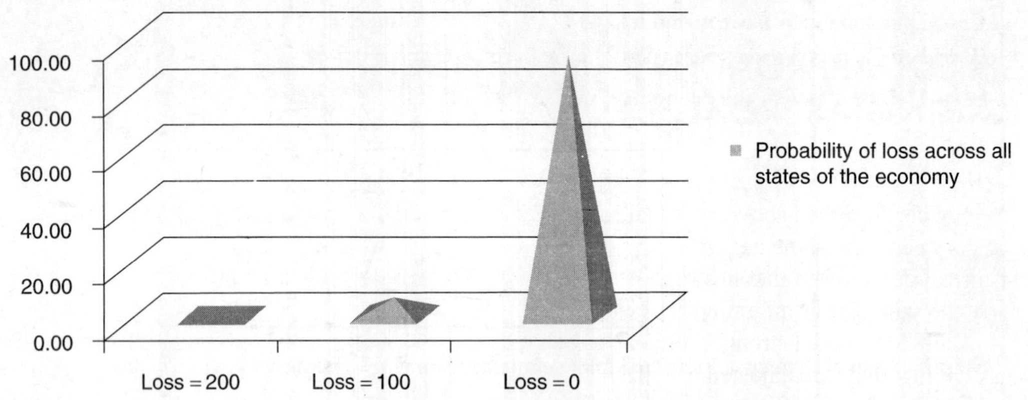

It can be seen from the above simple example that the 'conditional' probability of, say, a ₹200 loss in the growth state of the economy is 0.01 per cent, while, from the above graph the 'unconditional' loss of ₹200 across all states in the economy has a probability of 0.12 per cent.

Thus, ignoring the effect of the economy (systematic risk), it appears that X and Y are correlated. However, if the economic state is considered, the PD of X and Y as well as the joint conditional PD for X and Y is seen to be significantly higher during times of recession than during economic growth. This would imply more correlated defaults during recessionary periods, rather than an overall correlation between defaults of X and Y arising from the presence of both systematic and non-systematic risks.[32]

Therefore, the basic premise of the CPV is that credit migration probabilities show random fluctuations due to the volatility in economic cycles. It also assumes that different 'risk segments' into which borrowers are classified (in the above example, 'X' is a 'risk segment' and so is 'Y', and a bank can classify its borrowers into varying risk segments that could correspond with the 'ratings' given in the migration matrix in the previous example on Credit Metrics) react differently to economic conditions.

If we assume X and Y to be large 'risk segments' of borrowers whose non-systematic risks have been diversified away, then the systematic risks alone have to be considered to arrive at joint default correlations. Though this assumption is made implicitly by other models, this model extends the standard single factor approach to a multi-factor approach to capture country- and industry-specific shocks.

For each 'risk segment', CPV simulates a 'conditional migration matrix' as done in the simple numerical example above. Hence, in the three different 'states of the economy' envisaged in the 'risk horizon' (say, 1 year), the migration matrix will exhibit different characteristics, as in the simple two borrower example above: (1) in the 'growth state', it is likely that there are a lower number of probable downgrades and higher upgrade probabilities; (2) in the 'normal state', the conditional migration matrix is likely to be similar to the 'unconditional migration matrix' derived from historical observations (*i.e.*, similar to the migration matrix shown in the Credit Metrics example); and (3) in the 'recession state', the downgrades are more likely than upgrades. This concept of 'segment-specific risk' for each macro economic scenario gives the CPV flexibility to simulate a 'systematic risk model' with a large number of such scenarios and migration possibilities.

In practice, CPV uses simulation tools, such as 'Monte Carlo' methods to generate a systematic risk model and simulates the conditional default probabilities for each risk segment, using two different methods of 'calibration'[33]—CPV Macro and CPV Direct.

CPV Macro uses a 'macroeconomic regression model' using time series of historical data on macroeconomic factors, as described by Wilson in his papers quoted above.

CPV Direct was developed later to make the calibration easier, and derives default probabilities from a 'gamma distribution'.[34]

Finally, all conditional loss distributions are aggregated to arrive at the unconditional loss distribution for the portfolio. The technical documentation for CPV is not available freely, and will have to be obtained from McKinsey and company.

SECTION III

SELECT APPROACHES AND MODELS—THE OPTION PRICING APPROACH

The KMV[35] Model

The models discussed above have made three critical assumptions: (1) all borrowers included in a specified rating category carry the same default risk, (2) the actual default rate within a rating category would be the same as the historical default rate that has been observed over the years, and (3) all borrowers within each rating category carry the same PD or migration. These assumptions may not be totally valid in real world situations.

The KMV model strongly refutes these assumptions on the following grounds: (1) default rates are continuous, while ratings are adjusted in a discrete fashion by rating agencies; (2) rating agencies take time to upgrade or downgrade borrowers/counter parties, and such credit quality changes would be carried out at some point in time after the default risk is observed.

Further, KMV has demonstrated through simulation exercises that (a) the historical average default rate and transition probabilities can deviate significantly from the actual rates, (b) that substantial differences in default rates may exist within the same rating class, and (c) the overlap in default probability ranges may be quite large. In some cases, the historical default rate could, in reality, overstate the actual PD of a specific borrower. Such inconsistencies may lead to banks overcharging their better borrowers (since the loan pricing depends on the PD), which may endanger their banking relationship, or worse still, benefit riskier borrowers.

The KMV model relates the default probability of a firm to three factors:

The Market Value of the Firm's Assets The Market value is computed as the PV of the future stream of free cash flows that is expected to be generated by the firm. An appropriate 'discount rate'[36] is used to discount the future cash flows and arrive at the PV.

The Risk of the Assets The value computed above is scenario-based and can be impacted by business and other risks in future. The asset values can fluctuate in future, and could be higher or lower than expected. This 'volatility' is asset risk.

Leverage The firm would have to repay all its contracted liabilities. The relative measure of outstanding liabilities (this would typically be taken at book value) to the market value of assets is an indication of 'leverage'.[37]

Why are these three factors important? See Box 9.3 for a simplified explanation.

BOX 9.3 THE MAIN DETERMINANTS OF PROBABILITY OF DEFAULT

Assume a firm with only one asset on its balance sheet—1 crore shares (book value ₹100 crore) of a blue chip company—financed by ₹80 crore of debt due at the end of 1 year, and ₹20 crore of equity.

Over the next 1 year, analysts forecast that one of the two things could happen with equal probability—the market could do well, in which case the value of the investment could rise to ₹150 crore, or the market would do badly, in which case the value of the investment falls by 50 per cent to ₹50 crore. If the first event happens, the firm can pay off its debt of ₹80 crore (ignore interest for the time being) and add ₹70 crore to its equity value. If the market does badly, however, the firm will not have sufficient money to pay off its debt (equity + asset value will be ₹70 crore, while the debt will be ₹ 80 crore), and will default.

In a second scenario, assume the same firm with only ₹40 crore of debt on its balance sheet, ₹60 crore being equity. In this case, the firm would not default even when the investment value falls to ₹50 crore, since the debt can still be paid off. However, only ₹10 crore would be added to equity value.

In a third scenario, if other things remain as in the first scenario, but ₹80 crore of debt can be repaid after 2 years, the firm would not default at the end of the first year even when the market does badly.

We can infer from the above that

- Equity derives its 'value' from the firm's cash flows (determined by the market value of the firm's assets)
- The firm's cash flows (or market value) could fluctuate depending on various factors—this is called 'volatility'
- The lower the book value of liabilities as compared to market value of assets (leverage), the lower the likelihood of default by the firm

We are familiar with the 'book value' of assets and liabilities. Book values are those reflected in a company's financial statements, and the credit analyst uses them to make inferences about the firm's financial health, and also to assess if the cash flows the firm is likely to generate in future would be sufficient to service the debt taken. Present values (using time value of money concept) of future cash flows are arrived at, and compared with the debt – essentially, the asset values of the firm are being compared with its debt values. Though the accounting rules and computation of financial ratios ensure objectivity and comparability of the values, the approach is dependent on past values and trends, which may not be indicative of the firm's future growth prospects.

The market value balance sheet used in the structural credit risk model uses the same financial principle that the robustness of a firm's asset values determines its ability to service debt. However, the approach is more forward looking, as is shown in the following figure sourced from the Moody's Analytics website (Moody's Analytics, June 2012, 'Public Firm Expected Default Frequency (EDFTM) Credit Measures: Methodology, Performance, and Model Extensions' (Modelling Methodology), accessed at www.moodysanalytics.com, Figure 1, page 5)

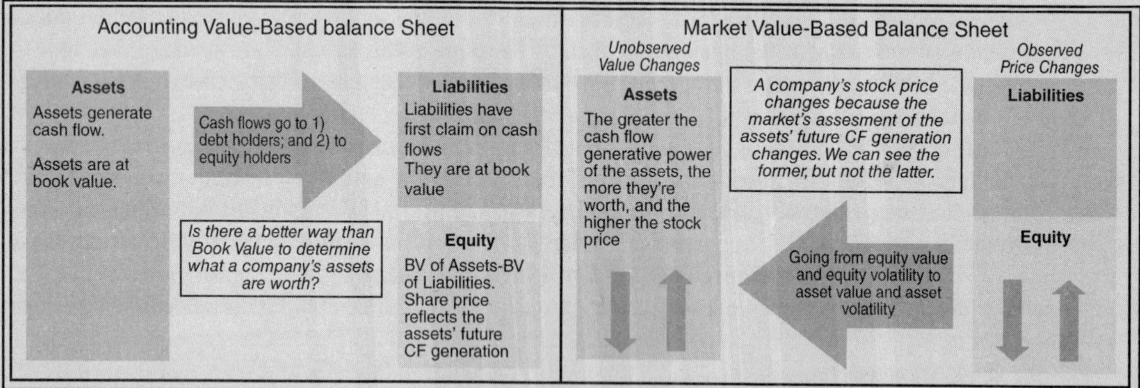

The above quoted paper lists the various advantages of the market value based balance sheet—the consideration of the firm's future prospects, easier updation of the assessment of firm's creditworthiness based on new information, and direct estimation of the economic variables driving a firm's default process such as asset value and asset volatility. However the challenge with the forward looking market value balance sheet is that asset value and asset volatility are not directly observable.

In other words, the lenders to the firm essentially 'own' the firm until the debt is fully paid off by the equity holders. Conversely, equity holders can 'buy' the firm (its assets) from the lenders as and when the debt is repaid. That is, equity holders have the 'right', but not the 'obligation' to pay off the lenders and take over the remaining assets of the firm.

Thus, simply stated, equity is a 'call option'[38] on the firm's assets with a 'strike price' equal to the book value of the firm's debt (liabilities). The value of the equity depends on, among other things, the market value of the firm's assets, their volatility and the payment terms of the liabilities. Implicit in the value of the option is an estimate of the probability of the option being 'exercised'—*i.e.*, for equity, it is the probability of not defaulting on the firm's liability. It is also obvious that the PD would increase if (1) the firm's market value of assets decreases, (2) if the volatility of the assets' market value increases or (3) the firm's liabilities increase. These three variables are therefore the main determinants of a firm's PD.

The approach in Box 9.3 follows one of the major pillars of modern finance—the Merton Model used in quantification of credit risk.

In 1973, Black and Scholes[39] proposed that equity of a firm could be viewed as a call option. This paved the way for a coherent framework in the objective measurement of credit risk. The approach, subsequently developed further by Merton in 1974,[40] Black and Cox in 1976,[41] and others after them, has come to be called 'the Merton model'.

Box 9.4 presents an overview of the 'Merton model'.

BOX 9.4 THE MERTON MODEL

The rationale behind Merton's 'Pricing of corporate debt' is as follows:

We know that a firm's cash flows are paid out to either debt holders (lenders) or equity holders. The lenders have priority over the cash flows till their debt to the firm (along with interest and other fees) is completely serviced. The remaining cash flows are paid to the equity holders.

Assume that the debt L of the firm has to be repaid only at the end of the term T, and there are no intermediate payments. If V is the value of the firm at T, the cash flow D to lenders can be expressed as

$$D = \text{Min}\,(L, V)$$

The remaining cash flows E accrue to equity holders who will receive at T

$$E = \text{Max}\,(V - L, 0)$$

Hence, the firm value at T would be

$$V = D + E = \text{Min}\,(L, V) + \text{Max}\,(V - L, 0).$$

The above implies that equity holders have the option to purchase the firm from lenders by paying the face value of debt L at time T—that is, they can 'exercise' the option to 'call' the firm away from the lenders at the 'strike price' L. In other words, given the firm value at a point in time, we can price its equity using an options pricing method, such as the Black–Scholes formula, in which E depends on the following factors: V the firm value, L the debt value, $T–t$ the time to expiration, r the risk-free rate of interest, and σ the volatility of the underlying asset (the firm).

What is the option that the lenders have? The lenders have taken a risk in lending to the firm. In the event that the firm value falls below the debt value at T, the lenders have a claim on all the assets of the firm. In other words, the lenders have given the firm the 'option' of 'buying' away the assets by repaying the debt, that is, the lenders are 'selling' the assets to the firm. This implies that the cash flow to the lenders is similar to those from a risk-free asset less the 'credit risk' of the firm. This credit risk is similar to a 'put option',[42] and, therefore, can be valued using the option pricing formula.

The classic Merton model (1974) makes use of the Black and Scholes option pricing model (1973—referred above) to value corporate liabilities. In doing so, it makes the following simplifying assumptions:

1. The (publicly traded) firm has a single debt liability and equity. It has no other obligations. Its balance sheet at time T appears as follows:

Liabilities	Assets
Debt L	Market value of Assets A
Equity E	
Total firm value V	Total firm value $V\,(=A)$

   Thus, we would have the equation $V = L + E$ at time T.

2. The firm's debt matures at time T and is due to the lender in a single payment. That is, the debt is 'zero coupon' debt.
3. The firm's assets are tradable and their market value evolves as a lognormal process.[43]
4. The market is 'perfect'—that is, there are no coupon or dividend payments, no taxes, no ban on short sales (selling the assets without owning them); the market is fully liquid, and investors can buy or sell any quantity of assets at market prices; trading in assets takes place continuously in time; borrowing and lending are at the same rate of interest; the conditions under which the Modigliani–Miller theorem[44] of firm value being independent of capital structure are present; the 'term structure'[45] is flat and known with certainty; and importantly, the dynamics for the value of the firm through time can be described through a diffusion-type stochastic process.[46] The last assumption requires that asset price movements are continuous and the asset returns are serially independent.[47]

Merton modelled his firm's asset value as a lognormal process and stated that the firm would default if the market value of the firm's assets, V, fell below a certain default boundary, X. The default could happen only at a specified point in time, T. The equity of the firm is a European call option[48] on the assets of the firm with a strike price equal to the face value of debt. The equity value of the firm at time T would therefore be the higher of the following scenarios: the positive difference between the market value of assets at T and the value of debt, or, if the difference is negative, zero (since the firm would default—see Box 9.3 titled 'Main determinants of PD').

We describe Merton's option pricing model through the following equations

$$E = \max\,(V - L, 0), \text{ at time } T$$

The current equity price is

$$E_0 = V_0 N(d_1) - Le^{-rt} N(d_2)$$

where E_0—Current market value of equity

A_0—Implied value of assets of the firm (= firm value)

$N(d_1)$—Standard Normal Distribution value corresponding to d_1

$N(d_2)$—Standard Normal Distribution value corresponding to d_2

T—Time horizon

L—Debt payable at the end of time horizon T

r—Risk-free rate of return

and

$d_1 = (\ln (V_0/L) + (r + \sigma_V^2/2) \times T)/\sigma_V T^{(1/2)}$

and

$d_2 = d_1 - \sigma_V T^{(1/2)}$

σ_V^2 being the implied variance of asset values (asset volatility)

$$\sigma_E E_0 = \frac{\sigma E}{\sigma V} \sigma_V V_0 = N(d_1) \sigma_V V_0$$

The above equation enables estimation of the firm value V (= market value of assets) and its volatility from the equity value and its volatility.

The 'distance to default' (DD) is given by the value of (d_2)

The PD is 1–the probability of the equity option being exercised. This is given by $N(-d_2)$ or $1 - N(d_2)$. From the lender's point of view, the model throws up the 'value' of debt for every unit change in firm value as $1 - N(d_1)$.

Oldrich Vasicek and Stephen Kealhofer extended the Black–Scholes–Merton framework to produce a model of default probability known as the Vasicek–Kealhofer (VK) model.[49] This model assumes the firm's equity is a perpetual option on the underlying assets of the firm, and accommodates five different types of liabilities—short-term and long-term liabilities, convertible debt, preferred and common equity.

Moody's KMV (MKMV) uses the option pricing framework in the VK model to obtain the market value of a firm's assets and the related asset volatility. The default point[50] term structure (for various risk horizons) is calculated empirically.

What is the 'default point'?

The Merton model assumption that a firm defaults when the market value of assets falls below the book value of its liabilities is modified by Crosbie and Bohn (2002) in their paper—'While some firms certainly default at this point, many continue to trade and service their debts. The long-term nature of some of their liabilities provides these firms with some breathing space. We have found that the *default point*, the asset value at which the firm will default, generally lies somewhere between total liabilities and current, or short-term, liabilities'.[51] Further, the 'market net worth' is assumed as the 'market value of assets less the default point', and a firm is said to default when the market net worth reaches zero.

How Merton's basic options framework is used in the VK Model of KMV is shown in Figure 9.7.

FIGURE 9.7 RELATING MERTON'S MODEL WITH KMV

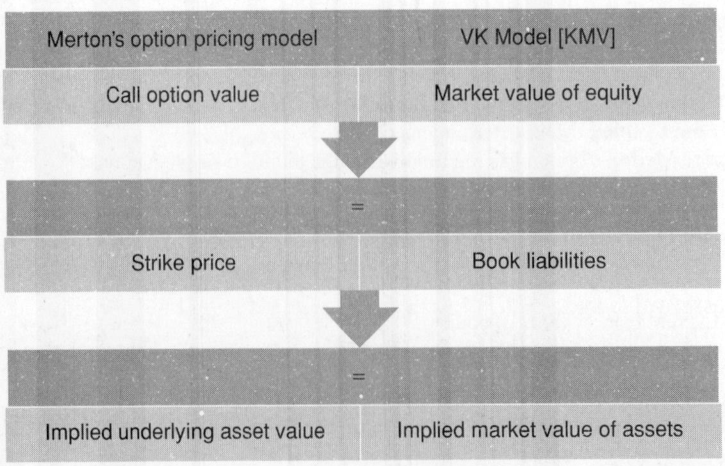

How the Black–Scholes–Merton model differs from the VK model is shown in Table 9.9[52]:

TABLE 9.9 KEY DIFFERENCES BETWEEN THE BSM AND VK MODELS

Black-Scholes-Merton	Vasicek–Kealhofer EDF model
Two classes of liabilities: Short Term Liabilities and Common Stock.	**Five classes of liabilities:** Short Term and Long Term Liabilities, Common Stock, Preferred Stock, and Convertible Stock.
No cash payouts	**Cash payouts:** Coupons and Dividends (Common and Preferred).
Default occurs only **at horizon**.	Default can occur **at or before horizon.**
Default barrier is total **debt**.	Default barrier is **empirically** determined.
Equity is a call option on Assets, **expiring** at the Maturity of the debt.	Equity is a **perpetual** call option on Assets.
Gaussian relationship between probability of default (PD) and distance to default (DD).	DD-to-EDF mapping **empirically** determined from calibration to historical data.

Source: Moody's KMV documents

MKMV combines market value of assets, asset volatility and default point term structure to calculate a DD term structure, which is then translated into a credit measure termed 'expected default frequency' (EDF). The EDF is the PD for the risk horizon (1 year or more for publicly traded firms)—and 'default' is defined by MKMV as the non-payment of any scheduled payment, interest or principal.

While the core methodology of the EDF model has remained consistent over the years,the model has undergone considerable version updates. The current version is 8.0. Table 9.10 shows the differences between the basic structural model described above and the public EDF model (simply, the EDF model) in its current version.

The public EDF model incorporates the two classic drivers of fundamental credit analysis as we have seen in earlier chapters. *Financial risk,* or leverage is measured in terms of the difference between the market value of assets and the book value of liabilities, and *business risk*,is measured by asset volatility—the higher the volatility, the higher the business risk. In addition, the EDF model framework allows for a clear understanding of the consequences of changes in these two primary drivers on a firm's default risk.

TABLE 9.10 KEY DIFFERENCES BETWEEN THE BASIC STRUCTURAL MODEL (BSM MODEL) AND THE CURRENT VERSION OF THE EDF MODEL

Basic Structural Model		Public EDF Model
Two classes of Liabilities: Short Term Liabilities and Common Stock	Theoretical Modification	Five Classes of Liabilities: Short Term and Long Term Liabilities, Common Stock, Preferred Stock, and Convertible Stock
No Cash Payouts		Cash Payouts: Coupons and Dividends (Common and Preferred)
Default occurs only at the horizon date		Default can occur any time
Default point is total debt	Empirical Advances	Default point is empirically determined
Estimation method of asset values and asset volatilities is not specified		Proprietary numerical routine to estimate asset value and asset volatility
Gaussian relationship between probability of default (PD) and distance to default (DD)		DD-to-EDF mapping empirically determined from calibration to historical data

Source: Moody's Analytics, June 2012, 'Public Firm Expected Default Frequency (EDFTM) Credit Measures: Methodology, Performance, and Model Extensions' (Modelling Methodology), Figure 6, page 10.

The procedure adopted by MKMV[53] for calculating the PD of a public firm can be described in the following three steps:

1. Estimate asset value and volatility from the market value and the volatility of equity and the book value of liabilities. This is done using the option nature of equity, as given in the Merton model in Box 9.4 The Market value of equity is observed and the market value of the firm (assets) is derived from it. The model solves the following two relationships[54] simultaneously:

$$\begin{bmatrix}\text{Equity}\\ \text{Value}\end{bmatrix} = \textit{Option Funtion}\left(\begin{bmatrix}\text{Asset}\\ \text{Value}\end{bmatrix}, \begin{bmatrix}\text{Asset}\\ \text{Volatility}\end{bmatrix}, \begin{bmatrix}\text{Capital}\\ \text{Structure}\end{bmatrix}, \begin{bmatrix}\text{Interest}\\ \text{Rate}\end{bmatrix}\right)$$

$$\begin{bmatrix}\text{Equity}\\ \text{Volatility}\end{bmatrix} = \textit{Option Funtion}\left(\begin{bmatrix}\text{Asset}\\ \text{Value}\end{bmatrix}, \begin{bmatrix}\text{Asset}\\ \text{Volatility}\end{bmatrix}, \begin{bmatrix}\text{Capital}\\ \text{Structure}\end{bmatrix}, \begin{bmatrix}\text{Interest}\\ \text{Rate}\end{bmatrix}\right)$$

The model solves for 'asset value' and 'asset volatility' based on the observed inputs of equity value and volatility and the capital structure. The 'interest rate' used in this model would be the 'risk-free' rate (option pricing theory).

2. Calculate the DD as = (market value of assets – default point)/(market value of assets × asset volatility)

   The numerator reinforces the fact that if the market value of assets falls below the default point, the firm defaults. Hence, the PD is the probability that this event happens.

   If the future distribution of the DD were known (over the relevant risk horizon), the default probability—called the expected default frequency (EDF)—would be the likelihood of the final asset value falling below the default point.

   In practice, however, it is difficult to accurately measure the DD distribution. MKMV uses the fact that defaults occur either due to large adverse changes in market value of assets or changes in the firm's leverage, or a correlation of these two factors, and measures DD as the number of standard deviations the asset value is away from default, and then uses empirical data to determine the corresponding PD.

   This process is pictorially depicted in MKMV documents[55] in figure 9.8.

   a. The current asset value.
   b. The distribution of the asset value at time *H*.
   c. The volatility of the future assets value at time *H*.
   d. The level of the default point, the book value of the liabilities.
   e. The expected rate of growth in the asset value over the horizon.
   f. The length of the horizon, *H*.

FIGURE 9.8 PROCEDURE ADOPTED BY MKMV FOR CALCULATING THE PD OF A FIRM

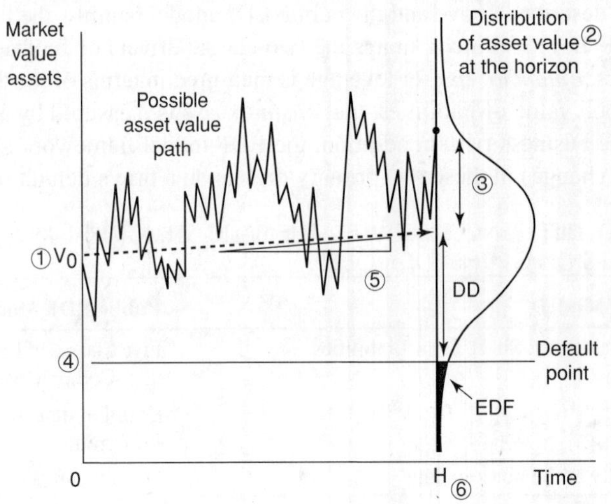

Source: Moody's KMV documents

3. Calculate the default probability

   As stated in the earlier paragraph, default probability is empirically determined from data on historical default and bankruptcy frequencies.

   Summarizing, the calculations for EDF are done in Table 9.11 using the relevant variables shown in step 2:

TABLE 9.11 CALCULATIONS FOR EDF USING THE RELEVANT VARIABLES

Sl. No.	Variable Description	How Calculated
a.	Market value of equity	Current value = current share price × no. of shares outstanding.
b.	Book value of liabilities	From the firm's balance sheet
c.	Default point	Liabilities payable within the risk horizon, say 1 year. KMV also computes a 'critical threshold' set as the aggregate of the firm's short-term debt and half of long-term debt value
d.	Market value of assets	Using the option pricing model
e.	Asset volatility	Using the option pricing model
f.	DD	[(d) – (c)]/(d × e)

Note: The asset growth rate has been ignored in this summary
Source: MKMV documents

The final step is to map the DD to actual probabilities of default over the determined risk horizon. These are the EDFs, which are calculated from a large sample of firms including those that defaulted. Based on this historical information, the model estimates, for each time horizon, the proportion of firms with say DD = 4 that actually defaulted after, say, 1 year. If this proportion were, say, 0.33 per cent,[56] it is taken to be the EDF of 33 bps. This PD is then assigned an implied rating by the model.

Improvements Made to the Basic Structural Model in the Current Version EDF8.0[57]

While the steps to calculating the PD remain as given above in the basic version, the current version has made improvements in the process to reflect a more realistic estimate of credit risk. The improvements are summarized below:

1. **Definition of default:**
   a. The basic structural models defined 'default' as the 'non payment of any scheduled payment, interest or principal. However, this is a static definition of default. In practice, identifying events of default can be challenging, and defaults vary in severity across different types of credit events. The range of credit events covered by the default definition would therefore have a direct impact on the credit risk model's estimation capability.
   b. In the current version of the EDF model, the range of credit events are considered defaults are (a) missed payments, (b) bankruptcy (as defined by local law), administration, receivership, or legal equivalent, (c) distressed debt restructuring, and (d) government bailoouts enacted to prevent a credit event.
2. **Estimation of asset value and volatility from equity value and volatility:**
   a. The basic structural model assumes a simplistic relationship between equity volatility and asset volatility.
   b. However, in practice, it was observed that application of the assumptions of the basic model showed asset volatility estimates to be much greater than actual empirical observations. Since unrealistic asset volatilities would distort PD estimates as well, a number of restrictive assumptions used by the basic model were relaxed, as depicted in Table 9.10 (showing the key differences between the current approach and the basic approach).
   c. For example, the unrealistic assumption that default can occur only at maturity was replaced by the assumption that default can occur at any time before maturity. While this assumption substantially increased the complexity of the theoretical relationship relating equity and asset values, it led to improvement in the model's ability to identify default risk. Similarly, the existence of several classes of liabilities was modelled, as well as the possibility of cash leakage over time in the form of dividend payments, coupons on bonds or interest on loans.
   d. The current EDF model employs a proprietary numerical procedure to incorporate both firm specific asset return information (for empirical volatility estimation), and information from comparable firms (for modelled volatility estimation). The two volatility estimates are combined to produce the total asset volatility measure used in the current version of the model. An iterative process is followed. Once the asset volatility is estimated and validated, the asset return equation in the basic model serves as the basis for obtaining asset returns. A detailed description of the methodology followed can be found in the quoted paper on the Moody's Analytics website, www.moodysanalytics.com
3. **Calculating the Default Point:**
   a. In the basic structural model, the determination of the default point is straightforward—it is simply the face value of a zero-coupon bond (assumed to be the only liability of the firm) whose maturity is the same as the default horizon.
   b. In practice, firms' liabilities are often comprised of multiple classes of debt with various maturities. This also means that the same amount of total liabilities for two otherwise identical firms may have different required debt payments for a given time horizon. So the default point is a function of both the prediction horizon and the maturity structure of liabilities. Further, the default point is dependent on the definition of default (see point 1 above). Additionally, there are balance sheet items that are included in a firm's stated liabilities, but that do not have the potential to force it into bankruptcy. Examples include deferred taxes and minority interests. Estimating default point realistically leads to the realistic estimation of the Distance to Default (DD), which in turn, maps to the PD estimation.
   c. The current version of the model therefore attempted empirical methods to reconcile the practical issues. In practice, it was observed that large firms do not always default when their asset values fall below their liability values, since they managed to survive through alternate sources of funding. In other cases, observations showed that some firms defaulted even when they could not service their short term liabilities. Hence the model proposed two algorithms—one for financial firms and the other for non financial firms.

d. For non-financial firms, the default point for a one-year time horizon is set at 100 per cent of short-term liabilities plus one-half of long-term liabilities (as in the earlier version).

e. For financial firms, it is more difficult to differentiate between long-term and short-term liabilities. As a consequence, the approach used in the EDF model is to specify the default point as a percent of total adjusted liabilities. This percentage differs by subsector (*e.g.*, commercial banks, investment banks, and non-bank financial institutions).

4. **Distance to default:**

As in the basic structural model given above, DD is calculated as = [Market value of assets – Default point]/[Market value of assets × asset volatility]

5. **DD to EDF mapping:**

a. The EDF model constructs the DD to PD mapping based on the empirical relationship (relationship evidenced by historical data) between DDs and observed default rates. The default database is maintained by Moody's Analytics.

b. The process for converting DD to EDF begins with the construction of a calibration sample (of large sample of corporate firms), and then grouping the sample into buckets according to firms' DD levels and fitting a nonlinear function to the relationship between DDs and observed default frequencies for each bucket. The EDF model produces not just a one-year horizon EDF for each firm, but also a term structure of EDF measures at horizons of up to ten years.

c. An additional feature of the current version of the model is that it accommodates the existence of 'jumps-to-default'. These are changes in asset values during a short time window, or due to unexpected events, such as corporate fraud or collapse of the business environment.

6. **EDF Measures:**

EDF metrics range from 1 basis point to 35 per cent. The interpretation of EDF measures is as given earlier.

7. **EDF term structures**:

Default probabilities over a longer period in time are necessary for pricing, hedging and risk management of long term obligations. In particular, portfolio models of credit risk, such as Moody's Analytics' Risk Frontier platform, require term structures of PDs as key inputs for the valuation of long-dated credit portfolios. The EDF model described above produces not just a one-year horizon EDF for each firm, but also a term structure of EDF measures at horizons of up to ten years. To build the EDF term structure, the starting point is the DD term structure. Instead of calibrating a separate DD-to-EDF mapping for each time horizon, the EDF model employs a credit migration based approach to build the EDF term structure. The DD transition function is evolved using empirical procedures.

8. **Model extensions:** Over the past two years three new EDF variants have been introduced to help manage differing risk variants, namely, CDS-implied EDFs, Through-the-Cycle EDFs, and Stressed EDFs. Brief descriptions of the methodologies behind these metrics are provided in Appendix A of the cited paper on Moody's Analytics website. Moody's Analytics also produces EDFs for private firms, *i.e.*, for entities without traded equity. These are delivered via the RiskCalc platform. Public EDFs (described in detail above) is also delivered on a variety of platforms—web platform, CreditEdge®, and through a daily Data File Service (DFS), an XML interface, and an Excel add-in is also being proposed.

What do the EDF measures indicate?

- EDF measures are not credit scores. They are actual probabilities.
- If a firm has a current EDF credit measure of 3 per cent, it implies that there is a 3 per cent probability of the firm defaulting over the next 12 months.
- That is, out of 100 firms with an EDF of 3 per cent, we can expect, on an average, three firms to default over the next 12 months.
- Further, a firm with 3 per cent EDF measure is 10 times more likely to default than a firm with 0.3 per cent EDF measure.

The above model is suitable for a publicly listed firm, where market value of equity would be readily available to estimate asset prices. If the firm is a private firm, whose market value of equity is not readily available, *KMV's private firm model* requires the following additional steps to precede estimation of the firm's DD:

Step 1 Calculate the Earnings before interest, taxes, depreciation and amortization (EBITDA) for the private firm P in industry I.

Step 2 Divide the industry average market value of equity by the average industry EBITDA. This yields the average 'equity multiple' for the industry.

Step 3 Multiply the average industry equity multiple from Step 2 by the private firm's EBITDA. This gives an estimate of the private firm's market value of equity.

Step 4 The private firm's asset value can now be calculated as the market value of equity (Step 3) + the firm's book value of debt.

From this point onwards, the calculation of EDF can proceed as for a public firm.

SECTION IV

SELECT APPROACHES AND MODELS—THE ACTUARIAL APPROACH

Credit Risk+™ Model

This model follows the typical insurance mathematics approach, which is why it is called the 'actuarial model'.

The insurance industry widely applies mathematical techniques to model 'sudden' events of default by the insured. This approach contrasts with the prevalent mathematical techniques used in financial modelling, which is typically concerned with modelling continuous price changes rather than 'sudden events'.

How does the actuarial model differ from other models outlined above—say, the Credit Metrics model, based on the credit migration approach?

In the credit migration approach, credit events (such as default or downgrade) are driven by movements in unobserved 'latent variables', which in turn give rise to 'risk factors'. In a credit portfolio, correlations in credit events occur since different borrowers/counter parties depend on the same risk factors. In the actuarial approach, on the other hand, it is assumed that each borrower has a 'default probability', but no latent variables. This PD changes in response to macroeconomic factors. If two borrowers are sensitive to the same set of macroeconomic factors, their default probabilities change together, which in turn, give rise to 'default correlations'.

Credit Risk+ has been developed based on the actuarial approach (insurance modelling techniques) by Credit Suisse Financial Products (CSFP).[58] In this model, only default risk is modelled, not downgrade risk. The model makes no assumptions about the causes of default. Each borrower/counter party can assume only one of two 'states' at the end of the risk horizon, say, 1 year— 'default' (0) or 'no default (1). The basic model setting is outlined in Box 9.5.

BOX 9.5 THE BASIC MODEL SETTING OF THE ACTUARIAL APPROACH IN CREDIT RISK+

1. Assume a portfolio of N borrowers where $n = 1,\ldots, N$, where the exposure to borrower n is E and the PD of borrower n is p_n.
2. Default of borrower n is represented by a 'Bernoulli'[59] random variable D_n such that at the end of the risk horizon, say, 1 year, the PD $P(D_n = 1) = p_n$ and the probability of 'survival' (no default) $P(D_n = 0) = 1 - p_n$.
3. If E_n is the exposure of the bank to borrower n, the total loss of the portfolio at the end of the year is given by

$$L = \sum_{n=1}^{N} En\ Dn$$

4. The objective is to determine the probability distribution of L under various sets of assumptions. Knowing the probability distribution of L will enable computing *VaR* and other risk measures for this portfolio.
5. There are two assumptions made under this model :
   a. For a loan or borrower or counter party, the PD during 1 year (the risk horizon) is the same as the PD for any other year; and
   b. Given a large number of borrowers/counter parties, the PD of any one borrower is small, and the number of defalts that occur during any 1 year is independent of the number of defaults that occur during (N) any other year.
6. The probability distribution for the number of defaults during 1 year is then modelled as a Poisson distribution.[60] The probability of realizing n default events in the portfolio in 1 year is given by the expression [61]

$$P[n\ defaults] = \frac{e^{-m}\mu}{n!}$$

where $n = 0,1,2,\ldots$, is a stochastic variable with mean μ and standard deviation$\sqrt{\mu}$

μ = average [expected] number of defaults per year. For example, if $\mu = 4$, over the next one 1 year,

$$P\ (0\ \text{defaults}) = \frac{e^{-4}4^0}{0!} = (0.018316 \times 1)/1 = 0.018 = 1.8\ \text{per cent,}$$

And

$$P\ (3\ \text{defaults}) \frac{e^{-4}4^3}{0!} = (0.018316 \times 64)/6 = 0.195 = 19.5\ \text{per cent,}$$

7. It can be noted from the above equation that the distribution has only one parameter, μ. The distribution does not depend on the number of exposures in the portfolio, or the individual probabilities of default, provided these probabilities are uniformly small.

Credit Risk+ models credit risk in two stages as shown in Figure 9.10. This approach is typically used in evaluating losses originated in insurance portfolios. The cumulative average EL is arrived at using the loss frequency average and the loss severity average. However, for a dynamic analysis of risks, it is necessary to quantify loss variability by computing the distribution of cumulative losses that would combine the effects of frequency and severity of losses.

Applied to a credit portfolio, the concepts are understood as follows:

a. Frequency—the number of defaults in a portfolio over the risk horizon (typically 1 year), and
b. Severity—the amount, in currency units, of each individual default, that is, the LGD.

FIGURE 9.10 CREDIT RISK+ STAGES IN MODELLING CREDIT RISK

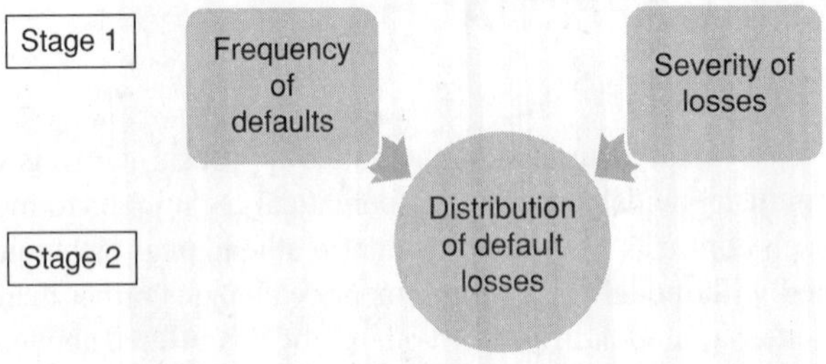

We will describe these processes briefly.

Stage 1 a. **Frequency of defaults:** There are two important inputs to estimate the frequency of defaults—the average (expected) default rates, and the volatility (standard deviation) of defaults. Since we have assumed that a standard Poisson distribution can be used to estimate the distribution of the number of defaults, it follows that the volatility (standard deviation) of the number of defaults would approximate to $\sqrt{\mu}$, where μ is the expected (average) default rate. However, this may not hold true in practice, since the default volatility changes over time, depending on business cycles and other factors, and the expected default rate would also change over time. In such a case, would the Poisson distribution still represent the default process? Yes, if we assume that the mean default rate is 'stochastic' with mean μ and standard deviation σ and that the mean default rate is 'gamma distributed'. (Please see our discussion on the KMV model for a brief definition of a gamma distribution).

b. **Severity of the losses:** This is given by the 'LGD'—the 'exposure' of the bank to the borrower, adjusted by the anticipated 'RR'.

c. **Distribution of default losses for a portfolio:** The model calculates the loss distribution under two scenarios, as shown in Figure 9.11.

FIGURE 9.11 LOSS DISTRIBUTIONS GENERATED BY CREDIT RISK+[62]

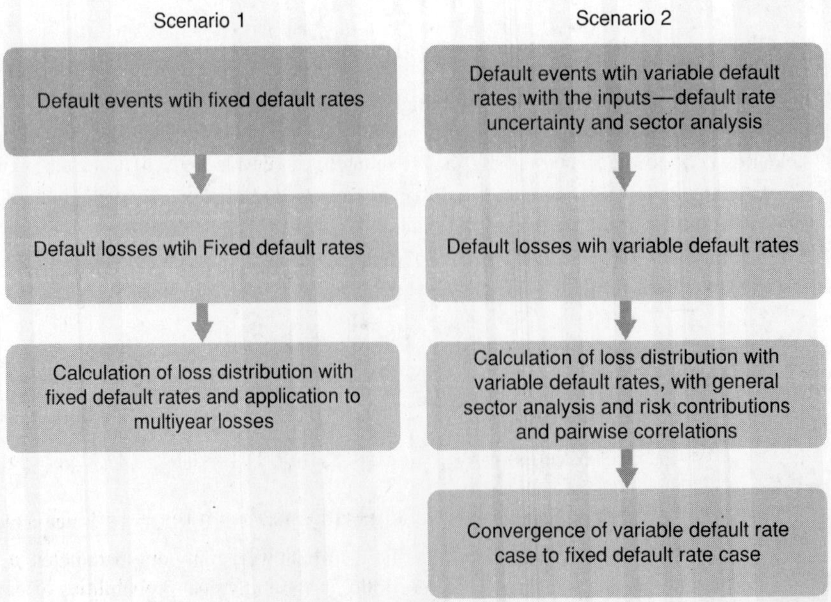

Box 9.6 summarizes the process and notations used by the model in arriving at the loss distributions.

BOX 9.6 PROCESS AND NOTATIONS USED IN CREDIT RISK+

Scenario 1
Default losses with fixed default rates

Step 1 Slotting exposures into independent 'bands'

Reference	Symbol
Obligor/borrower	A
Exposure	L_A
PD	P_A
Expected loss	λ_A

L is chosen as the base currency unit (*e.g.*, ₹ in lakh, \$1,00,000, etc.), such that for every borrower,

$$L_A = L \times v_A, \text{ and } \varepsilon_A = L \times \varepsilon_A$$

Where v_A and ε_A are the exposure and EL, respectively, of the borrower.
Each exposure v_A is then rounded off to the nearest whole number.
Thus, the portfolio gets divided into 'm' exposure bands, with $1 \leq j \leq m$.

Step 2 Calculating the expected number of defaults in each band
The following additional definitions are made:

Reference	Symbol
Portfolio exposure in band j in units of L	vj
EL in band j in units of L	ε_j
Expected number of defaults (mean) in band j	μ_j

The above implies that

$$\text{Expected loss } \varepsilon_j = v_j \times \mu_j \text{ and } \mu_j = \varepsilon_j / v_j$$

If μ is the total expected number of default events in a portfolio in 1 year (the risk horizon), then μ should be the sum of expected number of default events in each exposure band. That is,

$$\mu = \sum_{j=1}^{m} \mu_j = \sum_{j=1}^{m} \frac{\varepsilon_j}{v_j}$$

Step 3 To derive the loss distribution, calculate the Probability Generating function[63] (PGF) for each band, and then for the portfolio.

Step 3A Calculate the PGF for each band, j. This is done using equation (2) of the Credit Risk + technical document (Appendix A, page 34), where the PGF is defined in terms of an auxiliary variable z by[64]

$$F(z) = \sum_{n=0}^{\infty} p(n \text{ defaults}) z^n$$

Since the probability of n defaults is assumed to be a Poisson distribution, we can substitute this with the expression in item 6, Box 9.6. Hence,

$$F(z) = \sum_{n=0}^{\infty} \left(\frac{e^{-m} \mu^n}{n!} \right) z^n \quad \text{For each band '}j\text{'}$$

Step 3B Calculate the PGF for the entire portfolio. Since each band j is assumed to be a portfolio of exposures, independent from the other bands, the PGF of the entire portfolio is just a product of the PGFs of each band.

Step 3C Calculate the Loss distribution of the entire portfolio. The Credit Risk+ document (equation 25, page 38) derives the following formula:

$A_n = \sum_{j.v_j \leq n} \frac{\varepsilon_j}{n} A_{n-v_j}$, where A_n is the probability of loss of 'n' units of the portfolio. It should be noted here that the calculation depends only on knowledge of ε and v.

The above initial model, in which loss distribution has been calculated over a 1 year horizon, can be extended to multi-year periods by building a term structure of default for the portfolio. To achieve this, marginal rates of default must be specified for each future year in the portfolio, for each borrower. It can be seen from the

Credit Risk+ document (Equations 36, 37, page 40) that the PGF and the loss distribution have the same form as in the single year model described here.

Scenario 2
This scenario assumes variable default rates. The variability in default rates is assumed to result from 'background factors', each representing a sector of activity. The sectors are assumed to be independent. To arrive at the loss distribution in such cases, a 'Mixed Poisson' process is used.

Simply stated, the 'Mixed Poisson' is a two stage process—in the first stage, the external factor controlling the default is drawn from a 'gamma' distribution function, and in the second stage, the severity of this external factor is obtained from a conditional distribution that is assumed to be Poisson distributed. The 'Mixed Poisson' process is also called a 'Negative Binomial' distribution with μ and σ as its mean and standard deviation, respectively.

The 'gamma distribution' is a skew distribution that approximates to the Normal distribution when the mean is large. This continuous probability distribution that has two parameters—a scale and a shape parameter—called α and β. It is fully described by its mean μ and standard deviation σ such that $\mu = \alpha\beta$ and $\sigma^2 = \alpha\beta^2$. Hence, for every sector 'k', the parameters of the related gamma distribution are given by

$$\alpha = \frac{\mu_k^2}{\sigma_k^2} \quad \text{and} \quad \beta_k = \frac{\sigma_k^2}{\mu_k^2}$$

In this scenario, the portfolio is divided into n sectors with annual mean default rates following a gamma distribution defined by α and β as defined above. The PGF for each sector is given by the equation:

$$F(z) = \left[\frac{1 - p_k}{1 - p_{k(z)}}\right]^{\alpha_k}, \qquad \text{where} \qquad p_k = \frac{\beta_k}{1 + \beta_k}$$

This can be summed up to the PGF for n sectors, as in Equation 59 (in page 46) of the Credit Risk + document.

The loss distribution is then obtained as described in the Credit Risk + technical document, Section A10.

Source: Credit Risk + Technical Document, 1997.

A simple numerical example in Illustration 9.3 explains the calculation of loss distribution under Scenario 1.

ILLUSTRATION 9.3 CALCULATING THE LOSS DISTRIBUTION WITH FIXED DEFAULT RATES

A bank holds a portfolio of loans with 1000 different borrowers.

For simplicity, we will assume that the exposures fall between ₹50,000 and ₹10 lakh.

Scenario 1
Default Losses with Fixed Default Rates.

Step 1 Slotting Loans into Independent Bands.
We will consider, below, the first six borrowers.

Borrower	Actual Exposure in ₹ Lakh	Exposure in Units of ₹ 1 Lakh	Band
1	1.4	2	2
2	2.65	3	3
3	4.5	5	5
4	5.6	6	6
5	1.2	2	2
6	4.3	5	5

Step 2 Calculating the Expected Number of Defaults in Each Band.
Borrowers in each band are aggregated.
In Credit Risk + each band is viewed as an independent portfolio of loans.
Consider the hypothetical grouping of borrowers in various bands.

Band	Number of Borrowers	ε_j	μ_j
1	30	1.5	1.5
2	40	8	4
3	50	6	2
4	70	25.2	6.3
5	100	35	7
6	60	14.4	2.4
7	50	38.5	5.5
8	40	19.2	2.4
9	40	25.2	2.8
10	20	4	0.4

The loss distributions are then modelled using steps 3A, 3B and 3C outlined above.

Appendix B of the Credit Risk+ document (1997) provides an illustrative spreadsheet-based example.

SECTION V

SELECT APPROACHES AND MODELS—THE REDUCED FORM APPROACH

We have seen in the foregoing sections that two distinct classes of credit models exist—structural and reduced form.

The structural models discussed in the earlier sections focus on the borrower's/firm's fundamental financial variables—assets and liabilities—and link these to the PD. Since we assume complete knowledge of information related to the financial variables (from the firm's balance sheet), given the firm's capital structure, and having specified the stochastic process that drives the firm's asset value (assuming that the market value of the firm is the fundamental source of uncertainty that drives credit risk), the PD for any time horizon (1 year, 2 years, etc.) can be calculated. This implies that a firm's time of default is predictable. Further, Merton's model predicts default by allowing a gradual diffusion of asset values to the 'default point'—the level of debt (see Section III—the KMV model). Such a process would imply that the PD becomes almost zero as the debt approaches maturity—an assumption that may not be true in the real world.

In contrast, 'reduced-form' models assume 'default' to be an unexpected, sudden event (hence, unpredictable or inaccessible), and assume no explicit relationship between default and firm value. The models basically use the market prices of the firm's default-prone instruments, such as bonds or credit default swaps (CDS) to extract default probabilities. Thus they rely solely on market information to determine the firm's credit risk structure, which is much less detailed or complete (compared to the information available from the firm's financial statements). Since there is no observable link between the firm's credit risk and its financial situation, the firm's default time becomes 'inaccessible'.

The key difference therefore, between structural and reduced-form models, is in the 'information' available to model credit risk. While 'defaults' are specified 'endogenously' (the credit quality being determined by the assets and liabilities of the firm) in structural models, defaults are modelled exogenously from market data in the reduced-form approach. Another difference is in the treatment of RRs—structural models specify RRs based on the value of assets and liabilities within the firm, while reduced-form models look to the market to specify RRs.

Reduced-form models are also called 'intensity' models since the input for the models is the intensity of the random time of default within the risk horizon being considered. In practice, the 'intensity' of default can be inferred through observed prices of bonds. 'Default time' is assumed such that default occurs in a time interval $(0, T)$, where T is the risk horizon (as assumed in the structural models in the previous sections). The default time is driven by an intensity process that is stochastic in nature. These intensity processes define default events, or more generally, credit transitions (as in the structural models), but are directly calibrated to market prices. Though the terms 'reduced form' and 'intensity' models are used interchangeably, they are in fact two approaches based on the type of information required.

Reduced-form models go back to Artzner and Delbaen (1995),[65] Jarrow and Turnbull (1995)[66] and Duffie and Singleton (1999).[67] The earliest models dealt with just two credit states—default and no-default. Subsequently, various researchers extended the approach to the case of multiple, discrete credit states or ratings, leading to 'ratings-based' reduced-form models. The model was further extended to allow for stochastic credit 'spreads' (the indicator of credit risk), which were assumed to arise when the underlying default probabilities (intensities) and/or the RRs were stochastic. The theory underlying intensity models is mathematically complex, and will not be explained in this section.[68]

However, Box 9.7 sets out the basic mathematical premises on which the reduced-form approaches work.

BOX 9.7 BASIC MATHEMATICAL PREMISES OF REDUCED-FORM MODELS

There is no model definition of default in the reduced-form approach. If t, the random default time lies in the time interval (0, T), where T is the risk horizon, in the simplest case, the default process $N_T = \begin{pmatrix} 1, \textit{if } t \leq T \\ 0, \textit{if no default} \end{pmatrix}$. This is called a 'point process' with one 'jump' of size '1' at default. (Contrast this with the Merton structural model where there is a gradual fall—'diffusion'—in asset values to the 'default point'—the debt level).

Typically, reduced-form models characterize default as a Poisson process stopping at the 'first jump'. The corresponding 'default time'—called 'stopping time'—is usually totally unpredictable ('inaccessible') implying non-zero credit 'spreads' for short maturity debt. Defaults are assumed to occur randomly with a probability determined by the 'intensity' or 'hazard' function. From this viewpoint, the intensity model can be considered a time continuous extension of the actuarial framework embodied by Credit Risk+ introduced in the previous section.

The model works by decomposing observed 'credit spreads' on 'risky' debt (debt prone to default) to ascertain the PD and the LGD. This PD is a cumulative, conditional probability—conditional on there being no default before time t. Hence the observed credit spread can be expressed as follows:

$$CS = PD \times LGD,$$

where CS is the credit spread (calculated as the risky debt yield minus the risk-free rate),
PD is the probability of default, and
LGD is the Loss given default equal to 1—RR.

Intensity models, therefore, are basically empirical, since they use observable prices of risky debt (and therefore credit spreads).

The differences in the various reduced-form models arise from the assumptions made for calculating PD and LGD. In one of the earliest forms of the approach, Jarrow and Turnbull (1995) infer that the EL over a time period t would be the product of the conditional PD and the RR under the equivalent martingale (the risk neutral measure).[69] They assumed that the RR was a known fraction of the value at maturity of the debt. The other well known paper by Duffie and Singleton (1998) assumed that the RR was a known fraction of the value of debt just prior to default, while in their 1999 paper they modelled both PD and LGD as a function of economic state variables. Madan and Unal (1998)[70] and Unal et al. (2001) model different RRs on senior and junior debt.

The model developed by Jarrow, Lando and Turnbull in 1997[71] incorporates probabilities of rating transitions into the process. This can be viewed as a special case of the credit migration approach described earlier.

Kamakura Risk Manager Version 8.0 and Kamakura Public Firm Models Version 5.0[72]

Founded in 1990, with Dr. Robert Jarrow (who pioneered the reduced-form approach) as its Managing Director of Research, Kamakura Corporation (headquartered in Honolulu, Hawaii), provides daily default probabilities and default correlations for listed companies, as well as pricing services for collateralized debt obligations (CDO). The service is called KRIS—Kamakura Risk Information Services.

Kamakura's Public Firm Models currently offer four different quantitative approaches to modelling default probabilities: two versions of the Jarrow–Chava Model[73] (current version 5), the Merton Structural Model and the Jarrow—Merton Hybrid Model

A Brief Description of the Approaches Follows[74]

The Jarrow Chava Model

The Jarrow Chava Model is a statistical hazard model that relates the probability of firm default to several explanatory variables that include firm financial ratios, other firm attributes, industry classification, interest rates and information about firm and market equity price levels and behavior. In this model, firm default can occur randomly at any time with an intensity determined by the explanatory variables. The model was originally developed by Kamakura's Director of Research, Robert Jarrow. Both the fourth and fifth generation Jarrow-Chava models incorporate multiple equations for forecasting default at different forward time intervals, conditional on survival to that point in time.The current and forward conditional default probabilities are combined to derive the full default term structure out to five years.

Merton Structural Model

We have learnt in Section II of this chapter about The Merton Structural Model that uses option pricing methods to relate the probability of firm default to its financial structure and information about the firm's market price of equity.

Jarrow Merton Hybrid Model

The Jarrow Merton Hybrid Model is a statistical hazard model that relates the probability of firm default to the same explanatory variables as the Jarrow Chava Model, but it also incorporates the default probability of the Merton Structural Model as an additional explanatory variable. In this model, firm default can occur randomly at any time with an intensity determined by the explanatory variables.

Which Model is Better—Structured or Reduced Form?

Specific inputs required for structural models

a. Firm's asset value process
b. Firm's capital structure
c. LGD
d. Terms and conditions of debt issue

Specific inputs required for reduced-form models

a. Firm's default process (bankruptcy process)
b. LGD specified as a stochastic process

Common inputs required for both models

a. Risk-free interest rate process
b. Correlation between risk-free interest rates and asset prices

Thus it can be seen that the solutions/inferences from the models depend on the assumptions, restrictions and different techniques for calibration and solution.

It has, therefore, been claimed by Jarrow and Protter (2004)[75] that these models are not disconnected or disjoint model types as is typically assumed. The two types of models, in fact, are really the same model containing different informational assumptions. If information available to the modeller/bank is partial or incomplete, a structural model with default being a predictable 'stopping time' becomes a reduced-form model with default time being unpredictable.

To explain the concept further, we know from the Merton's model that default occurs when the value of the firm falls below a threshold level L. Once the firm defaults, it is assumed that it cannot recover. If we assume that the default barrier is constant (though it can be stochastic), then default occurs at time t, the stopping time, which is predictable. However, in reality, the firm value cannot be monitored continuously, nor is the value observable. Hence, information is not 'complete'. Even assuming we are able to observe asset values at discrete intervals, there is a likelihood of default occurring between two observations, quite unexpectedly. This implies that the predictable default time t has now become unpredictable. Therefore, the structural model, due to lack of partial information, has taken the form of an intensity-based, reduced-form model.

Hence, the purpose for which the model is to be used determines which model is more appropriate. Jarrow and Protter sum up thus: 'If one is using the model for risk management purposes—pricing and hedging—then the reduced-form perspective is the correct one to take.

Prices are determined by the market, and the market equilibrates based on the information that it has available to make its decisions. In mark-to-market (MTM) or judging market risk, reduced-form models are the preferred modelling methodology. Instead, if one represents the management within a firm, judging its own firm's default risk for capital considerations, then a structural model may be preferred. However, this is not the approach one wants to take for pricing a firm's risky debt or related credit derivatives'.[76]

SECTION VI

PRICING CREDIT DERIVATIVES

The previous chapter introduced some types of credit derivatives. Though there are several types, credit derivatives typically fall into three discernible classes, and structuring more complex derivatives can be achieved through a combination of the basic features.

FIGURE 9.12 MAJOR CLASSES OF CREDIT DERIVATIVES

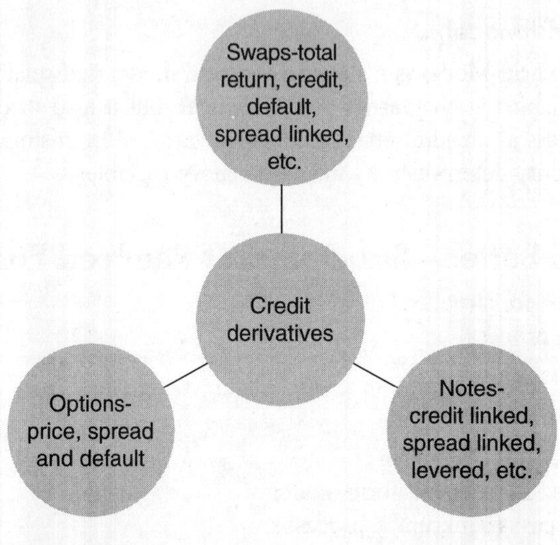

However, we have seen that the most popular is the CDS. We will therefore understand the pricing of CDS, an 'unfunded' credit derivative that works more like an insurance contract.

Pricing Credit Default Swaps—Understanding the Cash Flows

Understanding the valuation of a single entity (plain vanilla) CDS would provide insights into valuing variations of the CDS, such as binary CDS (where the payoff in the event of default is a specific amount), basket CDS (where more than one reference asset is specified, and the payoff happens when the first reference asset defaults), contingent CDS (where the payoff specifies a credit event as well as an additional trigger) or dynamic CDS (where the notional payoff is linked to a MTM value of a swap portfolio).

It is also important to understand CDS since it is a 'pure' credit risk derivative—default probabilities can be 'extracted' directly from default swap prices (credit spreads), which can then be used in pricing other credit risk-bearing instruments. Hence, CDS can be traded securities[77] as well as risk management tools. In our context, we are interested in valuing CDS as a credit risk management methodology.

Several formulas, using different approaches, have been developed for pricing or valuing CDS. However, the default probabilities that they yield are quite comparable, and the various pricing formulas are actually equivalent.[78]

Let us recap the basics of a single entity CDS.

A CDS is a contract that provides a lender or bank with 'insurance' against the risk of default by a specific borrower, firm or counter party. The borrower is called the 'reference entity'. The default is the 'credit event'.[79] If the credit event occurs, the bank, called the 'protection buyer', has the 'right' to sell the loan against whose default risk the insurance has been bought. The specific loan whose default risk is being protected against is called the 'reference obligation' or 'reference asset', and the total value of the loan for which the insurance contract has been created is called the 'notional principal'.

The cash flows in a CDS occur in two 'legs'. The 'protection seller' provides insurance against default risk. In return, the protection buyer makes a stream of periodical payments (usually quarterly, though semi-annual and annual payments can also happen), until the end of the CDS contract or till a credit event occurs. This is called the 'premium leg' (Figure 9.13). The size of these periodic payments are determined from quoted 'default swap spreads' to be paid on the notional principal on which default protection is sought.

Default swap spreads, (often simply called 'spreads', or sometimes referred to as 'credit swap premium',) are quoted in 'basis points per annum'[80] (bpa or bps) on the contracts' notional principal value. Another point to note that these 'spreads' are not the same concept as 'yield spread' of corporate bonds to government bonds, and not based on any risk free or benchmark interest rate.[81] Several large banks and other institutions are market makers in the CDS market. For example, when quoting on a 5-year CDS on firm F, a bank may 'bid' 250 bps and 'offer' 260 bps. This is called the 'bid-offer' spread and is the typical manner in which quotes are made. This means the bank is willing to 'buy' protection on F by paying 250 bps per year (or 2.5 per cent of the notional principal) and 'sell' protection at 260 bps per year (2.6 per cent of notional principal). This implies that if Bank A wanted to buy protection against exposure of ₹1 crore to firm F, it would have to pay 62.5 bps [(250/4) bps] per quarter on ₹1 crore or ₹62,500.

If the credit event does not occur till the maturity of the contract, the protection seller does not pay anything. However, if the credit event occurs *before* the maturity of the contract, the protection seller has to pay as specified in the contract—the swap is then settled either through cash or physical delivery. This is called the 'protection leg' and is shown in Figure 9.13.

FIGURE 9.13 CASH FLOWS IN A SINGLE ENTITY CDS

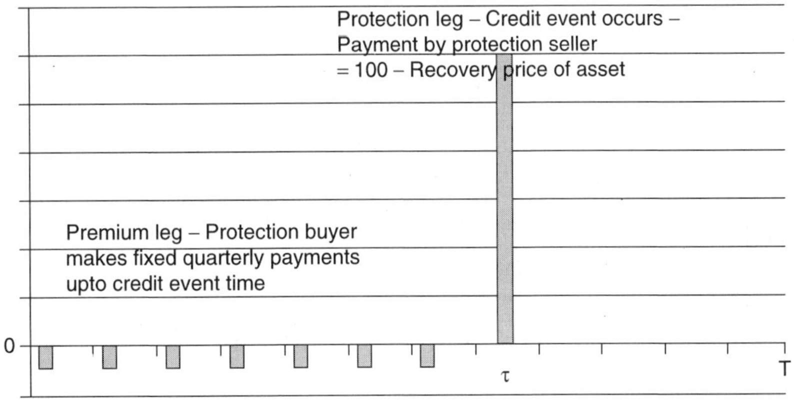

In a CDS settled through cash, the protection seller is required to compensate the loss suffered by the protection buyer by paying the amount of difference between the notional principal and the 'market price' of the defaulted bank credit (this approximates to the reduced recovery value). In the case of physical settlement, which is the prevalent market practice, the protection seller buys the defaulted loan from the protection buyer at par. Here the loan purchased by the protection seller is called the 'deliverable obligation'. The deliverable obligation may be the reference asset itself or one of a broad class of assets meeting certain specifications, usually in respect of seniority and maturity.[82] After a credit event, the value of the obligation may be different. Therefore, the protection buyer will deliver the 'cheapest' of all deliverable obligations. Hence, this is called the 'delivery option'. Typically, physical settlement takes place within 30 days of the credit event. Box 9.8 elucidates the 'cheapest-to-deliver' concept.

BOX 9.8 THE CHEAPEST-TO-DELIVER CONCEPT

The cheapest–to–deliver bond

The RR of a bond is defined as the value of a bond immediately after default as a percentage of face value. If the CDS is used to hedge the investment in a default prone bond, the payoff from the CDS in the event of default would be $(1 - R) \times$ notional principal.

Typically, a CDS specifies that a number of different bonds can be delivered in case of default. These bonds may have the same seniority, but may not be selling at the same proportion of face value immediately after default. This happens because the claim made on default is usually equal to the bond's face value plus the accrued interest up to default. If a bond has higher accrued interest at the time of default, it tends to have a higher price just after default. Another reason is because the market might feel that there would be differential treatment of bondholders in the event of the firm issuing the bonds being reorganized or restructured. Thus, in the event of default, the protection buyer would tend to choose for delivery the bond that can be purchased most cheaply in the market.

The cheapest–to–deliver loan

How does the above concept apply to bank loans? Bank A has made a senior, secured loan of ₹100 to borrower firm X and has bought protection through a long CDS position from Bank B. If the credit quality of the loan deteriorates and a credit event is triggered, then the buyer, under physical settlement, delivers the loan now valued at ₹70, down from ₹100 par, to the CDS seller. The seller pays ₹100 to the CDS buyer. Thus, the CDS buyer has made no loss (or profit) on the transaction. On the other hand, the buyer could instead sell the loan at ₹70 (making a loss of ₹30), and buy a junior ranking bond at, say, ₹50, to deliver to the seller (provided the deliverable obligation permits it). The CDS buyer would still receive ₹100 in settlement, and also make a gain of ₹20 (₹50 gain on CDS less ₹30 loss on loan). Such a practice is useful especially where restructuring is deemed a credit event, since Bank A may not want to sell the asset under restructuring.

In case of cash settlement the protection seller pays the protection buyer an amount equal to the notional principal × (1 − *R*). Cash settlement is less common since it is difficult to obtain market quotes for the distressed asset. In practice, cash settlement occurs within 5 days after the credit event, and the price will be determined through the Calculation Agent by reference to a poll of price quotations obtained from dealers for the reference obligation on the valuation date.[83] The assumption here is that defaulted loans will trade at a price reflecting the market's estimate of recovery value, irrespective of maturity or interest. In some cases, the cash settlement would be a sum predetermined by the counter parties, which is termed 'binary settlement'.

Though they seem different, the net value of asset transfer under physical settlement and the net transfer under cash settlement is the same. Under physical settlement, the protection buyer delivers the market value of the deliverable obligation (*R* × notional principal) and receives in return 100 per cent of the notional principal in cash. The total effect is that of being compensated for the notional principal. Under cash settlement, the asset is with the protection seller and can be realized at *R* × notional principal. The protection seller merely compensates the loss by paying (1 − *R*) × notional principal.

Illustration 9.4 clarifies through a numerical example.

Pricing Credit Default Swaps—Grasping the Basics

According to Duffie (1999),[84] pricing a CDS involves two issues.

The first issue is estimating the credit swap spread. We have seen in Figure 9.13 that, at the beginning of the contract, the standard credit swap involves no exchange of cash flows and, therefore, has a market value of zero. For convenience, we ignore dealer margins and transaction costs here. The market premium rate, therefore, is that for which the market value of the credit swap is zero.

ILLUSTRATION 9.4 UNDERSTANDING CDS CASH FLOWS

Basic inputs

a. Protection buyer, Bank A, wants protection against default risk of firm XYZ.
b. The notional principal (face value) on which protection sought for is ₹10 crore. (Bank A may have other exposures to firm XYZ but it wants protection only for ₹10 crore that it considers most vulnerable).
c. The protection is required for 2 years (*T* in Figure 9.13). (Again, the credit limit to firm XYZ may have a maturity period of 5 years, but Bank A needs protection only for the first 2 years).
d. The default spread is 300 bps over the risk-free rate (prime rate).
e. Bank A has to make quarterly payments to Bank B, the protection seller.

Cash flows

The quarterly payment would amount to 10 crore × 0.03 × 0.25 = ₹7,50,000.

Assume that at point τ, ($\tau < T$), the loan to firm XYZ suffers a credit event. At this point, the 'cheapest to deliver' (CTD) asset of the firm XYZ has a recovery price of ₹60 per ₹100 of face value.

The cash flows are as follows:

a. Bank A, the protection buyer, pays Bank B ₹7.5 lakh per quarter up to the time of the credit event, τ. If the credit event happens, say 1 month after the completion of a quarter, then a proportionate amount (₹7.5 lakh/3 months) of ₹2.5 lakh would be paid.
b. Bank B, the protection seller, compensates Bank A for the loss on the face value of the asset, by paying ₹10 crore × (100 per cent − 60 per cent) = ₹4 crore.

The second issue is that, with passage of time, interest rates or credit quality of the reference asset may change, and would impact the market value of the swap. Hence, for a given CDS, with defined periodic payments determined by the credit spread, the current market value would have to be ascertained. This market value would not be zero.

It should be noted that the default probabilities used to value a CDS are 'risk neutral' probabilities (and not 'real world probabilities').[85]

The simplest situation is where there is no counter party default risk.[86] The other simplifying assumption is that default probabilities, interest rates and RRs are independent. Box 9.9 outlines the basic equations to determine the single entity, CDS credit spread.

BOX 9.9 THE BASIC EQUATIONS TO VALUE A SINGLE ENTITY CDS

Assume Bank A has made a new loan *L* to firm *X*, an existing borrower. Bank A wants to transfer the risk of the new loan *N* (the Notional Principal) to Bank B through a CDS. Bank A is the protection buyer and Bank B, the protection seller. The protection against credit risk is sought for *T* years (the swap maturity, which need not be the same as the loan maturity). Bank A accepts to pay a fixed fee *f* for the protection provided by B. For understanding the basics, we will ignore, for the time being, accrued fee amount, if any, at the time of the credit event, and also assume that Bank B has zero PD on its contract with A.

At the time of the credit event (loosely, default), assume the value of the contract to be *RN*, where R is the already known RR. This means that Bank A would lose $(1 - R) \times N$ if it did not buy protection in case of default on the new loan by X. In other words, $(1 - R) \times N$ is the payoff of the CDS contract in the event of default. Assuming R as known, the fee *f* to be paid periodically by Bank A would depend on the market view of the PD by firm X.

Under the contract, Bank A pays f at predetermined periods (*e.g.*, every quarter) until the contract ends at *T* or until a credit event happens before *T*. Therefore, the PV of the cash payments by Bank A is the discounted value of each fee payment multiplied by the probability that X does not default up to the date of payment.

Assume that CDS premiums (fee payments) are paid on a set of predetermined dates represented by $\Gamma = t_1, t_2, \ldots, t_n$. In other words, in a CDS of *T* maturity starting time 0 (t_0) and having quarterly payments, the payment dates would be $t_1 = t_0 + 3$ (months), $t_2 = t_0 + 3 \times 2$ months, and so on, and $t_n = T$. If *p* is the PD of X, then $p(t_1)$ would be the probability (as seen at time t_0) that X will default at time t_1. That is, $1 - p(t_1)$ [call it $q(t_1)$] is the probability of no default by X at time t_1. If $d(t_1)$ is the discount factor pertaining to the prevailing risk-free rate, the expected *PV* of fee payments by Bank A can be obtained as follows:

$$PV_f = \sum_{i=1}^{n} d_{t_i} \times f \times q_{t_i} \times N$$

The *PV* of cash flow for Bank B, the protection seller, will be the discounted value of the recovered fraction of *N* multiplied by the PD at each fee payment date. This implies that for a default occurring at time $t_{(i+1)}$, it is necessary that the firm X has not defaulted up to time t_i, and that it defaults exactly at $t_{(i+1)}$. Hence, the weight to be used for calculating expected payment at time $t_{(i+1)}$ is the product of the probability of no default up to t_i and the conditional PD between t_i and $t_{(i+1)}$. The *PV* of expected cash flow for Bank B can be represented by the following equation:

$$PV_{\text{recovery}} = (1 - R) \sum_{i=1}^{n} \mathrm{d}_{t_{i+1}} \times \left(q_{t_i} \times p_{t_{i+1}}\right) \times N$$

However, since default does not occur on a predetermined date, and can occur at any time between t_i and $t_{(i+1)}$, we can rewrite the above equation as follows:

$$PV_{\text{recovery}} = (1 - R)\text{O}i = 1{:}n{:}\ \left[0.5\left(d_{t_i} + d_{t_{i+1}}\right)\right] \times \left(q_{t_i} \times p_{t_i t_{i+1}}\right) \times N$$

Here, the discount factor is the average of the discount factors of the periods within which default may occur, and $p_{t_i, t_{i+1}}$ is the conditional PD between times *i* and $i + 1$, given that default did not occur up to time *i*.

This implies that the 'value' of the CDS to the protection buyer is the difference between the *PV* of the expected payoff and the *PV* of payments made by the buyer.

Since we operate under the 'no arbitrage'[87] assumption, the two PVs should be equal at the beginning of the contract. Setting PV_f equal to PV_{recovery}, we can find the CDS rate or fee:

$$f = \frac{(1 - R)\,\Sigma_{i=1}^{n} 0.5\left(d_{t_i} + d_{t_{i+1}}\right) \times \left(q_{t_i} \times p_{t_i t_{i+1}}\right) \times N}{\Sigma_{i=1}^{n} d_{t_i} \times q_{t_i} \times N}$$

Here, *f* indicates the CDS 'spread'. This is an annualized spread.

In practice, CDS spreads are available in the market for different maturities based on the reference asset.

We can use the market CDS spreads to arrive at a term structure of default probabilities using the equation above. Assuming we have 1 year, 2 year,..., n year CDS spreads available from the market, we can value the PV of a CDS contract at any point in time using the above equation. For example, if we know that the mid-market CDS spread for a newly issued 5 year CDS is 100 bps, we can work backwards using the above equation and estimate the implied default probability.

One parameter required for valuing a CDS, but cannot be directly observed from the market, is the expected RR. So far, we have assumed the same RR for estimating PD densities, and for calculating the payoff, which means that the estimated CDS spread will not be very sensitive to the RR. This is because the implied probabilities of default are proportional to $(1/1-R)$ and the payoffs from a CDS are proportional to $(1-R)$.

However, the above will not be true in the case of a binary CDS. The payoff in a binary CDS is a fixed amount, regardless of the RR. Since implied probabilities are still proportional to $(1/1-R)$, but the payoff is independent of R, if we have the CDS spread of both a plain (vanilla) CDS and a binary CDS, we can estimate both the RR and the default probability.

The theory implicitly assumes that the reference asset is a floating rate asset, trading at par. However, where such floating rate assets are not available, the market often tries to estimate the CDS spread from a fixed rate asset, trading away from par, using an 'asset swap'. Asset swaps break down the asset's yield into a yield (say LIBOR) curve plus a spread. This spread is usually taken as an estimate for the CDS spread.[88]

Another complication is when the protection seller is prone to default risk.[89] In such cases, the CDS spreads reflect the default risk of the seller, or the protection buyers try to get additional/backup protection from the market.

There are other methodologies used to price CDS spreads. The reduced-form models (described in section V) are used extensively for this purpose. The Jarrow–Turnbull (1995)[90] model assumes recovery to be a fixed amount in the event of default, and is, therefore, called a 'fixed recovery model'. In a 'market standard' model based on the Jarrow–Turnbull model, O'Kane and Turnbull (2003)[91] propose that the PD occurring within the time interval $(t, t + dt)$, conditional on 'no default' up to time t, is proportional to a time-dependent function λ (called the 'hazard rate'), and the length of the time interval dt. Hence, the model uses a simple 'binomial tree'[92] where the probability of no default is $1-\lambda dt$, and if there is default the recovery value R is received with probability λdt. This model can be extended to multiple time periods and continuous time probabilities (as compared with discrete time probabilities used in Box 9.9) of default and no default can be arrived at.

The Duffie–Singleton (1999)[93] model assumes the amount of recovery is restricted and is, therefore, referred to as the 'fractional recovery model'.

The CDS market is largely over-the-counter (OTC). This means that the protection buyer and seller negotiate each CDS trade, at the time it is required—hence, each CDS will have a separate reference asset, notional amount, maturity, credit event definition, CDS spread, etc. Once the terms are agreed to by the counter parties, the trade is finalized through proper documentation. Default swaps are looked upon as a good source of expected return for protection sellers.

Credit derivatives are used by different groups of investors for a variety of reasons. Banks are understandably major protection buyers and sellers, in order to mitigate the credit risk in their large loan portfolios. Insurance firms are major protection sellers, who also provide protection against counter party risk for protection buyers.

We will illustrate estimation of CDS spread with a simple numerical example (Illustration 9.5).

ILLUSTRATION 9.5 CALCULATION OF CDS SPREAD—A SIMPLE EXAMPLE

Assumptions:

a. The notional principal is 1 (monetary value in any currency, *e.g.*, ₹1 or $1, etc.)
b. The PD p of a reference entity is assumed to be 2 per cent at the end of year 1, provided there is no earlier default. This is the conditional PD.[94]
c. The above implies that the probability of no default q at the end of year 1 is 98 per cent.
d. The protection buyer seeks protection for 5 years.

Step 1 Construct Table 9.12 of unconditional probabilities of default over 5 years (*i.e.*, PD viewed at time '0')

TABLE 9.12 UNCONDITIONAL PROBABILITIES OF DEFAULT OVER FIVE YEARS

Time	p	q
1	0.0200	0.9800
2	0.0196	0.9604
3	0.0192	0.9412
4	0.0188	0.9224
5	0.0184	0.9039

How did we obtain the above probabilities? For year 1, we know that $p = 2$ per cent and $q = 98$ per cent. For year 2, $p = q$ of year 1 $\times p = 0.9800 \times 0.02 = 0.0196$ and q (year 2) = probability of no default in both years = $0.9800 \times 0.9800 = 0.9604$. For year 3, p = probability of no default for 2 years (q of year 2) $\times p = 0.9604 \times 0.02 = 0.0192$ and q = probability of no default for 2 years $\times q = 0.9604 \times 0.9800 = 0.9412$ and so on.

Step 2 Calculate the cash flows of the protection buyer, assuming the risk-free rate[95] to be 6 per cent per annum. Since payments will be made by the protection buyer only in the case of no default, we take q over 5 years to estimate the expected fee payment. Let the fee to be paid be f.

Time	q	Expected Fee $f \times q$	Discount Factor @ 6%	PV of Expected Fee Payment
1	0.9800	0.9800f	0.9434	0.9245f
2	0.9604	0.9604f	0.8900	0.8548f
3	0.9412	0.9412f	0.8396	0.7902f
4	0.9224	0.9224f	0.7921	0.7306f
5	0.9039	0.9039f	0.7473	0.6755f
				3.9756f

The total expected cash flow of the protection seller over the 5 year CDS would be 3.9756f

Step 3 Cash flow of protection seller in case of credit event

We know that p is the probability of credit event (default) over the life of the CDS. If we assume 50 per cent RR, the protection seller will have to settle $100 - R$ or $100 - 50$ in case of a credit event (see Figure 9.13). We also assume that the credit event is likely to occur only at the end of the year.

Time	p	1−RR	Expected Pay-off	Discount Factor 6 per cent	PV of Expected Pay-off in Case of Default
1	0.0200	0.5	0.0100	0.9434	0.0094
2	0.0196	0.5	0.0098	0.8900	0.0087
3	0.0192	0.5	0.0096	0.8396	0.0081
4	0.0188	0.5	0.0094	0.7921	0.0075
5	0.0184	0.5	0.0092	0.7473	0.0069
					0.0406

The expected payoff is calculated as $p \times (1 - \text{RR})$ for each year. The PV of the expected payoff for the protection seller is seen to be 0.0406.

Step 4 Equate the two PVs in steps 2 and 3 and solve for f.

$3.9756f = 0.0406$

Hence, $f = 0.0102$ or 102 bps per year credit spread.

Note that the simple example is given to illustrate the calculation methodology. In practice, there are more complications, such as fee payments by the protection seller may be made quarterly or half yearly, or the credit event may occur at any time during the year. We have also assumed the protection seller will not default in settling the CDS.

Let us now turn to the second issue raised by Duffie (1999) outlined in an earlier paragraph.

At the time it is priced, the CDS, like most other swaps,[96] is worth almost nothing. Assume that the protection buyer in the Illustration 9.5 wants to value its position after 1 year. On the date of such revaluation, CDS spreads quoted in the market are 125 bps for a 4-year CDS (the 4-year spread is relevant since the protection was sought for 5 years in the example, and 1 year has since elapsed). What is the current market value of the position?

The MTM value = current market value of remaining 4-year protection *less* the expected PV of 4-year premium leg at the earlier calculated spread of 102 bps. It is to be noted here that the CDS contract has increased in value since the protection buyer is paying only 102 bps for something the market is now willing to pay 125 bps. Since the MTM of a new CDS is zero, the current market value of remaining 4-year protection becomes equal to the expected PV of the premium leg at 125 bps. It therefore follows that the MTM value to the protection buyer is the difference between the expected PV of 4-year premium leg at 125 bps and the expected PV of 4-year premium leg at 102 bps.

In Illustration 9.5, the expected PV of the protection buyer's fee payments would change to 3.9756 × 0.0125 = 0.0497. The PV of the payoff (assuming RR is the same) would remain at 0.0406. The market value of the swap would now be 0.0497 − 0.0406 = 0.0091 times the notional principal. In other words, the MTM value of the CDS to the protection buyer would now be −0.0091 times the notional principal.

In case of a binary default swap, the numbers in Illustration 9.5 would change as follows:

Time	*p*	Expected Pay-off	Discount Factor	PV of Expected Pay-off	
1	0.0200	0.0200	0.9434	0.0189	
2	0.0196	0.0196	0.8900	0.0174	
3	0.0192	0.0192	0.8396	0.0161	
4	0.0188	0.0188	0.7921	0.0149	
5	0.0184	0.0184	0.7473	0.0138	
				0.0811	
		PV of expected payment			3.9756 *f*
		PV of expected pay-off changes to			0.0811
		f is now estimated at			0.020408
				or	204 bps per year

In 2009, ISDA introduced the ISDA CDS standard model, the source code for CDS calculations, as a free download from its Web site, which can be accessed at www.cdsmodel.com

Pricing Collateralized Debt Obligations—The Basics

The CDS discussed above transfers the credit risk of a single entity from the protection buyer to the protection seller for a contracted period. Where protection buyers seek to securitize large portfolios of default risk prone loans, or even CDSs, the collateralized debt obligations (CDO) is used.

How is a loan portfolio different from a single loan? We have seen above that the individual firms (in a loan portfolio) could default, leading to losses in the portfolio value. This risk can be assessed by estimating the PD for each firm and the LGD (1 − RR). Additionally, the degree of dependence in the portfolio between firms' default probability, known as 'default correlation', has an impact on the timing of firms' default, and, therefore, on the portfolio loss.

Understanding the CDO We have seen in the previous chapter that a CDO, like securitization, is a way of creating securities with differing risk characteristics from a portfolio of debt instruments.

However in a CDO, the portfolio comprises of heterogeneous instruments, such as senior secured bank loans, CDSs or high yield bonds (in securitization, it is typically a homogeneous pool of, say, home loans, auto loans, etc.). The basic structure of a CDO is as given in Figure 9.14.

Bank A, owner of a loan portfolio, wants to protect itself against the possible losses in the portfolio, but it does not want to 'sell' the portfolio. One way is to buy CDS for each borrower/firm in the loan portfolio, but that would be quite expensive. Further, individual CDS contracts do not protect against correlated defaults.

Bank A decides to buy protection through a CDO. In a typical CDO, the portfolio's risk is 'sliced' into 'tranches' ('tranche' in French, means 'slice' and, in simple terms, every tranche is akin to tradable commercial paper) of increasing seniority and default risk of the underlying pool of loans (or CDSs).

Thus, each tranche in a CDO shows the priority of receiving payments from the underlying pool of assets, and also bearing the default risk. Each tranche is sold separately to investors according to their risk preferences, for a fee.

Cash flows are the critical link between the asset and liability sides of the CDO transaction. The asset side of the CDO is the underlying portfolio of reference assets—loans (or CDSs). The liabilities side comprises the securities issued by an issuer, which is typically a special purpose vehicle (SPV) that is a separate company or trust specially created for the transaction by the owner of the pool of assets. The SPV is created to insulate potential investors from the risk of failure of the CDO originator itself, say a bank.

Bank A, the originator of the CDO, sells the selected portfolio of assets whose credit risk is to be transferred, to the SPV, which in turn issues structured notes in the market backed by the portfolio of assets.

Let us now understand Figure 9.14. The first tranche (called the 'equity tranche') holds 5 per cent of the total notional loan principal, and absorbs all credit losses from the portfolio (during the life of the CDO) until the losses aggregate to 5 per cent of the notional principal. Hence the equity tranche is also called the 'first loss tranche', if the losses exceed 5 percent; the second tranche, which has 10 per cent of the loan principal, absorbs losses up to a maximum of 15 per cent (cumulatively). The third tranche holds 15 per cent of the principal and absorbs losses over 15 per cent up to a maximum of 30 per cent of the principal. The fourth tranche holds the bulk of the loan principal, 70 per cent, and absorbs all losses exceeding 30 per cent of the principal.

FIGURE 9.14 THE BASIC CDO STRUCTURE

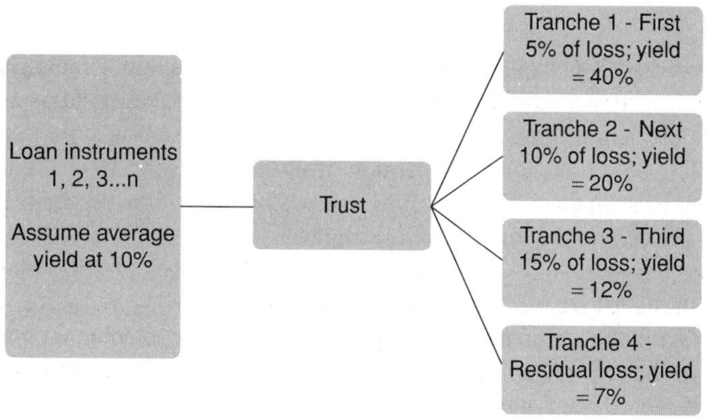

Now look at the yields (rate of interest paid) to the respective tranche holders. These rates are paid on the notional principal remaining in each tranche after the losses have been paid. Assume that tranche 1 suffers a loss of 1 per cent. The tranche holders, who were paid 40 per cent in case of no default, would now lose 20 per cent (1/5) of their investment, and would earn only on the remaining 80 per cent of their investment. Since they assume the first loss, taking the maximum risk, they are called the 'equity tranche holders'. If the default loss were to rise to 3 per cent, this tranche would lose up to 60 per cent of the notional principal. Compare this with tranche 4. Defaults on the portfolio must exceed 30 per cent if this tranche is to suffer losses. Hence, this tranche is usually given the top rating (say AAA) by rating agencies. Since this is relatively safe investment, the tranche earns less for its holders. It is usual for Bank A, the originator of the CDO, to retain the equity tranche. The remaining tranches are sold in the market.

The transaction in the above example is termed 'cash CDO'.

Typically, four broad types of CDOs are recognized—*cash flow CDOs, market value CDOs, managed CDOs and static CDOs*. The attributes of a specific CDO, such as MTM, rules related to trading of the underlying securities, etc., are determined by the type of CDO. For example, in a *cash flow* CDO, payments to investors are in the form of interest earnings and principal repayments from the underlying assets. Erosion in the underlying asset values would not usually have an impact on the cash flows to the investors in the CDO, unless the erosion is accompanied by a credit event. In this case, the interest/principal payments cease to flow from the asset originators to the SPV, leading to lower cash flow for the CDO investors. In the case of the *market value CDO*, changes in the MTM value are passed on to the CDO investors through the SPV.[97] In a *managed* CDO, the CDO manager actively trades the securities in the pool, with performance being monitored by the investors. In contrast, the *static CDO's* portfolio is determined upfront and does not change over time.

If the portfolio of loans in the example is replaced by a portfolio of CDSs, the CDO is termed 'synthetic CDO'. Cash inflows to the synthetic CDO are the underlying CDS premiums, and cash outflows are losses consequent to credit events related to the underlying assets. Each tranche in a synthetic CDO has a specified upper and lower 'detachment' (U) and 'attachment' (L) point. Defaults affect the tranche according to the seniority of the tranche in the capital structure. The buyer of the tranche with attachment point L and detachment point U will bear all losses in the portfolio value in excess of L and up to U per cent of initial value of the portfolio. Table 9.13 presents the typical tranching done in the iTraxx index (Please see Box 9.10 for an introduction to credit indices).

TABLE 9.13 A SAMPLE CDO TRANCHED STRUCTURE, ITRAXX[98]

Tranche Number	Tranche Description	Attachment L Per Cent	Detachment U Per Cent
1	Super senior	35	100
2	Junior senior	25	35
3	Senior mezzanine	15	25
4	Junior mezzanine	10	15
5	Equity	0	10

Source: www.markit.com

Assume that the above CDO experiences a 12 per cent loss of its initial value. This implies that the equity tranche holders will bear up to 10 per cent of the loss while the junior mezzanine holders would bear the remaining 2 per cent. The holders of more senior tranches (senior mezzanine, junior senior, super senior) will not suffer any loss. The super senior suffers only if the total collateral portfolio loss exceeds 35 per cent of its notional value.

Hence, it can be seen that CDO tranching enables holders of the respective tranches to limit their loss exposure to (U − L) per cent of the initial portfolio value.

For example,[99] assume a hypothetical CDS index comprises of 100 names with equal weight (1/100) for each name. The tranches are indicated in the market as follows: 0−5, 5−10, 10−15, 15−22, 22−100. In other words, the 10–15 tranche has an attachment point L of 10 and a detachment point U of 15 and so on. We assume a specific investor has bought protection on the 0–5 per cent tranche with a notional principal of ₹10 crore. If one name out of the 100 defaults, and recovery is set at 65 per cent, the LGD is 35 per cent. In such a case the payout from the protection seller would be calculated using the formula—(notional principal × LGD × weighting)/tranche size, *i.e.*, a payout of ₹70,000. Once the payout happens, the 0−5 tranche is recalculated to reflect the reduced notional principal. Hence 4.65 per cent (5 − 0.35 LGD) of the notional principal remains, which implies that the new detachment point should reflect that only 99 names now remain in the CDO. The new detachment point has to be now adjusted for the remaining names in the Index. It is to be noted that the original principal of the other tranches are not impacted due to this change, but have less protection against further losses.

The same concept can be used for determining the number of credit events at which the equity tranche stops covering losses, and the next tranche starts losing. The loss level in any given tranche depends on two random variables—the number of credit events in the entire portfolio and the related LGD. Assuming the LGD of 35 per cent in the previous paragraph applies to all defaulted firms in the portfolio (in reality LGD for each asset may be uncertain), the scenario under which the equity holders lose their entire notional principal (*i.e.*, when the equity tranche gets fully written down to zero) will be given by the equation *n* number of defaults × ₹10 lakh per name notional × 35 per cent loss rate = 5 per cent equity tranche width × ₹10 crore million total portfolio notional.

Solving for n yields 14—the number of defaults for the equity tranche to be written down to zero. This means that the portfolio would have lost ₹50 lakh, at which point the equity tranche would be fully written down to zero. The next tranche, say, the junior mezzanine, would start losing from the 15th default onwards, and so on.

Pricing the CDO The concept of 'default correlation' is important to determine the pricing of a tranched CDO, such as tranched iTraxx.

For any two given firms, their default correlation approximates to a measure of the correlation between the times at which they default. In other words, two reference assets or firms which are highly correlated (correlation close to 1) are likely to behave similarly—either defaulting or not defaulting, together. This implies that a portfolio with several reference assets, who bear a high default correlation with one another, will have higher probabilities of both higher and lower loss rates. Consequently, the emanating loss distribution is likely to have fatter tails.

As default correlation increases in a portfolio, it is easy to understand why the cash flows from the underlying asset pool of loans or CDS would exhibit higher volatility. As volatility increases, the market value of the equity tranche (the highest risk bearing tranche) increases (and the spread decreases). On the other hand, since increased volatility (risk) is not favoured by the senior most tranche, the market value declines with an increase in default correlation, leading to higher spreads. The mezzanine and other tranches in between these two can have exposures to correlation in either direction, depending on the degree of volatility.

The basic methodology is to average the discounted cash flows to a particular tranche over several independently simulated scenarios. This implies that cash flows for each underlying single name CDS in the CDO have to be simulated, with correlation in the default times of the various underlying firms as well. The widely used industry methodology for the correlated default time simulation is the 'Gaussian copula' (in Statistics, 'copula' is used to couple the behaviour of two or more variables—however, a discussion on this is outside the scope of this book).[100]

Box 9.10 introduces credit indices developed in credit derivative markets.

BOX 9.10 CREDIT INDICES

It is obvious from the discussion this far that CDOs were created and customized to meet specific needs of investors and credit risk transferring institutions. However, customization also means higher cost—creating exclusive SPVs, legal documentation and approvals, managers to design and oversee trade in the CDO and so on. The primary advantages of indices over customized CDOs are (1) liquidity, since issue sizes are large with varying credit spreads, (2) transparency (easier to obtain price quotes and information on pricing and spreads—rules, constituents, fixed coupon and daily prices are publicly available), (3) cost (lower transaction costs due to possibility of trading in portions of the market and standardization), (4) tradability, (5) operational efficiency (standardized terms, legal documentation and electronic processing) and (6) industry support (most major dealer banks and other players use and support the indices).

The standardization also contributed to better hedging patterns. For example, before the introduction of indices, issuers would hedge unbalanced positions of customized CDOs through even more complex, multi-tranche structures. This made the transaction even less transparent.

The Evolution

2001 saw the launch of synthetic credit indices by J. P. Morgan (JECI and Hydi), and Morgan Stanley (Synthetic TRACERS). Subsequently, in 2003, these indices were merged under the name Trac-x. At around the same time, credit derivative indices were introduced by iBoxx. Further consolidation took place in 2004 when Trac-x and iBoxx combined to form the CDX in North America, and the iTraxx in Europe and Asia. Since November 2007, Markit (www.markit.com), which had earlier been the administrator for CDX and the calculation agent for iTraxx, owns both families of credit indices. Markit owns the iTraxx, CDX, LevX and LCDX indices for derivatives and iBoxx indices for cash bonds.

The role of Delphi's bankruptcy in the evolution of new protocols

As CDS markets evolved, CDS indices were fast becoming the centre of trading activity. Simultaneously, the notional value of contracts written on insurers who found a place in these indices also increased rapidly. At times the notional value of CDS contracts began to exceed the bonds outstanding. This trend was more pronounced when CDS contracts were written on issuers who found a place in the major CDS indices. The result was a scramble by protection buyers to find CTD bonds when credit events happened.

When Delphi, a major supplier of auto parts to General Motors, filed for bankruptcy (Chapter 11 in the United States) in October 2005, it was reported to have $28 billion notional value of CDS contracts against $5.2 billion in outstanding bonds. The rush to find bonds to deliver to the CDS contracts led to a rise in the bond prices after the bankruptcy filing. This was followed by a steep fall in the bond prices.

The Delphi episode was one of the primary triggers for the ISDA, the trade organization for derivatives, to step in and set up protocols for settling derivative trades, as also determining, through auctions, the value of the obligations of the defaulted reference asset. The option to settle CDS contracts in cash (as opposed to physical settlement that led to complications as described) was popularized around this time.

The auctions happen in two stages. In the first stage, about 15 dealers submit bid and offer prices for the bonds of the reference asset, with a bid-offer spread of maximum 2 points. In the second stage, these bids and offers are bifurcated. Where the bids are higher than offers by other bidders, they are excluded from the calculation as 'tradeable'. The objective of this process is to prevent manipulation or misuse of the auction mechanism. The remaining bids are again bifurcated, and the best half of the two is selected. The average of the bids and offers in this best half is the auction settlement price or the 'inside market midpoint'. This process establishes the price of the instruments.

Market Participants

Apart from Markit, which owns and operates the indices, the other participants include all major banks dealing in derivatives, institutional investors, ISDA (responsible for globally approved legal documentation) and other parties who use and trade in the indices.

Trading Practices

Markit categorizes its tradable credit indices into three broad categories

a. Structured finance
b. Synthetic fixed income
c. Cash fixed income

The indices under 'structured finance' are the ABS, CMBX and the TABX, traded exclusively in the United States. 'Synthetic fixed income' indices form the largest category with the following sub-categories

FIGURE 9.15 CATEGORIES OF SYNTHETIC FIXED INCOME INDICES

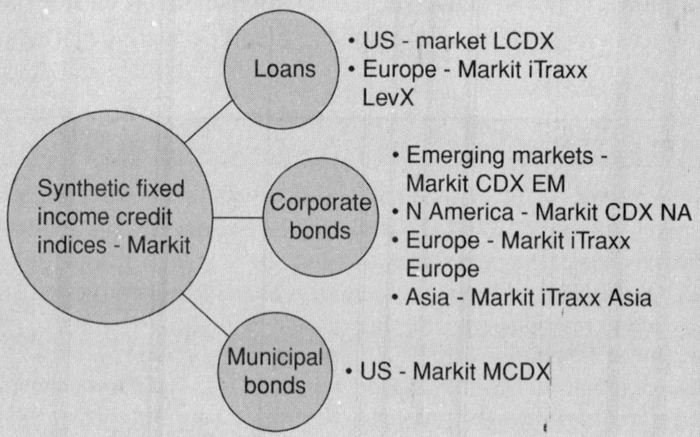

Each index has its unique features and notations. Indices roll every 6 months, and a new series is created with updated names. However, the previous series will continue trading.

The *CDX indices, e.g.*, are broken out between investment grade (IG), high yield (HY), high volatility (HVOC), crossover (XO) and emerging market (EM). The CDX.NA.HY is the notation to indicate an index based on a basket of North American (NA) single-name HY CDSs. The XO index includes names that are split-rated, meaning they are rated IG by one agency, and 'below IG by another. The CDX index rolls over every 6 months. There are 125 names in the IG index, with maturities of 1, 2, 3, 5, 7 and 10 years, and 100 names in the HY index, with a single maturity of 5 years. These names enter and leave the index as appropriate. For example, if one of the names is upgraded, it will move, say, from the HY index to the IG index when the rebalance occurs. The tranches for each index are standardized. For example, for the CDX, NA.IG, the tranches are 0–3, 3–7, 7–10, 10–15, 15–30 and 30–100. The significance of these tranches is as explained earlier using the hypothetical iTraxx example.

The LCDX basket is made up of 100 single-name, senior secured loans in the United States. Prices are quoted for maturities of 3 and 5 years, rolled over every 6 months.

The iTraxx Europe has 125 names, while the iTraxx Asia (Japan) has 50 names. Almost all the indices are rolled over every 6 months, but the maturities for which prices are quoted differ from index to index.

Payments from the protection buyer to the protection seller are made quarterly—the 20th of March, June, September and December—except in the case of CDX.EM, where payments are semi-annual. The payments accrue on an Actual/360 basis.

The 'cash-fixed income' category comprises of bonds. The index is iBoxx and is traded in Europe, Asia, United States and the emerging markets (EM).

More on trading rules can be found on Markit's Web site, www.markit.com. (May 2009)

Credit event fixings

The Credit Event Fixings have been developed by Creditex and Markit along with ISDA and major dealers in credit derivatives. The objective of credit fixings is to ensure a fair, efficient and transparent process for settlement of credit derivative trades following a corporate default. They are an integral part of ISDA's CDS Index protocols. Creditex and Markit have jointly acted as administrators of the Credit Event Fixings since their inception in June 2005.

Tradable credit fixings are determined based on a well-defined methodology for iTraxx Europe—iTraxx 5 year Europe, HiVol and XO indices. A North American version is shortly expected to be in the market. Credit fixings take place weekly on Fridays. More details can be accessed at www.creditfixings.com.

During a Credit Event Fixing, dealers place executable orders on the Creditex platform for the reference asset of a particular company in respect of which a credit event, such as filing for bankruptcy, has occurred. A market standard methodology is used to simultaneously execute these orders and generate a final cash settlement price for eligible credit derivative contracts in respect of this reference asset. Markit verifies the integrity of the process and calculates the final price which it publishes on the Credit Fixings Web site.

Source: www.markit.com, www.isda.org, www.creditfixings.com

SECTION VII

CREDIT RISK MEASUREMENT AFTER THE FINANCIAL CRISIS

The Financial Crisis—An Overview and Analysis[101]

When some of the world's largest banks folded up quietly overnight in 2007–2008, afflicted by the 'subprime crisis', shaking up powerful economies, leaving stock markets and investors in a state of panic, taking centre stage in the crisis were the 'villains'—structured products and the credit derivative.

The subprime crisis that began in mid 2007 is widely regarded as the first financial crisis in the age of mass securitization. It has unleashed a flurry of daunting questions on the very foundations of securitized finance and structured products. Just about everything related to the credit market is being questioned—is it right to originate and distribute? Is Basel II (to be discussed in a later chapter) adequate to control credit risks and ensure adequacy of bank capital? With its reliance on internal models and external credit rating agencies, can the credit risk be wished away by merely dispensing with complex derivatives? Is 'financial engineering' a dirty word?—and the debate goes on.

Funds and banks around the world purchased bonds or the risk related to bonds, backed by home loans, often bundled into CDOs. These CDOs were backed by pools of mortgages or other income-producing assets and considered essentially 'bond like' in that they offered investors a steady stream of returns. Investors found these securities attractive as they offered higher returns at a time when traditional fixed income or debt-related products were yielding lower returns. Investors also viewed these structured products to be quite 'risk free', when they were certified to be so by the top rating agencies of the world. The ability of 'structured finance' to repackage risks and create 'safe', tradable assets from risky, illiquid collateral was the reason for the meteoric increase in the issue of structured securities.

However, as low interest rates in many parts of the world fuelled a lending boom to less than creditworthy borrowers, banks looked for new avenues to package and sell these loans, so that they could get liquidity to lend more. By selling off risky loans, banks could maintain less regulatory capital commensurate with the risk. Hence banks and other financial institutions pooled these asset-backed securities into new pools, dividing them up and issuing securities against them, thus creating CDOs. The concept caught on pretty fast, with new combinations that were further and further removed from the original underlying asset. Such innovations included CDOs of CDOs or CDO-squared and even CDO-cubed.

According to J. P. Morgan, there are about $1.5 trillion in CDO, referring to those made up of bonds backed by subprime mortgages, slightly safer mortgages and commercial mortgage-backed securities.

Then what went wrong?

At the core of the crisis has been the housing boom in the United States since the beginning of the decade. Low interest rates meant home buyers could take larger loans, giving rise to a housing bubble marked by unrealistic optimism and a failure to consider the downside, since it was assumed that all foreseeable downside was taken care of while designing the securitized products. The cracks began showing in 2006, when subprime borrowers increasingly defaulted on monthly payments due to annual interest rate resets on their floating rate loans. Fears of recession caused bloated housing prices to dip alarmingly, and in 2007, prices of securities based on subprime loans were in free fall as investors feared that they would not get the promised payments from the structured securities. Lenders became wary and showed reluctance to lend.

With the underlying assets—the subprime mortgages—fast losing value, dangerous levels of leverage were revealed in the packaged securities, leading to the discovery that the 'safe' CDOs and other securities were actually far riskier than originally envisaged. As the complexity of these products increased, so did their opaqueness. The extent of losses that they have generated has surprised not only investors, but also the funds and bankers themselves. This was when weaknesses in the system were laid bare, including ratings that did not accurately reflect risk and faulty assumptions on how diversified pools would act on multiple layers of leverage.

The innovation in structured products was assisted by the rise of credit derivatives—especially CDSs. CDSs became staggeringly popular over the last few years throughout the developed world. CDSs resemble an insurance policy to the extent that they can be used by debt owners to hedge, or insure against a default on a debt. However, because there is no requirement to actually hold any asset or suffer a loss, CDSs could also be used for speculative purposes.

Thus, credit derivatives allowed banks to hedge their exposure to the subprime loans they had made, and also freed up capital—since they did not have to reserve capital for potential losses. The banks partnered with hedge funds—lightly regulated pools of capital with high fees—looking for better returns. Insurance companies and pension funds also sought the higher yields as interest rates hit historically low rates.

Annexure I presents a brief chronology of events leading to the crisis that hit the United States and Europe. Are structured products and credit derivatives really the villains of the high drama in the financial world? Who is responsible for the mammoth fiasco—Basel II, the rating agencies, the regulators or the banks themselves?

One possible inference is that the benefits of financial structuring and risk management are small compared to the huge costs they impose on financial stability and the reputation of banks. An alternative, therefore, is to return to 'good, old-fashioned banking' where banks create loans and hold them on their balance sheets and do not synthetically pool, package and distribute them.

Another argument advanced against credit risk transfer mechanisms is that they create the problem of 'moral hazard'. The originators of loans do not assess the credit quality with the same rigor that they would exercise were they to hold them on their balance sheets. This allegation seems to be true in the light of the findings of the 2008 and earlier surveys of credit underwriting practices in the United States.[102] The findings show that credit appraisal and delivery standards had in fact declined over the previous periods and banks have begun exercising more prudence in granting credit post the credit crisis. Table 9.14 summarizes the changes.

TABLE 9.14 TRENDS IN CREDIT APPRAISAL AND DELIVERY STANDARDS

	All Commercial Loans (in per cent)			
Underwriting Standards[103]	**2005**	**2006**	**2007**	**2008**
Eased	34	31	26	6
Unchanged	54	63	58	42
Tightened	12	6	16	52

Source: US OCC documents.

Basel II has also been squarely blamed for the incentive for banks to take risky assets off their balance sheet, or simply transfer the risk to willing sellers of protection—to comply with capital requirements. Theoretically, originators of loans can assume that assets or risks are off their balance sheet when they distribute them. Hence, the need to maintain capital on these assets is obviated. But for reputation, the originators may feel compelled to repurchase securities sold earlier. Then the assets come right back on the balance sheet—and when this would happen cannot be determined. For instance, Citigroup was seen to act responsibly when it included put options on CDOs backed by subprime mortgages that it sold to customers. The 'puts' gave the buyers the right to sell the securities back to the originator in case of financing problems. This contingency was not accounted for in the bank's balance sheet.

Sophisticated financial models of asset portfolios have been built and used by the banking system and these have now come under the scanner. Were the financial models flawed or was there too much reliance on the results that they threw up? For example, Northern Rock, one of the biggest casualties of the UK, had reportedly carried out extensive stress testing as stipulated by the UK Financial Services Authority only in the first half of 2007 and the results sounded no alarm. Evidently, the probability that all the bank's funding sources could dry up simultaneously was not one of the scenarios tested—since this looked highly improbable at that time!

The leading rating agencies of the world—S&P, Moody's, Fitch—have all drawn huge flak for their 'failure' to distinguish the riskiness of different securities. They have been accused of being too generous with their AAA ratings, and worse still, overlooking the potential downfall of the market as the underlying mortgage assets deteriorated in value. The worst cut of all—they reacted with wholesale downgrades when the market collapsed. The possible conflicts of interest arising from rating agencies being paid by the issuers and the same agencies offering advisory services to the issuers are also areas drawing criticism.

And there could be other reasons too—Was it the structured investment vehicles (SIVs, similar to special purpose vehicles/entities (SPVs) or (SPEs) and other mechanisms that used short-term bank funding to invest in long-term derivatives, or was it their opaqueness, or was it the lack of proper regulation?

The Way Forward There are two alternatives before banks.

They return to 'good, old-fashioned banking', where banks originate and hold the assets till they are liquidated. But this option ignores economic realities. Deregulation has already come to stay, and structured products and risk management are inexorably linked with the broader deregulation of the financial markets and financial technology, backed by the dramatic leap forward of information technology and communication. Even if we turn the clock back and launch the era of strict and restrictive regulation, the advances made in communication and technology would make it possible for banks to move risks and assets offshore, and securitization would take a different form.

The second alternative is to recognize the real benefits of securitization and financial innovation—after all, these innovations have shown us methods of packaging and redistributing risk, transforming illiquid assets on bank balance sheets to tradable ones with attractive income streams; they have shown banks how to reduce holding costly capital to absorb the credit risk; they have given liquidity to the system and lowered funding costs.

Innovation has its costs too—as the present crisis has shown. But this is a necessary though unwelcome cost of learning. Pioneering efforts in any industry have always run into rough weather for lack of prior experience. The global turbulence is a heavy price to pay for innovation, but central banks and governments have acted swiftly to soften the blow to the banking system and markets.

The present crisis can therefore be considered a maturity crisis of the credit market after the development of credit derivatives. At first glance, it looks like a massive failure of most used quantitative models of credit derivative pricing. However, we would have to remember here that there is a basic risk involved in lending money, and that this risk comes at a price, and credit derivatives have found a way to merely transfer this risk, but not to wish risk away! Probably, armed with a deeper understanding of the causality of the credit default process, deductive models with better and better predictive ability can take care of the changing environment.

The signals are now quite clear. The OCC Survey sums it up neatly. 'While the competitive environment will inevitably cause changes in credit underwriting standards, banks need to have risk management and control processes to signal when standards veer away from safe and sound banking practices. Banks should underwrite credit based upon an expectation that the borrower can repay the loan, regardless of whether the loan is intended for portfolio or for distribution. As recent events have clearly shown, liquidity conditions in credit markets can change abruptly. Banks originating credit for distribution should maintain underwriting standards reasonably consistent with the standards for their own portfolio holdings.'[104]

Current Developments and Regulatory Changes

In a bid to ensure the stability of the financial system, several regulatory and market-related changes are being introduced. One of the focus areas of these changes is credit derivatives. Even though public interest has turned towards the credit derivatives market only recently, the derivatives market has been focused on by regulators over the years. Regulatory attention is now most pronounced in the United States and Europe, where the crisis has taken its severest toll.

In the United States, far reaching changes are being brought about in both regulation of credit derivatives as well as market infrastructure for derivatives trading. Some of the important measures instituted include

- A comprehensive regulatory reform of the financial regulatory system, called the 'Treasury framework' (March 2009). This framework will cover four broad areas—systemic risk, consumer and investor protection, eliminating gaps in the US regulatory structure and international coordination—embedded in the 'core principles' of the framework.[105]
- One of the key elements of the above framework is the 'Derivatives framework', whose main components would be the oversight, protection and disclosures in the OTC derivatives market.
- The improvements in market infrastructure, as discussed by industry participants and the Federal Reserve of New York (April 2009)[106] would be consistent with the priorities in the President's Working Group (PWG) on Financial Markets and the Treasury framework mentioned above.
- The PWG's March 2008 'Policy Statement on financial markets' has been one of the most influential in deciding on regulatory issues. In this statement, the PWG outlines its diagnosis of the causes of the financial crisis, pointing out loosening lending standards, inadequate risk management systems, residential mortgage-backed securities (RMBS) and the lacunae in the functioning of the rating agencies as the most significant. The document also makes some recommendation for the OTC derivatives markets. The PWG consists of the Secretary of the Treasury (as Chairman), the Chairman of the Board of Governors of the Federal Reserve System, the Chairman of the Securities and Exchange Commission and the Chairman of the Commodity Futures Trading Commission.
- The important steps taken to improve market infrastructure include (a) establishing CDS central counter parties (CCPs) to mitigate counter party credit and operational risks, and (b) increasing market transparency, by expanding information publicly available on the credit derivative markets (such as release of periodical data on trading and prices of derivatives by the Depository Trust and Clearing Corporation (DTCC), dealers and the CCPs).
- The CDS contract itself and the trading of credit derivatives would soon undergo substantial changes. The changes to the CDS contract will be global changes. However, the convention changes would initially only apply to North American markets. In what is known as the CDS 'Big Bang', both contract and convention changes are to be introduced simultaneously.[107]
- The global changes to the CDS contract would be as follows:
  - The contract will be changed to 'hardwire' the auction mechanism for CDS following a credit event. The standard CDS document will incorporate this requirement in accordance with ISDA requirements. The current CDS contract deals only with physical settlement of trades. In 2005, an auction process was initiated to determine the final RR of a defaulted reference asset. The practice was for participants to sign up for a separate protocol (a legal document amending all previous trades) for each auction. Under this process, every time there was a credit event, the participants had to be tracked down to determine if they wanted to adhere to the protocol or not. This was a complex and time consuming process. Hardwiring the auction mechanism language into the protocol would make the process more efficient and reliable.[108]
  - Determination committees will be formed to make binding decisions on the terms of the auction as well as whether credit events have occurred.
  - The effective date for all CDS contracts will be current day less 60 days for credit events. The standardization of the effective date is to eliminate residual risk between two trades for participants.
- The contract and convention changes proposed are intended to support the CCP initiative by bringing in more standardization, and hence mitigate systemic risk.

SECTION VIII

A NOTE ON DATA ANALYTICS[109] AND BUSINESS SIMULATION

'Analytics will define the difference between the losers and winners going forward,'—Tim McGuire, a McKinsey director.

By this time, you would have understood that behind effective risk management, and a successful model that aids risk management, lies a very important ingredient – ***Information***. Valuable information, in turn, is embedded in data that is grouped and analyzed to yield information for decision making and management. Banks and firms now realize that data and its proper analysis can be used effectively to increase productivity, improve decision making, enhance risk management capabilities and thus gain competitive advantage. Experts call it the 'big data' revolution.

In the world of finance, we know that 'information' has value. However, voluminous and unstructured data or information that most banks and firms seem to have today cannot be managed or analyzed by traditional tools. For example, banks traditionally gather data for reporting purposes—to their head offices, to central banks, to the government, to the public and so on. However, today data signifies not only the traditional data, but also enormous amounts of data that converge from click stream sources from the web, social media, and videos. Banks' back offices generate voice data. Data is generated through the 'cloud'. (It is estimated that Google alone processes over 24000 terrabytes per day!). However, these unconventional information sources are not tabulated in typical rows and columns that one can read or interpret.

Banks, in particular, have access to enormous information—customer data, transaction details, performance data, credit information, and so on—from both internal and external sources.

So the first question is—what is the data that they want to use and for achieving what purpose? With the help of advanced technology, it is now easy to gather data and store it. But the challenge is to determine which data to use, the best source for the data, and how to put it together into an integrated form that can serve the objective across the bank.

Therefore, a key capability to utilize the information explosion for data analytics is to identify, integrate and manage diverse sources of data. Another key capability is to build or use the vast data in advanced analytics models that would realistically predict future trends and outcomes. Of course, the most important requirement is the capability of management to integrate the data analytics models into the firm's functioning so that better decisions can be made. The latter capability presupposes the existence of a clear strategy for transforming the way the firm works through data analytics, and the use of the most appropriate technology infrastructure and human skills. All this implies that the approach to using analytics for optimal decision making should be integrated with the sourcing of the correct and appropriate data. Information is costly, and lack of vision in collecting data and wondering how to use the data would lead to loss of productivity and undermine the firm's competitive ability.

Banks need data analytics in a big way for managing risks—be it credit risk, market risk, operational risks, liquidity risk, or the interplay of various risks on the financial system. While regulatory prescriptions for risk management are driving banks to 'big data' analytics, banks are using the data generated for internal management as well.

Banks can benefit from 'big data' in a big way. The following diagram illustrates.

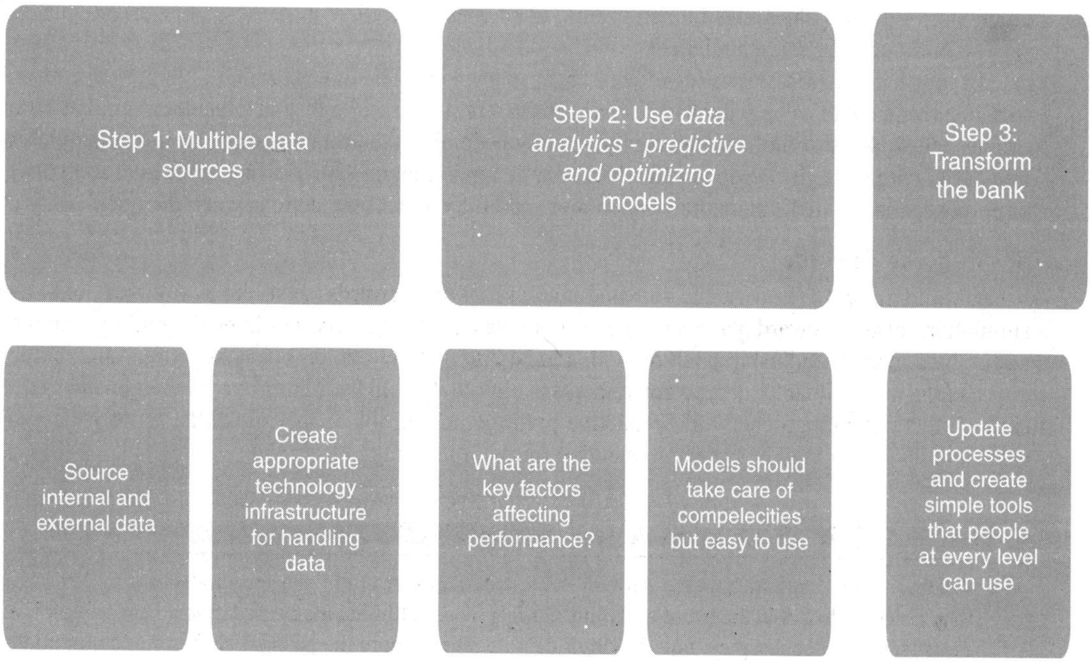

Business Simulations: 5 Reasons Why Business Simulations Are Great Learning Tools[110]

1. *Risk Free Learning*

One of the very foundations of the 'learning by doing' concept of business games is the acceptance of failures, and the ability of deriving valuable learning from them. This very basic principle is what made Silicon Valley become the unique and striving start-up hub it is today, and it is most valuable skill for students to get a complete hands on before embarking on their journey as working adults. Business management simulations are the safer ways of helping the students first learn how to navigate the landscape of a real company, than losing out all their savings on a badly executed business idea or venture.

One of the key differentiators of business simulation games is that it acts as an excellent tool to practice real world business decision-making skills as everything happens in a risk free simulated learning environment. This encourages the students to try out different strategies, observe the results, monitor market fluctuations, then pivot their direction, all without real-life repercussions.

2. *Multiplayer Environment*

With the massive surge of multiplayer online games, most college students today prefer an environment where they could interact with other players in either a cooperative or competitive fashion. Business Games brings people together in virtual worlds, mirroring the phenomenon of increased internationalization and cross-border cooperation between businesses as well, a need of the hour.

In business simulation games students form the management teams of a virtual company that competes against other companies in the same market for a slice of the consumer pie. Today business simulation games with a fully web-based platform supported by an in-game messaging system, enables these teams from anywhere in the world to improve cross-campus cooperation and create exciting competitions between partner universities.

3. *Interactive Game Play*

Another major appeal of many games would be their real time feedback on decisions made. This feature just not only makes participants more engaging, but also helps them practice a number of different strategies in a short period of time and discover what works best or better.

Most Business Simulation Games employ a round-based system which gives the students an opportunity to strategize with their teammates before coming to any final decisions, and also enabling the instructors/facilitators to schedule and manage his/her course better. The dynamic aspect is prevalent however in the decision-making areas, where students can immediately see the effect of their choices once they start experimenting with the decisions.

4. *Realistic Story Arc*

Good stories always captivates human brains, in business as well as in games, story driven game plays are very successful in enticing large audiences.

In higher education stories have been encapsulated in case studies, which although take students through a particular segment of a company's life, it happens in a non-interactive format. Business Simulations on the contrary enables the students to further immerse by actually becoming the protagonists of their company's story, and determining its faith through decisions made in a volatile environment. This not only does give students a greater sense of purpose, but also make them think much more carefully about their actions when they don't only exist in theory.

5. *In-game Rewards*

What would this entire experience be without any satisfying rewards? Just like in any traditional games, business simulations also do reward players in one or more ways, most notably would be the rankings on the leader board, and/or by a market leadership position with a great cumulative total on business profits, shareholder returns, etc.

But the most valuable rewards for students is ultimately help them improve on their business decision making skills, holistic thinking, teamwork, proactive pivoting, and problem solving skills, all of which will be retained substantially longer than by others, less active forms of learning.

CHAPTER SUMMARY

- Traditional methods such as the Altman's Z score and other credit scoring models try to estimate the PD, rather than potential losses in the event of default (LGD). The traditional methods define a firm's credit risk in the context of its 'failure'—bankruptcy, liquidation or default. They ignore the possibility that the 'credit quality' of a loan or portfolio of loans could undergo a mere 'upgrade' or 'downgrade'

- The credit risk of a single borrower/client is the basis of all risk modelling. In addition, credit risk models should also capture the 'concentration risk' arising out of portfolio diversification and correlations between assets in the portfolio. Typically, credit risk models are expected to generate (a) loss distributions for the default risk of a single borrower and (b) portfolio value distributions for migration (upgrades and downgrades of a borrower's creditworthiness) and default risks.
- Credit risk models have a wide range of applications. They are prevalently used for the following:
  a. Assessing the 'EL' of a single borrower.
  b. Measuring the 'economic capital' of a financial institution
  c. Estimating credit concentration risk
  d. Optimizing the bank's asset portfolio
  e. Pricing debt instruments based on the risk profile

  Credit risk models are valuable since they provide users and decision makers with insights that are not otherwise available or can be gathered only at a prohibitive cost.
- 'Creditmetrics™', the most well-known industry-sponsored credit migration model applies migration analysis to credit risk measurement. The model computes the full (1 year) forward distribution of values for a loan portfolio, where the changes in values are assumed to be due to credit migration alone, while interest rates are assumed to evolve in a deterministic manner. 'Credit *VaR*' is then derived as a percentile of the distribution corresponding to the desired confidence level.
- CPV is a ratings-based portfolio model used to define the relationship between macroeconomic cycles and credit risk in a bank's portfolio. It is based on the observation that default and migration probabilities downgrade when the economy worsens, *i.e.*, defaults increase, and the contrary happens when the economy strengthens. The model simulates joint conditional distribution of default and migration probabilities for non-IG borrowers whose default probabilities are more sensitive to credit cycles, which are assumed to follow business cycles closely, than those of highly rated borrowers in different industries and for each country, conditional on the value of macroeconomic factors.
- MKMV uses the option pricing framework in the VK model to obtain the market value of a firm's assets and the related asset volatility. The default point term structure for various risk horizons is calculated empirically. MKMV combines market value of assets, asset volatility and default point term structure to calculate a DD term structure, which is then translated into a credit measure termed (EDF). The EDF is the PD for the risk horizon (1 year or more for publicly traded firms).
- Credit risk+ has been developed based on the actuarial approach by Credit Suisse financial products (CSFP). In this model, only default risk is modelled, not downgrade risk. The model makes no assumptions about the causes of default. Each borrower/counter party can assume only one of two 'states' at the end of the risk horizon,—'default' (0) or 'no default' (1). All the above models are commonly known as 'structural models'.
- The other class of popular models is 'reduced-form' models. The key difference between structural and reduced-form models is in the 'information' available to model credit risk. While 'defaults' are specified 'endogenously' (the credit quality being determined by the assets and liabilities of the firm) in structural models, defaults are modelled exogenously from market data in the reduced-form approach. Another difference is in the treatment of RRs—structural models specify RRs based on the value of assets and liabilities within the firm, while reduced-form models look to the market to specify RRs. Reduced-form models are also called 'intensity' models. If information available to the modeller/bank is partial or incomplete, a structural model with default being a predictable 'stopping time' becomes a reduced-form model with default time being unpredictable.
- There are several methodologies used to price CDS spreads. The reduced-form models are also used for this purpose. The concept of 'default correlation' is important to determining the pricing of a tranched CDO, such as tranched iTraxx.
- 2001 saw the launch of synthetic credit indices by J.P. Morgan (JECI and Hydi), and Morgan Stanley (Synthetic Tracers). In 2003, these indices were merged under the name Trac-x. At around the same time, credit derivative indices were introduced by iBoxx. Further consolidation took place in 2004 when Trac-x and iBoxx combined to form the CDX in North America, and the iTraxx in Europe and Asia. Since November 2007, Markit owns the iTraxx, CDX, LevX and LCDX indices for derivatives, and iBoxx indices for cash bonds.
- The Credit Event Fixings have been developed by Creditex and Markit along with ISDA and major dealers in credit derivatives. The objective of credit fixings is to ensure a fair, efficient and transparent process for settlement of credit derivative trades following a corporate default. They are an integral part of ISDA's CDS Index protocols.

- The subprime crisis that began in mid 2007 is widely regarded as the first financial crisis in the age of mass 'securitization'. It has unleashed a flurry of daunting questions on the very foundations of securitized finance and structured products, as well as credit risk models and rating agencies.
- In a bid to ensure the stability of the financial system, several regulatory and market-related changes are being introduced. One of the focus areas of these changes is credit derivatives. Regulatory attention is now most pronounced in the United States and Europe, where the crisis has taken its severest toll.
- Banks and firms realize that data and its proper analysis can be used effectively to increase productivity, improve decision making, enhance risk management capabilities and thus gain competitive advantage. Experts call it the 'big data' revolution. Data analytics is transforming the way banks function.

TEST YOUR UNDERSTANDING

1. Which of the following loans is most risky? Assume that other things are equal—the borrowers are rated the same, are from the same industry and have the same risk profile.
   a. ₹30 crore loan with 50 per cent LGD
   b. ₹10 crore loan with no collateral
   c. ₹40 crore loan with 40 per cent RR
   d. ₹40 crore loan with 40 per cent LGD
2. Which of the following loans is likely to have the highest PD, other things being equal?
   a. The loan with the longest maturity
   b. The loan with the lowest LGD
   c. The loan whose value has the lowest volatility
   d. The loan whose borrower is assessed most creditworthy
3. Which of the following is NOT used to estimate the PD of a firm in the KMV model?
   a. Book value of equity
   b. Market value of equity
   c. Book value of debt
   d. Price volatility
   e. Time to maturity of loan to the firm
4. Using the KMV credit risk model, calculate the DD of a firm whose assets stand at ₹50 crore at current value, and whose liabilities are at ₹30 crore. Also assume the asset return volatility is 10, and the conditions of the Merton model are met.
5. Which of the following is NOT TRUE of MKMV's EDF?
   a. EDF measures are actual probabilities
   b. EDF measures are credit scores
   c. If a firm has a current EDF credit measure of 2 per cent, it implies that there is a 2 per cent probability of the firm defaulting over the next 1 year
   d. If there are 100 firms with an EDF of 4 per cent, we can expect, on an average, four firms to default over the next year
   e. A firm with 4 per cent EDF measure is 10 times more likely to default than a firm with 0.4 per cent EDF measure
6. For a portfolio of risky assets, Credit Metrics uses the following to estimate default correlations.
   a. Correlation of changes in corporate bond yields
   b. No default correlations are assumed
   c. Correlation of changes in corporate bond defaults
   d. Correlation of equity returns
7. In Illustration 9.3 (Credit Risk+), if in step 2, for the same bands and number of borrowers in each band, the expected number of defaults in each band doubles, what will be the effect on the EL in each band?

8. A 5-year CDS requires semi annual payment at the rate of 60 bps per annum. The notional principal is ₹30 crore. A credit event occurs after 4 years and 5 months. If the RR is 40 per cent, and the CDS is settled in cash, list the cash flows and their timing for (a) the protection buyer and (b) the protection seller.
9. What is the difference between (a) a plain vanilla CDS and a binary CDS, and (b) a plain vanilla CDS and a basket default swap?
10. How would the CDS fee (spread) change in Illustration 9.5 if (other things remaining constant)
    a. The fee payments were made quarterly
    b. The fee payments were made semi annually
    c. The default occurred mid way during the year
    d. The RR was more than 50 per cent
    e. The RR was less than 50 per cent
    f. It is a binary CDS.
11. Denote conditional default probability for a firm X as p per year, and the RR as R. The risk-free rate is 5 per cent per year. Default always occurs at the end of the year. The spread for a 5-year plain vanilla CDS is 120 bps and the spread for a similar 5-year binary CDS is 160 bps. What is the value of p and R?
12. How would p and R in the above example change if defaults always occurred mid way through every year? Would you be able to draw any conclusion about the relationship between the spreads of a similar plain vanilla CDS and binary CDS?

TOPICS FOR FURTHER DISCUSSION

- For a hypothetical loan/loan portfolio, apply the credit risk models and compare the results.
- MKMV publishes on its Web site, case studies on calculating EDF for several firms. Take a sample of these firms and trace their credit ratings as awarded by the top credit rating companies to these firms. Are the results consistent?
- Should credit derivatives be continued as credit risk transfer mechanisms, in the light of their role in the current global financial crisis?
- What are CDO-squared and CDO-cubed and how are they valued?
- What are the various types of exotic CDOs and how are they priced?

SELECT REFERENCES

1. Bluhm, Christian, Ludger Overbeck and Christoph Wagner (2003) *An introduction to credit risk modelling*. CRC Press LLC, USA, ISBN 1-58488-326-X.
2. Crouhy, M, Dan Galai and Robert Mark, (2000). 'A Comparative Analysis of Current Credit Risk Models', *Journal of Banking and finance* 24: 59–117.
3. Elizalde, Abel. (2005a) 'Credit Risk Models I: Default Correlation in Intensity Models', accessed at www.abelelizalde.com.
4. Elizalde, Abel. (2005b) 'Credit Risk Models II: Structural Models', accessed at www.abelelizalde.com.
5. Elizalde, Abel (2006), 'Credit Risk Models III: Reconciliation Reduced-Structural Models', CEMFI working paper 0607, accessed at *www.cemfi.es*.
6. Gordy, Michael (2000), 'A Comparative Anatomy of Credit Risk Models', *Journal of Banking and Finance* 24: 119–149.
7. Hull, John, and Alan White (2008), 'Dynamic Models of Portfolio Credit Risk: A Simplified Approach', *Journal of Derivatives* 15, 4 (Summer): 9–28.
8. Jarrow, Robert A. and Stuart M. Turnbull (2000), 'The Intersection of Market and Credit Risk', *Journal of Banking and Finance* 24: 271–299.
9. Merton, Robert C. (1974), 'On the Pricing of Corporate Debt: The Risk Structure of Interest Rates', *Journal of Finance* 39: 449–470
10. Uwe, Wehrspohn. (2002), 'Credit Risk Evaluation: Modelling–Analysis–Management', accepted as a doctoral thesis at the faculty of economics at Heidelberg University, Germany, available in e-book-format at http://www.risk-and-evaluation.com.
11. http://www.defaultrisk.com
12. http://www.bis.org

ANNEXURE I

THE GLOBAL CREDIT CRISIS—A BRIEF CHRONOLOGY OF EVENTS IN 2007–08

Months	2007	2008
January		A dismal dawn to the new year as bank losses continue to plague the market. Bear Stearns discloses subprime losses of $1.9 billion, leading to the exit of its CEO. Countrywide's shares plumb new depths and Bank of America steps in to buy it for $4 billion. Citigroup has a further $18 billion of losses to report in its mortgage portfolio, while Investment banker Merrill Lynch projects $15 billion of subprime losses. French bank Societe Generale takes a hit of 4.9 billion euros due to unauthorized activities of rogue traders. Financial losses translate into job losses. Lehman Brothers retires from wholesale mortgage lending and announces 1,300 job cuts. United States estimates 35,000 job losses in residential construction and mortgage lending. Rating downgrades also happen simultaneously. In a first of its kind move, Fitch downgrades Ambac, the second largest monoline insurer. In spite of successive cuts in fed funds rate to stand at 3 per cent, World Bank says that world economic growth will slow in 2008
February	US senate Banking committee holds first meeting on predatory lending in subprime sector after Ownit Mortgage Solutions filed for bankruptcy in December 2006. In the same month, HSBC loses over $10.5 billion, and the Head of HSBC US mortgage lending business is fired.	In an attempt to stem the rot, President Bush signs the Economic Stimulus Act of 2008. However, the downslide continues. UBS announces fourth quarter 2007 loss of CHF 12.4 billion ($12 billion). AIG, one of the largest insurers, announces fourth quarter 2007 losses of $5.3 billion due to more than $11 billion of losses on its CDS portfolio.
March	FDIC issues a cease and desist order against subprime lender Fremont Investment & Loan, which had been operating without adequate subprime mortgage loan underwriting criteria. The New York Attorney General announces investigation into subprime lending after lenders cut off credit lines to New Century Financial, a large subprime lender, and trading in its shares is sus pended, and Accredited Home Lenders decide to sell, at heavy discount, $2.7 billion of their subprime loans.	The delinquency rate on mortgages increases 87 bps to 5.82 per cent during fourth quarter 2007 over the same period previous year, according to MBA's National Delinquency Survey. Reflecting this trend, Carlyle Capital, a highly leveraged fund (30 times) mostly invested in agency-backed RMBS, defaults on $17 billion of debt. A larger shock comes later in the month, when a near insolvent Investment bank Bear Stearns is bid for by JP Morgan Chase at $2 per share. JP Morgan raises its bid to $10 per share and agrees to indemnify the Federal Reserve Bank of New York against the first 1 billion of losses, based on the latter's guarantee covering $30 billion of Bear Stearns assets, mostly mortgage-related,. To ease the situation further, The Federal Reserve Bank of New York announces TSLF, which lets primary dealers swap AAA-rated securities for Treasury securities. It also creates PDCF, to throw open the discount window to primary dealers and non-depository institutions. A further cut in the fed funds rate brings it to 2.25 per cent.

		The Federal Reserve, European Central Bank and Swiss National Bank also increase the size of their dollar swap lines to $30 billion and $6 billion, respectively.
April	New Century Financial, dealing in subprime loans, files for bankruptcy, while the National Association of Realtors announces a more than 8 per cent decline in existing home sales during a single month, the largest in 18 years	As losses continue, so does the scramble for funds by major banks. While Citigroup announces a further subprime loss of $12 billion, and UBS AG, the European bank hardest hit by the crisis announces further losses, Washington Mutual, one of the largest US mortgage originators, raises $7 billion from TPG, a private equity firm. National City Corp., a large regional US bank, seeks a $7 billion capital infusion from another private equity firm, Corsair Capital. And Royal Bank of Scotland announces that it will sell assets and approach investors to raise about £16 billion. Hedge funds rush in to make the most of the market tumble, by shorting the mortgage market, thus, worsening the situation. Fed funds rate is scaled down further to 2 per cent. IMF's Global Financial Stability estimates total credit losses of $1 trillion, of which $510 billion will be borne by banks. According to the IMF, the crisis has spread beyond the subprime, and has affected other mortgage bonds, securitized car and student loans, leveraged lending backing private equity buyouts and credit derivatives.
May	As GMAC, the finance arm of General Motors, reports home loan losses of $1 billion and UBS closes its US subprime business, the first comprehensive plan to help homeowners avoid foreclosures is presented in the US Senate. Some banks enter a sell off mode to raise long-term funds even as UK mortgage lender Kensington agrees to a $561 million takeover offer from South African bank, Investec.	Cities and towns rarely go bankrupt. But the city council of Vallejo, California, files for bankruptcy since its declining housing-related tax revenues are not enough to pay for basic services. Reports of first quarter 2008 losses continue to come in. UBS AG announces CHF 11.5 billion ($11.1 billion) loss, while monoline insurer MBIA announces a $2.4 billion loss. Fannie Mae also discloses $2.2 billion losses, but says it planned to raise $6 billion in capital, after the regulator gives it the go ahead to expand its activities even while being involved in the credit squeeze. Citigroup plans a massive wind down of $400 billion of assets over the next 3 years, after raising $44 billion in capital through stock sales and private offerings to investment funds abroad.
June	CDO prices fall, and Bear Stearns is forced to prop up two of its hedge funds with a $3.2 billion injection. At around the same time, fearing a backlash of the developing crisis in the United States, the Bank of England reduces the overnight bank rate by 25 basis points to 5.5 percent.	S&P downgrades Morgan Stanley, Merril Lynch and Lehman brothers, the second, third and fourth largest investment banks in the United States, and announces a 'negative' outlook on all four largest investment banks, including Goldman Sachs. The rating agency also downgrades MBIA and Ambac, US' large insurers. More and more banks in the United States announce dividend cuts and asset write downs. The UK's share of woes increases as Bradford and Bingley, UK's largest buy-to-let mortgage lender announces lower profits and sale of 23 per cent stake to US-based private equity firm, TPG.

July	As US housing prices plunge 20 per cent over the previous year, the three major credit rating agencies drastically lower their ratings of the subprime bonds, creating panic among investors. General Electric decides to sell WMC Mortgage, its subprime lending business. More serious, the two distressed Bear Stearns funds file for bankruptcy protection. As fear spreads, UK authorities take action against five brokers selling subprime mortgages	Freddie Mac and Fannie Mae fall by over 60 per cent over the year, on concerns that the capital they raised since December may not be sufficient to cover massive write-downs. The crisis throws up another casualty in the United States—Indymac Bancorp Inc. A run on the bank led to the bank's failure, estimated to cost the FDIC $4 to $8 billion to settle depositors' claims. Merrill Lynch liquidates $30.6 billion of assets at one-fifth of their original value. The tentacles of the crisis move into Australia, where the National Australia Bank, the country's second largest, discloses huge provisions on its CDO portfolio containing US residential mortgages
August	Things start happening at a rapid pace, not only in the United States but also in Europe. The S&P/Case-Shiller Home Price Index for second quarter 2007 shows a drop of 3.2 per cent over the previous year, the largest in the 17-year history of the index. While American Home Mortgage, one of the largest US home loan providers, and subprime lender Ameriquest file for bankruptcy, BNP Paribas suspends three investment funds hit by the crisis. Countrywide draws down its $11.5 billion credit line, and Bank of America buys 16 per cent stake in the company for $2 billion. German bank Sachsen Landesbank is sold to Landesbank Baden Wuerttemberg. Insurance giant AIG warns of increasing mortgage defaults even beyond the subprime segment. Even as the interest rate on 15 day AAA asset-backed commercial paper (ABCP) jumps to a historic high of 6.14 per cent, and Goldman Sachs decides to pump in $3 billion into prop up a hedge fund, Central banks step in to salvage the situation in their countries. The ECB provides 61 billion euros of funds for banks. The Fed and Japan's central bank assure provision of liquidity to markets. The Federal Reserve cuts the discount rate to 5.75 per cent and four large US banks announce coordinated borrowing of $2 billion from the Federal Reserve's discount window to gain liquidity.	Prospects of recovery of housing market in the United States appear bleak as the number of applicants for new mortgages fall to an 8 year low.
September	As delinquency rates on family mortgages soar, the Federal Reserve's annual Jackson Hole conference focuses on the link between housing and monetary policy. Global Alpha, a hedge fund managed by Goldman Sachs, reveals losses of 22 per cent over the previous month. The Federal Reserve cuts the discount rate by 50 basis points to 4.75 per cent. The US subprime crisis spreads its tentacles further as IKB, German regional lender, records $1 billion loss due to US subprime market exposure, and Bank of China discloses $9 billion in subprime losses. A big shake up is due as a run on deposits of British mortgage lender Northern Rock begins	High drama in the United States as Lehman, the fourth largest US investment bank, files for bankruptcy, the biggest bankruptcy filing in history. Moody's cuts its rating, bringing Lehman from IG to junk bond status overnight. In another equally startling development, Bank of America agrees to buy Merrill Lynch, the no. 3 investment bank in the United States, for $50 billion in stock. This is Bank of America's second acquisition in the credit crisis after it acquired Countrywide.

		In a third dramatic episode, the biggest US bank failure in history happens when Washington Mutual (the sixth largest mortgage bank and the 11th largest subprime lender) is seized by government regulators and sell its branches and assets to JP Morgan Chase In the wake of these dramatic developments, the Fed steps in to lend $85 billion (later increases to $152 billion) to AIG to save the world's largest insurer from failure. The US government takes custody of Freddie Mac and Fannie Mae, under a 'conservatorship', replacing their chief executives and eliminating their dividends. The Fed widens the collaterals it accepts for loans to securities firms to stocks to help weather the Lehman storm in the markets. At the same time a group of 10 banks (including Bank of America, JP Morgan, Goldman Sachs, Citigroup, Barclays, Credit Suisse, Merrill Lynch, Morgan Stanley, UBS AG) form a $70 billion fund to prop up market liquidity.
		Startling events in Europe as the UK government nationalizes Bradford and Bingley, the country's largest mortgage lender, in the second nationalization move after Northern Rock. The government assumes control over the bank's GBP 50 billion mortgages and loans, while its GBP 20 billion savings units and branches are bought by Abbey, part of Spain's Santander banking group. Lloyds TSB buys HBOS, one of UK's largest mortgage lenders. Banking giant Fortis is partially nationalized by the Dutch, Belgian and Luxembourg governments. The Icelandic government takes control of the country's 3rd largest bank, Glitnir
October	Even as the National Association of Home Builders confidence index hits 19, the lowest since the series began in 1985, banking losses continue unabated. UBS and Citigroup announce losses of $3.4 billion and $5.9 billion, respectively. Japanese bank Nomura discloses subprime losses of $621 million. Countrywide Financial reports a third quarter loss of $1.2 billion, its first loss in 25 years. Deutsche Bank reveals losses of $2.2 billion. Merrill Lynch announces losses of $7.9 billion and the resignation of its CEO.	Governments all over Europe are doing their best to bolster their faltering financial institutions, as the global banking crisis widens, and shows no signs of abating. European leaders pledge to bail out their own country's banks. France, Germany, Spain, the Netherlands and Austria commit 1.8 trillion euros to guarantee bank loans and take stakes in lending banks. Iceland's three biggest banks—Kauthing Kaup IC, Landsbanki and Glitnir—collapse under the weight of debt running into billions of dollars. The government takes over the banks, but the collapse shatters the currency, forcing Iceland to seek IMF aid. In Germany, Hypo real estate, the second largest property lender, is being rescued with a 50 billion euro package. BNP Paribas, France's largest bank, takes control over the Belgium unit of Fortis.

	The US government attempts to salvage the situation by launching Hope Now, an alliance with mortgage servicers and investors, with the objective of encouraging voluntary modification of adjustable-rate mortgages to fixed-rate. Leading banks take further initiatives—*e.g.*, Citigroup, JPMorgan Chase and Bank of America, with the support of the Treasury Department, announce a plan to form a Master-Liquidity Enhancement Conduit (MLEC) to purchase asset-backed commercial paper (ABCP) from liquidating SIVs. The Federal Reserve cuts the federal funds rate by 25 basis points to 4.5 per cent.	Dexia, the largest lender to governments, is on a 6.4 billion euro lifeline from the French and Belgian governments. The European Central Bank signals its willingness to extend help beyond the eurozone when it gave Hungary a 5 billion euro credit line. Switzerland's two major banks take emergency measures, with the government taking 10 per cent stake in UBS AG, while Credit Suisse seeks 10 billion francs from investors, including Qatar. Britain's largest banks are to be partly nationalized using 250 billion pounds of funds. Initially seven leading banks will increase their capital with the funds provided—Abbey, Barclays, HBOS, HSBC, Lloyds TSB, Royal Bank of Scotland, Standard chartered—with more banks and building societies expected to join in. The Australian government decides to guarantee all deposits as well as wholesale lending by banks for 3 years. In the United States, it is the turn of Wachovia, the 4th largest bank, to succumb, and be taken over by Wells Fargo in an all stock deal.
November	As US house prices hit a new 21 year low, the losses to the financial system seem unstoppable. Credit Suisse discloses a $1 billion loss even as Citigroup estimates that its $55 billion subprime portfolio has shed value drastically and stands between $8 and $11 billion, leading up to the resignation of its CEO. Morgan Stanley and BNP Paribas disclose mortgage losses of $3.7 billion and $197 million, respectively. Wachovia, one of	22 US lenders have failed in 2008, against 3 in 2007. FDIC states that the number of 'problem banks' (and thrifts) amount to 171 in the 3rd quarter of 2008, the highest since 1995. Ironically, the latest in the list is Franklin Bank, founded by Lewis Ranieri, often called the 'father of securitization' for popularising mortgage-backed securities in the 1980s.
	the largest US banks, announces $1.7 billion subprime loss, against Bank of America's $3 billion, HSBC's $3.4 billion and Barclays' $2.7 billion. Goldman Sachs forecasts subprime losses at $400 billion. Freddie Mac[111] reports $2 billion loss. Elsewhere in the world, Japan's second largest banking group, Mizuho reports fall of 13 per cent in annual operating profit. The insurers start feeling the heat as well. Reinsurance company Swiss Re loses about $1 billion on insurance of clients hit by subprime crises, while Insurance major AIG writes down $2 billion of mortgage investments. To partly redeem the situation, some institutions try to raise capital. Freddie Mac and Citigroup raise $6 billion and $7.5 billion of capital, respectively, while Fed injects $41 billion into the ailing financial sector. At the regulatory level, The US House of Re presentatives passes the Predatory Lending and Mortgage Protection Act.	However, Citigroup is 'too big to fail' and receives US government rescue package of $20 billion

December	British banks reel under the losses due to bad debts in the US housing market—Royal Bank of Scotland decides to write off GBP 1.25 billion, while Lloyds TSB reports GBP 200 million losses. The Bank of England responds with a cut in interest rates in the UK. The woes of UBS continue as it reports $10 billion losses.
	In the US, Washington Mutual, one of the largest banks, joins the subprime loss league with $1.6 billion. Citigroup takes $49 billion worth of SIV assets back on its balance sheet, and Morgan Stanley is forced to sell 9.9 per cent stake as its subprime losses touch $9.4 billion.
	Reflecting the market crisis and the scramble by banks for end of the year liquidity, the spread of 15-day AAA asset-backed commercial paper over equivalent duration AAA non-financial commercial paper soars to 173 bps (as compared to less than 10 bps under normal circumstances).
	The M-LEC plan to rescue struggling SIVs is abandoned by the sponsoring banks.
	The Federal Reserve announces measures to prop up the worsening liquidity—fed funds rate lowered by 25 bps to 4.25 per cent, $20 million liquidity made available to commercial banks, and creation of the term auction facility (TAF). It also tightens rules on subprime lending.
	Other central banks follow suit—ECB lends European commercial banks $500 billion, while Bank of England lends £10 billion to UK banks.
	The New York Attorney General sends subpoenas to major investment banks to investigate subprime mortgage securitization.
	Joint action is initiated by central banks—The Federal Reserve, the European Central Bank and the Swiss National Bank announce currency swaps of up to $20 billion to the ECB and $4 billion to the SNB; The Bank of England and Bank of Canada announce increase in their liquidity facilities.
	Moody's downgrades Citigroup's senior debt rating, based on 'worsening asset quality'.
	In the US, many regional banks, commercial lenders, insurers and card issuers decide over the last few months to convert into commercial banks to gain access to the $700 billion TARP. The latest to join this list is American Express company.
	Latvia, like Hungary, Belarus, Iceland and Serbia before it, turns to IMF and the European Union for financial support, after its economy and banking system are rolled by the credit crisis.

Sources: Gathered from various Web sites and published material.

ABBREVIATIONS EXPANDED

TPG—Texas Pacific Group; FDIC—The Federal Deposit Insurance Corporation; TSLF—Term Securities Lending Facility; PDCF—Primary Dealer Credit Facility; AIG—American International Group; TARP—Troubled Asset Relief Program; TAF—Term Auction Facility. BOX 9.10; *Source:* Credit Risk+ technical document, 1997.

ENDNOTES

1. The concept of 'economic capital' is discussed in the chapter titled 'Capital—risk, regulation and adequacy'.
2. This approach is taken by Stephanou, Constantinos and Mendoza, Juan Carlos, 2005, 'Credit risk measurement under Basel II: An overview and implementation issues for developing countries', World Bank Policy Research Working Paper 3556, 11.
3. Ibid, Figure 3, 11.

4. A detailed description of these methods is provided in Scheurmann, Til, 2004, 'What do we know about Loss given Default?', Wharton Financial Institutions Center Working Paper Series 04–01.
5. Altman, Edward I, Brooks Brady, Andrea Resti and Andrea Sironi, 'The Link Between Default and Recovery Rates: Theory, Empirical Evidence and Implications', *Journal of Business* 78, no. 6 (2005): 2203–2227.
6. Basel Committee on Banking Supervision (2006), 'International Convergence of Capital Measurement and Capital Standards: A Revised Framework, Comprehensive Version', www.bis.org
7. Department of the Treasury, Federal Reserve System and Federal Insurance Corporation (2006), 'Basel 2 Capital Accord—Notice of Proposed Rulemaking', 341–342.
8. Market risk is discussed in detail in chapter on bank investments.
9. Banks' capital requirements and the concept of 'economic capital' are discussed in detail in chapter titled 'Capital—Risk, regulation and adequacy'.
10. Discussed in Chapter as above.
11. The document is now available at www.msci.com, MSCI, a leading global provider of investment decision tools and Risk metrics merged in 2010.
12. Notable in this context are the published research work of Edward Altman (1991) of New York University, and Lucas and Lonski of Moody's Investor Service.
13. VaR is a commonly used abbreviation of Value at Risk, used prevalently in market risk determination. In simple terms, VaR measures the maximum expected loss for a given holding period (of a security or a portfolio of securities) for a given confidence level (as chosen by the portfolio manager). For example, a portfolio with daily VaR of ₹1 crore with 99 per cent confidence signifies that there is a 1 per cent chance that the portfolio will lose more than ₹1 crore over the next 24 hours. VaR is discussed in detail in the chapter on 'Investments'.
14. You can access the transition matrix on the Web site of CRISIL at http://www.crisil.com/credit-ratings-risk-assessment/crisil-rating-default-study-2007.pdf, accessed on 4 March 2009.
15. The other probability used in credit analysis is the 'risk neutral probability' of default, where the expected return required by all investors is the risk-free rate. See Box 9.1 for the distinction between risk neutral and real world probabilities.
16. CRISIL also measures 'accuracy ratios' reflecting the model's robustness and predictive ability.
17. Accessed at http://www.crisil.com/credit-ratings-risk-assessment/crisil-rating-default-study-2007.pdf on 19 March 2009.
18. It is also important to distinguish between the 'promised' return on a loan (which is the loan price), and the 'expected' return, which factors in expected losses.
19. The choice of the optimal time horizon is discussed in detail in the Technical document on Credit Metrics™, by J.P. Morgan, accessed at www.riskmetrics.com.
20. Several studies have been carried out for the construction of the 'transition matrix'. The first was a series of articles by Altman and Kao in 1991 (a&b) and 1992 (a&b), followed by special and periodical studies by Moody's and Standard and Poor's.
21. Credit Metrics™—Technical document.
22. Altman *et al.*, in their December 2001 report titled 'Analysing and explaining default recovery rates', submitted to International Swaps and Derivatives Association (ISDA), ascribe the following reasons for the relatively little attention to recovery rates. One, that credit pricing models and risk management applications tend to focus on the systematic risk component of credit risk, and two, credit risk models traditionally assume RR to be independent of PD.
23. Detailed explanations on forward zero curves can be found in the annexure to the chapter on 'Risk Management in Banks'.
24. Credit Metrics technical document, page 27, accessed at www.riskmetrics.com.
25. Credit Metrics Technical document, 2007 update, Appendix D, page 156.
26. The first percentile of a normal distribution M(m, σ^2) is (mean -2.33σ) which equals -18.46.
27. The primary motivation to develop quantitative portfolio models to manage credit risk is the need to address 'concentration risk', which has been discussed in an earlier section of this chapter, and in the previous chapter.
28. The normal distribution is the classic 'bell-shaped' curve described in statistics. The bivariate normal distribution has two variables which are possibly correlated. An extension of this is the multivariate normal distribution, features of which are covered in standard texts on statistics.
29. T. Wilson, 'Portfolio credit risk I', *Risk* 10, no. 9 (September 1987).

    T. Wilson. 'Portfolio credit risk II', *Risk* 10, no. 10 (October 1997).
30. Thomas C Wilson., 'Portfolio Credit Risk,' *FRBNY Economic Policy review* (October 1998): 71–82.
31. The illustration is based on the numerical example given in Wilson's paper quoted above.
32. In a large portfolio of borrowers, as more and more borrowers are added to the portfolio, the standard deviation of the portfolio losses (the variability in portfolio loss) would fall, up to a point. The residual risk that cannot be eliminated by diversifying the portfolio is called the 'market risk' or 'systematic risk'. This risk is considered non-diversifiable and arises due to market/industry or economy-related factors. The risk that can be diversified is called 'non-systematic' or 'idiosyncratic' or 'firm-specific' or 'non-diversifiable' risk. The following diagram clarifies:

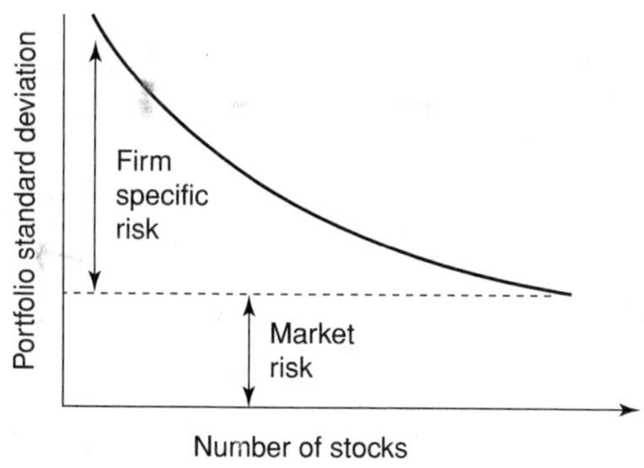

33. 'Calibration' is simply the process of assigning a default probability to a rating or a homogeneous segment of borrowers.
34. The 'gamma distribution' is a skew distribution that approximates to the normal distribution when the mean is large. This continuous probability distribution that has two parameters—a scale and a shape parameter—called α and β. It is fully described by its mean μ and standard deviation σ, such that $\mu = \alpha\beta$ and $\sigma^2 = \alpha\beta^2$. It is prevalently used in engineering, science and business to model continuous variables that are always positive and have a skewed distribution. Examples of its use include 'queuing' models—such as estimating the flow of material in manufacturing and distribution processes, assessing the load on web servers and applications in telecom exchanges. Its skewed profile makes it an appropriate model in climatology, say for rainfall pattern assessment, or in financial services, such as for modelling magnitude of loan defaults or insurance claims.
35. Stephen Kealhofer, John McQuown and Oldrich Vasicek founded KMV Corporation in 1989. Their credit risk models are based on a modification of Merton's asset value model. The firm was subsequently acquired by Moodys corporation, and details of various versions of the model can be accessed at www.moodysanalytics.com.
36. Please refer to any standard corporate finance textbook for an understanding of 'present value', 'free cash flows' and 'discount rate'.
37. For a discussion on the Equity Multiplier, a measure of 'leverage' and the impact of debt on a firm's balance sheet, please refer to chapters on 'Bank financial statements' and the annexure containing 'financial ratios' in the chapter on 'Uses of funds—the lending function'.
38. 'Options' are discussed in detail in the chapter on 'risk management'.
39. Fischer Black and Myron Scholes 'The pricing of options and corporate liabilities', *Journal of Political Economy* 81, no. 3 (May–June 1973): 637–659.
40. Robert C Merton, 'On the Pricing of Corporate Debt: The Risk Structure of Interest Rates.', *Journal of Finance*. 29, no. 2 (May 1974): 449–470.
41. Fischer Black and John Cox, 'Valuing Corporate Securities: Some Effects of Bond Indenture Provisions', *Journal of Finance* 31, no. 2 (May 1976):351–36
42. There are two basic types of options, 'call' and 'put'. A 'call' gives the option holder the right to buy the underlying asset for the strike price, whereas a 'put' gives the option holder the right to sell the underlying asset for the exercise price.
43. A random variable X is 'lognormal' if its natural logarithm $Y = \log(X)$ follows a normal distribution. This means that Y is a normal distribution with mean μ and variance σ^2. It is prevalently used in modelling stock or volatile asset prices where we assume that asset returns are normally distributed.
44. The Modigliani–Miller theorem is a Nobel Prize winning proposition that states that under perfect market conditions, the value of the firm is independent of its capital structure. Refer M. Miller and F. Modigliani, 'The cost of capital, corporation finance and the theory of investment,' *American Economic Review* (June 1958).
45. The term structure of interest rates is discussed in the chapter on 'Risk management'.
46. A 'stochastic process' is simply a collection of random variables—variables whose values change in an uncertain manner—taking values in a common time space. A diffusion type stochastic process is one modelled in continuous time. Many statistical inferential problems can be described in terms of diffusions, through forming stochastic differential equations.
47. Merton in his 1974 paper (page 450) refers to the stochastic differential equation $dV = (\alpha v - C)dt + \sigma V dz$, where α is the instantaneous expected rate of return on the firm per unit time, C is the total dollar payouts by the firm per unit time to either its shareholders or liabilities-holders (*c.g.*, dividends or interest payments) if positive, and it is the net dollars received by the firm from new financing if negative; σ^2 is the instantaneous variance of the return on the firm per unit time and dz is a standard Gauss—Wiener process. For more on the Gauss—Wiener process, please refer to a standard book on statistics.
48. European call options can be exercised only on the maturity date of the option. If the option can be exercised at any time before maturity, it is an 'American option'. Options basics are discussed in the chapter on 'risk management'.
49. Also called the KMV–Merton model, the KMV–Merton model was developed by the KMV Corporation in the late 1980s. It was successfully marketed by KMV until KMV was acquired by Moodys in April 2002. The model is now sold to subscribers by Moody's Analytics Enterprise Risk solutions.
50. Peter J Crosbie and Jeffrey R.Bohn 'Modelling default risk', KMV LLC, 2002.
51. Ibid, 3.
52. Moodys KMV company, 2006, 'Structural Modelling in Practice', presentation by Dr. Jeffrey R Bohn, Head of Research, Moodys KMV company.
53. Crosbie, Peter J, and Bohn, Jeffrey R, 2003, 'Modelling default risk—Modelling methodology'.
54. Ibid, 13

55. Ibid, 13, Figure 8.
56. Assume that firms with DD = 4 number 6000 at a particular point in time. Also assume that 20 firms out of these defaulted after one year. Then EDF 1st year = 20/6000 = 0.0033 = 0.33 per cent or 33 bps.
57. Sources: Moody's Analytics, June 2012, 'Public Firm Expected Default Frequency (EDFTM) Credit Measures: Methodology, Performance, and Model Extensions' (Modelling Methodology), and Dwyer, d, Qu S, 2007, EDFTM 8.0 MODEL ENHANCEMENTS, Modeling methodology
58. The technical document of Credit Risk+TM can be accessed at http://www.csfb.com/institutional/research/assets/creditrisk.pdf, accessed on 21 April 2009.
59. In the context of two state models, a typical approach is by means of Bernoulli random variables.
60. In its simplest form, a Poisson distribution assumes that every borrower can have multiple defaults, as contrasted with the Bernoulli distribution given earlier, which assumes that there are only two outcomes—the counter party either defaults or survives. One of the essential assumptions of the Credit Risk+ model is that the individual probabilities of default are sufficiently small for the compound Bernoulli distribution of default events to be approximated by a Poisson distribution.
61. Derived from the PGF for a portfolio of independent borrowers/counter parties, explained in the Credit Risk+TM document, Appendix A (1997): 34–35.
62. Based on the information in Credit Risk+TM document, Appendix A (1997): 33.
63. We can illustrate the PGF through a numerical example. If there is a portfolio X with only one borrower, who has a probability of default of, say, 5 per cent over the next 1 year, the number of defaults over the next 1 year will have a probability distribution as follows: P (X defaults, *i.e.*, $X = 1$) = 0.05 and P (X does not default, *i.e.*, $X = 0$) = 0.95. The PGF would be $P(z) = 0.95z^0 + 0.05z^1$. This is the PGF defined in Credit Risk+ technical document, Appendix A, equation (3), page 34. The same numerical example can be presented in a different way. If the portfolio value is defined as the expected exposure loss, then X will have the probability distribution at the end of one year as P(X defaults, recovery = 0) = 0.05 and P(X does not default, recovery = 5, say by way of interest + principal) = 0.95. Now the PGF would be $P(z) = 0.05z^0 + 0.95z^5$.
64. The numerical example in the previous footnote will help understanding this notation.
65. Philippe Artznerand and Freddy Delbaen 'Default Risk Insurance and In-Complete Markets', *Mathematical Finance* 5 (1995): 187–195.
66. Robert A. Jarrow and Stuart M. Turnbull, 'Pricing Derivatives on Financial Securities Subject to Credit Risk', *Journal of Finance* 50, no. 1 (1995): 53–86.
67. Darrell Duffie and Kenneth J. Singleton, 'Modelling Term Structures of Defaultable Bonds', *Review of Financial Studies* 12 (1999): 687–720.
68. The interested reader can access the mathematical derivations from the papers quoted above, as well as subsequent work and books by the above researchers and others.
69. If the default process N_T had a zero trend, that is, the expected future default given current information is exactly the current value of the process, it would be a 'fair game' or a 'martingale'.
70. D. Madan and H. Unal, 'Pricing the Risks of Default'. *Review of Derivatives Research* 2 (1998), 121–160.
71. Robert A. Jarrow, David Lando and Stuart M Turnbull, 'A Markov Model for the Term Structure of Credit Risk Spreads', *The Review of Financial Studies* 10, no. 2 (Summer 1997): 481–523.
72. These documents are available at http://www.kamakuraco.com.
73. The basic form of this model can be found in Chava, Sudheer and Robert A Jarrow (2004), 'Banruptcy prediction with industry effects', downloaded from http://ssrn.com, accessed on 2 May 2009.
74. Source: Kamakura Corporation, June 2011, 'Implied credit ratings- Kamakura public firm models', Version 5.0, pages 9, 10
75. Robert A. Jarrow and Philip Protter, 'Structural Versus Reduced Form Models: A New Information Based Perspective', *Journal of investment management* 2, no. 2 (2004): 1–10.
76. Ibid, 8
77. According to the British Bankers' Association (BBA) 2006 credit derivatives survey, the largest contributor to CDS growth has been CDS Index trading. The survey points out that about two-thirds of banks' derivatives volume is from trading activities. Unlike credit insurance contracts, credit derivatives are negotiable and attract large secondary trading. The Chicago Board of Trade has introduced CDR Liquid 50 NAIG Index futures contract, which enables the CBOT to facilitate growth of the CDS market. More information on CDS trading can be accessed at www.cbot.com. In addition, Creditex has online trading platforms for credit derivatives (www.creditex.com).
78. Wai-Yan Cheng, 'Recent Advances in Default Swap Valuation', *Journal of derivatives* (Fall 2001): 18–27.
79. Credit events that trigger a default swap may include one or more of the following: failure to meet payment obligations when due, bankruptcy, repudiation, material adverse restructuring of debt, obligation acceleration or obligation default. These are as defined by ISDA.
80. One basis point is (1/100) per cent.
81. Default swap spreads, though economically comparable to bond yield spreads, do not require specification of a benchmark risk-free yield curve. Second, changes in credit quality get reflected faster in CDS spreads than in bond yield spreads. Hence, CDS spreads are able to reflect credit risk with more speed and accuracy.
82. A loan (or bond) is a deliverable obligation if it has a maturity less than 30 years, is a G6 currency, and not

subordinated to the reference asset (for more details, see the ISDA Web site).

83. The final price is the market value of the reference obligation on the default date as computed by a specified calculation agent (by a specified valuation method). In practice, one or more dealers are asked for quotes on the reference obligation. Of the quotes obtained, the highest and the lowest quotes are ignored. The average of the remaining quotes is considered the value of the reference obligation.
84. D. Duffie, 'Credit Swap Valuation', *Financial Analysts Journal* (January/February 1999): 73–87.
85. Please refer to Box 9.1 in Section II of this chapter for the distinction between risk neutral and real world probabilities.
86. From here on, we follow the approach of Hull and White (2000) in their paper Hull J. and A. White, 'Valuing Credit Default Swaps I: No Counter party Default Risk', *Journal of Derivatives* 8, no. 1 (Fall 2000): 29–40.
87. Arbitrage is the simultaneous purchase and sale of an asset, in different markets or in different forms, in order to profit from a difference in the price. Arbitrage exists as a result of market inefficiencies; it provides a mechanism to ensure prices do not deviate substantially from fair value for long periods of time. The 'no arbitrage' argument in valuing CDS is explained in detail in Hull J. and A. White, 'Valuing Credit Default Swaps I: No Counter party Default Risk', *Journal of Derivatives*, (Fall 2000): 29–40.
88. In accordance with the practice in the interest rate swap market, the protection buyer is the 'fixed rate' payer, while the protection seller is the 'floating rate' payer. The protection buyer is also indicated by terminologies, such as (a) long CDS, (b) CDS buyer, (c) credit risk seller and, (d) fixed rate payer; while the protection seller is also called (a) short CDS, (b) CDS seller, (c) credit risk buyer and (d) floating rate payer. Another thing to remember is that with CDS, buying protection is 'short' the reference asset and selling protection is 'long' the reference asset. This is because buying protection implies 'selling' the reference asset. The market value of the premium leg acts like a short in that as the price of the CDS falls, the market value of the trade increases. The opposite is applicable to the protection leg.
89. J. C. Hull and Alan White, 'Valuing Credit Default Swaps II: Modelling Default Correlations', *Journal of derivatives* 8 (2001): 12–21.
90. R. A. Jarrow and S. M. Turnbull, 'Pricing Derivatives on Financial Securities Subject to Credit Risk', *Journal of Finance* 50 (1995): 53–85.
91. Dominic O'Kane and Stuart Turnbull, 'Valuation of Credit Default Swaps', Fixed Income quantitative research, Lehman Bros, QCR Quarterly, vol 2003-Q1/Q2 (2003): 1–19. The model is illustrated through easy to understand numerical examples.
92. Binomial tree is used in pricing options.
93. D. Duffie and K. J. Singleton, 'Modelling Term Structure of Defaultable Bonds', Review of Financial Studies. 12 (1999): 687–720.
94. Note that 'conditional probabilities' are also called 'default intensities', which form an important part of the reduced-form models discussed in the previous section.
95. There are two ways to price risky (defaultable) debt—one is to discount the risky (default-adjusted) cash flows by the risk-free rate, and the other, to discount risk-free cash flows by risk-adjusted (default spread) rates. Since we do not know the risky rates, it is easier to price the debt by discounting risky cash flows with the risk-free rate, which is easier to obtain or infer. On the other hand, calculating of risky cash flows is also simple—this is the expected cash flow based on probability of default. This is the reason for wide usage of the risk-free rate in the pricing methodology.
96. 'Swaps' in general is discussed in the chapter on 'Risk management in banks'.
97. A good resource to understand cash flow and market value CDOs is the 'CDO Handbook' published by J P Morgan Securities Inc (2002).
98. This sample CDO structure can be found in 'Markit Credit Indices: A Primer', Markit group Ltd., May 2009, accessed at www.markit.com on 16 May 2009.
99. Based on the example given in 'Markit Credit Indices: A Primer', published in May 2009, accessed at www.markit.com.
100. After the financial market collapse in 2007, this method too has drawn flak, and has been named as one of the reasons for the miscalculation by investors. However, for those interested in an analysis of this approach, please refer Christopher Finger , 'Issues in the Pricing of Synthetic CDOs', Risk metrics Group, working paper 04–01 (2004), at www.riskmetrics.com.
101. Summarized from Padmalatha Suresh 'Credit Derivatives—Still Relevant?', Treasury Management, The ICFAI University Press, (March 2009): 36–42.
102. 2008, Survey of credit underwriting practices, Office of the comptroller of currency, USA.
103. The term 'underwriting standards', as used in the above report, 'refers to the terms and conditions under which banks extend or renew credit, such as financial and collateral requirements, repayment programs, maturities, pricing and covenants. Conclusions about 'easing' or 'tightening' represent OCC examiners' observations during the survey period. A conclusion that the underwriting standards for a particular loan category have eased or tightened does not necessarily indicate that all the standards for that particular category have been adjusted.'
104. 'Survey of credit underwriting practices, 2008', Office of the comptroller of the currency, USA (June 2008).
105. Treasury Secretary Geithner's testimony can be accessed at www.ustreas.gov/press/releases/tg71.htm. A description of the four components of the Treasury Framework and a more detailed outline of the systemic risk component are available at www.ustreas.gov/press/releases/tg72.htm.
106. In the United States, the industry has been working closely with regulators, such as the Federal Reserve

Board (FRB). The FRB and fourteen dealer banks started working in 2005 to address operational inefficiencies and backlogs in the processing of OTC CDS trades. This group was known as the 'Fed 14'. Since then other banks have joined these efforts.

107. ISDA's big bang can be accessed at http://www.isda.org/bigbangprot/docs/Big-Bang-Protocol.pdf, accessed on 26 May 2009.
108. For more on credit event auctions, access www.markit.com/cds. The site also contains a useful document titled 'Credit event auction primer'.
109. Select references: McKinsey and Company, March 2013, 'Making data analytics work: Three key challenges; Burton, Dominic, and Court, David, 2012, 'Making Analytics work for you', Harvard Business Review, October 2012
110. Author: Ganesh S. About Author: Is a mentor of an Initiative named Campus Levers started by an alumni group of Indian Institute of Management, Calcutta (IIMC). The initiative is aimed at supporting academic institutes and the student community to understand the real business world with aid of systems and tools that impart business learning in a practical way.
111. Freddie Mac, the acronym for the 'Federal Home Loan Mortgage Corporation' (FHLMC), is a government-sponsored enterprise (GSE) of the US federal government. Its primary objective is to expand the secondary market for mortgages in the United States. It buys mortgages on the secondary market, pools and packages them, and sells them as mortgage-backed securities (MBS). In September 2008, consequent to its role in the credit crisis, the federal government took over Freddie Mac and Fannie Mae (Federal National Mortgage Association), the other mortgage loan purchaser in the private sector. In 2008, both institutions together owned or guaranteed about half of the US' $12 trillion mortgage market. Hence, both were at high risk from the subprime crisis.

CHAPTER TEN

Managing Market Risk—Banks' Investment Portfolio

CHAPTER STRUCTURE

KEY TAKEAWAYS FROM THE CHAPTER

- Understand the primary objectives of banks' investments.
- Know the functions of the bank treasury.
- Learn about conventional and contemporary treasury products.
- Understand risks associated with the treasury.
- Learn some tools for market risk measurement such as the VaR methodology and its implications.
- Understand how credit risk and market risk interact.

SECTION I

BASIC CONCEPTS

We have seen in the chapter 'Banks Financial Statements' that 'investments' constitute a major asset on banks' books and along with 'loans and advances,' take up a major share in banks' total assets. We have also seen in an earlier chapter the rationale for bank credit and its key role in a country's economic growth. If credit growth is a major driver of economic growth then what part do 'investments' play in banks' larger role as financial intermediaries?

Typically, banks invest in securities to meet the following objectives:

Safety of Capital We have seen that substantial credit risk is attached to the loan portfolio of banks. To offset this risk, banks invest in securities with low default risk thus preserving the capital.

Liquidity Banks need adequate liquidity to pay off unanticipated demands from the depositors and other liability holders, as well as meet the loan demands. In case a bank does not have liquid funds at the time these demands are made, it has two options—it can borrow from the market or it can sell off near cash assets. Market borrowings carry an inherent risk—interest rates at the time of borrowing may be more than the cost of deposits to be repaid or the contracted yield on the loans. This is called 'interest rate risk' and can lead to earnings volatility. On the other hand, banks can invest surplus funds in marketable securities, which can be liquidated in the short term. However, if the market value of these investments at the time of liquidation is less than the book value, the bank will have to report a loss. If the banks decide to invest in low rate securities with fairly stable market values, there is an opportunity loss in the form of reduced interest income.

Yield From the above point, it follows that banks will have to make investments in securities that will also yield reasonable returns. However, paradoxically, higher returns will flow from investments with higher risk. Portfolio managers will, therefore, have to look at risk return trade offs while building the investment portfolio of the bank.

Diversification of Credit Risk Over time, banks develop expertise in lending to a specific sector or industry and find it difficult to diversify their loan portfolios. Hence, banks invest in securities spanning diverse geographic areas or industries to offset credit risk, as well as ensure safety of the capital invested.

Managing Interest Rate Risk Exposure Banks can easily and quickly adjust the maturity or duration (refer chapter on 'risk management') of their securities portfolio in times of interest rate volatility. This flexibility will not be typically available with loan portfolios.

Meeting Pledging Requirements Most bank borrowings can be collateralized with assets and marketable securities are accepted as qualifying collateral.

From the foregoing discussion, it is evident that a bank's investment portfolio cannot satisfy all the objectives. There may be circumstances under which a bank looks for yield from security investments to bolster its dwindling spreads on loans made. There could be other times at which the bank's liquidity needs would be overarching. How should then the investment portfolio of banks be balanced? Regulators in most countries deal with this dilemma by stipulating that banks hold their investments in three classes to satisfy most of the objectives given above.

Typically, regulators stipulate that banks divide their security holdings into three categories, based on the objectives of such investment as given below.

- **Held to maturity (HTM):** These are securities purchased with the objective of holding till maturity. On the balance sheet, they are carried at a mortised cost (historical cost adjusted for principal payments). The capital gains or losses at the time of maturity will be taken to the income statement. However, during the period they are held, unrealized gains or losses due to market fluctuations have no impact on the income statement.
- **Held for trading (HFT):** These securities are purchased with the intention to sell in the near term. They are carried at market value on the balance sheet, and therefore, unrealized gains or losses could impact the income statement.
- **Available for sale (AFS):** Securities not classified under the above two categories will be included here. They too are carried at market value on the balance sheet.

It is evident that the above classification based on the motive of investment determine the accounting impact on banks' financial statements. For instance, a fixed rate bond (without options) will sell at par if the market rates and the coupon rate on the bond are the same. If market rates rise above the coupon rate, the market value of the bond falls below the par value. If market rates fall, the reverse would happen. Thus, the difference between the market value and par value would be the unrealized[1] gain or loss on the security.

However, if the intention is to hold the bond until maturity, changes in interest rates and the unrealized gains or losses will not affect the value of the security in the bank's financial statements.

Therefore, prudential treatment requires that adequate provisions are made in the income statements for unrealized gains or losses based on market values in the case of securities held by the trading categories.

The Treasury Functions

In much of the developed world, a bank's 'treasury' is a source of substantial profit to the bank and can therefore create substantial value to shareholders. In addition to managing liquidity, the treasury is responsible for managing assets and liabilities, trading in currencies and securities, and developing new products. High-performing treasuries systematically identify and mitigate profit from market risk—the risk arising from changes in interest rates, exchange rates and the value of securities and commodities. Banks' treasuries typically perform the following basic functions within their investment and trading activities.

- Investment advice and assistance to customers, including other banks, to manage their investment portfolios. Most treasury products are associated with the credit- and cash-management needs of corporate customers (for example, off balance-sheet and tax-efficient loans or project finance).
- The treasury can also play an important role in structuring products to hedge the bank's own capital. These products—typically derivatives contracts—protect the bank's capital exposure to a particular currency or to market factors such as, changing interest rates and commodity prices.
- The treasury buys and sells securities on behalf of the customers. The willingness of the treasuries to buy and sell securities is also called 'making the market'. While making the market, they also make profits on the transactions by maintaining a positive spread between the 'bid' (buy) and 'ask' (sell) prices. Large banks are also market makers in options and interest rate swaps.
- Banks, as traders, also speculate on short-term interest rate movements. The bank's treasury may borrow in US dollars and lend in the rupee inter-bank market or vice versa to take advantage of the domestic and foreign interest rates. Alternatively, the treasury could borrow in the short-term money market[2] and invest in 'commercial paper'. When the treasury expects interest rates to rise (bond prices to fall), it goes 'short' (sells securities) to avoid holding assets expected to depreciate in value. Conversely, when the Treasury expects interest rates to fall (bond prices to rise), it goes 'long' (buys securities).
- In developed markets, the treasury departments act as risk managers for banks. By using sophisticated internal transfer pricing, the treasury buys and sells funds among the bank's client-facing units, thus isolating and removing maturity and interest rate mismatches from corporate and retail business units. The treasury determines prices of 'buying' and 'selling' resources by business units of the bank on the basis of market rates of interest, the cost of hedging market risk and the cost of maintaining reserve assets of the bank. For instance, the bank branches may source deposits at, say, 6 per cent and transfer it to the treasury at 'market cost', which could be, say, 5 per cent after adjusting for hedging and liquidity. The difference of 1 per cent is borne by the deposit mobilizing units. Similarly, treasury 'sells' resources to the lending branches of the bank at 7 per cent, while the branches lend these resources at 10 per cent in the market. The difference of 3 per cent represents the risk premium earned by the lending units.

As markets develop, many credit products are being replaced by treasury products. An example is working capital credit being substituted by commercial paper. Since treasury products are more marketable, liquidity can be infused when required.

Features of Treasury Profit The following are the features of treasury profit:

- Treasury operates in markets that are almost free of credit risk.
- Treasury operates with little capital allocation, but the upside potential is unlimited, that is, the returns on capital could be very high.
- Operating costs are lower than for branch banking, whether corporate or retail.
- The treasury is manned by a few specialists, but the value of transactions could be very high.
- Business volumes are substantial to compensate for the thin spreads in trading.

Sources of Treasury Profit

1. **Foreign exchange business:** Buying and selling foreign currency to customers is a source of non-interest income for banks. The difference between the 'bid' and 'ask' rates, called the spread, constitutes the banks' profit. Banks buy foreign currency from exporter customers and sell the foreign currency in the inter-bank market. They can also sell the foreign currency to customers (importers), for which they can buy the currency in the inter-bank market or use the currency bought from exporter customers. Banks buy and sell in the inter-bank markets to square the foreign currency balances at the end of each day. Thus, banks do not maintain a stock of foreign currency at the end of each day. In case, a bank maintains an open position (overbought or oversold) at the end of any day, it exposes itself to exchange risk (adverse changes in the value of currency overnight).

New treasury products in the foreign exchange markets have considerably widened the range of services that the banks offer. These markets are the most liquid in respect of currencies that can be freely bought and sold, such as US dollars, Euros and Sterling pounds. These markets are also transparent markets, since information on currency movements are freely available. They are virtual markets with little or no physical boundaries and effective information dissemination. Hence, foreign exchange markets are likened to near-perfect markets with an efficient price discovery mechanism.

Some of the prevalent treasury products[3] in these markets are listed below:

- Spot trades, referring to current transactions, where mostly currency is bought and sold.
- Forward and futures trades, involving purchase or sale of currency at a future date.
- Swaps, which are a combination of spot and forward transactions. Though the swap is generally used for funding requirements, there is also a profit opportunity from interest rate arbitrage.
- Investment of foreign exchange surplus, which could arise out of profits from treasury or overseas branch operations, borrowings or deposits in foreign currency in global money markets or short-term securities.
- Loans and advances in foreign currency.
- Foreign bills rediscounting in the inter-bank market.

2. **Money market products:** These are securities with short maturities and durations, typically 1 year or less. They are held to meet liquidity and pledging requirements and also for a reasonable return.

Some of the prominent 'money market' products are as follows:

- *Repurchase agreements or repo*: These represent a loan transaction between two parties, typically securities dealers and banks. The lender (investor) buys securities from the borrower, simultaneously agreeing to sell the securities back on a predetermined date at a predetermined price plus interest. The borrower receives funds, while the lender earns interest on the investment. The underlying securities form the collateral for the loan. If the borrower defaults, the lender gets title to the securities. Banks operate both as lenders and borrowers in the repo market and the collaterals are typically government securities (though any security can serve as collateral) (Also refer chapter 'Monetary policy implications for bank management').
- *Treasury bills or T-bills*: These securities are marketable obligations of the government, carrying maturities of one year or less. They are attractive to banks because they are highly liquid, free of default risk, offer reasonable rates of interest and are tradable in the secondary market. The prices of T-bills are determined through an auction process in which banks participate. Banks can buy the bills directly for their own investment portfolios or for their trading activity. T-bills are purchased at a discount and the discount rate is quoted in terms of a 360 day year as being equal to (face value—purchase price) × (360/number of days to maturity)/face value.
- *Commercial paper (CP)*: These are unsecured promissory notes issued by corporations for the purpose of financing short-term working capital requirements. There are two types of CPs—'direct paper' and 'dealer paper'. Direct paper is issued primarily by finance companies and bank holding companies, while dealer paper (also called 'industrial paper') is issued primarily by non-financial firms through securities dealers. The CP issuers have to be highly creditworthy firms, since these instruments are not backed by any collateral. Most CP issues are rated by external rating agencies to signify the default risk. Banks invest in CPs since they typically yield more than T-Bills.
- *Certificates of deposit (CD)*: These are negotiable debt instruments similar to CPs, the difference being that they are issued by banks against deposit of funds. They are attractive because they yield more than T-bills do and if issued by a prime bank, can be sold in the secondary market before maturity. Even though CDs are issued by creditworthy banks, investors usually demand a risk premium over the deposit rates offered by safe banks. Recently, banks have also started offering stock market indexed CDs, where the interest rate is linked to the stock market index of the country.
- *Bankers' acceptances (BA)*: These are products predominantly used in international trade financing. A banker's acceptance simply represents a draft drawn on a bank by an exporter or importer of goods and services. The draft represents an order to pay a specified amount of money at a predetermined future date. When the bank 'accepts'[4] this draft, it represents a guarantee from the accepting bank to remit the face value of the draft at maturity. Bankers' acceptances are negotiable instruments and are mostly associated with letters of credit.[5] For the investor, BA represents a short-term interest bearing draft accepted by a prime bank. Due to the low default risk, the rate is only slightly above that of a T-Bill of comparable maturity.

3. **Securities market products:** Banks' investment portfolios are typically dominated by securities that can be bought and sold in the government securities and capital markets. Each of these securities exhibit varying risk and return features. In most countries, regulations restrict banks' investments to 'investment-grade'[6] securities only.

- *Government securities*: These are long-term securities issued by the governments of various countries for financing social programs. They are perceived as risk free, are highly liquid and carry attractive coupon rates. Like T-bills, government securities are sold through auctions and are actively traded in secondary markets. Box 10.1 outlines the salient features of some capital market instruments in the US.

BOX 10.1 US GOVERNMENT SECURITIES

There are four major types of marketable securities issued by the Department of Treasury in the US namely, bills, notes, bonds and treasury inflation protected securities (TIPS). These are direct obligations of the government and are considered free from default risk.

Treasury bills are issued for very short maturities, not exceeding a year. They are issued at a discount. The interest earned by the bank is the difference between the face value paid at maturity and the discount price.

The US treasury issues treasury notes, which are interest bearing notes with original maturities of 1–10 years. The prices and yields on these notes are set through auctions and investors include pension funds, insurance companies, financial institutions, corporate bodies and some foreign institutions. The secondary market for these securities is extremely deep, due to the large volumes being traded, low default risk and wide range of investors. In addition, thirty year bills or STRIPS (Separate trading of registered interest and principal of securities) are permitted by the US Treasury. STRIPS are created out of standard T-bills, treasury notes and bonds and are issued as bearer instruments. These instruments are 'stripped' into their interest and principal components and traded as 'zero coupon'[7] securities. Each zero coupon security is priced by discounting the promised cash flow at the appropriate interest rate. Banks find these instruments attractive since they are assured of fixed interest payment and yield for the selected maturity. Further, as there are no interim cash flows, there is no reinvestment risk. For example, a 10 year USD 10 million par value treasury bond that pays 10 per cent coupon interest (5 per cent semi-annually) pays USD 500,000 semi-annually. Thus, this security can be 'stripped' into 20 disparate interest payments of USD 500,000 each and a single USD 10 million payment at the end of 10 years or 21 separate zero coupon securities. If the market rate on the 3 year zero coupon security is 9 per cent, the associated price of the zero related to the sixth semi-annual payment would be $500{,}000/(1.045)^6$ or USD 383,949.

The US Treasury created TIPS in 1997. TIPS pay a fixed rate of interest semi-annually on the inflation adjusted principal amount. The amount paid out as interest will be calculated as the annual interest rate multiplied by the adjusted principal. Since the principal is adjusted for inflation, its value may fluctuate. But, at maturity, the greater of the face value or the inflation adjusted principal is paid. These securities are also eligible for the treasury's STRIPS.

In addition, banks in the US also invest in government agency securities, which exhibit characteristics similar to those of the US treasury securities. Agency securities are interest bearing and are issued at a discount to the face value. However, the agency securities are less liquid, since the issues are much smaller than treasury issues. Further, unlike treasury securities, agency securities may not be backed by federal government and may not be eligible for tax exemptions. Therefore, in order to compensate for these risks, the returns on agency securities are higher than treasury securities.

Other investments by banks in the US capital market include mortgage backed securities (MBS) that exhibit characteristics similar to corporate bonds. An MBS is a security that evidences an undivided interest in the ownership of mortgage loans. The most common form of MBS is the 'pass-through security',[8] in which homogenous mortgages are pooled and investors buy an interest in the pool in the form of securities. Other popular forms of MBS are: (a) Government National Mortgage Association, known as Ginnie Mae or GNMA pass-through securities, (b) Federal Home Loan Mortgage Corporation, popularly termed as Freddie Mac or FHLMC participation certificates, guaranteed mortgage certificates and collateralized mortgage obligations, (c) Federal National Mortgage Association, popularly termed as Fannie Mae or FNMA securities, and (d) other privately issued pass-throughs.[9]

Source: Federal Reserve documents.

- *Corporate debt paper, debentures and bonds*: These are debt instruments issued by the corporate bodies, mostly secured by specific assets. They may be issued with differing structures in order to enhance marketability and reduce cost of issue. Some of the common variations include structured obligations with put, call or convertibility[10] options, zero coupon bonds, floating rate bonds, deep discount bonds or instruments with step up coupons.
- *Equities*: While investing in equities, banks take direct exposure to the stock market. The risks involved in equity trading is matched by good returns but bank treasuries are circumspect while investing in equities.

Risks and Returns of Investment Securities

The primary objective of banks' investment portfolio and treasury operations is to maximise earnings while mitigating risks that are involved.

There are three predominant methods by which bank investments contribute to earnings, which are as follows:

- Interest income
- Income from reinvestment
- Capital gains or losses

However, the earnings are susceptible to the following risks:

- Interest rate risk is the potential volatility in returns caused by the changes in the interest rates. How do variations in earnings take place? If the bank holds fixed income securities, the market value of these securities would change in the direction opposite to the change in interest rates of comparable securities. If market interest rates (on comparable debt securities) increase after purchase, the market value of fixed-rate and option-free debt decreases.[11] Second, if the interest rates are decreasing, the investor will have to reinvest the coupon payments at lower rates. This is called reinvestment risk. In most cases, it is seen that interest rate risk is offset by reinvestment returns and vice versa. For example, if interest rates rise and the treasury decides to sell the bonds at less than cost, it can recoup part of the loss by reinvesting the proceeds to earn future coupon payments at the higher rates. When rates decrease, the treasury can sell the securities at a gain. However, part of the gain is offset by the lower rates earned by the reinvested amount. Hence, interest rate risk (also called price risk) will have to be viewed along with reinvestment risk.
- Credit risk arises in case when the bank's investment in debt securities does not yield the promised interest and principal payments. It is for this reason that many central banks require that banks invest only in 'investment grade'[12] securities, though these securities typically yield less than 'non-investment grade' securities. In many countries, regulators permit banks to invest in unrated securities as well, but the banks should maintain credit files on these issuers and be able to justify the economic rationale for the investment. Detailed analysis of the issuer's creditworthiness, as for credit expansion, is required for sound investment by the bank.
- Even though one of the important objectives of maintaining investment portfolios is liquidity, investment in securities could also be illiquid at times. Liquidity risk could arise from the lack of a market for securities held by the bank. Some securities, such as those in very small lots or unrated securities cannot be easily sold before maturity. The bank may have to sell off such securities by offering considerable discounts on the price. Second, securities used for pledging requirements are illiquid in the short term, since banks will have to substitute other collateral before reclaiming the security from the pledge for sale. Third, banks are expected to hold the 'HTM' securities till maturity and will have to show strong justification for the need to sell such securities before maturity.
- Of other general risks that could cause volatility in returns from the investment portfolio, the most important and visible is the inflation risk. Unanticipated rise in inflation would erode the purchasing power of the return from the fixed rate securities. Investors have deferred consumption to purchase these securities, but in inflationary conditions the returns, when they are actually received, buy less. Banks' profitability will take a hit when the banks' inflation expectations are lower than the inflation expectations of its depositors, but the actual inflation is high. When this happens, banks would be willing to accept lower returns on its investments, as compared with what they have to pay to the depositors. The higher is the actual inflation, the worse is the banks' spread.

SECTION II

MEASURING MARKET RISK WITH VaR

The increasing volatility of financial markets has necessitated design and development of more sophisticated risk management tools. Value at risk (VaR) has become one of the standard measures to quantify market risk.

The concept and use of VaR as a risk management tool gained prominence only about two decades ago. Major financial firms in the late 1980s were using the VaR to measure the risk of their trading portfolios. Since then, VaR has had a meteoric rise as a market risk management tool. Most derivative dealers around the world use the concept to measure and manage market risk. In 1994, J P Morgan released 'Risk Metrics'™ as a market standard and this provided further fillip to VaR usage.

VaR is defined as the *maximum* potential loss in the value of a portfolio due to adverse market movements for a given probability. The conceptual simplicity of this measure has made it immensely popular. VaR reduces the (market) risk associated with any portfolio to just one number, the loss associated to a given probability. VaR is a single, summary, statistical measure of possible portfolio losses. Specifically, it is a measure of losses due to 'normal' market movements. Losses greater than the value at risk are suffered only with a specified small probability.

VaR measures are used both for risk management and for regulatory purposes. For instance, the Basel Committee on Banking Supervision[13] at the Bank for International Settlements advocates VaR estimates as a basis for meeting capital requirements in banks. Box 10.2 describes the basic features of the VaR calculation.

BOX 10.2 THE RISK MEASUREMENT TOOL CALLED VaR

How the VaR evolved

It is said that J P Morgan Chairman Dennis Weatherstone used to call for a simple report at the end of each day, showing how the firm's position would be impacted by the market risk. Analysts of J.P. Morgan evolved the VaR concept and this number was included in the '4.15 report', as the report to the Chairman was called. In 1993, the Washington 'Group of thirty', headed by Weatherstone, recommended in its study on 'Derivatives: Practice and Principles' that VaR was an appropriate measure for measuring a firm's market risk. Since then, VaR has been a very popular measure adopted by almost all financial and other institutions for reporting on market risk.

Rationale of VaR methodologies

The statistical features of financial markets have been well documented[14]: (a) distribution of financial market returns are leptokurtotic (in other words, they have heavier tails and higher peak than the normal distribution), (b) equity returns are negative skewed, and (c) volatilities (as measured by squared returns or standard deviations) of market factors show a cluster tendency. One or more of these empirical features form the basis of the popular VaR models.

What is VaR?

VaR summarizes the predicted maximum loss (or worst loss) over a target horizon within a given confidence interval.

How is VaR computed?

Assume a bank holds ₹100 crore in medium-term investments. How much could the bank lose in a month? As much as ₹100,000 or ₹10 lakh or ₹1 crore? An appropriate answer to this question would enable the banks to decide whether the return they receive is an appropriate compensation for risk.

In order to answer this question, we first have to analyse the characteristics of medium-term securities. Let us do this in the following steps:

Step 1: Obtain, say, monthly returns on medium-term bonds over the last 40 years. It is possible that these returns could range from a low of −6 per cent to a high of +15.0 per cent.

Step 2: Construct regularly spaced 'buckets' going from the lowest to the highest number and count how many observations fall into each bucket (frequency distribution). Thus, we can construct a 'probability distribution' for the monthly returns, which counts how many occurrences have been observed in the past for a particular range.

Step 3: For each return, compute a probability of observing a lower return. This is done as follows. Pick a confidence level, say 95 per cent. For this confidence level, find on the graph a point such that there is a 5 per cent probability of finding a lower return. This number is, say, −2 per cent, which implies that all occurrences of returns less than −2 per cent add up to 5 per cent of the total number of months or 24 out of 480 months. (Note that this could also be obtained from the sample standard deviation, assuming the returns are close to normally distributed).

Step 4: Now, we can compute the VaR of a ₹100 crore portfolio. There is only a 5 per cent chance that the portfolio will fall by more than ₹100 crore times −2 per cent or ₹2 crore. The VaR is therefore, ₹2 crore.

Step 5: In other words, the market risk of this portfolio can be communicated effectively to a non-technical audience with a statement such as: Under normal market conditions, the most the portfolio can lose over a month is ₹2 crore.

Choosing VaR parameters

In the above example, VaR was reported at the 95 per cent level over a 1 month horizon. How do we choose these two quantitative parameters?

- *Horizon:* If the bank's trading portfolio is invested in highly liquid securities, even a 1 day horizon may be acceptable. For an investment manager with a monthly rebalancing and reporting focus, a 30 day period may be more appropriate. Ideally, the holding period should correspond to the longest period needed for orderly portfolio liquidation.
- *Confidence level:* The choice of the confidence level depends on how the bank wants to use VaR. The bank may intend to use the resulting VaRs directly for the choice of a capital cushion. In this case, the choice of the confidence level becomes crucial, as it should reflect the degree of risk aversion of the bank and the cost of a loss of exceeding VaR. Higher risk aversion or greater costs implies that a greater amount of capital should cover possible losses thus leading to a higher confidence level. On the other hand, if VaR numbers are just used to provide a yardstick to compare risks across different markets then the choice of the confidence level is not too important.

Changing VaR parameters

If we assume that portfolio returns follow the normal distribution then we can easily convert one horizon or confidence level to another.

As returns across different periods are close to uncorrelated, the variance of returns for 'n' days should be n times the variance of a 1 day return. Hence, in terms of volatility (or standard deviation), it can be adjusted as: VaR(n days) = VaR (1 day) × n

In order to convert from one confidence level to another, use standard normal tables. From these tables, we know that the 95 per cent one-tailed VaR corresponds to 1,645 times the standard deviation, the 99 per cent VaR corresponds to 2.326 times standard deviation and so on. Therefore, in order to convert from 99 per cent VaR to 95 per cent VaR,

$$\text{VaR (95\%)} = \text{VaR (99\%)} \times 1.645/2.326$$

Use of VaR

This single number summarizes the portfolio's exposure to market risk as well as the probability of an adverse move. It measures the risk using the same monetary units as the bottom line. Investors can, therefore, decide whether they feel comfortable with this level of risk.

If the answer is no, the same process that led to the computation of VaR can be used to decide where to trim risk. For instance, the riskiest securities can be sold or derivatives such as futures and options can be added to hedge the undesirable risk. VaR also allows users to measure incremental risk, that is, the contribution of each security to total portfolio risk.

Generalizing, using a probability of 'x' per cent and a holding period of n days an entity's VaR is the loss that is expected to be exceeded with a probability of only x per cent during the next n day holding period. In other words, it is the loss that is expected to be exceeded during x per cent of the n-day holding period. Typical values for the probability x are 1, 2.5 and 5 per cent while common holding periods are 1, 2, and 10 (business) days and 1 month. Values of x are determined primarily by how the user of the risk management system wants to view the VaR number is an 'abnormal' loss that occurs with a probability of 1 per cent or 5 per cent. For example, J P Morgan's Risk Metrics system uses 5 per cent, while there are others who use 0.3 per cent. The parameter n is determined by the entity's horizon. Those which actively trade their portfolios such as, financial firms typically use 1 day, while institutional investors and non-financial firms may use longer holding periods.

A VaR number applies to the current portfolio, so an implicit assumption underlying the computation is that the current portfolio will remain unchanged throughout the holding period. This may not be reasonable, particularly for long holding periods.

References: Jorion, Philippe, 2005, accessed at http://www.gsm.uci.edu/~jorion/oc/case.html and 'Value at Risk', Harvard Business School, (9-297-069), rev 15 July 1997.

TEASE THE CONCEPT

- A bank has a portfolio with daily VaR of ₹1 crore with 95 per cent confidence. This means that there is ...... per cent chance the portfolio will lose more than .... in the next .... hours/days/ months.
- Can we use the VaR for simple risk comparisons? Can we, for example, compare the risk of portfolios X and Y, where both portfolios have the same value, but portfolio X's VaR is ₹4 crore and Y's VaR is ₹2 crore? Assume both VaR have been computed for a holding period of one month and at 99 per cent confidence interval. If they can be compared, which portfolio is more risky?

Approaches to VaR Computation

There are various approaches to VaR computation. Therefore, it is likely that firms calculating VaR for the same portfolio using different approaches may arrive at different VaR figures. Of course, each approach has its advantages, disadvantages and limitations and hence, this aspect should be borne in mind while choosing the appropriate approach and interpreting the results.

However, the approaches follow a common structure, summarized in three steps: (a) mark to market the portfolio, (b) estimate the distribution of portfolio returns and (c) calculate the portfolio VaR. Depending on the method used to arrive at (b), the models can be grouped in three categories.[15]

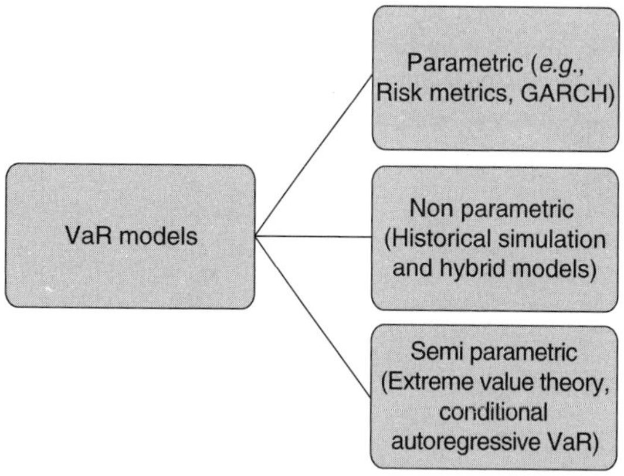

The more prevalent ones—historical simulation, the variance-covariance approach and Monte Carlo simulation—are briefly discussed below. The summary provided below is the approach for a typical, simple portfolio. The basic approach can be expanded to include more types of assets with diverse types of market risk.

The common features in all the approaches are: (a) they use historical (over long or short periods) data on the assets contained in the portfolio, (b) they value the portfolio in the next period and compare the future value with the current value and (c) they generate the distribution of the risk portfolios for the required period in future,

1. **The Historical Simulation Approach**

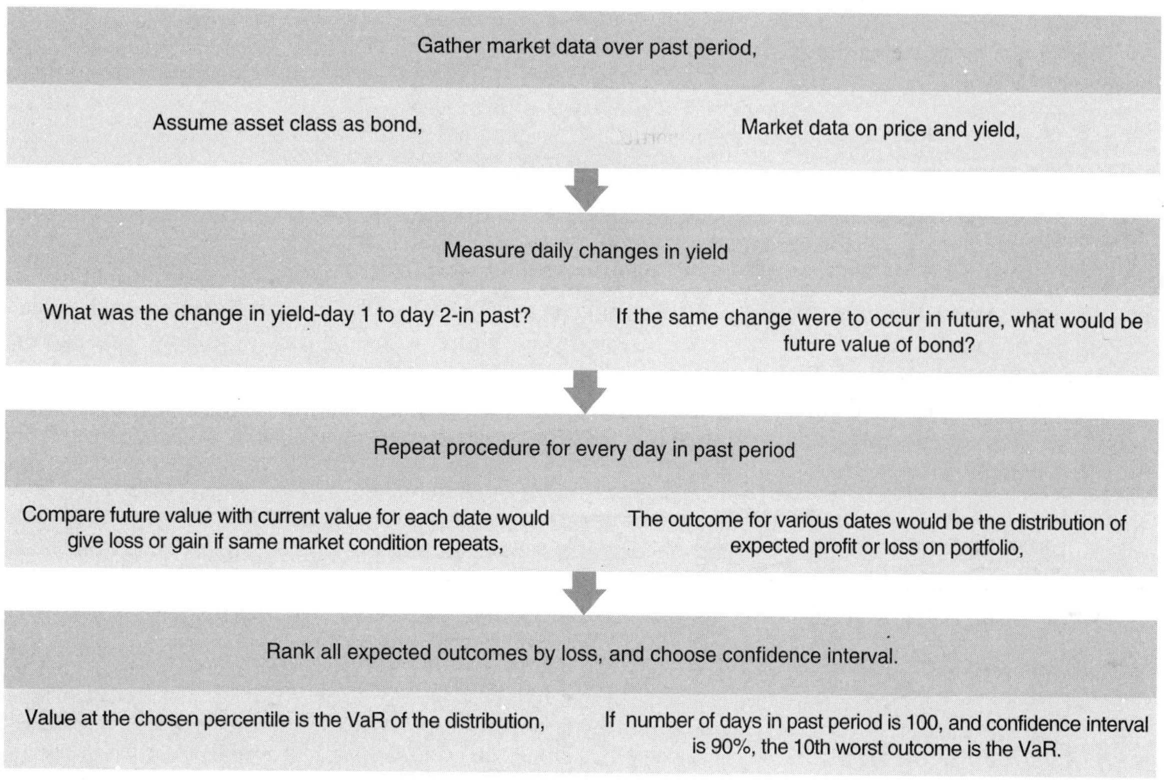

2. **The Variance-Covariance Approach (also called the 'analytic' or 'parametric' approach) and J.P. Morgan's Risk Metrics™**

The name 'variance-covariance' simply signifies the covariance[16] matrix of the distribution of changes in the values of the underlying market factors in the portfolio. It is based on the key assumption (there are also other assumptions) that the underlying market factors follow a multivariate normal distribution. With the normal distribution assumption, it is possible to determine the distribution of mark-to-market portfolio profits and losses, which is also normal (being a linear combination of normal variables). Return volatilities (measured by standard deviations) and correlations of risk factors are calculated using historical data. Once the distribution of expected portfolio profits and losses has been arrived at, standard mathematical properties of the normal distribution are used to determine the loss that will be equaled or exceeded *x* per cent of the time, *i.e.*, the VaR.

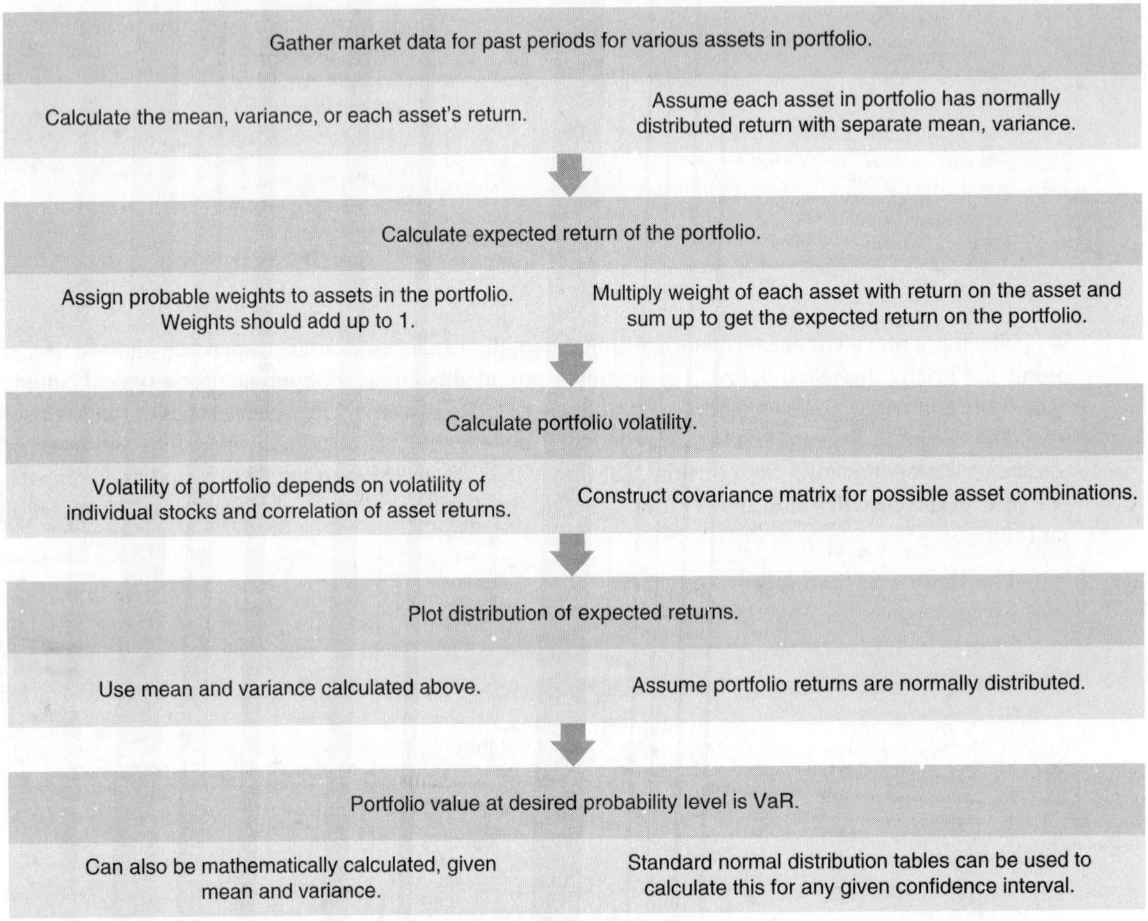

Note: As an example, the expected volatility (standard deviation) of a two-asset portfolio can be calculated using $\sigma_p^2 = w_1^2\sigma_1^2 + w_2^2\sigma_2^2 + 2w_1w_2\text{Cov}(r_1, r_2)$, where w_1 and w_2 are the respective asset weights in the portfolio and r and σ indicate the return and the standard deviation of the two assets, respectively. This formula can be extended to any number of assets in the portfolio.

The above approach forms the basis for the widely used Risk Metrics™ package[17] popularized by J P Morgan. Box 10.3

BOX 10.3 AN OVERVIEW OF RISK METRICS ™[18]

In 1994, J.P. Morgan developed a VaR model primarily to support the internal reporting system called the '4:15 report' that measured end of day portfolio risk. The Risk Metrics methodology was then standardized and published and developed into a software product in 1996. Two years later, Risk Metrics was spun out of J.P. Morgan as a separate company.

Risk Metrics group acquired institutional shareholder services (ISS) and Centre for Financial Research & Analysis (CFRA) in 2007. ISS was founded in 1985 to promote good corporate governance in the private sector and raise the level of responsible proxy voting among institutional investors and pension fund fiduciaries and in 1986, ISS launched its Proxy Advisory Service to assist institutional investors in fulfilling their fiduciary obligations with comprehensive proxy analysis. ISS gave Risk Metrics access to substantial data on pay, governance and other corporate practices at 41,000 companies, as well as 1,200 new clients who collectively manage $20 trillion in assets. **CFRA** was born in 1994 to provide institutional investors with early warning signs of business deterioration within portfolio companies. CFRA built a rigorous and proprietary forensic accounting research process for assessing the quality and sustainability of companies' reported financial results and expanded into specialty legal, regulatory and due diligence research.

Risk Metrics is widely recognized in VaR measurement. However, the industry has yet to settle on a single industry standard for VaR calculation.

In the variance-covariance methodology outlined above, we make a critical assumption that volatility is constant. However, in practice, volatility is not constant and varies from day to day. This problem has been recognized by researchers and a widely used solution was proposed in 1986 by Tim Bollerslev that generalized the pioneering and Nobel prize winning paper of Robert Engle in 1982.[19] The time varying volatility approach is commonly called the GARCH method,[20] and uses heavier weights for recent returns (and their variances), than for those more distant in time (whereas the constant volatility method outlined above assumes equal weights for all squared returns—variances—in the past). However, this process of weighting calls for a complex, computer intensive procedure.

Risk Metrics is a risk management system that includes techniques to approximate GARCH volatilities. Risk Metrics uses a similar method–Exponentially Weighted Moving Average (EWMA) estimates of daily volatility that represent the weighted average of past squared returns, with the more recent returns receiving heavier weights. However, the set of weights used by Risk Metrics are easier to compute than in the GARCH methodology, and the same set of weights can be used for any asset in the portfolio–say, bonds, stocks or currencies. Similarly, for calculating covariances in the portfolio, the Risk Metrics GARCH approximation can be used to estimate time varying covariances.

Since Risk Metrics is able to yield both volatility and covariance estimates, it can also handle Monte Carlo simulation of derivative portfolios. The general view is that Risk Metrics (as well as the GARCH methodology) tend to underestimate VaR, since the normality assumption made by the model is not consistent with financial market return characteristics.

Risk Metrics has periodically been updating its computation versions—known by the year they were updated in. For example, RM 1994 indicates the methodology proposed in the year 1994. RM 2006 is the latest updated version of the methodology.

RM 1994 methodology relies on the measure of volatilities and correlations given by the historical data, using the EWMA. The appeal of this methodology is its simplicity, conceptually and computationally. However, with more understanding of and experience with volatilities, RM 2006 has introduced a process leading to simple volatility forecasts, while retaining the appeal and advantages of RM 1994. The updated version can also deal with long term horizons.

In 2010, Risk Metrics group became part of MSCI, a leading provider of investment support tools, that include indices, portfolio risk and performance analytics and governance tools. The technical document of RM 2006 is now available on www.msci.com

Source: www.riskmetrics.com and the technical documents in footnotes

The appeal of the approach lies in the speed with which computations can be done and the ability to examine alternative assumptions about correlations and standard deviations.

However, the approach is limited by the normal distribution assumption, since movements in market returns do not always follow a normal distribution. The tendency of the market returns to exhibit 'fat tails' (extreme values or extraordinary events) can result in misleading conclusions due to the normal distribution assumption. Further, the approach has limited ability to capture the risks of portfolios containing derivatives such as options.

3. **The Monte Carlo Simulation Approach**

This simulation is much more rigorous than the historical simulation approach described above. It uses mathematical models to forecast future market shocks.

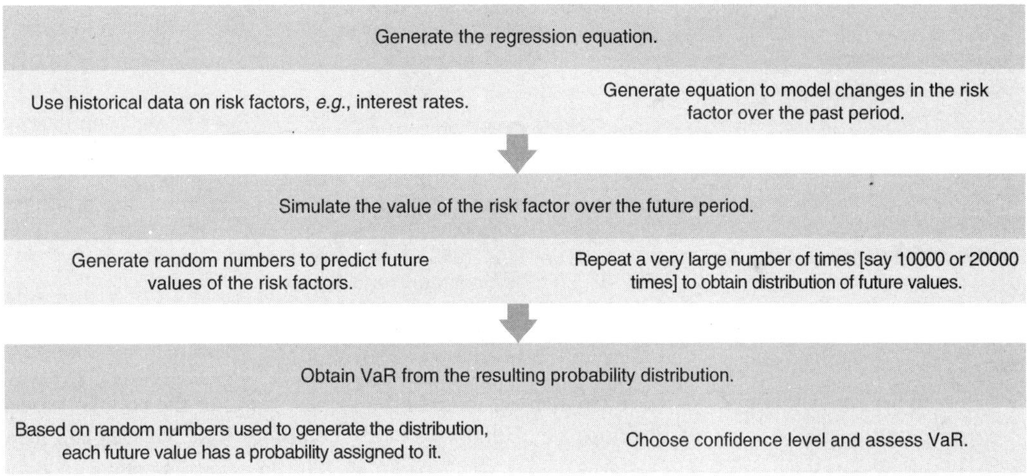

A comparative picture of the three most popular approaches is shown below:

Approach	Advantages	Disadvantages
Variance covariance (also called parametric or analytic approach)	The least complex, hence easy to understand.	Limited ability to capture the risks of portfolios which include options, hence may misstate non-linear risks.
	Easy to implement for portfolios covered by available 'off-the-shelf' software. Ease of implementation depends upon the complexity of the instruments and availability of data.	Unable to examine alternative assumptions about the distribution of the market factors, *i.e.*, distributions other than the normal.
	The least intensive computation and hence, can be done fast.	
Historical simulation	Can capture risks of portfolios which include options.	May produce misleading value of risk estimates when the recent past is atypical.
	Easy to implement for portfolios for which data on past values of market factors is available.	Difficult to perform scenario analysis under alternative assumptions.
	Performs well when back tested.	Can be computationally intensive.
Monte Carlo simulation	Easy to implement for portfolios covered by available 'off-the-shelf' software. Ease of implementation depends upon the complexity of the instruments and availability of data.	The model can produce misleading values of risk estimates when recent past is atypical. However, alternative estimates of parameters may be used.
	Can capture the risks of portfolios which include options.	
	Can handle statistical assumptions about risk factors	
	Various scenarios can be tested with the model.	

Although VaR is being used for multiple purposes—risk reporting, risk limits, regulatory capital, internal capital allocation and performance measurement—experts opine that VaR is not the answer for all risk management challenges. The perceived shortcomings of VaR are as follows:

- It does not measure 'event' (say, market crash) risks. Hence, portfolio stress tests are recommended to supplement VaR.
- It does not readily capture liquidity difference among instruments.
- It does not capture model risks.

However, it is a very popular and promising tool with wide use by practitioners, regulators and academicians. *Annexure I* to this chapter explores the sensational collapse of LTCM and its link with VaR.

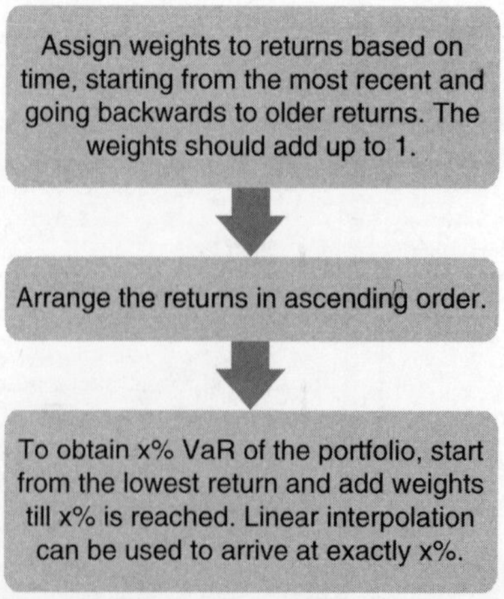

A hybrid model, which is believed to address some of the shortcomings of the popular models is also used by some practitioners. This model, developed by Boudoukh et al[21] combines Risk Metrics and historical simulation methodologies. According to proponents of the approach, the results are more precise than those obtained with the other methods. The approach is implemented in three steps, which are as follows:

Some simple numerical examples of VaR applications are given in *Illustrations* 10.1–10.3. However, before we understand the applications, we have to understand the basics of the normal distribution.

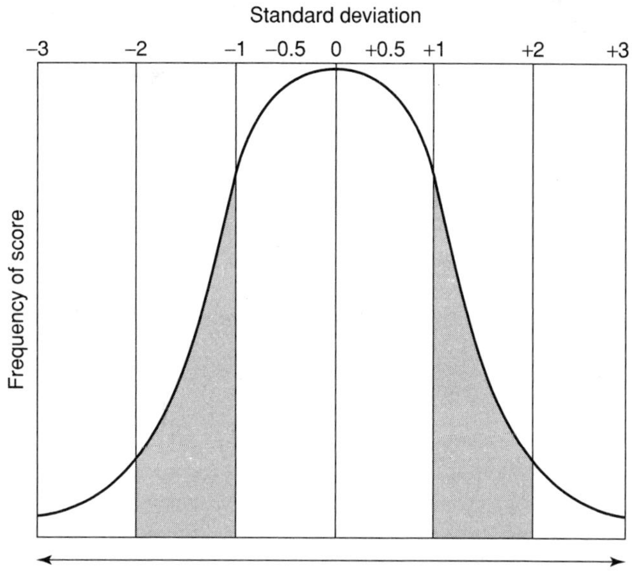

We can see from the diagram above that the normal distribution is a symmetric, bell shaped distribution, defined by its mean (μ) and standard deviation (σ). For simplicity, we assume that the mean is zero and the standard deviation is one—this is called the standard normal distribution. We also note that the distribution is symmetric around the mean—that is, the two halves of the curves are mirror images and the total area under the curve is 1 (or 100 *per cent*). Typically, the distribution exhibits the following characteristics:

- 68.3 per cent of the values fall within plus or minus 1 standard deviation from the mean of the distribution.
- 90 per cent of the values fall within plus or minus 1.65 standard deviation from the mean.
- 95.5 per cent of the values fall within plus or minus 2 standard deviation from the mean.
- 99.7 per cent of the values fall within plus or minus 3 standard deviation from the mean.

ILLUSTRATION 10.1 VAR FOR EQUITY SHARES OF A FIRM

A bank has recently added to its portfolio equity shares of firm ABC Ltd. The shares were bought at ₹500 per share. If the volatility of the share price is 20 per cent per annum and there are 250 trading days in a year, what is the 1 day VaR at 95 per cent confidence?

Stock price ₹500
Volatility 20%
Calculate daily volatility as 20/√250 = 1.26% = σ
At 95% confidence, VaR would be
500 (1 × 2*1.26) or 500 (1−2*1.26)
That is, ₹512.65 or ₹487.35, which translates into a potential gain or loss of ₹12.65 per day.

ILLUSTRATION 10.2 VAR FOR FOREIGN CURRENCY (SPOT)

A bank in India has bought USD 100 million in the spot market. It would like to assess the risk of holding this position for 1 day given the volatility of the currency to be at 10 per cent per year, at the exchange rate of USD1 = ₹50 (that is, ₹1 = 1/50 USD = .02 USD). Assume 250 trading days in a year and the required confidence level at 99 per cent.

The bank's position in ₹ is 50 × 100 million = ₹500 crore. The daily volatility is 10/√250 = 10/15.81 = .632%.

Hence, the value of the Re. to USD is likely to fluctuate between 0.02(1 + 3 × .00632) and 0.02(1−3 × .00632), that is between 0.0203 and 0.0196.

The bank's position may therefore result in a loss at 99 per cent confidence level as follows:

₹500 crore = USD 100 million
VaR= 500 × .0203 = ₹10.18 crore/day

ILLUSTRATION 10.3 VaR OF FIXED INCOME SECURITIES

The volatility of fixed income securities (such as bonds) is measured in terms of volatility in yield.

A bank has invested in fixed income bond with a price of ₹100 and coupon of 9 per cent. The market yield of a similar government security is also 9 per cent. with an annual volatility of 2 per cent. The holding period of the bank's security is 4 months. Assume the confidence interval to be 95 per cent.

Standard deviation for 4 months = $2/\sqrt{3}$ (since 4 months is 1/3rd of a year] = 1.15%

Hence, yields for 4 months at 95% confidence level would be

$$(9 + 2 \times 1.15) \text{ or } (9 - 2 \times 1.15) \text{ that is } 11.31\% \text{ or } 6.69\%$$

For simplicity, it can be assumed that 95 per cent of the values fall within $+/-2\sigma$ and that 99 per cent of the values fall within $+/-3\sigma$. As we have seen earlier, 95 per cent, 99 per cent, etc. represent confidence intervals in the VaR calculation.

Calculations of VaR for instruments such as forwards and options are somewhat more complex.

Supplementing VaR—Stress Testing and Scenario Analysis When the VaR is exceeded, how large can the losses be?

Stress testing attempts to answer this question by performing a set of scenario analyses to assess the effects of extreme market conditions. These extreme scenarios may be hypothesized using unexpected events and their impact on the prices of instruments in the portfolio is determined If the effects are unacceptable, the portfolio or risk management strategy needs to be revised or contingency plans prepared. However, the process is more intuitive and depends substantially on the judgment and experience of the risk manager.

Scenario analyses are also used to assess the impact of assumptions underlying VaR calculations being violated.

Alternative Measures to VaR VaR may not be appropriate for all situations or types of firms. The alternatives are sensitivity analysis, cash flow at risk and expected shortfall methodologies. Sensitivity analysis is considered less sophisticated than, and cash flow at risk more sophisticated than VaR.

Sensitivity Analysis: Sensitivity analysis are a reasonable alternative for simple portfolios. The approach in this ubiquitous methodology is to imagine hypothetical changes in the value of each market factor, compute the value of the portfolio given the new value of the market factor and determine the change in portfolio value resulting from the change in the market factor. The methodology works well when the magnitudes of likely changes in market factors can be realistically predicted.

Cash Flow at Risk: Risks inherent in operating cash flows are captured reasonably well by this measure and hence is preferred by non-financial firms

Cash flow at risk measures are typically estimated using Monte Carlo simulation but with differences from the use of Monte Carlo simulation to estimate VaR. First, the time horizon is much longer in cash flow at risk simulations. Second, the focus is on cash flows, not changes in mark-to-market values. Third, operating cash flows are the focus of the calculation. Hence, the factors included in the simulation are not the basic financial market factors included in VaR, but those factors affecting operating cash flows such as changes in customer demand or the outcomes of advertising programs. Finally, the primary emphasis is on planning (as opposed to control, oversight and reporting).

There is high degree of subjectivity involved in this approach since successful design and implementation of a cash flow at risk measurement system presupposes substantial knowledge and judgment in respect of the firm's operating cash flows and the important factors impacting these cash flows and then fitting these into an appropriate and workable model.

Expected Shortfall (ES): This method has been proposed as an alternative to VaR and is designed to measure the expected value of portfolio returns, given that the VaR (or some threshold) has been exceeded. The distinction between VaR and ES has been found to be not very important if the loss distribution is normal. However, for non-normal distributions, VaR and ES can yield quite different results.

As an example, assume that two firms A and B have invested in portfolios with 1 day VaR of ₹1 crore at 95 per cent confidence level. The ES is concerned with what happens on 5 per cent of the days when the loss exceeds ₹1 crore. For firm A, the loss during this period ranges between ₹1 crore and ₹3 crore with an average of ₹2 crore.

For firm B, the loss may range from ₹1 crore to ₹5 crore with an average of ₹3 crore. This implies that firm B's portfolio is riskier even though the two firms have the same VaR. The ES has brought out the comparative risks of both firms in absolute terms.[22]

Did VaR and Other Such Measures Fail During the 2007–2008 Global Financial Turmoil? It has been pointed out that banks, which used VaR as a primary tool of market risk management, failed, while derivative exchanges, which deal with more complex products, did not. Derivative exchanges have moved away from VaR and used the standard portfolio analysis of risk (SPAN) system. SPAN was developed by the Chicago Mercantile Exchange in 1988 and is used to calculate the portfolio loss under several price and volatility scenarios. *Annexure II* to this chapter outlines the regulatory responses to market risk measurement in the wake of the global financial crisis of 2007–2008.

SECTION III

THE INTERPLAY BETWEEN MARKET AND CREDIT RISK

In the chapter 'Managing credit risk – an overview', we have seen that though we isolate credit risk for mitigation and management, the interplay of various risks such as market and operational risks, could pose a challenge for risk management in banks.

In May 2009, the Basel committee on Banking Supervision (BCBS) published a working paper on the interaction of market and credit risk[23]. The paper mentions that market and credit risk have been treated as isolated or unrelated sources of risk—being measured and managed separately, and capital being assessed separately on each. The reasons for this are both historical and practical. However, we have seen in earlier chapters that illiquid credit assets can be turned into liquid traded assets through credit risk transfer mechanisms. These developments have blurred the distinctions between market and credit risks, and have led to the need for integrated measurement and management of the two risks. The financial crisis of 2007–08 has also highlighted the ways in which these two risks reinforce and interact with each other.

The working paper quoted above observes as follows (page 5): 'From a supervisory perspective, these developments raise important questions related to how the two types of risks can be defined and what relationships exist between them, how they should be aggregated and how precisely their joint risk is measured, what role liquidity plays in their interaction and under what conditions securitization—as one driver of the above developments—can work as a risk management approach.'

We will begin by defining 'market risk' and 'credit risk' in accordance with the definitions adopted by the Basel Committee. (*We will be learning more about the Basel committee and the regulatory definitions of risks and capital in the following chapter*).

Market risk is defined as the risk that a financial position changes its value due to changes of underlying market risk factors, like a stock price, an exchange rate or an interest rate.

Credit risk is defined as the risk of not receiving the promised payment on an outstanding claim, *i.e.*, due to changes of underlying credit risk factors, like default probabilities.

From the above definitions, it is clear that some risk factors may influence both market and credit risk. For example, interest rates are market prices that influence default risk of a borrower or default probabilities.

The Basel committee document describes a few 'trial' conclusions, after taking into consideration the research undertaken by various agencies. These conclusions fall into the following categories:

- Conceptual issues, especially those in respect of the distinction between market and credit risk.
  - Market and credit risks both tend to be driven by the same economic factors. Changes in the macroeconomic environment, for example, not only impacts stock and bond values but also business prospects, asset prices, and capital structure decisions of firms.
  - Since common risk drivers are present, it is difficult to distinguish these two risks clearly in practical risk measurement and management. Further, even if different risk drivers are responsible, the risks themselves might be correlated. Models that treat credit and market risks as independent of each other may not be adequate.
- Issues in aggregating the two types of risks, dealing with diversification of risks versus compounding of risks.
  - The 'top down' approach to risk aggregation believes that summing up separately measured credit and market risk components leads to 'conservative' estimates of overall risk. The rationale is that summing up

of components assumes perfect correlation between market and credit risks (which increases overall risk according to portfolio theory). However, if in reality, there is imperfect correlation between the same two risks (which decreases total risk, according to portfolio theory), then the total risk is overestimated. Hence, the top down approach is believed to provide a conservative cushion to deal with overall risk.

- However research findings show cases where the combined risk is actually higher than the sum of the components (and not as assumed in the earlier paragraph). The Basel committee paper illustrates through the example of a foreign currency loan. A loan denominated in a foreign currency availed by a domestic borrower carries both market (exchange rate) risk and credit (default of borrower) risk. If we assess both risks separately, the conclusion could be that the two risks offset each other—domestic currency depreciates value of the foreign currency loan in domestic currency increases, the probability of default by borrower increases. But the default risk of the borrower in this case is not linearly dependent on the exchange rate fluctuations. The home currency depreciation can erode the repayment probability of the foreign currency loan by a borrower who is not hedged against exchange risks. This effect would be much stronger than the summing up effect mentioned earlier. This is called the 'compounding effect'. The Basel paper mentions that there are other portfolios such as 'adjustable rate loans' and 'Over the counter (OTC) derivatives' where such compounding effects can be seen.
- In some other portfolios, 'diversification effects' can also occur, where the actual total risk decreases when market and credit risks interact.
- There are practical difficulties in building and operating totally integrated risk models. In an earlier chapter we have seen the difficulty in modelling credit risk distributions as compared with market risk distributions. Further, market and credit risks are assessed over different horizons. Hence building integrated models would make significant demands on the data collection, analytics, and the technology infrastructure

■ Issues of liquidity and the interaction of liquidity risk with market and credit risks, and the role of securitization.

- The Basel committee reports observes as follows (pages 15, 16). 'Liquidity conditions interact with market risk and credit risk through the horizon over which assets can be liquidated. In particular, deteriorating market liquidity often forces banks to lengthen the horizon over which they can execute their risk management strategies. As this time horizon lengthens, overall risk exposures generally increase, as does the contribution of credit risk relative to market risk. The liquidity of traded products can vary substantially over time and in unpredictable ways. Such liquidity fluctuations, all else equal, should have a larger impact on prices of products with greater credit risk. Conversely, as the current financial crisis illustrates, valuation uncertainties or other shocks that enhance actual or perceived credit risks can have adverse effects on liquidity and put in motion a downward spiral between market prices and liquidity of traded credit products.'
- Securitization is an important way in which credit risk is transformed into market risk. The Basel committee pays special attention to securitization in the report, as well as pricing of CDS.

SECTION IV

BANKS' INVESTMENT PORTFOLIO IN INDIA—VALUATION AND PRUDENTIAL NORMS'[24]

Similar to the loan policy that sets the direction for the credit portfolio of banks, an investment policy needs to be in place with the Board's approval. According to the RBI, the investment policy should be 'implemented to ensure that operations in securities are conducted in accordance with sound and acceptable business practices'.[25] Further, the central bank advocates that banks wanting to invest in the equity/bond markets should not only have a transparent policy for such investment but all direct investment decisions should be taken by the investment committee of the Board, which will be held accountable for the investment decisions. The central bank would like to see the banks build up adequate internal equity research capabilities.

In short, the RBI has prescribed that the investment policy of bank should clearly lay down the broad investment objectives to be followed while undertaking transactions in securities on their own investment account and on behalf of clients, clearly define the authority to put through deals, procedure to be followed for obtaining the sanction of the appropriate authority, procedure to be followed while putting through deals, various prudential exposure limits and the reporting system. Further, the RBI has spelt out the procedures to be followed by banks while transacting government securities.

Classification of the Investment Portfolio

The entire investment portfolio of banks (securities held to satisfy Statutory Liquidity Ratio (SLR)[26] requirements and those held outside the purview of SLR) are classified as HTM, AFS or HFT.).

However, in the balance sheet, the investments will continue to be disclosed with the following six classifications: (a) government securities, (b) other approved securities, (c) shares, (d) debentures and bonds, (e) subsidiaries/joint ventures and (f) others (CP, mutual fund units).[27]

The objective of the investment (*e.g.*, capital gains, trading profits) and the category–HTM, HFT or AFS should be determined and recorded by banks even at the time of acquisition.

Category 1: Held to Maturity (HTM)

- The securities acquired by the banks with the intention to hold them till maturity (permanent investments) will be classified under the HTM category.
- Investments in HTM category can be made up to 25 per cent of the bank's total investments. This ceiling does not include: (a) investment in recapitalization bonds issued by the Government of India, (b) investment in joint ventures and subsidiaries and (c) investment in the long-term bonds (with a minimum residual maturity of seven years) issued by companies engaged in infrastructure activities. (The minimum residual maturity of seven years should be at the time of investment in these bonds.)
- Banks can exceed the above stipulated limit of 25 per cent of total investments (since September 2004) under the HTM (permanent) category provided:
  - The excess comprises of only SLR securities
  - The total SLR securities held in the HTM category does not exceed 24.50 per cent by end-June 2013 and progress reduce to 23 per cent by end-March 2014; per cent of the demand and time liabilities (DTL)[28] as on the last Friday of the second preceding fortnight
- Banks can therefore hold the following securities under the HTM category:
  - SLR securities up to the prescribed proportion of their DTL as on the last Friday of the second preceding fortnight
  - Non-SLR securities included under the HTM category as on 2 September, 2004
  - Fresh recapitalization bonds received from the Government of India towards their recapitalization requirement and held in their investment portfolio
  - Fresh investment in the equity of subsidiaries and joint ventures (a joint venture would be one in which bank, along with its subsidiaries, holds more than 25 per cent of the equity)
  - Deposits of Rural Infrastructure Development Fund (RIDF), Small Industries Development Bank of India (SIDBI), and Rural Housing Development Fund (RHDF–of the National Housing Bank)
  - Investment in long-term bonds (with a minimum residual maturity of seven years) issued by companies engaged in infrastructure activities.

  Profit on sale of investments in this category should be first taken to the profit and loss account and thereafter be appropriated to the 'capital reserve account' net of taxes and transfer to statutory Reserve. Loss on sale will be recognized in the profit and loss account.

Categories 2 and 3: 'Available for Sale' and Held for Trading (AFS AND HFT)

- The securities acquired by the banks with the intention to trade by taking advantage of the short-term price/interest rate movements will be classified under the HFT category.
- The securities which do not fall within the other two categories will be classified under the AFS category.
- Banks have the freedom to decide on the extent of holdings under these two categories after careful consideration of various aspects such as, basis of intent, trading strategies, risk management capabilities, tax planning, manpower skills and capital position.
- The investments classified under the HFT category would be those from which the bank expects to gain from movements in interest/market rates. These securities are to be sold within 90 days.
- Profit or loss on sale of investments in both categories will be taken to the profit and loss account.

Shifting Among Categories

- Banks may shift investments to/from the HTM category once a year with the approval of the Board of directors.
- Banks may shift investments from the AFS category to the HFT category with the approval of their Board of directors Asset Liability Committe (ALCO) investment committee.

- Shifting of investments from the HFT category to the AFS is generally not allowed unless under exceptional circumstances such as, inability to sell the security within 90 days due to tight liquidity conditions or extreme volatility or market becoming unidirectional. Such transfer is permitted only with the approval of the Board of directors/ALCO/investment committee.
- Transfer of securities from one category to another should be done at the least of acquisition cost/book value/ market value on the date of transfer and the depreciation, if any, on such transfer should be fully provided for.

Valuation of Investments

Held to Maturity

- These investments are to be carried at acquisition cost and need not be marked-to-market unless the market value exceeds the face value. In such cases, the premium should be amortized over the period remaining to maturity.
- Any diminution, other than temporary, in the value of banks' investments in subsidiaries/joint ventures should be provided for.

Available for Sale

- The individual securities in the AFS category will be marked-to-market at quarterly or at more frequent intervals. Each security has to be valued and ultimately depreciation/appreciation shall be aggregated for each investment category. Net depreciation, if any, shall be provided for. Net appreciation, if any, should be ignored.
- Net depreciation is required to be provided for in any one category of securities (six broad categories defined earlier) cannot be set off against net appreciation in any other category. The book value of the individual securities would also not undergo any change after marking to market.

Held for Trading Individual securities in the HFT will be marked to market at monthly or more frequent intervals and provided for (as in the case of those in the AFS category). However, the book value of the individual securities in this category would not undergo any change after marking to market.

Investment Reserve

In case, the provision for depreciation on AFS and HFT categories is in excess of the required amount in a specific year, the excess should be credited to the P&L account of the bank and an equivalent amount (after tax) shown under 'Reserves and Surplus', which can be included as Tier 2 capital of the bank. Detailed instructions on the usage of the investment reserve (IRA) can be found in the quoted RBI circular.

Determination of 'Market Value' While Marking to Market (HFT and AFS Categories)

Quoted Securities The 'market value' for the purpose of periodical valuation of investments included in the AFS arid HFT categories would be the market price of the security available from the trades/quotes on the stock exchanges, price list of the RBI or prices periodically declared by the Primary Dealers Association of India (PDAI)[29] jointly with the Fixed Income Money Market and Derivatives Association of India (FIMMDA).[30]

Unquoted Securities

Central government securities: Banks should value the unquoted central government securities on the basis of the prices/YTM[31] rates published periodically by the PDAI/ FIMMDA. Treasury Bills are to be valued at carrying cost.

State government securities: State government securities will be valued through the YTM method, marked up by 25 basic points above the yields of the central government securities of equivalent maturity (advised periodically by PDAI/FIMMDA).

Other 'approved' securities: These will be valued applying the YTM method by marking it up by 25 basic points above the yields of the central government securities of equivalent maturity advised by PDAI/FIMMDA periodically.

The valuation of unquoted securities, not included under securities approved for investment under the SLR will be done as stipulated in Box 10.4.

BOX 10.4 VALUATION OF UNQUOTED NON-SLR SECURITIES

- What are non-SLR securities?

Those securities, which have not been approved as SLR securities are called non-SLR securities.

- What are 'rated' securities?

A 'rated' security would be assigned a rating after a detailed exercise by an external rating agency in India which is registered with the SEBI and is carrying a current or valid rating. This implies, inter alia, that the rating should not be more than a month old on the date of issue of the securities. 'Investment grade' ratings would be reviewed by the Indian Banks' Association (IBA) or the FIMMDA annually. Unrated securities are those which do not possess a valid rating.

- What are 'listed' or 'quoted' securities?

Listed securities are those listed on approved stock exchanges. Those securities which are not listed on approved stock exchanges are called 'unlisted'.

- Valuation of unquoted securities
    - Debentures/bonds of firms with varying ratings will be valued on the basis of their YTM with an appropriate mark up as suggested by PDAI/FIMMDA, with a minimum mark up of 50bps.
    - Quoted debentures and bonds will be valued at market rates, provided there have been transactions in these debentures in the previous fortnight.
    - Preference shares will be valued at YTM with appropriate mark up as suggested by PDAI/FIMMDA. The mark-up will be graded according to the ratings assigned to the preference shares by the rating agencies subject to certain conditions such as: (i) the YTM rate should be higher than that of a Government of India loan of equivalent maturity, (ii) the rate of YTM for unrated preference shares should be higher than that applicable to rated preference shares of equivalent maturity, the mark up reflecting the credit risk adequately, (iii) the preference share should not be valued above its redemption value or the value at which it has been traded on a stock exchange during the previous fortnight and (iv) specific guidelines have been provided for investments in preference shares as part of project finance or rehabilitation or cases in which preference dividends are in arrears.
    - Equity shares in the bank's portfolio should be marked-to-market preferably on a daily or weekly basis. Unquoted equity shares should be valued at break-up value (without considering 'revaluation reserves', if any) to be ascertained from the company's latest balance sheet (not more than 1 year prior to the date of valuation). In case, the latest balance sheet is not available, the shares are to be valued at ₹1 per company.
    - Mutual funds units should be valued as per stock exchange quotations. Investment in unquoted mutual fund units is to be valued on the basis of the latest repurchase price declared by the mutual fund in respect of each scheme. In case of funds with a lock-in period, where repurchase price/market quote is not available, units could be valued at NAV. If NAV is not available then these could be valued at cost, till the end of the lock-in period. Wherever the repurchase price is not available, the units could be valued at the NAV of the respective scheme.
    - Commercial paper should be valued at the carrying cost.
    - Investment in securities issued by securitization/reconstruction companies[32] (SC/RC) will be recorded at the lower of: (i) the redemption value of the security receipts/pass-through certificates, or (ii) the net book value of the financial asset.

Source: RBI. Detailed valuation guidelines can be accessed from section 3 of the RBI Master circular 'Prudential norms on investments' dated July 1, 2013.

'Non-Performing' Investments

As in the case of non-performing loans described in the chapter on credit risk, if interest or principal is not paid in respect of securities in any of the three categories, the banks should not recognise income from the securities. Appropriate provisions for the depreciation in the value of the investment should also be made. Banks cannot set off the depreciation requirement in respect of these non-performing securities against the appreciation in respect of other performing securities.

A non-performing investment (NPI) (similar to a non-performing advance (NPA)) is one, where:

- Interest/instalment (including maturity proceeds) is due and remains unpaid for more than 90 days.
- Fixed dividend on preference shares is not paid.
- Equity shares are valued at ₹1 per company on account of the non-availability of the latest balance sheet.
- The bank has invested in securities issued by a borrowing firm, credit facilities to whom is treated as an NPA.

- The investments in debentures/bonds, in the nature of advances, would also be subjected to NPI norms as applicable to investments.
- State government guaranteed investments where interest/principal/maturity proceeds remain unpaid for more than 90 days.

The RBI has also prescribed uniform accounting treatment for repo/reverse repo transactions. These instructions and numerical examples can be accessed on the website www.rbi.org.in as part of the Master Circular on 'Prudential norms for classification, valuation and operation of investment portfolio by banks, July 1, 2013.

Income Recognition

- Banks may book income on accrual basis on securities of corporate bodies/public sector undertakings in respect of which the payment of interest and repayment of principal have been guaranteed by the central government or a state government, provided interest is serviced regularly.
- Banks may book income from dividend on shares of corporate bodies on accrual basis provided dividend on the shares has been declared by the corporate body in its annual general meeting and the owner's right to receive payment is established.
- Banks may book income from government securities and bonds and debentures of corporate bodies on accrual basis where interest rates on these instruments are predetermined and provided interest is serviced regularly and is not in arrears.
- Banks should book income from units of mutual funds on cash basis.

Illustration 10.4 would serve to make the valuation computations clearer.

ILLUSTRATION 10.4 INVESTMENT VALUATION

Given below is the investment portfolio of Bank A at the end of March 2006.

		Face Value (₹)	Number of Securities	Total Face Value (₹)	Acquisition Price (₹)
I.	Govt. securities:				
	9.28% GOl 2012 (March)	100	7,000	7,00,000	7,19,000
	8.51 % State government loan 2014 (December)	100	3,000	3,00,000	3,16,000
	Sub total			10,10,000	10,30,000
II.	Approved securities:				
	7.55% 2009 February	100	35,000	35,00,000	36,70,000
	Sub total		35,00,000	36,70,000	
III.	Equity shares:				
	AB Financial Services Ltd.	10	44,000	4,40,000	4,40,000
	Bank G	10	23,700	2,37,000	8,87,000
	Sub total			6,77,000	13,27,000
IV.	Bonds and debentures:				
	7% 2009 (March) (Taxable)	100	50,000	50,00,000	49,85,000
	Sub total			50,00,000	49,85,000
V.	Subsidiaries				
	AG Caps	10	5,00,000	50,00,000	50,00,000
	Sub total			50,00,000	50,00,000
VI.	Mutual funds:	10	10,000	1,00,000	1,50,000
	Sub total			1,00,000	1,50,000
	Total			1,52,77,000	1,61,67,000

Note the following:

The bank classifies the entire government and approved securities into current investment category. The prices of government securities on the RBI list for sale are as follows:

Security	Maturity	Sale Price (₹)
5.25%	2010	98.90
6.10%	2012	102.25

For all other government securities (central and state), the following YTMs are applicable on 31 March, 2006.

Number of Years	YTM (%)
Less than 1	4.30
1	4.50
2	4.54
3	4.60
4	4.66
5	4.83
6	4.96
7	5.05
8	5.05
9	5.07
10	5.17

The shares of Bank G are traded in the market at ₹27. Since, AB Financial Services Ltd. is not a listed firm, the investment is valued, based on the latest audited accounts at ₹2.40 lakh.
For valuation of taxable bonds, 1 per cent above the applicable YTM rate is to be applied.
The net asset value (NAV) of the mutual fund is ₹10.75.
Provision made during the previous year stands at ₹18 lakh.
What would be the provision required to be made in respect of depreciation in investments during the current year?

Solution

The term to maturity of 9.28% GOI 2012 is 6 years and hence the corresponding YTM is 4.96 per cent from the table. We can use YTM formula[33] to calculate the sale price of the security.

$$\text{Sale price} \times n = \frac{1 \times n - F[(0.4nr) - 1]}{0.6nr + 1}$$

$$= \frac{700000 \times 0.0928 \times 6 - 700000[(0.4 \times 6 \times 0.0496) - 1]}{(0.6 \times 6 \times 0.0496) + 1}$$ [34]

= ₹8,53,951

Similarly, YTM for 8.51 per cent state government loan for 9 years term to maturity is 5.07 per cent (the term to maturity of 8.9 years is rounded off to 9 years).

$$\text{Sale price} = \frac{3,00,000 \times 0.0851 \times 9 - 300000[(0.4 \times 9 \times 0.0507) - 1]}{(0.6 \times 9 \times 0.0507) + 1}$$

= ₹3,72,917

Similarly, the price for 7.55 per cent security maturing February 2009 is

$$= \frac{3500000 \times 0.0755 \times 3 - 500000[(0.4 \times 3 \times 0.0460) - 1]}{(0.6 \times 3 \times 0.0460) + 1}$$

= ₹37,86,064

Since AB Financial Services Ltd. is not a listed company, no market quote is available for it. The break up value of ₹2.40 lakh can, therefore, be assumed as the appropriate value. In the case of Bank G, the value would be 27.00 × 23700 = ₹6,39,900
The valuation of 7 per cent bonds maturing March 2009 (taxable) is as follows:
Term to maturity = 3 years
YTM = 4.60 + 1.00% = 5.60%

$$\text{Sale price} = \frac{50,00,000 \times 0.07 \times 3 - 50,00,000[(0.4 \times 3 \times 0.0560) - 1]}{[(0.6 \times 3 \times 0.0560) + 1}$$

= ₹51,90,770

Investments in the subsidiary, being permanent in nature, will be shown at book value.
Mutual funds are valued at current NAV.

= 10,000 × 10.75 = ₹1,07,500

Now, we can recast the investment schedule as follows:

		Total Face Value (₹)	Acquisition Value (₹)	Market Value (₹)	Change Value (₹)
I.	Govt. securities				
	9.28% GOI 2012	7,00,000	7,19,000	8,53,951	1,34,95
	8.51% State government loan 2014 December	3,00,000	3,16,000	3,72,917	56,917
	Sub Total (I)	10,00,000	10,35,000	12,26,868	1,91,868
II.	Approved securities:				
	7.55% 2007 February	35,00,000	36;70,000	37,86,064	1,16,064
	Sub total II	35,00,000	36,70,000	37,86,064	1,16,064
III.	Equity shares				
	AB Financial Services Ltd.	4,40,00	4,40,000	2,40,000	(−)2,00,000
	Bank G	2,37,000	8,87,000	6,39,900	(−)2,47,100
	Sub total (III)	6,77,000	13,27,000	8,79,900	(−)4,47,100
IV.	Bonds and debentures				
	7% 2009 March (taxable)	50,00,000	49,85,000	51,90,770	2,05,770
	Sub total IV	50,00,000	49,85,000	51,90,770	2,05,770
V.	Subsidiaries				
	AG Caps	50,00,000	50,00,000	50,00,000	–
	Sub total V	50,00,000	50,00,000	50,00,000	–
VI.	Mutual funds	100000	150000	107500	−42,500
	Sub totals VI	100000	150000	107500	−42,500
	Totals (III + VI)				−4,89,600

Within an investment basket, appreciation is netted off against depreciation. However, the net depreciation is only considered and net appreciation is ignored. Thus, for the year the bank has to make a provision on the depreciated amount of ₹4,89,600 alone. (Baskets III + VI)

CHAPTER SUMMARY

- Typically, banks invest in securities to meet the following objectives: safety of capital, liquidity, yield, diversification of credit risk, managing interest rate risk exposure and meeting pledging requirements.
- Regulators stipulate that banks divide their security holdings into three categories based on the objectives of such investment like, held to maturity (HTM), held for trading (HFT), and available for sale (AES).
- In much of the developed world, a bank's 'treasury' is a source of substantial profit to the bank creating substantial value to shareholders. Banks' treasuries typically perform the following basic functions within their investment and trading activities like, (a) investment advice and assistance to customers, including other banks, in order to manage their investment portfolios, (b) an important role in structuring products to hedge the bank's own capital, (c) buying and selling securities on behalf of the customers and (d) as traders, also speculating on short-term interest rate movements.
- In developed markets, the treasury departments act as risk managers for banks. By using sophisticated internal transfer pricing, the treasury buys and sells funds among the bank's client-facing units thus isolating and removing maturity and interest rate mismatches from corporate and retail business units. As markets develop, many credit products are being replaced by treasury products. An example is working capital credit being substituted by commercial paper.
- There are three important sources of treasury profit: (a) foreign exchange business, (b) money market products and (c) securities markets products.
- The primary objective of banks' investment portfolio and treasury operations is to maximise earnings while mitigating risks involved. There are three predominant methods by which bank investments contribute to earnings: (a) interest income, (b) income from reinvestment, and (c) capital gains or losses.

- However, the earnings from investment are susceptible to the following risks: (a) interest rate risk, (b) credit risk in case the investment in debt securities does not yield the promised interest and principal payments, (c) liquidity risk that could arise from lack of market for the securities held and (d) other general risks that could cause volatility in returns from the investment portfolio, for example, inflation risk.
- Value at Risk (VaR) has become one of the standard measures to quantify market risk. VaR is defined as the maximum potential loss in the value of a portfolio due to adverse market movements for a given probability. VaR measures are used both for risk management and for regulatory purposes.
- The interplay or interaction of credit and market risks is becoming increasingly important. Hence measuring and managing these risks in an integrated manner is being explored, and the research into the integrated risk management has assumed special importance after the financial crisis of 2007.
- In terms of the existing guidelines from the RBI, banks will have to hold their investments under either of the following categories – permanent or current investment. The permanent category will be held to maturity and are also called investment securities as they are held for the benefits of long-term yields. The current category comprises of dealing securities and is held in the trading book to take advantage of short-term fluctuations in prices.
- These investments will be valued based on the following guidelines: (a) HTM investments are to be carried at acquisition cost and need not be marked to market unless the market value exceeds the face value – any diminution, other than temporary, in the value of banks' investments in subsidiaries/joint ventures should be provided for, (b) the individual securities in the AFS category will be marked to market at quarterly or at more frequent intervals. Net depreciation, if any, shall be provided for Net appreciation, if any, should be ignored. (Net depreciation is required to be provided for in any one category of securities (six broad categories defined) cannot be set off against net appreciation in any other category and (c) individual securities under the HFT category will be marked to market at monthly or more frequent intervals and provided for (as in the case of those 'available for sale').
- With the objective of building adequate reserves to guard against adverse interest rate movements, banks have to maintain an investment fluctuation reserve (IFR) at a minimum 5 per cent (maximum 10 per cent) of the investment portfolio. IFR should be computed with reference to investments in two categories – 'held for trading' and 'available for sale'. Banks maintaining capital of at least 9 per cent of the risk-weighted assets for both credit risks and market risks for both HFT and AFS categories may transfer the balance in excess of 5 per cent of securities included under HFT and AFS categories to Statutory Reserve, part of Tier I capital.

TEST YOUR UNDERSTANDING

1. Which of the following risks is present in a Repo transaction?
   a. Interest rate risk (b) liquidity risk (c) counter party risk
   Substantiate your answer.
2. 91 day T-bill of face value ₹100 is purchased at a yield of 5 per cent. What is the purchase price of the T-bill?
3. Under which of the following circumstances should a bank rebalance its investment portfolio?
   a. a change in interest rates b. a change in the bank's investment objectives c. a change in regulation
   Substantiate your answer.
4. How can banks assess the credit risk in their investment portfolio?
5. How can banks use their investment portfolio to speculate on interest rate movements?
6. What will be the VaR of a bond of 2 year maturity, whose price is ₹100 and whose yield and coupon are both at 5.8 per cent? The bank wants to hold the bond for one quarter. Assume that the annual standard deviation of 2 year treasury yields at 1.25 per cent and a confidence interval of (a) 95 per cent and (b) 99 per cent.
7. Bank A has recently added the listed company DEF Ltd. to its investment portfolio. The bank bought 100 shares of DEF Ltd. at ₹400 per share with the intention of holding the shares for one quarter. The annual volatility of the stock is assessed at 25 per cent. If there are 250 trading days in a year, compute the VaR of the bank at 95 per cent confidence interval for the equity investment in DEF Ltd. over the holding period.
8. VaR of ₹10 crore with 80 per cent confidence for bank A means –
   a. Bank A is 80 per cent certain that it will earn less than ₹10 crore
   b. Bank A's investment portfolio will yield a return of at least 20 per cent
   c. Bank A is 80 per cent sure that it will not lose more than ₹10 crore
   d. There is a 20 per cent chance that Bank A will earn more than ₹10 crore on its portfolio

9. What do you think will happen to the VaR of a portfolio when:
   a. The portfolio's volatility increases
   b. The portfolio's volatility decreases
   c. The portfolio's average returns are higher
   d. The portfolio's average returns are lower
   e. When the confidence level is increased
   f. When the confidence level is decreased
   g. When the holding period is increased
   h. When the holding period is decreased

TOPICS FOR FURTHER DISCUSSION

- The RBI website gives information on all banks. Study the investments patterns of banks in various categories – public sector, private sector and foreign. Do you notice any difference in their approach to investments? Has the approach been changing over time? What do you attribute the changes, if any, to?
- Study the current balance sheet of any bank in India, particularly its investment portfolio. Are there any risks that are inherent in the portfolio? Are there any potential risks that can arise in future?
- Did inappropriate VaR models mislead banks and contribute to the global financial crisis?

SELECT REFERENCES

1. Jorion, Philippe (2005). Access at http://www.gsm.uci.edu/~joriOfl/oc/CaSe.html
2. Koch, Timothy and Scott S MacDonald. *Bank Management*, Chapter 19, 765–817, 4th ed. The Dryden Press.
3. Linsmeier, Thomas J and Neil D Pearson (1996). *Risk Measurement: An Introduction to Value at Risk*. University of Illinois at Urbana-Champaign, July 1996.
4. Lopez, Jose A (1997). "Regulatory Revaluation of Value-at-Risk Models", Research Paper no. 9710, March, Federal Reserve Bank of New York. Managing Market Risk—Banks' Investment Portfolio

ANNEXURE I

CASE STUDY—LTCM COLLAPSE AND LINK WITH VaR

In 1998, LTCM, the world's largest hedge fund, failed and sent shock waves through the world's financial system. LTCM's size made the Federal Reserve Bank of New York step in to facilitate a bailout to the fund, fearing the negative impact of the liquidation on global financial markets.

It has been widely reported that the primary contributory factor to LTCM's failure has been its poor risk management.

With a capital base of USD 3 million, LTCM possessed derivatives whose value exceeded USD 5 trillion and controlled over USD 100 billion in assets, globally – making it one of the most highly leveraged funds in the history. To predict and mitigate its risk exposures, LTCM used a combination of different VaR techniques and claimed that its VaR analysis showed that investors might experience a loss of 5 per cent or more in about 1 month in 5 and a loss of 10 per cent or more in about 1 month in 10. Only 1 year in 50 should it lose at least 20 per cent of its portfolio. LTCM also estimated that a 45 per cent drop in its equity value over the course of a month was a 10 standard deviation event. In other words, this scenario had no likelihood of occurrence (Prabhu, 2001). However, this 'most unlikely' event happened in August 1998. In spite of sophisticated hedging strategies, LTCM went wrong in one basic assumption – that historical trends in securities movements were an accurate predictor of future movements. The VaR models used by LTCM relied on historical data to predict future price movements. Unfortunately, the future holds too many uncertainties that the past cannot predict was the lesson learned by the management and investors at a very great cost.

For example, on 18 October 1987, 2 month S&P futures contracts fell by 29 per cent, which under the hypothesis of a lognormal distribution with annualized volatility of 20 per cent (which was also the approximate historical volatility of this security) would have denoted a 27 standard deviation event. Experts opined that the possibility of such an event happening would have been virtually impossible. Again, 13 October 1989 saw the S&P 500 fall about 6 per cent, a 5 standard deviation event under similar assumptions as above. Again, experts opined that such an event would have the likelihood of occurring only once in 14,756 years!

In August 1998, some unexpected events occurred, which were beyond the 'predictive abilities' of the VaR models used by LTCM. The Russian crisis triggered drying up of liquidity in the global financial markets and derivative positions were quickly slackened. Yet, LTCM's VaR models continued to estimate that the daily loss would be no more than USD 50 million of capital. But the fund started losing around USD 100 million every day. On the fourth day in the wake of the Russian debacle, the fund lost USD 500 million in a single trading day.

While LTCM prepared to declare bankruptcy, the US Federal Reserve extended a USD 3.6 billion bailout to the fund, which was questioned by the experts who felt that such an action could create a moral hazard problem.

Hence, though perceived to be a highly effective risk measurement tool, VaR has to be used judiciously. At the end of August 1998, LTCM had USD 2.3 billion of equity capital and USD 1 billion excess liquidity. However, the firm was caught in a dilemma between reducing risk and raising additional capital. The magnitude of its positions rendered it unable to reduce its risk exposures immediately or attract new investors and it appeared that it had underestimated its capital needs. In retrospect, the fund was maximizing return while based on the simplistic assumption that volatility would remain constant, while in reality it could easily double in turbulent times.

The fund was not able to liquidate quickly enough in case of adverse market conditions, leading to a risk of liquidity and insolvency. Liquidity risk is not factored into VaR models since they assume that normal market conditions will prevail.

Therefore, it appears that LTCM's actual exposure to liquidity and solvency risks was not adequately exposed by its VaR model.

While VaR is seen as an invaluable tool to measure risks, complementary measures such as, stress testing could have probably offset the limitations and disadvantages of VaR While VaR could show fund managers what they could lose with a predetermined maximum probability, stress tests enable them to assess their possible loss if the worst case scenario materialized.

The case of LTCM serves to illustrate the practical dimensions of a popular risk measurement instrument like the VaR.

SELECT REFERENCES

1. Feridun, Mete (2005). "Value at Risk: Any Lessons from the Crash of Long Term Capital Management (LTCM)?". *Journal of Business Administration Online*, Spring 2005, vol. 4, no. 1. http://jbao.atu.edu.
2. Prabhu, Siddharth (2001). "*Long Term Capital Management: The Dangers of Leverage*". Duke University, Durham, May 2001.

ANNEXURE II

SUMMARY OF REGULATORY RESPONSES TO MARKET RISK MEASUREMENT PRACTICES BY BANKS AFTER THE GLOBAL FINANCIAL CRISIS

A series of bank failures in the 1970s prompted the setting up of the Basel Committee on Banking Supervision, with the intention to regulate financial institutions, particularly banks. A detailed discussion on the Basel Committee has been carried out in another chapter in this book.

Since its inception, the Committee has focused on regulation of bank capital globally. The measure of capital is based on the asset portfolio risks individual banks take, as well as operational risks in banking operations. An important part of the asset portfolio risk is 'market risk' caused by adverse fluctuations in market factors. The risk measure agreed upon for market risk measurement was the VaR.

The Basel II framework has taken its share of criticism for the global financial crisis. Though many of the regulatory responses were initiated even before the crisis erupted, they have now received final shape and are being recommended with vigour to member banks across the world.

The important policy measures are summarized below:

1. The Basel committee entered into an agreement with the International Organization of Securities Commission (IOSCO) in 2005 to make appropriate improvements in banks' capital requirements as well as for market risk assessment. One of the relevant outcomes was the decision (in March 2008) to improve the banks' internal VaR models for market risk. The improvement would specifically address recognition of credit risk related and often illiquid products in the investment portfolio of banks, whose risk was not reflected in their existing VaR models.
2. In June 2006, the committee published a comprehensive version of the Basel II Framework, which included, among others, the 1996 'Amendment to the Capital Accord to Incorporate Market Risks' and the July 2005 paper on 'The Application of Basel II to Trading Activities and the Treatment of Double Default Effects'.
3. The improvements in the Basel II Framework concerning internal value-at-risk models would, among others, specifically require banks to justify any factors used in pricing which are excluded in the VaR calculation. The banks would also have to carry out hypothetical back testing (for validation) and update market data once a month.
4. The committee stressed the importance of supervisory authorities being convinced that banks using models have market risk management systems that are conceptually sound and implemented with integrity. Accordingly, the supervisory authority will specify a number of 'qualitative criteria' that banks would have to meet before they are permitted to use a model-based approach.
5. The importance of routine and rigorous stress testing the model was stressed by the committee. The results of stress testing should be reviewed periodically by senior management and where stress tests reveal particular vulnerability to a given set of circumstances, prompt steps should be taken to manage those risks appropriately (for example, by hedging against that outcome or reducing the size of the bank's exposures or increasing capital).
6. The committee emphasized the need for specifying an appropriate set of market risk factors that impact the banks' trading positions. The risk factors should be sufficient to capture the risks inherent in the bank's portfolio of on- and off-balance sheet trading

positions. The committee has also proposed a set of guidelines for specifying the risk factors.

7. Though banks have the flexibility in choosing their VaR models, some minimum requirements are that (a) the VaR should be calculated daily, (b) a 99 per cent one tailed confidence interval is to be used, (c) the minimum holding period should be 10 days, (d) the historical period for calculating VaR should be at least one year, (e) data should be updated at least once every quarter, (f) banks can use the appropriate model such as, the variance-covariance, historical simulation or Monte Carlo simulation models, (g) banks can recognise empirical correlations within broad risk categories, (h) banks must accurately capture unique risks of options and (i) banks should calculate 'stressed VaR' based on the 10 day, 99th percentile one tailed confidence interval VaR of the current portfolio.
8. The VaR calculated as given in the guidelines should be validated by external experts.
9. For illiquid positions, especially those without market prices or observable inputs to valuation, valuation methodologies proposed include (a) marking to market, (b) marking to model and (c) independent price verification.
10. The 'Trading Book Group' of the committee has decided on an 'incremental default risk charge' (IRC) in response to the increasing amount of exposure in banks' investments to credit risk related products, which are often illiquid and whose risk is not reflected in the VaR. This decision was prompted by the credit market turmoil, where major losses were not captured by the banks' VaR. The IRC is expected to address many of the shortcomings of the current VaR framework. In essence, the IRC represents an estimate of the default and migration risks of unsecuritized credit products over a one-year horizon at 99.9 per cent confidence level, taking into account the liquidity horizons of individual positions or sets of positions.
11. Another important response by the committee is the 'Principles of sound stress testing practices and supervision' in May 2009. This has been triggered by the depth and duration of the financial crisis that led to questions on banks' stress testing practices before the crisis and also whether they were adequate for fast changing circumstances. The principles cover the overall objectives, governance, design and implementation of stress testing programs, as well as individual risks and products.

SELECT REFERENCES

1. *Sources*: Basel Committee on Banking Supervision, "Consultative document–Revisions to the Basel II market risk framework", January 2009, (points 1–9), "Consultative document–Guidelines for computing capital for incremental risk in the trading book", January 2009, (point 10) , "Principles of sound stress testing practices", May 2009 (point 11).

ENDNOTES

1. 'Unrealized' since the gain or loss would crystalise only if the bank decides to sell the bond in the market at that value.
2. Both the terms 'money market' and 'commercial paper' are being explained subsequently in this chapter.
3. More discussion on these products will be found in the chapter on 'International Banking'.
4. The bank stamps the word 'accepted' on the face of the instrument.
5. Letters of credit (LCs) are documents governed by the rules of the International Chamber of Commerce (ICC). These documents stipulate contract terms and duties of parties to the LC (the importer, exporter and the participating banks) and authorizes the exporter to draw a draft on a participating bank for payment to be received from the importer.
6. 'Investment grade' implies bonds that are likely to meet all payment obligations on time. According to Moody's, Aaa, Aa, A and Baa signify investment grade ratings, while according to Standard and Poor's, AAA, AA, A and BBB constitute investment grade ratings. For more on Credit Ratings, please refer earlier chapters on credit.
7. 'Zero coupon' implies that the bond does not pay periodic interest. Hence, the bond is sold at a discount from the face value.
8. Defined in the previous chapter. To recap, 'pass-throughs' constitute a pool of fixed income securities backed by a package of assets. A servicing intermediary collects the monthly payments from issuers and after deducting a fee, remits or passes them through to the holders of the pass-throughs. They are also known as a 'pass-through security' or 'pay through security'. The most common type of pass-through is a mortgage-backed certificate where homeowners' payments pass from the original bank through a government agency or investment bank to investors.

9. These and other securitized instruments were considered to be one of the leading causes of the global financial crisis. For a detailed discussion on the instruments and the crisis, please see chapters related to Credit.
10. Convertible bonds are a mix of debt and equity, where the bond holders are given the option to convert debt into equity on a predetermined date at a predetermined price.
11. The explanation for this is as follows: Bond value is measured as $\sum_{i+1}^{n} [c/(1 + r)^i] + M/(1 + r)^n$, where $i = 1$ to n years, C is the coupon rate, n is the number of years to maturity, r is the periodic required return, M is the maturity value, and i the time period when payment is received. If the interest rate falls during this period, investors start expecting less. Since the denominator would now decrease, the bond value would increase. If interest rates rise during this period, the reverse would happen and the bond value would decrease.
12. 'Investment grade' are those securities rated in one of their four highest ratings by nationally/internationally recognized external rating agencies such as Standard & Poor or Moody's.
13. More on the Basel Committee in Chapter, 'Capital – Risk, Regulation and Adequacy'.
14. In particular, please refer to Mandelbrot, B, (1963), 'The variations of certain speculative prices', *Journal of Business* 36, 394–419, and Fama, E, (1965), 'The behavior of stock market prices', *Journal of Business* 38, 34–105.
15. Manganelli, Simone, and Robert Engle, (2001), 'Value at risk models in finance', European Central Bank Working Paper no 75, August 2001. Page 7.
16. 'Covariance' is a statistical concept that measures how two or more assets move in tandem. A positive covariance signifies that the asset returns move together and a negative covariance moves inversely. Hence, the 'correlation' between two assets can be expressed as the covariance between the two assets divided by the product of the standard deviation (volatility) of the two assets.
17. 'Risk Metrics sells its VAR modeling and other services to 3,500 institutions, including the world's top ten investment banks and 70 of its 100 largest money managers. It also provides small investors free access to quick-and-dirty ways to X-ray their own holdings' (appearing in Forbes magazine, 13 October 2008, accessed at http://www.forbes.com/forbes/2008/1013/060.html on June 5, 2009).
18. Detailed description of the methodology can be found in 'Risk MetricsTM – Technical document', J.P. Morgan/Reuters, 4th edition, December 1996, 'Return to Risk Metrics: The Evolution of a Standard', Risk Metrics Group Inc., April 2001, and 'The Risk Metrics 2006 Methodology', Zimbach, Gilles, Risk Metrics Group, March 2007, all accessed at www.riskmetrics.com
19. Bollerslev, Tim. (1986), 'Generalized Autoregressive Conditional Heteroskedasticity', *Journal of Econometrics*, 31 , pp. 307–27, and Engle, Robert F.(1982) 'Autoregressive Conditional Heteroskedasticity with Estimates of the Variance of U.K. Inflation', *Econometrica*, 50, pp. 987–1008. The term 'heteroskedasticity' signifies 'different variances';, and more details can be found in statistics textbooks.
20. GARCH stands for 'generalized auto regressive conditional heteroskedasticity', and is a generalization of Engle's (1982) ARCH model, used to model financial time series that exhibit time variable volatility clustering – for example, periods of wild fluctuations followed by periods of relative calm. GARCH uses autoregressive moving averages.
21. Boudoukh, Jacob, Mathew Richardson and Robert Whitelaw,(1998), 'The best of both worlds', RISK 11, 64–67.
22. Verma, Jayanth R, (2009), 'Risk management lessons from the global financial crisis for derivative exchanges', Working paper no. 2009-02-06, Indian Institute of Management, Ahmedabad.
23. The Basle Committee on Banking Supervision, 2009, 'Findings on the interaction of market and credit risk', Working Paper no 16, accessed at www.bis.org.
24. RBI Master Circular–Prudential norms for classification, valuation and operation of investment portfolio by banks, July 1, 2013.
25. Ibid., Page 4
26. Statutory Liquidity Ratio. Please see Chapter 'Monetary Policy – Implications for Bank Management.'
27. All bank balance sheets should present the investment portfolio with the six classifications. We have seen this when we studied the financial statements of banks in India – refer Chapter 'Banks' financial statements'.
28. See Chapter 'Monetary Policy Implication for Bank Management' for composition of DTL.
29. Primary (PD) dealers are commercial banks or brokers/dealers authorized to buy and sell government securities, subject to minimum capital requirements.
30. The Fixed Income Money Market and Derivatives Association of India (FIMMDA), an association of commercial banks, financial institutions and primary dealers was incorporated as a company under section 25 of the Companies Act, 1956 on 3 June 1998. FIMMDA is a voluntary market body for the bond, money and derivatives markets. It has members representing all major institutional segments of the market. The membership includes State Bank of India and its associates, nationalized banks, private sector banks, foreign banks, financial institutions and all primary dealers.
31. YTM – Yield to Maturity. Academically YTM is defined as the market interest rate that equates a bond's present value of interest payments and principal repayment with its price. YTM can also be defined as the compound rate of return that investors will receive for a bond with a maturity greater than one year if they hold the bond to maturity and reinvest all cash flows at the same rate of interest. It takes into account purchase price, redemption value, coupon yield and the time between interest payments. The YTM is easy to compute where the acquisition cost of a bond is at par and coupon payments are effected annually. In such a situation, the yield to maturity will be equal to coupon payment. However, for other cases, an approximate YTM can be found by using a bond yield

table. In the absence of taxes, YTM would be an accurate measure of return if the yield curve were flat and interest rates remained constant over the life of the bond. It becomes a poorer measure as the yield curve becomes steeper or as the purchase price deviates further from par.

32. For more details on securitization/reconstruction companies, please refer chapter, 'Credit Risk—An Overview'.

33. Typically, YTM is calculated either by discounting the cash flows over the period remaining till maturity or by an approximation which equates the YTM to $(1 + (F-P)/n)/(0.4F + 0.6P)$, where I denotes the interest rate, F the face value, P the market price and n the term to maturity.

34. Calculated from the YTM formula given above.

CHAPTER ELEVEN

Capital—Risk, Regulation and Adequacy

CHAPTER STRUCTURE

KEY TAKEAWAYS FROM THE CHAPTER

- Understand why capital is so important for banks.
- Know what constitutes bank capital.
- Analyse what bank capital should be related to, if 'safety' of bank is to be ensured.
- Understand the difference between accounting capital, economic capital and regulatory capital.
- Learn to measure capital adequacy-Basel norms.
- Learn how Basel norms are applied in India.

SECTION I

BASIC CONCEPTS

Why Regulate Bank Capital?

Banking is undoubtedly one of the most regulated industries globally and the rules governing bank capital are one of the most prominent aspects of such regulation. Why should this be so?

There are two typical justifications presented for regulating banks—the risk of a systemic crisis and the inability of depositors (who are the primary creditors) to monitor banks. Bank failures[1] are often triggered by the inability of banks to honour repayment commitments to their creditors on time. *Modigliani and Miller*, in their seminal work of 1958, contended that in perfect frictionless markets with full information, the value of a firm is independent of its capital structure. Most research on firms' capital structure thereafter has studied the implications of deviations from the 'perfect'. Taxes, financial distress, transaction costs, agency costs and asymmetric information are the important 'imperfections' considered to explain a firm's capital structure. In the case of banks, research has added two other factors—banks' access to the safety net, in particular, deposit insurance and the fact that most of the bank debt originates from small, generally uninformed depositors.[1]

In the traditional corporate finance view, capital reduces risk of failure by providing protection against unexpected losses (ULs). This is applicable to non-financial firms with relatively low financial leverage and reliance on long-term debt. Is the same argument applicable to financial intermediaries as well?

Consider the balance sheets of the two hypothetical firms in Table 11.1. One is a manufacturing firm and the other, a bank.[2]

TABLE 11.1 BALANCE SHEET OF TWO HYPOTHETICAL FIRMS

Manufacturing Firm Assets	Percentage	Banking Firm Assets	Percentage
Cash	5	Cash	7
Debtors	25	Loans and advances	
Inventory	30	Short-term	40
Fixed assets	40	Long-term	10
Total	100	Investments	
		Short-term	30
		Long-term	10
		Fixed and other assets	3
		Total	100
Liabilities			
Owner's equity	40	**Liabilities**	
Long-term debt	30	Equity and reserves	10
Short-term debt	10	Deposits	80
Creditors	20	Borrowings	10
Total	100	Total	100

The following are the striking contrasts:

- The manufacturing firm has 60 per cent current assets and 40 per cent fixed assets. The bank has 77 per cent current assets and 3 per cent fixed assets.
- The manufacturing firm has a current ratio of 2, while the bank's current ratio is less than 1.
- The manufacturing firm finances its assets with 60 per cent debt and 40 per cent equity. The bank finances its assets with 90 per cent debt and 10 per cent equity.
- The manufacturing firm can tolerate a 40 per cent fall in the value of its assets before its equity value is reduced to zero. It would take a mere 10 per cent fall in asset values for the bank to default on its liabilities.
- Therefore, the higher the capital, the higher the number of problem assets that can default before the capital is fully depleted.

Then why are banks permitted to operate with much more financial risk than manufacturing firms? Is it because banks, with low fixed assets, exhibit low operating leverage? However, market values of bank assets are more volatile than those of the typical manufacturing firm. Interest rate changes, borrower defaults or force majeure happenings can trigger changes in market values of bank assets, which are essentially financial assets. Though, theoretically, financial assets are more liquid and less risky than real assets (that manufacturing companies hold), in practice, these very assets could turn illiquid due to a variety of influencing factors.

We have seen in earlier chapters that bank liabilities and assets vary greatly by tenor, rate and composition. The assets bear the credit risk (borrower default), market risk (interest rate fluctuations) and the operational risks (failure of internal systems or people). Any one or a combination of these risks or an unanticipated disastrous event (force majeure risk) could result in eroding the value of banking assets.

On the other hand, the bank needs liquidity to pay off its creditors in accordance with the various contracts it has entered into at various points in time. This liquidity will have to primarily come from the periodic liquidation of assets (*e.g.*, repayments, interest payments and sale of securities). If the assets start losing value, since assets = liability + equity, the bank would have to turn to its capital to keep up its liability commitments. If the capital is not augmented with fresh infusion of funds, the bank would run out of cash and face the most serious risk of all—liquidity and hence, solvency risk.

Diagrams 11.1 and 11.2 depict the relationship between asset value (cash flows) and the bank's solvency. In the first, book values of liabilities and assets are matched. However, in the second case, the market value of assets erodes and the bank faces a solvency risk.

DIAGRAM 11.1 BOOK VALUE BALANCE SHEET OF A BANK – ASSETS AND LIABILITIES MATCHED

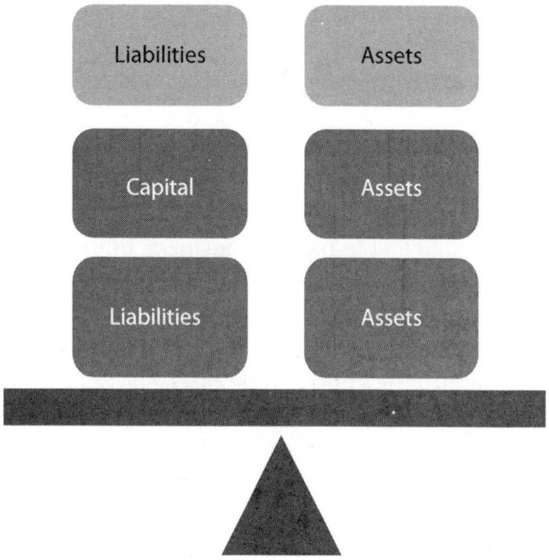

DIAGRAM 11.2 MARKET VALUE BALANCE SHEET OF A BANK – ASSET VALUE ERODES AND EQUITY USED TO MEET PART OF LIABILITIES

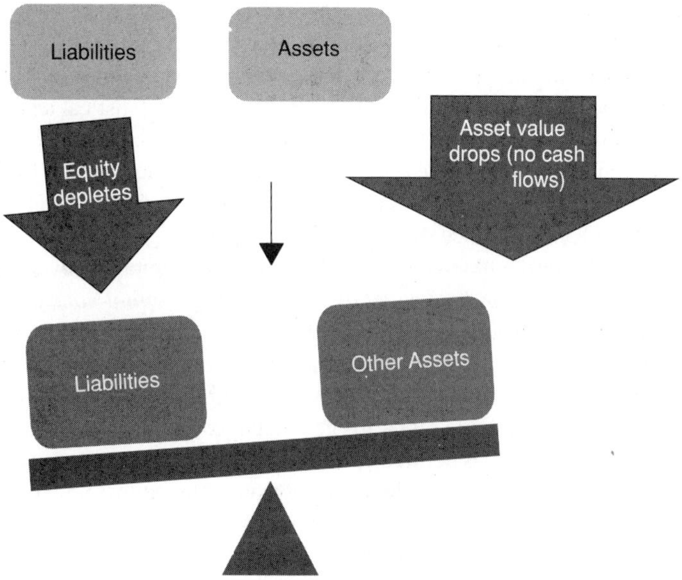

Thus, the greater the bank's capital funds, the greater the amount of assets that can default before the bank becomes technically insolvent and lower the bank's risk.

Apart from the vital function of absorbing losses as described above, which also ensures the long-term solvency of the bank, capital for a bank also serves other functions.

When a bank has adequate capital, it has ready access to the financial markets, since investors look upon it as a safe investment option. The bank can enter new businesses and can indulge in risk taking to boost earnings potential.

Thus, regulating the amount of capital that a bank should hold, though seen to constrain growth to some extent, is aimed at reducing the risk of banks expanding beyond their ability or taking undue risks.

To What Should Capital be Linked to Ensure Bank Safety?

How much capital is adequate? The debate goes on.

Take the hypothetical example given above. Let us assume that both the manufacturing firm and the banking firm have a return of 1 on their assets (ROA = 1). Which of the firms will have a higher return on equity (ROE)? Going by our analysis in the earlier chapter on 'bank financial statements', the ROE equals the product of the ROA and the equity multiplier (EM). The two firms' Equity multiplier are 2.5 (for the manufacturing firm) and 10 (for the banking firm), respectively. This implies that the bank's ROE is four times that of the manufacturing firm or that the latter should be able to flog its assets to produce an ROA, which is four times larger than what it is now!

What has contributed to this difference in the ROE? Financial leverage. Higher leverage improves profitability when earnings are positive.

More capital may ensure safety and stability, but may reduce profitability. Hence, bankers may prefer to operate with less capital.

Here lies the catch. What happens when the bank has risky or low quality assets whose earnings are being eroded either due to market factors or defaults? If the ROA slips to a negative slot, the bank's profits slide tenfold! This implies that only low risk firms should have high financial leverage.

However, financial risk is inherent to banking business, quite incomparable with the traditional manufacturing firms. Hence, the inference becomes quite clear. Only if banks have low-risk assets can they remain safe. In practice; however, banking assets are risky.

Therefore, banks should increase capital relative to the risks of the assets they hold.

In this connection, please recall the discussion in the chapter on Bank financial statements, where the implication of the inverse of the equity multiplier (Assets/Equity) was mentioned. The inverse, Equity/Assets, indicates the number of assets that can default before the equity of the bank is entirely eroded. The better the quality of assets, therefore, the more safe is the bank. In other words, when the bank's assets have low risk, the bank's capital, and hence the bank's solvency, is intact.

The Concept of Economic Capital[3]

If banks have to increase capital relative to the risk of the assets they hold, how should we determine how much capital would be adequate or required by banks to run the business, stay viable and survive?

We have seen that the risk associated with banking services depends on the type of service, that 'risk' is inherent in banking business and banks cannot survive by merely avoiding risk. Table 11.2 provides an overview of the risks that banks face in various facets of their operations.

Since 'risk' is statistically defined as the adverse deviation of actual results from expected results, the likelihood of potential adverse outcomes can be modelled using mathematical/statistical techniques. The capital that is estimated to cover the probabilistic assessment of potential future losses is called 'Economic Capital' and logically, banks themselves would be in a position to assess the amount of capital they require to absorb potential losses associated with all the risks they face. This estimate of capital is bound to be different from the traditional accounting capital measure that appears on banks' balance sheets. While the accounting capital represents book values, economic capital can be considered a forward looking measure of adequacy of capital to cover banking risks.

Thus, '*Economic Capital' can be defined as the amount of capital considered necessary by banks to absorb potential losses associated with banking risks*—such as credit, market, operational and other risks. In recent times, many banks have been using advanced modelling techniques that incorporate the internal allocation of economic capital considered necessary to support risks associated with individual lines of business, portfolios or banking transactions. Banks also use economic scenarios generated stochastically to model future business and risks.

Statistically, economic capital is defined as the difference between some given percentile of a loss distribution and the expected loss (EL) and can be understood as protection against unexpected future losses at a confidence level selected by the bank management. Usually the 99.9 per cent confidence level is used. We have seen from earlier chapters that selecting a high confidence level would imply lower probability of insolvency. Hence, the economic capital required would be higher for higher confidence levels (See Figure 11.1).

Maintaining economic capital at the 99.9 per cent confidence level implies that the capital is sufficient to cover all but one worst possible risk loss out of 1,000 possible risk scenarios, for a given time horizon. In other words, economic capital would cover most of the Unexpected Loss (UL) events, except catastrophic events. This possibility for 'ULs' necessitates holding of capital protection.

The Concept of Regulatory Capital

The widespread banking crises in the last two decades have resulted in a number of regulations to prevent such occurrences. These regulations were earlier based on the notion that banks are prone to default on their committed

TABLE 11.2 TYPES OF BANKING RISKS—AN OVERVIEW

Types of Risks	Definition
Credit risk	*Refers to the negative consequences associated with defaults or non-fulfillment of concluded contracts in lending operations due to deterioration in the counter party's credit quality.*
Counter party default risk	Refers to the possibility that the other party in an agreement will default.
Equity risk (participations)	Refers to the possibility of depreciation in the banks' investments in the stock market due to adverse price movements of the equity due to company-specific factors.
Securitization risk	Securitization is a process of distributing risk by aggregating debt instruments in a pool and then issuing new securities backed by the pool. There are two types of securitizations, viz., 'traditional' and 'synthetic' securtizations. A 'traditional' securitization is one in which an originating bank transfers a pool of assets that it owns to an arm's length special purpose vehicle. Conversely, a 'synthetic' securtization is one in which an originating bank transfers only the credit risk associated with the undertying pool of assets through the use of credit-linked notes or credit derivatives while retaining legal ownership of the pool of assets.
Concentration risk	A concentration risk is any single exposure or group of exposures with the potential to produce losses large enough (relative to a bank's capital, total assets or overall risk level) to threaten a bank's health or ability to maintain its core operations.
Market risk	*Market risk generally refers to risks which result from price changes in the money and capital markets. Market risk also results from sensitivity to foreign exchange fluctuations due to open foreign exchange positions and (in the broadest sense) open term positions.*
Interest rate risk (IRR)	Interest rate risk (IRR) is defined as the changes in a bank's portfoilo value due to interest rate fluctuations. The IRR management system is concerned with measurement and control of risk exposures both in trading book (*i.e.*, assets that are regularly traded and are liquid in nature) and in banking book (*i.e.*, assets that are usually held till maturity and rarely traded). IRR can be classified in following four categories: repricing risk (*i.e.*, fluctuations in interest rate levels that have differing impacts on bank assets and liabilities), yield curve risk (*i.e.*, changes in portfolio values caused by unanticipated shifts in the slope and shape of yield curve), basis risk (*i.e.*, imperfect correlation between index rates across different interest rate markets for similar maturties) and optionality (*i.e.*, risk artsing from interest rate options embedded in a bank asset, liabilities and off-balance-sheet positions).
Equity price risk	This risk arises due to fluctuations in market prices of equity due to general market-related factors.
Foreign exchange risk	This risk arises due to fluctuations in exchange rates.
Operational risk	*The risk of loss resulting from inadequate or failed internal processes, people and systems or from external events is called operatonal risk. This definition inclueds legal risk, but excludes strategic and reputational risk.*
Compliance/Legal risk	Compliance/Legal risk includes, but is not limited to, exposure to fines, penalties or punitive damages resuiting from superisory actions, as well as private settlements. Legal/compliance risk arises from an institution's failure to enact appropriate policies, procedures, or controls to ensure it conforms to laws, regulations, contractual arrangements, and other legally binding agreements and requirements.
Documentation risk	The unpredictabilty and uncertainty arising out of improper or insufficient documentation which gives rise to ambiguity regarding the characteristics of the financial contract is referred to as documentation risk.
Liquidity risk	*Liquidity risk arises from a bank's inability to meet its oblgations when they come due, and refers to situations in which a party is willing but unable to find counter party to trade an asset.*
Term liquidity risk	This risk arises due to an unexpected prolongation of the capital commitment period in lending transactions (unexpected delays in repayments).
Withdrawal/Call risk	The risk that more credit lines will be drawn or more deposits withdrawn than expected is refered to as withdrawal or call risk. This brings about the risk that the bank will no longer be able to meet its payment obligations without constraints.
Structural liquidity risk	This risk arises when the necessary funding transactions cannot be carried out (or can be carried only on less favourable terms). This risk is sometimes also called funding lquidity risk.
Contingent liquidity risk	Contingent liquidity risk is the risk associated with finding additional funds or replacing maturing liabilities under potential, future stressed market conditions.
Market liquidity risk	This risk arises when positions cannot be sold within a desired time period or can be sold only at a discount (market impact). This is especially the case with securities/derivatives in liquid markets, or when a bank holds such large positions that they cannot be sold easily. These market liquidity risks can be accounted for by extending the holding period in risk measurements (*e.g.*, the holding period for VaR) or by applying expected values derived from experience.

(*Continued*)

TABLE 11.2 (CONTINUED)

Other risks	
Strategic risk	Strategic risk refers to negative effects on capital and earnings due to business policy decisions, changes in the economic environment, deficient or insufficient implementation of decisions, or a failure to adapt to changes in the economic environment.
Reputation risk	Reputation risk refers to the potential adverse effects which can arise from bank's reputation deviating negatively from its expected level. A bank's reputation refers to its image in the eyes of the interseted public (investors, lenders, employees, customers, etc.) with regard to competence, integrity and reliability.
Capital risk	Capital risk results from an imbalanced internal capital structure in relation to the nature and size of the bank or from difficulties associated with raising additonal risk coverage capital quickly, if necessary.
Earnings risk	Earnings risk arises due to the inadequate diversification of a bank's earnings structre or its inability to attain a sufficient and lasting level of profitability.
Outsourcing risk	While there are many ways to categorize outsourcing risk, four of the most convenent are operational discruption risk, data risk, quality risk and reputation risk.

Source: RBI, Report on currency and finance, Chapter V, Table 5.1 (2006–2008): 180.

FIGURE 11.1 ECONOMIC CAPITAL AND HEDGING TECHNIQUES FOR LOSSES

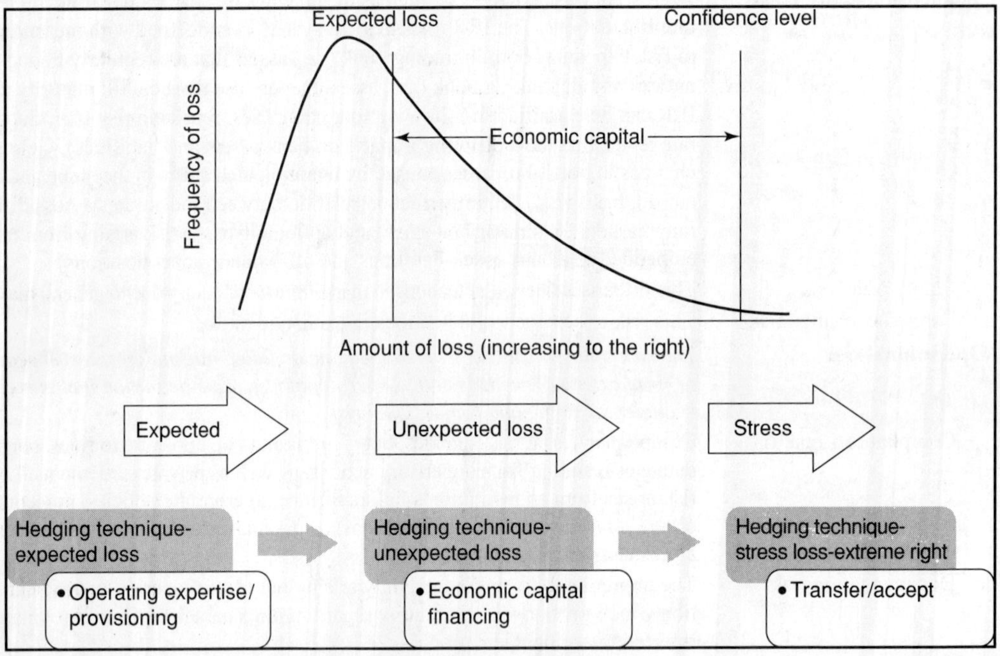

deposit payments because of the mismatch between the timings of the demand for withdrawals and the returns on the assets that banks create. The possibility of such a mismatch can encourage depositors to withdraw larger amounts than they would have, if such possibilities did not exist. On a large scale, such depositors' behaviour would result in a 'run' on the bank. Therefore, one aspect of bank regulation is to ensure that depositors who do not need to withdraw at present are given enough assurance that they will be paid in the future. Depositors need assurance that the bank has enough (claims on) liquid assets to meet all demands made by depositors. There are four ways to provide this assurance[4]—adequate bank equity capital, deposit insurance, lender of last resort and subordinated debt. Lack of assurance can lead to bank failures and outcomes that are not welfare maximizing. These assurances have an economic role in providing optimal outcomes and therefore, need to be formulated with utmost care.

Basically, both regulatory and economic capital are concerned with the bank's financial staying power. However, regulatory capital depends on the confidence level set by the regulator and therefore, does not respond in the same manner to changes in the common variables that affect both economic and regulatory capital, such as loans' Probability of Default (PD) and Loss Given Default (LGD). Hence, no direct relationship has been perceived between both capital levels.

The Basel Committee on Banking Supervision (BCBS) (see Section II) and the regulators however recognize that capital adequacy as determined by economic risk is imperative for the long term stability of banks. Therefore, apart from maintaining capital as stipulated by regulation, banks need to carefully assess their internal and future capital requirements based on the risks taken during the course of business.

Moreover, the two concepts reflect the needs of different stakeholders—the bank's shareholders look to economic capital, while the depositors look to adequacy of regulatory capital.

Illustration 11.1 depicts a simple example of how regulatory and economic capital might be different.

ILLUSTRATION 11.1

Please refer to Illustration 9.1 (Chapter 9 – Managing Credit Risk – Advanced Topics)

In the measurement of credit VaR for a single loan using the Credit Migration Approach (Credit Metrics), we will compare the regulatory requirement of capital for the loan with the economic capital requirement for the same loan.

Regulatory capital specifies that (Indian norms) 9% risk weighted capital has to be maintained. Though our loan in the example is A rated, we will assume 100% risk weight for the loan. Hence, for ₹100 crore of the loan, the bank has to maintain regulatory capital of ₹9 crore.

Economic capital can be calculated as the Credit VaR either by assuming 'normal' distribution, or using the values in the actual distribution in the example.

1. If we use normal distribution, we get the following results at 5% VaR and 1% VaR

5%	VAR	1.65*	₹12.89 cr
1%	VAR	2.33*	₹18.20 cr

2. If we use the actual distribution, we find that 5% VaR is approximated by 9.61% (adding the probabilities from the default state upwards *i.e.*, .009 + .007 + .002 + .044 + .072 + .827), and 1% VaR is approximated by 1.34% (add all probabilities except .827). At these values.

5% VAR	95% of actual distribution	(125.63 – 126.89)	₹–1.26 crore
1% VAR	99% if actual distribution	(125.63 – 125.67)	₹–0.04 crore

The VaR comes out negative in both cases, though, we can interpolate values to get to the 5% VaR level.

How do we interpret these results?

The results throw up some interesting observations, and in practice, challenges for banks when they have to maintain capital commensurate with the asset risk.

In our example of a ₹100 crore loan rated A, the bank would have to maintain ₹9 crore as capital to compensate for the credit risk in terms of the capital regulations. However, if the bank were to estimate the capital requirement based on its internal assessment of credit risk, it would have to maintain ₹18.20 crore as capital, if a normal distribution were assumed, or no capital at all, if the actual distribution were to be relied upon!

SECTION II

RISK-BASED CAPITAL STANDARDS[5]—REGULATORY CAPITAL

In the early 1980s, concern about international banks' financial health increased, as did complaints of unfair competition. It was then that the BCBS began thinking in terms of setting capital standards for banks.

Box 11.1 provides an overview of the Bank for International Settlements and the Basel Committee.

BOX 11.1 THE BIS AND THE BCBS

The Bank for International Settlements (BIS)

The Bank for International Settlements, the world's oldest international financial organization, was established in 1930 with its head office in Basel, Switzerland. It aims at fostering international monetary and financial cooperation and serves as a bank for central banks. The bank's capital is held exclusively by various central banks of the world. The BIS fulfils its mandate by acting as:

- a forum for discussion and decision-making among central banks and within the international financial and supervisory community,
- a centre for economic and monetary research,
- a prime counter party for central banks in their financial transactions and
- agent or trustee in connection with international financial operations.

Fifty-five central banks, including the RBI, currently (as of June 2009) have rights of voting and representation at general meetings.

To maintain exclusivity as a bank for central banks around the world, the BIS does not accept deposits from or provide financial services to private individuals or corporate bodies. It is also not permitted to make advances to governments or open current accounts in the name of governments. However, it offers a wide range of financial services to central banks and other monetary authorities, such as the following:

- Management of foreign exchange reserves, a service used by 135 monetary authorities (at end of March 2009), to manage total currency deposits of SDR 197 billion, amounting to about 4 per cent of the world's foreign currency reserves,
- Investment and asset management services for central banks, ranging from standard (such as sight/notice accounts and term deposits) to innovative, such as financial products to enable central banks to trade actively with BIS for increasing return on foreign assets, management of sovereign securities and other high grade assets and so on,
- Granting occasional collateralized short term credits to central banks and
- Acting as trustee for international government loans and performing collateral agent functions.

In order to further its objective of fostering international monetary and financial cooperation, the BIS undertakes the following activities:

- It organizes regular meetings of governors and other senior officials of central banks to enable them monitor global financial and economic developments and also discuss specific policy issues relating to monetary and financial stability.
- It hosts the secretariats of the BCBS (see below), the Committee on Payment and Settlement Systems, the Committee on the Global Financial System, the Markets Committee and several others.
- To support the meetings and the work of the committees, BIS undertakes extensive research in the economic, monetary, financial and legal areas. It also functions as a hub for sharing statistical information among central banks and for publishing statistics on global banking securities, foreign exchange and derivatives markets.
- The Financial Stability Institute has been set up by BIS to promote dissemination and implementation of robust financial sector supervisory standards.

The Basel Committee on Banking Supervision (BCBS)

The committee, established by central bank governors of the G10 countries in 1974, meets regularly four times a year. It has four main working groups, which also meet regularly.

The countries comprising the committee are represented by their central banks. The Committee reports to the governors of the central banks of the G10 countries. An important objective of the Committee is to tighten supervision of international banks towards achieving which the Committee has been working since 1975 and issuing a long series of documents. The Committee's Secretariat is provided by the BIS in Basel.

In 1988, the Committee introduced the bank capital measurement system popularly referred to as the Basel Capital Accord.

It should be noted that the Committee does not possess any formal supranational supervisory authority and its conclusions do not have legal force. Rather, it formulates broad supervisory standards and guidelines and recommends best practices to be customized and implemented suitably by individual authorities in various countries. In other words, the Committee encourages convergence towards common approaches and common standards.

Source: www.bis.org

The international convergence of bank capital regulation began with the 1988 Basel Accord on capital standards. The G10 countries signed the accord, which was then intended to apply to only internationally active banks. At that time, its focus was the measurement of capital and the definition of capital standards for credit risk. Since then the Accord has been amended several times, having been endorsed by the central banks of many countries and adopted by several banks across the globe. The first Basel Agreement (1988) contained some important features, which took into account the relationship between capital and the asset portfolio.

- It is directly linked by a simple formula, the capital requirement of a bank to the credit risk, determined by the bank's asset composition. The greater the default risk of the asset portfolio, the higher the required capital.
- Recognizing the vital role of owner's equity in capital it also prescribed, based on the risk profile of the assets, a minimum amount of equity capital.
- The capital norms were standardized across countries to 'level the playing field'.

Over time, the Accord has been fine-tuned to account for financial innovation and some other risks it had not considered earlier.

Basel Accords II and III seek to strengthen the resilience and risk management capabilities of global banks. Basel III, the latest version of the Accord, aims at reinforcing global capital and liquidity rules, in the wake of the financial crisis of 2007–08. The salient features of the three Accords are provided in the remaining part of this Section (See Figure 11.2).

FIGURE 11.2 THE BASEL ACCORDS – TIMELINES

1988: Basel I
1992: Fully implemented
1994: Market risk amendment issued.
1997: Implemented Market risk amendment

2004: Basel II
2006: Implemented
2007: Advanced approaches implemented
2009: Basel 2.5 trading book and securitization rules issued

2009: Basel III
2009: Consultative document
2010: G20 endorsement
2011: Implementation begins
2019: Proposed completion of implementation

Demystifying the Basel Accords I, II and III

What do the successive Basel Accords really say? They do not mean anything different from what we have simplistically stated earlier about the relationship between bank capital and the risks of the assets banks carry. Therefore, the basic Basel definition of capital adequacy remains 'Capital/Assets', that can be now expressed as $\frac{\text{(Regulatory capital)}}{\text{(Risk weighted assets)}}$.

The Numerator of 'Capital Adequacy' Ratio We will start with the ratio 'equity (capital)/assets' mentioned earlier. What defines capital of a bank? Is it the book value of equity and reserves shown on the balance sheet, or is it the economic capital described in the previous section required to support risks? This is what the successive Basel Accords seek to define and measure. We know that equity capital has the last claim on the cash flows or assets of a firm. Hence, any instrument that satisfies this criterion, namely, staking the last claim on residual cash flows after all commitments are met, can be a part of bank capital. 'Regulatory capital' as defined by the Basel Accords adopts this approach and specifies some 'equity like' instruments that can be considered part of 'capital' of a bank. This is the numerator of the 'capital adequacy ratio'. The ratio aims to ensure 'adequacy of capital' (in relation to asset risks) or simply measure 'capital adequacy' in regulatory terms. The successive Accords attempt to rigorously define and monitor the numerator.

The Denominator of the 'Capital Adequacy' Ratio Let us now look at the denominator – 'assets'. The discussion in the preceding section has established that rather than total assets of the bank the riskiness of the assets would determine how fast the bank's capital would be eroded, and the bank would become insolvent. Hence, the denominator of the 'capital adequacy ratio' is 'risk weighted assets'. Simply, each asset on the bank's balance sheet is assigned a 'risk weight' (either by the regulator or by the bank itself through its internal models). The risk weight is multiplied with the asset value to arrive at the total of risk weighted assets. Risk weights are applicable not only to assets on the balance sheet of the bank, but also to contingent liabilities of the bank, since these can become potential future liabilities for the bank. 'Credit conversion factors' are used to arrive at a credit equivalent of the off balance sheet items, and then multiplied by the appropriate risk weights to compute the consolidated 'risk weighted assets' in the denominator.

'Risk weighted assets' (RWAs) are an integral part of the regulatory norms since they can (a) provide a common measure for banks' risks, (b) ensure that capital maintained by banks is commensurate with the risks; and (c) potentially highlight where destabilizing asset class bubbles are arising[6].

Since banks deal with complex instruments and risks, the successive Basel Accords have been fine tuning the 'risk weighted assets' to consider risks of counter parties, securitizations, derivatives, foreign exchange and other market related risks. 'Operational risks' that impact asset value are also considered part of 'risk weighted assets'.

How Successive Basel Accords Have Treated 'Capital Adequacy' Basel I and Basel II (as well as Basel 2.5) concentrated on the measurement of the riskiness of assets in the denominator and the calculation of 'risk weighted assets'. The numerator, 'capital' was also defined to bring out the difference between permanent capital of the bank augmented by reserves, and other types of capital that would typically not be shown on the balance sheet as equity capital. As the Accords progressed, the various versions of the numerator, 'capital' and the denominator, 'risk weighted assets' aimed at fine tuning their definition and measurement

The manner in which the various versions have dealt with the concept is shown in Figure 11.3

FIGURE 11.3 EVOLUTION OF THE CAPITAL ADEQUACY RATIO OVER THE BASEL ACCORDS

(RWAs = Risk Weighted Assets)

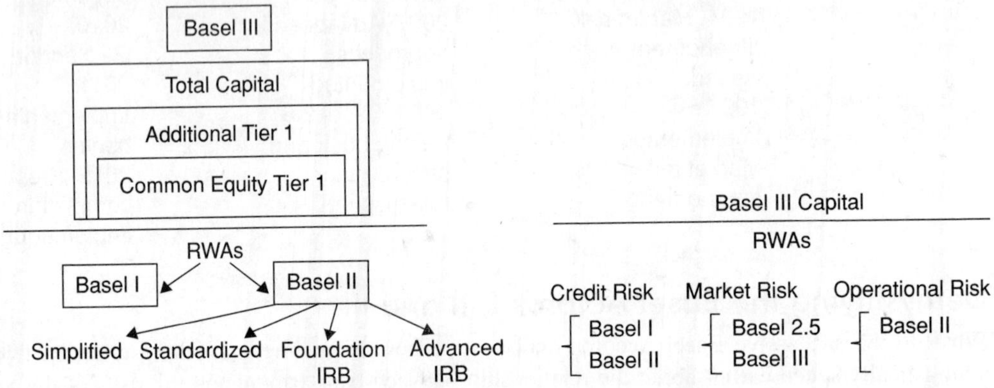

Source: BCBS, IMF staff

Source: IMF Working Paper WP/12/90, March 2012, 'Revisiting Risk weighted assets', prepared by Vanessa Le Leslé and SofiyaAvramova, Figure 1, page 5

It can be understood from the Figure 11.3 that in Basel III, the focus is on the definition and composition of the numerator, 'capital', and the denominator 'risk weighted assets' is largely being carried over from the previous approaches.

Basel I, II and III are briefly described in the remaining portion of this section.

Basel Accord I

The 1988 Basel Accord required internationally active banks in G10 countries to hold capital equal to at least 8 per cent of a basket of assets measured in accordance with their risk profiles. The definition of 'capital' is broadly set in two tiers—Tier 1 being shareholders' equity and retained earnings and Tier 2 being the additional internal and external sources available to the bank. The bank has to hold at least half of its measured capital in Tier 1 form.

A portfolio approach is taken to measure risk, with assets classified into four discrete buckets—10 per cent, 20 per cent, 50 per cent and 100 per cent—according to the quality of the assets. This means that some assets have no capital requirements, being considered riskless, while others have risk-weights attached to them. The two principal objectives of the Accord were: (a) to ensure an adequate level of capital in the international banking system and (b) to create a 'more level playing field' in competitive terms so that banks could no longer build business volumes without adequate capital backing.

The Accord was adopted as a world standard in the 1990s, with more than 100 countries applying the Basel framework to their banking systems.

However, the drawbacks in the framework were as listed below.

a. The regulatory measures were seen to be in conflict with increasingly sophisticated internal measures of economic capital.
b. The simple bucket approach with a flat 8 per cent charge for claims on the private sector resulted in banks moving high quality assets off their balance sheets, thus reducing the average asset quality.
c. The Accord did not sufficiently recognize credit risk mitigation techniques.

When the Accord was introduced in 1988, its very design was questioned since the capital ratios appeared to lack economic foundation, the risk-weights did not reflect the risk of the borrower, and it did not account for any benefits from diversification of the asset portfolio. Growing experience and research prompted development of various alternatives to the Accord's 'buckets' framework for setting capital standards.

Basel Accord II

It was recognized that the 'one-size-fits-all' framework of the Basel I Accord had to be upgraded, since each bank had its own unique way of measuring, mitigating and managing risks. The revised framework hence provides a spectrum of approaches ranging from simple to advanced for measurement of credit risks, market risks and operational risks, all of which could lead to asset quality and value deterioration. The framework also builds in incentives for better and more accurate risk management by individual banks.

The new Accord aims at a framework, which will maintain the overall 'safety' level of capital in banks through more comprehensive and risk sensitive approaches. It is less prescriptive than its predecessor and offers a range of approaches for banks capable of scaling up to more risk sensitive methodologies.

Structure of the New Accord The new Accord is based on three mutually reinforcing 'pillars', which together are expected to contribute to the safety and soundness of the international financial system (*see* Figure 11.4).

First pillar—Minimum capital requirement: The minimum capital requirement will now take into account market risks and operational risks, along with credit risks. It also proposes differentiated approaches to measurement of capital from basic to advanced.

1. *Capital for credit risk*
   a. Standardized approach
   b. Internal ratings based approach—Foundation and advanced
   c. Securitization framework
2. *Capital for market risk*
   a. Standardized approach (maturity method)
   b. Standardized approach (duration method)
   c. Internal models method
3. *Capital for operational risk*
   a. Basic indicator approach
   b. Standardized approach
   c. Advanced measurement approach (AMA)

The salient features of these three approaches to measuring 'risk weighted assets' are provided in the following paragraphs:

FIGURE 11.4 THE PILLARS OF BASEL II ACCORD

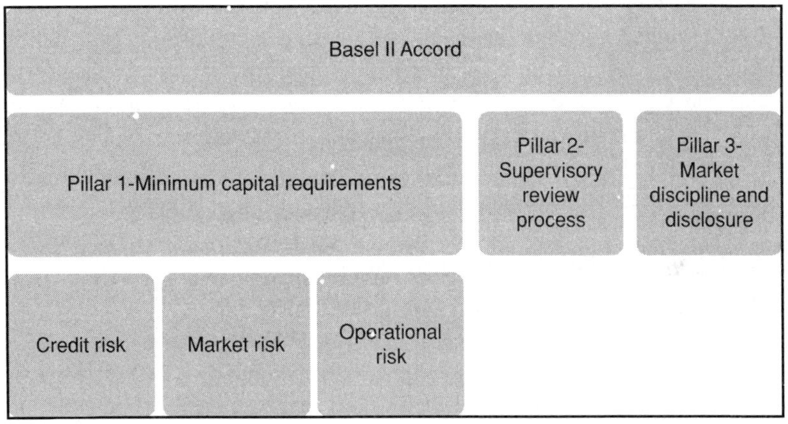

Credit Risk Measurement: Credit risk refers to the negative consequences associated with defaults or non fulfilment of concluded contracts in lending operations due to deterioration in the counter party's credit quality.

- In the 'Standardized' approach, the risk weight depends largely on external credit ratings provided by accredited credit rating agencies. (For more details on credit rating and credit rating agencies, please refer to the Chapter 'Uses of bank funds–the lending function')
    - In this case,
      regulatory capital = 8 per cent × risk weight × notional amount.

      For example, a BBB rated corporate borrower will attract 100 per cent risk weight. 8 per cent is the minimum capital that is to be maintained on the exposure to this corporate borrower. Hence, if the notional amount outstanding is ₹1000 crore, the regulatory capital to be maintained on this exposure would be
      8 per cent × 100 per cent × 1000 = ₹80 crore
- In the Foundation—Internal Ratings based approach (F-IRB), banks would use internal estimates of Probability of Default (PD), and regulatory values for Loss Given Default (LGD) and Exposure at Default (EAD). (For more details on PD, LGD and EAD, please refer to the chapters on 'Managing Credit Risk')
    - Banks can form their own assessment of 'risk components', after approval from their regulators/central banks. The risk components are—PD, LGD, EAD and M (Maturity—denoting effective maturity of every instrument).
    - The second key element of the IRB framework is definition of the 'risk weight functions'. These are the means by which risk components are transformed into risk weighted assets, the denominator of capital adequacy ratio. The risk weight functions are derived from the estimates of 'risk components'.
    - The third key element is definition of 'minimum requirements'—the minimum standards that must be met by a bank using the IRB approach for an asset class.
- Banks moving to Advanced Internal Ratings Based approaches (advanced IRB) would use internal estimates of PD, LGD and EAD.

Market Risk Assessment: Market risk is defined as the risk of losses in on and off-balance-sheet positions arising from movements in market prices. The risks pertaining to interest rate related instruments and equitiesin the trading book, foreign exchange risk and commodities risk throughout the bank are key components of market risk.

- The standardized approaches use risk weights provided by the supervisor.
- The Internal Models Method (IMM) allows banks to use risk measures derived from their own internal risk management models. (Please also refer to some market risk measurement tools mentioned in the previous chapter).
- Basel 2.5 is a complex package of rules that imposes higher capital charges on banks for the market risks they run in their trading books, particularly credit-related products.

Operational Risk Measurement: Operational risk is defined as the risk of loss resulting from inadequate or failed internal processes, people and systems or from external events (*e.g.*, fraud, system failures). This definition includes legal risk, but excludes strategic and reputational risk.

- Under the Basic Indicator Approach, capital is a fraction of gross income. Banks using the approach must hold capital equal to the average over the previous three years of a fixed percentage (termed $\alpha = 15$ per cent) of positive annual gross income.
- In the Standardized approach, capital is computed by lines of business using fixed percentages. Banks' activities are divided into eight business lines. Within each business line, the capital charge is calculated by multiplying gross income by a factor termed β assigned to that line of business. For example, the β factor for corporate finance is 18 per cent, for commercial banking is 15 per cent, for retail banking 12 per cent and so on.
- Advanced Measurement Approach requires banks to use statistical methods and data analytics to calculate capital. Under this approach, the regulatory capital requirement will equal the risk measure generated by the bank's internal operational risk measurement system using quantitative and qualitative criteria.

Calculation of Capital Adequacy Under Basel II

The 'Capital ratio' is expressed as follows:

$$\frac{\text{Aggregate of Capital components as defined by Basel II}}{\text{Aggregate of RWAs, } i.e., \text{ Credit risk} + \text{Market risk} + \text{Operational risk}}$$

The minimum ratio that a bank should maintain under the given formula is 8 per cent.

Credit risk is calculated as the aggregate of risk weighted assets under each applicable asset class. In the case of Market and Operational risks, risk-weighted assets are determined by multiplying the capital requirements (termed 'capital charge') for both risks by 12.5 (*i.e.*, the reciprocal of the minimum capital ratio of 8 per cent) and adding the resulting figures to the sum of risk-weighted assets for credit risk.

Comparison of Basel I and Basel II

	Basel I	Basel II
Complexity	Simple	High complexity
Approach	Top down—supervisor determines risk weights	Bottom up—Banks/external agencies determine risk weights
Approach to risk	No risk sensitivity	Increased risk sensitivity

A detailed description of the determination of Risk weighted assets under the above approaches, definition of 'capital' and calculating the capital requirement under Basel II and Basel 2.5, can be found in Annexure I.

Second pillar—Supervisory review process. Bank managements are expected to strengthen their internal processes to set targets for capital commensurate with the risk profile and control environment of each bank. The internal processes would be subject to more rigorous review and intervention by the country's central bank.

Third pillar—Market discipline. This aims at bolstering market discipline through enhanced disclosure by banks. The new framework sets out disclosure requirements and recommendations in several areas, including the manner in which a bank calculates its capital adequacy and its risk assessment methods. The core set of disclosure requirements is applicable to all banks.

How do the above approaches compare with the previous Accord? It can be seen that basel has shed the buckets approach which treated all banks alike, with no incentives for safer banks to differentiate themselves from riskier ones and thus save on capital. The present approach is an improvement since the buckets are now based on risk measures rather than on types of assets. This would bring regulatory capital for each exposure into closer alignment with the risk of the underlying asset and encourage banks to adopt better risk management practices.

Basel Accord III[7]

Shortcomings in Basel II

Some of the flaws pointed out in the Basel II proposals were as follows:

1. The main criticism against Basel I was that it had a 'one size fits all' and 'risk insensitive' approach. Basel II brought in 'risk sensitive' capital regulation. However, the risk sensitivity made Basel II blatantly 'procyclical'—that is, in good times, when banks are doing well, and the market is willing to invest additional capital in banks, Basel II does not demand more capital from banks. However, in bad times, when markets run out of or are unwilling to supply additional capital, Basel II requires that banks bring in more capital to support stressed assets. The happenings during the financial crisis of 2007, where major international banks could not bring in additional capital under pressure, bear out this observation about Basel II.
2. Basel II failed to promote frameworks for accurate and realistic measurement of risk. Thus, the regulations could not demand sufficient loss absorbing capital to mitigate the risks caused by changes in market dynamics. For example, the financial crisis happened when market risk models failed to factor in the real risk from complex derivative products, on the simplistic assumption that these were tradable instruments that could be sold readily in the market. Hence, banks did not adequately cover these risks with capital. Additionally, banks started converting their assets into tradable instruments (the 'originate and distribute' model) to minimize capital holding.

3. Basel II did not explicitly address the issues of excessive leverage and liquidity risk in banks. The assumption was that risk based capital would automatically mitigate the risk of excessive leverage. However, it was excessive leverage that triggered the financial crisis. The loss of liquidity that quickly followed excessive leverage led to banks becoming insolvent. The excessive leverage-liquidity risk–solvency risk relationship was not adequately recognized by Basel II.
4. Basel II also focussed on individual banks and financial institutions and failed to take into consideration the 'contagion' effect of failure of one large bank. The risks to the global banking system arising from the interconnectedness of large institutions was a major reason for the crisis spreading rapidly across the financial system.
5. Other issues that rendered Basel II ineffective against a major crisis were
    a. Pillar 1 does not penalize credit concentration. Instead, the issue of credit concentration risk is embodied as part of Pillar 2. In other words, the onus of identifying and penalizing credit concentration is left to supervisory review.
    b. All aspects of Counter party risk were not covered and there was no provision to include certain types of specialized derivative products in the risk measurement.
    c. On the issue of Pro cyclicality, it was noted that banks' risk measurements were more at a specific point in time rather than over the whole asset cycle. Also, profit recognition and compensation schemes were seen to encourage short term risk taking. The risk over the business cycle was ignored.

Annexure II to this chapter gives more viewpoints on Basel II and its role in the blame game for the financial crisis of 2007.

The Move to Basel III Basel III, as we can see from the following paragraphs, makes an effort to fix the lacunae in Basel II that came to light during the financial crisis as also to reflect other lessons of the crisis. It is also evident that Basel III does not jettison Basel II, but builds on the essence of Basel II—the link between the risk profiles and capital requirements of individual banks. In that sense, Basel III can be considered an enhancement of Basel II.

The enhancements of Basel III over Basel II are primarily in four areas: (i) augmentation in the level and quality of capital; (ii) introduction of liquidity standards; (iii) modifications in provisioning norms; and (iv) better and more comprehensive disclosures. It is noteworthy that Basel III has concentrated on capital definition (the numerator of the capital adequacy ratio), with minimal enhancements in the risk measurements (denominator of capital adequacy ratio).

Diagram 11.3 depicts the structure of Basel III guidelines and the comparison with Basel II.

DIAGRAM 11.3 BASEL III BASIC STRUCTURE AND BROAD COMPARISON WITH BASEL III

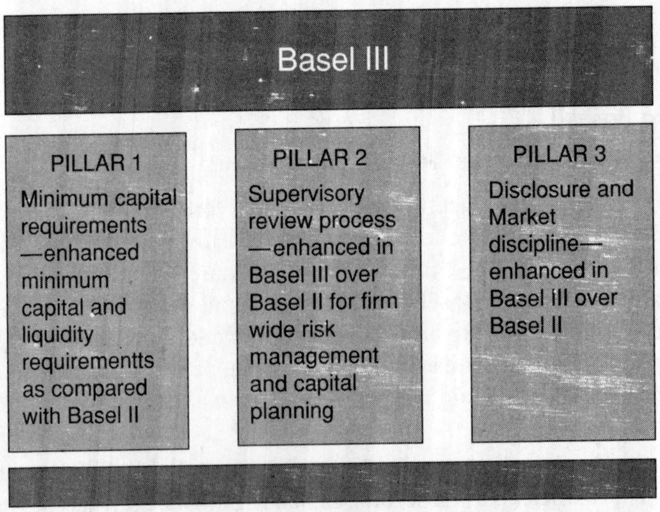

Objectives of Basel III According to the Basel committee, the Basel III proposals have two primary objectives:

- To strengthen global capital and liquidity regulations. The goal is to promote a more resilient banking sector
- To improve the banking sector's ability to absorb shocks arising from financial and economic stress

To achieve these objectives, the Basel III proposals have focussed on the areas of capital reform, liquidity reform and other reforms that would improve the stability of the global banking system. The key ingredients of these reforms are presented in Diagram 11.4

DIAGRAM 11.4 BASEL III – PROPOSED REFORMS TO ACHIEVE OBJECTIVES

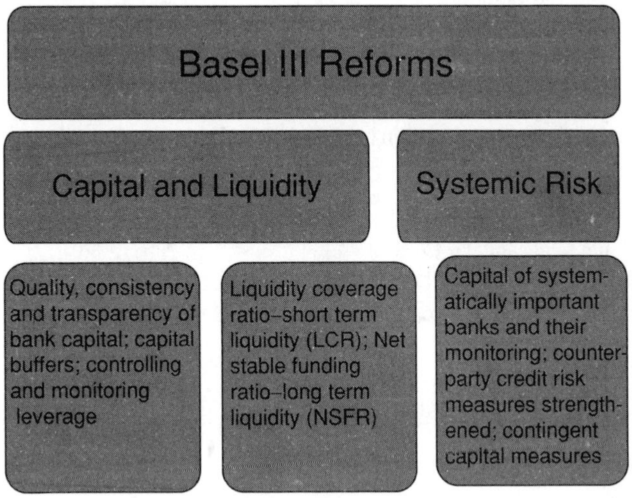

Each of the reforms are briefly discussed in the paragraphs below

Some Specific Enhancements Proposed in Basel III (Over Basel II)

1. **New definition of capital:**

   Table 11.3 distinguishes the capital requirements under Basel II and Basel III

TABLE 11.3 BASEL II AND BASEL III CAPITAL REQUIREMENTS COMPARED–THE QUANTITY OF CAPITAL

	Basel II/ 2.5			Basel III		
	Common Equity	**Tier I Capital**	**Tier II Capital**	**Common Equity**	**Tier I Capital**	**Tier II Capital**
Minimum capital required	2%	4%	8%	4.5%	6%	8%
Capital conservation buffer (additional)	Not required			2.5%		
Countercyclical buffer–range (additional)	Not required			0%-2.5% (in the form of common equity or any other fully loss absorbing capital)		
Required for Systematically Important Financial Institutions (SIFI) (additional)	Not required			1%–3.5% based on 'bucketing approach' given in BCBS document dated November 2011[8]		
Leverage ratio (additional)	Not required				$\frac{\text{Tier I capital}}{\text{Total exposure}} \geq 3\%$[9]	

It is not only the quantity of capital that has changed from Basel II as can be seen in the above table, but also the quality of capital required under the various categories of capital have undergone a change. Table 11.4 summarizes the key changes.

TABLE 11.4 BASEL II AND III CAPITAL REQUIREMENTS COMPARED – QUALITY OF CAPITAL

		Capital as % of Risk Weighted Assets	
		Basel II	**Basel III (as on Jan 1, 2019)**
A (= B + D)	Minimum total capital	8.0	8.0
B	Minimum tier 1 capital	4.0	6.0
C	Of which, Minimum Common Equity (tier 1 capital) (CET1)	2.0	4.5
D	Maximum tier 2 capital (within total capital)	4.0	2.0
E	Capital Conservation Buffer (CCB)	nil	2.5
F (= C + E)	Minimum Common equity tier 1 capital + CCB	2.0	7.0
G (= A + E)	Minimum total capital + CCB	8.0	10.5

Table 11.5 shows the composition of capital items under Basel II and Basel III

TABLE 11.5 BASEL II AND III CAPITAL REQUIREMENTS COMPARED – COMPOSITION OF CAPITAL

	Major Capital Components – Basel II	**Major Capital Components – Basel III**
Common Equity Tier I capital	• Basel II does not explicitly prescribe a minimum common equity Tier 1 capital. It is generally accepted that common equity should be the predominant part of Tier 1 capital *i.e.*, 50 per cent	• Equity shares issued by the bank • Share premium resulting from the issue of instruments included in Common Equity Tier 1 • Retained earnings • Accumulated other comprehensive income and other disclosed reserves
Tier I capital	• As in common equity Tier 1 capital above + hybrid debt capital instruments (maximum 15% of Tier 1 capital)	• Termed 'Additional Tier 1 capital' • Comprises of instruments that meet specific criteria of BCBS/regulator • Share premium resulting from the issue of instruments included above • Instruments issued by consolidated subsidiaries of the bank and held by third parties that meet the specific criteria for inclusion in Additional Tier 1 capital and are not included in Common Equity Tier 1. • Hybrid debt capital instruments held under Basel II requirements to be phased out
Tier 2 capital	• Limited to 100% of Tier 1 capital • Could be comprised of any or all of the following: undisclosed reserves, revaluation reserves, general provisions/loan loss reserves, hybrid debt capital instruments and subordinated term debt • Subordinated term debt maximum 50% of Tier 1 capital • Upper tier 2 capital maximum 50% of Tier 1 capital	• Instruments issued by the bank that meet the criteria for inclusion in Tier 2 capital (and are not included in Tier 1 capital) • Share premium resulting from the issue of instruments included in Tier 2 capital • Instruments issued by consolidated subsidiaries of the bank and held by third parties that meet the specific criteria for inclusion in Tier 2 capital and are not included in Tier 1 capital. • Certain loan loss provisions • No distinction between Upper Tier 2 and Lower Tier 2 instruments
Tier 3 capital	• Short term subordinated debt only to cover market risks • Tier 3 capital will be limited to 250% of a bank's Tier 1 capital that is required to support market risks	No Tier 3 capital

In essence, in order to qualify, the additional Tier 1 and Tier 2 instruments in Basel III must have the following features:

- They must be more loss absorbing
- They must not contain incentives to redeem prior to their stated maturity
- They must be written off or converted to equity at the determination by the supervisory authority—that either the bank would not be viable without the write off or that a public sector capital infusion is essential

All the above capital classes are also subject to 'regulatory adjustments'. Some of these adjustments are listed below:

- 'Goodwill' or other 'intangible assets on banks' balance sheets have to be deducted from Common Equity Tier 1 capital
- Deferred Tax Assets (DTAs) that rely on future profitability of the bank to be realize dare to be deducted in the calculation of Common Equity Tier 1.
- Gain on sale related to securitization transactions to be deducted from Common Equity Tier 1

Other adjustments mentioned by the Basel document related to 'cash flow hedge reserve', 'shortfall of stock of provisions to expected losses, 'cumulative gains and losses due to changes in own credit risk on fair valued financial liabilities', 'defined benefit pension fund assets and liabilities', 'investments in own shares', 'reciprocal cross holdings in banks and other financial entities', etc.

The essential difference between Basel II and III Tier 1 and Tier 2 capital is that:

- Under Basel II, qualifying Tier 1 and Tier 2 capital was determined on the basis of 'gross' instruments, before deduction of various items that could reduce the amount of capital available to withstand credit and other shocks
- Under Basel III, banks would determine available Tier 1 and Tier 2 capital only after deductions are made

2. **Additional requirements as part of capital—-the capital conservation buffer:**

As can be seen from the comparative data presented above, Basel III requires higher and better quality capital. The minimum total capital remains unchanged at 8 per cent of Risk Weighted Assets (RWA). However, Basel III introduces a *capital conservation buffer* of 2.5 per cent of RWA over and above the minimum capital requirement, raising the total capital requirement to 10.5 per cent against 8.0 per cent under Basel II.

This buffer is intended to ensure that banks are able to absorb losses without breaching the minimum capital requirement, and are able to carry on business even in a downturn without deleveraging. This buffer is not part of the regulatory minimum; however, the level of the buffer will determine the dividend distributed to shareholders and the bonus paid to staff.

According to the Basel committee, 'The framework reduces the discretion of banks which have depleted their capital buffers to further reduce them through generous distributions of earnings. In doing so, the framework will strengthen their ability to withstand adverse environments'. {page 55)

Table 11.6 from the Basel document shows the minimum capital conservation ratios a bank must meet at various levels of the Common Equity Tier 1 (CET1) capital ratios, and its impact on earnings distribution of banks

TABLE 11.6 IMPACT OF CAPITAL CONSERVATION BUFFER ON BANK CAPITAL AND EARNINGS DISTRIBUTION

Individual Bank Minimum Capital Conservation Standards

Common Equity Tier 1 Ratio	Minimum Capital Conservation Ratios (expressed as a percentage of earnings)
4.5% – 5.125%	100%
> 5.125% – 5.75%	80%
> 5.75% – 6.375%	60%
> 6.375% – 7.0%	40%
> 7.0%	0%

Source: Basel Committee on banking supervision, Basel III: A global regulatory framework for more resilient banks and banking systems, revised version, June 2011, page 56.

Let us interpret the table. A bank with CET1 capital ratio of say 5.5 per cent is required to pay out no more than 20 per cent of its net earnings as dividends or bonus payments or share buybacks in the following financial year. In other words, the bank has to conserve 80 per cent of its earnings over the following year. The motive is obvious—to curb excessive bonus and dividend payouts by banks at the cost of its stability and solvency.

If the bank still wants to make payments in excess of the prescribed limits, the bank has the option of raising more capital to equal the amount it wants to distribute over and above the limit. The option has to be discussed with the central bank/regulator as part of the bank's capital planning process.

3. **Countercyclical buffer:**

The financial crisis of 2007 came in the aftermath of a period of booming credit growth. A period of downturn succeeding excessive credit growth can destabilize not only the banking system but entire economies, as was evident from the events that followed the crisis. It is therefore important that the banking sector builds up additional capital defences to safeguard the macro-financial environment.

As the name suggests, this is an additional capital buffer. It is to be maintained in the proportion of 0–5 per cent of risk weighted assets that would be imposed on banks in periods of high credit growth. The buffer requirement should be met entirely from CET1 capital.

The National regulatory authorities would set the counter cyclical buffer, with the discretion of raising the buffer beyond 2.5 per cent of RWAs. The buffer would be set by public announcement. To enable banks build the buffer, a proposed increase in the buffer would have to be announced twelve months in advance. However, decisions to decrease the buffer would take effect immediately. Buffers would apply to banks based on geographic composition of credit exposures.

The implementation of this buffer is closely linked to the capital conservation buffer (CCB) described above. The following is an extract from the Basel III document, page 60.

Individual Bank Minimum Capital Conservation Standards

Common Equity Tier 1 (including other fully loss absorbing capital)	Minimum Capital Conservation Ratios (expressed as a percentage of earnings)
Within first quartile of buffer	100%
Within second quartile of buffer	80%
Within third quartile of buffer	60%
Within fourth quartile of buffer	40%
Above top of buffer	0%

For illustrative purposes, the following table sets out the conservation ratios a bank must meet at various levels of common Equity Tier 1 capital if the bank is subject to a 2.5 per cent countercyclical buffer requirement.

Individual Bank Minimum Capital Conservation Standards, When a Bank is Subject to a 2.5% Countercyclical Requirement

Common Equity Tier 1 (including other fully loss absorbing capital)	Minimum Capital Conservation Ratios (expressed as a percentage of earnings)
4.5% – 5.75%	100%
> 5.75% – 7.0%	80%
> 7.0% – 8.25%	60%
> 8.25% – 9.5%	40%
> 9.5%	0%

It is evident from the above that the capital conservation buffer and the countercyclical buffer combine to determine the required retained earnings and profit payouts of banks. If a bank breaches the buffer, the amount of profits it can distribute to shareholders and employees can be restrained.

4. **Leverage ratio:**

The 2007 financial crisis demonstrated that banks showing strong risk based capital ratios in accordance with Basel II, could also be excessively leveraged. The build up of excessive leverage was due to both on and off balance sheet activities. The Basel Committee has therefore introduced a 'simple, transparent, non risk based leverage ratio to act as a credible supplementary measure to the risk based capital requirements' (page 61).

The leverage limit is set at 3 per cent. This implies that a bank's total assets (including both on and off balance sheet assets) should not be more than 33 times the bank's capital.

The leverage ratio is proposed to be calculated as

$$\frac{\text{Tier 1 capital}}{\text{Total exposure}}$$

The ratio should be ≥3 per cent.

The leverage ratio is proposed to be calculated as the simple arithmetic mean of the monthly leverage ratios over the quarter, and is to be tested during the parallel run period of January 1, 2013 to January 1, 2017.

'Tier 1' capital in the numerator would include both CET1 and Additional Tier 1.

The 'exposure' in the denominator would follow the accounting measures for both on and off balance sheet items. While the asset values will be captured from the balance sheet, the off balance sheet items will be considered at their credit conversion factors, and derivatives with Basel II rules (of netting) and a simple measure of potential future exposure (using the Basel II framework). Hence both off balance sheet items and derivatives are converted to 'loan equivalents'.

5. **Liquidity requirements:**

Being 'liquid', or having enough cash to pay liabilities as and when they fall due and honour other commitments, is one of the most celebrated aspects of banking. This vital requirement was put to severe test during and just after the financial crisis of 2007.

Before the crisis struck, asset markets were buoyant and funding was available readily and at low cost. Liquidity conditions deteriorated rapidly as the crisis progressed, and the banking system faced severe stress. According to the Basel committee, the difficulties experienced by some banks were due to lapses in basic principles of liquidity risk management. These principles, published by BCBS (the following chapter contains a summary of these principles) in 2008, have been complemented with more stringent minimum standards for funding liquidity.

Basel III introduces a new liquidity standard through two liquidity ratios.

a. The Liquidity Coverage Ratio (LCR) is designed to improve the short term resilience of the liquidity risk profile of banks. It requires banks to hold a buffer of 'high quality' liquid assets to match net liquidity outflows during a 30 day period of stress. In other words, the ratio shows if the bank can survive an acute stress scenario lasting for a month.

$$\text{LCR} = \frac{\text{High quality liquid assets}}{\text{Total net liquidity outflows over a 30 day period}} \geq 100 \text{ per cent}$$

High quality liquid assets are defined by the Basel document as 'unencumbered, liquid in markets during a time of stress and, ideally, be central bank eligible.'

The reporting frequency for the LCR should be not less than monthly. The LCR would be mandatorily reported from January 1, 2015, while the observation period starts from January 1, 2013.

A detailed description of the ratio and its components can be found in the document '*Basel III: International framework for liquidity risk measurement, standards and monitoring*', published in December 2010, that can be accessed at www.bis.org

b. The Net Stable Funding Ratio (NSFR) is designed to promote resilience in the longer term. It requires that banks fund their activities with more stable sources of funding on an ongoing basis. More specifically, assets currently being funded and any other contingent obligations that may require funding must be matched by sources of stable funding over a one year horizon

$$\text{NSFR} = \frac{\text{Available stable funding}}{\text{Required stable funding}} \geq 100 \text{ per cent}$$

The numerator, 'Available Stable Funding' (ASF), is calculated using ASF factors of 100 per cent, 90 per cent, 80 per cent, 50 per cent, and 0 per cent, to reflect the stability of the funding sources, multiplied by the amount of available funding over the horizon. For example, Tier 1 capital will have an ASF factor of 100 per cent, while unsecured wholesale funding would have an ASF factor of 50 per cent.

The denominator, 'Required Stable Funding' (RSF), is also calculated using RSF factors ranging from 0 per cent (for example, cash) to 100 per cent (for example, loans to retail or SME customers with remaining maturity of less than one year would have an RSF factor of 85 per cent).

NSFR will be a required standard from January 1, 2018, and the reporting will be not less than quarterly.

A detailed description of the ratio and its components can be found in the document '*Basel III: International framework for liquidity risk measurement, standards and monitoring*', published in December 2010, that can be accessed at www.bis.org

6. **Additional requirement for Systemically important financial institutions (SIFI)[10]:**

The financial crisis of 2007 saw the fall or impairment of large, global institutions. The contagion that ensued affected global financial stability. The public sector intervention in many countries to restore financial stability imposed huge financial and economic costs, and also increased the moral hazard associated with too-big-to-fail institutions (by encouraging risky behaviour).

Basel III seeks to mitigate this externality by identifying global systemically important banks (G-SIBs) and global systemically important financial institutions (G-SIFIs), and mandating them to maintain a higher level of capital based on their importance in the global financial system. The Basel committee's approach is based on the Financial Stability Board's document endorsed by the G20 leaders in November 2010[11].

For assessing which banks should be considered as G-SIB, an indicator based measurement approach was adopted. The selected indicators reflect the size of banks, their interconnectedness, the lack of readily available substitutes or financial institution infrastructure for the services they provide, their global (cross-jurisdictional) activity and their complexity. The indicator-based measurement approach would be supported by supervisory judgment based on certain principles. The BCBS also identified several ancillary indicators which can support the supervisory judgment.

The Basel Committee grouped G-SIBs into different categories of systemic importance based on the score produced by the indicator-based measurement approach. GSIBs would be initially allocated into four buckets based on their scores of systemic importance, with varying levels of additional loss absorbency requirements applied to the different buckets as set out in Table 11.7.

TABLE 11.7 MAGNITUDE OF ADDITIONAL LOSS ABSORBENCY FOR G-SIBS

Bucketing Approach		
Bucket	**Score Range***	**Minimum Additional Loss Absorbency** (common equity as a percentage of risk-weighted assets)
5 (empty)	D	3.5%
4	C – D	2.5%
3	B – C	2.0%
2	A – B	1.5%
1	Cut-off point-A	1.0%

*Scores equal to one of the boundaries are assigned to the higher bucket.

Source: BCBS, 2011, Global systemically important banks: assessment methodology and the additional loss absorbency requirement-Rules text, November 2011, page 15

The additional loss absorbency requirement is to be met with Common Equity Tier 1 (CET1) capital. The requirements are only the minimum prescribed levels of capital required. The list of G-SIBs would be reviewed annually.

These requirementsare to be phased-in in parallel with the capital conservation and countercyclical buffers, *i.e.*, between 1 January 2016 and year end 2018, becoming fully effective on 1 January 2019.

7. **Enhancing risk coverage:**

In addition to raising the quality and level of the capital base, the Basel Committee has taken cognisance of other material risks that could impact capital. Failure to capture major on and off-balance sheet risks, as well as derivative related exposures, was a key factor that amplified the financial crisis of 2007.Based on the lessons learned from the crisis, revised metrics have been proposed in the Basel III document.

We know that total capital requirements are calculated relative to risk weighted assets. Under Basel III, the enhanced risk coverage in relation to capital market instruments and activities, could result in an increase in risk weighted assets. Further, Basel III addressed some concerns about the reliance on external credit ratings while determining risk weights, especially after the criticism that external credit rating agencies invited for their perceived role in the financial crisis.

a. Higher capital requirements for trading and securitization activities—In July 2009, the Basel Committee announced, among other things, higher capital requirements for trading and securitization activities under Basel II (also called Basel 2.5).The trading book[12] reforms, among other things, introduced new risk weights to better capture risks in trading portfolios. The securitization reforms also included an increase in the risk-weighting of certain securitizations and resecuritization exposures.

b. Capital requirements for certain counter party credit risk exposures—Basel III has enhanced capital requirements and risk management standards for counter party credit risk exposures arising from derivatives, repos and securities financing activities. It includes an additional capital charge for possible losses due to the deterioration in the creditworthiness of counter parties or increased risk weights on exposures to large financial institutions. The objectives were to reduce the risk of transmission of shocks between financial institutions whilst also creating incentives to move Over The Counter (OTC) derivative exposures to central counter parties and exchanges. The measures include additional capital requirements based on the following measures:

- Effective Expected Positive Exposure (EEPE), through the use of stressed inputs
- Credit Value Adjustment (CVA), that accounts for mark to market losses due to deterioration in the credit-worthiness of counter parties
- Specific 'wrong way risk' if future exposures to a specific counter party is highly positively correlated with the counter party's probability of default

c. External credit ratings in the Basel III framework—Basel III has incorporated elements of the International Organization of Securities Commissions' (IOSCO) Code of Fundamentals for Credit Rating Agencies that requires banks to carry out internal assessments of externally rated securitization exposures.

Table 11.8 shows the phase in arrangements for banks to completely adopt Basel III

TABLE 11.8 TIMELINES FOR MIGRATION TO BASEL III

	Phase-in Arrangements (shading indicates transition periods–all dates are as of 1 January)								As of 1 January 2019
	2011	**2012**	**2013**	**2014**	**2015**	**2016**	**2017**	**2018**	
Leverage Rato	Supervisory monitoring		Parallel Run 1 Jun 2013 – 1 Jan 2017 Disclosure Starts 1 Jan 2015					Migration to Pillar 1	
Minimum Common Equity Capital Ratio			3.5%	4.0%	4.5%	4.5%	4.5%	4.5%	4.5%
Capital Conservation Buffer						0.625%	1.25%	1.875%	2.50%
Minimum common equity plus capital conservation buffer			3.5%	4.0%	4.5%	5.125%	5.75%	6.375%	7.0%
Phase-in of deductions from CET 1 (including amounts exceeding the limit for DTAs, MSRs and financials)				20%	40%	60%	80%	100%	100%
Minimum tier 1 Capital			4.5%	5.5%	6.0%	6.0%	6.0%	6.0%	6.0%
Minimum Total Capital			8.0%	8.0%	8.0%	8.0%	8.0%	8.0%	8.0%
Minimum Total Capital plus conservation buffer			8.0%	8.0%	8.0%	8.625%	9.25%	9.875%	10.5%
Capital instruments that no longer qualify as non-core Tier 1 capital or Tier 2 capital			Phased out over 10 year horizon beginning 2013						
Liquidity Coverage Ratio	Observation period begins				Introduce minimum standard				
Net Stable Funding Ratio	Observation period begins							Introduce minimum standard	

Source: Basel Committee on banking supervision, Basel III: A global regulatory framework for more resilient banks and banking systems, revised version, June 2011, Annexure IV, page 69.

Annexure I provides an overview of the determination of risk weighted assets under select approaches of the Basel norms

Annexure II to this chapter examines why Basel II Accord takes a share of the blame for the financial crisis of 2007.

SECTION III

APPLICATION OF CAPITAL ADEQUACY TO BANKS IN INDIA[13]

In India, the Narasimham Committee, appointed by the government, had submitted its report on banking reforms in the early 1990s. The Committee had observed that the capital ratios of Indian banks were generally low and that some banks were seriously undercapitalized. The Basel framework was adopted by the RBI in 1992, prescribing a higher norm of 9 per cent on risk-weighted assets (as against 8 per cent by the Basel Accord) for all banks operating in India.

The RBI has adopted the BCBS Basel III framework (section II), and banks in India would be reporting minimum capital under Basel III beginning April 1, 2013. However, there are some significant deviations from the BCBS Basel III requirements in the context of banks in India. These deviations and the related guidelines have been published by the RBI in June 2013.[14] For better understanding, these guidelines have been regrouped and presented in the following paragraphs.

1. *Deviation 1–the minimum capital requirement*

   The Basel III total regulatory capital would be disclosed by banks in India as given below:

   i. Tier 1 capital (going concern capital)[15]
      a. Common equity tier I (CET1)
      b. Additional Tier I

   ii. Tier 2 capital (gone concern capital)

   The minimum total capital as a percentage of risk weighted assets (CRAR) would be at 9 per cent under Basel III. The RBI has been consistently stipulating higher minimum capital of 9 per cent (as against BCBS requirement of 8 per cent) for both Basel I and II for banks in India.

   Table 11.9 compares the various components of capital requirements in India and as proposed by BCBS Basel III framework

TABLE 11.9 MINIMUM CAPITAL REQUIREMENTS UNDER BASEL III FOR BANKS IN INDIA

		Capital as per cent of Risk Weighted Assets			
		Basel II (BCBS)	**Basel III (BCBS) (as on Jan 1, 2019)**	**Basel II–Banks in India – Existing**	**Basel III–Banks in India–required at End of March 2018**
A (= B + D)	Minimum Total Capital	8.0	8.0	9.0	9.0
B	Minimum Tier 1 Capital	4.0	6.0	6.0	7.0
C	Minimum Common Equity (Tier 1 Capital) (CET1)	2.0	4.5	3.6[16]	5.5
D	Maximum Tier 2 Capital (within total capital)	4.0	2.0	3.0	2.0
E	Capital Conservation Buffer (CCB)	Nil	2.5	Nil	2.5
F (= C + E)	Minimum Common Equity Tier 1 Capital + CCB	2.0	7.0	3.6	8.0
G (= A + E)	Minimum Total Capital + CCB	8.0	10.5	9.0	11.5
H	Leverage Ratio (Tier 1 Capital/Total Exposure)	Nil	3.0%	Nil	4.5%

RBI guidelines require banks in India to maintain 1 per cent more capital and 1.5 per cent more as leverage ratio, over and above the minimum requirements stipulated by BCBS.

The RBI would implement Basel III capital regulations from April 1, 2013 in a phased manner, with the plan of fully implementing the capital ratios by end March 2018. For the financial year ending March 2013, banks in India would disclose the capital ratios computed under both the Basel II and III guidelines.

During the period of parallel run for Tier 1 leverage ratio beginning from January 1, 2013 to January 1, 2017, banks in India should maintain the existing level of leverage ratio but, in no case it should fall below 4.5 per cent. Banks having leverage ratio below 4.5 per cent should achieve the target as early as possible.

2. *Deviation 2 – Transitioning to Basel III*

   The transitioning of banks in India to Basel III begins from April 1, 2013. Hence, from 2014 onwards, the target minimum capital and other ratios would be aligned with the financial year of banks–March 31. In this process, the capital and other requirements would be fully met by March 31, 2018 (BCBS specifies January 1, 2019). The phasing in plan for banks in India is shown in Table 11.10

TABLE 11.10 TRANSITIONING TO THE BASEL III REQUIREMENTS – BANKS IN INDIA

(per cent of RWAs)

Minimum Capital Ratios	January 1, 2013	March 31, 2014	March 31, 2015	March 31, 2016	March 31, 2017	March 31, 2018
Minimun Common Equity Tier 1 (CET)	4.5	5	5.5	5.5	5.5	5.5
Capital Conservation Buffer (CCB)	–	–	0.625	1.25	1.875	2.5
Minimum CET 1 + CCB	4.5	5	6.125	6.75	7.375	8
Minimum Tier 1 Capital	6	6.5	7	7	7	7
Minimum Total Capital*	9	9	9	9	9	9
Minimum Total Capital + CCB	9	9	9.625	10.25	10.875	11.5
Phase-in of all Deductions from CET 1 (in%)#	20	40	60	80	100	100

*The difference between the minimum totral capital requirement of 9 per cent and the Tier 1 requirement can be met with Tier 2 and higher forms of capital.
The same transition approach will apply to deductions from additional Tier 1 and Tier 2 capital.

Source: RBI Master circular–Basel III Capital regulations, dated June 1, 2013, p. 30.

Capital Components–Banks in India While the overall definitions of CET1, additional Tier 1 and Tier 2 capital have been retained, the RBI has spelt out the components of each type of capital relevant to Indian banks. Table 11.11 provides a comparative picture of capital components under Basel II and III is given below for clearer understanding

TABLE 11.11 BASEL II AND III CAPITAL REQUIREMENTS COMPARED – COMPOSITION OF CAPITAL

	Major Capital Components–Basel II	Major Capital Components–Basel III
Common Equity[17] Tier I Capital	Basel II does not explicitly prescribe a minimum common equity Tier 1 capital. It is generally accepted that common equity should be the predominant part of Tier 1 capital *i.e.*, 50 per cent	• Paid up Equity capital of the bank with features as given in Appendix of RBI circular • Share premium resulting from the issue of equity shares • Statutory reserves • Capital reserves representing surplus arising out of sale proceeds of assets • Other disclosed free reserves • Retained earnings;

(Continued)

TABLE 11.11 (CONTINUED)

		• At the consolidated bank level, shares issued by consolidated subsidiaries of the bank and held by third parties (minority interest), with features as provided in the RBI guidelines • Less regulatory adjustments or deductions from CET 1 capital
Tier I Capital	• Paid up capital • Statutory reserves • Other Disclosed free reserves • Capital reserves representing surplus arising out of sale proceeds of assets • Innovative Perpetual Debt Instruments [IPDI] • Perpetual non cumulative preference shares (PNCPS) In summary, as in common equity Tier 1 Capital above + hybrid debt capital instruments (maximum 15 per cent of Tier 1 Capital)	• Termed 'Additional Tier 1 Capital' • Share premium resulting from the issue of instruments included in Additional Tier 1 Capital • Perpetual Non-Cumulative Preference Shares (PNCPS), which complywith regulatory requirements as specified by RBI • Debt capital instruments eligible for inclusion in Additional Tier 1capital, which comply with RBI regulatory requirements • Instruments issued by consolidated subsidiaries of the bank and held by third parties that meet the specific criteria for inclusion in Additional Tier 1 Capital and are not included in Common Equity Tier 1. • Hybrid debt capital instruments held under Basel II requirements to be phased out
Tier 2 Capital	• Limited to 100 per cent of tier 1 capital • Could be comprised of any or all of the following—undisclosed reserves, revaluation reserves, general provisions/loan loss reserves, hybrid debt capital instruments and subordinated term debt • Subordinated term debt maximum 50 per cent of Tier 1 Capital • Upper tier 2 capital maximum 50 per cent of Tier 1 Capital	• Instruments issued by the bank that meet the criteria for inclusion in Tier 2 Capital (and are not included in Tier 1 Capital); • Share premium resulting from the issue of instruments included in Tier 2 Capital; • Instruments issued by consolidated subsidiaries of the bank and held by third parties that meet the specific criteria for inclusion in Tier 2 capital and are not included in Tier 1 Capital.; • Certain loan loss provisions • No distinction between Upper Tier 2 and Lower Tier 2 instruments
Tier 3 Capital	• Short term subordinated debt only to cover market risks • Tier 3 Capital will be limited to 250 per cent of a bank's Tier 1 Capital that is required to support market risks	No Tier 3 Capital

For detailed description of the types of capital funds, please refer to the latest RBI Master circular on Basel III, accessible on www.rbi.org.in

Pillar I-Implementation In accordance with the Basel II norms summarized in the BIS document 'International convergence of capital measurement and capital standards—a Revised framework' issued in June 2006 (please refer Section II), the RBI requires that all commercial banks in India (excluding local area banks and regional rural banks) adopt the

- Standardized approach for credit risk,
- Standardized approach (modified duration) for market risk and
- Basic indicator approach for operational risk.

All commercial banks were required to migrate to the above approaches by 31 March 2009. The revised capital adequacy norms will be applicable to commercial banks both at the global as well as the consolidated level.[18]

In order to enable banks to plan for migration to more advanced approaches, RBI has prescribed a time frame within which banks would obtain RBI approval for such migration, as shown below[19]:

Approach	The Earliest Date of Making Application by Banks to the RBI	Likely Date of Approval by the RBI
Internal Models Approach (IMA) for Market Risk	1 April 2010	31 March 2011
The Standardized Approach (TSA) for Operational Risk	1 April 2010	30 September 2010
Advanced Measurement Approach (AMA) for Operational Risk	1 April 2010	31 March 2014
Internal Ratings-Based (IRB) Approaches for Credit Risk (Foundation—as well as Advanced IRB)	1 April 2010	31 March 2014

The RBI has also permitted banks to migrate to the advanced approaches in a phased manner, where necessary.

Capital Funds owf Banks Operating in India

RBI requires banks in India to maintain at the minimum, a capital to risk-weighted assets ratio (CRAR) of 9 per cent (as against the international norm of 8 per cent prescribed by the Basel Committee).

Though the CRAR of 9 per cent will have to be held continuously by banks, RBI also expects banks to operate at a capital level well above the minimum requirement. Additionally, RBI would assess individual banks' risk profiles and risk management systems and call for additional capital infusion, where the capital is not found commensurate with the banks' overall risk profile.

Banks in India will continue to maintain minimum capital requirement under Basel II capital standards, under Tier 1 and Tier 2 capital (see Section II). Simultaneously, banks will have to ensure that their Basel II minimum capital is higher than 80 per cent of the minimum capital requirement computed in accordance with the Basel I framework for credit and market risks. The parallel run of Basel I and II would be till end March 2013, after which RBI would review the progress.

Banks in India are required to maintain a Tier 1 capital ratio of at least 6 per cent, and a total capital to risk weighted assets ratio of at least 9per cent. The Common Equity Tier 1 capital should be at least 5.5 per cent of risk weighted assets. These ratios are computed as follows

$$\text{Common Equity Tier 1 capital ratio (CET1)} = \frac{\text{Common Equity Tier 1 capital}}{\text{Credit RWA} + \text{Market RWA} + \text{Operational RWA}} \geq 5.5\%$$

$$\text{Tier I capital ratio (tier 1 CRAR)} = \frac{\text{Tier 1 capital funds}}{\text{Credit RWA} + \text{Market RWA} + \text{Operational RWA}} \geq 7\%$$

$$\text{Total Capital ratio (CRAR)} = \frac{\text{Total capital funds (Tier 1 + Tier 2 capital)}}{\text{Credit RWA} + \text{Market RWA} + \text{Operational RWA}} \geq 9\%$$

RWAs denote 'risk weighted assets'.

Some points to be noted are:

- The above equations signify that Tier 2 capital can be at a maximum of 2 per cent.
- In addition, banks should maintain a Capital Conservation Buffer (CCB) of 2.5 per cent of RWAs in the form of Common equity tier 1 capital.
- Only if a bank has complied with the CRT1 ratio – 5.5 per cent and the CCB of 2.5 per cent put together – can it admit additional tier1 and tier 2 capital in excess of the prescribed limits. The illustrative examples given in the RBI circular are self explanatory, and reproduced below: (Illustrations 11.2 and 11.3)

ILLUSTRATION 11.2

How to calculate admissible Tier 1 and Tier 2 capital (calculations pertain to March 2018)

Capital Ratios as on March 31, 2018

Common Equity Tier 1	**7.5% of RWAs**
CCB	2.5% of RWAs
Total CET1	10% of RWAs
PNCPS/PDI	3.0% of RWAs
PNCPS/PDI eligible for Tier 1 capital	2.05% of RWAs {(1.5/5.5) × 7.5% of CET1
PNCPS/PDI ineligible for Tier 1 capital	0.95% of RWAs (3–2.05)
Eligible Total Tier 1 capital	**9.55% of RWAs**
Tier 2 issued by the bank	2.5% of RWAs
Tier 2 capital eligile for CRAR	2.73% of RWAs {(2/5.5) × 7.5% of CET1}
PNCPS/PDI eligible for Tier 2 capital	0.23% of RWAs (2.73–2.5)
PNCPS/PDI not eligible Tier 2 capital	0.72% of RWAs (0.95–23)
Total available capital	**15.50%**
Total capital	**14.78% (12.28% + 2.55) (CET1 – 10% + AT1 – 2.05% + Tier 2 – 2.73)**

Note: PNCPS denotes 'Perpetual Non cumulative preference shares', and PDI denotes 'Perpetual debt instruments', both part of 'Additional tier 1 capital' under Basel III

ILLUSTRATION 11.3

How to calculate capital for market risk – Basel III

1.	**Capital Funds**	
	Common Equity Tier 1 capital	75
	Capital Conservation Buffer	25
	PNCPS/PDI	30
	Eligible PNCPS/PDI	20.5
	Eligible Tier 1 capital	95.5
	Tier 2 Capital available	25
	Tier 2 Capital eligibility	27.3
	Excess PNCPS/PDI eligible for Tier 2 Capital	2.73
	Total Eligible Capital	122.8
2.	**Total Risk Weighted Assets (RWA)**	
	RWA for credit and operational risk	900
	RWA for market risk	100
3.	Minimum Common Equity Tier 1 Capital required to support credit and opeational risk (900 × 5.5%)	49.5
	Maximum Additional Tier 1 Capital within Tier 1 Capital required to support credit and operational risk (900 × 1.5%)	13.5

	Maximum Tier 2 Capital within Total Capital required to support credit and operational risk (900 × 2%)	18
	Total Eligible Capital required to support credit and operational risk	81 (49.5 + 13.5 + 18)
4.	Minimum Common Equity Tier 1 Capital available to support market risk	25.5(75 – 49.5)
	Maximum Additional Tier 1 Capital within Tier 1 Capital available to support market risk	7 (20.5 – 13.5)
	Maximum Tier 2 Capital within Total Capital available to support market risk	9.3 (27.3 – 18)
	Total Eligible Capital available to support market risk	41.8 (122.8 – 81)

Source for both illustrations is the RBI Master circular on Basel III dated July 1, 2013, Annexure 14, pages 217, 218

- The Capital Conservation Buffer (CCB) will be transitioned during the Basel III implementation period as shown in Table 11.12 It may be noted that as against the Basel III international cut off of 7 per cent of CET1 ratio (please refer to the Basel III guidelines outlined in the previous section), Indian banks need a 7.375 per cent CET 1 ratio for maintaining the minimum CCB of 0 per cent.

TABLE 11.12 CCB TRANSITIONING PLAN FOR INDIAN BANKS

Common Equity Tier 1 Ratio after including the current periods retained earnings			Minimum Capital Conservation Ratios (expressed as % of earnings)
As on March 31, 2015	**As on March 31, 2016**	**As on March 31, 2017**	
5.5% – 5.65625%	5.5% – 5.8125%	5.5% – 5.96875%	100%
> 5.65625% – 5.8125%	> 5.8125% – 6.125%	> 5.96875% – 6.4375%	80%
> 5.8125% – 5.96875%	> 6.125% – 6.4375%	> 6.4375% – 6.90625%	60%
> 5.96875% – 6.125%	> 6.4375% – 6.75%	> 6.90625% – 7.375%	40%
> 6.125%	> 6.75%	> 7.375%	0%

Source: RBI Master circular -Basel III Capital regulations, dated June 1, 2013, page 154

- Table 11.13 compares the salient features of Additional Tier 1 instruments as stipulated by the RBI

TABLE 11.13 FEATURES OF ADDITIONAL TIER 1 INSTRUMENTS COMPARED

Feature of the Tier 1 Capital Instrument	PDI (Perpetual Debt Instruments)	PNCPS (Perpetual Non Cumulative Preference Shares)
Amount	Decided by bank's Board of directors.	Decided by bank's Board of directors.
Limit	PDI + PNCPS should not exceed 1.5 per cent of Risk weighted assets. The excess can be included in total Tier 1 Capital or Tier 2 Capital upto 2 per cent of risk weighted assets.	PDI + PNCPS should not exceed 1.5 per cent of Risk weighted assets. The excess can be included in total Tier 1 Capital or Tier 2 Capital upto 2 per cent of risk weighted assets.
Maturity	Perpetual	Perpetual. No maturity date.
Other features	Fully paid up, unsecured, free of any restrictive clause. Investments by FIIs outside the ECB limit. Progressive discount not to be applied for calculating capital adequacy.	Fully paid up, unsecured, free of any restrictive clause. Investments by FIIs outside the ECB limit. Progressive discount not to be applied for calculating capital adequacy.
Payment to investors	Interest at fixed or floating rate.	Dividend at fixed or floating rate, on a non cumulative basis.
Call Option	Yes, subject to certain conditions.	Yes, subject to certain conditions.
Put option	No	No
Step up option	Can be exercised once during the life of the instrument, along with call option, after 10 years from issue date.	No

(*Continued*)

TABLE 11.13 (CONTINUED)

Lock in clause	Yes. Interest should be non cumulative. Cannot pay interest unless conditions fulfilled.	Dividend cannot be paid unless conditions fulfilled.
Seniority of claim	Superior to claims on equity shares and PNCPS and subordinated to claims of all other creditors.	Superior to claims on equity shares and subordinated to claims of all other creditors and depositors.
Issue denominated in foreign currency.	Yes. Approval of RBI not required subject to conditions.	No
Reserve requirements.	Not applicable.	Not applicable.
Investment in instruments of other banks.	Permitted subject to conditions.	Permitted subject to conditions.
Grant of advances against instruments.	Not permitted.	Not permitted.

Source: Annexures 3 and 4 of RBI's Master circular–Basel III capital regulations, dated July 1, 2013.

- The RBI circular also provides detailed guidelines on treatment of investments in banks in capital instruments issued by other financial entities. The following Figure extracted from the circular (page 25) summarizes the instructions.

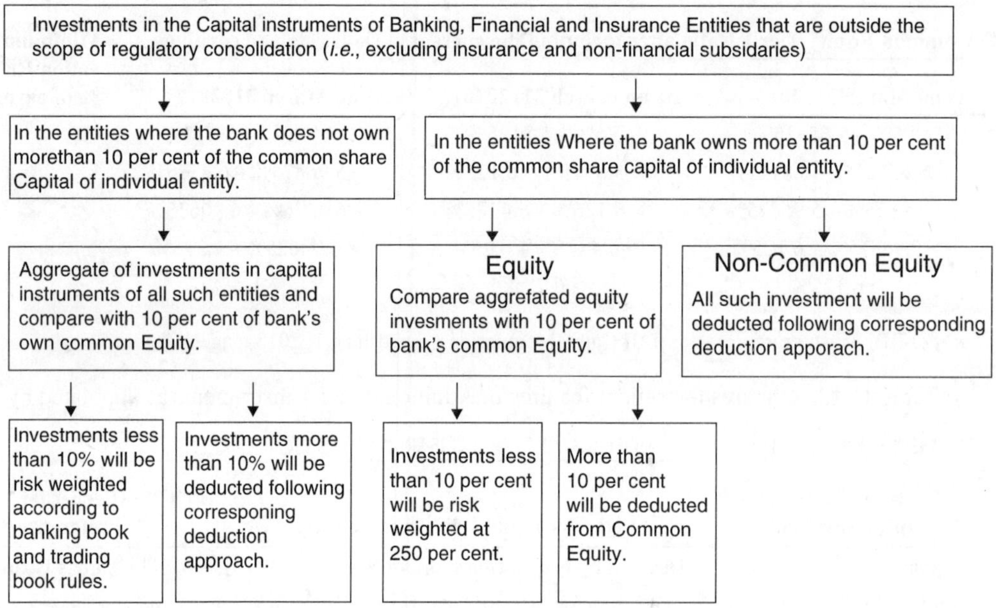

Tier 2 Capital—Some Features

For both Indian and foreign banks operating in India, Tier 2 capital can consist of the following:

- Revaluation reserves
  - These reserves often serve as a cushion against ULs. But they are less permanent in nature and cannot be considered as core capital. Revaluation reserves arise from revaluation of assets considered undervalued in the banks' books, typically bank premises and marketable securities. The extent to which revaluation reserves can be relied upon as a cushion for ULs depends primarily upon the level of certainty that can be placed on estimates of market values of the relevant assets, the subsequent deterioration in values under difficult market conditions or in a forced sale, potential liquidation at those values and tax consequences of revaluation. Hence, RBI prescribes that *revaluation reserves may be taken at a discount of 55 per cent while determining their value for inclusion in Tier 2 capital*. On the balance sheet, however, the entire value would continue to be reflected as revaluation reserves.
- General provisions and loss reserves
  - These reserves can be included in Tier 2 capital if they are available to meet ULs and are not attributable to actual diminution in value or potential loss in any specific asset. Banks are permitted to include under this

category (a) general provisions on Standard Assets, (b) floating provisions, (c) provisions held for country exposures, (d) Investment reserve account and (e) excess provisions on sale of NPAs. Such unencumbered reserves under this head will, however, be admitted as Tier 2 capital only up to a maximum of 1.25 per cent of credit risk-weighted assets.

- Debt capital instruments/Perpetual cumulative preference shares (PCPS)/ Redeemable non cumulative preference shares (RNCPS)/ Redeemable cumulative preference shares (RCPS)

  To be eligible for inclusion in Tier 2 capital, the instrument should be fully paid up, unsecured, subordinated to claims of other creditors, free of restrictive clauses and should not be redeemable at the instance of the holder or without the consent of the RBI. The instruments carry a fixed maturity and as they approach maturity, a progressive discount will be applied on their value.

  It is this discounted value that will be included as part of Tier 2 capital. Instruments with an initial maturity of less than 5 years or with a remaining maturity of 1 year, cannot be included in Tier 2 capital. Subordinated debt instruments eligible to be reckoned as Tier 2 capital will be limited to 50 per cent of Tier 1 capital. The rate at which discounts will be applied are as follows:

Remaining Maturity of Instruments	**Rate of Discount (per cent)**
Less than 1 year	100
1 year and more but less than 2 years	80
2 years and more but less than 3 years	60
3 years and more but less than 4 years	40
4 years and more but less than 5 years	20

The total amount of such Tier 2 capital instruments would be considered as part of NDTL for computing the bank's reserve requirements (CRR/SLR).

RBI approval has to be sought every time a bank issues subordinated debt in foreign currency.

The other conditions for accessing subordinate debt for Tier 2 capital by Indian banks and foreign banks in India are provided in Annexures 5 and 6 of RBI Master circular—Basel III regulations, dated July 1, 2013.

Similarly, criteria for Tier 1 and Tier 2 capital to be maintained by foreign banks operating in India are also spelt out in the quoted RBI circular.

TEASE THE CONCEPT

Why should 'Debt' be included in a Bank's 'Capital'?

Procedure for Computing Minimum Capital Requirements

- Degrees of credit risk expressed as percentage weightings are assigned to balance sheet assets and conversion factors to off-balance sheet items.
- Convert 'off-balance sheet' contingent liabilities to an on-balance sheet notional 'credit equivalent', by multiplying each contingent liability by the appropriate 'credit conversion factor' and classify in the applicable risk category.
- Multiply the rupee amount of assets in each category—funded and non-funded, converted into the credit equivalent—by the appropriate risk-weight.
- Risk-adjusted assets would mean the weighted aggregate of funded and non-funded items.
- The banks' overall minimum capital requirement will be the sum of:
  - Capital requirement for credit risk on all credit exposures excluding items comprising trading book and including counter party credit risk on all OTC derivatives on the basis of the risk-weights,
  - Capital requirement for market risks in the trading book and
  - Capital requirement for operational risks.

Calculating Capital Charges and Risk-Weighted Assets

I. Capital Charge for Credit Risk Banks in India currently follow the 'Standardized Approach' (described in Section II). Under this approach, ratings assigned by external credit rating agencies will largely support the credit risk measurement. The assets/credit facilities and other facilities provided by the bank would be rated by the approved credit rating agency and the risk-weighting of the asset or claim will be based on this rating.

The credit rating agencies identified by the RBI are given in the Master circular dated July 1, 2013, under Section 6. Once a bank decides on the credit rating agency, it should continue to use the ratings of the same agency for rating all claims to ensure consistency and prevent 'cherry picking'. Banks should also disclose the name of the credit rating agency and the rating should be publicly available. Section 6 of the RBI, 'Master Circular' stipulates stringent conditions in respect of external credit rating.

Under the Standardized approach of the Basel II framework, a mapping process would be required to link the ratings by external agencies to the risk-weights (reflecting the credit risk) to be applied to calculate capital adequacy. The mapping process has been described in detail in the RBI circular.

On the basis of the external credit ratings and the mapping process, credit risk-weights are assigned to the following counter parties: (described in detail under section 5 of the RBI circular).

- Claims on domestic sovereigns
- Claims on foreign sovereigns
- Claims on public sector entities
- Claims on multilateral development banks (MDB), Bank for International Settlements (BIS) and International monetary fund (IMF)
- Claims on banks
- Claims on primary dealers
- Claims on corporates, depending on short term or long term credit facilities and the related ratings
- Claims included in the regulatory retail portfolios. However this category excludes investment exposures (equity or bonds), mortgage loans (both residential and commercial real estate), staff advances, consumer credit such as personal loans and credit card receivables, capital market exposures and venture capital funds
- Claims secured by residential property
- Claims secured by commercial real estate
- Non-performing assets—bifurcated into unsecured and secured portions and assigned risk-weights
- Specified categories—will include venture capital funds, consumer credit, capital market exposures, non-banking financial companies (NBFC), investment in other banks and financial entities and other exposures considered 'high risk'
- Other assets—include advances to staff and central counter parties (CCP), such as Clearing Corporation of India (CCIL)
- Off balance sheet items—We know that off balance sheet items can be potential credit exposures. Hence, the risk-weighted amount of an off balance sheet item is arrived at through a two-step process:
  - The notional amount of the transaction is first converted into an 'on balance sheet credit equivalent' by multiplying by the appropriate 'credit conversion factor' (or by applying the 'current exposure method' briefly described later) and
  - The credit equivalent is multiplied by the applicable risk-weight to create a 'risk-weighted asset'.

  However, where the off balance sheet exposure is secured by eligible collateral or guarantee, the guidelines applicable to 'credit risk mitigation' (see section 7 of the RBI circular) will be used.

  While risk-weighting off balance sheet items, a further distinction is made between market related and non-market related exposures.

- Non-market-related off balance sheet items are those such as direct credit substitutes, trade and performance related contingent items or credit commitment with certain draw downs. In such cases, the credit equivalent is simply the contracted amount multiplied by the relevant credit conversion factor.

ILLUSTRATION 11.4

Assume a cash credit/short term loan facility of ₹100 lakhs. Of this, assume ₹60 lakhs has been drawn and is also the average utilization. The outstanding balance would be multiplied by the risk-weight applicable to the rating of the borrower. The remaining ₹40 lakhs would be treated as an undrawn commitment and would therefore have to be multiplied by the credit conversion factor. Assume the applicable conversion factor is 20 per cent. The credit equivalent would be 20 per cent of ₹40 lakhs, that is, ₹8 lakhs. This amount should be multiplied by the risk-weight applicable to the borrower to compute the risk-weighted asset value of the undrawn portion.

ILLUSTRATION 11.5

Assume a long term loan of ₹700 crores for a large project. The loan has been sanctioned such that the credit limit will be drawn in 3 stages, to coincide with the progress of construction. Assume that the loan can be drawn at every subsequent stage only with explicit approval from the bank and on completion of specified formalities. If the limit for stage 1 has been determined at ₹150 crores and the borrower has drawn ₹50 crores, the 'undrawn commitment' for applying the credit conversion factor will be restricted to stage 1 alone, that is, ₹100 crores. The conversion factor could vary depending on the period within which stage 1 is to be completed. Stages 2 and 3, which have not fallen due for disbursement would not be risk-weighted.

The illustrations provided in the RBI circular would make the treatment clear.

- Market-related off balance sheet items include market transactions that can potentially hold off balance sheet credit risk in the banking and trading books of banks. Examples are interest rate contracts (such as interest rate futures, interest rate swaps, forward rate agreements, etc. discussed in the following chapter) and foreign exchange contracts. The credit equivalent is determined by the 'current exposure method', which is the sum of current credit exposure and potential future credit exposure of the contracts. (The method, as well as special cases, such as 'failed transactions' are described in paragraphs 5.15.3 and 5.15.5 of the cited RBI, Master Circular).
- Securitization exposures resulting from securitization transactions have been defined in RBI's 'Guidelines for securitization of standard assets' (circular dated 1 February 2006) and Section 5.16 of the cited RBI, Master Circular on capital adequacy. Banks' securitization exposures include those (but are not restricted to) in roles such as investors, credit enhancers, liquidity providers, underwriters or providers of credit risk mitigation. This implies that if a bank invests in asset backed securities, provides liquidity facility or credit enhancement, retains a subordinated tranche or provides credit risk mitigation to other securitization transactions, the transactions would lead to securitization exposures. Further, securitization exposures would also include (a) credit enhancing interest only strips (I/O)[20], (b) implicit support provided by the bank in excess of its contractual obligation or (c) a gain on sale. If the originating bank in a securitization transaction fails to meet the minimum requirements of RBI (as given in the circular dated 1 February 2006), the bank will have to hold capital commensurate with the exposures, as if the exposures were not securitized and gain on sale, if any, would have to be deducted from capital. Illustration 11.5 clarifies the discussion.

ILLUSTRATION 11.6

Assume a securitization pool of ₹100 crores, with 80 per cent AAA rated, 10 per cent BB and 10 per cent unrated securities. If the transaction does not fulfil the criteria stipulated by the RBI, it would be assumed that the originating bank holds all the exposures in non-securitized form. Therefore, the risk-weight appropriate for AAA rated securities in the standardized approach would be applied to 80 per cent of the exposure. However, the value of lower rated and unrated securities (20 per cent in this case) would be deducted from capital.

Detailed guidelines for deduction of securitization exposures from capital funds can be accessed from Section 5.16 of the quoted RBI, Master Circular.

- Credit risk mitigation (CRM) techniques, historically in the nature of collateral securities and guarantees, have been undergoing a change with many banks shifting to 'originate to distribute' model. Under this model, banks transfer the credit risk of borrowers to other investors, as seen in earlier chapters. RBI follows the Basel II capital requirements under the standardized approach and makes it applicable to banking book exposures, as well as counter party risks in 'over the counter' (OTC) derivatives and 'repo style' transactions in the trading book. In order to mitigate possible legal risks in the CRM transactions, banks are required to meet minimum legal documentation standards.[21]

II. Capital Charge for Market Risk The RBI defines market risk as the risk of losses in on balance sheet and off balance sheet positions arising from movements in market prices. The market risk positions subject to capital charge requirement are as follows: (Please see Section 8 of RBI Master Circular)

- The risks pertaining to interest rate related instruments and equities in the trading book
- Foreign exchange risk (including open position in precious metals) throughout the bank (both banking and trading books)

Banks are required to maintain capital charge for interest rate related instruments in the trading book, equities in the trading book and foreign exchange risk (including gold and other precious metals) in both trading and banking books. Trading book for the purpose of capital adequacy will include the following:

- Securities included under the Held for Trading (HFT) category
- Securities included under the Available for Sale (AFS) category
- Open gold position limits
- Open foreign exchange position limits
- Trading positions in derivatives
- Derivatives entered into for hedging trading book exposures

Banks have to ensure that capital for market risk is maintained at the close of every business day and also manage intra day risks. Capital for market risk would not apply to securities that have already matured but remain unpaid, since these securities would attract capital only for credit risk.

Measurement of capital charge for interest rate risk in the trading book

Points to be Noted

- The measurement relates to debt securities and other interest rate related instruments held in rupees in the trading book.
- The capital charge would apply to current market values of these securities in the bank's trading book. The current market value will be determined in accordance with the RBI guidelines on valuation of investments.(See previous chapter)
- The capital requirement would be computed based on two separate charges—one, a specific risk charge for each security (comparable to the capital charge for credit risk), both for short[22] and long positions; and two, a general market risk charge towards interest rate risk in the portfolio.
- The capital charge for specific risk is to protect against adverse movements in prices of individual securities triggered by factors relating to individual issuers. Hence, the guidelines provide specific risk charges for various exposures related to broad categories of issuers such as government (central, state and foreign), banks (bonds) and others (corporate bonds and securitized debt). From Table 16 (Part A–I) in the quoted RBI Master Circular, it can be seen that the highest specific risk capital charges (as a percentage of exposures) are applicable to investments in low rated foreign government securities, banks whose performance is below the desired capital adequacy benchmark and other unrated securities or those with low ratings. Where the securities' risk is perceived as very high (as in unrated exposures), deduction from capital is stipulated.
- We have learnt from the earlier paragraphs on credit risk that counter party credit risk has to be computed on OTC derivatives. In addition, derivatives in the trading book carry a specific risk charge, the calculation of which is explained in detail in the quoted RBI circular.
- The capital requirements for general market risk are meant to capture the risk of loss arising from changes in market interest rates. The capital charge is the aggregate of four components:
    - The net short (not permitted in India except in derivatives) or long position in the trading book
    - A small proportion of the matched positions in each time band (the 'vertical disallowance')
    - A larger proportion of matched positions across different time bands (the 'horizontal disallowance')
    - A net charge for positions in options, where appropriate

Since banks in India are still in a nascent stage of developing internal risk management models, the RBI has stipulated that, to begin with, banks could adopt the standardized approach to market risk measurement. Under the standardized method, market risk could be measured by either the 'maturity' or the 'duration' method. Between the two, the duration[23] method is preferred over the maturity method due to better accuracy.

Accordingly, banks will be measuring the general market risk charge using the 'price sensitivity' or 'modified duration' in the following steps:

- Calculate the price sensitivity (modified duration)[24] of each instrument in the portfolio.
- Apply the assumed change in yield to the modified duration of each instrument between 0.6 and 1 percentage points, depending on the instrument's maturity (as given in Table 17 of the quoted RBI circular).

- Slot the resulting capital charge measures into a maturity ladder with fifteen time bands as in Table 17 of RBI circular
- Apply a 5 per cent vertical disallowance to long and short positions in each time band. This step is meant to capture basis risk.
- Finally, carry forward the net positions in each time band for horizontal off-setting subject to the horizontal disallowances set out in Table 18 of the quoted the RBI, Master Circular.

The illustrations provided in Section IV will be helpful in understanding the above procedure.

Capital charge for specific risk will be 9 per cent and specific risk is computed on the banks' gross equity positions (*i.e.*, the sum of all long equity positions and of all short equity positions—short equity position is, however, not allowed for banks in India). The general market risk charge will also be 9 per cent on the gross equity positions.

The aggregate capital charge for market risk is calculated in the following format:

Risk Category	(₹ in crore) Capital Charge
I. Interest rate (a + b)	
a. General market risk	
(i) Net position (parallel shift)	
(ii) Horizontal disallowance (curvature)	
(iii) Vertical disallowance (basis)	
(iv) Options	
b. Specific risk	
II. Equity (a + b)	
a. General market risk	
b. Specific risk	
III. Foreign exchange & gold	
IV. Total capital charge for market risks (I + II + III)	

III. Capital Charge for Operational Risk The RBI's definition of operational risk is the same as the Basel Committee's definition. The definition includes legal risk, but excludes strategic and reputation risk. Legal risk includes (but is not restricted to) fines, penalties or punitive damages as consequences of supervisory actions and private settlements.

Banks in India will be arriving at the capital charge for operational risk using the Basic Indicator approach. However, internationally active banks and banks with significant operational risk exposures are expected to use more sophisticated approaches. In its communication dated 31 March 2010, the RBI has issued guidelines to banks for migrating to the standardized approaches for measuring operational risk.

Pillars II and III of the Basel Accord and their application in the Indian context are summarized in *Annexure III* of this chapter, while *Annexure IV* provides information on the capital adequacy ratio of banks operating in India.

The application of the Basel III to Indian banks raises one more question. How would the capital adequacy ratio of Indian banks be impacted in future under Basel III? Box 11.2 provides some estimates.

BOX 11.2: BASEL III CAPITAL RAISING – IMPLICATIONS AND CHALLENGES

What is the size of the additional capital required to be raised by Indian banks? It depends on the assumption made, and there are various estimates floating around. The Reserve bank has made some quick estimates based on the following two conservative assumptions covering the period to March 31, 2018: (i) risk weighted assets of individual banks will increase by 20 per cent per annum; and (ii) internal accruals will be of the order of 1 per cent of risk weighted assets.

Reserve Bank's estimates project an additional capital requirement of ₹5 trillion, of which non-equity capital will be of the order of ₹3.25 trillion while equity capital will be of the order of ₹1.75 trillion (See Table on p. 398).

Additional (over and above internal accruals)Common Equity Requirements of Indian Banks under Basel III (estimates) (₹billion)

		Public sector banks	Private sector banks	Total
A	Additional Equity Capital Requirements under Basel III	1400–1500	200–250	1600–1750
B	Additional Equity Capital Requirements under Basel II	650–700	20–25	670–725
C	Net Equity Capital Requirements under Basel III (A-B)	750–800	180–225	930–1025
D	Of Additional Equity Capital Requirements under Basel III for Public Sector Banks (A)			
Government Share (if present shareholding pattern is maintained)		880 – 910		
Government Share (if shareholding is brought down to 51 per cent)		660 – 690		
Market Share (if the Government's shareholding pattern is maintained at present level)		520 – 590		

The additional equity capital requirement of the order of ₹1.75 trillion raises two questions. First, can the market provide capital of this size?

Second, what will be the burden on the Government in capitalizing public sector banks (PSBs) and what are its options?

Let us turn to the first question, whether the market will be able to provide equity capital of this size. The amount the market will have to provide will depend on how much of the recapitalization burden of PSBs the Government will meet. Data in the above Table indicate that the amount that the market will have to provide will be in the range of ₹700 billion –₹1 trillion depending on how much the Government will provide. Over the last five years, banks have raised equity capital to the tune of ₹520 billion through the primary markets. Raising an additional ₹700 billion - ₹1 trillion over the next five years from the market should therefore not be an insurmountable problem. The extended period of full Basel III implementation spread over five years gives sufficient time to banks to plan the time-table of their capital rising over this period.

Moving on to the second question of the burden on the Government which owns 70 per cent of the banking system. If the Government opts to maintain its shareholding at the current level, the burden of recapitalization will be of the order of ₹900 billion; on the other hand, if it decides to reduce its shareholding in every bank to a minimum of 51 per cent, the burden reduces to under ₹700 billion.

Clearly, providing equity capital of this size in the face of fiscal constraints poses significant challenges. A tempting option for the Government would be to issue recapitalization bonds against common equity infusion. But this will militate against fiscal transparency. In the alternative, would the Government be open to reducing its shareholding in PSBs to below 51 per cent? If the Government decides to pursue this option, an additional consideration is whether it will amend the statute to protect its majority voting rights.

Source: Excerpts from Inaugural Address by Dr Duvvuri Subbarao, Governor, Reserve Bank of India at the Annual FICCI–IBA Banking Conference at Mumbai on September 04, 2012, titled 'Basel III in International and Indian Contexts: Ten Questions We Should Know the Answers For', pp. 9–12, accessed at www.rbi.org.in.

SECTION IV

ILLUSTRATIVE PROBLEMS ON CALCULATING CAPITAL ADEQUACY

Illustration 11.6 will help to understand the mechanics. Note that, operational risk has been ignored for the purpose of these examples.

ILLUSTRATION 11.6[25]

A bank has the following position.

Details	Amount (₹ in Crores)
Cash and balances with RBI	200.00
Bank balances	200.00
Investments	
Held for trading	500.00
Available for sale	1,000.00
Held to maturity	500.00
Advances (net)	2,000.00
Other assets	300.00
Total assets	**4700.00**

The ₹2,000 crores investments of the bank relate to the following counter parties.

Government	₹1,000 crores
Banks	₹500 crores
Others	₹500 crores

Further break up of the investments is as follows:

Government securities

Date of Issue	Date of Reporting	Maturity Date	Amount (₹ in Crores)	Coupon (per cent)	Type
01/03/1992	21/03/2003	01/03/2004	100	12.50	AFS
01/05/1993	31/03/2003	01/05/2003	100	12.00	AFS
01/03/1994	31/03/2003	31/05/2003	100	12.00	AFS
01/03/1995	31/03/2003	01/03/2015	100	12.00	AFS
01/03/1998	31/03/2003	01/03/2010	100	11.50	AFS
01/03/1999	31/03/2003	01/03/2009	100	11.00	AFS
01/03/2000	31/03/2003	01/03/2005	100	10.50	HFT
01/03/2001	31/03/2003	01/03/2006	100	10.00	HTM
01/03/2002	31/03/2003	01/03/2012	100	8.00	HTM
01/03/2003	31/03/2003	01/03/2023	100	6.50	HTM
Total			**1000**		

Bank bonds

Date of Issue	Date of Reporting	Maturity Date	Amount (₹ in crores)	Coupon (per cent)	Type
01/03/1992	31/03/2003	01/03/2004	100	12.50	AFS
01/03/1993	31/03/2003	01/05/2003	100	12.00	AFS
01/03/1994	31/03/2003	31/05/2003	100	12.00	AFS
01/03/1995	31/03/2003	01/03/2006	100	12.50	AFS
01/03/1998	31/03/2003	01/03/2007	100	11.50	HFT
Total			**1,000**		

Others

Date of Issue	Date of Reporting	Maturity Date	Amount (₹ in Crores)	Coupon (per cent)	Type
01/03/1992	31/03/2003	01/03/2004	100	12.50	HFT
01/03/1993	31/03/2003	01/03/2003	100	12.00	HFT
01/03/1994	31/03/2003	01/03/2003	100	12.00	HFT
01/03/1995	31/03/2003	01/03/2006	100	12.50	HTM
01/03/1998	31/03/2003	01/03/2017	100	11.50	HTM
Total			**500**		

Step 1: Calculate risk-weighted assets for credit risk, which implies excluding securities held under trading book. In this case, the trading book would be ₹1,500 crores (₹700 crores of government securities + ₹500 crores of bank bonds + ₹300 crores of others—arrived at by excluding HTM securities). The credit risk would be computed after excluding the trading book as follows:

S. No.	Asset Details	Book Value (₹ in Crore)	Risk-weight (in per cent)	Risk-weighted Assets (Book value × Risk-weights)
1.	Cash and balances with the RBI	200	0	0
2.	Bank balances	200	20	40
3.	Investments			
	Government securities	300	0	0
	Banks	0	20	0
	Others	200	100	200
4.	Advances (Net)	2,000	100	2,000
5.	Other assets	300	100	300
6.	Total assets	3,200		
7.	**Total RWAs**			**2,540**

Step 2: Calculate risk-weighted assets for market risk. This comprises computing capital charge for specific risk for (see table on specific risks given in the RBI circular) the following:

- Government securities—₹700 crores-nil.
- Banks—to be grouped according to residual term to final maturity.
- Others—₹300 crores with capital charge of 9 per cent = ₹27 crores

Details	Capital Charge (per cent) (see table on capital charge)	Amount (₹ in crore)	Capital Charge (Capital Charge (per cent) (Amount)
For residual term to final maturity 6 months or less	0.30	200	0.60
For residual term to final maturity between 6 and 24 months	1.125	100	1.125
For residual term to final maturity exceeding 24 months	1.80	200	3.60
Total		500	5.325

Therefore, specific risk in trading book can be consolidated as (i) + (ii) + (iii) = 0 + 5.325 + 27 = ₹32.33 crores

Step 3: Compute general market risk.
Modified duration is used to arrive at the price sensitivity of an interest rate related instrument. For all the securities listed below, date of reporting is taken as 31 March 2003.

Counter Party	Maturity Date	Amount (Market Value)	Coupon (per cent)	(₹ in crore) Capital Charge for General Market Risk
Government	01/03/2004	100	12.50	0.84
Government	01/03/2003	100	12.00	0.08
Government	31/05/2003	100	12.00	0.16
Government	01/03/2015	100	12.50	3.63
Government	01/03/2010	100	11.50	2.79
Government	01/03/2009	100	11.00	2.75
Government	01/03/2005	100	10.50	1.35
Banks	01/03/2004	100	12.50	0.84
Banks	01/05/2003	100	12.00	0.08
Banks	31/05/2003	100	12.00	0.16
Banks	01/03/2006	100	12.50	1.77
Banks	01/03/2007	100	11.50	2.29
Others	01/03/2004	100	12.50	0.84
Others	01/05/2003	100	1200	0.08
Others	31/05/2003	100	12.00	0.16
Total		1500		17.82

Step 4: Consolidate general and specific risks to give the total capital charge for the trading book of interest rate related instruments. Thus, total capital charge for market risks = ₹32.33 crores + ₹17.82 crores = ₹50.15 crores.

Step 5: Compute the CRAR for the banking book as well as the trading book, in short, for the assets of the bank. For this purpose, the capital charge as above needs to be converted into equivalent risk-weighted assets. In India, the minimum CRAR is 9 per cent. Therefore, the capital charge is converted to risk-weighted assets by multiplying the capital charge by the factor (100/9). Accordingly, the risk-weighted assets for market risk in the example is 50.15 × (100/9) = ₹557.23 crores. The capital ratio would stand at 12.91 per cent, calculated as follows:

Sl. No.	Details	Amount (₹ in crore)
1.	Total capital	400
2.	Risk-weighted assets for credit risk	2,540.00
3.	Risk-weighted assets for market risk	557.23
4.	Total risk-weighted asses (2 + 3)	3,097.23
5.	CRAR [(1 ÷ 4) × 100]	12.91%

ILLUSTRATION 11.7

Assume that, in the above example, the assets of the bank include investments in 'equities' of ₹300 crores. The bank's modified balance sheet would appear as follows:

Details	Amount (₹ in crore)
Cash and balances with the RBI	200.00
Bank balances	200.00
Investments:	

Held for trading	500.00
Available for sale	1,000.00
Held to maturity	500.00
Equities	300.00
Advances (net)	2,000.00
Other assets	500.00
Total assets	**5,000.00**

Note that, the total assets have increased from the earlier ₹4,700 crores to ₹5,000 crores due to the investment in equities.

In addition, assume:

- foreign exchange open position limit at ₹60 crores
- gold open position at ₹40 crores and
- that the bank is having the following positions in interest rate related derivatives:
    - Interest rate swaps (IRS),[26] ₹100 crores-bank received floating rate interest and pays fixed, next interest fixing after 6 months, residual life of swap 8 years and
    - long position in interest rate future (IRF), ₹50 crores, delivery after 6 months, life of underlying government security 3.5 years.

Thus, in terms of counter parties, the investments are assumed to be as under:

- Interest rate related securities (as in Illustration 11.5)

  Government—₹1,000 crores

  Banks —₹500 crores

  Others—₹500 crores
- Equities

  Others—₹300 crores

Note: The composition of interest rate related securities remain as in Illustration 11.5.

Steps for Computing Risk-Weighted Assets

Step 1: Risk-weighted assets for credit risk

As per the guidelines, 'held for trading' and 'available for sale' securities are to be categorized as trading book. Thus, trading book in respect of interest rate related investments in this case would continue to be ₹1,500 crores as in Illustration 11.5. In addition, equities position of ₹300 crores would be in the trading book. The derivative products held by banks are to be considered as part of the trading book. Open position on foreign exchange[27] and gold also would be considered for market risk. While computing the capital charge for credit risk, the securities held under trading book would be excluded and hence, the credit risk based risk-weights would be as under:

Details of Assets	Book Value	Risk-weight (in per cent)	(₹ in crore) Risk-weighted Assets
Cash and RBI	200	0	0
Bank balances	200	20	40
Investment in (HTM category) Government	300	0	0
Banks	0	20	300
Others	200	100	200
Advances (net)	2,000	100	2,000
Other assets	300	100	300
Total	**4,700**	**2,540**	

Credit risk for OTC derivaties:			
IRS	100	1% + 1%	8.00
IRF	50	per year and 100% RW	4.00
Total	**4,850**	**2,552.00**	

Hence, the risk-weighted assets have increased from ₹2,540 crores in Illustration 11.5 to ₹2,552 crores, due to the credit risk in respect of OTC derivative.

Step 2: As in Illustration 11.5, we now calculate the risk-weighted assets for market risk.

- Specific risk

  We have seen in Illustration 11.5 that the specific risk for interest rate related instruments was ₹32.33 crores.

Additionally, we will now have to consider the capital charge of 9 per cent on equities of ₹300 crores held in the trading book, which amounts to ₹27 crores.

Thus, capital charge for specific risk in the trading book now stands at ₹59.33 crores (₹32.33 crores + ₹27 crores).

- General market risk

  As in Illustration 11.5, modified duration is used to arrive at the price sensitivity of interest rate related instruments and therefore, the capital charge remains at ₹17.82 crore.

  Additionally, we will have to calculate the capital charge for positions in respect of interest rate related derivatives.

- Interest rate swap

Counter Party	Maturity Date (*i.e.*, Market Value)	National Amount or Price Sensitivity	Modified Duration in Yield	Assumed Capital	Change Charge
GO!	30/09/2003	10	0.47	1.00	0.47
GO!	31/03/2011	100	5.14	0.60	(−) 3.08
					(−) 2.61

- Interest rate futures

Counter Party	Maturity Date	National Amount (*i.e.*, Market Value)	Modified Duration or Price Sensitivity	Assumed Change in Yield	Capital Charge
GOI	30/09/2003	50	0.45	1.00	(−) 0.45
GOI	31/03/2007	50	2.84	0.75	2.13
					1.68

- Example for computing the capital charge including the vertical and horizontal disallowances on interest rate related instruments. (Please see Box 11.6, for better understanding).

**0.45 × 5% = 0.02 @ 2.79 × 5% = 0.14 #0.29 × 30% = 0.09

		Zone 1				Zone 2					Zone 3					
Time-band	0–1 month	1–3 month	3.6 month	6m–1y	1–1.9y	1.9–2.8y	2.8–3.6y	3.6–4.3y	4.3–5.7y	5.7–7.3y	7.3–9.3y	9.3–10.6y	10.6–12y	12–20y	Over 20y	Capital charge
Position		0.72		2.51		1.35	1.77	2.29		2.75	2.79		3.63			17.82
Derivatives (long)			0.47					1.07								1.54

Derivatives (short)		(–) 0.22						(–) 3.08		(–) 3.30
Net Position	0.72	0.25	2.51	1.35	1.77	3.36	2.75	(–) 0.29	3.63	16.06
Vertical Disallowance (5%)		0.01**						0.14@		0.15
Horizontal Disallowance 1 (under zone 3)								0.09#		0.09
Horizontal Disallowance 2										
Horizontal Disallowance 3										

Note: Banks in India will generally not be subject to vertical or horizontal disallowance unless they have a short position in derivatives. However, conceptually, let us see how the disallowances are arrived at in Box 11.3.

BOX 11.3 COMPUTING VERTICAL AND HORIZONTAL DISALLOWANCE FOR INTEREST RATE DERIVATIVES

- **Calculation of vertical disallowance**

  While calculating capital charge for general market risk on interest rate related instruments, banks should recognize the basis risk (different types of instruments whose price responds differently for movement in general rates) and gap risk (different maturities within time bands).This is addressed by a small capital charge (5 per cent) on matched (off-setting) positions in each time band ('vertical disallowance'). An off-setting position, for vertical disallowance, will be the sum of long positions and/or the short positions within a time band, whichever is lower. In the above example, except for the time band 3 to 6 months in zone 1 and the time band of 7.3 to 9.3 years, where there are off-setting positions of (−) 045 and 2.79, there is no off-setting position in any other time band. The sum of long positions in the 3–6 months time band is +0.47 and the sum of short positions in this time band is (−) 0.45. This off-setting position of 0.45 is subjected to a capital charge of 5 per cent, *i.e.*, 0.0225. The sum of long positions in the 7.3 to 9.3 year time band is + 2,79 and the sum of short positions in this time band is (−) 3.08. This off-setting position of 2.79 is subjected to a capital charge of 5 per cent, *i.e.*, 0.1395. It may be mentioned here, that if a bank does not have both long and short positions in the same time band, there is no need for any vertical disallowance.

- **Calculation of horizontal disallowance**

  While calculating capital charge for general market risk on interest rate related instruments, banks must subject their positions to a second round of off setting across time bands with a view to give recognition to the fact that interest rate movements are not perfectly correlated across maturity bands (yield curve risk and spread risk), *i.e.*, matched long and short positions in different time bands may not perfectly off set. This is achieved by a 'horizontal disallowance'. An off-setting position for horizontal disallowance will be the sum of long positions and/or the short positions within a zone, whichever is lower. In the above example, except in zone 3 (7.3 to 9.3 years), where there is an off setting (matched) position of (−) 0.29, there is no off setting position in any other zone. The sum of long positions in this zone is 10.81 and the sum of short positions in this zone is (−) 0.29. This off setting position of 0.29 is subject to horizontal disallowance as under:

  Within the same zone (zone 3) 30 per cent of 0.29 = 0.09

  Between adjacent zones (zone 2 and 3) Nil

  Between zone 1 and zone 3 Nil

Similar to the case of vertical disallowance, if a bank does not have both long and short positions in different time zones, there is no need for any horizontal disallowance.

Banks in India are not allowed to take any short position in their books except in derivatives. Therefore, banks in India will generally not be subject to horizontal or vertical disallowance unless they have short positions in derivatives.

Source: RBI guidelines

- Total capital charge for interest rate related instruments

For over all net position	16.89
For vertical disallowance	0.16
For horizontal disallowance in zone 3	0.09
For horizontal disallowance in adjacent zones	Nil
For horizontal disallowance between zone 1 and 3	Nil
Total capital charge for interest rate related instruments	17.14

Let us summarize the above process:

- Price sensitivities have been slotted into a duration based ladder with 15 time bands.
- Long and short positions within a time band have been subjected to vertical disallowance of 5 per cent. In this case, vertical disallowance is applicable only under 3 to 6 month and 7.3 to 9.3 year time bands.
- Net positions in each time band have been arrived at for horizontal off-setting subject to the disallowances mentioned in tables given above. In this case, horizontal disallowance is applicable only in respect of zone 3 and not in respect of adjacent zones.

The total capital charge for general market risk for interest rate related instruments is thus computed as shown below.

Sl. No.	Capital Charge	Amount (₹)
1.	For the vertical disallowance (under 3–6 month time band).	2.25,000
2.	For the vertical disallowance (under 7.3–9.3 year time band).	13.95,000
3.	For the horizontal disallowance (under zone 3).	9,00,000
4.	For the horizontal disallowances between adjacent zones.	0
5.	For the overall net open position (17.82 − 2.61 + 1.68).	16,89,00,000
6.	Total capital charge for general market risk on interest rate related instruments (1 + 2 + 3 + 4 + 5).	17,14,00,000

Step 3: Compute capital charge for market risks by consolidating the following:

- Capital charge for specific and general market risks for interest rate related instruments.
- Capital charge on equities for specific and general market risks.[28]
- Capital charge for general market risk[29] in respect of open position of foreign exchange and gold.

Details	Capital Charge for Specific Risk	Capital Charge for General Market Risk
Interest rate related	32.33	17.14
Equities	27.00	27.00
Forex/Gold	9.00	
Total	**59.33**	**53.14**

Thus, total capital charge for market risk (general and specific) is ₹112.47 crores.

Step 4: We can now compute the capital ratio. To facilitate computation of CRAR for the whole book, this capital charge for market risks in the trading book needs to be converted into equivalent risk-weighted assets. Since a CRAR of 9 per cent is required, the capital charge could be converted to risk-weighted assets by multiplying the capital charge by (100/9), *i.e.*, ₹112.47 × (100/9) = ₹1,249.67 crores. Therefore, risk-weighted assets for market risk is ₹1,249.67 crores.

Sl. No.	(₹ in Crore)	
1.	Total capital	400
2.	Risk-weighted assets for credit risk	2,552,00
3.	Risk-weighted assets for market risk	1,249.67
4.	Total risk-weighed assets (2 + 3)	
5.	CRAR [(1 × 4) × 100]	10.52%

CHAPTER SUMMARY

- Banking is undoubtedly one of the most regulated industries globally and the rules governing bank capital are one of the most prominent aspects of such regulation. The higher the capital, the higher the number of problem assets that can default before the capital is fully depleted. Thus, greater the bank's capital funds, greater the amount of assets that can default before the bank becomes technically insolvent and lower the bank's risk.
- Capital for a bank also serves other functions. When a bank has adequate capital, it has ready access to the financial markets, since investors look upon it as a safe investment option. The bank can enter new businesses and can indulge in risk taking to boost earnings potential.
- Financial risk is inherent to banking business, quite incomparable with the traditional manufacturing firms. Hence, only if banks have low risk assets can they remain safe. In practice, however, banking assets are risky. Therefore, banks should increase capital relative to the risks of the assets they hold.
- One aspect of bank regulation is to ensure that depositors who do not need to withdraw at present are given enough assurance that they will be paid in the future. Depositors need assurance that the bank has enough (claims on) liquid assets to meet all demands made by depositors. There are four ways to provide this assurance—adequate bank equity capital, deposit insurance, lender of last resort and subordinated debt. Lack of assurance can lead to bank failures and outcomes that are not welfare maximizing. These assurances have an economic role in providing optimal outcomes and therefore, need to be formulated with utmost care.
- Accounting definition of bank capital is different from the definition of 'economic capital' and regulatory capital in banks.
- Economic Capital is the amount of capital considered necessary to absorb potential losses associated with banking risks.
- Regulatory capital, though seen to constrain growth to some extent, reduces the risk of banks expanding beyond their ability or taking undue risks. Regulators include certain forms of debt and loss reserves while measuring capital funds in banks.
- The international convergence of bank capital regulation began with the 1988 Basel Accord on capital standards. The G10 countries signed the accord, which was then intended to apply to only internationally active banks. At that time, its focus was the measurement of capital and the definition of capital standards for credit risk Since then the Accord has been amended several times having been endorsed by the central banks of many countries and adopted by several banks across the globe.
- The Accord currently under implementation in various countries is Basel III, which makes an effort to fix the lacunae in Basel II that came to light during the financial crisis as also to reflect other lessons of the crisis. Basel III builds on the essence of Basel II—the link between the risk profiles and capital requirements of individual banks. In that sense, Basel III can be considered an enhancement of Basel II.
- The enhancements of Basel III over Basel II are primarily in four areas: (i) augmentation in the level and quality of capital; (ii) introduction of liquidity standards; (iii) modifications in provisioning norms; and (iv) better and more comprehensive disclosures. It is noteworthy that Basel III has concentrated on capital definition (the numerator of the capital adequacy ratio), with minimal enhancements in the risk measurements (denominator of capital adequacy ratio).
- The minimum capital requirement will now take into account market risks and operational risks, along with credit risks. It also proposes differentiated approaches to measurement of capital ranging from basic to advanced. To calculate capital for credit risk, banks can adopt (1) the standardized approach, (2) the IRB foundation and advanced approach and (3) securitization approach depending on the strength of their internal risk management systems. Similarly, capital for market risk can be maintained on the basis of (1) the standardized approach (maturity method), (2) the standardized approach (duration method) and (3) the internal models method. Capital required for operational risk can be gauged through the following methods ranging from (1) the basic indicator approach, (2) the standardized approach, and (3) the advanced measurement approach (AMA).

- The essential difference between Basel II and III Tier 1 and Tier 2 capital is that: (a) Under Basel II, qualifying tier 1 and Tier 2 capital was determined on the basis of 'gross' instruments, before deduction of various items that could reduce the amount of capital available to withstand credit and other shocks, and (b) Under Basel III, banks would determine available Tier 1 and Tier 2 capital only after deductions are made.
- Further, within Tier 1 capital, there is a distinction made between the components of Common Equity Tier 1 and Additional Tier 1 Capital instruments.
- Basel III also requires buffers such as Capital conservation and countercyclical buffers to be kept as part of capital. A leverage ratio has also been introduced.
- Basel III introduces a new liquidity standard through two liquidity ratios.
  (i) The Liquidity Coverage Ratio (LCR) is designed to improve the short term resilience of the liquidity risk profile of banks. It requires banks to hold a buffer of 'high quality' liquid assets to match net liquidity outflows during a 30 day period of stress

$$\text{LCR} = \frac{\text{High quality liquid assets}}{\text{Total net liquidity outflows over a 30 day period}} \geq 100 \text{ per cent}$$

  (ii) The Net Stable Funding Ratio (NSFR) is designed to promote resilience in the longer term. It requires that banks fund their activities with more stable sources of funding on an ongoing basis.

$$\text{NSFR} = \frac{\text{Available stable funding}}{\text{Required stable funding}} \geq 100 \text{ pre cent}$$

- The capital ratio can be expressed as follows:

$$\frac{\text{Capital}}{\text{Credit risk} + \text{Market risk} + \text{Operational risk}}$$

- In India, the Narasimham Committee had submitted its report on banking reforms in the early 1990s. The Committee had observed that the capital ratios of Indian banks were generally low and that some banks were seriously undercapitalized. The Basel framework was adopted by the RBI. prescribing a higher norm of 9 per cent on risk-weighted assets (as against 8 per cent by the Basel Accord) for all banks operating in India. The aggregate of Tier 1 and Tier 2 capital forms the total capital funds for banks for the purpose of computing 'capital adequacy'.
- Banks in India are currently following the Standardized approach for credit risk, the Standardized approach (modified duration) for market risk and the Basic Indicator approach for operational risk.
- Banks in India are required to maintain a Tier 1 capital ratio of at least 6 per cent, and a total capital to Risk Weighted Assets ratio of at least 9 per cent. The Common Equity Tier 1 capital should be at least 5.5 per cent of Risk Weighted Assets.
- Banks in India would be reporting minimum capital under Basel III beginning April 1, 2013.

TEST YOUR UNDERSTANDING

1. Compare accounting capital, economic capital and regulatory capital. Which type of capital will reflect a realistic picture of the bank's capability of protecting itself against all risks? Support your choice with valid arguments.
2. Why does capital limit the ability of banks to make loans? Is risk-weighted capital a better measure of capital adequacy?
3. Analysts opine that risk-based capital requirements will force banks to raise their rates of lending. Let us assume that Bank A prices its loans to earn an ROE of 15 per cent. Will the allocation of capital to a loan affect loan pricing?
4. Consider the following shifts in asset composition in Bank A. How will the shift affect (a) the bank's capital requirement? (b) the bank's profit potential?
   a. From auto loans to home loans
   b. From investment in government securities to project financing
   c. From corporate lending to investment in government securities
   d. From investment in project bonds to investment in money market instruments
5. The capital of Bank B on 31 March 2009 was ₹1,000 crores. The bank's balance sheet carried total assets of ₹10,000 crores, which translated into risk-weighted assets of ₹7,000 crores. The bank desires an RCA of 2 per cent at the end of 31 March 2010. It also expects to add ₹2,000 crores of assets to the balance sheet during 2009–2010.

a. If the bank wishes to maintain the existing capital adequacy ratio, what is the probable maximum addition to the risk-weighted assets?

b. Assume that the incremental assets are totally financed by incremental liabilities of the same amount, which are subjected to reserve requirements of 5 per cent CRR and 25 per cent SLR. If the bank targets a capital adequacy ratio of 16 per cent by the end of March 2010, what would be the minimum addition to off-balance sheet items (non-funded assets) if the incremental assets carry 100 per cent risk-weight?

6. Bank C wants to grow during the next year, but does not want to add fresh capital. In the current year, it expects an ROA of 1.5 per cent and an Equity-to-asset ratio of 9 per cent. It also plans a dividend payout ratio of 25 per cent. By how much can the bank's assets grow under these expectations? If the bank plans to add capital to the extent of 1 per cent of its total assets, what would be the growth in assets? Assume that there is no change in the expected earnings.

TOPICS FOR FURTHER DISCUSSION

- Would increased regulatory capital requirements lead to more consolidation among banks?
- What are the possible consequences of Indian banks' need for huge capital in the next few years (as required by Basel III)?
- What are the consequences of bank failure?
- Compare the regulatory capital and accounting capital of all banks operating in India. What are your conclusions? Do you think regulatory capital provides an effective cushion against all risks?
- What would be the effects on government ownership in public sector banks as banks in India migrate to more advanced methods of capital adequacy calculations?

SUGGESTIONS FOR FURTHER READING

- The chapter provides a bird's eye view into the current regulatory aspects in banking. A thorough reading of the Basel Committee standards and the RBI's adaptation to banks in India through its Master Circulars would provide more insight into each of the aspects discussed in the chapter.

  Visit: http://www.bis.org; http://www.rbi.org.in

ANNEXURE I

DETERMINATION OF RISK WEIGHTED ASSETS UNDER THE BASEL NORMS[30]

The total minimum capital requirement for credit, market and operational risks is calculated using the definition of regulatory capital as defined above and risk-weighted assets. While Tier 2 capital is limited to 100 per cent of Tier 1 capital, the total 'capital to risk-weighted assets' ratio must be no lower than 8 per cent.

Total risk-weighted assets are determined by multiplying the capital requirements for market risk and operational risk by 12.5 (the reciprocal of the minimum capital ratio of 8 per cent) and adding the resulting figures to the sum of risk-weighted assets for credit risk.

Capital for Credit Risk The 'standardized approach' for credit risk retains some part of the 1988 Accord, such as the definition of 'capital'. Its novelty lies in replacing the existing risk-weighting scheme by a system where risk-weights are determined by the borrower's rating, defined by an external credit rating agency such as Standard and Poor's or Moody's or by Export Credit Agencies (ECAs) recognized by the respective country's central bank. Banking book[31] exposures are risk-weighted based on ratings by the external agencies in specified cases as follows: (See Chart 11.1)

- Claims on sovereigns and their central banks are assigned risk-weights ranging from 150 per cent for a below B-ratings[32] to 0 per cent for an AAA to AA rated country. Unrated sovereigns attract a risk-weight of 100 per cent.
- Claims on the Bank for International Settlements, the International Monetary Fund, the European Central Bank and the European Community may be assigned a 0 per cent risk-weight.
- Claims on public sector entities will be risk-weighted at the country's discretion or can also be treated at par with the risk-weight for claims on the sovereign.
- Multilateral development banks (MDBs) that are highly rated are eligible for a 0 per cent risk-weight.[33] Such eligibility will be evaluated on a case-to-case basis.

CHART 11.1 CREDIT RISK CALCULATIONS USING THE STANDARDIZED APPROACH

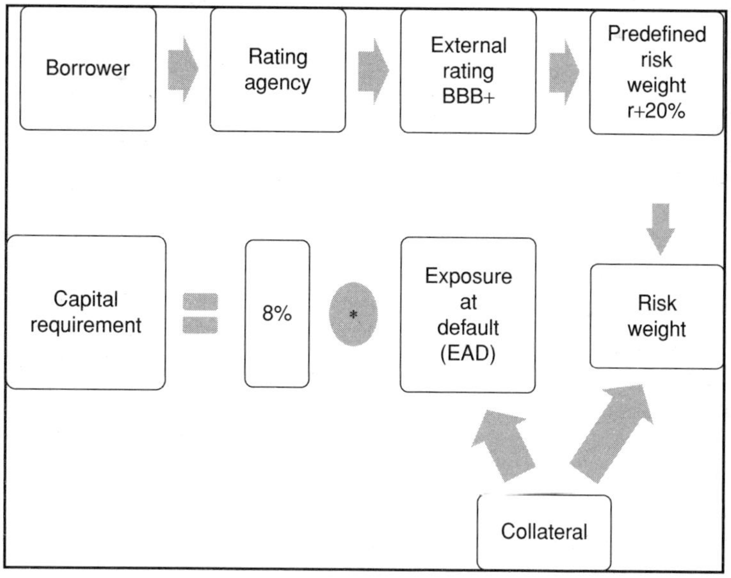

- In the case of claims on banks, there are two options presented for risk-weighting. Under the first option, all banks in a country will be assigned a risk-weight one category less favourable than that assigned to claims on the sovereign of that country. The second option bases the risk-weighting on the external credit assessment of individual banks in the country, with unrated banks risk-weighted at 50 per cent.
- Claims on securities firms are to be treated as claims on banks, provided such firms are subject to strict supervisory and regulatory arrangements. If not, such claims would follow the rules for claims on corporates.
- Claims on corporates, including insurance companies, cannot be assigned a risk-weight preferential to that of its country of incorporation. The central banks also have the discretion to permit banks to risk-weight corporate claims at 100 per cent without regard to external ratings.
- Retail exposures may be risk-weighed at 75 per cent on a uniform basis. However, central banks may increase these risk-weight based on the default experience.
- Claims on residential property may be assigned a risk-weight of 35 per cent only, provided the valuation is fair and substantial security exists over and above the loan amount. Based on prior default experience, central banks may increase the risk-weights appropriately. However, considering the volatility in commercial real estate, the Committee proposes a 100 per cent risk-weight for mortgages and commercial real estate loans.
- In addition, the Committee has proposed high risk-weights (ranging from 150 per cent to 350 per cent) on certain categories of claims.
- In all other cases not specified by the standardized approach, the risk-weights as presently applicable would continue.
- Off-balance sheet items under the standardized approach will be converted into credit exposure equivalents through Credit Conversion Factors (CCFs). Commitments with an original maturity of up to 1 year and those with original maturity over 1 year will receive a CCF of 20 per cent and 50 per cent, respectively. However, any commitments that can be unconditionally cancelled at any time by the bank without prior notice or that which can effectively provide for automatic cancellation due to deterioration in a borrower's creditworthiness will receive a 0 per cent CCF. A CCF of 100 per cent will be applied to the lending of banks' securities or the posting of securities as collateral by banks, including instances where these arise out of repo-style transactions (*i.e.*, repurchase/reverse repurchase and securities lending/securities borrowing transactions).
- Where Credit Risk Mitigation[34] (CRM) techniques such as (a) collateralized transactions, (b) on-balance sheet netting and (c) guarantees and credit derivatives exist, lower capital may be maintained, provided certain conditions are fulfilled. While the use of such risk mitigation techniques reduce or transfer credit risk, they may simultaneously increase other residual risks, which could include legal, operational, liquidity and market risks. Where

such residual risks are not adequately controlled, the central bank may impose additional capital charges under Pillar 2.

- To determine minimum capital requirement for a bank, a four step process is to be followed.
  - Classify assets into risk categories and assign risk-weights.
  - Convert off-balance sheet commitments and guarantees to a notional on balance sheet 'credit equivalent' (using CCF) and classify these in the appropriate risk categories.
  - Multiply the rupee amount of assets in each risk category by the appropriate risk-weight. The result equals 'risk-weighted assets'.
  - Multiply the risk-weighted assets by the minimum capital percentages required for it to be adequately capitalized. Compare this with the existing capital on the bank's balance sheet.

The process ensures that assets with the highest perceived risk have the highest risk-weights and hence require the most capital. Another important feature of the risk-based standards is that a bank's off-balance sheet items should be supported by adequate capital. These items, called 'contingent liabilities' are exposures that could arise in future if counterparties do not meet their commitments. Hence, banks that expose their operations to risk by offering letters of credit or guarantees or participating in forward or futures transactions must hold capital against the possible future exposure.

The Internal Ratings Based (IRB) Approach to Credit Risk Under this advanced approach, banks can use their internal estimates of borrower creditworthiness to assess the credit risk in their portfolio, subject to stringent methodological and disclosure standards. Distinct analytical frameworks are applicable to different types of loan exposures whose loss characteristics are different.

These banks may rely on their own internal estimates of risk components in determining the capital requirement for a given exposure. The risk components include measures of the following:

- Probability of Default (PD)
- Loss Given Default (LGD)
- Exposure at Default (EAD)
- Effective Maturity (M)

In some cases, banks may be required to use values prescribed by supervisors in lieu of internal estimates for some of the risk components. The IRB approach is based on measures of Unexpected Losses (UL) and Expected Losses (EL). The risk-weight functions account for capital for the UL portion.

Under the IRB approach, banks would categorize banking book exposures into broad classes of assets with different underlying risk characteristics, such as: (a) corporate, (b) sovereign, (c) bank, (d) retail, and (e) equity. Within each asset class, sub-classes of specialized lending are identified. For each of the asset classes covered under the IRB framework, there are three key elements.

- Risk components—estimates of risk parameters provided by banks some of which are supervisory estimates
- Risk-weight functions—the means by which risk components are transformed into risk-weighted assets and therefore capital requirements
- Minimum requirements—the minimum standards that must be met in order for a bank to use the IRB approach for a given asset class

For many of the asset classes, the Committee has made available two broad approaches: foundation and advanced. Under the foundation approach, banks generally provide their own estimates of PD and rely on supervisory estimates for other risk components. Under the advanced approach, banks provide more of their own estimates of PD, LGD and EAD and their own calculation of M, subject to meeting minimum standards.

For both the foundation and advanced approaches, banks must always use the risk-weight functions provided in this framework for the purpose of deriving capital requirements. The derivation of risk-weighted assets is dependent on estimates of the PD, LGD and EAD.

Credit Risk—The Securitization Framework The securitization framework should be used to determine regulatory capital requirements where banks have exposures to traditional or synthetic securitizations or similar structures. Since every securitization deal could be structured differently, the Committee requires banks and supervisors to determine the amount of capital based on 'economic substance' rather than the legal form of the structure. Some commonly known securitization structures are Asset Backed Securities (ABS), Mortgage Backed Securities (MBS), Credit enhancements and Liquidity facilities. However, securitization structures need not be restricted to the above forms and can be structured differently and innovatively.

Figure 11.5 lists the broad differences between traditional and synthetic securitizations. Banks are required to maintain capital against securitization exposures.

The exposures include those arising from providing credit risk mitigants to another securitization, investment in ABS, retention of a subordinated tranche, extension of a liquidity facility or credit enhancement or a repurchased securitization exposure.

Where such exposures are to be deducted from the regulatory capital, the deduction must be taken 50 per cent from Tier 1 and 50 per cent from Tier 2. However, where there is an increase in equity capital as a consequence of the securitization due to a gain on sale, the entire increase must be deducted from Tier 1 capital.

FIGURE 11.5 TRADITIONAL VERSUS SYNTHETIC SECURITIZATIONS

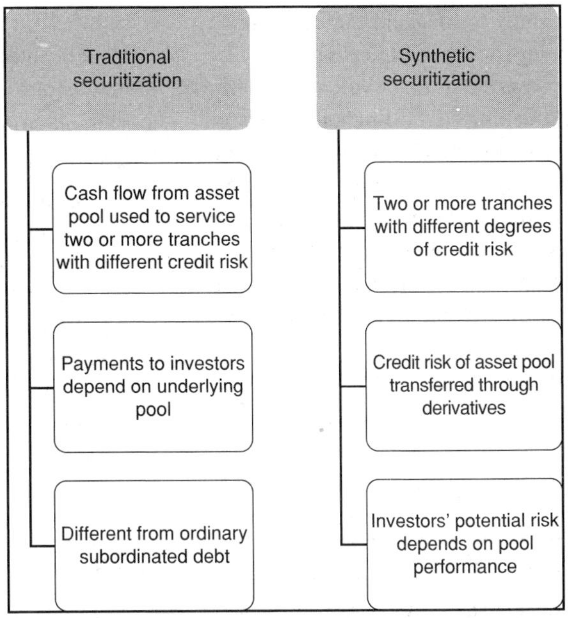

The BIS document also provides detailed guidelines on the computation of risk-weighted assets under securitized exposures in each of the approaches—Standardized and IRB.

Understandably, the lessons learnt from the financial crisis have led to further modifications/enhancements in the Basel II framework[35] and several such enhancements pertain to securitization exposures. Specifically, revisions have been proposed in determining resecuritization[36] risk-weights in the IRB approach and conversion factors in the case of liquidity facility under the Standardized and IRB approaches.

Capital Requirement for Interest Rate (Market) Risk

Credit risk or default risk is not the only risk borne by banks' assets. With banks resorting increasingly to treasury operations, they assume interest rate risk or market risk.

The Basel Committee defines market risk as "the risk of losses in on- and off-balance sheet positions arising from movements in market prices." The risks subject to this requirement are:

- The risks pertaining to interest rate related instruments and equities in the trading book.
- Foreign exchange risk and commodities risk throughout the bank.

Hence, market risk is the risk of loss to the bank from fluctuations in interest rates, equity prices, currency rates, commodity prices, as well as exposure to specific risk associated with the composition of the bank's investment portfolio. The sensitivity of the bank's trading assets (and liabilities) to the volatilities of the above rates and prices, exposes the bank to market risk.

Therefore, it is prudent for banks to measure market risk and hold adequate capital for exposure to market risk. Capital requirements should be designed to capture both general market risk as well as specific market risk. *General market risk* refers to the impact of broad market movements on the market value of on balance sheet assets and off balance sheet items and includes risks common to all securities, such as changes in the general level of interest rates, exchange rates, commodity prices or stock prices. *Specific market risks* arise from inherent risks of a particular security, such as the credit risk of the institution, which issued the security.

The capital charges for interest rate related instruments and equities would apply to the current market value of items in banks' trading books.

A trading book consists of positions in financial instruments[37] and commodities held with trading intent or in order to hedge other elements of the trading book. To be eligible for trading book capital treatment, financial instruments must either be free of any restrictive covenants on their tradability or able to be hedged completely. In addition, positions should be frequently and accurately valued and the portfolio should be actively managed.

In many banks the trading activities are carried out in quite separate units from the normal banking activities and so it is possible to identify the business, which falls within the trading book. Even where this is not the case, the trading activities tend to be readily identifiable because of their intent. Positions held with trading intent are those held intentionally for short-term resale and/or with the intent of benefiting from actual or expected short-term price movements. Other intentions can be to lock in arbitrage profits and may include for example proprietary positions, positions arising from client servicing (*e.g.*, matched principal broking) and market making.

Regulators also prescribe prudent valuation methods for trading book positions. The financial crisis of 2007 has prompted the Committee to revise its prudent valuation guidance to include valuations of positions accounted for by fair value, whether in the trading or banking book[38]. According to the Committee, "This guidance is especially important for positions without actual market prices or observable inputs to valuation, as well as less liquid positions."

A minimum framework for prudent valuation practices would include the following:

- Systems and controls should be adequate and sufficient, integrated with other risk management systems, such as credit analysis. Such systems are required to include documented policies and procedures for the valuation process and clear lines of accountability, with the ultimate reporting to a main Board Executive Director.
- The valuation methodologies to be used are:
  - Marking-to-market
  - Marking-to-model, only where marking to market is not possible. Marking-to-model is defined as any valuation, which has to be benchmarked, extrapolated or calculated from a market input. However, prudence and conservatism should be exercised while using this methodology. Box 11.4 lists out the criteria to assess the adequacy of the model adopted for valuation.

BOX 11.4 CRITERIA TO ASSESS THE PRUDENCE OF MARK-TO-MODEL VALUATION METHODOLOGIES

- Senior management should be aware of the elements of the trading book or of other fair valued positions, which are subject to mark-to-model and should understand the materiality of the uncertainty this creates in the reporting of the risk/performance of the business.
- Market inputs should be sourced, to the extent possible in line with market prices. The appropriateness of the market inputs for the particular position being valued should be reviewed regularly.
- Where available and possible, generally accepted valuation methodologies for particular products should be used.
- Risk management should be aware of the weaknesses of the models used and how best to reflect those in the valuation output.
- The model should be subject to periodic review to determine the accuracy of its performance (*e.g.*, assessing continued appropriateness of the assumptions, analysis of P&L versus risk factors and comparison of actual close out values to model outputs).
- Valuation adjustments should be made as appropriate for example, to cover the uncertainty of the model valuation.
- Where the model is developed by the institution itself, it should be based on appropriate assumptions, which have been assessed and challenged by suitably qualified parties independent of the development process. The model should be developed or approved independently of the front office. It should be independently tested. This includes validating the mathematics, the assumptions and the software implementation. There should be formal change control procedures in place and a secure copy of the model should be held and periodically used to check valuations.
- Independent price verification: While daily marking-to-market may be performed by dealers, verification of market prices or model inputs should be done by a unit independent of the dealing room.
- Valuation adjustments or reserves: Banks are expected to consider the following valuation adjustments/reserves at a minimum unearned credit spreads, close-out costs, operational risks, early termination, investing and funding costs and future administrative costs and where appropriate, model risk. Such adjustments/reserves will impact Tier 1 capital and may also exceed those under financial accounting standards.

Source: 'International Convergence of Capital Measurement and Capital Standards—a Revised Framework', Bank for International Settlements, (June 2006): 161.

Thus, a bank's overall minimum capital requirement will be based on:

- The credit risk requirements laid down in the present Accord, *excluding* debt and equity securities in the trading book and all positions in commodities, but *including* the credit counter party risk on all over-the-counter (OTC) derivatives whether in the trading or the banking books; *plus*
- The capital charges for operational risk; *plus*
- *Either* the capital charges for market risks summed arithmetically; or
- The measure of market risk derived from the models approach; or
- A mixture of the above two alternatives summed arithmetically.

Though reporting of market risk will be done periodically, banks are expected to manage the market risk in their trading book such that capital requirements are continuously being fulfilled.

Apart from the capital charge on specific and general market risk, banks should also calculate the counter party credit risk charge for OTC derivatives, repo style and other transactions in the trading book. For this purpose, the risk-weights will be consistent with those used in the banking book.

The credit market turmoil of 2007 in which major banks experienced large losses, especially in their trading books, prompted the Committee to introduce a new requirement for banks to hold capital against incremental default risk over and above the risk captured by banks' VaR model[39]. The reason for this was that banks' trading books were being increasingly exposed to credit risk and other illiquid products, which was not being reflected in the VaR. These losses could not be captured in the 99 per cent/10-day VaR, since the losses had been caused by credit migrations as well as widening credit spreads and loss of liquidity and not by actual defaults.

Therefore, the Incremental Risk Charge (IRC) represents an estimate of the default and migration risks on unsecuritized credit products over a one-year capital horizon at a 99.9 per cent confidence level. The Committee expects banks to develop internal models for calculating IRC. The July 2009 paper, 'Guidelines for computing capital for incremental risk in the trading book' provides guidelines on how the IRC model should be developed and how supervisors should evaluate the internal IRC models of banks.

Capital Requirement for Operational Risk

Operational risk is defined as the risk of loss resulting from inadequate or failed internal processes, people and systems or from external events. The Basel Committee definition includes legal risk, but excludes strategic and reputation risk.

The framework presents three methods for calculating operational risk capital charges in a continuum of increasing sophistication and risk sensitivity.

a. The basic indicator approach,
b. The standardized approach, and
c. Advanced measurement approaches (AMA)

The Basic Indicator Approach Banks using the basic indicator approach must hold capital for operational risk equal to the average over the previous 3 years of a fixed percentage (denoted alpha) of positive annual gross income. Figures for any year in which annual gross income is negative or zero, should be excluded from both the numerator and denominator when calculating the average. The charge is expressed as follows:

$$\Sigma K_{\mathrm{BIA}} = [\Sigma\,(GI_{1 \cdots n} \times \alpha)]/n$$

where K_{BIA} = the capital charge under the basic indicator approach

GI = annual gross income, where positive, over the previous 3 years

n = number of the previous 3 years for which gross income has been positive

α = 15 per cent, which is set by the committee, relating the industry wide level of required capital to the industry wide level of the indicator

Gross income is defined as net interest income plus net non-interest income. It is intended that this measure should: (a) be gross of any provisions (*e.g.*, for unpaid interest), (b) be gross of operating expenses, including fees paid to outsourcing service providers, (c) exclude realized profits/losses from the sale of securities in the banking book, and (d) exclude extraordinary or irregular items as well as income derived from insurance.

The Standardized Approach In the 'standardized approach', banks' activities are divided into eight business lines: corporate finance, trading and sales, retail banking, commercial banking, payment and settlement, agency services, asset management and retail brokerage. Within each business line, gross income is a broad indicator that serves as a proxy for the scale of business operations and thus, the likely scale of operational risk exposure within each of these business lines. The capital charge for each business line is calculated by multiplying gross income by a factor (denoted beta) assigned to that business line. Beta serves as a proxy for the industry-wide relationship between the operational risk loss experience for a given business line and the aggregate level of gross income for that business line. It should be noted that in the standardized approach gross income is measured for each business line, not the whole institution, *i.e.*, in corporate finance, the indicator is the gross income generated in the corporate finance business line.

Advanced Measurement Approach (AMA) Under the AMA, the regulatory capital requirement will equal the risk measure generated by the bank's internal operational risk measurement system using the quantitative and qualitative criteria for the AMA. Use of the AMA is subject to supervisory approval.

Annexure I also provides the salient features of the guidelines for operational risk measurement from the Basel Committee documents.

GUIDELINES FOR OPERATIONAL RISK MANAGEMENT

Relevant Excerpts from the Report on 'Sound Practices for the Management and Supervision of Operational Risk', Published by the Basel Committee on Banking Supervision in February 2003

Deregulation and globalization of financial services, together with the growing sophistication of financial technology, are making the activities of banks and thus their risk profiles (*i.e.*, the level of risk across a firm's activities and/or risk categories) more complex.

Developing banking practices suggest that risks other than credit, interest rate and market risk can be substantial. Examples of these new and growing risks faced by banks include the following:

- If not properly controlled, the greater use of more highly automated technology has the potential to transform risks from manual processing errors to system failure risks, as greater reliance is placed on globally integrated systems.
- Growth of e-commerce brings with it potential risks (*e.g.*, internal and external fraud and system security issues) that are not yet fully understood.
- Large-scale acquisitions, mergers, de-mergers and consolidations test the viability of new or newly integrated systems.
- The emergence of banks acting as large-volume service providers creates the need for continual maintenance of high-grade internal controls and back-up systems.
- Banks may engage in risk mitigation techniques (*e.g.*, collateral, credit derivatives, netting arrangements and asset securitizations) to optimize their exposure to market risk and credit risk, but which in turn may produce other forms of risk (*e.g.*, legal risk).
- Growing use of outsourcing arrangements and the participation in clearing and settlement systems can mitigate some risks but can also present significant other risks to banks.

The diverse set of risks listed above can be grouped under the heading of 'operational risk', which the Committee has defined as 'the risk of loss resulting from inadequate or failed internal processes, people and systems or from external events'. The definition includes legal risk but excludes strategic and reputation risk.

The Committee recognizes that operational risk is a term that has a variety of meanings within the banking industry and therefore, for internal purposes, banks may choose to adopt their own definitions of operational risk. Whatever be the exact definition, a clear understanding by banks of what is meant by operational risk is critical to the effective management and control of this risk category. It is also important that the definition considers the full range of material operational risks facing the bank and captures the most significant causes of severe operational losses.

Operational risk event types that the Committee—in co-operation with the industry-has identified as having the potential to result in substantial losses include the following:

- **Internal fraud.** For example, intentional misreporting of positions, employee theft and insider trading on an employee's own account.
- **External fraud.** For example, robbery, forgery, cheque kiting and damage from computer hacking.
- **Employment practices and workplace safety.** For example, workers' compensation claims, violation of employee health and safety rules, organized labour activities, discrimination claims and general liability.
- **Clients, products and business practices.** For example, fiduciary breaches, misuse of confidential customer information, improper trading activities on the bank's account, money laundering and sale of unauthorized products.
- **Damage to physical assets.** For example, terrorism, vandalism, earthquakes, fires and floods.
- **Business disruption and system failures.** For example, hardware and software failures, telecommunication problems and utility outages.
- **Execution, delivery and process management.** For example, data entry errors, collateral management failures, incomplete legal documentation, unapproved access given to client accounts, non-client counter party misperformance and vendor disputes.

Ten Principles for Operational Risk Management

Developing an Appropriate Risk Management Environment

Principle 1: The board of directors should be aware of the major aspects of the bank's operational risks as a distinct risk category that should be managed and it should approve and periodically review the bank's operational risk management framework. The framework should provide a firm-wide definition of operational risk and lay down the principles of how operational risk is to be identified, assessed, monitored and controlled/mitigated.

Principle 2: The board of directors should ensure that the bank's operational risk management framework is subject to effective and comprehensive internal audit by operationally independent, appropriately trained and competent staff. The internal audit function should not be directly responsible for operational risk management.

Principle 3: Senior management should have responsibility for implementing the operational risk management framework approved by the board of directors. The framework should be consistently implemented throughout the whole banking organization and all levels of staff should understand their responsibilities with respect to operational risk management. Senior management should also have responsibility for developing policies, processes and procedures for managing operational risk in all of the bank's material products, activities, processes and systems.

Risk Management: Identification, Assessment, Monitoring and Mitigation/Control

Principle 4: Banks should identify and assess the operational risk inherent in all material products, activities, processes and systems. Banks should also ensure that before new products, activities, processes and systems are introduced or undertaken, the operational risk inherent in them is subject to adequate assessment procedures.

Principle 5: Banks should implement a process to regularly monitor operational risk profiles and material exposures to losses. There should be regular reporting of pertinent information to senior management and the board of directors that supports the proactive management of operational risk.

Principle 6: Banks should have policies, processes and procedures to control and/or mitigate material operational risks. Banks should periodically review their risk limitation and control strategies and should adjust their operational risk profile accordingly using appropriate strategies, in light of their overall risk appetite and profile.

Principle 7: Banks should have in place contingency and business continuity plans to ensure their ability to operate on an ongoing basis and limit losses in the event of severe business disruption.

Role of Supervisors

Principle 8: Banking supervisors should require that all banks, regardless of size, have an effective framework in place to identify, assess, monitor and control/mitigate material operational risks as part of an overall approach to risk management.

Principle 9: Supervisors should conduct, directly or indirectly, regular independent evaluation of a bank's policies, procedures and practices related to operational risks. Supervisors should ensure that there are appropriate mechanisms in place which allow them to remain apprised of developments at banks.

Role of Disclosure

Principle 10: Banks should make sufficient public disclosure to allow market participants to assess their approach to operational risk management.

RBI Guidelines to Banks in India on Operational Risk Management On the basis of the Basel Committee's guidelines, the RBI has framed draft guidelines in March 2005 on operational risk measurement and management for adoption by banks in India by March 2007. Three options had been put forth by the Basel Committee for calculating capital charge for operational risk. These are, in the order of increasing complexity, (a) the basic indicator approach, (b) the standardized approach and (c) advanced management approaches (AMAs).

Though the RBI proposes to initially allow banks to use the basic indicator approach for computing regulatory capital for operational risk, banks are expected to move along the range toward more sophisticated approaches as they develop more sophisticated operational risk management systems and practices which meet the prescribed qualifying criteria.

Relevant Excerpts from the 'Draft Guidance Note on Management of Operational Risk' Published on 11 March 2005, by the RBI

The Basic Indicator Approach At the minimum, all banks in India should adopt this approach while computing capital for operational risk while implementing Basel II. Under the basic indicator approach, banks have to hold capital for operational risk equal to a fixed percentage (alpha) of a single indicator, which has currently been proposed to be 'gross income'. This approach is available for all banks irrespective of their level of sophistication. The charge may be expressed as follows:

$$K_{BIA} = (\Sigma\,(GI \times \alpha))/n,$$

Where, K_{BIA} = the capital charge under the basic indicator approach

GI = annual gross income, where positive, over the previous 3 years

α = 15 per cent set by the committee, relating the industry-wide level of required capital to the industry-wide level of the indicator.

n = number of the previous 3 years for which gross income is positive.

The Basel Committee has defined gross income as net interest income and has allowed each central bank to define gross income in accordance with the prevailing accounting practices. Accordingly, gross income has been defined as follows by the RBI.

Gross income = Net profit (+) Provisions and Contingencies (+) Operating expenses (Schedule 16) (−) Profit on sale of HTM investments (−) Income from insurance (−) Extraordinary/irregular item of income (+) Loss on sale of HTM investments.

Advanced Measurement Methodologies

The standardized approach. Under the standardized approach, banks' activities are divided into eight business lines against each of which, a broad indicator is specified to reflect the size or volume of banks' activities in that area. Table 11.14 shows the proposed business lines and indicator.

TABLE 11.14 PROPOSED BUSINESS LINES AS INDICATOR

Business Lines (in per cent)	Indicator	Beta Factors (in per cent)	Beta Values
Corporate finance	Gross income	β1	18
Trading arid sales	Gross income	β2	18
Retail banking	Gross income	β3	12
Commercial banking	Gross income	β4	15
Payment and settlement	Gross income	β5	18
Agency services	Gross income	β6	15
Asset management	Gross income	β7	12
Retail brokerage	Gross income	β8	12

Within each business line, the capital charge is calculated by multiplying the indicator by a factor (beta) assigned to that business line. Under this approach, the gross income is measured for each business line and not for the whole institution. However, the summation of the gross income for the eight business lines should aggregate to the gross income of the bank as computed under the basic indicator approach. The total capital charge under the standardized approach is calculated as the simple summation of the regulatory capital charges across each of the business lines.

The total capital charge may be expressed as follows:

$$K_{TSA} = \{\Sigma \text{ 1-3 } years\ max(\Sigma(GI_{1\text{-}8}\beta_{1\text{-}8}),0\} 1/3$$

Where K_{TSA} = the capital charge under the standardized approach

$GI_{1\text{-}8}$ = annual gross income in a given year, for each business lines

$\beta_{1\text{-}8}$ = a fixed percentage, set by the committee, relating the level of required capital to the level of the gross income for each of the eight business lines

The alternative standardized approach (ASA): At national supervisory discretion, a supervisor can choose to allow a bank to use the alternative standardized approach (ASA) provided the bank is able to satisfy its supervisor that this alternative approach provides an improved basis by, for example, avoiding double counting of risks. Once a bank has been allowed to use the ASA, it will not be allowed to revert to use of the standardized approach without the permission of its supervisor. It is not envisaged that large diversified banks in major markets would use the ASA. Under the ASA, the operational risk capital charge/methodology is the same as for the standardized approach except for two business lines-retail banking and commercial banking. For these business lines, loans and advances—multiplied by a fixed factor 'm'—replaces gross income as the exposure indicator. The betas for retail and commercial banking are unchanged from the standardized approach. The ASA operational risk capital charge for retail banking (with the same basic formula for commercial banking) can be expressed in the following way.

$$K_{RB} = \beta_{RB}\, xm \times LA_{RB}$$

Where K_{RB} = the capital charge for the retail banking business line

β_{RB} = the beta for the retail banking business line

LA_{RB} = total outstanding retail loans and advances (non-risk-weighted and gross of provisions), averaged over the past 3 years

m is 0.035

As under the standardized approach, the total capital charge for the ASA is calculated as the simple summation of the regulatory capital charges across each of the eight business lines.

Advanced measurement approaches (AMAs). The advanced measurement approaches would be based on an estimate of operational risk derived from a bank's internal risk measurement system and are, therefore, expected to be more risk sensitive than the other two approaches. Under the AMA, banks would be allowed to use the output of their internal operational risk measurement systems, subject to set qualitative and quantitative standards. For certain event types, banks may need to supplement their internal loss data with external industry loss data.

The approaches that banks in other territories are currently developing, fall under three broad categories. These are the internal measurement approach (IMA), loss distribution approach (LDA) and scorecard approach. The main features of these approaches, as outlined by the Basel Committee, are described as under.

Internal measurement approach (IMA): The approach assumes a fixed and stable relationship between ELs (the mean of the loss distribution) and ULs (the tail of the loss distribution). This relationship may be linear—implying the capital charge would be a simple multiple of ELs or non-linear—implying that the capital charge would be a more complex function of ELs.

The IMA calculations are generally based on a framework that divides a bank's operational risk exposures into a series of business lines and operational risk event types. In such a framework, a separate EL figure is calculated for each business line/event type combination. Typically, ELs are calculated by combining estimates of loss frequency and severity for various business line/event type combinations, based on internal and where appropriate, external loss data, along with a measure of the scale of business activities for the particular business line in question.

While these elements can be specified in a variety of ways, in general, they can be described as follows:

P_E: The probability that an operational risk event occurs over some future horizon

LGE: The average loss given that an event occurs

El: An exposure indicator that is intended to capture the scale of the bank's activities in a particular business line

Combining these parameters, the IMA capital charge for each business line (i)/event type (j) combination (Ki,j) would be:

$$Ki, j = \gamma i, j \times EIi, j \times PEi, j \times LGEi, j = \gamma i, j \times ELi, j$$

In this formula, a linear relationship between ELs and the tail of the distribution is assumed and the parameter γi,j translates the estimate of ELs for business line (i)/event type (j) (ELi, j) into a capital charge. The γ for each business line/event type combination would be specified by banks (possibly via consortia) and subject to acceptance by supervisors. The overall capital charge is generally calculated as the sum of the capital charges for individual business line/event type cells.

Loss distribution approach (LDA): Under loss distribution approaches, banks estimate, for each business line/risk type cell or group thereof, the likely distribution of operational risk losses over some future horizon (for instance, 1 year). The capital charge resulting from these calculations is based on a high percentile of the loss distribution. As with internal measurement approaches, this overall loss distribution is typically generated based on assumptions about the likely frequency and severity of operational risk loss events. In particular, LDAs usually involve estimating the shape of the distributions of both the number of loss events and the severity of individual events. These estimates may involve imposing specific distributional assumptions (for instance, a Poisson distribution for the number of loss events and lognormal distribution for the severity of individual events) or deriving the distributions empirically through techniques such as bootstrapping and Monte Carlo simulation. The overall capital charge may be based on the simple sum of the operational risk 'VaR' for each business line/risk type combination-which implicitly assumes perfect correlation of losses across these cells—or by using other aggregation methods that recognize the risk-reducing impact of less than full correlation.

At present, several kinds of LDA methods are being developed and no industry standard has emerged.

Scorecard approaches: A range of scorecard approaches is being developed with some banks already operating a system of economic capital allocation based on such an approach. In this approach, banks determine an initial level of operational risk capital at the bank or business line level and then modify these amounts over time on the basis of 'scorecards' that attempt to capture the underlying risk profile and risk control environment of the various business lines. These scorecards are intended to bring a forward-1ooking component to the capital calculations, that is, to reflect improvements in the risk control environment that will reduce both the frequency and severity of future operational risk losses. The scorecards may be based on actual measures of risk, but more usually identify a number of indicators as proxies for particular risk types within business units/lines. The scorecard will normally be completed by line personnel at regular intervals and are subject to review by a central risk function.

In order to qualify for the AMA, a 'scorecard' approach must have a sound quantitative basis, with the overall size of the capital charge being based on a rigorous analysis of internal and external loss data.

Other Issues

Overlap with credit and market risks: Certain operational risk loss events may overlap with those of credit or market risk related exposures. For the purpose of better operational risk management and to evolve internal policies in this regard, banks are expected to include all operational risks in the loss event database. However, for regulatory capital purposes, banks are expected to attribute operational risk related to credit and market loss events to those risk areas for the calculation of regulatory capital requirements.

Partial use: A bank may be permitted to use a combination of approaches, say, the standardized approach for some business lines and an advanced measurement approach for others, subject to a materiality requirement that at least a minimum percentage of the bank's business should be in the advanced measurement approach. However, with a view to prevent arbitrage of the capital charge, banks will not be allowed to choose to revert to simpler approaches once they have been approved for more advanced approaches.

ANNEXURE II

THE FINANCIAL CRISIS OF 2007—BASEL II AND THE BLAME GAME

Does the Basel II Accord deserve its share of the blame in the run up to the financial crisis of 2007?

Those who say 'no' however point to the shortcomings of Basel I Accord as a possible reason. At a time when countries had just begun implementing the Basel II Accord, the remnants of the Basel I era, with its lack of risk sensitivity and inflexibility to rapid innovations, could have created perverse regulatory incentives to simply move risky exposures off bank balance sheets, without really assessing the adequacy of capital to meet the risk exposures.

Those who say 'yes' feel that the financial crisis merely exposed the deficiencies in the 'vastly improved' Basel II Accord. What were the limitations of the Basel II Accord?

One, the Basel II Accord made a quantum leap from the relatively simple Basel I to include a degree of complexity that proved a challenge to both the regulators as well as banks.

Two, external ratings provided by rating agencies played a critical role in the Basel II Accord. Since rating agencies were assigned significant blame for the financial crisis, the basic premises of Basel II Accord were also questionable.

Three, the standardized and advanced approaches operated under certain assumptions may not be applicable to all countries adopting the Accord. Hence, the onus was on the regulator of each country to assess if the risk-weights assigned were applicable to the country's context.

Four, the Accord allocated higher capital to higher credit risk. This led to the concern that small businesses and the less prosperous sections of society, typically considered as high credit risk segments, would attract unaffordable rates of interest. This concern was especially true for developing countries.

Five, the risk modelling approaches in the advanced approaches had limitations. It is still unclear whether maintaining capital based on these risk models would ensure adequate amount of capital to cover risks. Further, these models require accurate and validated data to assess risks, which may not be available in all countries or for all instruments.

Six, the level of technological and computational competence that the approach presupposes may not be available with all banks or banking systems.

Seven, aligning disclosures under Pillar 3 (please refer to *Annexure II*) to international and domestic accounting systems would be a challenge.

Eight, effective implementation of the Basel II Accord would require tremendous upgrading in skills of both supervisors and banks.

Finally, an issue that has been discussed widely is that of pro-cyclicality. When economies are doing well, banks lend more, probably take more risks for better returns and maintain adequate capital. However, when business cycles take a downturn, banks downgrade the borrowers due to increased likelihood of default and therefore, have to maintain more capital. This leads to capital shortage, as well as restriction in credit and therefore, leads to further deterioration in the economy. The Basel Committee acknowledges that risk based capital requirements could inevitably lead to pro-cyclicality, but this problem could be addressed by different instruments.

In November 2008, the Basel Committee admitted that its proposed Accord had to be more comprehensive to address the fundamental weaknesses exposed by the financial crisis related to the regulation, supervision and risk management of internationally active banks. In 2009, the Committee has already brought out documents amending the Basel II Accord, as described in Section II of the chapter.

SELECT REFERENCES

1. RBI, "Report on Currency and Finance, 2006–2008"
2. www.bis.org

ANNEXURE III

PILLARS II AND III OF BASEL II AND III ACCORD[40] AND THEIR APPLICATION TO INDIAN BANKS[41]

The Second Pillar of the Basel II and III Accord—Supervisory Review Process

The supervisor's role would be not only to ensure that banks maintain adequate capital to cover all critical risks, but also to guide banks towards increasingly robust internal risk management systems. Increased capital should not be regarded as a substitute for fundamentally weak internal risk management and control processes. The Basel Committee points out areas where supervisory review becomes more important.

a. Risks under Pillar 1 not fully captured by the Pillar 1 (minimum capital requirements) process. An example would be 'credit concentration risk'.
b. Factors not taken into account in the Pillar 1 process. Examples would be interest rate risk in the banking book, business and strategic risks.
c. External factors, such as business cycles, over which banks have little control.
d. Assessment of compliance with minimum standards and disclosure requirements of the more advanced methods in Pillar 1, such as the IRB approach for credit risk or the AMA for operational risk.

Accordingly the Basel Committee has identified four key principles of supervisory review.

Principle 1. Banks should have a process for assessing their overall capital adequacy in relation to their risk profile and a strategy for maintaining their capital levels. (Note that the onus of maintaining adequate capital rests with individual banks.)

Principle 2. Supervisors should review and evaluate banks' internal capital adequacy assessments and strategies, as well as their ability to monitor and ensure their compliance with regulatory capital ratios. Supervisors should take appropriate supervisory action if they are not satisfied with the result of this process.

Principle 3. Supervisors should expect banks to operate above the minimum regulatory capital ratios and should have the ability to require banks to hold capital in excess of the minimum.

Principle 4. Supervisors should seek to intervene at an early stage to prevent capital from falling below the minimum levels required to support the risk characteristics of a particular bank and should require rapid remedial action if capital is not maintained or restored.

Thus, while principles 1 and 3 relate to the expectations of supervisors from banks, principles 2 and 4 delineate the role of supervisors under Pillar 2.

The Committee has emphasized that supervisory review should address risks not addressed under Pillar 1 such as those mentioned in the earlier paragraphs. In addition, supervisors should make rigorous assessments of the following aspects while carrying out their review process, to ensure proper functioning of Pillar 1. These aspects specifically include (a) interest rate risk in the banking book, (b) credit risk, especially with regard to stress tests under the IRB approaches, definition of default, residual risk (where credit risk mitigation techniques are used), credit concentration risk and counter party credit risk, (c) operational risk, and (d) market risk, with special reference to policies and procedures for trading book eligibility, valuation and stress testing and specific risk modelling under the internal models approach.

In view of its growing importance and the scope for innovation, the Committee has laid special emphasis on supervisory review process in securitization transactions.

Finally, as banks move towards greater sophistication in risk management, supervisors should be able to assess banks with greater transparency and accountability. This requirement assumes increased importance in the case of banks' international operations, where supervisors of the countries, where a bank operates, need to have an enhanced degree of cross border communication and co-operation.

Application of Pillar II to Indian Banks The RBI reiterates the Basel Committee principles and the specific areas for supervisory review as given above.

On the basis of the Basel Committee observations, the RBI has introduced unique nomenclatures (and abbreviations) in the implementation of Pillar 2 requirements. Some of these are as follows:

a. The process is known as the supervisory review and evaluation process (SREP) under Pillar 2.
b. An important component of SREP is the internal capital adequacy assessment process (ICAAP).

Banks in India are required to formulate an ICAAP (with Board approval). The ICAAP will be unique to the bank and will be commensurate with its size, level of complexity, risk profile and scope of operations. It is noteworthy that ICAAP will be, in addition to, the Bank's calculation of regulatory capital under Pillar 1. Foreign banks in India and Indian banks with international presence have operationalized their ICAAP from 31 March 2008 and all other commercial banks (excluding local area banks and regional rural banks) from 31 March 2009. The ICAAP document has to be sent to the RBI every year in the prescribed format. The RBI's July, 2013 Master Circular provides detailed guidelines on formulating, reviewing and using the ICAAP as a rigorous management control tool for both the bank and the supervisor.

The SREP will be conducted periodically by the RBI, generally coinciding with the annual financial inspection (AFI) by the RBI. Under this process, the RBI would carry out a comprehensive evaluation to assess the overall capital adequacy of each bank. The ICAAP would be an important input in this process.

The Third Pillar of the Basel II Accord—Market Discipline

Theoretically, regulation aimed at creating and sustaining competition among banks, notably through increased transparency, is believed to play an important role in mitigating bank solvency Problems[42].

Pillar 3—market discipline-serves to complement the requirements of the other two pillars. The key feature of this pillar is 'disclosure'. As banks move towards advanced methodologies of assessing risks, the discretionary element also increases. Market participants would therefore require more information on vital aspects of bank operations, especially those connected with risk exposures and assessment and capital adequacy.

Under this pillar, the Committee has recommended that supervisors use their powers to require banks to disclose information that would lead to a safe and sound banking system. Tables 1–14 of the quoted Basel document (pages 229–242) provide an illustrative list of specific disclosure requirements under various risk heads.

Application of Pillar III to Indian Banks The RBI has formulated disclosure requirements based on the Basel Committee recommendations. The effective dates of commencement of disclosures would be July 1, 2013.

ANNEXURE IV

CAPITAL ADEQUACY RATIOS OF INDIAN BANKS—SOME COMPARATIVE TABLES

TABLE 11.15 COMPARISON OF CAPITAL ADEQUACY RATIOS IN VARIOUS COUNTRIES

Country	2007	2008	2009	2010	2011	2012
			Advanced Economies			
France	...	10.5	12.4	12.7	12.3	14.5
Germany	12.9	13.6	14.8	16.1	16.4	17.9
Greece	11.2	10.0	11.7	12.3	–1.7	9.6
Italy	10.1	10.4	11.7	12.1	12.7	13.3
Japan	13.3	11.3	11.2	13.3	13.8	14.2
Portugal	10.5	9.4	10.5	10.3	9.8	12.6
Spain	11.4	11.3	12.2	11.9	12.1	11.4
United Kingdom	12.6	12.9	14.8	15.9	15.7	16.4
United States	12.8	12.8	13.9	14.8	14.7	14.5
			Emerging Market and Developing Economies			
Russia	15.5	16.8	20.9	18.1	14.7	13.7
China	8.4	12.0	11.4	12.2	12.7	13.3
India	12.3	13.0	14.3	15.2	13.1	13.1
Malaysia	14.8	16.1	18.2	17.5	17.7	17.6
Brazil	18.8	17.7	18.7	16.9	16.3	16.4
Mexico	15.9	15.3	16.5	16.9	15.7	15.9

Note: 2012 data for Italy pertain to June.

Source: RBI—Trend and Progress of Banking in India 2012–13, p. 18, Table II.3.

TABLE 11.16 CAPITAL TO RISK WEIGHTED ASSETS RATIO – BY BANK GROUPS

Item/Bank Group	Basel I 2012	Basel I 2013	Basel II 2012	Basel II 2013
1	2	3	4	5
Public sector banks	11.88	11.31	13.23	12.38
Nationalized banks*	11.84	11.39	13.03	12.26
SBI Group	11.97	11.14	13.70	12.67
Private sector banks	14.47	15.10	16.21	16.84
Old private sector banks	12.47	12.33	14.12	13.73
New private sector banks	14.90	15.71	16.66	17.52
Foreign banks	17.30	18.76	16.75	17.87
Scheduled commercila banks	12.94	12.77	14.24	13.88

Note: * Includes IDBI Bank Ltd.
Source: Based on off-site returns.

(Amount in ₹ Billion)

Item	Basel I 2012	Basel I 2013	Basel II 2012	Basel II 2013
1. Capital funds (i + ii)	7.810	8.906	7.780	8.879
i) Tier I capital	5.686	6.595	5.672	6.580
ii) Tier II capital	2.124	2.311	2.109	2.299
2. Risk-Weighted Assets	60.376	69.742	54.621	63.969
3. CRAR (1 as % of 2)	12.94	12.77	14.24	13.88
Tier I	9.42	9.46	10.38	10.29
Tier II	3.52	3.31	3.86	3.59

Source: RBI -Trend and progress of banking in India—2012–13, Tables IV.10 and IV.11, p. 65.

ENDNOTES

1. Jose A. C. Santos, 'Bank Capital Regulation in Contemporary Banking Theory: A review of literature', *BIS Working Papers* no. 90 (September 2000), Bank for International Settlements, Switzerland.
2. This portion is patterned on the discussion by Timothy, W Koch and S Scott, MacDonald in their book titled 'Bank Management', Chapter 13, pages 501–544, 4th edition, the Dryden Press, USA.
3. *Source*: RBI, 'Trend and Progress of Banking in India—2007–2008' and 'Report on Currency and Finance, 2006-2008', Chapter V titled 'Managing Capital and Risk', both accessed at *www.rbi.org.in*
4. Shubhashis Gangopadhyay and Gurbachan Singh 'Bank Runs, Capital Adequacy and Line of Credit', revised version of discussion paper presented at the Indian Statistical Institute (IST), Delhi Chapter (December 2003): 2.
5. Various documents of the Bank of International Settlements from the Web site http://www.bis.org
6. IMF Working Paper WP/12/90, March 2012, 'Revisiting Risk weighted assets', prepared by Vanessa Le Leslé and Sofiya Avramova, p. 5
7. Basel Committee on banking supervision, 2011, Basel III: A global regulatory framework for more resilient banks and banking systems, revised version, June 2011.
8. Basel committee on banking supervision, 2011, Global systemically important banks: assessment methodology and the additional loss absorbency requirement, Rules text, November 2011, accessed at www.bis.org
9. Will be disclosed by banks from January 1, 2015. Parallel run between January 1, 2013 and January 1, 2017.
10. BCBS, 2011, Global systemically important banks: assessment methodology and the additional loss absorbency requirement–Rules text, November 2011.
11. The FSB's document Reducing the moral hazard posed by systemically important financial institutions, FSB Recommendations and Time Lines, (20 October

2010) is available at www.financialstabilityboard.org/publications/r_101111a.pdf.

12. The banking book represents assets and liabilities of the bank, contracted with the intention of building a relationship or for steady income or statutory obligations and are generally held till maturity. In contrast, the trading book assets are primarily held for generating profits on short term differences between prices/yields. Thus while price risk is of prime concern to banks on the trading book, earnings or economic value changes are the main focus of the banking book.
13. This Section is based primarily on a) RBI Master circular—'Prudential Guidelines on Capital Adequacy and Market Discipline—New Capital Adequacy Framework (NCAF)' dated July 1, 2013, and b) Master circular-Basel III Capital regulations, dated June 1, 2013, both accessed at www.rbi.org.in
14. RBI Master circular—Basel III Capital regulations, dated June 1, 2013, accessed at www.rbi.org.in.
15. Both the Basel III document and the RBI guidelines call Tier 1 capital 'going concern' capital, and Tier 2 capital 'gone concern' capital. The rationale for this is that from regulatory capital perspective, going-concern capital is the capital which can absorb losses without triggering bankruptcy of the bank. Gone-concern capital is the capital which will absorb losses only in a situation of liquidation of the bank.
16. There is no direct prescription for minimum common equity. However, non-common equity elements in Tier 1 are restricted to a maximum 40 per cent of Tier 1 capital. Accordingly, indirectly minimum common equity is considered as 3.6 per cent of Tier 1 capital for banks in India.
17. Common Equity is recognized as the highest quality component of capital and is the primary form of funding which ensures that a bank remains solvent.
18. A consolidated bank is defined by the RBI in the above circular as 'a group of entities where a licensed bank is the controlling entity'. The RBI guidelines on consolidated banks issued in 2003 exclude group companies engaged in Insurance business and those *not* engaged in financial services.
19. RBI, Circular—'Introduction of Advanced Approaches of Basel II Framework in India-Time Schedule' (July 7 2009).
20. These are recorded as on balance sheet exposures by the originating bank, representing valuation of future cash flows related to margin income to be derived from the underlying exposures and is subordinated to the claims of other parties to the transaction in terms of priority of repayment. (RBI circular): 30.
21. Section 7 of the RBI Master Circular describes the guidelines to be followed by banks seeking capital relief for use of CRM techniques. An illustrative example for calculation of 'exposure' for calculating risk-weighted assets (RWA) is provided in Annexure 8.
22. Short positions not permitted in India except in the case of derivatives.
23. 'Duration' is not to be confused with the security's maturity. It is the measure of the price sensitivity of a fixed-income security to an interest rate change of 100 bps. It represents the time period within which the investment can be recouped and is calculated as the weighted average of the present values of all cash flows over the life of the instrument or asset. Duration is measured in years. However, this is not to be confused with the security's maturity. For all securities, duration is shorter than maturity except in the case of zero coupon bonds.
24. 'Duration' as defined above is also called 'Macaulay's duration'. However, to assess the effect of a 1 per cent change in interest rate on the price of the security, 'modified duration' is used. 'Modified duration' follows the concept that interest rates and bond prices move in opposite directions. It is used to determine the effect that a 1 per cent change in interest rate will have on the price of a bond. The concepts of 'duration' and 'modified duration' have been discussed in more detail in the chapter on 'Risk Management.'
25. The illustrations have been adapted from *Annexure II* of the RBI's 'Master Circular—Prudential Norms on Capital Adequacy—Basel I Framework' (1 July 2009).
26. For more discussion on interest rate derivatives, please refer to chapter on 'Risk Management'.
27. Any deal which has not been settled by physical payment or reversed by an equal and opposite deal for the same date.
28. Capital charge for general market risk for equities is 9 per cent. (Thus, general market risk capital charge on equities would work out to ₹27 crores).
29. Capital charge on forex/gold position would be computed at 9 per cent. (Thus, the capital charge works out to ₹9 crores).
30. Basel Committee on Banking Supervision, 'International Convergence of Capital Measurement and Capital Standards—A Revised Framework' (June 2006).
31. The banking book represents assets and liabilities of the bank, contracted with the intention of building a relationship or for steady income or statutory obligations and are generally held till maturity. In contrast, the trading book assets are primarily held for generating profits on short-term differences between prices/yields. Thus, while price risk is of prime concern to banks on the trading book, earnings or economic value changes are the main focus of the banking book.
32. The notations used by the Committee follow those used by Standard and Poor's (S&P). The use of S&P ratings is indicative and the ratings of other accredited rating agencies could also be used.
33. MDBs currently eligible for 0 per cent risk-weight are: the World Bank group which comprises the International bank for Reconstruction and Development (IBRD), the International Finance Corporation (IFC), the Asian Development Bank (ADB), the African Development Bank (AfDB), the European Bank for Reconstruction and Development (EBRD), the Inter American Development Bank (IADB), the European Investment Bank (EIB), the European Investment Fund (EIF), the Nordic

Investment Bank (NIB), the Caribbean Development Bank (CDB), the Islamic Development Bank (IDB) and the Council of Europe Development Banks (CEDB).

34. See chapters on 'Credit Risk' for a detailed discussion on CRM.

35. Basel Committee on Banking Supervision, 'Enhancements to the Basel II Framework', Bank for International Settlements, accessed at www.bis.org (July 2009), and Basel III June 2011.

36. The Basel II document proposing enhancements to the framework defines resecuritization as 'A resecuritization exposure is a securitization exposure in which the risk associated with an underlying pool of exposures is trenched and at least one of the underlying exposures is a securitization exposure. In addition, an exposure to one or more resecuritization exposures is a resecuritization exposure' (July 2009): 2, para 541(i).

37. A financial instrument is defined as any contract that gives rise to both a financial asset of one entity and a financial liability or equity instrument of another entity. Financial instruments include both primary financial instruments (and cash instruments) and derivative financial instruments. A financial asset is any asset that is cash, the right to receive cash or another financial asset or the contractual right to exchange financial assets on potentially favourable terms or an equity instrument. A financial liability is the contractual obligation to deliver cash or another financial asset or to exchange financial liabilities under conditions that are potentially unfavourable.

38. Basel Committee on Banking Supervision, 'Revisions to the Basel II Market Risk Framework' Bank for International Settlements, accessed at www.bis.org (July 2009).

39. Basel Committee on Banking Supervision, 'Guidelines for Computing Capital for Incremental Risk in the Trading Book', Bank for International settlements, accessed at www.bis.org (July 2009).

40. Detailed discussions on Pillar 2 and Pillar 3 can be found in pages 204–225 and 226–242, respectively of the Basel Committee document 'International Convergence of Capital Measurement and Capital Standards—A Revised Framework, Comprehensive Version', can be accessed at www.bis.org (July 2006). and Basel III June, 2011.

41. RBI Master circular – Basel III regulations, dated July 1, 2013

42. Observation made in RBI's 'Report on Currency and Finance—2006–2008,' Chapter V: 189

CHAPTER TWELVE

Managing Interest Rate and Liquidity Risks

CHAPTER STRUCTURE

KEY TAKEAWAYS FROM THE CHAPTER

- Understand why risk management is important for banks.
- Understand sources of asset liability risk, interest rate risk and liquidity risk.
- Learn how interest rate risk is managed.
- Learn how interest rate derivatives work.
- Learn how liquidity can be managed.

"The business of banking is the business of risk management; plain and simple, that is business of banking."

—Walter Wriston, Ex CEO, Citibank

SECTION I

THE CHANGING FACE OF BANKING RISKS

Consider a bank that borrows ₹100 crores at 5 per cent for a year, and lends the money at 5.5 per cent to a highly rated borrower for 5 years. For simplicity, let us assume interest rates are to remain fixed over the period of the loan; they are annually compounded and all interest accumulates to the maturity of the respective obligations. The net transaction appears profitable since the bank is earning a 50 basis point spread.

But the transaction is not without risks.

- At the end of a year, the bank will have to repay ₹100 crores to the depositor(s), and find new sources of financing for the loan, which still has 4 years to maturity. If the bank is not able to find sources for repayment, it runs a 'liquidity' risk, which could threaten the 'solvency' of the bank.
- At the end of the year, if interest rates have risen, the bank would have to pay a higher rate of interest on the new financing, thus narrowing the spread. Suppose, at the end of a year, an applicable 4-year interest rate is 6 per cent. The bank is in trouble. It is going to earn 5.5 per cent on its loan and pay 6 per cent on its financing. In short, the bank will be losing money on this transaction! Thus, the transaction has also entailed an 'interest rate' risk for the bank, which would impact the bank's net income

Also consider the following scenarios:

1. Ninety per cent of Bank A's liabilities mature within the next 12 months. Bank A has invested 80 per cent of these funds in securities maturing after 5 years.
2. Ninety per cent of Bank B's liabilities mature within the next 12 months. Bank B lends 75 per cent of these funds to various infrastructure projects, where the repayments will start after an initial payment holiday of 2 years.
3. Eighty per cent of Bank C's liabilities mature after 3 years and have been borrowed at fixed cost. Interest rates are on a downward trend, and 80 per cent of Bank C's loan portfolio consists of short-term loans to be fully repaid over the next 6 months.
4. Bank D has entered into dollar forward contracts at a premium for 6 months on behalf of its importer borrowers, who form about 60 per cent of the bank's loan portfolio. There is a fall in dollar value during this period.

What are the potential dangers in each of the above scenarios?

In the first two scenarios, the banks face a liquidity risk. When the liability holders demand their money in the next 12 months, the banks may not have enough cash to repay them, since the cash flow from the assets would be delayed beyond this period. In the third scenario, Bank C faces an interest rate risk. The short-term loans would be repaid, and the cash inflow will have to be lent by the bank at the prevailing lower rates, while the bank will have to continue paying interest on liabilities at the original contract rates till they mature. The bank's spreads would narrow further and impact the net earnings. Bank D, evidently, faces an exchange rate risk.

The primary problem in these examples was a 'mismatch' between the bank's assets and liabilities. Prior to the 1970s, many firms in developed countries intentionally mismatched their balance sheets, and borrowed short and lent long to earn a spread, taking advantage of the upward sloping yield curves. Interest rates in developed countries experienced only modest fluctuations, so losses, if any, due to asset-liability mismatches were trivial.

Things started to change in the 1970s, which ushered in a period of volatile interest rates that continued into the early 1980s. The 1980s and 1990s also saw a new wave of banking crises in the developed world and emerging markets. These events challenged the traditional view that 'runs' on solvent banks were at the heart of banking panics and that panics were the main causes for banking crises. The striking fact here was that 'bank runs' had played a negligible role in most of these events.

With new financial instruments such as derivatives, new participants such as hedge funds and new technologies such as e-banking, the informational efficiency of markets to match savings with investment opportunities improved substantially in the early years of the 21st century.

The growth in derivatives markets has no doubt increased the tools available to firms to take on and manage risks, but has also made risk exposure assessment tougher for regulators, as the financial crisis of 2007 has amply demonstrated. For example, a bank can take large risks through trading of derivatives, without making the exposure visible on its balance sheet. Traditionally, banks exposed themselves to interest rate risks by taking deposits, making loans or buying securities. With derivatives, banks can use swaps to take on the same interest rate risk as, say, in the case of buying bonds. However, the swaps are not recorded on the banks' balance sheets because the value of swaps at inception is typically zero. After inception of the swap, mark-to-market accounting requires the banks to record the market value of the swap, but that market value provides little indication of the magnitude of banks' interest rate exposure.

Moreover, banks could improve their traditional 'return on equity' measure through taking on risks for fee-based activities, without capital outlay.

Such developments have forced bank regulators and market participants to look for risk management approaches that would go beyond mere accounting numbers to capture realistic assessments of adverse outcomes, and reveal the actual risks borne by financial institutions. Figure 12.1 illustrates the sources of banking risks.

FIGURE 12.1 SOURCES OF BANKING RISKS

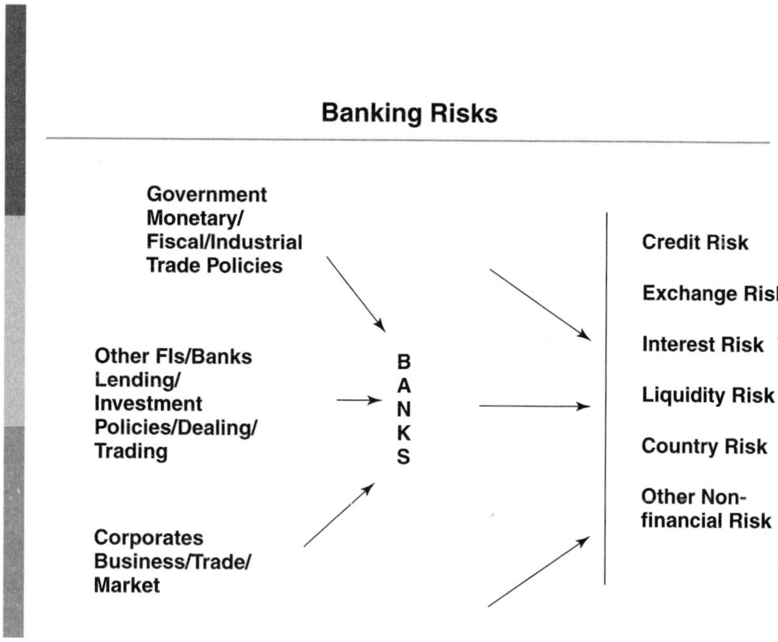

From Figure 12.1 and our discussions in earlier chapters, it is evident that banks are subject to various interdependent risks. Though, for convenience of measurement and analysis we isolate them, in reality, what starts off, say as a credit risk event, can snowball into a bundle of other risks as well. For the same reason, it appears difficult to conclude about the overwhelming cause of the financial crisis of 2007—was it subprime lending practices, or financial instruments, such as the Credit Default Swap or CDOs, or was it transactions such as securitization, or was it excesses in human greed and negligence?

However, one inference is clear—all banks and financial institutions will have to undertake a profound revision of their approach to risk management.

A relook at risk management does not imply that banks scale down their risk appetite, which is essential for future progress and survival in a competitive and developing environment. The implication only highlights the need for banks to state their risk policies more clearly and stringently, and ensure strict adherence to the policies and safeguards.

To complement the published work of a number of eminent bodies on the financial crisis of 2007, a unique private sector initiative termed the Counter party Risk Management Policy Group III (CRMPG III) was formed in April 2008, chaired by top bankers from HSBC and Goldman Sachs.[1] The Policy Group members are drawn from various leading multinational banks. The scope of this initiative was designed to focus primarily on the steps that the private sector should take to avoid future financial shocks.

The Policy Group identifies some common features characterizing the post 1980 financial crises—(a) credit concentrations, (b) broad-based maturity mismatches, (c) excessive leverage, and (d) the illusion of market liquidity. It also includes a 'wild card' in the form of macroeconomic imbalances. Overarching all these factors is collective human behaviour, where financial institutions tend to take on disproportionate risks on the upside of business or financial market cycles, and pull back fiercely when the cycle is on the downturn. In this context, the Group recognizes the need for private initiative to ably complement supervisory oversight to mitigate banking risks.

The Group has developed 'core precepts' to provide the broad framework for risk management in banks that focus on the basics of (a) corporate governance, (b) risk monitoring, (c) estimating risk appetite, (d) contagion effects, and (e) enhanced oversight. The salient features of the recommendations in respect of these precepts call for the highest quality of risk management and governance within the bank, and supervision by external administrators.

We have discussed credit, market and operational risks in earlier chapters. In the following sections of this chapter, we will discuss the 'wild card' risk that broadly translates into interest rate risk, and most important, liquidity risk, a product of the various factors listed above.

SECTION II

ASSET LIABILITY MANAGEMENT

Risk management is uniquely important for financial institutions because, in contrast to firms in other industries, their liabilities are a source of wealth creation for their shareholders.[2]

Over the years, banks have been focusing on 'asset-liability risk' to mitigate balance sheet weaknesses. The problem is not that the market value of assets might fall or that the value of liabilities might rise. It is that capital might be depleted by narrowing of the difference between assets and liabilities, since the values of assets and liabilities may not always move together, in the same direction. Asset-liability risk, therefore, is a 'leveraged' risk. As we have already seen, the capital of banks is small relative to the firm's assets or liabilities, so small percentage changes in assets or liabilities can translate into large percentage changes in capital.

The Asset-liability risk described above could manifest itself in more than one form, but what would concern bankers most would be two important risks—'interest rate' risk and 'liquidity' risk. While interest rate risk would directly impact the net income of the bank, the liquidity risk would endanger the very solvency of the bank.

The above need for risk management led to the evolution of *Asset-liability management* (ALM) in the 1980s. In a way, ALM was seen to substitute for market-value accounting[3] in a context of accrual (book value) accounting. Traditionally, banks and insurance companies have been using accrual accounting for essentially all their assets and liabilities. They would take on liabilities, such as deposits, life insurance policies or annuities. They would invest the proceeds from these liabilities in assets such as loans, bonds or real estate. All assets and liabilities were held at book values. Doing so did not recognize the possible risks arising from how the assets and liabilities were structured, or how the markets were moving. To overcome these shortcomings, a combination of ALM and market value accounting was advocated.

However, many of the assets and liabilities of financial institutions cannot be marked to market. A firm can earn significant mark-to-market profits but go bankrupt due to inadequate cash flow. Market-value accounting was therefore not the ideal solution.

However, where found suitable, banks are increasingly using market-value accounting for certain business lines. This is true of universal banks with trading operations, which find techniques of market risk management such as Value at Risk (VaR),[4] market risk limits, etc. more appropriate. On the other hand, ALM is associated with those assets and liabilities—those business lines—that are accounted for on an accrual basis. This includes bank lending and deposit taking.

In short, ALM is concerned with strategic balance sheet management. Risks caused by changes in interest rates and exchange rates, credit risk and the bank's liquidity position have to be monitored and mitigated. With profitability of banking operations and the long-term solvency of banks becoming key factors, it has now become imperative for banks to move away from partial asset management (credit, non-performing assets) and partial liability management (deposits) to integrated balance sheet management. In such an approach, all components of a bank's balance sheet, their maturity mix, their pricing and risks will be looked at not only from the angle of profitability, but also from the angle of solvency and long-term sustenance.

Techniques of ALM have been evolving over time. Banks typically have an Asset Liability Management Committee (ALCO) that comprises of a group of top or senior management personnel entrusted with the responsibility of managing the bank's assets and liabilities to balance the various risk exposures, to enable the bank achieve its operating objectives.

Table 12.1 depicts the shift from traditional ALM objectives and practices to modern ALM techniques.

TABLE 12.1[5] TRADITIONAL ALM OBJECTIVES AND PRACTICES TO MODERN ALM TECHNIQUES

Traditional ALM	Modern ALM
Focus on short-term earnings.	Focus on earnings and value.
Subjective scenarios based on parallel shifts.	Objective scenarios based on statistical models complemented by all manner of subjective scenarios.
Focus on home-currency interest-rate risk.	Include all risk factors including foreign exchange, basis, credit, commodities, and equity.
Assumption of static portfolio (or, at least dynamic behavior) that is scenario independent.	Dynamic evalution of the balance sheet encompassing growth forecasts, reinvestment and hedging strategies.

Source: Black, Richard, Brown, Karl, and Moloney, James, 2003, 'Asset and liability management: What does the future have in store?', Balance Sheet, Volume 11, No 2 (2003), page 33.

At present, in almost all banks, ALCO has the responsibility to devise broad strategies for handling banks' competing long-term needs, and also monitor and manage interrelated risk exposures on a daily basis. Therefore, the ALCO of a bank is the focal point for coordinating the bank's diverse activities to accomplish its operating objectives. Towards this objective, the ALCO receives and analyzes a wide variety of reports that bring together information on the bank's asset/liability positions, its capital level, its internal plans and current and projected external conditions. Some typical types of information and analyzes the ALCO might receive include (a) information on current and projected national and local economic conditions, (b) interest rate forecasts, (c) current loan and deposit positions, showing the asset and liability mix, highlighting concentrated exposures, (d) forecasts of cash inflows and outflows on account of assets and liabilities, based on commitments and likely trends, (e) the current and projected liquidity position for the bank, and (f) an analysis of the potential effects of interest rate risk on the bank's income and capital position.

Most ALCOs primarily focus on managing the bank's liquidity and interest rate risks, while a separate committee would be involved in managing credit risks. In practice, evaluating interest rate and liquidity risks involve the consideration of different possible scenarios. For example:

- What if the bank experiences an unexpectedly large volume of deposit withdrawals?
- What if loan repayments occur earlier than anticipated? Or later than due date? Or not at all?
- What happens if interest rates suddenly rise by *x* basis points?
- What happens if counterparties do not keep up commitments? Or off-balance sheet items turn into real cash outflows?

The ALCO's challenge is to assess the probability with which similar events would occur, and position the bank to handle the most likely scenarios with the minimum impact on the bank's expected performance and solvency.

The ALCO will therefore operate with the objectives of (a) assessing the probability of various liquidity shocks, (b) assessing the probability of various interest rate scenarios and their impact on the bank's net income, (c) positioning the bank to handle the most likely of these scenarios at minimum cost (impact on net income and the bank's capital), while achieving a reasonable profitability level, and (d) allocating the bank's remaining assets and liabilities to meet risk and profitability objectives.

ALM departments also handle foreign exchange and other risks. The growth of derivatives markets helped in ALM by facilitating a variety of hedging strategies, while securitization allowed banks to directly address asset-liability risk by removing assets from their balance sheets.

Of the important risks that ALM addresses, interest rate risk and liquidity risk are accorded paramount importance. We shall study these in detail in the following sections.

SECTION III

INTEREST RATE RISK MANAGEMENT

Simply stated, interest rate risk is the exposure of a bank's financial condition to adverse movements in interest rates. If accepted and managed as a normal part of banking business, interest rate risk can be used to enhance profitability and shareholder value. However, excessive interest rate risk could lead to substantial volatility in earnings and thus also affect the underlying value of the bank's assets, liabilities and off-balance sheet instruments. Hence, an effective risk management process that aims at sound financial health of a bank would have to maintain interest rate risk within prudent levels. The two most common perspectives for assessing a bank's interest rate risk exposure are (a) the *earnings perspective* that focuses on short-term earnings, and (b) the *economic value* perspective that looks at the long-term economic viability of the bank

Why are two approaches necessary? The 'earnings perspective' assesses the impact of changes in interest rates on the 'net interest income' (NII) (difference between total interest earned from loans and investments and total interest paid on deposits and borrowings) of the bank. This is the traditional method of risk assessment since reduced net interest earnings could threaten the financial stability of the bank and also impair market confidence. However, banks have been able to generate non-interest income from fee-based activities, such as loan servicing, transaction processing, off-balance sheet transactions or managing securitization pools, most of which depend on the way credit markets perform. Hence, a major portion of the fee-based income could also be interest rate sensitive, and banks would have to look at the impact of interest rate variations on net income as well.

'Value' or 'economic value' generally represents the present value of expected future net cash flows, discounted at appropriate market rates. For a bank, expected net cash flows would arise as the difference between expected cash flows on assets and the expected cash flows on liabilities, plus the expected net cash flows arising from off-balance sheet activities. We have seen earlier how variations in market interest rates can impact the economic value of banking assets, liabilities and off-balance sheet positions (contingent liabilities). Thus, the sensitivity of a bank's economic value to fluctuations in interest rates is of great importance to all stakeholders—investors, management and supervisors—since it reflects the sensitivity of the bank's 'net worth' to changes in interest rates. It is evident that the economic value perspective is more comprehensive and long term than the earnings perspective, since it considers the potential impact of interest rate fluctuations on future cash flows. This long-term perspective is valuable since short-term changes in earnings of a bank, which is the focus of the earnings perspective, cannot indicate realistically the impact of interest rate movements on the bank's overall positions, and hence, its financial health in the long run.

But it is not always future interest rates that impact a bank's financial performance. Past interest rates also have a continuing impact on future performance. For example, a long term, fixed-rate loan contract (as in the example quoted at the beginning of this chapter) may have to be refinanced at higher interest rates over the tenor of the loan. Securities not marked to market may contain embedded gains or losses due to past rate movements, which would be reflected over time in the bank's earnings. Hence, the impact of such 'embedded' losses or gains due to past interest rates would also have to be assessed realistically.

Assessment of the extent of a bank's interest rate risk by any of the perspectives given above would not be a simple exercise. Every asset on the bank's balance sheet has different risk and return characteristics, different possible sources, repricing[6] periods and so on. Box 12.1 presents some of the common sources of interest rate risk. The exercise would be rendered more complex by the discretion that the bank can exercise in adjusting the rates on assets and liabilities, or the likelihood of a change in bank customer behaviour (early repayment of loans or withdrawal of deposits) due to changes in market rates, or the interest rate sensitivity of fee-based income (non-interest income) and off-balance sheet exposures. In practice, banks will generally have a mix of all types of interest rate risk, with the effects potentially offsetting or reinforcing one another. It is the complexity of the resulting combination of factors that makes interest rate risk difficult to manage.

BOX 12.1 SOURCES OF INTEREST RATE RISK

As financial intermediaries, banks encounter interest rate risks arising from several factors fundamental to the business of banking. Some of the most discussed sources of interest rate risk are given as follows:

1. **Repricing risk:** The primary and frequently discussed form of interest rate risk arises when the average yield on a bank's assets or the average cost of its liabilities is more sensitive to changes in market interest rates. The difference in sensitivity could arise from possible mismatches in the asset and liability characteristics of the bank. First, fixed rate assets and liabilities could have different maturities. Second, floating rate assets and liabilities could have different repricing periods, with different base rates. For example, assets could reprice annually based on a 1-year rate and liabilities could reprice quarterly based on a 3-month base rate. Third, floating rate assets and liabilities could have base rates of different maturities, such as assets that reprice annually based on a long-term rate and liabilities that reprice annually based on a 1-year rate. Fourth, in countries with deregulated interest rates, banks can adjust pricing at will, and the rate-setting policies that banks follow determine the effective repricing behaviour of such instruments. The pricing decisions in these cases would then depend on a variety of factors in addition to market interest rates, such as the expected behaviour of bank customers and the extent of competition in the markets concerned. Finally, in some cases, bank customers have the option either to repay loans or withdraw their deposits at low (or no) cost, and the decisions of such customers would influence the response of the average pricing of such assets or liabilities to changes in market interest rates. Such repricing mismatches, though inherent to the business of banking, can expose a bank's income and underlying economic value to unanticipated fluctuations as interest rates vary. For instance, a bank that funded a long-term fixed-rate loan with a short-term deposit could face a decline in both the future income arising from the position and its underlying value if interest rates increase. These declines arise because the cash flows on the loan are fixed over its lifetime, while the interest paid on the funding is variable, and increases after the short-term deposit matures.
2. **Yield curve risk:** Even if, on an average, the yields on a bank's assets and liabilities adjust to changes in market rates to the same extent, a bank may still be subject to yield curve risk. Yield curve risk is the possibility that changes in the shape of the yield curve[7] could have differential effects on the bank's assets and liabilities. For example, if a bank's assets and liabilities reprice annually, it might want to balance a medium-term base rate for its assets with a mixture of

short-term and long-term base rates for its liabilities. In that case, increased curvature of the yield curve would boost medium-term yields relative to short- and long-term yields, and thus raise the rate on the bank's assets relative to the average cost of its liabilities, and reduce short-term earnings volatility.

Repricing mismatches can also expose a bank to changes in the slope and shape of the yield curve. Yield curve risk arises when unanticipated shifts of the yield curve have adverse effects on a bank's income or underlying economic value. *Annexure I* provides an overview of the theory of interest rates, to enable understand the concept of yield curves.

3. **Basis risk:** If the instruments have different base rates, the bank will be subject to basis risk. For example, yields on a bank's floating rate assets could be tied to government security yields, while those on its floating rate liabilities could be based on an interbank rate such as the Libor. There is a possibility that the two base rates will diverge unexpectedly owing to differing credit risk or liquidity characteristics, which might increase private yields relative to government yields. In that case, the cost of bank liabilities would increase, relative to the yield on assets, thus lowering the bank's earnings.
4. **Optionality:** An increasingly important source of interest rate risk arises from the options embedded in many bank assets, liabilities, and off-balance sheet portfolios. Simply stated, an option provides the holder the right, but not the obligation, to buy, sell, or in some manner alter the cash flow of an instrument or financial contract. Options may be stand-alone such as exchange-traded options and over-the-counter (OTC) contracts, or may be embedded within otherwise standard instruments. While banks use exchange-traded and OTC options in both trading and non-trading accounts, instruments with embedded options are generally more important in non-trading activities. For example, bonds/securities may include options. Call options are typically exercised by the issuers to redeem bonds before maturity, while put options are exercised by investors to seek redemption before maturity. Such options could expose banks to interest rate risk. For example, if call option on the bonds are exercised when interest rates are declining, the bank investing in these bonds would run a 'reinvestment risk', since the intermediate cash flows from bond redemption would have to be reinvested at a lower rate. If, on the other hand, the bank has issued bonds with a put option, and interest rates are rising, the bank would face a 'prepayment risk' when investors seek redemption before maturity. The bank, in such cases, may have to borrow from the market at higher rates to pay the bondholders. Both these options, therefore, would cause earnings volatility for the bank.

   Other examples of instruments with embedded options would be loans that give borrowers the right to prepay balances, or transaction deposit instruments that give depositors the right to withdraw funds at any time, often without any penalties.

   If not adequately managed, the asymmetrical payoff characteristics of instruments with optionality features can pose significant risk particularly to those who sell them, since the options held, both explicit and embedded, are generally exercised to the advantage of the holder and the disadvantage of the seller. Moreover, an increasing array of options can involve significant leverage which can magnify the influences (both negative and positive) of option positions on the financial condition of the firm.
5. **Other sources of risk:** Banks may also be subject to interest rate risk through interest sensitivity of their non-interest income. For example, lower interest rates could lead to prepayments (with the intention of refinancing the loans) that deplete the pool of loans serviced by a bank, thereby reducing its fee income, and also leading to a 'prepayment' risk. In a declining interest rate scenario, the cash inflows from prepayments could be invested only at lower rates, thus leading to more earnings volatility. More significant would be the substantial interest rate exposures embedded in the off-balance sheet positions of large banks, held either as a hedge for their on-balance sheet interest rate exposures or as a result of their trading activity in derivatives markets.

Source: Bank for International Settlements, Basel.

Managing Interest Rate Risk

In order to understand interest rate risk, one has to understand the nature of interest rates. The management of interest rate risk depends substantially on predicting how interest rates would behave in future. If interest rates can be forecasted with a great deal of accuracy, interest rate risk is mitigated to a very large extent. Predicting future interest rates essentially involves predicting the shape of the future 'yield curve'. *Annexure I* provides an overview of the various theories of interest rates, and how they could be used in predicting interest rate movements.

The Basel Committee on Banking Supervision[8] states that sound interest rate risk management involves the application of four basic elements in the management of assets, liabilities and off-balance sheet instruments:

- Appropriate board and senior management oversight.
- Adequate risk management policies and procedures.
- Appropriate risk measurement, monitoring and control functions.
- Comprehensive internal controls and independent audits.

The Committee further adds that 'the specific manner in which a bank applies these elements in managing its interest rate risk will depend upon the complexity and nature of its holdings and activities, as well as on the level of interest rate risk exposure'. Adequate interest rate risk management practices can therefore vary considerably.

The Committee also believes that interest rate risk monitoring should be done on a consolidated, comprehensive basis. Such monitoring should, therefore, include interest rate exposures in banks' subsidiaries. However, consolidation may also underestimate risk when positions in one affiliate may offset positions in another affiliate.

Box 12.2 sets out the 'Principles for interest rate Risk management' derived from the above-mentioned four basic elements delineated by the Basel Committee.

BOX 12.2 BASEL COMMITTEE FOR BANKING SUPERVISION—PRINCIPLES OF INTEREST RATE RISK MANAGEMENT—JULY 2004[9]

Board and senior management oversight of interest rate risk

Principle 1: In order to carry out its responsibilities, the board of directors in a bank should approve strategies and policies with respect to interest rate risk management and ensure that senior management takes the steps necessary to monitor and control these risks consistent with the approved strategies and policies. The board of directors should be informed regularly of the interest rate risk exposure of the bank in order to assess the monitoring and controlling of such risk against the board's guidance on the levels of risk that are acceptable to the bank.

Principle 2: Senior management must ensure that the structure of the bank's business and the level of interest rate risk it assumes are effectively managed, that appropriate policies and procedures are established to control and limit these risks, and that resources are available for evaluating and controlling interest rate risk.

Principle 3: Banks should clearly define the individuals and/or committees responsible for managing interest rate risk and should ensure that there is adequate separation of duties in key elements of the risk management process to avoid potential conflicts of interest. Banks should have risk measurement, monitoring and control functions with clearly defined duties that are sufficiently independent from position-taking functions of the bank and which report risk exposures directly to senior management and the board of directors. Larger or more complex banks should have a designated independent unit responsible for the design and administration of the bank's interest rate risk measurement, monitoring and control functions.

Adequate risk management policies and procedures

Principle 4: It is essential that banks' interest rate risk policies and procedures are clearly defined and consistent with the nature and complexity of their activities. These policies should be applied on a consolidated basis and, as appropriate, at the level of individual affiliates, especially when recognizing legal distinctions and possible obstacles to cash movements among affiliates.

Principle 5: It is important that banks identify the risks inherent in new products and activities and ensure these are subject to adequate procedures and controls before being introduced or undertaken. Major hedging or risk management initiatives should be approved in advance by the board or its appropriate delegated committee.

Risk measurement, monitoring and control functions

Principle 6: It is essential that banks have interest rate risk measurement systems that capture all material sources of interest rate risk and that assess the effect of interest rate changes in ways that are consistent with the scope of their activities. The assumptions underlying the system should be clearly understood by risk managers and bank management.

Principle 7: Banks must establish and enforce operating limits and other practices that maintain exposures within levels consistent with their internal policies.

Principle 8: Banks should measure their vulnerability to loss under stressful market conditions—including the breakdown of key assumptions—and consider those results when establishing and reviewing their policies and limits for interest rate risk.

Principle 9: Banks must have adequate information systems for measuring, monitoring, controlling and reporting interest rate exposures. Reports must be provided on a timely basis to the bank's board of directors, senior management and, where appropriate, individual business line managers.

Internal controls

Principle 10: Banks must have an adequate system of internal controls over their interest rate risk management process. A fundamental component of the internal control system involves regular independent reviews and evaluations of the effectiveness of the system and, where necessary, ensuring that appropriate revisions or enhancements to internal controls are made. The results of such reviews should be available to the relevant supervisory authorities.

Information for supervisory authorities

Principle 11: Supervisory authorities should obtain from banks sufficient and timely information with which to evaluate their level of interest rate risk. This information should take appropriate account of the range of maturities and currencies in each bank's portfolio, including off-balance sheet items, as well as other relevant factors, such as the distinction between trading and non-trading activities.

Capital adequacy

Principle 12: Banks must hold capital commensurate with the level of interest rate risk they undertake.

Disclosure of interest rate risk

Principle 13: Banks should release to the public information on the level of interest rate risk and their policies for its management.

Supervisory treatment of interest rate risk in the banking book

Principle 14: Supervisory authorities must assess whether the internal measurement systems of banks adequately capture the interest rate risk in their banking book. If a bank's internal measurement system does not adequately capture the interest rate risk, the bank must bring the system to the required standard. To facilitate supervisors' monitoring of interest rate risk exposures across institutions, banks must provide the results of their internal measurement systems, expressed in terms of the threat to economic value, using a standardized interest rate shock.

Principle 15: If supervisors determine that a bank is not holding capital commensurate with the level of interest rate risk in the banking book, they should consider remedial action, requiring the bank either to reduce its risk or hold a specific additional amount of capital, or a combination of both.

Source: Basel Committee on Banking Supervision.

We have seen earlier in this chapter that a bank's ALCO, alternatively known as the 'Risk Management committee' is responsible for measuring and monitoring interest rate risk. This brings us to the next important question: How do we *measure* interest rate risk, with all the complexities described above?

Measuring Interest Rate Risk[10]

Banks use various techniques to measure the exposure of earnings and economic value to changes in interest rates. These techniques range from simple calculations relying on basic maturity and repricing tables based on current and projected on- and off-balance sheet positions, to highly sophisticated dynamic modelling techniques. These measures can assess interest rate risk exposure from the earnings, or economic view perspectives or both. The methods also vary in their ability to capture different forms of interest rate exposure—the simpler methods aim at capturing risks arising from maturity and repricing mismatches, while the more sophisticated methods are designed to capture a fuller range of risk exposures.

An ideal approach to measuring interest rate risk would have to capture the entire range of potential movements in interest rates, taking into account specific characteristics of each interest rate sensitive asset and liability of a bank. However, this may not be possible in practice, and simplified assumptions will have to be incorporated into the approaches. Hence, the various measurement approaches would have their unique strengths and weaknesses in terms of accurately and realistically measuring interest rate risk exposure of a bank. For instance, in some approaches, positions may be aggregated into broad categories, rather than taken separately, injecting a degree of measurement error into the estimation of their interest rate sensitivity. In some approaches, the nature of interest rate movements that can be incorporated may be limited. In other approaches, only a parallel shift of the yield curve may be assumed or less than perfect correlations between interest rates may not be taken into account. Importantly, the various approaches differ in their ability to capture the optionality inherent in many positions and instruments.

Before we examine the various approaches, we will have to understand what determines interest rate 'sensitivity'. Typically, a bank's asset or liability is classified as rate sensitive *within a specified time interval* or 'bucket', if:

- It matures during the time interval.
- The interest rate applied to the outstanding advance changes contractually during the interval.
- It represents an interim or partial principal payment.
- The outstanding principal can be repriced when some base rate or index changes, and there is an expectation that the base rate or index may change during the interval.

We will elucidate further. For example, if the bank is considering interest rate risk that would arise in the 0–90 day time interval, the primary issue will be to identify the assets and liabilities on the balance sheet that will be repriced during the ensuing 90 day period, given the specific interest rate forecast or expectation. Any asset or liability that matures during this period will have to be repriced since the bank must reinvest the proceeds from the asset. Similarly, any deposit that matures for payment during this period will have to be replaced, or the deposit rate will have to be reset. Thus, any investment security, loan, deposit, or longer-term liabilities or assets that mature during this 90-day period would be 'rate sensitive'. In more general terms, any principal payment expected to be received during this 90-day period—final or interim—is rate sensitive. Further, some assets and liabilities earn or pay rates that are contractually linked to a changing index or base rate. These instruments are termed 'rate sensitive' if a change is expected in the index or base rate during the 90-day period, since any change in the index or base rate will lead to repricing. However, even when there is no definite knowledge of when the base rate will change, the instrument will remain rate sensitive, since there is a possibility that its yield can change at any time.

TEASE THE CONCEPT

Are these assets and liabilities rate sensitive during a 6-month period?

- 3–month treasury bills.
- Short term consumer loans.
- Savings bank deposits.
- a 7–year floating rate industrial loan with semi annual interest payments.
- a 15–year fixed rate housing loan with quarterly interest payments.

There are several modelling approaches to judge a bank's earnings and capital exposure to changing interest rates. The focus here is on three of the most popular of these approaches: Gap analysis, Earnings at Risk (EAR) models and Economic Value of Equity (EVE) models. Typically, Gap and EAR are used to assess earnings exposure to interest rate movements. EVE is used to assess capital risk.

Method 1: Measuring Interest Rate Risk—Traditional GAP Analysis Traditional GAP. models are the most basic interest rate risk exposure measurement techniques employed by banks. These models focus on GAP as a static measure of risk and NII as the target measure of bank performance.

This method requires preparation of a repricing gap report that distributes rate sensitive assets, rate sensitive liabilities and off-balance sheet positions into different time buckets according to their residual maturity or time remaining to their next repricing, whichever is earlier. The assets and liabilities that do not have contractual repricing intervals or maturities are assigned to maturity buckets based on statistical analysis or judgement. Interest rate risk is measured by calculating gaps over different maturity buckets. The GAP is defined as the absolute difference between Rate Sensitive Assets (RSA) and Rate Sensitive Liabilities (RSL) for each time bucket. Since interest rate risk is measured by calculating GAP over different time intervals based on aggregate balance sheet data at a fixed point in time, the measure is known as 'static GAP'.

The objective is to measure expected NII and then identify strategies to stabilize or improve it. The steps to static GAP analysis are as follows:

1. Forecasting interest rates for the time period during which interest rate risk is to be measured—based on historical experience, simulation of future interest rate movements, or management judgement.
2. Determining a series of sequential time intervals, called 'buckets'.
3. Grouping assets and liabilities of the bank, including contingent liabilities, into these time intervals, according to the time until the first repricing. The effects of off-balance sheet positions, such as those associated with futures, interest rate swaps and so on, are added to the grouping, based on whether the item effectively represents a rate sensitive asset or liability.
4. Calculating the bank's static GAP as the difference between RSAs and RSLs for each time bucket.
5. Multiplying the GAP by the forecasted interest rate to obtain expected NII.

Thus, there would be a periodic GAP and a cumulative GAP for each time bucket. For example, the cumulative GAP for the period 0–90 days would be the sum of, say, the periodic GAP of 0–28 days, 29–60 days and 61–90 days.

A negative, or *liability-sensitive GAP* occurs when liabilities exceed assets (including OBS positions) in a given time band. Conversely, a positive or *asset-sensitive GAP* occurs when the assets exceed liabilities.[11]

From Illustration 12.1, the effect of interest rate risk on the bank's earnings can be gauged:

ILLUSTRATION 12.1

Balance sheet composition and average interest rates over a specified time interval, say, 1 year, for a hypothetical bank (₹ in crore) can be explained as follows:

Case 1 Rate sensitive assets exceed rate sensitive liabilities, hence GAP is positive.

	Liabilities (₹ in Crore)	Interest Rate-present	Interest Rate-increase	Interest Rate-decrease	Assets (₹ in Crore)	Interest Rate	Interest Rate-increase	Interest Rate-decrease
Rate sensitive	550	0.1	0.11	0.09	700	0.12	0.13	0.11
Fixed rate	350	0.11	0.11	0.11	250	0.14	0.14	0.14
Non-earning/ non-paying	100	0	0	0	50	0	0	0
Total	1000				1000			
NII								
Earned from assets paid on liabilities (₹ in crore)		25.5	27	24				
RSA - RSL (₹ in crore)	150							

Case 2 Rate sensitive liabilities exceed rate sensitive assets, hence GAP is negative.

	Liabilities	Interest Rate-present	Interest Rate-increase	Interest Rate-decrease	Assets	Interest Rate	Interest Rate-increase	Interest Rate-decrease
Rate sensitive	800	0.1	0.11	0.09	700	0.12	0.13	0.11
Fixed rate	100	0.11	0.11	0.11	250	0.14	0.14	0.14
Non-earning/ non-paying	100	0	0	0	50	0	0	0
Total	1,000				1,000			
NII								
Earned from assets paid on liabilities		28	27	29				
RSA – RSL	–100							

The following inferences can be drawn from Illustration 12.1:

1. When GAP is positive, it indicates that the bank has more RSAs than RSLs across the time interval. Such a bank is termed as 'asset sensitive'
2. When GAP is positive, and interest rates rise by equal amounts at the same time for both assets and liabilities, NII increases. The bank would then be paying higher rates on all repriceable liabilities over the time horizon, and earning higher yields on repriceable assets. However, since more assets are repriced than liabilities, NII increases.
3. When GAP is positive, and interest rates decrease by equal amounts at the same time for both assets and liabilities, NII decreases for the reason discussed above.
4. When GAP is negative, it indicates that the bank has more RSLs than RSAs across the time interval. Such a bank is termed 'liability sensitive'.
5. When GAP is negative, and interest rates rise by equal amounts at the same time for both assets and liabilities, NII decreases. Though both interest income and interest expenses increase, the latter rise more because more liabilities are repriced.
6. When GAP is negative, and interest rates fall by equal amounts at the same time for both assets and liabilities, NII increases for the reason discussed in (5).

7. Therefore, the sign of a bank's GAP would indicate whether interest income or interest expenses are likely to change more when interest rates change.
8. It also follows that the bank can have a 'zero GAP' when RSAs equal RSLs. In this case, equal interest rate changes do not alter NII since changes in interest income equal changes in interest expenses.

These findings can be generalized in the Table 12.2.

TABLE 12.2 CHANGES IN GAP—SUMMARY OF RESULTS

When GAP is ...	And Interest Rates ...	Interest Income	More than/less than/equal to	Interest Expense	Leading to NII.
Positive	Increase	Increases	More than	Increases	Increase
Positive	Decrease	Decreases	More than	Decreases	Decrease
Negative	Increase	Increases	Less than	Increases	Decrease
Negative	Decrease	Decreases	Less than	Decreases	Increase
Zero	Increase	Increases	Equal	Increases	No change
Zero	Decrease	Decreases	Equal	Decreases	No change

The following simple formula summarizes the framework:

$$\Delta \text{NII}_{\text{[expected]}} = \text{GAP} \times \Delta r_{\text{[expected]}}$$

Where $\Delta \text{NII}_{\text{[expected]}}$ represents change in NII from an existing base over a specified period of time,
GAP represents cumulative GAP over the chosen time interval, and
$\Delta r_{\text{[expected]}}$ represents expected changes in the interest rates over the time period

The sign and magnitude of the gaps in various time buckets can be used to assess potential earnings volatility arising from changes in interest rates. A positive gap indicates that RSA are more than RSL and from an earnings perspective, the position benefits from a rise in interest rates. A negative gap on the other hand indicates that RSL are more than RSA and from an earnings perspective the position would benefit from a fall in interest rates. The size of the GAP indicates how much interest rate risk a bank assumes. The utility of this simple approach is that banks can take positions to improve NII for a given level of GAP and forecast of rise or fall in interest rates.

Strengths and weaknesses of this approach: Static Gap analysis is one of the most commonly used approaches to assessing interest rate risk exposure. The principal advantage of this approach is that it is easy to understand and compute. Specific balance sheet items responsible for the risk can be clearly identified, and, once cash flow characteristics of each instrument are determined, GAP measures can be easily calculated.

However, the approach has a number of shortcomings.

First, the analysis makes the simplifying assumption that all positions within a time band mature or reprice simultaneously, thus leading to aggregation that might impact precision of the estimates.

Second, the analysis ignores 'basis risk', which arises when loans and other instruments are tied to different base rates or indexes. It is not easy to forecast the frequency or magnitude of changes in market-driven base rates or indexes. This could lead to serious measurement errors.

Third, the analysis ignores the time value of money. The maturity buckets do not clarify whether cash flows arise at the beginning of the period or at the end. For example, if investment in a 1-month treasury bill is financed by an overnight borrowing in the money market, the 1-month GAP is zero, and suggests no interest rate risk. However, when overnight rates rise, the transaction exposes the bank to losses. Therefore, a bank's gains or losses could also arise from the timing of the repricing or the interest flows within each time interval. Thus even with a zero GAP, the bank's NII may fluctuate.

Fourth, the short-term focus of GAP measures ignores the long-term impact on fixed rate assets and liabilities. Interest rate changes could have long-term effects on the total risk of the bank's assets and liabilities.

Fifth, the rate sensitivity of liabilities that bear no interest is ignored. Many banks consider non-interest bearing demand deposits as non-rate sensitive. When interest rates fluctuate, customers' willingness to maintain demand deposits with banks also changes. It is thus difficult to estimate the exact rate sensitivity of such instruments.

Sixth, the analysis fails to account for differences in the sensitivity of income arising from options embedded in the securities and deposits that banks deal with. Depositors have the option of withdrawing their money before maturity. Similarly, long-term borrowers have the option of prepaying and foreclosing their loans. Such options have different probabilities of being exercised at different interest rate levels. If they are exercised, they can alter the GAP and, hence, the NII as well.

Finally, most GAP analyzes fail to capture variability in non-interest revenue and expenses due to interest rate fluctuations. Volatility in non-interest revenue and expenses is a potentially important source of risk to current net income of the bank.

Hence, GAP analysis, though prevalently used, would provide only a rough approximation of the actual change in NII resulting from the forecasted pattern of change in interest rates. The sign of the GAP does not impact the volatility of NII. It merely indicates whether NII rises or falls when interest rates are expected to fluctuate.

Measuring interest rate risk—Linking the GAP and net interest margin. Some ALM measures focus on the 'GAP ratio' while evaluating interest rate risk. The GAP ratio is defined as the ratio of RSAs to RSLs. Thus

$$\text{GAP ratio} = \frac{\text{RSAs}}{\text{RSLs}}$$

When the GAP is positive, the GAP ratio is greater than unity. When the GAP is negative, the GAP ratio will be less than unity.

However, the deficiency in this measure is that does not reflect the size of the interest rate risk a bank assumes. Illustration 12.2 depicts this feature.

ILLUSTRATION 12.2

	Bank A (₹ in Crore)	Bank B (₹ in Crore)
Total assets	1,000	1,000
RSAs	40	400
RSLs	20	200
GAP (RSAs – RSLs)	20	200
GAP ratio (RSAs/RSLs)	2	2
NII (assumed)	200	400
Decrease in interest rate	2%	2%
Change in NII (GAP × Δr)	–0.4	–4

In the above example, though the asset size and the GAP ratio are identical for both banks; it is evident that Bank B assumes greater risk since its interest income will be more volatile when interest rates change.

Since interest rate risk is more associated with the volatility in NII, a better risk measure would be one that relates the absolute value of a bank's GAP to its assets—particularly the earning assets. This ratio can be directly linked to the NIM[12] of the bank (*see* Box 12.3)—the greater this ratio, the greater would be the interest rate risk. The practical implications are that:

- the bank management can determine a target NIM based on the specific risk characteristics of its assets.
- it can determine an allowable variation in the NIM without affecting stakeholder interests.
- based on the above, an acceptable GAP is arrived at.

BOX 12.3 RELATIONSHIP BETWEEN TARGET GAP, EARNING ASSETS AND NIM

The relationship can be evolved as follows:

$$\text{NIM} = \frac{\text{NII}}{\text{earning assets}}$$

Hence,

$$\text{NII} = \text{NIM} \times \text{earning assets}$$

The bank determines the acceptable variation in NIM as Δc. Then, the acceptable variation in NII would be

$$\Delta\,\text{NII} = \text{NIM} \times \text{earning assets} \times \Delta c$$

Since

$$\Delta\,\text{NII} = \text{GAP} \times \Delta r,$$

$$\text{GAP} \times \Delta r = \text{NIM} \times \text{earning assets} \times \Delta c$$

Hence,

$$\text{the target GAP} = \frac{[\text{NIM} \times \text{earning assets} \times \Delta c]}{\Delta r}$$

and,

$$\frac{\text{Target GAP}}{\text{earning assets}} = \frac{[\text{NIM} \times \Delta c]}{\Delta r}$$

Effectively therefore, the relationship between Target GAP and Earning assets can be expressed as a ratio of the product of the expected NIM and the % variability in NIM that can be tolerated, to the expected change in interest rates.

For example, if a bank with earning assets of ₹100 crores expects NIM of 2.5 per cent, but can tolerate variability in the NIM to the extent of ±10 per cent during a year, NIM should fall between 2.25 per cent and 2.75 per cent. If, further, interest rates are forecasted to vary up to 2 per cent during the year, the bank's ratio of 1-year cumulative target GAP to its earning assets should not exceed 12.5 per cent, as given by the final equation in Box 12.3.

$$\frac{\text{Target GAP}}{\text{earning assets}} = \frac{(0.10) \times (0.025)}{0.02} = 0.125$$

Hence, the bank's decision to allow only a 10 per cent variation in NIM limits the variation in GAP from –₹12.5 crores to +₹12.5 crores, based on ₹100 crores of earning assets.

It is important to note here the close relationship between a bank's GAP and its NIM. Hence, in practice, banks limit the size of GAP as a fraction of earning assets, thus, limiting the variation in the NII.

Method 2: Measuring Interest Rate Risk—Earnings Sensitivity Analysis Earnings Sensitivity analysis is an extension of the static GAP analysis. It essentially assesses the impact on net income using 'what if' models, carrying out iterations of static GAP analysis assuming different interest rate forecasts and potential interest rate environments. The broad steps of the analysis are as follows:

Step 1 Forecast interest rates assuming various potential interest rate environments

Step 2 Assess the likely changes in the bank's assets and liabilities by volume and composition under each of these likely environments. The assessment will also examine which of the potential interest rate environments would lead to exercise of embedded options such as loan prepayments or premature deposit withdrawals

Step 3 Assess the likelihood that assets and liabilities would reprice under each of the identified environments. Similarly, identify the implications on off-balance sheet items

Step 4 Calculate the NII under each of the environments, and compare with the 'base case' and other scenarios.

The above framework thus helps evaluate the impact of different interest rate environments on the NII, and allows the bank management to set limits for variability of NII or NIM. This approach is sometimes termed as Earning-at-Risk (EAR).

Method 3: Measuring Interest Rate Risk—Rate-Adjusted GAP This method is a simpler variation of the Earnings Sensitivity analysis method described above, and is typically used under circumstances where the complexity and size of a bank's assets and liabilities and off-balance sheet items are not likely to change dramatically in the short run. The advantage of this approach is that, though simpler, it recognizes the existence of embedded options and different repricing timings. This method is also called 'Income Statement GAP' since it uses the balance sheet data to assess the differential impact of interest rate change on each asset and liability class of the bank.

The steps to adopting this approach are as follows:

Step 1 Assess the balance sheet GAP for all items in the balance sheet. This is done by including all balances whose rates are likely to change in, say, the next 12 months

Step 2 Compute the relevant 'Earnings volatility factor' (EVF) for each of the balance sheet items. The EVF would reflect the change in the rate applicable to a rate sensitive asset or liability for every 100 bps change in the base rate.

Step 3 The product of the balance sheet GAP and the EVF will reflect the 'Income statement GAP', which is the effective GAP estimate, were the interest rates to change as forecasted.

Step 4 Arrive at the impact on NII using the earlier formula

$$\Delta NII_{[expected]} = \text{Effective GAP} \times \Delta r_{[expected]}$$

Similarly, the effect on NIM can also be determined using the formula given earlier.

The important advantage of this approach is that it recognizes the value of options and repricing timing in bank assets and liabilities, while being simple to compute. However, the results will depend on the skill of the forecaster to accurately judge the impact of interest rate changes on each class of assets and liabilities.

Illustration 12.3 depicts a simplified usage of this approach. In the example given in Illustration 12.1, we impose differing EVFs on the rate sensitive assets and liabilities.

ILLUSTRATION 12.3

	Base Rate Falls by 100 bps			Base Rate Rises by 100 bps		
	Balance Sheet GAP (assumed from Illustration 12.1) (₹ in Crores)	**EVF (assumed)**	**Income Statement GAP (balance sheet GAP EVF) (₹ in Crores)**	**Balance Sheet GAP (assumed from Illustration 12.11) (₹ in Crores)**	**EVF (assumed)**	**Income Statement GAP (balance sheet GAP EVF) (₹ in Crores)**
Rate sensitive liabilities						
Demand liabilities	400	75%	300	400	0%	0
Other deposits /borrowings repricing within 1 year	400	85%	340	400	85%	340
Total RSL	800		640	800		340
Rate sensitive assets						
Loans	400	100%	400	400	100%	400
Investments	200	75%	150	200	75%	150
Other rate sensitive assets	100	95%	95	100	95%	95
Total RSA	700		645	700		645
Rate sensitive GAP	–100		5	–100		305
Total assets	1,000		1,000	1,000		1,000
GAP as % of total assets	10		0.5	10		30.5
Change in NII	1		– 0.05	–1		3.05

It is evident that assuming different responses to interest rate changes by different assets and liabilities of the bank lead to conclusions quite at variance with the conclusions reached in Illustration 12.1. The rate sensitive GAP is negative and the change in NII is in the opposite direction.

It is, therefore, important that assumptions regarding interest rate movements and their impact on changes in rate sensitive liabilities and assets are done with care and precision in order that misleading conclusions are avoided.

Box 12.4 explores if yield curves do matter for banks' profitability.

Method 4: Measuring Long-Term Interest Rate Risk—Duration GAP Analysis A fundamental criticism of the static GAP and Earnings Sensitivity analyzes pertain to their preoccupation with short-term interest rate risk in banks. A bank's assets and liabilities, however, may be mismatched beyond 1 or 2 years and thus expose the bank to substantial risk in the medium or long term. Such risks may go undetected by the traditional GAP approaches.

Hence, banks will also have to look at alternate methods of measuring interest rate risk over the entire life of the assets and liabilities. Duration gap (DGAP) analysis is one such method. As the name suggests, it incorporates estimates of 'duration' of assets and liabilities that reflect the value of promised cash flows up to maturity. Hence, it is considered a more comprehensive interest rate risk measure.

Stated in its simplest form, '*duration*' is the average life of an asset or liability, and is measured as the weighted average time to maturity using present value of the cash flows, relative to the total present value of the asset or liability as weights.

'Duration' measures the sensitivity of any instrument to a small change in any of the underlying risk factors. Simply, it is an elasticity measure, providing information on how much a security's price will change with changes in market interest rates. *Annexure II* provides the basic concepts, applications and measurement approaches for 'duration' and 'convexity'.

The reasons for using both static GAP and DGAP analyzes in estimating interest rate risk are outlined in Table 12.3.

BOX 12.4 DO YIELD CURVES MATTER FOR BANKS' PROFITABILITY?

According to theory, it appears logical that the NIM of banks—the difference between interest received and paid as a percentage of earning assets—should be impacted by the slope of the yield curve, *i.e.*, the spread between short- and long-term interest rates. Hence, a flattening yield curve would have an important macroeconomic impact—it may lead to slowing economic growth and consequent pressure on bank earnings. This relationship was seen to be true up to the 1990s. Figure 12.2 shows the trend in relationship in the case of banks in India.

FIGURE 12.2 TRENDS IN RELATIONSHIP BETWEEN YIELD SPREAD AND NIM IN INDIAN BANKS

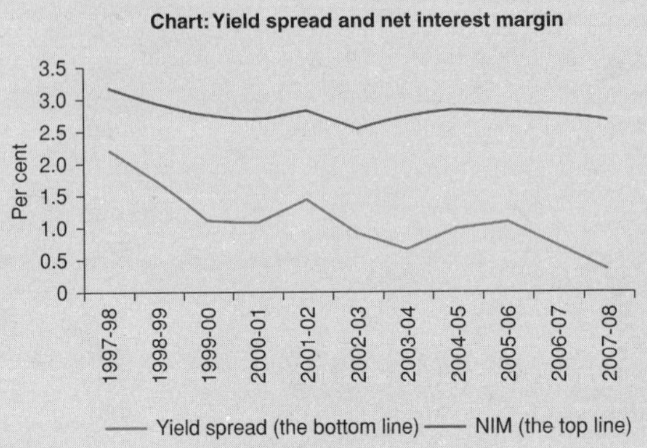

Source: RBI Report on currency and finance 0608—page 408, Box IX.4

Interestingly, in the recent past, banks' NIMs appear to show lower sensitivity to yield curve movements. The RBI report on currency and finance (2006–08) attributes the following reasons to this new trend:(a) banks' diversification into non-traditional activities, (b) banks' increasing use of derivatives to hedge interest rate risk and(c) banks' increasing use of non-interest bearing liabilities such as equity and demand deposits to fund assets, when interest yields on assets are declining.

In the case of India, the RBI report notes that there has been a flattening yield curve over the last decade (up to 2006–07). The reason attributed to this is the decline in long-term rates and relative stability of short-term rates. The report also points out that the NIM follows yield spreads with a lag, possibly because lending and borrowing rates of banks are not adjusted instantly to market rate movements.

Source: RBI report on currency and finance 2006–08, Chapter IX, 'Efficiency, productivity and soundness of the banking sector', page 408.

TABLE 12.3 COMPARISON OF BASIC FEATURES OF STATIC GAP AND DURATION GAP

Static GAP	Duration GAP
Uses 'rate' sensitivity	Uses 'price' sensitivity
Rate sensitivity is the ability to reprice the principal amount of an asset or liability	Price sensitivity reflects the extent of change in the value of an asset or liability when interest rates change
Highly rate sensitive assets may not be price sensitive. Example: short-term money market instruments. They are extremely rate sensitive since the maturity proceeds of these instruments will have to be frequently reinvested at the prevailing market rates	However, price sensitive assets may also be rate sensitive. For example, if the bank has invested in long-term zero coupon bonds for say, 15 years, it can reinvest the principal only after selling the bond in the market. The market value of the bond at any point of time is determined by the rise or fall in prevailing interest rates. Hence, the long-term bond is price sensitive.
Maturity of a loan measures, in absolute terms, the total number of periods in which the loan would be repaid	'Duration' is 'effective maturity' that takes into account the time periods at which repayments are made.

TEASE THE CONCEPT

As 'maturity' of a loan increases, what happens to its 'duration'?

DGAP analysis examines how interest rate changes would affect the market value of shareholder equity. Similar to the static GAP analysis, the duration of assets and liabilities of a bank are compared over different interest rate environments. After evaluating the impact of interest rate change on the market value of shareholder equity, the DGAP analysis also throws up options for bank management to immunize or insulate market value of equity (MVE) from rate changes.

The steps involved in DGAP analysis are as follows:

Step 1 Forecast interest rate changes for the planning horizon

Step 2 Estimate current market value of the bank's assets, liabilities and shareholders' equity

Step 3 Estimate the weighted average duration of assets and the weighted average duration of liabilities, also incorporating the effects of off-balance sheet items, based on the estimated market values.

Step 4 Calculate DGAP

Step 5 Forecast changes in the bank's MVE under various interest rate environments.

Step 6 Formulate strategies to insulate MVE from interest rate volatility

Box 12.5 derives the relationship between DGAP and the market value of assets and liabilities of a bank.

BOX 12.5 DERIVING THE RELATIONSHIP BETWEEN MVA, MVL AND MVE

The weighted average duration of a bank's assets is calculated as

$$\text{WADa} = \Sigma w_{ai}\,\text{Da}_i, \quad \text{where } i = 1 \text{ to } n$$

and the variables are defined as follows:

w_{ai} = the market value of each asset 'a_i' of the bank divided by the market value of all bank assets (MVA $= a_1 + a_2 + \cdots + a_n$)

Da_i = Macaulay's duration[13] of the ith asset

n = number of different bank assets

The weighted average duration of bank liabilities (Dl) is calculated as follows:

$$\text{WADl} = \Sigma w_{lj}\,\text{Dl}_j, \quad \text{where } j = 1 \text{ to } m$$

And the variables are defined as follows:

w_{lj} = the market value of each liability 'l_j' of the bank divided by the market value of all bank liabilities (MVL $= l_1 + l_2 + \cdots + l_m$)

Dl_j = Macaulay's duration of liability j and

m = number of different bank liabilities

We know that Duration is a measure of interest rate sensitivity or elasticity of a liability or asset, which can be represented as follows:

$$\left[\frac{\Delta P}{P}\right] \div \left[\frac{\Delta r}{(1+r)}\right] = -D$$

or equivalently,

$$\Delta P = -D\left[\frac{\Delta r}{(1+r)}\right] \times P$$

From the above basic equation, we can represent $\Delta A_i = -\text{Da}_i\left[\frac{\Delta r}{(1+r)}\right]A_i$, and $\Delta L_j = -\text{Dl}_j\left[\frac{\Delta r}{(1+r)}\right]L_j$, r representing the interest rate.

Since the focus is on insulating MVE from interest rate risk, let us define MVE as the difference between market value of assets and the market value of liabilities, *i.e.*,

$$\text{MVE} = \text{MVA} - \text{MVL; and}$$

$$\Delta\text{MVE} = \Delta\text{MVA} - \Delta\text{MVL},$$

implying that changes in MVE would result from changes in the market values of assets and liabilities.

In the same manner used to determine the change in price given above, we can find the change in the MVE using duration

$$\Delta\text{MVE} = -\,[\text{WADa} \times \text{MVA} - \text{WADl} \times \text{MVL}] \times \left[\frac{\Delta r}{(1+r)}\right]$$

or

$$\Delta\text{MVE} = -\,[\text{WADa} - \left(\frac{\text{MVL}}{\text{MVA}}\right)\text{WADl}] \times \left[\frac{\Delta r}{(1+r)}\right] \times \text{MVA}$$

The expression $[\text{WADa} - \left(\frac{\text{MVL}}{\text{MVA}}\right)\text{WADl}]$ is the *DGAP*, and hence

$$\Delta\text{MVE} = -\,\text{DGAP} \times \left[\frac{\Delta r}{(1+r)}\right] \times \text{MVA}$$

The important point to be noted from the expression denoting MVE are as follows:

- The weighted average duration of both assets and liabilities reflect the present value of all promised cash flows in future. Therefore, the need for classifying assets and liabilities into time buckets does not arise.
- The DGAP is 'leverage adjusted'. Note that DGAP is the difference between weighted average duration of assets and a 'leverage-adjusted' weighted average duration of liabilities. This implies that DGAP serves as a rough estimate of the sensitivity of MVE to interest rate changes. The leverage adjustment also denotes

how much equity is present to finance the assets and cushion unexpected losses. The interest rate *r* typically represents an average yield on earning assets. The interest rate assumed here would be an 'economic interest' that generates 'economic income' as contrasted with 'accounting income'. 'Economic Interest' is simply the product of the market value of each asset and liability and its market interest rate.

- The greater the DGAP, the greater would be the size of the 'interest rate shock'—the potential volatility in the MVE for a given change in interest rates. Therefore, DGAP serves as a measure of the interest rate risk assumed by the bank, as well as gains and losses to the bank arising from interest rate movements. For example, when DGAP is positive, an increase in interest rates would lower the MVE, while a decrease in interest rates would have an opposite effect and increase the MVE. And when DGAP is negative, an increase in interest rates would increase the MVE while a decrease in interest rates would lower the MVE. These results are in sharp contrast to those from similar static GAP analysis. It also follows that the closer the DGAP is to zero, the smaller the potential change in MVE.

Continuing with the example given in Illustrations 12.1 to 12.3, let us see how duration analysis can be applied to the data. This is demonstrated in Illustration 12.4.

ILLUSTRATION 12.4

Base case: Assumptions:

1. All values of assets and liabilities are market values
2. Principal is repaid on maturity
3. Interest paid yearly
4. No defaults, prepayments or early withdrawals

Rate Sensitive Liabilities	Market Value (₹ in Crores)	Rate %	Duration (years)
3-year term deposit	400	10	2.73
Other deposits/borrowings repricing within 1 year	400	6	1
Total RSL	800		
Rate Sensitive Assets			
3-year commercial Loans	400	12	2.69
5-year bonds	200	10	4.17
Other rate sensitive assets repricing in 1 year	100	6	1
Total RSA	700		
Total assets/liabilities	1000		
Of total liabilities, equity	90		

Workings

Weighted average duration of liabilities WADl $= \frac{400}{910} \times (2.73) + \frac{400}{910} \times (1) = 1.64$ years

Weighted average duration of assets WADa $= \frac{400}{1000} \times (2.69) \times \frac{200}{1000} \times (4.17) + \frac{100}{1000} \times (1) = 2.01$ years

DGAP $= 2.01 - \frac{910}{1000} \times 1.64 = 0.518$ years

Expected NII $= 400 \times 12 + 200 \times 0.10 + 100 \times 0.06 = 400 \times 10 = 400 \times 0.06 = 10$

Sample duration calculations using the basic concept of duration

$$D = \frac{\sum_{t=1}^{n}\left[\frac{Ct \times t}{(1+r)t}\right]}{\sum_{t=1}^{n}\left[\frac{Ct}{(1+r)t}\right]}$$

where, D = duration

t = number of periods in the future

C_t = cash flow to be delivered in t periods

n = term-to-maturity and r = yield to maturity (per period basis).

Sample duration calculations for the above example:

$$\text{3-year commercial loan} = \frac{\left[\left(\frac{48}{1.12.}\right) \times 1 + \left(\frac{48}{(1.12)(1.12)}\right) \times 2 + \frac{448}{1.12} \times 1.12 \times 1.12 \times 3\right]}{400}$$

$= 0.107(1) + 0.096(2) + 0.797(3) = 2.69$ years

$$\text{3-year term deposit} = \frac{\left[\left(\frac{40}{1.10}\right)\times 1 + \left(\frac{40}{1.10}\times 1.10\right)\times 2 + \left(\frac{440}{1.10}\times 1.10\times 1.10\right)\times 3\right]}{400}$$

$$= 0.090(1) + 0.083(2) + 0.826(3) = 2.73 \text{ years}$$

Case 1 Interest rates on both assets and liabilities rise uniformly by 100 bps

$$\text{MVA (new)} = -\text{D} \times \text{inc r} \times \frac{\text{current MVA}}{(1 + \text{current r})}$$

$$= -\left(2.69 \times .01 \times \frac{400}{1.12}\right) + \left(-4.17 \times 0.01 \times \frac{200}{1.10}\right) + \left(-1 \times 0.01 \times \frac{100}{1.06}\right)$$

MVA[new]	18.13	negative
MVL [new]	13.70	negative
MVE = MVA − MVL	4.43	negative

Thus, the positive DGAP has led to a fall in MVE when interest rates rise uniformly.

The NII is also seen to fall to ₹7.2 crores from ₹10 crores. [This is calculated using market values of assets and liabilities individually from the relationship:

$$\text{MVA (new)} = -D \times \text{inc } r \times \text{current MVA } (1 + \text{current } r)]$$

Case 2 Interest rates on both assets and liabilities fall uniformly by 100 bps

$$\text{MVA (new)} = \text{D} \times \text{inc } r \times \frac{\text{current MVA}}{(1 + \text{current } r)}$$

$$= \left(-2.69 \times -0.01 \times \frac{400}{1.12}\right) + \left(-4.17 \times -0.01 \times \frac{200}{1.10}\right) + \left(1 \times 0.01 \times \frac{100}{1.06}\right)$$

MVA[new]	18.13	positive
MVL [new]	13.70	positive
MVE = MVA − MVL	4.43	positive

The NII now increases to ₹12.8 crores from ₹10 crores.

Inferences from Illustration 12.4 are as follows:

1. Interest rate risk is evidenced by the mismatch between duration of assets and liabilities, as well as the DGAP of 0.518 years in the base case.
2. When there is a change in interest rates, the market values of assets and liabilities would change by different amounts. This would impact the NII in the short term as well as the MVE.
3. In the above example, the weighted average duration of assets exceeds the leverage-adjusted weighted average duration of liabilities. This implies that the change in market value of assets will be greater than the market value of liabilities, if all rates change uniformly. Case 2 demonstrates that with a uniform increase of 100 bps in interest rates, market value of assets declines by a greater margin (₹18 crores) than market value of liabilities (₹14 crores). MVE is estimated to fall by ₹4 crores.
4. In case 2, there is also a decrease in the expected NII when the interest rate increases. The explanation is simple—the bank will have to pay more for refinancing its assets when the liabilities mature (since the duration of liabilities is less than that of assets).
5. Further, the following table shows that there is an increase in the bank's overall risk with an increase in interest rates due to changes in the market values of assets, liabilities and consequently, equity.

(₹ in crores)	New (case 1 − interest rates increase)	Existing (base case)
MVA	983	1000
MVL	896	910
MVE	87	90
MVE/MVA	0.088	0.09
MVA/MVE	11.30	11.11

MVE/MVA is an approximate indicator of the bank's capital adequacy,[14] while the inverse of this indicator is the equivalent of the equity multiplier (EM).[15] The former shows a decline, and the latter an increase over the base case, in the wake of an interest rate increase—both pointers to increased risk for the bank.

6. Case 2, reflecting the impact of decrease in interest rates, shows opposite results. The duration mismatch leads to greater increase in market value of assets than market value of liabilities and, therefore, an increase in the MVE. NII also improves, and so do other indicators such as MVE/MVA and the EM, and it appears the bank is better off.

The above inferences are generalized in Table 12.4 as follows:

TABLE 12.4 CHANGES IN DGAP—SUMMARY OF RESULTS

When DGAP is ...	And Interest Rates ...	Market Value of Assets ...	Is More Than/Less Than/Equal to	Market Value of Liabilities	Causing Market Value of Equity to...
positive	increase	decreases	more than	decreases	decrease
positive	decrease	increases	more than	increases	increase
negative	increase	decreases	less than	decreases	increase
negative	decrease	increases	less than	increases	decrease
zero	increase	decreases	equal	decreases	No change
zero	decrease	increases	equal	increases	No change

Also note that the impact on NII is contrary to the results seen in the case of static maturity GAP.

How can duration be used as a tool to assess and manage interest rate risk? Though a static measure, DGAP can be employed in assessing the changes in MVE during periods of volatile interest rates. The greater the absolute value of the DGAP, the more is the interest rate risk. However, a bank would ideally desire to sustain the MVE or maintain an increasing trend, given the volatility of interest rates.

'Immunizing' Market Value of Equity From Table 12.4, a bank will have to operate with its DGAP at zero, if it desires to maintain its MVE while interest rates change. This implies that the bank's average asset duration should be slightly below the average liability duration. More specifically, the average asset duration for a bank with DGAP at zero should be equal to the product of the bank's liability duration and a factor that represents the 'leverage' (MVL/MVA).

To set DGAP to zero, three alternative courses of action can be followed:

- Adjust the duration of market value of assets
- Adjust the duration of market value of liabilities
- Adjust the market values of both assets and liabilities

In practice, it is easier to adjust the duration of the market value of assets. To do this, we would have to set DGAP = 0 in the equation WADa − (MVL/MVA)WADl = DGAP. That is,

$$\text{WADa} = \left(\frac{\text{MVL}}{\text{MVA}}\right) \times \text{WADl}$$

In Illustration 12.4, where the DGAP 0.518 arises from the difference between 2.01 (WADa) and 1.49 (WADl × MVL/MVA), DGAP can be made zero if: (a) the weighted average duration of assets is reduced to 1.49 years, or (b) the weighted average duration of liabilities is increased to 2.21 (2.01/0.91) years, or (c) use some combination of these adjustments.

Under (c), a deliberate mismatch is maintained to enable immunize the MVE. This is done by segregating the term WADa − WADl from the DGAP equation after setting DGAP = 0, as follows:

$$\text{WADa} - \left(\frac{\text{MVL}}{\text{MVA}}\right)\text{WADl} = \text{DGAP} = 0$$

Hence,

$$\text{WADa} - \text{WADl} = -\text{WADl}\left(\frac{\text{MVE}}{\text{MVA}}\right)$$ [16]

That is, from Illustration 12.4,

$$\text{WADa} - \text{WADl} = -\text{WADl}\left(\frac{90}{1000}\right)$$

$$\text{WADa} - 0.91\text{WADl} = 0$$

This implies that the bank in Illustration 12.4 can maintain the MVE if it can carry a duration mismatch, such that

$$\frac{\text{WADa}}{\text{WADl}} = 0.91$$

Other Target Variables Used for Immunizing Interest Rate Risk

Net interest income (NII) and market value of equity (MVE): Banks are sometimes interested in immunizing the market value of equity and NII simultaneously or independently. In such cases, variations of the immunization process are used. For instance, Toevs (1983)[17] sugggests that a bank can alternatively hedge or immunize its NII and MVE, as given below.

Since MVE = MVE − MVL, MVA × duration of assets (D_A) should equal MVL × duration of liabilities (D_L) if MVE is to be immunized.

It follows that if MVE should be positive, then D_L should exceed D_A.

$D_A = (MVA_{NS} \times D_{NSA} + MVA_{RS} \times D_{RSA})/MVA$ and $D_L = (MVL_{NS} \times D_{NSL} + MVL_{RS} \times D_{RSL})/MVL$, where NS, RS signify Non rate sensitive and Rate sensitive, respectively to immuise MVE.

Therefore, setting MVA × D_A = MVL × D_L to immunize MVE, the equation can be rewritten as

$$MVA \times (MVA_{NS} + D_{NSA} + MVA_{RS} \times D_{RSA})/MVA = MVL \times (MVL_{NS} \times D_{NSL} + MVL_{RS} \times D_{RSL})/MVL$$

or

$$MVA_{NS} \times D_{NSA} + MVA_{RS} \times D_{RSA} = MVL_{NS} \times D_{NSL} + MVL_{RS} \times D_{RSL}$$

Adding and subtracting MVE and MVL on the respective sides of the equation,

$$MVA_{NS}(D_{NSA} - 1) + MVA - MVA_{RS}(1 - D_{RSA}) = MVL_{NS}(DNSL - 1) + MVL - MVL_{RS}(1 - D_{RSL})$$

or

$$MVA_{NS}(D_{NSA} - 1) + MVE = MVL_{NS}(D_{NSL} - 1) + DGAP$$

According to Toevs, if a bank wishes to hedge NII and immunise MVE, DGAP should be set to Zero, and $MVA_{NS}(D_{NSA} - 1) + MVA$ equal to $MVL_{NS}(D_{NSL} - 1) + MVL$.

Alternatively, if the bank wishes to immunize MVE even at the cost of NII, it can select a non zero DGAP, while keeping the above eqality intact.

A bank can put its MVE at risk and hedge its NII by setting DGAP = 0 but not fulfilling the above equality.

Dynamic duration GAP analysis: As done in the static GAP earnings sensitivity analysis framework described above, a sensitivity analysis for MVE also called Economic Value of Equity (EVE) can be carried out through simulation models. The sensitivity analysis assesses the impact of various interest rate environments on MVE through 'what if' analysis. The volatility in the MVE compared with the base case or the most likely scenario would be the indicator of interest rate risk. Some of these models are also capable of assessing the impact of customers exercising embedded options, or shifts in the yield curve, or varying yield spreads.

TEASE THE CONCEPT

What is the expected impact on 'duration' if the following options were exercised?

- A large deposit is withdrawn before maturity
- A large loan is repaid before maturity

Strengths and weaknesses of the 'duration' approach: The primary strength of 'duration analysis' lies in its ability to provide a comprehensive measure of interest rate risk for the entire portfolio of the bank—assets, liabilities and surplus (equity). The smaller the absolute value of DGAP, the less sensitive the MVE is to interest rate changes.

The approach is considered more practical than the static GAP approach, since cash flows over the entire life of each asset and liability is taken into account while computing duration. Thus, the time value of each cash flow is recognized. Further, this feature obviates the need for classification of assets and liabilities into different time buckets.

Duration analysis enables the bank to match assets and liabilities at an aggregate level and assess the impact of interest rate risk, a feature that is not possible in static GAP analysis.

The long-term, aggregate view that duration analysis offers is valuable, since bank management acquires flexibility to adjust rate sensitivity using a variety of hedging instruments.

However, 'duration analysis' is not without *limitations*.

- First, duration measurement calls for several subjective assumptions, and, hence, the 'duration' may not be computed accurately.
- Duration is based on 'promised' rather than 'expected' cash flows. Exercise of embedded options, or change in default probabilities could render initial forecasts invalid. Hence, a bank should have systems in place to monitor whether actual cash flows conform to initial cash flow forecasts.
- Even while using sophisticated simulation models for sensitivity analysis, the need for forecasting customer behaviour on when embedded options would be exercised, or the value of these options, build in subjectivity and complexity into the model.
- Duration analysis requires that each cash flow be discounted by an appropriate discount rate, to arrive at the present value of future cash flows. Identifying appropriate discount rates for various cash flow streams, therefore, becomes a crucial but complex step in arriving at the likely impact of interest rate risk.
- We have seen that immunizing market value sensitivity requires continuous monitoring and adjustment of the portfolio's duration. Such adjustments could also mean potential restructuring of a bank's balance sheet, which may not be practically feasible.
- Theoretically, duration calculations have been found valid only for small changes in interest rates. In other words, with larger interest rate increases, duration over-predicts the fall in bond prices, while for larger interest rate decreases, it under-predicts the rise in bond prices. This is because the bond–price relationship is convex, and not linear, as assumed by the duration model.
- Duration of the market value of assets and liabilities are likely to keep changing over time and require continuous monitoring and balancing.
- Finally, it is a challenge to estimate the duration of assets and liabilities that do not earn or pay interest. For example, how will interest rate changes impact the level of non-interest bearing demand deposits maintained by borrowers? In the absence of fixed or promised cash flows in this important segment of bank liabilities, any assumptions made about cash flows could turn out to be inaccurate. However, fluctuations in these deposits have the potential to impact the DGAP and MVE sensitivity.

It can therefore be concluded that: (a) larger convexity of a security signifies larger interest rate protection, (b) the more the convexity, the larger the error of using just duration to immunize against interest rate changes, and (c) all fixed income securities are convex.[18]

Hence, bank management would prefer to capture the effect of such convexity in their interest rate risk management models

Managing Interest Rate Risk—A Strategic Approach

Let us begin with the understanding that financial risk and interest rate risk are an integral part of banking business. However, if these risks are not managed, the bank's profitability and solvency are at stake. The issues in managing interest rate risk, therefore, are to determine how much risk is acceptable to the bank, and the strategies to achieve and maintain a desired optimum risk profile.

We have seen that it is theoretically possible to manage interest rate risk by strategically varying static GAP or DGAP. How difficult is it to actually implement these approaches? For instance, can interest rates be forecasted accurately into the future? Even if such forecasting is possible, can the variations in GAP or DGAP be without other implications, such as the impact on the bank's profitability? How much control do banks have over a customer's selection of deposit or loan products?

Let us look at some of the strategies banks could follow to achieve the desirable GAP position. To reduce asset sensitivity, banks have the following alternatives. They could (a) extend the maturities in the investment portfolio, (b) increase floating rate deposits, (c) increase short-term borrowings, (d) increase long-term lending, (e) increase fixed rate lending and so on. Similarly, to reduce liability sensitivity, banks could do the opposite—such as, reducing the maturity of the investment portfolio, or increasing long-term deposits, or increasing short-term lending or increasing floating rate lending, and so on.

Hence, the basic balance sheet strategy to manage interest rate risk is to effect changes in portfolio composition. However, it has to be borne in mind that any variation in portfolio has a potential impact on NII.
Illustration 12.5 describes the possible impact of two specific strategies adopted by a bank.

ILLUSTRATION 12.5

Assumptions:

1. Bank A has a negative GAP over the time horizon of the next 1 year. This implies that the bank has a positive DGAP.
2. Bank A expects interest rates to rise

What should Bank A's strategy be for managing interest rate risk?

According to our earlier discussion, the bank would take measures to drive the GAP towards zero. Or, if the objective were a stable MVE, the bank would fine-tune its DGAP to shorten the average asset duration and lengthen the average liability duration.

Let us examine some of these strategies, say, where the bank shortens the maturity of its investment portfolio, and increases the rate on long-term deposits to attract more long-term depositors.

However, in implementing these strategies, the bank has explicitly decided to (a) sacrifice some yield from short-term investment, and (b) increase its interest costs in the short term. Both tend to reduce the bank's NII and NIM for the year. Then why is the bank embarking on this strategy? Since it expects to gain from stalling a potential NII or MVE fall when interest rates rise.

However, the bank has made a critical assumption here. Only if the interest rates rise above the current assumed forward rates,[19] will the bank's investment in short-term securities (versus long-term securities), or its preference for long-term deposits (over short-term deposits) translate into a gain for the bank. If the rates remain below the assumed forward rates, short-tcrm securities would yield much less than long-term investments, and the bank would end up paying more on its long-term deposits as well.

The inference from Illustration 12.5 is obvious. Bank A's management is adjusting GAP and DGAP, and basing such adjustments on its interest rate forecast, which could turn out to be accurate or inaccurate.

Interest Rate Risk or Model Risk?

Most banks prefer to develop and run their own models for interest rate risk measurement. Because different models tend to use much of the same information, but the results may be different, banks have to decide which model and results to use for its purposes.

A bank can get radically different results from the models by merely changing the assumptions on which the model is built. Therefore, it is important to be aware of the assumptions that were used to generate the results and the bank has to make some judgment about their plausibility. For instance:

- What interest rate assumptions have been made and what maturity assumptions have been used for deposit accounts without specified maturities?
- What assumptions were made with respect to the optionality in the bank's assets and liabilities? What business strategies were incorporated into the analysis?
- What assumptions were made regarding customer behaviour as interest rates change?
- Have assumptions changed since the last time the model was used? If so, why?

The best way to assess the reliability of the output of models is to ask questions about the assumptions to see if they seem realistic and cover all possibilities. Also, special attention should be paid to the worst-case scenarios, since worst-case situations often result in serious problems for banks in the unlikely event of their occurrence. Bank Management should always be thinking about new ways to hedge against these extreme situations.

Alternative Methods to Reduce Interest Rate Risk

According to Hingston (2002),[20] there are four basic methods to mitigate interest rate risk in financial institutions—(a) selling assets, (b) extending liabilities, (c) off-balance sheet hedging and (d) retaining status quo. While evaluating these alternatives, Hingston has concluded as follows:

- Selling fixed rate, long-term assets may reduce interest rate risk exposure, but could also lead to losses on such sale that may undermine the selling bank's capital
- By obtaining matching fixed rate, long-term liabilities to fund fixed rate and long-term assets, a bank may theoretically be able to reduce interest rate risk. However, this could create losses in a declining interest rate scenario;
- If the Board so decides, a bank may decide not to do anything about reducing interest rate risk.

This brings us to the final alternative strategy for managing interest rate risk—interest rate derivatives.

SECTION IV

MANAGING INTEREST RATE RISK WITH INTEREST RATE DERIVATIVES

Bank A in Illustration 12.5 can explore yet another alternative to mitigate the interest rate risk on its investments—it can use interest rate derivatives (IRDs) to transform some of its fixed rate investments into floating rate assets. It can also use IRDs to transform floating rate liabilities into fixed rate liabilities.

What do IRDs do? Simply, they are contracts that are used to hedge other positions that expose them to risk, or speculate on anticipated price moves. In most cases, banks use IRDs to replicate balance sheet transactions with off-balance sheet contracts, so that contingent positions are created.

Interest Rate Derivatives, as their name suggests, are financial instruments whose value depends on the value of other underlying instruments (such as the price of underlying fixed rate securities) or indices (such as interest rate indices). They have a variety of advantages over other interest risk mitigating approaches:

- They allow banks to completely customize their interest rate risk profile.
- Since the derivatives can replicate the interest rate exposure of fixed income securities without the requirement of an upfront investment, they may have lower credit risk and greater liquidity.
- Sometimes, use of IRDs could lower transaction costs.
- The accounting and regulatory treatment of IRDs are getting to be fairly streamlined.

The IRDs function as tools that banks can use to 'actively' manage interest rate risk. There are a variety of such tools, and we will be discussing the most important and prevalent among these in the ensuing paragraphs. Given that bank management would prefer to manage, rather than totally eliminate interest rate risk, these tools can be used to complement existing strategies (as discussed in earlier sections) aimed at immunizing the volatility of earnings and MVE to changes in interest rates.

In this chapter, we will focus on the most basic and widely used contracts—swap contracts, financial futures, forward rate agreements (FRAs), options, caps/floors/collars and 'swaptions' (swap options).

Swaps

A swap is an agreement in which two parties (counterparties) agree to exchange periodic payments. The monetary value of the payments exchanged is based on a *notional*[21] principal amount. Swaps are classified based on the characteristics of swap payments. There are four prevalent types of swaps—currency swaps, interest rate swaps, commodity swaps and equity swaps.

Traditionally, banks managed interest rate risk by adjusting the maturity or repricing schedules of their assets and liabilities. As described earlier in this chapter, a bank wishing to lengthen the duration of its assets can add long-term securities to its investment portfolio.

However, banks have now found that the same goal can be accomplished more efficiently and cost-effectively by entering into plain 'vanilla' swaps—where they pay a floating rate, usually based on the London Inter bank Offered Rate (LIBOR) or a market-determined prime rate of the country (where such a rate exists), and receive a fixed rate, which could typically be the treasury rate of equivalent maturity plus a premium. A liability sensitive bank, on the other hand, can enter into a swap where it pays a fixed rate and receives a floating rate. Banks can also use 'basis swaps' where both sides pay floating rates but the index rates are linked to the banks' cost of funds and yield on advances. In such cases, specifically, the banks would pay the prime lending rate and receive LIBOR.

In a 'pure' interest rate swap, one party X agrees to pay the other party Y, cash flows equivalent to a predetermined floating rate interest on a notional principal for a specified number of years. Simultaneously, Y agrees to pay X cash flows equal to fixed rate interest on the same notional principal for the same period of time. The currencies of the two sets of cash flows are also the same.

Interest rate swaps were basically developed to satisfy borrowers' need for fixed rate funds. Banks typically hesitate to fund less creditworthy borrowers on a fixed rate basis (simply because banks do not fund themselves on a fixed rate basis), but may be willing to lend at floating rates.

Illustration 12.6 would help to understand the concept better.

ILLUSTRATION 12.6 HOW DO INTEREST RATE SWAPS WORK?

Firm A, with credit rating less than investment grade, requires ₹100 crore fixed rate funding for a term of 7 years. The firm has two alternatives—(a) borrow 7-year, fixed rate funds at a sizeable premium, say, at 12 percent per annum, or (b) borrow floating rate funds for the 7-year period at a small premium, say at the market-determined prime rate (equivalent to LIBOR) plus 2 percent per annum

Firm B, which enjoys investment grade credit rating, requires floating rate funds. Moreover, it can issue 7-year fixed rate bonds in the same currency, at say, 10 per cent per annum. It can also acquire floating rate funds for an equivalent term at the market determined prime rate (equivalent to the LIBOR) plus 50 bps per annum.

The rates offered to the firms can be represented as follows:

	Fixed Rate	**Floating Rate**
Firm A	12%	LIBOR + 2%
Firm B	10%	LIBOR + 0.5%

The advantage enjoyed by Firm B is termed 'absolute advantage', since it is able to negotiate lower rates in both fixed and floating rate markets. It can also be seen that firm A's cost of funds is higher in the fixed rate market by 2 per cent [12% − 10%] and 1.5 per cent in the floating rate market [LIBOR + (2% − 0.5%)]. This is termed as A's 'relative advantage' in the floating rate market. This advantage is also called 'comparative advantage'. Thus, from the above argument, A has comparative advantage in the floating rate market. It follows that if A and B borrow in the markets where they enjoy comparative advantage, and then swap the borrowing, the cost of funds for both firms can be reduced.

Now, assume that Firm A wants to borrow funds at a fixed rate, and Firm B prefers to acquire funds at a floating rate linked to the LIBOR. Firm B appears to have comparative advantage in the fixed rate market. The fact that the difference between the two fixed rates is greater than the difference between the two floating rates, allows a profitable swap to be negotiated. This is done as follows:

Firm A would raise floating rate funds at LIBOR + 2%, and Firm B would raise an identical amount of fixed rate funds at 10 per cent. Next, A and B enter into a swap such that A ends up with fixed rate funds and B ends up with floating rate funds.

In most swap transactions in practice, a swap dealer serves as an intermediary. However, to understand the concept better, let us assume that A and B effect the swap directly without an intermediary. They might negotiate the following type of swap:

Firm A agrees to pay B fixed interest at, say, 9.75 per cent, and B agrees to pay A floating interest at LIBOR percent per annum.

How is the swap advantageous to both sides?

Let us consider B, which has three sets of interest rate cash flows: (a) it pays 10 per cent to outside lenders, (b) it receives 9.75 per cent per annum from A and (c) it pays the LIBOR to A. The net effect of cash flows (a) and (b) is a cost of 0.25 per cent per annum to B. The net effect of all three cash flows is that B pays LIBOR + 0.25%, or 0.25% less than what it would have had to pay to the floating rate markets if accessed directly.

Firm A also has three sets of cash flows: (a) it pays LIBOR + 2% to outside lenders, (b) it receives LIBOR from B and (c) it pays 9.75 per cent per annum to B. The first two cash flows aggregate to a cost of 2 per cent, and all three taken together implies that A pays 11.75 per cent per annum for obtaining fixed rate funds, or 0.25 per cent less than if it had gone directly to the fixed rate markets.

Therefore, it is evident that an interest rate swap benefits both A and B by 25 bps each, *i.e.*, an aggregate gain of 50 bps per annum. This figure of 50 bps is nothing but the difference between 2 per cent (the difference between the rates at which A and B could access funds in the fixed rate market) and 1.5 per cent (the difference between the rates at which A and B could access funds in the floating rate market).

Thus, generalizing, the total gain in an interest rate swap can be represented as $x - y$, where x is the difference between the interest rates facing the counterparties in the fixed rate market, and y the difference between the interest rates facing the counterparties in the floating rate markets.

The advantages to Firm B (inferred from Illustration 12.6) can be summarized as follows:

a. It could achieve a lower cost borrowing from the floating rate market
b. It could match its assets and liabilities
c. It eliminated interest rate and refinancing risks

The advantages to Firm A are summarized as follows:

a. It could achieve a lower cost of borrowing from the fixed rate market
b. Its capacity to access the fixed rate market in future remains intact
c. It saved the cost and time involved in a public issue
d. It constituted an off-balance sheet transaction
e. The higher cost of borrowing in the fixed rate market would have been accompanied by more stringent covenants, which the firm avoided by opting for the swap

Banks can serve as counterparties or intermediaries in swap transactions.

In Illustration 12.6, the swap involved only two parties. However, in practice, since it is difficult to find two entities with equal and opposite needs, intermediaries facilitate the transaction. Illustration 12.7 would serve to clarify the situation where the intermediary brings together the counterparties in a swap arrangement. In such a case, it is evident that the total benefit from the swap must be shared with the intermediary.

In Illustration 12.6, the total benefit from the swap was 50 bps. If the intermediary's fee is 10 bps, and the benefit of the swap is being shared equally by the two counterparties, each party will still be able to lower its cost of funds by 20 bps each. Banks can play the role of intermediaries effectively due to their strategic position and experience in the financial markets.

ILLUSTRATION 12.7

In Illustration 12.6, if the intermediary, say Bank X, demands a 10 bps fee, the cash flows would be as follows:

Firm A—(a) pays lenders in floating rate market at LIBOR + 2%, (b) receives LIBOR + 0.3% from Bank X and (c) pays 10.10 per cent to Bank X. The net effect of (a) and (b) is 1.7 per cent. Adding 10.10 per cent from (c) takes the total outflow to A to 11.8 per cent. If A had accessed the fixed rate markets it would have had to pay 12 percent. Thus, A has gained 20 bps from the swap transaction.

Firm B—(a) pays 10 per cent to lenders in the fixed rate market, (b) pays LIBOR + 0.3% to Bank X and (c) receives 10 per cent from Bank X. Its total outflow, therefore, is LIBOR + 0.3%. If it had accessed the floating rate market, B would have had to pay LIBOR + 0.5%. Therefore, B has gained 20 bps from the swap transaction.

Bank X—(a) receives 10.10 per cent from A, (b) receives LIBOR + 0.3% from B, (c) pays LIBOR + 0.3% to A and (d) pays 10 per cent to B. The net effect of the four transactions is a gain of 10 bps for Bank X.

It may be noted that the total gain from the swap remains at 50 bps, the difference between the net interest rates in the fixed rate and floating rate markets.

Illustration 12.8 introduces basic market terminologies in the swap market.

ILLUSTRATION 12.8 USING MARKET TERMINOLOGIES

Let us assume that in the swap market, firm A wants to enter into a swap transaction with Bank X for a period of 2 years. Firm A and Bank X enter into the contract on 1 June 2009. According to the contract, A will pay semi-annually the interest of 10.10 per cent per annum to X, while the bank will pay A semi-annually at the floating rate of LIBOR + 0.3%.

In this connection, the terminologies typically used in the swap market are as follows:

a. The 'trade date' is the date the parties agree to a swap. In this case, it is 1 June 2009
b. 'Value date' is the date on which the initial fixed and floating payments begin to accrue—that is, 2 days after the trade date. This is also called the 'effective date'. If the effective date is after 2 days of the trade date, it is called the 'spot date'. The maturity of a swap contract is computed from the effective or value date. In the example, if the value date is 3 June 2009, then the effective date, spot date and value date would be the same.
c. 'Maturity date' is the date on which interest accrual ceases
d. 'Reset date' is the date on which the applicable LIBOR will be determined for payment of semi-annual interest. In our example, the first payment is due on December 3, 2009, *i.e.*, 6 months from the value date and the second payment on 3 June 2010. The 6-month LIBOR relevant for calculating the second payment will be reset based on the rate prevailing 2 days before the first payment date, *i.e.*, on December 1, 2009. This sequence will be usually followed for the remaining period of the swap contract, unless otherwise specified in the contract.

How are swaps applied in practice to manage banks' interest rate risk?

- **Adjusting the rate sensitivity of an asset or liability:** Consider the following example. Bank C has made a loan of ₹100 crore with 5 year maturity to a prime customer at a rate of 10 per cent. The corresponding liability is a 6-month deposit of ₹100 crore, at a floating rate linked to the prevailing market-determined 6-month prime rate. Obviously, there exists an interest rate risk in this transaction. Every time the prime rate rises, the bank makes a loss on the transaction, apart from the bank having to seek refinance for the loan every 6 months (at higher rates, if interest rates are rising). Assume the bank wants to hedge this transaction through a swap, and it agrees to pay, say, 6 per cent, and receive 6-month prime rate against ₹100 crore for 5 years till the loan is fully paid. The net effect on the bank's balance sheet would be as follows—(a) the bank would earn 10 per cent from the loan + 6 month prime from the swap, and (b) the banks would pay 6 month prime for the rupee deposit + 6% from swap as agreed upon. The net spread on this transaction would therefore be 4 per cent (10% − 6%, the receipt and payment of prime cancelling out). The bank has thus locked in a liability cost of 6 per cent (the bank paying and receiving prime every 6 months). Thus, the use of the swap has helped the bank not only reduce interest rate risk, but also to lock in a spread of 4 per cent on this transaction. In general, a swap can help adjust the rate sensitivity of an asset or liability by converting a fixed-rate loan-floating rate, or a floating-rate liability fixed rate, and so on.

- **Creating synthetic transactions and securities:** Swaps are considered 'synthetic' since they are off the bank's balance sheet. Are off-balance sheet transactions less risky than balance sheet transactions? Capital adequacy requirements[22] mandate holding of capital against off-balance sheet positions, which implies that there are risks[23] associated with these positions. Of course, the bank can do away with the need for a swap and match the 5-year asset in the previous example with a long-term deposit with equal or longer tenor, or exit the swap midway. The decision to create a 'synthetic' security would, therefore, be dependent on whether the yield advantage of the swap exceeded the costs (and risks) of such transactions.
- **Adjusting the GAP or DGAP to immunize earnings or MVE:** A liability sensitive bank with a positive DGAP will resort to a swap that would produce profits even when interest rates increase. This can be achieved by adjusting asset duration or increasing RSAs. A swap that pays fixed and receives floating is comparable to increasing RSAs over RSLs. Similarly, a bank with a negative DGAP will want to hedge by taking a swap position that would produce profits when interest rates fall.

Box 12.6 summarizes the key points to be kept in mind in respect of interest rate swaps.

BOX 12.6 INTEREST RATE SWAPS—SUMMARIZING KEY POINTS

1. Interest rate swaps are off-balance sheet items.
2. A primary objective of the swap is to save on interest cost. Therefore, the prevailing relationship between borrowers and lenders does not change.
3. The major swap market players are banks or other intermediaries and corporate entities.
4. The swap contract is distinct from the original loan contract. Hence, the swap tenor is independent of the loan maturity.
5. Where the differential in fixed rate is greater than the differential in floating rate available to counterparties in a swap, a switch from fixed to floating rate is carried out.
6. Where the differential in floating rate is greater than the differential in fixed rate available to counterparties in a swap, a switch from floating to fixed rate is carried out.
7. The credit risk in a swap arrangement is restricted to interest payments only, and does not affect the notional principal amount agreed upon by the counterparties.
8. Pricing of the interest rate swap involves forecasting future benchmark rates. Some common techniques involve the use of yield curves of government securities, forward interest rates or zero coupon securities.
9. Swaps can be used for liability management, and could lead to speculative gains.

Interest Rate Futures

A futures contract is a legal agreement between a buyer (or seller) and an established exchange in which the buyer (or seller) agrees to take (or make) delivery of something at a predetermined price at the end of a predetermined period of time. The price at which the parties agree to transact in the future is the 'futures' price. The predetermined date at which the parties must transact is the 'settlement' or 'delivery' date.

Futures can be categorized as financial or non-financial futures. Commodity futures (which were the only known futures prior to 1972) are non-financial futures. Financial futures are contracts based on a financial instrument or financial index. The most commonly known financial futures are (a) stock index futures, (b) interest rate futures, and (c) currency futures.

When the underlying asset is an interest-bearing security, the contract is termed 'interest rate futures'. Interest rate futures contracts are typically classified by the maturity of the underlying security. Short-term interest rate future contracts are those whose underlying securities mature in less than 12 months. A long-term futures contract is, therefore, one whose maturity exceeds 1 year.

The major function of the futures markets is to transfer the interest rate risk from the 'hedger'[24] to the 'speculator'.[25]

In the futures market, hedging acts as a temporary substitute for a transaction to be made in the cash market, locking in a value for the cash position at some point of time. When cash and futures prices move together, a 'perfect hedge'[26] is possible where the profit in one market is equally offset by a loss in the other. Box 12.7 outlines some basic principles of hedging in the futures (and forward) markets.

BOX 12.7 BASICS OF FUTURES (AND FORWARD) CONTRACTS

Differences between futures and forward contracts

A forward contract, like a futures contract, is an agreement to deliver something at a predetermined price at the end of a predetermined period. Forward contracts differ from futures contracts in the following aspects: (a) futures contracts are standardized agreements in respect of delivery dates and quality of the deliverable, while forward contracts are essentially non-standardized, since the terms of each contract are negotiated individually between buyer and seller, (b) futures contracts are traded on recognized stock exchanges, while forwards are over the counter (OTC) instruments, (c) there is a very thin or non-existent secondary market for forward contracts, (d) forward contracts are intended for delivery, while futures may not be intended to be settled by delivery, (e) futures are marked to market at the end of each trading day, while the marking to market of forward transactions are by mutual agreement between the counter parties, (f) interim cash flows are possible in futures contracts, either as additional margin in case of adverse price movements or as cash withdrawn in case of favourable price movements, while such interim cash flows can occur in forwards not marked to market, and, importantly, and (g) the credit risk due to counter party default inherent in a forward contract is mitigated due to the transaction being guaranteed by the exchanges.

Simple examples of trading in interest rate futures

An interest rate futures contract is an agreement for buying or selling a standard quantity of specific interest-bearing instruments, at a price agreed upon by the parties, at a predetermined date in future.

Firm A has a fixed-rate loan contract with Bank B. It expects interest rates to fall. One alternative is to buy a futures contract. If the current interest rate is 10 per cent and the firm expects the rate to fall to 9 per cent, it can buy a futures contract at market price. If the interest rate does fall, the contract will quote higher (since when interest rates fall, instruments offering higher coupon rates rise in value). The firm sells the futures and gains.

Similarly, if the firm expects interest rates to rise, and it has a floating-rate loan contract, it would sell futures at market price. When interest rates rise, the futures contract will quote lower for the same reason stated above. The firm now buys the futures and gains.

In general, when a firm has an asset portfolio, it could:

a. buy interest rate futures if it expects interest rates to fall, and
b. sell interest rate futures if it expects interest rates to rise.

Similarly, when a firm has a liability portfolio, it could:

a. sell interest rate futures if it expects interest rates to fall, and
b. buy interest rate futures if it expects interest rates to rise.

A brief look at how futures trading takes place

Futures contracts are traded on organized exchanges[27] that also serve as clearing houses. The likelihood that the counter party to a forward contract defaults in his obligations is eliminated in futures contracts, since the exchange assumes all obligations at the end of each trading day, forcing members to settle their net positions.

In practice, a buyer and seller are found for each transaction, and the procedure enables any trader to offset an initial position by assuming the opposite position any time prior to the futures contract's delivery date. For example, a buyer of a T-Bill futures contract for, say, 90 days, can offset his position by selling the same contract, say, a fortnight later. The liquidity that this procedure affords is a feature of the futures market, not found in a forward contract. The liquidity is a result of trading standardized assets through the exchange.

Once the futures contract is entered into, there are cash flow obligations for buyers and sellers. While entering into the contract, traders must deposit an 'initial margin' with the exchange that serves as a cash margin that would partially offset losses arising from adverse rate movements.

Apart from the initial margin, the exchange also requires traders to meet a 'maintenance margin', specifying the minimum deposit required at the end of each trading day. These margins are not to be confused with margins for stocks discussed in earlier chapters on Credit Administration. The futures margin deposits are similar to performance bonds—the trader guarantees that mandatory payment obligations will be met. In case the margin deposit falls below the specified minimum requirement, the trader must deposit more funds.

The maintenance deposit varies with the movements of the underlying asset in the market, and, hence, the exchange identifies the change in the value of every trader's account at the end of every day, crediting the margin account of the trader with gains and debiting with losses. This daily settlement process is termed 'marking to market'.

On the date of contract expiration, trading is halted, and the traders settle their final positions. Contracts can be settled either through physical delivery or cash settlement. In the case of physical delivery, the seller of futures delivers the physical asset, while the buyer makes cash payment to the seller. In cash settlement, there is no physical delivery, and traders merely settle the final value of the position after the last trading day.

'Basis' risk of hedging

In practice, futures contracts may not work perfectly due to the following possibilities: (a) the hedge may require that the futures contract be closed before its expiration date, (b) the asset whose price is to be hedged may not be identical to the asset underlying the futures contract, or (c) the hedger may be unsure of the exact date when the asset would be bought or sold.

(a) is the result of futures contracts being standardized. An example for (b) would be using rupee futures to hedge price movements of commercial paper transactions. The situation in (c) could arise from the seller's uncertainty regarding delivery date of a product consequent to certain troubles experienced by the firm producing the product.

Any of the situations outlined above could give rise to 'basis risk'

'Basis' is simply the profit (or loss) on the hedge. It is determined by the difference between the cash price (also called the 'spot' price) of the asset to be hedged and the futures price when the hedge is placed, and when the hedge is lifted. Thus,

$$\text{Basis} = \text{Spot Price} - \text{Futures Price}$$

Theoretically, the basis is also the 'cost of carry' or the net cost of financing a position, *i.e.*, the difference between the rate of financing and the cash yield from holding the underlying asset.

If the asset to be hedged and the underlying asset of the futures contract are identical, the basis should be 'zero' when the futures contract expires. Before expiration, the basis can be positive or negative.

The above definition of basis shows that when the spot price increases more than the futures price, the basis will also increase or 'strengthen'. Similarly, when the futures price increases more than the spot price, the basis decreases or 'weakens'.

Basis risk in hedging arises when the basis changes at the time of removing the hedge. Hence, the actual risk in hedging interest rate movements is not that the level of interest rates will move against the cash position, but that the basis might change between the time the hedge is initiated and removed. The effective return from the hedge can be expressed as the difference between the initial cash rate and the change in basis.

Generally, movements in the basis are more predictable than movements in the spot market rates and the volatility of spot rates are typically more pronounced than the volatility of the basis. This explains why in most cases it is less risky to hedge than not hedge at all. Even where sizeable changes occur in the basis, it is to be noted that the predominant factors that influence the spot markets simultaneously influence futures markets as well. Further, with arbitrage activity, basis could be driven to zero levels as time to expiration approaches, if the cash instrument to be hedged is the same as the asset underlying the futures contract.

Basis risk and cross hedging

In not all cases is the asset to be hedged identical to the asset underlying the futures, as assumed above. In such circumstances, 'cross hedge' is used.

Though cross hedging is common in many hedging applications, the risk potential is also greater in cross hedges since futures and spot interest rates based on different underlying assets may not always move together in the same direction. According to the measure of effective return given above, the volatility of the return depends on the volatility of the basis.

In most cases, the effectiveness of a cross hedge is determined by (a) the relationship between the spot price of the underlying asset and its futures price when a hedge is initiated and when it is removed and (b) the relationship between the market value of the asset and the spot price of the underlying asset for the futures contract, when the hedge is initiated and when the hedge is removed

Short hedge and long hedge

In the case of interest rate futures contract, a short hedge serves to protect against a decline in the future spot price of an asset, which implies a rise in the interest rate. A short hedge is also called a 'sell hedge', since the hedger sells a futures contract (agrees to make delivery). By entering into a short hedge, the hedger has effectively frozen the future spot price, and also transferred the ownership risk to the buyer of the futures contract.

The strategy here is to sell futures contracts on securities similar to those carrying the interest rate risk. If spot rates increase, futures rates are also expected to increase. A loss in the spot position, therefore, is expected to be at least partially offset by a gain in the futures value. Similarly, if spot rates decline, the gain in the spot market is expected to be offset by a loss from futures.

Let us assume that a bank aims to protect its investment portfolio from future losses due to interest rate changes. It needs to sell a security from its investment portfolio in about 2 months' time. It expects an increase in interest rates and wants to protect itself against a decline in the value of the security at the time of sale. To hedge, the bank will want to sell futures, and buy it back at the time when it sells the security for cash.

In contrast to the above, a 'long hedge' is preferred when interest rates are declining. It is also known as a 'buy hedge' since the hedger buys a futures contract, *i.e.*, agrees to accept delivery. As for the short hedge, the appropriate strategy would be to buy futures contracts on securities similar to those facing interest rate risks. If interest rates decline, futures rates are also likely to decline, and the value of the futures position is likely to increase. Any loss in the spot market would be at least partially offset by a gain in futures. However, if spot rates rise, the investor may profit more from not hedging. Therefore, a hedger, in this case, foregoes gains arising from favourable price movements.

For example, a bank expects substantial loan repayment to flow in after 3 months. It would like to invest this cash inflow in high-yielding securities. The bank would like to invest the funds at spot rates, but obviousiy cannot have access to the cash inflow till 3 months later. If, during this period, interest rates move lower, the bank faces an opportunity loss. The bank hedges this risk by buying futures contracts. If interest rates fall, futures rates are also likely to fall, and the value of the security is likely to increase, which would offset cash losses.

The important point to note here is that the hedger's primary objective of trading in futures is mitigating intcrest rate risk, and not expected futures profits.

How Banks Apply Hedging Techniques to Mitigate Interest Rate Risk Banks can hedge at micro level (microhedging) or at the macro level (macrohedging). In microhedging, the bank can immunize itself against variations in asset or liability interest rates. For example, the bank can protect itself from an upward movement of the interest rate on its liabilities, by taking positions in futures contracts on, say, CDs or long-term deposits.

In macrohedging, the entire DGAP of a bank is hedged using futures contracts. Let us see how this is done.

Applying Hedging to GAP and DGAP According to Koch and Macdonald,[28] the hedging strategy of a bank using GAP and Earnings Sensitivity analysis to measure its interest rate risk is determined by: (a) whether a bank is asset or liability sensitive, and (b) the degree of impact of interest rate changes on the bank's NII. For example, in an asset sensitive bank, declining interest rates would cause NII to fall. Hence, the position will have to be offset by a 'long hedge' (see Box 12.7). Similarly, to overcome liability sensitivity, a bank would have to institute a 'short hedge'. In the case of a liability sensitive bank, if rates subsequently increase, leading to a fall in the NII, the sale of futures is expected to give rise to gains that at least partially offsets the dip in NII.

For example, take the negative cumulative GAP of ₹100 crore over a period of 1 year, as assumed in Illustration 12.1. The Illustration also shows that if interest rates were to increase by 100 bps, NII falls. Let us now assume that the bank wants to hedge ₹10 crore out of the ₹100 crore GAP over the next 6 months (180 days), and it chooses 90 day T-bill futures as the hedge instrument. The bank would have to sell 20 futures contracts [10 × (180 days/90 days)], assuming that the expected movement between the effective interest rate on the RSLs relative to the futures rate equals unity. This short hedge transaction has effectively fixed a rate, and has moved the GAP (and the earnings sensitivity) closer to zero.

DGAP lends itself more easily to hedging applications. A positive DGAP indicates that the MVE is likely to decline if interest rates were to increase equally for both assets and liabilities of the bank. We have already seen in the earlier paragraphs how MVE can be immunized by setting the DGAP to zero. The bank can also use futures to immunize MVE.

The appropriate value of the futures position can be derived as

$$\frac{\text{WADa [MVA]}}{(1+i_{\text{a}})} - \frac{\text{WADl[MVL]}}{(1+i_{\text{l}})} + \frac{\text{Df [MVF]}}{(1+i_{\text{f}})} = 0,$$

where WADa, WADl, MVA and MVL are as defined in the earlier paragraphs, interest rate measures (i) with subscripts 'a', 'l' and 'f' refer to 'assets', 'liabilities' and 'futures' and are expected to change by the same amount, and Df and MVF refer to the duration and market value of the futures contract used.[29]

The above concept can be used to hedge DGAP mismatches, without impacting the existing portfolio of the bank.

Routine Hedging and Selective Hedging A bank does 'routine' hedging when it reduces its interest rate risk to the lowest possible level by selling futures contracts to hedge its whole balance sheet. However, reduction in risk also succeeds in reducing returns.

Therefore, some banks may prefer to do 'selective' hedging. They may want to hedge only certain assets and liabilities, and bear the risk related to others. Thus, these banks take on selective risk to ensure that their profitability is maximized. According to Saunders,[30] banks may also want to hedge selectively to gain the arbitrage advantage that could arise between spot and futures price movements.

Forward Rate Agreements (FRAs)

The foregoing discussion had briefly introduced forward contracts in the context of comparing them with futures contracts. An FRA is one type of forward contract, which is based on interest rates. In this type of contract, the two counterparties agree to a *notional principal* amount to serve as a reference for determining relevant cash flows. The contract also provides for exchange of payments between the two counterparties over a single future contract period. While one party commits to pay a fixed rate of interest (agreed at the inception of the contract), the other party commits to pay a floating rate of interest (set at the inception of the contract) on the predetermined notional principal. An FRA can also resemble a swap agreement covering only one future interest payment period.

Typically, the 'buyer' of the FRA agrees to pay a fixed rate interest payment and receive floating rate payment against the notional principal on a predetermined future date. Similarly, the 'seller' of the FRA agrees to pay floating and received fixed rate payment against the same principal on the same specified date. Cash payment will be received or made by the buyer or seller only if the actual interest rate on the date of settlement differs from the forecasted rate. However, there would be no interim cash flows before the settlement date, margin or marking to market requirements, as in the case of futures contracts.

FRAs, like swaps, are traded in the OTC market. 'Bid' rates reflect the fixed rate the buyer is willing to pay versus receiving the reference rate (say LIBOR) flat, while 'ask' rates reflect the fixed rate the seller is willing to receive versus paying the reference rate (LIBOR) flat. Though the maturity of an FRA can typically be long (5 or more years), 3- or 0-month contract periods are more common.

Banks use FRAs to lock in a fixed interest rate expense on floating rate deposits, or lock in fixed interest rate revenues on floating rate loans. For example, if a bank has outstanding floating rate loans due for repricing in 6 months' time, it can mitigate the interest rate risk by 'fixing' the interest revenue in advance by selling an FRA with a notional principal equal to the outstanding principal on the loans. In return, the bank would pay the prevailing floating rate.

Illustration 12.9 clarifies the concept.

ILLUSTRATION 12.9

Firm A has contracted with Bank B for a 2-year loan of ₹100 crore priced at 300 bps over the existing benchmark rate (LIBOR or MIBOR). Assume that the loan is repriced every quarter. Firm A expects the benchmark rate to rise in future, and, hence, enters into a contract with the bank to pay fixed rate at 9 per cent per annum (called the exercise rate) over the next four quarters.

Note here that Bank B has 'sold' (receive fixed, pay floating) an FRA to Firm A. Bank B will call this '3 vs 12' FRA at 9 per cent on a notional principal amount of ₹100 crore. The term '3 vs 12' conveys that the FRA relates to a 3-month interest rate observed from the present for a security whose maturity falls 12 months later.

Case 1 Let us assume that in 3 months, the 3 month benchmark moves to 7 per cent. In this case, benchmark rate + 3% = 10%, while the fixed rate under FRA is 9 per cent. Hence, Firm A will receive the following amount of interest from Bank B.

$$(0.10 - 0.09) \times \left(\frac{90}{360}\right) \times ₹100 \text{ crore} = ₹25 \text{ Lakhs}$$

The above amount represents interest that would be paid 3 months later (on maturity). Hence, the actual payment is discounted at the prevailing 3-month benchmark rate:

$$\frac{₹25 \text{ Lakhs}}{1 + \left(\frac{90}{360}\right) \times 0.07} = ₹24{,}57{,}002$$

Case 2 Assume that the 3-month benchmark falls to 4 per cent. Now Firm A will have to pay Bank B:

$$(0.09 - 0.07) \times \left(\frac{90}{360}\right) \times ₹100 \text{ crore} = ₹50 \text{ Lakhs}$$

and the actual interest to be paid would be

$$\frac{₹50 \text{ Lakhs}}{\left(1 + \frac{90}{360}\right)} \times 0.04 = ₹49{,}50{,}495$$

In this illustration, the firm pays fixed and receive floating rate as a hedge since it wanted to avert loss in a scenario where interest rates were rising. (We can see that this is very similar to a short futures position.)

Similarly, Bank B would take its position as a hedge when interest rates are expected to fall. This is similar to a long futures position.

Risks Involved in Using FRAs

1. Their resemblance to forward contracts implies that FRAs are also subject to credit risk. There is a possibility that the counterparty may default when payment under the FRA is due.
2. The transaction depends on the integrity and creditworthiness of counterparties, and this has to be gauged by the parties themselves, without the guarantee or backing of exchanges/clearing houses as in the case of futures.
3. In practice, it may be difficult to find the counterparty that can take exactly the opposite position. There may also be disagreement between counterparties on the settlement date or the notional principal amount, and so on. This may lead to higher transaction costs as well.
4. Relative to other types of IRDs, FRAs are not very liquid. If one of the counterparties wants to exit the contract midway, compensation needs to be paid, as the contract has to be assigned to another party.

Interest Rate Options

Like all financial derivatives, interest rate options derive their value from an underlying security, which, in this case, would typically be a reference interest rate or an interest rate index. Interest rate options provide protection against adverse market moves, while enabling the holder to still benefit from favourable shifts in the market. Box 12.8 briefly explains the concept of 'financial options' and Box 12.9, the difference between options, forward and futures contracts.

To illustrate, assume that Bank A has lent ₹100 crore based on a floating rate. The rate is set at say LIBOR + 3%. Bank A is happy when LIBOR is increasing—but also wants to protect itself against drops in LIBOR. The level at which the bank would like to cover itself is, say, 9 per cent total. In other words, it wants to protect itself against LIBOR falling below 6 per cent.

The solution is to buy an 'interest rate put option'. This contract will specify a notional amount (say ₹100 crore – the loan amount), the strike rate (6% LIBOR) and a maturity date on which the option would expire.

Let us assume LIBOR does drop to 4 per cent. Bank A will exercise the option, and receives a payment from the option issuer as follows:

$$\text{Put option pay-off} = (\text{strike rate} - \text{actual rate}) \times \text{notional amount}$$

That is, the difference between strike rate (6 per cent) and actual rate (4 per cent) times ₹100 crore, which equals ₹2 crore.

Bank A will also receive from its borrower 7 per cent (LIBOR—4% + 3%) times ₹100 crore. In effect, the bank has received the desired minimum return of 9 per cent on ₹100 crore, of course, it would have had to pay a fee to the option issuer in return for the protection provided.

Similarly, Bank A could have entered into an interest rate call option to hedge against interest rate increases on its floating rate deposits. Assume that on a ₹100 crore deposit, the bank does not want to pay more than 9 per cent (LIBOR +3%). If the LIBOR does increase to 7 per cent, Bank A will have to pay its depositor ₹10 crore by way of annual interest. Bank A will now exercise the call option, and the option issuer pays (7% – 6%) × 100 crore or ₹1 crore, which taken with the ₹9 crore (9 per cent) the bank was willing to pay, would satisfy the depositor. If interest rates start dropping, the bank would not exercise the option and would still benefit since it has to pay less to the depositor.

Note that in the above example, we have made the simplifying assumption that all payouts are after a year.

Caplets and Floorlets In financial terms, the call option described above is called a 'caplet' and the put option, a 'floorlet'. The reason for the nomenclature is clear—a 'caplet' protects the bank against large increases in interest rates—it has effectively set a 'cap' on the bank's interest outgo. Similarly, the floorlet has ensured that drops in interest rate do not eat into the bank's earnings—it has effectively guaranteed a minimum level of income floor for the bank.

BOX 12.8 FINANCIAL 'OPTIONS'—THE BASICS

An option is a private contract between two parties, in which the holder has (a) the right to buy an underlying asset at a predetermined price, k, by a specified date, t, or, (b) the right to sell an underlying asset at a predetermined price, k, by a specified date, t.

Options form a unique type of financial contract since they give the buyer of the option the 'right', but *not* the 'obligation', to exercise the option. In other words, the buyer uses the option only if it benefits him/her; otherwise, the option can be discarded or allowed to lapse.

Some basic terminologies used in financial options are as follows:

a. The *writer* of the option is the seller of the option. The writer grants the right to buy or sell the underlying security to the buyer of the option.
b. The *holder* of the option is the buyer of the option. The buyer has the right to buy the underlying security from or sell it to the writer on or before a specified date.
c. The option with a right to buy the underlying security is the *call option.*
d. The option with a right to sell the underlying security is the *put option.*
e. The *option price* or *option premium* is the sum of money paid by the buyer of the option to the seller for gaining the right under the option.
f. The predetermined price at which the underlying security may be bought or sold is the *strike price* or *exercise price.*
g. The date specified in the contract is the *exercise date* or *expiration date* or *maturity*. After this date, the option contract becomes void.
h. The underlying assets in financial options can include stocks, stock indices, foreign currencies, debt instruments, commodities and futures contracts.
i. Options can be categorized according to when the buyer may exercise the option. *American options* can be exercised at any time up to (and including) the expiration date. *European options* can be exercised only on the expiration date. (It is to be noted that the terms 'American' and 'European' do not refer to the location of the option or the exchange)
j. The value of a call option on expiration date would not be known before expiration. If this value s is greater than the exercise price, k, the call is said to be *in the money*. If s is smaller than k, the call is *out of the money.*
k. The circumstances that establish the value of a put option are the opposite of those for a call option. The put option gives the holder the right to sell the asset, and hence it would not make sense for the holder to sell if the price at expiration s is greater than the exercise price k. In other words, the put option is worthless if s exceeds k. In this case, the put option is *out of the money*. The put option will be *in the money* if s is less than k.

Valuing the option

Consider the following example. An American call option contract on shares of firm V, has an exercise price of ₹600. Assume that the share sells at ₹700 today, a few days prior to expiration. The option price in this case is likely to be above ₹100, since investors would rationally pay more than ₹100 in the expectation that the share price would rise above ₹700 in the forthcoming days prior to expiration. (It is to be noted that the option cannot sell below ₹100 since this would result in 'arbitrage profit'—that is, profit from a transaction that has no risk or cost, but aimed at taking advantage of the price differential for the same stock in two different markets. If arbitrage profit did happen, the excess demand for this call option would quickly force the price to rise to at least ₹100.). However, the option price for buying the share cannot have a greater value than the market price of the share itself, since it would not make sense to buy a share with a call option, when the share itself can be purchased at a lower price.

It is, therefore, evident that the call option value will be bounded as follows—the upper bound of the call option will be the price of the stock itself s, and the lower bound for the option will be the difference between the stock price and the exercise price $(s - k)$.

Therefore, the following factors can be seen to determine the value of a call option—(a) exercise price (the higher the exercise price, the lower the value of the call option), (b) stock price (the higher the stock price, the more valuable the call option), (c) interest rate (the higher the interest rate, the more valuable the option), (d) expiration date, and (e) the variability of the underlying asset (the greater the variability of the underlying asset, the more valuable the call option). The value of a put option is determined by the same factors operating in the opposite direction.

If both the call and put options share the same expiration date and exercise price, it is seen that a relationship evolves between the prices at the time of the original position, which can be expressed as follows:

$$\text{Present value of exercise price} = \text{value of stock} + \text{value of put} - \text{value of call}$$

The above expression is commonly called the 'put call parity'

BOX 12.9 THE DIFFERENCES BETWEEN OPTIONS, FUTURES AND FORWARD CONTRACTS

Feature	Options	Futures	Forwards
Standardized?	Yes	Yes	No
Pricing Mechanism	Generally, option prices are market-determined and Strike prices are exchange-determined	Market-determined prices	Price determined between buyer and seller
Liquid?	Yes	Yes	No
Contracts are Closed....	• By delivery, or • By paying the price differential, or • By taking an offset-ting position	• By delivery, or • By paying the price differential, or • By taking an offset-ting position	Only by delivery
Margin Maintenance	Yes	Yes	No
Performance Obligations	Writer of the option	Both parties to a futures contract	Both parties to a forward contract
Guarantor	Clearing house	Clearing house	No guarantor
Profit Settlement	Option writer generally collects premium on T + 1	Daily	At the end of contract period

Interest Rate Caps and Floors In practice, it may so happen that both the depositor and borrower may want to invest/borrow for periods longer than a year, say, 9 years. In this case, the bank will have to buy a series of caplets and floorlets for 1, 2, 3 years and so on. To simplify the procedure, the option instruments of different maturities can be bundled together as one instrument.

A bundle of interest rate caplets with the same strike rate but different maturities is called an 'interest rate cap'. Similarly, a bundle of interest rate floorlets with the same strike rate and different maturities, is an 'interest rate floor'

What do interest rate 'Caps' do? They protect the bank (or the holder) against rising interest rates on its liabilities in the short term. If the underlying interest rate exceeds a specified ceiling rate, the option issuer (called 'cap issuer') makes payment to the bank. The payment will be equal to the difference between the actual rate and the strike rate times the notional amount specified in the option contract.

What do interest rate 'Floors' do? They protect the bank from interest rates falling below a desired minimum, the strike rate. The payment by the option issuer for a floor is determined by the difference between the strike rate and actual rate times the notional amount.

A series of payments—caplets or floorlets—are made during the period of the contract.

The benefits of buying caps or floors are similar to those of buying any option. The bank that buys a cap can set a maximum (cap) rate on its cost of borrowed funds. It can also convert a fixed rate liability to a floating rate liability. In the process, it gets protection when rates are increasing, and retains the benefits in case rates fall. The cost of such protection would be the upfront premium that the bank pays the option issuer. In an environment where interest rates are rising, such premiums could be quite high. Similarly, when interest rates are expected to fall, the premium for buying interest rate 'floors' would be high.

Interest Rate 'Collars' In some cases, to compensate for the premium paid on 'caps' and 'floors', banks buy interest rate 'collars' or 'reverse collars'.

When a bank purchases a 'collar', it is actually simultaneously buying an interest rate cap and selling an interest rate floor—the notional amount, maturity and index being the same. In buying a cap, the bank's objective is to protect against rising interest rates. By simultaneously selling the floor, the floor rate being set below the cap rate, the bank generates premium income.

Buying a collar would, therefore, be beneficial to a bank as long as interest rates are rising. When the actual interest rate (the index) rises above the cap (strike rate), the bank receives payment from the option issuer. If the actual index falls below the floor, the bank, as the collar buyer, would have to pay the option issuer the difference between the strike rate (floor) and the actual rate.

Therefore, a collar creates a 'range' within which the buyer's effective interest rates fluctuate.

Theoretically, it is possible to have a 'zero cost collar', where the cap and floor rates are so chosen that the premiums are equal, and there is no net premium outgo for the bank buying the collar.

When the bank wants to protect its earnings from assets when interest rates are falling, it buys a 'reverse collar'. This is the opposite of a collar, and refers to simultaneously buying an interest rate 'floor' and selling an interest rate 'cap'. The motivation for selling the cap is to compensate for the cost of buying the floor. When the actual rate falls below the floor, the bank, as the buyer of the 'reverse collar', receives payment from the option issuer. However, if interest rates rise above the cap, the bank will have to make cash payment to the option issuer. The net result is that the bank's interest rate fluctuates within a range.

Banks can also construct 'zero cost reverse collars' where they can find floor and cap rates with identical premiums that provide an acceptable interest rate band.

How do banks choose between swaps, caps and floors and collars?

Illustration 12.10 serves to clarify.

ILLUSTRATION 12.10

Assume that Bank A is asset sensitive, and a fall in interest rates would lead to a fall in NII. Also assume that the bank holds ₹100 crore of loans priced at prime +2%. The loans have been funded with a 5-year deposit costing 6.10 per cent to the bank. Interest rates may rise or fall over the next 5 years, but the bank wants to guard against a fall since its loans are at floating rate.

The bank is evaluating the following three alternatives:

1. It can enter into a plain interest rate swap, to pay LIBOR and receive a fixed rate,
2. It can buy an interest rate floor, or
3. It can buy a reverse collar.

All the alternatives are evaluated considering the following assumptions:

- The current loan rate has been assumed at 10 per cent, and the cost of deposit at 6 per cent.
- The loan rate is assumed to be linked to the bank's prime rate, and hence moves up or down based on prime rate changes. For ease of calculation, the rate movements have been assumed at 100 bps.
- LIBOR is assumed at 6 per cent and movements at 100 bps.

Case 1 Interest Rate Swap—The bank pays LIBOR and receives 6.05 fixed.

	Base Case LIBOR 6%	**Interest Rates Fall by 100 bps LIBOR 5%**	**Interest Rates Rise by 100 bps LIBOR 7%**
NII			
Loan interest earned	10%	9%	11%
Cost of deposit	6.10%	6.10%	6.10%
Spread	3.90%	2.90%	4.90%
Interest rate swap flows			
Fixed-inflow	6.05	6.05	6.05
LIBOR (floating)—outflow	6	5	7
Spread	0.05	1.05	– 0.95
Total spread	3.95	3.95	3.95

Case 2 Buy 6% Floor on LIBOR—The bank receives when LIBOR falls below 6%. For this, it has to pay a fee of 0.2% per year

NII			
Loan Interest earned	10%	9%	11%
Cost of deposit	6.10%	6.10%	6.10%
Spread	3.90%	2.90%	4.90%
Interest rate floor flows			
Payout—inflow	0	1	0
Fee—outflow	0.2	0.2	0.2
Spread	– 0.2	0.8	– 0.2
Total spread	3.7	3.7	4.7

Case 3 Buy Reverse Collar-Buy 5.5 % Floor On Libor, Sell 6.5% Cap On Libor-The bank will pay when LIBOR exceeds 6.5%, and will receive when LIBOR falls below 5.5%. The premium will be 0.05%.

NII			
Loan interest earned	10%	9%	11%
Cost of deposit	6.10%	6.10%	6.10%
Spread	3.90%	2.90%	4.90%
Reverse collar flows			
Payout-inflow	0	0.5	−0.5
Fee-inflow	0.05	0.05	0.05
Spread	0.05	0.55	−0.45
Total spread	3.95	3.45	4.45

Thus, it is evident that all three alternatives perform efficiently, and decision of the bank to prefer one instrument over the other depends on the objectives for which protection is sought for, and the risk appetite of the bank.

Interest Rate Guarantees

Interest rate guarantees (IRGs) are very similar to interest rate options, the only difference being that the hedging period is restricted to 1 year. In place of the option premium, the guarantor receives a guarantee commission.

Swaptions

Our earlier discussion introduced plain vanilla interest rate swaps. Financial innovation and the need for prudent risk management at least cost have been instrumental in expanding the types of instruments available for mitigating risks, as well the nature of their application.

One such innovation is the 'swaption', which as the name suggests, is an option on a swap. The holder of a swaption has the option of entering into a swap contract at a predetermined fixed rate during the agreed period. For example, a 1-year swaption gives the holder the right to purchase a swap within the year. However, at the end of the year, there is no obligation to enter into the swap arrangement. It follows that a receiver of a swaption has the right to receive the fixed rate, and a payer of a swaption has the right to pay the fixed rate.

As with options (see Box 12.8), there are 'calls' and 'puts' in swaptions as well. The buyer of a put or call swaption pays a premium to the option issuer.

A 'call swaption' gives the holder the right to enter a swap contract where the holder pays a fixed rate and receives a floating rate. The holder also has the right to terminate the swap after a fixed period of time. Similarly, a 'put swaption' gives the holder the right to put the security back to the issuer even before maturity. In this case, the party receiving the fixed payment has the option to terminate the swap after a certain period, which option is likely to be exercised when interest rates are increasing.

A 'callable' or 'puttable' swap is essentially a swap with an embedded option. Since a swaption effectively permits parties to terminate the swap, it is also referred to as a 'cancellable' or 'terminable' swap.

Swaptions have found applications in areas such as (a) anticipatory financing, (b) managing future borrowing costs and (c) changing existing swap terms. For example, if a borrower being charged floating rates fears that interest rates will not fall in future, he can reduce funding cost by selling a receiver swaption. Similarly, a borrower who is not sure if he wants to lock in interest rates for 1 year, can delay the decision by buying a payer swaption.

Arbiloans

Another recent innovation is 'Interest Arbitrage financing', also called 'Arbiloans'. These are useful to multinational corporations operating in high interest rate and low interest rate countries. Let us assume a subsidiary of this corporation is operating in a low interest rate country. The subsidiary borrows locally at the lower rate, converts into parent's home currency at spot rates, and lends the amount to the parent. The parent company guarantees to repay the principal along with interest, while hedging against adverse exchange rate movements.[31]

Derivatives Market Growth—The Issues

The market for interest rate and other derivative products is growing rapidly. Box 12.10 examines whether use of these risk management tools could create fresh risks for banks. Box 12.11 outlines the accounting standards adopted by the international community to make derivative transactions and their risks more transparent to the public.

BOX 12.10 ARE DERIVATIVES RISKY FOR BANKS?[32]

At around USD 344 trillion,[33] the notional amount of interest rate derivatives outstanding globally at the end of September 2009, may appear daunting. However, considering that this position had touched a peak of USD 600 trillion in 2007, and then plunged to a low of USD 294 trillion at the end of June 2009, the position in September 2009 appears to indicate stabilizing financial market conditions. However, we have to understand how risky this position is, and whether it renders the world's financial system vulnerable to further shocks!

While the notional amount is a proxy for the amount of derivatives activity, it does not reflect the riskiness of the activity. In the case of derivatives, the notional amount is seldom at risk of loss. It is the derivatives investor who is at risk of loss from changes in prices of or rates earned on the financial assets that the notional amount represents.

There are three broad kinds of derivative activities that banks involve in—hedging, dealing and speculating,

When used for 'hedging', a derivative is used to mitigate the risk associated with an existing balance sheet position. Banks use 'dealing' in derivatives to earn fees—the bank essentially functions as an intermediary and makes contracts available to customers for a fee. In turn, the bank may enter into offsetting positions with other customers or manage derivative risk in other ways. 'Speculating' in a derivative transaction would have the objective of earning profits from expectations about derivative price movements that differ from market expectations.

Most banks are involved in derivatives transactions as only 'hedgers' or 'dealers'. It is not easy to determine the extent of speculation—one, because speculation is not reported, and two, since speculative type risks could arise from certain dealer activities.

The three prevalent types of derivatives contracts banks enter into or facilitate are (a) interest rate derivative contracts, (b) foreign exchange derivative contracts and (c) equity, commodity and other types of derivative contracts.

Interest rate derivative contracts, which form the bulk of contracts banks enter into, are relatively less risky than other derivative types, say equity derivatives. This is because the magnitude of changes in short-term benchmark rate such as LIBOR is likely to be significantly lower than the changes in the stock market composite index. Hence, losses on the interest rate contract are more likely to be a small percentage of the notional amount. Exposures to equity or commodity for the same period are more likely to be a significant percentage of the notional value.

The risk in derivative activities also varies according to the objective for which the contracts have been created. Hedging, by definition, is a risk mitigating activity, and as already discussed, the risk of losses could be lower relative to other derivative activities. Derivative dealers are exposed to similar risks as hedgers, as well as 'operational risk' as a result of the huge volume of derivatives activity they undertake. A speculative objective, on the other hand, can lead to very high risk exposures, highly leveraged with minimum capital investment.

The risk of hedging primarily arises from the extent of variation in the value of the derivatives contract in relation to the value of the hedged item. This relationship is called 'correlation'. Accordingly, the least risky hedge exhibits relative price movements between the derivative value and the hedged item, which have been consistent over time and are close to completely opposite—implying that price movements have tended to offset one another over time.

Research by the Federal Deposit Insurance Corporation (FDIC)[34] reveals that most banks in the US that use derivatives hold them for hedging purposes. However, in terms of dollar volume, these hedging-related holdings amount to less than 0.5 per cent of the total notional amount. More noteworthy is the fact that almost 90 per cent of the derivatives held for hedging purposes are interest rate contracts—indicating that banks prevalently use derivatives to mitigate interest rate risk. More recent trends seem to support this observation—the BIS quarterly review quoted above estimated (page 24) the total turnover in derivatives markets at the end of September 2009 at USD 426 trillion (indicating a rebound from USD 366 trillion the previous quarter). Of this amount, about 80 per cent (USD 344 trillion) constituted interest rate derivatives.

The FDIC report also opines that it would be difficult to isolate and measure derivatives risk from total trading risk since most of the leading banks conduct derivatives activities as part their total trading activities. Even if a bank is speculating in derivatives, it occurs within the trading portfolio and hence cannot be measured separately.

Dealer banks face three critical risks from derivatives activities—market risk, credit risk and operational risk.

Market risks for banks in derivative activities

Banks use a combination of (a) matched trading, (b) market making and (c) positioning, while engaging in customer-related trading activities.

In matched trading, the dealer bank enters into a trade with a customer, and then enters into an equal offsetting position with counterparty. Although the bank could succeed in eliminating its market risk, it retains the credit risk, both from the customer and the counterparty.

Market makers, on the other hand, are ready to enter into certain contracts without an offsetting transaction. Though this approach exposes the bank to market risk, the bank compensates for the market, credit and liquidity risks through the intra day bid/ask spread, and rake in additional profits through intra day positioning. Generally, market makers try to offset intra day risks at the end of the trading day.

Positioning exposes the bank to speculation-like risks. Here, the bank takes on a transaction without establishing an offsetting position (called an 'open position'), probably expecting favourable market movements, or to maintain an inventory of financial instruments that customers may demand. These positions, unlike the market making positions, can be carried over for more than a trading day.

Hence, the magnitude of derivatives market risk in banks would bear a relationship to the extent to which the bank indulges in matched trading, market making and positioning.

Credit risks for banks in derivative activities

Even where market risk is under reasonable control, credit risk could arise out of current exposure or potential future exposure.

Current exposure represents the fair value[35] of the bank's derivative contracts with a positive value, and the 'exposure' is determined by the cost of replacing the contract in the event of non-performance by the counterparty.

Potential future exposure is more difficult to estimate, since it represents an estimate of the contract's replacement value.

Credit risk is generally mitigated by (a) netting positions open to the same counterparty, (b) carefully selecting creditworthy counterparties, and (c) ensuring that the counterparty is also hedging its earnings with derivatives.

Operational risks for banks in derivative activities

The largest derivative losses documented so far can be attributed to operational—arising from banks circumventing risk management controls. Since operational risks are typically expected to increase with the growth in volume of transactions, each derivative contract must be properly executed and managed throughout the contract period.

More research on the riskiness of derivatives

More new research on the benefits of derivative contracts serves to corroborate the arguments in the foregoing paragraphs. According to a University of Michigan study[36] of interest rate risk management in the banking sector, derivatives allow banks to maintain smooth operating policies and avoid unwanted costs, even when faced with external shocks.

BOX 12.11 ACCOUNTING FOR DERIVATIVES—INTERNATIONAL PRACTICES AND THE POSITION IN INDIA

Given the nature and risks of banks' involvement in derivatives, there is a growing concern that the present disclosures being made by banks in respect of their derivatives exposure need considerable transparency and fine tuning. In addition, international accounting practices are at present moving towards standardization and convergence in respect of all financial instruments including derivatives.

Background—International financial reporting standards and the international accounting standards

The International Accounting Standards Board (IASB) is an independent private sector body established to develop and approve international financial reporting standards (IFRS). The IASB replaced the International Accounting Standards Committee (IASC) in 2001. Now IASB functions under the oversight of the International Standards Committee Foundation (IASCF), an independent non-profit foundation created for this specific purpose. An International Financial Reporting Interpretations Committee (IFRIC) develops and solicits comments on the standards developed by the IASB.

IFRS is used in a narrow as well as broad sense. In the narrow sense, IFRS is the new set of numbered pronouncements being issued by the IASB, as distinguished from the IAS series issued by its predecessor, the IASC.

In the broad sense, IFRSs refer to the entire body of IASB pronouncements, including standards and interpretations approved by IASB, IASs and others.

The USA

Effective January 2001, the Financial Accounting Standards Board (FASB) of the US issued FASB 133—Accounting for Derivative Instruments and Hedging activities.

Both IAS 39[37] and FASB 133 require that all derivatives, including hedges, be recognized on the banks' balance sheet at their 'fair value', defined as 'value at which an asset could be exchanged or a liquidity settled between knowledgeable, willing parties in an arm's length transaction'.

We have seen that there are three broad types of derivatives contracts, classified according to objective—hedging, dealing and speculation. FASB 133 differentiates between hedging and speculative contracts, and sets forth three types of hedging relationships: (a) fair value, (b) cash flow, and (c) foreign currency.

A fair value hedge is a derivative contract entered into as a hedge against possible changes in the bank's balance sheet asset and liability values. The gain or loss in net income is recognized in the period of change together with the offsetting gain or loss on the hedged item attributable to the risk hedged. The effect of the accounting is to reflect in earnings the extent to which the hedge is not effective in achieving offsetting changes in fair value.

A derivative contract entered into as a cash flow hedge seeks to hedge the variations in cash flows of a forecasted transaction. A 'forecasted transaction' is that a bank expects to occur, but is not obligated to carry out in the course of its normal operations. The primary purpose of a cash flow hedge is to link a hedging instrument with a hedged item whose changes in cash flow are expected to offset each other. The gain or loss in such transactions are initially reported outside the profit and loss account, and subsequently included in earnings when the forecasted transaction actually affects the earnings. The ineffective portion of the gain or loss is immediately reported in earnings.

In the case of a hedging contract entered into to cover the foreign currency exposure, the gain or loss is reported outside the profit and loss account. The accounting for a fair value hedge described above applies to a derivative designated as a hedge of the foreign currency exposure of an unrecognized firm commitment or an available-for-sale security. Similarly, the accounting for a cash flow hedge applies to a derivative designated as a hedge of the foreign currency exposure of a foreign-currency-denominated forecasted transaction.

For a contract not designated as a 'hedging contract', gain or loss is recognized in the period of change.

The bank applying the hedge accounting standards is required to determine, even at the inception of the contract, the method it will use to assess the effectiveness of the derivative instrument. The method adopted should be consistent with the bank's overall approach to risk management.

However, the financial crisis of 2007 has prompted the FASB to introduce, effective November 2008, a new rule—FAS 161. The new rule requires the mark to market value of derivatives and their gains and losses to be shown in a table in company financial statements. The implication is that investors, regulators and other stakeholders would now have more information to estimate how complex derivatives and hedges affect companies' financial statements.

FAS 133 is non (Since 2013) codified in ASC 815 under US GAAP.

The UK

In 1998, the Accounting Standards Board (ASB) published Financial Reporting Standards (FRS) 13, 'Derivatives and other financial instruments: Disclosures', which became effective March 1999. The standards have laid down the requirements for disclosures of a bank's policies, objectives and strategies in using financial instruments, their impact on its risk, performance and financial condition, and details of how risks are managed.

In addition, Statement of Recommended Practice (SORP) supplements accounting standards. The latest version of the SORP on derivatives, issued in 2001, aims to ensure that derivatives held for trading purposes are measured at fair value. 'Fair value' is the amount at which the instrument could be exchanged in an arm's length transaction between informed and willing parties. All fair value calculations should also take account of counterparty credit quality, market liquidity, closeout costs and other administrative costs. Changes in fair value should be recognized in the profit and loss account immediately. The fair value of trading derivatives, where positive, should be included in 'other assets' on the bank's balance sheet, while the negative values should be included under 'other liabilities'.

Derivatives classified as 'non-trading' transactions should be measured on an accrual basis, equivalent to that used for the underlying asset, liability position or cash flow.

FRS 102 the current accounting standard for hedge accounting is proposed to be modified and converge to IFRS 9. The government is also preparing to implement an Indian version of IFRS (Ind-AS) from April 2015.

Position in India

The Institute of Chartered Accountants of India (ICAI) has committed to the convergence of IASs and the IFRS from 1 April 2011. The ICAI has also issued Accounting Standards (AS) 30, 31.and 32 which incorporate the norms for recognition and measurement, presentation and disclosure of all financial instruments in line with IAS 32, 39 (to be replaced by IASB) and IFRS 7. The Companies Act 2013 contains many requirement aligned to IFRS. The government is also preparing to implement an Indian version of IFRS (Ind-AS) from April 2015.

Basel Committee's guiding principles for replacement of IAS 39 (August 2009)

In response to the recommendations made by the G20 leaders at the April 2009 summit, the Basel Committee welcomes the replacement of IAS 39, provided the new standard avoids undue complexity, and takes into account the lessons from the financial crisis of 2007. IAS 39 will be superceded by IFRS 9 (Financial Instruments).

Sources: 1. www.iasb.org
2. www.icai.org
3. www.iasplus.com
4. www.bis.org

SECTION V

LIQUIDITY RISK MANAGEMENT AND BASEL III

The financial turmoil of 2007 has once again underscored the importance of liquidity to the functioning of both the financial markets and the banking sector. A cataclysmic change from buoyant, liquid markets just before the crisis, to an extended period of illiquidity put the global banking system under severe stress. In February 2008, the Basel Committee noted that many banks had failed to follow some basic principles of liquidity management during times of abundant liquidity. In its paper titled 'Liquidity risk management and supervisory challenges',[38] the Basel committee pointed out that:

a. Most of the banks which exposed themselves to severe liquidity risks did not have the requisite framework to support the risks inherent in individual business lines or products, and, therefore, did not align the risks to the banks' own risk tolerance.
b. Many banks did not account for the 'unlikely' event of a large part of their contingent liabilities having to be funded all at once.
c. To many banks the kind of severity or duration of the liquidity crisis (as it materialized later) seemed a remote possibility. Hence, these banks did not conduct stress tests to factor market wide liquidity strain and disruptions.
d. Even where contingency funding plans were made, they were not related to results of stress tests, or did not factor in the possible drying up of some potential funding sources.

Simply stated, liquidity is a bank's ability to generate cash quickly and at a reasonable cost. Liquidity risk is the risk that the bank may not be able to fund increases in assets or meet liability obligations as they fall due without incurring unacceptable losses. The problem may lie in the bank's inability to liquidate assets or obtain funding to meet its obligations. The problem could also arise due to uncontrollable factors such as market disruption or liquidity squeeze. Figure 12.3 illustrates how a bank's inability to generate cash is a manifestation of more serious problems.

FIGURE 12.3 ANATOMY OF LIQUIDITY RISK

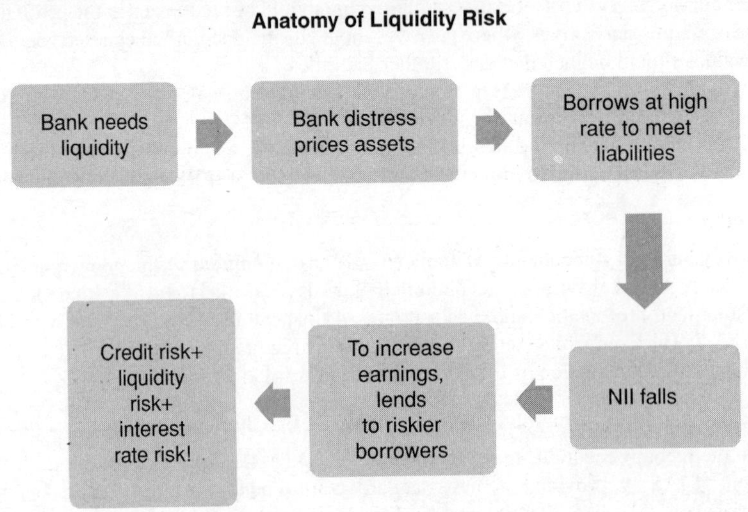

Liquidity problems can have an adverse impact on the bank's earnings and capital, and, in extreme circumstances, may even lead to the collapse of the bank itself, though the bank may otherwise be solvent. A liquidity crisis in a large bank could give rise to systemic consequences impacting other banks and the country's banking system as a whole. Liquidity problems can also affect the proper functioning of payment systems and other financial markets.

Sound liquidity risk management is, therefore, essential to the viability of every bank and for the maintenance of overall financial stability.

Recent trends in the liability profiles of banks pose further challenges to the industry and have made it increasingly important for banks to actively manage their liquidity risk. Some of these developments are: (a) the increasing proportion in bank liabilities of wholesale and capital market funding, which are more sensitive to credit and market risks; (b) the increase in off-balance sheet activities such as derivatives and securitization that have compounded the challenge of cash flow management; and (c) the speed with which funds can be transmitted and withdrawn, thanks to advanced technology and systems.

Why do banks need liquidity? They need liquidity in order to meet routine expenses, such as interest payments and overhead costs. More importantly, as financial intermediaries, they need liquidity to meet unexpected 'liquidity shocks', such as large deposit withdrawals or heavy loan demand. The most extreme example of a liquidity shock is a 'bank run'.[39] If all depositors attempt to withdraw their money at once, almost any bank will be unable to cover their claims and will fail—even though it might otherwise be in sound financial condition. However, individual institutions are rarely allowed to fail, thanks to the safety net existing in most countries in the form of deposit insurance, the central bank's role as lender of last resort, and stringent capital requirements. Poor liquidity may, therefore, lead to outright failure only in exceptional cases. However, if a bank does not plan carefully, it may be forced to turn to high-cost sources of funding to cover liquidity shocks, thus cutting into profitability, and ultimately, into its very existence.

It is also evident that to manage liquidity risk at the basic level, two sources of liquidity are equally important. One is the liquidity generated from liquidation of assets—this implies that in an adverse situation the bank needs excess liquidity from assets. The second is the funding liquidity—raised through liabilities.

Of the four specific forms of risk that impact banking operation—credit risk, market risk, operational risk and liquidity risk—the first three have been extensively studied and commonly incorporated into existing capital allocation frameworks. However, at present, there is no technique for modelling liquidity risk that has wide acceptance.

Though its importance is well recognized, at present there is no coherent definition of liquidity risk. This comes as no surprise. The term liquidity is used across the market for different purposes, which means that liquidity risk itself is defined differently and depends very much on the context in which it is used. For example, one quite popular definition of liquidity risk is the risk that a particular banking asset cannot be converted into cash within a specific time frame and at a specific price level. It refers directly to the 'liquidity' of this particular asset and yet this risk impacts the bank. Literature contains many more such contextual definitions.

Again, no single balance-sheet category or ratio is sufficient to assess liquidity risk. It involves the entire balance sheet and off-balance sheet activity as well. Liquidity management is largely about being sure that adequate, low-cost sources of funding are available on short notice. This might include holding a portfolio of assets that can easily be sold, acquiring a large volume of stable liabilities or maintaining lines of credit with other financial institutions. However, this effort must be balanced against the impact on profitability. In general, more liquid assets earn lower rates of return and certain types of stable funding may cost more than those that are more volatile. A bank can be perfectly liquid by holding only cash as an asset, but this would be an unprofitable strategy because cash does not earn any income.

Why is it so difficult to isolate and study liquidity risk?

First, unlike the other three risks that are bank-specific, liquidity risk can transcend the individual bank—liquidity shortfall at a single bank can have repercussions on the entire banking system of a country.

Second, liquidity risk is partly confounded with market risk as depositor behaviour can arise from perceptions of the market state.

Third, liquidity risk cannot be eliminated or transferred, as can be done with say, credit risk. It has to be borne and managed by the individual bank.

Fourth, liquidity risk can occur in perfectly normal times—as when a large number of depositors withdraw their deposits within a short period of time—or in crisis times when the most severe outcomes can be expected.

Fifth, liquidity risk can affect both the profitability of the bank in the short term, as well as the very survival of the bank in the long term.

Sources of Liquidity Risk

A bank that plans well can anticipate many of its internal liquidity needs (such as funding loan growth, meeting depositor demands and paying operating expenses) and structure its balance sheet accordingly. If the bank knows its market, it can plan for many external events (such as seasonal borrowing patterns, deposit run-off and business practices requiring bank funds).

Apart from such anticipated needs, unforeseen events can have serious implications for a bank's liquidity position. For example, frauds, natural disasters or resources malfunction could unexpectedly affect liquidity. Even with the most careful planning, banks need to maintain reserves of liquidity to sustain them when the unexpected occurs.

In general, factors that can influence bank liquidity include the following:

- **Access to financial markets:** Though most banks have some degree of access to financial markets for their funding requirements, larger banks have better access. Smaller banks may be equally creditworthy, but they lack the visibility and track record that larger banks enjoy in the markets. Tapping the market for funds could be expensive for smaller banks when the amount involved is not very large, since fixed transaction costs could be disproportionately high. Hence, smaller banks access the financial markets more infrequently or not at all.

- **Financial health of the bank:** Poor asset quality and earnings translate into adverse effects on a bank's liquidity. Low quality of assets (or high level of non-performing/impaired assets) stifles earnings growth. Earnings represent a flow of funds to help meet liquidity needs. Thus, when earnings are low, cash availability is also low. Both factors in combination may place the bank's solvency in doubt, which in turn, would deter potential lenders from providing funds.

- **Balance sheet structure:** Banks have to constantly trade off between liquidity and profitability. The most liquid bank would hold all its assets in cash or near cash investments, with most of its liabilities in stable core deposits. This bank can easily handle unexpected demand for funds and is not expected to face a liquidity problem in the foreseeable future. But such a bank would not be very profitable since its cash and near cash assets do not earn much income. The challenge for bank management is to, therefore, structure its balance sheet to earn a reasonable rate of return while maintaining a safe level of liquidity.

- **Liability and asset mix:** Many bank liabilities and assets have embedded options. Most short-term funding arrangements include option like structures where the provider of funds is permitted to withdraw on demand or at short notice. When such demands are large, the bank's liquidity comes under severe strain.

- **Timing of funds flow:** There is continuous flow of funds in and out of a bank. Inflows happen primarily from principal and interest payments, asset sales, deposits and other borrowings, and non-interest income. Similarly, outflows typically occur from interest payments, addition to assets, such as loans and investments, deposit and borrowing repayments, and other overhead expenses. The inflows and outflows occur at various points in time, which fact is not reflected in the balance sheet. The timing difference in cash inflows and outflows has liquidity consequences.

- **Exposures to off-balance sheet activity:** Banks make various non-funded commitments to their customers, which could result in potential liquidity drain if the counterparties default. These commitments are not reflected on the balance sheet, but are shown as 'contingent liabilities'. Further, a bank may have made loan commitments or unused lines of credit, which will have to be honoured on demand. Hence, the balance sheet alone may not convey the real picture of the liquidity strength of a bank.

- **Impact of other risks:** There is no single source for liquidity risk as there can be no single source for market or credit risk. Further, as we have seen earlier, any of the other risks can turn into liquidity risk—for example, credit risk affects cash inflow into the bank and, hence, affects liquidity. Similarly, volatility in market interest rates may affect the liquidity of a bank's investment portfolio.

Box 12.12 describes how one bank—Northern Rock of the UK—failed due to liquidity crisis.

BOX 12.12 CASE STUDY—NORTHERN ROCK LIQUIDITY CRISIS

Northern Rock in July 2007 was Britain's fifth largest mortgage lender. It had a robust credit book and analysts were positive on its medium-term outlook.

Less than 2 months later, Northern Rock collapsed. The run on Northern Rock was the first in over 100 years in the UK. Liquidity had dried up in the bank. How did it happen, so suddenly and so dramatically?

Northern Rock was not an international bank and did not have significant cross border operations. It was not a major bank either. It had been set up in 1965 as a building society, but subsequently enjoyed spectacular growth and expansion. Before the crisis, 80 per cent of the bank's liabilities were sourced from securitizations, covered bonds and wholesale sources of funding. Retail deposits comprised only about one-fifth of the liabilities.

When the sub-prime crisis spilled over from the US into securities and money markets of other countries, Northern Rock, with its low deposit to loan ratio, was unable to renew its other sources of short-term financing. It turned to the Bank of England for 'financial assistance' on 14 September 2007, in view of 'extreme conditions' in financial markets. When the news broke, most retail customers rushed to withdraw their savings from the bank. It was reported that the UK had not witnessed such panic-driven withdrawals since 1866.

In its report, 'The Run on the Rock', the House of Commons Treasury Committee stated that Northern Rock was a victim of its own funding structure. Its reliance on short term, wholesale funding was responsible for its inability to cope with the liquidity pressure placed on it when the international markets dried up after the credit crisis in the US.

In February 2008, the bank was nationalized after two unsuccessful bids for take over.

During the course of all this trouble, it is noteworthy that Northern Rock did not face a problem of inadequate capital! But its vulnerability to liquidity shocks in wholesale markets proved its undoing.

A key lesson flowing from the Northern Rock debacle is that bank capital and liquidity are equally important for regulation and solvency of banks.

Source: Various news items from related websites.

How to Measure Liquidity?

Historically, better practices for liquidity measurement and management focused on the use of liquidity ratios. These were static ratios, calculated from the bank's balance sheet. The thinking then welcomed the use of more and more such ratios.

Use of these ratios presupposed that past performance was a realistic indicator of the future. Banks discovered that this assumption may not be valid in a dynamic environment when bank failures happened, triggered by liquidity risk. For example, a large regional bank in the US, Southeast Bank, used over 30 liquidity ratios to manage its liquidity. When it failed in 1991, the second largest failure of the previous two decades in the US, the reason cited was 'liquidity risk'. It, therefore, became obvious that calculating more or different ratios was not the solution, since historical ratios, however well conceptualized, could say little about the future.

Now, better practices of liquidity measurement and management are evolving. These approaches focus on prospective liquidity, diversified funding and contingency planning. Such approaches can be used by all banks, irrespective of size and geographical area of operation.

The adage 'you manage what you measure' has been recognized by the regulators, as evidenced by the Basel III requirements for liquidity management, spelt out by the Basel Committee on Banking Supervision.[40] It is noteworthy that the principles for liquidity management as spelt out by the committee have undergone substantial changes and have taken into account lessons from the financial crisis of 2007.

The Basel document of 2000 and 2008 specifically mentions the key areas (quoted below) where more detailed guidance has been provided[41]:

- The importance of establishing a liquidity risk tolerance.
- The maintenance of adequate liquidity, including through a cushion of liquid assets.
- The necessity of allocating liquidity costs, benefits and risks to all significant business activities.
- The identification and measurement of the full range of liquidity risks, including contingent liquidity risks.
- The design and use of severe stress test scenarios.
- The need for a robust and operational contingency funding plan.
- The management of intraday liquidity risk and collateral.
- Public disclosure to promote market discipline.

The Basel document mentions two kinds of liquidity risk—funding liquidity risk and market liquidity risk. It defines the two kinds of risk as follows: (page 1) 'Funding liquidity risk is the risk that the firm will not be able to meet efficiently both expected and unexpected current and future cash flow and collateral needs without affecting either daily operations or the financial condition of the firm. Market liquidity risk is the risk that a firm cannot easily offset or eliminate a position at the market price because of inadequate market depth or market disruption.' The guidance in the document focuses primarily on 'funding liquidity risk'.

However, these two risks are not independent of each other. For example, under conditions of stress, investors in capital market instruments may demand higher compensation for increased risk, or simply refuse to lend. The need for funding liquidity may then increase, since the illiquidity in the market may make it difficult for banks to raise funds by selling-off assets.

In addition, Basel III has proposed liquidity coverage ratios described later in this section.

Modern Approaches to Liquidity Risk Management

It is evident that liquidity risk is closely linked to the nature of banking assets and liabilities. The assets and liability positions of a bank, in turn, are affected by the bank's investment and financing decisions, irrespective of whether they have short- or long-term implications.

It follows that banks should be able to manage their liquidity position both on an everyday basis as well as in the long term, to ensure that liquidity risk is effectively mitigated. This implies that a bank should preferably have two approaches to managing short-term and long-term liquidity.

Choosing the appropriate approach would depend on the bank management's 'liquidity policy'. What is important here is that board-approved policies address liquidity in some manner and that the board monitors both compliance with these policies and the need to change them as necessary.

The Liquidity Policy Similar to a bank's 'loan policy', which we saw in an earlier chapter, many banks have the practice of formulating a 'liquidity policy' for the bank.

Policies on liquidity are likely to vary from bank to bank based on individual operating environments, customers and needs. Also, policies will be subject to change over time as a bank's situation and environment change.

An illustrative list of typical features of a sound liquidity and funds management policy and some symptoms of potential liquidity problems are provided in *Annexure III*.

It should be noted here that the involvement of a bank's top management is extremely important in the process of 'liquidity risk management'.

Approach to Managing Liquidity for Long-Term Survival and Growth

Since the bank's long-term survival and growth are the driving factors, this approach tries to mitigate long-term liquidity risk by strategically controlling the bank's asset and liability positions. This could be achieved by (a) aligning the maturity of assets and liabilities so that cash flow timing risks are eliminated, or (b) diversifying the funding sources so that liquidity availability is ensured.

The alternative approaches prevalently used by banks are:

- Asset Management, and
- Liability Management.

Asset Management All bank assets are a potential source of liquidity. The asset portfolio of a bank can provide liquidity in the following circumstances—(a) on maturity of the asset; (b) on sale of the asset; and (c) the use of the asset as collateral for borrowing or repo transactions.

Typically, banks hold liquid assets such as money market instruments and marketable securities to supplement the conventional funding sources such as deposits and other liabilities. When the cash inflows from asset realization, either on maturity or through sale, are less than anticipated due to default risk or price volatility, the bank incurs liquidity risk. Similarly, secured funding, such as repos, may be affected if counterparties seek larger discounts on the collateral provided or demand better quality collateral. Additionally, concentrated exposure of the asset portfolio to specific counterparties, instruments, economic activity or geographical location, may heighten the level of liquidity risk.

We have seen in earlier chapters that the typical bank has very few fixed assets. Most of its assets are in the form of loans and investments. Though, theoretically, in an extreme situation, even the bank's building can be sold to provide funds, banks generally use shorter-term or readily marketable assets for liquidity purposes.

Of course, when the bank needs cash, the best thing to have on hand is cash. That is the reason vault cash, deposits at banks and other cash items are considered a bank's primary reserve. The problem with cash is that it does not earn a return. Therefore, banks often hold relatively little vault cash, keeping their liquidity reserves in assets that earn some interest.

We have also seen in an earlier chapter that many central banks insist on creating secondary liquidity reserve for banks through investing in approved securities. Securities can be liquidated quickly and at relatively little cost. Also, they provide interest income to the bank.

Secondary reserve securities used for asset management would typically exhibit the following characteristics: (a) they will be short-dated, with maturity periods below 1 year, (b) they will be high quality instruments with low default risk, (c) they will be highly marketable, and (d) have a low conversion cost.

For a bank resorting to 'asset management' as a strategy to mitigate liquidity risk, its investment portfolio is looked upon as a liquidity shock absorber. However, there is a trade off between asset liquidity and profitability for the bank, since short-term, liquid, risks-free assets yield relatively low returns.

How much of liquid assets should a bank maintain? The level of liquid assets is generally a function of the stability of the bank's funding structure and the potential for rapid expansion of its loan portfolio. Generally, if a bank has stable sources of funds and predictable loan demand, a relatively low allowance for liquidity may be required.

However, it is prudent to maintain higher allowance for liquidity to offset the factors described in the following illustrative list:

- The potential customer has a wide choice for investment in alternative instruments, due to the highly competitive environment.
- Recent trends also show that large liability account inflows are substantially lower.
- The bank's access to the capital market is limited due to various reasons.
- A sizeable portion of the loan portfolio consists of large impaired credits, with little potential for recovery.
- A sizeable portion of the loan portfolio consists of loans whose credit risk cannot be diversified through credit risk transfer or loan sales.
- A substantial amount of lines of credit and commitments already sanctioned are unused, and could be potential outflows at any time.
- The bank's credit exposure is concentrated in one or more industries with present or anticipated financial problems.

Hence, to balance liquidity and profitability, management must carefully evaluate the full return on liquid assets against the expected (risk-adjusted) return associated with less liquid assets. Adverse balance sheet fluctuations may lead to a forced sale of securities, in which case the potential higher income from securities may be lost.

Liability Management Liability management has been popular with larger banks since 1960s and 1970s. As the name suggests, the strategy focuses on sources of funds to mitigate liquidity risk.

Contrary to the practice in 'asset management', where surplus funds of the bank are parked in cash or near cash assets like readily marketable securities, a bank resorting to 'liability management' would invest its surplus funds in long-term assets. When there is a need for liquidity, the bank raises funds from external sources. Typically, the 'liability-managed' bank would manage its deposits and other borrowings judicially to meet its funding obligations.

In almost all banks, deposits constitute the largest component of liabilities. Of these, 'core deposits'[42] are generally the lowest-cost funding source because the presence of deposit insurance almost eliminates depositor concerns about the repayment of their funds.

Banks typically employ different liability funding strategies to manage liquidity risk. Those with large branch networks find it easier to garner relatively low-cost retail deposits. Banks concentrating on wholesale business may find borrowing in the money market the most efficient way of obtaining short-term liquidity. Others may issue medium-term certificates of deposit (CDs) or prefer term deposits with a spread of maturities to reduce liquidity risk.

Generally, banks that have a large and ready source of core deposits find liability management an easier task than those that must rely on more volatile, non-core deposits. Unfortunately, few banks have a large base of core deposits in the present competitive environment where investors are constantly seeking more profitable avenues to park their savings. Consequently, many banks now rely more heavily on non-core deposits and other non-deposit sources for funding. The greater volatility associated with these funds increases the rigour needed in a bank's liquidity management.

The underlying implication of this approach is that a bank will not depend on its liquidity position for credit commitments, since it intends raising the required funds from external or market sources. While the approach would benefit large, growth-oriented, aggressive banks by way of higher returns, it also involves greater risk for the bank.

One risk would be the sustenance of high spreads—while the yields could be high, the cost of borrowing could also be high and in some cases, out of the bank's control, since borrowing depends on market conditions.

The second would be the asset liability risk. Making long-term investments or loans also requires liabilities of matching maturity. It is likely that at the time the bank wants to source funds of a specific maturity, such sources may not be available, or available at a very high cost, or with embedded options.

The above factor would lead to a third risk—refinancing risk. If liabilities of shorter maturities are deployed in longer-term assets, the liability would fall due for payment before the asset flows come in completely. The bank would then have to seek more liabilities to match the remaining maturity of the assets. If interest rates are rising, there is likelihood that the new source of funds is priced much higher than the earlier one, which might render the transaction unviable.

A fourth risk—a critical one—cannot be ruled out. As the bank borrows more and more, it is vulnerable to credit risk. If a bank defaults on repayment of liabilities, it also runs a reputation risk.

Asset Management or Liability Management? Choosing between the strategies of 'asset management' and 'liability management' depends to a large extent on not only the size and nature of operations of a bank, but also expectations of how interest rates are going to move in the foreseeable future.

For example, consider a bank whose proportion of retail customers, both depositors and borrowers, is large. Though the amount per transaction, whether deposit repayment or loan disbursement, would be low, the volumes are likely to be large, and the payments would mostly be on demand. The surplus and deficits that arise on a periodic (depending on the liquidity planning horizon that the 'liquidity policy' has recommended) basis due to mismatch in cash inflows and outflows will have to be closely monitored. Surpluses, when they occur, will have to be accumulated carefully to take care of times of deficit, to ensure that the bank's liquidity is not impaired. Instead of maintaining the surplus inflows in the form of cash, the bank would find it more profitable to invest them in short-term securities that can be liquidated at short notice to yield cash. Such a bank, therefore, would prefer the asset management strategy.

On the other hand, the large bank with a substantial proportion of wholesale customers, typically also has large volatile deposits as liabilities. The need for funds would arise in this case for payment of balances in demand deposit accounts and large volatile accounts, as well as for the expected and unexpected needs of its large borrowers. The bank is also likely to have good credit rating in the market due to its large-scale lending and investing activities. In the case of this bank too, periodic mismatches in cash inflows and outflows are likely to arise. However, this bank, unlike the predominantly retail bank discussed above, would be more likely to invest its surplus in long-term loans or investments. The deficits would be met by borrowing in the market, which is facilitated by its market reputation.

Due to the short-term investment strategy, the bank opting for asset management may have to forego higher yields. An alternative this bank has is to invest in long-dated securities and liquidate them in the secondary market as and when the need arises. However, the transaction costs and characteristics of the secondary markets will play a major role in deciding for this alternative. In any case, marketable securities that are relatively risk-free do not yield high returns.

On the other hand, the bank opting for liability management may be looking for higher returns, which do not come without the attendant risks. First, the bank will have to access various types of lenders and markets in its bid to raise funds. Interest rate fluctuations in any of the instruments or markets increase interest rate risk. Second, the bank will have to operate in well-organized markets with credit rating capabilities. A default by the bank in any of these markets would lead to a downgrade of the bank by the rating agencies, which, in turn, would push up the bank's cost of borrowings. If the bank is not able to pass on the increased cost to its borrowers, its spreads weaken.

BOX 12.13 SOURCES OF CONTINGENT DEMAND FOR LIQUIDITY AND LIQUIDITY RISKS INHERENT IN OFF-BALANCE SHEET ACTIVITIES[43]

Off-balance sheet items, depending on the nature and size of transactions, can either supply or use liquidity. The following examples illustrate the effect of such items on a bank's liquidity:

1. It is common practice for a bank to obtain standby or committed facilities for funding from another bank or financial institution. However, the bank should be wary of restrictive covenants, if any, included in the facility agreement. Also, it should be able to test access to the promised funds regularly. Such testing would reveal the extent to which such facilities can be relied upon when the bank is in dire need or under stressed economic conditions.
2. Unused loan commitments can draw on the bank's liquidity at any time. The expected amount and timing of borrowers drawing on the unused commitments should be incorporated into the bank's cash flows.
3. Derivatives, options and other contingent items pose more challenges for liquidity risk management. The direction and amount of cash flows for such items will normally be affected by market interest rates, exchange rates and other special terms under the contract. For example, when a bank enters into an interest rate swap for paying a floating rate and receiving a fixed rate, it would receive a payment for the difference of the two rates only as long as the fixed rate is higher than the floating rate. In the event that interest rates increase, and the floating rate rises above the fixed rate, the bank will have to pay the difference of the two rates, thus incurring a cash outflow instead.
4. Credit derivatives may have a liquidity impact that is often difficult to forecast. For example, assume that a bank enters into a credit default swap (CDS) to compensate a counterparty for its credit losses. The bank has sold credit protection, and, hence, exposed itself to a contingent liability, the cash flow of which cannot be easily determined.
5. Special purpose vehicles (SPVs) can be a source or use of liquidity. Where a bank provides liquidity facility to an SPV under a contract or specific obligation, the bank's liquidity would be affected by the illiquidity of the SPV. For example, if a securitization SPV is considered a source of funding by the bank, under stressed liquidity conditions, this source may be restricted or not available to the bank. Where the bank itself has sponsored or administered the SPV, liquidity pressures in either the bank or the SPV can trigger liquidity risks in both the entities.
6. Foreign currency deposits as well as credit lines can be good sources of funding for banks. However, when market liquidity or exchange rates change suddenly, liquidity mismatches widen, which could even alter the effectiveness of the bank's risk management/hedging strategies.
7. Correspondent, custodian and settlement activities can lead to large cash flows, both on an intra day and overnight basis. Unexpected changes in these cash flows can impact the overall liquidity positions of banks, and the impact could be severe if banks fail to settle transactions on time.

Given the customized nature of the contingent contracts illustrated above, it is evident that triggering events for these contingent liquidity risks would be quite difficult to predict or model. Therefore, liquidity risk management in these cases would have to be based on analysis of assumptions and scenarios on the behaviour of both banks and counterparties under various conditions, even if there had been no adverse liquidity events in the past.

Source: FDIC and BIS documents.

We have been discussing the risks arising from balance sheet assets and liabilities of banks. What are the risks inherent in off-balance sheet activities (contingent liabilities) of banks? Box 12.13 outlines some of the liquidity risks in off-balance sheet activities.

Approach to Managing Liquidity in the Short Term—Some Tools for Risk Measurement

A single measurement of liquidity risk rarely suffices in the short term. Banks basically use two kinds of tools used by banks to measure liquidity risk—forward-looking and retrospective—since sound liquidity management requires a complement of measurement tools.

Forward looking or prospective tools project funding needs in the foreseeable future—the planning horizon in such cases could range from daily to quarterly to half yearly and so on. When based on sound assumptions, these tools provide a good basis for liquidity planning in the short term.

Retrospective tools analyze historical behaviour and try to draw inferences for the future, though this may not necessarily prepare the bank for the future.

Some of the forward-looking tools prevalently used by banks include:

- Projected sources and uses of funds over the planning horizon.
- The working funds approach.
- Cash flow or funding gap report.
- Funding concentration analysis.
- Funds availability report.

A few typical retrospective tools include:

- Ratio analysis, and
- Historical funds flow analysis.

As opposed to managing the asset and liability positions for long-term liquidity management, the short-term approach manages the actual cash flows.

A few of the above approaches are discussed as follows:

1. The Working Funds Approach The working funds typically constitute bank's capital and outside liabilities, such as deposits and borrowings as well as float funds.

In this approach, liquidity is assessed based on the working funds available with the bank. 'Liquidity needs' are typically estimated as a proportion of the working funds.

There are two ways in which a bank can estimate its liquidity requirements—one, as a proportion of total working funds. For example, the bank can decide to maintain 5 per cent of the total working funds as cash or near cash instruments for its liquidity requirements. A second approach is to segment the working funds and maintain separate liquidity limits for each segment.

In one commonly used segmentation approach, the bank classifies its liabilities based on their maturity profiles as follows:

- Owned funds of the bank are excluded from liquidity requirements since they have only residual claim
- Deposits and borrowings are segmented based on their withdrawal pattern.
  - Volatile funds can be withdrawn at any time in the foreseeable future. These would generally include large amounts of funds parked by corporate houses and government bodies in short-term deposits and certificates of deposit. They call for almost 100 per cent liquidity allowance
  - Vulnerable funds are those that can be withdrawn during the period for which liquidity planning is being undertaken. Most transaction deposits that are payable on demand fall under this category. Such deposits also call for almost 100 per cent allowance, or lower allowance depending on the bank's risk appetite
  - Stable funds have the least probability to be withdrawn during the period for which the liquidity planning is being done. These include the 'core' portion of savings deposits and time deposits not maturing during the planning period. The liquidity allowance for these funds would be much lower, based on the bank's previous experience with the withdrawal pattern in such deposits.
- Float funds are similar to volatile funds, since these are mostly funds in transit or meant for a particular short-term purpose. Usually, a 100 per cent liquidity allowance is maintained for these funds, since they are payable on demand.

Based on the above allowances for components of its working funds, the bank would assess its desired liquidity levels at any point in time during the planning period. The bank, again depending on its risk-return characteristics, would determine the allowable variance over the desired liquidity levels. The variance is called the 'acceptance range'. As long as the average cash or near cash balances fall within this acceptance range, the bank's profitability and liquidity would fall in line with its expectations. Any surplus or deficit over this range would be compensated by investing or borrowing. It is to be noted that both actions of the bank would have a potential impact on its profitability. However, the acceptance range changes along with the liability profile of the bank.

For example, if a bank's total working funds are ₹1,000 crore and the bank needs to maintain liquidity of 1 per cent on the working funds, the cash requirement would be ₹10 crore. In this case, an acceptance range of $\pm 5\%$ would imply that the cash balance can vary between 10 ± 0.5 crore, *i.e.*, between ₹9.5 crore and ₹10.5 crore.

The limitations of the approach are as follows:

- It is based on part historic, part subjective assumptions
- It focuses on the existing liability profile, and not the expected or potential liability profile, based on market changes.

2. ***The Ratios Approach*** Table 12.5 describes some key ratios and limits that could be employed by banks to assess and manage liquidity risk. The applicability of these ratios to a specific bank would depend on the nature of business and risk profile of the bank. For example, a ratio considered relevant for a predominantly retail bank would be less meaningful to a predominantly wholesale bank.

More liquidity ratios (with their significance) can be found in RBI's (2009) "Committee on Financial Sector Assessment" Report, pages 91–92.

TABLE 12.5 SOME KEY LIQUIDITY RATIOS

Ratio	Numerator	Denominator	Remarks
Loan to deposit ratio	Performing loans outstanding	Deposit balances outstanding	A simple measure to understand and compute. Indicates the extent to which relatively illiquid assets (loans) are being funded by relatively stable sources (customer deposits). It can also show overexpansion of the loan book. The limitation of this ratio is that it does not take into account the extent to which loans are funded by alternative stable funding sources, such as equity capital or long-term debt.
Incremental loan to deposit ratio	Incremental loans made during the period	Incremental deposit inflows during the same period	In addition to the above, the ratio also shows how additional sources of funds are being deployed. The differences between the above-mentioned overall ratio and the incremental ratio would throw up any significant shifts in the bank's funds utilization strategy.
Medium term funding ratio	Liabilities with maturity of over 1 year	Assets with maturity of over 1 year	The ratio focuses on the medium-term liquidity profile of a bank. It also highlights the extent to which medium-term assets are being funded by roll over of short-term liabilities. Hence a lower ratio would signify higher funding of medium-term assets, which could lead to liquidity risk.
Cash flow coverage ratio	Projected cash inflow	Projected cash outflow	A higher ratio indicates lower liquidity risk
Liquid assets ratio	Liquid assets	Short-term liabilities	
Liquid asset coverage ratio	Net liquid assets	Total volatile liabilities	
Net non-core funding dependence	Non-core deposits (+ borrowings) less short-term investments	Long-term assets	An increasing trend over time could signify that the bank's sources of funds are becoming more volatile, and more and more long-term assets are getting funded by volatile sources.
Net short-term liabilities to assets	Net-short term liabilities	Total assets	A variation of the medium-term funding ratio given above. If the ratio shows an increasing trend over time, the bank may be exposed to refinancing risk.
On hand liquidity to total liabilities	On hand liquidity – cash in hand + near cash assets	Total liabilities	A higher ratio signifies higher liquidity, but carries the risk of eroding profitability
Contingent liabilities ratio	Contingent liabilities to loans	Total loans	A higher ratio indicates higher potential risk

Can different banks have different liquidity positions despite having similar liquidity ratios? They can be due to the following factors:

- Cash flow from principal and interest payments could vary due to the types of loans on the balance sheet.
- Banks may have different existing relationships and procedures for loan sales.
- Banks may have large loans maturing at different points in time with different risk profiles.
- Banks specializing in short-term financing may generate significant liquidity from periodic pay offs, while banks lending to agriculture at the beginning of a growing season may receive little cash flow during a period when loan balances outstanding are increasing.
- Some banks may have borrowing lines collateralized by the loan portfolio.

All the above factors could dramatically affect the liquidity/cash flow of individual banks.

The limitations of balance sheet ratios are as follows:

- Ratios at best provide point-in-time measures.
- They cannot give an insight into how well existing or future funding sources can meet required funding needs and commitments.
- They cannot indicate available alternative funding sources.
- They cannot indicate the speed with which the assets can get converted into cash.

Apart from the above ratios, some banks fix limits for their volatile borrowings, in individual or all currencies, to reduce their dependence on market funding. Similarly, limits can also be fixed for unutilized commitments of customers. In this manner, banks use both the retrospective and prospective tools for liquidity management.

3. *Cash Flow Approach* This forward-looking approach forecasts the cash flows of the bank over a specified planning horizon, and estimates liquidity needs by identifying the likely gaps between sources and uses of funds. The bank then makes a decision on investing surplus funds and borrowing in case of a deficit.

The approach works well when two potentially conflicting parameters are reconciled—the planning horizon and the costs of forecasting. The shorter the desired planning horizon, the more will be the cost of forecasting.

The forecasting could be done in a format as follows:

Previous Estimate of Actual	Sources and Uses of Funds	Current Period Actual	Forecast One Period Ahead	Forecast Two Periods Ahead
(1)	(2)	(3)	(4)	(5)
	Beginning balance (cash)			
	Cash sources:			
	Core deposits			
	Non-core large deposits			
	Other time deposits			
	Borrowings, including foreign currency borrowings			
	Maturing investments			
	Loan repayments			
	Asset sales			
	Securitizations and SPVs			
	Any other source of funds			
	Total sources			
	Cash uses			
	Maturing deposits			
	Maturing borrowings			
	New loan commitments			
	Existing Loan commitments to be utilized			
	Investments in securities			
	—long term			
	—short term			
	Asset purchases			
	Financial derivatives			
	Guarantees and commitments			
	Other uses of funds			
	Total uses			
	Net cash sources (need)			
	Ending cash balance			

The ending cash balance could be a surplus or deficit at the end of the planning period.

What does the bank do in case of a surplus cash balance?

In case of a surplus, the bank has two options—(a) retain the surplus as cash; or (b) invest these funds in securities/loan assets. Though holding the surplus as cash would substantially reduce liquidity risk, the option would erode the bank's profitability. Hence, the bank should be investing the surplus funds.

Here again, the bank has two alternatives. In the first alternative, the surplus can be invested in short-term assets, so that liquidity is not impaired, and yet the bank would be able to earn a small return on the funds invested. In the second alternative, the surplus can be invested in long-term assets, and the bank would borrow when the need for liquidity arises.

The bank's decision would depend on whether it is an 'asset-managed' or a 'liability-managed' bank. An asset-managed bank would prefer to invest the surplus in low-yielding short-term assets, so that it can easily fund the liquidity deficits when they arise. A liability-managed bank would prefer to invest the surplus in high-yielding long-term assets and borrow to fund the liquidity deficit when it arises.

Illustration 12.11 will serve to clarify this.

ILLUSTRATION 12.11

Bank A wants to plan its liquidity, and has arrived at the cash inflows and outflows for the next 6 months as follows: (cash flows in ₹ crore).

Month	Cash Inflows	Cash Outflows	Net Cash Flows	Cumulative Cash Flows
1	100	80	20	20
2	90	100	– 10	10
3	95	90	5	15
4	100	110	– 10	5
5	95	98	– 3	2
6	110	90	20	22

Assumption:

a. All cash surpluses arise at the end of the relevant period.
b. All cash deficits arise at the beginning of the relevant period.
c. Additional information on expected yields on investments for different maturities is as follows:

Period (in months)	Yield (% per annum)
1	6%
2	6.25%
3	6.75%
4	7.25%
5	8%
6	8.75%

Case 1 The bank chooses to adopt asset management strategy.

It would, therefore, invest the surplus after meeting the deficit as follows:

a. It would invest ₹10 crore for 2 months (months 2 and 3)
b. It would invest ₹5 crore for 1 month (month 4)
c. It would invest ₹2 crore for 2 months (months 5 and 6)

The bank's *total returns* would amount to

$$\left(10 \times \frac{2}{12} \times 6.25\%\right) + \left(5 \times \frac{1}{12} \times 6\%\right) + \left(2 \times \frac{2}{12} \times 6.25\%\right) = ₹0.15 \text{ crore}$$

Case 2 The bank chooses to adopt liability management strategy

It would invest the surplus as and when it arises as follows:

a. It would invest ₹20 crore for 5 months.
b. It would invest ₹5 crore for 3 months.

It would also have to borrow to meet the deficits as follows:

a. It will borrow ₹10 crore for 2 months.
b. It will borrow ₹10 crore for 2 months.
c. It will borrow ₹3 crore for 1 month.

The *Bank's net returns* would amount to ₹0.53 crore, calculated as follows:

Income from investment: $\left(20 \times \frac{5}{12} \times 8\%\right) + \left(5 \times \frac{3}{12} \times 6.75\%\right)$

LESS

Cost of borrowing: $\left(10 \times \frac{2}{12} \times 6.25\%\right) + \left(10 \times \frac{2}{12} \times 6.25\%\right) + \left(3 \times \frac{1}{12} \times 6\%\right)$

Interpretation of the Result The above comparison seems to show that the bank benefits more by liability management. However, in reality, the decision will depend on the following:

i. The amount of time the surplus reserve position can sustain.
ii. The accuracy of yield forecasts.

It should also be noted that the cost of borrowing is assumed to be equal to the yield for the same period, a situation that may not be realistic in practice. Further, in a rising interest rate environment, the cost of borrowing may outpace the yield rate that has been locked in, thus, leading to refinancing risk for the bank.

Basel III—The International Framework for Liquidity Risk Measurements, Standards and Monitoring

In two documents published in December 2010 and January 2013 as part of the Basel III reforms described in earlier chapters, the Basel committee has presented reforms to strengthen liquidity risk management in banks. The latest documents build upon the Basel II framework for liquidity management as given in the 'Principles for Sound liquidity risk management and Supervision' (September 2008, accessed at www.bis.org) mentioned in an earlier paragraph.

The document published in December 2010, titled "Basel III: The International Framework for liquidity risk measurement, standards and monitoring", (accessed at www.bis.org), the Committee mentions that the objective is to set rules and timelines to implement the liquidity portion of the Basel III framework (which we have described in the earlier chapter). The document published in January 2013, titled "Basel III: The Liquidity Coverage Ratio and liquidity risk monitoring tools" (accessed at www.bis.org), describes in detail the Liquidity Coverage Ratio (LCR) and its implementation timelines.

To recap from the earlier chapter, the LCR is a short term measure of the liquidity profile of banks and is measured as:

$$\frac{\text{High-quality liquid assets}}{\text{Total net liquidity outflows over a 30 day period}}$$

The Committee states that this ratio should be more than 100%. This implies that banks should hold High Quality Liquid Assets (HQLA) to more than compensate for liquidity outflows expected over a 30 day period. HQLA should comprise of unencumbered cash and assets that can be converted into cash with little or no loss of value to meet the liquidity needs of the bank over a 30 day period.

Specifically, the LCR will be introduced as planned on 1 January 2015, but the minimum requirement will begin at 60%, rising in equal annual steps of 10 percentage points to reach 100% on 1 January 2019. This graduated approach is designed to ensure that the LCR can be introduced without disruption to the orderly strengthening of banking systems or the ongoing financing of economic activity.

	2015	**2016**	**2017**	**2018**	**2019**
Minimum LCR requirement	60%	70%	80%	90%	100%

A study of the components of the ratio as described in the document would show that the LCR builds on traditional liquidity coverage ratios and methodologies used internally by many banks (that have been outlined in earlier paragraphs of this section). However, the differences lie in the rigour of supervision by the regulator and the uniform definition for various classes of assets as well as cash inflows and outflows, taking into account off balance sheet items.

The summarized table given here (Basel III document of January 2013–Annexure IV) presents an illustrative list of the components of the numerator and denominator of the LCR.

The Numerator of the LCR – HQLA (The individual components of HQLA are to be multiplied by the factors given in the table)

Item	Factor
Stock of HQLA	
A. Level 1 assets:	
• Coins and bank notes.	
• Qualifying marketable securities from sovereigns, central banks, PSEs, and multilateral development banks.	100%
• Qualifying central bank reserves.	
• Domestic sovereing or central bank debt for non-0% risk-weighted sovereigns.	
B. Level 2 assets (maximum of 40% of HQLA):	
Level 2A assets	
• Sovereign, central bank, multilateral development banks, and PSE assets qualifying for 20% risk weighting.	
• Qualifying corporate debt securities rated AA, or higher.	85%
• Qualifying covered bonds rated AA, or higher.	
Level 2B assets (maximum of 15% of HQLA)	
• Qualifying RMBS.	75%
• Qualifying corporate debt securities rated between A+ and BBB.	50%
• Qualifying common equity shares.	50%
Total value of stock of HQLA	

The noteworthy feature of the above definition of HQLA is the recognition of the fact that all assets considered 'liquid' may not get converted to cash quickly without loss of value, due to their inherent risk and volatility factors. The Basel document contains detailed explanations of each of the above components.

The denominator of the LCR–net cash outflows over a 30 day period (The individual components of cash outflows and inflows are to be multiplied by the factors given in the table.)

Cash Outflows	
A. Retail deposits:	
Demand deposits and term deposits (less than 30 days maturity)	
• Stable deposits (deposit insurance scheme meets additional criteria)	3%
• Stable deposits	5%
• Less stable retail deposits	10%
Term deposits with residual maturity greater than 30 days	0%
B. Unsecured wholesale funding:	
Demand and term deposits (less than 30 days maturity) provided by small business customers:	
• Stable deposits	5%
• Less stable deposits	10%
Operational deposits generated by clearing, custody and cash management activities	25%
• Portion covered by deposit insurance	5%
Cooperative banks in an institutional network (qualifying deposits with the centralized institution)	25%
Non-financial corporates, sovereigns, central banks, multilateral development banks, and PSEs	40%
• If the entire amount fully covered by deposit insurance scheme	20%
Other legal entity customers	100%

C. Secured funding:	
• Secured funding transactions with a central bank counter party or backed by Level 1 assets with any counter party.	0%
• Secured funding transactions backed by Level 2A assets, with any counter party	15%
• Secured funding transaction backed by non-Level 1 or non-Level 2A assets, with domestic sovereigns, multilateral development banks, or domestic PSEs as a counter party.	25%
• Backed by RMBS eligible for inclusion in Level 2B	25%
• Backed by other Level 2B assets	50%
• All other secured funding transactions	100%
D. Additional requirements:	
Liquidity needs (eg collateral calls) related to financing transactions, derivatives and other contracts	3 notch downgrade
Market valuation changes on derivatives transactions (largest absolute net 30-day collateral flows realized during the preceding 24 months)	Look back approach
Valuation changes on non-Level 1 posted collateral securing derivatives	20%
Excess collateral held by a bank related to derivative transactions that could contractually be called at any time by its counter party	100%
Liquidity needs related to collateral contractually due from the reporting bank on derivatives transactions	100%
Increased liquidity needs related to derivative transactions that allow collateral substitution to non-HQLA assets	100%
ABCP, SIVs, conduits, SPVs, etc:	
• Liabilities from maturing ABCP, SIVs, SPVs, etc (applied to maturing amounts and returnable assets)	100%
• Asset Backed Securities (including covered bonds) applied to maturing amounts,	100%
Currently undrawn committed credit and liquidity facilities provided to:	
• retail and small business clients	5%
• non-financial corporates, sovereigns and central banks, multilateral development banks and PSEs	10% for credit 30% for liquidity
• banks subject to prudential supervision	40%
• other financial institutions (include securities firms, insurance companies)	40% for credit 100% for liquidity
• other legal entity customers, credit and liquidity facilities	100%
Other contingent funding liabilities (such as guarantees, letters of credit, revocable credit and liquidity facilities, etc.)	National discretion
• Trade finance	0-5%
• Customer short positions covered by other customers' collateral	50%
Any additional contractual outflows	100%
Net derivative cash outflows	100%
Any other contractual cash outflows	100%
Total cash outflows	

Cash Inflows	
Maturing secured lending transactions backed by the following collateral:	
Level 1 assets	0%
Level 2A assets	15%
Level 2B assets	
• Eligible RMBS	25%
• Other assets	50%
Margin lending backed by all other collateral	50%
All other assets	100%
Credit or liquidity facilities provided to the reporting bank	0%
Operational deposits held at other financial institutions (include deposits held at centralized institution of network of co-operative banks)	0%
Other inflows by counterparty:	
• Amounts to be received from retail counterparties	50%
• Amounts to be received from non-financial wholesale counterparties, from transactions other than those listed in above inflow categories	50%
• Amounts to be received form financial institutions and central banks, form transactions other than those listed in above inflow categories.	100%
Net derivative cash inflows	100%
Other contractual cash inflows	National discretion
Total cash inflows	
Total net cash outflows = Total cash ourflows minus min [total cash inflows, 75% of gross outflows]	
LCR = Stock of HQLA/Total net cash outflows	

It can be seen that the net cash outflows takes into consideration the possible cash outflows from off balance sheet commitments. Detailed definitions and explanations for each line item can be found in the Basel document of January 2013.

Some points to be noted are:

- It has been suggested that frequency of calculation and reporting of LCR by banks to supervisory authorities may be monthly or even more frequent. Under stressed situations, especially where the LCR falls below 100%, indicating that a bank does not have adequate liquidity to support its potential commitments, the supervisor should insist on immediate and more frequent reporting.
- The 2008 framework 'Principles for sound liquidity risk management and supervision' stipulates that a bank, at the consolidated level, should actively monitor and control liquidity risk exposures and funding needs at the level of individual legal entities, foreign branches and subsidiaries, taking into account the legal, regulatory and operational limitations to transfer of liquid funds within the group. This aspect continues to be relevant regardless of the scope of application of the LCR.
- For cross border banking groups, the LCR would be reported in the home currency. However, liquidity needs in each significant currency should also be calculated and reported. The rationale is clear. Banks and supervisors cannot assume that currencies will remain freely transferable and convertible in a stress period.
- In addition to the LCR, the document has identified metrics to enable consistent monitoring by banks themselves and their supervisors. These metrics, together with the LCR standard, is meant to enable supervisors assess the liquidity risk of a bank. Actions that supervisors can take in adverse situations are outlined in the Committee's 'sound principles' document of 2008 (paragraphs 141–153, "Principles for sound liquidity risk management and supervision", September 2008, accessed at www.bis.org).
- The metrics discussed in the January 2013 document include: (a) contractual maturity mismatch, (see Illustration 12.3 for a simple example); (b) concentration of funding; (c) available unencumbered assets; (d) LCR by significant currencies; and (e) market related monitoring tools. A detailed description of each of these metrics

can be found in the January 2013 document. It can also be understood that the approaches outlined in the earlier paragraphs have been rigorously formalized in the Basel III framework for liquidity risk management.

The Group of Governors and Heads of Supervision (GHOS) is the oversight body of the Basel Committee on Banking Supervision (BCBS). The above proposals for regulating the short term liquidity of banks through the LCR is an outcome of its long standing deliberations on Basel III reforms and liquidity risk management. Following the successful agreement of the LCR, the Committee will now press ahead with the review of the Net Stable Funding Ratio (NSFR), which is a medium term measure of liquidity. This is a crucial component in the new framework, extending the scope of international agreement to the structure of banks' debt liabilities. This will be a priority for the Basel Committee over the next two years.

To recap from the previous chapter:

$$\text{NSFR} = \frac{\text{Available stable funding}}{\text{Required stable funding}} \geq 100\%$$

NSFR will be a required standard from January 1, 2018, and the reporting will be not less than quarterly.

Annexure IV summarizes the key findings of a research conducted in May 2006 by the Bank for International Settlements[44] and the lessons flowing from the financial crisis of 2007 manifested as principles for measurement and management of liquidity risk by the BIS.[45]

SECTION VI

APPLICABILITY TO BANKS IN INDIA

Interest Rate Derivatives in India

Indian participation in the derivative markets has accelerated only since the late 1990s. After the introduction of currency forwards in the 1980s, the Indian banking system saw no new instruments till 1997 when long-term foreign currency swaps began trading in the OTC markets.

Thereafter, the rise of derivatives in India has been swift—Interest rate swaps and FRAs were introduced as OTC products in July 1999, followed by several exchange-traded derivatives such as equity index futures (2000), equity index options (June 2001), stock options and stock futures later in the same year, and interest rate futures in June 2003.

In India, the different derivatives instruments are regulated by various regulators, such as Reserve Bank of India (RBI), Securities and Exchange Board of India (SEBI) and Forward Markets Commission (FMC). Broadly, RBI is empowered to regulate the interest rate derivatives, foreign currency derivatives and credit derivatives.

There are two distinct groups of derivative contracts:

- **Over-the-counter (OTC) derivatives:** Contracts are traded directly between two eligible parties, with or without the use of an intermediary and without going through an exchange.
- **Exchange-traded derivatives:** Derivative products that are traded on an exchange.

Typically, participants in this market are broadly classified into two functional categories, namely, market-makers and users.

- **User:** A user participates in the derivatives market to manage an underlying risk.
- **Market-maker:** A market-maker provides bid and offer prices to users and other market-makers. A market-maker need not have an underlying risk.

At least one party to a derivative transaction is required to be a market-maker. (It is to be noted that the definition is purely functional. For example, a market making entity, undertaking a derivative transaction to manage an underlying risk, would be acting in the role of a user.)

In India, all commercial banks (excluding Regional rural banks) and primary dealers can act as market makers. They are governed by the regulations in force. The users are typically business entities with identified underlying risk exposures.

At present, the following types of derivative instruments are permitted, subject to conditions and regulations in force:

- **Rupee interest rate derivatives:** Interest Rate Swap (IRS), Forward Rate Agreement (FRA), and Interest Rate Futures (IRF). IRS and FRA are OTC products, while Interest rate futures are exchange traded
- **Foreign Currency derivatives:** Foreign Currency Forward, Currency Swap and Currency Option – (Separate guidelines regarding Foreign Currency derivatives are issued by the regulator).

OTC Derivatives in India Conventionally, OTC derivative contracts are classified based on the underlying into (a) foreign exchange contracts, (b) interest rate contracts, (c) credit linked contracts, (d) equity linked contracts, and (e) commodity linked contracts. The equity linked contracts and commodity contracts have been relatively insignificant and are absent in the domestic Indian OTC markets.

The structure of the OTC derivatives market (excluding equity and commodity linked derivatives) is broadly depicted in the chart below. (Instruments in bold face indicate that these are traded in the Indian market at present).

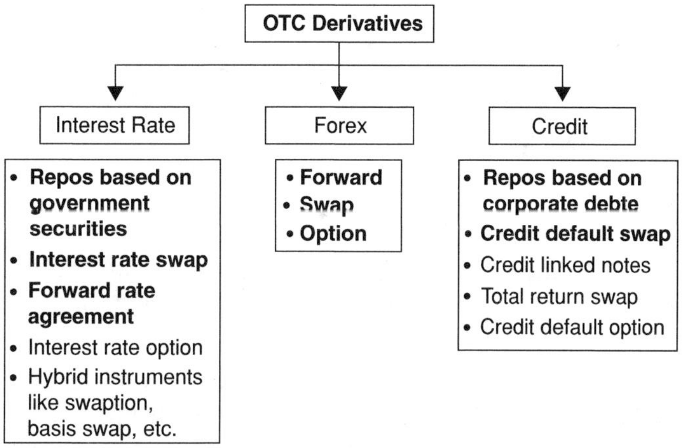

Source: RBI, 2011, Report of the Working Group on Reporting of OTC interest rate and forex derivatives, paragraph 3.8, page 16.

In the Indian markets, four OTC interest rate products are traded, *viz.*, Overnight Index Swap based on overnight MIBOR (Mumbai Inter Bank Offered Rate - a polled rate derived from the overnight unsecured inter-bank market), contracts based on MIFOR (Mumbai Inter-Bank Forward Offered Rate—a polled rate derived from London Interbank Offer Rate (LIBOR) and USD-INR forward premium), contracts based on INBMK (Indian Benchmark Rate—a benchmark rate published by Reuters that represents yield for government securities for a designated maturity), and contracts based on MIOIS (Mumbai Interbank Overnight Index Swap—a polled rate derived from the MIBOR rates of designated maturity)

A typical characteristic of the Indian interest rate market is that unlike in the overseas inter-bank funds markets, there is very little activity in tenors beyond overnight and as such there is no credible interest rate in segments other than overnight. Absence of a liquid 3-month or 6-month funds market has been a hindrance for trading in Forward Rate Agreements (FRA), as also in swaps based on these benchmarks. This is reflected in trading volumes of the products as shown in Table 12.6. It is seen that the market for OTC interest rate derivatives is predominated by Interest Rate Swaps (IRS) with no activity in FRAs. The total outstanding in terms of notional amounts as of end-March 2012 was 19,71,859 crore (MIBOR swaps), 2,93,310 crore (MIFOR swaps) and 25,910 crore (INBMK swaps). It is also evident that MIBOR swaps dominate the market.

TABLE 12.6 TREND IN OUTSTANDING VOLUMES IN INTEREST RATE SWAPS (IRS) MARKETS IN INDIA (MARCH 2012)

	MIBOR		MIFOR		INBMK	
Period	**Notioanl Amount**	**No. of Trades**	**Notional Amount**	**No. of Trades**	**Notional Amount**	**No. of Trades**
Mar-08	36,55,600	61,665	6,11,600	16,528	13,700	368
Mar-09	13,94,000	23,732	4,68,000	11,803	18,700	461
Mar-10	17,48,800	29,853	3,26,900	8,201	20,400	450
Mar-11	26,45,709	43,197	2,70,080	6,357	26,910	542
# Mar-12	19,71,859	27,541	2,93,310	6,348	25,910	520

up to March 22, 2012.

Source: RBI, 2012, Report of the Working Group on enhancing liquidity in the Government securities and Interest rate derivatives markets, Table 5, page 34.

Another aspect of the market, which is not unique only to India, has been the concentration of market participants. Share of foreign banks is about 80 per cent of the total market volume with virtual absence of nationalized banks. Activity in the IRS market is fairly spread across the swap curve between 1-10 years. There are no swap trades beyond 10 years.

All scheduled commercial banks (SCBs) excluding Regional Rural Banks, primary dealers (PDs) and all-India financial institutions (please refer to Chapter 1 for a list of financial institutions) have been allowed to use IRS and FRA for their own balance sheet management as also for the purpose of market making. The non-financial corporations have been allowed to use IRS and FRA to hedge their balance sheet exposures, with a caveat that at least one of the parties in any IRS/FRA transaction should be a RBI regulated entity. In addition to the RBI circular of 1999 (dated July 7,1999) which lays down principles for accounting and risk management for positions in IRS/FRA, RBI has, in 2007 (RBI circular dated April 20, 2007), released comprehensive guidelines on derivatives comprising general principles for derivatives trading, management of risk and sound corporate governance requirements along with a code of conduct for market makers. Some of the guidelines with regard to suitability and appropriateness policy for offering of derivative products to users, as outlined in paragraph 8.3 of the above circular, were reviewed in the light of the experience gained in implementation since then, and the revised version of the paragraph 8.3 was issued through RBI circular dated August 2, 2011, to take effect from January 1, 2012. All the current instructions can be accessed at www.rbi.org.in.

Reporting of OTC derivatives–CCP and TR

(*Sources: RBI, May 2011, Report of the Working group on reporting of OTC interest rate and forex derivatives, and RBI, 2012, Report of the Working Group on enhancing liquidity in the Government securities and Interest rate derivatives markets*)

The OTC derivatives market is characterized by large exposures between a limited number of market players. When the market is characterized by the existence of a few market makers, most of the activity takes place between these players and disruptions at any major dealer would soon transmit to other financial institutions and spread contagion to the entire market. The risk in the OTC derivative market also emanates from the opacity in the market that constrains the market participants from assessing the quantum of risk held with the counterparty. Further, with increase in volumes and complexities of the OTC derivatives, the non-standardized infrastructure for clearing and settlement also becomes a major impediment in containing risk, especially in the wake of the financial crisis of 2007-08. At the G 20 Toronto summit declaration of June 2010, Central banks and Market regulators agreed to initiate measures to enhance the post trading infrastructure in the OTC derivative markets.

Establishing Central counterparties (CCP) and Trade Repositories (TR) were two of the important commitments made at the above Summit.

A CCP is a financial institution that interposes as an intermediary between security (including derivatives) market participants. This reduces the amount of counterparty risk that market participants are exposed to. A sale is contracted between the seller of a security and the central counter party on one hand and the central counterparty and the buyer on the other. This means that no market participant has a direct exposure to another and if one party defaults, the central counterparty absorbs the loss. Settlement through a central counterparty has been progressively used on most major stock and security exchanges. However, a CCP based system can lead to concentration of risk with the CCP, which issue needed to be addressed.

On the other hand, the objective of TRs is simply to maintain an authoritative electronic database of all open OTC derivative transactions. It collects data derived from centrally or bilaterally clearable transactions as inputted/verified by both parties to a trade. An important attribute of a TR is its ability to interconnect with multiple market participants in support of risk reduction, operational efficiency and cost saving benefits to individual participants and to the market as a whole. The typical drawback of the OTC market is that the information concerning any contract is usually available only to the contracting parties. While expanding the scope of availability of information, it became pertinent to distinguish between information available to regulators, to market participants and to public at large. Post trade processing services is another important function of TR.

The reporting arrangement in interest rate derivatives in India follows a two tier system. Since at least one party to an OTC interest rate derivatives transaction is a RBI regulated entity, there has been an elaborate prudential reporting requirement in so far as the risk implication of the derivative positions for the entity is concerned.

In 2003, an internal Working Group of the RBI on Rupee derivatives had recommended a centralized clearing system for OTC derivatives through Clearing Corporation of India Ltd (CCIL). Preparatory to introduction of centralized clearing as also to get a better understanding of interest rate derivative market in India, RBI, in 2007, made it mandatory for the RBI regulated entities to report inter-bank/PD transactions in interest rate derivatives (FRAs and IRS) on a platform developed by the CCIL. Subsequently, all inter-bank/PD deals were required to be reported by the banks and PDs on the CCIL platform within 30 minutes of initiating the transaction. The information captured through this reporting system is comprehensive. Further, CCIL's evolution as a repository owed to a regulatory mandate, unlike repositories like DTCC which evolved out of a need to facilitate post trade processing.

As noted above, In India, RBI initiated measures for transaction-wise reporting of IRS Trades and mandated reporting of all inter-bank trades to Clearing Corporation of India Limited (CCIL) in August 2007. It is noteworthy that the Indian financial market has had a well-functioning CCP, *viz*., CCIL that has been offering CCP-guaranteed settlement for transactions in government securities, a few money market instruments, and forex *i.e*., dollar-rupee transactions. However, CCIL does not provide post trade services except aggregate data dissemination.

From April 2014, all entities regulated by the Reserve Bank should report their secondary market OTC trades in Corporate Bonds and Securitized Debt Instruments within 15 minutes of the trade on any of the stock exchanges (NSE, BSE and MCX-SX). These trades may be cleared and settled through any of the clearing corporations (NSCCL, ICCL and MCX-SX CCL). (RBI circular dated February 24, 2014)

The Need for TR

TRs help in obtaining a clear understanding of:

- the size and liquidity of the market.
- the scale of participation by various entities.
- the size and risk profile of outstanding positions and their potential impact in the event of a default.
- the evolution of price in the market which promotes transparency.

They also help in the development of tools that allow regulators and other stake holders to have access to more information and thereby identify emerging systemic risks.

Currently the major TRs globally are: (in order of their establishment)

1. CDS Trade Repository – DTCC & Markit (discussed in the chapters on 'Credit Risk')
2. IRS Trade Repository – TriOptima
3. REGIS-TR (promoted jointly by Clearstream and Bolsas y Mercados Espanoles
4. Equity Trade Repository – DTCC & Markit (since 2005, expanded to provide matching services for interest rate swaps and swaptions, equity swaps and variance swaps)
5. Credit Derivatives – DTCC Europe
6. All asset classes – Xtrakter owned by Euroclear

While DTCC contributes its Deriv/SERV matching and confirmation engine, Markit's data and valuation provides the much needed post trade valuation services. This alliance provides a **fully integrated system for processing OTC derivatives** across borders and asset classes to provide a service that helps a wide range of market participants achieve greater certainty in their transaction processing. It also addresses the challenges of rapid growth, increased cost and operational risks associated with the OTC derivative markets.

TriOptima, a Stockholm-based technology company was selected by ISDA to operate as an interest rate derivatives TR. A number of broker-dealers, buy-side firms and industry associations, committed to record all interest rate derivatives trades in this TR. The OTC Derivatives **Interest Rate Trade Reporting Repository (IR TRR)** launched by TriOptima in early 2010 was an important step towards improving transparency in the global OTC derivatives markets.

An important innovation in OTC derivative markets introduced during the last few years relates to portfolio compression services offered by TriOptima. Since the only way to exit a position in an OTC derivative is to enter into another with opposite pay off, the gross notional outstanding multiplies manifold as a result. Apart from the fact that this does not capture the economic essence of the portfolios, it increases the demand on capital for the regulated entities. TriOptima's TriReduce and TriResolve services reportedly offer multilateral netting with bilateral settlement whereby an entity can extinguish its OTC derivative positions without affecting its MTM value or the PV01(change in price of a bond for a change in yield in absolute monetary value rather than percentage as in modified duration. PV01 is measured as the product of the modified duration and price/value. For more on modified duration please refer to the Annexure to this chapter).

In India too, the service has been used by the IRS portfolio holders with significant reduction in the gross notional positions. The first such exercise was undertaken in July, 2011 wherein a compression of 94.30 per cent of the submitted trades was achieved. The second cycle of compression was carried out in March 2012 with a compression of 90.31 per cent. As already stated, 'Portfolio compression' reduces the overall notional size and number of outstanding derivatives contracts in the portfolio without changing the overall risk profile of the portfolio. During this period, RBI has also taken initiatives to strengthen the legal framework in respect of OTC derivatives in interest rates and forex.

The Exchange Traded Interest Rate Derivatives in India

Interest rate futures (IRF) were introduced in June 2003 when National Stock Exchange (NSE) launched three IRF contracts - futures on 10-year notional G-Sec with a coupon of 6 per cent, 10-year notional zero-coupon G-Sec and 91-Day T-Bills. However, these contracts did not attract enough market interest since its introduction and soon became defunct. The use of ZCYC to determine the daily settlement price and for MTM of the contract resulted in large basis risk for participants trying to hedge their cash market positions through the futures market thereby making the futures contract unattractive, if not risky (All the terms – ZCYC, MTM and basis risk – have been described in earlier chapters). Further, the prohibition of banks from taking trading positions in the futures market had resulted in very low/negligible liquidity in this market.

A second joint committee of the RBI and Securities and Exchange Board of India (SEBI) based its recommendations on the above findings in June 2009. Its primary suggestion was to introduce physically settled Interest rate futures contract on 10 year Government of India (GoI) coupon bearing security.

Subsequently, RBI issued Interest Rate Futures (Reserve Bank) Directions, 2009, on August 28, 2009, and followed it up with amendments upto December 2011. The latest Directions have come into effect in December 2013. The RBI has included cash settlement for 10 year Government of India (GoI) securities, which can also be settled by physical delivery. The other underlying securities included are 91 day Treasury bills, 2 year, 5 year and coupon bearing GoI securities, which are eligible for cash settlement.

Banks are permitted to participate in IRF both for the purpose of hedging the risk in the underlying investment portfolio and also to take trading position. However, banks are not allowed to undertake transactions in IRFs on behalf of clients. Similarly, stand-alone Primary Dealers are allowed to deal in IRF for both hedging and trading on own account and not on client's account.

However, experts attribute lack of activity in IRF to structural factors such as lack of liquidity in the underlying cash market, SLR prescriptions and HTM facility. Other factors normally cited for the lack of market activity are (a) banks and MFs have portfolio duration of less than 5 years; (b) IRF contract cannot be used as a perfect hedge; (c) the market hesitancy to take a view on long-term interest rates; and (d) lack of significant buy side interest in a rising interest rate cycle and over supply of G-secs.

The latest guidelines on exchange traded derivatives can be accessed at www.rbi.org.in

ALM Framework for Indian Banks

From 1 April 1999, banks in India were expected to implement an effective ALM system, the guidelines for which were contained in RBI circular dated 10 February 1999. The salient features of this system are as follows:

1. Banks were expected to form an ALCO headed by the bank's chief executive.
2. The ALM process rested on three pillars—ALM information system, ALM organization and the ALM process
3. The ALM information system emphasized the need for accurate and timely information to assess risks of individual banks.
4. The prerequisite for an effective ALM organization is strong commitment from the bank's senior and top management. The ALCO of the bank would be responsible for ensuring proper asset liability management as set by the bank's Board of directors.
5. Though the scope of the ALM process would encompass management of liquidity risk, market risk, trading risk, funding and capital planning and profit planning, the RBI guidelines primarily address liquidity and interest rate risks.

Liquidity Risk Management Guidelines Primarily, liquidity was to be tracked through maturity or cash flow mismatches. For this purpose, a standard tool was to be adopted, involving the use of a maturity ladder and calculation of cumulative surplus or deficit of funds at selected maturity dates. Within each specified time bucket, there could be mismatches between expected cash inflows and outflows. The main area of concern here would be the short-term mismatches—those up to 28 days. Hence, RBI had asked banks to keep the mismatches (negative gap) during this time period within 20 per cent of cash outflows in each time bucket. Bank assets and liabilities are grouped into different maturity profiles and presented in the statement of structural liquidity for decision making.

The statement of structural liquidity would essentially show all expected cash inflows and outflows during the specified period. *A maturing liability will be a cash outflow while a maturing asset would represent a cash inflow*. In determining the likely timing and magnitude of these cash flows, banks will have to make several assumptions based on whether they resort to asset management or liability management.

The guidelines also suggest a format that would enable banks to estimate short-term dynamic liquidity, *i.e.*, monitor their short-term (1 to 90 days) liquidity, as in the cash flow method described in *Section V*.

Interest Rate Risk Management Guidelines[46] RBI has proposed in April 2006 that the *Modified Duration Gap approach* be adopted for interest rate risk management. The steps to be followed for computing the Modified DGAP would be as follows:

1. Identify variables such as principal amount, maturity date/re-pricing date, coupon rate, yield, frequency and basis of interest calculation for each item/category of asset/liability (including off-balance sheet items).
2. Generate the bucket-wise (additional time buckets have been proposed for longer lending horizons) cash flows for each item/category of asset/liability/off-balance sheet item.
3. Determine the yield curve for arriving at the yields based on current market yields / current replacement cost for each item/category of asset/liability/off-balance sheet item.
4. Assume the mid-point of each time bucket as representing the maturity of all assets and liabilities in that time bucket.
5. Calculate the Modified Duration of each category of asset/liability/off-balance sheet item using the variables in (1).
6. Determine the weighted average Modified Duration of all the assets (DA) and similarly for all the liabilities (DL), including off-balance sheet items.
7. Derive the Modified Duration Gap as;

$$\text{DGAP} = \text{Modified DA} - \text{W} \times \text{Modified DL}$$

where $\text{W} = \dfrac{\text{RSL}}{\text{RSA}}\left(\dfrac{\text{Rate Sensitive Liabilities}}{\text{Rate Sensitive Assets}}\right)$.

DA = Weighted average Modified Duration of assets and

DL = Weighted average Modified Duration of liabilities.

8. Calculate the Modified Duration of Equity as = DGAP × Leverage, where Leverage = RSA / Equity. In this case, 'equity' will represent capital funds. It is proposed that banks report monthly to RBI the interest rate sensitivity as evidenced by the modified duration approach.

Illustration, 12.12 excerpted from the RBI guidelines, will serve to clarify the mechanics, which can be applied to assets, liabilities and equity:

ILLUSTRATION 12.12

EVE	(₹ in Crores) **Amount**
Net worth	1,350.00
RSA	18,251.00
RSL	18,590.00
Modified duration of gap	
DA (Weighted modified duration of assets)	1.96
DL (Weighted modified duration of liabilities)	1.25
Weight = RSL/RSA	1.02
DGAP = DA – W × DL	0.69
Leverage ratio = RSA / (Tier 1 + Tier 2)	13.52
Modified duration of equity = DGAP × Leverage Ratio	9.34
For a 200 bp Rate shock the drop in equity value is	18.68% (9.34 × 2)

Source: RBI Guidelines

The basic slotting of various assets and liabilities based on their maturity profile and interest rate sensitivity is shown in *Annexure V.* It is to be noted that these profiles are fine-tuned in subsequent RBI guidelines to refine the process of interest rate risk and liquidity risk management.

Liquidity Risk Management in Indian Banks

The global financial crisis of 2007 has highlighted, like never before, the role of prudent liquidity management as the cornerstone of financial stability. On November 7, 2012, RBI released guidelines for liquidity risk management, based on the documents *Principles for Sound Liquidity Risk Management and Supervision* as well as *Basel III: International Framework for Liquidity Risk Measurement, Standards and Monitoring* published by the Basel Committee on Banking Supervision (BCBS) in September 2008 and December 2010 respectively. Banks had to implement the guidelines immediately. However, these guidelines would be further refined based on the January 2013 document of the Basel committee titled '*Basel III: The Liquidity Coverage Ratio and Liquidity Risk Monitoring Tools*', the salient features of which were discussed in Section V. The details can be accessed at www.rbi.org.in

The approach of RBI in the latest guidelines[47] is to limit banks' exposure to liquidity risk in time buckets in the very near future—more specifically, up to the forthcoming 28 days. The RBI guidelines ask banks to fix 'tolerance limits' on the 'negative gap', to limit banks' exposure to liquidity risk.

As we have seen earlier, a 'negative gap' within a time bucket indicates that maturing assets during that time period are lower than the liabilities maturing during the same period. This implies that the cash flows from assets (say interest payments, principal repayments, etc., from loans, advances or investments) would not be sufficient to cover the demands made by depositors and other creditors during the period under consideration.

The simple Illustration 12.13 shows the impact of 'negative gap' on liquidity management through simple matching of 'maturities'.

ILLUSTRATION 12.13 MATURITY GAP MATCHING—A SIMPLE EXAMPLE

Bank D has the following assets and liabilities classified by maturity.[48] Note that these are maturing liabilities and assets in each time bucket.

Maturity Mths	Liabilities	Assets
Less than 1	7	10
1–3	13	8
4–6	11	10
7–12	9	20
13–24	24	27
25–36	29	19
Above 36	10	9

We will now find the GAP in each time bucket, affix a sign to this GAP, and then find the cumulative gap.

Matching assets and liability by maturity

Maturity Mths	Liability	Assets	GAP Absolute	GAP Positive/Negative	Cum GAP Positive/Negative
<1	7	10	3	3	3
3	13	8	5	–5	–2
6	11	10	1	–1	–3
12	9	20	11	11	8
24	24	27	3	3	11
36	29	19	10	–10	1
>36	10	9	1	–1	0

What can we conclude about the bank's liquidity risk from the above table?

We see that in the near term, *i.e.*, up to 6 months, the bank has two time buckets of negative gaps, which are not offset by the positive gap in the first time band, up to 1 month.

This implies that the bank is subject to liquidity risk even if all the assets yield cash flows as expected during this period. Further, if there is a shortfall in expected cash flows from maturing assets or if there is unexpected increase in demand from liability holders, the bank's liquidity position will deteriorate. Hence, the bank has to plan ahead for alternative sources of liquidity over the next 6 months.

This approach not only limits liquidity risk exposure in specific time buckets, but also recognizes the cumulative impact on liquidity over time periods in the near future, which is the most relevant for banks' liquidity.

According to these guidelines, banks have to undertake dynamic liquidity management. The guidance for slotting future cash flows is shown in *Annexure V*.

CHAPTER SUMMARY

- Prior to the 1970s, many firms in the developed countries intentionally mismatched their balance sheets, and borrowed short and lent long to earn a spread. Things started to change in the 1970s, which ushered in a period of volatile interest rates that continued into the early 1980s. The 1980s and 1990s also saw a new wave of banking crises that arose more from sharp movements in asset prices or sharp contractions in market liquidity or credit risk concentrations, defying the traditional regulatory prescriptions of deposit insurance or lender of last resort advances. The global financial crisis of 2007 has highlighted the need for policy makers and regulators to seek new preventive measures to handle banking risks.
- Risk management is uniquely important for financial institutions because, in contrast to firms in other industries, their liabilities are a source of wealth creation for their shareholders. Asset-liability risk is a 'leveraged' risk since the capital base of banks is small relative to its assets or liabilities. Hence, small percentage changes in assets or liabilities can translate into large percentage changes in capital.
- ALM is concerned with strategic balance sheet management. Risks caused by changes in interest rates and exchange rates, credit risk and the bank's liquidity position have to be monitored and mitigated. Techniques of ALM have been evolving over time.
- Banks typically have an ALCO, that comprises of a group of top or senior management personnel entrusted with the responsibility of managing the bank's assets and liabilities to balance the various risk exposures, to enable the bank achieve its operating objectives.
- Interest rate risk is the exposure of a bank's financial condition to adverse movements in interest rates. If accepted and managed as a normal part of banking business, interest rate risk can be used to enhance profitability and shareholder value. However, excessive interest rate risk could lead to substantial volatility in earnings and, thus, affect the underlying value of the bank's assets, liabilities and off-balance sheet instruments.
- The two most common perspectives for assessing a bank's interest rate risk exposure are (a) the *earnings perspective* that focuses on short-term earnings, and (b) the *economic value* perspective that looks at the long-term economic viability of the bank.
- Interest rate risk arises from several factors fundamental to the business of banking. Some of the most discussed sources of interest rate risk are: *Repricing risk, Yield curve risk, Basis risk and Embedded optionality.*
- Banks use various techniques to measure the exposure of earnings and economic value to changes in interest rates. These techniques range from simple calculations relying on basic maturity and repricing tables based on current and projected on- and off-balance sheet positions, to highly sophisticated dynamic modelling techniques. Some of the popular approaches include: Gap analysis, EAR models and EVE models, as well as DGAP analysis models used to immunize the MVE.
- A popular alternative to mitigate the interest rate risk on its investments is the use of Interest Rate Derivatives (IRDs). Banks use IRDs to transform some fixed-rate investments into floating-rate assets. They also use IRDs to transform floating-rate liabilities into fixed-rate liabilities. IRDs are simply contracts used to hedge other positions that expose them to risk, or speculate on anticipated price moves. In most cases, banks use IRDs to replicate balance sheet transactions with off-balance sheet contracts, so that contingent positions are created.
- Some of the most basic and widely used IRD contracts are—Swaps, Futures, FRAs, Options, Caps/Floors/Collars and 'Swaptions'.
- Liquidity risk is the risk that the bank may not be able to fund increases in assets or meet liability obligations as they fall due without incurring unacceptable losses. Of the four specific forms of risk that impact banking operation—credit risk, market risk, operational risk and liquidity risk—the first three have been extensively studied and commonly incorporated into existing capital allocation frameworks. However, at present, there is no technique for modelling liquidity risk that has wide acceptance. Basel III has introduced LCR in January 2013 for regulating liquidity.
- The alternative approaches prevalently used by banks for Liquidity Risk Management are (a) Asset Management, and (b) Liability Management.
- Some of the forward-looking tools for Liquidity Risk Management prevalently used include: (a) Projected sources and uses of funds over the planning horizon, (b) the working funds approach, (c) cash flow or funding gap report, (d) funding concentration analysis, (e) funds availability report and so on. A few typical retrospective tools include ratio analysis and historical funds flow analysis.

- Indian participation in the derivative markets has accelerated only since the late 1990s. A lion's share of banks' off-balance sheet exposures is attributable to derivatives activity. In December 2013, the RBI directives on interest rate futures has attempted to address some shortcomings of the earlier guidelines on interest rate derivatives.
- From 1 April 1999, banks in India were expected to implement an effective ALM system. The ALCO of the bank would be responsible for ensuring proper asset liability management as set by the bank's Board of directors.
- Though the scope of the ALM process would encompass management of liquidity risk, market risk, trading risk, funding and capital planning and profit planning, the RBI guidelines primarily address liquidity and interest rate risks.

TEST YOUR UNDERSTANDING

1. Why is refinancing risk an important interest rate risk?
2. How does a rise or fall in interest rates affect the market value of both assets and liabilities?
3. Which is the predominant risk in the following transactions carried out by a bank?
   a. It finances a 5-year fixed rate loan with a 1 year certificate of deposit
   b. A British bank uses deposits in GBP to lend in the euro market for fixed rates
4. What is the importance of 'maturity buckets' in the GAP models? Why is the length of time selected for repricing assets and liabilities important when using the models?
5. Calculate the Maturity GAP and the impact on NII for: (a) an increase in interest rates of 100 bps, and (b) decrease in interest rates of 100 bps, in each of the following positions:
   a. Rate sensitive assets ₹200 crore, rate sensitive liabilities ₹100 crore
   b. Rate sensitive assets ₹100 crore; rate sensitive liabilities ₹150 crore
   c. Rate sensitive assets ₹150 crore; rate sensitive liabilities ₹140 crore

   What conclusions can you draw from the above results?
6. A bank's ALCO is reasonably certain that interest rates are going to rise over the next 6 months. How should it adjust the bank's Maturity GAP to take advantage of this increase? Would the GAP be maintained differently if interest rates were expected to fall? How easy is it in practice to carry out adjustments in GAP?
7. In the above case, if the bank were using the Duration GAP, would the decision be any different? Substantiate your answer.
8. A Bank has the following assets and liabilities on its balance sheet—it has loans of ₹10,000 crore and no other assets; it has deposits of ₹8,500 crore and a capital of ₹1,500 crore. Assume that the average maturity of the loan is 4 years, and the average maturity of the deposits is 2 years. Also assume that the loan and deposit are at book value, and are repayable only at the end of the maturity period.
   a. If the interest rate on both the loan and deposit is at 9 per cent, what is the MVE?
   b. If the MVE is to be made zero in the above case, what should be the average maturity of the deposits?
   c. If MVE is to be zero, what should be the average interest rate on deposits that the bank should offer?
9. A bank's balance sheet has the following assets: cash of ₹50 crore and other assets of ₹150 crore. The corresponding liabilities are deposits of ₹140 crore, borrowings of ₹30 crore, and other liabilities of ₹30 crore. One of the bank's valued customers wants the sanctioned credit limit of ₹12 crore to be disbursed immediately. How will the bank's balance sheet look if (a) the bank adopts asset management and (b) the bank adopts liability management, in complying with the customer's request.
10. At March end, 2006, Bank X showed the following position:

(₹ in crore)

Liabilities	Amount	Average Interest (%)	Assets	Amount	Average Interest (%)
Capital and reserves	900	0	Cash and bank balance	500	0
Deposits	8,400	6	Advances	7,000	10
Borrowing	300	7	Investments	2,000	6
Other Liabilities	400	0	Fixed and other assets	500	0
	10,000			10,000	

a. Calculate the rate sensitive gap, assuming that all interest bearing assets and liabilities are rate sensitive.

b. If the interest rates were to move as follows over the next 1 year, what would the GAP be?

Deposits	6.75%
Borrowings	8.00%
Advances	11.00%
Investments	6.80%

c. If the average duration of assets were 4 years, and the average duration of liabilities were 3 years, and the current interest rate were at 10 per cent, what would be the change in the market value of the equity due to increase in interest rate by 100 bps?

d. How can Bank X immunize the MVE?

11. Bank Y's ALCO expects the interest rates to move as follows:

Change in Interest Rates	Probability
–0.5%	0.10
+0.5%	0.20
–1.0%	0.30
+1.0%	0.40

If the earning assets of the bank are at ₹50,000 crore, NII is ₹1,500 crore, and the bank expects a variation of 10 per cent in NII,

a. what is the Target GAP for each of the possible changes in interest rates?

b. what will be the change in NII be for different levels of GAP?

12. If RSA and RSL are decreased by the same amount, which of the following will be true?

a. Gap remains unchanged, gap ratio increases

b. Gap remains unchanged, gap ratio decreases

c. Gap and Gap ratio both remain unchanged

d. Gap and Gap ratio will change

e. None of the above is applicable

13. Bank B has the following position of assets and liabilities: ₹10 crore in short-term government securities, ₹6 crore line of credit to borrow in the short term and repo market, and ₹3 crore excess cash reserve with the central bank. It has also borrowed ₹5 crore in the call money market to meet urgent requirements.

a. What are the bank's total available sources of liquidity?

b. What are the bank's total uses of liquidity?

c. What conclusions do you draw from the net liquidity position of the bank?

14. How sensitive will a bank's MVE be to a change in interest rates under each of the following scenarios? Consider the effects of rising and falling interest rate environments.

a. Seventy per cent of the bank's assets are in 15 year housing loans and infrastructure loans

b. The bank is paying less than market rates on a major portion of its term deposits, and market interest rates move upwards

c. Eighty per cent of the bank's investment portfolio is in short-term investments, due to mature in the next two quarters

15. Bank Z is liability sensitive. The management seeks protection from interest rate risk. Which of the following would be a better hedge—interest rate cap, floor, collar or reverse collar? Would the management take a different stand if the bank were asset sensitive?

TOPICS FOR FURTHER DISCUSSION

- Study the financial statements of some large banks in the country. What are the risks they carry on their balance sheets, and in their off-balance sheet transactions? Can you quantify the risk?
- All banks in India mandatorily show the maturity profile of liabilities and assets on their financial statements. Analyze the maturity profiles. Can you arrive at conclusions regarding the interest rate and liquidity risks these banks carry?
- Study the derivative transactions entered into by major banks. What are the risks involved? How serious are these risks for the banks?
- Calculate LCR of major banks using Basel III guidelines of January 2013.

SELECT REFERENCES

1. Chacko, George, and Sjoman, Anders, 2006, 'Introduction to Interest rate options', Harvard Business School Publishing.
2. FDIC, 2005, 'Risk Management Manual of Examination Policies', Section 3.8, 'Off balance sheet activities' accessed at supervision@fdic.gov
3. Federal Reserve Bank of Kansas City and Federal Reserve Bank of St Louis, 'Insights for Bank Directors', The Federal Reserve Center for online learning.
4. Harvard Business School, 1995, 'Interest Rate Derivatives'.
5. Hong Kong Monetary Authority, 2004, Supervisory Policy Manual, 'Liquidity Risk Management'.

ANNEXURE I

THEORIES OF INTEREST RATES

Interest rate risk management can be effective only if interest rate forecasts are realistic and accurate. The forecasts are primarily based on the shape of the future yield curve.

The yield curve, simply stated, is a measure of the market expectations of movements in future interest rates, given the current market conditions. It is shown as a graph comparing yields on securities of different maturities, assuming other factors such as, default risk or marketability as identical for all the securities being compared. This is also known as the 'term structure' of interest rates.

Government securities are considered risk free and their yields are often used as the benchmark for other instruments with similar maturities. The yield curve is constructed as a graph in which the 'yield to maturity' is plotted on the vertical axis and the number of years to maturity on the horizontal axis. The two essential assumptions made while graphing are that the securities are noncallable and are akin to zero coupon bonds that mature on the common payment date. Typically, yield curves for risky bonds will be at a higher level on the graph than the yield curves for comparatively safe bonds.

The exact shape of the yield curve is closely scrutinized since it can be different at any point in time. An upward sloping yield curve is typical of economic recovery, where the long-term interest rates are expected to exceed the short-term interest rates and the spot rates are increasing. Similarly, when the yield curve tends to slope downward, indicating that long-term interest rates are less than short-term rates and the spot rates are declining, the economy could be heading for a recession. Hence, a change in the shape of the yield curve serves as a signal to the investors to change their outlook on the economy.

The slope of the yield curve is also seen as an important indicator—the greater the slope, the greater is the gap between short- and long-term interest rates.

In order to further elaborate, there are essentially three patterns created by the yield curves, which are as follows:

1. ***Normal Yield Curve*** This is the yield curve shape that is expected to form during normal market conditions, in which investors typically believe that the economy will grow at a reasonable rate in line with expectations and there will be no sudden or significant changes in critical indicators such as inflation rates. The yield curve will be generally upward sloping and the market expects longer-term fixed income securities to offer higher yields than short-term fixed income securities, due to the risks associated with time. With increase in the difference between short- and long-term yields, the curve becomes 'steep'.

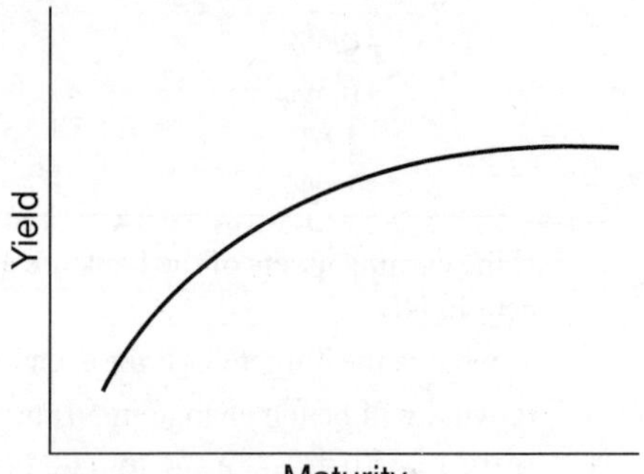

Source: investopedia.com

2. ***Flat (or Humped) Yield Curve*** This type of yield curve sends out varying signals, making it difficult for the market to determine the direction of interest rate movements in future. A flat yield curve usually occurs when the market is in a transition phase. Here, the shorter- and longer-term yields are very close to each other. When the yield curve is flat, the investors would prefer to invest in fixed income securities with the least risk or the highest credit quality. Under circumstances leading to a decline in the long-term interest rates, a flat curve can sometimes lead to an inverted curve.

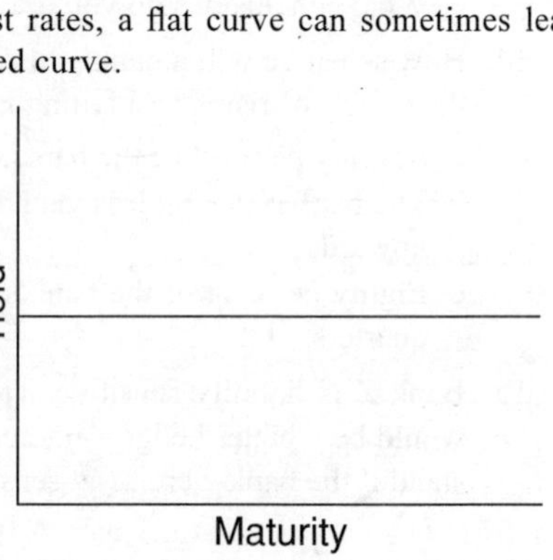

Source: investopedia.com

3. ***Inverted Yield Curve*** These yield curves, though rare, indicate abnormal market conditions where the expectations of investors are entirely in contrast with thoset demonstrated by the normal yield curve. The inverted yield curve signals that long-term bonds may yield less than short-term securities. This phenomenon happening in a growing economy could indicate upcoming recession.

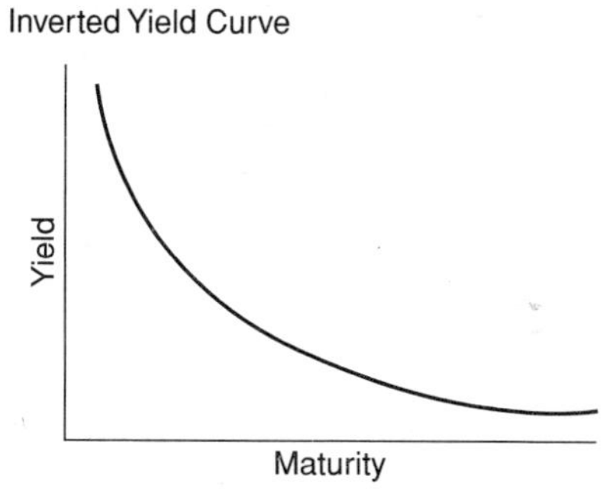

Source: investopedia.com

The Theories Behind Yield Curve Shapes

The shape of the yield curve is explained through a few popular theories. Before we describe the theories, we will have to understand the two terms – 'spot' rate and 'forward' rate.

The spot rate is the prevailing interest rate that can be obtained from the following equation:

$$\text{Loan amount } [L] = \text{Loan maturity value } [M]$$
$$[1 + \text{spot interest rate for a maturity t years } [S_t]]$$

The forward rate is the interest rate that is expected to prevail at some future specified dates. According to a popular theory (Pure Expectations Theory), the current forward rate is an unbiased predictor of future spot rates. In other words, a bank would earn identical yields on a two-year loan, irrespective of whether the loan tenure is of two years or one year, rolled over at the end of the first year. Such a rate, at which the rolled over loan would earn an identical yield is called the 'implicit forward interest rate'. Thus, the implicit forward interest rate would, in effect, represent the future rate of a short-term loan when rolled over and would be equal to the present long-term rate. In mathematical terms, the equation can be generalized as follows:

$$(1 + r_t)^t = (1 + r_{t-1})^{t-1} \times (1 + F_{t-1})$$

where r_t = yield on a loan with maturity 't'

r_{t-1} = yield on loan with maturity 't − 1'

F_{t-1} = implicit forward interest rate

We will now provide a brief overview of some of the popular theories.

Pure Expectations Theory This theory is also called the 'unbiased expectations theory' and the assumption here is that forward rates are unbiased estimates of expected spot rates. In other words, the theory attempts to explain the difference in yields on securities with different maturities arising due to varying investor expectations regarding interest rate movements in future. This implies that the investors will prefer securities with the highest return, regardless of the maturities. For example, an investor with a three-year planning horizon may choose one of the following alternatives to achieve his investment objective: (a) he can invest in a security with a maturity period of three years or (b) invest for one year and roll over twice or (c) invest for two years and roll over for one year or (d) invest for one year and roll over for two years thereafter. According to this theory, the interest rate that equates the return on a series of short-term securities with the return on a long-term security carrying the same final maturity would represent the market's expectation of the future interest rate. An inherent assumption is of course that the alternatives enumerated above can be carried through without cost. Therefore, after summarizing, the theory hypothesises that (a) the long-term interest rates are an average of the current and expected future short-term interest rates, (b) the expected short-term interest rate is the market forecast of future interest rates and (c) the investors would substitute maturities for better yields. Going by this theory, an upward sloping yield curve augurs an increase in interest rates, while a downward sloping yield curve is a signal that interest rates would dip in future. However, the interpretation could be too simplistic since an upward sloping curve can shift downwards in its entirety when rates decline, yet preserving the upward slope.

Liquidity Theory This theory is also called the 'liquidity premium theory' and is an extension of the pure expectations theory. The liquidity theory incorporates the additional factor of the investor's expectations of 'price risk' in forecasting the market rates. Even if expected returns are identical for long-term securities and a series of same maturity short-term securities, the investors would have to be induced into buying long-term securities due to the price fluctuations that could arise over a fairly longer term. That is, if an investor receives a return of 10 percent for securities with maturities of both one and two years' maturities, he may prefer to have the option of investing for a year and roll over for another, if interest rates are still favourable after a year. In other words, investors would expect additional return for investing in long-term securities in the form of a risk premium. Essentially, therefore, long-term rates would be set as the average of current and expected short-term rates plus a 'liquidity premium'. In effect, the forward rate, too, would then equal the expected rate plus a liquidity premium. The yield curve is theoretically expected to be upward sloping since the long-term rates are always expected to stay above the short-term rates and the imposition of a liquidity premium exerts an upward bias. However, in the very long term, the yield curve would tend to flatten out, since there is a little differential price risk at longer maturities. Further, if the yield curve becomes inverted, there would be expectation of a very sharp drop in the short-term rates to compensate for the heightened liquidity premiums.

Preferred Habitat Theory While not contesting the validity of the liquidity premium, this theory argues that it cannot be extended to cover all maturities. The maturity preference of borrowers and lenders depends on their unique needs, preferences and constraints. Hence, the presence of a premium might induce them to change maturity patterns only to a certain level, beyond which even enhanced premiums may not induce investors to change their maturity patterns.

Market Segmentation Theory This theory closely resembles the preferred habitat theory and states that the investors operate in different markets essentially due to their asset liability maturity patterns. The interest rates in each of these market segments are governed by the supply and demand forces within the segment. The investors in any segment are not induced by the presence of premiums to shift maturities. For example, most banks prefer to operate in the medium-term segment since the maturity profile of the bulk of their liabilities is medium term. On the other hand, insurance and pension funds are typically long-term investors and infrastructure funding has to be long term. Maturity restrictions can also arise from regulatory prescriptions as in the case of government securities or money market instruments. Under this theory, an upward sloping yield curve would result when, at each interest rate, the supply of funds exceeds the demand, more for short-term securities than for long-term securities. The smaller demand pressure on short-term funds would then push short-term rates below long-term rates and the curve would slope upward. Similarly, in the case of a downward sloping yield curve, the short-term rates outstrip the long-term rates, since at each interest rate, the demand for funds outstrips the supply, more for short-term securities than for long-term securities.

Riding the Yield Curve

The term signifies a 'buy and sell' strategy, where a portfolio manager purchases a medium- or long-term bond when the yield curve is upward sloping and sells it before maturity to make a capital gain.

The drawback with this strategy is the risk in riding the yield curve when it is changing. Further, frequent buying and selling (versus holding till maturity) entails higher transaction costs.

The Theoretical Spot Rate Curve

It is evident from the above discussion that the basic types of yield curves do not account for securities that have varying coupon rates. This is because the YTM is calculated with the assumption that coupons are reinvested at an interest rate equal to the coupon rate. For example, comparing a 10-year bond paying 12 per cent coupon with a 10-year government security with a coupon of 5 per cent may not be meaningful. That is, the bond paying 5 per cent may not be the most suitable benchmark for the bond yielding 12 per cent.

The spot-rate curve differentiates the yields from government securities from yields arising out of similar noncallable fixed income securities. It is formed by graphing the yields of zero coupon government securities like treasury bills and their corresponding maturities. The interest rate emerging from this graph is called the 'spot rate'. The spot rate given by each zero-coupon security and the spot-rate curve are considered in tandem to determine the value of each zero-coupon component of a noncallable fixed-income security. The implication is that the yield curve is graphed as though each coupon payment of a noncallable fixed-income security resembled a zero-coupon bond.

The Credit Spread

Also called the 'quality spread', this represents the additional yield from a corporate bond over a similar government security. The 'spread' reflects the yield curve of the corporate bond. Since the yield curve is used to forecast the direction that interest rates would take when inflation rates are increasing, the credit spread between corporate and government securities widens, indicating that all is not well with the economy. The widening of the credit spread also indicates that the investor would seek compensation in the form of higher coupon for taking on the higher risk of corporate bonds. When interest rates are declining, the credit spread between government and corporate fixed-income securities generally narrows, indicating that the economy is growing. Falling interest rates encourage firms to borrow at lower rates, thus increasing expectations of healthier cash flows and lowering default risk.

Thus, the yield curve, used in tandem with the credit spread, can also be used to price corporate fixed income securities.

SELECT REFERENCES

1. Koch, Timothy W, and MacDonald, Scott S, "Bank Management", Chapter 7, 4th edition, pp. 249–297, The Dryden Press, USA.
2. Kohn, Meir, "Financial Institutions and Markets", Chapter 7, pages 151–176, 5th reprint, Tata Mcgraw Hill Publishing Company Ltd., India.
3. http://www.investopedia.com

ANNEXURE II

CONCEPT OF DURATION AND CONVEXITY

When interest rates rise, bond prices fall. But to what degree do bond prices change when interest rates change? It depends on the bond's 'duration', its 'term to maturity' and 'yield to maturity'.

What is 'duration' in the context of bonds? Simply stating, 'duration' measures the number of years it takes for the price of the bond to be repaid by the cash flows. It is different from 'maturity' of the bonds. It is an important measure for investors, since bonds with higher durations are perceived as more risky and as having higher price volatility than bonds with lower durations. For example, between a zero coupon bond and a plain vanilla (or 'straight' bond that pays coupon at fixed periodicities) bond, a typical investor would prefer the latter, since its duration will always be less than its maturity. For a zero coupon bond, the duration is equal to its time to maturity. The reason is clear. In the case of a plain vanilla bond, cash flows (coupon payments) occur at fixed periods before maturity, enabling the investor to recoup his investment (price of the bond) earlier (using the time value of money, where earlier cash flows have greater weight). The zero coupon bond pays both coupon and original investment only at maturity and hence no interim cash flows occur.

In the case of a plain vanilla bond, as coupons are paid out, they no longer represent future cash flows to be paid to the investor and hence would not be included in computing the duration. Therefore, as more and more coupons get paid out, the duration changes and decreases as time moves closer to the bond's maturity. Eventually, duration converges with the bond's maturity. That is why a zero coupon bond's duration is the same as its maturity.

Besides the time to maturity, bonds with high yields (high coupon rates) tend to have lower durations than bonds with lower yields. This makes sense, since a higher yield translates into faster repayment of the investment made.

Types of Duration Measures

Though 'duration' is used as a common terminology in the market, there are at least three prevalent types of duration measures. These differ in the way they consider assumptions related to interest rate changes or the other features of securities such as options or maturity.

Macaulay's Duration Created by Frederick Macaulay in 1938, this concept gained popularity only in the 1970s. Macaulay's duration is calculated as the weighted average maturity of the cash flow stream of a security. The present value of each cash-flow interest and principal is used as the weight and it is multiplied by the time it is received. The aggregate is divided by the current value of the security. For calculating the present value of the cash streams, the yield to maturity is used as the appropriate discount rate. In effect, the 'duration' of a bond, calculated in this manner, represents the 'average' time taken to receive various parts of the cash flow of the security. In short, it represents the 'weighted average term to maturity' of security. In its simplest form, Macaulay's duration can be represented as follows:

$$D = \frac{1}{P}\left[\frac{1c_1}{(1+r)^1} + \frac{2c_2}{(1+r)^2} + \cdots + \frac{Tc_T}{(1+r)^T}\right]$$

where, 'c' represents the payments received at time periods 1, 2, etc.,

'P' represents the current value of the security,

'r' represents yield to maturity, and

'T' represents the number of periods for which cash flows are received.

The illustration given below will help clarify the point. Assume that you hold a three-year security with a face value of ₹1000 and coupon rate of 10 per cent. Assume that the interest rates are also at 10 per cent and the coupons are paid out annually. The duration is computed as follows:

Period	Cash flow	PV of cash flow	Proportion of cash flow received	Proportion of cash flow received × period
1	100	90.91	0.09091	0.09091
2	100	82.64	0.08264	0.16528
3	1100	826.45	0.82645	2.47935
		1000.00		2.73554

That is, the weighted average term to maturity of the above mentioned security is 2.73 years approximately.

The above simple example holds two important conclusions as well.

a. Assume that the coupon rate is 12 per cent instead of 10 per cent. The cash flows would improve and so would the present values, assuming the interest (discount) rate is still at 10 per cent. What would be the duration in this case? It would be shorter than 2.73 years.

b. Assume that the interest rate starts rising. The cash flows would remain the same since the coupon rate is the same, but the present value of nearer cash flows would tend to be higher than that of more distant cash flows. What would happen to the duration in this case? It would again be shorter than 2.73 years.

Hence, other things being equal, the higher the coupon rate and the yield to maturity, the shorter is the duration. It also follows that in the case of a zero coupon bond, the duration and the maturity of the bond would be identical.

Modified Duration It thus appears that the volatility or interest rate sensitivity of a security is approximately related to its duration.

That is,

$$\text{Volatility} = \frac{\text{Duration}}{(1 + \text{Yield})}$$

In the foregoing example, the volatility of the security would be (2.73/(1+.10)) or approximately 2.49. This implies that a change of 1 per cent in the required yield would result in a change of about 2.49 per cent in the price of the security. This is also called 'modified duration'. Thus,

$$\text{Modified duration} = \frac{\text{Macaulay's duration}}{1 + \text{yield}}$$

and is used to estimate the relative price volatilities of different securities. Rewriting the above equation, price volatility is represented as follows:

$$\frac{\Delta P}{P} = -\text{Modified duration} \times \Delta r$$

where, Δr is the estimated change in yield.

To sum up, modified duration is a different version of the Macaulay model and demonstrates the extent of change in duration for each percentage change in yield. It also follows that for fixed income securities without embedded options, prices and interest rates move in opposite directions and hence, there is inverse relationship between modified duration and an approximate one per cent change in yield.

Effective Duration The modified duration model assumes that expected cash flows from a security will not change even when interest rates change. However, when the security contains embedded options, expected cash flows would change when interest rates change. 'Effective duration' is used to estimate the price sensitivity of the security for the securities with embedded options. Effective duration typically requires the use of 'binomial trees' to arrive at the Option-Adjusted-Spread (OAS). One simple model for estimating effective duration is as follows:

$$\text{Effective duration} = \frac{(P_{i-} - P_{i+})}{P_0(i^+ - i^-)}$$

where, P_0 = initial price

P_{i+} = price when interest rates rise

P_{i-} = price when interest rates fall

i^- = initial market rate less decrease in rate

i^+ = initial market rate plus increase in rate

Therefore, effective duration compares the estimated price of a security in a rising and falling interest rate scenario.

The following are the key points to remember about duration:

1. The duration of a coupon bond is always less than its maturity.
2. Three important factors that determine how sensitive is the price of a bond to the interest rate movements are: (a) coupon rate, (b) term to maturity, and (c) yield to maturity.
3. The duration of a bond is lower when the yield of the bond is higher.
4. For a given coupon rate and yield, a longer maturity would typically increase the duration of the bond.
5. For a given coupon rate and maturity, a lower yield would increase the duration of the bond.
6. For a given yield and maturity, a lower coupon increases the duration of the bond.
7. Term to maturity and the initial price of a bond remaining constant, the higher the coupon, the lower is the volatility in the price of the bond and vice versa.
8. The coupon rate and the initial price of a bond remaining constant, the bond with a longer term to maturity has higher price volatility and a bond with shorter term to maturity will display lower price volatility.
9. A bond with a high yield to maturity will display lower price volatility than a bond with shorter yield to maturity.
10. The duration of a perpetuity is (1+y)/y, where 'y' denotes yield-to-maturity.

The Concept of Convexity

If the relationship between bond price and yield is graphed, typically the price of a 30 year bond changes more rapidly than that of a one-year bond. This implies that the graph is more a curve than a straight line. The degree of curvature represents the extent to which bond prices change in response to the yield. Technically, this curvature is termed as 'convexity'.

If we graph a tangent at a particular price of a bond (where the tangent meets the price-yield curve), the linear tangent is the bond's (Macaulay) duration. The slopes of these lines are negative due to the inverse relationship between bond duration and yields, but the bonds have positive duration. In mathematical terms, convexity is the second derivative of price with respect to yield. This also means that while the duration equation works well for small changes in yield, it may not work as well for large changes, since the duration also changes as yield changes.

Thus, convexity reveals an important limitation of duration analysis. Since different bonds exhibit different amounts of convexity, correcting convexity could be quite difficult.[49]

Therefore, rather than correcting bond convexity, we can estimate the extent of convexity using the following equation:

$$C = \frac{1}{(1+y)^2}\left\{(1 \times 2) \times \frac{CF_1/(1+y)}{\text{Bond price}} + (2 \times 3)\right\}$$

$$\times \frac{CF_2/(1+y)^2}{\text{Bond price}} + \cdots + (J \times (J+1))$$

$$\left\{\times \frac{CF_J/(1+y)^J}{\text{Bond price}}\right\}$$

where, CF_J is the value of the cashflow received in the year, j

We can also use a Taylor's series to estimate convexity. The series lays out the risk factors that affect the price of a security. The more such factors are estimated, the more accurate will be the estimate of price changes.

The convexity can then be incorporated into the modified duration equation as given below.

$$\% \text{ change in bond price} \cong -D^* \times \text{change in yield} + C \times (\text{change in yield})^2/2$$

In other words, for very small changes in yield, say, 10 basis points, the changes in convexity will be very small (the square of change in yield would be around .000001) and hence can be ignored. However, large changes in yield would yield large components of convexity.

Convexity has the following properties:

- It is useful in comparing bonds. Between two bonds with similar duration but different convexities, the bond with greater convexity is seen to be less affected by the interest rates than a bond with less convexity.
- Bonds with greater convexity would typically have a higher price than bonds with lower convexity, regardless of the changes in interest rates.
- Bonds with higher coupon rates would generally have a lower convexity.
- Bonds with embedded options such as, callable bonds can exhibit negative convexity at certain price-yield combinations. Negative convexity implies that duration decreases with the decrease in market yields.

Duration and Convexity Used in Immunization Strategies

Simply stating, when an investor with an identified future financial liability invests a specified amount today, such that its future value will equal the value of the liability when the liability falls due, the investor has immunized himself against future default in payment. For example, a person who wants to repaint his newly built house at a cost of ₹1 lakh in 10 years' time could invest in a 10 year ₹1 lakh zero coupon bond today at a discounted cost. In short, the investor is certain to have ₹1 lakh in 10 years to repaint his house.

Immunization utilizes the sensitivity of bond prices to changes in interest rates to create portfolios that will realize the yield at the time of purchase over the length of a planning period, regardless of the movements of interest rates during that period. In times of volatile interest rates, therefore, immunization theoretically restores a bond to its traditional role as a 'safe' financial asset.

Duration measures the percentage price change of a bond for a 1 per cent change in yield. Convexity measures the degree to which duration changes as the yield to maturity changes. Duration is additive, so the duration of a portfolio of bonds is the weighted sum of the duration of the individual bonds. Because duration and convexity measure price risk, they can be helpful in immunizing interest rate risk.

To immunize the portfolio to interest rate risk, assets or liabilities can be added to make the duration of the portfolio equal to zero. Other terms commonly used to denote immunization are 'hedging' and 'duration matching'.

When the weighted duration of assets does not equal that of the liabilities, derivatives (such as futures or swaps) can be employed to match the asset with liability duration.

Duration changes as time passes and as yields change. Therefore, in order to maintain an immunized position, the portfolio must be periodically rebalanced. A more precise form of immunization is dedication or cash flow matching. If a portfolio is perfectly matched in cash flow with projected liabilities, rebalancing will be unnecessary.

ANNEXURE III

FEATURES OF A SOUND LIQUIDITY AND FUNDS MANAGEMENT POLICY AND SYMPTOMS OF POTENTIAL LIQUIDITY RISK

Typically, sound liquidity and funds management policies will do all or most of the following factors:

- Establish goals or objectives for liquidity management. For example, monitoring liquidity requirements on a regular basis and meeting expected and unexpected funding needs at the least cost.
- Provide for the establishment of an asset/liability committee, which includes: (a) defining who will be on the committee, (b) the committee's responsibilities, (c) frequency with which the committee will meet, (d) its link to the board of directors, (e) mode of apprising the board of the committee's decisions and results and (f) clear delineation of lines of authority and responsibility in making liquidity and funds management decisions.
- Provide strategies for managing the liquidity position of the bank. For example, when in need of liquidity, should the bank liquidate investments, borrow in the market or securitize its loans?
- Identify and call for periodic review of the bank's primary sources of funds. Such primary sources for a bank would include core deposits (typically including demand deposits, savings accounts and small denomination time deposits) and other noncore sources such as, large certificates of deposit (CDs). For some banks, other funding sources such as, refinancing offered by the central bank or other apex financial institutions or loan sale mechanisms such as, securitizations could also be the critical sources of liquidity. In particular, an analysis of the bank's deposit structure would include: (a) the volume and trend of total deposits and various deposit products offered, (b) the maturity pattern of term deposits, (c) cost of each type of deposit to the bank and (d) competition analysis to study the interest rates and features of other deposit and savings products by other banks and agencies and any other information needed.
- Fix flexible limits on the liability mix in order to ensure against excessive reliance on one source of funding. This would be more applicable to volatile but large sources of funds. Similarly, set limits on the dependence on individual customers or market segments for funds. Also, flexible limits could be set on the minimum/maximum average maturity for different categories of liabilities, as follows:
  - Provide a method of pricing and computing the bank's cost of funds.
  - Determine, in conjunction with the bank's investment policy, which types of investments are permitted and desirable and the optimal mix among short- and long-term investments to ensure adequate liquidity from the investment portfolio when required.
  - Indicate the desired maturities and risk-return profile for loans and investments.
  - Establish target liquidity ratios and guidelines based on the board's risk tolerance. Examples of some typical guidelines/ratios would be as follows:
    - How much of the incremental deposits can be lent? (credit-deposit ratio)
    - How much of the bank's capital can be lent or invested? (credit/investment-capital ratio)
    - How much of the incremental liabilities should be kept as cash? (cash-deposit or cash-liabilities ratio)
    - How much of the longer term assets are being funded by less stable funding sources?
    - Establish an appropriate process for measuring and monitoring liquidity such as, generating simple cash flow projections or using models
    - Provide an adequate system of internal controls to ensure independent and periodic review of the liquidity management process and compliance with policies and procedures. The review would also include compliance with established limits and legal reserve requirements at the overall bank level.
    - Formulate contingency plans to include alternative sources of funds if initial projections of funding sources and uses are incorrect or if a liquidity crisis threatens.
    - Provide for handling policy exceptions; periodic review of policy effectiveness and adequacy by the board of directors.

A necessary prerequisite to sound liquidity management decisions is a sound management information system (MIS). Report formats and content would vary from bank to bank depending on the bank's strategy, its balance sheet structure and its funds management practices.

However, some basic details that should find a place in the MIS are as follows:

a. The liquidity needs of the bank over designated time horizons and the possible sources of funds to meet these needs. The maturity pattern of assets and liabilities and the likely funding of commitments would form the basis for this report
b. A report analyzing net interest margin and its variations over the period being reviewed. For this purpose, asset yields and liability costs should also be analyzed. This report can also contain forecasts of how NIM will behave in the longer term.
c. A report on large funds providers and their likely behaviour in future.
d. Projections of interest rates and other economic conditions that may trigger deviations from the proposed liquidity plan.
e. Exceptions to the policy guidelines of the bank and contingency plans.
f. Additional reports as decided by the ALCO/top management of the bank.

Symptoms of Potential Liquidity Problems—An Illustrative List

Some internal and market indicators could be useful to assess whether a potential liquidity problem is developing.

Internal indicators are as follows:

- Asset quality is deteriorating as evidenced by the growing proportion of impaired assets
- Excessive concentrations on certain assets and funding sources
- Declining spreads, interest margins and earnings
    - Increasing cost of borrowings
    - Rapid asset growth funded by volatile liabilities
    - Negative maturity mismatch in the short term, evidencing worsening cash-flow position
- Increasing currency mismatches
- Decrease in weighted average maturity of liabilities
- Repeated breach of internal or regulatory control limits of liquidity positions
- Negative publicity leading to reputation risk

Market indicators are as follows:

- Credit rating downgrades
- Gradual but persistent fall in the share prices of the bank
- Widened spread on the bank's senior and subordinated debt
- Reduction or elimination of available credit lines from correspondent banks
- Counter parties unwilling to extend unsecured or longer dated transactions to the bank, requesting for additional collateral or resist entering into new transactions with the bank
    - Widening default swap spreads
    - Difficulty accessing external funding
- Increasing trend of deposit withdrawals – both retail deposits and redemption of CDs before maturity

SELECT REFERENCES

1. Hong Kong Monetary Authority, 2004, *Supervisory Manual*, "Liquidity Risk Management", vol. 1 dated 20 August 2004.
2. Federal Deposit Insurance Corporation, USA, 2005, "Risk Management Manual of Examination Policies", Section 6.1 titled "Liquidity and Funds Management", accessed at superivision@fdic.gov
3. Federal Reserve Bank of Kansas City and Federal Reserve Bank of St. Louis, "Insights for Bank Directors", 6, "Asset & Liability Committee, Liquidity Policy", Federal Reserve Center for Online Learning.
4. Bank for International Settlements Document "Principles for Sound Liquidity Management and Supervision", September 2008.

ANNEXURE IV

MANAGEMENT OF LIQUIDITY RISK IN FINANCIAL GROUPS—KEY FINDINGS

(Research conducted in May 2006 by the Bank for International Settlements.[50])

The review, carried out by the Joint Forum's[51] Working Group on Risk Assessment and Capital, studied the funding liquidity risk management practices of 40 large conglomerates involved in banking, securities and insurance activities.

The review was designed to address five key questions, which are as follows:

- How large, complex banking, securities and insurance groups manage liquidity risks across jurisdictions, sectors and subsidiary units, particularly in times of stress?
- The impact of regulatory and supervisory approaches on liquidity risk management practices and structures.
- The nature of products and activities that give rise to significant demands for liquidity.
- Assumptions that firms make regarding available sources of liquidity.
- The scale of liquidity shocks that firms are prepared to address.

The review found that most of the conglomerates surveyed, monitored and managed liquidity risk primarily through the use of (a) risk limits, (b) monitoring systems and (c) scenario analyzes that are incorporated into contingency funding plans (CFPs).

The group inferred that the following factors appeared to exert significant influence on the approach of the conglomerates towards liquidity risk management: (a) scope of international operations, (b) level of complexity of activities undertaken in different jurisdictions in which the conglomerate is present, (c) types of foreign currency exposure, (d) supervisory requirements, (e) legal environment and restrictions, (f) commercial market environment and (g) national markets.

What is of more relevance to the present banking environment is that the group found a greater range of liquidity risk management practice within the banking sector, than within the securities and insurance sectors, especially in areas such as, liquidity risk measures and limits, types of scenarios, time considerations and underlying assumptions.

The study also found that though the metrics to measure liquidity risk varied, the basic approaches could be classified as follows:

a. **The liquid assets approach:** Under the liquid assets approach, the firm maintained liquid instruments on its balance sheet that could be drawn upon when required. A variation to this approach entailed maintaining a pool of unencumbered assets, usually government securities, which could be used as collateral in repurchase agreements and other secured facilities. In this approach, ratios were used as relevant metrics.

b. **The cash flow approach:** Under the cash flow matching approach, the firm attempted to match cash outflows with promised/expected cash inflows over a variety of near term maturity buckets.

c. **A hybrid approach that combined both the above:** In the hybrid approach, the firm attempted to match cash outflows in each time bucket with a combination of expected or contractual cash inflows, plus inflows that can be generated through sale of assets, repurchase agreements or other secured borrowing.

The study found that the banking sector used more of approaches (b) and (c).

Other interesting findings include the following:

- The conglomerates' CFPs reflected their assumptions about available liquidity sources in times of stress – almost all the firms expected to raise funds through secured borrowing. An interesting insight gained in this context is an implicit, sometimes explicit assumption of the conglomerates in their scenario analysis that the official sector would address any operational risk that could cause widespread disruption across multiple markets.
- Liquidity stress testing practices, especially in the banking sector, showed that about two-third of the banks surveyed simulate market events and firm specific events separately. About a third of the banks test the impact of a firm specific event within a disrupted market environment.
- A predominant section of the banking sector (nearly three-fourth) is expected to securitize loans and receivables. Securitization was considered more as a strategic means of raising funds rather than a means of getting liquidity under stress conditions.

However, all these 'best practices' were put to severe test during the financial crisis of 2007.

Lessons for Liquidity Risk Management Flowing from the Financial Crisis of 2007[52]

Principles 5 to 12 of the quoted BIS document have been framed in the aftermath of the global financial crisis of 2007. These principles are encapsulated in the following statements (pages 3,4):

Principle 5: A bank should have a sound process for identifying, measuring, monitoring and controlling liquidity risk. This process should include a robust framework for comprehensively projecting cash flows arising from assets, liabilities and off-balance sheet items over an appropriate set of time horizons.

Principle 6: A bank should actively monitor and control liquidity risk exposures and funding needs within and across legal entities, business lines and currencies, taking into account legal, regulatory and operational limitations to the transferability of liquidity.

Principle 7: A bank should establish a funding strategy that provides effective diversification in the sources and tenor of funding. It should maintain an ongoing presence in its chosen funding markets and strong relationships with funds providers to promote effective diversification of funding sources. A bank should regularly gauge its capacity to raise funds quickly from each source. It should identify the main factors that affect its ability to raise funds and monitor those factors closely to ensure that estimates of fund raising capacity remain valid.

Principle 8: A bank should actively manage its intraday liquidity positions and risks to meet payment and settlement obligations on a timely basis under both normal and stressed conditions and thus contribute to the smooth functioning of payment and settlement systems.

Principle 9: A bank should actively manage its collateral positions, differentiating between encumbered and unencumbered assets. A bank should monitor the legal entity and physical location where collateral is held and how it may be mobilized in a timely manner.

Principle 10: A bank should conduct stress tests on a regular basis for a variety of short-term and protracted institution-specific and market-wide stress scenarios (individually and in combination) to identify sources of potential liquidity strain and to ensure that current exposures remain in accordance with a bank's established liquidity risk tolerance. A bank should use stress test outcomes to adjust its liquidity risk management strategies, policies and positions and to develop effective contingency plans.

Principle 11: A bank should have a formal CFP that clearly sets out the strategies for addressing liquidity shortfalls in emergency situations. A CFP should outline policies to manage a range of stress environments, establish clear lines of responsibility, include clear invocation and escalation procedures and be regularly tested and updated to ensure that it is operationally robust.

Principle 12: A bank should maintain a cushion of unencumbered, high quality liquid assets to be held as insurance against a range of liquidity stress scenarios, including those that involve the loss or impairment of unsecured and typically available secured funding sources. There should be no legal, regulatory or operational impediment to using these assets to obtain funding.

ANNEXURE V

ALM IN INDIA—CLASSIFICATION OF BANK LIABILITIES AND ASSETS ACCORDING TO RATE SENSITIVITY[53] AND MATURITY PROFILE[54]

(Excerpted from RBI's 'Asset Liability Management (ALM) System', 1999, Appendix I and II.)

(Note that though the basic rate sensitivities and maturity profiles largely remain unchanged in respect of bank assets and liabilities, subsequent RBI circulars attempt to fine tune the classification for better analysis and control. Accordingly, rate sensitivity framework/classification into time buckets have been revised to suit the 'Modified Duration Approach' in April 2006. The revised framework can be accessed at Appendix I of the 'Draft Guidelines on Improvements to Banks' Asset Liability Management Framework' issued by the RBI on 17 April 2006.)

Interest Rate Sensitivity

The table given below shows the interest rate sensitivity.

Heads of Accounts Liabilities	Rate Sensitivity and Time Bucket
1. Capital, reserves and surplus	Non-sensitive
2. Current deposits	Non-sensitive
3. Savings bank deposits	Sensitive to the extent of interest paying (core) portion. This may be included in over 3–6 months bucket. The non-interest paying portion may be shown in non-sensitive bucket Where banks can estimate the future behaviour/sensitivity of current/savings bank deposits to changes in market variables, the sensitivity so estimated could be shown under appropriate time buckets
4. Term deposits and certificates of deposit	Sensitive and reprices on maturity. The amounts should be distributed to different buckets on the basis of remaining term to maturity. However, in case of floating rate term deposits, the amounts may be shown under the time bucket when deposits contractually become due for repricing
5. Borrowings – Fixed	Sensitive and reprices on maturity. The amounts should be distributed to different buckets on the basis of remaining maturity.
6. Borrowings – Floating	Sensitive and reprices when interest rate is reset. The amounts should be distributed to the appropriate bucket which refers to the repricing date
7. Borrowings – Zero coupon	Sensitive and reprices on maturity. The amounts should be distributed to the respective maturity buckets
8. Borrowings from the RBI	Upto 1 month bucket
9. Refinances from other agencies	(a) Fixed rate: As per respective maturity (b) Floating rate: Reprices when interest rate is reset
10. Other liabilities and provisions	
(i) Bills payable	(i) Non-sensitive
(ii) Inter-office adjustment	(ii) Non-sensitive
(iii) Provisions	(iii) Non-sensitive
(iv) Others	(iv) Non-sensitive
11. Repos/Bills rediscounted (DUPN), swaps (buy/sell), etc.	Reprices only on maturity and should be distributed to the respective maturity buckets
Assets	
1. Cash	Non-sensitive
2. Balances with the RBI	Interest earning portion may be shown in over 3–6 months bucket. The balance amount is non-sensitive
3. Balances with Other banks	
(i) Current account	(i) Non-sensitive
(ii) Money at call and short notice, term deposits and other placements	(ii) Sensitive on maturity. The amounts should be distributed to the respective maturity buckets

(Continued)

Heads of Accounts Liabilities	Rate Sensitivity and Time Bucket
4. Investments (Performing)	
(i) Fixed rate/Zero coupon	(i) Sensitive on maturity.
(ii) Floating rate	(ii) Sensitive at the next repricing date.
5. Shares/Units of mutual funds	
6. Advances (Performing)	
(i) Bills purchased and discounted (including bills under DUPN)	(i) Sensitive on maturity.
(ii) Cash credits/Overdrafts (including TODs)/Loans repayable on demand and term loans	(ii) Sensitive only when PLR/risk premium is changed. Of late, frequent changes in PLR have been noticed. Thus, each bank should foresee the direction of interest rate movements of funding options and capture the amounts in the respective maturity buckets which coincides with the time taken by banks to effect changes in PLR in response to changes in market interest rates.
7. NPAs (Advances and investments)*	
(i) Sub-standard	(i) Over 3–5 years bucket
(ii) Doubtful and loss	(ii) Over 5 years bucket
8. Fixed assets	Non-sensitive
9. Other assets	
(i) Inter-office adjustment	(i) Non-sensitive
(ii) Leased assets	(ii) Sensitive on cash flows. The amounts should be distributed to the respective maturity buckets corresponding to the cash flow dates.
(c) Others	(iii) Non-sensitive
10. Reverse repos, swaps (sell/buy) and bills rediscounted (DUPN)	Sensitive on maturity
11. Other products (interest rate)	
(i) Swaps	(i) Sensitive and should be distributed under different buckets with reference to maturity.
(ii) Other derivatives	(ii) Should be suitably classified as and when introduced.

* Amounts to be shown net of provisions, interest suspense and claims received from ECGC/DICGC.

Liquidity Risk Management[55]

The table below shows the various facts of liquidity risk management.

GUIDANCE FOR SLOTTING THE FUTURE CASH FLOWS OF BANKS IN THE REVISED TIME BUCKETS

Heads of Accounts	Classification into Time Buckets
A. Outflows	
1. Capital, reserves and surplus	Over 5 years bucket.
2. Demand deposits (Current and savings bank deposits)	Savings Bank and Current Deposits may be classified into volatile and core portion. Savings Bank (10%) and Current (15%) Deposits are generally withdrawable on demand. This portion may be treated as volatile. While volatile portion can be placed in the Day 1, 2–7 days and 8–14 days time buckets, depending upon the experience and estimates of banks and the core portion may be placed in over 1–3 years bucket. The above classification of Savings Bank and Current Deposits is *only a benchmark*. Banks which are better equipped to estimate the behavioral pattern, roll-in and roll-out, embedded options, etc, on the basis of past data/empirical studies could classify them in the appropriate buckets, *i.e.*, behavioral maturity instead of contractual maturity, subject to the approval of the Board/ALCO.

(*Continued*)

Heads of Accounts	Classification into Time Buckets
3. Term deposits	Respective maturity buckets. Banks, which are better equipped to estimate the behavioral pattern, roll-in and roll-out, embedded options etc. on the basis of past data/empirical studies could classify the **retail deposits** in the appropriate buckets on the basis of **behavioral maturity** rather than **residual maturity**. However, the wholesale deposits should be shown under respective maturity buckets. (wholesale deposits for the purpose of this statement may be ₹15 lakhs or any such higher threshold approved by the bank's Board).
4. Certificates of deposit borrowings and bonds (including sub-ordinated debt)	Respective maturity buckets. Where call/put options are built into the issue structure of any instruments, the call/put date/s should be reckoned as the maturity date/s and the amount should be shown in the respective time buckets.
5. Other liabilities and provisions	
(i) Bills payable	(i) The core component which could reasonably be estimated on the basis or past data and behavioral pattern may be shown under 'Over 1–3 years' time bucket. The balance amount may be placed in Day 1, 2–7 days and 8–14 days buckets, as per behavioral pattern.
(ii) Provisions other than for loan loss and depreciation in investments	(ii) Respective buckets depending on the purpose.
(iii) Other liabilities	(iii) Respective maturity buckets. Items not representing cash payables (*i.e.*, income received in advance, etc.) may be placed in over 5 years bucket.
6. Export refinance—availed	Respective maturity buckets of underlying assets.
B. Inflows	
1. Cash	Day 1 bucket.
2. Balances with RBI	While the excess balance over the required CRR/SLR may be shown under Day 1 bucket, the Statutory Balances may be distributed amongst various time buckets corresponding to the maturity profile of DTL with a time-lag of 14 days.
3. Balances with other banks	
(i) Current account	(i) Non-withdrawable portion on account of stipulations of minimum balances may be shown under 'Over 1–3 years' bucket and the remaining balances may be shown under Day 1 bucket.
(ii) Money at call and short notice, term deposits and other placements	(ii) Respective maturity buckets.
4. Investments (Net of provisions)[#]	
(i) Approved securities	(i) Respective maturity buckets, excluding the amount required to be reinvested to maintain SLR corresponding to the DTL profile in various time buckets.
(ii) Corporate debentures and bonds, PSU bonds, CDs and CPs, redeemable preference shares, units of mutual funds (close ended), etc.	(ii) Respective maturity buckets. Investments classified as NPls should be shown under over 3–5 years bucket (sub-standard) or over 5 years bucket (doubtful).
(iii) Shares	(iii) Listed shares (except strategic investments) in 2–7 days bucket, with a haircut of 50%, Other shares in 'Over 5 years' bucket
(iv) Units of mutual funds (open ended)	(iv) Day 1 bucket
(v) Investments in subsidiaries/joint ventures	(v) 'Over 5 years' bucket
(vi) Securities in the trading book	(vi) Day 1, 2–7 days, 8–14 days. 15–28 days and 29–90 days according to defeasance periods.

(*Continued*)

Heads of Accounts	Classification into Time Buckets
5. Advances (Performing)	
(i) Bills purchased and discounted (including bills under DUPN)	(i) Respective maturity buckets.
(ii) Cash credit/overdraft (including TOD) and demand loan component of working capital.	(ii) Banks should undertake a study of behavioral and seasonal pattern of availments based on outstanding and the core and volatile portion should be identified. While the volatile portion could be shown in the near-term maturity buckets, the core portion may be shown under 'Over 1–3 years' bucket.
(iii) Term loans	(iii) Interim cash flows may be shown under respective maturity buckets.
6. NPAs (Net of provisions, interest suspense and claims received from ECGC/DICGC)	
(i) Sub-standard	(i) 'Over 3–5 years' bucket.
(ii) Doubtful and loss	(ii) 'Over 5 years' bucket.
7. Fixed assets/assets on lease	'Over 5 years' bucket/Interim cash flows may be shown under respective maturity bucket.
8. Other assets	
Intangible assets	Intangible assets and assets not representing cash receivables may be shown in 'Over 5 years' bucket.
C. Off balance sheet items	
1. Lines of credit committed/available	
(i) Lines of credit committed to/ from instructions	(i) Day 1 bucket.
(ii) Unavailed portion of cash credit' overdraft/demand loan component of working capital limits (outflow)	(ii) Banks should undertake a study of the behavioral and seasonal pattern or potential availments in the accounts and the amounts so arrived at may be shown under relevant maturity buckets upto 12 months.
(iii) Export refinance – unavailed (inflow)	(iii) Day 1 bucket.
2. Contingent liabilities letters of credit/guarantees (outflow)	Devolvement of Letters of Credit/Guarantees, initially entails cash outflows. Thus, historical trend analysis ought to be conducted on the devolvement's and the amounts so arrived at in respect of outstanding Letters of Credit/Guarantees (net of margins) should be distributed amongst various time buckets. The assets created cut of devolvements may be shown under respective maturity buckets on the bass of probable recovery dates.
3. Other inflows/outflows	
(i) Repos/bills Rediscounted (DUPN)/CBLO/ Swaps INR/USD, maturing fore forward contracts etc. (outflow/inflow)	(i) Respective maturity buckets.
(ii) Interest payable receivable (outflow/ inflow) –Accrued interest which are appearing in the books on the reporting day	(ii) Respective maturity buckets.

D. Financing of Gap

In case the net cumulative negative mismatches during the Day 1, 2–7 days, 8–14 days and 15–28 days buckets exceed the prudential limit of 5%,10%, 15% and 20% of the cumulative cash outflows in the respective time buckets, the bank may show by way of a foot note as to how it proposes to finance the gap to bring the mismatch within the prescribed limits. The gap can be financed from market borrowings (call/term). Bills Rediscounting. Repos, LAF and deployment of foreign currency resources after conversion into rupees (unsnapped foreign currency funds), etc.

Provisions may be netted from the gross investments provided provisions are held security-wise. Otherwise provisions should be shown in over 5 years bucket.

Notes:

(i) Liability on account of event cash flow, *i.e.*, short fall in CRR balance on reporting Fridays, wage settlement, capital expenditure, etc which are known to the banks and any other contingency may be shown under respective maturity buckets. The event cash outflows, including incremental SLR requirement should be reported against 'Outflows–Others'.

(ii) All overdue liabilities may be placed in the Day 1, 2–7 days and 8–14 days buckets, based on behavioral estimates.

(iii) Interest and installments from advances and investments, which are overdue for less than one month may be placed in Day 1, 2–7 days and 8–14 days buckets, based on behavioral estimates. Further, interest and installments due (before classification as NPAs) may be placed in '29 days to 3 months bucket' if the earlier receivables remain uncollected.

ENDNOTES

1. The complete report can be accessed at www.crmpolicygroup.org
2. Merton, Robert C., and André F. Perold. 'Theory of Risk Capital in Financial Firms' *Journal of Applied Corporate Finance* 6, No. 3 (fall 1993): 16–32.
3. Many use the term 'market value accounting' when evaluating how to account for a bank's investment portfolio. But it is more than reporting investments at market value. In a technical sense, market value accounting is the valuation of an item at the price for which it can be sold. In a fundamental sense, market value accounting is the actual accounting for transactions, events and other activities at their current or fair market value instead of their original historical cost. At any particular balance sheet date, those transactions, events and other activities create both on-balance sheet and off-balance sheet assets and liabilities. Under market value accounting, these on-balance sheet and off-balance sheet assets and liabilities would be marked to market at each balance sheet date. Moreover, under market value accounting, changes in the market value of those items from balance sheet date to balance sheet date would be reported either in net income or as a separate component of stockholders' equity.
4. See Chapter on 'Investments' for a detailed description of VaR.
5. Black, Richard, Brown, Karl, and Moloney, James, 'Asset and Liability management: What does the future have in store?', Balance Sheet, Volume 11, No. 2 (2003), pages 32–38.
6. In general, any occasion on which interest rates are to be reset—either due to maturities or floating rate resets—is called a 'repricing'. The date on which it occurs is called the 'repricing date'; if a portfolio has assets repricing earlier than liabilities, it is said to be 'asset sensitive'. This is because near term changes in earnings are going to be driven by interest rate resets on those assets. Similarly, if liabilities reprice earlier, earnings are more exposed to interest rate resets on those liabilities, and the portfolio is called 'liability sensitive'.
7. The 'yield curve' is a line that plots the interest rates, at a set point of time, of bonds of equal credit quality, but differing maturity dates. The benchmark yield curve compares, say, the 3 month, 2 year, 5 year and 30 year Treasury debt, and is then used to compare other debt in the market, such as home loan rates or bank lending rates. The curve is also used to predict changes in economic output and growth. The shape of the yield curve is closely scrutinized to gain an idea of future interest rate change and economic activity. There are three main types of yield curve shapes—normal (where longer maturity bonds have higher yields compared to short-term bonds), inverted (where short-term yields are higher than long-term yields, which could signal imminent recession), or flat or 'humped' (where short- and long-term yields are very close to one another, signifying economic transition). The slope of the yield curve is also seen as significant—the greater the slope, the greater the gap between short- and long-term rates.
8. Bank for International Settlements, Basel committee on Banking Supervision, 'Principles for the Management and Supervision of Interest Rate Risk', July 2004.
9. ibid, pages 3, 4.
10. This section broadly follows the approach taken by Timothy W Koch and S Scott MacDonald in their book 'Bank Management', chapters 8 and 9, 4th edition, The Dryden Press, USA.
11. This is easily explained if one considers that a maturing liability is a cash outflow and a maturing asset is a cash inflow.
12. NIM is defined as the ratio of a bank's NII to its earning assets.
13. Macaulay's duration and other concepts of duration are described in *Annexure II*.
14. For more detailed discussion on 'capital adequacy', please see chapter titled 'Capital–Risk, regulation and adequacy'.
15. For more detailed discussion on the equity multiplier, please see chapter titled 'Banks' financial statements'.
16. This is derived quite easily from the existing equation as follows: WADa – (MVL/MVA) WADl = 0

    or, WADa – WADl + WADl – (MVL/MVA) WADl = 0

    or, WADa – WADl = (MVL/MVA) WADl – WADl;

    the RHS can be rewritten as WADl ((MVL – MVA)/MVA) or WADl(–MVE/MVA)
17. Toevs, Aldenl (1983). "GAP Management: Managing: Interest Rate Risk in Banks and Thrifts", pp. 30-31, Spring 1983 *Economics Review*, Number 2, Federal Reserve Bank of San Francisco.
18. Mahshid, Deniz, and Naji, Mohammad Raiszadeh, 2003, 'Managing interest rate risk—A case study of four Swedish savings banks', page 30.
19. See the discussion on 'Theory of Interest Rates' in *Annexure I* for better understanding of this concept.
20. Hingston, Roy (2000), 'Reducing interest rate exposure', Community Banker, volume 9.7, pages 44–45, as quoted by Mahshid, Deniz and Naji, Mohammad Reiszadeh, 2003, 'Managing interest rate risk—a study of four Swedish savings banks', page 33, Master's Thesis, Goteborg University.
21. 'Notional' denotes that the amount of principal is used only for calculation of interest payments, and the principal as such does not change hands.
22. Please see chapter on 'Capital—Risk, regulation and adequacy' for a detailed discussion on capital adequacy requirements for off-balance sheet positions of banks.
23. For example, though the amount to be paid on its liabilities is locked in at 6 per cent in the previous example, if the market perceives higher risk over time and revises

its risk premium, the bank may end up paying more on subsequent deposits.

24. A 'hedger' is one who is willing to pay to avoid risk. Typically, a hedger has an existing or anticipated position in the 'cash' market, and trades futures contracts to reduce the risk arising from unexpected changes in the value of the hedger's cash position. To elaborate further, 'cash' or 'spot' transactions represent the exchange of any asset with specific features and price between a buyer and seller, the former making payment to take possession of the asset from the latter.
25. Traders are classified by their trading strategies. The 'speculator' assumes the risk of the 'hedger' in the hope of gaining from the transaction. Speculators try to guess price movements, and time their trading to sell at a price higher than the purchase price.
26. Theoretically, in a market where the futures contract is priced correctly, a perfect hedge would provide a return tending to equal the risk-free rate.
27. For instance, in the US, interest rate futures are traded on the Chicago Mercantile Exchange (www.cmegroup.com), one of the world's largest and most diverse marketplaces for derivatives. Interest rate futures can be based on both short-term and long-term debt obligations. Short-term obligations are typically for less than 1 year, and those above 1 year constitute long-term obligations.
28. Koch, Timothy, and Macdonald, Scott, 'Bank Management', Chapter 10, 4th edition, The Dryden Press.
29. Arguably, futures contracts have no fixed price or cash flows, and, hence, there can be no duration ascribed to these contracts. However, research has shown that under certain assumptions, the duration of a futures contract can be assumed to equal the duration of the underlying asset.
30. Saunders, Anthony, and Millon Cornett, Marcia, 2005, 'Financial Markets and Institutions—A modern perspective', chapter 24, 2nd edition, Tata McGraw Hill Publishing Company Ltd., India.
31. Note that an 'External Commercial Borrowing' (ECB) raised by an Indian firm could be termed an 'arbiloan' if the firm's foreign subsidiary takes a loan in its country at lower rates, converts into INR and lends it to the Indian parent. The Indian firm, in turn, has to guarantee repayment to the foreign lender.
32. Based on research by Federal deposit Insurance Corporation (FDIC), 26 March 2003, 'Derivatives Risk in Commercial Banking'.
33. Bank for International Settlements, Quarterly Review, September 2009, Chapter 2 titled 'Highlights of International Banking and Financial Markets Activity', pages 24–25.
34. FDIC, 26 March 2003, 'Derivatives Risk in Commercial Banking'.
35. International accounting standards define 'fair value' as the 'value at which an asset could be exchanged or a liquidity settled between knowledgeable, willing parties in an arm's length transaction'.
36. Study conducted by Amiyatosh Purnandam, Assistant Professor of Finance at the Ross School of Business, quoted in 'Commercial Banks Benefit by Using Derivatives for Hedging Risk', 2005, by Claudia Capros, on the University of Michigan website, www.umich.edu
37. IAS 39 is the standard pertaining to financial instruments. More information can be accessed at www.iadb.org
38. This paper can be accessed at www.bis.org
39. A 'bank run' could have a snowballing effect on the entire economy. When a large number of depositors withdraw their deposits at the same time from a bank, triggered by a fear that the bank's assets are so eroded in value that their combined worth may not be sufficient to repay their deposits, the bank will run out of cash to repay them. If the bank recalls the loans made in a distress measure, it may realize only a part of the value of the assets, since the bank's borrowers may be unable to pay or the securities invested in may not yield their full value.
40. January, 2013, Basel Committee on Banking supervision, 'Basel III: The Liquidity Coverage Ratio and Risk Monitoring Tools.'.
41. September 2008, Basel Committee on Banking Supervision, 'Principles for Sound Liquidity Management and Supervision', Bank for International Settlements, page 2.
42. 'core ' deposits typically constitute demand deposits, savings deposits and small denomination term deposits. These deposits are looked upon as stable sources of funds, as opposed to volatile sources of funds from non-core deposits and other funding avenues.
43. FDIC, The USA, 2005, 'Risk Management Manual of Examination Policies', Section 3.8, 'Off balance sheet activities' accessed at supervision@fdic.gov, and Bank for International Settlements, September 2008, 'Principles for sound liquidity management and supervision', pages 12–14.
44. May 2006, The Joint Forum, Bank for International Settlements, 'The Management of Liquidity Risk in Financial Groups'.
45. September 2008, Bank for International Settlements, 'Principles for Sound Liquidity Management and Supervision', pages 10–30.
46. The guidelines are excerpted from RBI's 'Draft Guidelines for improvements to banks' Asset Liability Management Framework', 17 April 2006. Also see Annexure 1–4 of BCBs document on interest rate risk (2004).
47. RBI, 'Liquidity Risk Management by Banks', November 7, 2012.
48. It is mandatory for banks to disclose the maturity profile of their assets and liabilities in their financial statements. The classification can be found in the Notes to Accounts of banks' financial statements.
49. Note that for a zero coupon bond, the graph could be almost flat, while the graph related to coupon bonds can be quite convex.

50. May 2006, The Joint Forum, Bank for International Settlements, 'The Management of Liquidity Risk in Financial Groups'.
51. The Joint Forum consists of the Basel Committee on Banking Supervision, International Organization of Securities Commissions and International Organization of Insurance Supervisors, under the aegis of the Bank of International Settlements, Basel, Switzerland.
52. September 2008, Bank for International Settlements, 'Principles for Sound Liquidity Management and Supervision', pages 10–30.
53. For the purpose of interest rate risk measurement.
54. For the purpose of liquidity risk measurement.
55. RBI, 'Guidelines on Asset Liability Management (ALM) System—Amendments' dated 24 October 2007.*Source*: RBI documents.

CHAPTER THIRTEEN

Banking Functions, Retail Banking and Laws in Everyday Banking

CHAPTER STRUCTURE

Section I Basic Concepts
Section II Retail Banking—Nature and Scope
Section III Customer Relationship Management (CRM)
Section IV Laws in Everyday Banking
Chapter Summary
Case Study
Test Your Understanding
Topics for Further Discussion

KEY TAKEAWAYS FROM THE CHAPTER

- Understand the basic banking terms.
- Examine the banking functions and obligations of banks to customers.
- Understand the scope and SWOT analysis of retail banking.
- Information on CBM in banking.
- Examine the laws in everyday banking.

SECTION I

BASIC CONCEPTS

Commercial banking activities can be broadly categorized as retail banking and corporate banking. Retail banking refers to the banking functions undertaken by individuals whereas corporate banking refers to the banking services offered to the firms irrespective of their size (small, medium and large-scale organizations). The distinction has already been elucidated in our earlier chapter on banks' lending function.

A third type of banking—investment banking—has been in the news during the last two decades. How is investment banking different from retail and corporate banking?

Pure investment banks typically do not accept deposits from or make loans to individuals, as commercial banks do. They provide fee-based financial services such as acting as advisors, managers or underwriters to public share issues, facilitating mergers and acquisitions, corporate restructuring, private equity deals, or corporate bond placements, or acting as brokers/dealers/custodians in the capital markets, and so on.

Negotiable Instruments

Negotiable instruments have a great significance in the modern business world. These instruments have gained prominence as the principal instruments for making payment and discharging business obligations. Negotiation implies transfer by endorsement if payable to the order or by delivery if payable to bearer. 'Instrument' implies a documentary means of transferring ownership.

Section 13 of the Negotiable Instruments Act, 1881 defines a negotiable instrument to be 'a promissory note, bill of exchange or cheque, payable either to order or to bearer'.

The major negotiable instruments are bill of exchange and cheque payable either to order or bearer. For example, when a cheque is transferred to any person, the cheque (instrument) is said to be negotiated.

Bill of Exchange It is an instrument in writing, containing an unconditional order, signed by the maker, directing a person to pay a certain sum of money to a certain person or to the order of that certain person or to the bearer of the instrument (Refer to the Negotiable Instrument Act (N. I. Act), Section 5, India, for more information and also the earlier chapters on bank lending. In the United States, the Uniform Commercial Code Article 3 covers the use of such negotiable instruments.).

Cheque The characteristic features of a cheque can be specified as follows:

- As per the Negotiable Instrument Act, a cheque is a bill of exchange.
- It is always drawn on a bank and is payable on demand.
- It has three parties:
  1. **Drawer:** A person who draws the cheque on a bank.
  2. **Drawee:** A bank on whom the cheque is drawn.
  3. **Payee:** A person to whom the payment is to be made by the bank.
- A cheque can be payable either to order or to bearer.
- When a cheque is crossed, the banker shall not pay the amount over the counter.
- When a payee accepts a cheque and if it is dishonoured, he can claim the money from the drawer.
- A customer has the right to 'stop payment' before the due date, after he issues the cheque.

It is a common practice to return cheques where the amount differs in words and figures. The customer is not expected to draw cheques by leaving any blank space that would facilitate insertion of words/figures.

The banker has to cross-check the signature, with the specimen available in the branch, when a cheque is presented for payment.

Difference Between Cheque and Bill of Exchange Every cheque is a bill of exchange. However, every bill of exchange is not necessarily a cheque. The essential differences are as follows:

- A bill of exchange need not necessarily be drawn on a banker.
- A bill of exchange may be payable on demand or payable on a future date.
- A bill of exchange payable on a future date is called usance bill.

Types of Deposits

Deposits[1] can be classified into demand deposits and time deposits.

Demand Deposits These are of two types:

1. Saving deposits
2. Current deposits

1. **Saving deposits:** As saving accounts are meant to encourage savings habit, organizations whose purpose is profit are not allowed to open such accounts. Interest is paid on a half-yearly basis in these accounts. A minimum balance is stipulated by each bank. A balance amount above the minimum stipulated amount is eligible for a 3.5 per cent interest rate in India at present.
2. **Current deposits:** Since this account is to meet the transaction needs of the customer, there is no restriction on the number of transaction in the account or in the type of customers eligible to open these accounts. Account holders are not entitled to any interest from the bank.

Time Deposits These are also called as fixed deposits or term deposits. These are repayable after the expiry of a specified period varying from 7 days to 120 months.

Senior citizens get higher interest rates. Hence, joint deposits with them make sense.

Non-Resident Indian (NRI) Accounts

The present menu of bank accounts for Non-Resident Indians (NRIs) has three categories:

- Non-resident (external) rupee accounts (NRE)
- Non-resident (ordinary) rupee accounts (NRO)
- Foreign currency non-resident (banks) accounts [FCNR] (B)

These accounts can be distinguished as follows:

- While NRO and NRE accounts can be kept in the form of current, savings or term deposit accounts, FCNR (B) deposit can be kept only in the form of term deposits, for periods ranging from 6 months to 3 years.
- Remittances from abroad can be credited to any of these accounts. But earnings of NRIs on the property held by them in India, which are non-repatriable, can be credited only to NRO accounts.
- Money from an NRO account is non-repatriable, but NRE and FCNR deposits are repatriable.
- The entire interest earned on NRO accounts is eligible for repatriation. Persons of Indian nationality who have been NRIs for a period of not less than 1 year and have returned to India are eligible to open a RFC (Resident Foreign Currency) account.
- An NRO account may be jointly held with residents.
- NRE and FCNR (B) accounts cannot be jointly held with residents. But resident power of attorney is permitted for local payments and investments in India.
- Balances held in NRE/FCNR accounts are exempted from wealth tax and interest earned is exempted from income tax. There are no tax exemptions on interest earned on NRO accounts.

Mandates and Power of Attorney

An account holder can appoint a third person to act on his behalf to do certain acts like drawing cheques or instructing bank to debit the account for various purposes like issuance of drafts.

Mandates The following are the salient features of mandates:

- It is an unstamped letter signed by the customer, authorizing a person to operate the account on his behalf.
- Signature of the mandatory should be obtained in the letter of mandate.
- A letter of mandate is generally issued for a short and temporary period.

Power of Attorney The following are the salient features of power of attorney:

- It is a stamped document and generally executed in the presence of a notary/magistrate of a court.
- Two types of powers are granted—special and general powers of attorney. Special power of attorney is often for a single transaction and general power of attorney confers an agent very extensive powers.

Lien Lien is the right of the creditor to retain possession of the goods and securities owned by the debtor until the debt due from the latter is paid. General lien gives a right to possess the goods, banker's lien adds to it, the right of sale in case of default by the latter. Therefore, it is called an implied pledge.

SECTION II

RETAIL BANKING—NATURE AND SCOPE

Retail banking encompasses retail deposit schemes, retail loans, credit cards, deposit cards, insurance products, mutual funds, depository services including demat facilities. It includes various products and services forming a part of the assets as well as the liabilities segment of the banks. A simplistic definition could be 'banking catering to the multiple requirements of individuals relating to deposits, advances and associated services'. See Figures 13.1 and 13.2.

FIGURE 13.1 BANK'S FUNCTIONS

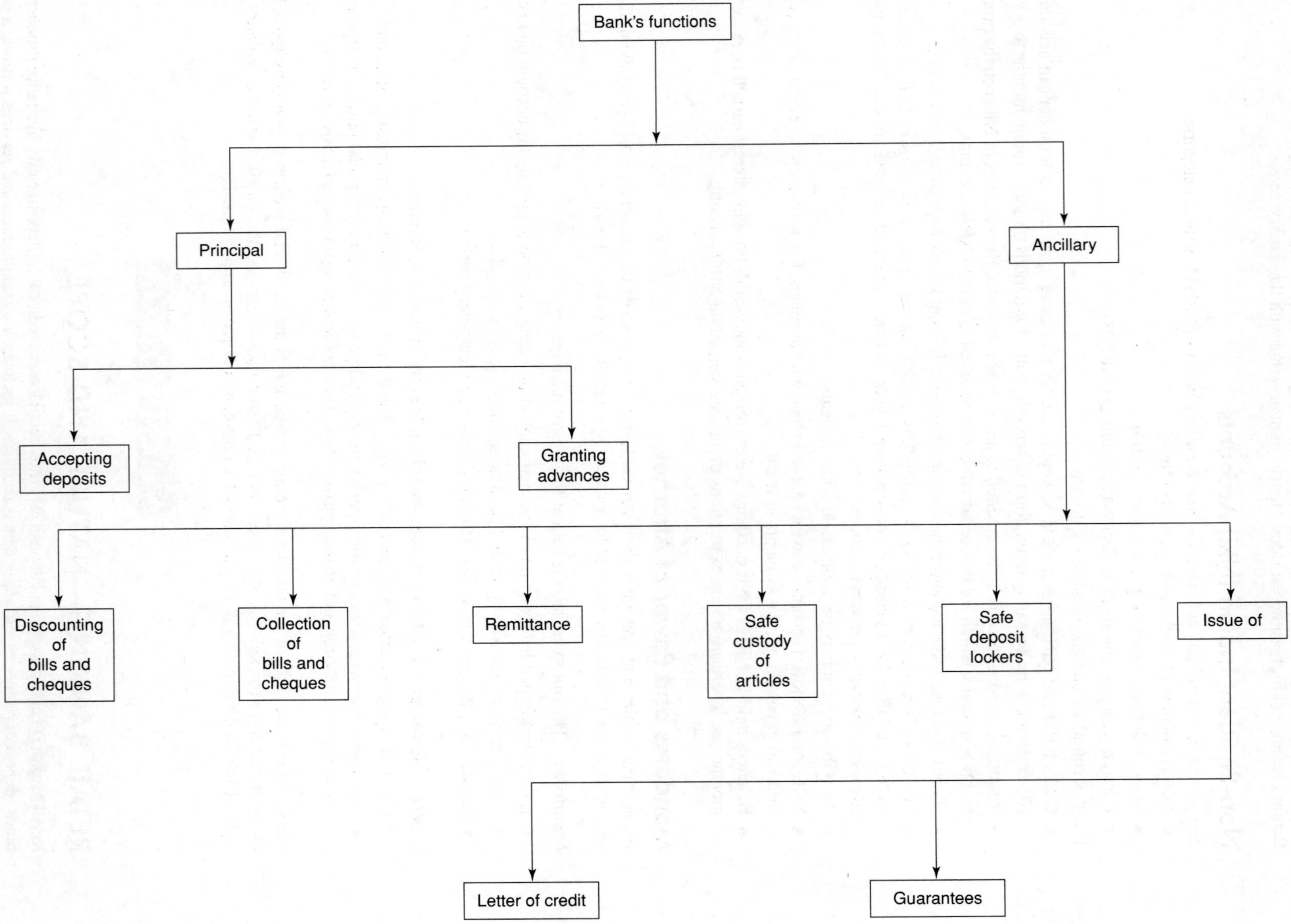

FIGURE 13.2 OBLIGATIONS OF A BANK TO ITS CUSTOMER

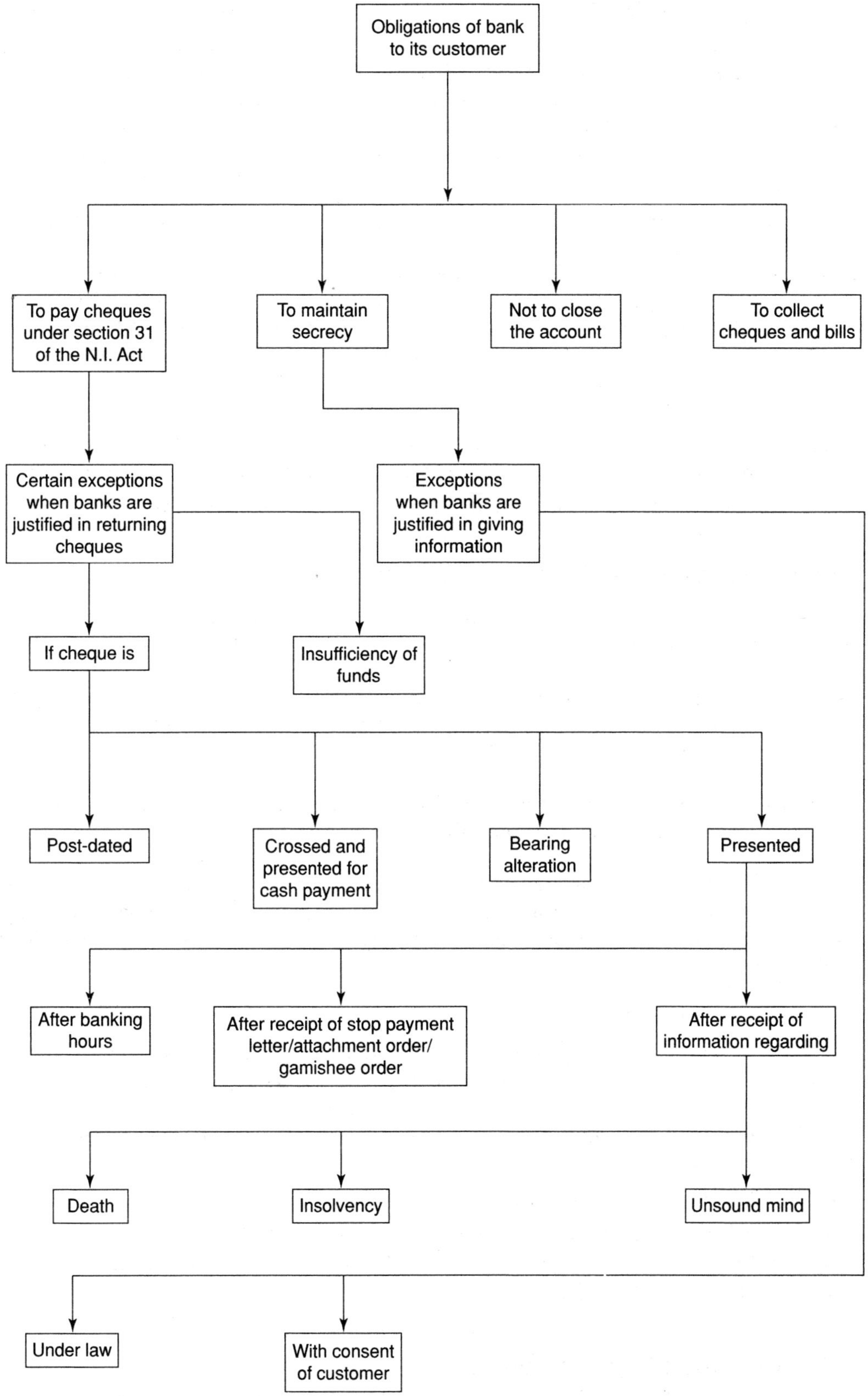

Why Banks Focus on Retail Business?

Financial Disintermediation

Traditionally, banks have been catering to demands of economic developments; finance for manufacturing activities had a greater priority. Reliance of commercial banks was on blue-chip companies for deployment of funds.

A scenario has emerged wherein there is a lack of demand for credit from large corporates, primarily due to two reasons:

- Near demise of working capital requirements due to enhancement in activities like productivity and increased sales realization.
- Corporates have their own avenues, *e.g.*, tapping public deposits and issuance of shares and debentures.

Advent of Economic Liberalization Privatization and globalization has opened the gate for a lot of new players in the banking sector, which has resulted in competition with each other for market share. The confluence of increased purchasing power, consumerism and competition with the banks has resulted in a retail chase. The identity of banks has changed from those known for their roles in development of business/economy to the ones helping in the development of the family.

Instant Solution for the Ills in the Banking Business Retail banking has the potential to provide decent returns for banks with an extended clientele base in an era of thinning margins and non-performing advances.

Retail banking is based on the principle 'banking for the people, by the people and of the people'.

Emerging Issues in Handling Retail Banking

Knowing the Customer A concept which is easier said than practised. Each branch should set up data warehouse wherein meaningful data on customers, their preferences, spending patterns, etc. can be mined.

Technology Issues Retail banking calls for huge investments in technology, *e.g.*, providing anytime, anywhere convenience to vast number of customers and delivery channels through asynchronous transfer modes (ATMs), which requires a huge investment by the banks.

Product Innovation All new products may not become successful. Products should be introduced to create value, not amusement. The days of selling products on the shelves are gone in the banking sector.

Pricing of Products The banking sector is witnessing a pricing war with each bank wanting to have a larger slice of the market share. The much needed transparency in pricing is also missing with many hidden charges. For example, 'minimum amount due' and 'total amount due' in the credit card application form and processing charges are not advertised.

Issues Related to Human Resources

- Motivating the front line staff by projecting them as sales managers of products rather than as clerks at work.
- Changing the image of the bank from a transaction provider to a solution provider.

Low-Cost and No-Cost Deposits Bank managers are in need of more savings bank and current accounts so that their cost of liability would be less.

- Three AAAs (anytime, anywhere and anyhow banking).
- With the advent of ATMs, 'anytime banking' has become a reality.
- Satellites and telecom networks across the world have made 'anywhere banking' possible.
- Now, it is the turn of 'anyhow banking'.

SWOT Analysis of Retail Banking

The strengths, weaknesses, opportunities and threats of retail banking have been analyzed and given in Table 13.1.

TABLE 13.1 SWOT ANALYSIS OF RETAIL BANKING

Strengths	Weaknesses	Opportunities	Threats
Low level of NPAs			In times of recession, the NPAs can rise manifold, as witnessed during the financial crisis of 2007.
Tendency to default a retail loan is low as these are backed by mortgages of houses in case of housing loans and post-dated cheques in case of other loans like vehicle loans.			However, defaults even in housing loans can be triggered by macro economic factors or tax lending procedures, as shown by the 2007 financial crisis.
The housing loan has been proved as a safe advance as a house is considered as the most sensitive and essential asset of a family.	Longer tenure of loans, ranging from minimum 3 years to 15/20 years (for housing loans) as against the average deposits of less than 3 years.	Growth in retail lending has outperformed other segments in recent years and is expected to continue at much higher rates. Banks have the opportunities to offset the demand of funds from the corporate sector. Banks have more opportunities for cross-selling of products.	Incidences of concurrent borrowings are on an increase in case of retail loans through credit card/other routes. Shrinkage in the kitty of no cost (current account) deposits, thereby increases the average cost of deposits for the bank. Retail loans can be risky when individuals lack purchasing power.

Strategies for Success in Retail Banking

Banks can formulate the following strategies in order to achieve success in the retail banking segment:

- Advanced techno logy and adoption of this latest technology
- Skilled manpower in all branches and offices
- Balanced and sustained growth in deposits and advances
- Strategic cost management
- Market research and market intelligence, in order to formulate competitive and innovative products
- Risk management
- Customers relationship management
- Universal banking/financial supermarkets
- More delivery channels
- Service quality with a human touch

SECTION III

CUSTOMER RELATIONSHIP MANAGEMENT (CRM)

The objectives of this section are:

- To highlight the importance of Customer Relationship Management (CRM).
- To provide inputs on how to market bank products.
- To discuss the increased relevance of CRM in light of the growing competition in the banking sector with the entry of foreign and new generation banks.

Marketing—Coin

Head — CRM
Tail — Advertisement

Customer relationship management and advertising are an integral part of marketing. However, CRM and advertising are two different sides of the coin called marketing. Advertising is too expensive. On the other hand, CRM is based on word of mouth. Hence, meeting customer needs is most important in the competitive banking sector.

Although CRM is a recent concept, its tenets have been around for some time. CRM has three application areas:

1. Customer acquisition
2. Customer value maximization
3. Customer retention

A banker must keep CRM in mind from the time he acquires a new customer and each time the customer is serviced. CRM is based on word of mouth, hence, a pleasant experience for the customer would ensure retention and possibly, new customers. Furthermore, how a bank handles complaints also goes a long way in building an image in the customer's mind.

CRM Strategies/Steps

Some of the important CRM strategies/steps are as follows:

- Appeal to the self-interest of the customer, during discussions. Steer conversation to topics like areas of interest, profession, native place and hobbies. 'Recognize' the customer. All human beings need recognition. Most of us seek recognition in the company of others. Managers can give customers individual recognition with some small talk and friendliness. It is worth noting that the correlation between the enthusiasm of manager and customer satisfaction is always high. It would be useful for bankers to know the preferences of customers (time/service/money) and treat them accordingly.
- Make use of logic and emotional appeal to motivate the customer. Courtesy and concern are prime necessities for a bank. Offering a seat, bidding farewell, using the right blend of formality and informality, demonstrating civility to aged people are all important.
- Be patient (have self-control) with difficult customers. It will pay-off in the long run.
- Know the strength and weaknesses of competitors so that you will be prepared to face competition. The competition in the sector is escalating day by day. PSU banks, private banks, foreign banks have all formulated strategies for more customers.
- Smile while serving the customer. The smiling face of a banker brings reassurance to the customer who develops goodwill for the bank.
- Importance of 'Greeting and Meeting.' All banks offer identical products and polite service. Customers go back to the bank, where officers greet him/her with a smile. Marketing efforts and CRM have to be laced with humour and smile.

Three Tip Questions for Managers

Managers can do self-introspection by way of asking a set of questions as follows:

- Can I recall the names of customers and people?
- Do I mingle with the customers?
- Did I appear active and cheerful or do I present a gloomy appearance?

Image-Building Exercises

Officers and staff in a bank normally undertake the following exercises to build the image of their organization in their efforts to build brand.

- Marketing activities are closely tied to the cleanliness and aesthetic aspects of bank premises.
- Marketing activity would be incomplete without making 'customer calls' and gathering their perception about products offered by the bank.
- Cultivating relationship is the specialty of the modern day banker. From college days, banks give credit cards free of cost to students of reputed institutes.
- Some banks undertake payment of phone and electricity bills for clients.
- Bank of Tokyo Mitsubishi, one of the leading banks in Japan does not advertise, but relies on the word of mouth of its customers.

Blending Tradition with Technology

All banks focus on automating and improving business with customers in the areas of sales, marketing and support. Today, with the use of information and communication technology, banks can offer personalized service. Services like anywhere banking to their customers, mobile banking and loan *melas* for customers have been implemented by all banks.

Customers are becoming more dynamic in their behaviour. Banks use CRM tools to identify which customers are to be 'targeted.'

CRM is based on the idea 'banking for the customers, by the customers and with the customers'.

Historically, banking had a limited standard product range. Currently, it is moving with a larger range of products, aimed at specific customer base segments to a future where marketing will deal with customers as individuals, providing 'tailor-made' solutions to cater to their needs (*e.g.*, monthly/quarterly installments, 1/2/3/4/5 year loans for car purchase).

Banks are moving from a product-focused, mass marketing approach to a customer-focused micro-marketing approach. CRM is based on database-driven marketing to communicate with a customer in response to his behaviour. Success depends on attitude and culture of employees to serve the customer better.

SECTION IV

LAWS IN EVERYDAY BANKING

Key Acts That Govern the Functioning of the Banking Sector[2]

The Reserve Bank of India Act, 1934

Establishment and preamble

The Reserve Bank was established on 1 April 1935 in accordance with the provisions of the Reserve Bank of India Act, 1934, with its central office at Mumbai since inception.

The preamble of the act prescribes the objective of the Reserve Bank as follows:

'... to regulate the issue of bank notes and keeping of reserves with a view to securing monetary stability in India and generally to operate the currency and credit system of the country to its advantage'.

The Reserve Bank of India Act, 1934 has defined the main functions of the RBI as follows:

- Monetary authority
- Regulator and supervisor of the financial system
- Manager of exchange control
- Developmental role
- Related functions

The Negotiable Instrument Act, 1881

A few key points regarding the act are as follows:

- This act was passed to define the law relating to promissory notes, bills of exchange and cheques. The act was originally drafted in 1866 by the Law Commission of India. The bill was redrafted in 1877, because of the objections.

  But the bill could not reach the final stage. In 1880, by the order of the secretary of state, the bill had to be referred to a new law commission. On the recommendation of the new law commission, the bill was redrafted.
- The draft thus prepared for the fourth time was introduced in the Council and was passed into law in 1881 as the Negotiable Instruments Act, 1881 (26 of 1881).

The Banking Regulation Act

The Banking Regulation Act was passed as the Banking Companies Act, 1949 and came into force with effect from 16 March 1949. Subsequently, it was changed to the Banking Regulation Act, 1949 with effect from 1 March 1966.

Some important sections of this act are given as follows:

- Banking means accepting for the purpose of lending or investment of deposits of money from the public repayable on demand or otherwise and withdrawal by cheque, draft order or otherwise [5(I) (b)].

- Banking company means any company which transacts the business of banking [5(I) (c)].
- Demand liabilities are the liabilities which must be met on demand and time liabilities means liabilities which are not demand liabilities [5 (I) (f)].
- A banking company may be engaged in businesses, like borrowing, lockers, letter of credit, travellers cheque and mortgages [6(1)].
- Cash reserve—Scheduled banks to maintain 3 per cent of the demand and time liabilities by way of cash reserves with themselves or by way of balance in a current account with the RBI (18).
- Every bank is to maintain a percentage of its demand and time liabilities by way of cash, gold, unencumbered securities 25–40 per cent as on the last Friday of second—the preceding fortnight (24)—known as the Statutory Liquidity Ratio (SLR).
- Every bank has to publish its balance sheet as on 31st March, (29).
- The balance sheet is to be audited by qualified auditors (30(I)).
- A published balance sheet and auditor's report should be available to the public within 3 months from the end of the period to which they refer. The RBI may extend the period by a further 3 months (31).

Different Customers—Different Laws

There are different laws that apply to different groups which are classified as follows:

- Joint hindu family
- Societies
- Trust
- Company
- Sole proprietor/partners

Joint Hindu Family A Hindu undivided family (HUF) or joint family possesses ancestral properties and carries on an ancestral business. The ownership of such property passes on to the member of the family according to Hindu Law. In the case of a joint Hindu family governed by the *Mitakshara* school of Hindu Law, every male member of a family acquires an interest in the joint property by birth.

Societies Voluntary societies committed to promotion of art, science, literature or to charitable purpose may be incorporated under the following acts:

- The Societies Registration Act, 1860
- The Companies Act, 1956
- The Co-operative Societies Act

A society gets the legal recognition as an entity separate from its members only after its incorporation under one of these Acts.

A registered society is governed by the provision of the act under which it is registered. It may have its own constitution, character, memorandum of association, rules and by-laws to carry on its activities.

Trusts According to the Indian Trusts Act, 1882, a trust is an obligation annexed to the ownership of the property, arising out of a confidence reposed by the owner, or declared and accepted by the owner for the benefit of the author, or of the author and the owner.

- **Author:** The person who reposes the confidence.
- **Trustee:** The person on whom the confidence is reposed.
- **Beneficiary:** The person for whose benefit the trust is formed.
- **Trust deed:** The document by means of which the trust is formed.

Joint Stock Company A joint stock company is an artificial entity with perpetual section succession brought into existence under the provision of the Companies Act. Legally, a company is considered as an entity separate from its member and hence possesses all powers to enter into a valid contract.

A joint stock company has to submit the following important documents while giving an application to open a bank account.

- Certificate of incorporation and certificate of business
- Memorandum of association
- Articles of association
- Board resolution

Sole Proprietor and Partnership An individual running a business or commercial activity under a name other than his/her own is known as a sole proprietor.

Partnership is defined as relation between two or more persons who have agreed to share the profit of business run by all or any of them acting for all.

Bankers will have to take precautions while opening an account in the name of a partnership firm. These precautions can be specified as

- Partnership letter or mandate

It is a letter signed by all partners and contains the following details:

- Name of all partners
- Nature of business

- Limitation on the number of partners
    - Minimum two
    - Maximum for banking business—10; others—20

Bank–Customer Relationship

A customer's deposit is a debt given to a bank for the bank's use, repayable on demand. The bank becomes the customer's debtor and the customer becomes the unsecured creditor with no claim over the bank's assets as security.

When the customer takes a loan, he/she becomes the bank's debtor. As the bank normally obtains security for the loan it gives, the bank becomes a secured creditor for the customer.

When the customer deposits securities or other valuables with the bank for safe custody, the bank becomes the trustee of these assets. The customer remains the owner.

When the bank buys or sells securities on behalf of the customer or pays the utility bills of the customer, it acts as the customer's agent. Such services are rendered for the convenience of the customer.

So what is the relationship between the banker and customer when a cheque is sent for collection to another banker? The answer is Trustee.

Rights of a Banker

The important rights of a banker are as follows:

- Right of general lien
- Right of setoff
- Right of appropriation
- Right to change interest, levy charges, etc.

Let us now understand each of these rights.

Right of General Lien The right of a general lien is as follows:

- Lien is the right of a creditor to retain the goods and securities owned by his debtor until the debt is repaid.
- This right has some important features and conditions. When a lien applies to a specific debt, it is known as a particular lien. When a tailor retains the clothes stitched by him till his tailoring charges are paid, the tailor is exercising a particular lien. A general lien applies to all amounts due from the debtor.

Right of Setoff The right of a setoff is as follows:

- Under this right, the bank may use the credit balance in another account, when both accounts belong to the same customer. The accounts may be held in different branches.
- Normally, the bank takes a letter in advance from the customer authorizing the setoff without prior notice to the customer.

The main condition of right of setoff is 'same name, same right'. Both the accounts must be held in the same name and in the same capacity. This is to avoid misuse of funds belonging to someone else but standing in the name of the customer.

Right to Appropriation: Who and How The right to appropriation is as follows:

At times, a customer takes several loans from the bank. When the banker receives the payment from the customer, against which loan should the deposit be appropriated? Who is the deciding authority on this? According to the Indian Contract Act, the right of appropriation vests with the debtor. Alternatively, the payment may be made under circumstances clearly implying the debt to be discharged. In the absence of such circumstances and instruction from the debtor, the bank, as the creditor can exercise the right.

Right to Charge Interest and Levy Charges As a creditor, the bank has the implied right to charge interest on loans given to customers. Periodically, the customer account is debited with the interest due. The banks may also levy charges to meet incidental expenses incurred on a current account.

Obligations of a Banker

The banker is essentially a debtor or creditor to the customer. However, such a relationship imposes certain obligation on the bankers.

Honour Cheques The following points are related to honour cheques:

- There must be sufficient funds.
- They must be properly applicable to a cheque.
- They must be properly presented in proper time.

Wrong Dishonour of Cheque This may happen due to following causes:

- The mistake in posting that reduces the correct balance to the customer's credit.
- Fraud committed by employee.
- Honouring a post-dated cheque.

The banker is responsible not only for the monitory loss but also for the injury to the customer's reputation. The latter is more important to a customer.

Maintain Confidentiality A customer account reflects his/her true financial position. This information is very sensitive and may directly reflect on the customer's reputation. Therefore, the banker should:

- not disclose any information regarding the account to a third party.
- ensure no such information leaks out of the account books.
- prevent such disclosure even after the account is closed.

The exceptions are as follows:

- When required by the law.
- Practice and usage among bankers.

Premature Closure A bank may allow premature encashment of a fixed deposit at the request of customer. In this case, the banker's obligations are as follows:

- Ensure that the customer has the information about the bank's penal interest rates for the premature withdrawal of term deposits, if the bank charges such an interest.
- Inform the customer while opening the account whether the bank disallows premature withdrawals of large deposit held by entities other than individuals and HUF.

Act in Good Faith Without Negligence The banker collects numerous cheques on behalf of the customers and cannot verify the validity of each instrument. The Negotiable Instrument Act protection to the banker can be specified as follows:

- The cheque must be crossed before it is deposited.
- The cheque must be received as an agent of the customer whose account is to be credited with the amount of the cheque.

- Payment is received in good faith and without negligence.

Examples of negligence of bankers are as follows:

- Opening an account without proper instruction.
- Overlooking irregularity of endorsement (*e.g.*, spelling, signature).
- Collecting 'account payee' cheques for another person.

Deceased Depositors The key points to be considered regarding deceased depositors are as follows:

- If depositor dies, the banker is obliged to pay the amount to the credit of a deposit account to the nominee survivor or claimant.
- If death occurs before maturity of the deposit, the interest is payable at the rate applicable to the deposit up to the actual date of payment. If death occurs before maturity, the claimants may be paid at the saving rate of interest prevalent on maturity date for the period from maturity to the payment date.
- A succession certificate is not mandatory; however, the bank may obtain an indemnity bond. Where there is a dispute among legal heirs who are unable to provide a unanimous indemnity bond, the bank should obtain the succession certificates.
- If there are doubts about the claimants, the bank should insist on succession certificates.

Payment to Nominee The payment to the nominee is made in the following conditions:

- Nomination may be made in the name of individuals.
- In case of a joint account, there can only be one nominee and the nominee may receive the dues only after the death of all the depositors.
- Nomination may be altered at any time in the prescribed manner.

Closure of Accounts The banker must comply with a written directive from the customer to dose his/her account. The customer must be asked to return unused cheques.

Other possible occasions on which a bank can close the accounts are on receiving notice of a customer's insanity or death or when the customer becomes insolvent.

CHAPTER SUMMARY

Commercial banks have been relying on corporates for a long time as their main source of income because the latter have not had access to any other avenues like capital markets. In the last few decades, the focus of commercial banks has changed from corporate banking to retail banking. The retail banking segment offers an extended client base which, in turn, minimizes the risk for banks. It is evident that the banks that formulate strategies and implement practices like Customer Relationship Management emerge as winners in this era of competition and globalization.

CASE STUDY

SAVINGS ACCOUNT IS NOT AN INVESTMENT TOOL[3]

The Mumbai suburban Borivali-bound fast local train was overcrowded and Ravi Kumar had boarded the train from the starting point CST station after his work. He had to get down at Andheri which is located before the last station. He thought it would be better to stand at the door. However, when the train halted, Kumar as usual, got pushed out. As a matter of habit, he checked if his wallet was in place. To his horror, he realized it was not. His wallet was already stolen by someone. Though Kumar was carrying a little cash, he had a debit card, linked to his savings account, which had ₹65,000. Now, he had to act fast and get his debit card blocked. This was tough as the bank would have closed down for the day by now.

With the extra cash he always kept aside for days like this, he managed to reach home. He frantically searched for the 'welcome kit' he had received from the bank on opening the account. The kit contained a detailed booklet on debit card usage. He had to call up the 24-hour customer service number of the bank and report the loss. From that moment on, he would be insured against fraudulent purchase transactions. But his insurance would not be available for ATM transactions as he was the only one who had the password and there was no way anyone could withdraw money from his account using the ATM. Having done this, Kumar had a bigger question to answer—Why did he has so much money in his savings account that gave him a miniscule interest of 3.5 per cent? He knew he had been extremely lazy about putting his money to better use, despite the fact that the requirement of a minimum average quarterly balance of ₹5,000 in the account was driving him paranoid.

His laziness had been costing him dearly. The interest rate of 3.5 per cent was on the minimum balance in the account between the tenth and the last day of the month. Also, banks could pay this interest either monthly or quarterly, and his bank chose to pay quarterly.

Even the interest on a 15-day fixed deposit was somewhere around 5.5 per cent. All one needed to do was log on to the net and do a fixed deposit. And the certificate would be delivered at the specified address with in a few days.

Further, with all the money in the savings account, there was always the danger of carrying too much money in the wallet.

When Kumar opened this savings account, he had been told about the requirement of maintaining a minimum quarterly average balance of ₹5,000. In the good old days, all one needed to do was have a balance of ₹500 and if one went under the limit, most public sector banks simply slapped a fine of ₹10. Things had become far more complicated since then.

In order to calculate the average quarterly balance, his bank considered the period between the 25th day of the last month of the previous quarter to the 24th day of the last month of the present quarter. In other words, Kumar was expected to maintain an average balance of ₹5,000 in his savings account on each day of this 90-day period. Alternatively, he could have ₹4,50,000 in the account for a single day to meet the average quarterly balance requirement of ₹5,000 (₹4,50,000/90 = ₹5,000).

In case he did not maintain the minimum average quarterly balance, the bank would charge for non-maintenance. The charge in his case was ₹250 if the average quarterly balance was between ₹2,500 and ₹5,000 and ₹500 if it was below ₹2,500.

Kumar felt the charges were too high, but he had the satisfaction of knowing that there were other banks which charged as high as ₹750 for non-maintenance. Indeed, wasn't it for charges like these that the fee-based incomes of new generation private sector banks had gone up dramatically in the last few years?

Case Questions

1. Why does a savings account offer low interest rates?
2. Distinguish between minimum balance, average quarterly balance and average monthly balance.
3. Discuss the methods of calculating average quarterly balance.

TEST YOUR UNDERSTANDING

1. Banker's lien is a (n) ____________________.
   a. hypothecation b. mortgage
   c. implied pledge d. pledge
2. Mandate is (a) n ____________________.
   a. stamped agreement b. order of the court of law
   c. memorandum of understanding d. unstamped letter to the bank
3. Power of Attorney is a ____________________.
   a. signed letter to the bank b. promissory note
   c. garnishee order d. stamped documents
4. Person to whom a power of attorney is given is called ____________________ and the person who gives the power of attorney is called ____________________.
   a. Debtor-Creditor b. Bailor-Bailee c. Agent, Principal (donor, donee)
5. Negotiate instrument (N I) are easily ____________________.
   a. transferable b. gifted c. sold
6. A cheque is drawn on a (n) ____________________.
   a. owner of a ship b. agent of a principal c. bank
7. Two parallel transverse lines across the cheque is called ____________________.
   a. endorsement b. transfer
   c. assignment d. crossing
8. When a cheque is drawn on a bank, the bank is called the ____________________.
   a. drawer b. endorser
   c. acceptor d. drawee

9. The crossing in a crossed cheque can be cancelled by ________________.
   a. drawer b. endorser
   c. acceptor d. drawee
10. When a banker makes payment of a cheque after banking hours, he will be held ________________.
   a. liable b. reasonable c. acceptable
11. One of the conditions to honour a cheque by the paying banker is that amount in words and figures should ________________.
   a. differ b. tally c. be clear
12. Where a customer, by a letter, has advised the bank directing the banker not to honour or pay a particular cheque, such a letter is called a ________________.
   a. letter of authority b. letter of credit
   c. stop-payment letter d. letter of continuity
13. Where the signature of the drawer of a cheque is not genuine, such a cheque is called a ________________.
   a. post-dated cheque b. forged cheque
   c. clearing cheque d. stale cheque
14. Demand deposits are those which can be withdrawn ________________.
   a. on demand b. at any future date
   c. after 1 year d. after 5 years
15. Current deposits are not entitled to ________________.
   a. a cheque book b. statements
   c. customer service d. interest
16. Introduction in all deposit accounts is ________________.
   a. optional b. compulsory c. at the discretion of the bank
17. A bank has the obligation to maintain confidentiality of customers' accounts. The only exceptions are
   a. no exceptions as bank is liable for financial loss
   b. with the concurrence of the Reserve Bank of India
   c. when the different laws warrant so
   d. the banker has to use its discretion and selectively reveal the balance
   e. both 'a' and 'b'
18. Which of the following is NOT a feature of a recurring deposit product?
   a. Amount periodicity and tenure of investment fixed
   b. Identical to fixed deposit in terms of interest rates
   c. TDS as per the applicable rates
   d. Loan against deposits available
   e. All of these
19. Which of the following is NOT one of the functions of the RBI?
   a. monetary authority b. manager of exchange control
   c. corporate finance d. supervisor of financial system
   e. developmental role
20. A 'society' cannot be incorporated under one of the following acts:
   a. The Societies Registration Act, 1860 b. The Companies Act, 1956
   c. The Co-operative Societies Act d. The Partnership Act, 1932
21. NRNR and FCNR (B) accounts can be kept in the form of ________________.
   a. term deposits b. current deposits
   c. saving deposits d. recurring deposits
22. Accounts jointly with residents can be opened in the case of ________________ accounts.
   a. FCNR (B) and NRE b. NRO and NRNR

True or False

1. Payment of a post-dated cheque by a banker is in order.
2. Right of setoff is not a discretionary right with the bank.
3. A forged cheque is a valid cheque.
4. In savings deposits, interest is paid on the minimum balance in the account between the 10th and the last working day of the month.
5. A FCNR (B) account can be kept in the current, savings and recurring deposits.
6. Credit card offers revolving credit for a certain period.

TOPICS FOR FURTHER DISCUSSION

- A holds ₹820 to his credit in a bank. He presents five cheques of ₹200 each for payment at the same time. Can the banker refuse payment of all the cheques?
- A payee of a cheque informs the bank, on which it is drawn, that the cheque drawn in his favour is lost and requests the bank to stop payment of the cheque pending an advice from the drawer. But before the stop-payment instructions are received from the drawer, the cheque is presented through clearing. How should the drawee bank act?
- A teacher deposits into his account an outstation cheque for ₹800 issued by the state education authorities. He demands immediate credit in his account against the cheque. Explain your reply.
- Mr. A opens a well-introduced savings account with you. He deposits a cheque crossed 'account payee' in the account and withdraws the amount. A few days later, the paying banker informs you that the drawer of the cheque has learnt that the real Mr. A has not received the cheque and it was stolen in transit. On further inquiry, it appears that the man who opened the account with you is not traceable at the address given. The paying banker calls upon you to pay back the amount as the cheque was wrongly collected by you. As the branch manager how would you deal with the above situation?
- Distinguish between
    a. Cheque and bill of exchange
    b. Mandate and power of attorney
    c. NRE, FCNR (B) and NRO accounts
    d. Savings bank account and current account
- Analyze the strengths, weaknesses, opportunities and threats of retail banking.

SELECT REFERENCES

1. Aleida, R. A. (2003). 'Retail banking—A Focus', *IBA Bulletin,* November, pp. 5–8.
2. Manoj, P. K. (2003). 'Retail Banking—Strategies for Success', *IBA Bulletin,* November, pp. 18–21.
3. Pathrose, P.P. (2003). 'Marketing Retail Products: Strategic Perspectives for Banks', *IBA Bulletin,* November, pp. 29–34.
4. Sood, Rajesh Kumar (2003). 'Retail Banking—Growth Drivers and Analysis of Associated Risks', *IBA Bulletin,* November, pp. 9–17.
5. Indian Institute of Banking and Finance (2005). *Legal Aspects of Banking Operations*, MacMillan. India.

ENDNOTES

1. More details on bank deposits can be found in the chapter on 'Sources of bank funds'.
2. An illustrative list of legal provisions can be found in the chapter on 'Sources of bank funds'.
3. This is a substantially modified version of the write-up published by Vivek Kaul, 'Personal Finance', *DNA Money.*

CHAPTER FOURTEEN

Banking System—Services and Innovations

CHAPTER STRUCTURE

Section I Commercial Banking System and Structure
Section II Case Studies of Bank
Section III Case in Detail—HSBC Bank
Chapter Summary
Test Your Understanding
Case Study

KEY TAKEAWAYS FROM THE CHAPTER

- Look at a precise picture of the modern banking system and structure.
- Examine services offered by leading banks like ICICI, HSBC and State Bank of India.
- Analyse innovations in retail and corporate products.

SECTION I

COMMERCIAL BANKING SYSTEM AND STRUCTURE

This chapter is an outcome of the effort to document the effect of globalization on commercial banking and discuss key facts based on the comparison of services offered by leading banks. Through this, an attempt has been made to highlight the business environment in which banks operate and its importance for society based on cases of ICICI Bank, HSBC and State Bank of India.

Commercial banks are the oldest and largest financial intermediaries, compared to insurance or mutual funds. They are also the most important depositories of public savings and the most important disbursers of finance. Commercial banking in India is a unique system, the likes of which exists nowhere in the world. The truth of this statement becomes clear as one studies the philosophies and approaches that have contributed to the evaluation of banking policy, programmes and operations.

Commercial banks are fractional reserve banks and they, unlike other financial institutions, can create money in certain multiples of their deposits, which is known as a money multiplier. Commercial banks ordinarily are simple businesses or commercial concerns which provide various types of financial services to the customers in return for payments in one form or another, such as interest, discount, fees and commission. Their objective is to make profits. However, what distinguishes them from other business concerns is the degree to which they have to balance the principle of profit maximization with certain other principles. Banks deal in other people's money, a substantial part of which is repayable on demand. That is why for banks, unlike other business concerns, liquidity management is as important as profitability management.

Commercial banks are in the business of providing banking services to individuals, small businesses and large organizations. While the banking sector has been consolidating, it is worth noting that far more people are employed in the commercial banking sector than in any other part of the financial services industry.

Globalization and Innovations

The World Trade Organization (WTO) was established on 1 January 1995 when the implementation of the Uruguay round results began. Since its inception, the WTO has been moving towards becoming a universal organization. The International Monetary Fund (IMF) and the WTO have extended considerable pressure on the Indian government to undertake economic reforms towards a more liberal order. As a result, the Indian economy saw the introduction of market forces and a new era of competition. The banking sector was subject to disinvestments, deregulation of interest rates and had to accept internationally accepted norms.

All banks are now to abide by some predetermined international standards. Transparency of information and flexibility of operations is becoming increasingly necessary. Increase in the number of banks will ease the credit scenario and customers will be able to enjoy better services. The increased competition arising from the WTO entry and the introduction of new banks will only help the banking industry to mature. Since inception, public sector banks have been operating in a monopolized market, which have rendered them inefficient and subject to client complaints. It is obvious that after becoming a WTO member, the government has developed legislation and administration rules that comply with the WTO rules thus making conditions ripe for the banking industry to pursue its development.

CHART 4.1 STRUCTURE OF THE BANKING SYSTEM[1]

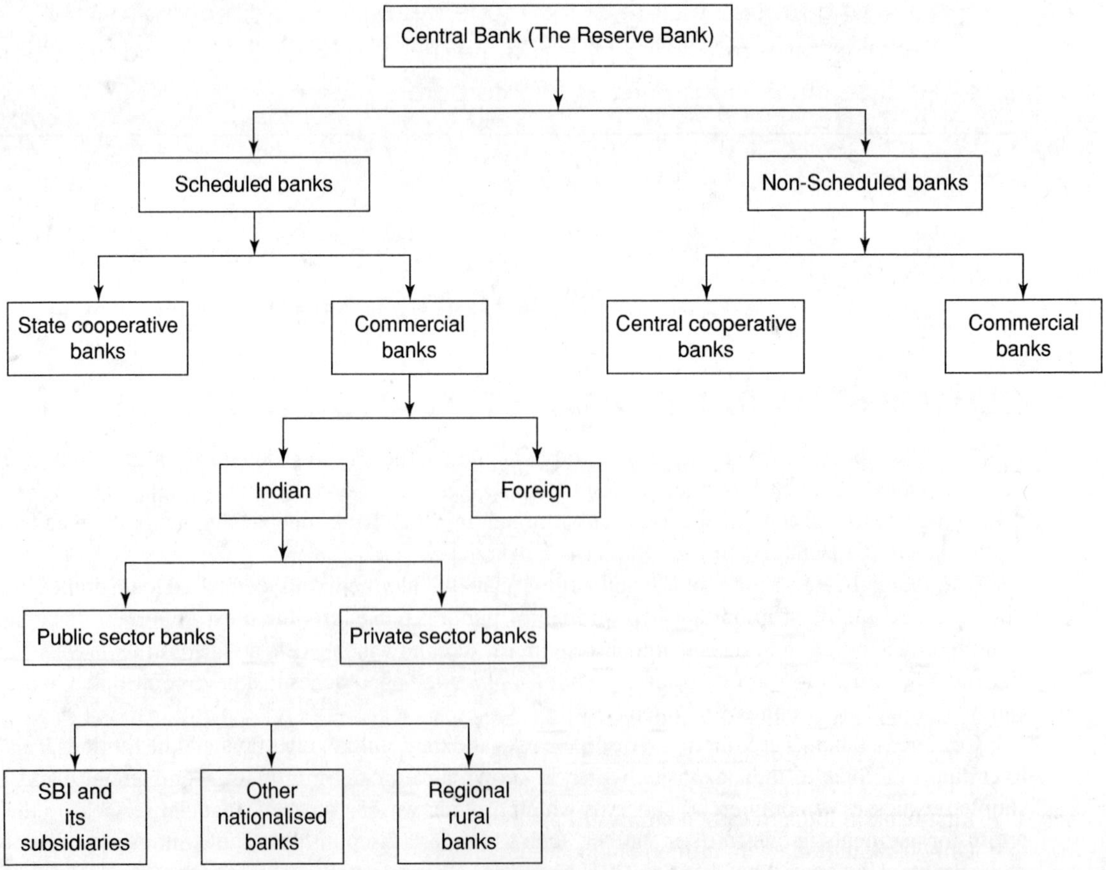

Globalization has brought about structural changes in the world economy. This includes services, particularly banking and financial services. Although the service sector contributes significantly to national output, the impact of globalization on services is yet to capture the attention of researchers and policymakers in many countries.

With the entry of more and more foreign sector banks in the country, the very set-up of the banking industry has been shaken up. State-owned banks have lost their market monopolies and face stringent competition in their contention with new giants. Public sector banks have been left with no alternatives but to rise to the occasion and reform themselves.

Since the mid-1990s, there has been a big increase in the number of branches and ATMs opened by foreign banks in emerging economies. Most of this foreign entry has been through two routes—acquisition of domestic banks in the host country and strategic alliances.

Banks conduct business in foreign countries also and this business has grown slowly over time. The overseas business of banks include provision of trade-related banking services such as negotiation and collection of bills, opening of letters of credit, channelising foreign inward remittances and mobilising savings abroad. They also provide import and export finance to local businessmen, arrange for foreign currency loans, promote project exports, joint ventures and provide merchant banking services.

SECTION II

CASE STUDIES OF BANKS[2]

This section is designed to provide information based on the case studies of three banks based in India. The ICICI Bank, the HSBC Bank and the State Bank of India (SBI)—with a focus on innovative products of these banks. These banks were selected for case analysis to analyse the effects of recent changes on commercial banks based on the representative character, *i.e.*, the ICICI Bank, which represents the private sector, the HSBC Bank, which is a foreign bank, and the SBI, which is a public bank. Retail banking products have been focused on in the three cases.

The ICICI Bank

The ICICI Bank was established by the ICICI in the year 1994. The bank's activities have gained momentum with the reverse merger of the parent company, ICICI, with the bank. ICICI Bank is India's largest private bank with about USD 21 billion in assets and the second largest Indian bank including all public enterprises. The ICICI Group comprises the ICICI Bank and various subsidiaries in the area of life insurance, general insurance, asset management, investment banking and venture capital. ICICI Bank is well known as the first Indian company to be listed on the New York Stock Exchange (NYSE). ICICI Bank has created global benchmarks through its US GAAP audit processes, the Securities and Exchange Commission (SEC) compliance practice and corporate governance standards. The bank's business has been driven by the multichannel distribution through hundreds of branches and ATMs, mobile, telephone and Internet banking facilities. ICICI Bank pioneered Internet banking in India and more than 30 per cent of its retail customers are on the Internet. The bank has set up representative offices and branches in countries such as the United Kingdom and the UAE.

ICICI Bank has introduced a wide spectrum of innovative domestic and international banking products to facilitate trade, investment, cross-border business and foreign exchange services. The different innovative services and products offered by the bank are savings account, fixed deposit (FD), quantum optima, recurring deposit, ICICI select, roaming current account, kid-e-bank, Bank@campus, power pay and locker facility.

Features in Savings Bank Account The salient features of the savings account are given below:

- The ICICI Ncash debit card is a debit-cum-ATM card providing their customers with the convenience of acceptance at merchant establishments and cash withdrawals at ATMs. Besides this card, ICICI bank also offers a credit card.
- Internet banking is offered free of cost. Given below are some achievements by ICICI bank in this respect.
    - First bank in India to launch a Web site—1996
    - First bank in India to launch Internet banking—1997 through www.icicibank.com
    - First bank in India to launch online bill payment—1999
    - Only bank in India with million online customers

- Anywhere banking enables the customer to bank at any of their branches across India. This too is offered at no additional cost.
- Besides these features the bank also offers PhoneBanking standing instructions, and nomination facilities. In addition, ICICI Bank Demat Services boasts of an ever-growing customer base of 16.29 lacs as on 30 September 2009. This bank offers various innovative products in their endeavour to offer world-class services to its customers.

HSBC Bank

The HSBC Group is one of the world's largest multinational banking and financial services organizations, with major commercial and investment banking and insurance businesses in Europe, the Asia-Pacific region, the USA the Middle East and Africa. The group's name is derived from one of its founder members, the Hong Kong and Shanghai Banking Corporation Limited, which was established in Hong Kong and Shanghai in 1865. The HSBC Group, headquartered in London, has more than 5,000 offices in 80 countries and territories.

Retail Banking—Products and Services HSBC Bank offers a wide range of financial products and services, from current and savings account to term deposits, automobile and home loans, mutual funds, loans against shares, gold and silver, Master and Visa credit or debit cards. It provides latest self-service banking technology including ATMs in each branch and at off-branch locations and 24-hour telephone banking. Innovative products like Smart Money accounts have been introduced by the bank in different countries including India (a deposit product for 400 days with many add-on facilities).

Corporate Banking Being a multinational organization, HSBC Bank stands for fostering long-term relationships with corporate clients based on its global connections and extensive knowledge of Asian business. The bank provides services including working capital, term finance, syndications, import and export finance.

Treasury HSBC, through one of the most advanced systems provides a comprehensive range of services to clients, including foreign exchange, money markets and financial instruments. HSBC's treasury is open until midnight in both Europe and North America on a real-time basis.

Investment Banking HSBC investment banking is a trade name for merchant banking, stock broking and fund management activities of the HSBC group.

HSBC Securities and Capital Markets Limited, headquartered in Mumbai, is considered a specialist in research and distribution of Indian securities to both Indian and international institutions.

The State Bank of India (SBI)

The State Bank of India (SBI) was constituted on 1 July 1955. The bank, in its drive for deployment of ATMs, had put in place a record number of over 2,000 ATMs by 2004 and the number has gone up further during the recent years. It is worth nothing that SBI did so much expansion work in the last 5 years by opening ATMs everywhere in record time. SBI was one of the first banks to create this 24-hour user-friendly banking channel across the country—from metros to small towns to remote places. The biggest gainer in this drive is the customer in small towns and remote corners—the latest technology is now made available to each and everyone.

Innovation Through Networked ATMs SBI had realized the need for more ATMs by the end of the 1990s. In order to retain customers, the bank started implementing its ATM Networking Project in 2001 and within a short period it deployed the largest number of networked ATMs. The bank has procured state-of-the-art Compaq's Tandem Switch and ACI's Base 24 software which enables them to scale up to meet the growing requirement.

Innovation—Depository Participant Services and Dematerialization (Demat) Depository is an organization, which holds customers' securities in the form of electronic book entries. This is being done at the request of shareholders through a depository participant (DP). An investor has to open an account with the DP, if he wants to avail services of the depository. A depository can transfer securities as per the investor's instructions without actually handling securities, through the electronic mode. The DP maintains the account balances of securities bought and sold by the investor from time to time. The DP also gives the investor a statement of holdings, which is similar to a passbook given to an SBI account holder. SBI introduced this facility immediately after the launch of electronic trading in securities.

Dematerialization is the process by which an investor gets his physical certificates converted into electronic form into his account with the DP. The customer has to fill in a dematerialization request form available with his

DP and submit his share certificates along with the above form. If one wishes to convert his electronic shares back to physical shares at a later stage, he can still do so by applying for rematerialization through a request form available with his or her DP.

Internet Banking The Internet banking service of the SBI is being offered through the Web site http://www.onlinesbi.com. Through this site, one can

- Access information about transactions and balance status
- Request for a transfer of funds
- Ask for issue of cheque books
- Give instructions to stop payment of cheques
- Request for issue of drafts from the funds in account
- Request for issue and renewal of term deposits
- Issue-standing instructions

Portfolio Management Services SBI has set up a Portfolio Management Services (PMS) section to handle investment-related concerns of institutional investors. The PMS forms part of the integrated treasury department of the SBI, and is based at Mumbai. The officers of the PMS section are highly experienced officers of the SBI who have an in-depth knowledge of how to handle large investment portfolios.

Innovation Through STEPS State Bank Electronic Payment System (STEPS) is a highly innovative and effective payment solution developed and implemented by the SBI in selected fully computerized branches (FCBs). STEPS provides an end-to-end electronics funds transfer (EFT) with speed and efficiency. STEPS facilitates credit of funds to the beneficiary's account at the other branch on the next day.

SECTION III

CASE IN DETAIL—HSBC BANK[3]

HSBC is one of the largest banking and financial services organizations in the world. HSBC is headquartered at London. Its international network comprises over 10,000 offices in more than 80 countries and territories in Europe, the Asia-Pacific region, the USA the Middle East and Africa.

HSBC is listed on the London, Hong Kong, New York, Paris and Bermuda stock exchanges; shares in HSBC Holdings Plc are held by nearly 2,00,000 shareholders in some 100 countries and territories. Shares are traded on the NYSE in the form of American Depository Receipts (ADRs).

The HSBC came into existence in India by the acquisition of the Mercantile Bank of India, Mumbai, in 1959. After the Mercantile Bank was acquired by the HSBC, the Mumbai Flora Fountain building of the bank became the head office of the HSBC Group in India. In recent years, HSBC has become a major bank and financial services provider in the world. Its strategy of 'managing for value' emphasizes the group's unique balance of business and earnings between older, mature economies and faster-growing emerging markets. The first ever ATM in India was established by HSBC way back in 1987. The organization's adaptability, resilience and commitment to its customers have further enabled it to survive through turbulent times and prosper through good times over the years.

HSBC's governing objective is to provide a satisfactory return on shareholders' capital. HSBC does this by having a talented and motivated staff and competitive services and products. The policy of the HSBC is not to make contributions to political parties or partisan organizations. HSBC works co-operatively with host governments and regulators while remaining politically neutral in all jurisdictions.

The HSBC Group is committed to five core business principles:

- Outstanding customer service
- Effective and efficient operations
- Strong capital and liquidity
- Prudent lending policy
- Strict expense discipline

Salient features of the retail products offered by HSBC in India are discussed in following sections.

Accounts

Savings Account The HSBC savings account offers interest at the rate fixed by the central bank, *i.e.*, the Reserve Bank of India. As it is targeted primarily at the upper classes, a very high quarterly average balance is required.

Benefits offered to savings account holders are listed below.

- A joining fee waiver on the credit card.
- Special rates on home loans, personal loans and Assetlink (overdraft against shares).
- Automatic transfer of extra savings from savings account to a FD to enable the customer to earn a higher interest.
- Demat account services with no account opening charges.
- Free quarterly account statement.
- Free personalized cheque book.
- Insurance and mutual fund services.
- ATM access—ATMs can be used to withdraw cash, transfer funds, deposit cheques and cash, request for a bank statement, cheque book or mini-statement and check balances.
- Credit card users can withdraw cash from their HSBC current or savings accounts at any of the VISA/Master Card ATMs worldwide.

Fixed Deposit HSBC offers a FD option that provides a fixed rate of return on an amount deposited with the bank for a fixed tenure. The amount (principal + interest) is repayable (or renewable at the option of the customer) at the end of the tenure period.

The salient features of this deposit scheme are

- Free savings account
- 90 per cent overdraft facility on the amount in FD
- Internationally valid debit card

Certificate of Deposit A certificate of deposit is somewhat similar to a FD. It is a fine opportunity to earn interest in advance for funds invested from 15 days to 1 year. It is available to individuals (other than minors), corporations, banks, companies, trusts, funds and associations.

The salient features of this scheme are the following:

- Holders receive interest in advance—the certificate of deposit facility works just like a FD, with one feature being that interest is received in advance. (The minimum marketable lot for a certificate of deposit is ₹1 lakh.)
- Transfer mechanism—certificates of deposit held in a physical form are freely transferable by endorsement and delivery. Those in demat form can be transferred as per the procedure applicable to other demat securities.

Demat Accounts HSBC provides depository services where shares are held in dematerialized (demat) form. Demat is the process of converting the physical (paper) shares into electronic form. With demat trading, customers will not need to worry about forgery and duplicate or stolen share certificates. Apart from safety, transaction costs are significantly lesser too. Under demat trading, every security has an ISIN (International Security Identification Number) that uniquely identifies that particular security, and provides a convenient form of ID.

The salient features of a demat account are

- Holding statement every 3 months, showing current portfolio of shares
- Overdraft available against demat shares
- No account opening charges and no minimum balance requirements
- No stamp duty on transfers and immediate transfers possible

A total of 10 sale transactions per month are free of cost for each demat account. Further, HSBC will receive new issues, rights and bonus issues in demat form on behalf of the customer. Interest rates for loans against demat shares are lower than the rates for loans against physical scrips.

Smart Money Account Smart Money account is a unique FD linked to a savings or current account where the customer can enjoy the higher returns of a FD and yet retain the flexibility of using money through the linked account. A Smart Money account can be opened with a minimum of ₹25,000 and customers also get high returns and a free savings or current account. Access to funds is anytime through ATMs, PhoneBanking, Internet banking or personalized cheque books.

The salient features of a Smart Money account are

- Withdrawal up to 90 per cent through an overdraft facility yet continues to earn interest on 100 per cent of your FD.
- Debit card with a withdrawal limit of ₹25,000 per day (higher limits for PowerVantage and HSBC Premier).
- Interest is calculated on a daily outstanding debit balance and is charged monthly to the account. Interest is charged at 2 per cent over the interest rate being paid on the deposit. The interest is charged only for the amount utilized and for the number of days in debit. The interest rate on an overdraft limit over ₹200,000 is linked to the bank's Prime Lending Rate (PLR). FDs will remain untouched and will continue to earn interest at the rate fixed at the time of placement. Customers get a personalized cheque book for their savings account.

Current Accounts There are three types of current accounts offered by HSBC Bank.

- Business Select
- BusinessVantage
- Business Account

Business Select: This is a premium service designed to look after business and personal needs. Financial services, wealth management solutions, personalized banking and, most importantly, the recognition that a Business Select customer deserves. HSBC provides the customer a personal relationship manager, dedicated to understanding his financial needs.

The salient features of this product are given below:

- Preferential pricing on trade services.
- HSBC offers local expertise and global reach in handling the account, including services in export and import. These include letter of credit confirmation, export bill negotiation, documentary collection and remittances.
- Preferential pricing of foreign exchange rates.
- Business centre facilities at all branches.
- Cluster deposits where idle money earns the interest rate of a FD while allowing free withdrawal any time.
- Smart Money account where the customer can take advances (overdrafts) against FDs with HSBC.
- 'Business Select' that ensures all cheques up to ₹2,00,000 will be honoured irrespective of the balance in the account.
- Customers can view account statements, pay bills, make drafts or transfer funds round the clock.
- PhoneBanking ensures that access to bank balances can be made 24 hours a day, 7 days a week, without actually stepping into the bank. Funds transfer, payment for suppliers, FDs and a cheque book request all can be carried out through PhoneBanking.
- Cash, cheques and drafts can be picked up from or delivered to office absolutely free of cost.
- Withdrawal up to ₹2,00,000 per day with the special Business Select ATM card.
- Preferential foreign exchange rates for all 'Business Select' customers, preferential rates on large volume trade services requirements, efficient processing of requests, rapid cheque clearance, faster remittances, salary accounts, investment services and much more ensure flexibility, leaving you with time and energy to focus on your business.

BusinessVantage: BusinessVantage is a current account that gives businessmen a superior service advantage. In the BusinessVantage account, an average quarterly balance of ₹1,00,000 is required. A host of benefits, such, as the 'no bounce' cheque protection facility, and a wide range of free services, such as 'Business PhoneBanking', 'Business Doorstep Banking' and more, are available too.

A BusinessVantage account holder is eligible for the following facilities:

- E-banking
- Complete range of services through PhoneBanking
- Free business Doorstep Banking
- No bounce cheque protection
- Free cheques payable at par
- Special ATM withdrawal limit of ₹10,00,000 per day

- Free personalized cheque book
- Preferential pricing on trade services
- Expertise and global reach in handling trade business
- Preferential pricing of foreign exchange rates
- Make payments to any part of the country with free telegraphic transfers, free auto sweeps to transfer excess cash to a FD, free standing instructions

Business Account. A Business Account is a cost-effective current account. An average quarterly balance of ₹25,000 is required in a business account.

A 'Business Account' holder is eligible for the following facilities:

- Free Internet banking for businesses
- Free business PhoneBanking
- Business Doorstep Banking
- Multi-branch banking
- Free special ATM card for cash withdrawal of up to ₹75,000 per day
- Fast and efficient collection services
- Up-country cheques drawn on any location across the country can be collected through the payments and cash management set-up
- Savings accounts for employees
- Simplified salary payments by using autopay to directly credit salaries to employees' accounts

Business banking customers can also invest in mutual funds, enjoy up to 48 days' interest-free credit on an internationally valid credit card and convert shares into electronic form with HSBC's depository services.

Credit Cards

Classic Credit Card The classic credit card from HSBC offers much more than just credit facilities. It is designed to maximize the value of the customer's hard-earned money through a combination of money-saving features and value-added benefits as given below.

Internet banking for credit card customers: The customer can get an instant review of his credit card transactions, know his credit card balances, opt for e-statements, redeem his bonus points online, benefit from these and more facilities with online@hsbc.com

Comprehensive insurance: All insurance benefits other than lost card cover are for primary active classic cardholders only. A primary active classic credit cardholder for the purpose of an insurance cover claim is defined as having a classic credit card that has been utilised at least three times for the purpose of customer initiated purchase and/or cash advance transactions within 89 days of the occurrence of the event.

- Personal accident insurance upto ₹15 lakh for loss of life due to air accidents and ₹1,50,000 due to any other accident.
- Purchase protection upto ₹30,000 for 180 days from the date of purchase for items bought using your HSBC classic card.
- Zero lost card liability.
- Cover upto USD 600 for loss of checked-in baggage.
- Credit shield facility involving waiver of payments of outstandings upto ₹20,000 for accidental death.

Credit shield extension: HSBC has structured a special life insurance cover for Classic credit cardholders for ₹20,000 in association with Tata AIG Insurance Company Ltd for non-accidental death. This insurance cover is utilized, to first offset any balance remaining on the customer's HSBC card in the event of non-accidental death, with any part of the cover remaining after that going to the cardholder's nominee.

Standard Privileges for HSBC Card Holders

Global access to bank account: The customer can withdraw cash from his bank account with HSBC India from any VISA Plus/MasterCard Cirrus ATM in India or overseas. He can also perform banking transactions like cash withdrawal, balance enquiries and fund transfers from any HSBC ATM in the world.

Cash advance: He can avail of this facility at over 700,000 ATMs in the world.

Bonus rewards programme: For every ₹100 the customer spends on his card, he receives 1 bonus reward point. He can choose from an exciting range of redemption options including jewellery, fashion accessories, garments, cosmetics, and much more.

Global calling card: Enables the customer to make long distance calls, while travelling overseas and get billed through HSBC credit card.

Gold Card The Gold credit card from HSBC is globally recognized as a symbol of success and achievement. The holder is eligible for all the facilities offered to Classic card holders such as 0 per cent balance transfer from other credit cards and 0 per cent fuel surcharge.

In addition, the bank provides some other facilities to Gold card holders like

- 5 per cent off on all international and domestic leisure packages.
- 10 per cent off on car rentals at domestic locations.
- Upto 20 per cent off on room rack rates at premium hotels.

A Gold card holder gets superior insurance benefits as mentioned below:

- Personal accident insurance upto ₹40 lakhs for loss of life due to air accidents and ₹400,000 due to any other accident
- Purchase protection up to ₹50,000 for 180 days from the date of purchase for items bought using the HSBC Gold credit card
- Zero lost card liability for accidental death
- Cover up to USD 500 for loss of passport or travel documents
- Cover up to USD 1,200 for loss of checked-in baggage while flying.
- Credit shield facility involving waiver of payments of outstanding up to ₹40,000 for accidental death.

Loans

Home Loans—Smart Home With the Smart Home product, the customer gets a bank account. The customer then needs to put his usual savings, from other accounts, into the Smart Home account. Depending on the savings put into the Smart Home account, the customer can reduce the quantum of interest paid by up to 50 per cent. That's because the principal on which loan interest is calculated, is the principal outstanding minus the savings deposited in the Smart Home account every month, over and above the equated monthly installment (EMI). The key benefits are as follows:

- Reduction of the tenor of loan to own the house quicker
- Flexibility to use the Smart Home account as the main account where full access to the account is given through cheque book, debit card and Internet Banking.

The Smart Home account is categorized as a PowerVantage relationship. The interest will be calculated on this debit balance in the account on a daily basis, *i.e.*, if the customer pays an excess amount over the EMI, the excess amount will remain available for use in the Smart Home account but helps save the amount of interest cost. Loans can be repaid by depositing at least the EMI amount into the Smart Home account every month.

Loan Against Property In this scheme, the loan tenor ranges from 1 to 10 years. The customer can opt for floating interest rates and the residential property would be the collateral.

Other features are

- Loan transfer—there is an option to transfer an existing loan against residential property from another bank.
- Banking benefits—loan against property account will be categorized as a PowerVantage relationship.

Personal Loan HSBC offers its customers four ways by which they can repay a personal loan.

- Lower EMIs in the first year and after that higher EMIs can be paid.
- Interest on utilized loan amount only and not on the entire loan. It requires the customer to estimate the maximum loan amount needed. Money can then be withdrawn as and when needed.
- Last EMI waiver: This repayment option gives the benefit of getting the last EMI refunded by paying a marginally higher interest rate.
- Standard EMI repayment.

Features of the personal loan facility are

- A flexible loan tenor of up to 4 years.
- Loans available from a minimum of ₹50,000 up to a maximum of ₹6,00,000.
- Easy monthly repayment through EMIs with either post-dated cheques or direct debit to the bank account.
- Flexibility of choosing the EMI dates.
- Transfer of an existing personal loan from another bank to HSBC, at attractive interest rates.
- Existing HSBC customers are entitled to special relationship discounts on processing fees.
- No collateral or guarantor required.
- Hassle free loan based on 12 months credit card or retail loan track record.
- Special schemes for corporate salary accountholders.

Educational Loans HSBC offers comprehensive educational loans that go beyond just providing the fee. A funding ranges from a ₹50,000 to ₹25,00,000 to support education in India and abroad. There is flexibility to opt for loans up to 4 years for unsecured loans and 7 years for secured loans. HSBC offers competitive interest rates on education loans with a choice between fixed and a floating rate.

Flexi Finance This flexible overdraft facility lets the customer draw money against assets such as balance sheets, salary slips, FDs, shares and cars. Interest is paid only on what is withdrawn and for the period of withdrawal of funds. Flexi Finance is offered as a floating interest rate product, to give the benefit of changing PLRs.

Wealth Management

HSBC Premier The HSBC bank offers this product to the following individuals:

- Residents of India with a minimum relationship value of ₹25 lakhs held in a combination of deposits, investments and loans.
- Non-resident Indians with a minimum relationship value of an equivalent of ₹25 lakhs in deposits.

HSBC Premier is a global relationship banking package and has been designed for a one-to-one banking relationship. The customer enjoys the following benefits:

- Relationship management: There is a dedicated HSBC Premier relationship manager who will be 'single-point' contact with the bank.
- 24-hour banking: As an HSBC Premier customer, access to the bank is given through personal telephone banking service, 24/7.
- Investment services: These include execution of investment in mutual funds, and assessment of risk-profile.
- Broking services: Broking services are made available through HSBC Securities and Capital Markets Limited.
- HSBC Premier global services: Access to a wide range of special facilities and services while travelling across the world such as free encashment of traveller's cheques and exchange of foreign currency, free of commission, at any branch of HSBC.
- HSBC Premier service centre: This is available in selected branches to provide confidentiality and comfort during banking and financial transactions.
- The debit card gives free, unlimited 24-hour access to all HSBC ATMs across the world and at other bank VISA ATMs in India.
- High cash withdrawals up to ₹1,00,000 per day from any HSBC ATM in India.
- HSBC Premier MasterCard credit card with a pre-approved credit limit of at least ₹2,00,000.

PowerVantage The holder of this product gets the following services from the bank:

- Unlimited free transactions at over 15,000 VISA ATMs using the PowerVantage debit card
- Dedicated service desk and teller counters
- Financial planning services
- Free cheque books with cheques payable at par in all cities where HSBC has branches
- No-bounce cheque protection
- Joining fee waiver and 50 per cent off on the annual fees of credit card
- Preferential pricing on home loans and personal loans
- Higher cash withdrawal limit of ₹50,000 and funds transfer up to ₹1,00,000 with Power Vantage debit card

GenNext Account GenNext Account is an exclusive account for children of PowerVantage and HSBC Premier customers. It helps secure a child's future through a systematic investment plan made with the help of consultants. Pocket money can be transferred to the child's account. The child gets a debit card which gives him the financial freedom within the spending limits controlled by the parent. This account comes to PowerVantage and HSBC Premier customers absolutely free and with no minimum balance requirement.

Financial Planning Services (FPS) HSBC has launched FPS for people who may not have the time or the expertise to plan their finances properly even for durations as long as 20 years or after retirement. This exclusive service is available free of charge to high net worth HSBC customers.

Mutual Funds These services are available for both resident and non-resident Indians. The process of investing through HSBC starts with an investor risk profile exercise. This helps HSBC understand customer's investment goals and recommend most suitable options from a variety of carefully selected funds. HSBC provides independent performance-based rankings of funds and regular performance updates to help through selection and tracking of your portfolio.

Insurance

Unfortunately, life is full of surprises. An accident or illness could seriously impair one's lifestyle, either temporarily or permanently. It is never too early to plan for the future considering the benefits of starting early; hence, the need for insurance.

The various insurance plans offered by HSBC are as follows:

- **Health first:** provides for all hospitalization needs.
- **Personal injury insurance plan:** provides for the medical needs of the customer and immediate family.
- **Auto secure:** a comprehensive auto insurance policy that provides protection in case of car damages and against third party liabilities.
- **Home secure:** insurance plan that protects home, from a host of natural and other calamities.
- **Home loan protection plan:** takes care of a home loan if something unfortunate were to happen to the loan bearer.
- **Educare:** provides the customer's child with the finance for the higher education he or she desires.
- **MahaLife gold:** guaranteed income for the child for a lifetime.
- **Golden years:** plans for a long retirement living with financial independence.

Some of the insurance schemes available from HSBC are:

- **Life insurance plans** include Nirvana pension, loan repayment protection, Tata AIG health first
- **Non-life insurance plans** include auto secure, accident guard, home secure, travel guard, personal injury insurance

Special Offers

These are the offers that HSBC comes out with every now and then. Presently, the following are the special offerings of HSBC.

Lifestyle Offer There is a certain offer running in 'Lifestyle' stores across metros which is offering upto 50 per cent off on selected items. Producing HSBC credit cards at the counter at these stores would enable a person to get an extra 6 per cent discount.

IT Offers In partnership with various manufacturers like Dell, Zenith and BenQ, HSBC empowers its customers to get discounts on certain models.

Holiday Deals HSBC has tie-ups with several hotel chains and several big travel agents which enable an HSBC card holder to get great deals and get discounts. Some hotels and resorts have also got strategic alliance with HSBC.

Dining Offer HSBC has come out with a concept of 'Palate'—a collection of some of the choicest restaurants across the country those serve authentic Indian and international cuisine. The customer will also enjoy a significant discount when he or she uses his or her HSBC debit or credit card at any of the selected restaurants which HSBC has tie-ups with.

Case Questions

1. Why does HSBC bank offer differentiated savings bank accounts?
2. Discuss the salient features of Business Select, BusinessVantage and Business Account. Distinguish between these three accounts.
3. Is there any difference between, the Classic Card and the Gold Card?
4. Discuss the characteristic features of loan products of HSBC bank.

CHAPTER SUMMARY

Globalization of the economy has resulted in modernization and innovations in banks. The importance of sophisticated or high technology for improving the customer service, productivity and operational efficiency of banks is well recognized. As a part of their action plans, banks have introduced many new techniques and also a considerable degree of mechanization and computerization in their operations. Banks have set up exclusive data communication network for banks known as Banknet. For this, the Reserve bank and 36 other banks have become members of the Society for Worldwide Inter-bank Financial Telecommunications (SWIFT) and have installed the SWIFT regional processor at Bombay. Through this network, any bank will be able to establish a connection with its own offices and with any other banks/offices/computers in the national and international network.

Another change taking place is the use of alternatives to cash by most of the constituents of banks. The large scale use of cards for settlement of financial transactions—whether credit cards or debit cards or even the new smart cards-proves beyond doubt that cash is slowly losing the prominence of the yesteryears. Banks are quickly adapting to provide non-cash-based services. Transactions through ATMs or through electronic mode are gaining importance.

TEST YOUR UNDERSTANDING

1. Name the first Indian bank that was listed at the New York Stock Exchange?
2. Specify the Internet banking portal of the State Bank of India.
3. Write the full form of the follows abbreviations:

   a. ATM b. HSBC c. ICICI
4. Distinguish between the following HSBC products:

   a. Business Vantage b. HSBC Premier c. Smart Money Account
5. Discuss the innovative products of HSBC.

CASE STUDY

INTEREST RATES AND PROF BOND[4]

As Prof. Bond (short for Bondop) entered the class, he found a heavy silence. 'What's the matter of the class? Friday morning blues?' the professor asked in a jovial tone. Confucious (because he was always confused), a student, seemed as usual perplexed and showed the Prof. an article on interest rates, 'I cannot figure out the fuss about interest rates and monetary policy,' he said. Prof. Bond looked at the article in his usual manner; a frown on his face leading to a grin at the end of the article. He rolled up his sleeves and said, 'Ok, let's start with the basics. What are interest rates? Interest rate is simply the cost of money. Just like we need to pay a price for buying our movie tickets or burger at McDonalds, we need to pay a price for borrowing money. This is what we call cost of funds from the point of view of borrower and for the person lending, it is the price received, which we call yield on capital'.

The Boy Lost in the Back Row (BLITBR), suddenly, as if he had found what he was looking for read out aloud, 'despite the implementation of reforms, structural rigidities remained in interest rate structure distorting the true market-determined rates. Rates had been kept artificially high by offering high-administered rates on small savings and provident funds. The gap between the short- and long-term rates tended to remain high on account of this'. The Prof. nodded his head. 'You are right. But we should be aware of the linkage between interest rates, its role in banking system and other asset prices'. Sanjay (the topper of the class), who was listening silently till now, remarked, 'But interest rates in developing countries like India and Brazil still continue to be very high relative to the rates prevailing in global markets'.

'Can't disagree with you Sanjay, I get what you are leading at', the Prof. remarked. Confucious was a little dumb-founded, 'Will you care to clarify?' Sanjay explained, 'Against the backdrop of a slowing Indian economy, bank rate and administered rates on small savings were cut in the 1990s. Added to this, the RBI proclaimed the policy of pursuing a lower interest rate regime. However, the recent hike in interest rates shows that the rate would go up and down depending upon the market requirements'.

It was then that Miss Dreamy Eyes decided to enter the discussion, 'But Sir, what does the RBI have to do with interest rates? Why can't it just let interest rates move on their own?' Prof. Bond was now on song and explained, 'Industrial growth is a pre-requisite for economic development. Every industry requires finance for the establishment, expansion and working capital management Bank credit is considered as the most important source of industrial finance. The dependence on bank for finance could vary according to the size of the companies and to the availability of the credit at a lower cost'.

Confucious jumped and chipped in, 'Monetary policy aims to influence the overall level of monetary demand in the economy so that it grows broadly in line with the economy's ability to produce goods and services'. He was proud for finally getting the linkage between interest rates, price level and monetary policy. 'Bingo,' said the Prof. and explained, 'This stops output from rising too quickly or slowly. Interest rates are increased to moderate demand and inflation (an increase in the general price level in an economy).

Miss Dreamy Eyes was now in a little fix, 'What do the interest rates have to do with demand?' The class was now in full swing. And the Prof. enjoyed questions from his students. He calmly explained, 'When interest rates are changed, demand can be affected in various ways. A change in the cost of borrowing affects spending decisions. Interest rates will affect the attractiveness of spending today relative to spending tomorrow'. 'You mean that an increase in interest rates will make saving more attractive and borrowing less so. This will tend to reduce current spending, by both consumers and firms,' said Confucious. 'Absolutely right!' the Prof. exclaimed and added, 'this spending includes both spending by consumers in shops and spending by firms on new equipment, *i.e.*, investment. Conversely, a reduction in interest rates will tend to increase spending by consumers and firms'.

Prof. Bond smiled and went on, 'Monetary policy operates by influencing the price of money, *i.e.*, the cost of borrowing and the income from saving. The RBI sets the bank rate. This is an interest rate for the Reserve Bank's own market transactions with financial institutions—the rate at which the Reserve Bank will make short-term loans to banks and other financial institutions.

'And why is this bank rate so important?' quipped BLITR. 'That is because changes in the bank rate affects, a whole range of interest rates set by commercial banks, and other financial institutions, for their own savers and borrowers. It will influence interest rates charged for overdrafts and mortgages, as well as savings accounts. A change in the bank rate will also tend to affect the price of financial assets such as bonds and shares'. Prof. Bond read the quizzical look on the face of his students. He went on, 'These changes in the financial markets affect consumer and business demand and, in turn, output. Changes in demand and output then have an impact on the labour market-employment levels and wage costs—which, in turn, influence producer and consumer prices'.

'You mean that there is a positive correlation between a cut in the bank rate and movement in the interest rate?' asked Sanjay. 'Precisely', said the Prof., 'most banks make downward adjustment in their respective lending and deposit rates following a slash in the bank rate'.

Confucious was getting to where the Prof. was trying to lead them. He chipped in excitedly, 'and while the cut in lending rate would bring down the interest income, it is only logical that most banks would try to compensate for the loss of income by bringing down the interest out-go through adjustment in deposit rates so as to neutralize the impact on their net interest income'.

'Exactly and to that extent, this would definitely reduce their cost of funds as also bring down the interest income'.

Miss Dreamy Eyes continued, 'Sir, the article also mentioned something about the asset prices and exchange rates'. Sanjay looked at her teasingly and said, 'That's just like substitution effect of the simple law of demand. Higher interest rates increase the return on savings in banks and PPFs. This might encourage savers to invest less of their money in alternatives, such as property and company shares'.

The Prof. smiled at Miss Dreamy Eyes and continued his point, 'And any fall in demand for these assets is likely to reduce their prices. This reduces the wealth of individuals holding these assets, which, in turn, might influence their willingness to spend. Again, lower interest rates have the opposite effect; *i.e.*, they tend to increase asset prices. Similarly, a significant fall in interest rates can be expected to reflect in higher stock prices'. BLITBR, came out of *hi reverie* and pulled out some facts, 'But Sir, long-term interest rates have declined more than 25 per cent in the last 3 years. However, a commensurate increase in stock prices has failed to happen. Why is that so?'

'Well, a probable reason for this phenomenon can be that given the uncertainty in the Indian as well as global markets, the investors prefer to stay liquid'.

Prof. Bond decided it was time to wrap up the session. He looked at his watch and announced that the time was over.

Case Questions

1. Discuss the importance of interest rates.
2. Elucidate the learnings from this case.

SELECT REFERENCES

1. Indian Institute of Bankers, *Principles of Banking*. (New Delhi: Macmillan, 2005).
2. L. M. Bhole, *Financial Institutions and Markets*. (Tata McGraw-Hill, 2004).
3. IBA, *IBA Bulletin*, special issue, Indian Banking 2010. (January 2004).
4. ICFAI, *Professional Banker*. (May–June 2005).
5. Web site and product brochures of HSBC, ICICI and SBI.

ENDNOTES

1. Figure drawn based on the information from the book *Principles of Banking*, India Institute of Banking, Macmillan, 2005.
2. These cases are developed solely as the basis for class discussion. Cases are not intended to serve as endorsements, sources of primary data or illustrations of effective or ineffective management.
3. This case is developed solely as the basis for classroom discussion. This is not intended to serve as endorsements, sources of primary data or illustrations of effective or ineffective management.
4. This case was co-authored by Professor Justin Paul with Prasoon Agrawal and Srikant Rajagopal.

CHAPTER FIFTEEN

International Banking—Foreign Exchange and Trade Finance

CHAPTER STRUCTURE

KEY TAKEAWAYS FROM THE CHAPTER

- Learn the concept and terms pertaining to international banking.
- Understand the practical aspects of foreign exchange operations.
- Know the basics of exchange rates and foreign exchange markets in India.
- Understand basics of letters of credit.
- Understand various aspects of trade finance.

INTRODUCTION

Central banks do not deal with customers who have international banking requirements. Therefore, commercial banks have been authorized as dealers to undertake foreign exchange transactions. Since it would be extremely difficult for a person to search for an individual who has foreign currency for supply or sale, foreign exchange market has been developed by designating certain banks as authorized dealers (AD). Banks normally classify their international banking operations into the following two segments:

- When the dealing is between a bank and a merchant (could be importer, exporter, individuals).
- When the dealing is between banks (inter-bank segment). 'Forex Dealing Room' is a part of this segment.

The transactions pertaining to the first segment are carried out through select branches of the bank that have foreign exchange facility. At the same time, banks trade with each other in different currencies in the inter-bank market in order to square-up their positions undertaken for their customers in branches. One has to get a clear idea about the basic terms used in the foreign exchange market, in order to understand the international banking operations.

SECTION I

BASIC CONCEPTS

Exchange Rates

Exchange rate is the price of one currency in terms of another. The rate varies from time to time depending upon the supply of and demand for foreign exchange (FOREX) in the inter-bank market, which is based on the transactions in the merchant segment. The exchange rate of a currency appreciates if the general demand for that currency at any moment exceeds the current supply. It is worth noting that the exchange rates of active currencies fluctuate every four seconds.

You would have come across the data on buying and selling exchange rates in newspapers and televisions. The selling rate is the rate at which the banks sell a foreign currency against the local currency. The buying rate is the rate at which banks buy a foreign currency against the local currency. The margin between the selling and buying rates constitutes the exchange profit for the bank.

FOREX Market

Foreign exchange market can be defined as an over-the-counter market in which retail individuals, business firms and banks purchase and sell FOREX. The transactions include sale and purchase of currencies, demand drafts (DD), cheques, transfer of money from one country to another and can be through telegraphic transfer (TT), mail transfer (MT), etc. Banks form the cream in the market and quote the rates to the customers as 'price makers'. The characteristic features of the FOREX market are as follows:

- 24-hour open-market (inter-bank segment, because of the time difference between countries)
- World-wide market: No single location and no geographical constraint
- Large capital and trade flows

Transfer Systems

While undertaking transactions with their retail and corporate clients, banks use the following modes for inward/outward FOREX remittances:

- **Telegraphic transfer (TT):** Banks transfer funds from one country to another by way of instructions through Telex. With the advent of software 'SWIFT' (Society for Worldwide Inter-bank Financial Telecommunication), most banks use SWIFT for international fund transfer. The payments are made the very next day by the banks.
- **Mail transfer (MT):** A mail transfer is an agreement between two banks in writing, to pay to the beneficiary the sum mentioned therein. This can be issued to the correspondent bank/branch abroad and normally being sent by post. MT is not as quick as TT, but it is a cheaper mode.
- **Demand draft (DD):** A foreign DD is a written order issued by a bank on another bank (correspondent) or its own branch in a different country.

Types of Rates There are different types of exchange rates. These are briefly discussed as follows:

(i) TT (Buying)
(ii) TT (Selling)
(iii) Bill (Buying)
(iv) Bill (Selling)
(v) Currency (Buying)
(vi) Currency (Selling)
(vii) Traveller's Cheque (TC-Buying and Selling)

A specimen quotation from a bank would look like this[1]:

Currency	TT-SELL	TT-BUY	BIL-SELL	BIL-BUY	CUR-SELL	CUR-BUY	TC-SELL	TC-BUY
US	43.66	43.35	43.75	43.36	44.15	42.80	43.90	43.05
EUR	70.59	70.01	70.68	70.02	71.10	69.50	70.85	69.75

The authorized dealers (banks) have to apply the relevant rate depending on the nature of transactions. Some of them can be illustrated as follows:

TT-selling rate: For (1) outward remittance in foreign currency (TT, MT or DD), (2) cancellation of purchase, *e.g.*, bill purchased earlier is returned unpaid, (3) a forward purchase contract cancelled and (4) import documents received directly by the importer.

Bill-selling rate: For transactions involving transfer of proceeds of import bills (except for [4] above). Even if proceeds of import bills are to be remitted in foreign currency by way of TT, MT or DD, the rate to be applied is the bill selling rate and not the TT-selling rate.

TT-buying rates: For (1) clean inward remittance (TT, MT or DD for which the cover amount has already been credited to NOSTRO account of the bank abroad), (2) conversion of proceeds of instruments sent on collection basis, (3) cancellation of earlier outward remittance (TT, MT or DD, etc.) and (4) cancellation of forward sale contract. Generally, if the NOSTRO account has been credited, the TT-buying rate is applied.

Bill-buying rate: For the purchase/discounting of export bills.

Direct and Indirect Quotations

There are two ways of quoting exchange rates—direct and indirect.

- For direct quotation, the value of one unit of the foreign currency is expressed in terms of the domestic currency. For example, in the United States, the rate for the euro against dollar might be stated as $1.0571 per euro.
- For indirect quotation, a foreign currency's value is expressed in terms of one unit of domestic currency. For example, in UK, the sterling/euro rate could be quoted as euro 1.4875 per one pound sterling.

The direct quotation method is used in most countries for dealings between banks and their customers. In the case of a forward transaction, the purchase or sale is agreed, but will take place at some time in the future, thereby fixing the rate for a future exchange of currencies.

Functioning of Foreign Exchange Market

A FOREX transaction is a contract to buy or sell a quantity of one currency in exchange for another at a specified time for delivery and settlement and at a specified price or rate of exchange. The FOREX market consist of FOREX dealing rooms within commercial banks where trading takes place by computer and telephone for their customers. Despite its lack of a physical centre, the FOREX market is still a market in the sense that it is a system for bringing buyers and sellers together and for supplying information about prices and trading activity to participants. The FOREX dealers responsible for setting the prices at which their banks will exchange currencies must have access to the latest prices in the market.

The important FOREX dealing centres in the world, each operating within a specified time zone, are in London, New York and Tokyo. Historically, London has been the major centre for FOREX trading. There are two types of FOREX transaction:

- **Trade transactions:** This is a transaction between a bank and a non-bank customer where the customer wishes to buy or sell a quantity of currency to complete a trading transaction or occasionally, speculates for profit by anticipating future charges in the exchange rates.
- **Inter-bank transactions:** This is a transaction where two banks trade currencies between themselves.

Banks buy and sell huge quantities of foreign currencies. They also accept currency deposits and lend in foreign currency. Banks are subjected to exposure if they sell more or less of a currency than they buy. Most of the FOREX deals are transacted between banks. This is partly to hedge their exposures to customer business. Banks, these days, maintain accounts in foreign currencies with different banks for international fund transfer and settlement (NOSTRO account). For example, Corporation Bank maintains NOSTRO account in US dollar with Bank of America and in GBP with Barclays Bank.

In the early days of the FOREX market, transactions were purely trade or investment-related and there was little dealing between banks operating in the FOREX markets. But now, the exchange rates in major currencies such as, dollar/yen, euro/dollar and sterling/dollar have become increasingly volatile as the volume of FOREX transactions has increased. With the advent of electronic trading mechanism, a bank can eliminate its exposure instantly with another bank and lock in a profit. In addition to trade-related transactions, there are speculative transactions in the forward market. These are outright gambles on future exchange rate movements, conducted by bank dealers, investment managers and brokers or by companies.

SECTION II

INTER-BANK MARKET AND FOREX DEALING

FOREX Dealing Room Operations

FOREX dealing room of a bank occupies an important place since the strategic international banking transactions are carried out by the 'dealers' engaged in trading of currencies. International banking division, particularly the officers designated as 'dealers' enter into positions—purely selling and buying FOREX—to minimize profit because of the fluctuations in exchange rates. The inter-bank market operates on a professional basis with the integrity of the dealers.

Dealing room is the nodal point for all the FOREX activity of a bank. Most of the banks classify the organizational structure of dealing room into three segments, which are as follows:

1. Front office
2. Mid office
3. Bank office

The front office, which forms the main hub of the operations, consists of the dealing room made up for inter-bank and corporate desks. While the inter-bank desk engages in management of exposures arising on account of transactions from branches by trading with other banks, the corporate desk quotes the exchange rates for merchant transactions emanating from branches. The mid-office shall be responsible for administration of the risk management policy of the bank. The bank office is responsible for a follow-up of every transaction entered into by the bank till it reaches its logical end, *i.e.*, settlement of currencies. The bank office functions include maintenance of parallel exchange position, cross checking the deal entered into by dealers, settlement data and so on.

The FOREX dealing rooms of banks are connected through electronic network. The rate quotations are always available on the screen meant for trading currencies. A discussion between the dealers of different banks, sitting in Mumbai, London, Singapore and Dubai takes place and in the same way, an 'Internet chat' takes place between people sitting at different locations. The conversations would go something like this:

Bank A: Hi Hi Bank A Here
Spot USD/GBP please, 2,000
Bank B: Hi there, 1.6945/53
Bank A: OK at 45 yours 2,000
Bank B: Agreed. I buy USD 2,000 at 1.6945 value spot
My USD to my account with my New York City
Where your GBP please
Bank A: My GBP to my account with my London
Barclays Bi Bi

Heavy responsibility rests on the FOREX dealers of a bank. The dealers meet before the work starts and arrive at tentative conclusions valid for the day. They are supposed to concentrate on the market rates by maintaining contacts with other banks.

When a dealer buys or sells foreign currency, the bank gets into a position and if the purchases are more than the sales in a given day, it is said to be in an overbought/long/plus position. If the sales are more than the purchases, it is said to be in an oversold/shot/minus position. That is, an excess of assets over liabilities is called an overbought position and excess of liabilities over assets results into a short/oversold position.

Spot, Forward, Cash, TOM Rates in an Inter-Bank Market

A FOREX transaction to buy or sell currency can be broadly categorized as a spot transaction or a forward transaction. A spot transaction is a contract to buy or sell a quantity of a foreign currency for immediate settlement or value. The exchange rate for such a transaction is known as spot rate.

There could also be cash and TOM-based dealings in the inter-bank market. The settlement date (value date) in the case of spot transaction would be on the second working day, that for cash on the same day and for TOM— the next day; and forward means any day beyond the spot.

Every forward contract has three main elements.

- It is a binding agreement to buy or sell a specific quantity of one currency in exchange for another.
- The rate of exchange is fixed when the contract is made.

- The contract is for delivery of the currency, at an agreed future time, either a specific date or any time between two specific dates, depending on the contract terms.

However, a spot transaction in the merchant segment of the FOREX market refers to conversion and remittance of money on the same day from one country to another. Anything beyond the spot is known as forward.

In the case of a forward transaction, the purchase or sale is agreed; but will take place at some time in the future, thereby fixing the rate for a future exchange of currencies.

Bid and Offer Rates

Exchange rates are commonly quoted by banks as two-way rates—the bid price and the offer price.

USD/EUR 0.9670/0.9682
USD/GBP 0.7121/0.7126

However, sometimes, the financial press shows the mid-point (average) of the bid and offer rates. The bid rate is the price at which the bank will buy base currency from a customer. In the case mentioned above, a bank will buy 1 USD against 0.9670 euro and 0.7121 pound sterling, respectively. The difference between the bid price and the offer price is called the spread.

Premium and Discount A currency is said to be at a premium, when it is costlier for a forward value date. In the case of direct quotes, the premium is added to the spot rate for both buying and selling to arrive at the forward rate. A currency is said to be at a discount when it is cheaper for a forward value date.

Pips and the Big Figure Exchange rates are usually quoted up to five figures by banks. The first three digits of the quote are the big figure.

Example:

0.9567

USD/EUR. Big

In the above case, 0.95 is known as 'big' and 67 is called as 'pip'.

The dealers often assume that everyone knows what the big figure is in major currencies at the time. Deals are often conducted without any mention of the big figure; only the pips are quoted.

Cross Rate It is an expression of the value of one foreign currency versus another foreign currency, neither of which is a domestic currency. For example,

USD/JPY = 114.28 EUR/USD = 1.1625, etc.

Then, USD/INR = 45.6251

Here, you are required to calculate EUR/INR rate based on the information given above. EUR/INR rate, in this case, is called as the cross rate.

FIGURE 15.1 VOLATILITY IN THE INR/USD MARKET—APRIL 2006 TO SEPTEMBER 2009[2]

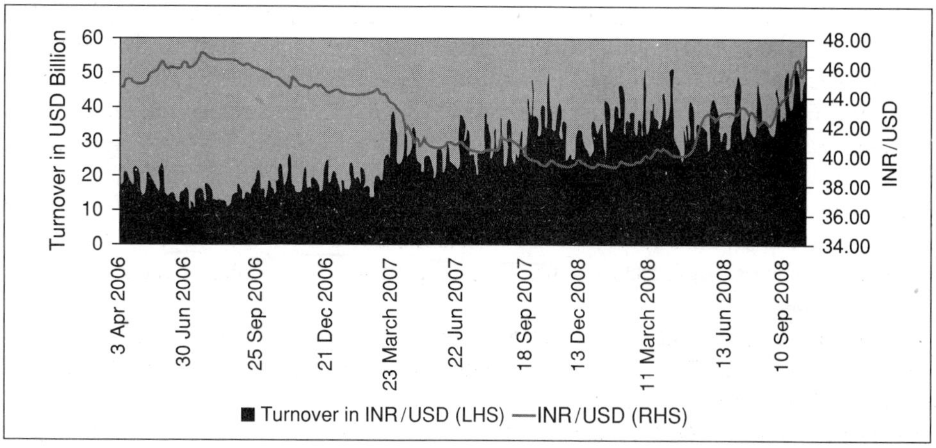

Source: RBI database

Volatility The exchange rate fluctuation is referred to as volatility. Figure 15.1 shows how the INR/USD rates have moved between April 2006 and September 2008. The turnover signifies the volume of business transacted during this period. It can be seen from the chart that although turnover has been increasing, the volatility in exchange rates is high. Table 15.1 substantiates the increase in volatility.

TABLE 15.1 USD VERSUS OTHER CURRENCIES—EXTENT OF APPRECIATION (+) AND DEPRECIATION (−) (IN %)

Currency	End-March 07 @	End-March 08 @	End-March 09 @	13 August 2009*
1	2	3	4	5
Euro	−9.12	−15.77	18.82	−6.89
Pound Sterling	−11.40	−1.53	38.67	−13.74
Japanese Yen	0.21	−14.92	−2.00	−2.04
Chinese Yuan	−3.53	−9.25	−2.61	−0.02
Russian Ruble	−6.06	−9.68	44.25	−5.18
Turkish Lira	3.23	−5.75	27.69	−11.87
Indian Rupee	−2.46	−8.30	27.47	−5.52
Indonesian Rupiah	0.47	1.09	25.58	−14.04
Malaysian Ringgit	−6.24	−7.77	14.42	−3.52
South Korean Won	−3.65	5.47	38.86	−11.15
Thai Baht	−9.90	−10.16	12.85	−4.21
Argentine Peso	0.65	2.08	17.32	3.29
Brazilian Real	−6.41	−16.99	31.20	−17.83
Mexican Peso	1.27	−3.48	32.90	−9.09
South African Rand	17.24	11.34	17.22	−16.38

@: Year-on-year variation.
* : Variation over end-March 2009.

Source: RBI Annual Report, 2008–2009, Table 2.59, page 138

Foreign Exchange Market

Banks in India were first permitted to undertake intra day trading in FOREX in 1976. In the early 1990s, the exchange rate was pegged to a basket of currencies, which can be considered as the first step towards current account convertibility. In August 1994, current account convertibility was permitted.

Under current account convertibility, residents of India can make or receive foreign currency payments related to export and import trade, sundry remittances and gain access to foreign currency for education, travel, medical treatment, gifts and so on. On the other hand, when investments and borrowings in foreign currency are also freely permitted at market determined exchange rates, it is called capital account convertibility. This essentially means that anyone can move freely from local to foreign currency and back. Residents of India are even now subject to capital controls, even though a gradual process of liberalization has been initiated.

Though the FOREX market has seen a substantial increase in average daily turnover from the 1990s, the market is dominated by spot transactions. This, coupled with the global financial turmoil of 2007, resulted in increased volatility.

The exchange traded currency futures platform in India has been setting global benchmarks since its introduction. Apart from India, Brazil is the only country where the currency futures market has exhibited more liquidity than the OTC currency market.

The players in the FOREX markets are the ADs, FOREX brokers and individuals/corporate firms.

SECTION III

TRADE FINANCE—LETTERS OF CREDIT

Financing International Trade Through Letters of Credit

A letter of credit (LC) is an instrument for settling trade payments and is an arrangement of making payment against documents. Under this arrangement, a bank, at the request of a customer, undertakes to pay a third party by a given date, according to agreed stipulations and against presentation of documents, the counter-value of goods or services shipped. An LC is a commitment on the bank's part to place an agreed sum at the seller's disposal on behalf of the buyer under precisely defined conditions. The importer knows that the negotiating bank will not effect payment to the seller unless and until the latter tenders the documents strictly in accordance with the terms of the LC. The seller is assured of getting payment as long as he presents the documents as per LC terms to the negotiating bank.

Box 15.1 introduces ICC, uniform customs and practice (UCP) and their connection to the LC.

BOX 15.1 THE ICC, UCP AND THE LC

As trade between nations rapidly increased in the early part of the 20th century, conflicting laws governing LC among countries acted as a major barrier to trade expansion. In 1933, members of the ICC created the first uniform customs and practice for documentary credits (UCPDC), a set of rules that brought uniformity to documentary LC.

About the ICC (www.iccwbo.org)

- The ICC is a non-profit, non-governmental, self financed, private international organization that works to promote and support global trade.
- It was founded in 1919 with the objective to serve world business by promoting trade and investment, opening markets for goods and services, and ensuring free flow of capital.
- Its international secretariat was established in Paris and its international court of arbitration was created in 1923.
- Initially, representing the private sectors of Belgium, Britain, France, Italy and the USA, it has expanded to represent worldwide business organizations in more than 175 countries.
- ICC has direct access to national governments worldwide through its national committees.

About the UCP

UCP plays a pivotal role in the world of international business and trade finance. It is a set of standardized rules that was first put together in 1933 to facilitate international trade transactions. The UCP has since then gone through seven versions. The current version, UCP 600, came into force in July 2007.

Since inception, the UCP has become the most successful private set of rules for trade ever developed. Now firmly established, the UCP remains an essential component in international trade. It establishes the conditions under which the majority of banks operate in documentary commercial credit transactions. The current version, UCP 600, has been officially endorsed by the UN commission on international trade law (UNCITRAL) in 2009. Where a credit is issued subject to UCP600, the credit will be interpreted in accordance with the entire set of 39 articles contained in UCP600.

About 'documentary credits'—The letter of credit

A 'documentary credit'—an agreed method of settlement in international trade—is one where the buyer's bank pays the seller against presentation of 'documents', after ensuring compliance with conditions stipulated in the documentary credit.

A documentary credit is a conditional undertaking of payment given by a bank. It is a written conditional undertaking issued on behalf of the importer (applicant) by the issuing bank to the exporter of goods (beneficiary) to pay for the goods or services, provided the documents submitted conform strictly to the terms and conditions of the credit.

The advantages of settlement of payment through documentary credits accrue to both buyer and seller. The buyer is confident that payment will be made to the seller only if the documents strictly comply with the terms of credit as agreed to by the buyer and seller. The seller will ensure payment by complying with the terms and conditions of the credit.

Now the connection...

All documentary LC are subject to the provisions of UCP (currently UCP 600) issued by the ICC, wherever it is incorporated into the text of the credit as such. UCP600 does not automatically apply to a credit if the credit is silent as to which set of rules it is subjected to.

For example, a credit issued by SWIFT MT700 is not subject by default to the current UCP.

The different parties involved in an import transaction with a LC can be the following:

- **Applicant:** Normally, an applicant is the buyer of the goods or the importer who approaches the bank for opening the LC.
- **Issuing bank or opening bank:** The bank which issues the LC, *i.e.*, the bank which opens the LC and undertakes to make the payment.
- **Beneficiary (Exporter):** A beneficiary is the seller of the goods, who has to receive the payment from the applicant. An LC is issued in the seller's favour in order to enable him or his agent to obtain payment on submission of the stipulated documents.
- **Advising bank:** An advising bank is one which advises the LC to the beneficiary, thereby assuring the genuineness of the LC. It is normally situated in the country/place of the beneficiary. The advising bank could also be the beneficiary's bank.
- **Confirming bank:** A confirming bank is one which adds guarantee to the LC opened by another bank, thereby undertaking the responsibility of payment/negotiation/acceptance under the credit, in addition to that of the issuing bank. LC confirmation is not mandatory and is desirable in some cases where the parties and the banks are not internationally reputed. For example, sometimes, the seller abroad may not be aware of the standing of the LC opening bank and, hence, may ask for the credit to be guaranteed for payment by a bank in his own country against presentation of documents without recourse.
- **Reimbursing bank:** This is the bank which is authorized to honour the reimbursement claim in the settlement of negotiation/acceptance or payment lodged with it by the paying, negotiating or accepting bank. It is normally the bank with which the issuing bank has an account from which payment is to be made (NOSTRO account).

These and other relevant definitions can be found under Article 2 of UCP 600.

Flowchart Depicting a Typical Import Transaction with Letter of Credit

(i) The importer signs a purchase contract for buying certain goods. The contract would also include, among others, specific clauses relating to means of transport, credit period offered (where applicable), latest date of shipment, Incoterms (see Box 15.2) to be used, etc.

(ii) The importer requests his bank to open an LC in favour of the exporter.

(iii) The importer's bank opens an LC as per the application.

(iv) The opening bank forwards the original LC to the advising bank in the exporter's country.

(v) The advising bank, after satisfying itself about the authenticity of the credit, forwards the same to the exporter.

(vi) The exporter scrutinizes the LC to ensure that it conforms to the terms of the contract.

(vii) In case any terms are not as agreed, the importer would be asked to make the required amendments to the LC.

(viii) In case the LC is as required, the exporter proceeds to make arrangements for the goods.

(ix) The exporter effects the shipment of goods.

(x) The exporter prepares export documents and submits to his bank.

(xi) The exporter's bank (negotiating bank) verifies all the documents with the LC.

(xii) If the documents are in conformity with the terms of LC and all other conditions are satisfied, then the bank negotiates the bill.

(xiii) The exporter receives the payment in his bank account if he wants post-shipment finance.

(xiv) The LC issuing bank receives the bill and documents from the exporter's bank.

(xv) The importer receives the bill from the LC issuing bank and checks the documents. He then accepts/pays the bill. On acceptance/payment, he gets the shipping documents covering the goods purchased by him.

(xvi) The LC issuing bank reimburses the amount to the negotiating bank, if the documents are found in order.

(xvii) Exporter receives the payment upon realization, if he has not availed post-shipment finance.

BOX 15.2 INCOTERMS RULES

'Incoterms' can be expanded to international commercial terms. They are standard trade definitions most commonly used in international sales contracts.

ICC has updated the Incoterms rules six times since 1936, when the first version was introduced. ICC has introduced Incoterms 2010.

The scope of Incoterms rules is limited to matters relating to the rights and obligations of the parties to the contract of sale with respect to the delivery of goods sold, but excluding 'intangibles' like computer software.

Each Incoterms rule is referred to by a three-letter abbreviation. There are 13 Incoterms, which are given below. (The common abbreviation is followed by the expansion).

EXW (EX WORKS)
FCA (FREE CARRIER)
FAS (FREE ALONGSIDE SHIP)
FOB (FREE ON BOARD)
CFR (COST AND FREIGHT)
CIF (COST, INSURANCE AND FREIGHT)
CPT (CARRIAGE PAID TO)
CIP (CARRIAGE AND INSURANCE PAID TO)
DAF (DELIVERED AT FRONTIER)
DES (DELIVERED EX SHIP)
DEQ (DELIVERED EX QUAY)
DDU (DELIVERED DUTY UNPAID)
DDP (DELIVERED DUTY PAID)

Incoterms 2000 groups the above terms in four categories, denoted by the first letter of the three-letter abbreviations given above; for example, those abbreviations beginning with C are called the 'C' terms and so on. How are these terms helpful?

- Under the 'E'-term (EXW), the seller makes the goods available to the buyer only at the seller's own premises. It is the only one of that category.
- Under the 'F'-terms (FCA, FAS and FOB), the seller is called upon to deliver the goods to a carrier appointed by the buyer.
- Under the 'C'-terms (CFR, CIF, CPT and CIP), the seller has to contract for carriage, but without assuming the risk of loss or damage to the goods or additional costs due to events occurring after shipment or dispatch.
- Under the 'D'-terms (DAF, DES, DEQ, DDU and DDP), the seller has to bear all costs and risks needed to bring the goods to the place of destination.

It can be seen that all terms list the buyers' and sellers' obligations. The listing helps the users to compare buyers' and sellers' respective obligations under each Incoterms rule. Subsequent revisions of Incoterms rules are adapted to contemporary commercial practice. The revisions also clearly indicate the loading and unloading requirements of both buyer and seller.

In order to illustrate, the explanation for the abbreviations seems to show a clear trend—the 'D' terms are the most risky to the seller or exporter, the 'C' terms, less risky and so on. Hence, in international trade, exporters would typically prefer refraining from dealing in trade terms that would hold the seller responsible for the import customs clearance and/or payment of import customs duties and taxes and/or other costs and risks at the buyer's end; for example, the trade terms DEQ (Delivered Ex Quay) and DDP (Delivered Duty Paid). This is understandable, since the charges and expenses at the buyer's end may cost more to the seller than anticipated. The current revision of Incoterms rules specifies that under DEQ the buyer (and not the seller) is required to clear the goods for import and to pay for all formalities, duties, taxes and other charges upon import. This is a clear deviation from the previous stipulation under DEQ, which required the seller to arrange for import clearance.

Similarly, importers prefer not to deal in EXW (Ex Works) or FAS (Free Alongside Ship), which would hold the buyer responsible for the export customs clearance, payment of export customs charges and taxes, and other costs and risks at the seller's end. The current revision stipulates that under FAS, the seller (and not the buyer) is required to clear the goods for export.

Source: www.iccwbo.org/incoterms

Types of LC

Banks issue several types of LC to suit the need of their trading clients. The most common types are briefly introduced as follows:

- **Irrevocable LC:** This is a basic form of LC, most commonly used in foreign trade. An irrevocable LC cannot be revoked or amended without the consent of all parties thereto. Under UCP, all LCs are deemed irrevocable.
- A **confirmed LC** is confirmed/guaranteed by a bank other than the issuing bank.
- An **unconfirmed LC** is one where the advising bank or another bank forwards the LC to the exporter without adding its own undertaking to make payment or accepting responsibility for payment on due date, but confirming the LC's authenticity
- **Revolving LC:** Under the terms and conditions of a revolving LC, the amount under the revolving LC can revolve in relation to time or value. This type of LC provides for delivery of goods in installments and at intervals. Such a credit would stipulate certain ceiling amount in addition to the date of expiry.
- **Deferred payment LC:** This type of LC allows the issuing bank to make the payment to the beneficiary in installments. The timing and the amount of these installments are predetermined. The buyer accepts the documents and agrees to pay the issuing bank on a fixed maturity date. Thus, the buyer gets an extended period for payment.
- **Transferable LC:** In some cases, the seller or beneficiary may not be the actual producer of the goods. In such cases, the seller (exporter) may request the buyer (importer) to open a transferable irrevocable LC. On receipt of the same, he will instruct his bank to transfer the credit in favour of the actual third party supplier. The other features of this type of LC are (a) at the request of the (first) beneficiary, it may be made available in whole or in part to another (second) beneficiary and (b) a credit may be transferred in part to more than one second beneficiary.
- **Back to back LC:** This is a variant of the transferable LC. In this case, instead of transferring the original LC to the third party supplier, the exporter uses the LC as security to establish a second LC issued by the advising bank in favour of the third party supplier. In other words, when an inland LC is opened by a bank in the exporter's country backed by the security of another LC (original LC by importer), it is known as 'back to Back credit'. This is useful for merchant exporters.

  Many banks may be reluctant to issue back to back LC due to the level of risk to which they are exposed, whereas a transferable credit will not expose them to risk higher than that under the original credit.
- **Anticipatory LC:** It provides for payment to beneficiary at the preshipment stage. Under this type of LC, a 'red clause' LC (it is called so because the referred clause is normally incorporated in red ink) provides for payment up to processing and packing goods for shipment, while a 'green clause' LC provides for payment up to point of loading for shipment.
- **Standby LC:** We have seen the use of bank guarantees in the earlier chapters on bank lending. Standby LCs are used in lieu of bank guarantees in some countries, *e.g.*, the USA. They are secondary payment mechanisms used as support where an alternate, less secure method of payment has been agreed upon. They can be used to guarantee financial payments (like a financial guarantee) or guarantee performance (as in performance guarantee). The ICC rules for operating standby LCs are UCP600 and ISP98 International Standby Practices.

It is important to note that all parties in the LC transaction deal with 'documents' and not with 'goods'.

Documentary collections under the LC may be carried out in two different ways:

- **Documents against payment:** Documents are released to the importer only against payment. These are also known as a 'sight collection' or 'cash against documents' (CAD), and correspond to cash.
- **Documents against acceptance:** Documents are released to the importer only against the acceptance of a draft. They are also known as a 'term collection', and correspond to 'credit sales'.

SECTION IV

TRADE FINANCE—FINANCING EXPORTERS

The Export Credit Scheme

The export credit scheme to finance exporters was introduced in 1967. It is intended to facilitate exports through providing working capital finance to exporters at internationally competitive interest rates. Banks are permitted to decide appropriate rates of interest based on the current guidelines, borrower's creditworthiness, risk perception and market practices.[3]

Pre-Shipment Finance Pre-shipment credit is a short-term working capital finance provided by a bank to an exporter enabling the latter to procure raw materials, to process/manufacture the goods, arrange for transport and warehouse and for shipment of the finished goods. Pre-shipment credit is usually extended as packing credit (PC). It is also granted as advance against incentives receivable from the government, advance against duty drawback and advance against cheques/drafts received as an advance payment. The exporter can avail the PC either in rupees or in a foreign currency.

Features of Packing Credit in Local Currency

Normally, banks extend PC to exporters on production of either an LC or a confirmed order. A confirmed order is a purchase order issued by a reputed foreign buyer to the exporter, mentioning the terms of purchase, such as the price, quality, quantity, the date within which the shipment is to be effected and so on.

(a) The PC availed against an LC/order will be adjusted by the bank from out of the proceeds of the export made against that LC/order. The bank makes an endorsement in the original LC/order to prevent the exporter from availing a PC with another bank, while allowing the credit.

(b) Running account facility: This is a facility granted to exporters with good track record to avail PC without lodging an LC/order. The borrower will have to produce the LC/order to the bank within a reasonable time. The liquidation of PCs outstanding in the running account is done on a 'first in first out' basis.

(c) A PC can be given for a period not exceeding 360 days.

(d) This type of credit is generally granted at a concessional rate of interest. If the credit is not adjusted within 180 days, the concession could be withdrawn.

(c) Refinance can be available by banks from the RBI against the PC granted to the exporters, up to a period not exceeding 180 days.

(f) PC is available for both cash exports and deemed exports. In cash exports, goods are exported outside the country and the full value is realized within the prescribed period.

Features of Pre-Shipment Credit in Foreign Currency (PCFC)

The following are the features of PCFC:

(a) The foreign currency loans (FCL) granted to exporters by the banks are known as PCFC. The salient features of PCFC are similar to rupee export credit. However, PCFC is available only for cash exports in foreign currencies. The facility will be made available in one of the convertible currencies—USD, GBP, JPY and Euro.

(b) The lending rate to the exporter, under the current guidelines, should not exceed 200 bps above LIBOR (London interbank offered rate)/EUROLIBOR/EURIBOR[4] Even though the interest rate is less in PCFC, compared to that of PC in rupees, exporters may not prefer PCFC when they expect a fall in the value of rupees. For example, if rupee depreciates against US dollar subsequent to availing of PCFC, say, from 1 USD = ₹43 to ₹48, the exporter will not get the benefit of such depreciation as the export proceeds in US dollar will be adjusted against the PC which is already accounted in dollar. The exporter will get the benefit of depreciation, if PC was availed of in rupees, as the bank will convert the export proceeds in dollar to rupee @ 1 US dollar = ₹48 for adjusting the PC outstanding and crediting the balance to the party's account.

(c) For lending under the PCFC scheme, banks can use the foreign currency balances available with them, in exchange earners foreign currency (EEFC) account/resident foreign currency (RFC) accounts, foreign currency non-resident (FCNR) account, foreign currency borrowings, etc.
(d) PCFCs can be maintained as running accounts.
(e) PCFC is self-liquidating in nature and is liquidated by purchasing/discounting of related bills.
(f) Refinance from the RBI is not available to banks against PCFC.

Post-Shipment Finance

Post-shipment credit is defined as any loan or advance granted by a bank to an exporter of goods/services from the date of extending the credit after the shipment of goods/services to the date of realization of the export proceeds. It is a working capital finance extended against the evidence of a shipping document for the purpose of financing the export receivables. Post-shipment finance is extended in the following manner.

(a) Negotiation (*i.e.*, payment of export bill and documents under LC)
(b) Purchase (*i.e.*, providing finance against export documents without LC, covered by drafts drawn 'at sight' at spot bill buying rate)
(c) Discount of export bill under confirmed order/export contracts (*i.e.*, providing finance against export documents covered by drafts without LC, drawn 'on usance' at the usance bill buying rate)
(d) Advances against export bills sent on collection basis

After making the shipment, the exporter presents to his bank the set of export documents, such as bill of lading/airway bill, invoice, bill of exchange, insurance policy, certificate of origin, inspection certificate, packing list, etc. The bank then verifies the documents and confirms that the shipment of goods is as per the terms of LC/confirmed order. Thereafter, the bank negotiates the bill (if against LC) or purchases (sight bills without LC)/discounts (usance bills without LC). The bill is drawn in foreign currency and the proceeds credited in rupees, to the exporter's account, after adjusting the PC outstanding against it.

SECTION V

FOREIGN CURRENCY LOAN (FCL)

Companies prefer to borrow money in a currency where interest rate is low. For example, many multinational corporations all over the world have borrowed in Japanese yen and other low interest rate currencies for a relatively long period.

Till October 1996, the commercial banks in India were permitted to give FCL to exporters only by way of granting PCFC. In 1996, the RBI permitted banks in India to use FCNR (B) funds to extend foreign currency denominated loans to their resident constituents (including non-exporters) for meeting their term loan needs too.

Features of Foreign Currency Loans

The following are the features of FCL:

(a) The FCL can be extended for a period ranging between 6 months and 3 years normally. Banks are free to determine the tenor.
(b) Purpose: The FCL can be extended for meeting working capital/capital expenditure needs of the clients subject to precautions taken by banks relating to prudential norms, credit discipline and credit monitoring. Banks do not offer FCL as personal loans and loans for purchase of consumer durables. The loans can be used for many other purposes, including expansion projects or diversifying into another sector. There are many cases where private educational institutes and hospitals have borrowed money as FCL for 2 or 3 years for their requirements like constructing new buildings, etc.

(c) Loans would be denominated in foreign currency irrespective of the fact whether the loan is utilized in foreign currency for payment of imports or in rupee for domestic expenditure. Repayment can be made by remitting rupee or foreign currency. Exporters can repay the loan in foreign currency or by way of proceeds of export bills, if they so desire.

(d) Banks are free to decide the interest rate on FCL. Most of the banks have adopted a system where interest rates are linked to prevailing LIBOR plus margin. In FCL, there is exchange risk factor due to possible depreciation of rupee against foreign currency at the time of repayment, say after 6 months or 3 years.

(e) FCLs are available at a lower interest rate. When depreciation is not anticipated, forward booking can be avoided and thus forward premium is saved. In such cases, FCLs will be a cheaper source of financing.

(f) There is no maximum ceiling on FCL.

(g) A customer can repay loans even before the due date, if he desires, by paying a nominal penalty.

Example: A customer takes FCL of USD 50,000 for 6 months, at 2 per cent interest, when USD–INR Rate is 1 USD = ₹45. If the rate becomes 1 USD = 50 INR on the due date, then the customer will have to pay an amount equivalent to the principal and the interest at the rate of ₹50. In order to hedge the exchange rate risk, banks permit the borrower to have forward contract booked for repayment of the FCL, especially in respect of non-exporters. So, the effective cost of FCL will be LIBOR + margin + forward premium.

CHAPTER SUMMARY

- The volume in the FOREX has witnessed a surge in the recent years because of rapid growth in foreign trade and foreign investment. Although multinational banks have got an edge in this segment, small banks are also trying to capture their own market share in the FOREX business. Since the exchange rate is becoming increasingly volatile, banks have been permitted to offer FOREX derivative products like options, swaps and forward rate agreement to their customers.
- The FOREX market in India comprises of the spot and derivatives markets. Although the OTC derivatives instruments dominate the derivatives markets in the form of forwards, rupee and cross currency swaps and options, the introduction of exchange traded currency futures in October 2008 has gained rapid popularity.
- Financing international trade is an important function of a commercial bank. Banks extend trade finance products through their selected branches located in towns, designated as 'FOREX' specialised branches. With the increase in the volume of foreign trade, many banks have identified 'trade finance' as a focus area.
- LCs are the important financing tools for firms involved in trade, especially international business and trade. A bank agrees to open LCs on behalf of creditworthy customers alone. The bank, on behalf of the customer or trader, and for a fee, promises through the LC, to pay the purchase price to a seller (or the seller's bank) if the stipulated and highly detailed conditions are fulfilled.

  How are these conditions and rules stipulated? The most widely accepted 'rules' for LC business across the world are those drafted by the International Chamber of Commerce (ICC).
- The trade finance functions of a bank can be broadly classified as:
  - Financing the importers
  - Financing the exporters
  - Pre-shipment finance
  - Post-shipment finance

TEST YOUR UNDERSTANDING

1. An exporter has a requirement of ₹2,40,000 to meet his expenditure at the pre-shipment stage. He has a choice of availing PC in Indian rupees or a PCFC in US dollar. He is planning to apply for a loan on 1 January. Assume that the exchange rate is ₹48 = 1 USD. He gets an offer from his bank for PCFC of USD 5,000 (equivalent of ₹2,40,000 for 6 months at LIBOR + 120 basis points (LIBOR on USD = 2.5 per cent) on 1 January. He has to pay 8.5 per cent interest rate, if he has to avail pre-shipment loan in Indian rupees.

   a. How much would he have to pay back, if he avails ₹2,40,000 as rupee loan?

   b. Calculate his repayment liability, if he goes for FCL, if exchange rate becomes 1USD = ₹50.

c. State which one would be profitable for him.

d. What would be his liability, if he gets a forward contract @ 1 USD = 49.50 for repayment?

2. USD = INR 48.79/83. Forward rates are quoted as one month 0.31/33. At what rate can you sell USD as an exporter? At what rate, can you buy USD as an importer?
3. Exchange rate of Swiz Franc against Indian rupees (CHF/INR) in the Inter-bank market is 26.8967/9235. An exporter requests bank to purchase a bill for CHF 3,50,000.

   a. What rate would the bank quote to the exporter, if the bank requires an exchange margin of 0.20 per cent?

   b. What would be the interest on export finance to be recovered from the exporter, if the transit period of the export bill is 25 days and the rate of interest is 8 per cent?

   c. What would be the rupee amount payable to the exporter?
4. An exporter based in UK submits a sight bill for US Dollar 20,000 for post-shipment finance in his bank. How much his bank will credit to his account, taking into account the following given particulars?

   Inter-Bank US $1 = 0.75 GBP

   Exchange margin to be taken by the bank = 0.15%

   Transit period: 15 days (from the date of financing to the date of realization of export bill)

   Interest rate: 3% per annum on GBP
5. An exporter in France has the requirement of EURO 5,000 to meet his expenditure at the pre-shipment stage. He has a choice of availing PC in EURO or a FCL in Japanese Yen. He is planning to apply for the loan on 1 January. Assume that the exchange rate is Euro 1 = 150 Yen. He gets an offer from his bank for FCL of 7,50,000 Yen (equivalent of Euro 5,000/–) for 1 year at LIBOR + 70 basis points (LIBOR on JPY + 0.20%) on 1 January. He has to pay 2.5% interest rate, if he has to avail pre-shipment loan in Euro. How much he has to pay back, if he avail Yen as loan, if the currency is stable? Calculate his repayment liability, if he goes for FCL if exchange rate becomes 1 Euro = JPY 144. State which one would be profitable for him? What would be his liability, if he gets a forward contract @ 1 Euro = JPY 149 for repayment?
6. Society for inter-bank worldwide financial telecommunication is known as_____.

   a. SFIWFT   b. SIBWFT   c. SWIFT   d. none of these
7. _____make the price in the foreign exchange market.

   a. Importers   b. Exporters   c. Brokers   d. Banks   e. Central bank
8. A bank's account in a foreign currency, with a bank in the said foreign country for international fund transfer and settlement is called as_______.

   a. TT   b. NOSTRO   c. premium   d. forward
9. Importers do not prefer ___________.

   a. advance payment   b. documentation   c. payment in Euro
10. Import LC is issued by an __________.

   a. exporter   b. importer's bank   c. exporter's bank   d. advising bank

SELECT REFERENCES

1. Paul, Justin (2006). *International Business*. 4th ed. Delhi: Prentice Hall of India.
2. Apte, P. G. (2005). *International Financial Management*. New Delhi: Tata McGraw-Hill.
3. Paul and Aserkar (2009), Export-Import Management, Oxford University Press.

ENDNOTES

1. Rates quoted are 1 USD = ______ Indian Rupees and 1 Euro = ______ Indian Rupees.
2. RBI, 2009, Committee on financial sector assessment, Chapter 4, Table 4.5, page 203, accessed at www.rbi.org.in
3. For a full text of the RBI guidelines, please refer 'Master circular on rupee and foreign currency export credit and customer service to exporters' dated 1 July, 2009, accessed at www.rbi.org.in
4. RBI circular 'Interest rates on export credit in foreign currency' dated February 19, 2010, accessed at www.rbi.org.in. The circular also stipulates that where the pre-shipment credit in foreign currency is outstanding beyond 180 days, an additional interest of 200 bps over the existing rate would be applicable.

CHAPTER SIXTEEN

High-Tech Banking—E-Payment Systems and Electronic Banking

CHAPTER STRUCTURE

KEY TAKEAWAYS FROM THE CHAPTER

- Understand how technology helps banks and customers.
- Learn about electronic payment and settlement systems.
- Understand e-banking—the concepts and the benefits.
- Understand retail payment systems and their benefits to banks and customers.
- Learn the concepts and usage of plastic money such as credit cards, debit cards, etc.
- Be aware of the security issues in e-banking.

SECTION I

BASIC CONCEPTS

Why Do We Need Technology in Banking?

Welcome to the digital age in banking. Over the last couple of decades, technology has assumed the vital role of not only a facilitator, but also a source of competitive advantage for banks. During the 1990s, efficiency and cost-cutting used to be the primary objectives of banks turning to new technology. At present, banks have evolved a strategic approach towards their investments in technology, since they have found that both revenue enhancement and cost-effectiveness count in their constant endeavour to improve their ROA and ROE.

The business of banking—especially financial services/retail banking—is undergoing a sea change, as business shifts increasingly to the online environment. The increasing number of customers transacting online would move the 'market place' to 'market space', where banks would be forced to expand their product range to competitors' products, while rapidly innovating their own value-added products.

Technology, and more specifically, the Internet, has evolved into an essential access channel. For banks, the Internet offers a cost effective means of innovating, publicizing and delivering services to the customer, as well as maintaining customer relationships. For the customer, the Internet has opened up enormous possibilities of convenience and choice.

Let us understand the role of technology as an enabler for improved transaction efficiency through the categorization provided in Figure 16.1.

FIGURE 16.1 CATEGORIZING FINANCIAL TRANSACTIONS THROUGH TECHNOLOGY

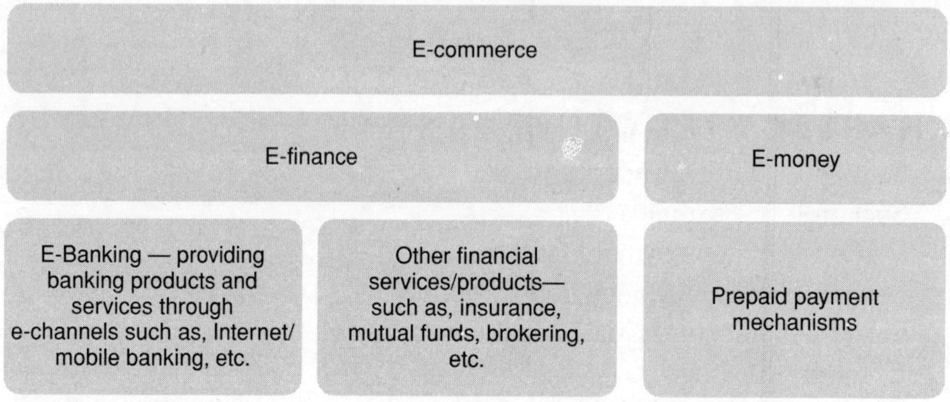

The effect of technology in banking has been dramatic. The bank-to-customer relationship has changed significantly, with open standards replacing proprietary front ends, and many-to-many networks substituting for single-line links. Most banks, today use Internet as their global expansion platform, offering an increasing array of financial services online.

Benefits of Electronic Banking

For Banks

The benefits of electronic banking (e-banking) for banks are as follows:

- **Price:** In the long run, a bank can reduce expenses by not paying for tellers or for managing branches. Also it is cheaper to make transactions over the Internet.
- **Customer base:** The Internet allows banks to reach new markets and high net worth individual, because there are no geographic boundaries with the Internet. The Internet also provides a level playing field for small banks who want to add to their customer base.
- **Efficiency:** Banks can become more efficient by providing Internet access for their customers. The Internet provides the bank with an almost paperless system.
- **Customer service and satisfaction:** Banking on the Internet not only allows the customer to access full range of available services but it also provides some services not offered at any of the branches. The customers can print information, forms and applications via the Internet and search for information efficiently instead of waiting in line and asking bank employees. With better and faster options, a bank will surely be able to create better customer relations and satisfaction.
- **Image:** A bank seems more state-of-the-art to a customer if they offer Internet access. A person may not want to use e-banking but having the service available gives a person the feeling that the bank is on the cutting edge.

For Customers

The benefits of e-banking for customers are as follows:

- **Systematically Important Payment Systems (SIPS):** High value clearing and Real Time Gross Settlement (RTGS) are classified under this category since they benefit large corporate and high net worth customers. Steps have already been initiated to merge the two payment services—the high-value clearing threshold has been raised from ₹1 lakh to ₹10 lakh, with the intention of progressively discontinuing the service, due to the availability of alternate channels for high-value transactions.
- **Financial markets clearing and other important retail payment facilities:** Financial markets clearing is intended primarily for government securities and foreign exchange markets. Retail payment systems, such as e-banking, give customer the control over nearly every aspect of managing his bank accounts. The customers can, buy and sell securities, check stock market information, check currency rates, check balances, see which cheques are cleared, transfer money, view transaction history and avoid going to an actual bank. The best benefit is that e-banking is free. At many banks the customer does not have to maintain a required minimum balance.

SECTION II

E-PAYMENTS

The Importance of Payments and Settlement Systems

An important ingredient of an efficient and deep financial system is the ability of intermediaries to effect smooth and secure transfers of money and exchange financial claims embedded in financial instruments. The security of payment and settlement systems is critical for sustaining public trust in the financial intermediaries. (Please also see Chapter 1 where we discussed the role of 'trust' as the backbone of the financial system).

Hence central banks, as supervisors and regulators of payments and settlement systems through financial intermediaries, have to ensure development of efficient and secure systems to match the explosion in needs and sophistication of the financial sector.

Technology has been a primary contributor to new and innovative products and methods of payments and settlement in various countries around the world. Similarly, the power of technology has been harnessed to enable central banks to carry out their regulatory and supervisory roles as well.

International Standards and Codes for Payment and Settlement Systems

The Committee on Payment and Settlement Systems (CPSS) was set up by the Bank for International Settlements (BIS, www.bis.org, please also refer to chapter on Capital Adequacy) as a standing committee, with the objectivet of strengthening financial market infrastructure through promoting sound and efficient payment and settlement systems.

CPSS was formed by G 10 central banks in 2001 with the specific objective of formulating broad supervisory standards and guidelines for payment and settlement systems. It serves as a forum for central banks to monitor and analyse developments in domestic payment, clearing and settlement systems as well as in cross-border and multicurrency settlement schemes. The membership of CPSS has widened beyond the G10 countries, to include about 25 central banks in 2009. The RBI is a member of CPSS.

The Committee has also forged relationships with many non-CPSS central banks in order to help strengthen payment systems globally. Apart from setting standards, the CPSS also publishes reference works on payment systems in select countries—widely known as the 'Red book'.

After formalizing the 'Core Principles of Systemically Important Payment Systems' in 2001, CPSS published in 2002, along with IOSCO, its 'Recommendations for Securities Settlement Systems (SSS)'. This was followed up with the CPSS-IOSCO 'Recommendations for Central counter parties (CCP)' in 2004. Box 16.1 summarizes the CPSS core principles and recommendations.

BOX 16.1 CPSS—CORE PRINCIPLES AND RECOMMENDATIONS

- **CPSS core principles for Systematically Important Payment Systems (SIPS)**

  The CPSS defines payment systems as a 'set of instruments, procedures and rules for the transfer of funds among system participants'. SIPS is further defined as the 'payment systems which, if it is insufficiently protected against credit, liquidity, legal, operational and other risks, the disruptions within the system could trigger or transmit further disruptions among its participants, or generate systemic disruptions in the financial markets or more widely across the economy'. Accordingly, a system is considered SIPS if at least one of the following conditions is met—(a) it is the only or the principal payment system or the principal system in terms of the aggregate value of payments, (b) it handles mostly payments of high individual value, and (c) it is used for the settlement of financial market or other payment systems.
- **CPSS–IOSCO Recommendations for Securities Settlement Systems (SSS)**

  The 19 recommendations for SSS can be construed as 'standards' to enhance safety and efficiency. The recommendations/standards cover all aspects of securities settlements, particularly, the legal framework, settlement cycles, central counterparties, operational reliability, governance, transparency, regulation and oversight.
- **CPSS–IOSCO Recommendations for Central Counter Parties (CCP)**

  We have seen in earlier chapters that the role of a CCP is to reduce risk to market participants by interposing itself between counterparties to financial contracts, imposing controls and enhancing liquidity. However, failure of risk management of a CCP could have catastrophic consequences on markets as well as payment and settlement systems. The 15 recommendations (in the nature of standards) for CCPs broadly cover the legal and participation requirements, risk management procedures, operational reliability, efficiency, governance, transparency, regulation and oversight.

  It is to be noted that CPSS has not set specific standards for Retail Payment Systems.

Source: www.bis.org

Payment and Settlement Systems in India

The RBI has spearheaded a vast change in the use of technology for making banking in India safer, more secure, smoother and more efficient. RBI was empowered in 2007 through the enactment of the Payment and Settlement Act, 2007, to regulate and supervise payment and settlement systems in India, formulate relevant policies and provide a legal basis for multilateral netting and settlement finality. To operationalize the Act, RBI framed the 'Board for Regulation and Supervision of Payment and Settlement Systems Regulations, 2008' and 'Payment and Settlement Systems Regulations, 2008'.

Payment systems in India can be bifurcated into 'paper-based' and 'electronic' payment systems. Another classification, based on users, can be into 'large-value payment systems' and 'retail payment systems'. See Figure 16.2 for the components of each classification.

FIGURE 16.2 ALTERNATE CLASSIFICATION OF PAYMENT SYSTEMS

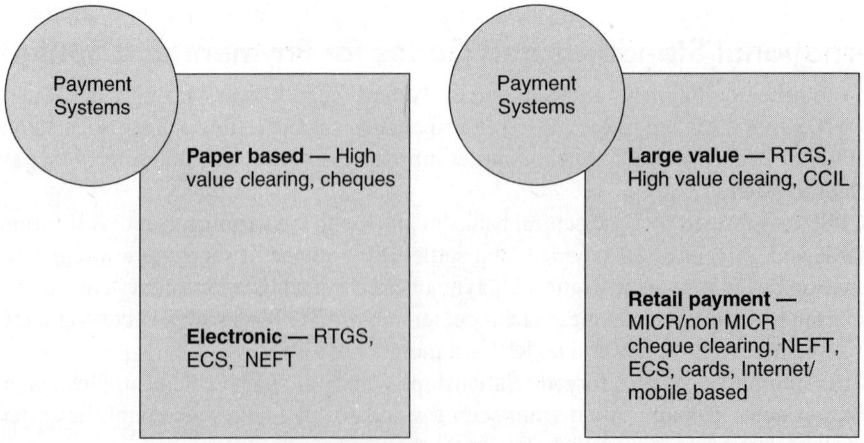

We can infer from Figure 16.2, that while the classification 'paper-based' versus 'electronic' conveys the mode of payment and settlement, the alternate classification—'large value' versus 'retail'—convey their relative importance to the stability of the financial system.

The large-value system (sometimes also termed 'bulk payment system') is characterized by relatively low volumes but high values, as contrasted with retail payment systems where high volumes (number of transactions) and low values are typical. Being high value, the large value payment system carries systemic risks that could affect the stability of the payment systems of the financial sector as a whole. Therefore, according to the BIS (CPSS) standards, both high-value clearing and RTGS would be classified as SIPS.

Though retail payments are not termed 'SIPS', their relative importance to the economy cannot be undermined due to the sheer volume and geographical coverage that these systems demand.

Box 16.2 describes the salient features of RTGS, the fastest growing segment of SIPS.

BOX 16.2 SALIENT FEATURES OF RTGS

The Rationale

The traditional payment system involves settlement of payments on a settlement day (next day, 2 days after and so on) and interest is invariably computed to accrue on a daily basis. Even in the inter-bank foreign exchange and money market contracts, spot transaction means 2 business days. Settlement for clearing cheques presented to clearing houses takes place on a netting basis at a particular time either on same day or on the next day. These conventions make sense, when book-keeping is done manually. However, this system gives rise to risks, such as credit risk, liquidity risk, operational risk, legal risk and systemic risk. Such risks could cause widespread liquidity problems.

The RTGS, was introduced to solve these problems in the banking sector. It is a software package which provides an online settlement of payments between financial institutions, *i.e.*, bank to bank fund transfer and settlement same day. In this system, payment instructions between banks are processed and settled individually and continuously throughout the day. This is in contrast to net settlement that takes place only afterwards, typically at the end of the day. Under the RTGS system, payee banks and their customers receive funds during the day, enabling them to use the funds immediately without exposing themselves to risk. To initiate a fund transfer, the bank has to send a payment message, which is subsequently routed to the central bank and to the receiving bank as the system processes and settles the transfer. The RTGS system settles payments on a transaction-by-transaction basis as soon as they are accepted by the system. It is a large-value fund transfer system whereby financial intermediaries can settle inter-bank transfers for their own account as well as for their customers.

RTGS in India

Operationalized as part of SIPS in March 2004, the RTGS began with four banks settling only interbank transactions. In 2006, it was expanded to customer transactions (multilateral net settlement). The RTGS operated with 105 members in 2009.

The first transaction was put through by the State Bank of India, which made an interbank payment. The RTGS system now allows high-value customer payments to happen through this system. High value for the purpose of RTGS is defined as transactions of ₹1 lakh (0.1 million) and above. Subsequently, all customer payments would be enabled on the RTGS system.

The RTGS system is owned and operated by the RBI. Direct membership is restricted and open to commercial banks, primary dealers, clearing houses and others as decided by RBI. The commercial banks are called 'type A' members, which enables them to submit customer-based transactions. Primary dealers are 'type B' and clearing houses 'type D' members. RTGS membership and operations are governed by RTGS Membership Regulations and Business Operating guidelines, 2004 (and subsequent amendments).

Settlement of RTGS transactions are done in the RBI books. To enable them transact, members open an 'RTGS settlement account' with the RBI, Mumbai. The member has to fund this account at the beginning of every RTGS processing day from the member's current account with RBI. At the end of the day, the balance in the account is swept back to the member's current account.

Members are provided with a participant interface gateway server with which participants/members connect to the RBI system through the INFINET.[1] The software is supplied by the RBI. The banks procure the hardware, which is specified by the RBI. Participants are advised to get a dedicated lease line link between PT gateway and the local hub of the RBI.

RTGS is a gross settlement system in which both processing and final settlement of fund transfer instructions take place continuously (*i.e.*, in real time). As it is a gross settlement system, fund transfers are settled individually, without netting debits against credits. RTGS systems are able to minimize or eliminate the inter-bank risks in the settlement process.

The RTGS system has reduced the time for processing payments from 24 hours (which could go up to a week) for cheques at present, to a matter of a few minutes. The launch of the system is expected to phase out cheques from the banking system in due course. Importantly, RTGS systems can offer a powerful mechanism for reducing systemic risk. As central banks have a common interest in limiting systemic risk, this capability has often been the key motive for many central banks to adopt the RTGS system for larger-value money transfer.

Source: RBI documents.

SECTION III

RETAIL PAYMENT SYSTEMS

Retail payment systems are required primarily for purposes such as payments for goods and services, bill payments, cash payments and so on. Figure 16.3 shows the major purposes for individuals to require e-banking facilities, and the instruments available to satisfy the requirements.

FIGURE 16.3 E-BANKING—PURPOSE AND INSTRUMENTS AVAILABLE

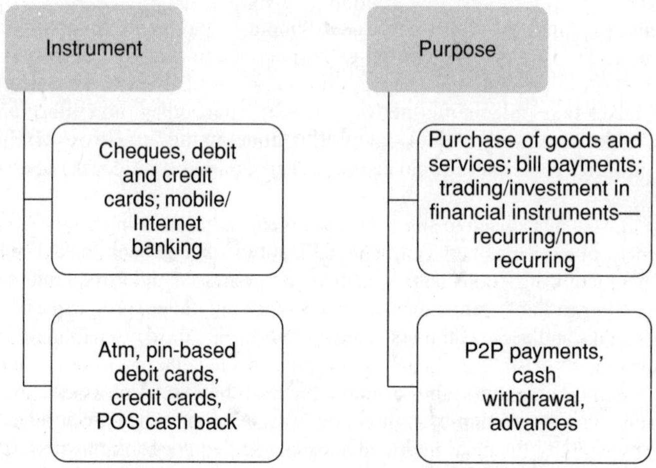

To achieve the purposes shown in Figure 16.3, retail customers can resort to paper-based clearing and settlement or electronic payment and settlement, as shown in Figure 16.2.

The paper-based payment and settlement mechanisms in vogue in India are as follows:

- Magnetic Ink Character Recognition (MICR) and non-MICR cheques
- High-value clearing
- Speed clearing of cheques drawn on outstation CBS branches of drawee bank processed in local clearing
- Cheque truncation

The Electronic clearing and settlement systems being operated are as follows:

- Electronic Clearing Service (ECS), National Electronic Clearing Service (NECS)
- Electronic Funds Transfer (EFT)
- National Electronic Funds Transfer (NEFT)

Chart 16.1 shows the progress of electronic transaction over paper-based transactions. While the volume of electronic transactions has grown over the years, the value of electronic transactions has far exceeded paper-based transactions during this period. One obvious inference is that electronic transactions have become more popular in high-value transactions than in retail payment systems.

CHART 16.1 PAYMENT AND SETTLEMENT SYSTEMS IN INDIA—GROWTH IN PAPER-BASED VERSUS ELECTRONIC TRANSACTIONS

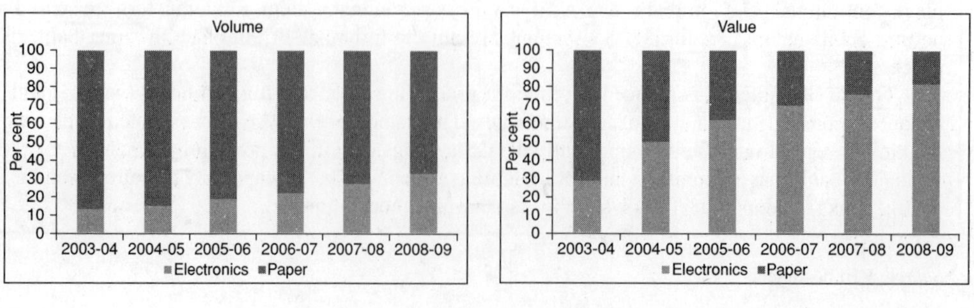

Paper-Based Instruments in Retail Payment Systems—An Overview

1. **Cheques**: The most common form of notational money[2] is an account with cheque facility. A cheque is an order authorizing the transfer of money from one account to another. When a cheque is accepted as payment, the recipient's bank collects the value of the cheque after presenting it to the bank on which it is drawn. Cheques can be returned for insufficient funds. The person who wrote the cheque can stop payment on it by notifying the bank that holds the account if a cheque is lost or stolen. Apart from cheques as described above, there are *banker's cheques* and *demand drafts*, which are special kinds of cheques. A banker's cheque is drawn by a bank on its own funds. It is a direct obligation of the bank—hence individual consumers cannot write banker's cheques. A demand draft is guaranteed to be good by the bank on which it is drawn. Both banker's cheques and demand drafts are considered insured deposits.

   Traveller's cheques are also included in a bank's net transaction accounts and are subject to reserve requirements.[3] Traveller's cheques issued by a bank are covered by deposit insurance.

   The clearing and settlement of cheques drawn on different banks necessitates banks in the area coming together for transfer of funds and final settlement. This is done through 'clearing houses' at various centres. Further, where the process was manual hitherto, as in the 1029 non-MICR clearing houses at various centres, Magnetic Media-based clearing system is also implemented.

   The clearing and settlement process takes two days—on day 1, the cheques are presented at the clearing house, and on day 2, the funds are settled or cheques returned.

   The volume and value of paper-based cheques have been increasing over the years, but at a declining rate, presumably due to the impact of electronic payment systems (see Table 16.1).
2. **Magnetic Ink Character Recognition (MICR)**: Magnetic Ink Character Recognition is a character recognition system that uses special ink and character. The cheque, which contains this ink, needs to be read, and passed through a machine, which magnetizes the ink and then translates the magnetic information into characters. Banks use MICR technology on cheques, which provides secure, high-speed method of scanning and processing information.
3. **Speed clearing**: This new clearing arrangement was introduced in India in 2008 for collection of outstation cheques through local clearing, provided such cheques were drawn on 'core banking'[4] solution (CBS) enabled branches of paying banks. Cheques drawn on outstation CBS branches of a bank can be processed in local clearing, thus, reducing the time taken for realization of outstation cheques, thus enabling payment on a (T + 1) or (T + 2) basis. Speed clearing had been introduced at 53 centres as of March 2009.
4. **High-value clearing**: This is a paper-based clearing for large value payments, currently operational at 27 major cities. The clearing process is completed on the same day for cheques of ₹1 lakh and above payable in the same city. This means that the cheque proceeds will be received and can be withdrawn by the beneficiary the same day. Table 16.1 shows the volume of transactions in SIPS in India. It can be seen that while the value of transactions handled is much lower compared with RTGS, the number of transactions is much higher. However, with RTGS picking up, high-value clearing process may be gradually phased out. As a first step, a decision has been taken by the RBI that no new high-value clearing centres would be opened.

TABLE 16.1[5] COMPARISON OF TRANSACTIONS UNDER SIPS

System	Name of the System	Number of Participants	Daily Volume of Transactions Handled (Number)	Average Value per Transaction Settled (in ₹ lakh)	Daily Value of Transactions Handled (in ₹ crore)
1.	High Value	All participants in paper-based clearing systems	91,438	284	26.042
2.	RTGS	105	23.481	4.620	1,08,700

Source: Reserve Bank of India.

5. **Cheque truncation**: We have seen from the discussion above that the use of electronic payment systems is increasing due to the advantages that such systems offer to the customer. However, since paper-based payment systems continue to be used in a big way, cheque truncation was introduced to speed up the process of cheque clearing, and thus reduce the cost of transit or possibility of loss of cheque in transit, thus enhancing customer service.

Truncation is the process of stopping the transit of a paper-based cheque from the drawer to the drawee branch of a bank. The physical cheque will be 'truncated' at some point en route to the drawee branch, and would be replaced by an electronic image of the cheque. Cheque truncation, thus is a more secure alternative to the actual movement of physical instruments from place to place.

Cheque truncation has been introduced in the national capital region (NCR), New Delhi on a pilot basis, and will be extended to more centres. The process is expected to be more efficient and cost effective, especially in the case of clearing and settlement of outstation cheques.

Member banks of clearing house in the NCR and INFINET can participate in the cheque truncation system.

Electronic Retail Payment Systems—An Overview

Electronic Clearing Service (ECS)

Bulk and repetitive payments like interest/dividend are mostly paper-based involving printing of warrants (in costly MICR format), dispatching them by post and reconciliation thereof after payment by the agency banks. The difficulties are as follows:

- It requires an expensive administrative machinery for printing, dispatching and reconciliation.
- Bunching of a large number of instruments in clearing results in operational bottlenecks and pressures on the cheque processing system.
- Chances of loss of instruments in transit and their fraudulent encashment.
- The customer has also to keep track of the receipt/non-receipt of the instrument and take efforts to deposit the instrument with the bank on receipt of the same.
- Banks find processing of such a large volume of instruments not only error prone and monotonous, but also a strain on the cheque clearing system.

ECS is a retail payment system that facilitates bulk payments (such as dividend payment) and bulk receipts (such as utility payments). These two aspects are handled by two components of the system—ECS (credit) and ECS (debit). The facility is available at 75 major centres as of 2009.

- **ECS (Credit):** ECS (Credit) facilitates bulk payments, where an institution makes payment to several retail customers. Examples are payment of dividend/interest warrants to investors, payment of salaries to employees and so on. In such cases, it follows that the account of the institution remitting the payment should be debited and the payments remitted to beneficiaries' accounts. Hence, the company or entity making the payment has to have the bank account details of the individual beneficiaries.
- **ECS (Debit):** ECS (Debit) is the opposite of ECS (credit). Here, many individuals/ firms pay to one firm or utility. Thus, the accounts of various customers of the utility in different banks have to be debited and the amounts have to be credited to the utility company's account with designated banks. Using a specific mandate, the utility can also advise the customers' banks to debit payments on due dates.

  Settlement in this system currently takes place on (T + 0) basis and the cycle gets completed on (T + 1) basis. The clearing and settlement transactions through ECS occur at the respective centres.
- **ECS (Centralized):** A third facility called the NECS is centralized and available at the Reserve Bank, Mumbai. NECS-Credit, like ECS (credit), facilitates multiple credits to beneficiary accounts at destination branches across the country against a single debit in the account of a user with the sponsor bank from a single central location at Mumbai. Similarly, the NECS-Debit would facilitate multiple debits to destination account holders across the country against a single credit to the user account at Mumbai. The NECS is a nationwide system leveraging on CBS of member banks. All CBS bank branches are participants in the system, irrespective of their location. As of 31 March 2009, as many as 114 banks with 26,275 branches participated in NECS.

The ECS systems works in the following steps:

Step 1: The corporate body institution (called user) which has to make payments to a large number of customers/ investors would prepare the payment data on a magnetic media (*i.e.*, tape or floppy) and submit the same to its banker (sponsor bank).

Step 2: The sponsor bank would present the payment data to the local bankers' clearing house (managed by the Reserve Bank of India at 15 centres and by the State Bank of India or associate banks at 31 other centres) authorizing the manager of the clearing house to debit the sponsor bank's account and credit the accounts (destination bank) of the banks where the beneficiaries of the transactions maintain their accounts.

Step 3: On receiving this authorization, the clearing house will process the data and work out an inter-bank funds settlement.

Step 4: The clearing house will furnish to the service branches of the destination banks branch-wise credit reports indicating the beneficiary details, such as the names of the branches where the accounts are maintained, the names of the beneficiaries, account type, account numbers and the respective amounts.

Step 5: The service branches will, in turn, pass on the advices to the concerned branches of their bank, which will credit the beneficiaries' accounts on the appointed date.

Benefit to an organization: The ECS system offers following benefits to an organization.

- Savings in administrative cost presently being incurred for printing of paper instruments in MICR format and dispatching them by registered post.
- Loss of instruments in transit or fraudulent encashment thereof totally eliminated.
- Reconciliation of transactions is made automatic. By the time the ECS cycle is completed, the user institution gets an electronic data file from its bank with the date of payment and banker's confirmation thereon.
- Cash management becomes easier as arrangement for funds is required to be made only on the specified date.
- Ensuring better customer/investor service.
- Paying the way the best companies in the world pay to their shareholders/investors and customers.

Benefit to the customer: The ECS system offers following benefits to the customers.

- Payment on the due date.
- Effortless receipt—no need to visit the bank to deposite the dividend/interest warrant.
- Probability of loss of instrument in transit or fraudulent encashment thereof and consequent correspondence with the company are completely eliminated.

Electronic Funds Transfer (EFT) and National Electronic Funds Transfer (NEFT)

Electronic funds transfer system was introduced by RBI in 1997 as an inter-city, intra-city and inter-bank, intra-bank fund transfer mechanism by which funds can be transferred by any bank branch to any other bank branch from one city to another. EFTs process pre-authorized debits or credits from one bank account to another within a 48-hour period. It is similar to standing instructions maintained in customers' accounts, which are carried out automatically at pre-appointed dates.

First, customers have to sign a form that authorizes the bank to deduct their payment on a certain date. Details, such as the payee and beneficiary's account, amount and date are programmed into the account. According to the billing cycle, the amount of customers' bill is then automatically debited from their checking account and deposited into the payees' account. In the case of payroll, the account is debited and employee's account is credited for each pay period.

The key benefits of EFTs are as follows.

- For receivables, benefits include prompt payment of customers' bills each month and early notice of insufficient funds. While there is a small fee per transaction for this service, EFTs eliminate the need to print, process and send a monthly bill in many instances. It is estimated that an EFT can save as much as USD 2.25 to USD 3.00 or more per customer. Thus, it lowers labour cost to prepare statements as well as postage and the cost of paper used to print statements. EFTs also reduce late payments and the need to send out reminder notices.
- EFTs can actually increase customer retention. This is most likely to occur in businesses that bill the same amount on a month-to-month basis for ongoing services, such as pest control companies, newspapers, pool services, security companies and the like. Having the fee automatically deducted from the customer's checking account increases the retention of those who might otherwise let the service lapse.
- It saves on billing and administrative costs, dramatically improves cash flow and eliminates many collection hassles.

The EFT system was replaced in November 2005 by the NEFT, an electronic message-based payment system using Public Key Infrastructure[6] technology to ensure end to end security. NEFT uses the INFINET to connect bank branches for electronic transfer of funds. NEFT was available at about 63,000 branches of various banks at the end of 2009. To make NEFT more retail customer friendly, RBI has permitted initiation of transactions by accepting cash from walk in customers (earlier account to account transfers were mandatory), permitting credit card payments and extending settlement time. These measures have yielded tangible results in the forms of sizeable increase in retail electronic fund transfers during 2008–09 (please see Table 16.1). Several changes/upgraded versions of the software and security features are being released periodically by RBI.

Participants in the clearing and settlement process: Information technology has revolutionized the way payments and settlements are being done throughout the world. The Indian system has also seen several innovations, in line with international recommendations and standards (see Box 16.1), though some of them are yet to penetrate the entire market.

Box 16.3 provides an overview of the various participants in the clearing and settlement process

BOX 16.3[7] MAIN PARTICIPANTS IN THE CLEARING AND SETTLEMENT PROCESS

Clearing corporation: The clearing corporation is responsible for post-trade activities such as the risk management, confirmation, delivery and settlement of trades executed on a stock exchange.
Clearing members: Clearing members are responsible for settling these obligations as determined by the clearing house/ clearing corporation. They do so by making available funds and/or securities in the designated accounts with clearing bank/ depositories on the date of settlement.
Custodians: Custodians are clearing members but not trading members. They settle trades on behalf of trading members, when a particular trade is assigned to them for settlement. The custodian is required to confirm whether he is going to settle that trade or not. If he confirms to settle the trade, then clearing corporation assigns that particular obligation to him.
Clearing banks: Clearing banks are a key link between the clearing members and clearing corporation/house to effect settlement of funds. Every clearing member is required to open a dedicated clearing account with one of the designated clearing banks. Based on the clearing member's obligation as determined through clearing, the clearing member makes funds available in the clearing account for the pay-in and receives funds in case of a pay-out.
Depositories: Depository holds securities in dematerialized form for the investors in their beneficiary accounts. Each clearing member is required to maintain a clearing pool account with the depositories. He is required to make available the required securities in the designated account on settlement day. The depository runs an electronic file to transfer the securities from accounts of the custodians/clearing member to that of clearing corporation/house and viceversa as per the schedule of allocation of securities.
Professional clearing member: NSCCL admits special category of members known as professional clearing members (PCMs). PCMs may clear and settle trades excuted for their clients (individuals, institutions, etc). In such cases, the functions and responsibilities of the PCM are similar to that of the custodians. PCMs also undertake clearing and settlement responsibilities of the trading members. The PCM in this case has no trading rights, but has clearing rights, *i.e.*, he clears the trades of his associate trading members and institutional clients.

Source: RBI documents.

SECTION IV

PLASTIC MONEY AND E-MONEY

Plastic money refers to substitution of currency at the time when a payment is taking place by using a card normally made of plastic (hence the name, plastic cards) representing such substitution.

There can be several objectives for such substitution. Most important among these would be the need to postpone actual payment, or pre-purchase payment on the card that is issued. Whatever be the objective, the most important advantage of plastic money is protection to the user from the risks of carrying cash. Since it is the exclusive property of the cardholder, it means that it can be used only by him.

The prevalent types of plastic money are:

- Credit Cards
- Debit Cards
- Other payment channels/products

Credit Cards

Credit cards started off as a type of payment cards issued by some merchants for the convenience of their customers. It is believed that the first such card was issued by Sears in 1910, which was quickly emulated by other retailers who issued cards containing vital information about the customer, which was recorded when the card was put through a processing device. The popular 'Diner's Club' card was introduced in 1949 to be used in multiple restaurants that were willing to participate in the scheme. It is to be noted here that these cards had to be paid in full each month, and, therefore, had very little 'credit' or 'loan' component to them.

Today, credit cards are synonymous with a form of short term, revolving credit to the cardholder. As pointed out in the chapter on bank lending, a revolving credit replenishes automatically when loan installments are met. For typical card accounts in the form of revolving credit, the cardholders are billed monthly for purchases made with the credit card. Every month, cardholders have the option of paying back the entire outstanding amount on the credit card, or the minimum payment stipulated, say 2 per cent or 3 per cent of the outstanding balance. Typically, a grace period of about a month or more is granted, during which no interest will be charged on the 'loan'. Cardholders who pay the minimum amount every month are considered current on their account. If one payment is not made on time, the account would be considered delinquent after a predetermined period. Hence, it is evident that credit card is very similar to a loan account with a bank.

Credit cards can be issued through various channels. The most common are 'general purpose' cards, such as Visa or MasterCard. These are accepted by most merchants/retailers. It is also the practice of individual banks to issue co-branded cards with Visa or Master network.

Credit cards can be broadly classified into three types. These are as follows:

1. Bank cards, *i.e.*, MasterCard, Visa, Maestro, etc.—This type of cards are sponsored by individual banks and considered all-purpose cards. Each bank decides credit limits, annual fees, terms and conditions.
2. Travel and Entertainment cards, *e.g.*, American Express or Diner's Club—This type of cards are used by people for travel and entertainment expenses. In many cases, unlike credit cards, cardholders are expected to pay the balance outstanding in full every month. Hence, while credit cards permit users to carry balances over several months, provided the minimum payment is made every month, 'travel and entertainment' cardholders will have to pay back the 'credit' in 1 or 2 months at most.
3. Company or Retail Store cards, such as Walmart, Reliance, BP, Shell or Mobil—This type of cards are used in the retail store or gas station. These are issuer-specific and cannot be used for all purposes as can be done for bank-issued credit cards.

The Parties to Credit Card Transactions

The following are the principal players in credit card transactions:

- Card issuers
- Card holders/users
- Member establishments (MEs)
- Member affiliates (MAs)
- Clearing agencies
- Credit card affiliates

The role of each party in credit card transactions is described briefly in the following paragraphs:

- **Card issuers:** Card issuers are predominantly banks. Almost all banks today offer credit card services to retail customers. Credit card business is attractive to banks because of the potentially high returns. For example, banks charge member establishments (ME) a commission of about 2 per cent. To customers, banks offer a credit period of about 45 days, but charge at the rate of say 2.5 per cent per month on the entire outstanding amount at the end of the credit period. Thus, on a single purchase through a credit card, assuming the customer does not pay within the credit period, the bank can earn up to 4.5–5 per cent per month, which is a significant 55–60 per cent per year. From our discussion on corporate lending in earlier chapters, it is clear that banks do not earn such high returns on other types of advances.

  Of course, credit cards also mean cost to the bank—the cost of marketing the credit cards, making of the card with tamper proof features, credit information, processing, investigation, follow up to recover receivables, bad debt losses at the other end of the spectrum—that can be quite high.

- **Card holders:** The cardholders or users could be individuals or business entities. As for other types of lending, the amount that can be drawn against the credit card is based on creditworthiness criteria. After his account gets approved by the credit issuer bank, the customer is issued a credit card, with which the customer would be able to make purchases from merchants accepting that credit card up to a pre-established credit limit.
- **Member Establishments (ME):** These are the establishments/ merchants who accept valid credit cards as payment for goods/services, in place of cash. MEs can be large retail establishments, restaurants, hospitals, gas filling stations, travel agencies—in short, any entity which can generate a good volume of business to justify usage of credit cards. As mentioned earlier, MEs will have to pay a 'fee' in the form of commission for every credit card payment they accept. Sometimes, this fee is passed on to the cardholder, which implies that the cardholder pays more for usage of the card.
- **Member Affiliates (MA):** A large organization that wishes to issue credit cards in its name without investing in the elaborate infrastructure for servicing credit cards may opt for the 'affiliate' route. The affiliate enters into an agreement with a card issuer, who authorizes the affiliate to issue credit cards in its name, along with that of the original issuer. Many large hotel chains are MAs. The other kind of affiliate arrangement could happen between banks as well.
- **Clearing agencies or card associations:** Mastercard international and Visa international are the two leading international card issuers who also act as clearing agencies. The card issuers associate themselves with one of these agencies to enable the cardholder of one affiliate to use the card at the member establishment of another affiliate. They are also called 'credit card affiliates' when the logos of both the clearing agency and the issuer are embossed on the face of the card.

Box 16.4 describes how credit card settlements are made in practice where affiliates are involved.

BOX 16.4 SETTLEMENTS PROCESS THROUGH CREDIT CARD NETWORKS

When a purchase is made, the credit card holder agrees to pay the card issuer. The cardholder gives his or her consent to pay, by signing a receipt with a record of the card details and indicating the amount to be paid or by entering a Personal Identification Number (PIN). Also, many merchants now accept verbal authorizations in person or via telephone and electronic authorization using the Internet, known as a Card Not Present (CNP) transaction.

Electronic verification systems allow merchants to verify, almost immediately, that the card is valid and the credit card customer has sufficient credit to cover the purchase. The verification is performed using a credit card payment terminal or Point of Sale (POS) system with a communications link to the merchant's acquiring bank. Data from the card is obtained from a magnetic stripe or chip on the card.

The process works as follows:

Step 1: A Visa or MasterCard cardholder makes a purchase from an ME.
Step 2: The ME transmits the transaction information to his bank—called the 'acquirer'. The acquirer contacts the card-issuing bank with the details through the card association (Master or Visa) requesting authorization of the transaction.
Step 3: The card-issuing bank verifies that the transaction is bona fide, and passing the transaction would keep the outstanding balance on the card within sanctioned limits. Thereafter, the transaction is authorized.
Step 4: The ME now requests for payment from his bank, which in turn, routes the request to the card association.
Step 5: The card association processes the request for payment with the acquirer and the issuer, and requests the issuer to make payment.
Step 6: The card association forwards payment to the acquirer, after deducting its fees for mediation, as well as the issuer's fee for the transaction
Step 7: The issuing bank transmits funds (less its fee) to the card association
Step 8: The acquirer pays the ME for the cardholder's purchase, after deducting its fee.
Step 9: The cardholder gets his monthly statement from the issuing bank at the end of the billing cycle, reflecting the payment to the ME.

How Do Credit Card Issuers Make Money?

There are three main sources of income for credit card issuers—fees paid by MEs, interest on cardholder balances and other fees charged to cardholders. A Visa or Mastercard affiliation involves more than a simple transaction between customer and the ME, as we can see from the process described above. In this case, the issuing bank takes a major share of the merchant's discount (say ₹1.50 out of ₹2 on every ₹100 transaction), while the acquiring bank would take ₹0.50. Apart from interest payable by the cardholder on unpaid balances on the credit card, the issuing bank earns from other charges, such as annual charges, penalty fees for late payments, over the limit transactions, fees for cash advances and so on.

The 'expenses' of credit card issuers can be classified into four main categories—(a) marketing and operations that account for a bulk of the expenses; (b) cost of funds (see chapter on loan pricing); (c) losses due to delinquencies or write-offs where outstanding balances could not be recovered; and (d) losses due to frauds. (We will discuss 'Internet frauds' in the following section.).

The marketing and operations expenses increase as card issuers compete to differentiate themselves in the market. It is not uncommon to see and own cards with additional benefits such as insurance coverage, purchase protection, rewards or points-based programmes and cash back offers.

It can thus be seen that while credit card companies do levy hefty charges on their customers, their profitability will have to be monitored closely due to the possibility of expenses shooting up due to competition and other factors. As discussed in our earlier chapter on 'Loan pricing,' since the delinquency rates are high, they have to be compensated by higher risk premiums, translating into higher interest rates.

Credit Cards—Benefits

To summarize, the following benefits accrue to customers from the usage of credit cards:

(a) Deferred payment of bills
(b) Revolving credit
(c) Rewards from card issuers

The benefits to merchants are as follows:

(a) Immediate payment
(b) Assured payment
(c) Increased consumer spending

Debit Cards

To a customer, credit and debit cards may be look-alikes. Both are almost the same size, provide the same payment function and may also carry the Master/Visa card logo that makes them acceptable at merchant establishments where credit cards are accepted. But debit cards are quite different from credit cards.

If credit cards advocate 'pay later', debit cards signify 'pay now'. The debit card is a product through which the customer's own account with the card issuer is debited immediately to the extent of the transaction value. Further, the debit card does not allow the customer to 'borrow', nor does it provide 'revolving credit'.

Since debit cards do not provide the 'benefits' provided by credit cards, why would customers prefer them?

Customers who prefer debit cards do so because they do not want to go into debt for their necessary or luxury purchases. Customers cannot spend beyond what their account holds. More importantly, there is no monthly billing or interest charges.

The debit card programme requires a 'POS' terminal at the member establishment. The debit card, behind which there is a magnetic strip, is inserted into the machine by the customer at the time of billing for purchases made. The merchant keys in the transaction amount. There are two types of debit system followed at the point of payment—one a 'signature-based' card, where the customer swipes the card and signs the sales receipt, and the second a 'PIN-based' transaction.

The PIN is known only to the cardholder and the issuing bank. Once the PIN is entered, the machine places an automatic call to the bank, checks the balance in the customer's account, and reduces the balance to the extent of the transaction value. The merchant's account is credited for the transaction value.

Benefits to Customers

The following are the benefits enjoyed by the customers:

- Payment convenience and safety: The customer does not have to carry a cheque-book or large sums of cash.
- Wide acceptance: Debit cards are more widely accepted than cheques. They are suited for online shopping and travel.
- Easier qualification: Since debit cards use the customer's own money, not his credit, they are often easier to get than credit cards.

Benefits to Merchants

Benefits to the merchants are as follows:

- Fast approvals: Authorized transactions in seconds.
- Fraud prevention: Purchase amounts are 100 per cent authorized at the POS, reducing losses due to fraudulent checks
- Increased sales: Statistics show the average ticket sale is increased with debit acceptance.
- Minimum investment and charges: Involves adding a low-cost PIN pad that works with existing equipment. Merchants prefer PIN-based debit cards since the charges are lower.
- Security: Online debit transactions are encrypted to protect the integrity of the cardholder's personal banking information.
- Cash management: Funds are available sooner than with personal cheques. Debit transactions are funded within 2–3 days of batch settlement

The key differences between debit and credit cards are summarized in Table 16.2.

TABLE 16.2 KEY POINTS OF DIFFERENCE BETWEEN CREDIT AND DEBIT CARDS

Feature	Credit Cards	Debit Cards
Payment terms	Deferred	Immediate debit to customer's account
Credit	Around 45 days; typically structured as revolving credit	No credit, immediate debit
Account with issuing bank	Not required	Essential
Access to deposit account with card-issuing bank	No access	Direct access to current or savings account
Technology	Required	POS terminal at merchant's establishment
Risks	Default risk; fraud risk	Risk minimized through PIN-based system

Credit and Debit Cards in India

The data shows a deceleration in growth rates of both credit and debit cards (volume and value) in 2008–09, presumably a reflection of the global credit crisis and the consequent economic slowdown. More remarkable is the fact that the decline is more marked in the case of credit cards than in debit cards, evidencing the reluctance of the Indian consumer to spend on consumer goods on credit. Another noteworthy feature is that debit cards are primarily value-added ATM (ATM, defined later in the chapter) cards. As a result, while the number of debit cards in circulation are substantially higher than the number of credit cards, the number of transactions recorded using debit cards at POS terminals (used for purchases) are very low. The debit cards are mainly used as ATM cards. This is reflected in the fact that the monthly usage of debit cards at ATM machines is around 179 million and the number of transaction at POS terminals is 8.7 million in March 2008.

Other Payment Channels/Products

Automated Teller Machines (ATM)

Despite the development of electronic payment systems, customers still prefer cash for various transactions. Cash delivery is increasingly being done on the huge base of Automated Teller Machines (ATMs), which are being increasingly networked together to permit customers to collect cash from different banks as well as in other countries. ATM and credit card networks are linked in, and VISA and MasterCard holders have long enjoyed the facility to draw cash from ATMs. ATM networks are increasingly being developed by non-banking organizations as well.

As ATMs gain popularity, banks in India have started looking at alternative uses for the investment made. Some banks have tapped the vast potential of ATM structures to provide innovative and value-added services to customers, such as funds transfers, bill payment services, mobile phone recharge and so on.

Mobile Banking

The rapid spread of the 'mobile phone' era has helped banks use this mode for transactions. Mobile banking can be used for small-value payments at relatively lower costs, and, therefore is being used in many developing countries as a delivery channel to facilitate financial inclusion.[8] In countries where mobile banking has been introduced, there are two distinct models that can be operated—the bank-led and telecom company-led models. India has adopted the bank-led model, while the telecom company led-model may be preferred in countries with relatively lower coverage of formal banking facilities (an example of this being Kenya).

RBI provided guidelines for mobile banking transactions in India in October 2008. The salient features of these guidelines are (a) banks have to obtain RBI approval for providing mobile banking facility to customers, (b) the facility can be provided only in Indian rupees to the banks' own customers, or holders of debit/credit cards, and (c) banks should adhere to prescribed technology and security standards and limits set. The guidelines also mandate inter-operability among service providers, so that monopolistic practices by a few operators are avoided.

Prepaid Payment Instruments

These are payment instruments, such as smart cards, magnetic strip cards, Internet accounts, Internet wallets, mobile accounts, mobile wallets and so on, where value is stored in advance to be used when required. The 'value stored' is the value paid by cash, debit or credit card by the instrument holder. Purchase of goods and services is made against the stored value in the prepaid instruments. Hence, these instruments serve as a convenient and relatively risk-free mode of payment in lieu of cash, and for e-payments through Internet/mobile. More than convenience or efficiency, the safety and security of these payment instruments and the underlying technology have to be ensured.

The flow of information and funds for a generic stored value card is provided in Box 16.5.

BOX 16.5 FLOW OF INFORMATION AND FUNDS IN A GENERIC 'STORED-VALUE' CARD (SMART CARDS)

Assume the customer buys a stored-value card, say a Petro card, with cash or with a debit or credit card. The purchase of the card sets off a chain of settlement transactions. When the customer pays with a stored-value card, the system transfers electronic notations, or tokens, from the card to the merchant's electronic cash register. The merchant periodically contacts the computer network connected to the bank issuing the stored-value cards and presents the tokens for payment. The network then informs the customer's bank to pay the amount of purchase to the merchant's bank, and the two banks make a net settlement. The banks keep a percentage of the payment (the discount) as compensation for the services they and the networks have provided.

These and other issues have been addressed in the RBI guidelines for 'Issuance and operation of prepaid instruments in India' dated 27 April 2009 that can be accessed at the RBI Web site.

The salient features of these guidelines are summarized as follows:

- The prepaid instruments are categorized as: (a) closed payment instruments; (b) semi-closed instruments (c) semi-open; and (d) open payment instruments.
- Closed system payment instruments, for which examples are gift vouchers issued by certain merchants, or prepaid mobile services or telephone-calling cards. It is evident that these instruments are intended for exclusive use at the specified establishment or for availing services from a service provider. These instruments typically cannot be reloaded (except mobile services) or redeemed, nor do they permit cash withdrawals. As these instruments do not facilitate payments and settlement for third party services, issue and operation of such instruments are not classified as payment systems.
- Semi-closed system payment instruments are similar to closed instruments, except that they have wider scope of operation. Examples are instruments generally issued by third party service providers, such as those redeemable at a group of establishments (associated say with a particular shopping mall, or tourist resorts or

other establishments) specified by the issuer. The establishments have entered into specific contracts with the issuer to accept the payment instruments. These instruments can be issued in reloadable or non-reloadable formats but do not permit cash withdrawals.

- Semi-open and open system payment instruments are basically in the nature of credit/debit cards that can be used for purchase of goods and services at any card-accepting merchant locations/POS terminals. They can be issued in reloadable and non-reloadable formats. The essential difference is that semi open instruments do not provide the option of cash withdrawal, while open payment systems do.
- Banks can issue all categories of prepaid cards, and non-banks/NBFCs can issue semi closed system prepaid instruments, provided the preconditions stipulated by RBI are fulfilled. Other eligible issuers can issue only closed system instruments.
- Semi-open and open instruments are vulnerable to frauds and misuse. Hence, safeguards should be in place to prevent money laundering and other types of misuse.
- The prepaid card should have minimum validity of 6 months from date of issue/activation.
- The maximum value for which a prepaid card can be issued is ₹50,000.
- The money collected against issue of such instruments would be substantial. But, since it is payable to merchants and others with whom the instrument holders transact, the money received by the issuer should be treated as 'float' money and invested in liquid, near cash and safe investments. Where banks are the issuers, the money collected is treated as part of NDTL for the purpose of reserve maintenance.[9] If the issuers are non-banks, they will have to maintain the outstanding balance in an 'escrow account'[10] with a commercial bank. The escrow account is intended only for making payments to participating merchant establishments—hence, banks do not pay interest on these balances, and cannot grant loans against these funds.

SECTION V

SECURITY ISSUES IN E-BANKING

It is evident that e-banking is here to stay. However, the advent of high technology has also brought with it new operational risks in the form of security risks. The safety of banks, the integrity of the country's payment and settlement systems, and the trust that customers impose in the safety of the system are all intertwined to ultimately contribute to financial stability. The challenge for the future will be to identify and address risks to banking safety and security without hampering technological innovations in banking.

Internet-banking has evolved into a mass market product—an essential service whose quality can affect the customers' loyalty to and satisfaction with their bank. And, not surprisingly, it is Internet-banking that is posing the gravest risk to banks' viability and sustenance. Hackers and fraudsters have realized the immense potential of Internet-banking to give them ill-gotten monetary gains.

Therefore, as new technologies evolve to make banking faster and more convenient for customers, the concerns about e-payment security have increased. The 'conventional' risks of unauthorized access, identity theft or network attacks have been exacerbated by 'contemporary' threats—phishing and pharming, spear phishing, carding and skimming, crimeware and spyware, money laundering, mules, scams, spams, Nigerian advance fee fraud—and still counting.

Real Life Example 1

Nordea lost more than $1,000,000 in aggregate due to a sophisticated malware attack, which recorded user's account details and sent them to fraudsters. These transfers were made in several small amounts between 2005 and 2007, in order to circumvent the bank's fraud detection mechanisms

Often inadequately protected, personal computers are the first point of attack for cyber criminals. Users are attracted to various offers that seem to be coming in from their banks and fall prey to Internet fraud.

Source: The example was accessed at www.cronto.com

The most prevalent types of Internet frauds are discussed as follows:

1. ***Identity Thefts*** In the virtual world, a person's identity is defined by the user name, passwords or account names. Identity theft is the misuse of personal data or documents in order to impersonate another individual to carry out illegal or fraudulent activities, *e.g.*, to abuse the victim's banking facilities or other assets. Especially affected are popular transaction types, such as card transactions at ATMs, online banking transactions or the use of credit card numbers for Internet payments.

   Some of the largest identity thefts have happened in the US (Table 16.3), as reported by McAfee.

TABLE 16.3[11] LARGEST DATA LOSS INCIDENTS IN THE US (MCAFEE)

Records Exposed	Duration	Date Reported	Organizations	Origin
94,000,000	July 2000–December 2006	17 January 2007	TJX Companies	Deficiencies in the wireless network allowed the data theft
40,000,000	September 2004–May 2005	19 June 2005	CardSystems, Visa, Master-Card, American Express	Malicious script injected via a web application
50,000,000	April 2003–April 2004	24 June 2004	America Online	Data stolen by employees and sold to spammers
26,500,000	3 May 2006	22 May 2006	U.S. Department of Veterans Affairs	Personal data on a laptop computer stolen during a burglary
25,000,000	October 2007	20 November 2007	HM Revenue and Customs, TNT	Loss of two CDs
17,000,000	2006–2008	5 October 2008	T-Mobile, Deutsche Telekom	Data stolen and found online for sale
12,500,000	27 February 2008	7 May 2008	Archive Systems, Bank of New York Mellon	Loss of unencrypted tapes
11,000,000	July–Aug. 2008	6 September 2008	GS Caltex	Employees made copies of personal data to sell
8,637,405	May 2001–March 2006	12 March 2007	Dai Nippon Printing Company	Data stolen by a former contract worker and sold to a criminal group
8,500,000	2002–June 2007	3 July 2007	Certegy Check Services, Fidelity National Information Services	Data stolen by employee and sold to a third party for marketing purposes

Source: McAfee Avert Labs.

Real Life Example 2

Stephen Watt was a member of a conspiracy which, between 2003 and 2008, unlawfully gained electronic access to corporate computer networks using various techniques, downloaded customers' credit and debit card information, and fraudulently used that information and sold the information to others for fraudulent use. Watt modified and provided a 'sniffer' program used by the conspirators to monitor and capture the data crossing TJX's computer network.

Watt pleaded guilty to conspiracy charges on 28 October 2008. He was sentenced to 2 years' imprisonment, to be followed by 3 years of supervised release, a condition of which was electronic monitoring of any computer use. He was ordered to pay restitution in the amount of $171.5 million dollars.

Source: US Department of Justice, accessed at www.usdoj.gov/criminal/cybecrime

2. ***Carding/Skimming*** 'Carding' sites can be found on the Internet, where fraudsters buy and sell access to bank accounts, stolen card numbers, dumps from magnetic strips and even personal profiles.

   'Skimming' constitutes the unnoticed duplication of electronic data from a payment card. A copying device is installed in front of the original card slot of an ATM, which transcribes the information from the magnetic stripe on a card inserted by a customer. Sometimes these devices could be a camera or a fake touch pad to duplicate the keystrokes used for password entry.

The vital information obtained by these methods enables fraudsters to easily create duplicate cards and withdraw money from the accounts in question. Instances of skimming can also occur at cash registers.

Real Life Example 3

In May 2008, McAfee[12] found a set of bank accounts for sale. The most expensive was also the most highly funded: an account at European bank BNP Paribas with a balance of €30,792, selling online for just €2,200. In addition to the discounted rate, the seller offered a 24-hour guarantee: if the buyer could not log in within that period or if the account no longer contained the money, a replacement account would be provided!

Source: McAfee

3. ***Phishing*** 'Phishing' is a famous word these days—signifying fraudulent capture and recording of customers' security details, to be used later for committing fraud. It originates from the analogy that Internet fraudsters are using email lures to 'fish' for passwords and financial data from myriads of Internet users.

   Phishing can take on several forms such as the following:

   - *Email phishing* signifies creation of email messages and web pages that exactly resemble existing sites in order to deceive users to part with financial, personal or password data to fraudsters.
   - *Pharming* is the use of malware/ spyware to redirect Internet users from genuine Web sites to fraudulent ones. It carries out modifications in the name resolution system, such that when a user opens the Web site of his bank, it actually takes the user to the fraudulent Web site.
   - *Spear phishing* is a highly targeted phishing attack that focuses on a whole group—such as employees of a certain firm, government agency or organization. The message would appear as though it is generated by the employer, asking for updating of passwords or any other personal information. Spear phishing could, therefore, gain access and wreak havoc on an entire company's computer system.
   - *Phlash phishing* uses Macromedia Flash to build an entire Web site. The use of Flash is intended to make it more difficult to determine whether or not the page is malicious, and could also bypass antiphishing toolbars.
   - *Vishing* (voice phishing) may begin with an email or telephone call. The email warns that the user's bank account has been cyber attacked and, therefore the user has to call a certain telephone number, which will ask for the account number and other details. The phone call version purports to be even more authentic. The caller already knows the user's credit card number and asks for the valuable 3-digit code at the back of the card. Such calls can be set up quickly and automatically by voice over Internet protocols (VoIP).
   - *Man in middle* attacks (phishing in sessions) is a rapidly growing threat to online banking security. Fake Web sites are set up to closely replicate the bank's authentic Web sites. The bank customer receives an email purportedly from the bank, asking the customer to click on a link provided on the bank 'Web site'. Once this is done, the customer is automatically taken to the fake bank Web site. In another approach, the customer's Internet connection is already tampered with; hence, when the customer tries to visit the genuine bank Web site, he invariably gets connected to the fake Web site. The noteworthy feature is that, to the customer, the fake Web site will appear identical to the genuine Web site, including encryption symbols. However, details entered by the customer will reach the fake Web site and not the real one. Once the details are received, special software connects to the real bank Web site, impersonates the customer, and carries through financial transactions. Even the bank cannot discern the difference since all details are in place. While both the bank and the customer believe that they are communicating directly with each other, the fraudster can easily put through and modify any information that is transmitted.
   - *Man in the browser* attacks have reached an even higher level of sophistication. In these cases, rather than intercepting communication between the customer's computer and the bank Web site, the malicious software (malware) installed on the customer's computer intercepts communication between the customer and his web browser.

The malware (such as 'trojans') gets installed when a customer opens an email attachment or downloads a file from a Web site. Just visiting a web site, or viewing an email, may be sufficient for a fraudster to install malware without the customer's permission or knowledge. In some cases, criminals tamper with existing genuine Web sites, so that they will infect their visitors. The customer is unlikely to notice the difference, as it is believed that as much as 80 per cent of new malware is undetected by anti-virus software. Normal web browsing will be unaffected, but the malware will recognize when the customer visits their online bank Web site. Then, the malware can freely alter the web page as it is displayed to the customer, and modify the requests sent back to the bank. For example, in case of funds transfer made by the customer, the malware could change the amount transferred and the destination account number to that of the fraudster. Similarly, once the bank confirms that the transfer has occurred, the malware will change what is displayed to the customer, making the customer believe that the intended original transaction has been executed.

Real Life Example 4

In 2006, Citibank customers were targeted by a Man in the Middle attack. An email asked customers to confirm their address, stating that suspicious activity was detected. The site asked for account details, including the one-time password from the tokens issued to customers. If they were incorrect, the customers were asked to re-enter them.

Source: www.cronto.com

Real Life Example 5

AT&T's back-end systems were broken into by attackers. This system stored data on customers who had ordered certain equipment. The attackers sent emails to many of these customers, quoting authentic information already provided by them to create confidence, and then asking them to provide further personal information.

Source: www.cert-in.org.in

Real Life Example 6

In 2007, ABN AMRO's online banking service suffered a malware-based attack. Customers were sent emails with attachment, claiming to be from the bank itself. The customers responding to the email would visit the bank site that would redirect them to a fake site that asked for account details. Even though ABN AMRO deployed two-factor card reader-based authentication, the fraudsters were able to get away with transactions while the one-time password was still valid.

Source: www.cronto.com

It can be seen that this fraud technique can circumvent security measures since it is more sophisticated than simply gathering details from the customer. This technique has already been instrumental for large amounts of losses, and has gone to such levels of sophistication that 'kits' are available from the Internet, enabling even relatively unskilled fraudsters to launch advanced attacks.

Phishing activities as well as anti phishing measures have reached such levels of frenzied activity, that an Anti Phishing Working group (APWG) has been formed as a 'global pan industrial and law enforcement association, focussed on eliminating the fraud and identity theft that result from phishing, pharming and email spoofing of all types'. The APWG publishes periodical research reports on phishing activity, as well as customer guidance and other helplines that can be accessed at *www.antiphishing.org.*

4. ***Mules*** 'Mules' are individuals 'recruited' over the Internet with the sole purpose of being intermediaries for illegally acquired funds. These funds could have been acquired through methods such as phishing and other types of scams. The name 'mule' is suggestive of the transport method that smugglers are believed to have adopted for moving their illegally acquired goods.

   Mules earn sizeable sums of money—deducting 5 per cent to 10 per cent of the transferred amount as fee for their 'services'. The money is transferred through anonymous transfer services, such as Western Union or e-gold.[13]

   Contrary to popular belief, mules are not innocent people tricked into illegal business. They are typically mercenary volunteers with scant respect for the law—and for this very reason, they are turning 'professionals.'

Real Life Example 7—Money Mules in India

As the number of online job seekers increase exponentially in India, so do online frauds. Many 'money mules' are individuals desperately seeking jobs online, and are lured into the 'profession' due to their greed to make quick money. They are 'recruited' as money mules, and follow 'instructions' without being aware of their implications, and ultimately end up in prison.

The recruitment operation takes place as follows. A foreign company, pretending to have clients in India, calls for application for an India branch manager responsible for 'collections'. When an online job seeker expresses interest, an online interview is conducted and the job seeker is appointed with the responsibility of transferring money deposited into his personal account by the foreign company's clients. In the bargain, the 'recruit' earns around 10 per cent commission apart from the monthly 'salary' promised to him. The 'recruit' is the 'money mule'.

The action then moves to other gullible people lured either by promises of lottery wins or job offers abroad. They are instructed to contact the money mule and deposit a specified amount in the mule's bank account. The mule then transfers say 90 per cent to the fraudster abroad. Both the mule and the deceived persons may land in trouble later with the Indian authorities for illegal acts.

The police confirm that online frauds are increasing, and many of them originate in Nigeria (see 'Nigerian advance fee fraud' in Real life example 9).

Source: The Economic Times dated 17 February 2010.

Real Life Example 8—Nigerian Advance Fee Fraud (419 fraud)

The fraud is named after the Nigerian law that covers it. The fraud begins with the arrival of an email from a family member of an (usually) African dignitary, who claims that following the death of an influential family member, a huge sum of money is locked up in a bank account at some location. The sender of the email solicits the recipient's help to release the money, and lures the recipient with hefty compensation for the help. Once the unwitting recipient is tempted, the fraudsters demand an 'advance'—either in the form of a bank account opened for this purpose or a fee. Once this is accomplished, there may be a series of expenses the victim has to contend with, sometimes leading to physical threats. The victim realizes after some time that the blocked money does not exist, and that he has been hoodwinked.

Source: McAfee

McAfee and other e-security experts predict heightened security threats in 2010 and thereafter. An illustrative description is given as follows:

- Banking Trojans[14] are predicted to become even more sophisticated—for example, they could interrupt legitimate transactions and make unauthorized withdrawals, even where security systems are tight.
- Malware via email attachments are expected to increase, targeting all types of banking customers—corporate houses, individuals and other entities.
- Botnets, the infrastructure that launches nearly every type of cyber attack, are predicted to grow in 'stature' to operate a peer-to-peer architecture, *i.e.*, connecting computer to computer without a centralized control point. Hence, detection becomes very difficult.
- HTML 5 and the evolution of new programming languages are expected to provide new avenues for cyber criminals to write malware targeting specific users.

The examples and discussion so far show that security issues pose grave threats to users and stiff challenges to those responsible for tackling and controlling them. Cyber crime also poses systemic risk. A single user's loss may be limited but the consequences of such attacks would entail indirect costs—identification and legal proof of fraudulent transactions, cleaning of records, issuing/devising new instruments/payment systems, the threat of contagion to other payment systems—all of which would involve system-wide responses.

CHAPTER SUMMARY

- Over the last couple of decades, technology has assumed the vital role of not only a facilitator, but also a source of competitive advantage for banks. The business of banking—especially financial services / retail banking—is undergoing a sea change, as business shifts increasingly to the online environment. The increasing number of customers transacting online would move the 'market place' to 'market space', where banks would be forced to expand their product range to competitors' products, while rapidly innovating their own value-added products.
- The Internet has evolved into an essential access channel. For banks, the Internet offers a cost effective means of innovating, publicizing and delivering services to the customer, as well as maintaining customer relationships. For the customer, the Internet has opened up enormous possibilities of convenience and choice.
- The security of payment and settlement systems is critical for sustaining public trust in banks and other parts of the financial system. Hence, central banks, as supervisors and regulators of payments and settlement systems through financial intermediaries, have to ensure development of efficient and secure systems to match the explosion in needs and sophistication of the financial sector.

- The Committee on Payment and Settlement Systems (CPSS) was set up by the Bank for International Settlements with the objective of strengthening financial market infrastructure through promoting sound and efficient payment and settlement systems. The membership of CPSS has widened to include about 25 central banks in 2009. The RBI is a member of CPSS.
- RBI was empowered in 2007 through the enactment of the Payment and Settlement Act, 2007, to regulate and supervise payment and settlement systems in India. To operationalize the Act, RBI framed the 'Board for Regulation and Supervision of Payment and Settlement Systems Regulations, 2008' and 'Payment and Settlement Systems Regulations, 2008'.
- Payment systems in India can be bifurcated into 'paper-based' and 'electronic' payment systems. Another classification, based on users, can be into 'large-value payment systems' and 'retail payment systems'.
- The paper-based payment and settlement mechanisms in vogue in India are MICR and non-MICR cheques, high-value clearing, speed clearing, cheque truncation, etc.
- The electronic clearing and settlement systems being operated are ECS/NECS, EFT/NEFT.
- Though retail payments are not termed Systematically Important Payment Systems (SIPS), their relative importance to the economy cannot be undermined due to the sheer volume and geographical coverage that these systems demand.
- Retail payment systems are required primarily for purposes, such as payments for goods and services, bill payments, cash payments and so on.
- Plastic money refers to substitution of currency at the time when a payment is taking place, by using a card normally made of plastic representing such substitution. There can be several objectives for such substitution. Most important among these would be the need to postpone actual payment, or pre-purchase payment on the card that is issued. Whatever be the objective, the most important advantage of plastic money is protection to the user from the risks of carrying cash. Since it is the exclusive property of the cardholder it means that it can be used only by him. The categories are (a) credit cards, (b) debit cards and (c) other payment channels and products. Some of the popular channels under (c) are ATMs, Mobile banking services and prepaid instruments.
- However, the advent of high technology has also brought with it new operational risks in the form of security risks. The safety of banks, the integrity of the country's payment and settlement systems, and the trust that customers impose in the safety of the system are all intertwined to ultimately contribute to financial stability. The challenge for the future will be to identify and address risks to banking safety and security without hampering technological innovations in banking.
- The 'conventional' risks of unauthorized access, identity theft or network attacks have been exacerbated by 'contemporary' threats—phishing and pharming, spear phishing, carding and skimming, crimeware and spyware, money laundering, mules, scams, spams, Nigerian advance fee fraud—and still counting.

TEST YOUR UNDERSTANDING

1. Why do countries require technology in banking?
2. Are e-payments a necessity? Whom do they benefit? What are the risks?
3. What are the essential differences between credit cards, debit cards and other prepaid cards? Rank the three types of cards on the following parameters:

Feature	Credit Cards-rank	Debit Cards-rank	Prepaid Cards-rank
Which card is the safest for the user?			
Which card is the safest for the banker/ issuer?			
Which card is the safest for the merchant?			
Which card is the most convenient for the user?			
Which card is the most convenient to the merchant?			
Which card is the most convenient to the issuer?			

4. What is 'systemic risk' and why are SIPS important in this context?
5. Which of the variants of 'phishing' could you be faced with if you encounter the following while banking online?
   a. A voice says 'Welcome to account verification. Please enter your account number'.
   b. A flash player pops up urging you to install the update.
   c. Your mail id is used as the salutation on your bank site, urging you to update confidential information.
   d. You receive an email with a link to your bank Web site asking you to open the link and update personal information.
   e. A seemingly genuine bank site opens with the security 'lock' icon in the login space, but no lock sign in the status bar.
6. In an attempt to make the e-payment system more secure, Bank A makes a basic assumption that all customer computers are not safe. It, therefore asks customers to use virtual keyboards and additional transaction security systems. Would the bank succeed in fending off e-attacks?
7. What will be your course of action if you suspect phishing? Whom will you report the incident to?

8. Can a 'payment risk' due to security lapses translate into 'reputation risk' for a bank? What are the consequences of reputation risk?
9. You are on a foreign posting and are looking for a house on rent. You find a prospective house online. The landlord asks for your details but refuses to give you his address, and does not permit you to see the house unless you transfer some funds in foreign currency to his Western Union account. What will be your reaction and subsequent action?

TOPICS FOR FURTHER DISCUSSION

- What is the status of the RTGS system in other countries? How can a system like RTGS be successful in preventing systemic risk?
- Access the site www.antiphishing.org. What are the kinds of action being taken by the international community to fend off cyber attacks?
- Make a country study of anonymous payment methods and related laws. What conclusions can you draw?

ENDNOTES

1. INFINET stands for Indian Financial Network—the communication backbone for the Indian banking and financial sector. All banks and financial institutions are members of the INFINET, which functions as a closed user group.
2. Most money exists not as cash but as notations in the ledgers of depository institutions (banks and other financial institutions). Debiting one party's account and crediting another party's account execute notational money transactions. Banks must be prepared to convert notational demand deposits into cash on demand by the customer.
3. Please refer to chapter 'Monetary Policy Implications for Bank Management' for a discussion on 'reserve requirements'.
4. Core banking applications help provide complete front- and backend automation of banks. These applications also help banks achieve centralized processing and provide anywhere, anytime 24 × 7 non-stop services, not possible with traditional localized branch automation systems that are available only during their working hours. Core banking applications help integrate the enterprise to existing in-house applications to offer a single customer view. These applications provide automation across multiple delivery channels.
5. RBI, (2009) Committe for financial sector assessment, Vol. V Chapter V, Table 1, page 265.
6. Public Key Infrastructure (PKI) offers authentication of online transactions, by providing each user with an electronic identity in the form of a digital certificate and a private cryptographic key. It is usually stored in a secure media, such as a smart card or an i-key. The person could make use of the identity to digitally sign documents or transactions.
7. RBI, (2009), Committee for financial sector assessment, Vol. V, Chapter V, Box 2, page 276
8. Studies indicate that formal banking reaches 37 per cent of the population, while mobile phones are owned by more than 50 per cent of the population. For every 10,000 people, these countries on an average have one bank branch and one ATM, but 5,100 mobile phones.
9. NDTL and reserve requirements are dealt within the chapter 'Monetary Policy Implications for Bank Management'
10. Escrow is a legal agreement created for a specific purpose and period, and deposited with a third party. It is valid until the performance of an act or the happening of an event specified in the agreement. Before making the deposit of the money paid by holders of prepaid instruments with the bank, the agreement between non-banks and the cardholders should specify the terms of the agreement, and more specifically, when the agreement is to be released. The bank holding the escrow account will not be a party to the agreement, but will function as a 'custodian' who has no right to alter the terms of the agreement. The custodian bank is also bound by duty to act according to the trust placed in it and therefore would be liable for wrong payments.
11. McAfee Report titled 'Financial Frauds and Internet Banking: Threats and Countermeasures', (2009), page 6, by Francois Paget, McAfee Avert Labs, US, accessed at www.mcafee.com, can also be accessed at www.avertlabs.com
12. Ibid, page 8.
13. Cyber criminals prefer anonymous (and convenient) services, such as these to carry out their activities. There are currently about 20 such known services in operation. Many countries are now cracking down on such services through appropriate legislation. For example, e-gold's founders are currently under investigation. Web money is a Russian entity with 4 million customers, whose customers' integrity is under question. Western Union, the American money transfer agent with presence in more than 200 countries, set up to facilitate fund transfers to family members, is also allegedly being misused. (*source*: www.mcafee.com)
14. The Trojan.Satiloler family monitors traffic sent and received by web browsers. It can inject malicious code into web pages received even before the user can read them. For example, in an online banking Web site, the Trojan can replace all the functions with its own functions. This enables the Trojan to control information flow on the site without the user's knowledge, sometimes irrespective of the authentication mode used. Hence, a clean and trusted system is the first prerequisite to avoid this malware attack. A variation, called the Banbra Trojan, targets those using virtual keyboards provided on banking Web sites to enter passwords and confidential information. It captures the movement of the mouse as the user types in the password and sends a video file to the cyber criminal, thus enabling online frauds. (*source*: www.cert-in.org.in)

CHAPTER SEVENTEEN

Understanding Financial Services

CHAPTER STRUCTURE

Section I Non-Banking Financial Company
Section II Venture Capital and Private Equity
Section III Credit Cards
Section IV Housing Finance
Section V IPO
Section VI Microfinance
Section VII Pension Funds
Section VIII Alternative Investments
Section IX Consumer Rights and Protection Applicable to Financial Services
Chapter Summary
Test Your Understanding
Annexures I

KEY TAKEAWAYS FROM THE CHAPTER

- Non-Banking Financial Company (NBFC) does not include any institution whose principal business is of agriculture activity, industrial activity, sale or purchase or construction of immovable property. It cannot accept deposits and cannot issues cheques. Under automatic route, 100 per cent FDI is permitted.
- With effect from December 6, 2006, they are classified as Asset Finance Company, Investment Company, Loan Company and Infrastructure Finance Company.
- Venture capitalist provides funds to new start-ups facing the problem of lack of funds.
- Against providing, they take some ownership rights of the business entity.
- There are five stages in VC Seed, Early Stage, Formative Stage, Later Stage and Last Stage.
- PE acquires mostly 100 per cent of the company (large investments), whereas VCs acquire 50 per cent of the company (new business start-ups).
- Credit card transaction is divided into two parts—one is authorization (when issuer bank authorizes the transaction after swipe of the card) an other is clearing and settlement (when the merchant is paid for the sale).
- Interchange fee is around 1–2 per cent of the transaction value.
- The purpose of a housing finance system is to provide the funds which home-buyers need to purchase their homes.

- Housing finance market's performance and changes are routinely monitored.
- HF is considered one of the leading indicators of economic development.
- Securitization is a process through which an issuer creates a financial instrument by combining other financial assets and then marketing different tiers of the repackaged instruments to investors.
- Reverse mortgage is a financial product accessible for senior citizens who own a house. It facilitates them to mortgage their property with a lender and convert fraction of the home equity into tax-free income.
- An Underwriter is an Investment firm that plays the role of liaison between the organization selling its shares/securities and the investing public.
- Underwriter purchases shares from corporation and sells it to investors.
- Underwriters mostly make money from the spread between the price paid by investors and price paid to issuers. There are two main types of underwritings:
    - Firm commitment underwriting (underwriter buys the entire issue)
    - Best efforts underwriting (underwriter does not bear the risk of unsold shares)
- Microfinance includes farming, trifling trade, livestock, food processing, vending, small-scale labour incentive productions like weaving, craft, artisans, street vendors, small shops, services, etc.
- Microfinance is often confused with Microcredit. Microcredit is a subset of Microfinance.
- A pension scheme is simply a saving scheme with deferred return as the source of saving.
- Pension schemes that are arranged by government for the entire or segment of labour force are referred to as social security schemes.
- Schemes arranged by employers or other organizations are referred to as employer pension schemes.
- Commodities, Hedge funds, Real assets, Private equity, Structured products are the examples of alternative investment and they acts as a tool to diversification.
- Hedge funds can be defined as privately organized investment vehicle that generates investment opportunities by leveraging.
- Consumer protection consists of laws and organizations designed to ensure the rights of consumers as well as fair trade competition and the free flow of truthful information.
- The Banking Codes and Standards Board of India (BCSBI) develops standards, enhances transparency and improves relations between banks and customers.

SECTION I

NON-BANKING FINANCIAL COMPANY

A Non-banking Financial Company (NBFC) is a company registered under the Indian Companies Act, 1956, and is engaged in the business of loans and advances, acquisition of shares/stock/bonds/debentures/securities issued by the Government or a local authority or other securities of marketable nature, leasing, hire-purchase, insurance business, chit fund business, but does not include any institution whose principal business is that of agricultural activities, industrial activities, sale/purchase/construction of immovable properties. A non-banking institution which is a company with its principal business of receiving deposits under any scheme/arrangement/any other manner, or lending in any manner is also considered as a non-banking financial company (residuary non-banking company).[1]

Most of the functions of NBFCs are akin to that of banks; however, there are a few differences:

1. NBFC cannot accept demand deposits. Demand deposits are funds deposited at a depository institutions that are payable on demand, immediately or within a defined short notice like current or savings account.
2. NBFC is not a part of the payment and settlement system. Therefore, NBFC cannot issue cheques drawn on it.
3. Deposit insurance facility of Deposit Insurance and Credit Guarantee Corporation (DICGC) is not available for NBFC depositors, unlike in case of banks.

Hundred per cent FDI is permitted under the Automatic Route subject to minimum capitalization norms of:

FDI Stake	Minimum Capitalization
Up to 51 per cent	USD 0.5 mn; to be brought upfront
Above 51 per cent and up to 75 per cent	USD 5 mn; to be brought upfront
Above 75 per cent	USD 50 mn; USD 7.5 mn; to be brought upfront and balance in 24 months

NBFCs registered with RBI were classified as:

1. *Equipment leasing company* is any financial institution whose principal business is that of leasing equipments or financing of such an activity.
2. *Hire-purchase finance company* is any financial intermediary whose principal business relates to hire-purchase transactions or financing of such transactions.
3. *Loan company* means any financial institution whose principal business is that of providing finance, whether by making loans or advances or otherwise for any activity other than its own (excluding any equipment leasing or hire-purchase finance activity).
4. *Investment company* is any financial intermediary whose principal business is that of buying and selling of securities.[2]

However, with effect from December 6, 2006, the NBFCs registered with RBI have been reclassified as[3]:

1. Asset Finance Company (AFC)
2. Investment Company (IC)
3. Loan Company (LC)
4. Infrastructure Finance Companies (IFC)

Asset Finance Company (AFC) Can be defined as any company which is a financial institution carrying on as its principal business 'financing of physical assets supporting productive/economic activity' such as automobiles, tractors, lathe machines, generator sets, earth moving and material handling equipments, moving on own power and general purpose industrial machines.

Principal business for this purpose is defined as aggregate of financing real/physical assets supporting economic activity and income arising there from is not less than 60 per cent of its total assets and total income respectively. They are further classified as those accepting deposits or those not accepting deposits.

Investment Company (IC) Is a company which is a financial institution carrying on as its principal business 'acquisition of securities'.

Loan Company (LC) Means any company which is a financial institution carrying on as its principal business 'providing of finance whether by making loans or advances or otherwise for any activity other than its own' but does not include an Asset Finance Company.

Infrastructure Finance Companies (IFC) Are in long term funding for developing or operating and maintaining or developing, operating and maintaining any infrastructure project in road, highway, port, airport inland port, waterways, water supply, irrigation project, water treatment, sanitation and sewage system or solid waste management, telecom services (basic or cellular), network and internet services, transmission or distribution of power, laying down and maintenance of gas, crude oil and petroleum pipelines.

The above-mentioned types of NBFCs are further classified into:

1. NBFCs accepting public deposit (NBFCs-D)
2. NBFCs not accepting/holding public deposit (NBFCs-ND)

Funding sources of NBFCs include debentures, borrowings from banks and FIs, Commercial Paper and inter-corporate loans.

NBFCs are typically into funding of:

- Construction equipment
- Commercial vehicles and cars
- Gold loans
- Microfinance
- Consumer durables and two wheelers
- Loan against shares, etc.

List of major products offered by NBFCs in India are:

- Funding of commercial vehicles
- Funding of infrastructure assets
- Retail financing
- Loan against shares
- Funding of plant and machinery
- Small and Medium Enterprises Financing
- Financing of specialized equipment
- Operating leases of cars

Funding transactions of banks have inbuilt exposure on corporate; whereas in case of NBFCs, the benefit is that in most of the transactions, there is exposure on the asset and not on the corporate. Also, NBFCs are able to provide fund to non-banking regions (or where banks are not aggressive due to various constraints and reasons) on providing financial assistance. Thus, NBFCs have an edge over banks.

NBFCs have been playing a very significant role both from the macroeconomic perspective and the structure of the Indian financial system. With the gamut of services, they account for around 9 per cent of financial sector assets, have become an integral part of the financial system in India, playing a crucial role in broadening access to financial services, enhancing competition and bringing in greater risk diversification[4]. This intricate participation calls for strict vigilance and policy checks. Gaps in the regulation of the non-banking financial sectors are being continuously identified and plugged and the oversight mechanism strengthened. In cognition of the risks posed to the banking system on account of their exposure to NBFCs extending gold loans, exposure limits of banks to NBFCs have been tightened while loan to value (LTV) ratios have been prescribed on gold loans extended by NBFCs[5].

SECTION II

VENTURE CAPITAL AND PRIVATE EQUITY

During your market research and analysis, you come up with innovative idea of software that can bridge the gap in university communication system. Filled with zeal, you design a prototype with two other friends. But when it comes to developing the running actual software, you need to hire developers/programmers, invest on hardware and development software. Arranging money for this becomes a big challenge. To pursuit your idea, you need source of financing. Approaching bank may come up as a spontaneous solution, but banks need assets for security, but you need finance to purchase those assets. In order to come out of this deadlock, you need OPM (other people's money) who are willing to invest on your idea being the only asset. Venture Capital market is the answer to this search for investment and capital.

The term, 'venture capital' generally refers to financing for new, often high-risk ventures. Venture capital funds pool investors' cash and loan to start-up firms and small businesses with perceived, long-term growth potential. In exchange of the high risk that venture capitalists assume by investing in smaller and less mature companies, they usually gain significant control over company decisions, in addition to a significant portion of the company's ownership (and subsequently value). For start-ups that do not have access to other capital, venture capital is a highly significant source of funding and it typically entails high risk (and potentially high returns) for the investor. The underlying sources of funds for venture capital firm include individuals, pension funds, insurance companies, large corporations, and even university bequest funds[6].

FIGURE 17.1 BASIC FLOW OF FUNDS—IN AND OUT OF A VENTURE CAPITAL COMPANY.

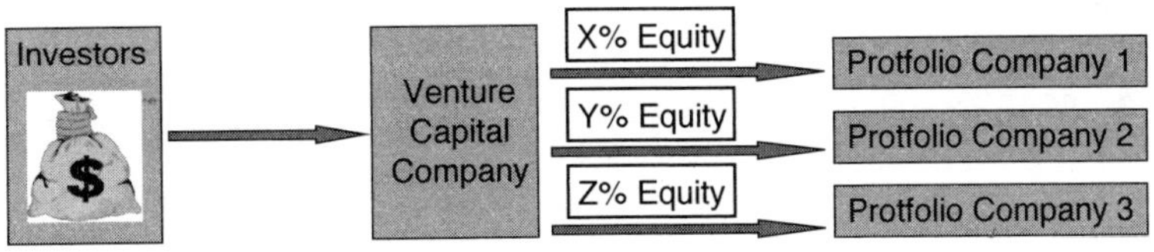

Stages in Venture Capital (VC) Investing

Angel investors are individuals who help entrepreneurs get their businesses off the ground, and earn a high return on their investment. Mostly, they are the bridge for self-funded entrepreneurs that take their business ahead to the stage that they need venture capital. They typically offer expertise, experience and contacts in addition to money.

Stage 1: *Seed*: Seed-stage financing is the first stage, often involving a modest amount of capital provided to entrepreneurs to finance the early development of a new product or service. These early financings are infused for product development, market research, building a management team and developing a business plan. Seed-stage financing company has not actually set up operations yet, and R&D is the major cost centre.

Stage 2: *Early Stage*: For companies at a stage wherein they are able to begin operations but are not yet at the stage of commercial manufacturing and sales, early stage financing supports a step-up in capabilities. Business, being new, can consume vast amounts of cash at this stage.

Stage 3: *Formative Stage*: Financing includes both seed stage and early stage.

Stage 4: *Later Stage*: Capital provided after commercial manufacturing and sales have embarked on, and before any initial public offering falls in this stage. The operations have begun; product or service is in production and is commercially available. The company exhibits noteworthy revenue growth, but may or may not be showing a profit.

- *Third Stage:* Capital provided for major expansion such as physical plant expansion, product improvement and marketing.
- *Expansion or Mezzanine Stage:* Financing refers to the second and third stages.
- *Bridge Financing:* Finances the step of going public and represents the bridge between expanding the company and the IPO.

Stage 5: *Balanced-stage*: This refers to all the stages, seed through mezzanine[7].

Private equity consists of investors and funds that make investments directly into private companies or conduct buyouts of public companies that result in a delisting of public equity. Capital for private equity is raised from retail and institutional investors, and can be used to fund new technologies, expand working capital within an owned company, make acquisitions, or to strengthen a balance sheet.

Venture capital is a subset of private equity. Therefore, all venture capital are private equity, but not all private equity are venture capital.

TABLE 17.1 DIFFERENCES BETWEEN PRIVATE EQUITY AND VENTURE CAPITAL[8]

	Private Equity	Venture Capital
Structure	Has both Equity and Debt involved.	Uses only Equity.
Percentage Acquired	Mostly acquire 100 per cent of a company.	Relatively have lesser stake of less than 50 per cent.
Company Size	PE firms make large investments.	VC investments are comparatively smaller.
Stage	Buy mature companies.	Invest mostly in early-stage companies.
Risk–Return	Invest in mature business, so Lesser risk. Expect 2x return.	High risk in investment, as invest in initial stages. Expect 10x return.

FIGURE 17.2 ROLE OF VENTURE CAPITAL AND PRIVATE EQUITY IN BUSINESS LIFECYCLE.

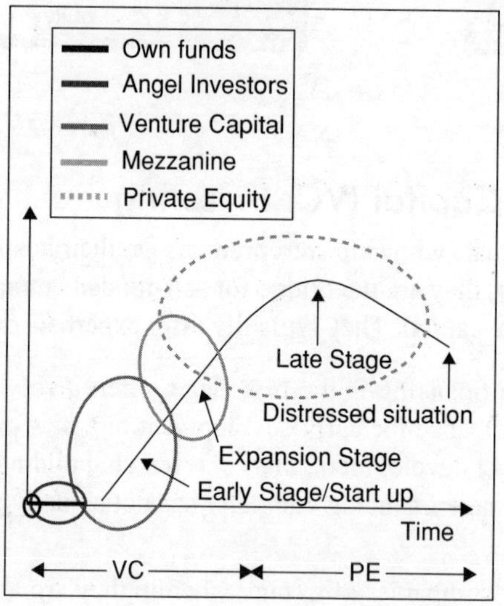

SECTION III

CREDIT CARDS

Selling goods or services on credit, relying on the credibility of the consumer has been a custom of merchants since past. This practice has been mutually beneficial for both the merchant and the consumer. Introduction of credit cards has been an extension of this idea, with better defined terms and conditions and involving regulatory bodies for vigilance.

Credit Card is a card issued by a financial company giving the holder an option to borrow funds. Credit cards charge interest and are primarily used for short-term financing[9]. They are issued by banks or credit unions, and have shape and size according to the specification of ISO/IEC 7810 standards as ID-1 (defined as 85.60 × 53.98 mm in size)[10]. Credit cards are usually used at point of sale. This plastic card entitles its holder to buy goods and services based on holder's promise to pay for these goods and services availed now, in near future. It is also known as 'Plastic Money'.

Institutions issuing these credit cards need to use with due diligence while processing the applications of consumers. The critical step in the process is credit history check. This mainly includes validating the consumer's ability to repay debts based on the responsibility and sincerity demonstrated in repaying previous debts. Though this check is not a guarantee that similar response would be repeated in future transactions too, it provides a primary check when carried meticulously. The consumer's credit report thus prepared contains information, like number and types of credit accounts, duration for which each account has been opened, amount of available credit used and whether bills are paid on time. Information regarding whether the consumer has any bankruptcies, liens or judgments are also a part of the report that supplements the decision whether to extend credit to that consumer and also the credit limit to be granted.

Major Parties Involved in Credit Card Transaction

1. **Cardholder:** Owner of credit card, who uses it to make a purchase of goods or services.
2. **Merchant:** The individual or business who accepts credit cards for payment of the product or services sold to the consumer or cardholder.
3. **Issuer Bank**[11]**:** The responsibilities of issuer bank are majorly administrative. The functions it handles covers various aspects of cardholder relationship, including card marketing, credit processing of applications, card issuance, cardholder billing, payment collection from cardholder, fraud control, collection from defaulters, and so forth.
4. **Acquirer Bank:** Receiving side of the transaction, *i.e.*, Merchant is managed by acquirer bank. It is the financial institution accepting payment on behalf of the merchant.

   Operations of processing and reconciling all the credit transactions made at merchant's end are also acquirer banks' responsibility. They perform sales and marketing functions too by soliciting and signing up new merchants. Merchant's application processing and authorization is done by acquirer bank. Institutions like J P Morgan Chase, Bank of America, HSBC, etc., are the bigger players in this role, accompanied by many more.
5. **Credit Card Association:** Association of issuer banks like MasterCard, Visa, American Express, etc., is made to monitor, control, and manage transaction terms for all parties involved in transaction (merchants, issuer banks, acquiring banks).
6. **Transaction Network:** It is the technology part of the transaction that enables the electronic transaction.

Working of Credit Cards

FIGURE 17.3 CREDIT CARD TRANSACTION PROCESSING DIAGRAM[12]

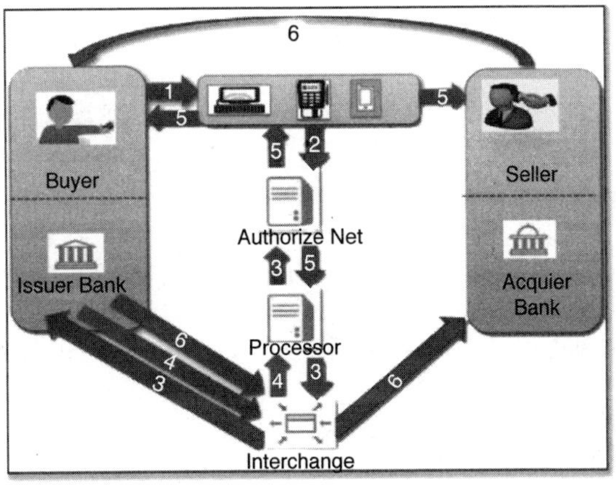

The credit card transactions can be majorly divided into two parts:

1. *Authorization:* It is the process that happens immediately after each purchase transaction. Once the card is swiped at register for payment, issuer bank authorizes the transaction by validating the card and its outstanding limit.
2. *Clearing and Settlement:* This is the second part of transaction cycle, wherein merchant is paid for the sales. Issuer bank gets interchange fee[13], and acquirer bank earns discount fee as their share of profit in the transaction.

A typical credit card transaction involves the following steps:

Step 1: Consumer swipes his card at POS for payment of the purchases made.

Step 2: An intermediary, Authorize.Net, supports the intricate routing of data forward for authorization and processing.

Step 3: The secured transaction network passes the information via defined connection and finally submits the transaction information to the credit card network (like Visa or MasterCard) which further relays the transaction to the issuer bank that issued the credit card to the consumer.

Step 4: The issuing bank either authorizes or declines the transaction based on the customer's available credit limit and passes the results back to the credit card network which is finally routed to Authorize.net.

Step 5: Authorize.net sends the results of authorization to the merchant and consumer (at website, in case of online transaction).

Step 6: After this authorization, merchant delivers the goods or services to the consumer.

Step 7: The issuer bank sends the calculated funds for the transaction to the credit card network, which passes the funds to the merchant's bank (acquirer bank). The bank then deposits these funds into the merchant's bank account. This process is called 'settlement'.

Respective interchange fee and discount fee are also deducted by issuer bank and acquirer bank. Consumer pays outstanding credit card consolidated bills at defined interval, defined in the terms of contract.

Charges and Profits in Credit Card Transactions

1. ***Issuer Bank*:** They issue cards to consumers and represent them during transaction. They bear the risk of default that cardholder or consumer might commit. In return, they charge; and therefore are benefitted in case of no defaults by *interchange fees* (generally 1–2 per cent of the total transaction value[14]) to merchants with every transaction.
2. ***Acquirer Bank*:** They are the intermediary between Issuer bank and Merchant. They receive all credit card transactions from issuers, and present all payments in a time period to the merchant in lump sum. In exchange, the acquirer bank charges merchants a fixed amount for its services, as well as a variable sum dependent on the volume of the merchant's sales[15].

SECTION IV

HOUSING FINANCE

'The purpose of a housing finance system is to provide the funds which home-buyers need to purchase their homes. This is a simple objective, and the number of ways in which it can be achieved is limited. Notwithstanding this basic simplicity, in a number of countries, largely as a result of government action, very complicated housing finance systems have been developed. However, the essential feature of any system, that is, the ability to channel the funds of investors to those purchasing their homes, must remain.'

Source: (1985) Mark Boleat, National Housing Finance Systems—A Comparative Study, p. 1.[16]

Housing Finance in simple terms implies financing or loans for meeting array of needs relating to housing, including:

- Purchase of a house/flat
- Acquisition of land
- Construction/ extension of house/flat
- Renovation, repair or upgradation of house/flat
- Taking over of housing loans from other banks or housing finance companies

Housing finance market's performance and changes are routinely monitored as it is considered one of the leading indicators of economic development. In case of emerging economies with population growth and rapid urbanization, robust financing systems are required. Considering these issues primarily focussing on growing middle-class, World Bank in its conference in October, 2012 has suggested five key strategic areas (Fig. 17.4) to be worked on[17]:

FIGURE 17.4 FIVE KEY-STRATEGIC AREAS OF HOUSING FINANCE RECOMMENDED BY THE WORLD BANK.

Source: www.siteresources.worldbank.org/FINANCIALSECTOR/Resources/Housing_Finance_Introduction.pdf

The aforementioned strategic areas in macro-perspective are intended to bridge the demand-supply gap that exists in the housing and housing finance sector.

Every country has its own regulatory framework and body, with variations in norms depending on the economic condition and demand of the country. National Housing Bank is such apex level institution for housing finance in India. The National Housing Policy, 1988, envisaged the setting up of NHB. NHB was set up in July 9, 1988, under the National Housing Bank Act, 1987. NHB is wholly owned by Reserve Bank of India, with the entire paid-up capital contributed by RBI[18]. Rural Housing Microfinance launch is one of the major milestones of NHB.

Housing finance sector in India has been growing at a remarkable pace. [Refer Annexure 1.] Indian housing finance has developed from a stage where it was solely government-driven to present stage of growth and multiple players. The structure of the financing system has been cited bellow:

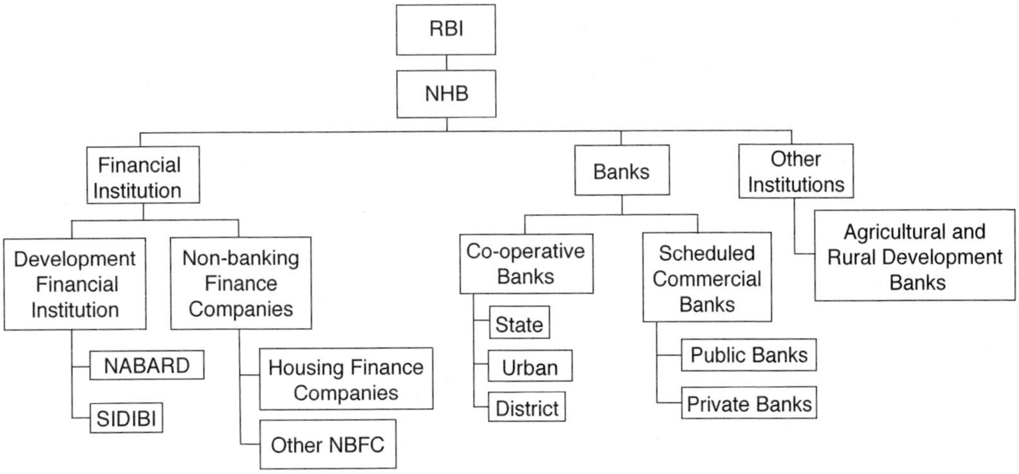

Currently, housing finance in India in the organized sector is provided majorly by following institutions:

- Scheduled Commercial Banks
- Scheduled Co-operative Banks
- Agricultural and Rural Development Banks
- Housing Finance Companies
- State Level Apex Cooperative Housing Finance Societies

Funding Sources of these Housing Finance companies consist of:

- Public deposits
- Term deposits
- Domestic and International Institutional borrowing
- Capital Markets
- Securitization
- Refinance from NHB

Securitization: It is a long-term way of raising resources for housing finance organizations.

> Securitization is a process through which an issuer creates a financial instrument by combining other financial assets and then marketing different tiers of the repackaged instruments to investors. The process can encompass any type of financial asset and promotes liquidity in the marketplace.[19]

Securitization creates liquidity in the market as is makes, otherwise unaffordable, big asset pool of mortgages approachable for retail investors. This also distributes the risks, previously confined to housing sector, among a greater number of players.

The process of processing loan application is tedious and complex for the institutions. For countries, like USA, where such records are centralized and easily available, it is a process driven procedure. Whereas in developing countries, like India, gathering all information of the loan applicant, like outstanding, other loans taken, etc., is slightly complex because of unorganized financial sector. Developing a central repository of this information would bring significant improvement in the process. Easy availability of verified land records and property data is also crucial and inevitable.

Reverse mortgage is a financial product accessible for Senior citizens who own a house. It facilitates them to mortgage their property with a lender and convert fraction of the home equity into tax-free income. They retain ownership of house. Unlike other loans, in this case, the lender makes payments to those senior citizens. There is no compulsion to service the loan as long as the borrower is alive and in occupation of the property. Later, through sale of property, the loan can be repaid.[20]

SECTION V

IPO (INITIAL PUBLIC OFFERING)

Venture capital and Private Equity supports start-ups in their initial stages to set-up their operations, grow and turn to a profitable venture. Beyond this stage, when a privately held company needs financing to expand its business, or the existing stakeholders want to monetize their investment, they opt for IPO. IPO stands for 'Initial Public Offering'. An IPO is the first time an organization introduces their shares to general public for sale to outside investors on securities exchange. Companies get an option of raising cash, after IPOS, by trading additional stocks in future.

There is a gamut of activities to be performed before IPO can be executed and after the IPO is offered. These tasks include, among many others, analytical working of the price to be offered, preparing processes and documents for statuary compliances, marketing the new issue, and stabilizing the stock performance after-market offering. These are the key activities performed by Underwriters.

> An Underwriter is an Investment firm that plays the role of liaison between the organization selling its shares/securities and the investing public.[21]

Some of the leading IPO Underwriters are Goldman Sachs, Morgan Stanley, Merrill Lynch.[22] Underwriters are the primary players in entire IPO process. Apart from supporting, guiding issuer organization to prepare for IPO, they are meticulously involved in the most critical step of IPO. The basic transaction that happens between issuer/corporation, Investment bank/underwriter and Investor is that underwriter purchases shares from corporation and sells it to investors. Investors pay for these shares to underwriters who further give cash to issuers. Underwriters mostly make money from the spread between the price paid by investors and price paid to issuers, apart from their fee.

FIGURE 17.5 SIMPLISTIC DIAGRAM OF TRANSACTIONS IN IPO ISSUE PROCESS.

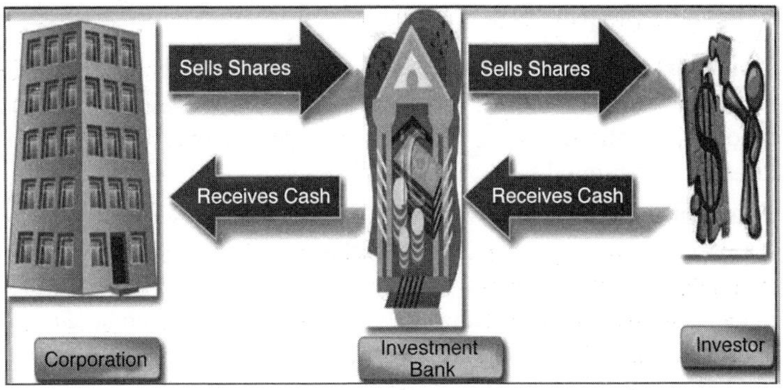

There are two main types of underwriting:

1. Firm commitment underwriting
2. Best efforts underwriting

Firm Commitment Underwriting This is the prevalent type of underwriting, wherein the underwriter buys the entire issue. They take up the full risk and responsibility for unsold shares. They purchase all the shares from organization and sell them to investors at a higher price. So, underwriter makes profit on the spread between price paid to issuer organization and price received from public investors.

Best Efforts Underwriting This underwriter has reduced risks. Though they sell as much of issues as possible, they don't bear the risk of unsold shares. The unsold issues can be returned to the issuer. Although underwriter doesn't have financial responsibility for unsold shares, they must make their best efforts to sell the shares at the agreed offering price. In situation where issuer doesn't find enough investors showing interest at the offered price, they can pull back the offer, as the company won't make sufficient capital. They would have incurred significant flotation costs.

FIGURE 17.6 OVERVIEW OF PROCESSES INVOLVED IN IPO ISSUING PROCESS[23]

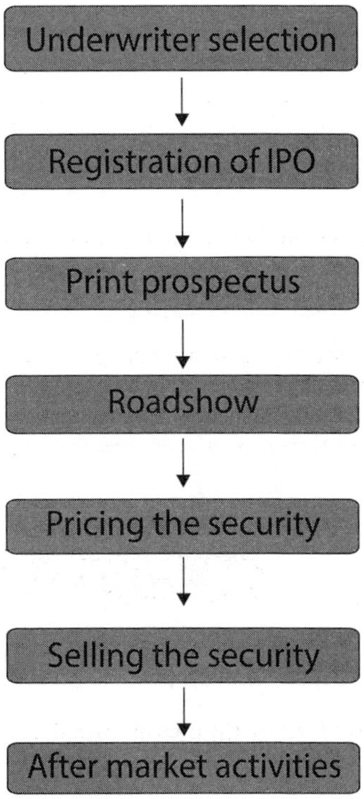

1. **Underwriter Selection:** Once organization decides to go public, they select an underwriter. Selection criteria is based on their experience as underwriters, management fees and other anticipated expenses, proposed roles and strategies and general structure of the deal.
2. **Registration of IPO:** Company needs to register with Public Exchange such as the Securities and Exchange Commission (SEC) in the United States. The issuer firm needs to prepare a registration statement that is to be registered with Public Exchange. The registration statement discloses all material information about the corporation making an initial public offering.
3. **Printed Prospectus:** The prospectus is a legal document describing details of the corporation issuing IPO and also the proposed offering to potential investors. Most of the information in prospectus about the organization is contained in the registration statement. The initial prospectus is also often called a 'red herring', because it contains a passage in red that states the corporation is not endeavouring to sell its shares before the registration is sanctioned by the Public Excahnge.[24]
4. **Present Road-show:** It is more of a marketing, as well as marketing research activity. Road-show is for potential institutional investors. It helps firm to generate interest in investors about the corporation. At the same time, it gives opportunity to firms and underwriters to collect information and interest level of potential purchasers.
5. **Pricing the Securities:** Determining the price of security is instrumental in the success or failure of IPOs. Over-pricing would lead to lower acceptance of IPO; thereby, underwriter would be stuck with shares as well as would hit underwriter's reputation and credibility. Under-pricing on the other hand might bring more investors, but in essence would generate lesser capital than it could have. Issuing firm would bear the burden of expenses associated with IPO, without reaping the possible benefits. The two critical factors in determining the price of IPO are:
   a. Value of the company
   b. Expected demand for the securities
6. **Selling the Shares/Securities:** All the possible efforts are done on the effective date of the registration statement. It is a part of underwriter's duty to ensure that participating investors get their share on the issue date. Securities must be supplemented with a final prospectus.
7. **After Market Activities:** Underwriters are responsible for sustaining and supporting the stock price by trading. If stock prices decline, they purchase the share to control the falling price. Whereas in case stock price goes up, they use over allocation alternative to cover short position. Only after '25 calendar days' of IPO, also known as 'quiet period', underwriters and other syndicate members reach a state to analyse and comment on value of firm and convey earnings estimates.

TABLE 17.2 ADVANTAGES/DISADVANTAGES OF IPO

Advantages	Disadvantages
Source of interest-free capital.	Process of IPO is expensive and time-consuming.
Open option of trading additional stock offerings in future.	Stringent disclosure rules under Sarbanes-Oxley Act and demand of periodic reporting.
Enhanced liquidity for shareholders and investors, as they cash out anytime.	Intense pressure post IPO to perform in the short term.
Better monitoring and control by external capital markets.	Limits on management's freedom to act.
Unlike debt, corporations are not under compulsion to repay capital to its investors. They can focus on performance and growth, and investors would get their return automatically.	Competitors might gain access to certain information.

SECTION VI

MICROFINANCE

According to estimates, there are 500 million economically active poor people in the world operating micro-enterprises and small businesses.[25] Active entrepreneurs who are running microenterprises not only address unemployment by option of self-employment, but also contributes to the economic growth of the country by increasing per capita income and prudent utilization of unproductive human resource. The lamentable fact is that these microenterprise entrepreneurs always don't have access to sufficient finance. Though experts in developing and developed nations suggest promotion of self-employment, glaring problem is the inadequacy they face in fixed and working capital. Banks have a constraint as source for them, as banks ask for collateral as a prerequisite, which is not available to microenterprises. The evident resort for them is to avail credit services of local moneylenders and pawnbrokers who ask for high interest rates with stringent rules. Therefore to support self-employment, it gets imperative for government and other agencies to provide financial services to them at a subsidized rate.

Microfinance has evolved with intend to benefit microenterprises, small businesses, low-income households, and thereby support economic development. 'These financial services may include savings, credit, insurance, leasing, money transfer, equity transaction, etc., that is, any types of financial services, provided to customers to meet their formal financial needs: lifecycle, economic opportunity and emergency' (Dasgupta and Rao 2003).[26] In generic terms, it is financial services in form of small-sized financial transactions for people who fall outside the range of formal finance. Activities that are mostly financed by Microfinancing include:

- **In rural areas:** Farming, trifling trade, livestock, food processing, vending, small-scale labour incentive production like weaving, craft, etc.
- **In urban areas:** Artisans, street vendors, small shops, services, etc.

Microfinance is often confused with Microcredit. Microcredit is a subset of Microfinance that includes gamut of activities like savings, insurance, market assistance, technical assistance, etc. Key features of Microfinance can be summed up as:

- Lends to poor
- Doesn't ask for security or collaterals
- Uses group guarantees and appraisal as a substitute to security
- Gives preference to saving over borrowing
- Loans are short-term

Microfinance, though not restricted, is preferred source for women. Primary reason for this is the available evidences that demonstrate that women are less to default in repayment of loans, than men. The main incentive foreseen in doing so is that development of women has ripple effect on family and eventually on society. Empowerment of women results in improved in nutrition an education of their family, which is also an indirect aim of MFIs. As per the statistics on Nov 5, 2007, since 1996, the World Bank has reached more than 6 million poor in Bangladesh through microfinance projects; 90 per cent of these microcredit borrowers are women. Microfinancing has improved their lives in various aspects:[27]

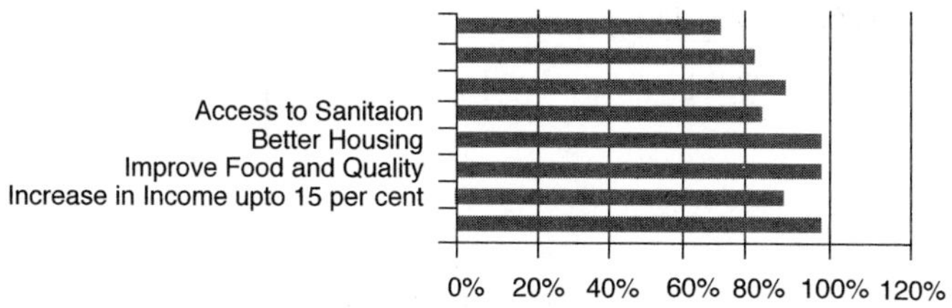

Microfinance programs are financed by loans, grants, guarantees and investments from individuals, philanthropists, social investors, local banks, foundations, governments, and international institutions.[28] Major providers of Microfinance are categorized in 3 major categories:

1. Formal sector
2. Semiformal sector
3. Informal sector

Informal sector is also specified in the category because it contributes a descent fraction to microfinance lending, and the drawbacks or limitations of informal lenders have, over a period of time, instigated the need of formal/semiformal sectors. Few key contributors to Microfinance are:

Grameen Group: Pioneered by Mohammed Yunus in Bangladesh, it targets poor women in rural areas to setup a microenterprise. A bank branch, covering 15–22 villages, is set up with a field manager and bank workers. Their prime objective for successful operations is to develop an understanding of the local environment, clientele and their business. To begin with, they form a group of 5 prospective borrowers, of which 2 are given loan. The performance and loan repayment of these 2 borrowers is observed over a period of time (mostly 50 weeks) to decide the eligibility of other borrowers. Peer pressure and peer support drive these groups.

Rotating Savings and Credit Associations (ROSCAs): It is a type of Combined Saving and Credit Association. It is a group of individuals who unite and make cyclical contribution to a common fund, shared by them all. This fund is given to involved members cyclically, *i.e.*, lump-sum amount of the saving is given to one individual member in each cycle. This amount is paid back in regular monthly contributions.

Self-Help Groups: It's a voluntary association of 10-20 people, made to attain common collective objectives. It is a homogenous group of people who save portion of their emergent credit needs and revolve resources among the group members. Period and other term of loans are decided by members by consensus. If the group is not formally registered, it should not have more than 20 members.

A slightly detailed sub-categorization of these microfinance providers has shown below:[29]

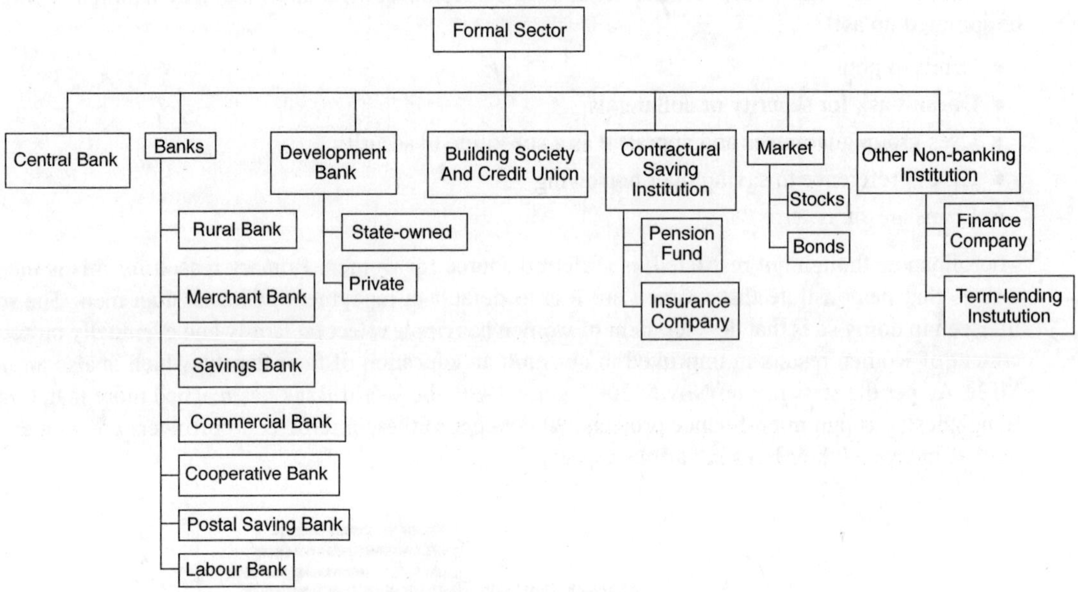

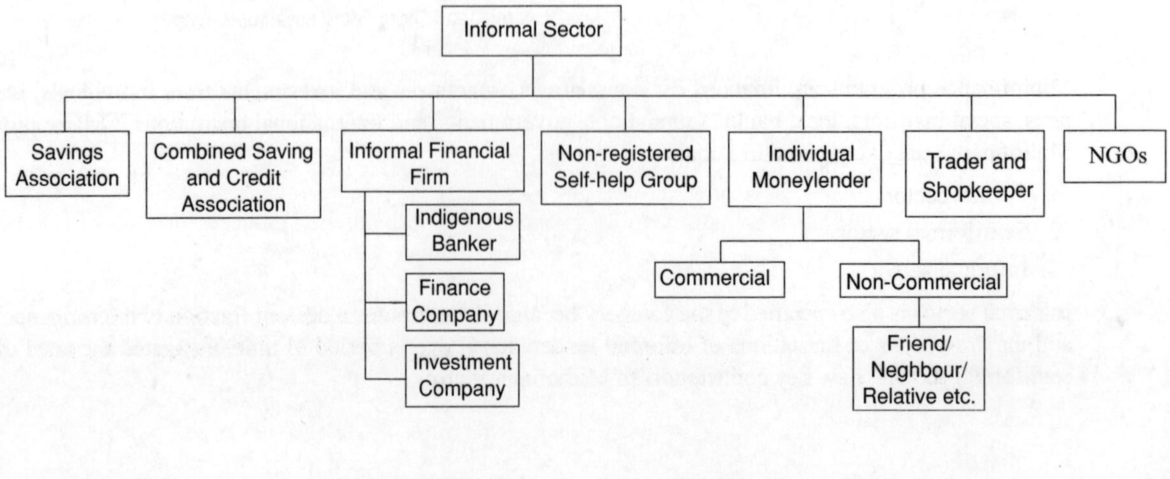

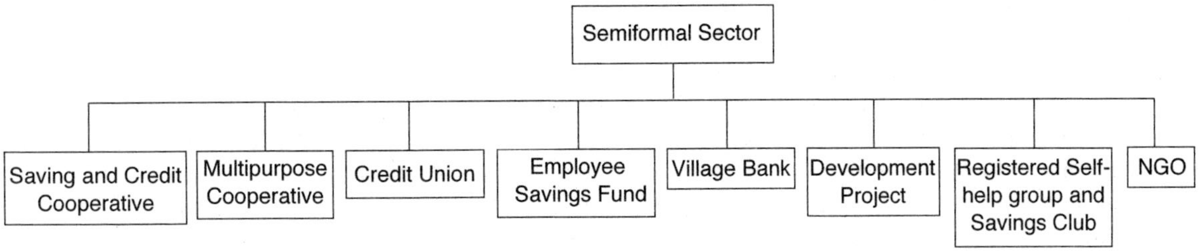

Challenges

1. The key challenge for lending organization is the Credit Risk involved in these transactions, and various factors that contribute in increasing this risk are:
   - Dependency on Seasonality: The traditional activity of agriculture, the major fraction among all, have high seasonal dependency and variation, thereby making loan recovery schedule dependent on these factors, and not on the planning.
   - Uncertain Market Conditions: The market, on which borrowers count for to sell their output and repay the loans, has high level of uncertainty of demand, price and competitors.
   - Deficiency of Skills: The borrowers take loans for, and are dependent on, one particular skill they possess to repay loans. Failure of that skill to generate desired result would lead neither borrowers nor lenders with alternates.
   - Lack of tangible history for income evaluation: Unavailability of income history makes it tough to predict future income.
2. It is extremely difficult to monitor the diversion of funds in unproductive activities, instead of purpose loan was taken.
3. A main disadvantage to microfinance is that the deal is too small for the lender to devote ample time and money to doing proper due diligence. The smaller deal size makes transaction cost comparatively higher. As the capital is low, the profits are also low.
4. Lesser technology and doorstep service for loan initiation and monitoring makes the operational cost very high.
5. The inability to reach the poorest of the poor is the biggest challenge and failure of such programs. As Gresham's law reminds us, if the poor and non-poor are combined within a single program, the non-poor will always drive out the poor.[30] To be effective, the system must ensure that it reaches the poor.
6. Due to lesser default, women are preferred and targeted over men in microfinancing programs. This may result in men requiring wife to get loans for them.

SECTION VII

PENSION FUNDS

When employees reach the end of their working tenure and embark retirement phase, a series of monetary payments are paid to worker or worker's survivor. Pension funds contribute on large scale to overall institutional investments. For instance, as quoted by *Organization for Economic Co-operation and Development,* pension fund assets in OECD countries contributes a record value of USD 20.1 trillion in 2011.

> A **Pension Scheme** is the set of financial, administrative, legal, social, and other arrangements established for the purpose of providing pensions to a designated group of workers and their survivors.[31]

More generally, a pension scheme is simply a saving scheme with deferred return as the source of saving. Pension schemes can be organized in several ways with various organizers including:

- Employer
- Government
- Trade union
- Other type of organization

Pension schemes that are arranged by government for the entire or segment of labour force are referred to as *social security schemes*. Based on government's overall fiscal policy as well as actuarial considerations, these schemes are created by, contribution made by and benefits are set by government.

Schemes arranged by employers or other organizations are referred to as *employer pension schemes*. These schemes are mutual agreements between employees and employer. The terms of such schemes are typically in the form of a legal contract. The terms of these schemes can be altered by mutual consensus of both the parties, by forming a new contract or agreement. Through employment, employees become eligible for participation in employer pension schemes. Employee's right to pension begins right away, and he/she begins to accumulate or contribute to the fund, but the right becomes vested only after a specified years of employment. After specified time period, the employee becomes eligible to pension benefits.

Pension Schemes are categorized mainly on the type of benefits and contributions:

1. *Defined-contribution Scheme*: In defined-contribution scheme, the employer is obliged by agreement to contribute a definite amount to the scheme on behalf of its employees. Normally this amount is derived as a percentage of the employee's wages and salaries, but it can be a fixed or variable sum if different formulas are agreed upon for calculation. This amount can be matching employee's contributions or according to legal limits. Employees also contribute to individual accounts and get tax advantage apart from future savings. The amount contributed by employee is excluded from current taxable income. These contributions are deposited in individual accounts for each employee. Since upon retirement, the employee or survivor receives benefits based on the contribution, employers invest these contributions in long-term financial assets in the meanwhile. These funds are invested in variety of assets, including shares, bonds, other financial assets, land, buildings, and valuables. The pension funds thereby have a liability to provide the committed pension benefits. The counterpart of the liability is a financial asset owned by the employees. This asset and its counterpart liability are classified as *insurance technical reserves*.
2. *Defined-benefit Scheme*: In defined-benefit scheme, the employer is obligated to provide specific benefits. The level of benefits offered is typically defined by a formula centred on the years of employment, the wages and salaries earned. There is no obligation of contribution on either employee or employer. Either party may or may not make contributions to the scheme. In case contributions are made, the amount deficit to provide an agreed benefit is borne by employer.

Pension Funds in India

Pension funds in India, like in other countries, are structured and controlled by Government Regulatory bodies. PFRDA, established by Government of India on August 23, 2003, is the regulator for the pension sector development and regulation in India.

Pension funds and related norms have modified and improved over a period of time to find justifiable solutions to the problem of providing satisfactory retirement income. One of the major amendment introduced by the New Pension System for the reform was complete shift from a defined benefit pension to a defined contribution-based pension system, making it mandatory for new recruits (except armed forces) from January 1, 2004.[32]

There are two broad categories of pension schemes in India:

1. *Tier-I Account*: In this option, a contribution of {10 per cent of basic + DA + DP components} in every month is mandatory. Though employees can contribute more than 10 per cent, government's contribution is 10 per cent. Any withdrawal of saved amount before retirement (at age of 60) is not allowed. These contributions also help in tax advantages as it is exempted from taxable income, subject to certain defined range by government. Once the saving is withdrawn post-retirement, it's taxable.
2. *Tier-II Account*: It is a voluntary savings facility. Neither does it provide tax benefits, nor there is any restriction on the time period after which withdrawals be done. These savings can be withdrawn on need basis.

SECTION VIII

ALTERNATE INVESTMENTS

As is evident from the name, an alternative investment is an investment product other than traditional investments, such as stocks, bonds, cash or real estate. They are mostly short-term investments, unlike traditional sources. These investments include[33]:

1. Commodities
2. Hedge funds
3. Real assets
4. Private equity
5. Structured products

It provides alternate source of investment and acts as a tool of diversification. These investments are expected to have low correlation with traditional financial investments, thereby reducing portfolio risk and diversifying investments. Initially, there was demand of retail investor to get into commodities, but it was difficult. The common way to trade commodities and currencies is through the futures and options market. However, trading futures is much more complicated than the ease of investing in equities. ETPs (Exchange-Traded products) were created with a familiar structure, thereby making investments in commodities and currencies easier to understand and more accessible like stocks.

Exchange Traded Funds: They are shares of a portfolio, not of any individual company. They are traded on stock market as common share.

Commodities

Commodities are raw materials, mostly natural resources that are sold in bulk, like silver, gold, oil, wheat, etc. The items traded as commodities are largely raw materials that are ultimately used to produce other goods. Commodities can be broadly categorised as[34]:

- Precious metals (*e.g.*, silver, gold)
- Livestock (*e.g.*, cattle, hogs)
- Agricultural products (*e.g.*, wheat, sugar, rice, corn)
- Soft commodities (*e.g.*, coffee, cocoa, cotton)
- Industrial metals (*e.g.*, copper, aluminium)
- Energy commodities (*e.g.*, crude oil, natural gas, gasoline)

Unlike traditional instruments, they cannot be evaluated using CAPM (Capital Asset Pricing Model) or NPV (Net Present Value). It is countercyclical asset, *i.e.*, its performance is reverse of market instruments like bonds and stocks. Commodities and inflation have positive correlation, whereas inflation and stock/bonds have negative correlation. So, commodities help in diversification.

There are various ways of getting exposure to commodity market:

1. Spot Market
2. Pure Play
3. Commodity Futures
4. Commodity Indices

1. **Spot Market:** It provides access to either the producer directly, or intermediary. In this case, the investor has to bear the storage cost too. This is feasible for some commodities, like precious metals, but not for all, like gas. It requires full payment at initial level itself. Its storage and other overheads are feasible and under control of investors. These markets provide better hedge against hostile price movements.
2. **Pure Play:** This involves buying shares of the company or organization producing the commodity investor wants to deal with. For example, an investor wishing to trade in natural gas would trade in company producing natural gas. The movement of the stocks of those companies are expected to move in sync with the commodity market. But the assumption has an inherent operational risk of the company and its management's performance.
3. **Commodity Futures:** These contracts are well-defined standardized agreements. They are backed by faith of exchange on defined terms mentioned in agreement. The future written on these commodities is another way of gaining exposure in commodities. Unlike Spot market, there is no need of full initial payment. Commodity futures require an initial margin only. Depending on direction of spot prices, future calls are determined.
4. **Commodity Indices:** Commodity indices provide access to commodities or commodities of a specific sector. Based on the total return on commodities, Commodity-linked Notes can also possible option to gain exposure in commodity.

Hedge Funds

Hedge funds can be defined as privately organized investment vehicle that generates investment opportunities by leveraging on its less controlled nature, unlike stringent and complicated requirements of mutual funds. They do not perform relative to some specific or index and seek to maximize returns in all market scenarios. Most hedge funds are in the form of either limited partnership or limited liability corporation or offshore corporation. The manager of the fund receives compensation, which has two components—base fee (independent of hedge fund performance) and incentive fee (percentage of the actual return of the fund). Hedge funds can be classified as follows:

- *Long/Short*: These funds take long and short common stock positions. They are not market-neutral but seek to make profit from greater returns on the long position that on the short positions.
- *Market Neutral*: They are modified long/short fund as they attempt to hedge against general market moves.
- *Global Macro*: These funds make bets on the direction of a market, interest rate or such factors.
- *Event Driven*: These funds attempt to capitalize on some distinctive chances in the market. This may be investment in a distressed company or in a probable merger and acquisition.

Real Assets: This involves direct ownership of nonfinancial assets. These assets have lesser dependence on value-creating factors, unlike for organizations where management performance and market acceptability determine the valuation. In prior times, land was the only valuable asset. Buying and selling occurs intermittently in local market. Transaction cost involved is comparatively high.

Private Equity: Private equity includes both equity and debt that is not publicly traded. Debt, in short-term, has high risk and thereby cash flow is uncertain. So, in highly leveraged company, debt behaves more or less like equity, especially in short-term. In a typical transaction, a private equity firm buys majority control of a firm, can be mature firm too. This is different from a venture capital wherein the investors invest in young or emerging companies, and seldom gain majority control.

Structured Products: Structured products are synthetic investment tools created to meet definite needs that cannot be met from the standardized financial instruments available in the markets. They can be used to reduce risk exposure of a portfolio or to leverage on the existing market trends. The investment for structured products might focus on a single security, on specific asset classes, or on a related sub-sector. Examples of Structured products are Collateralized Debt Obligation (CDO) and credit derivatives.

SECTION IX

CONSUMER RIGHTS AND PROTECTION APPLICABLE TO FINANCIAL SERVICES

'Consumer protection' consists of laws and organizations designed to ensure the rights of consumers as well as fair trade competition and the free flow of truthful information in the marketplace. Consumer protection laws are government regulations formulated to protect the rights of consumers. The laws are intended to prevent businesses that engage in fraud, scams or unfair practices. Consumer protection can also be asserted via non-government organizations and individuals as consumer activism.

Financial sector has been growing at a fast pace. This growth has led to increase in competition, advances in information technology, which in turn steered devising of highly complex financial products introduced in marketplace. These products demand deep understanding of their operations which is lacking in nascent financial consumers. There is a continually widening gap between the complex financial offering and consumer's skill to comprehend them. Consumer protection and financial literacy in developing countries are still in their initial stages. This leaves them vulnerable to unfair practices.

Economies of all countries across the world are deeply intertwined. The financial crisis of 2007–09 has been the recent demonstration of this. World Bank has been working upon the issue of Consumer Protection and Financial Literacy for the countries of the Europe and Central Asia Region, since 2005, by a pilot program. World

Bank's analysis suggests that the need for consumer protection arises from an imbalance of power, information and resources between consumers and their financial service providers, placing consumers at a disadvantage. It suggests that a set of good practices should be followed, which requires financial sector players to provide their consumers with:[35]

- *Transparency* by providing complete, accurate and simplistic comparable information about the prices, terms and conditions of financial products. The inherent risks should also be disclosed.
- *Choice* by ensuring impartial, non-coercive and rational practices in the selling and advertising of financial products, and collection of payments.
- *Redress* by providing economical and prompt mechanisms to address complaints and resolve issues.
- *Privacy* by guaranteeing control over access to personal information.

Consumer Protection and Regulation in India

Consumer protection in India is shielded by both statutory regulation and voluntary membership bodies (also called consumer activism). Strategic players in consumer protection in India are:[36]

- Reserve Bank of India (RBI)
- Banking Codes and Standards Board of India (BCSBI)
- Banking Ombudsman
- Indian Banking Association
- Consumer Courts
- Banks with Internal Customer Service Mechanisms

Reserve Bank of India, the main regulator for all financial institutions (like banks, NBFCs), establishes regulation and policy for consumer protection. The policy includes various aspects with provisions on pricing, transparency, recovery methods, and avoidance of multiple-borrowing. Financial institutions, like banks, adhere to these regulations. For instance, the Grievance Redressal Mechanism in Banks of 2008 recommends banks to implement an internal customer service mechanism that accepts and addresses customer complaints and resolves them with an unbiased and competent manner. These RBI guidelines are also specified by the BCSBI. Reserve Bank of India has set up local Banking Ombudsmen in majority of states in India. These Ombudsmen act as impartial watchdogs. In case of consumers' disputes with banks, these arbiters handle them at an appellate level. These complaints and grievances have either not been fully resolved by the banks or not been satisfactorily resolved in the opinion of the consumer. The Banking Codes and Standards Board of India (BCSBI), started as a collective venture between the banking industry and the RBI in 2005, serves as an autonomous authority for the industry. The BCSBI develops standards, enhances transparency and improves relations between banks and customers. The BCSBI has developed:

- Banking Code Rules—covering member bank obligations to BCSBI
- Code of Bank's Commitment to Customers Code—covering member bank commitments to customers

The Rules, also mentioned as the Fair Practices Codes, have to be complied by all member banks. The BCSBI also requires all banks to spread information to customers and manages a web-based helpline for customers. On a broader perspective, all those involved with regulation and protection of consumer rights work on set of good practices discussed by World Bank.

CHAPTER SUMMARY

- In NBFCs, most of the exposure is given to assets and it is a great help in non-banking regions.
- NBFCs are also playing a very important role for macroeconomic perspective and Indian financial system.
- NBFCs accounts for around nine per cent of financial assets and is continuously broadening the financial services with bringing in the high competition.
- Gaps in non-banking services are continuously been bridged up to strengthening its potential.
- Venture capitalist deals with the new and small business start-ups and bridges the gap of funds needed.

- VC allows business to open its wings completely by allowing it to execute each and every business activity.
- Private equity players always deal with large investments and mostly take 100 per cent of the ownership. It also helps in making new acquisitions.
- Basically, credit cards help you to buy goods and services even when you do not have money but for that you have to pay a certain amount to your issuer bank.
- A typical credit card transaction involves huge steps which are executed in couple of minutes only.
- Housing finance enables a person to buy, renovate and expand his house. The National Housing Policy, 1988, envisaged the setting up of NHB.
- NHB was set up on July 9, 1988, under the National Housing Bank Act, 1987. NHB is wholly owned by Reserve Bank of India with the entire paid-up capital contributed by RBI. Rural Housing Microfinance launch is one of the major milestones of NHB.
- Housing finance sector in India has been growing at a remarkable pace. Indian housing finance has developed from a stage where it was solely government-driven to the present stage of growth and multiple players.
- As IPO is interest free capital but the whole IPO process is very much expensive. Here, the corporate sectors are not forced to repay the debt but they can put limit on management freedom.
- IPO enhances liquidity for shareholders and investors as they cash out anytime but there is intense pressure on IPO to perform in the short term so that the shareholders can get their profit.
- Though microfinance is developing which is changing and developing business opportunities in context to Indian economy, it has got a lot of challenges also like dependency on seasons where the agricultural activities do not take place throughout the year along with the deficiency of skills as the borrower can only repay when he performs, otherwise he can repay the amount back.
- Pension funds in India, like in other countries, are structured and controlled by Government Regulatory bodies. PFRDA, established by Government of India on August 23, 2003, is the regulator for the pension sector development and regulation in India.
- There are two broad categories of pension schemes in India. Tier-I account in this option is a mandatory contribution of {10 per cent of basic + DA + DP components} in every month. Though employees can contribute more than 10 per cent, government's contribution is 10 per cent. Any withdrawal of saved amount before retirement (at the age of 60) is not allowed.
- Tier-II account is a voluntary savings facility. Neither does it provide tax benefits, nor there is any restriction on the time period after which withdrawals be done. These savings can be withdrawn on need basis.
- Alternate investment provides alternate source of investment and acts as a tool of diversification. These investments are expected to have low correlation with traditional financial investments by reducing portfolio risk and diversifying investments.
- The Banking Codes and Standards Board of India (BCSBI) started as a collective venture between the banking industry and the RBI in 2005 serves as an autonomous authority for the consumer rights and protection applicable to financial services.

TEST YOUR UNDERSTANDING

1. What is a NBFC and how is it different from banks?
2. What are the recent classifications of NBFCs under RBI?
3. Difference between VCs and PE.
4. How the Credit card transaction can be divided?
5. What is Securitization and Reverse mortgage?
6. Define Underwriters and their role.
7. What are the challenges in Microfinance?
8. What are the two broad categories of Pension schemes in India?
9. Comment on BCSBI.
10. What are the advantages of Alternative Investment?

ENDNOTES

1. http://www.rbi.org.in/home.aspx
2. http://business.gov.in/business_financing/non_banking.php
3. http://rbi.org.in/scripts/PublicationReportDetails.aspx?UrlPage=&ID=586#OVE
4. http://rbi.org.in/scripts/PublicationReportDetails.aspx?ID=671
5. Fundamentals of Corporate Finance, Vol. 1, Sixth Edition, Ross et al.
6. CFA Level 1 Study Guide
7. http://www.mbaknol.com/business-finance/stages-of-venture-capital-financing/
8. http://www.mergersandinquisitions.com/private-equity-vs-venture-capital/
9. http://www.investopedia.com/terms/c/creditcard.asp#axzz2E7esUwli on 12/04/2012
10. http://www.dimensionsinfo.com/credit-card-dimensions/ on 12/04/2012
11. Financial Services, 2E By Gurusamy
12. http://www.authorize.net/resources/howitworksdiagram/ on 12/04/2012
13. http://www.wikinvest.com/wiki/Interchange_fee on 12/05/2012
14. http://www.mastercard.com/us/wce/PDF/MasterCard%20Interchange%20Rates%20and%20Criteria%20-%20April%20 2008.pdf on 12/05/2012
15. http://www.wikinvest.com/industry/Credit_Services on 12/05/2012
16. http://www.housingfinance.org/housing-finance/what-is-housing-finance
17. http://www.nhb.org.in/AboutUs/about_us.php#Genesis
18. http://web.worldbank.org/WBSITE/EXTERNAL/TOPICS/EXTFINANCIALSECTOR/0,,contentMDK:22217029~pagePK:210058~piPK:210062~theSitePK:282885,00.html
19. http://www.investopedia.com/terms/s/securitization.asp#axzz2EOf6uMLj
20. http://nhb.org.in/RML/RML_Index.php
21. http://www.allbusiness.com/glossaries/investment-banker/4944014-1.html#axzz2Eg5TRBcR
22. http://www.investopedia.com/terms/l/leadunderwriter.asp#axzz2EgDV7eWy
23. http://www.investopedia.com/terms/r/redherring.asp#ixzz2EhC1uOAk
24. Introduction to Corporate Finance, by William L. Megginson, Scott B. Smart
25. http://external.worldbankimflib.org/uhtbin/cgisirsi/x/0/0/5/?searchdata1=643870%7Bckey%7D#_
26. Microfinance: Concepts, Systems, Perceptions, and Impact: A Review of SGSY operations in India, by Soumitra Sarkar and Samirendra Nath Dhar
27. http://web.worldbank.org/WBSITE/EXTERNAL/NEWS/0,contentMDK:21153910~pagePK:34370~piPK:34424~theSitePK:4607,00.html
28. http://www.grameenfoundation.org/what-we-do/microfinance-basics
29. http://www.csa.com/discoveryguides/microfinance/review3.php
30. Microfinance Handbook: An Institutional and Financial Perspective: By Joanna Autor Ledgerwood
31. http://www.investopedia.com/terms/p/pensionfund.asp#ixzz2FMYXJK9e
32. http://www.docstoc.com.lax.llnw-trials.com/docs/1009228/The-Treatment-of-Pension-Schemes-in-Macroeconomic-Statistics-a-discussion-paper-by-John-Pitzer-IMF-November-2002
33. http://www.pfrda.org.in/indexmain.asp?linkid=100
34. CAIA Level I: An Introduction to Core Topics in Alternative Investments, 2nd series, Mark J. P. Anson, PhD, CFA, Donald R. Chambers, Keith H. Black, Hossein Kazemi
35. Alternative Investment Strategies and Risk Management, by Raghurami Reddy Etukuru, MBA
36. http://siteresources.worldbank.org/INTECAREGTOPPRVSECDEV/Resources/GoodPractices_August2010.pdf

ANNEXURE I

(Amount in ₹ crore)

Year Ended 30th June	2006	2007	2008	2009	2010	2011
Sanctions	9,076	9,101	13,362	15,729	12,715	14,293
Disbursements	5,998	5,672	9,036	10,889	8,160	12,035
Net Owned Fund	1,730	1,831	1,999	2,230	2,485	2,770
Gross NPAs	27	27	Nil	Nil	Nil	Nil
Net NPAs	Nil	Nil	Nil	Nil	Nil	Nil
Profit After Tax (PAT)	86	101	170	236	280	279
PAT Per Employee	1.05	1.41	2.13	2.62	3.15	3.21
CRAR (per cent)	22	23	24	18	20	21

CHAPTER EIGHTEEN

18

Insurance Services

CHAPTER STRUCTURE

Section I Basic Concepts
Section II The Insurance Sector—An Overview
Section III Banks and Insurance Services—Bancassurance in India
Section IV The Global Insurance Industry—Opportunities and Challenges
Chapter Summary
Test Your Understanding
Topics for Further Discussion

KEY TAKEAWAYS FROM THE CHAPTER

- Understand the principles on which insurance is based on, and the broad classification of insurance products.
- Review the past, present and future of insurance sector.
- Look at the functioning of organizations like LIC, GIC and ECGC.
- Learn the process of liberalization in the insurance sector and look at new private sector firms.
- Learn why bancassurance adds value.

SECTION I

BASIC CONCEPTS

Insurance is a protection against a financial loss, arising on the happenings of an unexpected event. Insurance is a contract between two parties whereby one party called insurer takes a fixed sum called premiums, in exchange to pay the other party on the happening of a certain event. A loss is paid out of this premium collected from the insuring public. The insurance company acts as a trustee for the amount collected through these premiums. Insurance is generally classified into three main categories—life insurance, health insurance and general insurance. In order to get insured, an individual or an organization can approach an insurance company directly, through an insurance agent of the concerned company or through intermediaries.

In legal terms, insurance is a 'uberrimae fidae' contract—a contract of 'utmost good faith'. The compensation is contingent upon happening or non happening of a certain event. Insurance provides monetary compensation for the loss, damage or death, provided it falls within the framework of the specific terms of the insurance contract.

What will the amount of compensation of 'loss' be based on? The most important factor is 'value' – perceived value of the insured object or its potential value in future, or the value for which insurance has been taken. This implies that only those entities or activities that have ascertainable value can be insured. Assessment of 'value' is possible in all 'non life' (general insurance) contracts – say, insurance on property or vehicles – where the current market price as well as the future revenue generating capacity of the asset can be evaluated with reasonable data or assumptions.

But how does one value 'life' – and hence 'life insurance'? Unlike general insurance, no compensation can be considered adequate for loss of life. In fact, what is compensated is the loss of future income of the individual whose life was insured. Of course, this value would again depend on the age, health and earning capacity of the individual. Once a value is placed on these factors, the policy 'insures' the life. Hence, the essential difference between life and general insurance is that life insurance considers the future stream of cash that the insured person would be able to generate over his/her lifetime, while general insurance considers the present value of future cash flows possible from the asset.

Box 18.1 provides an illustrative list of the important terminologies used in respect of Insurance.

BOX 18.1 AN ILLUSTRATIVE LIST OF UNIQUE INSURANCE TERMINOLOGIES

Policy: The contract sold by the Insurance company

Policy falling due: Date of payment by insurance company—either due to contract terms or because the insured risk has translated into actual loss. Once a policy falls due for payment (as in the case of life insurance), the 'life' of the policy is over and insurance cover under the policy is no more available.

Premium: The amount to be paid by the insured person to enter into the contract or to maintain continuity of the policy.

Sum insured: The amount promised by the insurance company in case of claim at maturity, as in the case of life insurance or when actual loss occurs.

Surrender value: This term is applicable to life insurance policies. In case the person who has taken insurance decides to discontinue paying premiums after a few years before maturity, the insurance company would pay back 'surrender value', a value less than the actual amount of premiums already paid.

Assurance versus insurance: Though both terms are often used interchangeably, there is a subtle difference. Insurance refers to protection against loss that may or may not happen, as in the case of fire or theft. Assurance is protection against an event that is bound to occur sooner or later. Hence, 'life assurance' is possible, but not 'fire assurance'.

Basic Features of Insurance Contracts

A contract of insurance should contain certain essential features. Though some of these features may be found in contracts other than insurance, the following are the characteristic features that every insurance contract should contain:

1. **Insurable interest**: The person entering into the contract (buyer of insurance or policyholder) should have valid interest in the item being insured. This is called 'insurable interest'. This implies that the policyholder should be able to establish that a loss incurred in the item being insured would lead to direct monetary loss to the policyholder. Any insurance contract without insurable interest is considered in the nature of 'wagering contracts'. (In terms of Section 30 of the Indian Contracts Act, 1872, all wagering contracts are 'null and void').

   Generally, one rule to establish insurable interest is through ownership of the assets being insured. However, in special cases, such as mortgagees and mortgagors, agents, executors and trustees or bailees, partial ownership of assets insured is recognized as insurable interest. There are also certain classes of insurance that do not demand proving insurable interest, such as accident insurance and certain life insurance contracts. For example, in the case of insurance taken on the life of the spouse, the relationship itself is sufficient to prove existence of insurable interest.
2. **Utmost good faith**: As mentioned earlier, insurance contracts are 'uberrimae fidae' contracts. Voluntary disclosure of all information pertinent to the contracts is expected of both the insurer and the insured. Any material fact not disclosed at the time of entering into the contract, which is relevant to the contract, can render the contract null and void. Since it may not be possible in practice to conduct a thorough due diligence on every person or entity wishing to enter into an insurance contract, the agreements contain express 'warranties' from the insured and 'disclosures' from the insurer.
3. **Indemnification**: Under a contract of indemnity, the indemnifier provides assurance to save the counterparty from loss, caused by the action of indemnifier or a third party. Hence, every contract of insurance is a contract of indemnity. However, the party, whose loss is being compensated, should seek compensation for the loss alone and not attempt to make a profit on the compensation. It is noteworthy that the principles of insurable interest and indemnification are complementary, since the entity receiving insurance should prove that it will suffer a loss to the extent of the sum assured.

4. **Subrogation**: This is a corollary to the indemnification feature. It is the right of the insurer to take the place of the insured, after settlement of a claim (by the insurer) to enforce the right of recovery from the source that caused the loss. This means that if the insured suffers a loss due to the action of a third party and the insurance company has settled the insured's claim, the insurance company can step into the shoes of the insured to recover the loss from the third party that caused the loss. Subrogation therefore ensures that all rights in respect of the insured asset are transferred to the insurance company once the loss in indemnified. However, if after subrogation, the insurance company is able to recover from the third party more than the indemnified value, the excess amount will have to be paid back to the insured.

   It is to be noted that both 'indemnification' and 'subrogation' are not applicable to life insurance contracts.
5. **Warranties**: These are corollaries of 'uberrimae fidae', and are written as conditions in insurance contracts. These are explicit or express warranties. There are also 'implicit' or 'implied' warranties, such as 'affirmative' or 'promissory' warranties. For example, in marine insurance, an express warranty may be that the ship is seaworthy for a particular journey, or it would take a specified route to its destination. The implied warranties in this case would be that the ship is in perfect working condition, adequately equipped with machinery, supplies and skilled workers and is not overloaded. The insurance company will not be liable to compensate loss to the ship if the express or implied warranties are violated.
6. **Proximate cause**: This important feature of an insurance contract looks at the 'immediate cause' of the event that caused the loss. For example, if a machine is insured against floods and damage is caused due to collapse of the factory building in which the machine was kept, the insurance company is not liable to compensate even if the building collapse was due to floods. The proximate cause of damage in this case was 'building collapse' and not 'floods' as specified in the contract. However, if building collapse was included as an insured peril, the insurance company would have to compensate the loss.
7. **Assignment and nomination**: Both these aspects have been briefly discussed in the chapters on 'Credit'. Both life and general insurance policies can be assigned as securities for loans granted to the insured. Nomination refers to the procedure by which the nominee (in whose favour the nomination is made) to receive the proceeds of the policy without cumbersome legal documents. However, if an assignment is made, the assignor (the insured) ceases to be the owner of the policy. Hence, once the purpose for which the policy has been assigned is achieved and the insured becomes the owner of the policy once again, he would have to carry out a fresh nomination procedure.

Benefits of Insurance

Insurance is an instrument of security, savings and peace of mind. By paying a small amount of premium to an insurance company, one can avail of several benefits as follows:

- Safeguard oneself and one's family for future requirements
- Peace of mind in case of financial loss
- Encourage savings
- Get a tax rebate
- Protection from claims made by creditors
- Security against a personal loan, housing loan or other types of loan
- Provide a protection cover to industries, agriculture, women and children

Life insurance is universally acknowledged to be an institution which eliminates 'risk' and provides timely aid to the family in case of an unfortunate event like the death of the breadwinner. It is a contract for payment of a sum of money to the person assured (or the nominee) on the happening of the events insured against. The contract provides for the payment of premium periodically to the insurance company by the insured. The contract provides for the payment of an amount on the date of maturity or at specified dates at periodic intervals or at unfortunate death, if it occurs earlier. Some benefits of life insurance are as follows:

Protection Life insurance guarantees the full protection against risk of death of the assured. In case of death, the full sum assured is payable.

Long-Term Saving By paying a small premium in easy installments for a long period, a handsome saving can be achieved.

Liquidity A loan can be obtained against an assured policy whenever required.

Tax Relief Tax relief in income tax and wealth tax can be availed on the premium paid for life insurance.

Health insurance polices ensure guarding a holder's health against any calamities that may cause long-term harm to his life hampering his earning ability for a lifetime. These health policies cover individuals and groups.

There are several types of health policies as given below.

- Mediclaim policy
- Personal accident–individual
- Personal accident–family
- Group accident insurance
- Traffic accident policy

Types of Insurance Products

Broadly, insurance products can be classified as given in Figure 18.1.

FIGURE 18.1 BROAD CLASSES OF INSURANCE PRODUCTS

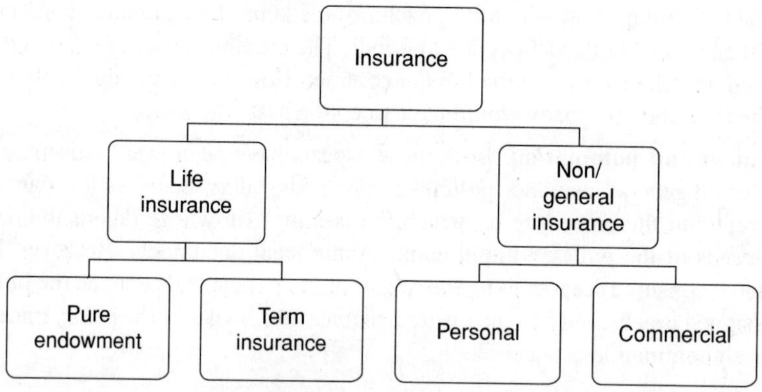

Life insurance: This is a contract between the insurance company and the insured person, whose terms specify that the insurer pay a specified amount of money at the end of the term of the policy, or in case of the death of the insured. The insured periodically pays a premium, the amount of which is determined based on the insured's age and health. At the end of the term or on the death of the insured, whichever is earlier, the amount along with bonus is paid to the insured or his family.

As shown in Figure 18.1, there are two basic types of plans under life insurance—pure endowment and term assurance. These are considered the building blocks of life insurance, and the other plans, schemes and annuity plans of life insuring companies are variants of these basic plans. Under the pure endowment plan (and its variants), the sum assured is paid on survival of the life assured for the term of the policy. Under the term insurance plan, in contrast, the insurance sum is paid only on death of the insured during the term of the policy.

An illustrative list of general insurance products is as follows:

- **Motor insurance:** There are two types of motor insurance.
  - Third party—which only insures the party/parties other than the owner in the case of an accident.
  - Comprehensive—which insures the owner as well as the third party involved. The premium for motor vehicles is decided on the value of the vehicle and location where it is to be registered. The premium for a heavy commercial vehicle is decided on the value of the vehicle and gross laden weight.
- **Property insurance:** This insurance covers land, building and the contents of the building.
- **Fire insurance:** This is a comprehensive policy. This policy, besides covering loss on account of fire, also covers loss on account of earthquake, riots, strikes, malicious intent and floods.
- **Burglary:** This insurance covers all losses arising out of burglary committed in one's premises.
- **Health insurance:** The holder can claim reimbursement of medical expenses.

SECTION II

INDIA'S INSURANCE SECTOR—AN OVERVIEW

The Insurance Sector

The economic growth and increase in population have made the countries, such as India and China as the most lucrative insurance markets in the world. Before 1999, Indian market was a monopoly with the state-run Life Insurance Corporation of India (LIC), the major player in life insurance sector and the General Insurance Corporation of India (GIC), with its four subsidiaries in the general sector. In the wake of the reform process and the passing of the Insurance Regulatory Development Act (IRDA) by the parliament in 1999, the Indian insurance sector was opened for private companies.

History The insurance industry has a long history. Life insurance, in its existing form, came to India from the UK in 1818. The Indian Life Insurance Companies Act of 1912, was the first measure to regulate the life insurance business. Later in 1928, the Insurance Companies Act was passed, which the government amended in 1950. On 1 September 1956, all the insurance companies were nationalized. The LIC of India was formed in September 1956, by the passing of the LIC Act by the Indian parliament in 1956.

The first general insurance company, Triton Insurance Company Ltd, was established in Calcutta in 1850. In 1957, the General Insurance Council, a wing of the Insurance Association of India, formed a code of conduct. In 1961, an insurance act was passed to form the GIC Ltd, which was amended in 1968. The general insurance business was nationalized with effect from 1 January 1973 by the General Insurance Business Act of 1972. 107 Indian and foreign insurance companies operating prior to 1973 were amalgamated and grouped into four operating companies under the GIC.

- National Insurance Company Limited
- New India Assurance Company Limited
- Oriental Insurance Company Limited
- United India Insurance Company Limited

All the above four subsidiaries of the GIC operate all over India. The GIC and its four subsidiary companies were government companies registered under the Companies Act.

The GIC as a holding company of the above four companies, super intends, controls and carries on the business of general insurance. The GIC undertakes mainly reassurance business and aviation insurance. The general insurance business of fire, marine, motor and miscellaneous is undertaken by the four subsidiaries. The general insurance industry has been growing at a rate of 17 per cent per annum.

Globalization and Liberalization The wave of globalization and liberalization is in full swing in the Indian markets. The insurance sector, being one of the most affected markets, has experienced a plethora of new relationships in the last couple of years. There are a few forces acting on the industry that have brought about significant changes in the behaviour of insurance policies.

India has become the second largest emerging market in the world. Emerging markets are characterized by low penetration and high growth.

Tables 18.1 and 18.2 provide basic information on the life and general insurance companies operating in India.

Though liberalization has led to an increase in the number of players, there is immense potential to increase insurance penetration in India. One study states that only about a quarter of India's population has life insurance. 'Insurance penetration' is defined as the ratio of insurance premium to GDP, and is considered a key indicator of the spread of insurance coverage and insurance culture.

People purchase insurance for various reasons—old age security, risk coverage, tax rebate, money for child's marriage and money for child's education in that order with diminishing importance. In terms of insurability, the market penetration and coverage of human life value of policyholders are both less than 20 per cent. To harness the full force of Indian potential for contractual savings like insurance, the industry must learn a differential technique for rural business in areas like product development and pricing, marketing, development of sales channels, sales process, service to customers and financial management with a rural bias.

TABLE 18.1 LIFE INSURANCE COMPANIES OPERATING IN INDIA (UPDATED UP TO THE END OF 2009)

Sl. No.	Date of Registration	Name of the Company
1.	23 Oct. 2000	HDFC Standard Life Insurance Company Ltd.
2.	15 Nov. 2000	Max New York Life Insurance Company Ltd.
3.	24 Nov. 2000	ICICI Prudential Life Insurance Company Ltd.
4.	10 Jan. 2001	Om Kotak Mahindra Life Insurance Company Ltd.
5.	31 Jan. 2001	Birla Sun Life Insurance Company Ltd.
6.	12 Feb. 2001	Tata AIG Life Insurance Company Ltd.
7.	30 Mar. 2001	SBI Life Insurance Company Ltd.
8.	02 Aug. 2001	ING Vysya Life Insurance Company Pvt. Ltd.
9.	03 Aug. 2001	Allianz Bajaj Life Insurance Company Ltd.
10.	06 Aug. 2001	Metlife India Insurance Company Pvt. Ltd.
11.	03 Jan. 2002	Reliance Life Insurance Company Ltd.
12.	14 May 2002	AVIVA Life Insurance Company Ltd.
13.	06 Feb. 2004	Sahara India Insurance Company Ltd.
14	17 Nov. 2005	Shriram Life Insurance Company Ltd.
15.	14 Jul. 2006	Bharti AXA Life Insurance Company Ltd.
16.	04 Sep. 2007	Future Generali India Life Insurance Company Ltd.
17.	19 Dec. 2007	IDBI Fortis Life Insurance Company Ltd.
18.	08 May 2008	Canara HSBC Oriental Bank of Commerce Life Insurance Company Ltd.
19.	27 Jun. 2008	Aegon Religare Life Insurance company Ltd
20.	27 Jun. 2008	DLF Pramerica Life Insurance Company Ltd.
21.	2008–2009*	Star Union Dai-ichi Life Insurance Company Ltd.
22.	05 Nov. 2009	India First Life Insurance Company Ltd.

Source: http//www.irdaindia.org
*(exact date not available)

TABLE 18.2 GENERAL INSURANCE COMPANIES OPERATING IN INDIA (UPDATED UP TO THE END OF 2009)

Sl. No.	Date of Registration	Name of the Company
1.	23 Oct. 2000	Royal Sundaram Alliance Insurance Company Ltd.
2.	23 Oct. 2000	Reliance General Insurance Company Ltd.
3.	04 Dec. 2000	IFFCO Tokio General Insurance Company Ltd.
4.	22 Jan. 2001	TATA AIG General Insurance Company Ltd.
5.	02 May 2001	Bajaj Allianz General Insurance Company Ltd.
6.	03 Aug. 2001	ICICI Lombard General Insurance Company Ltd.
7.	15 Jul. 2002	Cholamandalam General Insurance Company Ltd.
8.	27 Aug. 2002	Export Credit Guarantee Corporation Ltd.
9.	27 Aug. 2002	HDFC-Chubb General Insurance Company Ltd.
10.	03 Aug. 2007	Apollo Munich Health Insurance Company Ltd.
11.	04 Sep. 2007	Future Generali India Insurance Company Ltd.
12.	16 Nov. 2007	Universal Sompo General Insurance Company Ltd.
13.	27 Jun. 2008	Bharti AXA General Insurance Company Ltd.
14.	15 Dec. 2008	Raheja QBE General Insurance Company Ltd.

Source: http//www.irdaindia.org

Some of the discernable trends for a healthy industry in India are a change of strategy from a technology focus to an integrated business focus, management style from a functional control to leadership based on team-work, organization from a rigid hierarchical structure to a flexible team-based structure, performance measurement from a weak internal job orientation to a result-based business, funding from incremental induction to business value-based commitment and relationship with customer from 'sell what can be sold' to 'retain the customer for life'.

Changing Scenario of the Life Insurance Sector

Consider the following facts. Only 22 per cent of the insurable population in India possesses life insurance. What's more, in a country of over 1 billion people, life insurance premia forms only 1.8 per cent of the GDP, indicating the extent of underinsurance. Recognizing the huge potential in the market and the need to make insurance, particularly life insurance, available on a wider scale, the government opened the industry to private players in 1999 and was flooded with applications. Major international insurers—Prudential and Standard Life of UK, Sun Life of Canada and AIG, MetLife and New York Life of the US, to name a few, tied up with leading companies in India to reach out to this vast mass (see Table 18.3). Today, the Indian life insurance industry has many private players, each of which are making strides in raising awareness levels, introducing innovative products and increasing the penetration of life insurance in the vastly underinsured country. Several of the private insurers have introduced revamped products to meet the needs of their target customers in line with their business objectives. Some insurers, such as ICICI PruLife have fulfilled their mission to be a scale player in the mass market by introducing a slew of products to meet the need of each customer. Others have taken a more focused approach, introducing select products that they believe hold potential and fill market gaps. Whatever the case may be, each life insurer has approached the category with a fresh perspective. The success of the efforts is noteworthy—private players captured over 20 per cent of the premium income in less than 4 years since the beginning of operations, a figure that is growing each month.

Undoubtedly the biggest beneficiary of the competition amongst life insurers is the consumer. A wide range of products, customer-focused service and professional advice has become the mainstay of the industry, and the consumer forms the pivot of each company's strategy. On the back of advertising campaigns, seminars and workshops, one can see a dramatic increase in customer awareness. Penetration of life insurance is beginning to cut across socio-economic classes and attract people who have never purchased insurance before.

Life insurance is no longer a poorly understood product that is pushed on to people. Nor is it a product that is only to be bought hurriedly at the time of filling taxes. It is now catching on as an important element of the overall financial basket; one that is purchased to fulfil specific rational and emotional needs and has clear benefits and advisors are being trained to sell insurance as a solution to meet these needs.

Life insurance is now also being regarded as a versatile financial planning tool. Research indicates that Indians have four basic financial needs during their life—asset accumulation (house, car), protecting their family, securing their children's education and provision for their retirement. So, while there are three basic types of insurance, these have been structured with increased flexibility to meet focused requirements. Furthermore, these can be enhanced with riders to protect one against disability and provide monetary compensation at times of critical illness or surgeries. Apart from protection, life insurance policies are also ideal vehicles to save for retirement, because of their expertise in long-term fund management. By starting, say in one's early thirties, and saving regularly through a pension plan for say, 25–30 years, a person can accumulate a large amount at the time of retirement. This can then be invested in an annuity to provide a regular income.

In addition to innovation, there are two trends that stand out on the products front. The days of high guaranteed return products, which were unsustainable, are over. Products are now priced flexibly, realistically and sustainably. What does this mean for the consumer? With greater awareness, they are in a better position to understand the benefits and are accepting new products.

Another area of vast improvement is in the service attitude and delivery. From a system that left policyholders running from pillar to post to get policy serviced, service levels are steadily rising to make the customer the focus of each initiative.

Multiple touch-points have emerged—contact centres, email, facsimile, web sites and of course snail-mail—which enable the customer to get in touch with insurance companies quickly, easily and directly. In the process, response time has come down dramatically and information availability has become immediate.

As with privatization in any industry, the benefits are not restricted to the customer alone, but extend to society at large by generating employment for thousands. Over the past 2 years, insurance companies—both life and non-life—have collectively hired thousands of employees to staff their operations across the country. Most of them have been appointed as life insurance advisors who counsel and recommend products to insurance buyers. One of the most promising outcomes of this trend is that a job as an insurance advisor has become a practical career option for thousands of people who would otherwise not work—housewives, retirees, even those with just basic educational qualifications! Success levels are determined by the amount of effort one puts in, and the advantages are several—flexible hours, continuous learning and training, little or no investment, the pride of working with some of the most respected names in the financial services industry and an income stream that can continue for several years.

It is clear that the face of life insurance is changing. But with the changes, there come a host of challenges, and it is only the credible players with a long-term vision and a robust business strategy that will survive. Whatever be the developments, the future and the opportunities in the industry will surely be exciting.

Insurance Regulatory Development Authority (IRDA)

On the recommendation of the Malhotra Committee, the Insurance Regulatory Development Act (IRDA) was passed by the Indian Parliament in 1993. Its main aim was to activate an insurance regulatory apparatus essential for proper monitoring and controlling of the insurance industry. This Act helped several private companies to enter into the insurance market and some companies even joined hands with foreign partners. In this economic reform process, insurance companies could boost the socio-economic development process also. The huge amount of funds at the disposal of insurance companies could be directed towards desired avenues like housing, safe drinking water, electricity, primary education and infrastructure. The growth of the debt market also got a boost. Above all, the policyholders got better pricing of products from competitive insurance companies.

IRDA is responsible for the proper monitoring and controlling of the insurance industry. The IRDA is headed by a chairman, who is also the controller of insurance.[2]

IRDA, for the time being, prohibits 100 per cent foreign equity in insurance. It requires Indian promoters to invest either wholly in an insurance venture or establish a joint venture with a foreign partner. IRDA is the sole authority responsible for awarding of licenses.

IRDA Regulations

Due to the IRDA regulations, foreign players have to cultivate and develop long-term relations with potential Indian partners. The IRDA encourages domestic insurers to maintain maximum retentions commensurate with their financial strength and premium volume. Further, insurers must satisfy minimum obligations to serve specific rural and social sectors with phased operational targets. The IRDA also has tight controls and regulates rates, minimum capitalization and solvency, as well as advertisements, disclosure requirements, contract terms and conditions. Insurers must also satisfy minimum investment requirements in national government, state or approved securities (*i.e.*, not less than 50 per cent of the total invested assets for life insurers and 30 per cent for non-life and reinsures). Minimum investment in infrastructure and social sector assets also apply (*i.e.*, at least 15 per cent of life assets and 10 per cent for non-life and reinsures).[4] The general intent is to keep as much business in the country as possible, a somewhat questionable action given the potentially substantial economic benefits of greater geographic diversifications.

Tax Concession An investment in life insurance is not only a safety net, but also a great way to reduce tax burden. An illustrative list of income tax benefits available under various plans of life insurance is provided in Table 18.3.

TABLE 18.3 AN ILLUSTRATIVE LIST OF IT BENEFITS CURRENTLY APPLICABLE (2009–2010) IN RESPECT OF LIFE INSURANCE

Section of IT Act	Deductions Allowed in Respect of	Maximum Deduction Allowed from Taxable Income
80C	1. Life insurance premia, in respect of assessee, spouse, children or HUF member. 2. Deferred annuity plan payments in respect of assessee, spouse or children, with no option for cash payment in lieu of annuity. 3. Payments to pension annuity plans.	₹1 lakh (in aggregate under sections 80C, 80CCC, 80 CCD).
80CCC	Amount paid or deposited from taxable income in designated annuity plans for receiving pension from fund set up by the insurance company under the Pension Scheme.	₹1 lakh (in aggregate under sections 80C, 80CCC, 80 CCD).
80D	Amount paid to keep in force insurance on health of assessee and other members of family.	1. Deduction allowable up to ₹15,000 if an amount is paid to keep in force an insurance on health of assessee or his family (*i.e.*, spouse and children).

(Continued)

TABLE 18.3 (CONTINUED)

		2. Additional deduction up to ₹15,000 if an amount is paid to keep in force an insurance on health of parents. 3. In case of HUF, deduction allowable up to ₹15,000 if an amount is paid to keep in force an insurance on health of any member of that HUF.
80DD	Amount deposited for maintenance of handicapped dependent.	Up to ₹50,000 on amount deposited with LIC for maintenance of an handicapped dependent (₹1,00,000, where handicapped dependent is suffering from severe disability).
10(10 A)(iii)	Payment received by way of commutations of pension under select plans.	
10(10D)	Maturity/Death claims proceeds of life insurance policy (including bonus), with some exceptions.	

Life Insurance Corporation of India

Life Insurance Corporation of India (LIC) was formed in September 1956 by the Government of India. Its main duty was to spread the message of life insurance in the country and mobilize people to save for nation-building activities.

Over time, LIC became very popular in India. The central office of LIC is in Mumbai and it has seven zonal offices located at Mumbai, Delhi, Kolkata, Chennai, Hyderabad, Kanpur and Bhopal. There are over 100 divisional offices and 3,000 plus branch offices. There are more than half a million active agents of LIC. It also has offices in different countries for business transactions. LIC has entered into joint ventures abroad with several companies in the field of insurance.

LIC has a variety of insurance plans which helps all categories of people and their diverse needs. The funds generated through the premium of policyholders are divested to a number of socio-economic projects in the country. The LIC insurance plan is categorized as individual insurance plan, group insurance schemes, pension plans and capital market linked plans.

LIC Plans for Individuals The important insurance plans offered by the LIC are as follows:

- Whole life schemes
- Endowment schemes
- Term assurance plan
- Periodic money back plans
- Plan for high-worth individuals and key men
- Medical benefits linked insurance
- Plans for the benefit of the handicapped
- Joint life plan
- Plans for children's needs
- Investment plans

Export Credit Guarantee Corporation of India (ECGC)

The Export Credit Guarantee Corporation of India, the fifth largest credit insurer of the world was established in 1957 by the Government of India. Its main purpose is to cover the risk of companies on export credit. It is managed by a board of directors comprising representatives of the government, the Reserve Bank of India, the banking sector and insurance and exporting firms.

Major Functions The major functions of ECGC can be discussed as under.

- To provide a range of credit risk insurance, which covers exporters against loss in export of goods and services.
- To offer guarantees to banks and financial institutions to enable exporters obtain better facilities from them.

- ECGC also help exports by providing insurance protection to export-related activities, guidance in export-related activities, information on credit-worthiness of overseas buyers and information on about 180 countries with its own credit ratings, making it easy to obtain export finance from banks/financial institutions.
- Assisting exporters in recovering bad debts.

Policies issued by the ECGC can be divided into the following categories:

1. **Standard policy**: Shipments (comprehensive risks) policy, which is commonly known as the standard policy, is the one ideally suited to cover risks in respect of goods exported on short-term credit, *i.e.*, credit not exceeding 180 days. The policy covers both commercial and political risks from the date of shipment.
2. **Specific policies**: Specific policies are designed to protect Indian firms against payment risks involved in exports on deferred terms of payment, including services rendered to foreign parties and construction works and turnkey projects undertaken abroad.
3. **Financial guarantees**: Financial guarantees are issued to banks to protect them from risks of loss involved in their extending financial support at pre-shipment and post-shipment stages. These cover a host of non-fund based facilities that are extended to exporters.
4. **Some special schemes**: Transfer guarantee is meant to protect banks that add confirmation of letters of credit opened by the foreign banks.
   - Insurance cover for buyers' credit
   - Exchange fluctuation risk insurance

Overseas Investment Risk Insurance The ECGC has evolved a scheme to provide protection for Indian investments abroad. Any investments made by way of equity capital or untied loan for the purpose of setting up or expansion of overseas projects will be eligible for cover under investment insurance. The investments may be either in cash or in the form of export of Indian capital goods and services. The cover will be available for the original investment together with annual dividends or interest receivable.

SECTION III

BANKS AND INSURANCE SERVICES—BANCASSURANCE IN INDIA

Gradually all over the world, the separation of commercial banking activities from other financial services is blurring. In many countries, where such compartmentalization did exist, the barriers are being broken down through appropriate legislation and regulation. Financial liberalization and innovation have brought the worlds of banking and insurance closer.

Bancassurance refers to selling insurance products through banks' established distribution channels. Given India's size, its low insurance penetration, low insurance density and a very large bank branch network, it was only natural that banks entered the insurance business—since insurance is a financial product required by all banking customers.

The term 'bancassurance' stems from French origins (banc + assurance). In France, traditionally, a large part of insurance selling is being done by banks, and the term first appeared in 1980. Banks selling insurance products became common in other European countries too. Even in the United States, where there was a strict division between banking and non-banking activities, there is increased preference—post the Gramm-Leach-Blailey Act 1999—for banks dealing in non-banking financial products, especially insurance products. Several Asian countries too have adopted the 'financial supermarket' theme.

Following the Malhotra Committee recommendations,[1] the Government of India specified in August 2000 that 'Insurance' is a permissible form of business that could be undertaken by banks under Section 6(1)(o) of the Banking Regulation Act, 1949. Subsequently, the RBI issued the guidelines on banks conducting insurance business.

How Does Bancassurance Help Banks?

Bancassurance helps banks in the following ways:

- Banks are experiencing narrowing 'spreads' or 'net interest margins (NIM)' due to increasing competition. Hence, banks are being forced to look for alternate sources of income in the nature of 'fee based income' (Also see the chapter 'Sources of Bank funds').

- Such fee-based income should be stable and free of default risk. Bancassurance promises enhancement in earnings without the problem of NPAs. (See chapter 'Managing credit risk' for more on NPAs).
- Bancassurance requires little or no investment in additional infrastructure.
- Banks can take advantage of the low insurance penetration and density (both terms were defined earlier in this chapter), as well as their very large branch network to generate substantial income.
- Banks have the advantage of customer interface even in the age of automation. This is an advantage to enable banks understand customers' specific needs and design and market insurance and other financial products accordingly.
- Studies have revealed that adding life insurance activities to banking operations enabled banks not only to diversify their earnings but also increase assets under management substantially.

How Does Bancassurance Help Insurance Companies?

Bankassurance helps insurance companies in the following ways:

- Competition increased manifold with a number of foreign insurance companies in both life and non-life segments entering India through joint ventures. The huge market potential could be tapped only by increasing the distribution channels from the traditional 'agency' model.
- Insurers, especially those who were not subsidiaries to large commercial banks (*e.g.*, SBI Life, HDFC Chubb or ICICI Prudential), and those in the private sector, benefitted through collaborative arrangements with specific banks to reach a huge client base.
- In a study, Swiss Re noted that Greenfield start up operations would be easier without the need to recruit and train a large number of insurance agents. At best, insurance companies need to train existing frontline bank staff. Insurer's own agents could also act upon the client database obtained from banks. Thus, insurance companies can realize better earnings through cost effective operations and increased revenues.
- The proximity of bank staff to customers would help in understanding customer needs, which would lead to timely innovations or improvement in existing products to ensure better risk management.
- IRDA regulations require that a certain proportion of insurance revenues[2] should flow from the rural and social sector. Banks, with their extensive rural reach, would help achieve this objective, cost effectively.

How Does Bancassurance Help Customers?

Bancassurance helps customers in the following ways:

- We have seen that insurance rests on the 'uberrimae fidae' pillar. For a long time, customers have built long-term trust and relationship with the public sector insurance companies, such as the LIC. With several new private sector insurance players, many of them with foreign collaborations entering the fray, the customer is confused about their trustworthiness. Bancassurance can bring in trust, since customers have long standing relationships with banks who are selling the insurance provided by the new players.
- Customers can now enjoy almost all types of financial services at a single window provided by the banks.
- The single window financial supermarket concept relieves customers from having to scout for good deals for various financial products.
- Even if they do get good deals, many customers may not have sufficient expertise to evaluate the deal or product. The financial supermarket concept lends comfort to customers since the bank recommends the product.
- The 'one stop shop' for the customer's financial needs could also lead to cost effective products for customers; for example, a reduced premium rate due to economies of scope, as well as expert financial counselling.
- Banks take the role of financial advisors to the customer, since the relationship between the insurer and the insured is different from the relationship between the banker and the customer. Since customers trust banks due to their long standing relationship, the bankers' advice could be a source of reassurance to the customers.

Let us look at the typical models of bancassurance.

a. **The referral model:** This is the path of least risk for banks. They merely part with their client database for a commission. The client contact and deal closing is carried out by the insurance company or its agents.
b. **The corporate agency model:** Here, the bank assumes the role of an 'agent'. As a 'corporate agency', the bank trains its staff to assess customer needs for insurance and sell products. Understandably, the commission earned by the bank will be higher than for the referral model. However, the issues that could arise with

this model can be easily foreseen—the bank may run a reputation risk if its staff does not provide appropriate advice,[3] or specially trained staff would be required to handle the business, or the chosen employees may resist the change in their portfolio. However, many believe that this model can be made to work with proper training and incentives.

c. **The fully integrated financial service model:** Recall the concept of the 'operating subsidiary' model from Chapter 1 (Managing Banking and Financial Services—Current Issues and Future Challenges), as one of the alternative models for a financial conglomerate. In this case, insurance business is just one more line of business for the bank. This includes banks having fully owned insurance subsidiaries, with or without private/foreign participation. Indian banks, such as the SBI, ICICI Bank and HDFC Bank have already established and are successfully operating this model. For relatively large banks like these, this model could yield the benefits of synergy and economies of scope. International experience also finds that such fully integrated bancassurance performs better than other models.

Both the referral and corporate agency models are in vogue in India. The current regulations stipulate that banks can opt to become either referral providers or corporate agents, but they are permitted to do so only for one life and one non-life insurance company in India. Variants of these practices can be found in various parts of the world, as shown in Table 18.4.

TABLE 18.4 ILLUSTRATIVE PRACTICES ADOPTED BY VARIOUS COUNTRIES FOR BANCASSURANCE

Attributes	Variations in Practice
Ownership	• Independent operation (distribution agreements) • Joint venture • Subsidiary (captive)
Point of sales	• Insurance agents located in the bank's branches • The bank acts as a licensed broker • Bank staff are qualified insurance agents • Sales through mixed channels-direct mailing, Internet, branches
Products	• Simple products sold on an opportunistic basis • Simple products that are bundled with existing bank offers (for example credit life) • Advice-intensive product tailored to customer needs • Integrated financial products geared towards life cycles/key events of customers
Client database	• Limited sharing of the bank's customer database • Bank actively shares database with insurance partner(s)
Product supplier	• Products manufactured by the bancassurer • The bank is responsible for distribution only, products supplied by one (exclusive agreement) or multi-supplier
Policy administration	• Done by the insurance partner • Done by the bank's insurance subsidiaries • Outsourced to third parties

Source: Report of the committee on distribution channels, pages 23–24, accessed at http//www.irda.gov.in

SECTION IV

GLOBAL INSURANCE INDUSTRY, OPPORTUNITIES AND CHALLENGES

The Industry After the Financial Crisis[4]

The performance of the insurance sector since 2007 has been largely influenced by the sub-prime crisis that originated in the United States, and later engulfed most of the major world economies. However, except for a few major insurance companies, most insurance companies were not affected. Nevertheless, for the first time since 1980, insurance premiums declined in real terms. Life premiums appeared to be impacted more by a fall of about 3.5 per cent, while non-life premiums fell by 0.8 per cent. Profitability of insurance companies were further eroded due to losses on investments in volatile capital markets and higher cost of guarantees as well as lower revenues from management fees.

The United States of America accounts for 35 per cent of the global life and non-life insurance premiums. This reflects the concentration of wealth and high risk-awareness in that market. Japan has a global share of 21 per cent, mainly due to the public's strong reliance on life insurance products as an investment vehicle. The UK contributes to about 10 per cent of the world's total premium. Together, the three markets account for 66 per cent of world insurance premiums. It is worth noting that insurance industry too has its plate full of miseries. Non-life insurance companies suffered more than the life insurance ones. They were called upon to bear the loss due to the terrorist attacks; reinsurance companies had also doled out billions of dollars taking a severe hit in the process.

Challenges

There is tremendous potential for growth in the insurance industry because of the diversity and depth of the market. Amidst challenges of liberalization, intense competition and convergence of financial institutions, global insurers have called for greater cooperation among themselves and with the regulators. The life market is coping with challenges of new regulations, widened competition from banks and pressure to expand distribution channels. In recent years, insurers have expanded the frontier of insurability to include previous unfamiliar areas like political, gene and financial risk and would necessarily face greater challenges than before. In general, the key challenges are as follows:

Catastrophes Natural catastrophes include storms, floods and earthquakes. In recent years, the magnitude of catastrophic property—casualty disaster has become a major topic of debate. An approach based on traditional insurance according to the solidarity principle is better for all concerned and is feasible from an underwriting point of view.

Opportunities

Both life and non-life insurers see real challenges and opportunities in the market. Non-life insurers welcome the hardening cycle as a forcing factor to the industry to return to prudent underwriting basics, while life insurers feel there is greater scope for players with stress on financial planning, retirement planning, asset management and healthcare insurance. The key strength of the market is a strong consumer demand for insurance products, which is expected to continue for a long time.

Convergence

One conception of convergence is that the lines between banking, finance and insurance are increasingly blurred. For example, bancassurance, the provision of insurance products through banks, has developed into a major insurance distribution channel in Europe, where regulatory barriers are less restrictive than in other markets. Life products are more easily sold through banks than non-life products. The growth of bancassurance reflects several broad industry trends, including growing competition, a desire to expand existing distribution networks through cross-selling, a bank's desire for diversification, financial deregulation and the pursuit of cost efficiencies.

The Growth of Insurance Demand

Globally, insurers are increasingly pressured by the demands of their clients. The development of the global insurance industry over the past few years was considerably influenced by the booming stock markets, which enabled considerable capital gains to be made in the non-life business. This strengthening of insurers' equity capital increased underwriting capacity, while demand did not develop at the same pace, resulting in a dramatic fall in insurance prices. The stock market boom of the past few years led to a soaring demand for unit-linked insurance products in life business.

CHAPTER SUMMARY

The key areas for the IRDA for developing the emerging Indian insurance market are given below.

- In this world of continuous relationship marketing, the regulator has to strive to establish deep and direct linkages between the insurance companies and the policyholders in order to build a sustainable market.
- Achieving rapid sustainable growth requires that companies manage three horizons simultaneously, which are: growing current business, expanding into related businesses and seeding options for future growth.
- Delivering high-quality products, given the state of India's fragmented retail trade and extreme weather conditions, is often viewed as a challenge. To ensure growth of the insurance business, the regulator has to develop innovative business systems.

- Insurance would assist businesses to operate with less volatility and risk of failure and provide for greater financial and societal stability.
- The government has arranged for disaster management funds. NGOs and public institutions assist with fund raising and relief assistance. Besides, government provides for social security programs. Insurance substantially steps in to provide these services. The effect would be to reduce the strain on the taxpayer and assist in efficient allocation of societal resources.
- Insurance firms facilitate trade, business and commerce by flexible adaptation to changing risk needs particularly of the burgeoning services sector.
- Like any other financial institution, insurance companies generate savings from the insurance sector within the economy and make available the same in well-directed areas of the economy deserving investments.
- It enables risk to be managed more efficiently through risk pricing and risk transfers and this is an area which provides unlimited opportunities in the Indian context for consulting and education in the post-privatization phase with newer employment opportunities.
- The insurance firm's functions are based on the theory of 'loss minimization'. The expertise in understanding losses would enable better loss control.

TEST YOUR UNDERSTANDING

1. Which of the following is not a general insurance product?
   a. Motor insurance b. Life insurance c. Fire insurance
   d. Property insurance e. Health insurance
2. Which organization/agency gives a license to new private players?
   a. GIC b. IRDA c. SEBI
   d. ECGC e. None of these
3. Name three new players in the insurance sector in India.
4. Name three firms offering services in the general insurance segment in India.

TOPICS FOR FURTHER DISCUSSION

- Why did the government privatize the insurance sector?
- Do you think that the new players would survive in the insurance industry?
- Do you agree with the idea of tax rebate for investment in insurance products?

SELECT REFERENCES

1. Khan, M. Y. (1997). *Financial Services,* 2nd ed. Chapter 11. New Delhi: Tata McGraw-Hill.
2. Ray, Alok (2001). *Pros and Cons of Insurance Liberalisation,* in K. Seethapathi (ed.) *'Financial Services: Emerging Trends,* Chapter 22. Hyderabad: ICFAI Publication.
3. Bhusnurmath, Mythili (2001). 'Insurance Sector Reforms', in K. Seethapathi (ed.), *Financial Services,* Chapter 23. Hyderabad: ICFAI Publication.
4. Karunagaran, A.,(2006), "Bancassurance: A feasible strategy for banks in India", Reserve Bank of India Occasional Papers, Vol. 27, No. 3, Winter 2006, accessed at http//www.rbi.org.in
5. Report of the committee on IRDA distribution channels, (2008), accessed at http//www.irda.gov.in

ENDNOTES

1. In 1993, the Government set up a committee under the chairmanship of R. N. Malhotra, former Governor of the RBI, to propose recommendations for reforms in the insurance sector. The objective was to complement the reforms initiated in the financial sector. The committee submitted its report in 1994 wherein, among other things, it recommended that the private sector be permitted to enter the insurance industry.
2. IRDA notification dated 16.10.2002 and amendments can be accessed at http//www.irda.gov.in
3. IRDA annual report 2008–2009 provides information on major types of grievances/complaints against insurance companies, and the most prevalent complaint relates to 'wrong plan and term allotted'.(page 50, Table 53), accessed at http//www.irda.gov.in
4. IRDA annual report, 2008–2009, accessed at http//www.irdaindia.org

CHAPTER NINETEEN

Mutual Funds, Securities Trading, Universal Banking and Credit Rating

CHAPTER STRUCTURE

Section I Mutual Funds
Section II Trading in Securities/Shares
Section III Universal Banking
Section IV Credit Rating Services

KEY TAKEAWAYS FROM THE CHAPTER

- Understand the basics of financial services, such as mutual funds, bancassurance, securities trading.
- Learn the mechanism of universal banking.
- Understand the trends and progress of financial services sector.

SECTION I

MUTUAL FUNDS

A mutual fund is a trust that pools the savings of a number of investors who share a common financial goal. The money, thus, collected is then invested in capital market instruments, such as shares, debentures and other securities. The income earned through these investments and the capital appreciation realized is shared by its unit holders in proportion to the number of units owned by them. Thus, a mutual fund could be considered as one of the most suitable investment for the common man as it offers an opportunity to invest in a diversified, professionally managed basket of securities at a relatively low cost. Mutual funds can be broadly divided as open-ended and closed-ended funds. Companies, such as Franklin Templeton, Prudential, Unit Trust of India, Nomura Securities, etc. offer mutual funds for investors.

Advantages of Mutual Funds

- **Professional management and research:** Mutual funds are managed by professional fund managers who regularly monitor market trends and economic trends for taking investment decisions. They also have dedicated research professionals working with them who make an in-depth study of the investment option to take an informed decision.

- **Convenience:** With features like dematerialized account statements, easy subscription and redemption processes, availability of Net Asset Values (NAVs) and performance details through journals, newspapers and updates and lot more; mutual funds can be considered as a convenient way of investing.
- **Liquidity:** One of the greatest advantages of mutual fund investment is liquidity. Open-ended funds provide option to redeem on demand, which is beneficial during rising or falling markets.
- **Tax advantages:** Investment in mutual funds also enjoys certain tax advantages. Dividends from some specific mutual funds are tax-free in the hands of the investor in many countries. Also capital gain accrued from mutual fund investment for a period of over 1 year is treated as long-term capital appreciation and is tax-free in most of the countries.

**Systematic Investment Plan: Many companies offer systematic investment plan in which investors can deposit their money systematically every month or every week, instead of investing lump sum amount at a time.*

Types of Mutual Funds

- **Equity-based funds:** The investments of these schemes will predominantly be in the stock markets. The purpose is to provide investors the opportunity to benefit from the higher returns which stock markets can provide. However, they are exposed to the volatility of stock markets. Therefore, investors should choose this type of mutual funds based on their risk-taking capacities and willingness to think long term.
- **Debt funds:** Debt Funds invest only in debt instruments, such as corporate bonds, government securities and money market instruments. They completely avoid investments in the stock markets. Hence, they are safer than equity funds. At the same time, the expected returns from debt funds would be lower. Such investments are advisable for the risk-averse investor.
- **Hybrid funds:** Hybrid funds invest in a mix of equity and debt investments. Hence, they are less risky than equity funds, but at the same time provide lower returns. Some people prefer this type of funds because they believe hybrid funds offer optimum returns.

Important Terms

Net Asset Value Net asset value is the market value of the assets of the scheme minus its liabilities. The per unit NAV is the NAV of the scheme divided by the number of units outstanding on the valuation date.

Sale Price The Sale price refers to the price you pay when you invest in a scheme. Also called 'offer price', it may include a sales load (also known as Entry Load).

Repurchase Price Repurchase price refers to the price at which a close-ended scheme repurchases its units and it may include a back-end load. This is also called 'bid price'.

Redemption Price This is the price at which open-ended schemes repurchase their units and close-ended schemes redeem their units on maturity. Such prices are NAV-related.

Sales Load Sales load is a charge collected by a scheme when it sells the units. It is also called 'front-end' load. Schemes that do not charge a load are called 'no-load' schemes.

Exit Load or Repurchase Exit load refers to a charge collected by a `mutual fund` company when it buys back the units from the holders.

SECTION II

TRADING IN SECURITIES/SHARES

The rapidly advancing technology, particularly the Internet, has drastically changed the economic landscapes and every aspect of our daily life. In the securities industry, the Internet has facilitated online trading, changing the way the market works, as well as the way the investors access the market.

'Online trading' is broadly defined as a trading mechanism where investors place orders and confirm trading results via electronic communication channels, such as the Internet, mobile phones and personal digital assistants. The whole process of securities transactions, from order placement and execution to trade confirmation, is fully automated, thus, enabling the investors who have placed orders to confirm their trading results within a few seconds in many countries.

Factors Behind Growth of Online Trading

The drastic growth of online trading in the world did not happen by chance. Initially, online trading was not well received by investors, as the concept of e-commerce was new to them. Once the investors recognized its advantages, however, online trading flourished rapidly, especially among individual investors.

Key factors that have fostered the growth are as follows:

1. First, the rapid growth of Internet-using population
2. Liberalization of brokerage commissions allowing securities companies to determine their own rates autonomously. The liberalization of brokerage commission triggered a price competition among securities companies, ending up with the reduction of fees for online trading.
3. The speed and lower transaction costs of online trading encouraged investors to trade frequently in pursuit of short swing profits, making day trading prevalent in the market.

Impact on Securities Market

The prevalence of online trading had significant impacts on the trading patterns of investors and trading volume. Let us see the extent of impact one-by-one.

1. Online trading has significantly contributed to the growth in trading volume.
2. Transaction costs have been significantly lowered after online trading was introduced. Initially, a 0.5 per cent of brokerage commissions were applied to both online and traditional transactions. Due to the price competition, brokerage commissions for online trading continued to be lowered to as low as 0.2 per cent charged by a few broking houses.
3. Lowering of the capital requirements for the establishment of broking-only securities firms prompted establishment of several broking-only securities firms, which are exclusively engaged in online trading businesses. The low fee strategies of these securities firms further accelerated price competition.
4. Lastly, after online trading was introduced, individual investors could have an easy and speedy access to market information. The number of securities market-related Web sites increased rapidly, providing a variety of information, including quotation information, corporate disclosure, financial information, research papers and financial news, on a real-time basis.
5. Excessive day trading increased the price volatility and some devious large investors attempted to mislead investors by placing fake orders.

SECTION III

UNIVERSAL BANKING

The term 'universal banking' in general refers to the combination of commercial banking and investment banking, *i.e.*, issuing, underwriting, investing and trading in securities. In a very broad sense, however, the term 'universal banks' refers to those banks that offer a wide range of financial services, beyond commercial banking and investment banking, such as insurance. However, universal banking does not mean that every institution conducts every type of business with every type of customer. In the spectrum of banking, specialized banking is on the one end and the universal banking on the other.

Financial institutions with focus on 'universal banking' offer the entire range of financial services. They sell insurance, underwrite securities and carry out securities transactions on behalf of others. In other words, a 'universal bank' is a 'one-stop' supplier for all financial products and activities like deposits, short-term and long-term loans, insurance, investment banking, etc.

There are multi-product firms in the financial services sector whose complexity is difficult to manage. In their organizational structure and strategic direction, universal banks constitute multi-product firms within the financial services sector. This profile of universal banks presents shareholders with an anagram of distinct businesses that are linked together in a complex network.

The structural form of universal banking appears to depend on the ease with which operating efficiencies and scale and scope economies can be exploited—determined in large part by product and process technologies—as well as the comparative organizational effectiveness in optimally satisfying client requirements and bringing to bear market power.

Many bankers argue that 'bigger is better' from a shareholder perspective, and usually point to economies of scale as a major reason for 'universal banking' activity.

It seems that banks of roughly the same size and providing the same range of services may have very different cost levels per unit of output. The reasons may involve efficiency—differences in the use of labour and capital, effectiveness in the sourcing and application of available technology and perhaps in the acquisition of skilled labour, strategy, organizational design, compensation and incentive systems—and just plain better management.

Size and Market Power

Universal banks are able to extract economic rents from the market by application of market power. However, in many national markets for financial services, these types of organizations suppliers have shown a tendency towards oligopoly, but may be prevented by regulation or international competition from fully exploiting monopoly positions.

Diversification—Insurance and Securities

There are potential risk-reduction gains from diversification in universal financial service organizations. Indeed, these gains increase with the number of activities undertaken. The main gains appear to arise from combining commercial banking with insurance activities, rather than with securities activities.

Core of Universal Banking

A bank uses its lending power activities to tie-in a customer and uses it as an opportunity for cross-selling securities and insurance products.

Impartial Investment Advice

There is a lengthy list of problems, involving potential conflicts between banks' commercial and investment roles. For example, there may be possible conflict between the investment banker's promotional role and commercial banker's obligation to provide impartial advice.

Benefits to Banks

'Universal Banking' enables banks to leverage from economies of scale and scope. What it means is that a bank can reduce average costs and, thereby, improve spreads if it expands its scale of operations and diversifies its activities.

By diversifying, a bank can use its existing expertise and infrastructure in one type of financial service to provide the other types of services. So, it entails less cost in performing all the functions by one entity instead of separate specialized organizations. A bank possesses information on the risk characteristics of its clients, which it can use to pursue other activities with the same clients. This again saves cost compared to the case of different entities catering to the different needs of the same clients. A bank has an existing network of branches, which can act as shops for selling products like insurance. This way a big bank can reach the remotest client without having to appoint many agents. Many financial services are inter-linked activities, *e.g.*, insurance and lending. A bank can use its instruments in insurance to borrower and vice versa, and exploit the other, *e.g.*, lending to the same firm which has purchased insurance from the bank.

Benefits to Customers

The idea of 'one-stop-shopping' saves a lot of transaction costs and increases the speed of economic activity. Another manifestation of universal banking is a bank holding stakes in a firm (sometimes, banks undertake this kind of activity). A bank's equity holding in a borrower firm acts as a signal for other investors on the health of the firm, since the lending bank is in a better position to monitor the firm's activities. This is useful from the investors' point of view.

Challenges

Having explained the benefits, let us talk about the problems of 'universal banking'. These benefits have to be weighed out against the problems. The obvious drawback is that 'universal banking' leads to an imperfectly competitive market structure like oligopoly.

SECTION IV

CREDIT RATING SERVICES

Credit rating has become a benchmark criterion for investors, borrowers, banks and financial institutions while taking decisions. The 'rating' mechanism helps the organizations to compare the performance of financial service providers, and work as a basis for strategy formulation in this era of competition. This section is an outcome of an attempt to look at the prospects and consequences of 'credit rating' system in the financial sector. The goal is to discuss the rationale for credit rating, benefits of the system for investors, issuers, regulators and the functioning of rating agencies.

Credit Rating—An Overview

The trend of establishing local credit rating agencies started only in the 1970s. Prior to this, the two international rating agencies, namely, Standard & Poor's and Moody's Investors Service, dominated the rating world. However, since the establishment of the first known local rating agency, the Canadian Bond Rating Services in 1972, local rating agencies have proliferated across the globe, both in the developed markets (Australia, France and Japan) and also in a large number of emerging markets. Currently, there are ratings agencies in Argentina, Brazil, Chile, Columbia, India, Israel, Korea, Malaysia, Mexico, Pakistan, Peru, Philippines, Portugal, Sri Lanka, South Africa, Thailand, Tunisia and Venezuela, which are duly recognized and are in operation. It is interesting to note that in several other important emerging markets in the East European countries and republics of the former Soviet Union, rating agencies still have to be established or are in the process of being established. The main motivation for the establishment of local rating agencies is the recognition of their critical role in promoting bond or other fixed-income securities markets. At the same time, there is increasing realization that rating agencies are likely to impart efficiency to the financial and capital markets. The experience of these emerging markets provides ample evidence of the positive impact of rating agencies. Credit rating provides an important tool for guiding the decisions of investors, issuers as well as regulators.

Information to Investors

Traditionally, ratings were used mainly for investment decisions covering acquisition of fixed-income securities in the primary market. As long as the risk level of the security, indicated by the rating, conformed to the investor's risk preference, there was a tendency to acquire and hold to maturity. However, this traditional approach has changed since the credit rating mechanism came to be recognized as a continuing evaluation rather than a one-time exercise. Currently, all rating agencies feel obliged to continuously monitor the ratings and upgrade or downgrade them as warranted by any significant developments. This process provides added advantage to investors to adjust their portfolio by maintaining a consistent risk profile.

Credit ratings are often used by banks and other financial intermediaries to support decisions on their own corporate lending. Banks, *e.g.*, may use bank deposit ratings to guide their decisions on inter-bank loans, trade finance, swap agreements and other counterparty risks. Increasingly, corporate treasurers are also using ratings to evaluate the credit risk of banks, securities firms and other counterparties.

As the credit rating agencies develop organizationally and their coverage includes a critical mass, they acquire the capacity to provide vital information to the market through dissemination of ratings. It is generally recognized that information available in credit rating reports is of greater value than that generally available through other sources of corporate financial data. Rating agencies are, therefore, being increasingly viewed as providers of professional credit research services that major institutional investors use to supplement their internal credit evaluation.

Benefits to Issuers

Although the principal beneficiaries of credit rating are investors, the cost of this service is borne by the issuers of fixed-income securities. It follows, therefore, that unless corporate issuers see any measurable benefit, there would be little interest in exposure to additional scrutiny and cost that a rating process involves.

Cost savings with rated debt instruments may also show up in comparison with other forms of financing alternatives. For example, some investors who otherwise could have required a bank guarantee to purchase a given debt security may instead accept a sufficiently high rating from a recognized agency. Depending on the situation, the cost of the credit rating may be less than that of a bank guarantee. As the credit rating culture develops, it is likely that the cost of issuing rated short-term commercial paper is lower than the cost of bank credit facilities.

The ratings and associated analysis of an independent agency can also help debt issuers to manage investor perceptions of credit risk over time—and consequently to maximize access to the capital market even in times of stress. For example, a news item could adversely affect the prices of a company's outstanding bonds, and some investors may, thus, be disinclined to make further investments in new issues by the company. An appropriate rating action by an independent rating agency—accompanied by an analytical statement about how the new situation will affect the company's financial strength—could help to maintain investor confidence.

Benefit to the Regulators

Financial regulators have also found that ratings may service a variety of uses. In the United States, *e.g.*, many state and federal agencies use ratings as an independent yardstick to regulate the eligibility of some issuers to offer new debt securities. Many regulators also use independent credit ratings to help them monitor the financial soundness of the insurance companies and public utilities. While there is no consistent pattern about the extent of reliance by regulators on ratings in different countries, there is increasing recognition that use of ratings facilitates the regulatory role. In countries like France, Japan, India, Malaysia, Thailand and Australia, regulators of the financial capital markets can use different variants of mandatory ratings. The mandatory ratings of all local rating agencies are, therefore, not unique and are generally in line with the current global practice.

Differences of Opinion in the Credit Rating Industry

Some studies have suggested, that among the many variables considered, only size and bond issuance history are consistently related to the probability of having third ratings. These variables probably reflect differences in the relative costs of third ratings across firms.

Rating-dependent financial regulators assume that the same letter ratings from different agencies imply the same levels of default risk. Most 'third' agencies, however, assign significantly higher ratings on average than Moody's and Standard & Poor's. Contrary to the claims of some rating industry professionals, sample selection bias can account for at most half of the observed average difference in ratings.

An attempt has been done to investigate the economic rationale used by multiple rating agencies. Among the many variables considered, only size and bond-issuance history are consistently related to the probability of an issuer seeking third ratings. The probability appears unrelated to uncertainty over default risk or firms' opportunities to improve their standing under rating-dependent regulations.

Regulators, like investors, value the cost savings achieved through the use of credit ratings in credit evaluation. As a result, they have come to rely on a variety of specific letter ratings as thresholds for determining capital charges and investment prohibitions. The regulatory use of ratings, however, does not account for the fact that some rating agencies appear to have different absolute scales, some rating bonds higher or lower on average on jointly rated issues than Moody's and Standard and Poor's (S&P), the two leading agencies. At present, the ratings of the four major U.S. agencies are used interchangeably in regulations issued by the Securities and Exchange Commission (SEC) and the National Association of Insurance Commissioners. Critics of the current system have recommended that regulatory usage be limited only to those agencies that have demonstrated a market impact, or that ratings should not be used at all by financial regulators.

While for decades, Moody's and S&P's have automatically assigned ratings to all corporations issuing in the U.S. public bond markets, Fitch and Duff & Phelps—the two other major agencies—have issued ratings only upon request. These 'third' agencies have argued that their ratings have often been sought when there is a strong expectation by issuers of improving upon Moody's and S&P's ratings. However, whenever Fitch and Duff & Phelps would have rated lower, their ratings would not have been purchased.

Certainly, the mechanism of reputation should serve as a powerful incentive to maintain ratings that are not too out-of-line with established standards. The rationale for obtaining credit ratings has traditionally been viewed in the finance literature to be the economies of scale in information collection and the reduction of agency costs in the issuance of debt. If investors were to lose confidence in an agency's ratings, issuers would no longer believe they could lower their funding costs by obtaining its ratings. To this extent, we might expect the credit rating agency's reputation in the bond market to play a role similar to that of the underwriter's in the initial public offering market, where reputation checks the degree to which low-quality issues are brought to the market.

It is possible that the reputation mechanism works imperfectly in a credit rating industry characterized by regulation-related demand. Firms may purchase an agency's ratings in order to meet regulatory guidelines independent of how that agency's ratings are viewed in the marketplace. As a result, concerns over 'rating shopping' have prompted the SEC to reconsider the use of ratings in regulations and its procedures for identifying with agencies' ratings it recognizes.

Ultimately, whether observed rating differences reflect different credit standards is an empirical question. Are the default risks associated with a particular letter grade higher for some agencies than for others? Or, do the third agencies appear to have lower credit standards just because they provide ratings only upon request? In addition, do firms systematically employ credit rating agencies to clear regulatory hurdles?

The bond ratings of the four agencies are comparable in the sense that they attempt to measure the likelihood of the default or delayed payment of a security. But while each agency's ranking of relative default risks is fairly straightforward, the correspondence between their symbols and absolute levels of default risk has not been made explicit by the agencies. Standard & Poor's, Duff & Phelps and Fitch use the same basic set of rating symbols, but Moody's uses a slightly different system.

As ratings have gained greater acceptance in the marketplace, regulators of financial markets and institutions have increasingly used them to simplify the task of prudential oversight. The reliance on ratings extends to virtually all financial regulators, including the public authorities that oversee banks, thrifts, insurance companies, securities firms, capital markets, mutual funds and private pensions.

CHAPTER SUMMARY

- The creation of bancassurance operations has a material impact on the financial services industry at large. Banks, insurance companies and traditional fund management houses are converging towards a model of global retail financial institution offering a wide array of products. It leads to the creation of 'one-stop shop' where a customer can apply for mortgages, pensions, savings and insurance products.
- Banks' desire to increase fee income works as motivating factor for them to look at insurance. Insurance carriers and banks can become part of the vision through strategic partnerships.
- Online trading can flourish when certain conditions are in place and interact with each other positively. Among others, large Internet-using population, well-established communication infrastructure, the provision of incentives for online trading, deregulation and favourable market conditions are necessary to encourage online trading. It should be kept in mind that online trading has both positive and negative effects on the securities market. It is necessary to address the negative effects. Ignoring the risks involved, one might be drowned while sailing the ocean.

TEST YOUR UNDERSTANDING

1. Name three companies offering mutual fund services.
2. Mutual funds offer the following types of funds:
   a. Equity, debt and hybrid types,
   b Equity and debt funds
   c. Only equity-based funds
   d. Only hybrid funds
3. The market value of the assets of a mutual fund scheme minus its liabilities is known as:
   a. NAV
   b. GAV
   c. Entry load
   d. Exit load
4. Bancassurance in its simplest form is the distribution of insurance products through a bank's distribution channels. State whether this statement is true or false.

TOPICS FOR FURTHER DISCUSSION

- Discuss the synergies of universal banking.
- Compare and examine different type of mutual fund products.
- Discuss the scope of credit rating services.

SELECT REFERENCES

1. Seethapathi K (2001), Financial Services, edited, ICFAI Hyderabad.
2. Masahiko Egami and Hideki Iwaki (2008), An Optimal Life Insurance Policy in the Investment-Consumption Problem in an Incomplete Market, Paper Presented at the Asian Finance Association 2008 International Conference held during 6–9 July 2008, Tokyo, Japan.
3. AMFI (2007–08), Annual report.
4. Paul, Justin (2009), *Business Environment*, 2nd edition, McGraw-Hill.
5. Ravi Mohan R (2000), 'Credit Rating: A Paradigm Shift', Chartered Financial Analyst, December, pp 71–73.
6. Reddy Y. V (2000), 'Credit Rating: Changing Perspectives', RBI Bulletin, May, P 507.
7. Rating Scan (2004), CRISIL publication.
8. www.crisil.com, accessed on 30 January, 2009.
9. www.icraindia.com, accessed on 15 December 2008.

CHAPTER TWENTY

Cash Management and Demand Forecasting in ATMs[1]

CHAPTER STRUCTURE

KEY TAKEAWAYS FROM THE CHAPTER

- Learn how to determine the cash flow from banks and ATMs.
- Analyze forecasting methods to decide optimum cash in ATMs to avoid a stock-out situation.
- Analyze data from the ATMs of two banks in Mumbai city.

SECTION I

INTRODUCTION

All retail banks including leaders are competing for a larger share of customers' financial transactions. Their efforts are directed toward attracting and retaining customers by offering them a basket of tailor-made schemes supported by a state-of-the-art distribution system (the ATMs). The whole exercise is helping the banks to serve their customers fast and avoid human intervention totally. And for the customers, ATMs offer hassle-free cash withdrawal. There are no more fighting with the bank's teller for change and fresh notes. The ATM has become a medium for non-cash transactions, such as payment of bills, insurance payments, printing of statements or even accessing the Internet.

Cash management service (CMS) is a new product off the block, which facilitates the banks to source cheaper funds and serve its clients (having widespread networks across the country) more efficiently. The analysis is based on the cases of two banks, namely Bharath Bank and Global Bank[2] and the data from their ATMs in Mumbai city.

The product in this chain is cash. The objective of this chapter is to primarily study the information flow and the fund flow in the supply chain of the retail banks in the country.[3] The supply chain in retail banks needs to be more responsive to the needs of the customers in comparison to the traditional FMCG industry. All the intermediaries in the supply chain play an important role in making the supply chain more efficient. The various aspects involved are the logistics involved in ATM operations, role of forecasting in retail outlets and ATMs and the parameters that are taken into consideration, scope of network sharing and issue of having the right mix of currency denomination to be able to satisfy the demand. The chronic problem faced in such a scenario is cash stock-outs and banks are increasingly trying to synergize their supply chain with that of the external agents (ATM vendors, outsourcing agents and VISA network) involved in this process.

The players in a retail bank's supply chain are the RBI, the corporate branch of the bank in the city, the retail branches, the delivery channel coordinators, outsourced agents who take care of physical cash movement, ATMs and ATM vendors.

The key elements in the supply chain are cash flow, information flow and IT infrastructure, lead time of cash replenishment, payments and receipts, different denominations of currencies and geographical locations and status of accounts (corporate accounts and salary accounts).

In case of financial services and banks, it is presumed that the demand drivers for cash are those factors which increase the propensity of cash withdrawal (retail as well as ATMs) and cash deposits. Certain demand drivers having a substantial effect on the final level of demand are the following:

- Location of the branch/ATM
- Number of current accounts
- Resident accounts and their age profile (for example, some banks have a captive audience of pension holders)
- Number of salary accounts
- Seasonal factors including weekends and festivities

In order to understand this concept, two banks were selected—Bharath Bank and Global Bank. Their cases will be discussed in detail in the following sections.

SECTION II

THE CASE OF BHARATH BANK

Let us assume that Bharath Bank has 22 branches and 120 ATMs in Mumbai. Like any bank in the country, it does maintain an account with the RBI for cash reserve rates (CRR) requirements. In addition to this, the RBI also offers a 'currency chest' facility to the banks. Under this facility, the banks can operate their accounts for their daily requirements of cash ensuring that the CRR is maintained at the end of the day. However, Bharath Bank has not subscribed to this facility. It uses its Nariman Point branch as the central point for all cash issuance to the branches and ATMs in Mumbai. Figure 20.1 describes the flow of funds in the entire retail banking segment of the bank.

In the case of Bharath Bank, the corporate accounts and taxation department at Bandra Kurla Complex (BKC) has worked out a certain retention limit for all the branches as well as the ATMs. The factors on which such a limit is calculated by the department are as follows:

- Total deposits of the branches
- Total advances (amount lent to the customers)
- Branch location

FIGURE 20.1 STRUCTURE OF BHARATH BANK ATMs AND BRANCHES IN MUMBAI

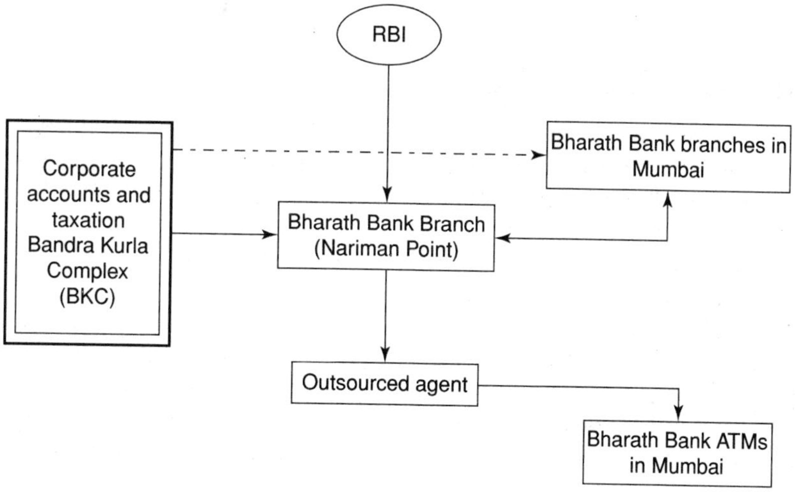

- Number of salary account holdings
- Corporate accounts, if any
- Total receipts/payments of the branch in the last three months

This figure of retention limit is shared across all the branches in Mumbai including the Nariman Point branch. Based on the retention limits as set by the bank's BKC office, the cash management centre is responsible for distributing the funds to various branches (retail outlets) and the outsourced agents for ATMs. It needs to be mentioned here that all correspondence with the RBI regarding any kind of shortfall is carried out by the Nariman Point branch. However, Bharath Bank does not have any currency chest account with the RBI as it requires immense procedural hassles and formalities. Thus, at the end of the day, all branches are notified to return the excess cash above the retention limit to the Nariman Point branch, which remains in Bharath Bank's custody.

Outsourced Agents for ATMs

Bharath Bank has only one outsourced agent—M/s Brinks Arya, for depositing cash in their 120 ATMs across Mumbai. Unlike in Global Bank, Brinks Arya does not maintain any vault cash account, *i.e.*, it does not maintain certain cash balance/overdraft account with Bharath Bank. The outsourcing agent's account gets debited when it collects cash from the bank and it gets adjusted when the money is transferred to the ATMs.

Bharath Bank ATMs The ATM operation is coordinated by a delivery channel coordinator and it is similar to the functioning of Global Bank. The ATM switch is located at BKC and all forecasting is carried out in BKC. Bharath Bank deploys only one outsourced agent for the 120 ATMs.

Bharath Bank Retail Branches Each of the 22 retails outlets are aware of the retention limits set upon them by BKC and are also notified by the main branch at Nariman Point that any excess cash above the retention limit should be returned to the main branch.

The Reserve Bank of India The RBI is known as the banker's bank in India. This is so because the banks fulfill all their excess cash requirements by borrowing from the RBI. Most of the banks have a currency chest option wherein they are able to put in cash and withdraw it as and when required as part of its maintenance of its CRR. The RBI has already outsourced its coinage division to a player so that they can cut costs in this process.

SECTION III

THE CASE OF GLOBAL BANK

For Global Bank, to cater to its needs and demand of 33 ATMs and branches in Mumbai, cash is centrally distributed from its Bandra office. For the ATMs, there are three vendors which have been outsourced to replenish cash at the ATMs in Mumbai. These are: Brinks Arya (which looks after 22 ATMs), CMS Securities (which looks after 6 ATMs) and Writer's Safeguard (which looks after 5 ATMs).

The maximum limit that Global Bank normally keeps in an ATM is ₹20 lakh, since each ATM is insured for an equivalent amount. This amount varies with each bank.

Brinks Arya has a vault whereby they maintain a certain cash balance, whereas, the other two vendors have accounts with Global Bank and they are allowed to go in for an overdraft (OD). This amount is settled by the end of the day by a reverse entry. The OD account is essential as banks cannot allow cash to lie idle with the outsourced agents. Vault cash account necessitates the replenishment of the cash from the outsourced agents to the ATMs in case of some major shortfall in cash. The intention of the entire ATM management is to ensure that there is no cash out situation at any point of time.

Information Flow in the Supply Chain—Role of IT Infrastructure

Global Bank has 33 ATMs in Mumbai city. They have changed over to switch technology from star technology. The server is located at Hyderabad and can handle 1000 ATMs at one go. All the ATMs are directly connected to the server (Base-24 systems, also called Tandom) and all the transactions across all the ATMs in the country are recorded out there. Every two hours, a report is generated to analyze the amount of cash withdrawal and idle cash lying in each of the ATMs.

Global Bank has a wide number of ATM networks across the country. The back office operation is maintained by the Finacle server which is the main database of all the customers of the bank. The ATM switch controls the functioning of all the ATMs and validates the operations of the customers by linking up with the financial server.

If there is a break in connectivity between the Finacle server and the ATM server, there is a cash memory that takes control of the operations of the ATMs. All transactions taking place at that point of time are recorded in the cash memory in a file called the positive balance file. Once the Finacle server is up-linked, the transactions are debited from the respective accounts of the customers.

Card Operation Centre There is a VISA server at the Global Bank corporate office at Hyderabad. This server is connected to the main VISA server at Singapore. Once a VISA card holder logs into any Global Bank ATM, the Global Bank server at Hyderabad passes on the link to the VISA server at the corporate office which transfers the information to the main server for validation of the transaction. Here, Global Bank has no direct role in controlling the operations and is just a part of the supply chain of information. This is a classic case of how two independent information hubs can collaborate to deliver better customer service to its customers.

FIGURE 20.2 ATM IT CHAIN OF GLOBAL BANK IN INDIA

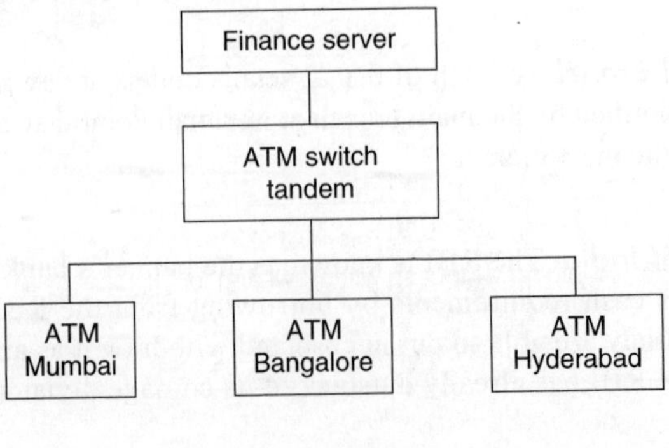

Source: Global Bank

For efficient functioning of the supply chain, the following factors have to be kept in mind in order to ensure minimum lead time and minimum breakdown time:

- The way vendors are integrated in the supply chain of the banks for maintenance management.
- Actual time required by the vendor to physically go to the branch/ATM to replenish the stock.
- Physical replenishment of items like rolls and stationary.

TEASE THE CONCEPT

How does the information flow place between ATMs and the VISA network?

The time lag between a breakdown of the ATM machine either due to a cash out situation or a technical snag and the information getting passed onto the delivery channel coordinator is about 20 minutes. Any problem with the ATMs gets captured first by the switch at Hyderabad and the information is then passed over to the respective individual in the city looking after the distribution system. The message is acted upon by informing the outsourced agency looking after that particular ATM to go and replenish the cash. This process takes another one hour. Hence, on an average, thc lead time for cash replenishment or ATM machine maintenance takes about one and a half hours. Stationary/rolls are sent by the corporate office at Hyderabad to the head office at Mumbai and are then distributed to the respective ATMs through the outsourced agents like Brink's Arya.

Payments and Receipts The inflow of cash to a bank takes place either through deposits of the customers, borrowings from the RBI or other commercial banks. The banks only go to the RBI when their expected outflows in a particular day exceed the available cash-on-hand on that day. The difficulty out here is that if the demand and supply for cash is not synchronized, it leads to a dead weight loss since there is an opportunity cost of holding back idle cash. Banks often face the situation whereby a customer wanting to withdraw a hefty amount does not turn up on that particular day leading to the bank holding more cash than what is permitted by the retention limit. Hence, the issue is to decide to what extent should the supply chain of a retail bank be efficient or should it be more responsive even if the total costs are not minimized.

FIGURE 20.3 INFORMATION FLOW FOR CASH REPLENISHMENT AND WITHDRAWAL IN GLOBAL BANK

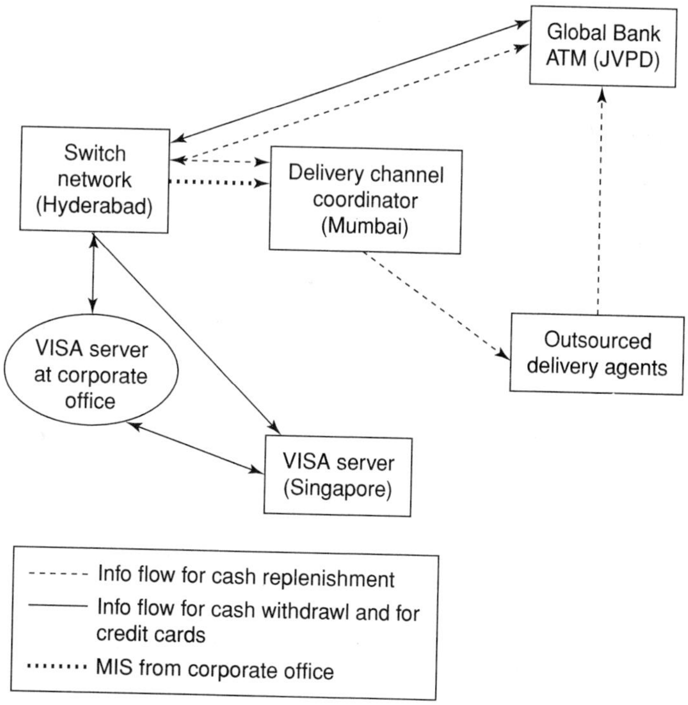

Source: Global Bank

Geographical Locations The geographical location of the branches and the ATMs are of vital importance in order to ensure either responsiveness of efficiency of the supply chain. While analyzing the 'cash dispensed figures' for the various ATM locations for Global Bank, certain locations show a significant amount of variability in the amount of cash dispensed. Depending on the high volume of transaction or high value of transaction, this could be attributed to the change in withdrawal pattern of the customers in the catchment area. The ATMs around shopping complex and malls have enormously large withdrawals in weekends and festival times.

Status of Accounts The asymmetry in the nature of accounts is one main factor that leads to wide fluctuations in the demand for/or supply of cash. The catchment area can necessarily have resident individuals, shopping malls or a large chunk of salaried people (in a typical downtown location). In such a scenario, the withdrawal of cash recurs on a fixed slot every month. Naturally, banks should take cognizance of this fact and accordingly plan the replenishment at these counters so as to avoid any excess cash holding situation.

SECTION IV

CASH DEMAND FORECASTING

There are four steps in any market forecast undertaken by an organization:

- Defining the market for the product/basket of products
- Dividing total industry demand into its main components
- Forecasting the drivers of demand in each segment and projecting how they are likely to change
- Conducting sensitivity analysis to understand the most critical assumptions and to gauge risks to the baseline forecast

The selection of a forecasting method depends on the following factors:

- The context of the forecast
- Relevance and availability of historical data
- Time period to be forecasted
- Degree of accuracy desirable
- Cost benefit or value of the forecast to the bank
- Time available for making the analysis

The following are the factors that are kept in mind while forecasting tools for demand management of cash for the branches as well as the ATMs.

- There is no stock-out situation in any of the branches as well as the ATMs.
- There is not much of idle cash lying since the opportunity cost of holding cash is quite high.

FIGURE 20.4 LINK BETWEEN THE CENTRAL SERVER, ATM AND VENDORS

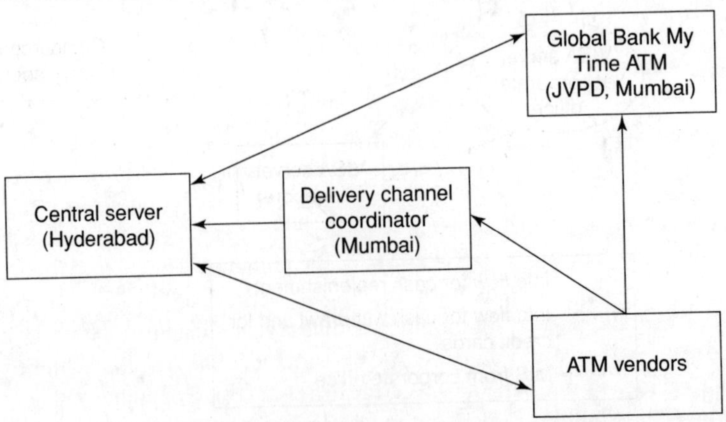

Source: Global Bank

- The cost of delivering cash to the branches and ATMs through the outsourced agents is minimized.
- The lead time to deliver cash is minimized.
- The architecture of the supply chain also becomes an endogenous variable since it has a direct relationship with the efficiency/responsiveness of the supply chain. The nature of information flows, the lead times in every step of the chain, the relationship with the outsourced agents and the geographical location of the branches and the ATMs all play an important factor in zeroing in on the most appropriate demand forecasting tool.

Both time series data as well as judgmental forecasting is used by all the retail banks to predict the demand for cash. Based on the demand forecasting tools, used by Global Bank and Bharath Bank, it was observed that location-wise daily data were captured to forecast demand for the next month.

Time Series Analysis of Cash Withdrawals from ATMs

In most banks, demand is forecasted for a period of one month at a time. Therefore, the demand for the month of October 2002 gets forecasted on 30 September 2002. Table 20.1 is a representative table highlighting the methodology of data calculations.

The data from Global Bank (for the period of July–August 2003) on the basis of the monthly cash dispensed from each of the ATMs aggregated over a month were collected.

TABLE 20.1 CASH WITHDRAWALS FROM ATMs OF GLOBAL BANK IN SEPTEMBER

(Figures in ₹)

	1	**2**	**3**	**...**	**28**	**29**	**30**	**31**	**Total**
S V Road	55,000	52,000	65,000	...	55,000	32,000	45,000	28,000	A
Khar	52,000	...	...	...	...	...	...	...	...
JVPD	75,000	...	...	...	...	...	...	...	...
Ghatkopar	51,000		...	...	...	...	...	...	...
Kandivilli	55,000	...	...	...	...	...	...	...	...
Chembur	45,000	...	...	...	...	...	...	...	...
Seepz	1,50,000	...	...	...	...	...	...	...	...
Church Gate	3,00,000	...	...	...	...	...	...	...	...
Vashi	2,50,000	...	...	...	...	...	...	...	...
Malad	1,00,000	...	...	...	...	...	...	...	...
Thane	2,45,000	...	...	...	...	...	...	...	...
Breach Candy	25,000	...	...	...	...	...	...	...	...
Opera House		65,000	...	...	...	...	...	...	...
Fort Branch	2,00,000	...	...	...	...	...	...	...	...
Total	16,68,000	...	...	...	...	...	...	...	...
Total for August									X
Total for July									Y
									Z

The figure X shows the total withdrawal of cash that has taken place in the month of September. Similarly, such tables are constructed for the last three months. Y and Z show the corresponding totals for the months of July and August. Therefore, the demand planner will have the cash withdrawal data for the last three months before him and will be able to find out what has been the growth in the total cash outflow in this period of time. Using linear growth trends, one can initially predict that the total cash outflow for the month of October also grew at a similar rate and a total figure is arrived at. But this figure in itself is erroneous since only the trend is taken into consideration without paying heed to seasonality and judgmental factors. This growth which was calculated was the overall growth expected for the month of October. One can also take the site specific data and analyze the monthly growth based on the ATMs or the branches. The overall trend can be increasing, decreasing or stagnant.

Corrected: The present trend for month is with last year's data to analyze the difference in the growth rates. This difference is then added into the forecasted trend. Once the trend is achieved, the list of festivities for the forecasted month is looked into. The dates are identified and then over and above the normal trend, the seasonality is factored in. (For example, 15 per cent to 18 per cent growth in outflow was factored in all major ATMs of Global Bank during Ganesh Puja).

Sales Trends and Other Factors

There are many salary accounts that banks have in their fold. These are those accounts where the salaries of the employees directly get credited to their respective accounts. From the day of the salary payment, within next four to five days, it has been observed that normally 50 per cent to 70 per cent of the money is withdrawn by the account holders. Therefore, if the salary accounts get credited by the bank on the first of every month, then for the next five days there has to be more cash that needs to be provided at the ATMs as well as the branches. To predict the outflow, a simple iteration is carried out whereby the number of salary accounts holders (say 500) is multiplied by the average salary that is deposited in their respective accounts (say ₹15,000). This would help the planner to arrive at a figure representing the expected demand for cash in the next few days exclusively because of the salary issue.

Judgmental factors in demand forecasting of cash by banks are stated as follows:

- Safety margin—Banks take into consideration the lead time that they will take to reach cash to the branches as well as the ATMs. The time to procure that cash from the RBI or from other branches is also factored in while deciding the amount of cash that needs to be sent out. Also, in those ATMs which are situated far off, cash is disbursed there sufficiently in order to cater to the demand for the next two days. These calculations are reached at after undertaking cost-benefit analysis at each ATM and branch. Even in case of weekends (Saturday and Sunday), many of the banks are closed and hence the money which is disbursed on Friday takes into account the expected demand in the weekends too. This type of system is primarily followed by smaller banks and in those ATMs where the volume of transactions is at a low level.
- Cash inflows that are expected to take place—Inflows from the RBI from their own branches, cash position maintenance as well as exogenous factors that effect the final decision of cash disbursal.
- ATMs are categorized by some of the banks depending on the volume of transaction that takes place from the outlets. Table 20.2 shows the method of categorization used by Global Bank to grade its ATMs.

TABLE 20.2 CATEGORY OF ATMs

'A' Category	Average cash dispensed per day is greater than ₹7.5 lakh
'B' Category	Average cash dispensed per day is between ₹5 lakh and ₹7.5 lakh
'C' Category	Average cash dispensed per day is between ₹1.5 lakh and ₹5 lakh
'D' Category	Average cash dispensed per day is less than ₹1.5 lakh

Once the ATMs are categorized, a maximum cash retention limit is set on the basis of the following calculation shown in Table 20.3.

TABLE 20.3 SETTING LIMITS FOR EACH CATEGORY OF ATMs

'A' Category	₹7.5 lakh × 3 = ₹22.50 lakh
'B' Category	₹(7.5 + 5) lakh/2 = ₹6.25 lakh × 3 = ₹18.75 lakh
'C' Category	₹(5 + 1.5) lakh/2 = ₹3.25 lakh × 3 = ₹9.75 lakh
'D' Category	₹1.5 lakh × 3 = ₹4.5 lakh

The average volume of transaction is taken into consideration in each of the categories. This value is multiplied by a factor of 3. This factor 3 has been derived after taking the data of the maximum withdrawals that has taken place from each of the ATMs in the last three months and measuring the deviations, and then applying judgment to the factor in any unexpected swings in demand and other external variables.

CHAPTER SUMMARY

The findings and the observations based on the discussion in this chapter can be summarized below:

- In the following areas in Mumbai, significant variability in the average cash dispensed over a month was observed (Table 20.4) in the case of Global Bank.

TABLE 20.4 LOCATION-WISE VARIABILITY IN CASH TRANSACTIONS (MUMBAI CITY LOCATIONS)

Locations	% chg. cash	% chg. transaction
Kandivilli	−11%	−2%
Silver Line Tech	58%	−45%
Malad	−8%	−1%
Opera House	−13%	−13%
Versova	11%	−2%
Sion	−17%	−1%
CBD Khargar	−73%	−85%

It is worth noting that in the ATM counters where variability is high, it can lead to either a cash-out situation or an idle cash situation. If such wide variability is observed over a considerable period of time, then such changes in the demand pattern has to be immediately incorporated in the forecasting system.

- Maximum value withdrawn in the weekend is 1.5 to 2 times the normal withdrawal.
- If there is an increase in the number of transactions, it implies greater volume of transactions. On the contrary, an increase in the cash transactions implies a higher value of transaction. The cause of variability is either rooted in a higher volume of transactions or a higher value. The forecasting strategy of the bank can take this vital information into account to put in their judgmental part in the forecast If, for example, there is a higher volume of transaction noticed for a significant period in any ATM, it could be necessarily inferred that there has been an upsurge in the number of customers operating the ATM. This phenomenon is further analyzed by looking into the account numbers of the transactions from the Finacle server. The local addresses and the office addresses of the account holders can be looked into to verify whether the upsurge in demand is because of any significant change in the catchment area (which can be taken to be the area around, say, five kms. in the vicinity of the ATM). The chances should be noted as an endogenous variable in the regression model and has to be carried out in future so that such changes, once noticed can be factored into the model to avoid cash-out situations.
- On the other hand, if there is a high value of transaction noticed where the volume is not commensurately high, it can be inferred that the account holders are withdrawing more cash than they used to in the recent past. If this trend is witnessed for say three consecutive months, then there is surely a change in the withdrawal pattern of the customers. This needs to be further introspected to see if the base composition of the accounts operating the ATM is the same or has there been some change out there. If the composition happens to be the same, then the total volume of money that those specific accounts are having needs to be looked into. Finally, the amount of withdrawal as a percentage of the total holdings of the accounts can give the planner a better insight into the customer's withdrawal pattern. If this change becomes a constant factor over a few periods, then the trend is considered to be a part of adaptive forecasting where level, trend and seasonality are updated after each demand observation.

  From Table 20.4 it is evident that in Kandivali, the percentage change in number of transaction is significantly less than the percentage change in cash dispensed. This clearly indicates the high volume of transactions that have taken place from this ATM outlet. Similar inferences can be drawn for Sion and Malad. However, the Versova ATM shows that there is an increase in the number of transactions but a decrease in the value. If this trend persists, then it could be attributed to a change in withdrawal patterns at Versova ATMs. It is to be mentioned here that ATMs in Global Bank have currency denominations of ₹100 and ₹500 only. So for low value and high number of transactions, we could also study the flow of each of this currency from the ATMs. In scenarios such as this, the movement of the 100-rupee denomination might be significantly more than the 500-rupee currency so as to support a low value of transaction.
- Banks are highly overenthusiastic in setting retention limits of each of the counters, and so while setting up limits they have used a factor of 3, which arises due to an element of judgement. The intention is always to avoid any cash-out situation, but at times, it may lead to idle cash in the counters. No sophisticated forecasting tools are being used in any of the ATMs and retail branches; rather, banks take atleast two or three months to arrive at a figure for retention limits.
- The forecast horizon that is considered by a few banks is for a period of one month. This can be further subdivided into weekly forecasts so that better tracing of fluctuations is done leading to sound forecasting.

- The bankable consumer population in India is 300 million and the number of ATMs required for this population is supposedly more than two lakh. An ATM will have to be installed for every 1,489 cards issued. This seems to be an uphill task for private banks considering the expansion spree of the retails banks.
- On an average, an ATM costs around ₹8–14 lakh, while the annual maintenance varies between ₹12 and 20 lakh. An ATM is profitable if 50 – 100 transactions are carried per day on it. If the number of transaction are 260 – 270, the bank recovers its investment within a year. Bharath Bank claims that its ATMs execute over 300 transactions per day, hence justifying its expansion spree. But the moot point lies in the fact that the urban market is getting saturated in the days to come. In a crowded location in any of the metros, it would be prudent on the part

FIGURE 20.5 ATM—POST- AND PRE-INSTALLATION ACTIVITIES

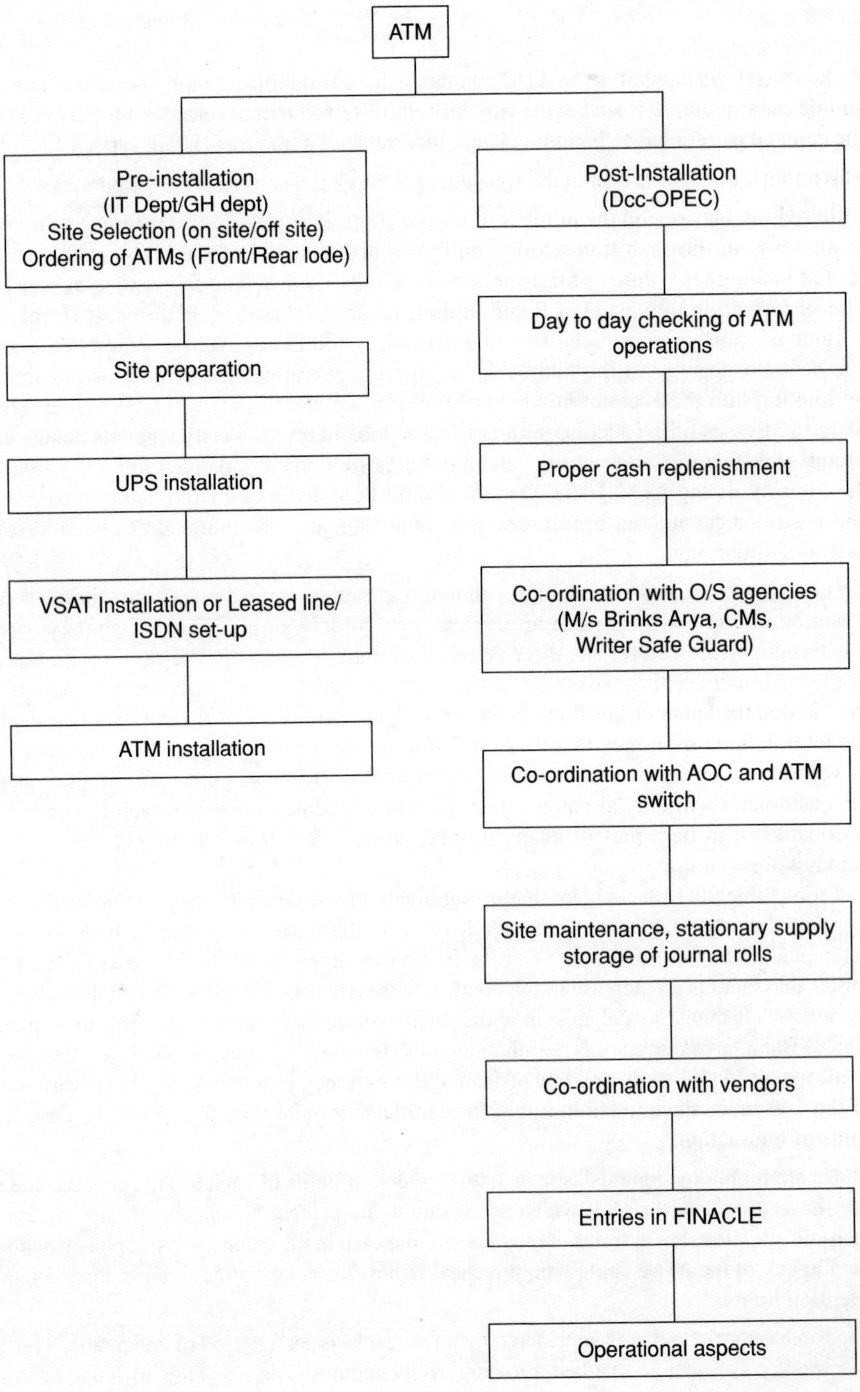

of the bank to have a shared network, and given the number of transaction and the prevailing IT infrastructure they have, it is quite feasible.

- The flip side of this would be that a particular bank would loose out on its marketing edge when its network is shared, but on the other hand, it will gain free income from other banks for the use of its ATMs and hence recover its costs. Many banks have already entered into this kind of collaborative networking sharing as it gives them immediate access to a widespread market with minimal cost involved in infrastructure.
- The biggest problem that banks are facing today is deciding the optimal mix of denominations that they must keep in order to ensure that there is maximum customer satisfaction. All those banks which have harped strongly on CRM look forward to satisfying customers by supplying them with the denominations they look for. But in this process, at times, demand gets skewed for a particular denomination leading to short supply. This can still be managed by demanding the specific denominations from the RBI or from other commercial banks. However, the reverse case is the banker's worst nightmare. For example, Bharath Bank once faced a situation whereby they are left with ₹2 crore in ₹10 denominations. Their predicament was such that they could not push this cash through the ATMs since the machines accepted only ₹500, ₹100 and ₹50 denominations. Another example is of HLL which holds an account with Bharath Bank. HLL gives only a day's notice to the bank regarding the exact denominations it needs for paying off its members in its supply chain. At times, it so happens that the RBI also runs short of such denominations and hence has to look forward to get the specified denominations from its other branches. Therefore, it is not only forecasting what would be the level of demand but also the nature of demand that is important to understand.

TEST YOUR UNDERSTANDING

1. How would you forecast the demand for cash in ATMs?
2. What are the judgmental factors, you would take into account, while forecasting demand for cash in ATMs?
3. Do you think that the complications would be more with the new system of shared ATM networks of banks like cash net and cash tree?

TOPICS FOR FURTHER DISCUSSION

- How does Bharath Bank manage the daily requirement in ATMs in Mumbai?
- Discuss the factors on which the retention limit for cash is set in branches and ATM of Bharath Bank.
- Analyse the case of cash management in ATMs based on the Global Bank case.

ANNEXURE I

ATM—POST- AND PRE-INSTALLATION ACTIVITIES

Operational Aspects

- Daily end of day (EOD) reports from outsourced agencies
- Collection and processing of ATM deposit envelopes everyday at 6 p.m. at OPEC
- Disposing captured cards
- Checking and proper storing of journal rolls
- MIS to corporate office
- Electronic data capture (EDC) storing
- Informing respective agency at any time if there is any problem with the ATM

ATM Departments in Global Bank

AOC (ATM Operation Centre)

- Taking care of all the ATMs in India 24 hours
- Coordination of respective delivery channel coordinator
- Checking of ATM transactions and reconciliation
- MIS to Q and OPS department

CMC (Card Management Centre) Preparing ATM cards as per the application from the respective branches (FATM).

PMC (Pin Management Centre) Preparing PIN (Personal Identification Number) for all the ATM cards prepared by CMC.

COC (Card Operation Centre)

- Taking care of all the VISA transaction all over India in Global Bank ATMs
- Coordination with VISA—Bangalore and Singapore
- Maintenance and proper care of VISA server at corporate office

SELECT REFERENCES

1. Patnaik, Santosh (2004). 'Shared ATMs—The Way Foreward', *IBA Bulletin*, December, pp. 24–27.
2. Geetha, D (2005). "A Study on the Performance of ATM Services in Malaysia and Coimbatore City" in Justin Paul and S. Ganesan, *Management: Strategies and Policies*. Allied Publishers, New Delhi.
3. Indian Institute of Banking and Finance (2005). *General Bank Management*. Delhi: MacMillan.
4. Indian Banks Association (2004). 'Technology as Competitive Edge', *IBA bulletin*, March, special issue.

ENDNOTES

1. This chapter has been co-authored by Dr Justin Paul, IIM Indore with Anirban Mukherjee, Arindya Roy and Dr Rakesh Singh.
2. The names of the banks have been changed based on the request from the respective organizations.
3. Author Dr Justin Paul is thankful to Anirban Mukherjee for collecting data and drafting the article that provided the preliminary source for this chapter.

CHAPTER TWENTY ONE

Mergers and Acquisitions in the Banking Sector

CHAPTER STRUCTURE

KEY TAKEAWAYS FROM THE CHAPTER

- Understand the mergers and acquisition scenario in the banking sector.
- Get informed about the strategies of a bank, while thinking about a merger or acquisition.
- Analyze the classic case of the Bank of Madura Merger with ICICI Bank.
- Discuss the case of major bank merger in Japanese banking sector.

SECTION I

MERGERS AND ACQUISITIONS

Business combinations which may take the form of mergers, amalgamations and takeovers are important features of corporate restructuring and governance. They have played an important role in the growth of a number of leading companies in the world over. Subsequent to the structural adjustment programmes in the Indian economy, restructuring of companies in the form of collaborations, mergers and acquisitions have taken place in most of the industries including banking, information technology, fast-moving consumer goods and pharmaceuticals.

The principal factors behind the corporate restructuring activity in India have been the policy changes that were announced in the form of economic reforms. These include removal of restrictions on corporate investments and growth contained in the Monopolies and Restrictive Trade Practices Act (MRTP Act), extensive trade reforms involving lowering of tariff and physical barriers on imports, financial sector reforms permitting public sector banks and financial institutions to tap capital markets, a policy to encourage the inward flow of foreign direct investment and foreign portfolio investment.

Mergers and acquisitions are results of business strategy. While mergers are a result of the decision of two organizations, acquisitions are a takeover of one organization by another. A 'forced' merger or a merger due to a survival problem is normally known as an amalgamation.

Although amalgamation, merger and acquisition are principal tools of corporate restructuring, they bring with them a sense of uncertainty. Despite the restructuring frenzy, such strategic transactions in the banking sector could fail or perform far below potential because of mistakes in post-merger integration. On the other hand, it could also be arousing success.[1]

Mergers and acquisitions have been the principal tools of corporate restructuring in India after the implementation of economic reforms since 1991. The Indian corporate sector has experienced a major restructuring through mergers and acquisitions with the changes brought about in the MRTP Act as well as in the Industrial Policy Resolution of June 1991, which relaxed the norms for licensing and growth. There are some factors that motivate executives to think about a merger or acquisition. Many executives think it is good to be big in a globalizing economy. Companies seem to be combining at a rate almost unprecedented in history on a global scale. In the automobile industry, Daimler-Benz and Chrysler have joined hands, and Ford has taken over the automobile operations of Volvo and so on. In the banking industry, Grindlays merged with Standard Chartered Bank. Similar merger examples can be found in industries as diverse as entertainment, telecommunication and the oil sector. In India, recent mergers in the banking sector have been the merger of Times Bank with HDFC Bank and merger of Bank of Madura (BoM) with ICICI Bank.

The possible outcomes of mergers and acquisitions in banking sector are downsizing, relocations, technological changes and an insecure feeling among employees. The most common attitude that prevails in 'bank mergers' is the attitude of 'us versus them' due to issues like seniority. This attitude gets further aggravated if there are cultural differences and lack of acceptance of each other's processes if one bank is superior in terms of tasks and methodologies than the other.

Merger seems to lead to financial and strategic growth. The strategic management aspect of merger has been analyzed in this chapter on the basis of factors such as shareholder value, competition, geographical base and market share of companies in the mergers deal. Ghemawat and Ghadar (2000)[2] have found that the rush towards huge mergers is based on a faulty understanding of economics. They have pointed out better ways to address globalization than relentless expansion through merger. Venkitesware (1997)[3] has analyzed the emerging scenario in the context of restructuring corporate India. Pawaskar (200l)[4] studied the impact of mergers on corporate performance by comparing the post-merger performance of the acquirer with its pre-merger performance, taking a sample of 36 cases of merger between 1992 and 1995. The regression results in the study showed that there are no significant differences in the financial characteristics of the two firms involved in merger. It is worth noting that the concept of `too big to fail` has been criticised by experts in the context of global financial crisis 2008–2010, with the collapse of big firms in the banking and financial services industry.

In his research study, Pandey (2001)[5] has analyzed the stock price performance of target firms in the context of change in management control in the case of takeover announcements and shown that the target firm valuations increase in the run up to announcement. There is a dearth of literature on mergers and acquisitions in the Indian context, which could potentially look at the factors influencing merger decision, and the impact of the swap ratio announcement on the share price. This chapter is a modest attempt to contribute to the literature on mergers and acquisitions in the Indian context.

'Survival of the fittest' has become a reality in the case of commercial banks. In this era of globalization, banks will have to be competitive in order to face challenges and leverage opportunities. With the decision taken by the RBI to implement the Basel Committee recommendations on banking supervision (Basel II), commercial banks are required to follow prudential norms and maintain sound financial ratios like higher capital adequacy ratio (CAR) and low non-performing assets (NPA). This implies that 'small is no longer beautiful' in Indian banking industry.

Although the merger of a bank can be considered as a barrier to perfect competition, it makes the acquiring bank stronger organization that can face competition from aggressive multinational banks.[6] A bank merger could happen due to different reasons. One reason could be lack of resources, both capital and labour, that are required for competing with the big players, forcing the 'small' ones to merge with the 'big wigs'. This could happen if a bank finds it difficult to make a profit due to an increase in NPA or other such reasons. This phenomenon is known as amalgamation, *e.g.*, the GTB amalgamation with Oriental Bank and Nedungadi Bank's amalgamation with Punjab National Bank. A merger could also happen because a bank's board of directors agrees for a single new company if their shareholders get a better price in the form of the swap ratio, *e.g.*, Bank of Madura's merger with ICICI Bank.

SECTION II

CASE OF BANK OF MADURA MERGER WITH ICICI BANK[7]

On Friday, 8 December 2000, BoM and ICICI Bank decided to work out a merger of the former with the latter. The news was published in the daily newspapers on 9 December and the merger decision with swap ratio was officially announced on 11 December 2000. The shareholders approved the decision on 19 January 2001 and the banks got an approval from the RBI on 1 March 2001.

In this chapter, an analysis of the synergies of the merger of BoM with ICICI Bank in the Indian banking industry and the strategic factors to be considered while taking a merger or an acquisition decision have been discussed. The objective is to look at the valuation of the swap ratio (ratio at which shareholders of the old company receive shares of the new company in exchange for shares in the old company), the announcement of the swap ratio, share price fluctuations of the banks before the merger decision announcement and the impact of the merger decision on the share prices. An attempt has also been made to look at the suitability of BoM to merge with ICICI Bank.

Profiles of Banks

Profile of Bank of Madura The profile of BoM is listed as follows:

- A South India-based well-established bank with a track record of 57 years with strong brand equity, established in the year 1943.
- Asset base: Over ₹4,400 crore with a CAR of 14.25.
- Distribution reach (financial year 2000) and automation: A total of 263 banking branches, 182 branches in Tamil Nadu with 1.2 million customer accounts, 132 computerised branches that account for 90 per cent of the business, 47 branches networked through VSATs.
- Employees: Total strength of 2,577, of which 2,000 employees are computer literate.

Profile of ICICI Bank The profile of ICICI Bank is listed as follows:

- The first Indian bank to list on the New York Stock Exchange with US GAAP accounting. It was established in the year 1994 by Industrial Credit and Investment Corporation of India (ICICI) as a new generation private sector bank.
- Asset base: It is one of the largest private sector banks based in India with an asset base of over ₹12,000 crore with strong CAR of 19.6 per cent.
- Distribution reach and automation: Technology-driven business growth with 104 branches, 366 ATMs (as on 7 December 2000) and the largest ATM network in India. Total number of ATMs has been increased to more than 1,000 by ICICI Bank in the year 2001 along with ten call centres. All branches have been computerised, and Internet banking facility has been provided to the customers.
- Employees: Total strength of around 1,500, all of whom are computer literate.

TABLE 21.1 COMPARISON OF BALANCE SHEETS

	(Figures in ₹ Million)	
Balance Sheets (By 2000)	**ICICI Bank**	**Bank of Madura**
Liabilities	1,20,726	44,437
Equity capital	1,968	118
Reserves and surplus	9,527	2,361
Deposits	98,660	36,310
Borrowings	4,915	1,836
Other liabilities and provisions	5,656	3,812
Assets	1,20,726	44,437
Cash and balances with the RBI	7,219	4,561
Balances with banks and call	26,933	3,072
Investments	44,167	17,128
Advances	36,573	16,655
Fixed assets	2,221	1,788
Other assets	3,613	1,233

Source: Annual Report of the ICICI Bank 2000–01 and www.icicibank.com

A comparison of balance sheets of ICICI Bank and BoM (financial year 2000) shows that ICICI Bank has got more assets (both fixed and other) than BoM (see Table 21.1). They have given more advances (₹36,573 million) than BoM (₹16,655 million), and they have mobilised amount of deposits a higher (₹98,660 million) than BoM (₹36,310 million).

The income statements of ICICI Bank and BoM for the financial year 2000 are given in Table 21.2. ICICI Bank's interest income was ₹8,528 million whereas BoM's interest income was much lower at ₹3,702 million. Total income of ICICI Bank (₹10,470 million) was more than twice of that of BoM (₹4,689 million).

Profit after tax of ICICI Bank was also more than twice of that of BoM.

TABLE 21.2 COMPARING INCOME STATEMENTS OF ICICI BANK AND BANK OF MADURA (FINANCIAL YEAR 2000)

(Figures in ₹ Million)

	ICICI Bank	Bank of Madura
Interest income	8,528	3,702
Other income	1,942	987
Total income	10,470	4,689
Interest expense	6,670	2,661
Operating expense	1,534	1,074
Provisions and taxes	1,214	498
Total expenses	9,417	4,233
Profit after tax	1,053	456

Source: www.icicibank.com, on 11 December 2000.

Swap Ratio and Stock Price Fluctuations

The competition for more business volume and the motivation to increase the shareholder value with the desire to become a big player have motivated banking executives in India to think about the mergers and consolidations. Though the Indian banking industry witnessed the emergence of new private banks like Times Bank, IndusInd Bank, ICICI Bank, HDFC Bank, UTI Bank and Global Trust Bank in the early 1990s, many executives felt the need for consolidation of operations in the late 1990s in order to compete with other strong players. There were talks between banks (even with the old private sector banks) to arrive at an acceptable swap ratio for a possible merger.

On 8 December 2000, Friday, ICICI Bank and BoM came together to work out a merger of the two banks. swap ratio announcement was postponed to 11 December, Monday, by the board of directors of the banks. However, on hearing the news (before it appeared in newspapers on 9 December 2001, Saturday) about the merger decision between these banks, ICICI bank's stock shot up 12 per cent to ₹170 and BoM's by 8 per cent to ₹131.6 on 8 December at the Bombay Stock Exchange (Saturday and Sunday are holidays in the stock market). The expectation that the acquiring bank would become a strong player, motivated people abroad too, on the same day, to purchase shares of ICICI bank at the New York Stock Exchange in bulk, and the price of the American Depository Share of ICICI bank shot up 17 per cent on the same day, from the previous day's closing value of USD 8.12.

It is interesting to look at the factors influencing swap ratio in a merger deal. The swap ratio announced in the case of the BoM–ICICI Bank merger was 1:2, *i.e.*, the shareholders of BoM got two shares of ICICI Bank for each BoM share (Table 21.3). The market price of ICICI bank share on 7 December 2000 was ₹152.95 and BoM's price was ₹122.45 (National Stock Exchange [NSE] closing price. See Annexure I). They could have derived a swap ratio in favour of ICICI bank on the basis of the market price of the shares of both the banks, had they not considered other factors (both financial and strategic). It could have been 10 shares of ICICI bank for 13 shares of BoM, if the valuation was done on the basis of balance sheets of both the banks. Again, the swap ratio could have been in favour of ICICI Bank, if they had done valuation on the basis of NPA of both banks. The net NPA to net advances was 1.3 per cent for ICICI Bank, while it was 4 per cent in the case of BoM. To quote from *The Economic Times* (as published on 9 December 2000), 'swap ratio could be 10 shares of ICICI Bank for 13 shares of BoM (Table 21.4). The ratio could be influenced by NPA level of the two banks.' The swap ratio was derived on the basis of strategic and financial ratios. Financial ratios, such as book value of the share of both the banks as on 30 September 2000, earning per share (net profit/shares outstanding), last dividend paid by both of them and the per cent of NPAs were taken into consideration for deriving the swap ratio.

TABLE 21.3 SWAP RATIO ANNOUNCED (NUMBER OF SHARES)

Bank of Madura	ICICI Bank
1	2

TABLE 21.4 IMPORTANT DATES

Rapid round of negotiations	24 November–8 December
Newspaper reports on merger decision	9 December 2000, Saturday
Merger decision and swap ratio announcement	11 December 2000, Monday
Shareholder's approval	19 January 2001
RBI approval	1 March 2001
US GAAP Recasting	31 March 2001

Source: Compiled from *The Economic Times* 7 December to 15 December 2000 and ICICI Bank Annual Report 2000–01.

TABLE 21.5 IMPORTANT FINANCIAL RATIOS TO BE ANALYZED FOR SWAP RATIO DERIVATION

	Bank of Madura	ICICI Bank
NPA	4%	1.3%
Last dividend paid	55%	15%
Earning per share	₹44	₹7
Book value (as on 30 September 2000)	₹206	₹62
Market price of share before the merger (7 December at NSE closing price)	₹122,45	₹152.95
Profit after tax (financial year 2000)	₹456 million	₹1,053 million

Source: The Hindu Business Line 10, 11 and 12 December 2000.

Bank of Madura had an edge while analysing the earning per share, book value and percentage of last dividend paid (see Table 21.5) whereas ICICI bank had more assets earned, higher market price of share (pre-merger announcement phase), low NPA and high-tech image. The swap ratio for BoM–ICICI Bank merger could have been in the range of 1:1–1:1.5 as most of the advantages of the BoM get neutralised by the disadvantages (*e.g.*, high NPA level, low market price). In our case, the swap ratio was announced in favour of the BoM, mainly because of the desire of ICICI Bank to acquire a good bank from south India where they did not have strong presence and geographical advantage.

The ICICI Bank could have got a better swap ratio, if the valuation was done only on the basis of market price of the shares of both the banks and with the 'ceteris paribus' (other things being same) assumption. ICICI Bank should have got the swap ratio 1: 1.35 (1 share ICICI Bank equal to 1.35 share of BoM on the basis of market price of the shares traded at NSE (₹165: ₹122) on 7 December 2000. But this is not the way the swap ratio is to be calculated in any merger decision. The companies need to analyze other factors like book value, earning per share, dividend paid, profit after tax as well as the need for merger and the motivation for acquisition. The range of possible swap ratios (theoretical and practical) based on various parameters have been given in the Table 21.6.

TABLE 21.6 RANGE OF POSSIBLE SWAP RATIOS

Bank of Madura	ICICI Bank	Basis Parameters
1.35	1	Market price of the shares on 7 December 2000
1.8	1	Market price of the shares on 15 November 2000
1.3	1	Economic Times prediction (as published on 9 December 2000)
1	3–3.5	EPS, book value and last dividend paid
1	1.5	NPA, profit after tax, EPS, book value, last dividend paid and market price of the shares
1 (Announced)	2 (Announced)	All factors mentioned above and strategic factors like motivation for acquisition

There was speculation in the stock market that the BoM would get a favourable swap ratio for about 2 weeks, when the discussions were going on between the banks. The shares of BoM had gained sharply by around 70 per cent in the past fortnight (last week of November and first week of December 2000), expecting a better swap ratio and merger. The swap ratio for the BoM/ICICI Bank merger was announced as 1:2 (1 share of BoM = 2 shares of ICICI Bank) on 11 December, Monday. This proved that a higher swap ratio is the only way an acquisition can be accomplished in the Indian banking sector. The BoM shareholders got a better deal as they could exchange 1 share worth approximately ₹120 and get approximately ₹304 (average of ICICI Bank share price during 4–8 December 2000, *i.e.*, ₹152 multiplied by 2).

The impact of the announcement of the swap ratio on share prices of the acquiring bank (ICICI Bank) and the acquired bank (BoM) shows that the investors in stock market reacted immediately with acumen (on hearing the news of swap ratio, before it appeared in the next day's newspaper). The share price of BoM at Bombay Stock Exchange and National Stock Exchange shot up on 11 December 2000 on the same day after the announcement of the swap ratio, and ICICI Bank's share price slipped down (see Tables 21.7 and 21.8). An extract from *The Economic Times* dated 12 December 2000 stated 'The Bombay Stock Exchange share price of ICICI Bank fell into ₹165.30 on 11 December Monday, against the Friday's close of ₹169.85, however, closed at ₹165.30 (down ₹4.55 from Friday's close). Bank of Madura scrip, on the other hand, gained from ₹131.6 (8 December 2000 Friday's close) to touch at ₹142.1 (11 December, Monday's close)'. The same trend was seen at the NSE as well.

TABLE 21.7 CLOSING SHARE PRICE OF THE BANK OF MADURA (BEFORE AND AFTER THE ANNOUNCEMENT OF SWAP RATIO)

Date	Bombay Stock Exchange	National Stock Exchange
8 Dec. 2000	131.6	132.25
11 Dec. 2000	142.1	142.85

Source: Compiled from *The Economic Times,* dated 12 December 2000 and Business Line, 10 December 2000.

TABLE 21.8 CLOSING SHARE PRICE OF ICICI BANK (BEFORE AND AFTER THE ANNOUNCEMENT OF SWAP RATIO)

Date	Bombay Stock Exchange	National Stock Exchange
8 Dec. 2000	169.85	168.95
11 Dec. 2000	165.30	164.50

Source: Compiled from *The Economic Times*, dated 12 December 2000 and Business Line, 10 December 2000.

TABLE 21.9 CRUCIAL PARAMETERS AS ON THE DATE OF ANNOUNCEMENT OF THE MERGER AND SWAP RATIO

Name of the Bank	Book Value of Bank on the Day of Merger Announcement	Market Price on the Day of Announcement (Opening Price at National Stock Exchange)
Bank of Madura	183.0	142.85
ICICI Bank	58.0	176.00

Source: *The Hindu Business Line*, dated 10 December 2000 and nseindia.com.

The share price and volume data for the BoM and ICICI Bank traded at the NSE of India from 15 November 2000 to 29 December 2000 are given in *Annexure I*. The data show that BoM scrip was traded at 79.20 on 15 November 2000 and increased sharply over the period from 15 November 2000. The closing value of BoM scrip on 30 November 2000 was ₹90.50 (up from 79.20) and touched ₹122.45 on 7 December 2000 (around a 70 per cent increase over a fortnight). This could be linked to the rounds of negotiations held between BoM and ICICI Bank during this period for a possible merger. (ICICI Bank had held negotiations with other banks too, for a possible acquisition). The closing price of ICICI Bank scrip at NSE on 15 November 2000 was ₹142.30 and increased to ₹142.95 (closing price of 30 November 2000) and ₹168.95 on 8 December 2000 before the announcement of merger. This shows that the share price of both the banks increased in the pre-merger announcement period, but the percentage price increase of BoM scrip was much more than the increase in the ICICI bank share price. A quotation from *The Hindu Business Line* (Stock Focus column, 10 December 2000, 1 day before the announcement of the swap ratio) is reproduced here to substantiate the point mentioned above. 'It is quite likely that the swap ratio may be fixed in a manner that holds out a good deal for shareholders of BoM. The scrip has gained sharply by around 70 per cent in the past fortnight, expecting a favourable swap ratio and merger'.

Though the merger swap ratio was announced on 11 December 2000, by the board of directors of the banks, the scripts were available for trading till the date the decision was approved by the shareholders of both the banks. Hence, it is important to look at the impact of the swap ratio announcement on the share prices of both the banks. The NSE data given in *Annexure I* shows that BoM scrip shot up from ₹132.25 (closing price on 8 December 2000) to ₹142.85 and ₹154.30, ₹166.65, ₹180, ₹194.40, ₹209.95, ₹226.75 and ₹244.90 on 11, 12, 13, 14, 15, 18, 19 and 20 December, respectively. On the other hand, ICICI Bank scrip dropped from ₹168.95 (closing price on 8 December 2000) to ₹165.30, ₹160.05, ₹159.10, ₹157.60, ₹157.20 and ₹157.05 on 11, 12, 13, 14, 15 and 18 December, respectively. Though the ICICI Bank share price increased to ₹158.00 on 19 December, it slipped down further to ₹143.35 and ₹141.10 on 26 and 27 December 2000. The increased demand for BoM scrip resulted in the increase in the price of BoM scrip, because of the expectation of the investors to make money by exchanging the share in future against the ICICI bank share at the 1:2 swap ratio, after the shareholders and the RBI approved the merger decision. (The shareholders can swap the scrip only if the decision of boards gets approval in the meeting of the shareholders and from the central bank of the country, if it is a bank). The stock price fluctuations have been shown in the graph in Figure 21.1 (before the announcement of the merger and swap ratio from 15 November 2000 to 11 December 2000) and Figure 21.2 (after the announcement of merger decision and swap ratio—from 12 December to 29 December 2000) using daily data on share prices of BoM and ICICI Bank scrip traded at NSE.

Strategic factors like immediate strength of customer base, geographical base and enhancement of future shareholder value were also taken into account for derivation of the swap ratio. To quote P. H. Ravi Kumar, Senior Vice President, ICICI Bank (as appeared in *The Economic Times* dated 12 December 2000), 'Three issues were considered for the merger, customer base, geographical base and enhancing shareholder value. We had been looking for such an activity. South is high economic activity area where BoM had strong presence.' In fact, ICICI Bank had negotiated with other South India-based banks including Karnataka-based Vysya Bank, Kerala-Based Federal Bank and South India Bank for a possible merger with the latter with the intention of expanding its operations to south India. But the negotiations were not successful. The statement of Mr. Sinor, Chairman and Managing Director of ICICI Bank is as follows. 'Bank was looking at a branch network of 350–400, which would have taken at least 5 years to achieve. Moreover, to get an additional 1.2 million customers (BoM's client base) would have required a minimum 2 years. On the other hand, Mr K. M. Thiagarajan, the then Chairman and Managing Director of BoM released a statement which is reproduced here: 'The financial consolidation was becoming necessary for the growth of the bank. Shareholder value is more important than anything else. The decision is based on value creation.'

Suitability Analysis

Suitability analysis was undertaken to ascertain the suitability of BoM merger with ICICI Bank. The Bank of Madura represented the culture of a 57-year-old organization whereas ICICI Bank represented a 6-year-old 'new

FIGURE 21.1 SHARE PRICE FLUCTUATIONS OF ICICI BANK AND BOM (PRE-SWAP RATIO ANNOUNCEMENT)

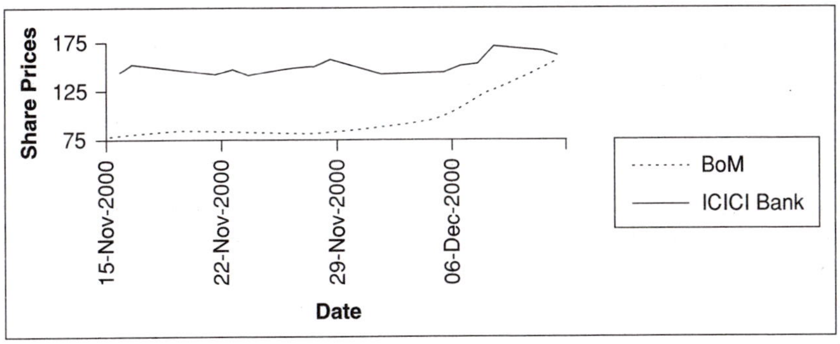

FIGURE 21.2 SHARE PRICE FLUCTUATIONS OF ICICI BANK AND BOM (PRE-SWAP RATIO ANNOUNCEMENT)

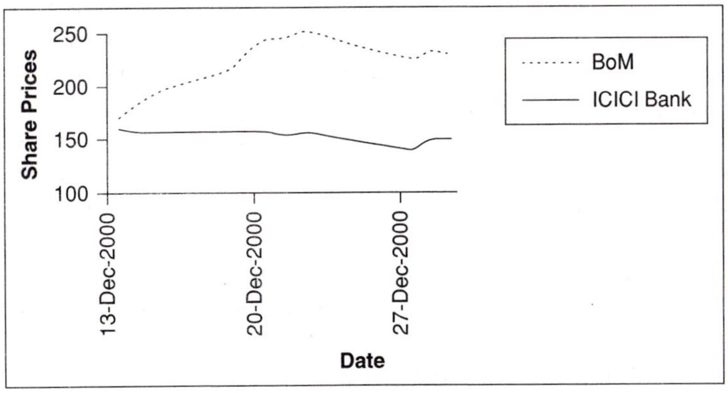

age' organization. Hence, an attempt was made to position both banks in context of the new trends in the banking sector. The emerging trends in the banking sector are summarised in the form of what's in and what's out format given in Table 21.10. Being an old private sector bank, BoM laid emphasis on the parameters listed under the title 'what's out' in the banking sector. They had, traditionally focused on mass banking strategies based on the social objectives, whereas ICICI Bank, had been emphasizing on parameters like profitability in the interests of shareholders. Being a newborn private bank, ICICI Bank had a credit recovery management cell, whereas BoM had a cell working like a credit monitoring department.

ICICI Bank has been a leading private player emphasizing more on 'What's In' rather than 'What's Out' in the banking sector. Thus, this merger is beneficial for the parties concerned since BoM was also trying to focus on new strategies in the banking sector, after the implementation of banking sector reforms in India. It was not a mammoth task for them to position them with the functional styles of ICICI Bank. However, integrating the human resources of BoM with ICICI Bank's employees was a difficult process for ICICI bank.

TABLE 21.10 NEW STRATEGIES (IN) AND OLD PRIORITIES (OUT) IN THE BANKING SECTOR

	What's in	What's out
Objective	Profitability	Developmental and social
Interests of	Shareholders	Priority sector
Strategies	Pro-active	Passive
Segment	Target banking	Mass banking
Business	Fee-based	Fund-based
NPA mgt.	Recovery mgt. Cell	Credit monitoring cell
Concentration	Investments	Advances
HR policy	Hire and fire	Job security

Synergies of the Merger

The synergies of the merger of BoM with ICICI Bank can be summarised as follows:

- Network of over 360 branches.
- Reduced time for setting up new branches.
- Combined customer base of 2.7 million.
- Combined asset base of ₹16,000 crore, which makes the ICICI bank amongst the largest private sector banks in India.

In detail, the synergies can be discussed on the basis of the following parameters:

- **Financial capability:** The merger has enabled them to have a stronger financial and operational structure, which is supposed to be capable of greater resource/deposit mobilization. ICICI Bank will emerge as one of the largest private sector banks in the country.
- **Branch network:** ICICI Bank's branch network not only increased by 264, but also increased the geographic coverage as well as convenience to its customers.
- **Customer base:** The largest customer base (combined) enabled ICICI bank to offer banking, and financial services and products and also facilitate cross-selling of products and services of the ICICI group.
- **Tech edge:** The merger will enable ICICI Bank to provide ATMs, phone and Internet banking, and financial services and products to a large customer base, with expected savings in costs and operating expenses.
- **Priority sector advances:** Commercial banks are required to lend money to people in the priority sector which include farmers, people in rural areas and small-scale industry. ICICI Bank did not have many branches in rural areas whereas BoM had lot of branches in rural and semi-urban areas. The enhanced branch network enabled ICICI Bank to lend for micro-finance activities through self-help groups, and for the agricultural sector in its priority sector initiatives through its acquired 87 rural and 88 semi-urban branches.
- **Equity capital and EPS:** The swap ratio approved was in the ratio of 1:2—two shares of ICICI Bank for every one share of BoM. The deal with BoM diluted the current equity capital by around 12 per cent, and the merger brought about 20 per cent gains in the EPS of ICICI Bank. Also the bank's comfortable CAR of 19.64 per cent declined to 17.6 per cent (Table 21.11).

TABLE 21.11 FINANCIAL STANDINGS OF ICICI BANK AND BANK OF MADURA (₹ in Crores)

	Parameters	ICICI Bank	Bank of Madura	
	1999–2000	**1998–99**	**1999–2000**	**1998–99**
Net worth	1,129.90	308.33	247.83	211.32
Total deposits	9,866.02	6,072.94	3,631.00	3,013.00
Advances	5,030.96	3,377.60	1,665.42	1,393.92
Net profit	105.43	63.75	45.58	30.13
Share capital	196.81	165.07	11.08	
Capital adequacy ratio	19.64%	11.06%	14.25%	15.83%
Gross NPAs/ Gross advances	2.54%	4.72%	11.09%	8.13%
Net NPAs /Net advances	1.53%	2.88%	6.23%	4.66%

Source: Compiled from Annual Reports (1999–2000) of ICICI Bank and BoM.

- **Managing human resources:** One of the greatest challenges before ICICI Bank was managing human resources. When the head count of ICICI Bank was taken, it was less than 1,500 employees; on the other hand, BoM had over 2,500. The merged entity had about 4,000 employees which made it one of the largest banks among the new generation private sector banks. The staff of ICICI Bank is drawn from various banks and business schools, mostly young qualified professionals with a computer background who prefer to work in metros or big cities with good remuneration packages. While under the influence of trade unions, most of the BoM employees have low career aspirations. Many of them have already availed of the voluntary retirement scheme and left. On the other hand, pay of most of the BoM employees were revised upwards. It was a herculean task to integrate two work cultures.
- **Managing a client base:** The client base of ICICI Bank after merger, was as big as 2.7 million from its past 0.5 million, an accumulation of 2.2 million from BoM. The nature and quality of clients was not uniform. The BoM had built up its client base for a long time, in a hard way, on the basis of personalised services. In order to deal with BoM's client base, ICICI Bank needed to redefine its strategy to suit to the new culture. If the sentiments or a relationship of small and medium borrowers was hurt, it would have been difficult for them to re-establish the relationship, which could also hamper the image of the bank.
- **Managing rural branches:** ICICI's major branches were in major metros and cities, whereas BoM had spread its wings mostly in semi-urban and rural segments of south India. There was a task ahead lying for the merged entity to increase dramatically the business mix of rural branches of the BoM. On the other hand, due to geographic location of its branches and level of competition, ICICI Bank would have a tough time to cope with. For example, an account holder needed to maintain a minimum of ₹5,000 in the savings bank account with ICICI Bank, whereas BoM's requirement to open a savings bank account was just ₹500. The branches in the rural area had a number of customers from low-income and middle-income groups who could not have maintained ₹5,000 in their savings bank account. Also, most of the BoM employees who were working in the rural branches were likely to retire soon, as the average age of the BoM employees was almost twice that of ICICI Bank. The ICICI Bank employees, mostly youngsters, would not prefer to get transferred to the rural branches because of their preference for city life and culture.

CHAPTER SUMMARY

In this era of globalization, organizations will have to be competitive in order to face challenges. Survival of the fittest has become a reality in most sectors, including banking with the entry of foreign players. On the other hand, mergers can be considered as barriers to perfect competition. But the inclination to create a monopoly and the desire to become a champion in their respective industrial sectors motivate the big players to take over the small ones. Small companies tend to look at the short-term (immediate) gain through mergers and let the 'big wigs' acquire them. Lack of resources, both capital and labour that are required to compete with the big players sometimes force the 'small' to merge with the 'big.' In the case of BoM–ICICI Bank merger; the BoM got a better deal in the form of a higher swap ratio. Therefore, one finds that the BoM has not compromised in the negotiation with ICICI bank. At the same time, the desire of ICICI bank to achieve more strength within a less span of time and their urge for relentless expansion have led them to agree upon a higher swap ratio with the BoM shareholders. Therefore, the BoM shareholders benefited from the merger in the short run and 100 banks could increase the number of customers, branches and business, which would be helpful to them in the long run to raise new challenges to other competitors in the Indian banking industry.

After viewing the merger syndrome, there could be a possibility that permutations and combinations of mergers in the Indian banking industry may take place in future. Public sector banks, which will shortly be losing their public sector nature (as the Government of India is planning to reduce its stake from 100 per cent to 33 per cent) are strong contenders to take over old generation private sector banks. Foreign banks will not stay behind in the takeover bids.

TOPICS FOR FURTHER DISCUSSION

- What are the implications of mergers in banking sector?
- Why did BoM agree for merger with ICICI Bank?
- Do you think that the 'business strategy' of ICICI Bank played a more important role than financial ratios, while deciding the swap ratio?
- What are the synergies of the BoM merger with ICICI Bank? Analyse the effect of the swap ratio on share prices?
- Had you been the CEO of ICICI Bank, what decision you would have taken?

ANNEXURE I

SHARE PRICE VOLUME DATA

Share Price Volume Data (National Stock Exchange)

DATA FOR BANK OF MADURA—FROM 15 NOVEMBER 2000 TO 12 DECEMBER 2000

Date	Previous Closing	Open	High	Low	Close	Traded Quantity	Turnover (₹ in Lakh)
15-Nov-2000	78.85	83.00	83.00	79.20	79.20	2,200	1.78
16-Nov-2000	79.20	79.75	81.40	79.00	79.60	3,150	2.52
17-Nov-2000	79.60	80.95	81.40	79.20	79.20	2,450	1.96
20-Nov-2000	79.20	78.85	83.00	78.85	82.35	4,400	3.61
21-Nov-2000	82.35	81.50	83.65	81.00	83.15	3,150	2.60
22-Nov-2000	83.15	82.45	83.00	82.25	82.95	1,700	1.41
23-Nov-2000	82.95	80.00	83.75	80.00	83.45	3,650	3.00
24-Nov-2000	83.45	83.05	84.35	83.05	84.25	1,500	1.26
27-Nov-2000	84.25	83.50	85.00	83.50	84.25	6,100	5.15
28-Nov-2000	84.25	85.00	88.50	85.00	87.20	5,200	4.52
29-Nov-2000	87.20	85.15	92.50	85.10	87.85	7,550	6.79
30-Nov-2000	87.85	87.00	90.50	87.00	90.50	5,250	4.69
01-Dec-2000	90.50	90.40	95.00	88.50	89.95	13,700	12.51
04-Dec-2000	89.95	90.00	97.15	90.00	97.15	23,100	21.79
05-Dec-2000	97.15	104.95	104.95	104.95	104.95	2,650	2.78
06-Dec-2000	104.95	113.35	113.35	113.35	113.35	18,000	20.40
07-Dec-2000	113.35	122.45	122.45	122.45	122.45	14,850	18.18
08-Dec-2000	122.45	132.25	132.25	126.35	132.25	89,400	117.75
11-Dec-2000	132.25	142.85	142.85	142.85	142.85	3,450	4.93
12-Dec-2000	142.85	154.30	154.30	154.30	154.30	2,200	3.39

Share Price Volume Data

DATA FOR THE BANK OF MADURA—FROM 13 DECEMBER 2000 TO 30 DECEMBER 2000

Date	Previous Closing	Open	High	Low	Close	Traded Quantity	Turnover (₹ in Lakh)
13-Dec-2000	154.30	166.65	166.65	166.65	166.65	150	0.25
14-Dec-2000	166.65	180.00	180.00	180.00	180.00	200	0.36
15-Dec-2000	180.00	194.40	194.40	194.40	194.40	1,350	2.62
18-Dec-2000	194.40	209.95	209.95	209.95	209.95	3,000	6.30
19-Dec-2000	209.95	226.75	226.75	226.75	226.75	7,900	17.91
20-Dec-2000	226.75	244.90	244.90	240.10	244.90	4,34,600	1,062.42
21-Dec-2000	244.90	249.90	259.90	240.50	242.35	3,45,350	854.02
22-Dec-2000	242.35	245.70	258.00	238.10	250.00	2,65,850	661.52
26-Dec-2000	250.00	250.00	251.00	230.00	230.15	1,20,200	283.50
27-Dec-2000	230.15	220.00	225.00	213.00	220.45	67,100	146.30
28-Dec-2000	220.45	216.00	237.90	206.50	231.00	1,25,350	285.02
29-Dec-2000	231.00	232.95	235.00	225.05	231.00	51,650	118.82

Share Price Volume Data

DATA FOR ICICI BANK—FROM 15 DECEMBER 2000 TO 12 DECEMBER 2000

Date	Previous Closing	Open	High	Low	Close	Traded Quantity	Turnover (₹ in Lakh)
15-Nov-2000	122.65	124.75	142.30	124.75	142.30	2,95,465	404.25
16-Nov-2000	142.30	143.00	162.00	143.00	151.15	4,94,907	758.46
17-Nov-2000	151.15	151.90	151.90	140.15	147.20	3,03.,746	441.25
20-Nov-2000	147.20	149.50	149.50	139.55	141.25	1,61,529	230.31
21-Nov-2000	141.25	143.00	152.00	138.25	142.35	1,93,952	277.77
22-Nov-2000	142.35	147.00	153.00	145.00	145.65	1,43,503	211.11
23-Nov-2000	145.65	143.10	143.10	139.15	141.65	71,117	100.52
24-Nov-2000	141.65	142.00	144.50	142.00	143.15	53,625	76.72
27-Nov-2000	143.15	146.00	152.00	144.15	150.35	2,04,631	304.89
28-Nov-2000	150.35	149.80	157.90	145.00	156.10	2,78,024	431.28
29-Nov-2000	156.10	153.00	155.95	151.00	152.15	54,639	83.46
30-Nov-2000	152.15	152.05	154.00	147.20	147.95	50,807	76.00
01-Dec-2000	147.95	145.00	147.95	140.15	142.00	1,17,359	168.23
04-Dec-2000	142.00	141.40	146.30	141.40	144.75	78,897	114.65
05-Dec-2000	144.75	144.40	146.50	144.05	144.45	68,577	99.73
06-Dec-2000	144.45	147.60	156.00	147.60	150.10	2,08,424	314.08
07-Dec-2000	150.10	151.55	156.25	148.50	152.95	2,03,511	309.51
08-Dec-2000	152.95	153.85	171.90	152.50	168.95	4,90,187	796,51
11-Dec-2000	168.95	176.00	182.00	158.60	165.30	8,46,339	1,430,87
12-Dec-2000	165.30	163.15	163.15	152.10	160.05	7,39,518	1,162.20

DATA FOR ICICI BANK—FROM 13 DECEMBER 2000 TO 31 DECEMBER 2000

Date	Previous Closing	Open	High	Low	Close	Traded Quantity	Turnover (₹ in Lakh)
13-Dec-2000	160.05	161.00	161.00	151.05	159.10	2,75,203	433.87
14-Dec-2000	159.10	159.00	160.00	156.50	157.60	1,94,739	307.42
15-Dec-2000	157.60	156.55	158.70	153.05	157.20	351,909	548.59
18-Dec-2000	157.20	157.00	158.50	153.25	157.05	1,49,768	234.84
19-Dec-2000	157.05	156.55	159.50	156.15	158.00	1,82,074	286.61
20-Dec-2000	158.00	157.00	157.95	152.00	157.05	2,28,654	354.12
21-Dec-2000	157.05	155.00	156.00	152.10	153.75	3,16,820	488.52
22-Dec-2000	153.75	153.20	157.00	153.20	155.25	1,89,770	294.14
26-Dec-2000	155.25	154.30	155.70	139.00	143.35	2,44,325	357.55
27-Dec-2000	143.35	140.50	145.00	132.10	141.10	1,43,202	198.35
28-Dec-2000	141.10	138.10	154.00	138.00	150.30	2,34,139	346.80
29-Dec-2000	150.30	152.00	154.50	147.05	150.50	1,90,248	286.22

Source: http://nseindia.com.

ANNEXURE II

THE MERGER OF BANK OF TOKYO MITSUBISHI AND UFJ BANK[8]

On 9 September 2005, Mitsubishi Tokyo Financial Group (MTFG) and United Financial of Japan (UFJ Holdings) announced that they had received the approval for the merger and began joint operations as merged entity with the new name Mitsubishi Tokyo UFJ Financial Group, Inc. (MUFG) from 1 October 2005. The commercial banks within the two financial groups, Bank of Tokyo Mitsubishi Ltd (BTM) and UFJ Bank Limited were merged on 1 January 2006 and the new bank was named as Bank of Tokyo Mitsubishi–UFJ Bank. The new bank, in short, is also known as MUFJ Bank. After the merger, MUFJ Bank became one among the world's largest financial groups in terms of assets amounting to 1,97,001.6 billion Japanese yen. This merger captured the attention of the business world because it helped both the organizations to create monopolistic power in the Japanese banking industry. Nobuo Kuroyanagi (President/CEO MTFG), a 63-year-old lifetime committed employee who had worked for MTFG from the age of 23 in a range of positions, was the main focal person to press the button to open the curtains for the merger drama.

MTFG had set an aspiration of being one of the top five financial groups in the world. They had aimed to achieve this by creating a premier, comprehensive, financial group that can succeed against competitors globally. They wanted a bank with an extensive and a well-balanced financial network, locally and internationally.

Major Banks in the Japanese Banking Industry

As on 2004, before the merger between MTFG and UFJ, The Mizuho Financial Group (Mizuho), MTFG, Sumitomo Mitsui Financial Group (SMFG) and UFJ Holdings were the four major leading banks in the Japanese banking industry. MTFG and SMFG were the 2nd and 3rd largest banks while UFJ holding was the 4th largest bank. (Refer Exhibit 21.1).

- **The Mizuho Financial Group (Mizuho)**

  Mizuho Bank belongs to the Mizuho Financial Group as a core retail banking unit and was the largest mega bank in Japan until the year 2005 and its headquarters were located in Chiyoda, Tokyo. Mizuho Bank was formed by a merger of Dai-Ichi Kangyo Bank with retail operations of Fuji Bank and the Industrial Bank of Japan, which were major financial institutions. Fuji Bank had been one of the major banks during the post-war era and was formed in 1948 as part of the Yasuda Zaibatsu. During the last half of the 20th century, Dai-Ichi Kangyo Bank was one of the largest banks in the world and was formed in 1971 by merging Dai-Ichi and Nippon Kangyo Banks. When merging the three banks, the Bank Dai-Ichi Kangyo was renamed Mizuho Bank and inherited the groups' individual, small businesses and local/regional government services, while individual banking services were consolidated into the Fuji bank and is being renamed as Mizuho Corporate Bank. Then the two banks, namely, Mizuho Bank and the Mizuho Corporate Bank were consolidated under Mizuho Holdings on October 2005 and were transferred to the Mizuho Financial Group. Mizuho Financial Group was initially formed in January 2003 and was financed by Mizuho Holdings by using share exchange. In March 2003, it became sole shareholder of Mizuho Holdings Inc.

- **The Mitsubishi Tokyo Financial Group**

  The Mitsubishi Tokyo Financial Group (MTFG) had divided into different subsidiaries, such as Bank of Tokyo–Mitsubhishi, Mitsubhishi Trust, Nippon Trust and Tokyo Trust. Bank of Tokyo–Mitsubhishi was the flagship organization within the group.

  This bank (Bank of Tokyo–Mitsubhishi) was the financial wing of the Mitsubishi Group of Companies, but they also expanded their business which covered many Japanese industries ranging from small-, medium-sised companies to individuals. The Mitsubishi Group of Companies were engaged in a broad range of activities including manufacturing, trading, natural resources, transportation, real estate, banking and insurance and were managed and operated individually. They had been able to build a worldwide network and were involved in a range of commercial banking activities locally and internationally.

- **Sumitomo Mitsui Banking Financial Group**

  Sumitomo Group of Enterprises has been one of the oldest surviving business entities in the world and dates back to 1600. Sumitomo Bank was established as a subsidiary of the Sumitomo Group of Enterprises in 1895 and experienced smooth and rapid growth. After World War II, due to some laws Sumitomo Bank was renamed as Bank of Osaka and it was again restored as Sumitomo Bank in 1952. In 1965, it merged with Kaiwachi Bank and in 1986 with Heiwa Sogo Bank. Due to the crisis in the banking sector in 1990s, the financial situation continued to worsen, and Sumitomo Bank had also made an unprecedented move of writing off 100 billion (US$895 million)[9] in bad loans. In April 2001, Sumitomo Bank merged with Sakura Bank and formed Sumitomo Mitsui banking corporation (SMBC). In December 2002, SMBC established a holding company by the name Sumitomo Mitsui Banking Corporation Inc. through a share transfer and became a wholly-owned subsidiary of SMFG. In 2003 again, SMBC merged with Wakshio Bank and the same name was kept. During this period, Sumitomo Bank was one of the leading providers of highest quality financial products and services by maintaining their respect and confidence, providing quality service to its worldwide clients. Its expansion ranges all over Japan as well as nearly hundred overseas branch offices, and subsidiaries in about 30 countries

- **UFJ Group**

  UFJ group was headquartered in Osaka. UFJ Bank was the flagship firm within the group, which was formed by merging Sanwa Bank and Tokai Bank in 2001. Sanwa bank had an extensive branch network in Tokyo and

Osaka, and it had been providing innovative financial services with a well-established service network. Tokai Bank, which was one of the leading banks in Nagoya, had a considerable presence in Tokyo and Osaka.

Financial Times had ranked UFJ as 392 among the Global 500 companies, during the pre-merger period. During this period, UFJ Group was ranked 14th in the world and 4th in Japan among banks in terms of assets. Operations were being broadly classified into retail banking and corporate banking. Retail banking business were handled by providing housing and consumer loans. Corporate banking division mainly catered for medium and small companies providing services, such as electronic banking, sales of derivatives and corporate finance services, global banking and trading, trust operations, securities and investment banking, and asset management. UFJ had been able to establish a wide global network covering the US, Canada, Europe, the Middle East and Oceania. However, during the three fiscal years 2002–2004 (pre-merger period), UFJ had been facing losses.

Need for Mega Banks

Global financial industry had turned into a major battle field among the major mega banks by the end of 20th century. Merging banks and forming mega banks was not only common to Japan but had been a worldwide trend in 1990s, even though it has been criticised in the context of global financial crisis in 2008–2010.

Japanese banks were ranked in higher positions among the banks in the world during 1980s. Japanese yen had appreciated more than 50 per cent in 1980s (mainly because of excessive exports and surplus in trade account) which caused deflationary effects in Japan. The government and the central bank, *i.e.*, the Bank of Japan relaxed the rules for providing credit (loan) to counteract the deflationary pressure. Loans and share prices had risen and touched peak points. Japanese firms had become cash-rich by mid-1980s with remarkable export growth rate and high share prices. Banks also started investing lot of money (lent money for borrowers who invested in real estate), in order to compensate for the lowered demand for loans by the companies to meet their working capital requirements.

In early 1990s, there were signs that Japanese economy was slowing down. Bank of Japan introduced new measures to control the credit and tightened monetary policy. As a result, share and land prices went on a down spin and the individual borrowers defaulted the loan repayments. This was instrumental in creating large amount non-performing loans (NPL) in Japanese banks during 1990s. Major banks began to crumble with the collapses and bankruptcies. In order to reduce their NPL and to earn sustainable revenues and profits recovering from the exiting problems, banks tried to merge and get stronger with their capital and assets. Japanese financial service sector triggered due to economic bubble during the 1990s.

Due to the inability of securing sufficient revenues from its conventional loan operations, Japanese banks made effort to expand their revenues made through service charges and commissions while others were seeking to obtain profit stream in securities services through investment banking services. They also started to focus on small-scale consumer loans which were let out for consumer finance companies up to this period. Therefore, many banks tried to associate and attach business by way of merger proposals.

Compared to the banks in many other countries during this period of time, Japanese banks had been lagging behind in terms of high-risk financial products such as derivatives. In order to perform banking activities, such as investment banking services, massive capital base was required. Also, in order to expand their international operations, merging and forming into mega banks gave them the necessary strength to compete with their international competitors.

The Establishment of Mitsubishi Tokyo UFJ Financial Group Inc. and MUFJ Bank The merger and the establishment of Mitsubishi Tokyo Financial Group Inc. (MUFG) and the combined new bank named as Bank of Tokyo Mitsubhishi–UFJ (MUFJ Bank) were fully completed on 1 January 2006. The new group's asset base was regarded as the world's largest asset base in the global banking sector. The deposit base was also significantly higher than other Japanese banks.

The new group established its corporate governance based on a dual system which comprised of a system of voluntary committees, corporate auditors and directors supplemented by external perspectives. In order to fully and appropriately preview their responsibility of accountability to shareholders and to enhance management transparency, they appointed independent directors on the board. They also had appointed outside corporate auditors. An advisory board had been established, which composed of external experts. This helped them to build up a proper framework for risk management and internal audit across the entire group to strengthen oversight of management. They also listed their bank in the New York Stock Exchange.

Synergies of the Merger

The synergies and the impact of the merger between Bank of Tokyo Mitsubhishi and UFJ Bank Ltd can be analyzed as follows.

- **Impact on loans and deposits**

  • *Pre-merger period (until 2005).* Loans and bills discounted for the physical year 2004 (including trust accounts) had recorded an amount of 85 trillion yen and had increased for the physical year 2005 by 1.1 trillion to 86.1 trillion yen, mainly due to the growth in lending by overseas branches and subsidiaries. Total amount of deposits for the physical year 2004 amounted to 118.2 trillion yen, which had got increased by 1.1 trillion yen than that of the previous year. For the physical year 2005, the amount got increased by 0.7 trillion to record 118.9 trillion yen.[10] (see Exhibit 21.1 to 21.5)

  • *Post-merger (2006 onwards).* For the physical year 2006, loans and bills discounted decreased by 0.6 trillion yen than that of the previous year and amounted to 85.1 trillion yen.[11] During year 2007, loans and bills discounted had increased by 3.6 trillion yen than the previous year and amounted to 85.1 trillion yen.[12] For the physical year 2008, the above amount again got increased by 3.4 trillion to record 92 trillion yen.[13] This increment was mainly due to the factors such as increase in domestic corporate lending. Deposits for the year 2006 amounted to 118.7 trillion yen. The amount for the year 2007 got increased from 2.5 trillion yen and recorded an amount of 121.3 trillion yen. This was mainly due to the increase in deposits in overseas offices. Deposits got again decreased by 1.1 trillion to 120 trillion yen in the year 2008 due to decrease in deposits at overseas offices (refer Exhibit 21.6).

- **Non-performing loans**

  • *Pre-merger.* Non-performing loan (NPL) ratio for the fiscal year 2004 was 3.33 per cent, and for the year 2005, the percentage values decreased by 1.26 points to 2.07 per cent. This was a result of decline in newly arising NPLs and progress in the disposal of NPLs.

  • *Post-merger.* In the fiscal year 2006, disclosed NPL ratio was 1.46 per cent and had decreased by 0.60 points than that of the previous year. The ratio again got decreased for the year 2007 by 0.31 points to 1.15 per cent. This was mainly due to credit rating improvements of obligors and progress in the disposal of NPLs. For the year 2008, the ratio got increased by 0.09 per cent to record 1.24 per cent.

- **Domestic and overseas branches of MUFG**

  Before the merger, MTFG had 306 domestic branches and UFJ bank had 546 branches all over Japan. By the year 2008, the total number of domestic branches of MUFJ Bank had increased to 1,244. Before the merger, MTFG had 81 overseas branches and UFJ had 26 overseas branches. Both holding companies altogether had 107 overseas branches. After the merger, they opened new overseas branches, and at the end of the fiscal year 2006, the total number of overseas branches was 429. The number of overseas branches increased in the year 2007 to 456 branches, and in the year 2008 to 459 branches. MUFG is the largest current global network than any of the Japanese financial group with over 400 locations in more than 40 countries and has a solid domestic customer base with approximately 40 million retail accounts and 5,00,000 corporate clients.

- **Share price** In this section, we compare the Tokyo stock market share prices of the combined financial group MUFJ (also known as Bank of Tokyo Mitsubishi–UFJ) during the post-merger period with that of MTFG bank during the pre-merger period. The price data were collected from Yahoo finance portal and were given in US dollar terms. A comparison exercise with NIKKEI 225 (*Stock market index* for the *Tokyo Stock Exchange*) has also been undertaken. From the year 2002 to end of 2004 (prior to the merger), there was no clear improvement/increase in the share prices of MTFG bank. From the second half of 2004, particularly during the second half of 2005, MTFG share price had risen. This could be because of rumours and the news pertaining to the discussion for merger between MTFG and UFJ group.

  While considering as a whole, share prices had improved than that of the past during the first 1 year of post-merger period, but there was no stable improvement after that. The extent of fluctuation was greater than the fluctuations in the benchmark index NIKKEI 225. From October 2001 to November 2002, market closing share price had fluctuated between 6.15 and 7.15 USD. During December 2002 to September 2003, the share price had fallen down much more and had lowered down to less than 4 USD, continuously for about 3–4 months. The share price had gone up during October 2004 to January 2006 but had fluctuated between 8.75 and 13.7 USD (see Exhibit 21.7).

  After the completion of the merger in January 2006, there had been an improvement in share prices until October 2006, but since then up to March 2009, share prices had declined. At the end of the year 2007, the value had decreased down to about 9.8 USD. At the end of year 2008, the value had decreased to about 6.5 USD (This could be because of the global financial crisis). During the year 2008, the share price had fluctuated between 5.5 and 11 USD. In the year 2009, on a specific day, this had fallen down to around 4.5 USD. Therefore, one can say that from the merger, there had been no visible positive effects of merger on the share prices of the merged entity (refer Exhibits 21.6–21.9).

Strategies for the Future

Getting stronger with earnings and profits has been a major target for the MUFJ Bank. They have been trying to concentrate more on to demonstrate sustainable growth strategies in their core business areas, including retail, corporate and trust assets businesses. They have the ability to strengthen their investment product sales by responding well to each customer segment in the retail business segment. But, the challenges remain as it is, whether it is possible for them to upgrade activities in all categories and main sources of earnings in retail operations, such as investment product sales, consumer finance and housing loans. Would it be difficult to reinforce internal management systems, execute a strategy to increase distribution channels, etc. are some of the actions that can take place to increase retail earnings. Recently MUFG had made a US$9 billion strategic investment in Morgan Stanley and had come up with a strategic alliance and had also signed a memorandum of understanding for integration of their respective security firms in Japan, creation of marketing joint ventures for corporate finance operations in America, developing a cooperative framework in Asia, etc.

Does it make sense to use this alliance to advance their corporate and investment banking strategies as well as to expand their businesses globally?

Another question is how to take advantage of their strong capital base for investments? Do they have to look forward and review for possible business opportunities such as services that use Internet and which can deliver solid returns that enhance their profitability and growth?

EXHIBIT 21.1 RANKINGS: JAPANESE BANKING INDUSTRY (2004—PRE-MERGER)

1	Mizuho Financial Group	12,85,471	1
2	Mitsubishi Tokyo Financial Group	9,74,950	2
3	Sumitomo Mitsui Financial Group	9,50,448	3
4	UFJ Holdings	75,36,31	4
5	Norinchukin Bank	5,53,720	5
10	Resona Holdings	3,81,994	6
6	Shinkin Central Bank	2,59,265	7
7	Sumitomo Trust & Banking	1,44,107	8
8	Shinsei Bank	60,822	17
9	Shoko Chukin Bank	1,15,070	10
14	Mitsui Trust Holdings	1,18,506	9
11	Aozora Bank	49,626	24
12	Shizuoka Bank	76,654	13
13	Bank of Yokohama	99,264	11
16	Chiba Bank	77,733	12
15	Joyo Bank	67,657	14
17	Chugoku Bank	53,867	21
18	Hachijuni Bank	54217	20
19	77 Bank	51032	23
21	Gunma Bank	54485	19

Source: The banker Web site www.thebanker.com Accesses on 18 January 2010.
Asset base in terms of US Dollar (Millions) is given in 3rd column.

EXHIBIT 21.2 NUMBER OF BRANCHES WITHIN JAPAN AND OVERSEAS (2004—PRE-MERGER)

	Overseas	Total in Japan	Central Japan	Western Japan	Eastern Japan
MTFG	81	366	22	81	263
UFJ	26	546	148	186	212

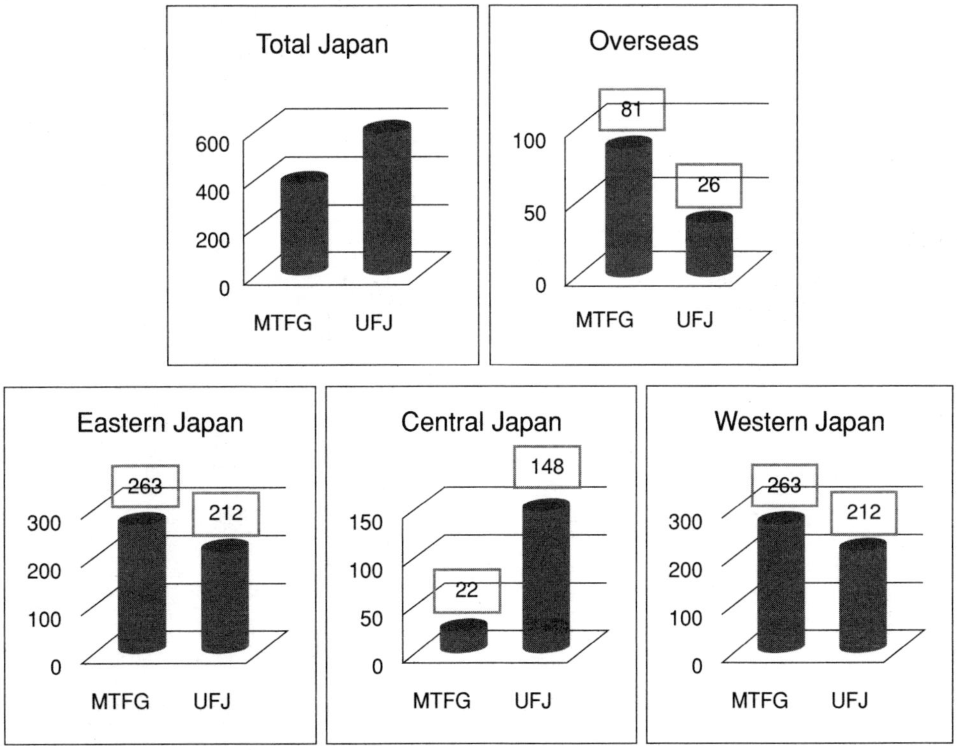

Source: http://www.secinfo.com/d14D5a.147gw.htm

EXHIBIT 21.3 SYNERGIES OF CONSOLIDATED STATEMENTS OF OPERATIONS: EARNINGS (2004–05 INCLUDES PRE-MERGER STATISTICS AND 2006–08 INCLUDES POST-MERGER STATISTICS)

TABLE 21.12 GROSS PROFITS

Year	Gross Profits (Billions of Yen)
2004	3401.9
2005	3610.9
2006	3726.7
2007	3512.7
2008	3272.9

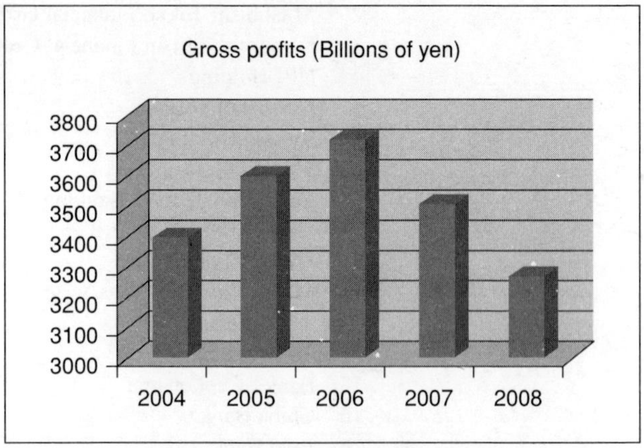

Drawing based on Table 21.12

TABLE 21.13 NET PROFITS

Year	Net Profits (Billions of Yen)
2004	1716.3
2005	1685.5
2006	1652.7
2007	1396.9
2008	1189.1

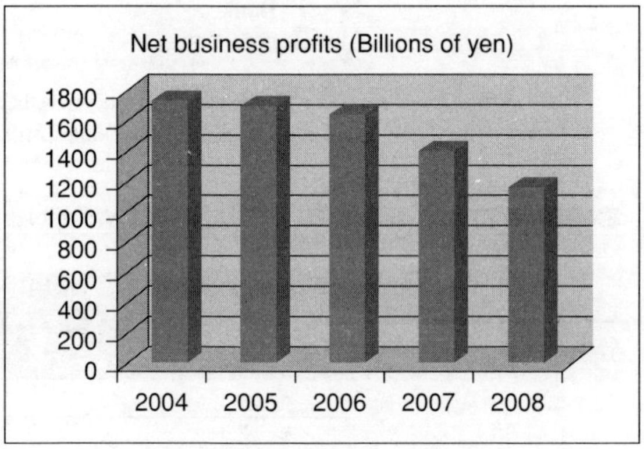

Drawing based on Table 21.13

EXHIBIT 21.4 NET INCOME

TABLE 21.14 NET INCOME

Year	Net Income (Billions of Yen)
2004	216.1
2005	1181.7
2006	880.9
2007	636.6
2008	256.9

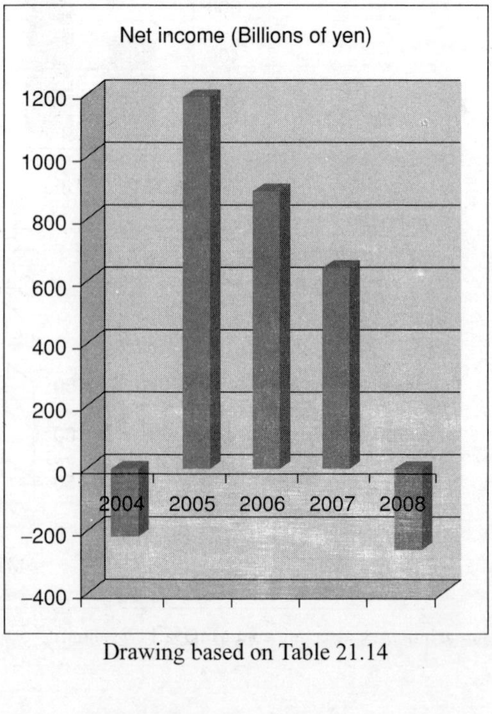

Drawing based on Table 21.14

EXHIBIT 21.5 IMPACT ON LOANS AND DEPOSITS (2004–05 INCLUDES PRE-MERGER STATISTICS AND 2006–08 INCLUDES POST-MERGER STATISTICS)

TABLE 21.15 LOANS

Year	Loans (Billions of Yen)
2004	85.0
2005	86.1
2006	85.1
2007	88.7
2008	92.2

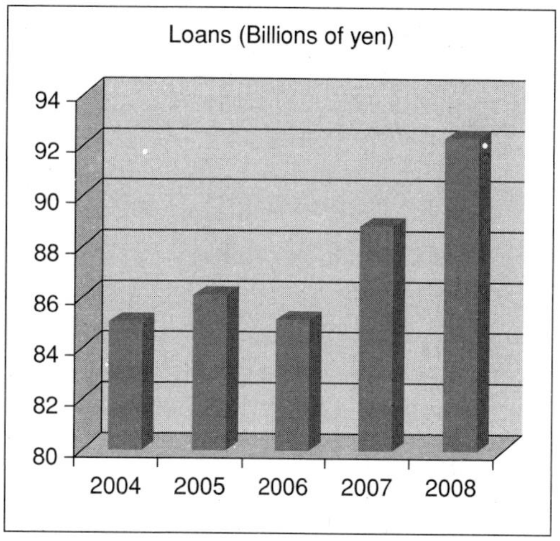

Drawing based on Table 21.15

TABLE 21.16 DEPOSITS

Year	Deposits (Billions of Yen)
2004	118.2
2005	118.9
2006	118.7
2007	121.3
2008	120.1

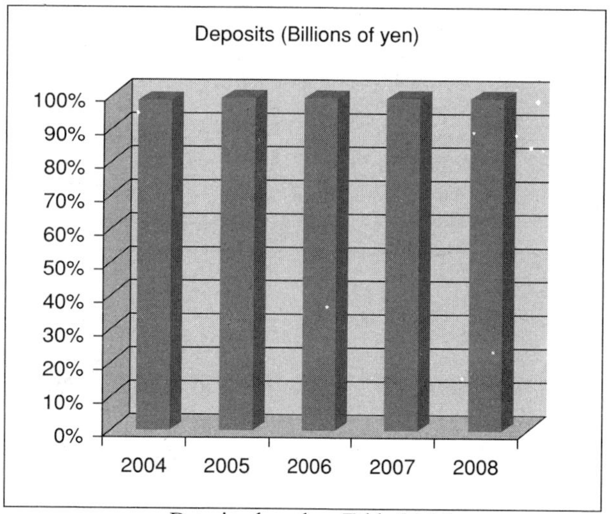

Drawing based on Table 21.16

EXHIBIT 21.6 PRE-MERGER MONTHLY SHARE PRICES OF MTFG (01/2006–03/2009)

Date	Market Open	Market High	Market Low	Market Close	Market Volume	Adj. Close
3-Jan-2006	13.8	14.4	13.18	13.25	17,62,600	13.19
1-Dec-2005	13	14.48	12.83	13.69	13,91,200	13.62
1-Nov-2005	13	14.19	12.57	12.65	20,02,600	12.59
3-Oct-2005	12.54	13.13	11.67	12.69	19,54,000	12.63
1-Sept-2005	10.15	13.05	9.99	13.03	19,30,100	12.97
1-Aug-2005	8.4	10.41	8.33	10.35	11,33,600	10.28
1-July-2005	8.39	8.57	7.95	8.3	5,14,400	8.24
1-June-2005	8.36	8.78	8.3	8.48	4,64,600	8.42
2-May-2005	8.74	8.88	8.16	8.3	6,40,300	8.24
1-Apr-2005	8.64	8.83	8.16	8.65	4,93,000	8.59
1-Mar-2005	9.18	9.47	8.6	8.65	8,74,200	8.59
1-Feb-2005	9.53	9.66	8.95	9.17	7,76,500	9.04
3-Jan-2005	10.26	10.27	9.4	9.52	5,77,500	9.39
1-Dec-2004	9.6	10.24	9.04	10.22	4,91,400	10.08
1-Nov-2004	8.49	9.66	8.4	9.48	6,20,200	9.35

(*Continued*)

EXHIBIT 21.6 (CONTINUED)

1-Oct-2004	8.48	8.84	8.02	8.49	5,44,200	8.37
1-Sept-2004	9.09	9.1	8.11	8.34	5,49,200	8.23
2-Aug-2004	8.87	9.55	8.31	9.06	6,14,200	8.94
1-July-2004	9.2	10.4	8.36	9.06	10,70,600	8.94
1-June-2004	8.64	9.37	8.08	9.37	4,27,600	9.24
3-May-2004	8.9	9.21	7.12	8.72	9,06,700	8.6
1-Apr-2004	9.93	10.4	8.64	8.9	8,56,800	8.78
1-Mar-2004	7.84	10.12	7.79	9.93	13,20,500	9.79
2-Feb-2004	7.75	8	7.34	7.8	4,66,600	7.65
2-Jan-2004	7.83	8.15	7.43	7.73	6,44,600	7.58
1-Dec-2003	7.55	7.87	6.93	7.83	4,77,000	7.68
3-Nov-2003	7.31	7.5	6.31	7.39	8,21,700	7.25
1-Oct-2003	7.16	8.42	6.6	7.34	9,78,300	7.2
2-Sept-2003	6.03	6.6	5.59	6.44	8,47,000	6.32
1-Aug-2003	4.5	5.99	4.03	5.87	4,55,800	5.76
1-July-2003	4.63	5.28	4.39	4.47	5,46,700	4.38
2-June-2003	4	4.63	3.94	4.58	5,69,400	4.49
1-May-2003	3.45	4.05	3.4	3.89	3,89,900	3.82
1-Apr-2003	3.72	3.82	2.98	3.52	3,20,800	3.45
3-Mar-2003	4.12	4.34	3.65	3.72	4,86,000	3.65
3-Feb-2003	5.3	5.51	4.42	4.43	3,42,600	4.31
2-Jan-2003	5.32	6.2	5.11	5.25	2,98,100	5.11
2-Dec-2002	6.07	6.12	5.08	5.35	2,53,800	5.2
1-Nov-2002	6.45	6.66	5.26	6.15	2,03,100	5.98
1-Oct-2002	7.34	7.34	6.15	6.41	2,52,100	6.23
3-Sept-2002	6.25	7.4	5.98	7.34	5,88,100	7.14
1-Aug-2002	6.5	7	6.5	6.83	1,12,100	6.59
1-July-2002	6.75	7.64	6.53	6.75	2,51,000	6.51
3-June-2002	8.2	8.42	6.2	6.8	2,99,600	6.56
1-May-2002	7	8.16	6.63	7.88	2,70,300	7.6
1-Apr-2002	6.01	7.14	5.91	6.96	2,19,600	6.72
1-Mar-2002	6.13	7.4	6.05	6.15	2,49,100	5.94
4-Feb-2002	5.55	6.35	5.15	6.11	2,22,200	5.85
2-Jan-2002	6.47	7.06	5.65	5.72	2,82,000	5.48
3-Dec-2001	6.8	6.98	5.95	6.47	6,55,100	6.2
1-Nov-2001	7.45	7.8	6.6	6.95	4,47,600	6.66
15-Oct-2001	7.74	8.05	7.35	7.49	2,02,100	7.17

Source: www.yahoo.com—finance section. Price in US dollars.

EXHIBIT 21.7 COMPARISON OF SHARE PRICE FLUCTUATIONS MTFG VERSUS NIKKEI (PRE-MERGER 2002–12/2005)

*Drawn based on Monthly share Prices of MTUFG (01/2006–03/2009)

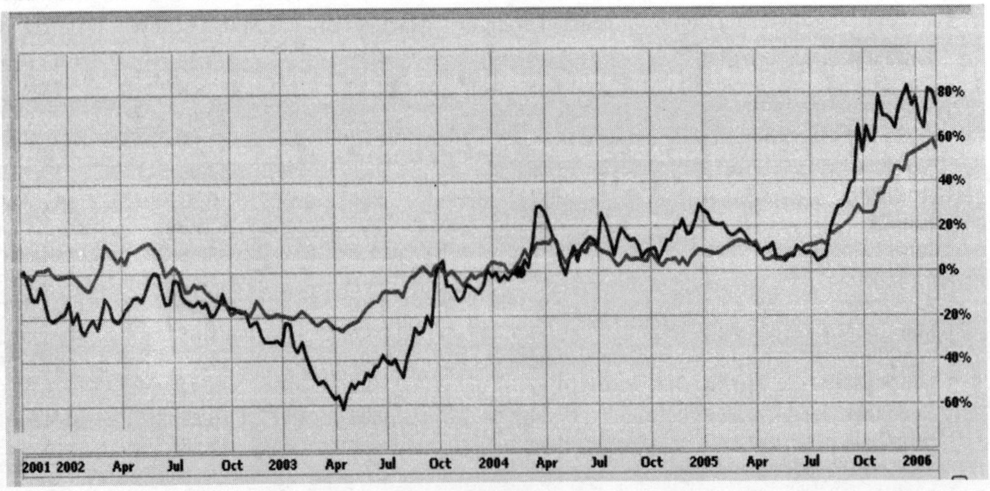

EXHIBITS 21.8 POST MERGER SHARE PRICE FLUCTUATIONS

Share Prices of Merged entity (New one) MUFJ Bank (01/2006–03/2009)

Date	Market Open	Market High	Market Low	Market Close	Volume	Adj. Close
2-Mar-2009	4.27	4.43	3.71	4.28	39,28,400	4.28
2-Feb-2009	5.38	5.56	4.26	4.47	31,74,200	4.47
2-Jan-2009	6.22	6.34	5.15	5.5	35,88,000	5.5
1-Dec-2008	5.11	6.41	4.53	6.21	73,68,600	6.21
3-Nov-2008	6.31	6.92	4.5	5.48	31,74,200	5.48
1-Oct-2008	8.57	9.14	5.18	6.29	38,78,300	6.29
2-Sep-2008	7.63	9.21	6.87	8.74	46,96,500	8.74
1-Aug-2008	8.7	8.78	7.21	7.64	27,45,700	7.64
1-July-2008	8.77	9.67	8.51	8.78	41,43,100	8.78
2-Jun-2008	10.69	10.94	8.66	8.8	34,11,500	8.8
1-May-2008	10.69	11.1	9.45	10.15	28,54,000	10.15
1-Apr-2008	8.87	11.11	8.87	10.99	18,85,100	10.99
3-Mar-2008	8.69	9.28	7.95	8.7	23,84,200	8.7
1-Feb-2008	9.45	9.69	8.46	8.81	23,97,200	8.81
2-Jan-2008	9.33	9.9	8.2	9.87	29,34,200	9.87
3-Dec-2007	9.96	11.22	8.84	9.33	35,36,400	9.33
1-Nov-2007	9.54	10.05	8.04	9.79	31,19,300	9.79
1-Oct-2007	9.15	10.27	8.49	9.96	23,27,400	9.96
4-Sep-2007	9.46	9.55	8.28	9.08	21,20,000	9.08
1-Aug-2007	10.33	10.61	9.03	9.6	20,34,400	9.6
2-July-2007	11.2	11.48	10.6	10.64	17,80,600	10.64
1-Jun-2007	11.5	11.7	10.7	11.02	15,36,600	11.02
1-May-2007	10.49	11.72	10.41	11.53	22,68,100	11.53
2-Apr-2007	11.21	11.72	10.42	10.45	15,22,600	10.45
1-Mar-2007	12	12.14	11	11.26	19,39,000	11.26
1-Feb-2007	12.15	12.7	11.49	12.22	17,99,400	12.22
3-Jan-2007	12.59	12.85	12	12.15	16,59,300	12.15
1-Dec-2006	12.82	12.89	12.35	12.45	13,15,400	12.45
1-Nov-2006	12.81	12.84	11.73	12.74	19,84,600	12.74
2-Oct-2006	12.94	13.24	12.45	12.75	12,54,100	12.75

EXHIBIT 21.9 COMPARISON OF SHARE PRICE FLUCTUATIONS MTUFG VERSUS NIKKEI (POST-MERGER—01/2006–03/2009)

*Drawn based on Monthly share Prices of MTUFG (01/2006–03/2009)

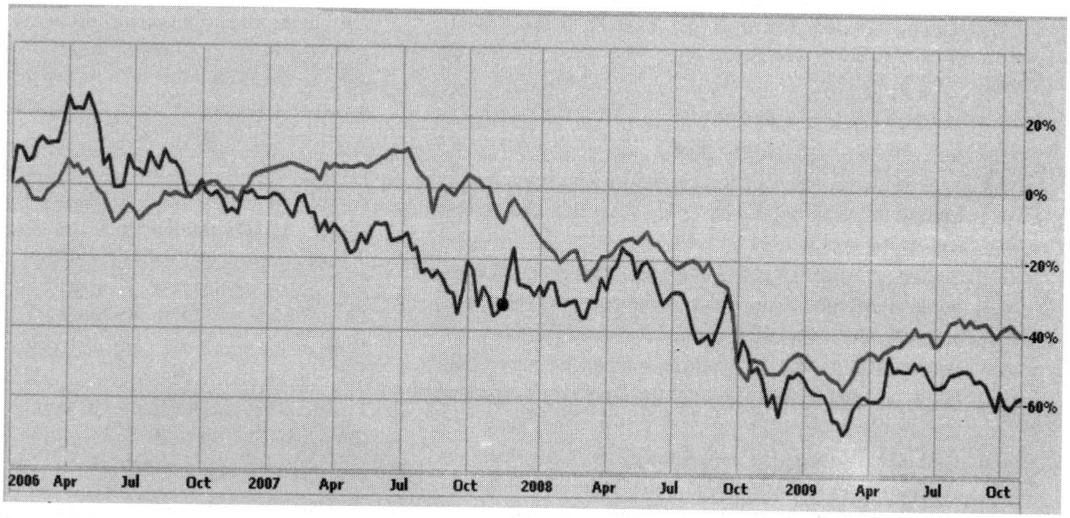

Source: Tokyo stock exchange, yahoo finance.

EXHIBIT 21.10 TOP 10 BANKS IN THE WORLD IN TERMS OF ASSETS $MILLION (2009)

Rank	Bank	Country
1	JP Morgan Chase & Co	U.S.
2	Bank of America crop	U.S.
3	Citigroup	U.S.
4	Royal Bank of Scotland	U.K.
5	HSBC Holdings	U.K.
6	Wells Fargo & Co	U.S.
7	Mitsubishi UFJ Financial Group	Japan
8	ICBC	China
9	Credit Agrico Group	France
10	Stander Central Hispano	Spain

Source: The banker website—www.thebanker.com

EXHIBIT 21.11 TOP 10 BANKS IN THE WORLD IN TERMS OF MARKET CAPITALIZATION $ MILLION (2009)

Rank	Bank	Country
1	China Construction Bank	China
2	HSBC Holdings	U.K.
3	JP Morgan Chase & Co	U.S.
4	Wells Fargo & Co	U.S.
5	Stander Central Hispano	Spain
6	Bank of America	U.S.
7	Mitsubishi UFJ Financial Group	Japan
8	BNP Paribas	France
9	Royal Bank of Canada	Canada
10	ICBC	China

Source: The banker website—www.thebanker.com

SELECT REFERENCES

1. Basant, Rakesh (2000). 'Corporate response to Economic Reforms', *Economic and Political Weekly*, 4 March, pp. 813–822.
2. Paul, Justin (2003). 'Bank of Madura Merger with ICICI Bank: An Analysis', *IIM-B Management Review* vol. 15, no. 3, July–September, pp. 10–17.

Newspapers

The Economic Times 7 December to 15 December 2000.
The Hindu Business Line, 7 December to 15 December 2000.
Business Standard, 7 December to 15 December 2000.

ENDNOTES

1. Walter, Ingo (2004). *Mergers and Acquisitions in Banking and Finance—What Works, What Fails Why?* New Delhi: Oxford University Press.
2. Ghemawat, Pankaj and Fariborz Ghadar (2000). 'The Dubious Logic of Global Megamergers' *Harvard Business Review*, July–August, pp. 65–72.
3. Venkiteswaran (1997). 'Restricting of Corporate India, Emerging Scenario', Vikalpa, vol. 22, no. 3, July–September, pp. 3–13.
4. Pawaskar, Vardhana (2001). 'Effect of Mergers on Corporate Performance in India', Vikalpa, vol. 26, no. 1, January–March, pp. 19–31.
5. Pandey, Ajay (2001). 'Takeover Announcements, Open Offers and Shareholders' Returns in Target Firms' Vikalpa, vol. 26, no. 3, July–September, pp. 19–26, IIM Ahmedabad
6. Paul, Justin (2003). 'Business Strategy for Niche structure: A Case Study of Acquisition from Indian Commercial Banking Market', Award Winning Paper, 25th Bank Economist Conference (BECON-2003), 11–12 December.
7. This case was prepared by Professor Justin Paul solely for the purpose of classroom discussion. This case is not intended to serve as endorsements, sources of primary data or illustrations of effective or ineffective management. Statistics reported in this case were, unless otherwise, specified as on 2000.
8. Professor Justin Paul and Yasiru Vikrama, Nagoya University of Commerce and Business co-authored this case study. This case is not intended to serve as endorsements, sources of primary data or illustrations of effective or ineffective management. The case is prepared solely as the basis for classroom discussion.
9. *Source*: *International Directory of Company Histories*, Vol. 26. St. James Press.
10. Financial review for the fiscal year ended on 31 March 2006, MUFJ Group.
11. ibid as on 31 March 2007.
12. ibid as on 31 March 2008.
13. Financial review for the fiscal year ended on 31 March 2009.

CHAPTER TWENTY TWO

Innovations in Products and Services—Cases of Three Banks[1]

CHAPTER STRUCTURE

Case Study I Barclays Bank
Case Study II ING Vysya Bank
Case Study III State Bank of India

KEY TAKEAWAYS FROM THE CHAPTER

- Understand the recent changes in the banking sector with reference to a UK-based multinational bank (Barclays Bank), joint venture bank (ING Vysya Bank) and India's no.1 public sector bank (the State Bank of India).
- Learn the process of product differentiation in the banks.
- Gain knowledge about the features of similar products.

CASE STUDY I

BARCLAYS BANK[2]

(By, Radhika Basu and Prof. Justin Paul)

Barclays is an international financial services group engaged primarily in banking, investment banking and asset management. In terms of market capitalization, Barclays is the third largest financial services group in the UK.

The group operates in many other countries with a very large international presence in Europe, the USA, Africa and Asia. It is a leading provider of global services to multinational corporations and financial institutions in the world's main financial centres.

With over 300 years of history and expertise in banking, Barclays Plc has five major divisions. The functions of these five divisions are discussed as follows:

UK Banking

This provides solutions to Barclays' UK retail and business banking customers. Customers are served through a variety of channels comprising the branch network, cash machines, telephone banking, online banking and relationship managers.

It is managed through two business areas: UK retail banking and UK business banking.

Barclay Card

This is one of the largest global credit card companies with 14.9 million credit card customers around the world.

Barclays Capital

This is a leading global investment bank which provides large corporate, institutional and government clients with solutions to their financing and risk management needs.

Barclays Global Investors

This is one of the world's largest asset managers and a leading provider of investment management products and services.

Barclays Wealth Management

This has over £74 billion of customer funds under management. Businesses include the following:

Barclays Stockbrokers It is the largest 'execution only' stockbroker in the UK. Barclays Private Bank offers a full service private bank to high net worth clients in the UK and abroad.

Barclays Financial Planning This provides regulated financial planning advice on life, pensions and investment products. Its financial planning managers can offer customers expert advice and access to leading financial providers from across the market. International banking provides offshore banking services for individuals and corporate customers.

International Retail Banking This provides a range of banking services, including current accounts, savings, investments, mortgages and loans, as well as services to corporate customers across Spain, France, Portugal, Italy, Africa and the Middle East. Barclays operates in over 800 international branches under its own name.

Performance and Governance

Since corporate governance continues to be a subject of intense interest to shareholders, regulators, companies and the press, Barclays has complied with the provisions of the new combined code. They have taken a number of steps to further enhance their corporate governance practices.

The financial performance is built on a clear and simple understanding of what Barclays exists to do—lend, invest and protect money—for customers and clients of all kinds. By doing this, they achieve the overall business purpose—to help customers and clients achieve their goals and, thereby to create value for them and earn their loyalty.

Products and Services

A summary of various products and services offered by the Barclays Bank are provided in the chapter. Barclays Bank has specific current account products for each and every need in the current account segment. Various accounts offered by the bank are highlighted here.

Barclays Bank Account (BBA) The basic Barclays Bank Account is known as BBA and can be applied over the web or several means including manual. Basic accounts like BBA can be later upgraded to add other facilities easily. All current accounts are by nature, eligible instantly for cheque books. Also there are no charges when in credit and for the regular statements.

The other features of the BBA would vary from country to country. The salient features of BBA in UK are as follows:

- Personal overdraft of up to £5,000 depending on the account status and agreed terms.
- In case of overdraft, the account owner need not pay any interest till he/she uses the facility.
- Debit card facility: Through this, an account holder can get up to £50 at supermarkets or shops offering cash back.
- An account holder can withdraw up to £300 per day at Barclays and Woolwich cash machines, provided the customer has sufficient funds.
- No transaction charges when using the debit card in cash machines abroad belonging to the bank's global alliance.

Young Persons Account (YPA) Young Persons Account is a current account facility tailor-made for the age group of 16–19 with extra benefits. The product features are provided as follows:

- The account holder can hit the high street or shop online with the Visa Electron card wherever you see the Visa Electron sign.

- He can withdraw up to £300 a day with a Visa Electron card at any Barclays or Woolwich cash machine or wherever he sees the Plus sign.
- An account holder can arrange to have paid an allowance or salary direct into his account from another.

Barclay Plus Account (BPA) The Barclay Plus Account is designed for the people in the age group of 11–15 who want to manage their money better. The most important features of this type of account are as follows:

- Easy to open with just £1.
- Tiered interest rates: The more the account holder saves, the more he earns.
- Debit card: Customers could use a Visa Electron card to shop on the high street if he gets his guardian's permission.

Cash Card Account (CCA) The Cash Card Account is for someone who wants an account and does not want a cheque book. The CCA is a bank account offering basic banking facilities without a cheque book. This concept is working well in countries like UK and Japan. Salient features of the product are as follows:

- Customers can withdraw up to £300 a day at Barclays or Woolwich cash machines. They can use the cash card to withdraw money in post offices.
- Customers can transfer money to other accounts by phone, 24 hours a day.

Student Account Student accounts are designed to help students make maximum out of student life. The product comes with a range of offerings and features.

Attractive features of the 'student account' include the following:

- Free mobile phone insurance for the first year of study.
- Twenty per cent discount on restaurants.

Student Barclay Card This product is designed to help students manage their money throughout their university life. Significant features of the product include:

- Up to £600 opening credit limit with regular reviews.
- 56 days interest-free credit on purchases for payment of balance in full and on time.
- Optional payment breaks for when students are stretched.

Graduate Package This product is designed to help graduates when they are starting off their careers. The basic account in this package is called as 'Graduate Additions', which comes with features worth up to £382 all for just £5 a month, including the following:

- Green Flag Roadside Assistance including 'home-call'.
- Comprehensive mobile phone insurance.
- Twenty per cent discount at selected restaurants.

Higher Education Account This is a current account with no monthly fee and is designed for students who are pursuing their higher education. The account helps students bridge the gap till they settle in their lives.

Career Development Loan This is for people who want to take a career development course (either full-time or part-time) to improve their career prospects. Important information about the loan is mentioned as follows:

- One can borrow from £300 up to £8,000.
- Payments remain fixed when the loan is agreed upon.
- Interest-free for up to 1 month after the end of the course. After the interest holiday, the rate would go up two or three times roughly.
- Customer need not pay back until 2 months after the course is complete.
- One can repay the loan over a period of 12–60 months.

Professional Studies Loan This loan is for students who want to study a full-time course to gain a professional qualification. The students need not pay anything up to 9 months after the completion of the course. Salient features of the product are follows:

- Repayment terms range from 1–5 years or up to 9 years for loans over £10,000.
- Customer can borrow up to £25,000.

Barclays Personal Loans

Barclays unsecured personal loans: Barclays Bank offers various loan schemes each of them tailor-made to suit a particular need. The broad categories of the loans are secured loans and unsecured loans. Most of the bank's customers are pre-selected for unsecured as well as secured loans.

Barclay secured loans: These loans are designed to help home owners or any other property owners who are looking for a loan in the range of £20,000–100,000. Some of the product features are as follows:

- The product is available for home owners, employed people, self-employed people.
- Early repayment charge of two months additional interest.

Other Services

Insurance Products Various Barclays insurance products are summarized as follows:

Online banking: Barclays' online banking services enable every account holder to use all the facilities online. Various features of online banking include the following:

- Pay bills to bank accounts
- Pay money into other UK bank accounts.
- Check statements and account balances.
- Set up or change standing orders and cancel direct debits.
- Set up or increase overdraft.
- Apply for a Barclay loan.
- Open an e-savings account and apply for a savings bond.
- Apply for and amend any part of open plan.
- Download account information to software packages.
- Get e-mail updates.

Mortgages: Barclays offers mortgages in simple terms for a value-seeking customer. Simple features of mortgage products would include no higher lending charge, mortgages are subject to valuation (maximum loan-to-value 95 per cent, re-mortgages 95 per cent or less than 90 per cent with a mortgage reserve), a first charge over property is required, a strongly recommended life assurance in place to cover the full amount of all sums that may be borrowed under this facility, mortgage is available on an interest only and/or repayment basis. Complete set of services are provided for all customers whether they are first time buyers, existing customers, re-mortgaging or moving homes.

The rates offered are both fixed and discount rates. Fixed rate is one where the interest rate remains the same during a fixed period of a loan. The customer gets peace of mind as monthly payments will stay the same for the period during which the rate is fixed. The customer has the flexibility to pay off up to a set amount per year with no early repayment charges or take a payment holiday, subject to the availability of a mortgage reserve.

Open plan: Innovative products like 'open plan' have been made for the convenience of the customer so that he can save money. Money manager helps in taking the spare cash from the current account and moves it into a savings reserve account where it earns extra interest. Open plan savings helps create a number of savings 'pots' to help save for specific things. All the balances in the pots are combined to give the best possible interest. Offset mortgage helps by offsetting the spare cash in the current and savings accounts.

Protection and pensions: These plans are designed with the help of legal and general experts to offer the best covers for the customer and his family. The packages are in the form of life cover, which provides a lump sum in case of death; stakeholder pension, which gives a pension with low charges and flexibility; Critical illness, where a cash lump sum is given if one suffers from a specified illness; income protection, which provides regular income in case of inability to work apart from other financial advices for the needs of the customer.

Travel services: These cater to the customers travel and international needs. Travel-related products would include getting commission-free foreign currency and travellers cheques with free home delivery, travel insurance with preferential rates for both single and multi-trip policies online. Global alliance, which helps save money when withdrawing money from cash machines around the world, comprehensive international banking solutions, assistance in buying property in Europe and expert advice on all travel-related questions.

Barclays Platinum card: This card allows a zero per cent balance transfer from 10 months after opening the account. Emergency card advance and emergency card replacement, fraud protection, optional payment protection insurance, online account management, 24-hour customer service and optional everyday cover are also being offered.

Platinum banking: Platinum banking is for customers who hold a number of products with Barclays Bank. There is no charge—it is the bank's way of saying thank you for banking with them. They get valuable extra benefits, including preferential rates and higher spending limits.

Savings and Investment

Easy Access Savings The easy access accounts cover short-term savings. The customer does not have to give notice to get his money and interest rates reflect the way he saves.

The 'easy access savings' are classified as follows:

- **E-savings:** It provides instant access to funds and instant transfers online between Barclays online accounts.
- **Reward saver:** It provides instant access and also a higher interest for the fewer withdrawals one makes.
- **Regular savings:** An account that rewards the customer for saving regularly. It can be opened with as little as £25 and restricts one to two withdrawals a year.
- **Tracker savings:** It links the interest rate the customer receives to the Barclays' base rate, so his savings keep pace with the latest changes. Balances of £10,000 and over will track the Barclays' base rate by the guaranteed percentage rate.

Open Plan Savings One can pool his savings to get better rates. Open plan savings lets the customer create a number of savings 'pots' for specific purposes, such as a wedding or new car. The pots' balances are combined to give the customer a potentially higher interest rate on total savings. The customer can combine open plan savings with 'money manager' to automatically move spare cash from his Barclays current account into open plan savings. The customer could also use open plan savings to offset an open plan mortgage. This could cut years and thousands of pounds off his mortgage instead of earning interest on savings.

Savings Bonds The bonds provide guaranteed fixed interest rates for the term of the bond. The customer can open a bond with just £2,000 over a term ranging from 1 to 3 years. However, he can withdraw money during the term of the bond.

Children Savings Barclays provides several ways to save for children, including the Government's Child Trust Fund and Junior BPA for children up to 10 years old.

Recent Initiatives

Barclays has constantly tried to educate its customers about its financial products and services, and how it will benefit them. Some of the new initiatives worth mentioning are outlined as follows:

Comprehensive Mobile Phone Insurance Its cover includes loss, theft, accidental damage, water and liquid damage, electrical and mechanical breakdown, unauthorized calls up to £2,000 per claim; accessories up to the value of £250 per claim alongside cover wherever you are in the world.

Green Flag Roadside Assistance This service that include home call, covers roadside assistance for 30 minutes at the side of the road. If vehicle is not able to be repaired, transportation will be arranged with another vehicle to drop up to five passengers to the destination of the customer's choice within a 10 mile radius.

Legal Helpline Legal helpline provides access to a helpline, 24-hours a day, covering a wide range of subjects by an independent team of solicitors and legal executives on call. Advice on English and Scottish law is also available over the phone.

Insurance Products Barclays is urging shoppers to be aware of how much their suitcase will be worth on their return to the UK and how much they stand to lose if their uninsured or under-insured luggage gets lost. Barclays has launched a range of competitive insurance products for holidaymakers who can have access to a range of cover for less money—perhaps making a saving of over £26 on a single trip travel policy. Barclays' single and multi-trip policies can cover personal baggage up to £1,500. These are backed up by service guarantees and improved access and distribution. Barclays general insurance is available at over 2,000 branches, the telephone and the Internet, which features a 'quote and buy' facility.

Barclays Strategy

Long-Term Barclays aims to be one of the most admired financial services organizations in the world in the eyes of shareholders, customers, colleagues and the communities in which they work.

The bank believes that the best measure of long-term performance is the total return they give to their shareholders—the increase in the price of their shares, assuming that any dividends are used to buy more shares, known as 'total shareholder return'.

They are aware that only by comparing themselves to their closest competitors, can they clearly understand how well they are doing. They measure long-term success by looking at how good their total shareholder return is, compared with eleven of their closest competitors.

Medium-Term They aim to focus their energy where it will create the most value and, therefore, get them closer to achieving their goals. They believe this will be best achieved by concentrating on four medium-term themes that are as follows:

- Defend and extend UK banking
- Build new international markets
- Grow world-class global product businesses
- Develop operational excellence

Case Questions

1. Find out whether Barclays bank offers any unique product.
2. Distinguish between BBA, YPA and BPA.
3. Discuss the retail banking strategy of Barclays Bank.

CASE STUDY II

ING VYSYA BANK[3]

The origin of the Vysya Bank (ING Vysya Bank) was pretty humble. It was in the year 1930 that a team of visionaries came together to establish a bank that would extend a helping hand to those who were not privileged enough to enjoy banking services. It has been a long journey since then and the bank has grown in size and stature to encompass every area of present-day banking activity and has carved a distinct identity of being India's premier private sector bank.

The bank has made rapid strides to reach the coveted position of being the number one private sector bank. In 1990, the bank completed its diamond jubilee year.

Milestones of the Bank Over the Long Years of Its Services

The major milestones achieved by the bank since its inception are as follows:

1930 Vysya Bank was set up in Bangalore.
1948 Scheduled bank.
1985 Largest private sector bank.
1987 The Vysya Bank Leasing Ltd commenced.
1988 Pioneered the concept of company branding of credit cards.
1990 Promoted Vysya Bank Housing Finance Ltd.

1992 Deposits cross ₹1,000 crore.
1993 Number of branches crossed 300.
1996 Signs strategic alliance with BBL, Belgium.
1998 Cash management services, and commissioning of VSAT. Golden Peacock Award—for the best HR practices by the Institute of Directors.
2000 State-of-the-art data centre at ITPL, Bangalore. The RBI clears setting up of ING Vysya Life Insurance Company.
2001 ING-Vysya commences life insurance business.
2002 The bank launches a range of products and services like the Vys Vyapar Plus, the range of loan schemes for traders, ATM services; Smartserv, the account that comes with a personal assistant service; Save and Secure, an account that provides accident hospitalization and insurance cover; Sambandh, the international debit card and the mi-bank net banking service.
2002 ING takes over the management of the bank from 7 October 2002.
2002 The RBI clears the new name of the bank as ING Vysya Bank Ltd.
2003 Introduced customer-friendly products like Orange Savings, Orange Current.
2004 Introduced Protected Home Loans—a housing loan product.

The Origin of ING Group

The ING group was originated in 1990 from the merger between Nationale–Nederlanden NV, the largest Dutch insurance company, and NMB Post Bank Groep NV. Combining roots and ambitions, the newly formed company was called 'Internationale Nederlanden Group'. Market circles soon abbreviated the name to I-N-G. The company followed suit by changing the statutory name to 'ING Group N.V'.

ING has gained recognition for its integrated approach to banking, insurance and asset management. Furthermore, the company differentiates itself from other financial service providers by successfully establishing life insurance companies in countries with emerging economies such as Korea, Taiwan, Hungary, Poland, Mexico and Chile. Another specialization is ING Direct, an Internet and direct marketing concept with which ING is rapidly winning retail market share in mature markets. Finally, ING distinguishes itself internationally as a provider of 'employee benefits', *i.e.*, arrangements of non-wage benefits, such as pension plans for companies and their employees.

ING's mission is to be a leading, global, client-focused, innovative and low-cost provider of financial services through the distribution channels of the client's preference in markets where ING can create value.

The New Identity: ING Vysya Bank

Performance over the decades ING Vysya Bank Ltd is an entity formed with the coming together of the erstwhile Vysya Bank Ltd, a premier bank in the Indian private sector, and a global financial powerhouse ING, of Dutch origin.

Customer Relationship Management

The Citizen Charter The success of the banking industry in achieving its socio-economic and growth objectives will depend upon the ability to provide satisfactory service of high standard to the customers at an affordable cost. For any business for that matter, a satisfied customer is a key factor for its growth and development.

In order to achieve the twin objectives of socio-economic responsibilities and growth, ING Vysya Bank Ltd has come out with a 'citizens' charter' which clearly defines and lays down the rules, regulations, terms and conditions governing its products and services, the commitment and responsibilities of its employees towards the customers, the redressal procedure in case of unsatisfactory service and the rights and obligations which customers are entitled for.

ING Vysya Bank maintains constant touch with their clientele through seminars, customer meets and personal contact in order to evaluate, improve and widen the range of products and services to the customers. The bank requests all its customers to keep it informed of their banking experience with it and also to provide their valuable comments/suggestions to enable it to improve the existing processes and procedures so that it could provide customer service of a very high standard.

The charter helps in providing transparency in customer transactions and adds to the banks credibility.

IT Implementation for Quick Customer Response

Tie-up with IBM IBM, along with its business partners Avaya Global Comment and Talisma, has implemented 'Customer Service Line', a customer relationship management (CRM) solution for ING Vysya Bank.

The ING Vysya Bank customer service line CRM solution ensures a 24 × 7 availability of phone banking service to its customers across the country and enables the bank to increase customer penetration, while improving customer response time.

IBM Global Services managed this CRM project and integrated it in addition to setting up the LAN infrastructure and IT infrastructure for this project. The ING Vysya customer service line provides full service phone banking solutions to its customers and handle customer requests.

Tie-up with iGate Solutions iGate Global brings together the best technology and domain expertise in the banking spacc to offer the full spectrum of services that include process consulting IT strategy, managed operations and back-office solutions, and transaction processing. ING Vysya Bank benefits from iGate Global's expertise in automating core banking operations, and implementing innovative multi-channel customer touch points that include online alerts, electronic bill payment and presentment. iGate Global also offers a unique business services provisioning model for specific banking processes. iGate Global plays a key role in the entire value chain—from hardware identification to procurement, to defining and implementing the technology strategy for the bank. iGate Global also takes responsibility for all data centre operations, systems and network management, and local or remote support at ING Vysya locations. This contract is worth around $20 million over 5 years.

Retail Banking

The retail banking division of ING Vysya Bank has classified its products and services in the following main categories:

- Smartserv
- Demand deposits
- Term deposits
- Loans
- Cards

Smartserv Smartserv is a comprehensive personal assistance service provided by ING Vysya Bank to its customers. The core benefits offered by this service are as follows:

- Save time and effort.
- Avail a range of services with a single call.
- Pay for various kinds of services easily.

The various services one can avail of under this scheme are as follows:

- Entertainment: Dining reservations and suggestions, concert, sport, theatre tickets, planning parties and picnics.
- Gifts: Delivery of flower baskets, cakes, chocolates and bouquets.
- Travel: Tickets and hotel bookings, car rental, leisure tours, travel information and tips and weekend getaways.
- Errands: Electricity and telephone bills, credit card bills, insurance and tax payments and school/college fees.
- Home services: Household appliance repairs, pest control and LPG cylinder booking.
- Emergency services: Non-fee based services like doctor, towing service and pharmacies.
- Information services: Regular services like restaurant services and reservations.

Demand Deposits It can take one of the following forms:

- Savings bank account
- Orange savings account
- Current account
- Access Plus

Savings bank account: At present interest rate is 3.5 per cent per annum, payable half yearly on all savings bank deposits. Free and concessional transfer of funds between accounts spread across branches is available. ING Vysya Bank has a large number of outlets which are networked, providing the facility of AAA Banking; one can operate an account from a remote place.

Orange savings account: This is a special type of account initiated by ING Vysya to provide added convenience to the customer and also to make banking as simple and hassle free as possible.

This account offers customers' free access to the bank's own ATMs and free ATM transactions at over 9,000 non-ING Vysya Bank ATMs.

Some of the salient features include:

- Free personal accident insurance cover of ₹3 lakh for 3 years.
- Free annual accident hospitalization cover of ₹35,000 for 3 years.
- Free international debit card.
- Free opening of a demat account to buy/sell/hold stocks and shares in electronic format.
- Cash/cheque pick-up and delivery at select locations.
- Internet banking convenience through mi-b@nk.

Current account: This type of account is offered, like other banks.

Access Plus: The salient features of this special product launched by ING Vysya Bank are as follows:

- A single current account with access from eight cities in India.
- Separate cheque-books for each centre for easy reconciliation.
- Pooling of funds in the city of residence.

Access Plus current account can be opened in any one of the following three categories.

Category	**I**	**II**	**III**
Minimum balance (in ₹)	10,000	50,000	100000
Cheque-book (No. of cities)	1 to 8	1 to 8	1 to 8
Charges for cheque leaf (in ₹)	3.00	1.50	Nil
DD/PO charges	As per tariff	75% of tariff	5% of tariff
Non-maintenance of minimum balance charges (in ₹)	100	250	500

Term Deposits

The term deposits products offered have been differentiated as follows:

- Akshaya deposits
- Fixed deposits
- VysUnit deposits
- Prashanti
- Cumulative deposits

Let us try to understand the features of these similar, but differentiated products.

Akshaya deposits: The salient features of this product are given as follows:

- Type of account: Individual account, joint account.
- Period of deposit: 6 months to 10 years
- Payment of interest: Interest, compounded quarterly, along with interest accrued, plus principal amount, on maturity of the deposit.
- Loans: Loan of up to 75 per cent of the accrued value of the deposit can be taken.
- Premature closure: Permissible, however, with a marginal loss (1 per cent) of interest.

Fixed deposits: The salient features of this product are given as follows:

- Period of deposit: 15 days to 10 years
- Payment of interest: Monthly interest, on discounted value basis.

- Loans: Loan of up to 75 per cent of the value of the deposit can be taken
- Premature closure: Permissible, however, with a marginal loss (1 per cent) of interest.

VysUnit deposits: The salient features of this product are given as follows:

- VysUnits offer the depositor functional short-term disinvestments, without effecting change on the contracted rate of interest.
- Loan of up to 75 per cent of the value of the deposit can be availed of.
- Cost-free transfer between branches.

Prashanti: This is an exclusive deposit scheme from ING Vysya Bank for senior citizens. Under this scheme, the deposits of 1 year and above maturities earn extra interest over and above the normal rates. Under this scheme one can avail of the following features.

- One can deposit minimum of ₹2,000 and in multiples of ₹1,000 thereafter up to any amount less than ₹30 lakh. The holder gets an additional 0.50 per cent interest. This is over and above the normal rate of interest.
- Easy to operate: The deposit can be in individual or joint names. The first name being the senior citizen's, the second applicant need not be a senior citizen.
- The scheme is applicable to both fixed deposits as well as re-investment deposits. You can choose between interest credits to be effected on monthly, quarterly, half-yearly or yearly modes.

Loans The ING Vysya Bank offers the following types of loans:

- Personal loans
- Against demat securities
- Auto loans
- Two-wheeler loans
- Home loans
- Truck loans

Personal loans: This type of loans is available for a wide range of amount. The loan eligibility depends upon net monthly income excluding all other statutory and financial commitments.

Loans	Eligibility
For 1 year	4 times net monthly income
For 2 years	8 times net monthly income
For 3 years	11 times net monthly income
For 4 years	13 times net monthly income
For 5 years	15 times net monthly income

For the purpose of calculating financial eligibility, the spouse's income can be added.

Loans against demat securities: In this scheme, the minimum limit is ₹50,000 and maximum limit is ₹20,00,000. The interest rate is very competitive, charged monthly on the amount drawn only.

Auto loans: The salient features of the auto loan are given as follows:

- Loan amount depends on the amount of margin money and the model. It varies between ₹1,00,000, and ₹20,00,000.
- For used cars, the loan amount varies between ₹75,000 and ₹7,50,000 based on the valuer's report and the amount of margin money.
- Up to 90 per cent of the invoice value.

Home loans: Most home loans help you build or buy a home. However, an ING Vysya protected home loan makes sure that customer gets free life insurance for the full loan term and for the full loan amount. In the event of something unfortunate happening, not only will the loan amount be paid off, but the nominee will also receive the principal amount that has already been repaid on the loan. It has a requirement of a minimum monthly income of ₹7,500.

Other facilities provided by the bank for home loan borrowers are given as follows:

- Options—fixed rate and floating rate
- Equated monthly installments (EMI)—Daily reducing balance
- Option to convert the type of loan
- Free property insurance—1 year
- Free demat account
- DD concession facility

Cards The following are the types of cards offered by the ING Vysya Bank to the customers:

Credit card: The benefits for credit card holder are as given as follows:

- No petrol transaction fee: As an introductory offer, the ING Vysya Bank credit card provides the exclusive benefit of no transaction fee on petrol purchases at any petrol pump that accepts the cards in India, as against the normal fee of 2.5 per cent as charged by some other banks.
- Reduced service charge on emergency cash: Every time you withdraw cash, a reduced service charge of 1.5 per cent will be levied from the date of withdrawal to the date of billing, as against the normal service charge of 2.95 per cent per month charged by some other banks.
- Revolving credit facility: Card members can opt for a revolving credit facility by remitting 5 per cent of their liability making it more convenient to utilize the credit limit.
- ING Vysya Bank credit card can be used for making down payments for investments, and payment of telephone and electricity bills.
- Customer loyalty by rewarding points: One point, equivalent to ₹1, is rewarded to every Re. 1 spent. It can be accumulated and redeemed for free gifts.
- Insurance protection: Personal accident insurance cover, baggage loss protection, 18 days protection on purchase of articles bought through card.

Debit cards: ING Vysya Bank issues ATM cum debit card in association with MasterCard International.

- Also, this card is very secure as it is a PIN-based card (at merchant locations, the payment has to be authorized using the PIN only) and the PIN cannot be used fraudulently as it is unique and only known to the cardholder.
- ING Vysya Bank has a daily limit of ₹15,000 and ₹25,000 for SB and current account holders, respectively, at ATMs (at merchant locations there is no transaction limit), and this is subject to the available balance in the account.

ING Vysya Bank's Retail Banking Strategy

Retail banking has many advantages like stable deposits, low cost of funds and large customer database on the resources side. On the asset side, the advantages are better yields and higher profitability, larger volumes of credit absorption, well-diversified risk and lower NPAs. These benefits, supplemented with the availability of surplus lendable resources, resulted in ING Vysya Bank focusing on the retail lending, portfolio.

Prospects of Retail Credit as a Market Segment for ING Vysya Bank One of the prominent features of retail banking and in particular retail credit is that it is a volume-driven business. Further, retail credit ensures that the business risk is widely dispersed among a large customer base, unlike in the case of corporate lending where the risk is concentrated on a few selected clients. ING Vysya is banking on its following abilities to administer a large portfolio of retail credit products.

- Strong credit assessment capability.
- Sound documentation.
- Strong processing capability.

Asset Portfolio In order to maximize the benefits flowing out of retail credit, it is very essential that a lot of thought and effort are put towards building volumes. There are several strategies for sustained business growth and profitability. Let us look at a few that ING has formulated.

Maximizing total relationship value: Banks are nowadays coming out with more and more features to add value to retail banking products and services. Few of the value-added services being offered by banks are free collection of outstation cheques, concession in commission on demand drafts/POs, free personalized cheque-books and accident insurance cover. While offering these value-added services, banks take into account the concept of total relationship value (TRV) of the customer to the bank through the various accounts or services being availed by him. This is simply done by offering a one-page brochure along with deposit account opening kits which give insight into the various retail credit facilities and competitive interest rates and also offer him a special concession on interest rate which is flowing out of the existing TRV, thus, letting the customer know that they truly appreciate his relationship with ING and that it wants to further expand it. This would generate a desire, which might result in availing the credit made available to him at softer terms.

Pro-action from a reliable customer database: 'Data mining' and 'data warehousing' have come to play a crucial role in the marketing strategy of cross-selling. It is imperative that banks build on this function, since data mining is essential in cross-selling of products, managing asset risk and improving per customer profitability. Data mining enables ING Vysya Bank to understand and predict client behaviour and develop an actionable consumer strategy. They plan to use this to great effect in promoting retail credit. It could be sending loan offer letters to existing borrowers especially those with an excellent 12-month plus track record or it could simply mean sending a 'thank-you letter' to the borrower on his loan maturing and getting closed. In addition, a fresh offer could be made to him.

Branding retail products: The strategy of branding at ING Vysya Bank is to separate products from those of competitors or stand out from the crowd. It is a means to communicate clear and competitive advantages to the customers. Traditionally retail product brands have proved to be particularly difficult to build. However, there is definitely room for retail products to establish powerful and winning brands. Winning brands have two things in common.

- A powerful consumer insight: Understanding and anticipating the customer.
- Intense focus: Focusing on a few products having strong appeal and real potential for growth.
- In order to build a retail assets portfolio, ING has taken lot of efforts like advertising and marketing campaigns.

Cross-selling: ING Vysya firmly believes that amongst all factors, cross-selling should take centre stage as a logical marketing approach to expand their retail segment. Cross-selling considerably reduces customer acquisition costs, servicing costs, and marketing and communication costs, thereby substantially increasing spread for banks. One such area is bancassurance which they have already ventured into. This enables better product bundling.

Cross-selling enhances customer loyalty. As the number of products that a customer purchases from a bank increases, the chance of loosing that specific customer to a competitor decreases.

Case Questions

1. Discuss the retail banking products of ING Vysya Bank?
2. ING Vysya Bank offers unique and attractive services to their customers. Do you agree with this statement? Debate.

CASE STUDY III

STATE BANK OF INDIA

(By, Sreyas Agarwal and Prof. Justin Paul)

Banking originated at a time when indigenous bankers played a very important role in lending money and financing foreign trade and commerce. During the days of the East India Company, it was the turn of the agency houses to carry on the banking business. The General Bank of India was the first joint stock bank to be established in 1786. The others which followed were the Bank of Hindustan and the Bengal Bank.

In the first half of the 19th century, the East India Company established three banks—the Bank of Bengal, 1809; the Bank of Bombay, 1840; and the Bank of Madras, 1843. These three banks, also known as presidency banks, were amalgamated in 1920 and a new bank, the Imperial Bank of India, was established in 1921. With the passing of the State Bank of India (SBI) Act in 1955, the undertaking of the Imperial Bank of India was taken over by the newly constituted SBI.

Features of the State Bank of India

The salient features of the SBI include:

- It is India's largest bank in terms of assets, net earnings, number of branches, market capitalization and market share.
- It has a vast distribution network of over 13,600 branches in India and 54 overseas offices in 28 countries.
- SBI is the preferred vehicle of the Government of India for raising funds abroad by way of NRI Bonds/India Millennium Deposit.
- It has a dominant corporate and retail banking franchise serving more than 90 million customers.
- SBI also has 200 years of continuous profitability.
  - Central banker prior to formation of the Reserve Bank of India.
  - It holds record of continuous dividend payment.
- It is also best positioned to leverage the resurgence in the Indian economy.
- Critical size achieved by the State Bank Group—USD 100 billion plus size, and profit crosses USD 1 billion mark.
  - Consolidated group presents a formidable entity.
  - Seven associate banks (ABs) considered together are the second largest bank in the country.

SBI has nearly one-fifth of the market share of total deposits and advances; along with the seven ABs, the State Bank Group enjoys more than one-fourth market share.

Primary Activities

The primary activities can be listed as follows:

- Treasury operations
- Corporate banking group
- National banking group
- NPA management
- Internal controls
- Cross-selling
- Management information system
- Community services

These activities have been discussed in brief below:

Treasury Operations The State Bank is the largest player and market mover in both the rupee and FOREX markets in India. Treasury operations have expanded significantly beyond the conventional role of liquidity management and regulatory compliance to emerge as a major profit centre. The implementation of the Treasury Solutions Software has facilitated online trading, accounting, valuation and portfolio risk management. Real-time gross settlement systems have also been implemented. Trading in derivatives, both rupee and FOREX, was introduced after putting in place requisite policies and risk management systems.

Corporate Banking Group The bank's corporate banking group (CBG) consists of three strategic business units (SBUs), namely Corporate Accounts Group (CAG), Leasing SBU and Project Finance SBU.

Leasing SBU: Compared to CAG and the Project Finance SBU, the Leasing SBU is not active in the market.

Project finance SBU: The bank's project finance SBU focuses on core and infrastructure sectors which are seen as drivers of future growth, like telecommunications, oil and gas, roads, bridges, ports and urban infrastructure. The SBU has also played an advisory role to the government through various committees, particularly in the power sector.

Secondary Activities

Associates and Subsidiaries

Associates: SBI has the following seven associate banks with controlling interest ranging from 75 per cent to 100 per cent.

- State Bank of Bikaner and Jaipur
- State Bank of Hyderabad

- State Bank of Indore
- State Bank of Mysore
- State Bank of Patiala
- State Bank of Saurashtra
- State Bank of Travancore

These seven ABs have a combined network of 4,596 branches in India which are fully computerized and 1,070 ATMs networked with SBI ATMs, providing value-added services to clientele.

Foreign subsidiaries: The foreign subsidiaries of SBI are as follows:

1. *SBI International (Mauritius) Ltd, Offshore Bank:* It is one of the first offshore banks to be established in Mauritius in 1990, with a paid up capital of USD 10 million. The bank has had a consistent record of having earned profits since its very first year of operations.
2. *State Bank of India (California):* A wholly owned subsidiary in California is a California State Chartered Bank and a member of the Federal Deposit Insurance Corporation. With four full-service branches and a money transfer office, the bank caters to the banking needs of the community, ethnic and non-ethnic alike, through various deposit and loan schemes. The bank also provides Internet banking, telebanking, ATM service and credit cards.
3. *State Bank of India (Canada):* A wholly owned subsidiary of SBI has been operating in Canada at four locations—Toronto, Vancouver, Surrey and Mississauga—extending various facilities to Indians settled in Canada such as remittance of funds through a network of over 9,000 offices of SBI, the largest commercial bank in India and through the branches of its ABs. SBI(C) has also been instrumental in fostering trade ties between India and Canada by extending financial, advisory and logistic support to Canadian and Indian corporates.
4. *INMB Bank Ltd., Lagos:* A subsidiary of SBI, INMB Bank Ltd, (formerly Indo–Nigerian Merchant Bank Ltd) was incorporated on 26 November 1981 under the Banking Act, 1969. The principle activity of the bank is providing banking services, mainly to corporate clients. Such services include the granting of loans and advances, equipment leasing, corporate finance activities and financial advisory services.

Products and Services

SBI has a vibrant range of products and services ranging from personal banking, international banking and corporate services.

Personal Banking SBI has a wide range of products in personal banking which are designed with huge flexibility to meet every customer's needs. The personal banking products are listed as follows:

- SBI term deposits
- SBI recurring deposits
- SBI housing loan
- SBI car loan
- SBI educational loan
- SBI personal loan
- SBI loan for pensioners
- Loan against mortgage of property
- Loan against shares and debentures
- Rent Plus scheme
- Medi Plus scheme

SBI term deposit: SBI offers attractive term deposit schemes that range from 15 days to 10 years and that can be opened with as low as ₹1,000.

Recurring deposit: The recurring deposit schemes of SBI feature high flexibility in periods of deposit with maturity ranging from 6 months to 10 years which can be opened with amounts as low as ₹100.

Housing loan: SBI housing loans come with features like no hidden costs or unnecessary documentation. They have the longest tenors and repayment terms are amongst the most flexible. SBI offers a totally transparent process. SBI even gives an in-principle approval prior to identifying a house/flat, relieving the customer of the tension of anticipating the approved amount. And to show the importance which SBI gives to housing loans, SBI has specialized housing loan branches to serve the needs better. A special short-term housing loan scheme for loans of repayment period up to 5 years has been launched by SBI. This scheme carries still lower rates of interest.

Other features of SBI housing loans are as follows[4]:

- Low EMI.
- Low interest rates, currently between 8–9.25 per cent per annum on daily reducing balances.
- A nominal processing fee of 0.25 per cent.
- No hidden costs or administrative costs.
- No prepayment penalties as compared with penalties of up to 2 per cent charged by others.
- In-principle approval given prior to customer's identifying a house/flat, giving flexibility in choice.

SBI Car loan: The SBI car loans come with the following features:

- Lowest interest rates.
- Longer repayment period of up to 84 months.
- Zero processing charges.
- No hidden costs or administrative charges.
- Finance for one-time road tax, registration fee and insurance premium.
- No advance EMIs.
- Complete transparency: SBI levys interest on the daily reducing balance method. When customers pay one installment, the interest is automatically calculated on the reduced balance thereafter. When customers pay interest on an annual reducing balance, as charged by many other companies/banks, the interest amount for the coming year is determined on the amount outstanding at the beginning of the year. Customers continue to pay interest even on the amounts they repay during the year.
- The interest rates offered are floating rates and fixed rates.

SBI Educational loan: The SBI educational loans include loans for the following expenses:

- Fees payable to college/school/hostel.
- Examination/library/laboratory fees.
- Purchase of books/equipment/instruments/uniforms.
- Caution deposit/building fund/refundable deposit.
- Travel expenses/passage money for studies abroad.
- Purchase of computers considered necessary for completion of course.
- Cost of a two-wheeler up to ₹50,000.

Amount of loan: Amount of loan offered to students by SBI in India and abroad are as follows:

- For studies in India, maximum ₹10 lakh.
- Studies abroad, maximum ₹20 lakh.

Processing fees: The processing fees charged by SBI are as follows:

- No processing fee/upfront charges.
- Deposit of ₹5,000 for education loan for studies abroad, which is adjusted in the margin money.

Repayment tenure: Repayment commences 1 year after completion of course or 6 months after securing a job, whichever is earlier.

EDUCATION LOAN—PARTICULARS

Place of Study	Loan Amount	Repayment Period in Years
In India	Up to ₹7.5 lakh	5–7
	Above ₹7.5 lakh	5–10
Abroad	Up to ₹15 lakh	5–7
	Above ₹15 lakh	5–10

Up to ₹4 lakh	No security	No security
Above ₹4 lakh to ₹7.50 lakh	Third party guarantee	Third party guarantee
Above ₹7.50 lakh to ₹10 lakh (India)/₹15 lakh (Abroad)	Tangible collateral security for full value of loan	Tangible collateral security of suitable value of loan or third party guarantee
₹15 lakh to ₹2 lakh	—	Tangible collateral security for full value of loan

SBI Personal loan: SBI personal loans are available across the country from more than 3,000 branches and come with the following features:

- Lowest interest rates.
- Lowest processing charges—no hidden costs or administrative charges.
- No security required which means minimal documentation.
- No prepayment penalties—reduces the interest burden and customers can optimally utilize their surplus funds by prepaying the loan.
- Long repayment period of up to 48 months.
- The important feature is processing charges which are 1 per cent of the loan amount. This is amongst the lowest fees in the industry. Processing fees have to be paid upfront. There are no hidden costs or other administrative charges.

SBI Loan for pensioners: These loans are available to central or state government pensioners drawing pension through one of the SBI branches. Loans can be availed of up to a maximum of 6 months pension, subject to a ceiling of ₹40,000 and come with easy documentation. The loan may be repaid over 2 years and will carry a low interest rate of 13.1 per cent.

There are no processing fees, no hidden costs and no prepayment penalties. Whenever customers have some surplus funds, they can credit their loan account, thereby reducing the loan liability and interest burden.

Loan against mortgage of property: This loan comes with features like minimum amount of 1 lakh and maximum amount of 50 lakhs and margin of up to 50 per cent. The loan amount can be repaid in maximum of 60 installments and customers can opt to divert any surplus funds towards prepayment of the loan without attracting any penalty.

Loan against shares and debentures: SBI offers loans up to ₹20 lakh with the following features:

- Lowest interest rates.
- Lowest processing charges.
- No hidden costs or administrative charges.
- No pre-payment pen.

Rent Plus scheme: This is a term loan available for 7 years or the residual lease period, whichever is lower.

Medi Plus scheme: This loan is available for specialized medical treatments which not only do the cost implications run into several lakhs of rupees, but more often than not, these liquid funds also need to be generated at a very short notice, in order to be able to make prompt hospital bill payments. With this in mind, Medi Plus is specially designed to make life simpler for customers.

Medi Plus scheme covers the cost of treatments such as follows[5]:

- Corneal implant
- Orthodontic treatment (fixed tooth implant)
- Congenital heart surgery
- Angioplasty
- Heart valve replacement surgery

- Serious accidents and multiple injuries surgery
- Hip and knee replacement surgery
- Coronary artery bypass/graft surgery
- Reconstructive nose surgery with face lifting
- Penile implant surgery

NRI Accounts The following types of NRI accounts are offered by SBI:

- NRE rupee accounts.
- Savings bank.
- Current accounts.
- Term deposits (interest paid out quarterly).
- Special term deposits (interest compounded quarterly).
- Non-resident (ordinary) account: Rupee accounts for crediting income from India for Non-residents.
- Foreign currency non-resident accounts: Fixed deposits in pound, sterling, US dollar and euro currencies.
- Resident foreign currency accounts.
- All these accounts come with features like ATM, Internet banking, easy swipe facility between fixed deposit and current accounts.

Agricultural Accounts The important types of agricultural accounts offered by SBI are given as follows:

- Crop loan
- Produce marketing loan scheme
- Loan against warehouse receipts/cold storage receipts
- Kisan credit card scheme
- Agricultural term loans
- Land development schemes
- Minor irrigation schemes
- Kisan gold card scheme
- Land purchase scheme
- Dairy plus scheme
- Broiler plus scheme
- Finance to horticulture
- Lead bank scheme

International Banking In international banking segment, SBI offers the following services:

- Trade finance
  - Export
  - Import
- Correspondent banking
- Corresponding banking—categorization
- Swift operations centre (SOC)
- Nostro accounts
- Standard settlement instructions FOREX trading account
- Merchant banking
- Project export finance
- Exporter gold card
- Treasury

The points which differentiate the bank from other banks in these accounts are the following:

- The SBI offers an exhaustive range of financial products and services that answer any business or market circumstance, backed by an expertise in customizing the product to meet the most sensitive specificities of each client and each business.
- Commanding unsurpassed respect and legacy in the Indian financial expanse, the SBI is committed to offer financial solutions that extract maximum value from business and market situations.
- While the bank is strongly positioned to structure financial packages that anticipate the changing business environment, its branch network—the world's largest—ensures delivery channels of unmatched reach.

SME Schemes SBI has been playing a vital role in the development of small-scale industries since 1956. It has over 50 specialized SSI branches and more than 400 branches.

Case Questions

1. State Bank of India offers very attractive product for all types of customers. Do you agree with this statement? Validate your argument with points.
2. Although State Bank of India has better products, they lag behind banks like Barclays Bank and ING Vysya Bank in marketing efforts. Do you think so? Compare, discuss and debate.

SELECT REFERENCES

1. www.SBI.co.in/in/viewssection. jsp?id=0,16,393,395.
2. www.statebankofindia.com
3. www.onlinesbi.com

ENDNOTES

1. Cases in this chapter are developed solely as the basis for class discussion. Cases are not intended to serve as endorsements, sources of primary data or illustrations of effective or ineffective management.
2. The information given in the case—Barclays bank is in the context of United Kingdom, unless otherwise specified.
3. This case was co-authored with Abhishek Bhatewara, Achal Panda and Anshuman Goswami. Arpita Saha and Jayendran Rajappa also helped.
4. Holders of 'student' and 'young person`s' accounts will not be able to access these services.
5. www.SBI.co.in/viewsection.jsp?id=,1,2,125.

CHAPTER TWENTY THREE

Innovations in Products and Services in Banking—Cases of Public and Private Sector Banks

CHAPTER STRUCTURE

KEY TAKEAWAYS FROM THE CHAPTER

- Learn about the recent changes in the banking sector in the context of a public sector (Corporation Bank) and old private sector (South Indian Bank) bank.
- Understand how banks differentiate their products.
- Gain knowledge about the features of similar products to take wise decisions.

CASE STUDY I

CORPORATION BANK[1]

Corporation Bank has a tradition of excellent performance and service and is one of India's top state-owned banks. It is headquartered at Mangalore and was originally formed as a small *nidhi* in pre-independent India in 1906.

Corporation Bank constantly tries to upgrade its operations to take advantage of the latest technology and has formed a well-connected network of over 1000 branches. This has enabled the bank to provide the latest in banking service to its customers. Several new IT initiatives such as cluster banking, phone banking, any branch banking, Internet banking and networked automated teller machines (ATMs) have been implemented. The bank has been successful in retaining its premier position of having the lowest non-performing assets.

Personal Banking

Deposit Schemes

Corporation Bank offers a wide range of deposit schemes catering to the varied needs of the customers. The bank offers a range of schemes which encompass recurring, one-term, short-term, long-term and high-interest, high liquidity or both. These deposit schemes are discussed as follows:

Savings account: Corporation Bank offers the following products and facilities to its account holders:

- *Any branch banking*: Account can be accessed from more than 500 branches of the bank across the country.
- *Corp Power Cheq (Multi-city cheque facility)*: The cheques are payable at par, at over 170 cities.

- *Free international debit card (Corp Convenience)/ATM card*: It allows the customer to shop at merchant establishments and to withdraw cash at all Visa ATMs worldwide. It can also access the bank's network of online interconnected ATMs across the country.
- Facility of Internet banking.
- *Corp Senior Account*: This account is for monthly remittances to parents/elderly dependents.
- *Corp Elite Account*: It is a premium savings account with free add on facilities. This is an innovative product.
- *Corp Classic Account*: It is a savings bank account with the facility to earn interest at term deposit rates.
- *Corp Jeevan Raksha*: This account provides life insurance cover from the Life Insurance Corporation of India to the deposit account holders of the bank.
- *Corp Anytime Premium*: The payment of the Life Insurance Corporation of India (LIC) premium can be made through any of the Corporation Bank's ATMs.

Current account: Current account is primarily meant for businessmen, firms, companies, public enterprises, etc. that have numerous daily banking transactions. In a current account, a customer can deposit any amount of money at any number of time and withdraw any amount as many times as he wants, as long as he has funds to his credit. Current accounts are meant neither for the purpose of earning interest nor for the purpose of savings but only for convenience of the business.

Apart from the services which are commonly offered, there are additional offers made to these account holders. There are four types of current accounts offered by the bank called Corp Business, Corp Business Premium, Corp Business Club and Corp Business Privilege. Explanation of these accounts, *i.e.*, their product has been differentiated into four categories.

Term deposit: The following are the term deposits offered:

- *Kshemanidhi Cash Certificates (KCC)*: KCC is a money multiplier deposit or reinvestment term deposit scheme that can be opened for a period ranging from six months to 10 years. It is a money multiplier deposit where the deposit amount grows rapidly as interest is compounded quarterly. The rate of interest depends on the period of deposit.
- *Money flex*: The flexible term deposit is a flexible fixed deposit scheme that do not block the customer's money for the full term of the deposit. The scheme allows the customer to withdraw his money whenever he wants. The deposit can be made for a period ranging from 6–120 months. The minimum deposit is ₹5,000. Additional deposits can be made in multiples of ₹1,000. The rate of interest depends on the period of deposit. The customer can earn interest on his fixed deposit as per applicable rates. He can also withdraw a part of the deposit without having to permanently close the entire deposit.
- *Fixed deposit*: It is a term deposit scheme and interest can be paid at regular intervals namely monthly, quarterly, half yearly or yearly. The deposit can be made for periods ranging from 15 days to 10 years.
- *Corp classic*: High returns and total liquidity are the two major advantages of this account. It is an innovative technology-based account that combines the high liquidity of a savings bank account and the high returns of a term deposit to give customer the best returns for his money. It is fully computerized, carrying out all transactions based on standing instructions.

  The account works simply by fixing and unfixing the customer's savings from a savings bank account to a term deposit and vice versa. Corp classic 'fixes' term deposit in units of ₹1,000 each on a 'period', 'interest rate' or 'due date' basis, whichever the customer prefers. The interest can either be withdrawn or compounded as required.
- *Continuous deposit*: This product is also called the cluster deposit. Here the customer can choose between simple interest and compound interest while keeping the deposits in a cluster form. All deposits are recorded in one account in a pass book, thus making it easy to keep track of deposits.
- *Ready cash deposit*: This high returns, high liquidity deposit is a fixed deposit scheme with a cheque facility to withdraw whenever funds are required by the customer. Under this scheme, a customer can deposit a minimum of ₹5,000 for a period ranging from 12 to 36 months. While the deposit earns at the agreed rate of interest, he can withdraw the money through cheques. There is a requirement to pay interest on the amount withdrawn as per the rates fixed by the bank.
- *Recurring deposit*: This account has a fixed sum to be deposited every month for a period ranging from 12 to 120 months. The rate of interest depends on the period of deposit and it is compounded quarterly. Accounts can also be opened in the name of minors.

- *Premium deposit*: It requires savings of a minimum of ₹100 per month for a period ranging from 1 to 10 years. On completion of that period, the deposit alongwith the interest is reinvested in minimum blocks to give maximum interest at the rate prevailing then and converted into a corpus.
- *Janatha deposit*: This deposit is for a period of 1–5 years. The bank's collection agent is called at the place to collect savings at regular intervals, even daily if required. The small savings thus accumulate into a substantial amount over the deposit period.

Loan Schemes

Corporation Bank offers housing loans, education loans, consumer loans for purchase of consumer durables, loans against future rent receivables like leased out building/premises, loans to purchase two-wheelers and four-wheelers, loans against shares, loans for purchase of medical and other such sophisticated equipments, loan to acquire office premises/building and furniture, personal loans, loans to women to buy pure gold/jewellery and loan against mortgage of property.

Home Loan and Insurance Corporation Bank in association with LIC of India presents life insurance cover to the housing loan taken by the customer.

Cards

Debit Card: Corp Convenience

The following are the features offered by the debit card:

- Worldwide acceptance: Corp Convenience can be used to make purchases worldwide.
- Money management: Every purchase and ATM withdrawal appears on the monthly checking account statement, including the date, place and amount so that the customers can track their method of spending.

Credit Card

The following are the important features of the credit card offered by the Corporation Bank:

- Accepted at thousands of merchant establishments.
- Can be used for booking railway and air tickets.
- ATM facility at select centres.
- Cash withdrawal facility at the branches of eight banks.
- Free credit for upto 45 days.
- Free personal accident insurance cover for the customer and his spouse, baggage insurance cover and purchase protection cover.

High-Tech Banking Products and Services

Internet Banking

Corporation Bank has introduced a series of products and services for different consumer segments. CorpNet is one such product offered by the bank to its customers. On 1 January 2001, the bank had launched its Internet Banking (CorpNet) facilities for the corporate customers of its collection and payment services (CAPS), *i.e.*, cash management services. Subsequently, the bank introduced the CorpNet facility for both corporate and retail customers of its computerized branches effective 28 March 2002.

The various online services provided by CorpNet are as follows:

- Verification of account balance.
- Viewing and downloading statements.
- Making payments to third parties and transfering funds using Corp E-cheque.
- Requesting for cheque books, demand drafts (DD), stop payments.
- Paying utility bill payments online.

CorpNet is a browser-based application and can be accessed through an Internet browser. CorpNet can be accessed at any time of the day irrespective of the location.

In the niche area of CAPS, Corporation Bank has a leadership presence in the country and caters exclusively to the cash management requirements of the corporates. The bank, within its network, has ten specialized CAPS branches which are fully automated and currently provide services to over 900 companies.

Functional Modules

Account information: Using this module, the user can view the account-related information like balance enquiry, transactions, statement of account, loan details and deposit details. Report and download options are also provided. The consolidated balance of all the accounts in all the branches with date and time of last updation is also available.

Funds transfer: This module enables the user to request the branch to transfer funds from one of his running accounts to his other running account. The requested transfer can be viewed by using the review option.

Payments: This module can be used for third party payments. For effecting payment using this module, users need to have beneficiaries approved by the bank. While applying for CorpNet, the customers shall mention the beneficiary details required to be created. It can be created later on also by giving a request through the branch.

Services: This module can be used to put request for cheque books, stop payment of cheques and remittances. The users can register for messages using the option alert message registration. The messages can be viewed using the option of message center.

Corp E-Cheque

Corporation Bank has launched Corp E-Cheque facilitating remittance of funds to pre-approved beneficiaries across banks within 48 hours.

Corp E-Cheque is an innovative product developed by Corporation Bank by combining the power of CorpNet with electronic funds transfer (EFT) scheme of the Reserve Bank of India (RBI).

The customers of Corporation Bank can make a remittance request to the branch where he maintains his account through an Internet banking transaction. The customer's account gets debited at concerned branch of Corporation Bank and the remittance details are transmitted to RBI-EFT system through the service branch of Corporation Bank at the destination center.

RBI will debit Corporation Bank's account and credit the beneficiary's bank and pass on the remittances details to the service branch of the beneficiary's bank through EFT.

The service branch of the beneficiary's bank will send the information to the beneficiary's branch for crediting the amount to the beneficiary's account.

The facility is now available through Internet Banking enabled branches of Corporation Bank. Individuals, sole proprietorship concerns, partnership firms, companies and corporates having Internet banking account with the Corporation Bank can also avail of this facility.

How Corp E-Cheque is different from normal remittance? The features of Corp E-Cheque is as follows:

- Funds transfer can be effected across banks without visiting the branch by passing an instruction through the Internet.
- Remittance instructions can be issued from anywhere in the world.
- Credit to the account of pre-approved beneficiaries within 48 hours.

Tele-Banking

Tele-banking service offers the convenience of anytime, anywhere banking to the customers. The customer can check his account balance and have his latest transactions faxed. Tele-banking is available 24 hours a day, 7 days a week. The system is easy to use and secure. The customer can easily obtain information guided by the interactive voice response system.

Even a person who is not a customer of Corporation Bank can obtain general information about deposit interest rates, foreign exchange rates and gold selling rates.

Products and Services for Non-Residents

High level of customer satisfaction is ensured through computerized operations, interconnectivity between major centres through satellite-based communication system. Bank has an elaborate network of branches in non-resident Indians (NRI) belts like Kerala, Goa, South Karnataka, Gujarat, Mumbai and New Delhi. The bank maintains foreign currency accounts (called as Nostro) with reputed international banks in 15 major currencies.

Deposit Schemes

Schemes without repatriation facility: Non-resident ordinary (NRO) accounts (Current earnings repartriable)

- Savings: Normally operated for crediting rupee earnings/income, such as dividends, interest. Currently the interest rate is 3.5 per cent.
- Term deposits: Banks are free to determine their interest rates.

Schemes with repatriation facility: Non-resident external (NRE) deposits (Principal/interest repatriable)

- Savings: Interest is paid at par with the domestic deposits.
- Term deposits: Fixed or floating rates of interest within the ceiling rate announced by the RBI from time to time. Foreign currency non-resident. [FCNR(B)] deposits (Principal/interest repartriable)
- Term deposit can be placed with banks in India in five specific foreign currencies (USD, GBP, EUR, AUD, CAD).

RFC deposits (on return)

- Resident foreign current accounts can be opened by those people who return to their country in the following forms:
  - Current accounts (not in FCNR (B))
  - Savings Bank accounts (not in FCNR (B))
  - Fixed Deposits
  - Cash Certificates
  - Money-flex deposits
  - Recurring deposits (not in FCNR (B))

Payquik.com: It provides banks and other financial institutions with a complete front-end interface which enables their NRI customers to remit funds through a customized web-enabled interface. Corporation Bank has tied up with this company to process the online remittance instructions of its NRI clients. This product is the most modern technology-oriented facility which provides the NRIs a means to transfer funds quickly, securely, conveniently and in a cost-effective manner.

NRI remittances made easy: Corporation Bank is taking the advantage of modern means of communication and technology to make funds transfer in India secure, speedy, economical and convenient.

The options are as follows:

- DDs in rupees: A DD denominated in Indian rupees from any bank or Exchange House abroad, having arrangement with banks in India and made payable at a place nearest to the Corporation Bank branch where an account is maintained, and then mailed it to the branch.
- DD/personal cheques in foreign currency: Remittances can be sent by way of DDs/personal cheques in foreign currency and made payable abroad.

Telegraphic Transfer Telegraphic transfer (TT) or wire transfer is the most popular medium for quick money transfers. Corporation Bank offers the facility of speedy money transfer with unique features. Most of the city-based branches of Corporation Bank are provided with SWIFT connectivity. If the three-digit branch code of the beneficiary branch is mentioned alongwith the swift code of the Bank—CORPINBB***—the branch will receive an advice immediately on credit of funds into the bank's account thereby facilitating the money transfer.

In the normal course, credit of international TT amount to the beneficiary's account would be received on the same day/next day if remitted to a branch dealing in foreign exchange and 3 days in the case of other branches.

Portfolio Services Investment in shares, *i.e.*, buying and selling shares through secondary market is called 'portfolio investment'. NRIs can invest in shares/securities in terms of guidelines issued under portfolio investment scheme (PIS).

Important Services

Some of the product and services introduced with innovative features has been elaborated in the following sections:

Any Branch Banking Any branch banking (ABB) is a facility for customers to operate their account from any networked branch. The branch where the customer maintains his account is the base branch and the branch from where he carries out his transactions is referred to as the remote branches. Presently, more than 465 branches of the bank offer this facility.

Facilities available under ABB are as follows:

- **Cash withdrawal:** Withdrawal of cash from an account from any of the core-connected branches by presenting a self-drawn cheque. This facility is not extended for withdrawals by any third party.
- **Cash deposit:** Deposit cash for credit of an account through any of the core connected branches.
- **Fund transfers:** Instant transfer of funds between accounts or between an account and any third party account maintained at different core-connected branches.

- **Purchase of DDs/pay orders:** Purchase DDs/pay orders at any remote branch by debiting an account maintained at the base branch.
- **Deposit of local cheques:** Cheques can be tendered at remote branches for crediting the proceeds after realization to an account maintained at remote branches.

Corp Powercheq—Multi City Cheque Facility (MCC) Multi City Cheques is a facility wherein the customer can issue cheques drawn at the base branch and payable at selected remote centers. These cheques will thus be treated as local cheques in the remote centre selected by the customer. The facility of MCC is available in all core-connected branches (more than 200 centres) of the bank.

Corp Mediclaim Corporation Bank offers a group mediclaim scheme in association with New India Assurance Company Ltd., the bank's partner in general insurance. This product was devised to meet the medical insurance needs of the customers, who may be unexpectedly burdened with expenses to meet sickness requirements for themselves and their family members. The salient features of the scheme are as follows:

- Cashless claim settlement with a wide network of hospitals all over the country.
- Dependent members in the family up to a maximum of four members including self can be covered on a floater basis, *i.e.*, cover floats among the family members without the need to pay separate individual premium for each member.
- Savings on actual mediclaim policy premiums.

Corp E-rail Corporation Bank has e-enabled railway reservation booking. It has entered into a tie-up with the Indian Railway Catering and Tourism Corporation Ltd. (IRCTC) for online booking of railway tickets. All customers who are availing of CorpNet Internet banking service and Corp Convenience international debit card can now book their tickets online over the Internet, by direct debit to their Corporation Bank account.

Corp Billpay At Corp Billpay one can pay bills and make other payments online. Instead of writing a cheque each time, one can use any device connected to the Internet (*e.g.*, computer and kiosk) and make payments with the click of a mouse.

Corp Mobile Recharge Electronic recharge of pre-paid mobile phones is a facility which enables customers having prepaid mobile phones to electronically recharge their mobile phone cards by debiting their account through Corporation Bank ATMs or through SMS from their mobile phone. The facility is offered to all the ATM/Debit card holders of the bank free of any service charge.

Corp Anytime Premium Corporation Bank has introduced the Corp anytime premium facility to pay LIC premium through its ATM network spread throughout the country for its customers, holding a tie-up with Life Insurance Corporation, its strategic partner. Corporation Bank has become the first bank in India to introduce such a facility.

Through this facility, all ATM/debit card (Corp Convenience) holders of Corporation Bank can remit their LIC premium through Corporation Bank ATMs. The bank had already enabled the payment of LIC premium through its Internet banking facility CorpNet.

Corporation Bank now acts as a corporate agent for selling bank assurance products of LIC through its branch network. The bank has set up 100 service units including branches, extension counters and ATMs in LIC premises throughout the country.

Corp Junior Corp Junior leverages on the power and convenience of the free Corp Bank ATM card and the vast nationwide online interconnected ATM network of the bank. Corp Junior enables parents with children studying away from them to remit money at periodic intervals in a hassle free manner.

Mutual Funds The bank is aiming to become a financial supermarket where its customers are able to purchase a wide range of quality financial products under one roof. The bank offers a wide range of mutual fund products, be it equity, diversified or sectoral, debt or liquid or for that matter balanced funds.

Depository Services Majority of the security related transactions in the Indian capital market have shifted to the dematerialized form. Therefore, it has become all the more necessary for investors to maintain depository accounts. Corporation Banks also offers 'demat' account for investors.

Case Questions

1. Discuss the retail banking marketing strategy that the Corporation Bank follows
2. Has the corporation bank adapoted some innovative techniques to differentiate their products from other banks?

CASE STUDY II

SOUTH INDIAN BANK[2]

Introduction

The South Indian Bank (SIB) was incorporated 76 years ago in 1929 at Thrissur (Trichur), the cultural capital of Kerala with the view to establish a safe, efficient and service-oriented bank and also to free the business community from the clutches of greedy money-lenders by providing need based credit at reasonable rates of interest. The bank was converted into a public limited company in 1939 and became a scheduled commercial bank in 1946. It also took over 15 other small regional banks in the 1960s. SIB was listed on the domestic bourses after its initial public offering in 1999. Prior to its IPO, the bank had privately placed equity with the ICICI Group and UTI in 1995. It has now transformed itself into a vibrant, fast growing and trend setting financial intermediary. The bank has many firsts to its credit. It is the first private sector bank to open a NRI branch in November 1992; the first bank in the private sector in India to open a currency chest on behalf of the RBI in April 1992; the first bank in the private sector to start an industrial finance branch in March 1993 and many more.

Established by a small group of local citizens, SIB caters to the banking needs of traders and residents of the region. Over time, as a large proportion of the local population migrated to other countries, especially the Middle East, the bank has tied up with foreign banks to meet the banking needs of these expatriates.

The bank has tied-up with three banks and eight exchange houses in the Middle East and one exchange house in Singapore for providing foreign currency remittance facility to its customers. It has also tied-up with the ICICI Group to undertake distribution of life insurance and mutual fund products, and has an arrangement with the public sector general insurance company, United India Insurance, for distribution of non-life insurance products. The bank is also active in offering 'gold loans', a popular retail product in south India.

Over the years, SIB has enhanced its reach and visibility by expanding its branch network. Nearly 60 per cent of the bank's branches are located in its home state of Kerala and given the high concentration of its business in the state, SIB can be viewed as a regional player.

SIB Deposit Schemes

South Indian Bank offers the following main products:

- Current account
- Savings account
- Fixed deposit

In addition to that, the bank has launched various innovative products. These schemes, some of them very unique to SIB are discussed at length in the following sections.

SIB Flexi Deposit Scheme This deposit scheme offered by SIB uses the positive features of both a fixed deposit as well as a saving account. In flexi deposit, a fixed deposit and the savings account are linked by a common identity number for the consumer. A fixed amount needs to be maintained in the savings account for this scheme to be activated. The amount above that minimum limit is automatically transferred (sweeped) by the bank in units of ₹1,000 to a fixed deposit.

The main advantage of this scheme is flexibility, *i.e.*, it allows withdrawals of deposit without any restriction on the amount, even before the maturity of the deposit, without having a charge for premature withdrawal.

Kalpakanidhi Deposits It is a reinvestment plan with cumulative interest. The interest is added to the principal on quarterly basis, and hence, there is a scope for higher returns. Principal along with interest is paid only on the maturity date. This product offers a range of maturity periods ranging from 6 months to 10 years.

Fast Cash Deposits This is a facility provided by SIB where it allows the consumers to enjoy the interest rates of a fixed deposit for ultra short-term duration. Deposits can be made for as short as 30 days. The various schemes available in fast cash are of duration of 30, 46 and 91 days. Partial withdrawal from this deposit is permitted and the balance continues to earn interest at no penalty.

Recurring Deposits This scheme by the bank is targeted at people living on a monthly salaried income. Recurring deposit aims to improve the long-term savings for these salaried people. Since they would not have a large amount to deposit in the fixed deposit, this scheme allows people to deposit small amount of money on a monthly basis over a period in which it will reach maturity and they would get a large amount in hand when they withdraw the money. The interest rates on this scheme are similar to that of the fixed deposits. There is an added incentive in the form of no tax deduction at source for the amount deposited in this scheme.

Mangala Deposits This is a unique scheme offered by SIB. Mangala deposits are a kind of recurring deposit scheme in which the bank gives the customer the option to change the monthly installments at the beginning of every new financial year so that they can synchronize these payments with the new income. By the time, if a customer's income increases substantially in a year, he/she can save more money that year without starting a new recurring deposit account and other hassles. This is a benefit for salaried employees in private companies, especially IT and BPO companies, whose salaries change significantly over the years. The scheme is offered for period between 24 and 120 months.

Holiday Recurring Deposit Holiday recurring deposit scheme is offered by the SIB for a period of 12 months. This is aimed at the customers who want to save some amount every month for going on a holiday or tour at the end of a year. In this scheme, the bank allows the customer to withdraw after a year-long deposit alongwith the maturity amount and an equal amount given by the bank as a repayable holiday loan.

Loans and Advances

The various products available under 'the credit' category are given below.

SIB Planters Choice It targets individuals and/or jointly with family members/firms/companies with traditional plantations—tea, coffee, rubber, coconut and cardamom. The purpose of the loan is for purchasing agricultural land/existing plantation and development. The rate of interest and the processing fee depends on the size of the land being acquired. The maximum repayment period is 15 years including gestation period. However, the loan has to be closed within the economic life of the crop.

SIB Utsav It is a family specific loan, intended to establish and retain a long-term relationship with the members of more than two generations of each family, who avail of this facility to celebrate auspicious occasions. The target group for this product is salaried class with adequate take-home pay and others with sufficient income to repay the loan, as reflected in their tax return.

The Retreat The Retreat home loan scheme details in a nutshell are as follows:

- Target group: Only those who are drawing pension from state/central government/banks/insurance companies and have completed the age of 55 years.
- Purpose: It is granted for the construction of house in own plot/purchase of land and construction of house/purchase of ready-built house with plot/purchase of flat/repairs and/or renovation of existing houses owned.
- Rate of interest: 0.5 per cent less than the rate applicable for normal housing loans.
- Quantum of loan: Maximum 50 times of the monthly pension drawn at the time of application, subject to the condition that EMI should not exceed 50 per cent of the monthly pension.
- Repayment period: The maximum repayment period is 15 years or till the borrower attains the age of 75 years, which ever is earlier.

Consumer Delight This scheme is meant for the purchase of consumer durables. The target is any person having regular income and profit-making firms with 2 years of existence. The maximum loan amount granted is ₹2 lakh and margin is 25 per cent. The repayment period is 12–48 months as equal monthly installments (EMI).

Flexi Loan The purpose of the flexi loan is not limited by the bank. However, the purpose should not be for hoarding, speculation or activity restricted by the Government of India or state governments or local bodies. The purpose of the loan should be made by simple declaration on white paper.

The rate of interest is less than that of 'consumer delight' and the repayment period of the loan is minimum 6 months and maximum 84 months without holiday under EMI.

Gold Power The scheme in a nutshell is as follows:

- Target group: Individuals, partnership and proprietary firms
- Type of facility: Overdraft against pledge of gold ornaments

- Loan limit: ₹0.25 lakh to ₹25 lakh
- Security: Pledge of 22 ct gold ornaments
- Rate of advance: Maximum ₹500 per gram
- Period of sanction: 12 months

Gold Rush The scheme in a nutshell is as follows:

- Period of advance: 12 months
- Minimum amount of advance: ₹10,000
- Cut-off date for redemption auction: 13 months
- Rate per gram of 22 ct. gold ornament: ₹450
- Minimum interest: For 5 days or ₹50 whichever is higher

Home Loan The home loan is given for single or joint account holder. The loan for new construction/purchase and take over is maximum ₹50 lakh while for renovation/additions/major repair and improvement is maximum ₹5 lakh. The period of loan (including holiday) is minimum 5 years and maximum 20 years. The rate of interest could be fixed or floating.

Mercantile Credit It targets traders for the purpose of providing working capital. The quantum of finance is minimum ₹1 lakh and maximum ₹50 lakh.

NRI Flexi Loan It targets NRIs for investment in residential/commercial buildings except for investment in non-banking business, in agricultural or plantation, real estate business and construction of farm house for trading in transferable development rights (TDRs). The loan amount is maximum ₹25 lakh. The repayment of loan is to be done within 84 months as EMI without holiday. The loan amount will be 50 per cent of the property as security assessed by a valuer from the bank's panel.

Overdraft Facility for NRI It provides a facility of overdraft up to ₹25,000 in NRE SB account. The criteria is an equal amount of NRE/FCNR deposit with the bank. The rate of interest is deposits rate plus 1 per cent irrespective of the size of the loan/overdraft. The period of sanction is 1 week and repayment is through fresh inward remittance from abroad through normal banking channel or out of transfer of funds held in other NRE/FCNR accounts.

Personal Loans It targets permanent employees of government PSUs, blue chip companies and reputed institutions where salary deduction undertaking is available. It also provides line of credit to SB account holders, whose salary is being credited to the account, subject to a maximum of 11/2 times the monthly salary credited or ₹50,000 whichever is less. It is for personal purpose like repairs to house, medical treatment of self and family, consumption and purchase of consumer items. The mode of installment is through EMI and the repayment period is 60 months. Processing charges are ₹100 per loan.

Rental Loan Scheme It provides loan against lease rent receivables. Repayment is through EMI equal to unexpired lease period or extended lease period subject to a maximum of 7 years. Loan repayment period will be the remaining period of lease period or extended lease period. Upfront fee is 1 per cent with minimum ₹5,000 and maximum ₹2.50 lakh and processing charges are 0.25 per cent with minimum ₹5,000 and maximum ₹2.50 lakh. There are no other hidden charges and the primary security is the assignment of lease rentals.

Vitjan Pradan The borrowers of this loan scheme are students who have completed 18 years. In the case of minor students, parents will be the borrowers. The maximum amount is ₹5 lakh for domestic studies and ₹15 lakh for foreign studies. Margin is nil up to ₹25,000 and 15 per cent above ₹25,000 and 25 per cent for overseas studies. Repayment starts after holiday period of 6 months after obtaining employment or 1 year from the date of qualifying the exam whichever is earlier. For overseas studies, it is 6 months from the date of qualifying the exam.

SIB Life Line It is a unique family health care loan package with insurance cover designed to support financially for timely medical treatment of various ailments. The financial parameters are as follows:

Treatment	Minimum Loan	Maximum Loan	Margin
In India	₹25,000	₹3,00,000	10%
Abroad	₹1,00,000	₹10,00,000	25%

First installment starts 1 month after full availment of the loan. The rate of interest will be fixed, based on the repayment schedule, *i.e.*, from the date of availment of the loan to the date of closure.

SIB Sthree Shakthi The targets of this loan scheme are the employed women and housewives whose husbands are employees, agriculturists, professionals or businessmen. Eligible amount of loan is total emoluments/income of permanent nature received by self/husband, as the case may be, for the past 1 year. Loan amount may range between ₹25,000 and ₹1,00,000 (100 per cent of the value without margin) and the repayment is within 60 months as EMI. The purpose of this scheme is to provide financing for the purchase of gold/platinum/diamond ornaments, electric/electronic equipments and modernising the kitchen.

SIB Help-Line for Nurses It is a special loan scheme for nurses proceeding for employment abroad. The purpose of the loan is to meet expenses like one way ticket charges, initial expenses with recruiting agency, initial expenses abroad till first salary is received and clothing to be purchased from India. Maximum amount provided through this loan is ₹2 lakh. The repayment period is 24 months as EMI/bulk payment. The candidates having passed general/B.Sc (Nursing) from a recognized college are eligible for the loan.

Agriflex The target group of this loan scheme is individuals and/or jointly with spouse/parents or joint property owners. The net worth in landed property should be at least twice the loan amount. The purpose of the loan is any agricultural and allied activity. The quantum of loan is minimum ₹1 lakh and maximum ₹25 lakh.

NRI Schemes

NRIs contribute a large number of the South Indian Bank customer base—this especially includes the residents of Kerala who are located in the Middle East. The various schemes, facilities and services offered for NRIs are elaborated below.

NRI Deposit Schemes The various schemes are NRE, NRO, FCNR (B) and RFC. For NRE, accounts can be in the form of current, savings, term deposit and recurring deposit. Joint accounts are also permitted.

FCNR (B) deposit is accepted in USD, GBP and Euro for various maturities insulated against exchange rate fluctuations. Balance and interest is repatriable.

NRO accounts are maintained in Indian rupees for routing bonafide local remittance like rent. Joint accounts are permitted. Interest earned in this type of account is subject to Indian income tax.

A person of Indian origin who returns to India for permanent settlement after a stay of a minimum period of one year abroad is eligible to open RFC account. Accounts can be maintained in USD, GBP and EURO. The assets acquired or held at the time of return are eligible for credit to RFC account.

Swift Centres SIB is the one among the few banks in India using new version of IP based SWIFT network. It is the fastest way for transfer of funds.

Online Money Transfer It can be done through various schemes like TT remittance, Xpress money, Wall Street instant cash and SIB express.

Loans and Advances Various types of loans are available for NRIs. Loan against deposits is available up to 90 per cent of the deposit amount against security of fixed deposits under NRE and NRO. The rate of interest for loan against NRE/NR deposit is deposit rate + 1 per cent. Foreign currency and rupee loans are available up to 75 per cent of FCNR (B) deposits.

Housing loans are available for purchase of ready-built house/flat or for construction of new house/flat. The rate of interest is less than that of the other loans. Floating rate is also available.

NRI Family Welfare Scheme This scheme provides reimbursement of hospitalization expenses for NRI and his family and also personal accident cover for the NRI at a reduced rate of premium. All NRIs who maintain account with SIB within the age limit of 3–75 years are eligible for this scheme. Hospitalization expenses up to a maximum of ₹2 lakh and personal accident insurance up to ₹10 lakh are covered. It is valid for 3 years from the date of the payment of premium.

Special Services SIB offers special services for NRIs. The bank has 13 NRI branches and NRI newsletter.

Tele-Transfer For tele-transfer of funds to India, NRIs can instruct their banks abroad to remit the amount directly to the correspondent bank, giving SIB account number to the correspondent bank and the name of SIB branch where the account is maintained.

Draft Drawing Arrangements NRIs can send remittance through DD through any bank/exchange companies abroad for credit of account with SIB. SIB has inward rupee drafts drawing arrangements with the following banks/exchange companies.

Banking Channels SIB's motto of 'blending tradition with technology' can be very well seen in 'Sibertech', an initiative to connect its 264 key branches electronically and hence providing 'anywhere banking'. The bank uses the Infosys' banking solution software called Finacle for this purpose. The project was started in January 2001. Using this robust network, facilities like networked ATMs, Internet banking, mobile banking, global debit cum ATM card operations and other facilities are offered by the SIB in addition to its branch banking facilities.

Branch Banking SIB has over 650 branch offices across 14 states in India with the head office at Thrissur, Kerala. Almost all services are offered at the branch. However, the bank is increasingly trying to reduce the branch usage by providing anywhere, anytime banking facilities, since in that way it can increase its customer base at reduced cost and also expand its geographical reach.

Internet Banking Services Sibernet is now used to describe the Internet banking service provided by SIB. Using Sibernet, users can conduct banking operations from whatever location be it home, office, cyber-cafe or anywhere in the world where there is Internet connection and the service is available round the clock for 365 days a year.

The security of the site is done through a 128 bit encryption, which is certified by Verisign, a global pioneer in e-security. The software used is developed by Infosys. These facilities are offered to retail customers as well as corporate customers.

ATM SIB has its ATMs which allow the customers to enjoy the facilities of anywhere, anytime banking using SIB ATM card. It is present in all major cities in India and operating 24 hours a day.

SIB has also joined the National Financial Switch (NFS) network system on 4 May 2005. The NFS network is owned and managed by the Institute for Development and Research in Banking Technology (IDRBT) which is the technical arm of the RBI. This facility helps SIB customers to do ATM transactions from other bank ATMs at reduced charge rates.

With the providing of this facility, SIB is in a better position to serve its customers through more number of ATMs in the country. Moreover, the customers of other member banks of NFS will be able to transact their business through the bank's ATMs located in all major centers.

SIB Premium This product is targeted towards current account and overdraft account holders who may require frequent transfer of funds in their course of business. Some of its features are as follows:

- Current deposit accounts are categorized as D-standard, C-silver, B-gold and A-platinum, based on the monthly average balance, for the purpose of collection of charges. D-standard category has to maintain a monthly average balance of ₹10,000, C-silver—₹50,000, B-gold—₹1,00,000 and A-platinum—₹5,00,000.
- One ordinary ATM card will be issued to individual and proprietary current accounts. They can draw cash up to ₹20,000 per day through any of the banks online ATMs.

SIB's Global ATM-cum-Debit Cards SIB's global ATM-cum-debit cards are now acceptable in the Master Card International (MCI) network system as well as in the domestic NFS network system. SIB's debit cards are supported in more than 8,30,000 ATMs together within India and worldwide and also in around seven million point of sale (POS) terminals across the globe.

MCI is a leading global payment solutions company that provides a broad variety of innovative services in support of their global members' credit, deposit access, electronic cash, business-to-business and related payment programs. MCI manages a family of well-known, widely accepted payment cards brands including MasterCard®, Maestro® and Cirrus® and serves financial institutions, consumers and businesses in over 210 countries and territories.

SIB Mobile Service As a registered user of SIB mobile service, a customer can send pull requests and/or receive push alerts.

Pull Requests Customers send simple, standard SMS messages to a published number of the bank to get online information on his/her account(s). The requests which can be sent by the customers are as follows:

- Get the balance in any of his SB/CA/CC/OD account/s instantaneously
- Fetch the last five transactions in any of his SB/CA/CC/OD accounts

- Inquire on the status of a cheque issued by him in any of his SB/CA/CC/OD accounts
- Change his mobile banking PIN
- Disable his SIB mobile service temporarily
- Re-enable his SIB mobile service temporarily

These requests are known as pull requests.

SIB Privilege Card This is a multi-purpose photo card which can be used in all the ATMs of the bank and also at all the networked branches. The privilege card holders can withdraw money up to ₹25,000 at the networked branches.

Other Service Features Offered by SIB

General Insurance Business SIB entered into a MOU on 29 November 2002 with United India Insurance Company, a south-based general insurance major in public sector to act as their corporate agent. SIB is the first corporate agent of the United India Insurance Company. Through the corporate agency, SIB has already started distributing various general insurance products to the customers through its own branches (Bancassurance).

Exporter's Credit Insurance Export credit guarantee corporation (ECGC) of India, a Government of India enterprise, established to promote export/import, has appointed SIB as its corporate agent to market their exporter's credit insurance policies. As SIB is already extending the life and non-life insurance facilities, it is now equipped to cover the entire range of insurance products under one roof. ECGC provides a range of credit risk insurance covers to exporters against loss in export of goods.

RTGS for Customer Transactions Real Time Gross Settlement (RTGS) is an electronic payment system, which provides online settlement of payments between financial institutions. The SIB started RTGS operations since 16 July 2004. All the networked branches of the bank are RTGS enabled. Customers of all SIB's networked branches can avail RTGS services for transferring funds to accounts of other banks; provided those bank branches are also RTGS enabled.

SIB Collect It was introduced by the bank to facilitate the fast collection of cheques and other outstation instruments.

SIB Cash Passport Cash Passport is offered by the SIB in agreement with Interpayment Services Limited (a subsidiary of Travelex Global and Financial Services, UK, formerly The Thomas Cook Group of England). Cash Passport card is to be loaded in US dollar, post which customers can use the card to withdraw money from VISA ATMs all over the world in the local currency or US dollar. Another attractive feature of the card is that the money can be loaded on it without the customer being physically present at the bank. Another feature of this product is that the customer need not maintain an account with the bank to own this card because the card is not linked to any account.

Case Questions

1. Do you think that the South Indian Bank has adopted some new innovations to improve their product offerings?
2. Discuss the retail banking strategy that the South Indian Bank follows.

ENDNOTES

1. This case was co-authored by Professor Justin Paul with Adarsh Mohta, Nikhil Gupta and Varun Kabra. The contribution by Vandana Mohan are also acknowledged. Cases in this chapter are developed solely as the basis for class discussion. Cases are not intended to serve as endorsements, sources of primary data or illustrations of effective or ineffective management.
2. Dr. Justin Paul co-authored this case study with Pramod Potti, Pallab Mukherjee and Parvez Qazi. Cases in this chapter are developed solely as the basis for class discussion. This case is not intended to serve as endorsement, sources of primary data or illustrations of effective or ineffective management.

APPENDIX

Objective-Type Questions on Commercial Banking

Tick √ YES or NO for the following statements.

1. Retail banking means managing of individual customers on both assets and liabilities side.
   Yes No
2. Customer segmentation refers to classification of customers into different groups for the purpose of identifying their financial requirements.
   Yes No
3. The Basel II Accord deals in capital adequacy norms to be fulfilled by the banks.
   Yes No
4. Bundling of products means availability of various options within the main product/service.
   Yes No
5. The success of retail lending depends on assessment of future requirements of customer needs and to prepare for the same now.
   Yes No
6. Housing loan can be sanctioned to a property situated in any industrial area.
   Yes No
7. Housing loan can also be considered for the purchase of a plot.
   Yes No
8. The maximum moratorium under a housing loan is 30 months.
   Yes No
9. Stamp duty/registration charges do not form a part of the project cost in housing loans.
   Yes No
10. Under the flip method, the installments are graduated with a rise in the income level of the borrower.
    Yes No
11. The maximum IRR (installment to recovery ratio) to be considered is 25 per cent under housing loans.
    Yes No
12. A third party can join as co-applicant in the case of housing loans.
    Yes No
13. There is no restriction on the number of co-applicants in housing loans.
    Yes No
14. The house/property proposed to be purchased/constructed on banks finance need not be held jointly by all the applicants.
    Yes No
15. Cross guarantee under group housing scheme can be permitted.
    Yes No
16. Delay in payment or instalment attracts penal interest in the case of housing loans.
    Yes No
17. Second charge on house/property for extending finance under housing loan scheme can be permitted, subject to certain terms and conditions.
    Yes No
18. Finance to state-owned corporations and involved housing projects and statutory bodies like housing boards can be treated as 'direct housing finance'.
    Yes No

19. Finance to firms/companies under the vehicle loan scheme may be permitted.
    Yes No
20. Consumer durable loans backed by hypothecation of assets can be termed as 'secured' personal loan.
    Yes No
21. Margin under clean personal loan is 25 per cent.
    Yes No
22. Loan against mortgage (LAP) can be permitted to meet any purpose/requirement.
    Yes No
23. The minimum margin under loan against mortgage is 50 per cent.
    Yes No
24. The maximum quantum of loan under the education loan scheme is ₹15 lakh.
    Yes No
25. Loans above ₹4 lakh under education loan require tangible security.
    Yes No
26. Minimum margin under education loan in 25 per cent.
    Yes No
27. The repayment period under education loan is study period plus one year or study period plus 6 months after securing employment, whichever is earlier.
    Yes No
28. The allowable expenses under education loans include the amount paid towards development fund.
    Yes No
29. A loan of ₹100 lakh to a corporate or firm for business purposes fall within the definition of retail lending (as per Basel II norms).
    Yes No
30. Loan against shares will be considered only if the shares are in the demat form.
    Yes No
31. Loan can be granted against pledge of share of any company.
    Yes No
32. Maintaining pension account is not mandatory in case loan is to be considered for a senior citizen.
    Yes No
33. Top-up loans are a kind of supplementary finance extended to home loan borrowers.
    Yes No
34. Loan against rent receivables is granted against total rent receivable for the unexpired lease period.
    Yes No
35. Recovery in loans against rent receivables is ensured by debiting the customers account.
    Yes No
36. The security under loan against rent receivable, the collateral security should necessarily be the same property from which the lease rentals are derived.
    Yes No
37. The maximum repayment tenure allowed in the case of loan against rent receivables is to the extent of unexpired period of lease or 84 months, whichever is earlier.
    Yes No
38. Banks' individual credit policy governs the internal policies and control with regard to credit dispensation.
    Yes No
39. Finance can be extended even to those activities which are declared as low priority in credit policy of individual banks.
    Yes No
40. Rating of the borrower is one of the risk mitigating tools and therefore it is mandatory in respect of all credit proposals.
    Yes No
41. Verification of authenticity of various documents is a part of due diligence exercise.
    Yes No
42. The EMI can be permitted up to 50 per cent of gross monthly income.
    Yes No
43. Floating rate of interest varies as and when there is change in interest rate without a change in the BPLR.
    Yes No
44. Credit monitoring function is to ensure constant vigil on conduct and operations of loan account.
    Yes No

45. By crediting the loan amount to the account of the customer, end use of funds can be ensured.
    Yes No
46. Management information system (MIS) can be used as one of the credit monitoring tools.
    Yes No
47. Drawing the sanctioned limit to full extent and operating the account near sanctioned limit is an indication of diversion of funds and low level of activity.
    Yes No
48. Non-security documents, such as application forms and letters of undertaking can be admitted as the main documents of evidence in the court of law.
    Yes No
49. In the case of DP note executed by a partnership firm, the words jointly and severally need to be inserted.
    Yes No
50. The liability of guarantor arises only in the event of failure of the principal borrower.
    Yes No
51. The limitation period in the case of guarantee commences from the date of execution of the guarantee itself.
    Yes No
52. Even if the principal borrower is absolved of his liability by virtue of the DP noted getting time barred, the guarantor shall continue to be liable for the debt.
    Yes No
53. Equitable mortgage does not attract any stamp duty, though, of date, some of the state governments introduced stamp duty even on equitable mortgage to increase revenue.
    Yes No
54. Search report and non-encumbrance certificate are not required for creation of mortgage.
    Yes No
55. Security charged as prime security in the case of one loan account can be extended as collateral security in the case of another loan.
    Yes No
56. Physical inspection of assets charged to the bank is necessary to corroborate with the information furnished by the customer.
    Yes No
57. If two mortgages are created on the same property—one is by way of simple mortgage and another by way of equitable mortgage, the second mortgage can enforce his right only after the debt secured by the first mortgage is fully satisfied.
    Yes No
58. NEFT is an electronic fund transfer facility and came into force with effect from 1 June, 2006.
    Yes No
59. Facility under NEFT is available only at select branches.
    Yes No
60. NEFT is distinct from RTGS.
    Yes No
61. Transaction under NEFT is on a gross settlement basis.
    Yes No
62. ECS facilitates bulk payment system easier.
    Yes No
63. Transactions under ECS are cleared through the National Clearing House of the RBI.
    Yes No
64. RTGS is an electronic fund transfer system amongst different bank's branches.
    Yes No
65. RTGS system eliminates settlement system deficiencies.
    Yes No
66. Transaction under RTGS are materialises the very next day.
    Yes No
67. Each bank is allotted a code under RTGS called 'IFS code'.
    Yes No
68. Service under RTGS is not available on three national holidays namely 26 January, 15 August and 25 December.
    Yes No
69. The settlement under RTGS is carried through a settlement account called the RTGS settlement account.
    Yes No

70. In the case of shortfall in the RTGS settlement account, the RBI will not give any liquidity support.
Yes No
71. The first ATM was installed in 1967 in the USA.
Yes No
72. The present day ATMs in many of the places are only cash dispensing machines.
Yes No
73. Motorized card system is convenient from the customer's point of view as it enables transaction in a row without requiring the card to be inserted every time.
Yes No
74. The transaction in the ATM is routed through the ATM switch of the individual bank.
Yes No
75. The transactions effected through service provider like VISA/MasterCard/AMEX are settled on a monthly basis.
Yes No
76. Alliance with other banks for sharing ATMs is a part of the strategic management of banks.
Yes No
77. Considering the ATM network in China and South-East Asian countries like South Korea, the ATM network in India is adequate.
Yes No
78. All settlements of transactions through VISA are settled through a 'settlement account opened for this purpose'.
Yes No
79. ATM-cum-debit card tagged to VISA/MasterCard can be used in any ATM without any extra charge.
Yes No
80. Credit card business is not a profitable venture.
Yes No
81. The full form of CVV is credit value verification and being a secret code, it should neither be disclosed nor made accessible to others.
Yes No
82. The credit card contains 18 digits on the fact of it eight digits of which are allotted by VISA/Master Card/AMEX and the rest by the individual bank concerned.
Yes No
83. Card limit will be fixed on the basis of the income level of the customer.
Yes No
84. The cash withdrawal limit does not exceed 10 per cent of the total limit of the credit card.
Yes No
85. The POS will be provided by the card-issuing bank at the merchant establishments.
Yes No
86. Commission earned through POS will be passed on to the card issuing bank in full.
Yes No
87. Details of customer name, card limit and cash withdrawal limit are encrypted on the magnetic tape on the back side of the card.
Yes No
88. Customers enjoy 2 months credit under credit cards.
Yes No
89. Transaction cost and finance charges under credit card are low.
Yes No
90. USP stands for Unique Selling Proposition, which refers to distinct features of a product, which are not available in the contemporary market with the competitors dealing in the same product or service.
Yes No

Correct answers for these objective-type questions are available on the web site of the book.

INDEX

D

E

F

NOTES